Street by Street

CW00326376

LEEDS BRADFORD

BRIGHOUSE, DEWSBURY, HALIFAX, ILKLEY, KEIGHLEY, WAKEFIELD, WETHERBY

Batley, Bingley, Castleford, Garforth, Guiseley, Haworth, Normanton, Otley, Pontefract, Tadcaster

2nd edition January 2003

© Automobile Association Developments Limited 2003

Ordnance Survey® This product includes map data licensed from Ordnance Survey® with the permission of the Controller of Her Majesty's Stationery Office. © Crown copyright 2003. All rights reserved. Licence No: 399221.

Published by AA Publishing (a trading name of Automobile Association Developments Limited, whose registered office is Millstream, Maidenhead Road, Windsor, Berkshire SL4 5GD. Registered number 1878835).

The Post Office is a registered trademark of Post Office Ltd. in the UK and other countries.

Schools address data provided by Education Direct.

One-way street data provided by:

Tele Atlas   © Tele Atlas N.V.

Mapping produced by the Cartographic Department of The Automobile Association. A01539

A CIP Catalogue record for this book is available from the British Library.

Printed by G. Canale & C. S.P.A., Torino, Italy.

Ref: MX015z

Key to map pages	ii-iii
Key to map symbols	iv-1
Enlarged scale pages	2-19
Street by Street	20-191
Index – towns & villages	192
Index – streets	193-240
Index – featured places	240-246

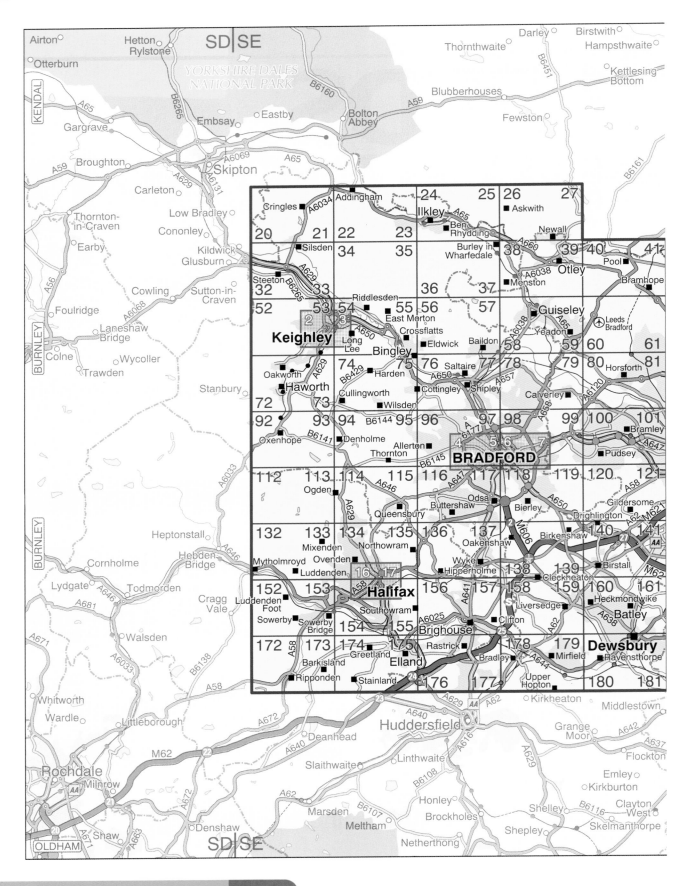

SD | SE

YORKSHIRE DALES NATIONAL PARK

Airton
Hetton
Rylstone
Otterburn
KENDAL
Gargrave
Broughton
Skipton
Carleton
Thornton-in-Craven
Earby
Cononley
Low Bradley
Kildwick
Glusburn
Foulridge
Cowling
Sutton-in-Craven
Laneshaw Bridge
BURNLEY
Colne
Wycoller
Trawden
Stanbury
Embsay
Eastby
Bolton Abbey
Cringles
Addingham
Ilkley
Ben Rhydding
Silsden
Burley in Wharfedale
Steeton
Riddlesden
East Morton
Crossflatts
Eldwick
Keighley
Long Lee
Bingley
Oakworth
Harden
Haworth
Cullingworth
Wilsden
Oxenhope
Denholme
Allerton
Thornton
Ogden
Queensbury
Buttershaw
Heptonstall
Cornholme
Hebden Bridge
Mixenden
Ovenden
Luddenden
Mytholmroyd
Lydgate
Todmorden
Cragg Vale
Luddenden Foot
Sowerby
Sowerby Bridge
Walsden
Halifax
Southowram
Barkisland
Greetland
Ripponden
Stainland
Elland
Whitworth
Wardle
Littleborough
Rochdale
Milnrow
Denshaw
OLDHAM
Shaw
Deanhead
Slaithwaite
Marsden
Meltham
Huddersfield
Honley
Brockholes
Netherthong
Shepley

Darley
Birstwith
Thornthwaite
Hampsthwaite
Kettlesing Bottom
Blubberhouses
Fewston
Askwith
Newall
Otley
Pool
Bramhope
Menston
Guiseley
Leeds Bradford
Yeadon
Baildon
Calverley
Shipley
Saltaire
Cottingley
BRADFORD
Bramley
Pudsey
Odsal
Bierley
Gildersome
Drighlington
Oakenshaw
Birkenshaw
Wyke
Hipperholme
Cleckheaton
Birstall
Liversedge
Heckmondwike
Batley
Clifton
Brighouse
Rastrick
Bradley
Mirfield
Dewsbury
Ravensthorpe
Upper Hopton
Kirkheaton
Middlestown
Grange Moor
Flockton
Emley
Kirkburton
Shelley
Clayton West
Skelmanthorpe

SD | SE

20 21 22 23 24 25 26 27
32 33 34 35 36 37 38 39 40 41
52 53 54 55 56 57 58 59 60 61
72 73 74 75 76 77 78 79 80 81
92 93 94 95 96 97 98 99 100 101
112 113 114 115 116 117 118 119 120 121
132 133 134 135 136 137 138 139 140 141
152 153 154 155 156 157 158 159 160 161
172 173 174 175 176 177 178 179 180 181

2
3
4 5 6 7
16 17

Enlarged scale pages   **1:10,000**   6.3 inches to 1 mile

0   1/4   miles   1/2   3/4
0   1/4   1/2   kilometres   3/4   1   1 1/4

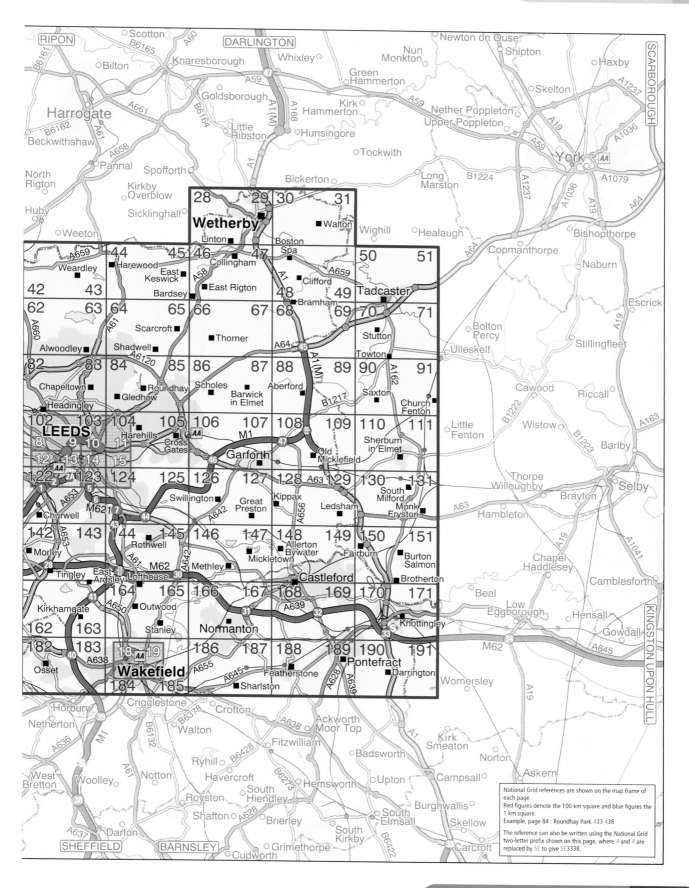

4.2 inches to 1 mile **Scale of main map pages 1:15,000**

National Grid references are shown on the map frame of each page.
Red figures denote the 100 km square and blue figures the 1 km square.
Example, page 84 : Roundhay Park 433 438

The reference can also be written using the National Grid two-letter prefix shown on this page, where 4 and 4 are replaced by SE to give SE3338.

Junction 9	Motorway & junction		⊖	Underground station
Services	Motorway service area		——⊖——	Light railway & station
	Primary road single/dual carriageway		+++++++++++++	Preserved private railway
Services	Primary road service area		*LC*	Level crossing
	A road single/dual carriageway		•—•—•—•—•	Tramway
	B road single/dual carriageway		- - - - - - - - -	Ferry route
	Other road single/dual carriageway		··················	Airport runway
	Minor/private road, access may be restricted		– · – · – · –	County administrative boundary
← ←	One-way street		ⱽⱽⱽⱽⱽⱽⱽⱽⱽⱽⱽⱽ	Mounds
	Pedestrian area		**93**	Page continuation 1:15,000
- - - - - - - -	Track or footpath		**7**	Page continuation to enlarged scale 1:10,000
▪▪▪▪▪▪▪▪▪	Road under construction			River/canal, lake, pier
⌐ - - - - ⌐	Road tunnel			Aqueduct, lock, weir
AA	AA Service Centre		465 ▲ Winter Hill	Peak (with height in metres)
P	Parking			Beach
P+🚌	Park & Ride			Woodland
🚌	Bus/coach station			Park
	Railway & main railway station		††††††	Cemetery
	Railway & minor railway station			Built-up area

	Featured building			Abbey, cathedral or priory
	City wall			Castle
A&E	Hospital with 24-hour A&E department			Historic house or building
PO	Post Office		Wakehurst Place NT	National Trust property
	Public library			Museum or art gallery
i	Tourist Information Centre			Roman antiquity
	Petrol station Major suppliers only			Ancient site, battlefield or monument
†	Church/chapel			Industrial interest
	Public toilets			Garden
	Toilet with disabled facilities			Arboretum
PH	Public house AA recommended			Farm or animal centre
	Restaurant AA inspected			Zoological or wildlife collection
	Theatre or performing arts centre			Bird collection
	Cinema			Nature reserve
	Golf course		V	Visitor or heritage centre
▲	Camping AA inspected			Country park
	Caravan site AA inspected			Cave
	Camping & caravan site AA inspected			Windmill
	Theme park			Distillery, brewery or vineyard

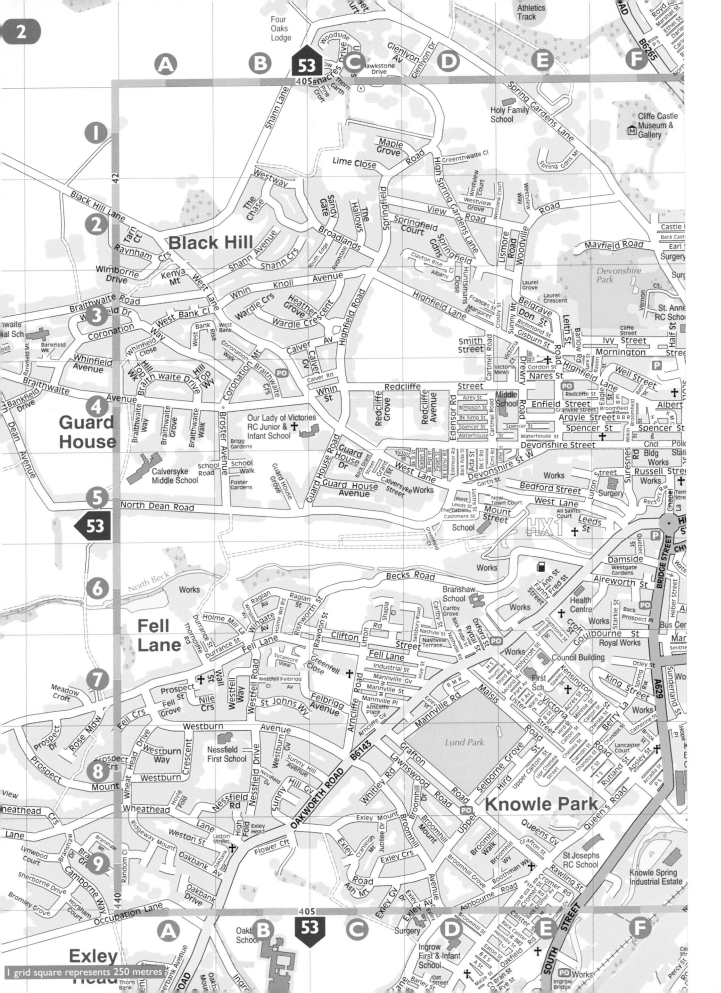

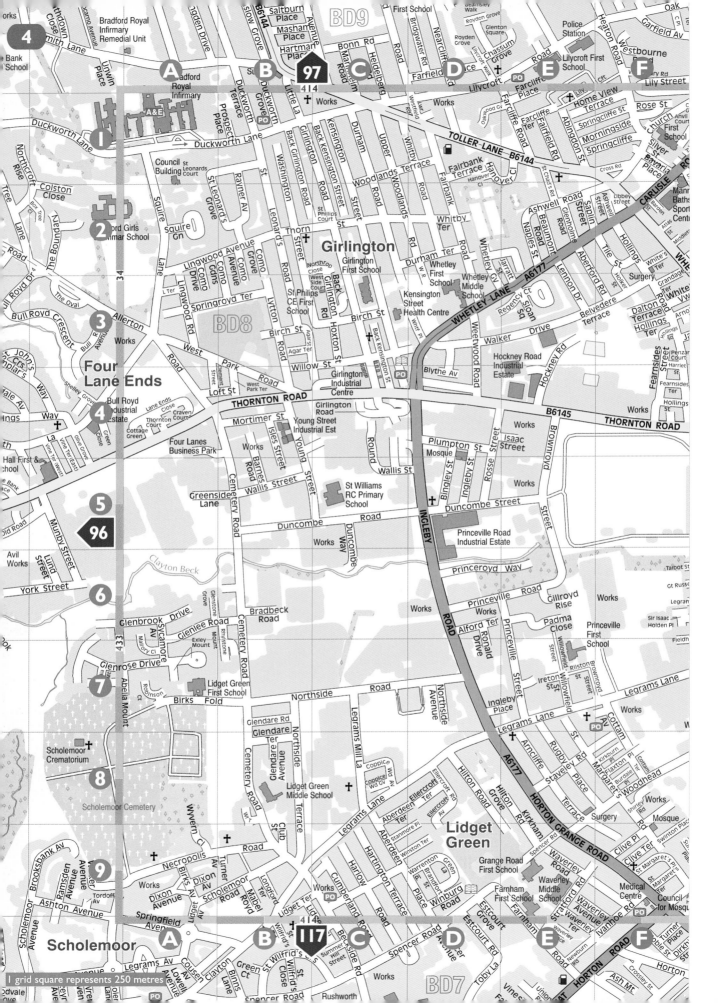

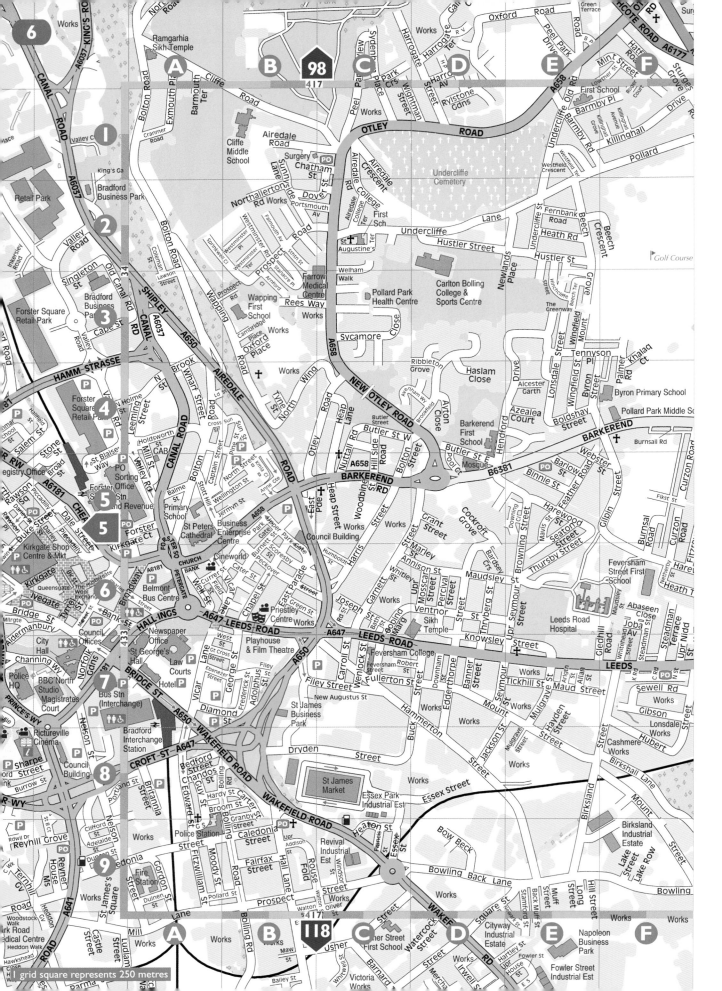

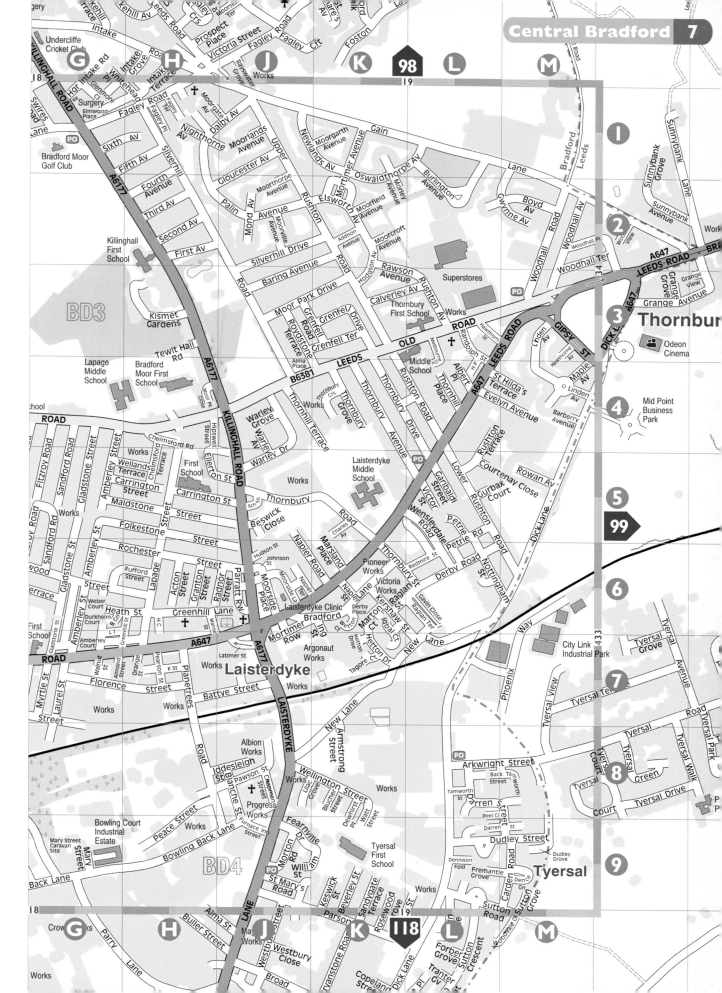

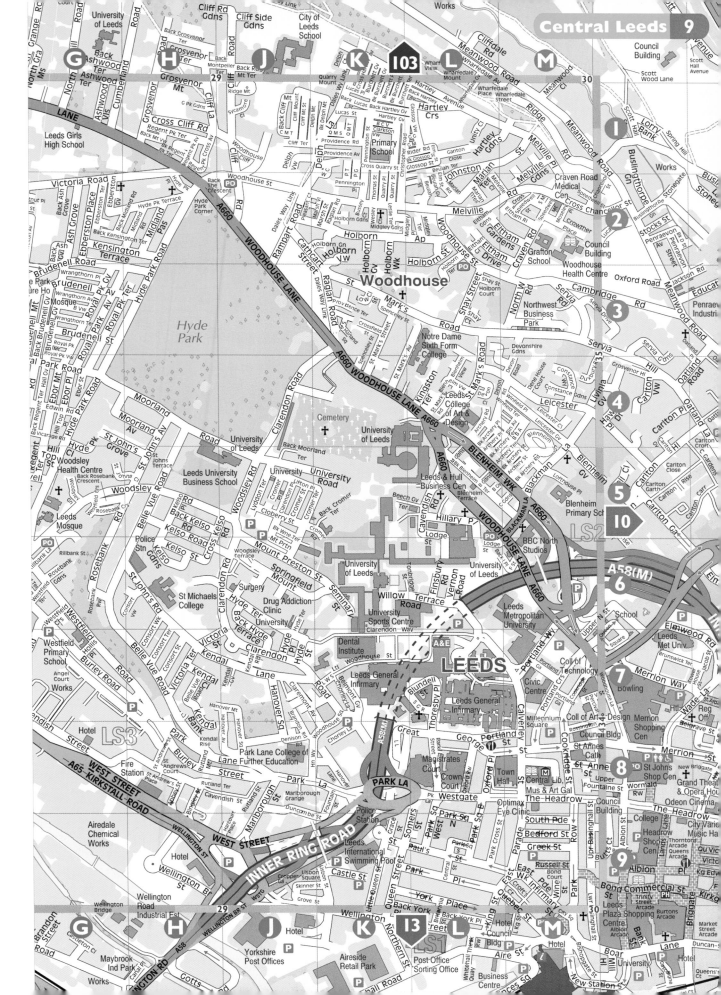

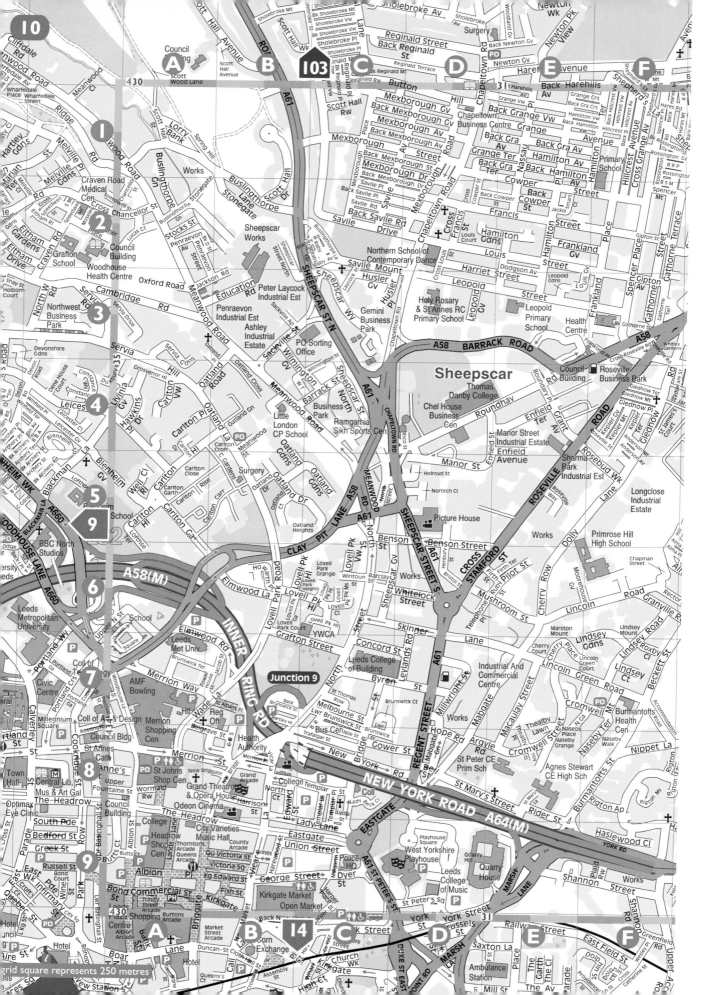

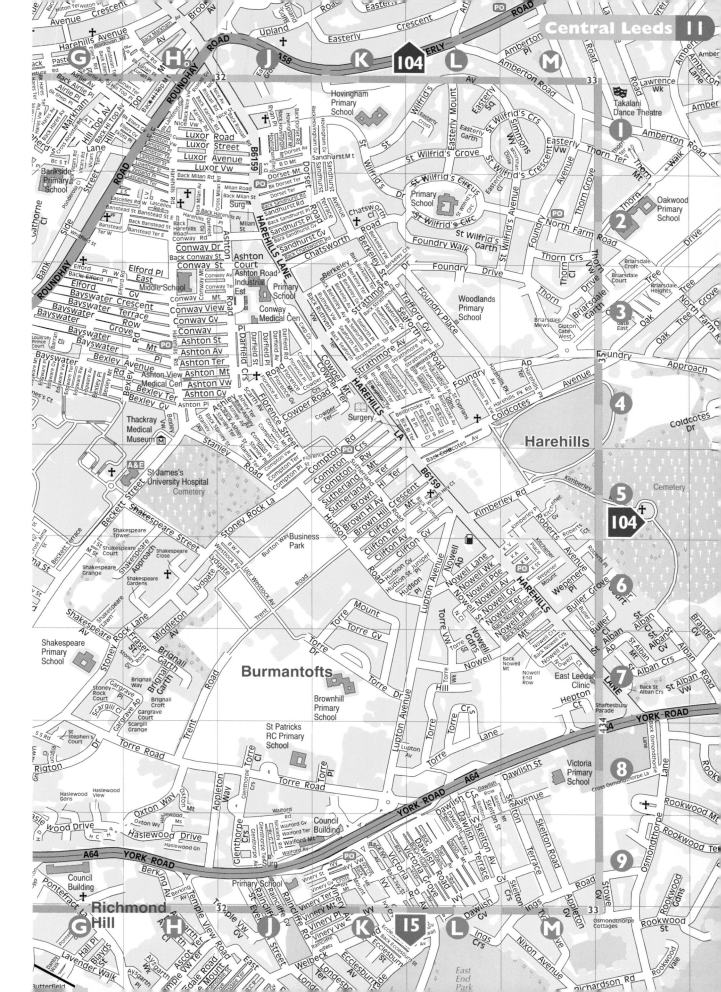

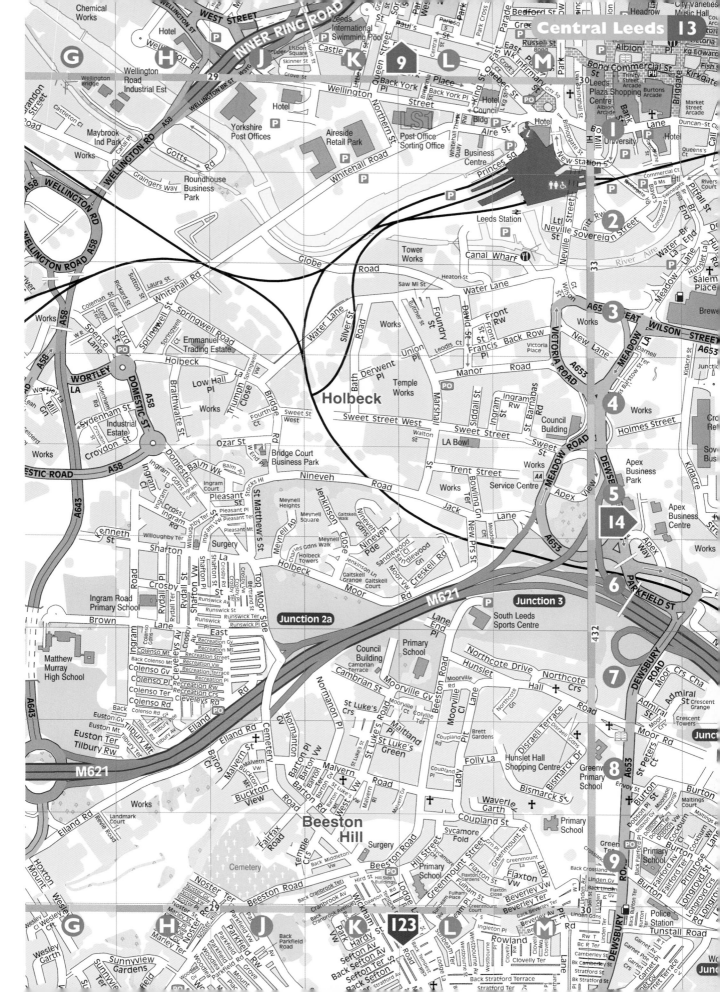

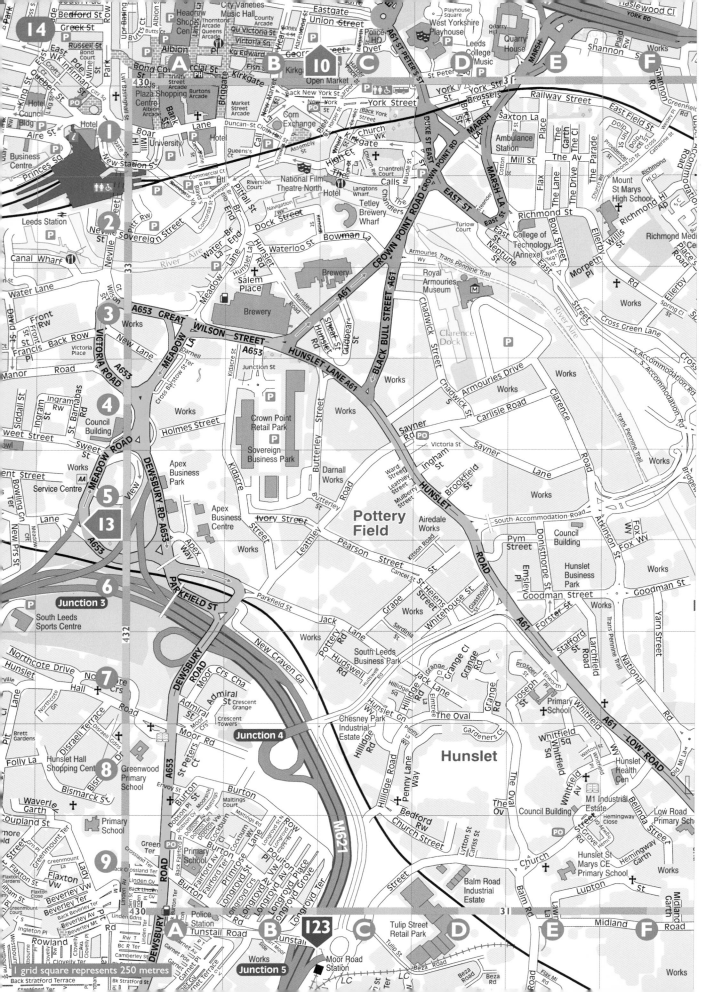

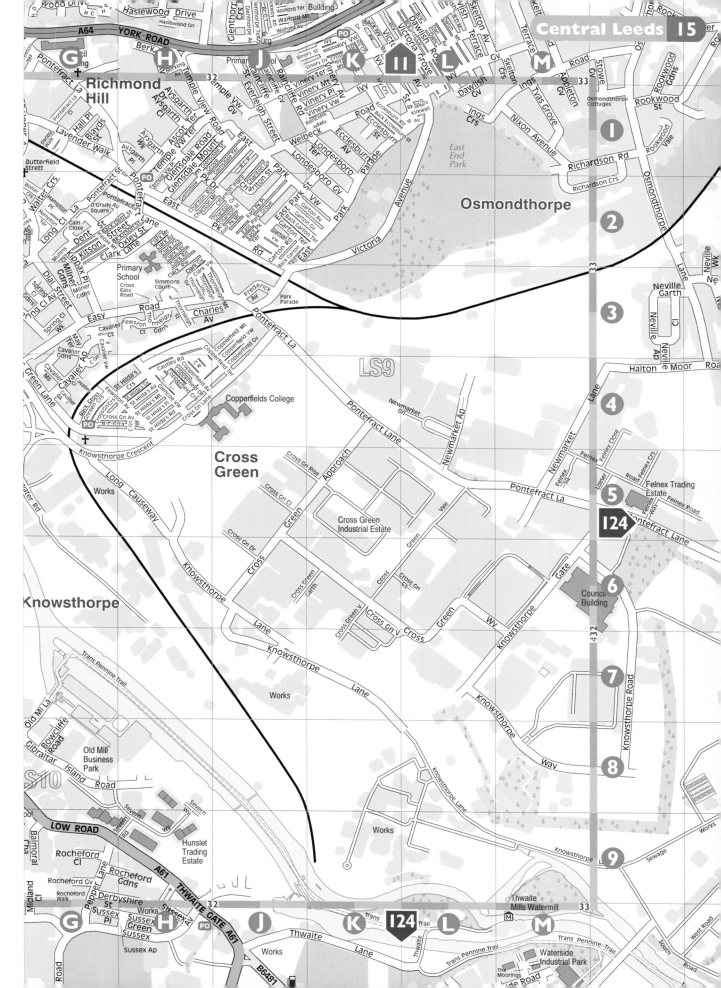

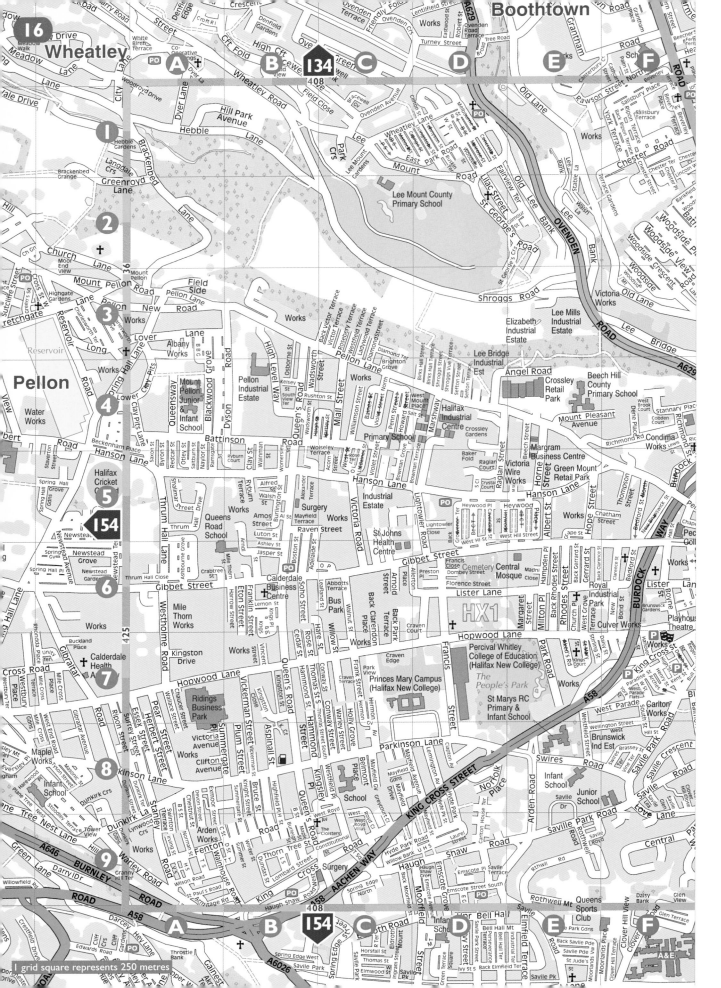

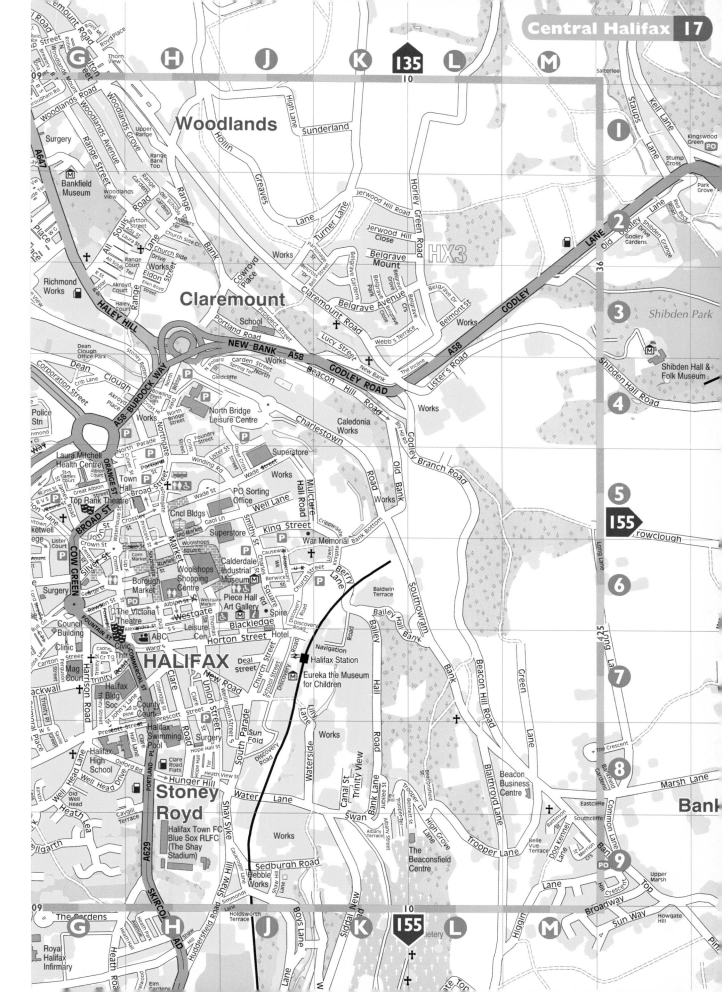

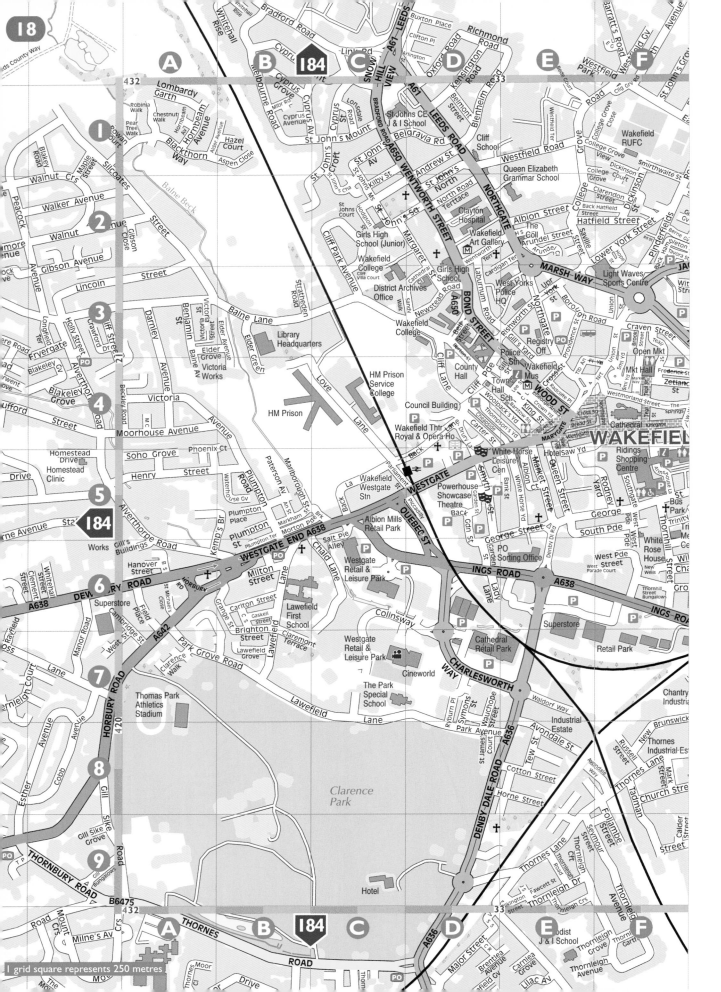

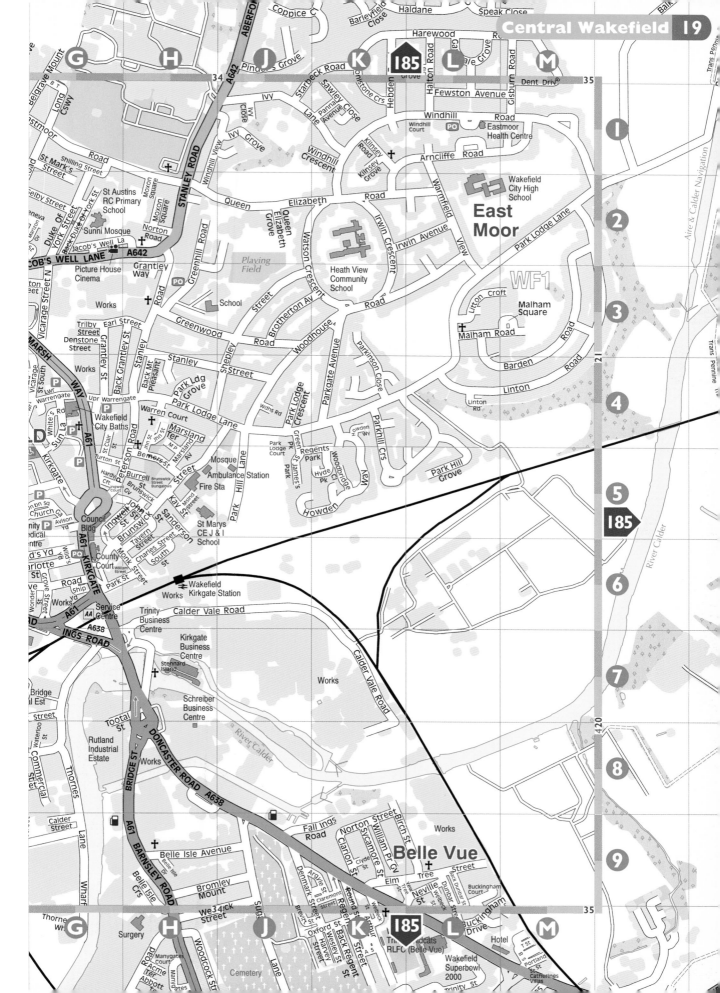

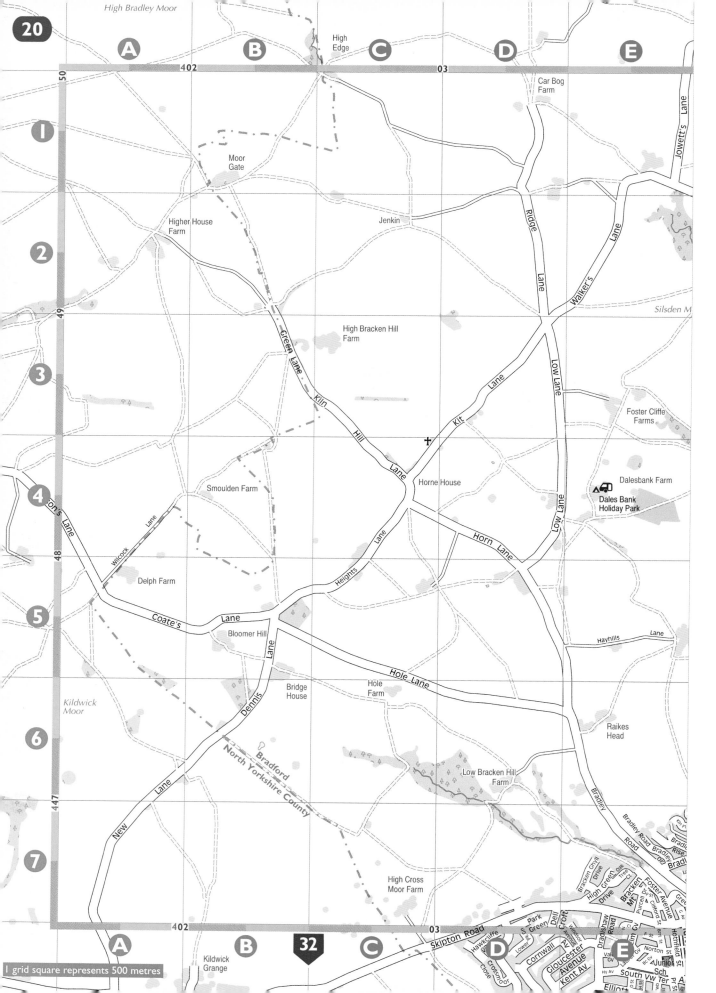

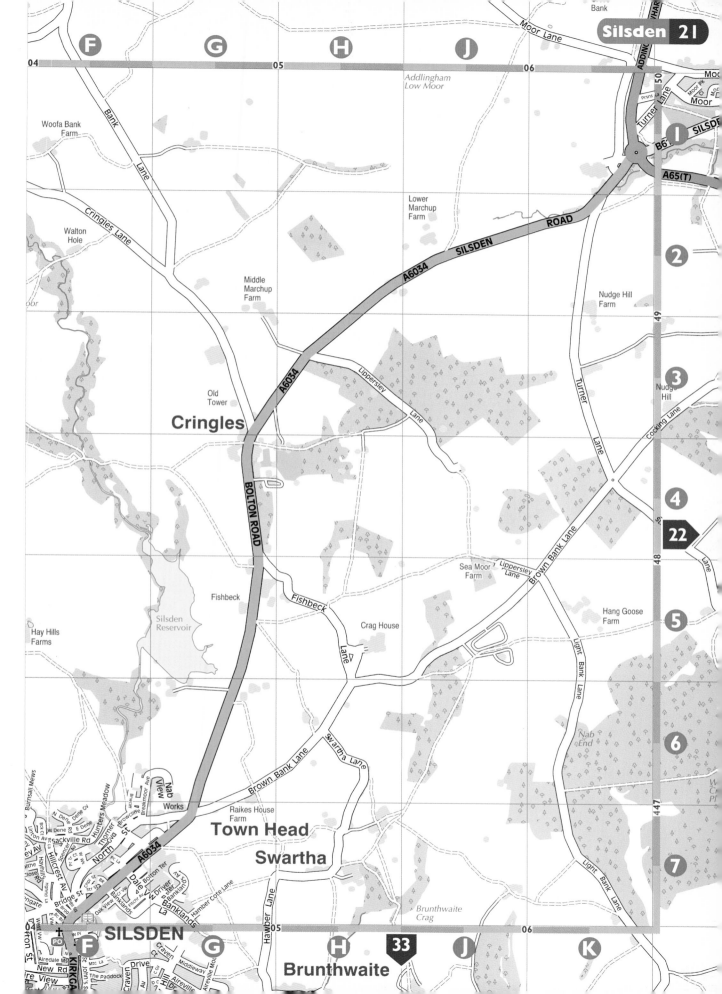

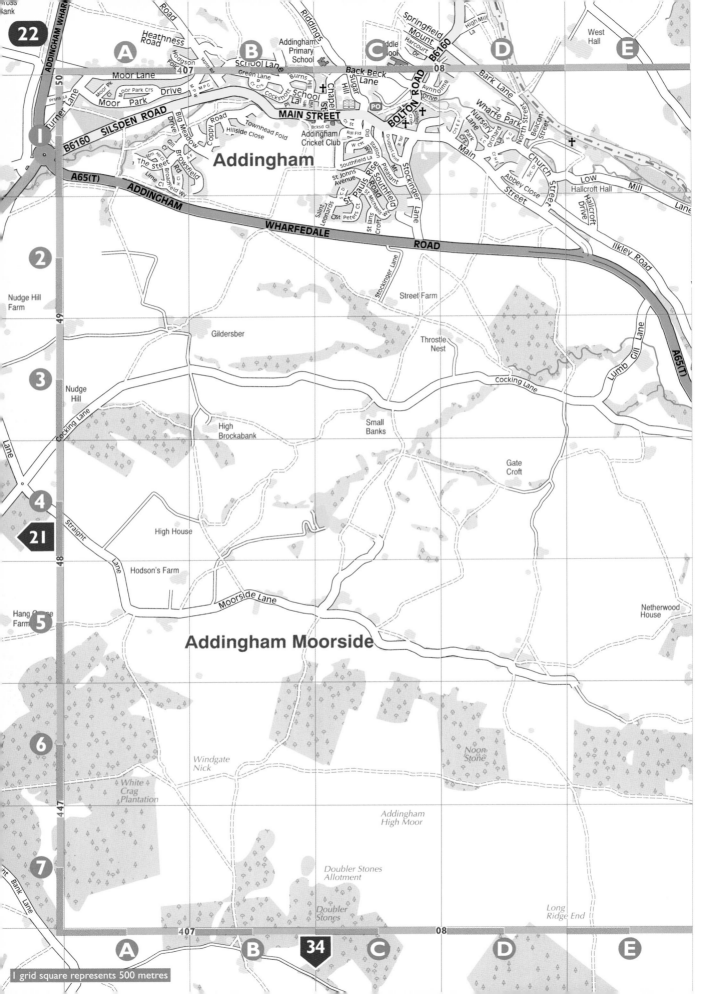

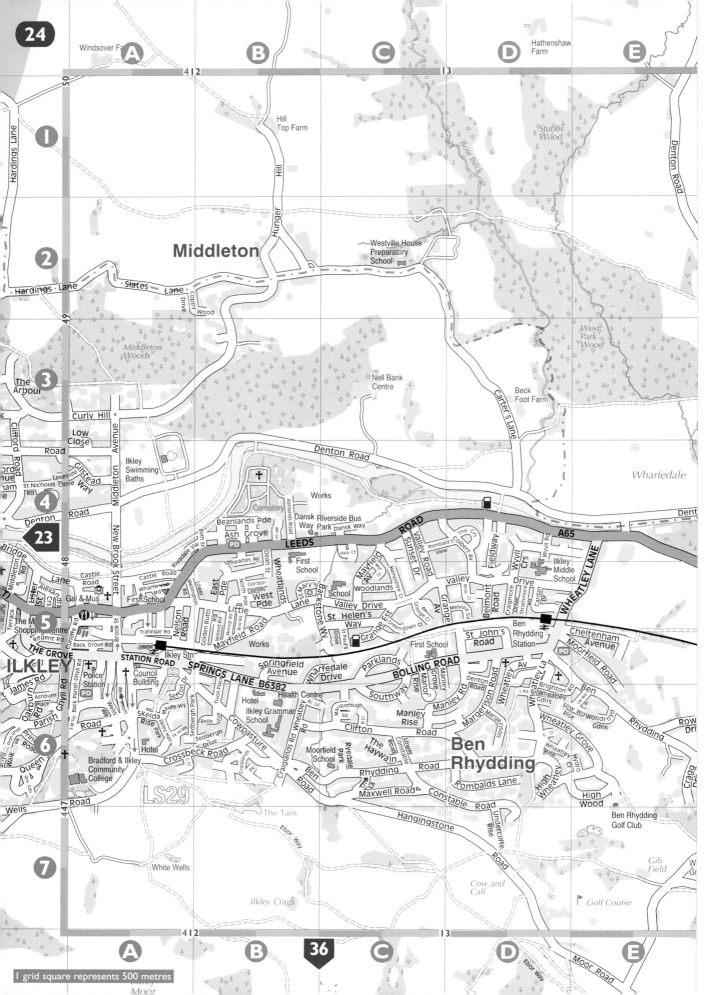

Yarnett House Farm

Smithy Lane

F **G** **H** **J**

14 15 16 50

Carrow Bank

Willow Hill Farm

I

Hole House Beck

Quarry House Farm

Scales House Farm

Moors

2

49

Denton †

Whitbeck Manor

3

Hall Lane

Denton Park

Denton Road

West Lane

4

on Road

Low Park Road

Carr House Farm

As

26

Crook

48

Ben Rhydding Sports Club

5

River Wharfe

West Beck

COUTANCES

North Yorkshire County

Bradford

Manor Park

6

ley ve

Green La

Leather Bank

Gre ne Farm

WAY

ILKLEY ROAD A65(T)

Esscroft

Green La

447

Great Pasture

Drive

Low House Farm

Woodpecker Rd

Ilkley Road

Well La

Tanfield Dr

Croft

7

harfedale ange Farm

Clevedon House School

Ben Rhydding Drive

Maria St

Sun Lane

Wrexham Road

Mansfield Road

West View Av

Main St

North Pde

Long Mdw

Old Mill

Willow Tree Gdns

F **G** **H** **J** **K**

14 15 **37** Stirling Road Terrace Surgery

Hall Drive

Manse

Grange Road

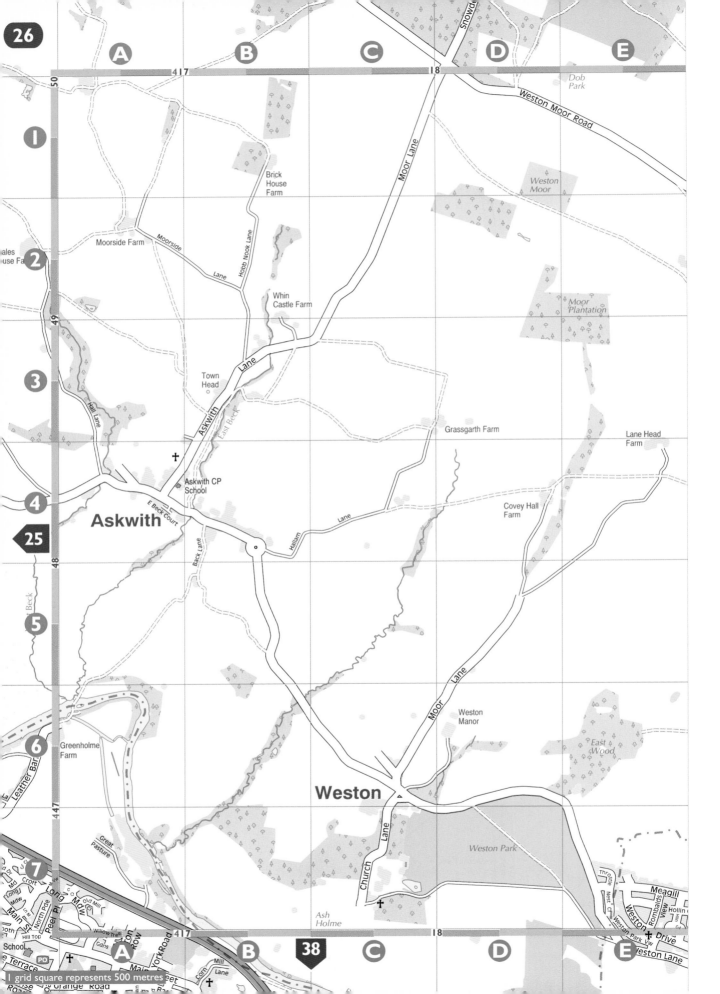

A   B   C   D   E

417
50

I

Dob
Park

Weston Moor Road

2   Moorside Farm   Moorside   Brick
House
Farm
Weston
Moor

Hobb Nook Lane   Whin
Castle Farm

Moor Lane

49

3   Town
Head   Grassgarth Farm   Moor
Plantation
Lane Head
Farm

Askwith   East Beck

†   Covey Hall
Farm

4   Askwith CP
School

E Beck Court

Askwith

Lane

Hallam

48

Back Lane

Beck

5

6   Greenholme
Farm
Leather Ban   Moor
Lane   Weston
Manor   East
Wood

Weston   Weston Park

Great
Pasture   Church Lane

7   Long   Croft   School   †

Willow Tree   Ash
Holme   †

417   18

A   B   C   D   E

Main St   York Road   Corn
Mill
Lane

PO   Meagill
Throstle
Nest   Hollin
Weston Park Vw
Rombalds View
Weston Lane

Weston Park
Drive

1 grid square represents 500 metres

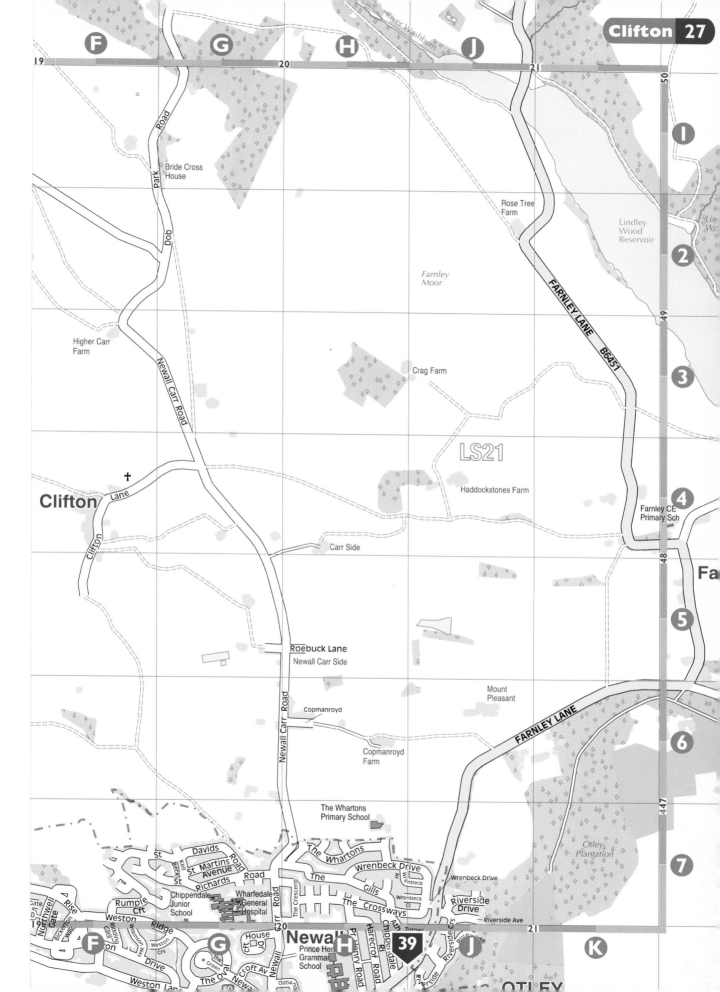

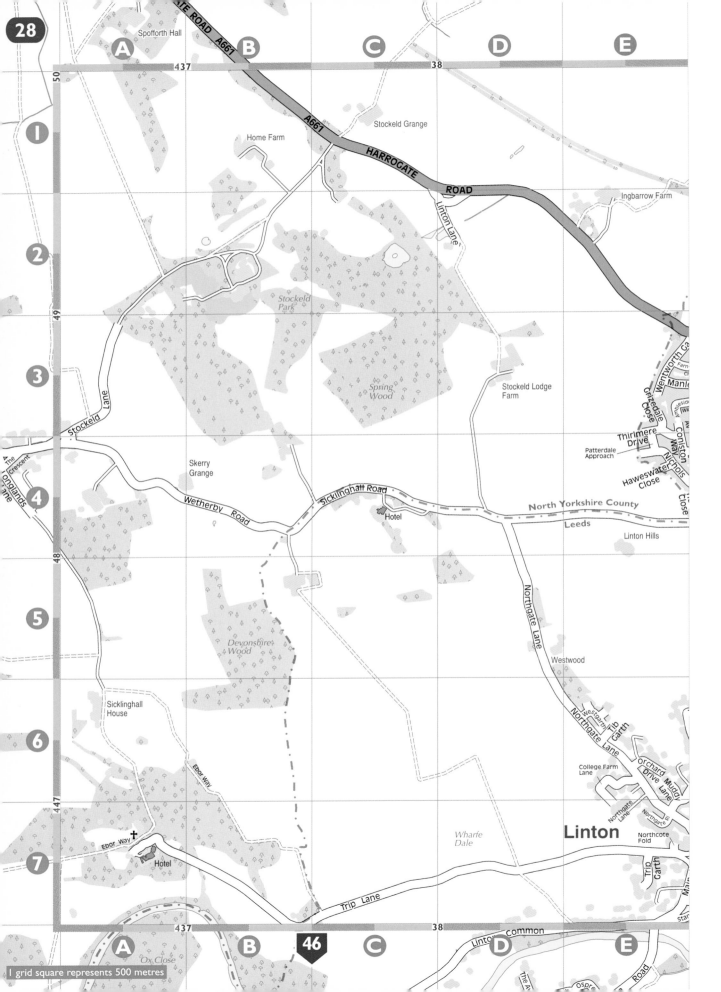

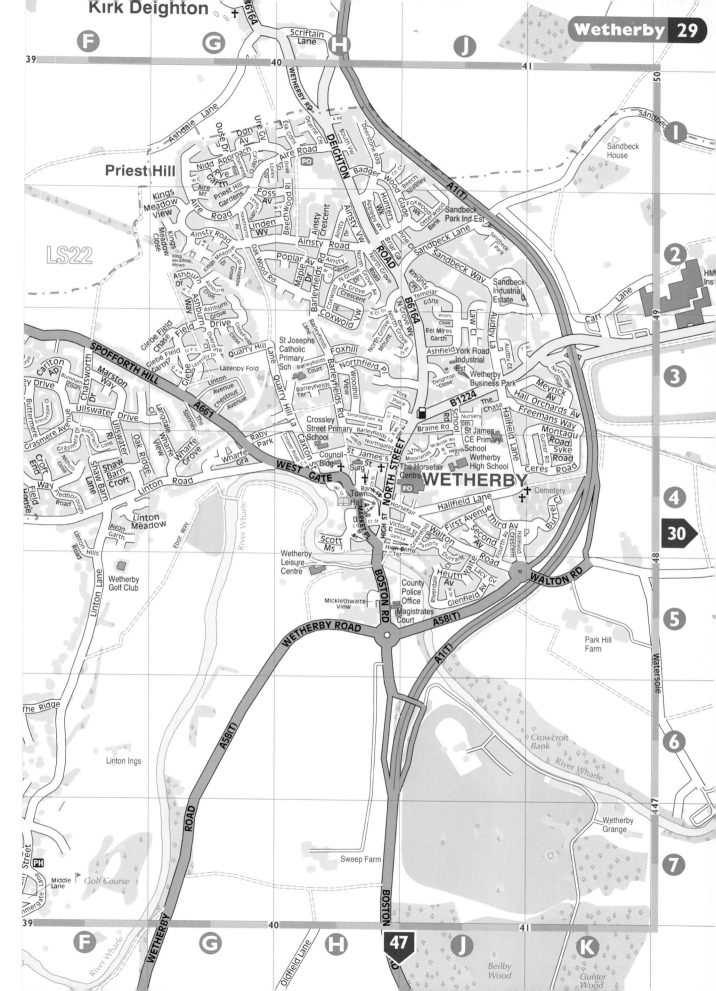

A   442   B   C   43   D   E

50

Ingmanthorpe Park

Sandbeck Lane

1

Sandbeck
House

Moss Carrs
Farm

Swinnow Park

2

HM Young Offender
Institution

YORK ROAD — B1224

Works

49

Springs Lane

3

Wetherby
Racecourse

Sykes House
Farm

Moor Lane

4

Spring Lane

29

48

5

Park Hill
Farm

Walton Road

Watersole

Wetherby   Road

School
Lane

6

Lane

Flint Mill
Grange

Flintmill Lane

Wood Lane

Walton
Chase

447

Wetherby
Grange

Leys Lane

7

Wood Lane

Walton

A   442   B   48   C   43   D   E

Deep Dale

Hall
Wood

Dowkell   Lane

Causeway

I grid square represents 500 metres

B1224 YORK ROAD

F G H J

Wharton
Lodge

Tinkingfield Lane

Tinkingfield La

Bilton
Haggs

North Yorkshire County
Leeds

Rudgate

Featherbed Lane

Syningthwaite
Farm

Hall Parks
Farm

Hall Park Road

Walton
Wood

Wighill
Lodge

Croft
Lane
Street
Main

Walton

Smiday Hill

Inholmes
Lane

Rudgate

Rudgate

Leeds

North Yorkshire County

Vehicle Testing
Centre

Grange
Avenue

Northfields

The British Library
Document Supply Centre

Walton
Lodge

Rudgate
Park

Thorp Arch
Trading
Estate

Avenue A

Road

Street 7

Wighill Lane

HM Prison

Street 5

Av C East

Street

Avenue G

Avenue C West

Street 7

Street F

F G H **49** J K

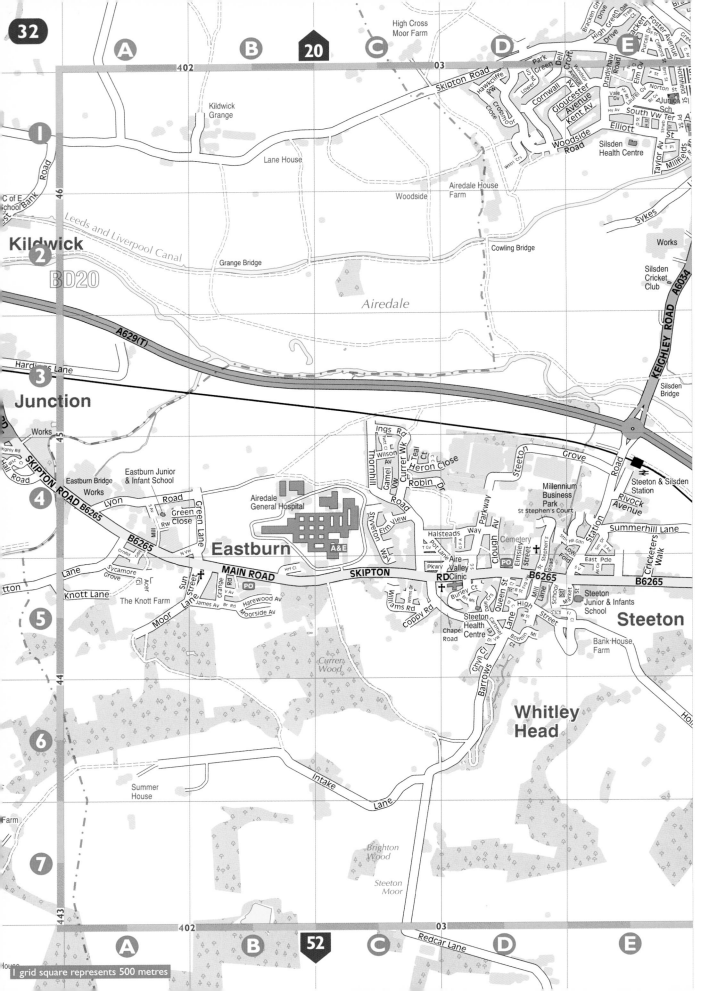

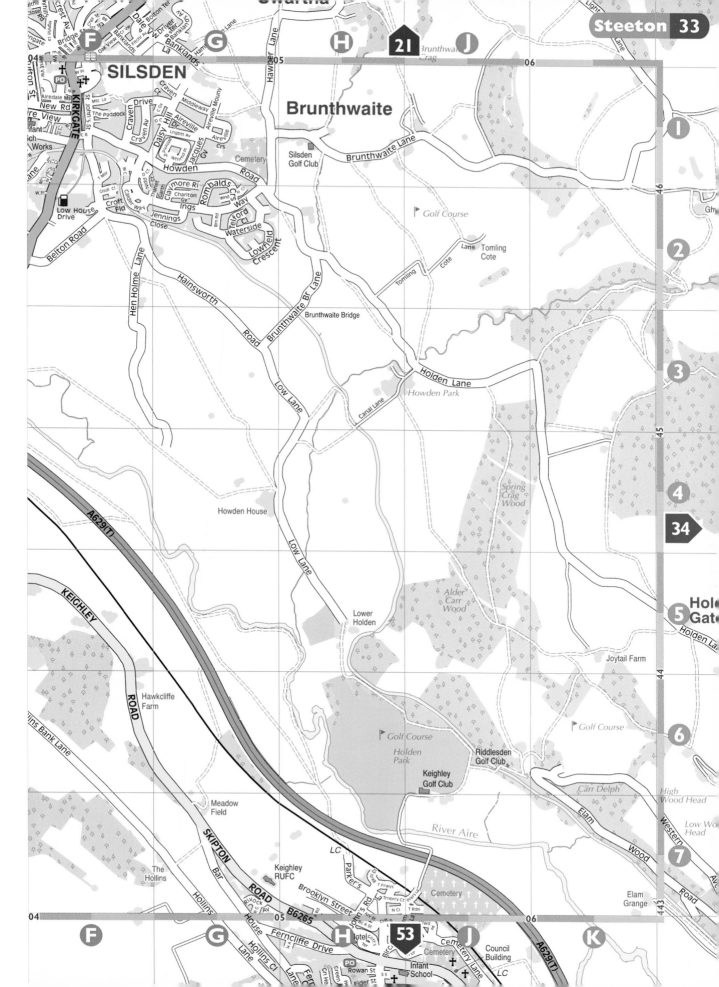

SILSDEN

Brunthwaite

Silsden Golf Club

Cemetery

Golf Course

Tomling Cote

Tomling

Brunthwaite Lane

Brunthwaite Crag

Brunthwaite Br Lane

Brunthwaite Bridge

Holden Lane

Howden Park

Canal Lane

Howden House

Spring Crag Wood

Lower Holden

Alder Carr Wood

Holden Gate

Holden Lane

Joytail Farm

Hen Holme Lane

Hainsworth Road

Low Lane

KEIGHLEY ROAD

Hawkcliffe Farm

Hollins Bank Lane

Golf Course

Holden Park

Riddlesden Golf Club

Golf Course

Keighley Golf Club

Carr Delph

High Wood Head

Low Wood Head

Elam Wood

Western Road

A629(T)

Meadow Field

SKIPTON ROAD B6265

Hollins Bar

The Hollins

Keighley RUFC

Brooklyn Street

Parker's

River Aire

LC

Ferncliffe Drive

Rowan St

Infant School

Cemetery

Cemetery Lane

Council Building

Elam Grange

LC

A629(T)

Craven Drive

Craven Av

Daisy Hill

Aireville

Middleway

Areville Mount

Howden

Claymore Ri

Rombalds

Charlton

Telford Cl

Way

Ings

Jennings Close

Waterside

Lowfield Crescent

Croft Fld

Calder Way

Low House Drive

Belton Road

New Rd

KIRKGATE

PO

21

34

53

34

A   B   **22**   C   D   E

407   08   Long Ridge End

1

46

Ghyll Grange

Jerry Lane

Black Pots

2

Rombalds Moor

High Moor

3

45

Rough Holden

Rivock Oven

4

High Bradup

33

Rivock

5

Holden Gate

Brass Castle

Holden Lane

Bradu

Joytail Farm

44

Course

6

Banks Lane

Silsden Road

Delph

High Wood Head

Low Wood Head

Moorcock Farm

Ilkley Road

7

Western

Avenue

Elam Grange

Road

443

407   Malvern Crs   08   **West Morton**

A   B   **54**   C   D   E

Coles Way

Scott

Dunkirk Rise

Slade La

W. Bank Rd Crs

La

W Bn

Ridge

Aire Vw

Bank Top Dr

Ilkley

Barley Cote Rd

Barley Cor

Bank Top Road

W. Bank Rd

1 grid square represents 500 metres

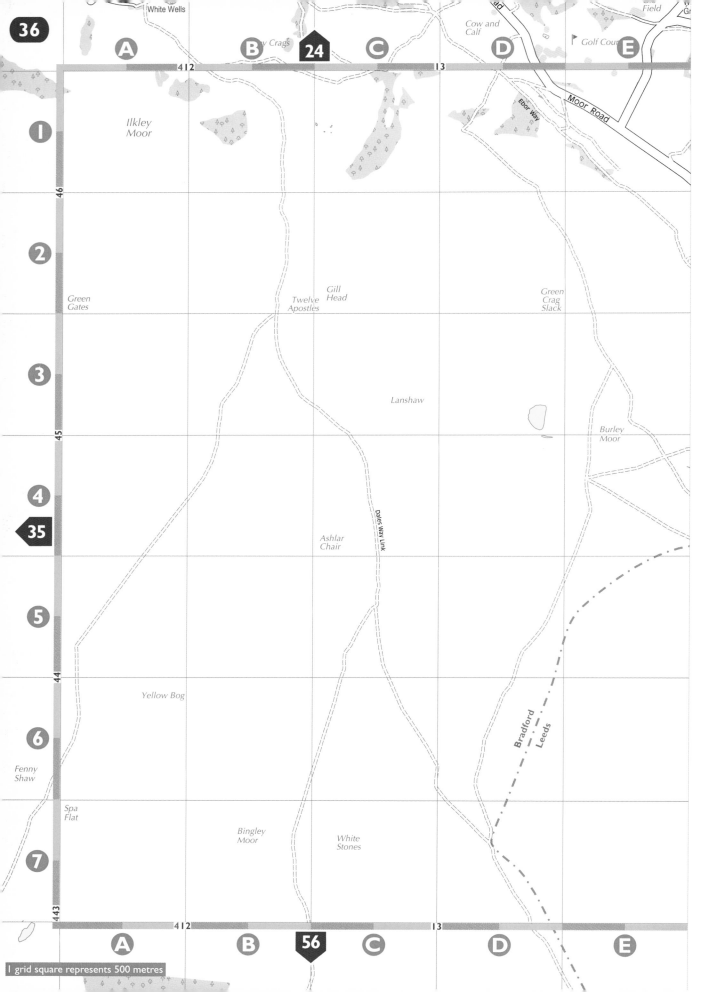

36

A   B   **24**   C   D   E

412   13

White Wells

Cow and
Calf

Golf Cour

Moor Road

Ebor Way

I   46
Ilkley
Moor

2

Green
Gates   Twelve
Apostles   Gill
Head   Green
Crag
Slack

3   45
Lanshaw   Burley
Moor

4

35   Ashlar
Chair   Dales Way Link

5   44

Yellow Bog

6   Bradford
Leeds

Fenny
Shaw

Spa
Flat

Bingley
Moor   White
Stones

7   443

412   13

A   B   **56**   C   D   E

`1 grid square represents 500 metres`

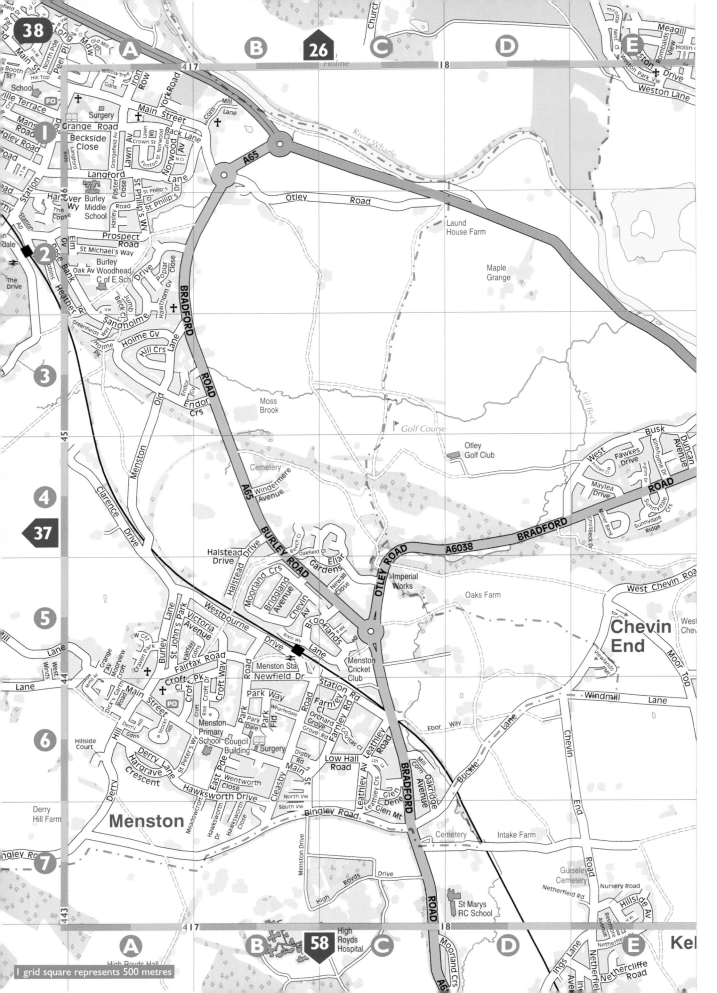

A B C D E

North Yorkshire County
Leeds

1

46

2
Pool Rd
Otley Town FC &
Old Otliensians
RUFC
Busk
Lane
Foulcauseway Lane

Moor Drive

A659
POOL ROAD

B6161

Leathley
Hall

Leathley Bridge

The Golf

Midgley Farm

3

45

Stubbings Farm

Caley Hall
Farm

4
A660(T)

The
Deals

39

Chevin
Forest Park

Ebor
Way
Way
Dales
Link

Leeds ROAD
Caley Crags

Quarry Road
Park Ter
Park Mt

Old

Cabi

5
East Chevin Road

44

Link

Way

Dales
Fells
Plantation

Quarry Farm Road

Old Pool Bank

6
ate

East
Chevin Farm
Bramhope Old Lane

A658
POOL
BANK

Hilton
Court
Dales
Way

Carlton Lane

H M
Old Lane
Hilton
Grange

Old Bramhop

7

443

†
East
Carlton

Occupation

Carlton
Manor

A B **60** C ROAD D 23 E

422 60 422

Brewery Farm

I grid square represents 500 metres

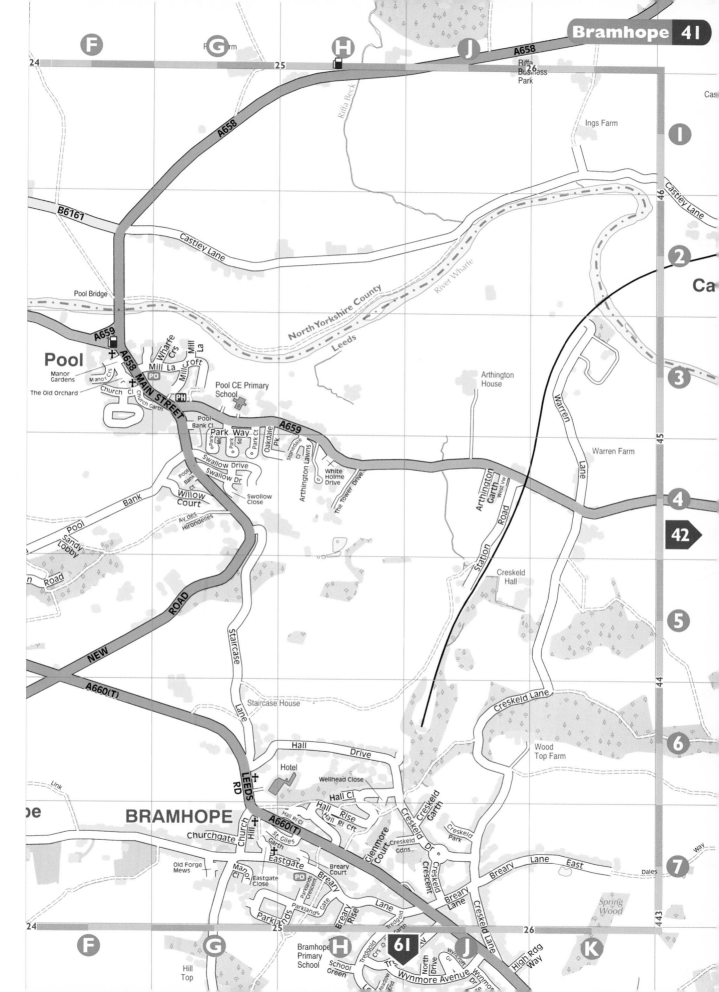

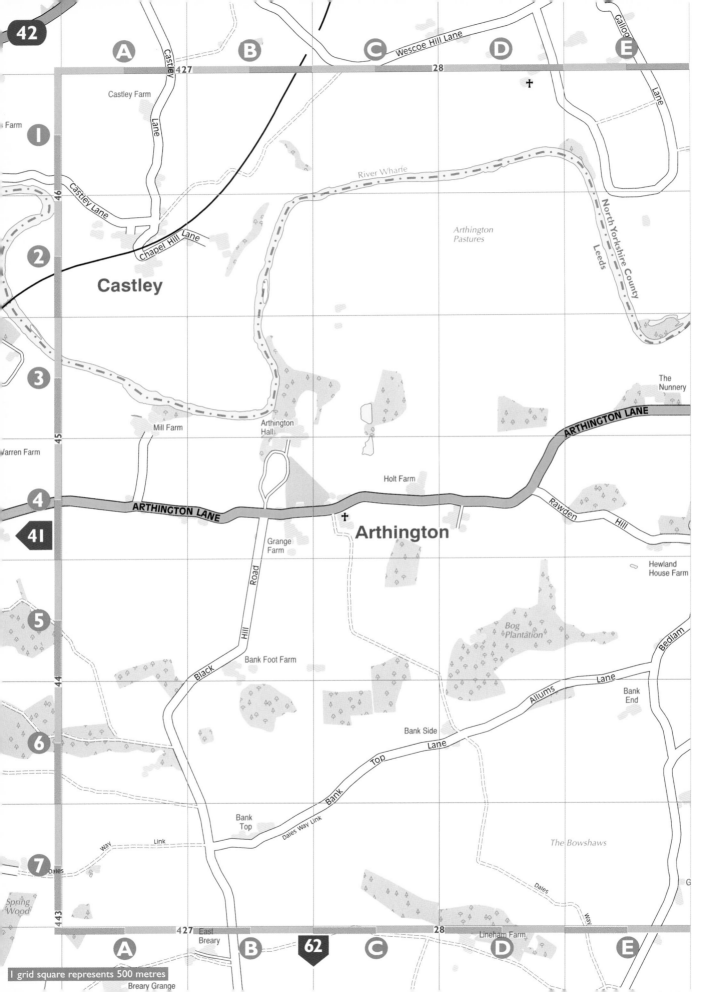

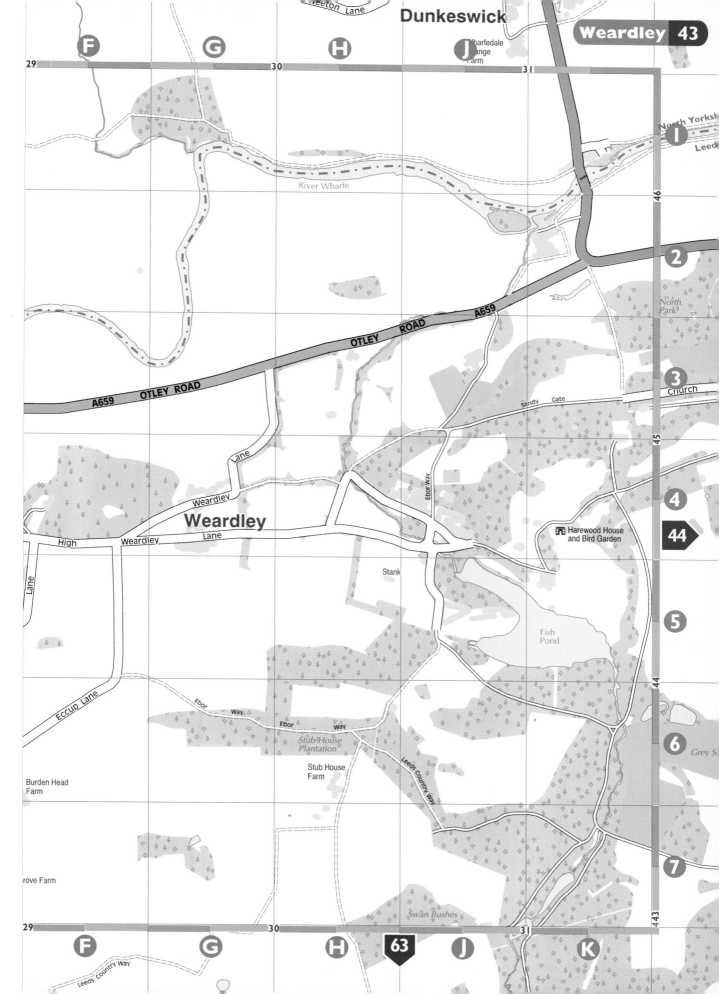

Chapel Hill

Carlshead House

Carlstonhill Farm

Paddock House

Carthick Wood

Pasture Lane

River Wharfe

North Yorkshire County

Leeds

Ebor Way

Middlefield Farm

Farfield Farm

HAREWOOD ROAD

A659

Crabtree Lane

Field House

Cleavesty Lane

Allerton Drive

Vicarage Farm

Lumby Lane

Rose Croft

South Mount

Whitegate

South Bank

East Kes 46

Moor Lane

The Grove

PO

The Close

The Paddock

Main St

A M

Meadow Cft

Church Drive

St Mary's Garth

Paddock Gn

School Lane

Laurel Close

Keswick Gra

Burn's Farm

Keswick Lane

Woodacre Green

Bankfield

Gateon House Farm

Gateon House Lane

Rigton Grange

Rigton Grange

Bardsey Primary School

Woodacre Lane

Bardsey

Grange

Cornmill Close

Cas C

Rigton Carr Farm

Leeds Country Way

Woodacre Crescent

Gle Gv

Biggin Farm

Bingley Bank

Smithy Lan

Leeds Country

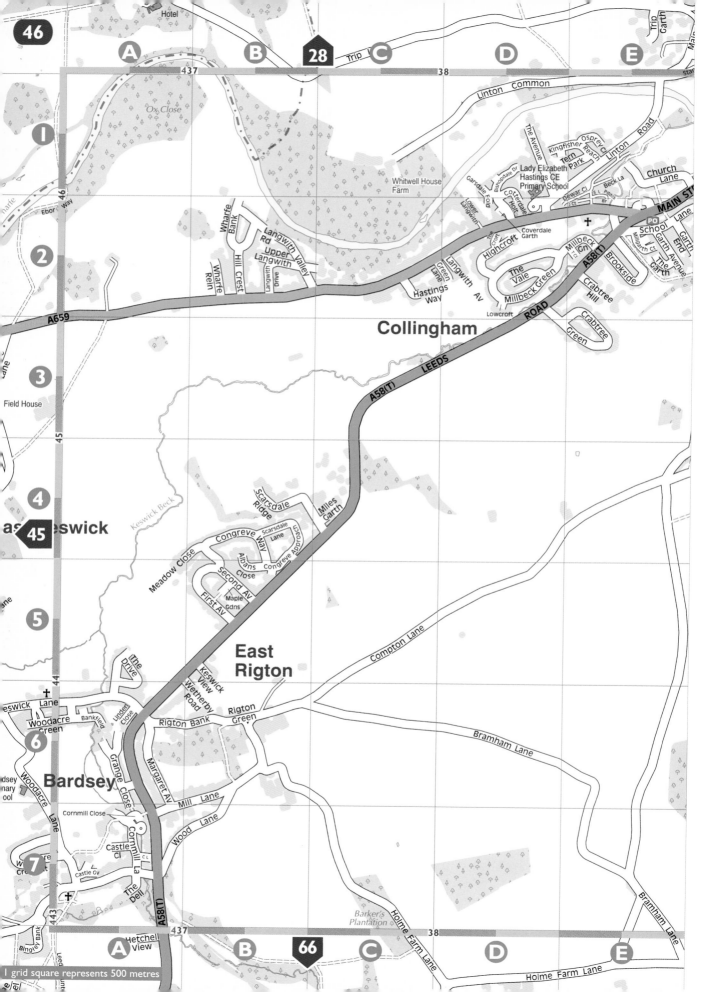

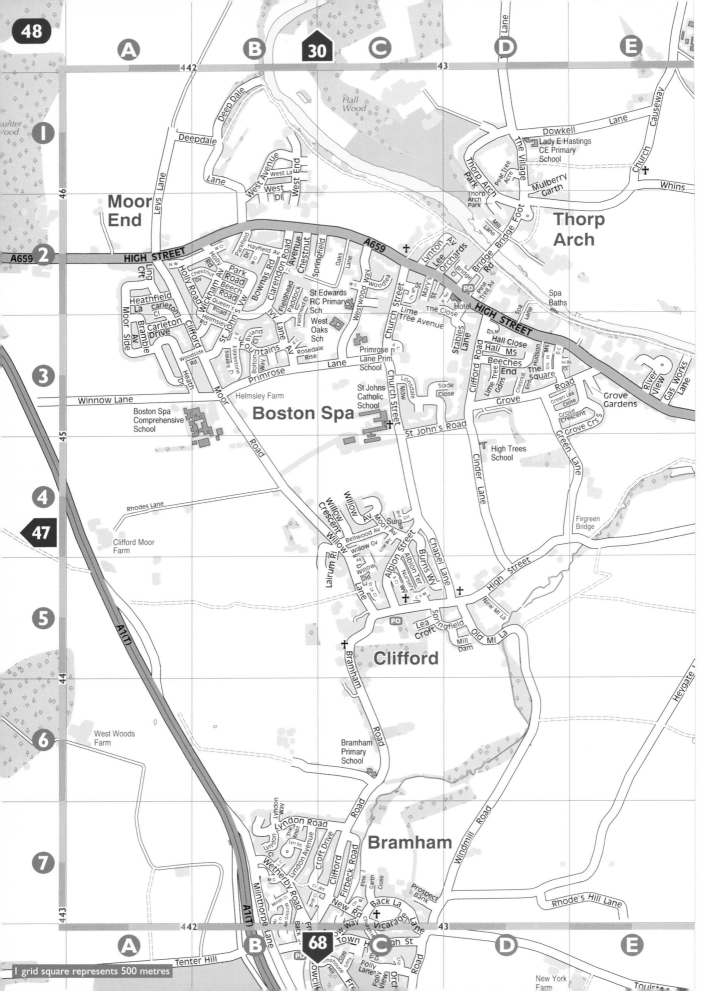

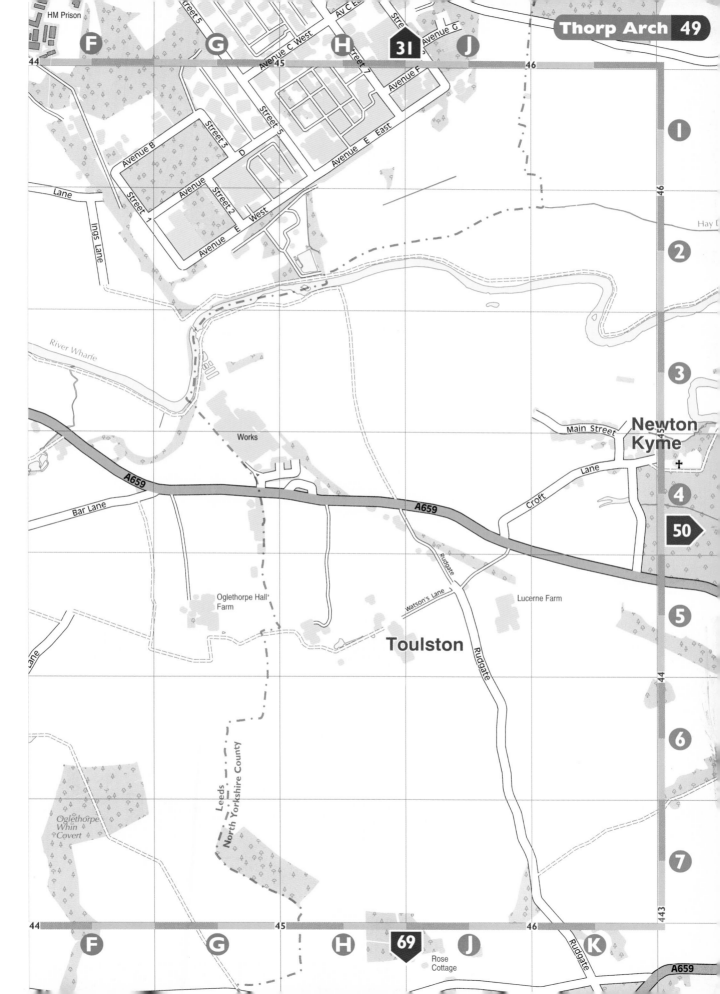

HM Prison

F **G** **H** **31** **J**

44 Avenue C West 45 Avenue F 46

Avenue G

Street 7

Stre

Av C Ea

I

46

Hay

2

Avenue B

Street 3

Street 5

Avenue

D

Avenue E East

Street 1

Avenue

Street 2

Avenue E West

Lane

Ings Lane

3

River Wharfe

Main street

Newton
Kyme

Works

Lane

Croft

4

A659

A659

50

Bar Lane

Rudgate

Lucerne Farm

5

Oglethorpe Hall
Farm

Watson's Lane

44

Lane

Rudgate

Toulston

6

Leeds

North Yorkshire County

Oglethorpe
Whin
Covert

7

443

F **G** **H** **69** **J** **K**

44 45 46

Rose
Cottage

Rudgate

A659

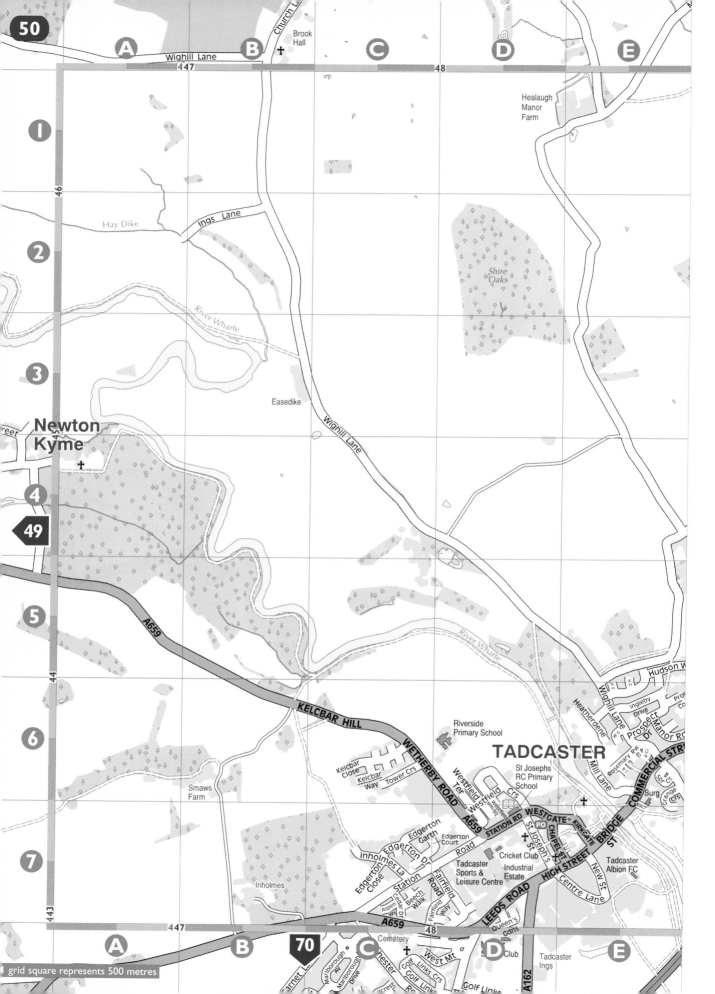

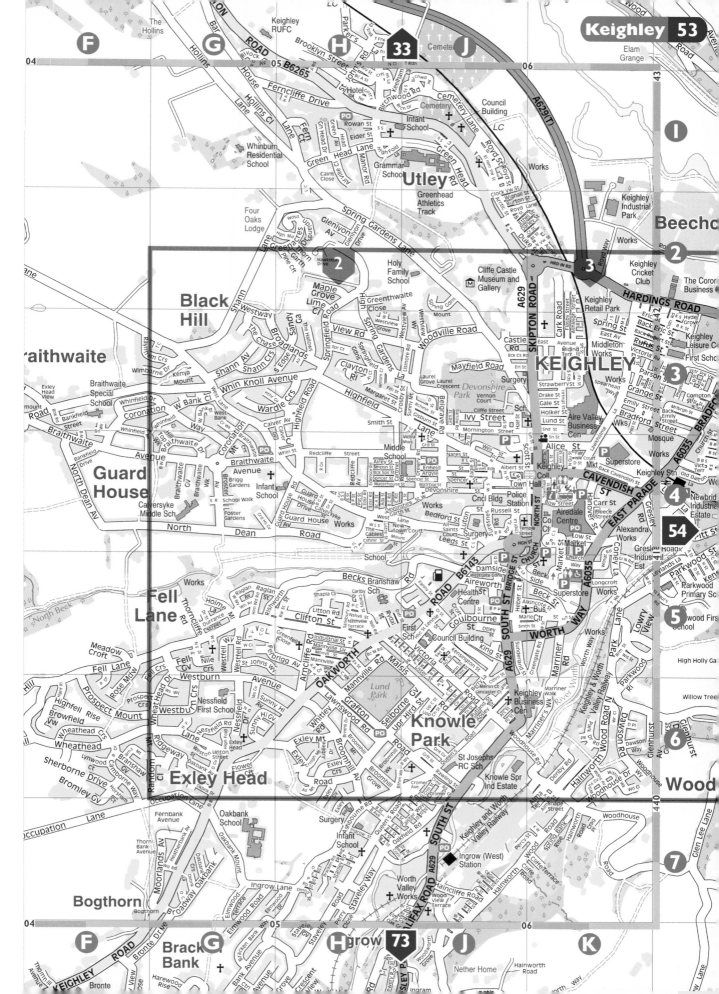

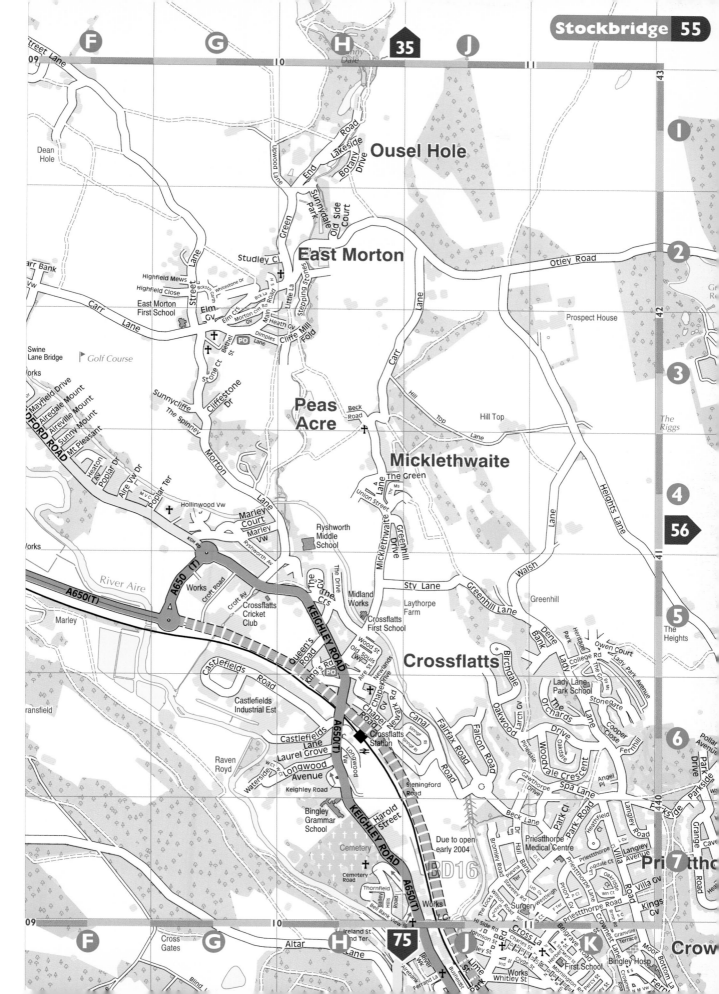

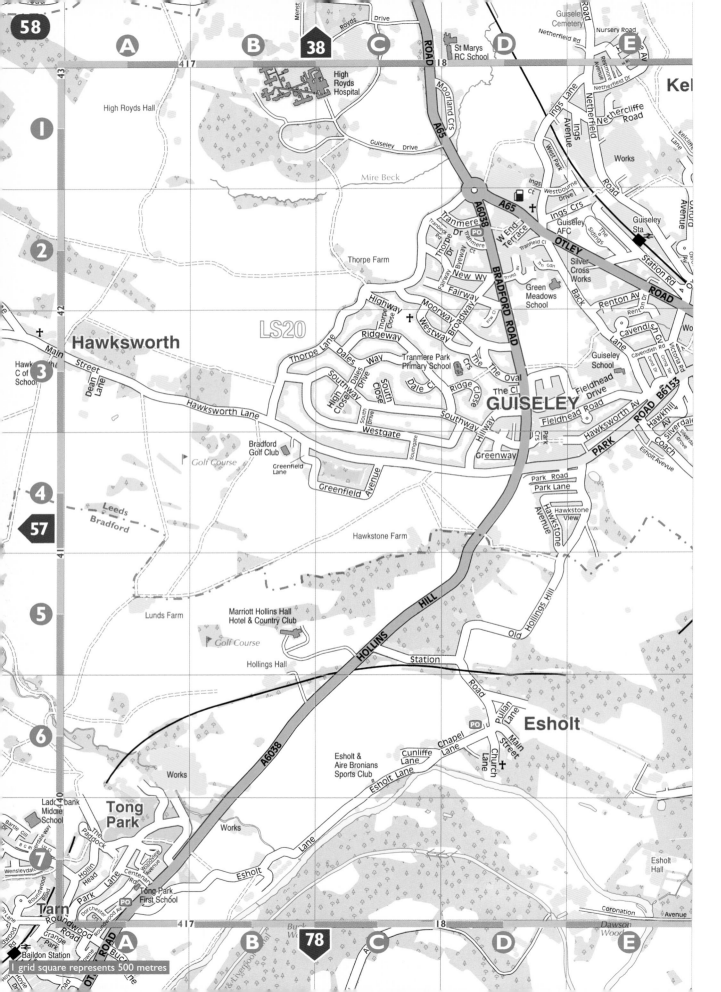

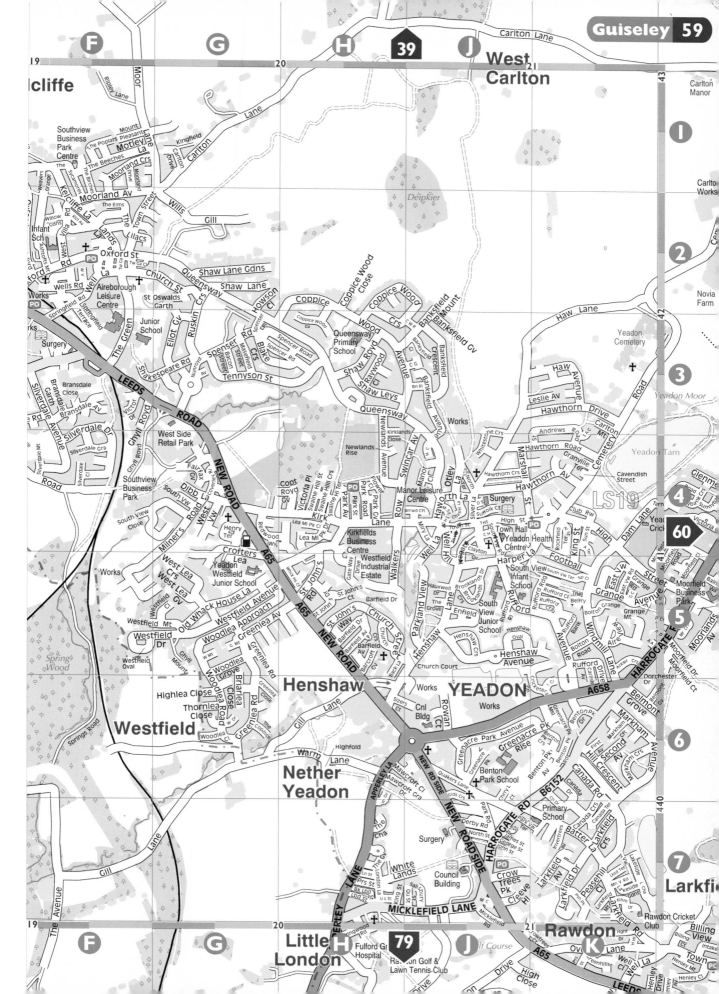

Woodacre Crescent

Leeds Country Way

F   G   Rigton Carr Farm   H   45   J

34   35   36   43

Biggin Farm

Smithy Lane

The Ginnel

Bingley Bank

Tithe Barn Lane

Blackmoor Lane

Wike Whin

Gill Beck

Spear Fir

Gill Lane

ckstone

Wayside Gardens

Wayside Crescent

Wayside Mt

Wayside Av

I

Sheepcote Farm

Glenfield Caravan Park

Moor Lodge Park

The Village Golf Course

Scarcroft

2

Moss Syke

Malthouse Close

Green Vw

North Hill

The Croft

Scarcroft Co

PO

Golf Course

Scarcroft Golf Club

Green WN Syke Gn

Woodlands Park

Woodlands Close

Stonefield

3

Golf Course

Coal Road

Moor Allerton Golf Club

Syke Lane

Bracken Park

Fern Way

Fern Croft

Fern Chase

The Glade

Heather Vale

The Firs

Heather Gardens

Larch Wood

Bracken Park

Ling Lane

Ling Lane

Manor Pk

Hellwood

4

66

Tarn Lane

Brandon Crescent

Brandon Lane

Bay Horse Lane

Manor Cottage Mews

41

Brandon Lodge

5

Brandon Crescent

Beech Grove

A58(T)

6

Eltofts

dle Path Road

Stoney Lane

LEEDS ROAD

440

Avon Court

Cricketers Fold

C Vw

Old Brandon Lane

Old Brandon La

Ash Hill Drive

Ludolf Dr

Ash Hill Lane

Strickland Av

Strickland Cl

Strickland Grs

Crofton Ter

Crofton Rise

Bay

Carr Lane

Carr La

Carr

7

Shadwell

Main Street

Gateland Dr

Colliers Lane

Blind Lane

Churchfarm Garth

Ash Hill Gardens

Avon Close

Manor court

Hastings Ct

Shadwell Primary School

Main Street

Crofton

Coal Rd

WETHERBY ROAD A58(T)

Birkby Grange

F   G   Charville Gdns   H   85   J   K

34   35   Hobbe   36

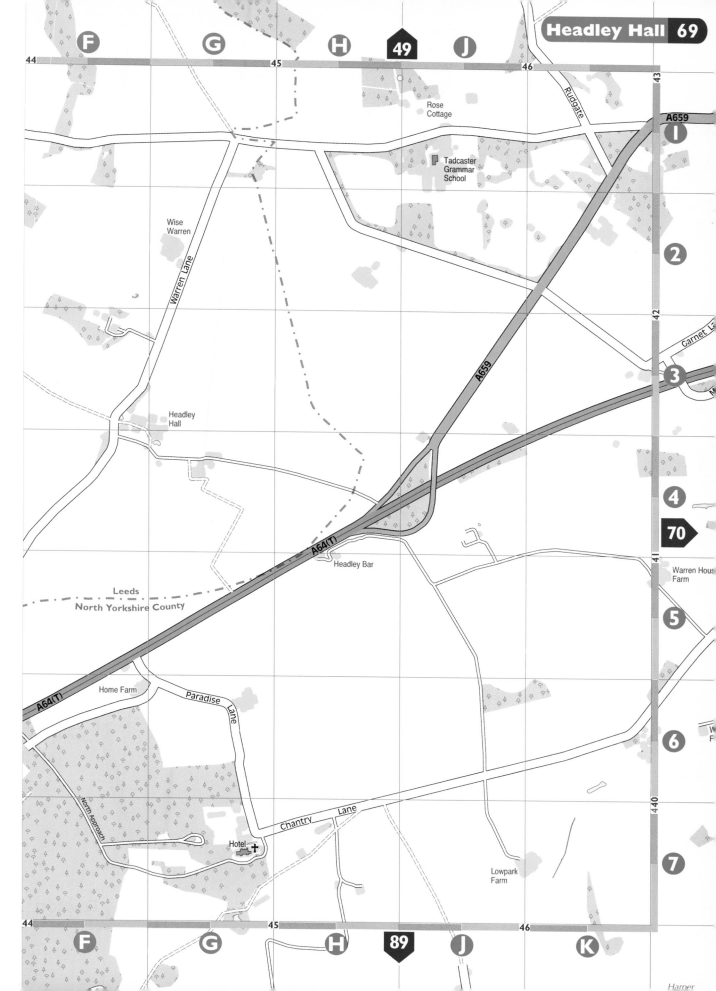

F G H 49 J

44 45 46 43

A659

Rudgate

Rose
Cottage

Tadcaster
Grammar
School

I

2

Wise
Warren

42

Garnet L

A659

3

Warren Lane

Headley
Hall

4

70

A64(T)

41

Warren Hous
Farm

Headley Bar

Leeds
North Yorkshire County

5

6

Home Farm

Paradise Lane

A64(T)

440

North Approach

Chantry Lane

7

Hotel

Lowpark
Farm

44 45 46

F G H 89 J K

Harper

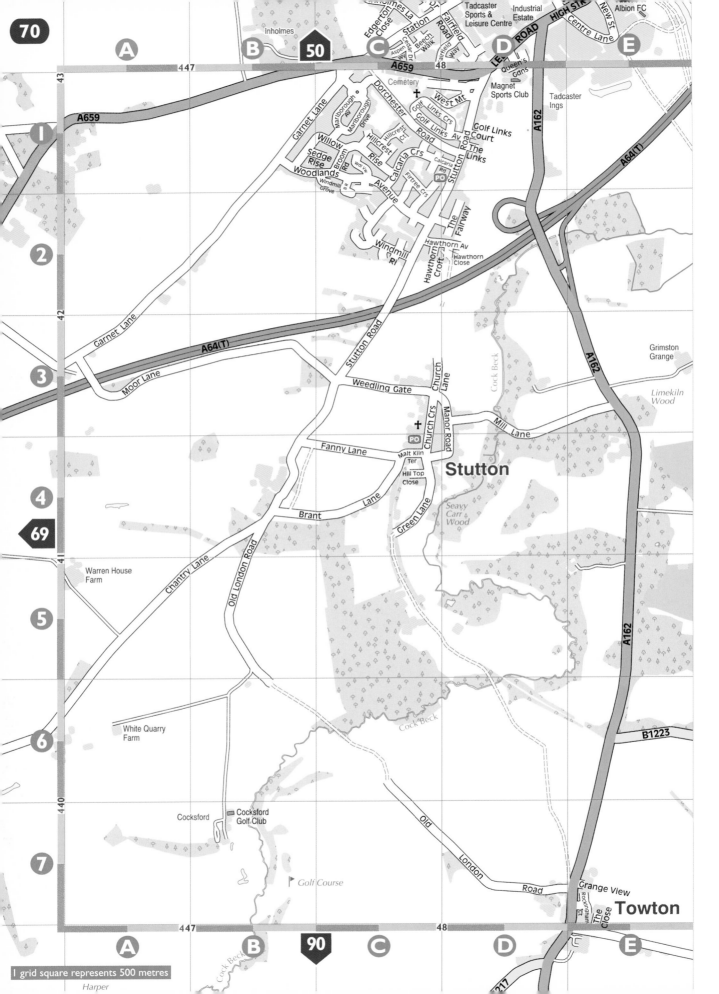

A **B** **50** **C** **D** **E**

I grid square represents 500 metres

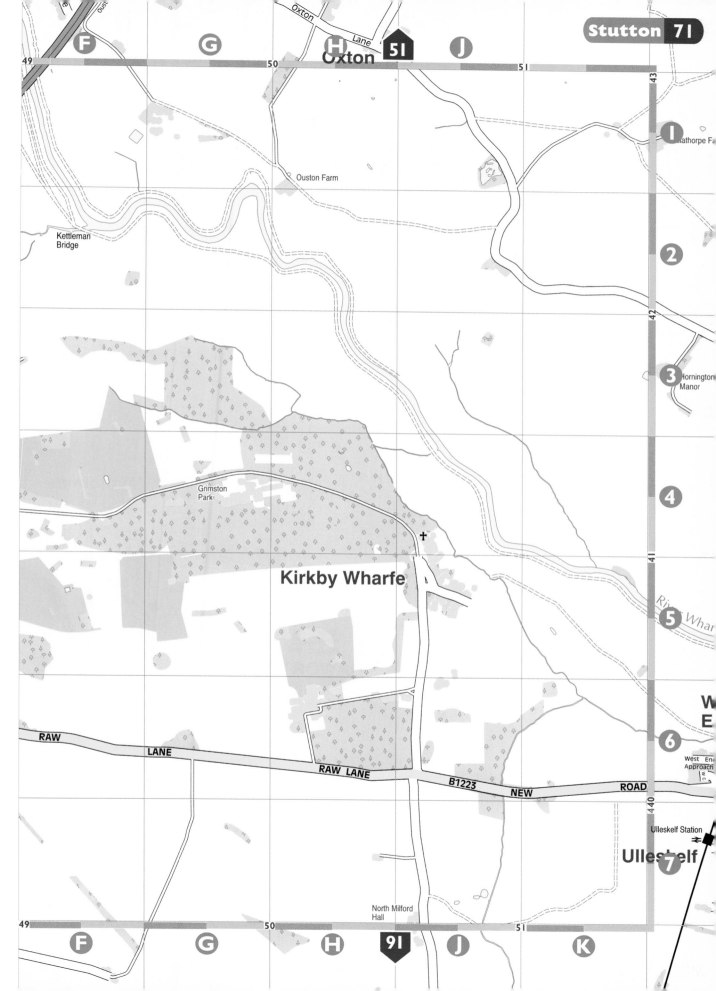

F
G
H
J

51

Oxton
Oxton Lane

49
50
51

43

I
Mathorpe Fa

Ouston Farm

2

Kettleman
Bridge

42

3
Hornington
Manor

Grimston
Park

4

41

Kirkby Wharfe

River Wharfe

5

W
E

6

West End
Approach

RAW
LANE

RAW LANE
B1223
NEW
ROAD

1440

Ulleskelf Station

Ulleskelf

7

North Milford
Hall

49
50
51

F
G
H
9I
J
K

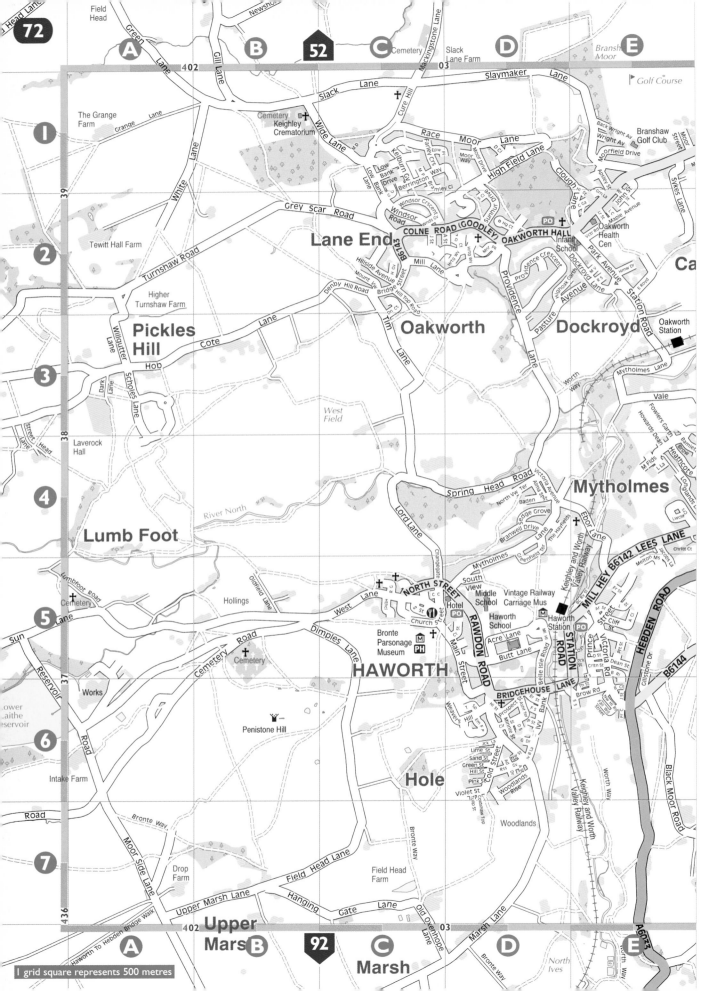

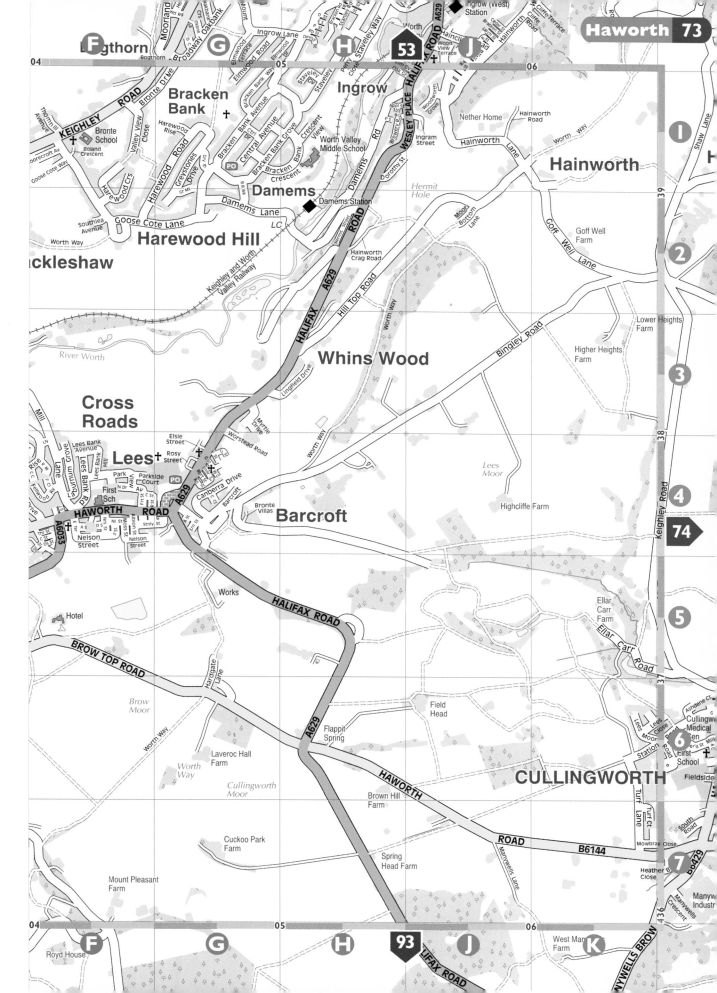

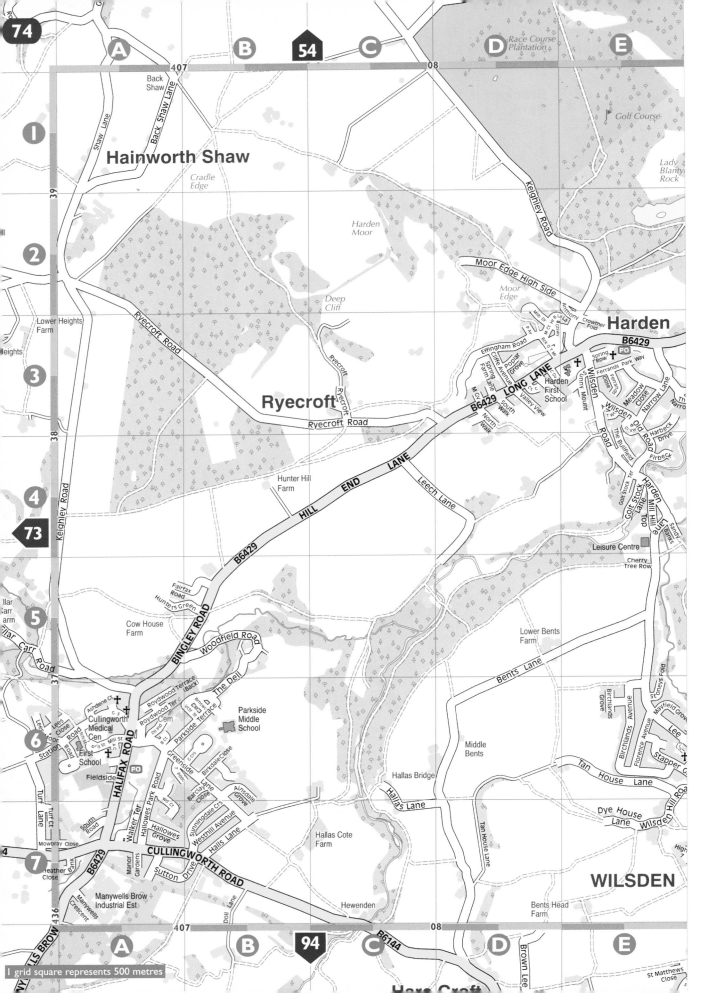

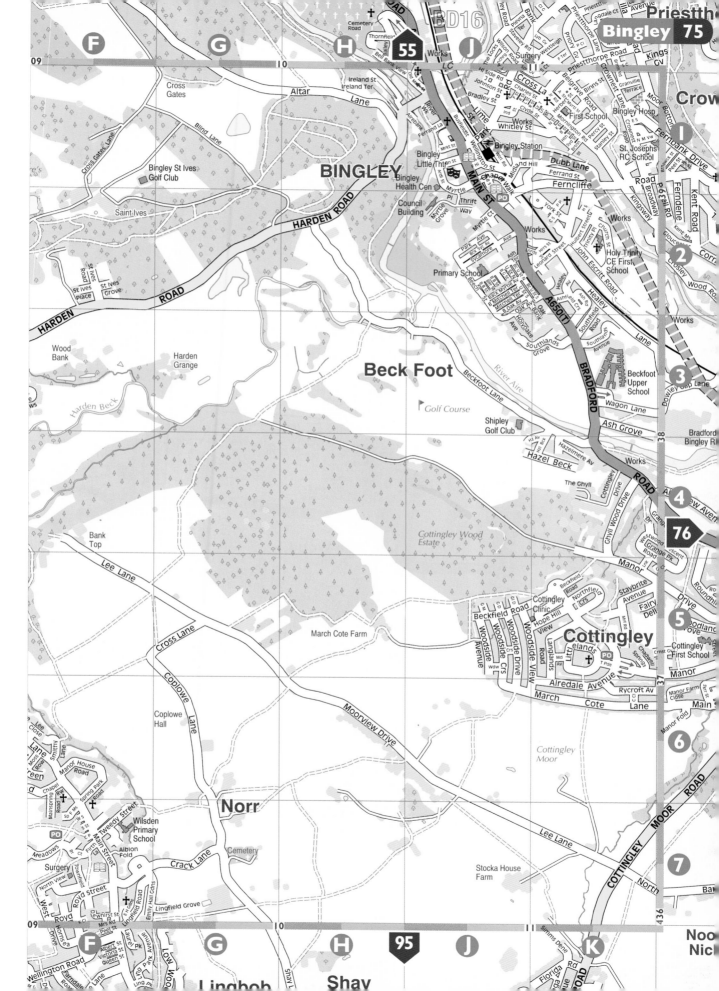

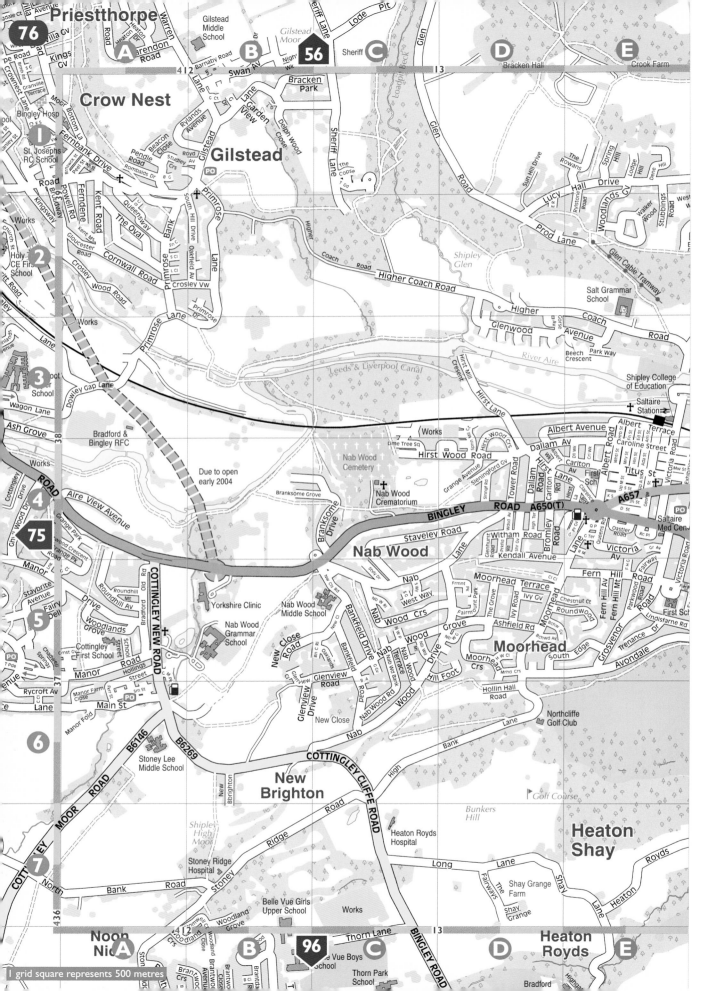

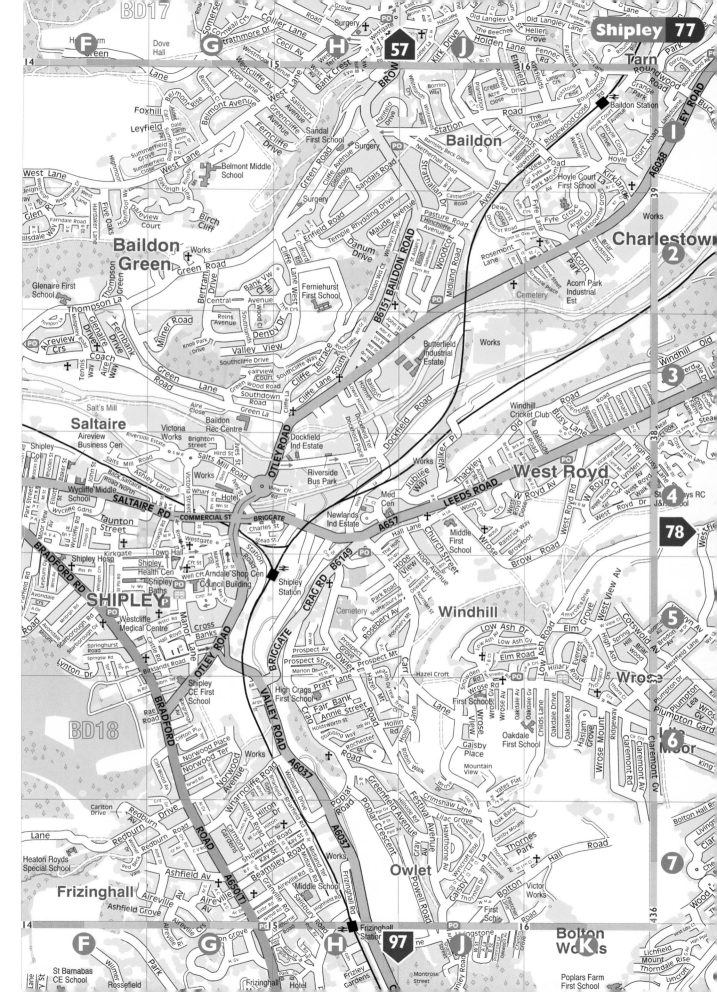

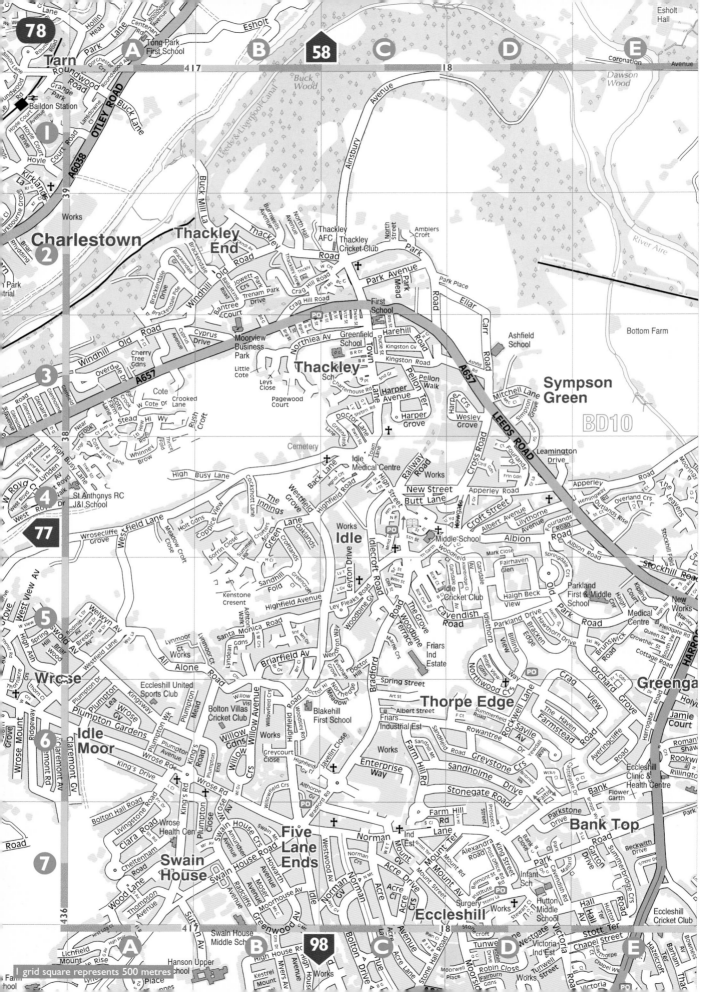

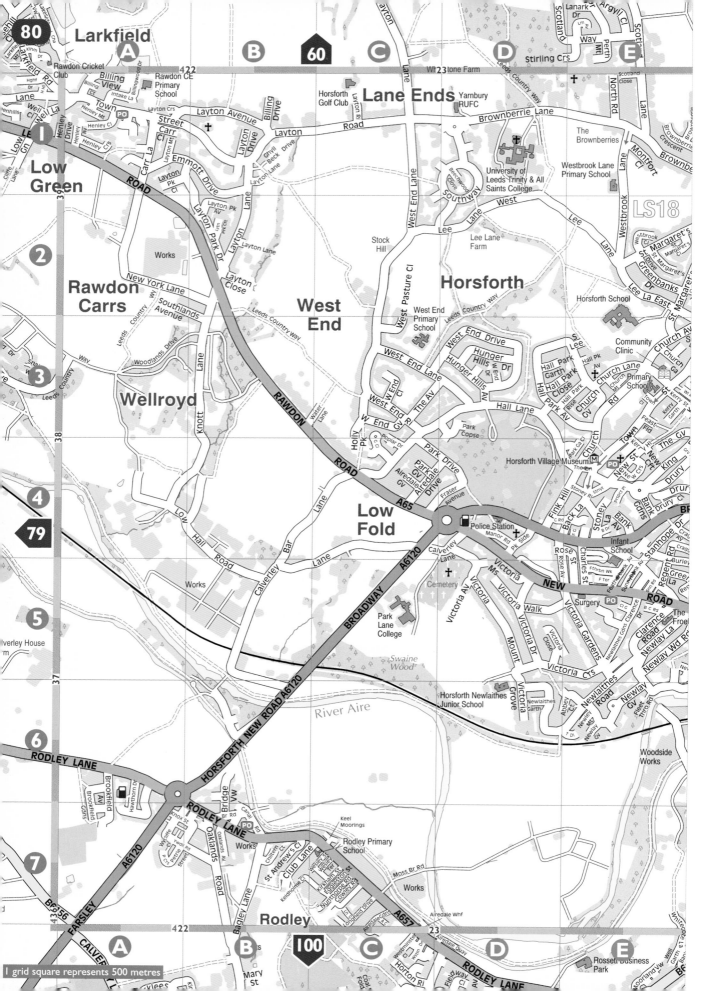

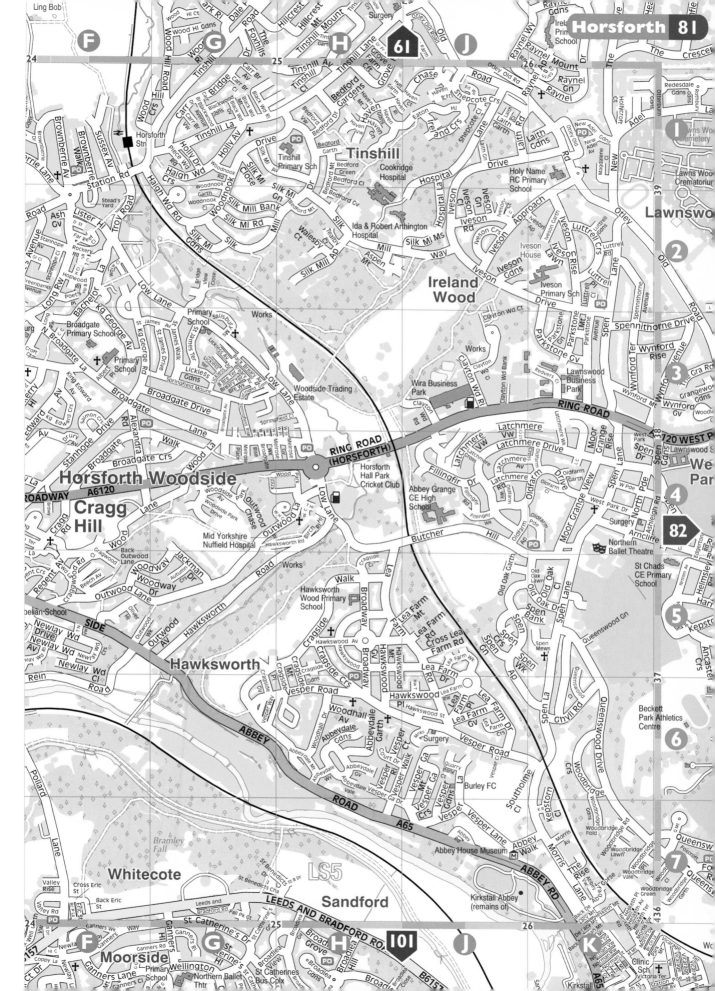

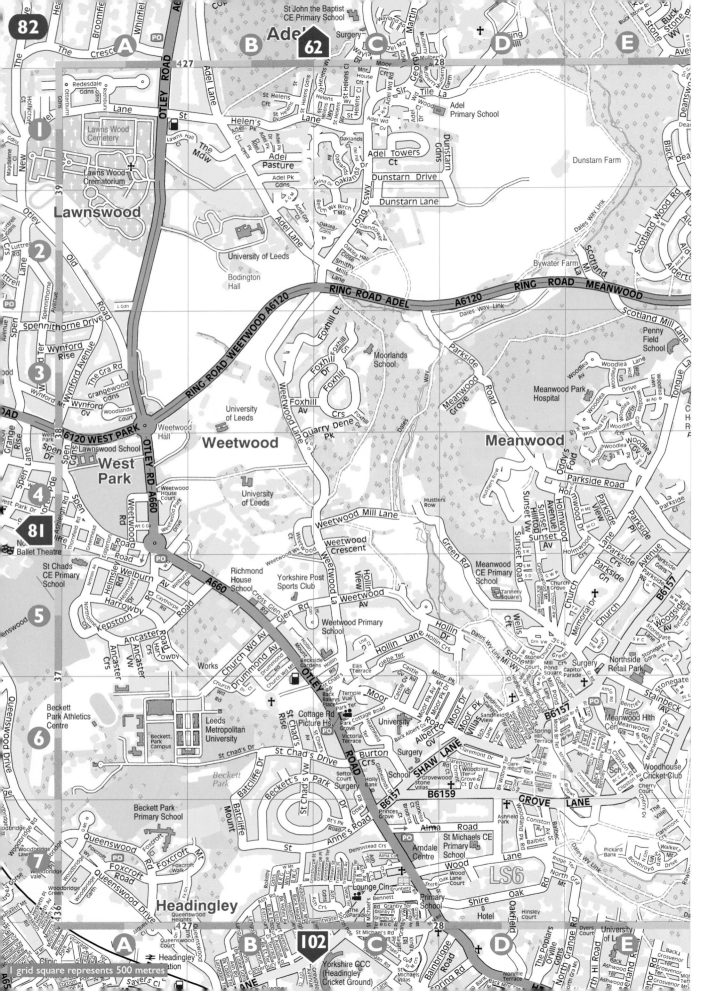

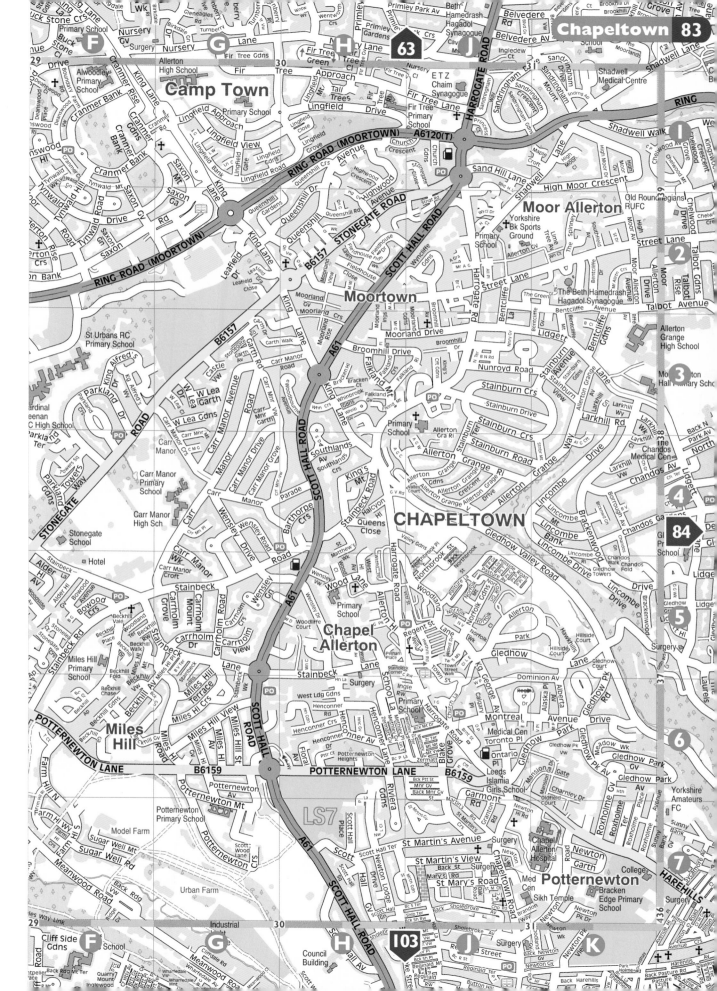

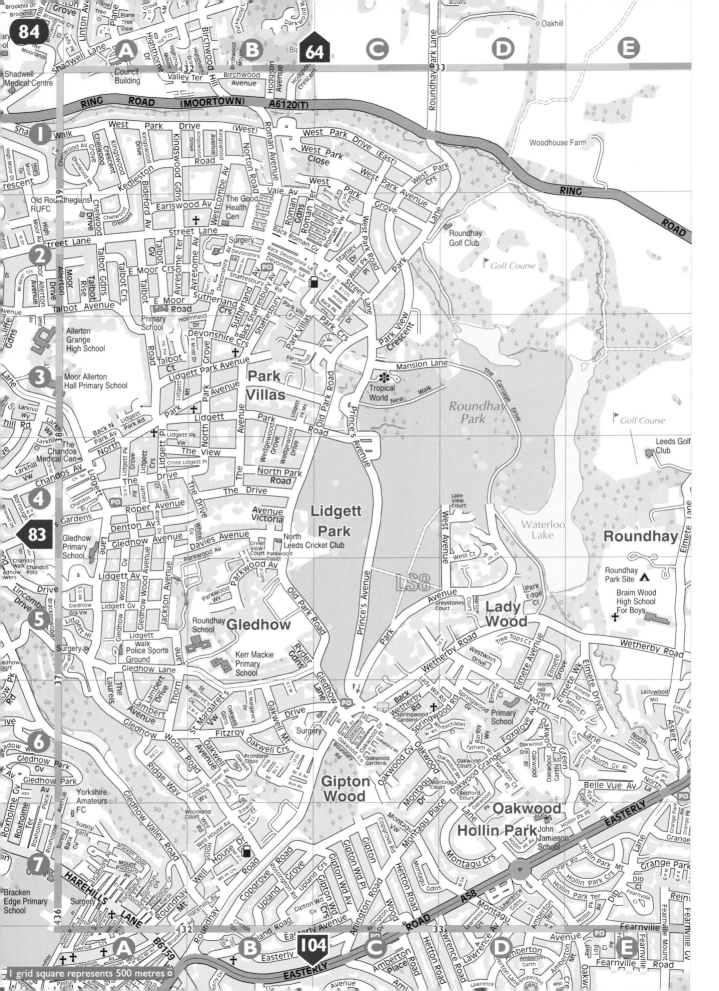

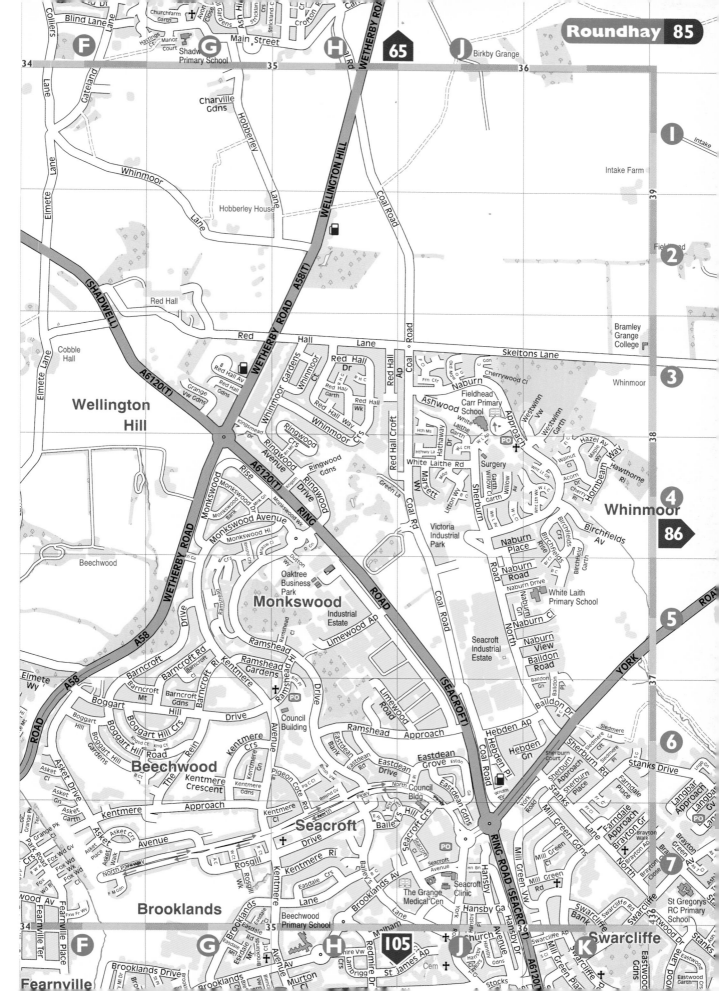

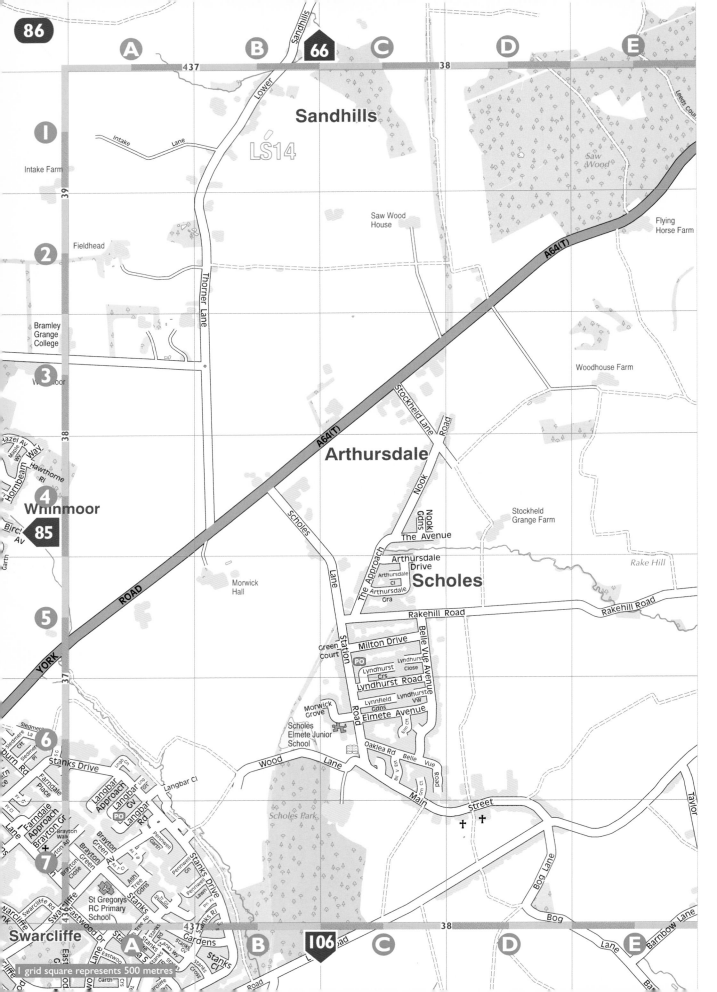

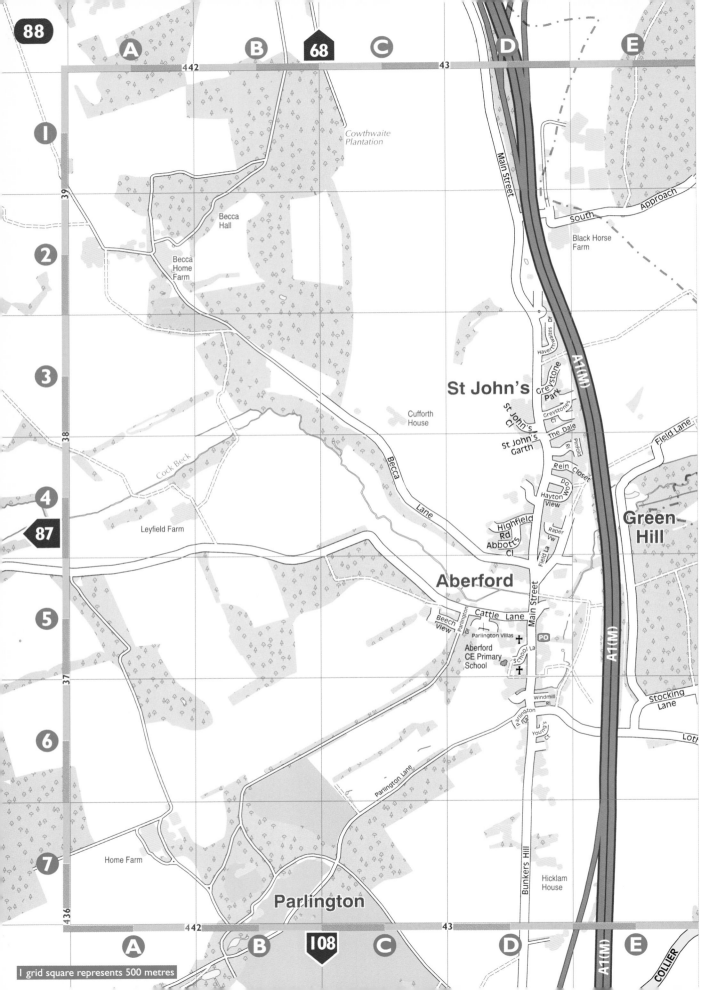

A B 68 C D E

1
39
2
3
38
4
87
5
37
6
7
436

442 43

Cowthwaite
Plantation

Becca
Hall

Becca
Home
Farm

Cock Beck

Leyfield Farm

Cufforth
House

Becca
Lane

St John's
St John's Ct
Park
Greystone
Greystones
Cl
St John's
Garth
The Dale
Pinfold
Rein Closet
DOW
Hayton
View
Highfield
Rd
Abbotts
Cl
Raper
VW
Field La

Aberford

Green
Hill

Field Lane

Main Street

A1(M)

Haverthwaites Dr

South
Approach

Black Horse
Farm

Main Street

Beech
View
Parlington
Dr
Cattle Lane
Parlington Villas
Aberford
CE Primary
School
School La
PO

Windmill
Rl
Parlington
Young's
Ct

Stocking
Lane

Loth

Parlington Lane

Home Farm

Parlington

Bunkers Hill

Hicklam
House

A1(M)

A B 108 C D E

442 43

COLLIER

A1(M)

Lowpark
Farm

F
G
H
69
J

44
45
46

I
per
Nash

South Approach

39

Lodge
Farm

2

Hayton
Wood

3

Bullen
Wood

Newstead
Farm

38

Hayton House

Cock Beck

4

90

North Yorkshire County

Leeds

Woodhouse
Grange

The
Rein

5

Stocking Lane

Lead Hall
Farm

37

†

herton Lane

B1217

6

LOTHERTON
LANE

Lotherton
Lane

B1217

Copley Lane

7

LANE

436

† Lotherton
Hall

44
45
46

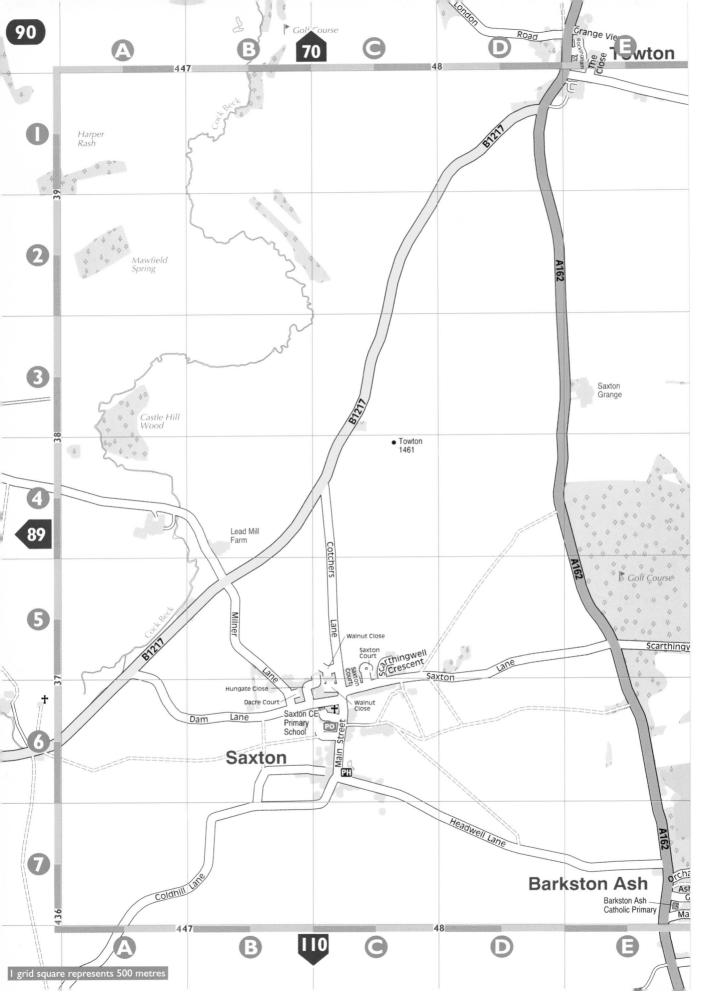

Ⓐ Ⓑ **70** Ⓒ Ⓓ Ⓔ

447 48

▶ *Golf Course*

London Road

Grange View

Rockingham

The Close

Towton

Ⅰ *Harper Rash*

Cock Beck

B1217

A162

Ⅱ *Mawfield Spring*

Ⅲ *Castle Hill Wood*

Saxton Grange

● Towton 1461

Ⓐ **89**

Lead Mill Farm

Cotchers Lane

A162

▶ *Golf Course*

Cock Beck

B1217

Milner Lane

Walnut Close

Saxton Court

Saxton Court

Scarthingwell Crescent

Scarthingwell

Saxton Lane

Ⓐ Hungate Close

Dacre Court

Walnut Close

Dam Lane

Saxton CE Primary School

PO

✝

Saxton

Main Street

PH

Headwell Lane

Orcha

Barkston Ash

Ash

Barkston Ash Catholic Primary

Ma

A162

Ⓐ Coldhill Lane

✝

37

436

38

39

Ⓐ Ⓑ **110** Ⓒ Ⓓ Ⓔ

447 48

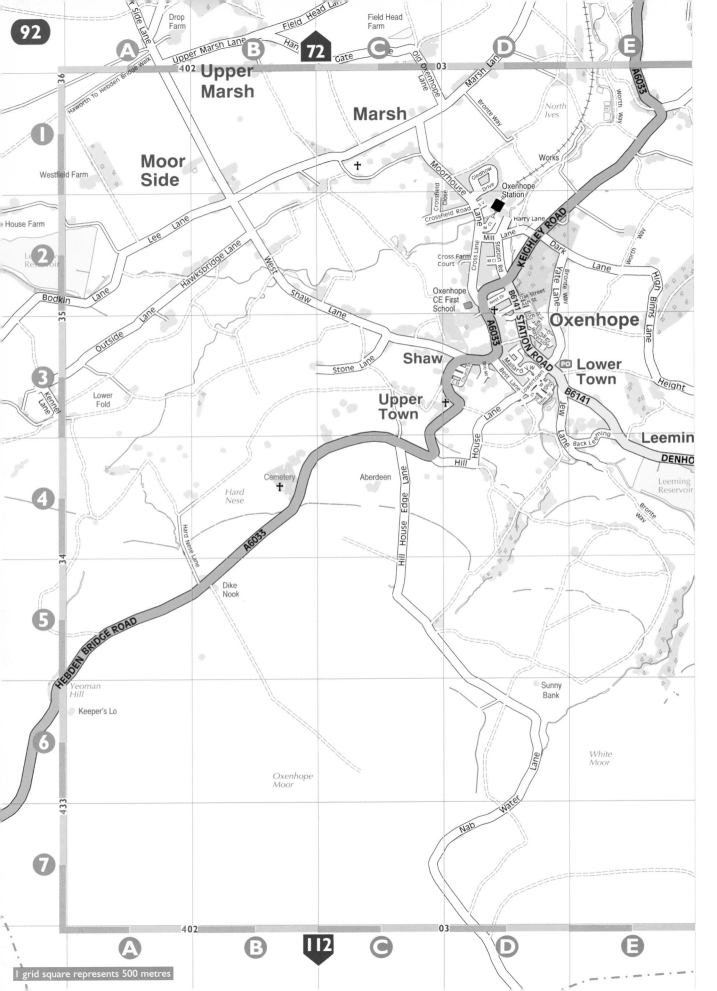

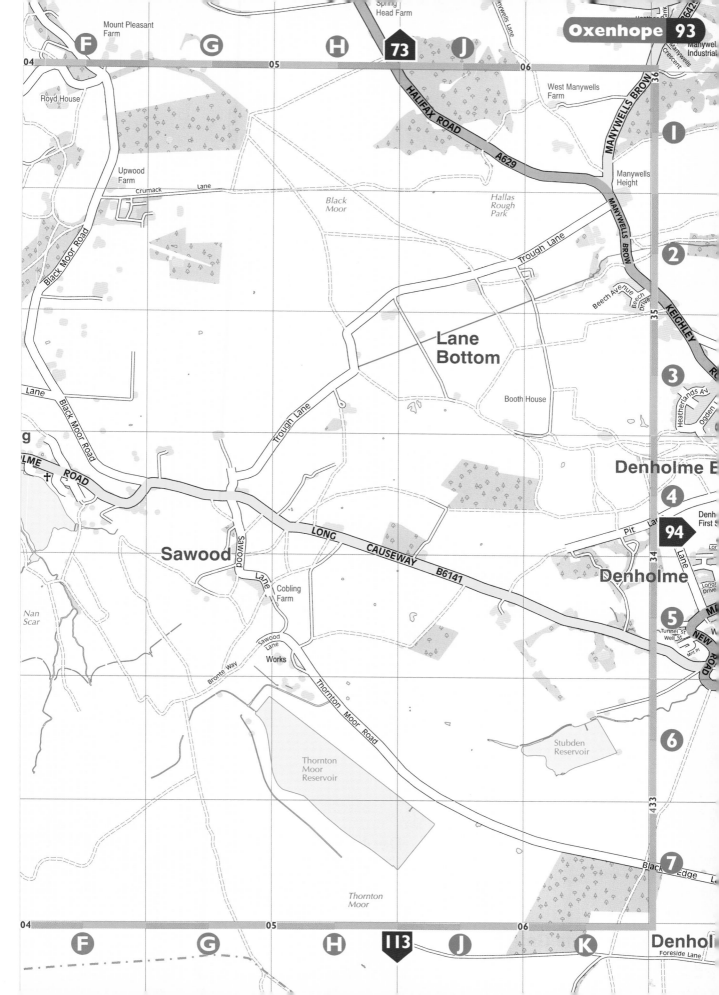

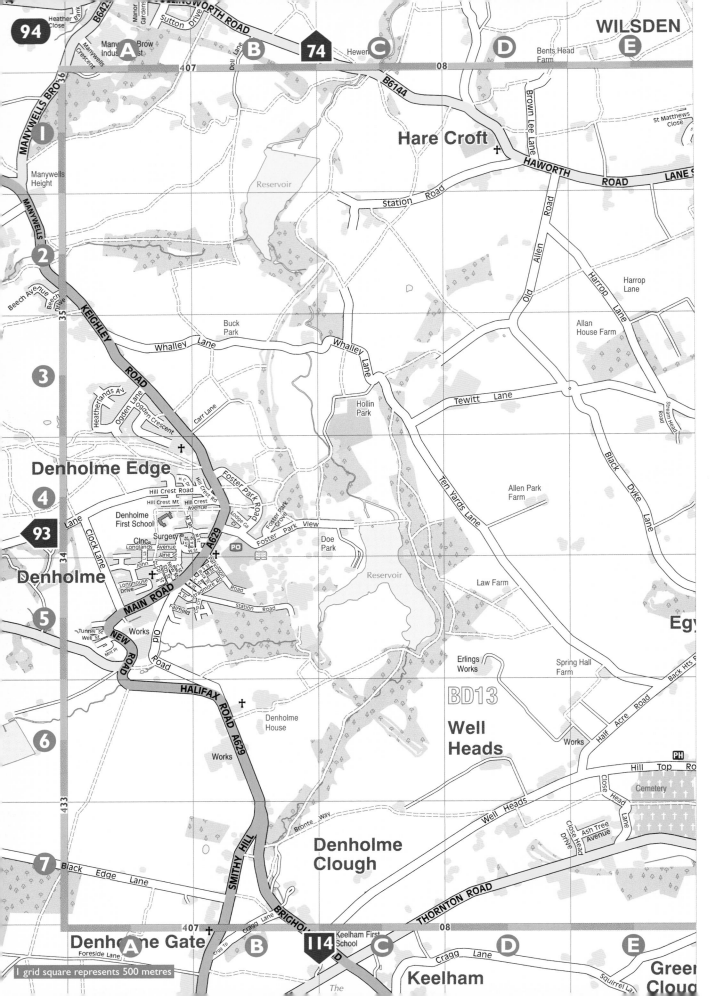

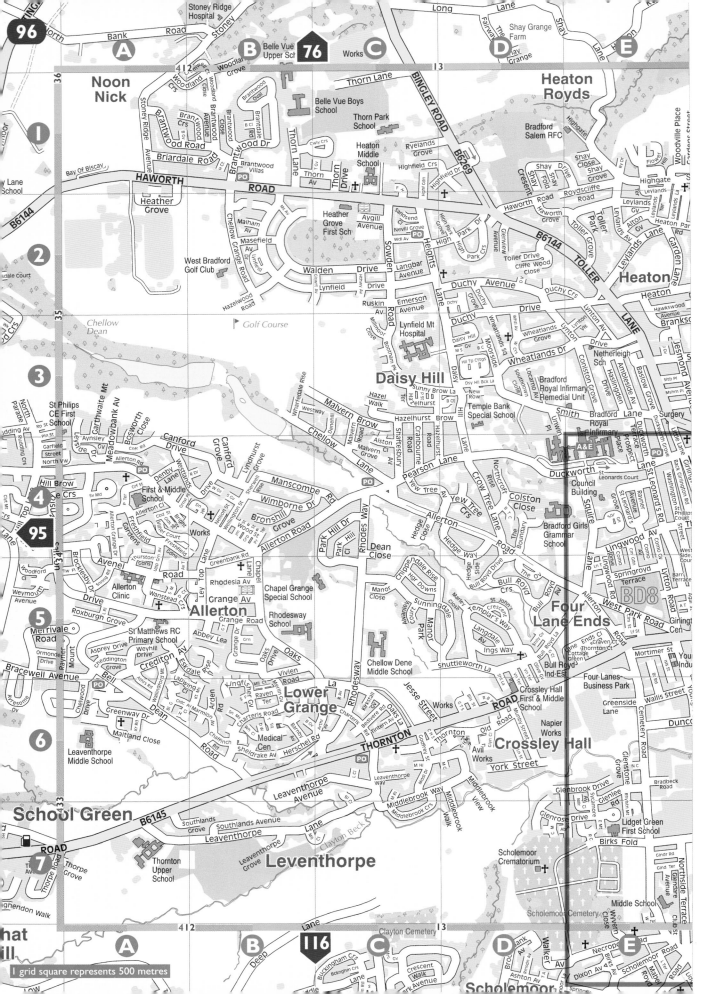

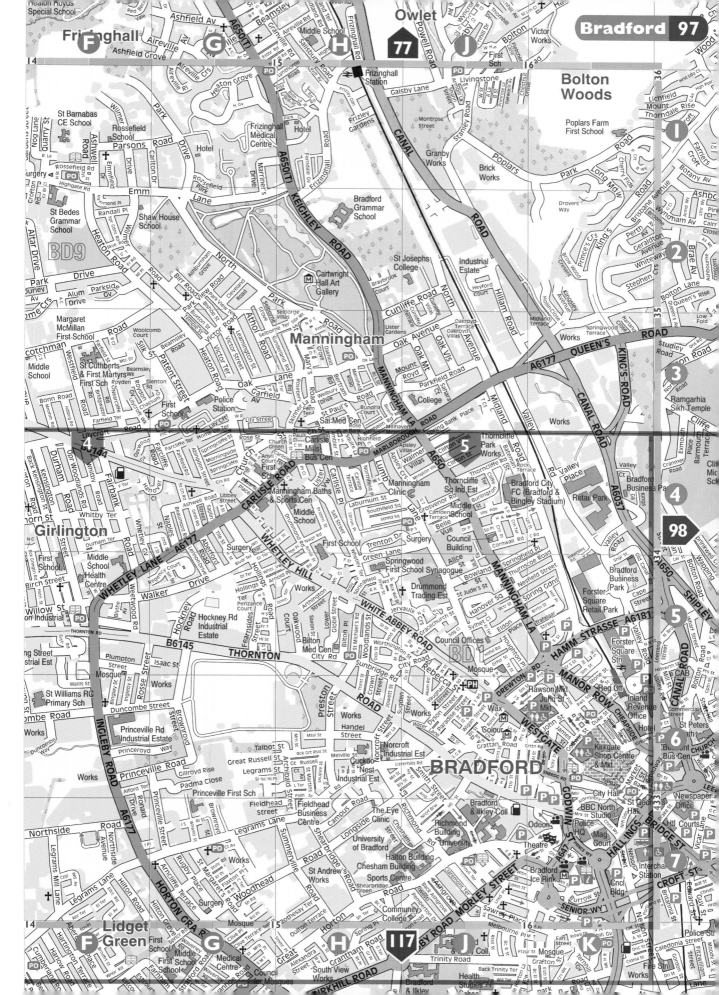

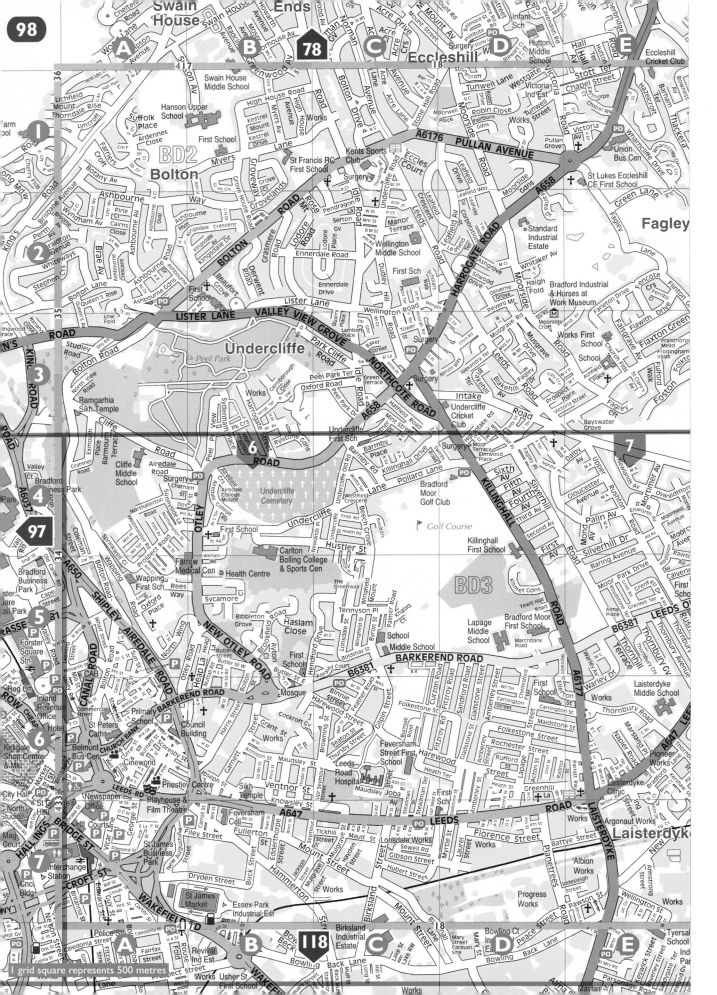

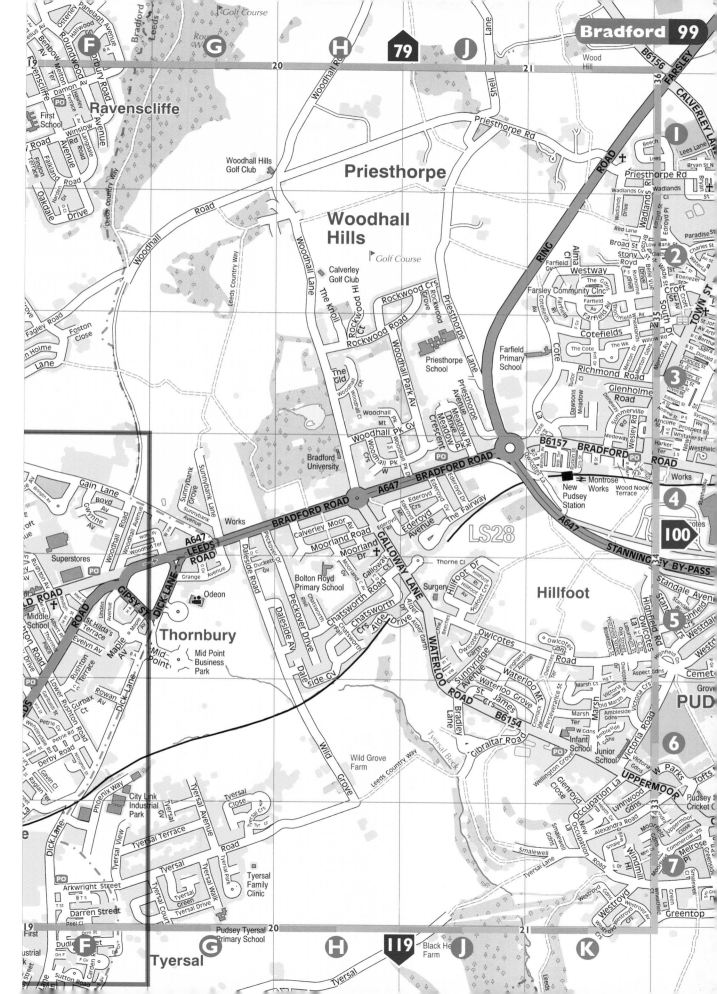

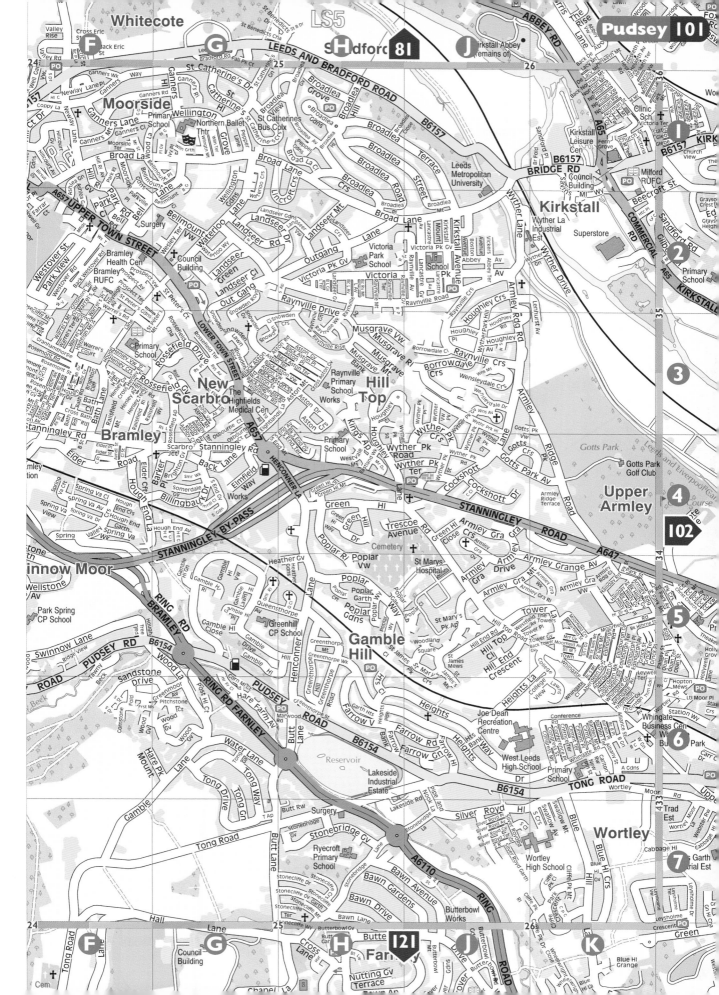

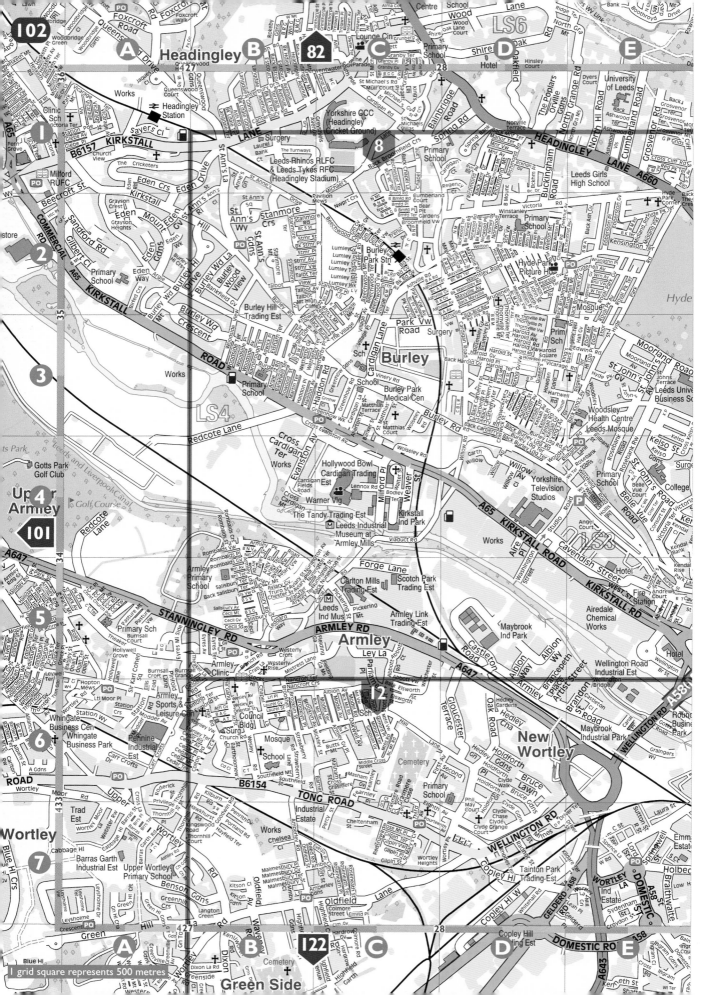

I grid square represents 500 metres

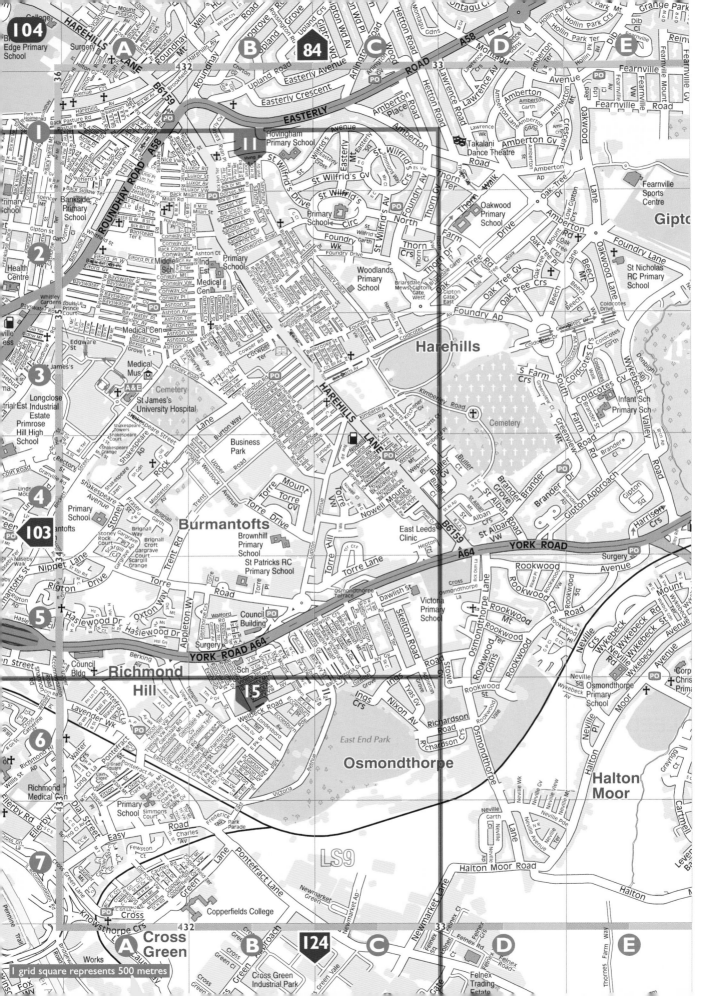

F B1217 G Lotherton H Copley Lane 89 J
Hall

44 45 46 36

1

2
Coldhill Farm

Bragdale Ringhay 35
Wood

3

Weet
Wood 4

Daniel
Hartly's 110
Wood 34

5

North Yorkshire County

Churchville Churchville Dr Churchville Ter Great N. Rd Hartly Huddleston
PO Wood Old Wood

Leeds

Mary's 6
Walk

Micklefield 33
CE Primary LS25
School

Garden Village

Lane Pit Lane

Village 7
age

Micklefield Station West
View Newthorpe
Sunnybank Rd Barrack
Pit Lane Prospect Ter

New Micklefield

44 45 46

F G 129 J K Mill Dike

The Crescent

Woodlands Hall

Barkston Ash

A   447   B   **90**   C   48   D   **E**

Barkston Ash
Catholic Primary   Ma

LONDON R

1

Garlic Flats

Oldgate Lane

2   Coldhill Farm

35

Coldhill Lane

Coldhill Lane

3

Stream Dike   Stream Farm

4

34

◄109

**SHEF
IN EL**

Sir John's Lane

5   Laith Staid Lane

†

uddleston
ld Wood

Garden
Tom
Garden

6

433

LS25

Low
Grange

7

Mill Dike

New

CHURCH HILL   B1222

Corse Lane

Mill Dike

A   447   B   **130**   C   48   D   **E**

Hall   Lane

I grid square represents 500 metres

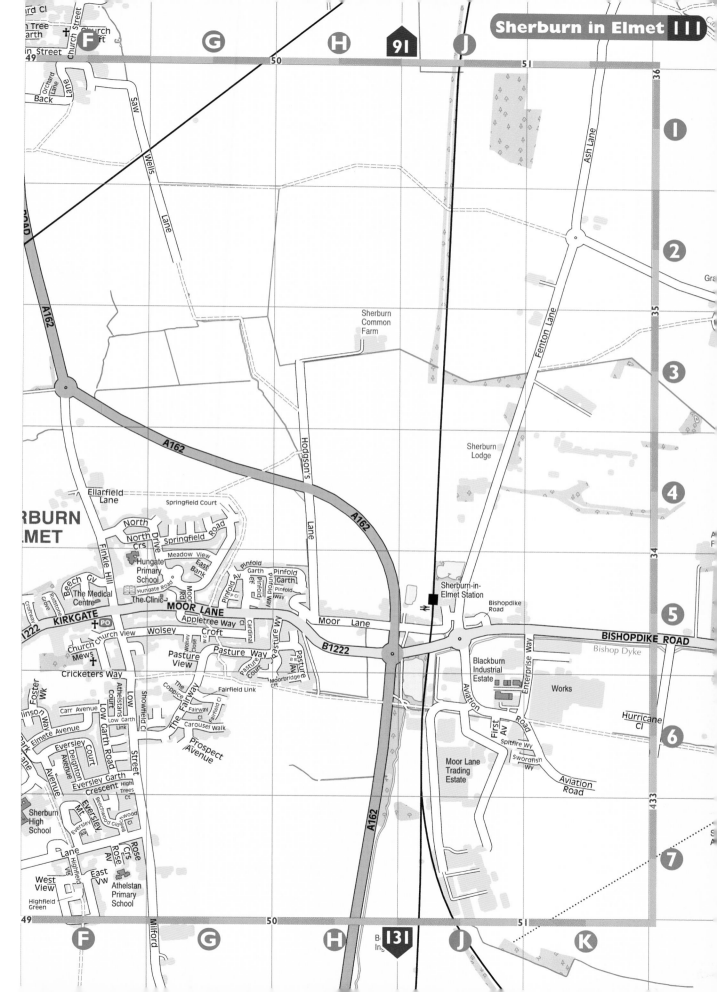

A 402 B 92 C 03 D E

1

Bradford
Calderdale

32

Spa
Clough
Head

Warley
Moor
Reservoir

447
▲

2

Cold Edge Road

3

31

Dean
Head
Reservoir

4

Warley
Moor

Castle Carr Road

5

Rocking
Stone

30

Castle Carr Road

6

Gate

Castle

Ray

Lane End Shore

Carr

Road

Sleepy
Lowe

7

Dimmin Dale

429

402 B 03 D

Low

Lane

Catherine House Lane

A B 132 C D E

Castle Carr Road

Castle C

1 grid square represents 500 metres

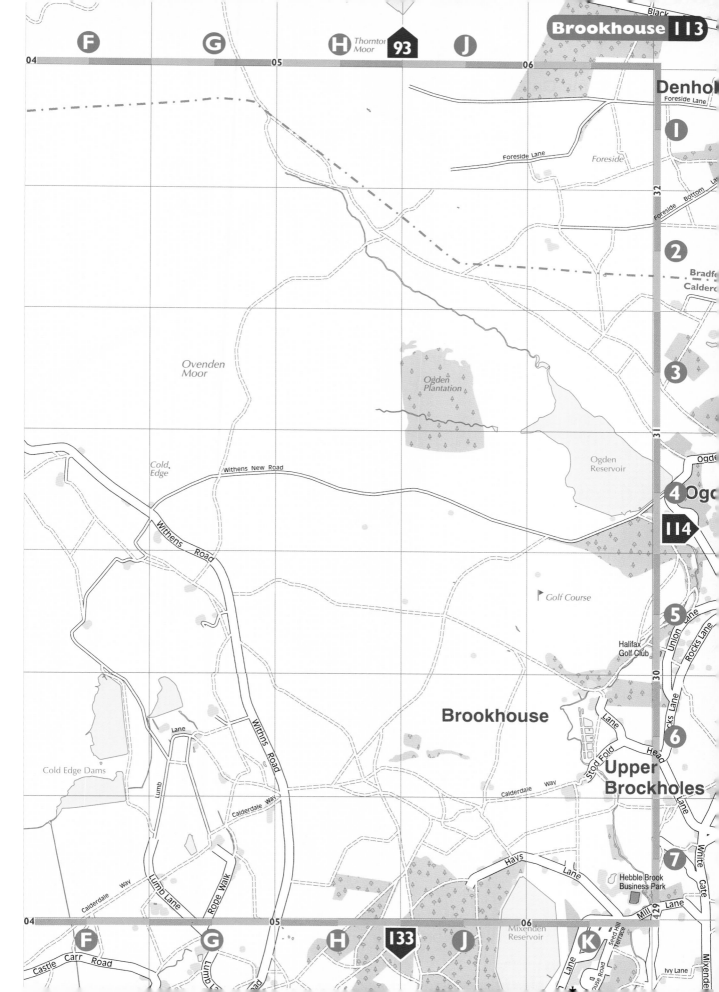

F **G** **H** Thornton Moor **93** **J**

04 05 06

Denho

Foreside Lane

I

Foreside Lane

Foreside

32

Foreside Bottom Lane

2

Bradfo
Caldero

3

Ovenden
Moor

Ogden
Plantation

31

Ogde

Cold.
Edge

Withens New Road

Ogden
Reservoir

4 Ogd

114

Withens Road

Golf Course

5

Union Lane

Rocks Lane

Halifax
Golf Club

30

cks Lane

Brookhouse

Lane

6

Lane

Head

Stod Fold

**Upper
Brockholes**

Lane

Cold Edge Dams

Lumb Lane

Withins Road

Calderdale Way

Calderdale Way

White Gate

7

Calderdale Way

Lumb Lane

Rope Walk

Hays Lane

Hebble Brook
Business Park

429 Lane

Mill

04 05 06

F **G** **H** **133** **J** **K**

Mixenden
Reservoir

Seed Hill
Terrace

Castle Carr Road

Lumb Lane

use Road

Lane

Ivy Lane

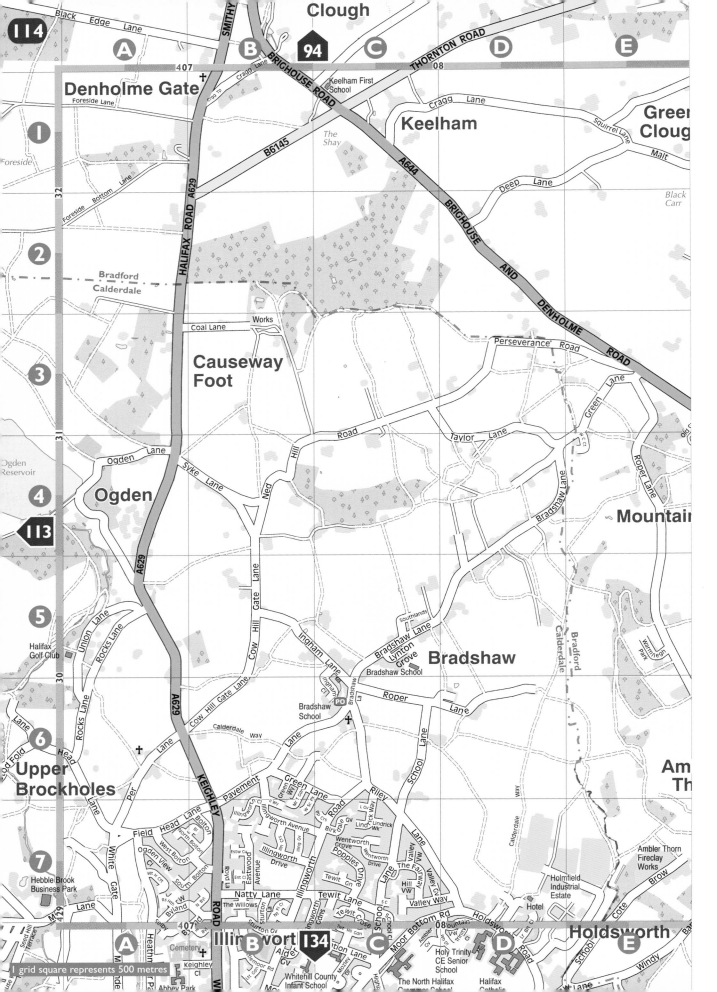

Ⓐ Ⓑ 94 Ⓒ Ⓓ Ⓔ

Clough

Black Edge Lane

Denholme Gate

Foreside Lane

THORNTON ROAD 08

Keelham First School

Keelham

Cragg Lane

Squirrel Lane

Green Clough

Malt

1

Foreside

Foreside Bottom Lane

SMITHY

BRIGHOUSE ROAD

B6145

A629

HALIFAX ROAD

The Shay

A644

Deep Lane

Black Carr

32

2

Bradford Calderdale

3

Coal Lane

Works

Causeway Foot

Road

Perseverance Road

Taylor Lane

BRIGHOUSE AND DENHOLME ROAD

Green Lane

Bradshaw Lane

Roper Lane

31

Ogden Reservoir

Ogden Lane

Ogden

Syke Lane

Ned

Hill

Bradford Calderdale

Mountain

4

113

A629

Cow Hill Gate Lane

Southlands

Bradshaw Lane

Lynton Grove

Bradshaw

Warm Yegn Park

5

Halifax Golf Club

Union Lane

Rocks Lane

Ingham Lane

Bradshaw School

Roper Lane

School Lane

Calderdale

30

6

Upper Brockholes

Head Lane

Rocks Lane

A629

KEIGHLEY ROAD

Cow Hill Gate Lane

Calderdale Way

Bradshaw School

PO

Ingham Cl

Bradshaw La

Roper Lane

Ambler Thorn

7

Hebble Brook Business Park

Field Head Lane

White Gate Lane

Bolton

West Bolton

North Bolton

South Bolton

Ogden View Cl

Pavement

Illingworth Avenue

Green Lane

Illingworth Drive

Eastwood Avenue

Illingworth Road

Wentworth Grove

Poppies Drive

Riley Lane

Lindrick Wk

Wentworth Drive

The Fairway

Valley Gv

Ambler Thorn Fireclay Works

Holmfield Industrial Estate

Calderdale Way

Cote Brow

M429

Seed Hill Terrace

Natty Lane

The Willows

Sturton Lane

Byland

Tewit Lane

Tewit Close

Hill VW

Valley Way

Holdsworth Rd

Moor Bottom Rd 08

Hotel

Holdsworth

407

Cemetery

Illingworth 134

Whitehill County Infant School

Holy Trinity CE Senior School

The North Halifax Grammar School

Halifax Catholic

Keighley Cl

Ⓐ Ⓑ Ⓒ Ⓓ Ⓔ

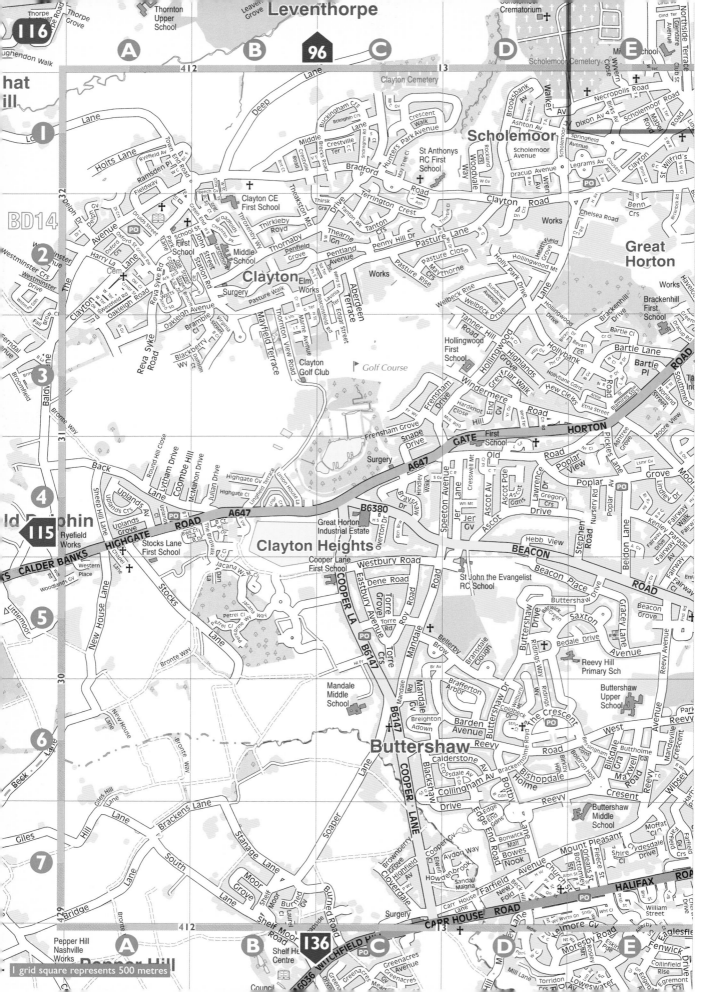

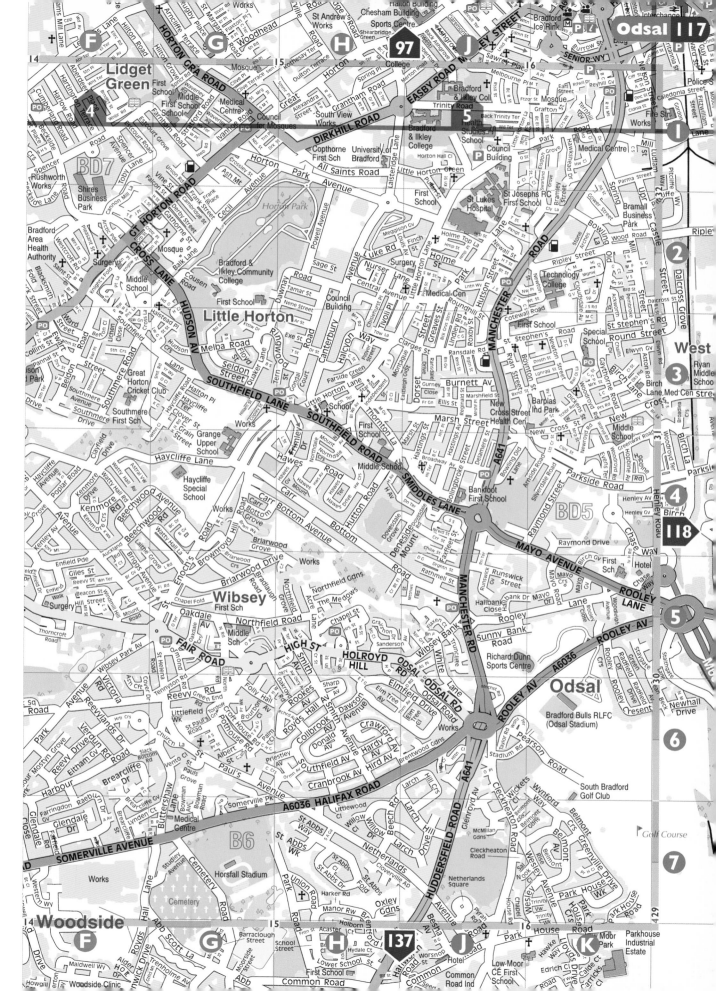

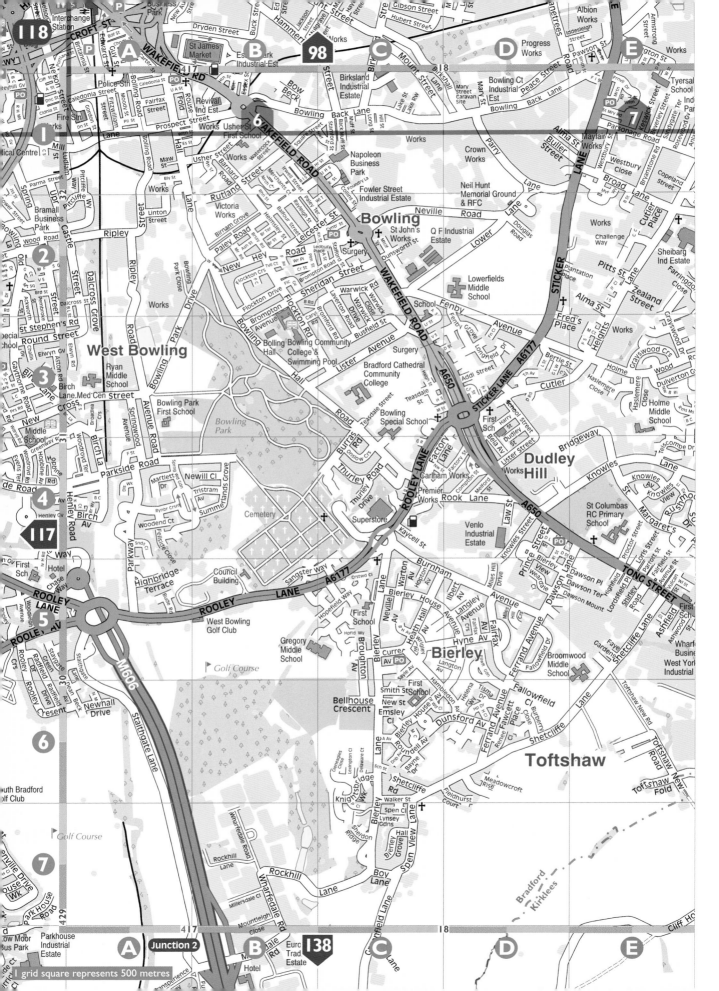

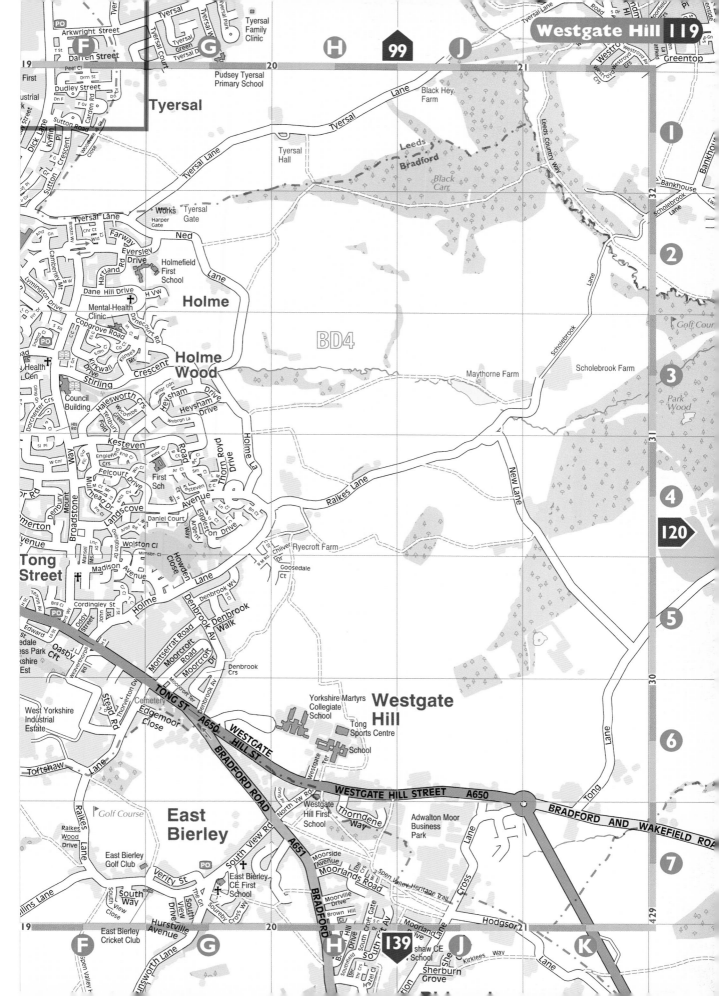

120

A Greentop
B Primary School
100
C
D Troydale
E

Station Street

Fulneck

Fulneck School
Fulneck Golf Club

Golf Course

Golf Course

Park Wood

Business Centre

Hotel

119

Tong

Corn Mill Farm

Leeds Country Way

Cockers Dale

Upper Moor Side

Cockersdale

Dale Road

New Lane

GILDERSOME LANE B6126

Moorland

BRADFORD AND WAKEFIELD ROAD

BRADFORD ROAD

Blind Lane

WHITEHALL ROAD

Lumb Bottom

Old Lane

Leeds Country Way

Junior School

Manor Park Industrial Estate

A **B** **140** **C** **D** **E**

The Medical Centre

Drighlington

1 grid square represents 500 metres

Farnley

New Farnley

Gildersome

Moor Head

LS12

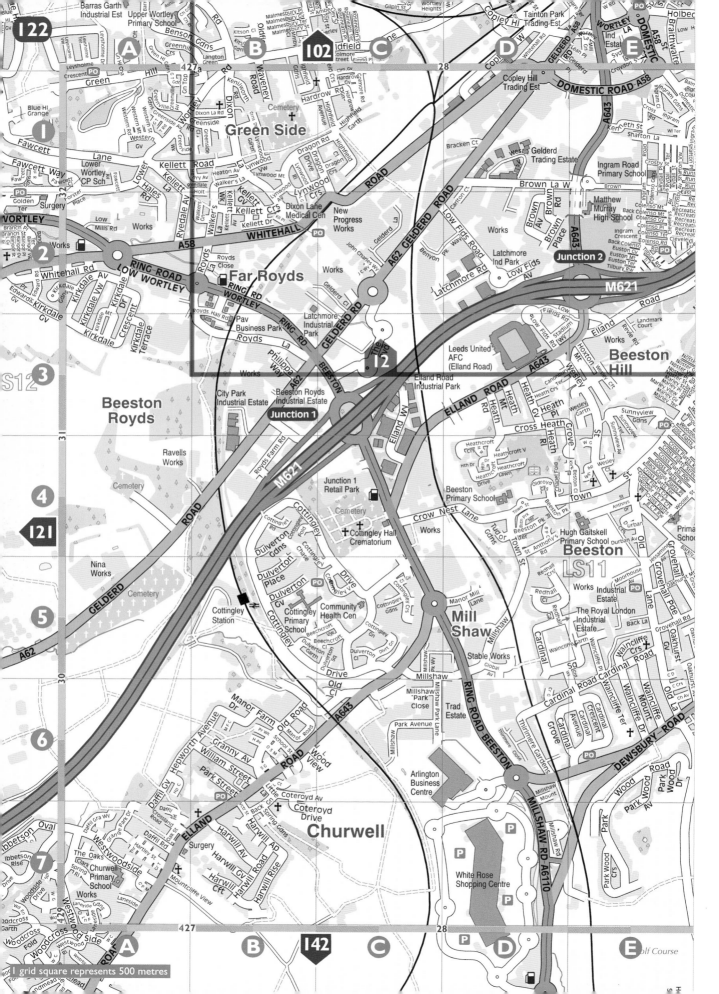

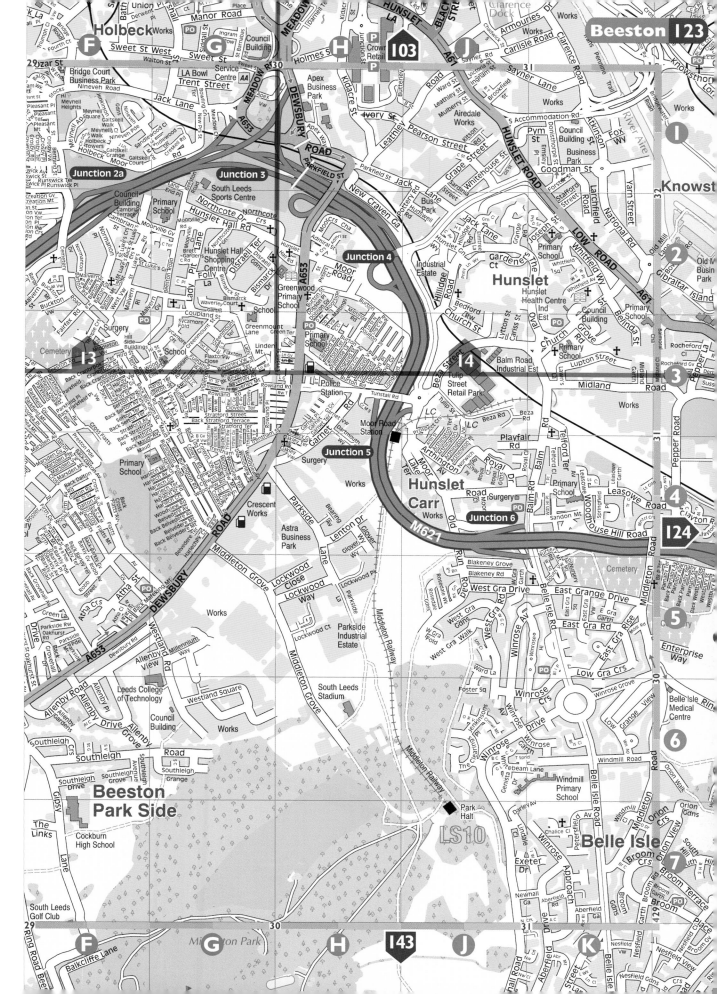

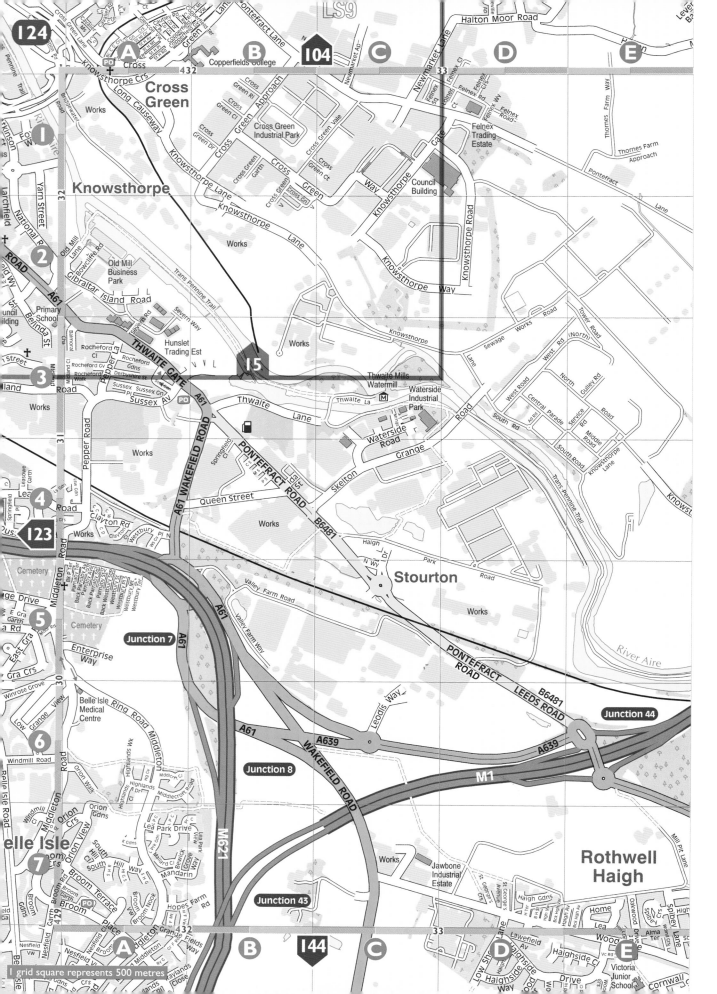

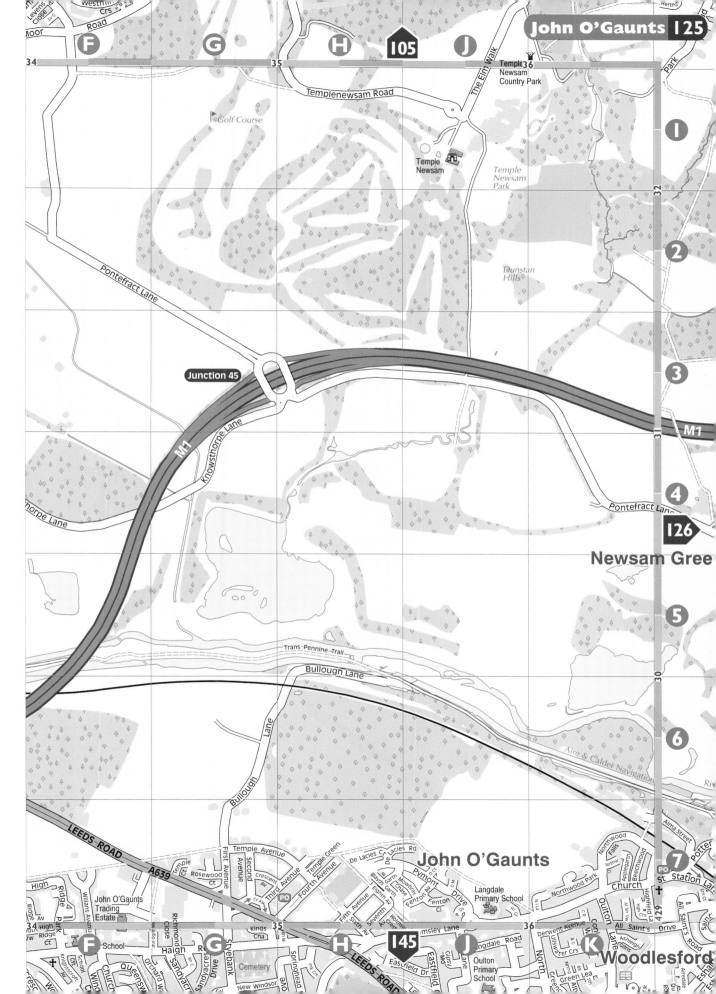

F G **105** H J

34 35 36

Temple
Newsam
Country Park

I

Templenewsam Road

The Elm Walk

Golf Course

Temple
Newsam

Temple
Newsam
Park

32

2

Dunstan
Hills

Pontefract Lane

3

M1

Junction 45

Knowsthorpe Lane

M1

31

4

Pontefract Lane

126

Newsam Gree

5

30

Trans-Pennine-Trail

Bullough Lane

Aire & Calder Navigation

6

Lane

Bullough

LEEDS ROAD A639

Temple Avenue

First Avenue

Second Avenue

Crescent

Third Avenue

Fourth Avenue

Temple Green

De Lacies Ct

De Lacies Rd

Pymont Drive

John O'Gaunts

Northwood Falls

PO

Ri

7

Alma Street

St Station La

Potter

John O'Gaunts
Trading
Estate

Rosewood
Ct

Temple

Richmond
Close

PO

Blairds Garth
Mowbray Chase
Fenton Cl
Fenton Ci
Eighth Av
Holmse
Fifth Avenue
Sixth Av
Seventh Av

Langdale
Primary School

Northwood Park

Oulton Lane

429

PO

Church

Highfield La

All Saint's Drive

All Saints

High
Ridge
Av

High
Ridge

Wilans Avenue

Park

School

Haigh

Styebank

Kings
Cha

Cr Av

msley Lane

145

LEEDS ROAD

Eastfield Dr

Eastfield

Langdale Road

Derwent Avenue

North Green

Green Lea

All Sn'

Ashleigh
Gdns

Cemetery

Springhead

New Windsor

Oulton
Primary
School

Gipsy
Md

Lane

K

Woodlesford

34 35 36

F G H J

lton

A B 106 C Swillington D SELBY E ROAD
Common

437 38

M1

I

32

The Avenue

Avenue
Wood

2 Hollinthorpe

Bullerthorpe Lane

Leeds Lane

The Avenue

Leeds Country Way

3

31

M1

The Avenue

Swillington

4 Swillington Lane

Pontefract Lane

125

Neville Grove

Newsam Green Lowther Drive Whitecliffe Rd Crescent Whitecliffe Rd
Church Avenue Church Cl Swillington
Lower Crs Smeaton Gv Primary School Works
Church Wakefield Road
Lane Goody
Newsam Green Road Hillcrest Cl The Pleasance Church Crs The Grove
5 Crest Hill The Crest St Mary's Surgery Primrose Hall Road
The Drive Av Av
Leventhorpe Bullerthorpe Lane The Link Springwell Scott Cl PO Preston
Hall Crs Rd Park Vw
Road Woodland Dr Woodland A642 Av
Woodland Gv Woodland Astley Park
Av Wakefield Rd Av View Park
Gv

30

6 Jinny Astley Astley Lane
Way Industrial
Lane Estate

Ider Navigation Leeds Country Way

River Calder

Alma Street Pottery Lane WAKEFIELD ROAD A642
Northwood New
Falls Farmers
7 PO Hill
Church St Station Lane Woodlesford
Station
429 Minerva
Industrial Trans Pennine Trail
Estate Leeds Country Way

Woodesford A B 146 C D E

437 38

1 grid square represents 500 metres

128

GARFORTH

Kippax

Ledston Luck

Green Lane Primary School

Fosse Way
Witham Way
Thames Drive
Kentmere Av
Severn Drive
Hammerton Dr
Chester Drive
Trent Avenue
Cherwell Croft
Ribbesdale Av
Riddesdale Close
Denesway
Eastwood Grove
Leabank Avenue
Eskdale

Warren Farm

Pit Lane

Crescent
Newfield East Dr
Newfield Dr

A63(T)

BY ROAD

A63(T)

Peckfield Bar

Sandgate Lane

Ridge Road

Shuttocks Close
Shuttocks Fold
Baildon Av
Ashgrove
Moorgate Rd
PO
Moorgate Av
Ashgrove Crs
Birla Cl
Bldn Av
Sandgate Drive
Grange Lane
Manor Garth
Rutland Close
WC
Medhurst Av
Clayton Av
Holland Rd
Lincoln Wk
Merton Close

Grange Avenue
each Grange
Moorgate Close

B6137

Gibson Road
Moorgate Av
Kippax Health Centre
Greenfield Cl
Greenfield Av

127

Mount View
Greenfield Primary School
Westfield Avenue
Robinson La
Rutland
West View
West View East

Moorleigh
Sandall Close
Pondfields Drive
Parkfield Cl
Pondfields Rise
Pondfields Close
Pondfields Crest
Keble Garth
Pembroke Rd
Sandgate Rise
Sandgate Crs

Church View

Gibson Lane Junior School

The Close
Infant School
Well Lane
Cross Dr
Church Lane
Chapel La
Hopewell Ter
PO
HIGH STREET
Cross Hills
Surgery
Butt Hill
Tateshield Pl
Ashtree Gn
Bargess Ter
New Street
Gibson Lane
Cliff Crs
Sandgate Ter
Coronation Avenue
Lime-Tree Crs

Coronation Bungalows

B6137
Surgery
Brigshaw La
Cromwell Rise
Hall Park Cl
Hall Pk Mdw
Hall Pk Crt
Hall Park Croft
Mount Pleasant
The Intake
Malt Kiln
Park Avenue
Woodlands Grove
Park La
Woodlands View

LONGDIKE LANE
B6137

A656

A656
RIDGE ROAD

Spartal Lane

Ledston Mill Lane

148 Home Farm

Dovecote Dr
Hall Dr

Green

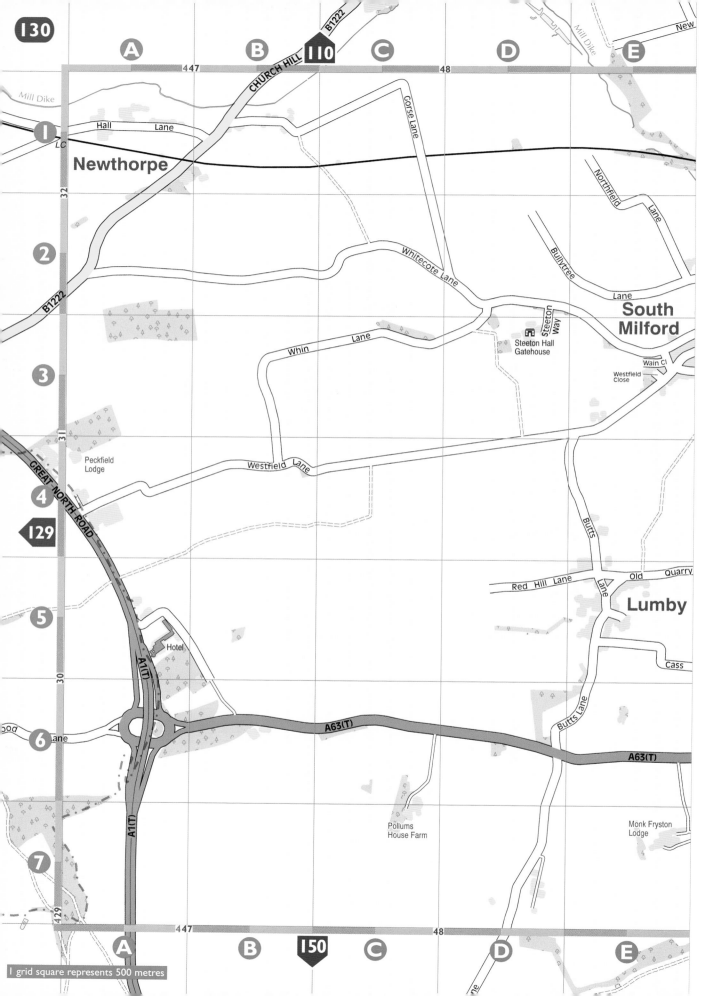

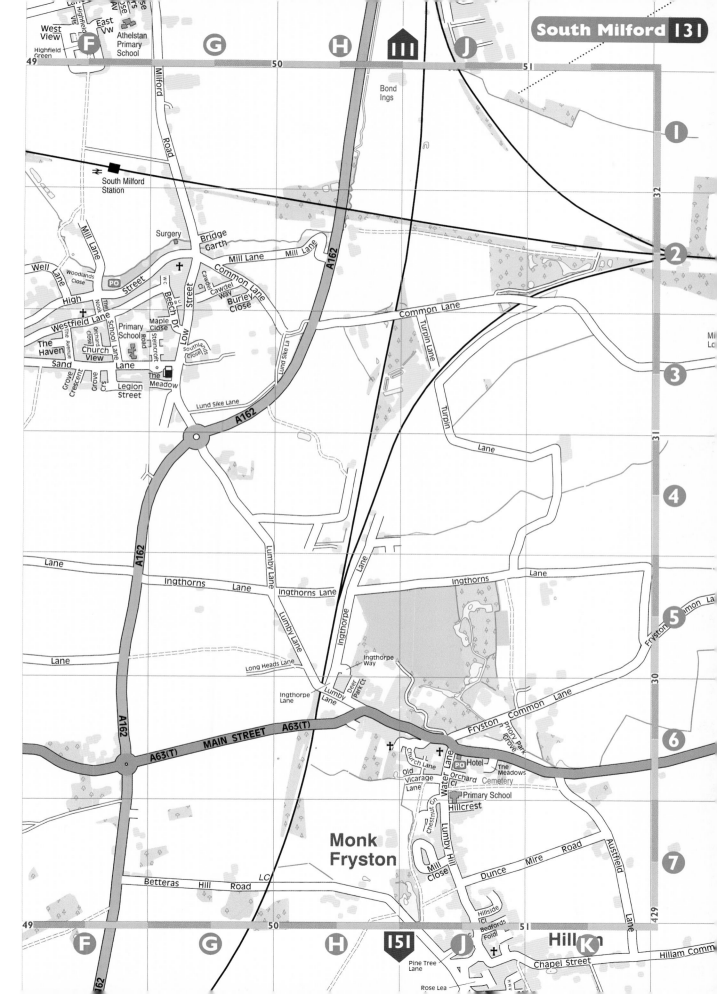

West View
Highfield Green
East Vw
Athelstan Primary School

49
50
51

Milford Road

South Milford Station

Bond Ings

Surgery

Bridge Garth

Mill Lane
Mill Lane

Mill Lane

A162

Common Lane

Common Lane

Turpin Lane

Well Lane
Woodlands Close
PO
High Street
Cawdel Ct
Cawdel Way
Burley Close
The Nook
WC
B C
Beech Dr

Westfield Lane
School Lane
Orchard Close
Primary School
Maple Close
Steincroft Road
Southlands Close
Lund Sike La

The Haven
Church View
Sand
Grove Crescent
Grove Cl
Lane
The Meadow
Legion Street

Lund Sike Lane

A162

Turpin

Lane

Lane

Lane

Lumby Lane

Ingthorns Lane

Ingthorns Lane

Ingthorns Lane

Lane

Ingthorpe

Ingthorns Lane

Lane

A162

Lane

Lumby Lane

Long Heads Lane

Ingthorpe Way

Fryston Common Lane

Ingthorpe Lane

Lumby Lane

Deer Park Ct

A162

MAIN STREET   A63(T)

A63(T)

Fryston
Priory Park Grove

Old Vicarage
Church Lane
Water Lane
PO Hotel
Orchard Cl
The Meadows
Cemetery

Lane
Chestnut Gn
Primary School
Hillcrest

Monk Fryston

Lumby Hill

Mill Close

Dunce Mire Road

Austfield Lane

Betteras   Hill   Road

LC

Hillside Cl
Bedfords Fold

49
50
51

Lane

Hillam Comm

Pine Tree Lane

Chapel Street

Hill m

Rose Lea

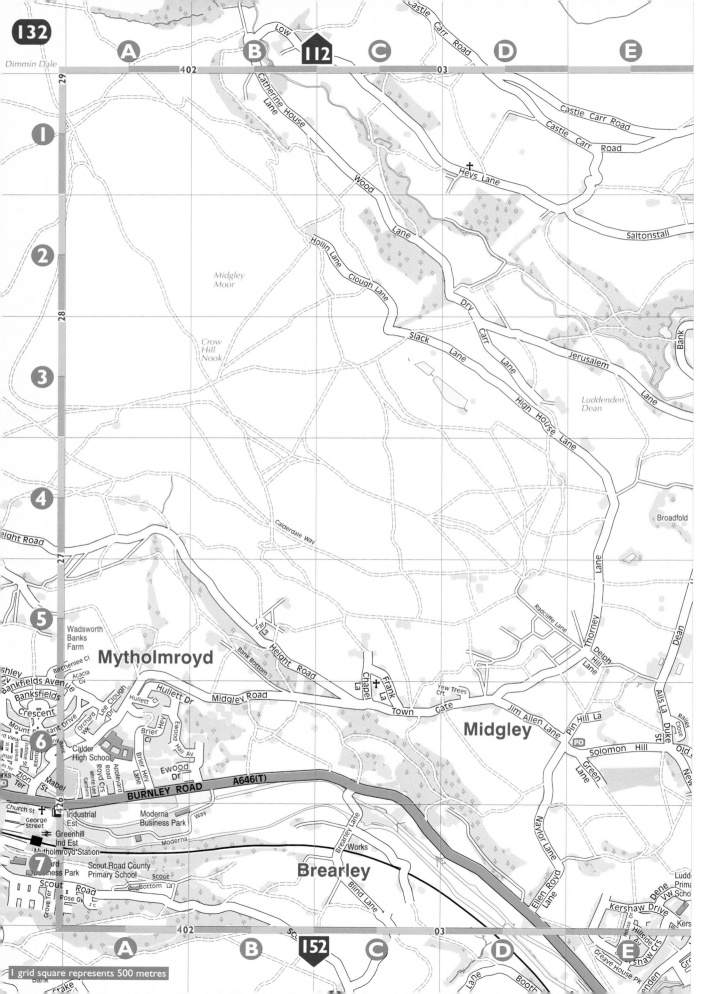

132

Dimmin Dale

A 402 B 112 C 03 D E

29
1

28
2

Midgley Moor

3
Crow Hill Nook

4
Calderdale Way

27
5
Wadsworth Banks Farm

Mytholmroyd

Bank Bottom

Height Road

Catherine House Lane

Wood Lane

Hollin Lane

Clough Lane

Slack Lane

Dry Carr Lane

High House Lane

Jerusalem Lane

Luddenden Dean

Broadfold

Castle Carr Road

Castle Carr Road

Heys Lane

Saltonstall

Lane

Radcliffe Lane

Thorney Lane

Delph Hill Lane

Allis La

Duke St

Dean

Railes Close

Old

Midgley

Birchenlee Cl

Acacia Gv

Bankfields Avenue

Banksfields

Banksfields Crescent

Mount Pleasant Drive

Orchard Gv

Lee Clough Drive

Hullett

Hullett Dr

Hullett Cl

Brier Hey

Brier Cl

Midgley Road

Chapel La

Frank La

Town Gate

Yew Trees Cft

Jim Allen Lane

Pin Hill La

PO

Solomon Hill

Green Lane

6
View

Mount Ter

Zion Ter

Ribsto

Calder High School

Ewood Hall Av

Royd Crs

White Lee Gardens

Appleyard

Ewood Dr

Mabel St

426

BURNLEY ROAD A646(T)

Naylor Lane

Church St

George Street

Industrial Est

Moderna Business Park

Way

Moderna

Greenhill Ind Est

Mytholmroyd Station

7
Business Park

Scout Road County Primary School

Scout Bottom La

Scout Road

Rose Gv

Grove Ter

Brearley Lane

Works

Brearley

Blind Lane

Ellen Royd Lane

Kershaw Drive

Greave House Pk

Dene

VW Scho

Hillside

Kers

A 402 B 152 C 03 D E

1 grid square represents 500 metres

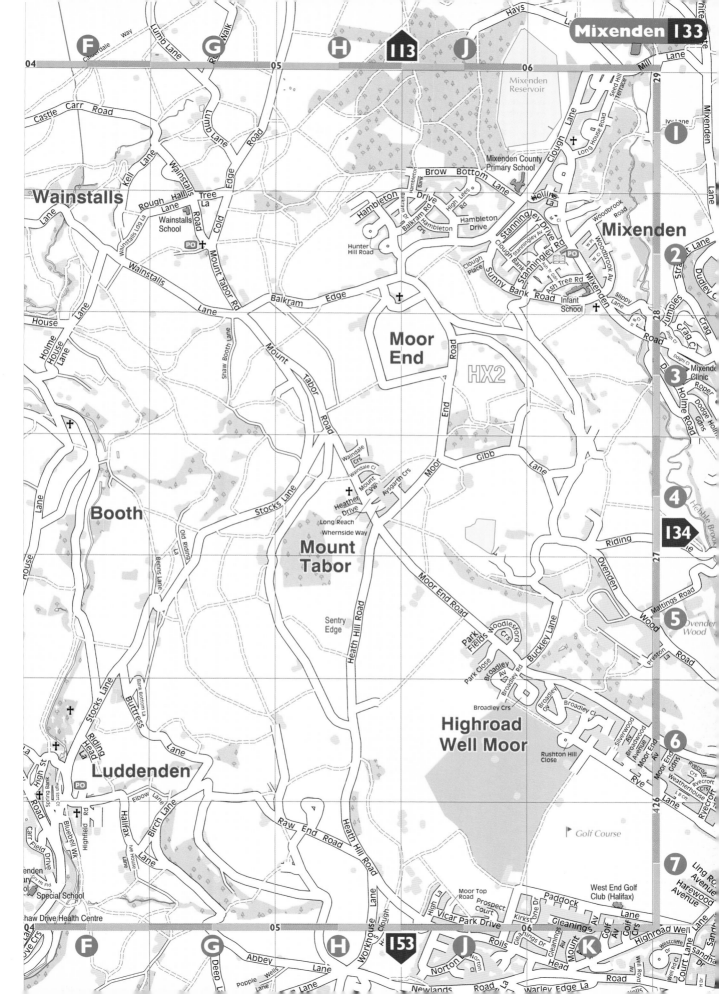

Calderdale Way
Lumb Lane
Walk

F
G
H
113
J

04
05
06
29

I

Mixenden
Reservoir

Castle Carr Road
Keil Lane
Lumb Lane
Wainstalls Lane
Edge Road
Cold

Seed Hill Terrace
White
Mill Lane
Ivy Lane
Mixenden Lane

Mixenden County
Primary School
Clough Lane
Long House Road
Woodbrook Road

Wainstalls
Rough Hall La
Lane
Tree La
Wainstalls
School
PO

Brow Bottom Lane
Hollins La
Hambleton Dr
Balkram Dr
High Lees Rd
Hambleton

Mixenden

Street Lane
Dudley C
Crag Cl
Jumples
Crag Cl

Wainstalls Ldg La
House Lane
House Lane
Holme
House
Lane

Wainstalls Lane
Mount Tabor Rd
Balkram Edge Lane
Shaw Booth Lane

Hunter
Hill Road
Hambleton Crs
Hambleton
Drive

Stanningley Rd
Clough Bank
stanningley Av
Sunny Bank Road
Clough Place

PO
Ash Tree Rd
Mixenden
Infant
School

Jumples Road
28

Slippy Lane

**Moor
End**

Mount Tabor Road
End Road
HX2

Mixenden
Clinic
Roper
Holme Road
3
Dodge Holme Gdns

Booth

Old Riding La
Berns Lane
Stocks Lane

Walndale Crs
Walndale Cl
Mount
Heather Drive
Long Reach
Whernside Way

Moor Lane
Aysgarth Crs
Gibb Lane

Ovenden
Henble Brook
le
4
134

**Mount
Tabor**

Sentry
Edge

Moor End Road
Riding

Maltings Road
Wood Road
Preston La
5
Ovender
Wood

Heath Hill Road

Park Fields
Woodlesford Crs
Buckley Lane
Broadley Rd

Silverwood
Broadwood
Avenue
Broadley Gv
Broadley Cl
Broadley Crs

Moor End
Ryecroft Crs
Ryecroft
6

Stocks Lane
Riding Head La
Buttress
Luddenden
PO

Park Close
Broadley Av

**Highroad
Well Moor**

Rushton Hill
Close

Rye Lane
L&CR
Weatherhouse

High St
Spring Bank High
Carr Field Drive
Bluebell Wk
Highfield Rd
Halifax Lane
Birch Lane
Ive House Lane

Raw End Road
Heath Hill Road

Golf Course

Ling Ro.
Avenue
Harewood
Avenue
7

Special School
Shaw Drive Health Centre

Moor Top Road
High La
Prospect Court
Vicar Park Drive
Paddock
Lane
One Dr
Kirkst
Gleanings
Golf Av
Golf Mount
Golf Road

West End Golf
Club (Halifax)

Highroad Well
Westcliffe
Well Royd
Court La
Sandhall Dr

F
G
H
153
J
K

04
05
06
426

Abbey Lane
Deep L
Popple Wells Lane
Norton Head
Roils
Gleanings Dr
Glenings Dr
Newlands Road
Warley Edge La

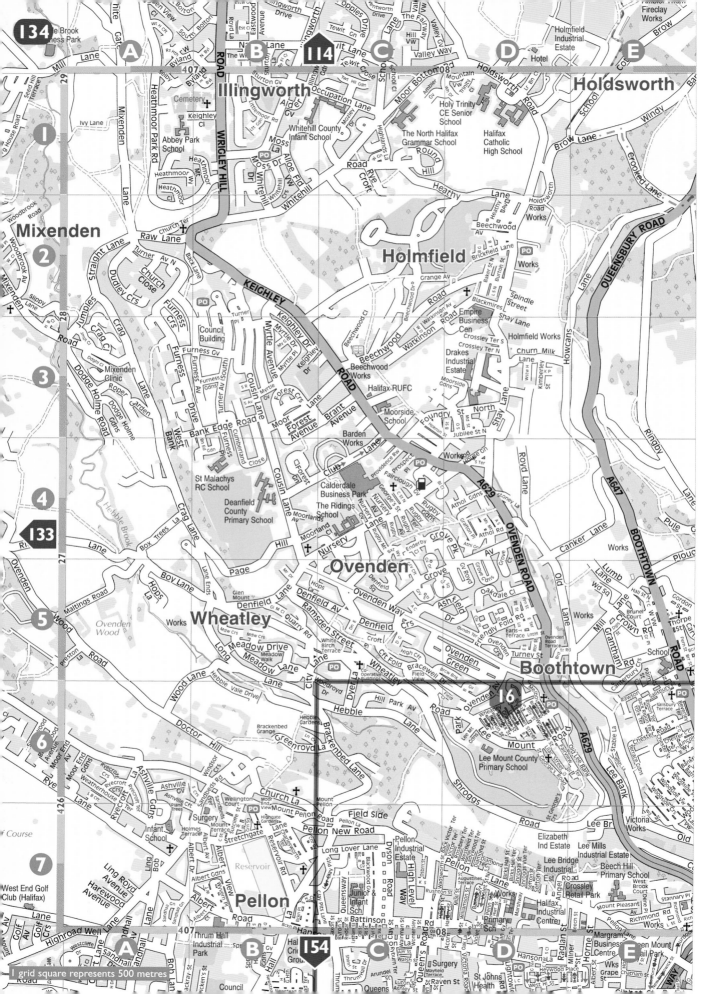

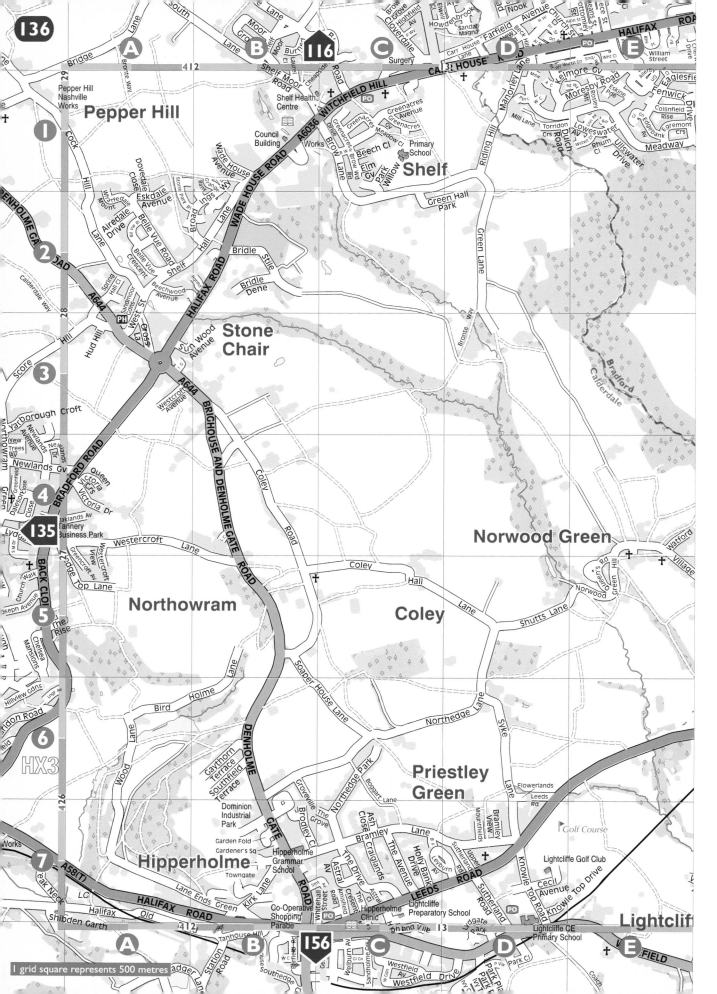

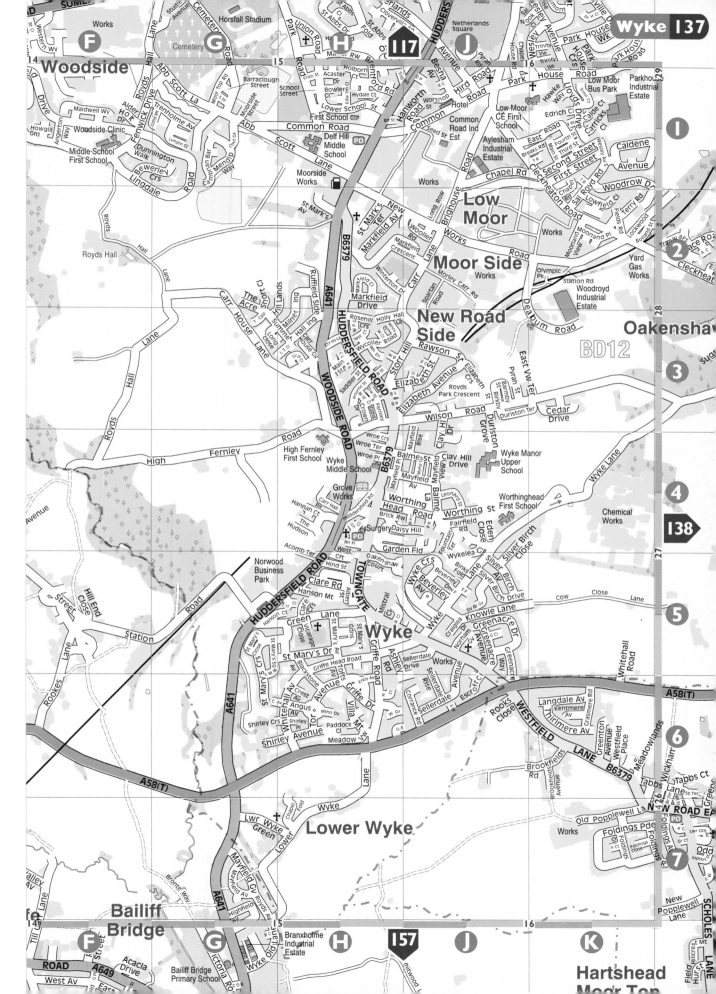

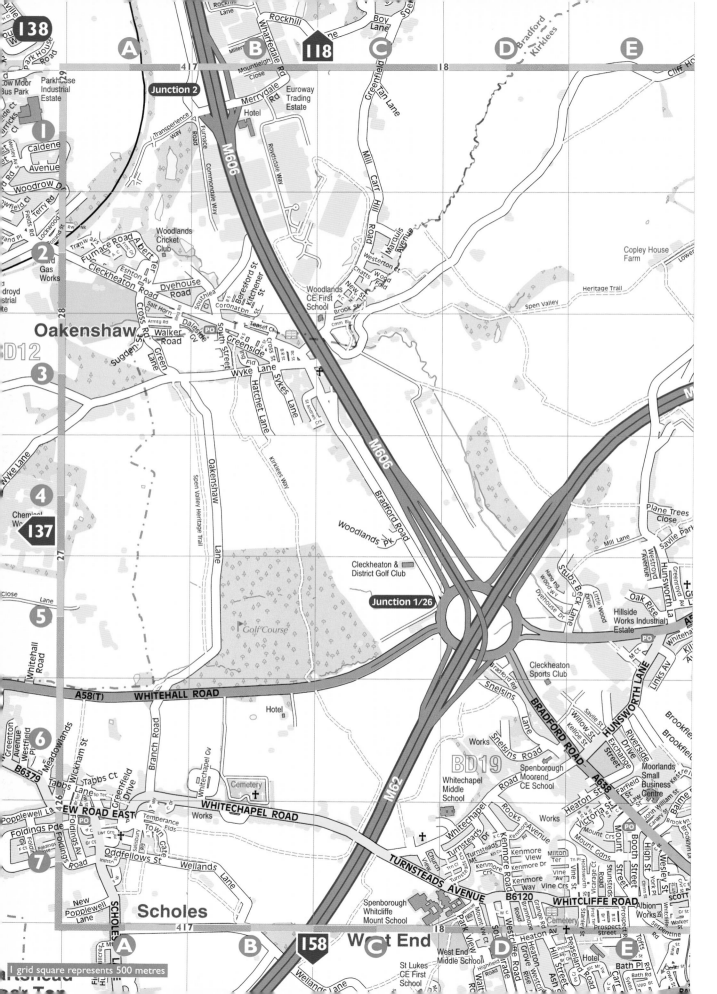

A B 118 C D E

Junction 2

Parkhouse Industrial Estate
Low Moor Bus Park
Park House Road

Rockhill Lane
Wharfedale Rd
Mountleigh Close
Merrydale Rd
Hotel

Boy Lane
Bradford Kirklees
Cliff

Caldene Avenue
Woodrow Dr

Transpennence Way
Furnace Road
Commondale Way

Euroway Trading Estate
Roydsdale Way

Greenfield
Tan Lane
Mill Carr Hill Road
Marquis Avenue
Westerton Ct
Chatts Wood Fold
New St

Copley House Farm

Heritage Trail
Spen Valley

Woodlands Cricket Club
Furnace Road
Albert Ter
Tramway
Eshton Av
Cleckheaton Road
Dyehouse Road
Salt Horn
Southlea
Beresford St
Kitchener St
Coronation St
Teasel Ct

Woodlands CE First School
Brook St

Oakenshaw
BD12

Sugden
Green Lane
Walker Road
Greenside
South Street
Cross St
Daleside Gv
PO

Wyke Lane
Hatchet Lane
Sykes Lane

Wyke Lane

Oakenshaw Lane
Kirklees Way
Spen Valley Heritage Trail

Bradford Road
M606

Woodlands Pk

Chemical Works
137

Cleckheaton & District Golf Club

Junction 1/26

Plane Trees Close
Mill Lane
Saville Pk
Westroyd Avenue
Hunsworth La
Greenroyd

Close
Lane

Golf Course

Hamp Hg
Wood Wy
Stubs Beck Lane
Dyehouse Dr
Little Wood

Hillside Works Industrial Estate
Oak Rise
Links Av
PO

Whitehall Road
A58(T) WHITEHALL ROAD

Bradford Rd
Cleckheaton Sports Club
Snelsins

HUNSWORTH LANE
BRADFORD ROAD A638
Riverside Drive
Exchange Street
Brookfield

Hotel

Greenton Avenue
Westfield Pl
B6379
Tabbs Ct
Wickham St
Tabbs Ct
Lane
So Ter
Greenfield Drive
Branch Road
Meadowlands

Works
Snelsins Road
Snelsins Lane
Willow St
Kenloe St
Saville St

BD19
Whitechapel Middle School
Spenborough Moorend CE School
Road

Moorlands Small Business Centre
Farfield St
Law Pl

Popplewell La
NEW ROAD EAST
Foldings Pde
Foldings Av
PO
Foldings Gr
Foldings Road
Oddfellows St
Temperance Town Gate
Whitechapel Gv
Cemetery
Whitechapel Road
Works
Wellands Lane

WHITECHAPEL ROAD

M62

Whitechapel Dr
Turnsteads
Kenmore Rd
Kenmore Av
Kenmore Ter
Kenmore Dr
Kenmore Cres
Kenmore Way
Vine Cres
Milton Ter
Victoria St
Mount Crs
Mount Gdns
Heaton St
High St
Booth Street

New Popplewell Lane
Scholes

TURNSTEADS AVENUE

Spenborough Whitcliffe Mount School
B6120
WHITCLIFFE ROAD

A B 158 C W t End D E

West End Middle School
St Lukes CE First School
Hotel
Heaton Av
Heaton Grove Road
Highfield Rd
Hill Street
Ash Gv
Bath Pl
Bath Rd

Albion Works
Scott
Prospect Street
Stanley St
Walker
Serpentine
Carr
Toft

1 grid square represents 500 metres

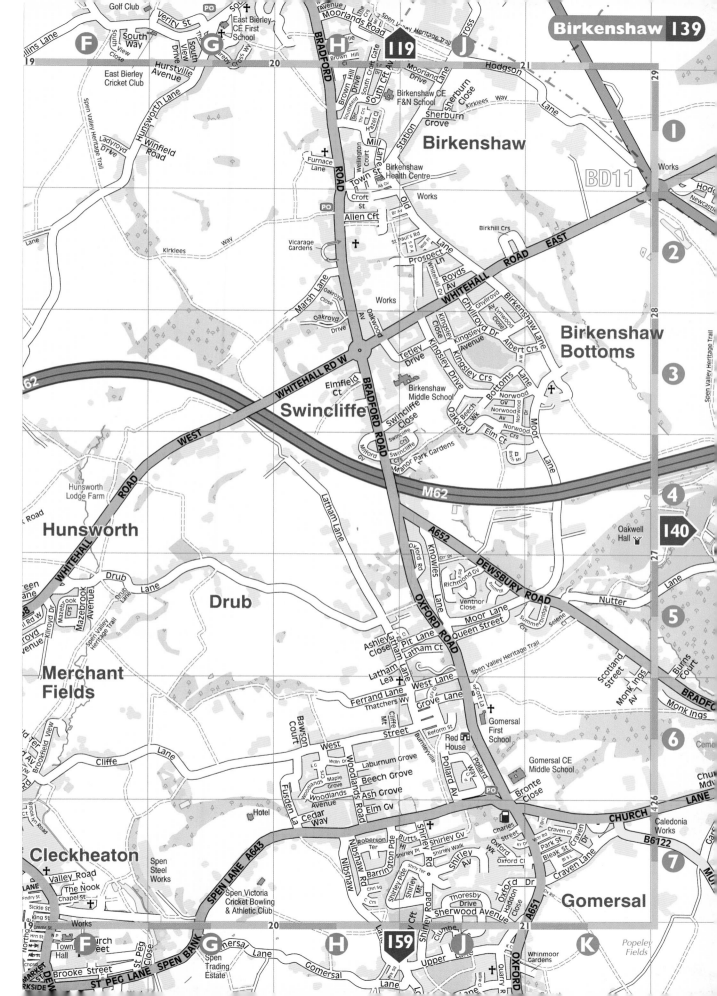

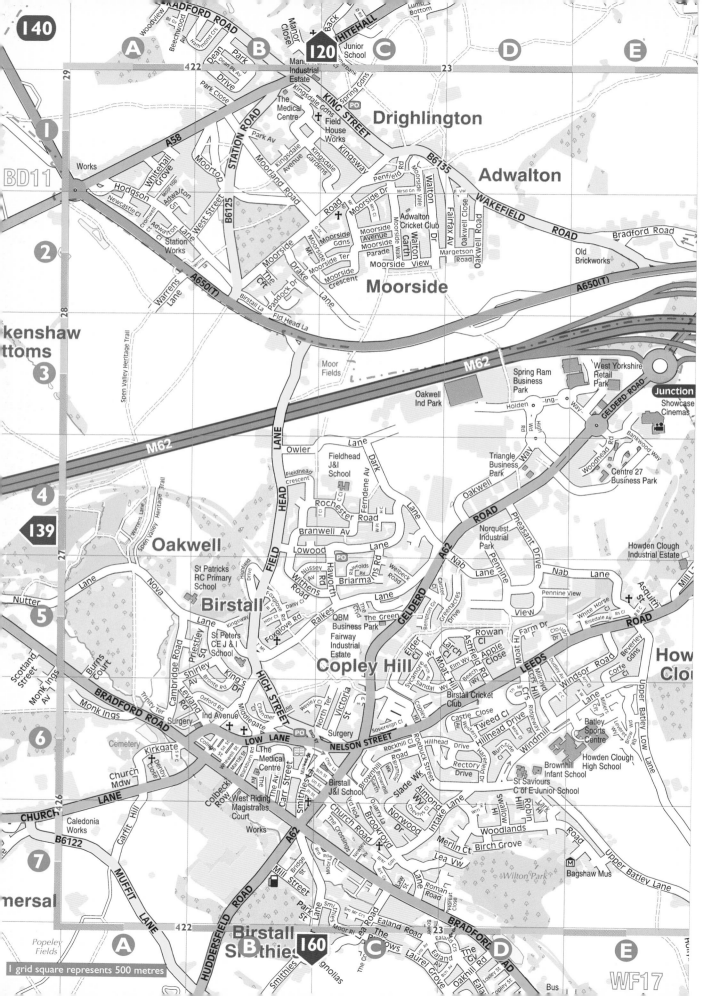

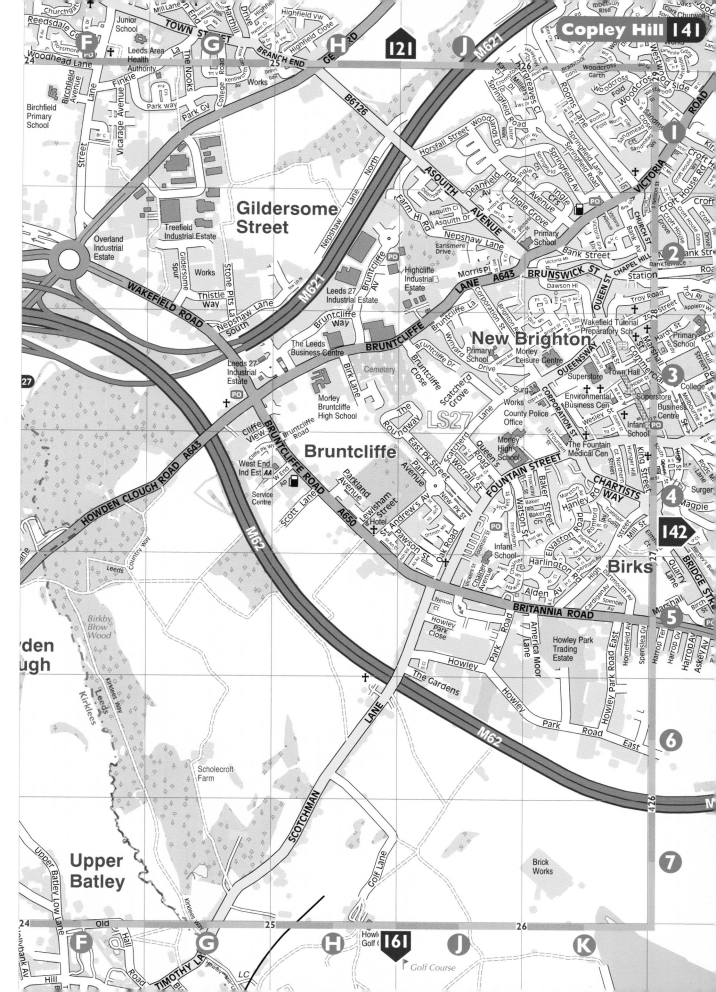

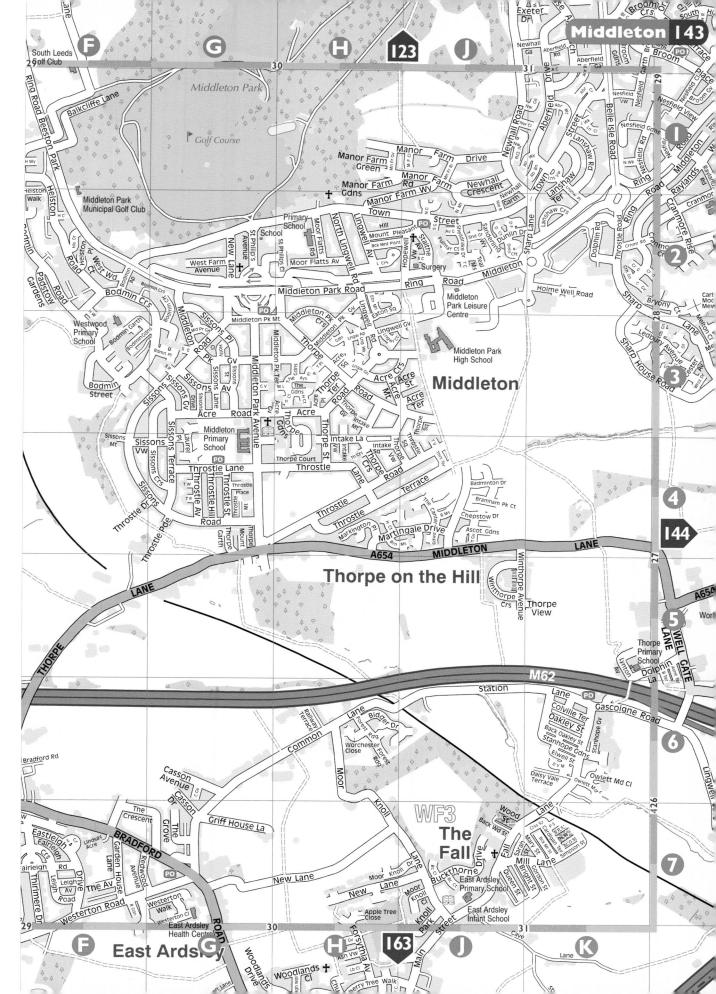

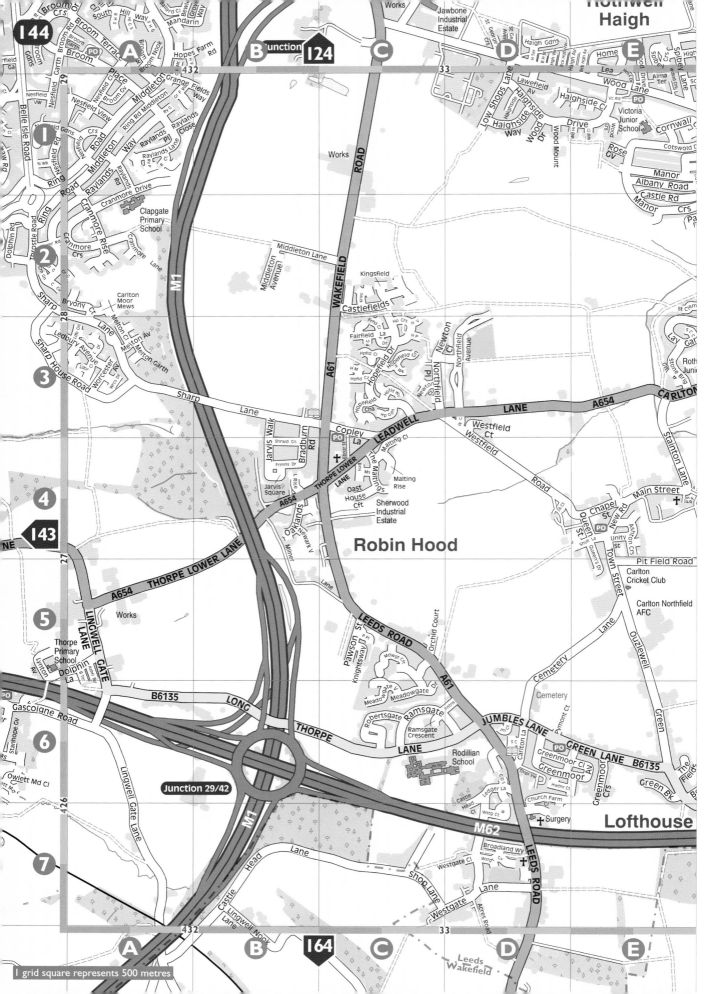

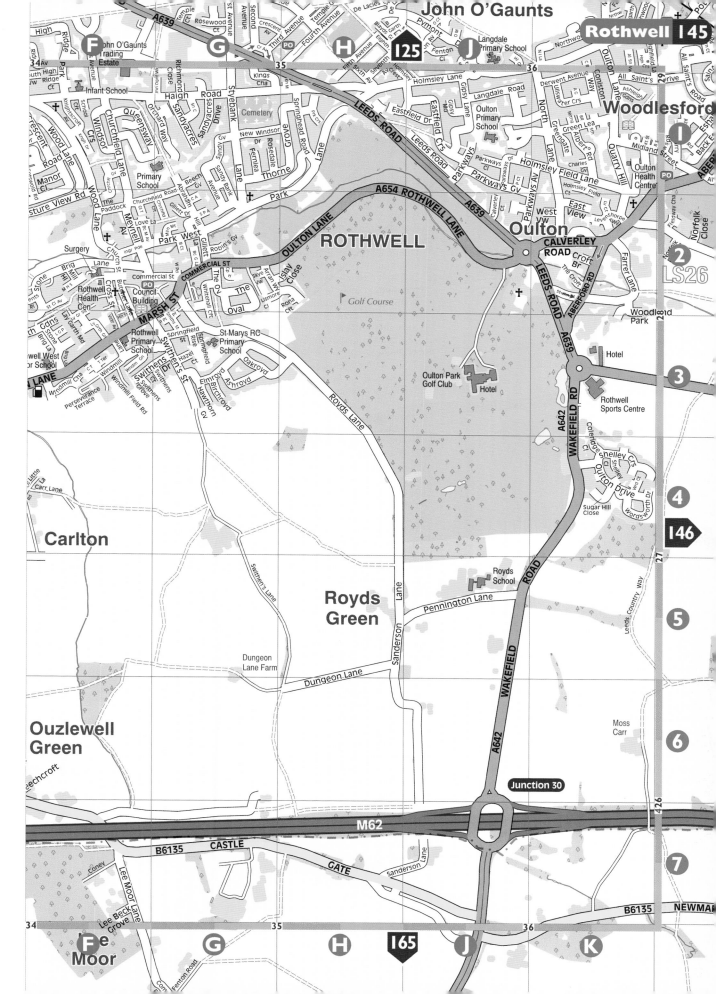

146

Woodlesford

126

166

A · B · C · D · E

LS26

Woodlesford Station

Minerva Industrial Estate

St station Lane
Farmers Hill

Leeds Country Way

Juniper
Yew Tree Dr
Rowan Ct
Chestnut
Redwood Cl

Lynwood Crs
Lynwood Avenue
Sydney St
Bernard st
Airedale Road

ABERFORD ROAD

Eshald
Back Eshald Pl
Eshald Rd

Norfolk Close
Norfolk Drive
Eshald Lane

Fleet Lane

Fleet Lane

Woodland Park

Leeds Country Way

Hotel

Rothwell Sports Centre

METHLEY LANE

A639

Methley Park Hospital

Fleet Lane

Trans Pennine Trail

Woodrow Crs
Station Rd
Wood Row
The Hollings

LEEDS ROAD

Woo

Mulberry Gdns

145

Shelley Crs
Shelley
Oulton Dr
Wordsworth Dr
ar Hill

Clumpcliffe

Leeds Country Way

Moss Car

Leeds Country Way

Hungate Lane

Park Lane

WATERGATE

B6135

Hungate

Scholey Hill

B6135 **NEWMARKET**

M62

LANE
437

Bleth Lanes

Trans Pennine Trail

Leeds Wakefield

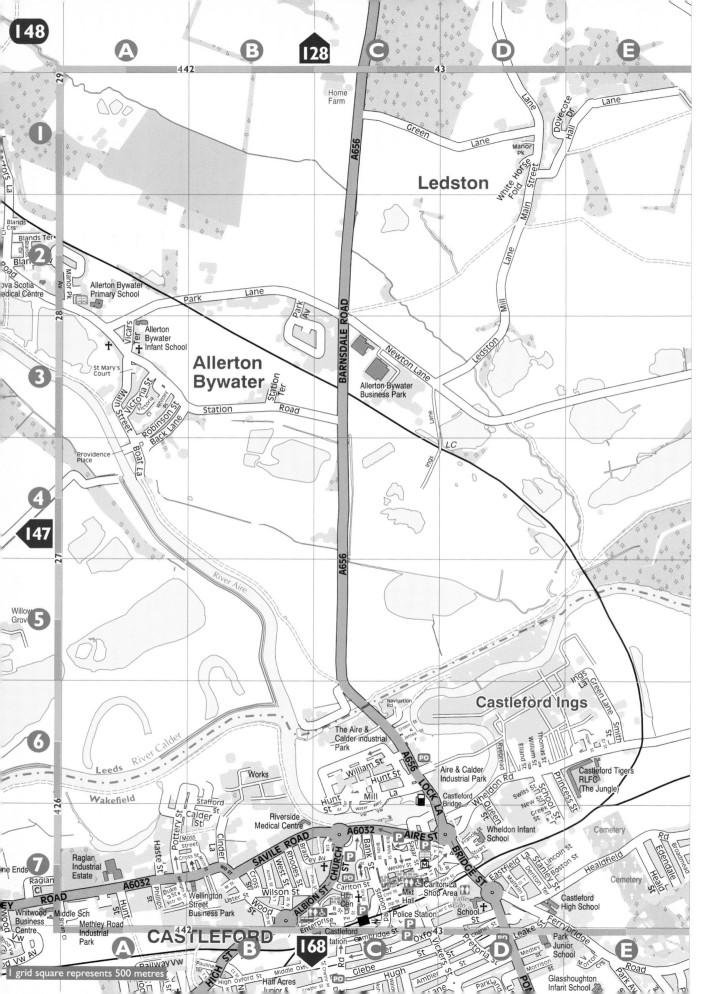

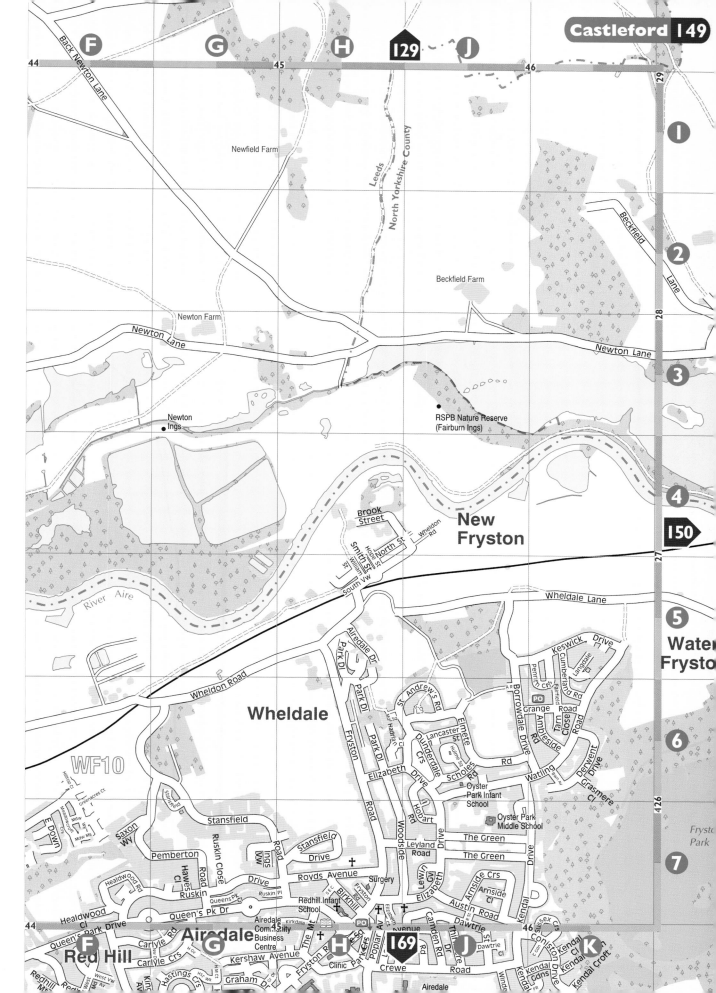

F G H **129** J

I

2

Newfield Farm

Leeds

North Yorkshire County

Beckfield Lane

28

Beckfield Farm

Newton Farm

Newton Lane

Newton Lane

3

Newton Ings

RSPB Nature Reserve
(Fairburn Ings)

4

150

Brook Street

Wheldon Rd

New Fryston

27

Smith St

Hope St

North St

William St

South Vw

Wheldale Lane

5

Water Fryston

Airedale Dr

Park Dl

Keswick Drive

Langdale

Cumberland Rd

Penrith

St Andrew's Rd

Wheldon Road

Park Dl

Fairfield

Borrowdale Drive

PO

Grange

Tarn Close

Ambleside Road

Wheldale

Park Dl

Fryston Road

St Hadrian Cl

Lancaster St

Elmete St

Dunderdale Crs

Scholes Rd

Watling Rd

Denwent Drive

Grasmere Cl

6

WF10

Elizabeth Drive

Hobart

Oyster Park Infant School

Oyster Park Middle School

Drive

Fryston Park

Saxon Wy

Stansfield

E Down

Mdw

Greenacres Ct

Ruskin Close

Stansfield Drive

Ings Mw

Woodside

Leyland Road

The Green

The Green

7

Pemberton

Hawes Cl

Ruskin Road

Drive

Royds Avenue

Surgery

Lewin Gv

Elizabeth Drive

Arnside Crs

Arnside Cl

Kendal

Healdwood Rd

Ruskin Pl

Queens Pk

Redhill Infant School

Birkhill

Fryston Rd

Elizabeth Rd

Austin Road

Kendal

Healdwood Cl

Queen's Pk Dr

Aredale Community Business Centre

Kirkdale

The Mt

PO

Poplar Av

Camden Rd

Dawtrie

Coniston Drive

Kendal Gdns

426

44 F **Red Hill**

Carlyle Rd

Carlyle Crs

Kershaw Avenue

Graham Dr

45 G

Clinic

Parkers

H **169**

Crewe

Airedale

Thilere Road

J

Dawtrie

Winder

Sussex Crs

46 K

Kendal Croft

Redhill Mt

150

130

A   B   C   D   E

1

2

Fairburn

3

4

149

Water Fryston

5

6

7

A   B   C   D   E

170

Beckfield Lane

Newton Lane

Caudle Hill

Manor Ct

Piper Hl

Cut Road

Cross Hl

Gauk St

Old Carth

Cft

PO

Top Fold

Fairburn Sports & Recreation Centre

Silver Street

Fairfield

Orchard Dr

Fairburn Community School

Lunnfields Lane

Lunnfields Lane

Rawfield Lane

A1(T)

A1(T)

A1(T)

A162

A162

A162

New Lane

Ledgate

LC

North Yorkshire County

Wakefield

River Aire

Fryston Park

Drive

smere

Fryston Lane

Old High Street

Great Street

Cut Rd

Norfolk Close

Hall Cft

Gauk St

North Road

Church St

School Cft

Brotherton & Byram CP School

Selby Gas & Leisure Centre

OLD CT N RD

Qu Margaret's Dr

Foxcliff

Byram Industrial Park

Wood Lea

Brothe

West Acres

Marsh Cft

Hillside

Sandringham Rd

LC

447   48

29

28

27

426

I grid square represents 500 metres

Fryston

Betteras Hill Road

F G H 131 J

Mill Close

Dunce Mire

LC

49 50 51 29

A162

Hillside Cl

Bedfords Fold

Lilac Oval

Pine Tree Lane

Chapel Street

Hillam

Hillam Comn

Rose Lea Close

Hillam Hall Lane

Hillam Hall Close

Hillam Lane

Stocking Lane

1

Hillam Lane

2

Woo

Hillam Lane

Fairfield Lane

28

Burton Salmon

3

Burton Salmon Primary School

The Paddock

Burton Common Lane

Burton Common Farm

Main St

Top Stone Cl

Clarkson Dr

4

Poole Lane

27

5

Byram Hall

6

Byram Farm

426

rton

7

Byram Pk Av

Byram Park Road

Byram Park Road

Sutton Lane

49 50 51

E Acres

St Edwards Cl

F G H 171 J K

Byram **Sutton**

Tippaty Lane

Smeathalls

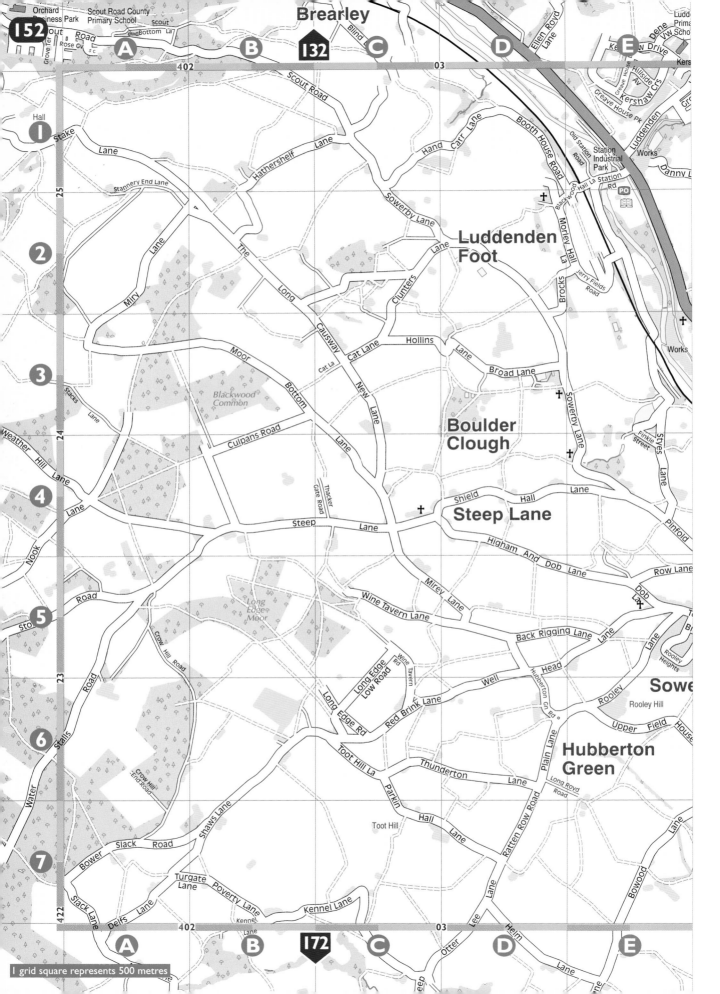

Brearley

132

Luddenden Foot

Boulder Clough

Steep Lane

Hubberton Green

Sowe

Rooley Hill

Orchard Business Park

Scout Road County Primary School

Hall

Blackwood Common

Long Edge Moor

Toot Hill

Kennel

172

Stake Lane

Stannery End Lane

Scout Road

Hathershelf Lane

Hand Carr Lane

Booth House Road

Sowerby Lane

Clunters Lane

Hollins Lane

Broad Lane

Sowerby Lane

Morley Hall La

Brocks

Old Station Road

Station Industrial Park

Ellen Royd Lane

Kershaw Crs

Creave House Pk

Kershaw

Danny L

Works

Works

Miry Lane

The Long Causeway

Moor Bottom Lane

Cat La

Cat Lane

New Lane

Thacker Gate Road

Culpans Road

Weather Hill Lane

Stacks Lane

Nook

Sto

Stalls

Road

Crow Hill Road

Crow Hill End Road

Water

Bower

Slack Road

Shaws Lane

Steep Lane

Shield Hall Lane

Higham And Dob Lane

Row Lane

Pinfold

Mirey Lane

Wine Tavern Lane

Back Rigging Lane

Dob La

Wine Tavern Rd

Long Edge Low Road

Long Edge Rd

Red Brink Lane

Well Head

Hubberton Gn Rd

Rooley

Rooley Heights

Upper Field House

Toot Hill La

Thunderton Lane

Plain Lane

Long Royd Road

Parkin

Toot Hill Hall Lane

Ratten Row Road

Lee Lane

Helm Lane

Otter Lane

Bowood Lane

Turgate Lane

Poverty Lane

Kennel Lane

Slack Lane

Delfs Lane

Jerry Fields Road

Finkle Street

Styes Lane

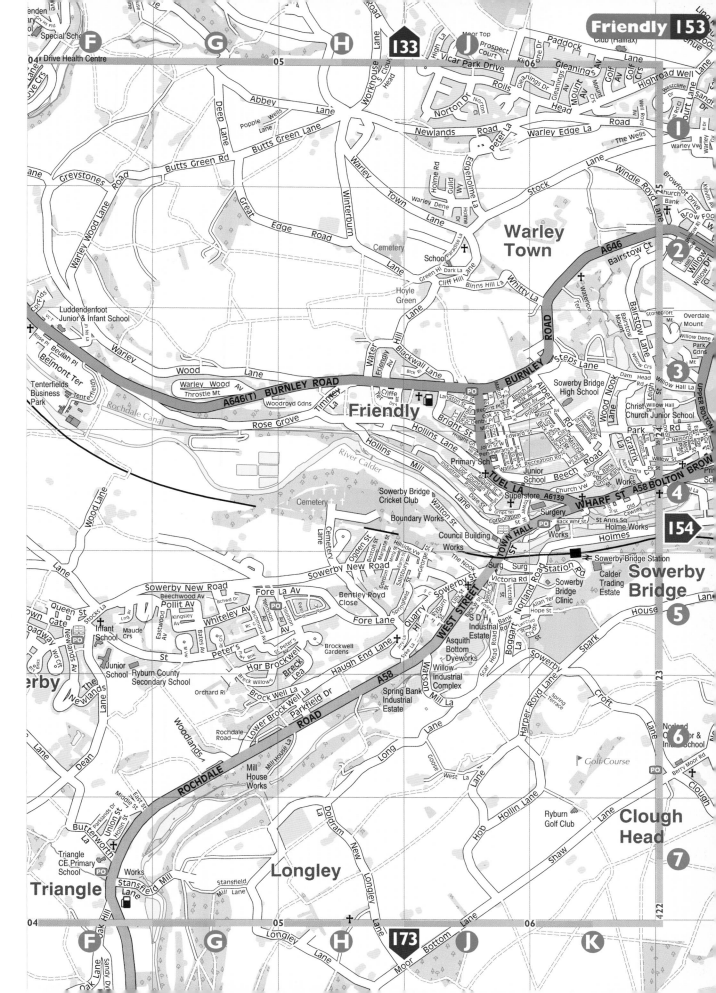

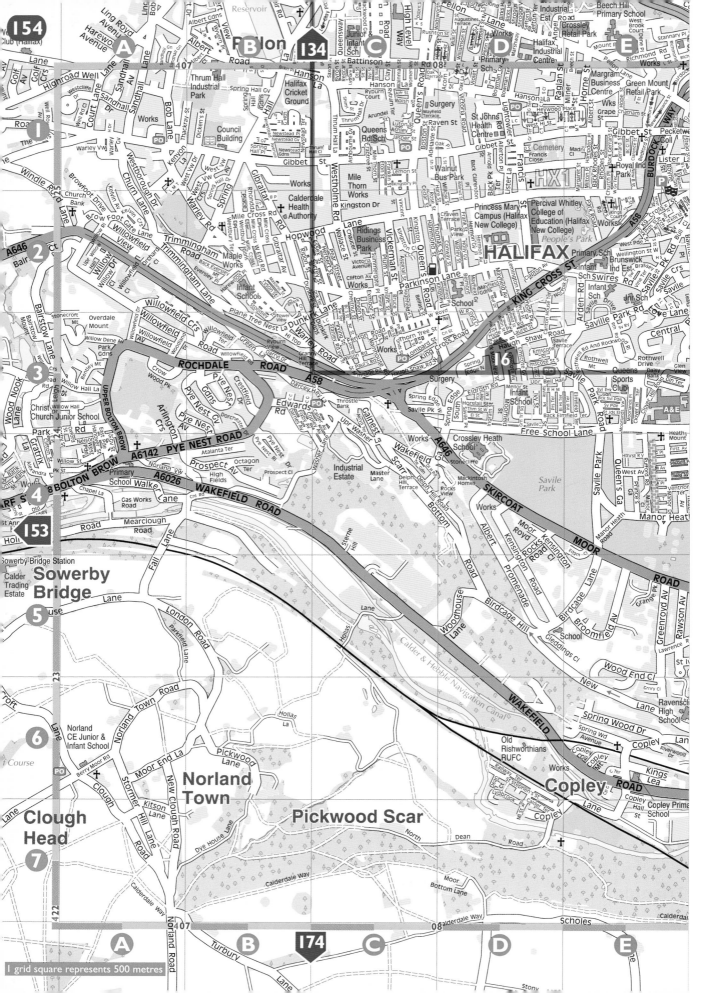

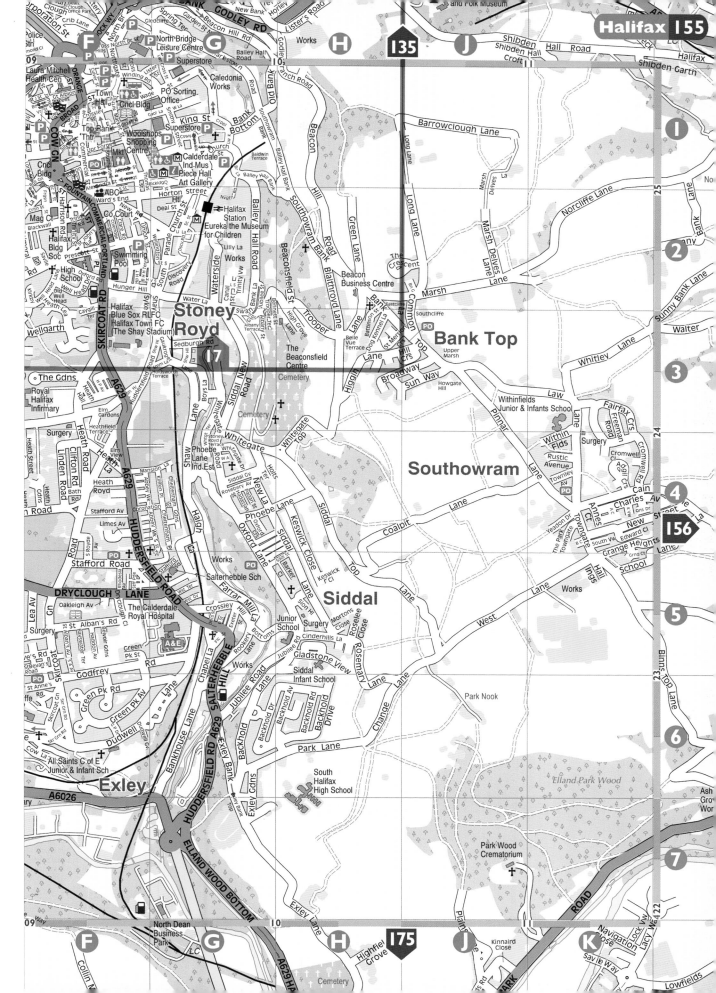

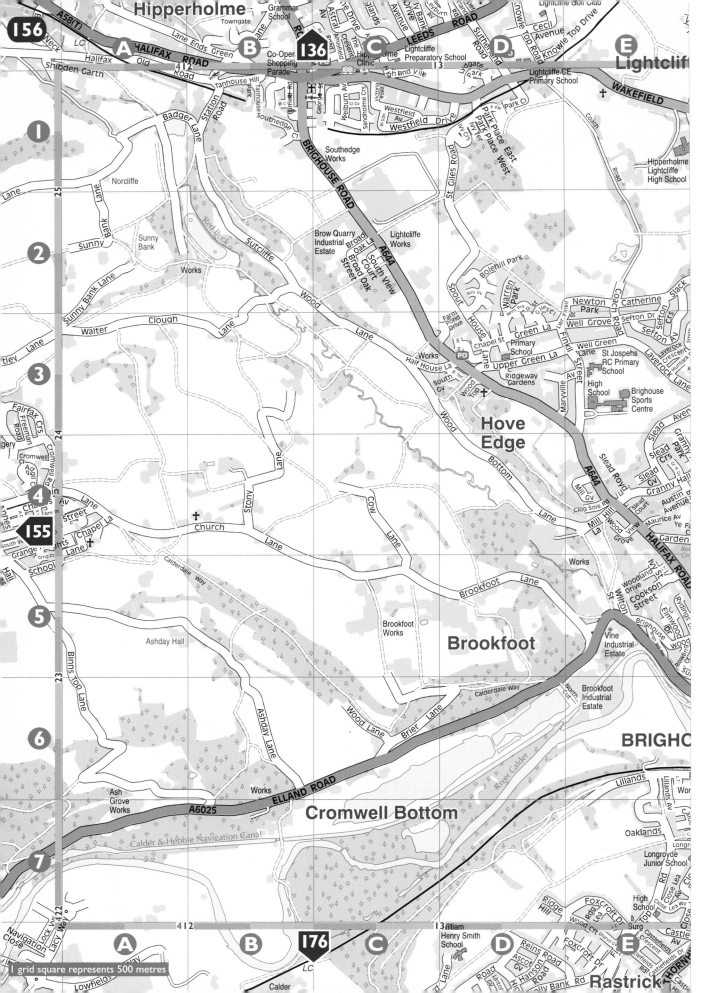

Bailiff Bridge

Hartshead Moor Top

Birkhouse

Thornhills

Clifton

Junction 2

Sickheaton

Littletown

Rawfolds

Liversedge

Norristhorpe

Roberttown
Castle Thorpe

Moor Top

WF15

Westfie

Spen Valley Industrial Park

Princess Mary Stadium

Spen Valley High School

Liversedge Cricket Club

Norristhorpe Primary School

Spenborough Industrial Estate

BMK Industrial Estate

Crosslane Industrial Estate

Cross Lane Business Park

Owlet Hurst

139

179

160

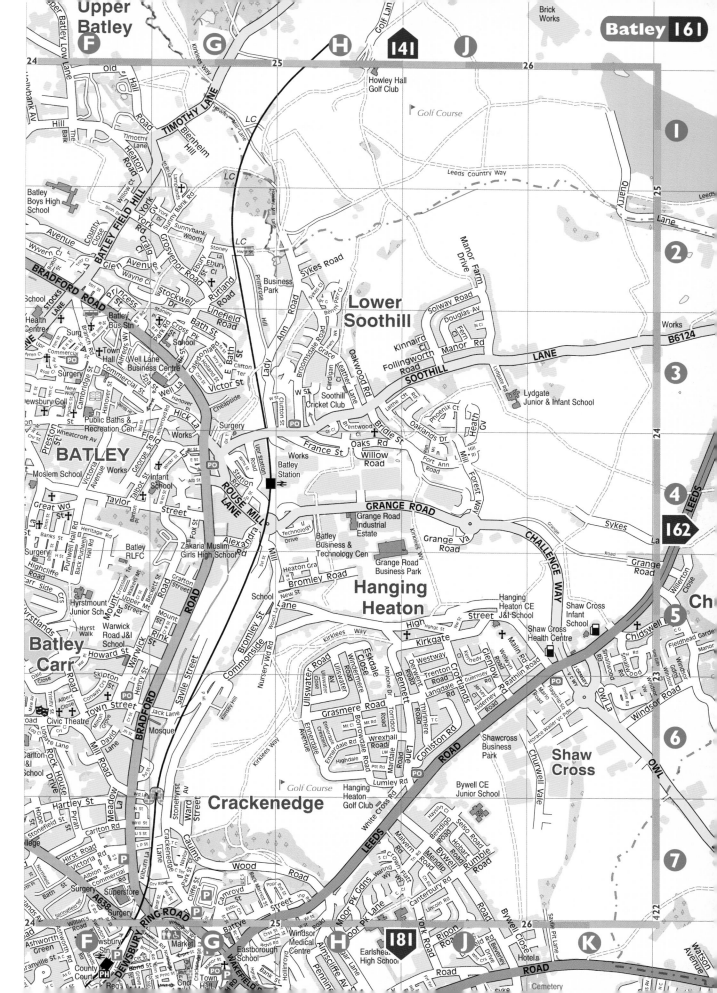

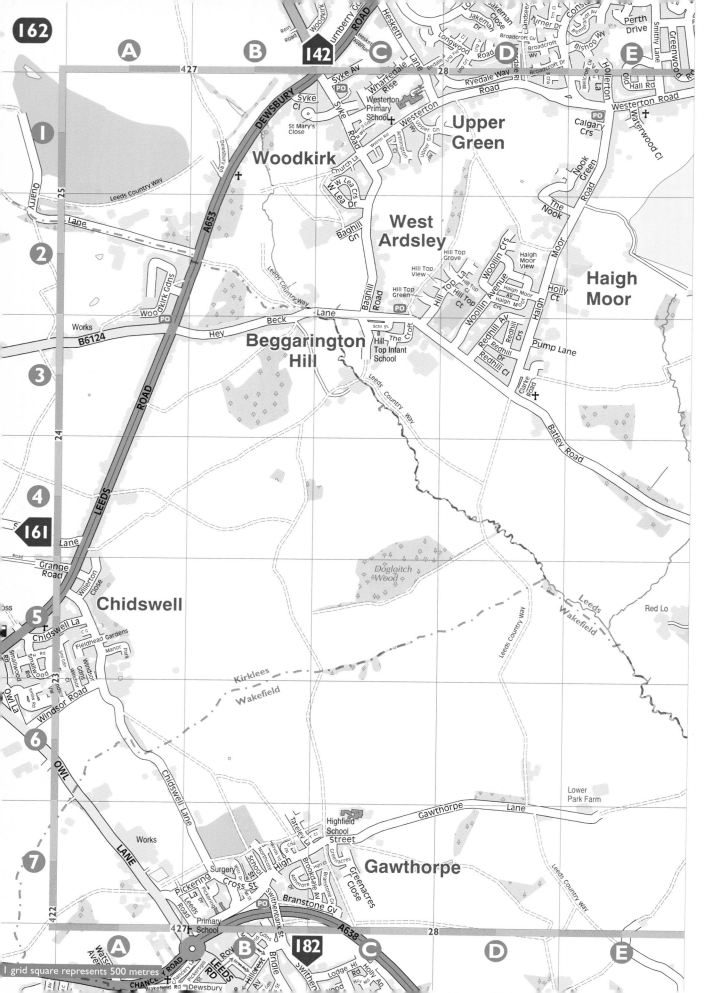

A 427 **B** **142** **C** 28 **D** **E**

1

Quarry

Lane

25

24

23

422

2

3

4

161

5

Chidswell

6

7

DEWSBURY

Syke Cl

St Mary's Close

Dewsbury Rd

A653

LEEDS

ROAD

Woodkirk Gdns

PO

Works

B6124

Hey

Beck

Lane

Grange Road

Willerton Close

Chidswell La

Fieldhead Gardens

Manor

Windsor

Gdns

Smithy Rd

Smallwood Rd

Smithy Rd

OWL La

Windsor Road

OWL

LANE

Works

Woodkirk

Leeds Country Way

W Lea Crs

W Lea Dr

Church La

Baghill Gn

Baghill Road

Leeds Country Way

Beggarington Hill

Syke Av

Syke Road

PO

Westerton Primary School

Westerton

Upper Gn

Upper Gn

Armington Wy

Westn Rd

Upper Green

West Ardsley

Hill Top View

Hill Top Green

Hill Top

Hill Top Cl

PO

Schl St

The Croft

Hill Top Infant School

Hill Top Grove

Woollin Crs

Woollin Avenue

Haigh Moor View

Haigh Moor

Haigh Mo

Redhill Av

Redhill Dr

Redhill Crs

Redhill Cl

Clarke Road

Haigh

Holly Ct

Pump Lane

Battey Road

The Nook

Nook Green Road

Moor

Haigh Moor

Calgary Crs

PO

Westerton Road

Waterwood Cl

Hollerton La

Old Hall Rd

Perth Drive

Greenwood

Smithy Lane

Wharfedale Rise

Hesketh Lane

Hesketh Avenue

Rein Road

Woodkirk

Turnberry Ct

ROAD

Syke Av

Ryedale Way

Road

Longwood Rd

Bedale Dr

Broadcroft Gv

Broadcroft Wy

Broadcroft Dr

Jakeman Dr

Jakeman Close

Consd Av

Turner Dr

Bishop Wy

Landseer Av

Wellcroft

Dogloitch Wood

Leeds Country Way

Leeds Wakefield

Red Lo

Kirklees

Wakefield

Lower Park Farm

Gawthorpe Lane

Highfield School Street

Gawthorpe

Greenacres Close

Tateley Cl

Northcote

Chancery La

High

Surgery

School St

Cross St

Pickering La

Pickering Leeds Road

Primary School

CHANCERY ROAD

LEEDS RD

Wakefield Rd Dewsbury

427

A Watson Ave **B** **182** **C** **D** **E**

A638

28

Swithenbank St

Branstone Gv

Brookdale Av

Ashmore

Hilltop

Bridle

Lodge Hl

Holly Ap

Swithen

Hillcrest

PO

1 grid square represents 500 metres

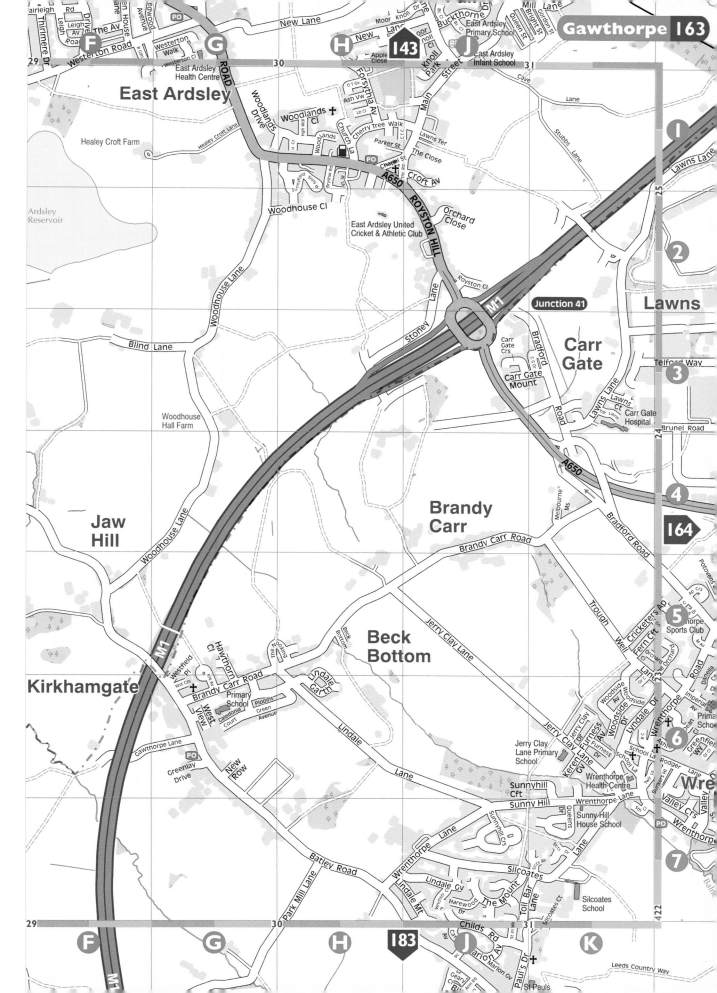

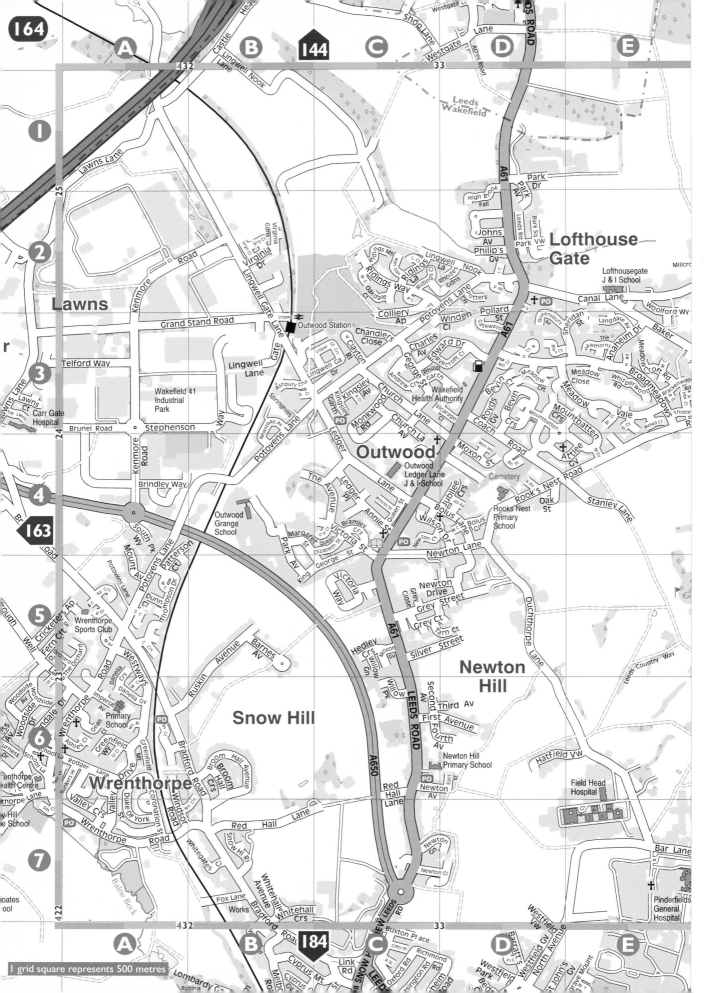

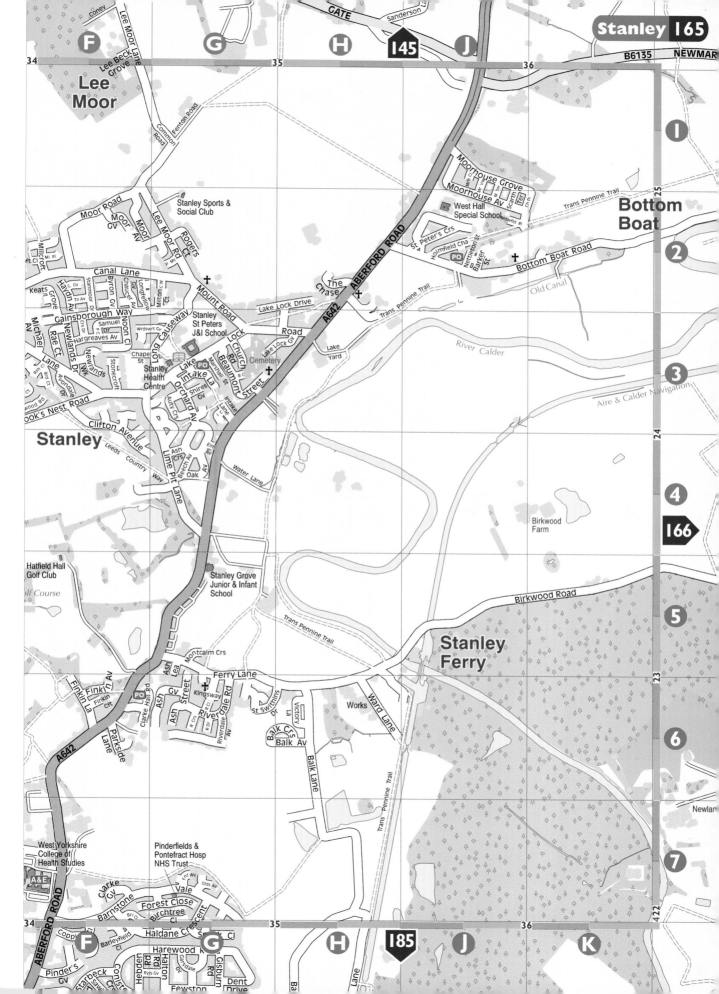

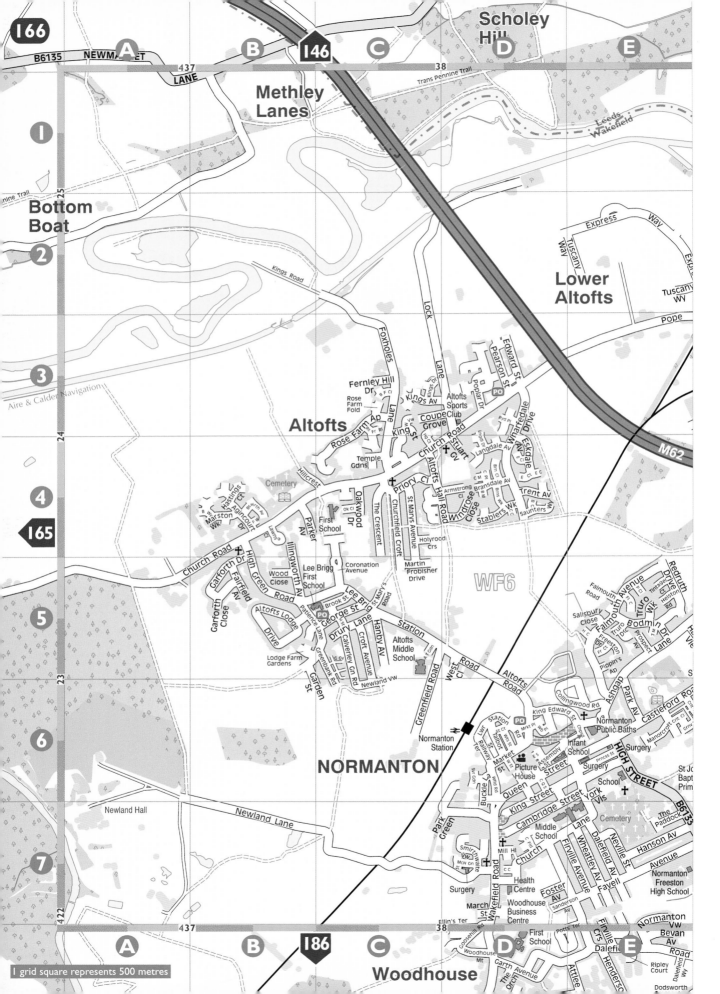

B6135 NEWMARKET

A 437 LANE B 146 C 38 D Scholey Hill E

Trans Pennine Trail

Methley Lanes

Leeds Wakefield

1

Bottom Boat

25

Express Way
Tuscany Way

2

Kings Road

Lower Altofts

Tuscany Wy

Pope

3

Aire & Calder Navigation

24

Foxholes Lane

Fernley Hill Dr
Rose Farm Fold
Rose Farm Ap

Altofts

Kings Av
Altofts Sports Club
Coupe Grove

Edward St
Pearson St

PO

Wharfedale Drive

Eskdale Drive

M62

Temple Gdns

King St

Church Road

Stuart Gv

Poplar Dr

Langdale Av

Rose Farm Lane

Cemetery

Hillcrest

Oakwood Dr

The Crescent

St Marys Avenue

Churchfield Croft

Altofts Hall Road

Priory Cl

Armstrong Cl
Windrose Close
Bransdale Av
Stablers Wk
Saunters Wy
Trent Av

4

165

Hastings
Marston
Agincourt Dr

First School

Parker Av

Church Road

Garforth Dr
Garforth Close
Fairfield Av

High Green Road

Wood Close

Illingworth Av

Lee Brigg First School

Coronation Avenue

Holyrood Crs

Martin Frobisher Drive

WF6

Falmouth Road

Truro Wk
Redruth Drive
Tintagel
Helston Rd

23

5

Altofts Lodge Drive

Brook St

Lee Brigg

PO

George St

Drury Lane

St Mary's Road

Hamby Av

Croft Avenue

Station Road

Altofts Middle School

Salisbury Close

Falmouth Avenue

Bodmin Dr

Truro

Fleeton

Prospect

Park Av

Ashgab

Pippin's Ap

Lodge Farm Gardens

Calverley Gn Rd
Greenbank Rd

Newton Vw

Garden St

West Cl

Greenfield Road

Altofts Road

Collingwood Rd

Castleford

422

6

Newland Hall

Newland Lane

NORMANTON

Normanton Station

Railway St
Station Rd
Market St

PO
Mrkt Pl

King Edward St

Normanton Public Baths

Surgery

Manorcroft

7

Surgery

Park Green

Buckle

Queen St
King Street

Cambridge Street

Mill Hl

Church

Middle School

York Vls
Dalefield Av
Finvill Avenue
Favell

School

HIGH STREET

Cemetery

Hanson Av

The Paddock

Normanton Freeston High School

B6133

Smithywaite
McH Gn

Surgery

Health Centre

Woodhouse Business Centre

March St

Wakefield Road

Foster Av
Sanderson

Neville St
Wheatley Av

Finvill Crs
Bevan Av
Daleif

Normanton Vw

Ripley Court

A 437 B 186 C 38 D First School E

Woodhouse

Henderson Av
Attlee

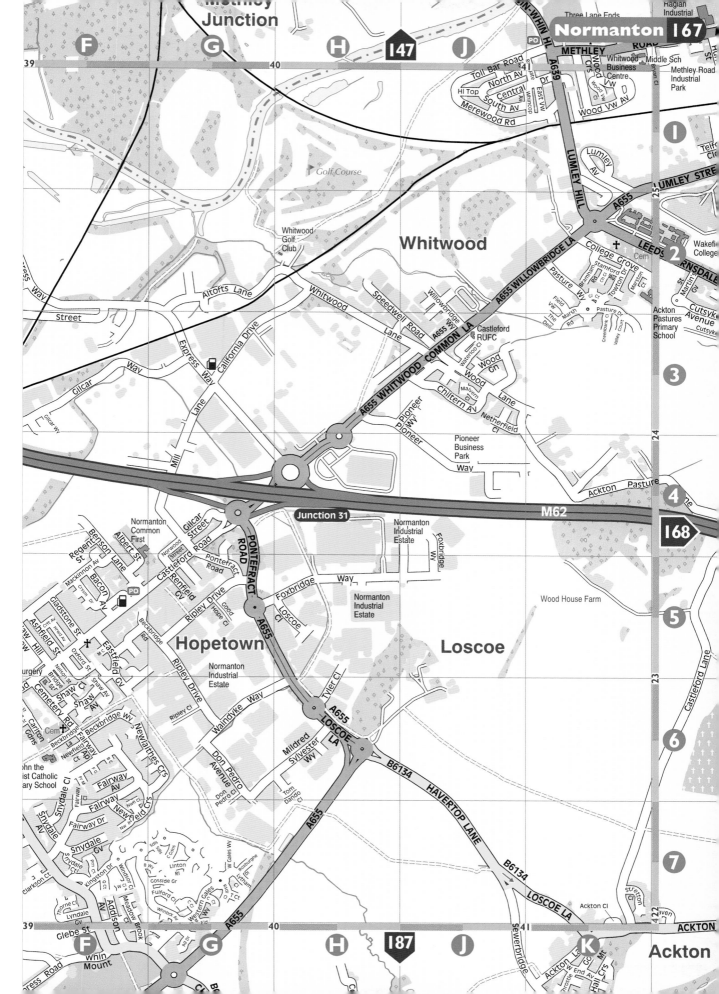

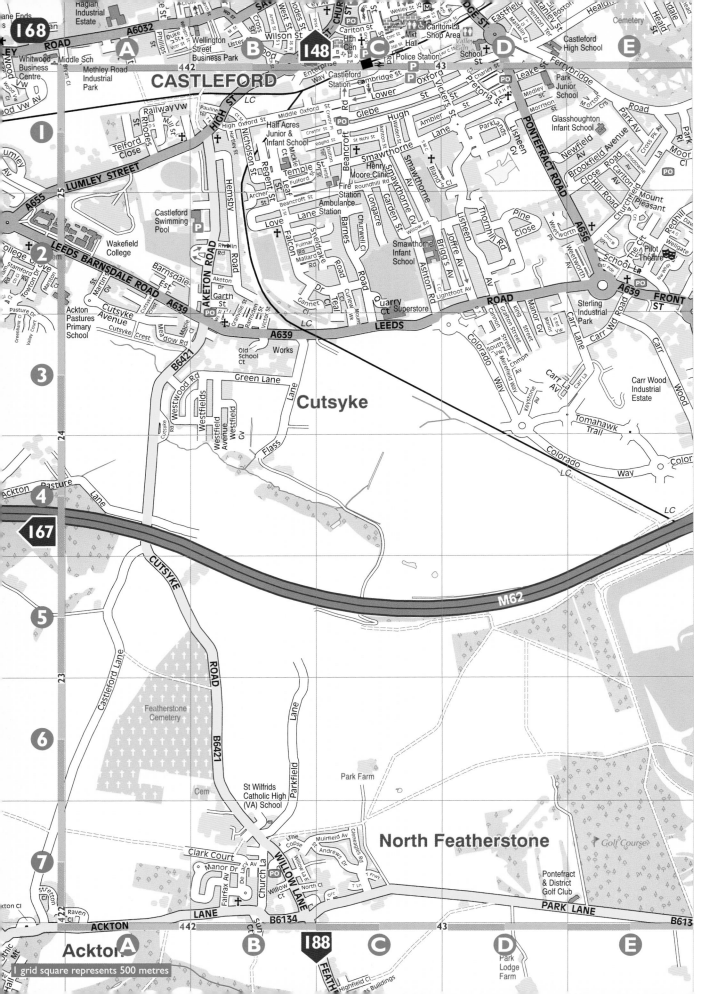

Byram Park Road

F   G   H   151   J

49   50   Sutton   Lane   51

I

Byram   Sutton   25

Smeathalls Farm

St Edwards Cl

Byram Pk Av

E Acres

ckingham Wy

Marsh   La

2

West Ings Crescent

West Ings Mews

West Ings Lane   West Ings Way   3

West Ings Court

River Aire   Aire St   Croftlands   Aire Street   Marsh End   24

Bridge La   The Croft   Marsh Lane   Stocking La   Trundles La

North Vw   Middleton Wy   Garden Lane   Sunny Bank   Fernley Green Close   Works

Forge Hl La   Grafton   Belvoir Dr   Rope Walk   Sunny Bank   Fernley Green Rd

Holes   Fisher   Saltersgate Av   HILL TOP   A645   Knottingley CE (C) J&I School   Racca   Fernley Green Rd   Surgery   4

6136   Bleasdale Av   Holderness Rd   Superstore   Surgery   Racca Avenue   Fernley Green Industrial Estate   Works

Malvern Rd   Marine Vila   Chilterns Av   Grove La   Cheviot Pl   Lamb Rd   Harker Street   Low Green

Pentland   Cleveland Av   Banks La   Gillann Street   Springfields   Works

KNOTTINGLEY   Middle Lane   Springfields

La   Northfield Av   LC   England La   Womersley Road   Broomhill Grove

Bone   Gv   Elmhurst   Westfield Rd   Quarry Avenue   Broomhill Avenue

Spawd   Hilgarth   Oakfield Crs   Eastfield Av   Broomhill Cl   5

Health Centre   The Ridgeway   England Lane J&I School   Broomhill Crescent   Common La

Hazel Rd   Cherry Tree Av   The Paddock   Middle Lane   Cemetery   The Poplars   Blackburn Lane

Works   LC   Broomhill Drive   Southmoor Lane   23

Elm Pl   Poplar Gv   Throstle Farm J&I School   Leys Lane   Downland Crescent   6

Carsdale Walk   Ryedale Av   Road

Windermere Drive   Derwent Pl   Hawswater Pl   Womersley Road   7   M62

M62   M62   422

49   50   51

F   G   H   191   J   K

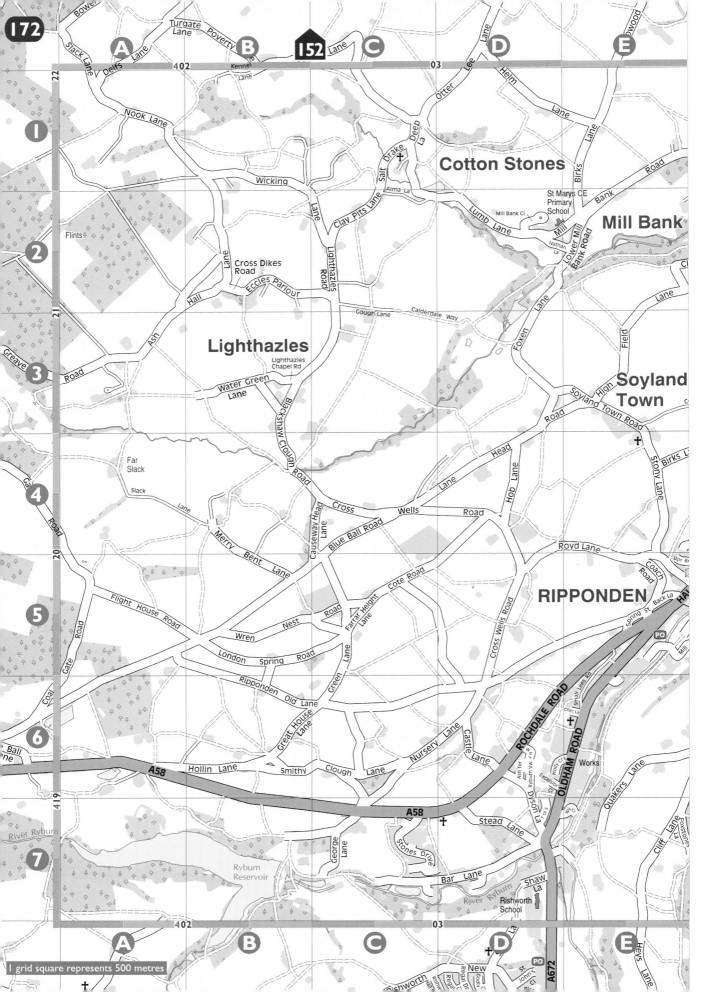

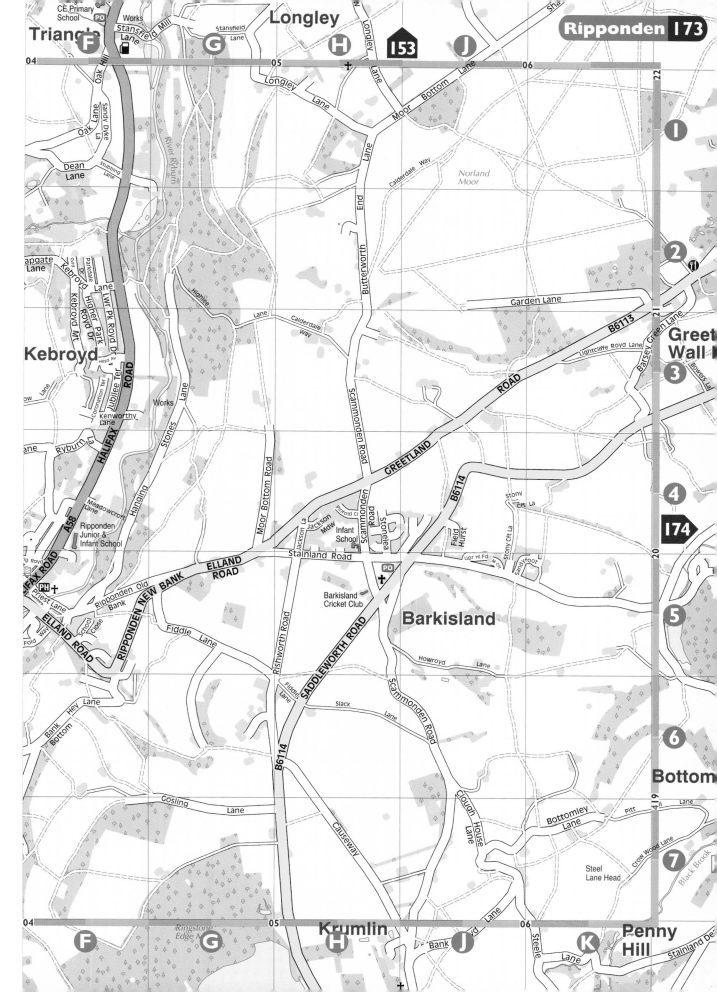

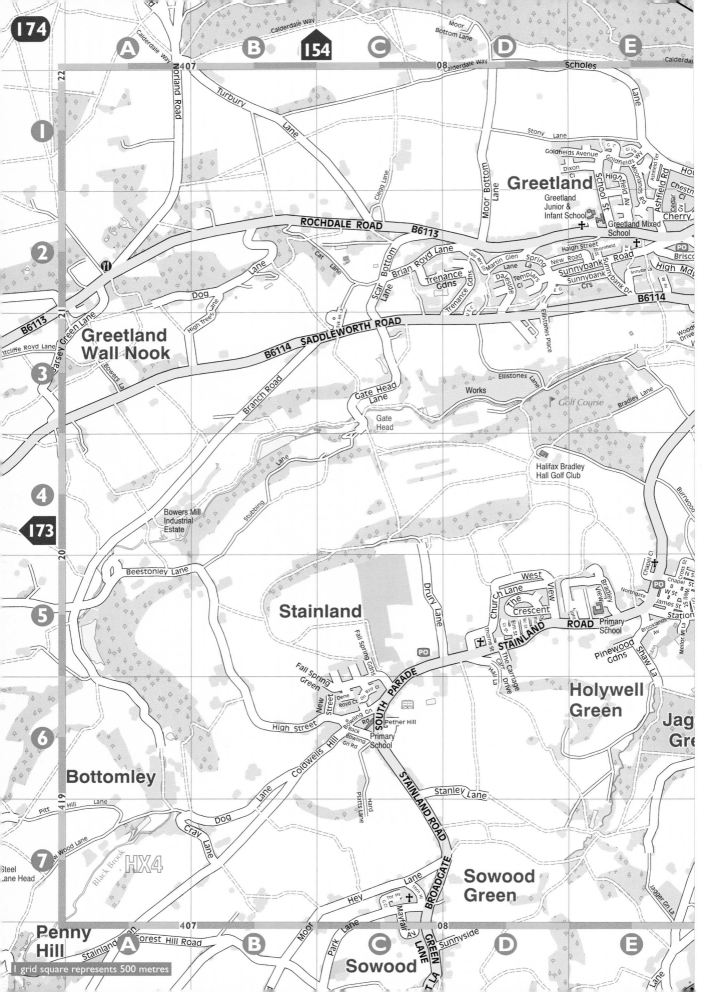

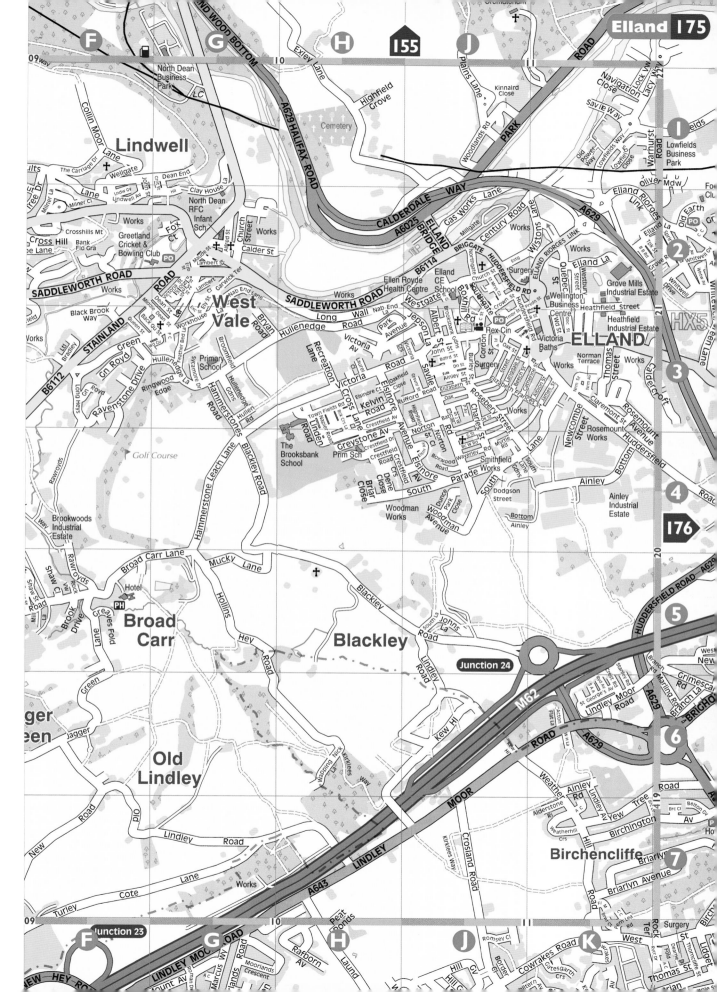

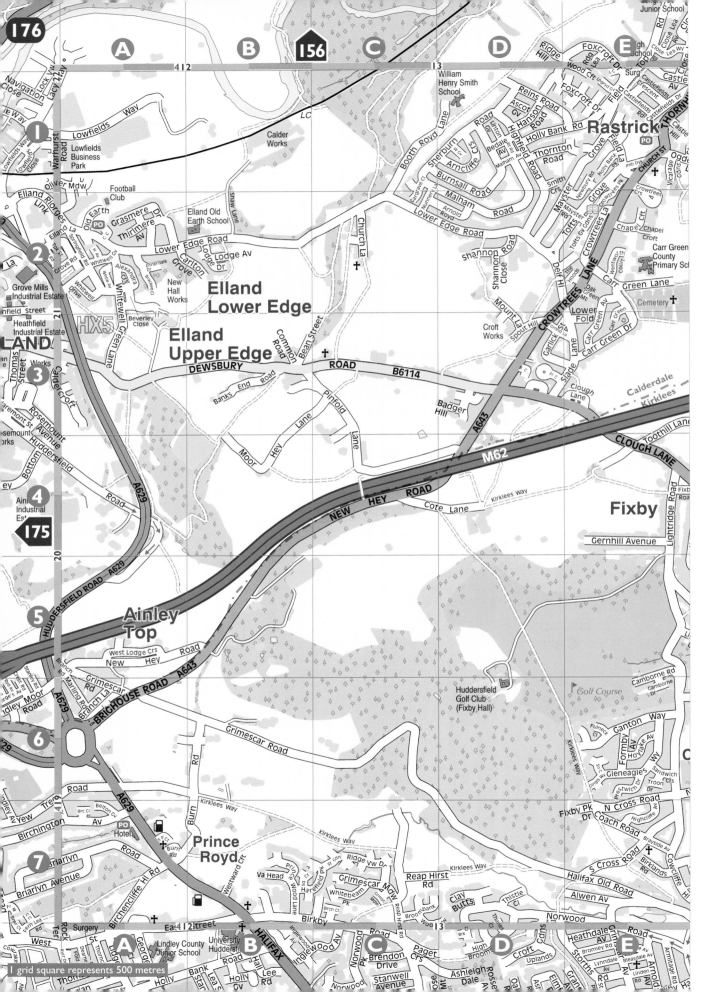

156

A B C D E

1 grid square represents 500 metres

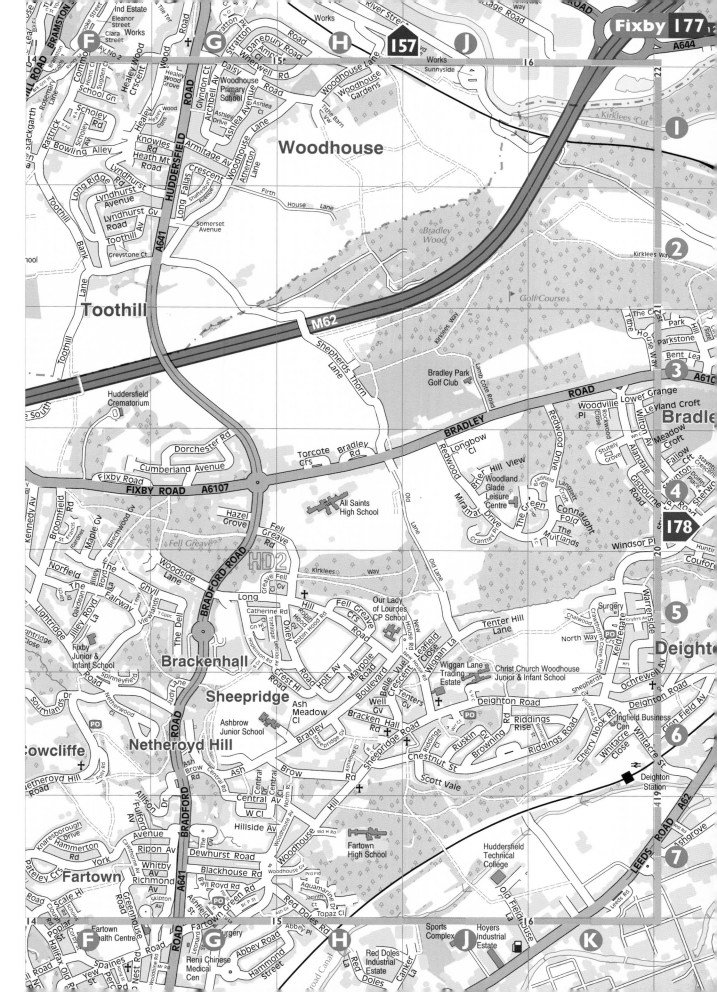

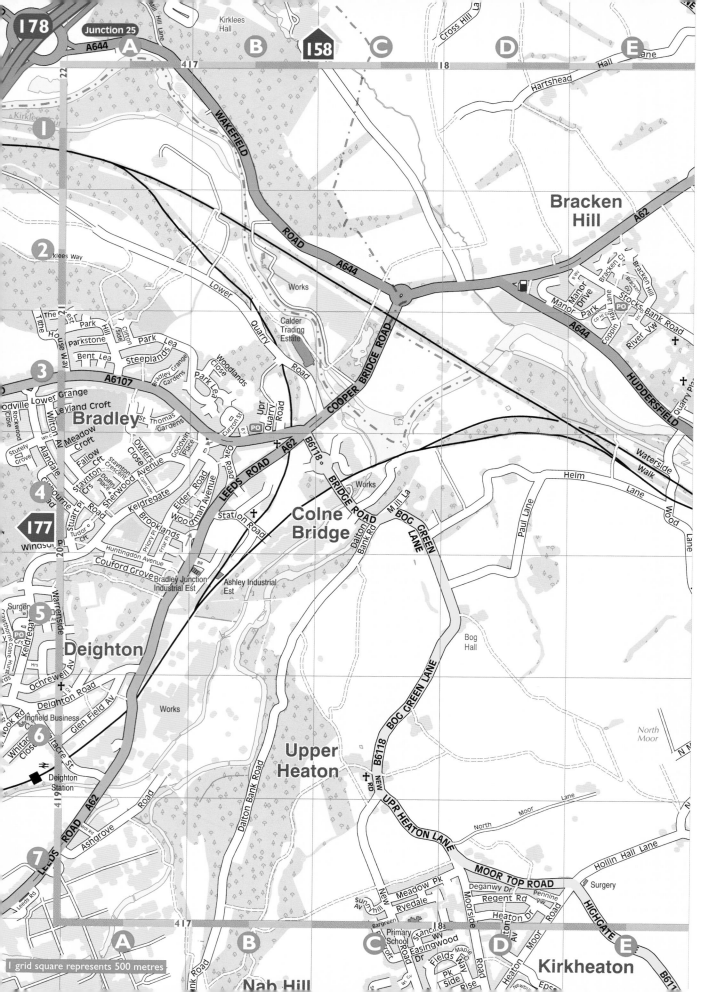

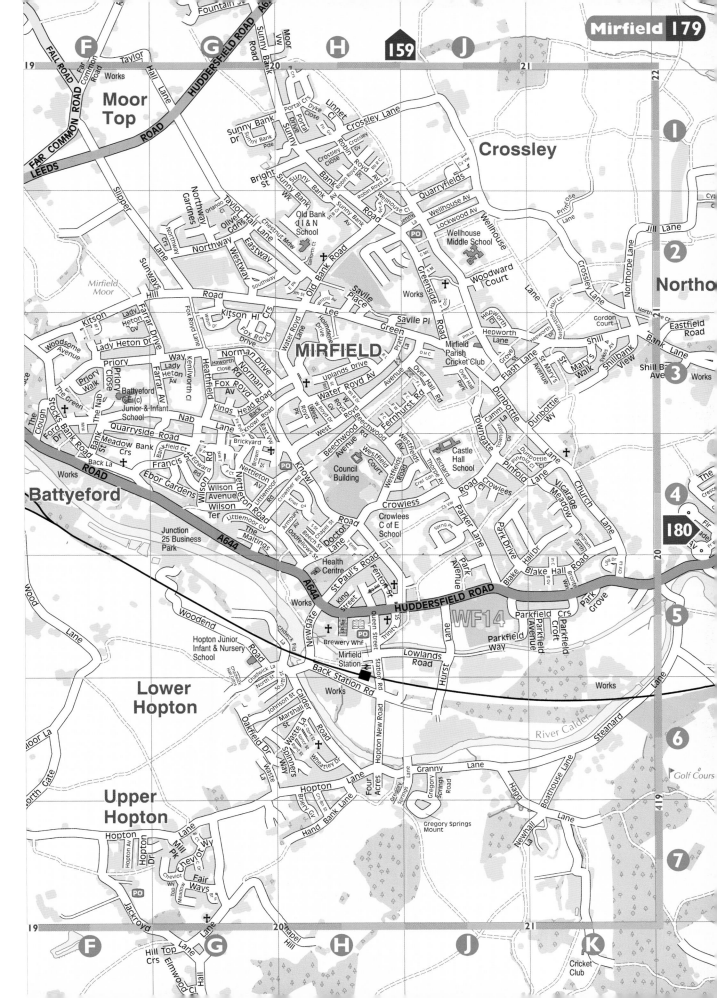

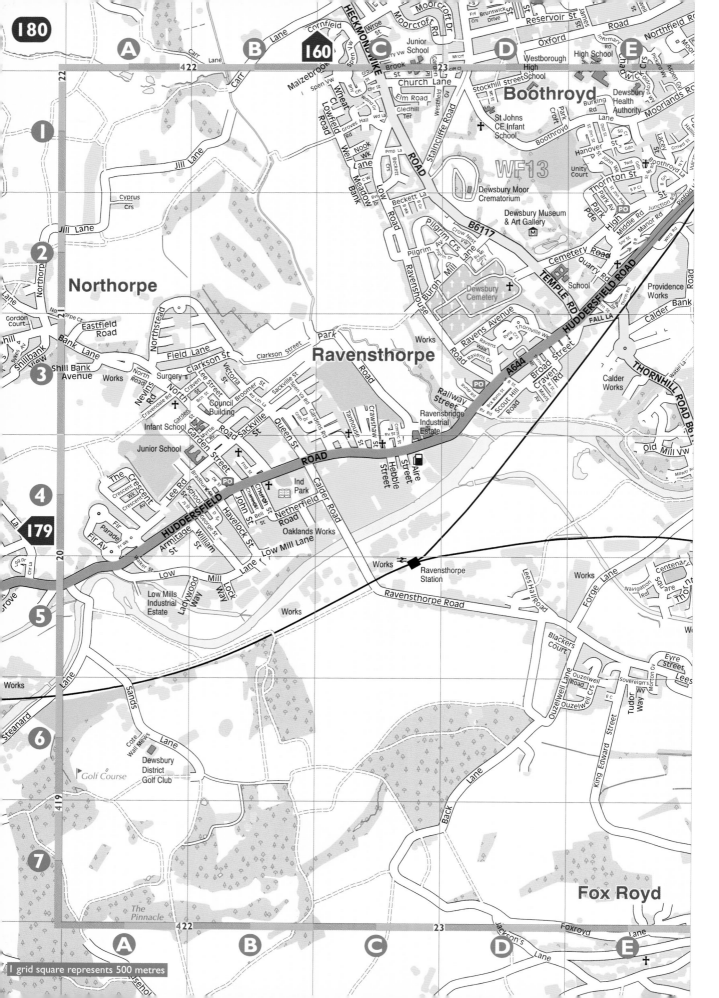

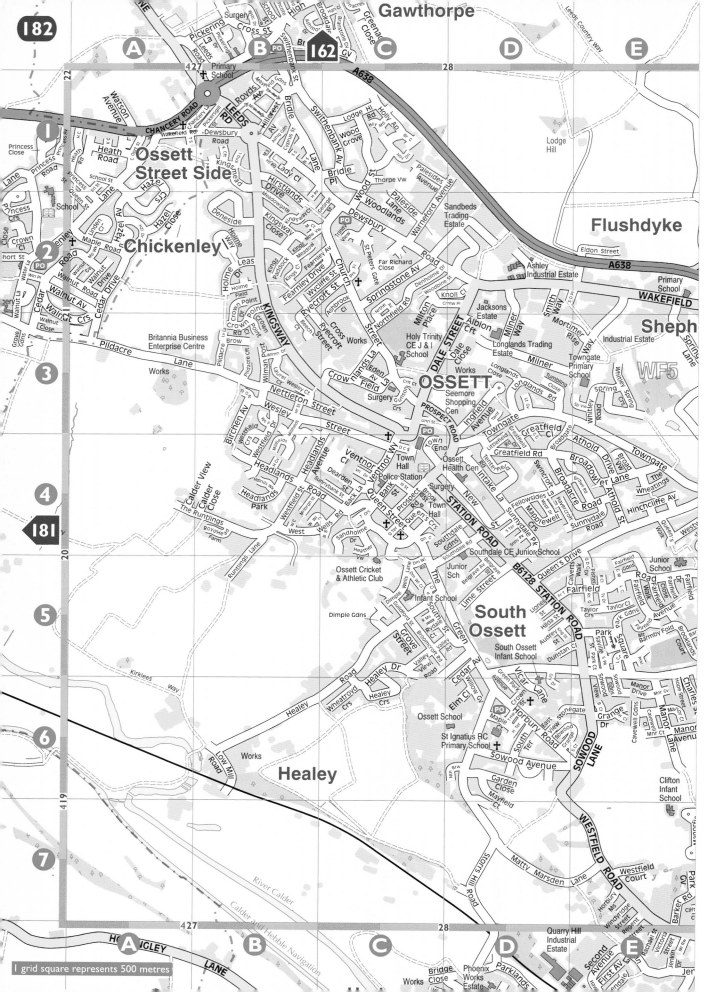

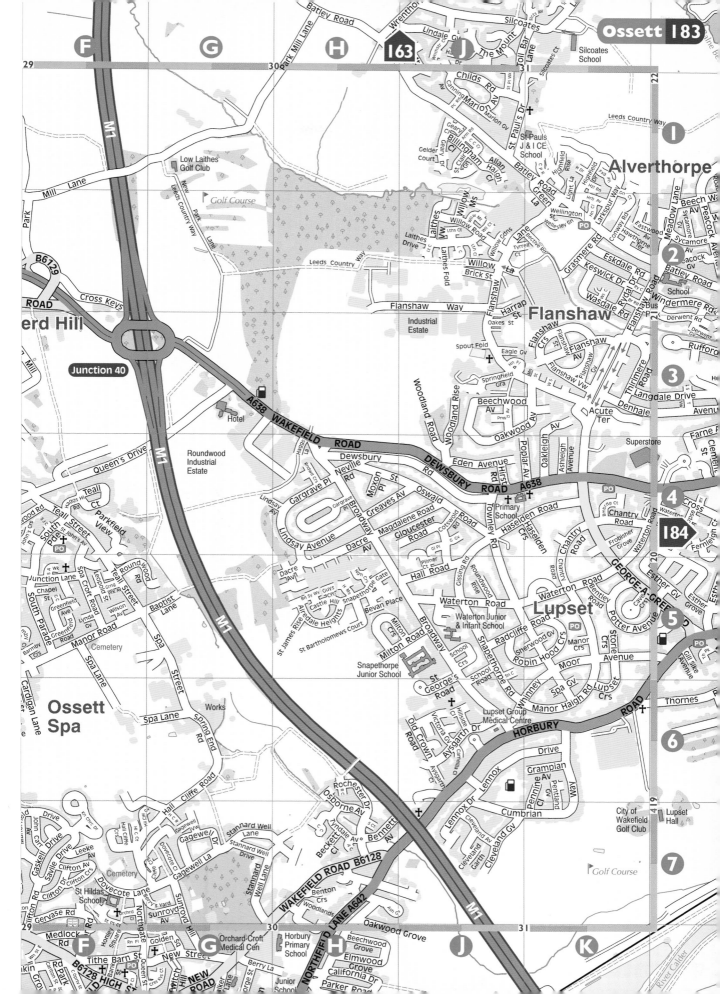

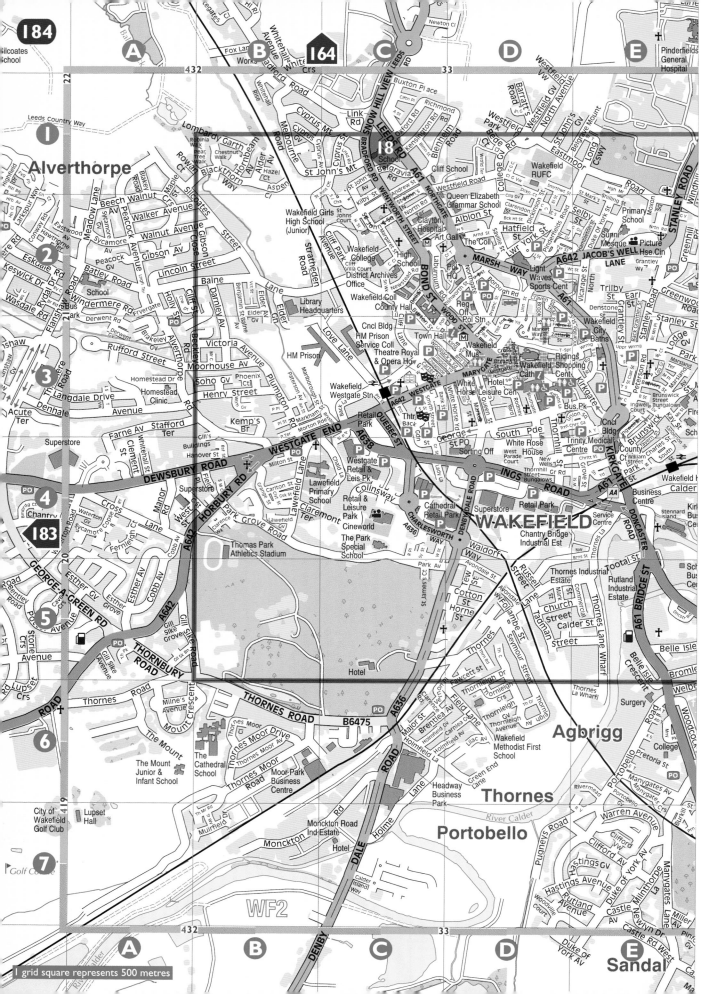

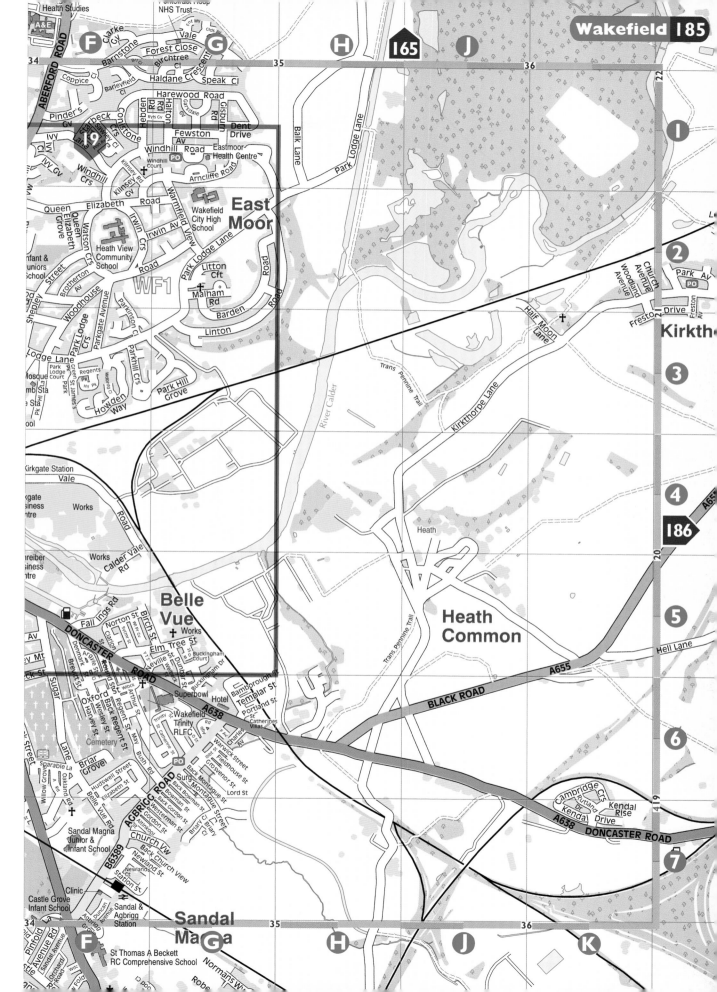

Health Studies
Pontefract Hoop
NHS Trust

A&E

F Clarke Gv
Barnstone
Forest Close
Birchtree Cl
Haldane Crescent
Speak Cl

G

Coppice
Pinder's Gv
Barleyfield
Harewood Road
Fewston Av
Windhill Road
Windhill Court
Arncliffe Road

Starbeck
Constone
Hebden Rd
Halton Rd
Garsdale
Gisburn Rd
Dent Drive
Eastmoor Health Centre
PO

19

Ivy Gv
Windhill Crs

Queen Elizabeth Grove
Queen Elizabeth Road
Elizabeth Road
Irwin Crs
Irwin Av
Park Lodge Lane
Wakefield City High School

Watson Crs
Brotherton Av
Woodhouse

East Moor

Infant & Juniors School
Park Lodge Crs
Parkgate Avenue
Parkinson Cl
Parkhill Crs
Heath View Community School
Road

WF1

Litton Cft
Malham Rd
Barden
Linton

Lodge Lane
Park Lodge Court
Regents Pk
Green St James's Park
Park Hill Grove
Howden Way
Parkhill Cl

Kirkgate Station
Vale
Works
kgate Business Centre

Schreiber Business Centre

Works
Calder Vale Rd
Road

Belle Vue

Fall Ings Rd
Norton St
Birch St
Elm Tree St
Neville St
Dunbar St
Works
Clarion St
Denmark St
Brent St
Buckingham Court
Buckingham Dr

Bamborough St
Templar St
Portland St
Catherines Villas

DONCASTER ROAD
Oxford St
Wesley St
Harvey St
Regent St
May St
Bush Rd
Arthur St
Wilbck
A638
Superbowl
Hotel
Wakefield Trinity RLFC
PO

Sparable La
Oakland Rd
Briar Grove
Hudswell Street
Elizabeth St
Willow Grove
Belle Vue Road

AGBRIGG ROAD

Warwick Street
Fieldhouse St
Grosvenor St
Lord St
Montague Street
Charles Av
Trinity Rd
Surg
Back Montague St
Back Bowman St
Bowman St
Gordon St
Westerman St
Kittlewood
Briary Cl
Briary
Back Gordon St

Sandal Magna Junior & Infant School
Church Vw
Back Church View
Newland St

B6389

Clinic
Station St
Castle Grove Infant School

St Thomas A Beckett RC Comprehensive School

Sandal Magna

Sandal & Agbrigg Station

F

G

Normans W

165

H

J

Balk Lane
Park Lodge Lane

River Calder

Trans Pennine Trail

Half Moon Lane

Church Avenue
Woodland Avenue
Park Av
PO
Freston Drive
Freston Av

Kirkth

Kirkthorpe Lane

2

3

Heath

Heath Common

Trans Pennine Trail

4

186

A65

5

Hell Lane

BLACK ROAD
A655

6

Cambridge Crs
Rutland Dr
Kendal Rise
Kenda Drive
Kendal Drive
A638 DONCASTER ROAD

7

H

J

K

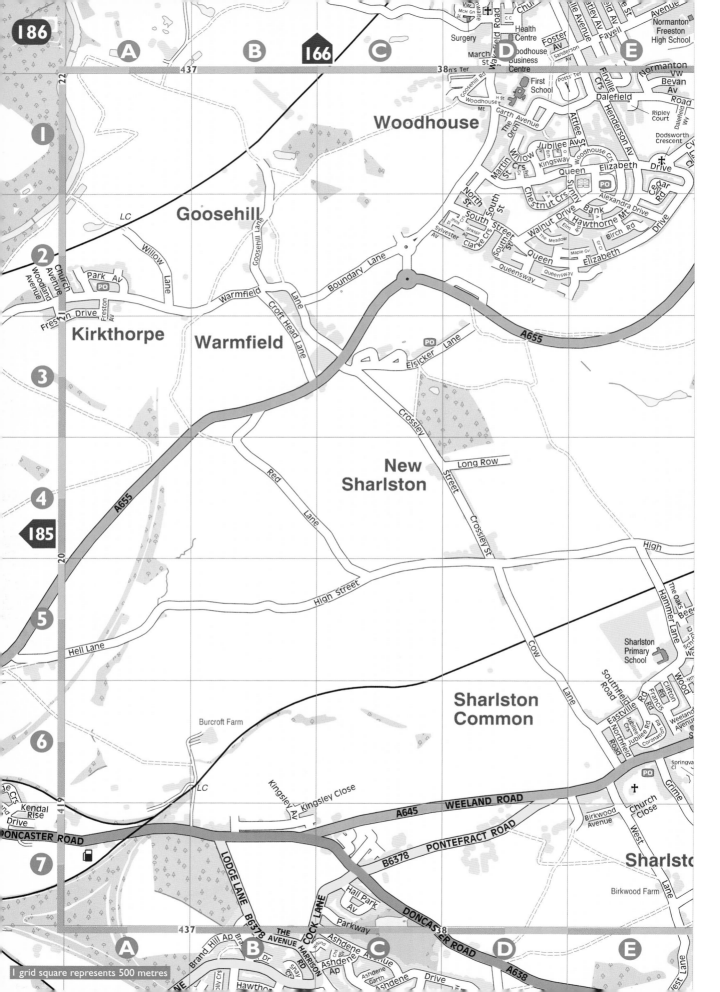

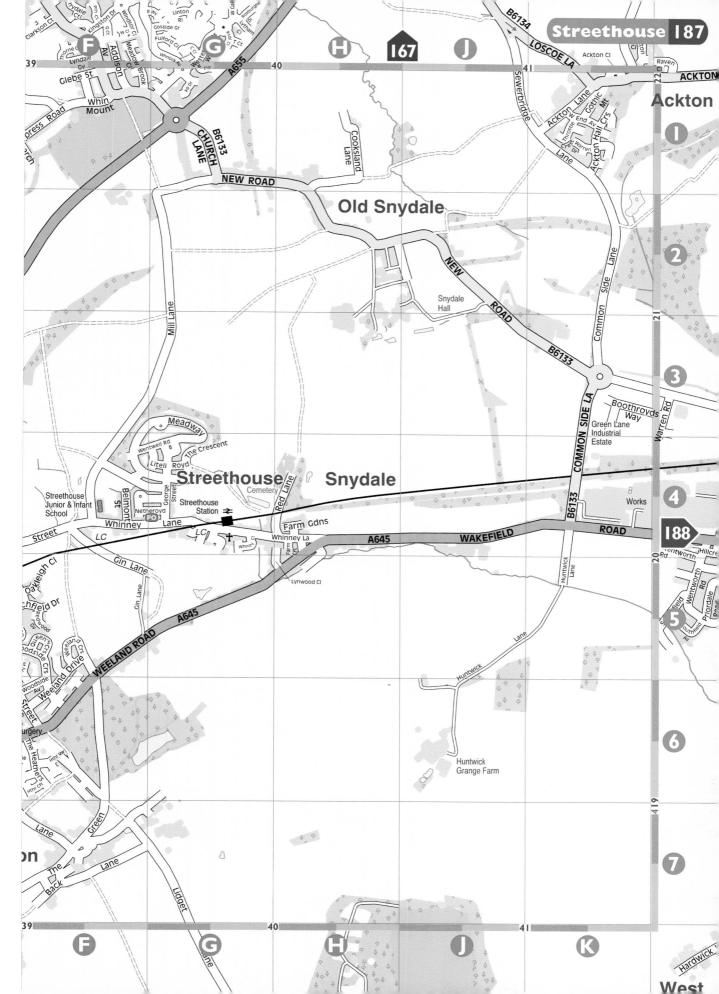

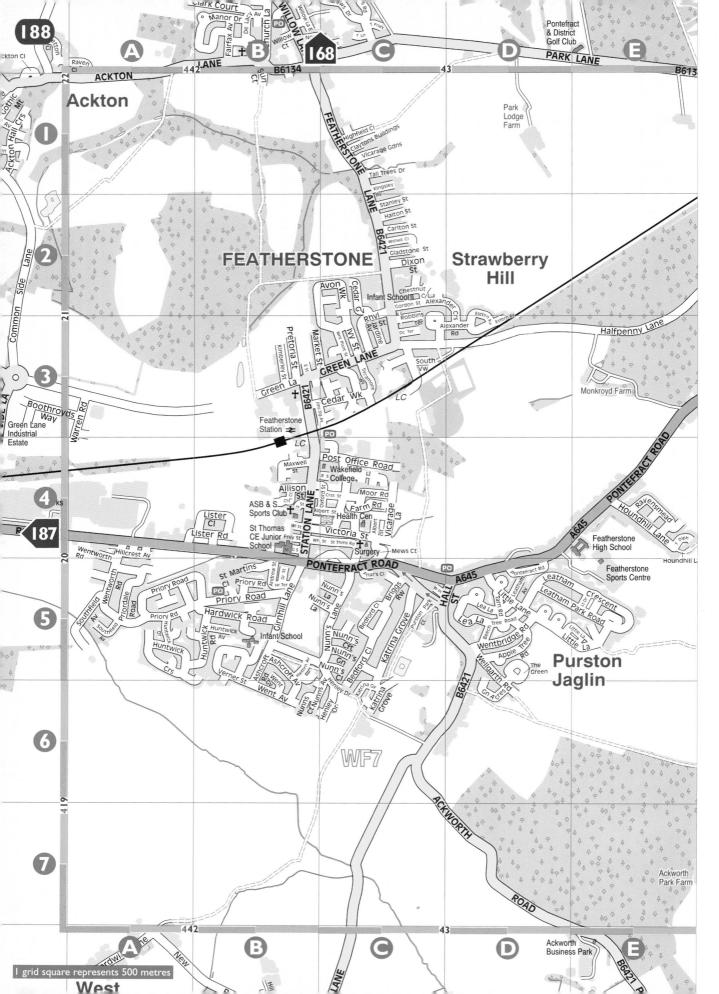

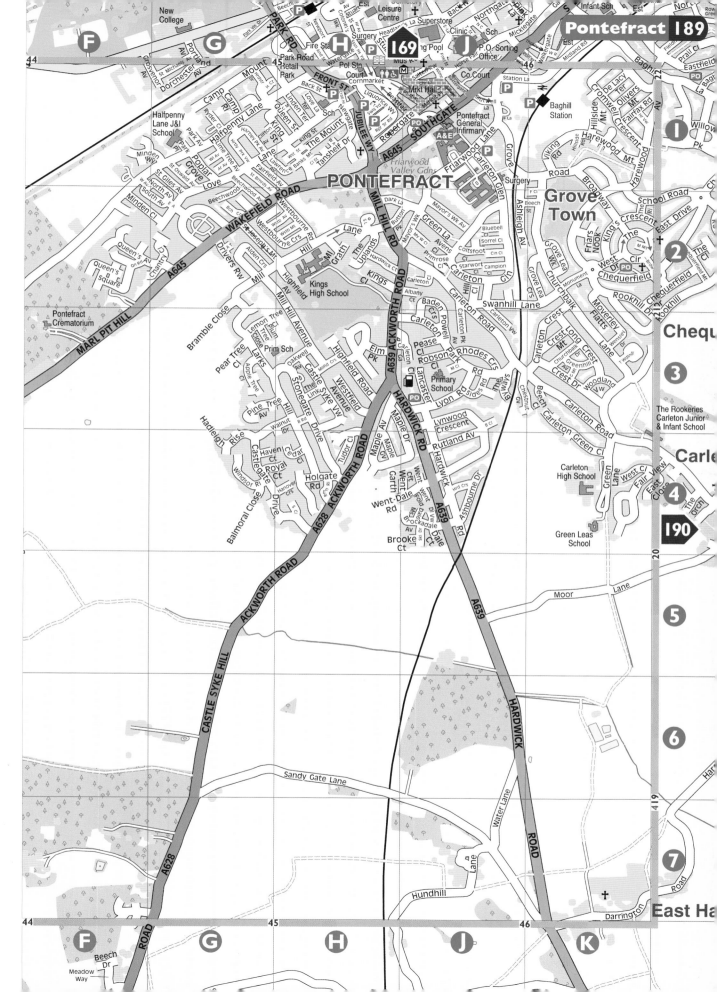

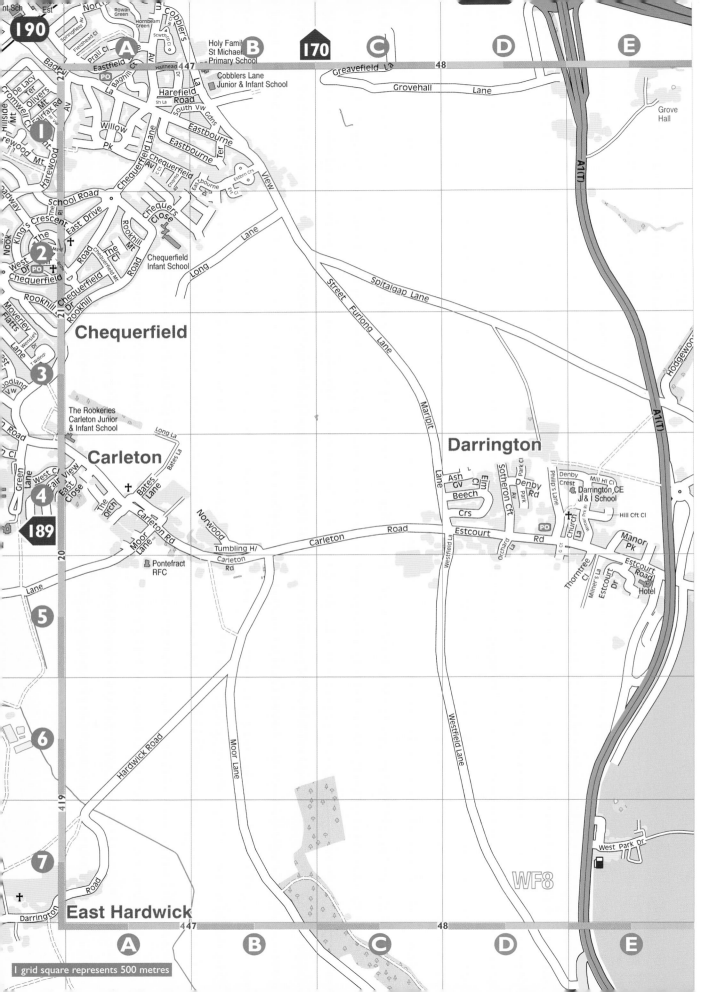

190

170

Chequerfield

Carleton

Darrington

189

East Hardwick

WF8

1 grid square represents 500 metres

M62

M62

171

F   G   H   J

49   50   51   22

I

2

LC

12

3

Leys

North Yorkshire County

Wakefield

Stubbs Lane

Hodgewood
Farm

Lane

Golf Course

Leys Road

Wake
Wood

Scrombeck
Farm

4

20

Havercroft

Mid Yorkshire
Golf Club

Lane

Valley
Gdns

Valley

Road

Bank Wood Road

North Lodge Lane

Works

5

Stapleton Park Farm

6

61

New Road

Stapleton
Park

7

F   G   H   J   K

North Yorkshire

Wakefi

Aberford ... 88 C5
Ackton ... 187 K1
Addingham ... 22 B1
Addingham Moorside ... 22 A5
Adel ... 62 B7
Adwalton ... 140 D1
Agbrigg ... 184 D6
Ainley Top ... 176 A5
Airedale ... 169 G1
Allerton ... 96 B5
Allerton Bywater ... 148 B3
Altofts ... 166 B3
Alverthorpe ... 183 K1
Alwoodley ... 63 H6
Alwoodley Gates ... 63 K5
Alwoodley Park ... 62 E5
Ambler Thorn ... 114 E6
Apperley Bridge ... 79 F3
Armley ... 8 C9
Arthington ... 42 C4
Arthursdale ... 86 C4
Askwith ... 26 A4
Austhorpe ... 106 B5
Bagley ... 100 B1
Baildon ... 77 J1
Baildon Green ... 77 F2
Bailiff Bridge ... 137 F7
Bank Top ... 78 D7
Bank Top ... 155 J3
Bantam Grove ... 142 C3
Barcroft ... 73 G4
Bardsey ... 45 K6
Barkisland ... 173 J5
Barkston Ash ... 90 D7
Barnbow Carr ... 87 F7
Barwick in Elmet ... 87 F6
Batley ... 161 F4
Batley Carr ... 161 F5
Battyeford ... 179 F4
Beck Bottom ... 163 H5
Beck Foot ... 75 H3
Beechcliffe ... 54 A2
Beechwood ... 85 F6
Beeston ... 122 D4
Beeston Hill ... 13 J9
Beeston Park Side ... 123 F6
Beeston Royds ... 122 A3
Beggarington Hill ... 162 B3
Belle Isle ... 123 K7
Belle Vue ... 19 K9
Ben Rhydding ... 24 D6
Bierley ... 118 C5
Bingley ... 75 H1
Birchencliffe ... 175 K7
Birkenshaw ... 139 J1
Birkenshaw Bottoms ... 139 K3
Birkhouse ... 157 H2
Birks ... 141 K5
Birstall ... 140 B5
Birstall Smithies ... 160 B1
Black Hill ... 2 A2
Blackley ... 175 H5
Black Moor ... 63 F7
Bogthorn ... 53 F7
Bolton ... 98 A1
Bolton Woods ... 97 K1
Booth ... 133 F4
Boothroyd ... 180 D1
Boothtown ... 134 D5
Boston Spa ... 48 B3
Bottom Boat ... 165 K2
Bottomley ... 174 A6
Boulder Clough ... 152 D3
Bowling ... 118 C2
Bracken Bank ... 73 G1
Brackenhall ... 177 C5
Bracken Hill ... 178 D2
Bracken Park ... 65 G4
Bradford ... 5 K6
Bradley ... 178 A3
Bradshaw ... 114 C5
Bradup ... 34 E5
Braithwaite ... 52 E3
Bramham ... 48 C7
Bramhope ... 41 F7
Bramley ... 101 F4
Brandy Carr ... 163 J4
Brearley ... 132 B7
Brighouse ... 156 E6
Broad Carr ... 175 F5
Brookfoot ... 156 D5
Brookhouse ... 113 J6
Brooklands ... 85 F7
Brotherton ... 150 E7
Brown Moor ... 106 C6
Bruntcliffe ... 141 H4
Brunthwaite ... 33 H1
Burley ... 8 D4
Burley in Wharfedale ... 37 J1
Burley Woodhead ... 37 H4
Burmantofts ... 11 J7
Burton Salmon ... 151 F3
Buttershaw ... 116 C6
Byram ... 171 F1
Cackleshaw ... 72 E2
Calverley ... 79 K6
Cambridge ... 39 K3
Camp Town ... 83 G1
Carleton ... 190 A4
Carlinghow ... 160 C1
Carlton ... 145 F4
Carr Gate ... 163 K3
Castleford ... 168 A1
Castleford Ings ... 148 D6
Castley ... 42 A2
Catherine Slack ... 135 F1
Catterton ... 51 K2
Causeway Foot ... 114 B3
Chapel Allerton ... 83 H5
Chapel Allerton ... 83 H5
Chapeltown ... 83 H4
Charlestown ... 77 K2
Chat Hill ... 115 K1
Chequerfield ... 190 A3
Chevin End ... 38 E5
Chickenley ... 182 A2
Chidswell ... 162 A5
Churwell ... 122 B7

Claremount ... 17 H3
Clayton ... 116 B2
Clayton Heights ... 116 B4
Cleckheaton ... 139 F7
Clerk Green ... 160 D4
Clifford ... 48 C5
Clifton ... 27 F4
Clifton ... 157 J6
Clough Head ... 153 K7
Cockersdale ... 120 C6
Coley ... 136 C5
Collingham ... 46 C3
Colne Bridge ... 178 B4
Colton ... 105 K7
Combs ... 181 G6
Compton ... 47 C3
Cookridge ... 61 G5
Copley ... 154 D6
Copley Hill ... 140 C5
Cottingley ... 75 K5
Cotton Stones ... 172 D1
Cowcliffe ... 176 E6
Crackenedge ... 161 G7
Cragg Hill ... 81 F4
Cringles ... 21 G3
Cromwell Bottom ... 156 B7
Crossflatts ... 55 J5
Cross Gates ... 105 H4
Cross Green ... 15 J3
Crossley ... 179 J1
Crossley Hall ... 96 D6
Cross Roads ... 73 F3
Crow Nest ... 76 A1
Cullingworth ... 73 J6
Cutsyke ... 168 B3
Daisy Hill ... 96 C3
Daisy Hill ... 142 B1
Damems ... 73 G2
Dam Head ... 135 J4
Darrington ... 190 D4
Deighton ... 178 A5
Denholme ... 93 K5
Denholme Clough ... 94 B7
Denholme Edge ... 93 K4
Denholme Gate ... 114 A1
Denton ... 25 F3
Dewsbury ... 181 F2
Dewsbury Moor ... 160 B7
Dockroyd ... 72 D3
Drighlington ... 140 C1
Drub ... 139 G5
Dudley Hill ... 118 D4
Earlsheaton ... 181 H2
East Ardsley ... 163 F1
East Bierley ... 119 G7
Eastburn ... 32 B4
East Carlton ... 40 B7
East Garforth ... 108 B5
East Hardwick ... 190 A7
East Keswick ... 45 K4
East Moor ... 19 L2
East Morton ... 55 H2
East Rigton ... 46 B5
Eccleshill ... 78 C7
Eccup ... 63 F2
Egypt ... 94 E5
Eldwick ... 56 C6
Elland ... 175 K3
Elland Lower Edge ... 176 B2
Elland Upper Edge ... 176 A3
Esholt ... 58 D6
Exley ... 155 F6
Fagley ... 98 E2
Fairburn ... 150 A2
The Fall ... 143 J7
Farnley ... 121 H1
Far Royds ... 12 A8
Farsley ... 100 A2
Farsley Beck Bottom ... 100 B2
Fartown ... 177 F7
Fearnville ... 105 F1
Featherstone ... 188 B2
Fell Lane ... 2 A6
Ferrybridge ... 170 D2
Five Lane Ends ... 78 B7
Fixby ... 176 E4
Flanshaw ... 183 K3
Flushdyke ... 182 E2
Four Lane Ends ... 96 D5
Fox Royd ... 180 E7
Friendly ... 153 H3
Frizinghall ... 77 F7
Fulneck ... 120 A1
Gamble Hill ... 101 H5
Garden Village ... 108 E7
Garforth ... 128 A1
Gawthorpe ... 162 C7
Gildersome ... 121 G6
Gildersome Street ... 141 G2
Gilstead ... 76 B1
Gipton ... 104 E2
Gipton Wood ... 84 C6
Girlington ... 4 C2
Glass Houghton ... 169 F3
Gledhow ... 84 B5
Gomersal ... 139 K7
Goose Eye ... 52 C5
Goosehill ... 186 A2
Great Horton ... 116 E2
Great Preston ... 127 H6
Green Clough ... 114 E1
Greengates ... 78 E6
Green Hill ... 88 E4
Green Side ... 12 A6
Greetland ... 174 D1
Greetland Wall Nook ... 174 A3
Grove Town ... 189 K2
Guard House ... 53 F4
Guiseley ... 58 D3
Haigh Moor ... 162 E2
Hainworth ... 73 K1
Hainworth Shaw ... 74 A1
Halifax ... 17 H7
Halton ... 105 F5
Halton Moor ... 104 E6
Hanging Heaton ... 161 H5
Harden ... 74 E3
Hare Croft ... 94 C1

Harehills ... 11 M4
Harewood ... 44 B3
Harewood Hill ... 73 F2
Hartshead ... 158 D7
Hartshead Moor Side ... 158 B2
Hartshead Moor Top ... 157 K1
Hawksworth ... 58 A3
Hawksworth ... 81 G5
Haworth ... 72 C5
Headingley ... 82 A7
Healey ... 160 D3
Healey ... 182 B6
Heath Common ... 185 J5
Heaton ... 96 E2
Heaton Royds ... 96 D1
Heaton Shay ... 76 E7
Heckmondwike ... 160 A4
Henshaw ... 59 H6
Highroad Well Moor ... 133 J6
Hightown ... 158 E3
Hightown Heights ... 158 D3
Hillam ... 151 K1
Hillfoot ... 99 K5
Hill Top ... 95 F6
Hill Top ... 101 H3
Hipperholme ... 136 A7
Holbeck ... 13 K4
Holden Gate ... 34 A5
Holdsworth ... 134 E1
Hole ... 72 C6
Hollin Park ... 84 D7
Hollinthorpe ... 126 D2
Holme ... 119 G2
Holme Wood ... 119 G3
Holmfield ... 134 C2
Holt Park ... 61 J6
Holywell Green ... 174 E6
Hopetown ... 167 G5
Horsforth ... 80 C2
Horsforth Woodside ... 81 F4
Hough Side ... 100 E5
Hove Edge ... 156 D3
Howden Clough ... 140 E5
Hubberton Green ... 152 D6
Hungate ... 146 C7
Hunslet ... 14 D8
Hunslet Carr ... 123 J4
Hunsworth ... 139 F4
Idle ... 78 C4
Idle Moor ... 78 A6
Ilkley ... 23 K5
Illingworth ... 134 B1
Ingrow ... 53 H7
Intake ... 100 C2
Ireland Wood ... 81 J2
Jagger Green ... 174 E6
Jaw Hill ... 163 F4
John O'Gaunts ... 125 J7
Kebroyd ... 172 E3
Keelham ... 114 C1
Keighley ... 3 J2
Kelcliffe ... 58 E1
Kiddal Lane End ... 67 H7
Killingbeck ... 105 F3
Kippax ... 128 A4
Kirkby Wharfe ... 71 H5
Kirkhamgate ... 163 F6
Kirkstall ... 101 K2
Kirkthorpe ... 186 A3
Knottingley ... 171 F4
Knowle Park ... 2 D8
Knowsthorpe ... 14 F6
Lady Wood ... 84 D5
Laisterdyke ... 7 J7
Lane Bottom ... 93 J3
Lane End ... 72 B2
Lane Ends ... 80 C1
Larkfield ... 60 A7
Lawns ... 163 K2
Lawnswood ... 81 K2
Laycock ... 52 D4
Ledsham ... 129 J6
Ledston ... 148 C1
Ledston Luck ... 128 C4
Leeds ... 9 L7
Leeming ... 92 E4
Lee Moor ... 165 F1
Lees ... 73 F4
Leventhorpe ... 96 B7
Lidget Green ... 4 D9
Lidgett Park ... 84 B4
Lightcliffe ... 156 E1
Lighthazles ... 172 B3
Lindwell ... 175 F1
Lingbob ... 95 G1
Linton ... 28 D7
Little Horton ... 117 G3
Little London ... 79 H1
Little Preston ... 127 F5
Little Thorpe ... 158 E7
Littletown ... 159 H3
Liversedge ... 159 H4
Lofthouse ... 144 E7
Lofthouse Gate ... 164 D2
Long Lee ... 3 L8
Longley ... 153 G7
Loscoe ... 167 J5
Lower Altofts ... 166 D2
Lower Grange ... 96 B6
Lower Hopton ... 179 F6
Lower Mickletown ... 147 J5
Lower Soothill ... 161 H2
Lower Town ... 92 E3
Lower Wyke ... 137 H7
Low Fold ... 80 C4
Low Green ... 79 K1
Low Moor ... 137 J2
Luddenden ... 133 F6
Luddenden Foot ... 152 D2
Lumb Foot ... 72 A4
Lumby ... 130 E5
Lupset ... 183 K5
Manningham ... 97 H3
Manor Park ... 25 J6
Manston ... 106 B3
Marsh ... 92 C1
Meanwood ... 82 D4
Menston ... 38 A7

Merchant Fields ... 139 F6
Methley ... 147 F5
Methley Junction ... 147 G7
Methley Lanes ... 166 B1
Micklefield ... 108 E7
Micklethwaite ... 55 H4
Middleton ... 24 A2
Middleton ... 143 J3
Midgley ... 132 D6
Miles Hill ... 83 F6
Mill Bank ... 172 E2
Mill Shaw ... 122 D5
Mirfield ... 179 H3
Mixenden ... 133 K2
Monk Fryston ... 131 H7
Monkhill ... 169 J6
Monkswood ... 85 G5
Moor Allerton ... 83 J2
Moor End ... 48 A2
Moor End ... 133 H3
Moorhead ... 76 D5
Moor Head ... 121 F6
Moor Side ... 92 A1
Moorside ... 101 F1
Moor Side ... 137 J2
Moorside ... 140 C2
Moor Top ... 179 F1
Moortown ... 83 H2
Morley ... 142 A4
Mountain ... 114 E4
Mount Pleasant ... 160 D4
Mount Tabor ... 133 H4
Mytholmes ... 72 E4
Mytholmroyd ... 132 A5
Nab Wood ... 76 C4
Netheroyd Hill ... 177 F6
Nether Yeadon ... 59 H6
Newall ... 39 H1
New Brighton ... 76 B6
New Brighton ... 141 J3
New Farnley ... 121 H3
New Fryston ... 149 J4
New Holland ... 95 F2
New Micklefield ... 109 G7
New Road Side ... 137 J3
Newsam Green ... 125 K5
New Scarbro ... 101 G3
New Sharlston ... 186 C4
Newsholme ... 52 B7
Newthorpe ... 130 A1
Newton Hill ... 164 D5
Newton Kyme ... 49 K3
New Town ... 169 J4
New Wortley ... 12 F2
Noon Nick ... 96 A1
Norland Town ... 154 A6
Normanton ... 166 C6
Norr ... 75 G7
Norristhorpe ... 159 J6
North Featherstone ... 168 C7
Northorpe ... 180 A2
Northowram ... 136 A5
Norwood Green ... 136 D4
Oakenshaw ... 137 K3
Oakwell ... 140 A4
Oakwood ... 84 D7
Oakworth ... 72 C3
Odsal ... 117 K6
Ogden ... 114 A4
Old Bramhope ... 40 E7
Old Dolphin ... 115 K4
Old Lindley ... 175 G6
Old Micklefield ... 108 D5
Old Snydale ... 187 H2
Osmondthorpe ... 15 L2
Ossett ... 182 C3
Ossett Spa ... 183 F6
Ossett Street Side ... 182 A1
Otley ... 39 J1
Oulton ... 145 J2
Ousel Hole ... 55 H1
Outwood ... 164 C6
Ouzlewell Green ... 145 F6
Ovenden ... 134 C5
Overthorpe ... 181 F7
Owlet ... 77 H7
Oxenhope ... 92 D3
Oxton ... 51 H7
Parklands ... 105 G1
Park Villas ... 84 B3
Parlington ... 88 B7
Peas Acre ... 55 H3
Pellon ... 134 B7
Pendas Fields ... 106 C2
Pepper Hill ... 136 A1
Pickles Hill ... 72 A3
Pickwood Scar ... 154 B7
Pontefract ... 189 H1
Pool ... 41 H1
Portobello ... 184 C7
Potternewton ... 83 K7
Potterton ... 87 H1
Pottery Field ... 14 C5
Priest Hill ... 29 F1
Priesthorpe ... 99 H1
Priestley Green ... 136 C6
Priestthorpe ... 55 K7
Prince Royd ... 176 B7
Pudsey ... 100 A6
Pule Hill ... 135 F4
Purston Jaglin ... 188 D5
Queensbury ... 115 F5
Rastrick ... 176 E1
Ravenscliffe ... 99 F1
Ravensthorpe ... 180 B3
Rawdon ... 79 K1
Rawdon Carrs ... 80 A2
Rawfolds ... 159 F3
Red Hill ... 169 F1
Richmond Hill ... 15 G1
Riddlesden ... 54 D2
Ripponden ... 172 C5
Roberttown ... 158 E7
Robin Hood ... 144 C4
Rodley ... 80 B7
Rothwell ... 145 H2
Rothwell Haigh ... 124 E7
Roundhay ... 84 E4

Royds Green ... 145 H5
Ryecroft ... 74 B3
St John's ... 88 D3
Saltaire ... 77 F3
Sandford ... 81 H7
Sandhills ... 86 B1
Sandy Lane ... 95 J2
Savile Town ... 181 G4
Sawood ... 93 G5
Saxton ... 90 B6
Scarcroft ... 65 K2
Scarthingwell ... 91 F5
Scholemoor ... 116 D1
Scholes ... 86 C5
Scholes ... 138 A7
Scholey Hill ... 146 D7
School Green ... 95 K7
Seacroft ... 85 H7
Shadwell ... 65 G7
Sharlston ... 186 E7
Sharlston Common ... 186 D6
Shaw ... 92 C3
Shaw Cross ... 161 K6
Shay Gate ... 95 H1
Sheepridge ... 177 G6
Sheepscar ... 10 D4
Shelf ... 136 C1
Shepherd Hill ... 182 E3
Sherburn in Elmet ... 110 E4
Shibden Head ... 135 G1
Shipley ... 77 F5
Siddal ... 155 H5
Silsden ... 33 F1
Snow Hill ... 164 B6
Snydale ... 187 H4
South Milford ... 130 E2
South Ossett ... 182 D5
Southowram ... 155 J4
Sowerby ... 152 E6
Sowerby Bridge ... 153 K5
Sowood Green ... 174 D7
Soyland Town ... 172 E3
Staincliffe ... 160 D4
Stainland ... 174 B5
Stanks ... 106 A2
Stanley ... 165 F4
Stanley Ferry ... 165 J5
Stanningley ... 100 C3
Stead ... 37 F1
Steep Lane ... 152 D4
Steeton ... 32 E5
Stockbridge ... 54 A1
Stone Chair ... 136 B3
Stoney Royd ... 17 H8
Stourton ... 124 C5
Strawberry Hill ... 188 D2
Streethouse ... 187 G4
Stutton ... 70 D4
Sutton ... 171 G1
Swain House ... 78 A7
Swarcliffe ... 105 K1
Swartha ... 21 G7
Swillington ... 126 C3
Swillington Common ... 106 C7
Swincliffe ... 139 H3
Swinnow Moor ... 100 E5
Sympson Green ... 78 D3
Tadcaster ... 50 D6
Tarn ... 57 K7
Thackley ... 78 B3
Thackley End ... 78 A2
Thornbury ... 99 G5
Thorner ... 66 C6
Thornes ... 184 D6
Thornhill ... 181 J7
Thornhill Lees ... 181 F5
Thornhills ... 157 H4
Thornton ... 95 H7
Thorp Arch ... 48 D2
Thorpe Edge ... 78 C6
Thorpe on The Hill ... 143 H5
Thwaites ... 54 C4
Thwaites Brow ... 54 C5
Tingley ... 142 D6
Tinshill ... 81 H1
Toftshaw ... 118 D6
Tong ... 120 B5
Tong Park ... 58 A7
Tong Street ... 118 E5
Toothill ... 177 F3
Toulston ... 49 H5
Town Head ... 21 G7
Towton ... 70 E7
Triangle ... 153 F7
Troydale ... 100 D7
Tyersal ... 7 M9
Tyersal ... 119 G1
Ulleskelf ... 71 K7
Undercliffe ... 98 B3
Upper Armley ... 101 K4
Upper Batley ... 141 F7
Upper Brockholes ... 113 K6
Upper Green ... 162 D1
Upper Heaton ... 178 B6
Upper Hopton ... 179 F7
Upper Marsh ... 92 B1
Upper Moor Side ... 120 E5
Upper Town ... 92 C3
Upwood ... 35 F6
Utley ... 53 J1
Wainstalls ... 133 F2
Wakefield ... 18 E4
Walton ... 31 F5
Warley Town ... 153 J2
Warmfield ... 186 B3
Water Fryston ... 150 A5
Wayside Gardens ... 65 K2
Weardley ... 43 G4
Weetwood ... 82 B4
Well Heads ... 94 D6
Wellington Hill ... 85 F3
Wellroyd ... 80 A3
West Ardsley ... 162 C2
West Bowling ... 118 A3
West Carlton ... 39 J7
West End ... 80 B2
West End ... 158 C1
Westfield ... 59 F6

Westfield	160 A3	West Vale	175 G3	Whitkirk	105 K6	Woodhouse	3 H9	Wood Row	146 E4
West Garforth	127 G1	Wetherby	29 J4	Whitley Head	32 D6	Woodhouse	9 K3	Woodside	137 F1
Westgate Hill	119 H6	Wheatley	134 A5	Whitwood	167 H2	Woodhouse	177 H1	Wortley	101 K7
West Morton	54 D1	Wheldale	149 G6	Wibsey	117 G5	Woodhouse	186 C1	Wrenthorpe	164 A6
Weston	26 C6	Whinmoor	85 K4	Wike	64 E2	Woodkirk	162 B1	Wrose	77 K6
West Park	82 A4	Whins Wood	73 H3	Wilsden	74 E7	Woodlands	17 H1	Wyke	137 H5
West Royd	77 J4	Whitecote	81 F7	Windhill	77 J5	Woodlands	135 F5	Yeadon	59 J6
West Scholes	115 G3	White Lee	160 B1	Woodhall Hills	99 H2	Woodlesford	145 K1		

USING THE STREET INDEX

Street names are listed alphabetically. Each street name is followed by its postal town or area locality, the Postcode District, the page number, and the reference to the square in which the name is found.

Standard index entries are shown as follows:

Aachen Wy *HFAX* HX1 ....16 C9

Street names and selected addresses not shown on the map due to scale restrictions are shown in the index with an asterisk:

Abbotside Cl *IDLE* * BD10 ....78 D6

GENERAL ABBREVIATIONS

ACC	ACCESS	CTYD	COURTYARD	HLS	HILLS	MWY	MOTORWAY
ALY	ALLEY	CUTT	CUTTINGS	HO	HOUSE	N	NORTH
AP	APPROACH	CV	COVE	HOL	HOLLOW	NE	NORTH EAST
AR	ARCADE	CYN	CANYON	HOSP	HOSPITAL	NW	NORTH WEST
ASS	ASSOCIATION	DEPT	DEPARTMENT	HRB	HARBOUR	O/P	OVERPASS
AV	AVENUE	DL	DALE	HTH	HEATH	OFF	OFFICE
BCH	BEACH	DM	DAM	HTS	HEIGHTS	ORCH	ORCHARD
BLDS	BUILDINGS	DR	DRIVE	HVN	HAVEN	OV	OVAL
BND	BEND	DRO	DROVE	HWY	HIGHWAY	PAL	PALACE
BNK	BANK	DRY	DRIVEWAY	IMP	IMPERIAL	PAS	PASSAGE
BR	BRIDGE	DWGS	DWELLINGS	IN	INLET	PAV	PAVILION
BRK	BROOK	E	EAST	IND EST	INDUSTRIAL ESTATE	PDE	PARADE
BTM	BOTTOM	EMB	EMBANKMENT	INF	INFIRMARY	PH	PUBLIC HOUSE
BUS	BUSINESS	EMBY	EMBASSY	INFO	INFORMATION	PK	PARK
BVD	BOULEVARD	ESP	ESPLANADE	INT	INTERCHANGE	PKWY	PARKWAY
BY	BYPASS	EST	ESTATE	IS	ISLAND	PL	PLACE
CATH	CATHEDRAL	EX	EXCHANGE	JCT	JUNCTION	PLN	PLAIN
CEM	CEMETERY	EXPY	EXPRESSWAY	JTY	JETTY	PLNS	PLAINS
CEN	CENTRE	EXT	EXTENSION	KG	KING	PLZ	PLAZA
CFT	CROFT	F/O	FLYOVER	KNL	KNOLL	POL	POLICE STATION
CH	CHURCH	FC	FOOTBALL CLUB	L	LAKE	PR	PRINCE
CHA	CHASE	FK	FORK	LA	LANE	PREC	PRECINCT
CHYD	CHURCHYARD	FLD	FIELD	LDG	LODGE	PREP	PREPARATORY
CIR	CIRCLE	FLDS	FIELDS	LGT	LIGHT	PRIM	PRIMARY
CIRC	CIRCUS	FLS	FALLS	LK	LOCK	PROM	PROMENADE
CL	CLOSE	FLS	FLATS	LKS	LAKES	PRS	PRINCESS
CLFS	CLIFFS	FM	FARM	LNDG	LANDING	PRT	PORT
CMP	CAMP	FT	FORT	LTL	LITTLE	PT	POINT
CNR	CORNER	FWY	FREEWAY	LWR	LOWER	PTH	PATH
CO	COUNTY	FY	FERRY	MAG	MAGISTRATE	PZ	PIAZZA
COLL	COLLEGE	GA	GATE	MAN	MANSIONS	QD	QUADRANT
COM	COMMON	GAL	GALLERY	MD	MEAD	QU	QUEEN
COMM	COMMISSION	GDN	GARDEN	MDW	MEADOWS	QY	QUAY
CON	CONVENT	GDNS	GARDENS	MEM	MEMORIAL	R	RIVER
COT	COTTAGE	GLD	GLADE	MKT	MARKET	RBT	ROUNDABOUT
COTS	COTTAGES	GLN	GLEN	MKTS	MARKETS	RD	ROAD
CP	CAPE	GN	GREEN	ML	MALL	RDG	RIDGE
CPS	COPSE	GND	GROUND	ML	MILL	REP	REPUBLIC
CR	CREEK	GRA	GRANGE	MNR	MANOR	RES	RESERVOIR
CREM	CREMATORIUM	GRG	GARAGE	MS	MEWS	RFC	RUGBY FOOTBALL CLUB
CRS	CRESCENT	GT	GREAT	MSN	MISSION	RI	RISE
CSWY	CAUSEWAY	GTWY	GATEWAY	MT	MOUNT	RP	RAMP
CT	COURT	GV	GROVE	MTN	MOUNTAIN	RW	ROW
CTRL	CENTRAL	HGR	HIGHER	MTS	MOUNTAINS	S	SOUTH
CTS	COURTS	HL	HILL	MUS	MUSEUM	SCH	SCHOOL

SE	SOUTH EAST
SER	SERVICE AREA
SH	SHORE
SHOP	SHOPPING
SKWY	SKYWAY
SMT	SUMMIT
SOC	SOCIETY
SP	SPUR
SPR	SPRING
SQ	SQUARE
ST	STREET
STN	STATION
STR	STREAM
STRD	STRAND
SW	SOUTH WEST
TDG	TRADING
TER	TERRACE
THWY	THROUGHWAY
TNL	TUNNEL
TOLL	TOLLWAY
TPK	TURNPIKE
TR	TRACK
TRL	TRAIL
TWR	TOWER
U/P	UNDERPASS
UNI	UNIVERSITY
UPR	UPPER
V	VALE
VA	VALLEY
VIAD	VIADUCT
VIL	VILLA
VIS	VISTA
VLG	VILLAGE
VLS	VILLAS
VW	VIEW
W	WEST
WD	WOOD
WHF	WHARF
WK	WALK
WKS	WALKS
WLS	WELLS
WY	WAY
YD	YARD
YHA	YOUTH HOSTEL

POSTCODE TOWNS AND AREA ABBREVIATIONS

AIRE	Airedale	CLECK	Cleckheaton	HDGY	Headingley	LDS	Leeds
AL/HA/HU	Alwoodley/Harewood/Huby	COP/BISH	Copmanthorpe/Bishopthorpe	HECK	Heckmondwike	LDSU	Leeds University
BAIL	Baildon			HFAX	Halifax	LM/WK	Low Moor/Wyke
BEE/HOL	Beeston/Holbeck	CUL/QBY	Cullingworth/Queensbury	HIPP	Hipperholme	LUD/ILL	Luddenden/Illingworth
BFD	Bradford	DEWS	Dewsbury	HOR/CROF	Horbury/Crofton	LVSG	Liversedge
BFDE	Bradford east	EARD/LOFT	East Ardley/Lofthouse	HORS	Horsforth	MID	Middleton (W.Yorks)
BGLY	Bingley	EARL	Earlsheaton	HTON	Heaton	MIRF	Mirfield
BHP/TINH	Bramhope/Tinshill	ECHL	Eccleshill	HUD	Huddersfield	MOR	Morley
BIRK/DRI	Birkenshaw/Drighlington	ELL	Elland	HUDE	Huddersfield east	MSTN/BAR	Manston/Barwick in Elmet
BOW	Bowling	FEA/AMT	Featherstone/Ackworth Moor Top	HUDN	Huddersfield north	NORM	Normanton
BRAM	Bramley			HUDW	Huddersfield west	OSM	Osmandthorpe
BRIG	Brighouse	GFTH/SHER	Garforth/Sherburn in Elmet	HWTH	Haworth	OSS	Ossett
BULY	Burley	GIR	Girlington	IDLE	Idle	OT	Otley
BVRD	Belle Vue Road	GSLY	Guiseley	ILK	Ilkley	PBR	Pateley Bridge
CAS	Castleford	GTHN	Great Horton	KGHY	Keighley	PDSY/CALV	Pudsey/Calverley
CHAL	Chapel Allerton	GTL/HWG	Greetland/Holywell Green	KNOT	Knottingley	PONT	Pontefract
CLAY	Clayton	HBR	Hebden Bridge	KSTL	Kirkstall	RHAY	Roundhay

RPDN/SBR	Ripponden/Sowerby Bridge
RTHW	Rothwell
RYKW	Rural York west
SCFT	Seacroft
SHPY	Shipley
TAD	Tadcaster
WBOW	West Bowling
WBSY	Wibsey
WBY	Wetherby
WIL/AL	Wilsden/Allerton
WKFDE	Wakefield east
WKFDW/WTN	Wakefield west/Walton
WOR/ARM	Wortley/Armley
YEA	Yeadon

A

Aachen Wy *HFAX* HX1 ....16 C9
Abaseen Cl *BFDE* BD3 ....6 F6
Abbey Av *KSTL* LS5 ....101 J2
Abbey Cl *ILK* LS29 ....22 D1
Abbey Ct *HORS* LS18 ....80 E6
Abbeydale Gdns *KSTL* LS5 ....81 H6
Abbeydale Garth *KSTL* LS5 ....81 H6
Abbeydale Gv *KSTL* LS5 ....81 H6
Abbeydale Mt *KSTL* LS5 ....81 H6
Abbeydale V *KSTL* LS5 ....81 H6
Abbeydale Wy *KSTL* LS5 ....81 H6
Abbey Gdns *PONT* WF8 ....169 K5
Abbey Gorse *KSTL* LS5 ....81 K7
Abbey La *LUD/ILL* HX2 ....153 C1
Abbey Lea *WIL/AL* BD15 ....96 B5
Abbey Ms *PONT* WF8 ....169 J4
Abbey Rd *BTLY* WF17 ....160 C4
  KSTL LS5 ....81 G6
Abbey St *BVRD* LS3 ....9 H8
Abbey Ter *KSTL* LS5 ....101 J2
Abbey Vw *KSTL* LS5 ....81 K7
Abbey Wk *HIPP* HX3 ....155 F4
  KSTL LS5 ....81 J7
  PONT WF8 ....169 J4
Abbey Wk South *HIPP* HX3 ....155 F4
Abbotside Cl *IDLE* * BD10 ....78 D6
Abbotsway *GFTH/SHER* LS25 ......107 G2
Abbott Ct *WOR/ARM* LS12 ....8 D9
Abbott Rd *WOR/ARM* LS12 ....8 D9

Abbotts Cl *GFTH/SHER* LS25 ....88 D4
Abbotts Ter *HFAX* HX1 ....16 C6
Abbott Ter *WKFDE* WF1 ....184 E6
Abbott Vw *WOR/ARM* LS12 ....8 D9
Abb Scott La *LM/WK* BD12 ....137 G5
Abelia Mt *GTHN* BD7 ....96 D7
Abel St *LM/WK* BD12 ....137 H3
Aberdeen Dr *WOR/ARM* LS12 ....101 K6
Aberdeen Gv *WOR/ARM* LS12 ....101 K6
Aberdeen Pl *GTHN* BD7 ....4 C3
Aberdeen Rd *WOR/ARM* LS12 ....101 K6
Aberdeen Ter *CLAY* BD14 ....116 C2
  GTHN BD7 ....4 C3
Aberdeen Wk *WOR/ARM* LS12 ....101 K6
Aberfield Bank *MID* LS10 ....143 K1
Aberfield Cl *MID* LS10 ....123 K7
Aberfield Crest *MID* LS10 ....143 K1
Aberfield Dr *MID* LS10 ....143 K1
Aberfield Ga *MID* LS10 ....123 K7
Aberfield Mt *MID* LS10 ....143 K1
Aberfield Ri *MID* LS10 ....143 K1
Aberfield Rd *MID* LS10 ....123 K7
Aberfield Wk *MID* LS10 ....143 J1
Aberford Rd *BSPA/BRAM* LS23 ....68 C2
  GFTH/SHER LS25 ....107 J5
  GIR BD8 ....4 E2
  MSTN/BAR LS15 ....87 H5
  RTHW LS26 ....145 K3
  WKFDE WF1 ....185 F1
Abingdon St *GIR* BD8 ....4 E1
Abraham Hl *RTHW* LS26 ....145 G1
Acacia Cl *CAS* WF10 ....169 J2
Acacia Dr *BRIG* HD6 ....157 F1

CAS WF10 ....169 H2
WIL/AL BD15 ....95 K1
Acacia Gv *HBR* HX7 ....132 A5
Acacia Park Crs *IDLE* BD10 ....79 G2
Acacia Park Dr *IDLE* BD10 ....79 G2
Acacia Park Ter *IDLE* BD10 ....79 G2
Acaster Dr *GFTH/SHER* LS25 ......127 K1
  LM/WK BD12 ....137 H1
Accommodation Rd *OSM* LS9 ......10 F7
Acer Cl *AIRE* BD20 ....32 A5
Acer Wy *CLECK* BD19 ....138 E2
Ackroyd Ct *CUL/QBY* * BD13 ......95 C7
Ackroyd St *MOR* LS27 ....142 A3
Ackton Cl *FEA/AMT* WF7 ....167 K7
Ackton Hall Crs *FEA/AMT* WF7 ..187 K1
Ackton La *FEA/AMT* WF7 ....187 K1
Ackton Pasture La *CAS* WF10 ....167 K4
Ackworth Av *YEA* LS19 ....59 K5
Ackworth Crs *YEA* LS19 ....59 K5
Ackworth Dr *YEA* LS19 ....59 K5
Ackworth Rd *FEA/AMT* WF7 ......188 C6
  PONT WF8 ....189 G5
Ackworth St *WBOW* BD5 ....117 K2
Acme Ter *WKFDE* WF1 ....184 E6
Acomb Ter *LM/WK* BD12 ....137 H4
Acorn Cl *WBSY* BD6 ....136 D1
Acorn Dr *SCFT* LS14 ....85 K4
Acorn Pk *BAIL* BD17 ....77 K2
Acorn St *HFAX* HX1 ....16 C5
The Acre *LM/WK* BD12 ....137 H5
Acre Av *ECHL* BD2 ....78 C7
Acre Cl *ECHL* BD2 ....78 C7
Acre Crs *ECHL* BD2 ....78 C7

MID LS10 ....143 H3
Acre Dr *ECHL* BD2 ....78 C7
Acre Fold *ILK* LS29 ....22 A1
Acre Gv *ECHL* * BD2 ....78 C7
  MID LS10 ....143 H3
Acrehowe Ri *BAIL* BD17 ....57 J7
Acre La *ECHL* BD2 ....98 C1
  HUD BD22 ....72 D5
  WBSY BD6 ....117 H5
Acre Mt *MID* LS10 ....143 H3
Acre Pl *MID* LS10 ....143 H3
Acre Ri *BAIL* BD17 ....57 H7
Acre Rd *MID* LS10 ....143 H3
Acres Hall Av *PDSY/CALV* LS28 ..100 D7
Acres Hall Crs *PDSY/CALV* LS28 ..100 D7
Acres Hall Dr *PDSY/CALV* LS28 ..100 D7
Acre Sq *MID* LS10 ....143 H3
Acres Rd *EARD/LOFT* WF3 ....144 D7
Acres St *KGHY* BD21 ....2 E7
Acre St *MID* LS10 ....143 H3
Acre Ter *MID* LS10 ....143 J3
Acton Flat La *HUDW* HD3 ....175 K6
Acton St *BFDE* BD3 ....7 H6
Acute Ter *WKFDW/WTN* WF2 ....183 K3
Adam Cft *CUL/QBY* BD13 ....74 A1
Adams Gv *MSTN/BAR* LS15 ......106 B1
Adam St *WBSY* BD6 ....117 G5
Ada's Pl *PDSY/CALV* LS28 ....100 B3
Ada St *BAIL* BD17 ....77 K2
  CUL/QBY BD13 ....115 G5
  HIPP HX3 ....17 H2
  KGHY BD21 ....2 D5
  SHPY BD18 ....76 E4

MID LS10 ....143 H3
Acre Dr *ECHL* BD2 ....78 C7
Addingham Gdns
  WOR/ARM LS12 ....101 K6
Addingham Wharfedale Rd
  ILK LS29 ....22 A1
Addison Av *BFDE* BD3 ....7 K2
  NORM WF6 ....167 F7
Addison Ct *HOR/CROF* WF4 ......183 H7
  MSTN/BAR LS15 ....106 A7
Addison Dr *HWTH* BD22 ....72 D6
Addi St *BOW* BD4 ....118 D3
Adelaide St *HFAX* HX1 ....16 B6
  WBOW BD5 ....5 M9
Adel Garth *BHP/TINH* LS16 ....62 C6
Adel Grange Cl *BHP/TINH* LS16 ..82 B2
Adel Grange Cft *BHP/TINH* * LS16 ..82 B2
Adel Grange Ms *BHP/TINH* LS16 ..82 B2
Adel Gn *BHP/TINH* LS16 ....62 C7
Adel La *BHP/TINH* LS16 ....62 B7
Adel Md *BHP/TINH* LS16 ....62 C7
Adel Ml *BHP/TINH* LS16 ....62 C5
Adel Park Cl *BHP/TINH* LS16 ......82 B1
Adel Park Ct *BHP/TINH* LS16 ......82 B1
Adel Park Cft *BHP/TINH* LS16 ......82 B1
Adel Park Dr *BHP/TINH* LS16 ......82 B1
Adel Park Gdns *BHP/TINH* LS16 ..82 B1
Adel Pasture *BHP/TINH* LS16 ......82 B1
Adel Towers Ct *BHP/TINH* LS16 ..82 C1
Adel V *BHP/TINH* LS16 ....62 C7
Adel Wood Dr *BHP/TINH* LS16 ..82 C1
Adel Wood Gv *BHP/TINH* LS16 ..82 C1
Adel Wood Pl *BHP/TINH* LS16 ..82 C1
Adel Wood Rd *BHP/TINH* LS16 ..82 C1
Adgil Crs *HIPP* HX3 ....155 K4

Administration Rd *OSM* LS9 ....124 D3
Admiral St *BEE/HOL* LS11 ....6 A7
Adolphus St *BFD* BD1 ....6 B7
Adwalton Cl *BIRK/DRI* BD11........140 A2
Adwalton Gn *BIRK/DRI* BD11........140 A2
Adwalton Gv *CUL/QBY* BD13 ....115 J5
Adwick Pl *BULY* LS4........................8 B4
Agar St *GIR* BD8 ....4 B3
Agbrigg Gv *WKFDW/WTN* WF2 ...185 F7
Agbrigg Rd *WKFDE* WF1.................185 F7
Agincourt Dr *NORM* WF6...............166 B4
Agnes St *KGHY* BD21.....................53 K2
Ails La *LUD/ILL* HX2....................132 E6
Ainley Bottom *ELL* HX5..............175 K4
Ainley La *HUDW* HD3....................175 K7
Ainley Rd *HUDW* HD3...................175 K6
Ainley St *ELL* HX5.........................175 J3
Ainsbury Av *IDLE* BD10................78 C1
Ainsdale Gv *CUL/QBY* BD13 ....74 B6
Ainsty Crs *WBY* LS22....................29 H2
Ainsty Dr *WBY* LS22......................29 H2
Ainsty Garth *WBY* LS22................29 H2
Ainsty Rd *WBY* LS22......................29 H2
Ainsty Vw *WBY* LS22.....................29 H2
Aintree Cl *GFTH/SHER* LS25.......127 J4
Airebank *BGLY* BD16......................75 J1
Aire Cl *BAIL* BD17...........................77 G3
Airedale Av *BGLY* BD16................75 K6
Airedale College Mt *BFDE* * BD3...6 C1
Airedale College Rd *BFDE* BD3....6 C1
Airedale College Ter *BFDE* BD3...6 C2
Airedale Ct *SCFT* LS14..................85 G7
Airedale Cft *BRAM* LS13...............100 C1
Airedale Crs *BFDE* BD3 ....6 C1
Airedale Dr *CAS* WF10.................149 H5
  GFTH/SHER LS25........................108 A7
  HIPP HX3...................................136 A2
  HORS LS18....................................80 C4
Airedale Gdns *BRAM* LS13...........100 C1
Airedale Gv *HORS* LS18.................80 C4
  RTHW * LS26...............................146 A1
Airedale Hts
  WKFDW/WTN WF2.....................183 H5
Airedale Ms *AIRE* BD20................33 F1
Airedale Mt *AIRE* BD20..................55 F3
Airedale Pl *BAIL* BD17...................77 K2
Airedale Quay *BRAM* LS13...........100 D1
Airedale Rd *BFDE* BD3 ....6 B1
  CAS WF10..................................169 G1
  KGHY BD21..................................54 C3
  RTHW * LS26...............................146 A1
Airedale St *BGLY* BD16..................75 J3
  ECHL BD2...................................98 C2
  KGHY BD21....................................3 M3
Airedale Ter *MOR* LS27...............142 A3
  RTHW * LS26...............................146 A1
Airedale Vw *RTHW* LS26..............146 A1
Airedale Whf *BRAM* LS13..............80 C7
Aire Gv *YEA* LS19............................59 K5
Aire Mt *WBY* LS22...........................29 G2
Aire Pl *BVRD* LS3...............................8 F7
Aire Rd *WBY* LS22............................29 G2
Aire St *BGLY* BD16..........................55 H6
  BRIG HD6...................................157 G7
  CAS WF10..................................148 C7
  DEWS WF13...............................180 C4
  HWTH BD22..................................72 E5
  IDLE BD10....................................78 B3
  KGHY BD21....................................3 K3
  KNOT WF11................................171 H3
  LDS LS1...13 L1
Aire Ter *CAS* WF10.......................148 C7
Airevalley Rd *KGHY* BD21..............3 L2
Aire Vw *AIRE* BD20.........................32 E1
  AIRE BD20....................................54 C1
  YEA LS19......................................59 K5
Aire View Av *BGLY* BD16..............76 A4
  SHPY BD18...................................77 F4
Aireview Crs *BAIL* BD17.................77 F3
Aire View Dr *AIRE* BD20.................55 F4
Aire View Ter *KGHY* BD21...............3 M6
Aireville Av *SHPY* BD18..................77 G7
Aireville Cl *AIRE* BD20....................53 H1
  SHPY BD18...................................77 G7
Aireville Crs *AIRE* BD20..................33 G1
  HTON BD9.....................................77 G7
Aireville Dr *AIRE* BD20....................33 G1
  HTON BD9.....................................77 G7
Aireville Gra *SHPY* BD18...............77 G7
Aireville Gv *HTON* BD9...................77 G7
Aireville Mt *AIRE* BD20....................55 F4
Aireville Mouny *AIRE* BD20...........33 G1
Aireville Ri *HTON* BD9....................97 C1
Aireville Rd *HTON* BD9...................77 H7
Aireville St *AIRE* BD20....................53 H1
Aireville Ter *ILK* LS29.....................37 K1
Aire Wy *BAIL* BD17.........................77 F3
Aireworth Cl *KGHY* BD21...............3 M2
Aireworth Gv *KGHY* BD21..............3 M3
Aireworth Rd *KGHY* BD21..............3 M2
Aireworth St *KGHY* BD21...............2 F6
Airey St *KGHY* BD21.........................2 D4
Airlie Av *RHAY* LS8.......................104 A1
Airlie Pl *RHAY* LS8..........................11 G1
Akam Rd *BFD* BD1............................5 J5
Aked's Rd *HFAX* HX1.......................16 E7
Aked St *BFD* * BD1...........................6 B7
Aketon Cl *CAS* WF10.....................168 B2
Aketon Rd *CAS* WF10....................168 B2
Akroyd Cl *HIPP* HX3.........................17 G3
Akroyd Pl *HFAX* HX1........................17 G4
Akroyd Ter *LUD/ILL* HX2..............154 C3
Alabama St *HFAX* HX1.....................16 B5
Alan Crs *MSTN/BAR* LS15............105 H6
Alandale Crs *GFTH/SHER* LS25....107 G7
Alandale Dr *GFTH/SHER* LS25......107 J7
Alandale Gv *GFTH/SHER* LS25......107 G7
Alandale Rd *GFTH/SHER* LS25....107 G6
  HUDN HD2..................................177 K4
Alaska Pl *CHAL* LS7........................83 K6
Albans Cl *AL/HA/HU* LS17.............46 B4
Alban St *BOW* BD4.......................118 C2
Albany Rd *RTHW* LS26..................144 E1
Albany Rw *ILK* * LS29......................38 A6
Albany St *HIPP* HX3.........................17 K9

  WBOW * BD5................................117 K2
  WBSY BD6....................................117 H5
  WOR/ARM LS12..........................101 K6
Albany Ter *HIPP* HX3.......................17 K9
  WOR/ARM * LS12.......................101 K6
Alberta Av *CHAL* LS7.......................83 K6
Albert Av *IDLE* BD10.......................78 D4
  LUD/ILL HX2...............................134 B7
  SHPY BD18...................................76 D3
Albert Ct *LUD/ILL* HX2..................134 B7
Albert Crs *BIRK/DRI* BD11............139 J3
  CUL/QBY BD13...........................115 H5
Albert Dr *LUD/ILL* HX2..................134 A7
  MOR LS27...................................142 C2
Albert Gdns *LUD/ILL* HX2............134 B7
Albert Gv *HDGY* LS6........................82 C6
Albert Pl *BFDE* BD3...........................7 L4
  HORS LS18....................................81 F3
Albert Prom *HIPP* HX3..................154 D4
Albert Rd *CUL/QBY* BD13.............115 G4
  LUD/ILL HX2...............................134 B7
  MOR LS27...................................142 A2
  RPDN/SBR HX6...........................153 F1
  RTHW LS26.................................145 K1
  SHPY BD18...................................76 E4
Albert Sq *BFD* BD20.........................33 F1
Albert St *BAIL* BD17........................77 H3
  BRIG HD6....................................157 H5
  CAS WF10..................................148 D7
  CLECK * BD19............................138 E7
  CUL/QBY BD13.............................95 G7
  CUL/QBY BD13...........................115 J5
  ELL HX5......................................175 J3
  FEA/AMT WF7............................188 C4
  HFAX HX1......................................16 B5
  HWTH BD22..................................73 C4
  IDLE BD10.....................................78 C6
  KGHY BD21....................................2 F4
  LM/WK BD12...............................137 H5
  LVSG WF15.................................159 K5
  NORM WF6..................................167 H4
  PDSY/CALV LS28........................100 A7
  WBSY BD6....................................117 G6
  WIL/AL BD15.................................95 F1
Albert Ter *LM/WK* BD12................138 A2
  SHPY BD18...................................76 E3
Albert Vw *LUD/ILL* HX2.................134 B7
Albert Wk *SHPY* BD18.....................76 D4
Albert Wy *BIRK/DRI* BD11............139 J3
Albion Ar *LDS* LS1............................14 A1
Albion Av *WOR/ARM* LS12.............12 C1
Albion Cl *BSPA/BRAM* LS23...........48 C5
Albion Ct *HFAX* HX1.........................17 C5
  WKFDE WF1..................................18 E5
Albion Cft *OSS* WF5......................182 D3
Albion Fold *WIL/AL* BD15..............75 F7
Albion Pl *LDS* LS1............................10 A9
Albion Rd *IDLE* BD10.......................78 D4
  PDSY/CALV LS28........................100 B3
Albion St *BRIG* HD6.......................157 F5
  BSPA/BRAM LS23.........................48 C5
  BTLY WF17..................................161 G4
  CAS WF10..................................148 B7
  CLECK BD19................................159 F1
  CUL/QBY BD13.............................94 B5
  CUL/QBY BD13...........................115 C5
  DEWS WF13...............................161 F7
  DEWS * WF13............................180 C4
  EARD/LOFT WF3.........................144 E4
  ELL HX5......................................175 K3
  HECK WF16.................................159 K4
  HFAX HX1......................................17 H6
  HWTH BD22..................................73 F4
  LDS LS1...10 A9
  LVSG WF15.................................159 H4
  MOR * LS27................................141 K3
  OT LS21...39 J3
  PDSY/CALV LS28........................100 C6
  WBSY BD6....................................116 D7
  WKFDE WF1..................................18 E2
Albion Wy *WOR/ARM* LS12.............8 F9
Alcester Garth *BFDE* BD3.................6 E4
Alcester Pl *RHAY* * LS8...................11 G1
Alcester Rd *RHAY* * LS8..................11 G1
Alcester St *RHAY* * LS8...................11 G1
Alcester Ter *RHAY* LS8....................11 G1
Aldams Rd *EARL* WF12..................181 F2
Alden Av *MOR* LS27.......................141 K5
Alden Cl *MOR* LS27.......................141 K5
Alden Ct *MOR* LS27.......................141 K5
Alden Crs *PONT* WF8......................189 G2
Alden Fold *MOR* * LS27................141 K5
Alder Av *KGHY* BD21........................3 K8
  WKFDW/WTN WF2.......................18 A1
Alder Carr *BAIL* BD17......................77 G1
Alder Dr *PDSY/CALV* LS28..............99 H5
Alder Garth *PDSY/CALV* LS28.........99 J5
Alder Gv *LUD/ILL* HX2..................134 B1
  NORM WF6..................................186 D2
Alder Hill Av *CHAL* LS7...................83 F5
Alder Hill Gv *CHAL* LS7...................83 F5
Alder Holt Dr *WBSY* BD6..............137 F1
Aldermanbury *BFD* BD1....................5 L7
Alderney Rd *EARL* WF12...............161 J6
Alderscholes Cl *CUL/QBY* BD13.....95 G7
Alderscholes La
  CUL/QBY BD13...........................115 F1
Alderson St *WBSY* BD6.................116 D7
Alderstone Hl *HUDW* HD3.............175 K7
Aldersyde *BTLY* WF17...................140 B6
Alderton Bank *AL/HA/HU* LS17......82 E2
Alderton Crs *AL/HA/HU* LS17.........82 E2
Alderton Mt *AL/HA/HU* LS17.........82 E2
Alderton Pl *AL/HA/HU* LS17...........82 E2
Alderton Ri *AL/HA/HU* LS17...........82 E2
Alegar St *BRIG* HD6.......................157 H6
Alexander Av *MSTN/BAR* LS15.....105 H4
Alexander Crs *FEA/AMT* WF7........188 C2
Alexander Rd *FEA/AMT* WF7.........188 C3
Alexander Sq *CLAY* BD14..............116 A2
Alexander St *LDS* * LS1.....................9 M8
  WBSY BD6....................................117 G6
Alexander Ter *HFAX* HX1................16 B5
Alexandra Cl *RPDN/SBR* HX6.......153 K4
Alexandra Crs *ELL* HX5.................176 A1
  ILK LS29..23 K5

  HTON BD9.......................................97 F2
Alexandra Dr *NORM* WF6.............186 E2
Alexandra Gv *HDGY* LS6..................8 F5
  PDSY/CALV LS28..........................99 K6
Alexandra Rd *BTLY* WF17.............161 G4
  BFD BD7...78 D7
  HDGY LS6..8 E5
  HORS LS18....................................81 F3
  PDSY/CALV LS28..........................99 K7
  SHPY BD18....................................77 F5
Alexandra St *CUL/QBY* BD13.......115 H5
  GTHN BD7...................................116 C1
  HFAX HX1......................................17 G7
  LVSG WF15.................................159 H4
Alexandra Ter *ECHL* BD2................98 D3
  YEA LS19......................................59 K4
Alford Ter *GTHN* BD7........................4 D6
Alfred St East *HFAX* * HX1.............17 J6
Alfred St *BRIG* HD6........................157 G5
  BTLY WF17..................................160 E4
  EARL * WF12...............................161 H7
  GTL/HWG HX4.............................175 G2
  HECK WF16.................................160 A5
  HFAX HX1......................................16 B5
  LVSG WF15.................................159 J4
  MOR * LS27................................122 B6
Alfreds Wy *BTLY* WF17.................161 F3
Alice St *CLECK* BD19.....................138 E7
  GIR BD8...5 J3
  HWTH BD22..................................72 D6
  KGHY BD21....................................3 G4
Alkincote St *KGHY* BD21..................2 F6
All Alone Rd *IDLE* BD10..................78 A5
Allanbridge Cl *IDLE* BD10...............78 D5
Allandale Av *WBSY* BD6...............117 F7
Allandale Rd *WBSY* BD6...............117 F7
Allan Haigh Cl
  WKFDW/WTN WF2.....................183 J1
Allan St *BFDE* BD3.............................6 F7
Allan Ter *RPDN/SBR* HX6.............153 K5
Allenby Crs *BEE/HOL* LS11...........123 F6
Allenby Dr *BEE/HOL* LS11............123 F6
Allenby Gdns *BEE/HOL* LS11........123 F6
Allenby Gv *BEE/HOL* LS11............123 F6
Allenby Pl *BEE/HOL* LS11.............123 F6
Allenby Rd *BEE/HOL* LS11............123 F6
Allenby Vw *BEE/HOL* LS11...........123 F5
Allen Cft *BIRK/DRI* BD11..............139 H2
Allerby Gn *WBSY* BD6...................136 E1
Allerton Cl *WIL/AL* BD15.................96 A4
Allerton Dr *AL/HA/HU* LS17...........45 K4
Allerton Grange Av
  AL/HA/HU LS17............................83 K3
Allerton Grange Cl
  AL/HA/HU LS17............................83 H4
Allerton Grange Crs
  AL/HA/HU LS17............................83 J4
Allerton Grange Cft *RHAY* LS8.....83 K4
Allerton Grange Dr
  AL/HA/HU LS17............................83 J4
  WIL/AL BD15.................................96 A4
Allerton Grange Gdns
  AL/HA/HU LS17............................83 J4
Allerton Grange Ri
  AL/HA/HU LS17............................83 J4
Allerton Grange V
  AL/HA/HU LS17............................83 J4
Allerton Grange Wk
  AL/HA/HU LS17............................83 J4
Allerton Grange Wy *RHAY* LS8.....83 J4
Allerton Gv *AL/HA/HU* LS17...........83 J2
Allerton Hl *CHAL* LS7.......................83 H5
Allerton La *WIL/AL* BD15.................95 K6
Allerton Pk *CHAL* LS7......................83 J5
Allerton Pl *AL/HA/HU* LS17............83 J2
  HFAX HX1......................................16 C6
Allerton Rd *GIR* BD8........................96 C4
  WIL/AL BD15.................................95 G4
  WIL/AL BD15.................................96 A4
Allerton St *BULY* LS4........................8 C5
Alliance St *WOR/ARM* LS12..........101 K6
Allinson St *WOR/ARM* * LS12.........12 C1
Allison Dr *HUDN* HD2....................177 H6
Allison La *ECHL* BD2.........................97 J1
Allison St *FEA/AMT* WF7...............188 B4
Alloe Field Vw *LUD/ILL* HX2.........134 B1
All Saint's Cir *RTHW* LS26............126 A7
All Saints Ct *KGHY* BD21..................2 E6
All Saint's Dr *RTHW* LS26.............145 K1
All Saints Rd *GTHN* BD7................117 H1
  RTHW LS26.................................126 A7
All Saints Ter *KGHY* BD21................2 E4
All Saint's Vw *RTHW* LS26............125 K7
All Souls' Rd *HIPP* HX3....................17 G2
All Souls' St *HIPP* * HX3..................17 G2
All Souls' Ter *HIPP* HX3...................17 G2
Allums La *OT* LS21...........................42 D6
Alma Cl *PDSY/CALV* LS28...............99 K2
Alma Cottages *HDGY* LS6...............82 C7
Alma Gv *OSM* LS9............................10 F5
Alma La *HECK* WF16.....................160 A2
  RPDN/SBR HX6...........................172 C2
Alma Pl *BFDE* BD3.............................7 J4
  KGHY BD21....................................3 G9
  OSM LS9.......................................10 F5
Alma Rd *HDGY* LS6.........................82 C7
Alma St *BOW* BD4.........................118 C2
  CUL/QBY BD13...........................115 C5
  HWTH BD22..................................72 C4
  KGHY BD21....................................53 K7
  OSM LS9.......................................10 F6
  RTHW LS26.................................126 A7
  SHPY BD18....................................77 J4
  YEA LS19......................................59 K4
Alma Ter *KGHY* BD21.......................53 K7
  RTHW LS26.................................144 E1
Almondroyd *HECK* WF16..............159 K3
Almond St *BFDE* BD3........................7 G7
Almond Wy *BTLY* WF17.................140 C6
Almscliffe Av *EARL* WF12.............181 H1
Almshouse Hl *BSPA/BRAM* LS23....68 C1
Almshouse La *WKFDE* WF1.............18 F5
Alnwick Dr *ECHL* BD2........................5 F1
Alpine Cl *BTLY* WF17.....................160 E4
Alpine Ri *CUL/QBY* BD13.................95 G6
Alston Cl *HTON* BD9........................96 C4
Alston La *SCFT* LS14.....................105 H2
Alston Rd *KGHY* BD21.......................3 L1
Altar Dr *AIRE* BD20..........................54 D2

  HTON BD9.......................................97 F2
Altar La *BGLY* BD16.........................54 D7
Althorpe Gv *IDLE* BD10...................78 B6
Altinkool St *WKFDE* WF1..............185 F7
Altofts Hall Rd *NORM* WF6...........166 C4
Altofts La *CAS* WF10......................167 G2
Altofts Lodge Dr *NORM* WF6........166 B5
Altofts Rd *NORM* WF6...................166 D5
Alton Gv *HTON* BD9.........................96 E2
  SHPY BD18....................................77 G7
Alum Ct *HTON* BD9..........................97 F2
Alum Dr *HTON* BD9..........................97 F2
Alvanley Ct *GIR* BD8........................96 C5
Alverthorpe Rd
  WKFDW/WTN WF2.....................184 A3
Alwen Av *HUDN* HD2....................176 E7
Alwoodley Cha
  WKFDW/WTN WF2.......................63 K6
Alwoodley Court Gdns
  AL/HA/HU LS17............................63 F5
Alwoodley Gdns
  AL/HA/HU LS17............................63 F5
Alwoodley La *AL/HA/HU* LS17.......62 E5
Amberley Ct *BFDE* BD3.....................7 L4
Amberley Gdns *WOR/ARM* LS12.....12 B4
Amberley Rd *WOR/ARM* LS12.......12 B4
Amberley St *BFDE* BD3......................7 G5
  WOR/ARM LS12.............................12 B4
Amber St *BTLY* WF17.....................160 D2
Amberton Ap *RHAY* LS8...............104 D1
Amberton Cl *RHAY* LS8...................84 D7
Amberton Crs *RHAY* LS8..............104 D1
Amberton Gdns *RHAY* LS8...........104 D1
Amberton Garth *RHAY* LS8..........104 D1
Amberton Gv *RHAY* LS8................104 D1
Amberton La *RHAY* LS8................104 D1
Amberton Mt *RHAY* LS8................104 C1
Amberton Pl *RHAY* LS8.................104 C1
Amberton Rd *RHAY* LS8................104 D1
Amberton St *RHAY* LS8.................104 D1
Amberton Ter *RHAY* LS8...............104 D1
Ambler Gv *LUD/QBY* BD13...........115 F7
Ambler St *CAS* WF10.....................168 C5
  GIR BD8...97 H3
  KGHY BD21....................................3 K5
Amblers Ct *PDSY/CALV* LS28.......100 B7
Amblers Cft *IDLE* BD10....................78 D7
Amblers Ter *HIPP* HX3.....................17 H2
Ambleside Av *HTON* BD9................96 E3
Ambleside Gdns
  PDSY/CALV LS28..........................99 K6
Ambleside Gv *RTHW* LS26............145 K1
Ambleside Rd *CAS* WF10..............149 K6
Ambleside Wk *WBY* LS22................28 E3
Ambleton Wy *CUL/QBY* BD13......115 F6
Amelia St *SHPY* BD18......................76 E4
America La *BRIG* HD6....................157 H6
America Moor La *MOR* LS27.........141 K5
Amisfield Rd *HIPP* HX3..................136 C7
Amos St *HFAX* HX1..........................16 B5
Amport Cl *BRIG* HD6.....................157 G7
Amspool Ct *EARD/LOFT* WF3.......144 D4
Amundsen Av *ECHL* BD2.................78 B7
Amyroyce Dr *SHPY* BD18................77 K5
Amy St *BGLY* BD16...........................75 K1
  HIPP HX3.....................................134 D5
Anaheim Dr *WKFDE* WF1...............164 E3
Ancaster Crs *BHP/TINH* LS16.........82 A5
Ancaster Rd *BHP/TINH* LS16..........82 A5
Ancaster Vw *BHP/TINH* LS16.........82 A5
The Anchorage *BGLY* BD16............55 J7
Anchor Bridge Wy *EARL* WF12.....181 F2
Andersen Ct *CAS* WF10.................169 H5
Anderson Av *RHAY* LS8....................10 F4
Anderson Mt *RHAY* LS8....................10 F4
Anderson St *GIR* BD8.........................5 G1
  PONT WF8...................................169 H7
  WKFDW/WTN WF2.......................18 B5
Anderton St *WKFDE* * WF1...........185 F6
Andover Gn *BOW* BD4...................119 F2
Andrew Cl *HIPP* HX3......................155 K4
Andrew Crs *WKFDE* WF1...............164 C3
Andrew St *FEA/AMT* WF7..............188 B5
  PDSY/CALV LS28........................100 A3
  WKFDE WF1..................................18 D2
Angel Ct *BVRD* LS3...........................9 G7
Angel Pl *BGLY* BD16.........................55 K6
Angel Rd *HFAX* HX1..........................16 D4
Angel St *BAIL* BD17..........................57 J7
Angel Wy *BFD* BD1............................5 J6
Angerton Wy *WBSY* BD6...............137 F1
Angus Av *LM/WK* BD12.................137 H6
Anlaby St *BOW* BD4.......................118 E1
Anne Ga *BFDE* BD3...........................6 B5
Annes Ct *HIPP* HX3........................155 K4
Anne St *BTLY* WF17.......................160 D1
  GTHN BD7...................................116 E3
Annie St *KGHY* * BD21.......................3 C1
  MOR LS27...................................142 A3
  RPDN/SBR HX6...........................153 J3
  SHPY BD18....................................77 H6
  WKFDE WF1..................................164 C4
Anning Fold *GFTH/SHER* LS25......108 A5
Annison St *BFDE* BD3........................7 G6
Ann Pl *WBOW* BD5............................5 L9
Ann St *CUL/QBY* BD13.....................94 A4
  KGHY BD21....................................2 E6
Anroyd St *DEWS* WF13..................160 D7
Anson Gv *GTHN* BD7......................116 E4
Anthony La *BGLY* BD16....................74 E2
Anvil Ct *GIR* BD8................................4 F1
Anvil St *BRIG* HD6.........................157 F5
Apex Vw *BEE/HOL* LS11..................13 M5
Apex Wy *BEE/HOL* LS11..................14 A6
Apperley Gdns *IDLE* BD10..............79 F4
Apperley La *IDLE* BD10....................79 F4
Apperley Rd *IDLE* BD10...................78 E4
Appleby Cl *CUL/QBY* BD13...........115 F5
Appleby La *GFTH/SHER* LS25........108 A4
Appleby Pl *MSTN/BAR* LS15.........105 F5
Appleby Wk *MSTN/BAR* LS15.......105 F5
Appleby Wy *MOR* LS27..................142 A2
Apple Cl *BTLY* WF17.......................140 D5
Applegarth *RTHW* LS26..................125 K7

Appleshaw Crs
  WKFDW/WTN WF2.....................164 A5
Apple St *HWTH* BD22.......................73 H1
  HWTH * BD22...............................92 D3
Appleton Cl *BGLY* BD16...................56 A6
  LM/WK BD12..............................138 A2
Appleton Gv *OSM* LS9...................11 M9
Appleton Wy *OSM* LS9.....................11 J8
Appletree Cl *BSPA/BRAM* LS23......48 C3
Apple Tree Cl *EARD/LOFT* WF3.....143 H7
  PONT WF8...................................189 G3
Apple Tree Ct
  EARD/LOFT * WF3.......................163 H1
Apple Tree Gdns *ILK* LS29..............23 J5
Apple Tree Rd *FEA/AMT* WF7........188 D5
Appletree Wy *GFTH/SHER* LS25....111 G5
Appleyard Rd *HBR* HX7..................132 A6
The Approach *MSTN/BAR* LS15......86 C5
April Ct *LVSG* WF15.......................159 H6
Apsley Crs *GIR* BD8............................5 H1
Apsley St *HWTH* BD22.....................72 E1
  KGHY BD21....................................2 F8
Apsley Vls *GIR* BD8...........................5 H1
Aquamarine Dr *HUDN* HD2...........177 H7
Aquila Wy *LVSG* WF15..................158 E3
The Arbour *ILK* LS29........................23 K3
Arcadia St *KGHY* BD21.......................2 F8
Archbell Av *BRIG* HD6...................177 G1
Archer Rd *BRIG* HD6......................157 J7
Archer St *CAS* WF10......................168 B2
Archery Pl *LDSU* LS2..........................9 L5
Archery Rd *LDSU* LS2..........................9 L4
Archery St *LDSU* LS2.........................9 M5
Archery Ter *LDSU* LS2.........................9 L5
The Arches *HIPP* * HX3.....................17 H1
Arches St *HFAX* HX1..........................16 F7
Archibald St *GTHN* BD7.....................5 G6
Arctic Pde *GTHN* BD7.....................117 G5
Arctic St *HWTH* BD22......................73 F4
  KGHY BD21....................................53 J2
Ardennes Cl *ECHL* BD2....................98 A1
Arden Rd *GIR* BD8.............................96 B6
  HFAX HX1......................................16 E9
Ardsley Cl *BOW* BD4.....................119 G4
Argent Wy *BOW* BD4....................119 G4
Argie Av *BULY* LS4.........................102 A2
Argie Gdns *BULY* LS4.........................8 B4
Argie Rd *BULY* LS4.............................8 B4
Argie Ter *BULY* LS4.............................8 B4
Argyle Ms *AL/HA/HU* LS17.............45 K5
Argyle Rd *KNOT* WF11...................170 D3
  OSM LS9.......................................10 D8
Argyle St *BOW* BD4.......................118 C2
  KGHY BD21....................................2 E4
  SHPY BD18....................................77 G6
  WKFDE WF1..................................19 J9
Argyll Av *PONT* WF8......................189 G1
Argyll Cl *BAIL* BD17.........................77 K2
  HORS LS18....................................60 E7
Arkendale Ms *GTHN* * BD7............116 D3
Arksey Pl *WOR/ARM* LS12................8 B8
Arksey Ter *WOR/ARM* LS12..............8 B8
Arkwright St *BOW* BD4.....................7 L8
  CLAY BD14..................................116 A2
Arkwright Wk *MOR* LS27...............141 K1
Arlesford Rd *BOW* BD4..................119 F4
Arley Gv *WOR/ARM* LS12..................8 B8
Arley Pl *WOR/ARM* LS12....................8 B8
Arley St *WOR/ARM* LS12....................8 B7
Arley Ter *WOR/ARM* LS12..................8 B8
Arlington Crs *LUD/ILL* HX2............154 A3
Arlington Gv *CAS* * WF10..............168 E1
  RHAY LS8....................................104 C1
Arlington Rd *RHAY* LS8.................104 C1
Arlington St *BFDE* BD3.......................6 E7
  WKFDE WF1.................................184 C1
Armadale Av *BOW* BD4.................118 C6
Armgill La *SHPY* BD18......................97 J1
Armidale Wy *ECHL* BD2...................98 A2
Armitage Av *BRIG* HD6..................177 G1
Armitage Rd *HFAX* HX1....................16 A9
  LM/WK BD12..............................138 A3
  WKFDW/WTN WF2.....................183 J1
Armitage Sq *PDSY/CALV* LS28......100 A7
Armitage St *CAS* WF10..................148 B7
  DEWS * WF13............................180 A4
  RTHW * LS26...............................145 F3
Armley Gra *WOR/ARM* LS12..........101 J5
Armley Grange Av
  WOR/ARM LS12..........................101 J5
Armley Grange Crs
  WOR/ARM LS12..........................101 J4
Armley Grange Dr
  WOR/ARM LS12..........................101 J5
Armley Grange Mt
  WOR/ARM LS12..........................101 J5
Armley Grange Ov
  WOR/ARM LS12..........................101 J4
Armley Grange Ri
  WOR/ARM LS12..........................101 J5
Armley Grange Vw
  WOR/ARM LS12..........................101 J5
Armley Grange Wk
  WOR/ARM LS12..........................101 J5
Armley Grove Pl
  WOR/ARM LS12.............................12 C2
Armley Lodge Rd
  WOR/ARM LS12..............................8 A8
Armley Park Rd
  WOR/ARM LS12..............................8 A7
Armley Ridge Cl
  WOR/ARM LS12..........................101 K5
Armley Ridge Rd
  WOR/ARM LS12..........................101 J3
Armley Ridge Ter
  WOR/ARM LS12..........................101 K4
Armley Rd *WOR/ARM* LS12..............8 C9
Armouries Dr *MID* LS10....................14 D4
Armouries Wy *MID* LS10..................14 C7
Armoury Av *MIRF* WF14................179 H4
Armstrong Cl *NORM* WF6..............166 D4
Armstrong St *BOW* BD4....................7 K8
  PDSY/CALV LS28........................100 A3
Armstrong Ter *PONT* WF8..............189 G2
Armytage Rd *BRIG* HD6.................157 H6
Armytage Wy *BRIG* HD6................157 J7
Arncliffe Av *HWTH* * BD22...............2 C7
Arncliffe Crs *BRIG* HD6..................176 D1

MOR LS27 .....142 B5
Arncliffe Dr KNOT WF11 .....170 C4
Arncliffe Gdns BTLY WF17 .....160 E3
Arncliffe Garth
  PDSY/CALV LS28 .....100 A3
Arncliffe Gra AL/HA/HU LS17 .....83 J2
Arncliffe Gv HWTH BD22 .....2 C8
Arncliffe Pl HWTH BD22 .....2 C7
Arncliffe Rd BHP/TINH LS16 .....81 K4
  BTLY WF17 .....160 D3
  HWTH BD22 .....2 C8
  WKFDE WF1 .....19 L1
Arncliffe St PDSY/CALV LS28 .....100 A3
Arncliffe Ter GTHN BD7 .....4 E8
Arnford Cl BFDE BD3 .....6 B3
Arnold Pl GIR BD8 .....4 F3
Arnold Royd BRIG HD6 .....176 D2
Arnold St GIR BD8 .....5 G2
  HFAX HX1 .....16 C6
  LVSG WF15 .....159 H4
  RPDN/SBR * HX6 .....153 J4
Arnside Av AIRE BD20 .....54 B2
Arnside Cl CAS WF10 .....149 J7
Arnside Crs CAS WF10 .....149 J7
Arnside Rd WBOW BD5 .....117 J4
Arran Ct GFTH/SHER LS25 .....127 J1
Arran Dr GFTH/SHER LS25 .....127 J1
  HORS LS18 .....60 E7
Arran Wy RTHW LS26 .....145 G2
Arthington Av MID LS10 .....123 J4
Arthington Cl EARD/LOFT WF3 .....162 C1
Arthington Garth OT LS21 .....41 H3
Arthington Gv MID LS10 .....123 J4
Arthington La OT LS21 .....41 H3
Arthington Lawns OT LS21 .....41 H4
Arthington Pl MID LS10 .....123 J4
Arthington Rd BHP/TINH LS16 .....62 B2
Arthington St GIR BD8 .....5 G3
  MID LS10 .....123 J4
Arthington Ter MID LS10 .....123 J4
Arthington Vw MID LS10 .....123 J4
Arthur Av GIR BD8 .....96 C6
Arthursdale Cl MSTN/BAR LS15 .....86 C5
Arthursdale Dr MSTN/BAR LS15 .....86 C5
Arthursdale Gra
  MSTN/BAR LS15 .....86 C5
Arthur St BGLY * BD16 .....75 J1
  BRIG HD6 .....157 H6
  HWTH BD22 .....72 C2
  IDLE BD10 .....78 C6
  PDSY/CALV LS28 .....100 B3
  WKFDE WF1 .....185 F6
Artillery St HECK WF16 .....160 E4
Artist St WOR/ARM LS12 .....12 F1
Arum St WBOW BD5 .....117 H3
Arundel Cl BTLY WF17 .....140 E5
  WKFDE WF1 .....18 E2
Arundel St GFTH/SHER LS25 .....108 A5
  HFAX HX1 .....16 B5
  PDSY/CALV LS28 .....100 B5
  WKFDE WF1 .....18 E2
Arundel Wk BTLY WF17 .....140 E6
Ascot Av GTHN BD7 .....116 D4
Ascot Dr WBSY BD6 .....116 D4
Ascot Gdns EARD/LOFT WF3 .....143 J4
  GTHN BD7 .....116 D4
Ascot Gv BRIG HD6 .....176 D1
Ascot Pde GTHN BD7 .....116 D4
Ascot Rd GFTH/SHER LS25 .....127 J4
Ascot Ter OSM LS9 .....15 H1
Ash Av HDGY LS6 .....82 C7
Ashbourne Av CLECK BD19 .....158 E2
  ECHL BD2 .....98 A2
Ashbourne Bank ECHL BD2 .....98 A2
Ashbourne Cl ECHL BD2 .....98 A2
Ashbourne Crs CUL/QBY BD13 .....115 G5
  ECHL BD2 .....98 A2
  GFTH/SHER LS25 .....127 J1
Ashbourne Cft CLECK BD19 .....158 E2
Ashbourne Dr CLECK BD19 .....158 E2
  ECHL BD2 .....98 A2
  PONT WF8 .....189 J4
Ashbourne Gdns CLECK BD19 .....158 E2
  ECHL BD2 .....98 A2
Ashbourne Garth ECHL BD2 .....98 B1
Ashbourne Gv ECHL BD2 .....98 A2
  HFAX HX1 .....16 A6
Ashbourne Hvn ECHL BD2 .....98 A2
Ashbourne Mt ECHL BD2 .....98 A2
Ashbourne Ov ECHL BD2 .....98 A2
Ashbourne Ri ECHL BD2 .....98 A2
Ashbourne Rd ECHL BD2 .....98 A2
  HWTH BD22 .....53 H7
Ashbourne Vw CLECK BD19 .....158 E2
Ashbourne Wy CLECK BD19 .....158 E2
  ECHL BD2 .....98 A2
Ashbrook Cl OSS WF5 .....182 C3
Ash Brow Rd HUDN HD2 .....177 G6
Ashburn Cl WBY LS22 .....29 G2
Ashburn Cft WBY LS22 .....29 G2
Ashburn Dr WBY LS22 .....29 G3
Ashburn Gv BAIL BD17 .....57 H7
  WBY LS22 .....29 G3
Ashburnham Gv HTON BD9 .....97 G2
Ashburn Pl ILK LS29 .....23 K6
Ashburn Wy WBY LS22 .....29 G2
Ashbury Cha WKFDE WF1 .....164 B3
Ashby Av BRAM LS13 .....101 G3
Ashby Cl LVSG WF15 .....159 G7
Ashby Crs BRAM LS13 .....101 G3
Ashby Mt BRAM LS13 .....101 G3
Ashby Sq BOW BD4 .....118 B2
Ashby Ter BRAM LS13 .....101 G3
Ashby Vw BRAM LS13 .....101 G3
Ash Cl HIPP HX3 .....136 C7
  ILK LS29 .....23 H5
Ashcombe Dr KNOT WF11 .....171 G1
Ash Ct CLECK BD19 .....138 A7
Ash Crs EARD/LOFT WF3 .....165 G4
  HDGY LS6 .....82 B7
Ash Cft WBSY BD6 .....117 F6
Ashcroft Av FEA/AMT WF7 .....188 B5
Ashcroft Cl BTLY WF17 .....160 D5
Ashcroft Rd FEA/AMT WF7 .....188 B5
Ashdale La WBY LS22 .....29 G1

Ashday La HIPP HX3 .....156 B6
Ashdene WOR/ARM LS12 .....121 G3
Ashdene Cl PDSY/CALV LS28 .....120 B1
Ashdene Ct CUL/QBY BD13 .....74 A6
Ashdene Crs PDSY/CALV LS28 .....120 B1
Ashdene Gv PONT WF8 .....170 A4
Ashdown Rd WKFDE WF1 .....185 H6
Ashdown St BRAM LS13 .....101 F3
Ashfield BOW BD4 .....118 E5
  EARL WF12 .....181 G5
  WBY LS22 .....29 J3
Ashfield Av MOR LS27 .....141 J5
  SHPY BD18 .....77 G7
Ashfield Cl HIPP HX3 .....134 C7
  MSTN/BAR LS15 .....106 A2
  WOR/ARM LS12 .....121 H2
Ashfield Crs BGLY BD16 .....75 K2
  PDSY/CALV LS28 .....100 A4
Ashfield Dr BAIL BD17 .....57 J7
  HIPP HX3 .....134 D5
  SHPY BD18 .....77 G7
Ashfield Gv PDSY/CALV * LS28 .....100 B4
  SHPY BD18 .....77 F7
Ashfield Pk HDGY LS6 .....82 C6
Ashfield Pl ECHL BD2 .....98 E3
  OT LS21 .....39 G3
Ashfield Rd BTLY WF17 .....140 D5
  CUL/QBY BD13 .....95 G7
  GTL/HWG HX4 .....174 E2
  IDLE BD10 .....78 D3
  MOR LS27 .....141 J5
  PDSY/CALV LS28 .....100 A4
  SHPY BD18 .....76 D5
Ashfield St HUDN HD2 .....177 G7
  NORM WF6 .....167 F5
Ashfield Ter EARD/LOFT WF3 .....144 A5
  GTL/HWG HX4 .....174 E1
  HWTH BD22 .....72 C6
  MSTN/BAR LS15 .....106 A1
Ashfield Wy WOR/ARM LS12 .....121 J2
Ashford Dr PDSY/CALV LS28 .....100 C3
Ash Ford Gv WBSY * BD6 .....116 E5
Ashgap La NORM WF6 .....166 E6
Ash Gdns HDGY LS6 .....82 C7
Ash Ghyll Gdns BGLY * BD16 .....55 J7
Ash Gn PONT WF8 .....170 A7
Ash Gv AIRE BD20 .....32 E5
  BGLY BD16 .....75 K3
  BIRK/DRI BD11 .....139 H1
  BRIG HD6 .....157 H6
  CLECK BD19 .....139 H6
  EARD/LOFT WF3 .....165 G6
  HDGY LS6 .....9 G2
  HORS LS18 .....81 F2
  HWTH BD22 .....53 H7
  ILK LS29 .....24 B4
  OT LS21 .....39 G3
  PDSY/CALV LS28 .....100 B7
  PONT WF8 .....190 D4
Ashgrove ECHL BD2 .....98 D2
  GTHN BD7 .....5 J8
  IDLE BD10 .....79 F5
Ashgrove Av HIPP * HX3 .....155 H5
Ashgrove Crs
  GFTH/SHER LS25 .....128 A3
Ashgrove Cft
  GFTH/SHER LS25 .....127 K4
  GFTH/SHER * LS25 .....128 A4
Ashgrove Ms BRAM LS13 .....100 C1
Ashgrove Mt GFTH/SHER LS25 .....127 K3
Ashgrove Rd AIRE BD20 .....53 H1
  HUDE HD5 .....178 A7
Ash Hall La RPDN/SBR HX6 .....172 A3
Ash Hill Dr AL/HA/HU LS17 .....65 G7
Ash Hill Gdns AL/HA/HU LS17 .....65 G7
Ash Hill La AL/HA/HU LS17 .....65 G7
Ashington Cl ECHL BD2 .....98 E2
Ashlands Rd ILK LS29 .....24 B4
Ash La GFTH/SHER LS25 .....107 K5
  TAD LS24 .....91 K7
Ashlar Cl HWTH BD22 .....72 E5
Ashlar Gv CAS WF10 .....168 E2
  CUL/QBY BD13 .....115 G7
Ash Lea EARD/LOFT WF3 .....165 G4
Ashlea Av BRIG HD6 .....177 G1
Ashlea Cl BRIG HD6 .....177 G1
  GFTH/SHER LS25 .....127 J1
Ashlea Dr BRIG HD6 .....177 G1
Ashlea Ga BRAM LS13 .....101 F1
Ashlea Gn BRAM LS13 .....101 F1
Ashleigh Av PONT WF8 .....189 J2
  WKFDW/WTN WF2 .....183 K4
Ashleigh Gdns OSS WF5 .....182 B1
  RTHW LS26 .....145 K1
Ashleigh Rd BHP/TINH LS16 .....81 K4
Ashleigh St KGHY BD21 .....3 G2
Ashley Av OSM LS9 .....11 J4
Ashley Cl CLECK BD19 .....139 H5
  WKFDW/WTN WF2 .....164 A6
Ashley La BAIL BD17 .....77 F4
Ashley Park Ms
  GFTH/SHER LS25 .....108 A5
Ashley Rd BGLY BD16 .....75 K2
  LM/WK BD12 .....137 H5
  OSM LS9 .....11 H4
  WOR/ARM LS12 .....102 A7
Ashley St HFAX HX1 .....16 B6
  SHPY BD18 .....77 G4
Ashley Ter OSM LS9 .....11 J4
Ashmead BSPA/BRAM LS23 .....48 C5
  BTLY WF17 .....160 D5
Ash Meadow Cl HUDN HD2 .....177 H6
Ashmere Cl HUDN HD2 .....177 G7
Ashmews IDLE * BD10 .....79 F5
Atha Cl BEE/HOL LS11 .....123 F5
Atha Crs BEE/HOL LS11 .....123 F5
Atha St BEE/HOL LS11 .....123 F5
Ashmore Dr OSS WF5 .....162 B3
Ashmore Gdns BOW * BD4 .....118 C6
Ashmount CLAY BD14 .....116 C2
Ash Mt GTHN BD7 .....117 C1
  KGHY BD21 .....2 C9
Ash Rd HDGY LS6 .....82 B7
Ashroyd RTHW LS26 .....145 G3
Ash St CLECK BD19 .....158 D1
  EARD/LOFT WF3 .....165 G6
  HWTH BD22 .....92 D2
Ash Ter BGLY BD16 .....75 J2
  HDGY LS6 .....82 C7
  RPDN/SBR HX6 .....172 D6
Ashtofts Mt GSLY LS20 .....59 F2

Ashton Av GTHN BD7 .....116 D1
  RHAY LS8 .....11 H4
Ashton Clough Rd LVSG WF15 .....159 H4
Ashton Ct RHAY LS8 .....11 J2
Ashton Crs PDSY/CALV WF3 .....144 E4
Ashton Gv OSM LS9 .....11 H4
Ashton Mt OSM LS9 .....11 H4
Ashton Pl OSM LS9 .....11 H4
Ashton Rd CAS WF10 .....168 C2
  RHAY LS8 .....11 J2
Ashton St BFD1 BD1 .....5 J5
  CAS WF10 .....168 C1
  RHAY LS8 .....11 H3
Ashton Ter RHAY LS8 .....11 H4
Ashton Vw OSM LS9 .....11 H4
Ashton Wk IDLE BD10 .....78 B5
Ash Tree Ap SCFT LS14 .....106 A1
Ash Tree Av CUL/QBY BD13 .....94 E7
Ash Tree Bank SCFT LS14 .....86 A7
Ash Tree Cl SCFT LS14 .....86 A7
Ash Tree Gdns LUD/ILL HX2 .....133 K2
  NORM WF6 .....166 C5
  SCFT LS14 .....86 A7
Ash Tree Garth TAD LS24 .....90 E7
Ashtree Gv GFTH/SHER LS25 .....128 A5
  GTHN BD7 .....116 E4
Ash Tree Gv SCFT LS14 .....86 A7
Ash Tree Pk GFTH/SHER * LS25 .....128 A5
Ash Tree Rd LUD/ILL HX2 .....133 K2
Ash Tree Wk SCFT LS14 .....37 K1
Ash Vw EARD/LOFT WF3 .....163 H1
Ashville Av HDGY LS6 .....8 D3
Ashville Cft LUD/ILL HX2 .....134 A6
Ashville Gdns LUD/ILL HX2 .....134 A6
Ashville Gv HDGY LS6 .....8 D3
  LUD/ILL HX2 .....134 A6
Ashville Rd BULY LS4 .....8 D3
Ashville St HIPP * HX3 .....16 D1
Ashville Ter HDGY LS6 .....8 D3
Ashville Vw HDGY LS6 .....8 D4
Ashwell Rd GIR BD8 .....4 E2
  HTON BD9 .....97 F1
Ashwell St GIR BD8 .....4 F1
Ashwood SCFT LS14 .....85 J3
Ashwood Dr AIRE BD20 .....54 D2
  MOR LS27 .....120 E7
Ashwood Gdns MOR LS27 .....120 E7
Ashwood Gv HOR/CROF WF4 .....183 H7
  MOR LS27 .....121 F7
Ashwood St BOW BD4 .....118 C5
Ashwood Ter HDGY LS6 .....9 G1
Ashwood Vls HDGY LS6 .....9 G1
Askam Av MOR LS27 .....142 A5
Asket Av SCFT LS14 .....85 F6
Asket Cl SCFT LS14 .....85 F6
Asket Crs SCFT LS14 .....85 F6
Asket Dr SCFT LS14 .....85 F6
Asket Gdns RHAY LS8 .....84 E6
Asket Gn SCFT LS14 .....85 F7
Asket Garth SCFT LS14 .....85 F7
Asket Hl RHAY LS8 .....84 E6
Asket Pl SCFT LS14 .....85 F7
Asket Wk SCFT LS14 .....85 F7
Askew Av MOR LS27 .....142 A5
Askey Crs MOR LS27 .....142 A5
Askham Rd CAS WF10 .....149 J6
Askwith La OT LS21 .....26 B3
Aspect Gdns PDSY/CALV LS28 .....99 K5
Aspen Cl KGHY BD21 .....3 L8
  WKFDW/WTN WF2 .....18 E1
Aspen Ct EARD/LOFT WF3 .....142 B6
Aspen Gv DEWS WF13 .....160 E7
Aspen Mt BHP/TINH LS16 .....81 H2
Aspen Ri WIL/AL BD15 .....95 J1
Aspen Wy TAD LS24 .....50 C7
Aspinall St HFAX HX1 .....16 B8
Asprey Dr WIL/AL BD15 .....96 A5
Asquith Av MOR LS27 .....141 J1
Asquith Cl MOR LS27 .....141 J1
Asquith Ct LUD/ILL * HX2 .....154 A1
Asquith Dr MOR LS27 .....141 J2
Asquith St BTLY WF17 .....140 E5
Assembly St LDSU LS2 .....14 B1
  NORM WF6 .....166 D6
Astley Av RTHW LS26 .....126 D5
Astley La RTHW LS26 .....126 E6
Astley Wy RTHW LS26 .....126 E6
Aston Av BRAM * LS13 .....101 G3
Aston Cl LVSG WF15 .....159 G6
Aston Crs BRAM LS13 .....101 H3
Aston Dr BRAM LS13 .....101 H3
Aston Gv BRAM LS13 .....101 H3
Aston Mt BRAM LS13 .....101 H3
Aston Pl BRAM LS13 .....101 G3
Aston Rd BRAM LS13 .....101 G3
  WBOW BD5 .....117 K3
Aston St BRAM LS13 .....101 G3
Aston Ter BRAM LS13 .....101 G3
Aston Vw BRAM LS13 .....101 G3
Astor Gv BRAM LS13 .....100 D3
Astor St BRAM LS13 .....100 D3
Astral Av HIPP HX3 .....136 C7
Astral Cl HIPP HX3 .....136 C7
Astral Vw WBSY BD6 .....117 F4
Astra Pk BEE/HOL * LS11 .....123 H4
Atalanta Ter LUD/ILL HX2 .....154 B4
Athelstan La OT LS21 .....27 H7
Athelstanes Ct GFTH/SHER LS25 .....111 F6
Atherstone Rd WIL/AL BD15 .....96 A5
Atherton La BRIG HD6 .....177 G1
Athlone Gv WOR/ARM LS12 .....12 A1
Athlone Ri GFTH/SHER LS25 .....108 A6
Athlone St WOR/ARM LS12 .....12 A1
Athlone Ter WOR/ARM LS12 .....12 A1
Athol Gdns HIPP HX3 .....134 D4

Athol Gn HIPP HX3 .....134 D4
Athol Rd HIPP HX3 .....134 D4
  HTON BD9 .....97 G3
Athol St HIPP HX3 .....134 D4
  KGHY BD21 .....3 M1
Atkinson Ct NORM * WF6 .....166 D7
Atkinson La PONT WF8 .....170 A6
Atkinson St MID LS10 .....14 E5
  SHPY BD18 .....77 G4
Atlanta St BRAM LS13 .....100 D3
Atlas Mill Rd BRIG HD6 .....157 F6
Atlas St GIR BD8 .....4 F2
Attlee Gv WKFDE WF1 .....164 D4
Attlee St NORM WF6 .....186 E1
Auckland Rd WBSY BD6 .....117 F5
Audby Ct WBY LS22 .....29 J5
Audby La WBY LS22 .....29 J4
Audrey St OSS WF5 .....182 D5
Augusta Dr NORM WF6 .....187 G1
Auster Bank Av TAD LS24 .....51 F6
Auster Bank Crs TAD LS24 .....51 F6
Auster Bank Rd TAD LS24 .....51 F6
Auster Bank Vw TAD LS24 .....51 F5
Austfield La GFTH/SHER LS25 .....131 K7
Austhorpe Av MSTN/BAR LS15 .....106 B6
Austhorpe Ct MSTN/BAR LS15 .....106 B6
Austhorpe Gdns
  MSTN/BAR LS15 .....106 C5
Austhorpe Gv MSTN/BAR LS15 .....106 B6
Austhorpe La MSTN/BAR LS15 .....106 A4
Austhorpe Rd MSTN/BAR LS15 .....106 A3
Austhorpe Vw MSTN/BAR LS15 .....106 A3
Austin Av BRIG HD6 .....156 E4
Austin Rd CAS WF10 .....149 J7
Austin St KGHY BD21 .....3 J1
Authorpe Rd CHAL LS7 .....82 E6
Autumn Av HDGY LS6 .....8 F5
  WBY LS22 .....29 H1
Autumn Crs HORS LS18 .....81 G5
Autumn Gv HDGY LS6 .....8 F5
Autumn Pl HDGY LS6 .....8 F5
Autumn St HDGY LS6 .....8 F5
  HFAX * HX1 .....16 B9
Autumn Ter HDGY LS6 .....8 F5
Auty Crs EARD/LOFT WF3 .....165 G3
Auty Sq MOR LS27 .....142 A4
Avenel Rd WIL/AL BD15 .....96 A5
Avenel Ter WIL/AL BD15 .....96 A5
Avenham Wy BFDE BD3 .....6 C4
Avens Cl PONT WF8 .....189 J2
The Avenue AL/HA/HU LS17 .....44 B4
  AL/HA/HU LS17 .....63 F6
  BGLY * BD16 .....76 A4
  BTLY WF17 .....140 B6
  BTLY WF17 .....160 D1
  CLAY BD14 .....116 A2
  DEWS WF13 .....160 C5
  EARD/LOFT WF3 .....143 F7
  GFTH/SHER LS25 .....131 F3
  HIPP HX3 .....136 C7
  HORS LS18 .....80 C3
  IDLE BD10 .....79 F1
  MSTN/BAR LS15 .....86 C4
  MSTN/BAR LS15 .....106 A2
  MSTN/BAR LS15 .....126 A4
  OSM LS9 .....14 E1
  RHAY LS8 .....84 B4
  WBY LS22 .....46 D1
  WKFDE WF1 .....164 B4
Avenue A BSPA/BRAM LS23 .....31 G6
Avenue B BSPA/BRAM LS23 .....49 G1
Avenue C BSPA/BRAM LS23 .....31 J7
Avenue Crs RHAY LS8 .....104 A1
Avenue C West
  BSPA/BRAM LS23 .....49 G1
Avenue D BSPA/BRAM LS23 .....49 G2
Avenue Des
  Hirondelles OT LS21 .....41 G1
Avenue E East BSPA/BRAM LS23 .....49 H1
Avenue E West
  BSPA/BRAM LS23 .....49 G2
Avenue F BSPA/BRAM LS23 .....49 H1
Avenue G BSPA/BRAM LS23 .....31 J7
Avenue Gdns AL/HA/HU LS17 .....62 E6
Avenue Hl RHAY LS8 .....104 A1
Avenue No 2 BRIG HD6 .....157 F7
Avenue Rd WBOW BD5 .....118 A3
Avenue St BOW BD4 .....118 E5
Avenue Victoria RHAY LS8 .....84 B4
Averingcliffe Rd IDLE BD10 .....78 E6
Aviary Rd RTHW LS26 .....126 D5
Aviary Mt WOR/ARM LS12 .....8 B8
Aviary Pl WOR/ARM LS12 .....8 B8
Aviary Rw WOR/ARM LS12 .....8 B8
Aviary St WOR/ARM LS12 .....8 B8
Aviary Ter WOR/ARM LS12 .....8 B8
Aviary Vw WOR/ARM LS12 .....8 B8
Aviation Rd GFTH/SHER LS25 .....111 K6
Avison Yd WKFDE WF1 .....19 G5
Avocet Garth MID LS10 .....143 J2
Avon Cl AL/HA/HU LS17 .....65 G7
Avon Ct AL/HA/HU LS17 .....65 G7
Avondale KGHY BD21 .....2 C3
Avondale Crs SHPY BD18 .....77 F5
Avondale Dr EARD/LOFT WF3 .....165 F5
Avondale Gv SHPY BD18 .....77 F5
Avondale Mt SHPY BD18 .....77 F5
Avondale Pl HIPP HX3 .....154 E4
Avondale Rd SHPY BD18 .....76 D5
Avondale St BRAM LS13 .....101 F4
  WKFDW/WTN WF2 .....18 E8
Avondale Wy
  WKFDW/WTN WF2 .....18 E8
Avon Dr GFTH/SHER LS25 .....107 J7
Avon Garth WBY LS22 .....29 F4
Avon Wk FEA/AMT WF7 .....188 C2
Axis Ct MOR * LS27 .....141 H2
Aydon Wy WBSY BD6 .....116 D3
Aygill Av HTON BD9 .....96 C2
Aylesbury St HWTH * BD22 .....53 H7
Aylesford Mt MSTN/BAR LS15 .....106 C2
Aynholme Dr ILK LS29 .....22 C1
Aynsley Gv WIL/AL BD15 .....96 A4
Ayresome Av RHAY LS8 .....84 B4
Ayresome Ovl WIL/AL BD15 .....95 K6
Ayresome Ter RHAY LS8 .....84 B4

Aysgarth Av BRIG HD6 .....157 F2
Aysgarth Cl LM/WK BD12 .....137 H5
  OSM LS9 .....15 H1
  WKFDW/WTN WF2 .....183 J6
Aysgarth Crs LUD/ILL HX2 .....133 H4
Aysgarth Dr OSM LS9 .....15 H1
  WKFDW/WTN WF2 .....183 J6
Aysgarth Fold MID LS10 .....143 H3
Aysgarth Pl OSM LS9 .....15 H1
Aysgarth Rd BTLY WF17 .....160 D3
Aysgarth Wk OSM LS9 .....15 H1
Ayton Cl BFDE BD3 .....6 E4
Azealea Ct BFDE BD3 .....6 E4

B

Bachelor La HORS * LS18 .....81 F2
Back Ada St KGHY BD21 .....2 D5
Back Aireview Ter KGHY * BD21 .....3 M6
Back Aireville St AIRE BD20 .....53 H1
Back Airlie Av RHAY * LS8 .....104 A1
Back Albert Gv HDGY LS6 .....82 C6
Back Albert Ter HDGY LS6 .....8 E5
Back Alcester Pl RHAY * LS8 .....11 G1
Back Alcester Rd RHAY * LS8 .....11 G1
Back Alcester Ter RHAY * LS8 .....11 G1
Back Ann St CUL/QBY * BD13 .....94 A4
Back Archery Pl LDSU LS2 .....9 L4
Back Archery Rd LDSU LS2 .....9 M5
Back Archery St LDSU LS2 .....9 M5
Back Archery Ter LDSU LS2 .....9 L5
Back Ash Gv HDGY LS6 .....9 G2
Back Ashgrove (West) GTHN BD7 .....5 J8
Back Ashley Av OSM LS9 .....11 J4
Back Ashley St OSM LS9 .....11 J4
Back Ashville Av HDGY LS6 .....8 D4
Back Ashville Gv HDGY LS6 .....8 D3
Back Ashville Rd HDGY LS6 .....8 D3
Back Ashville Ter HDGY LS6 .....8 D3
Back Ashwood Ter HDGY LS6 .....102 E1
Back Aston Pl BRAM LS13 .....101 H3
Back Aston St BRAM LS13 .....101 G3
Back Aston Ter BRAM LS13 .....101 G3
Back Aston Vw BRAM LS13 .....101 G3
Back Athlone Av
  WOR/ARM * LS12 .....12 A1
Back Athlone Gv
  WOR/ARM * LS12 .....12 A1
Back Athlone Ter
  WOR/ARM * LS12 .....12 A1
Back Atlanta St BRAM * LS13 .....100 D3
Back Austhorpe Rd
  MSTN/BAR * LS15 .....106 A3
Back Autumn Rd HDGY LS6 .....8 E5
Back Autumn Ter HDGY LS6 .....8 E5
Back Aviary Rd WOR/ARM LS12 .....8 B8
Back Aylesbury St HWTH * BD22 .....53 H7
Back Baileys Pl HDGY LS6 .....82 C6
Back Baker St SHPY * BD18 .....77 F4
Back Baldovan Ter RHAY LS8 .....104 A1
Back Balfour St BGLY BD16 .....75 J2
  KGHY * BD21 .....2 E7
Back Bank St CAS WF10 .....148 C7
Back Bank Ter PDSY/CALV LS28 .....100 B3
Back Banstead St RHAY LS8 .....11 H3
Back Barden Pl
  WOR/ARM LS12 .....101 K6
Back Barkly Gv BEE/HOL LS11 .....123 F4
Back Barkly Pde
  BEE/HOL LS11 .....123 F4
Back Barkly Ter
  BEE/HOL LS11 .....123 F4
Back Barrowby Vw
  MSTN/BAR LS15 .....106 B6
Back Bath Rd BRAM * LS13 .....101 F3
Back Beamsley Gv HDGY * LS6 .....8 E4
Back Beamsley Mt HDGY LS6 .....8 E4
Back Beamsley Ter HDGY * LS6 .....8 E4
Back Beaumont St
  BTLY * WF17 .....161 F5
Back Beech St BGLY BD16 .....75 J2
Back Beechwood Gv BULY LS4 .....8 D3
Back Beechwood Rd BULY * LS4 .....8 D3
Back Bellbrooke Gv OSM LS9 .....11 L4
Back Bellbrooke Pl OSM LS9 .....11 L4
Back Bellbrooke Ter OSM LS9 .....11 K4
Back Belvedere Av
  BEE/HOL LS11 .....123 G4
Back Belvedere Mt
  BEE/HOL LS11 .....123 G4
Back Bentley Av HDGY LS6 .....82 E6
Back Bentley Gv HDGY LS6 .....82 E6
Back Berkeley Av RHAY LS8 .....11 K3
Back Berkeley Ter RHAY LS8 .....11 K3
Back Beverley Ter
  BEE/HOL LS11 .....123 G3
Back Blackwood Gv HFAX HX1 .....16 A1
Back Blenheim Av GIR * BD8 .....2 M4
Back Blenheim Mt GIR * BD8 .....97 H3
Back Blenheim Ter LDSU LS2 .....9 L5
Back Boundary Ter BVRD LS3 .....8 F6
Back Bower Rd ELL HX5 .....175 K2
Back Bowling Green Rd
  GTL/HWG HX4 .....174 C6
Back Bowman St WKFDE WF1 .....185 G6
Back Breary Av HORS LS18 .....81 G3
Back Breary Ter HORS LS18 .....81 G3
Back Briggate AIRE BD20 .....21 F7
Back Broad La BRAM * LS13 .....101 G1
Back Broomfield Crs HDGY LS6 .....8 C1
Back Broomfield Pl HDGY LS6 .....8 D2
Back Broomfield Rd HDGY LS6 .....8 D2
  KGHY BD21 .....2 C3
Back Broomfield St KGHY * BD21 .....2 F1
Back Broughton Av OSM LS9 .....11 K4
Back Broughton Ter OSM LS9 .....11 K4
Back Brudenell Gv HDGY LS6 .....9 G4
Back Brudenell Mt HDGY LS6 .....8 F3
Back Brudenell Rd HDGY LS6 .....8 E4
Back Brunswick St
  DEWS * WF13 .....160 D7
  LDSU LS2 .....10 B7
Back Burchett Gv HDGY LS6 .....9 K1
Back Burchett Pl HDGY LS6 .....9 K1
Back Burley Hl BULY LS4 .....8 B4

Back Burley Lodge Rd
HDGY LS6 ....8 F5
Back Burley Lodge Ter
HDGY LS6 ....8 E6
Back Burley St *BVRD* * LS3 ....9 J8
Back Burlington Pl
BEE/HOL LS11 ....123 G4
Back Burlington Rd
BEE/HOL LS11 ....123 G4
Back Burton Ter
BEE/HOL LS11 ....123 H3
Back Buxton St *KGHY* BD21 ....3 J4
Back Byrl St *KGHY* * BD21 ....3 H1
Back Caister St *KGHY* * BD21 .....53 H7
Back Caledonia Rd *KGHY* BD21 ....3 J2
Back Camberley St
BEE/HOL * LS11 ....123 H3
Back Carberry Pl *HDGY* LS6 ....8 E5
Back Carberry Rd *HDGY* * LS6 .....8 E5
Back Carberry Ter *BULY* LS4 ....8 E6
Back Carter Ter
MSTN/BAR * LS15 ....105 K4
Back Cartmel Rd *KGHY* BD21 ......2 D5
Back Castle Rd *KGHY* BD21 ....2 F2
Back Cavendish St *IDLE* BD10 ....78 C5
Back Cavendish Rd *KGHY* BD21 ....3 H4
Back Cavendish Ter *HFAX* HX1 ...16 D5
Back Chapel La *HDGY* LS6 ....8 D1
Back Charles St *BRIG* HD6 ....157 F5
Back Charlton Rd *OSM* LS9 ....15 J1
Back Chatsworth Rd *RHAY* LS8 ...11 J2
Back Chestnut Av
MSTN/BAR LS15 ....106 A3
Back Chiswick Ter *HDGY* LS6 ....8 E6
Back Christ Church Vw
WOR/ARM LS12 ....102 A5
Back Church La *BHP/TINH* LS16 ..62 B6
KSTL LS5 ....101 K1
Back Church Vw *WKFDE* WF1 ....185 F7
Back Claremont Av *BVRD* * LS3 .....9 J7
Back Clarence Rd *HORS* LS18 .....80 E5
Back Clarence St *HFAX* HX1 ....16 E6
Back Clarendon Pl *HFAX* HX1 ......16 C6
Back Clarkson Vw *HDGY* LS6 ....9 K1
Back Clayton St *RTHW* LS26 ......145 G2
Back Cliff Mt *HDGY* LS6 ....9 J1
Back Clifton Ter *OSM* LS9 ....11 L5
Back Clipston Av *HDGY* LS6 ....82 E6
Back Clock View St
KGHY * BD21 ....53 J1
Back Close Lea *BRIG* HD6 ....157 F7
Back Close Lea Dr *BRIG* * HD6 ...157 F7
Back Clough *HIPP* HX3 ....135 K5
Back Coldcotes Av *OSM* LS9 ......11 L5
Back Colenso Mt *BEE/HOL* LS11 ..13 H7
Back Colenso Rd *BEE/HOL* LS11 ..13 G7
KGHY BD21 ....3 M1
Back Colton Rd *WOR/ARM* LS12 ..12 A2
Back Colwyn Pl
BEE/HOL * LS11 ....123 G4
Back Colwyn Vw
BEE/HOL * LS11 ....123 G4
Back Compton St *KGHY* * BD21 .....3 J3
Back Conway St *RHAY* LS8 ....11 H2
Back Cowper Gv *OSM* * LS9 ....11 J3
Back Cowper St *CHAL* LS7 ....10 D2
Back Cranbrook Av
BEE/HOL * LS11 ....123 F3
Back Cranbrook Ter
BEE/HOL LS11 ....13 J9
Back Croft House La
AIRE * BD20 ....53 H1
Back Cromer Av *KGHY* * BD21 .....53 J7
Back Cromer Ter *LDSU* LS2 ....9 K5
Back Cromwell Ter *HFAX* HX1 .....16 E5
Back Cross Flatts Av
BEE/HOL LS11 ....123 F4
Back Cross Flatts Crs
BEE/HOL LS11 ....122 E4
Back Cross Flatts Gv
BEE/HOL LS11 ....123 F4
Back Cross Flatts Mt
BEE/HOL LS11 ....123 F4
Back Cross Flatts Pl
BEE/HOL LS11 ....122 E4
Back Cross Flatts Rw
BEE/HOL LS11 ....122 E4
Back Cross Green *OSM* LS9 ....15 G4
Back Cross Green La *OSM* LS9 ....15 G4
Back Crossland Ter
BEE/HOL LS11 ....13 M9
Back Cross La *ELL* HX5 ....175 H3
Back Dalton Av *BEE/HOL* LS11 ...123 F4
Back Dalton Gv *BEE/HOL* LS11 ...123 F4
Back Dalton Rd *BEE/HOL* LS11 ...123 F4
Back Dargai St *CHAL* LS7 ....10 A2
Back Dawlish Mt *OSM* LS9 ....11 L9
Back Dawlish Rd *OSM* LS9 ....11 L9
Back De Lacy Mt *KSTL* LS5 ....81 K7
Back Delph Mt *HDGY* LS6 ....9 K1
Back Dent St *OSM* LS9 ....15 G2
Back Devonshire La *RHAY* LS8 ....84 B2
Back Dorset Rd *RHAY* LS8 ....11 J1
Back Dorset St *RHAY* LS8 ....11 J1
Back Dorset Ter *RHAY* LS8 ....11 J2
Back Dudley Hill Rd *ECHL* * BD2 ..98 C1
Back Duke of York St
WKFDE WF1 ....19 G2
Back Duke St *FEA/AMT* * WF7 ....188 B3
Back Dunbar St *WKFDE* WF1 ......19 L9
Back East Park Rd *OSM* * LS9 .....15 J2
Back Eaton St *HWTH* BD22 ....53 H7
Back Ecclesburn Gv *OSM* LS9 ....15 L1
Back Ecclesburn St *OSM* LS9 .....15 L1
Back Edensor Rd *KGHY* BD21 ....2 D5
Back Elford Pl *RHAY* LS8 ....11 G3
Back Elizabeth St *WBOW* BD5 ....5 L9
Back Ellers Gv *RHAY* LS8 ....11 G1
Back Ellers Rd *RHAY* LS8 ....104 A1
Back Elmfield Ter *HFAX* HX1 ......154 D3
Back Elsworth St
WOR/ARM LS12 ....12 D1
Back Emily St *KGHY* * BD21 ....3 J3
Back Eric St *BRAM* LS13 ....81 F7
KGHY BD21 ....3 H2
Back Eshald Pl *RTHW* LS26 ....146 A1

Back Esmond Ter
WOR/ARM LS12 ....102 A6
Back Estcourt Av *HDGY* LS6 ......82 B7
Back Eversley Mt *LUD/ILL* HX2 ...154 B2
Back Fairford St *BEE/HOL* LS11 ..14 A9
Back Ferguson St *HFAX* * HX1 .....17 C1
Back Field Ct *CUL/QBY* * BD13 ....95 C7
Back Florist St *KGHY* BD21 ....3 M1
Back Fold *CLAY* BD14 ....116 A1
Back Foster Rd *KGHY* BD21 ....2 E9
Back Garden St *WKFDE* WF1 ......18 D5
Back Garton Rd *OSM* LS9 ....15 J3
Back Garton Ter *OSM* LS9 ....15 J2
Back Gathorne St *RHAY* LS8 ....10 F3
Back Gerrard St *HFAX* HX1 ....16 E6
Back Giles Street Sout
WBOW BD5 ....117 J1
Back Giles St South
WBOW * BD5 ....117 J1
Back Gillett La *RTHW* LS26 ....145 G2
Back Girlington Rd *GIR* BD8 ....4 B7
Back Gladstone St *BGLY* BD16 ....75 J2
Back Glenthorpe Ter *OSM* LS9 .....11 J9
Back Glossop St *HDGY* LS6 ....9 L1
Back Gooder La *BRIG* * HD6 ....157 G7
Back Gordon St *WKFDE* WF1 ......185 G6
Back Gordon Ter *HDGY* LS6 ....82 E6
Back Graham Gv *BULY* LS4 ....8 C2
Back Granby Gv *HDGY* LS6 ....102 C1
Back Grange Av *CHAL* LS7 ....10 E1
Back Grange Crs *CHAL* LS7 ....10 E1
Back Grange Ter *CHAL* LS7 ....10 D1
Back Grange Vw *CHAL* LS7 ....10 D1
Back Grantley St *WKFDE* WF1 .....19 G6
Back Grant St *HWTH* BD22 ....2 C5
Back Graveley St
MSTN/BAR LS15 ....105 H5
Back Great Russell St
GTHN BD7 ....5 C6
Back Greaves Streen
WBOW BD5 ....117 J3
Back Gn *MOR* LS27 ....122 B7
Back Greenhow Wk *BULY* * LS4 ....8 C5
Back Greenmount Ter
BEE/HOL * LS11 ....13 M9
Back Greenwood Mt
HDGY LS6 ....82 D5
Back Grosvenor Ter *HDGY* LS6 ..102 C1
HFAX HX1 ....16 D6
Back Grouse St *KGHY* * BD21 ....3 J3
Back Grovehall Av
BEE/HOL LS11 ....123 F5
Back Grovehall Dr
BEE/HOL LS11 ....123 F5
Back Grove Rd *ILK* LS29 ....24 A5
Back Haigh Av *RTHW* LS26 ....124 E7
Back Haigh Rd *RTHW* LS26 ....124 D7
Back Haigh Vw *RTHW* LS26 ....124 D7
Back Halliday Gv
WOR/ARM * LS12 ....101 K5
Back Halliday Pl
WOR/ARM LS12 ....101 K5
Back Hambleton St
WKFDE WF1 ....18 F3
Back Hamilton Av *CHAL* LS7 ....10 E1
Back Hamilton Vw *CHAL* LS7 ....10 E1
Back Harehills Av *CHAL* LS7 ....103 J1
Back Harehills Pl *RHAY* LS8 ....11 H2
Back Harehills Rd *RHAY* LS8 ....11 G1
Back Hares Av *RHAY* LS8 ....11 G1
Back Hares Mt *RHAY* LS8 ....10 F1
Back Hares Ter *RHAY* LS8 ....104 A1
Back Hares Vw *RHAY* LS8 ....11 G1
Back Hartley Av *HDGY* LS6 ....9 L1
Back Hartley Gv *HDGY* LS6 ....9 L1
Back Hartley St *MOR* LS27 ....142 A4
Back Hatfeild St *WKFDE* WF1 ......18 E2
Back Headingley Av *HDGY* LS6 ....82 B7
Back Headingley Mt *HDGY* LS6 ....82 B7
Back Heddon St *HDGY* LS6 ....82 D6
Back Heights Rd *CUL/QBY* BD13 ...92 B7
Back Henrietta St *BTLY* WF17 ....161 F3
Back Hessle Av *HDGY* LS6 ....8 F3
Back Hessle Mt *HDGY* LS6 ....8 F3
Back Hessle Ter *HDGY* LS6 ....8 F3
Back Hessle Vw *HDGY* LS6 ....8 F2
Back Highbury Ter *HDGY* LS6 ......82 D6
Back Highfield Rd *BRAM* LS13 ....101 G3
Back High St *CUL/QBY* BD13 ....95 G7
Back Highthorne Gv
WOR/ARM * LS12 ....101 K5
Back Highthorne St
WOR/ARM LS12 ....101 K5
Back Hillcrest Av *CHAL* LS7 ....10 F1
Back Hillcrest Vw *CHAL* LS7 ....10 F1
Back Hill Top Av *RHAY* LS8 ....11 G1
Back Hill Top Mt *RHAY* LS8 ....11 H1
Back Hilton Gv *RHAY* * LS8 ....104 A1
Back Hilton Pl *RHAY* LS8 ....104 A1
Back Hilton Rd *RHAY* LS8 ....104 A1
Back Hird St *KGHY* * BD21 ....2 E7
Backhold Av *HIPP* HX3 ....155 H6
Backhold Dr *HIPP* HX3 ....155 H6
Backhold La *HIPP* HX3 ....155 G6
Backhold Rd *HIPP* HX3 ....155 H6
Back Hollyshaw Ter
MSTN/BAR LS15 ....105 K5
Back Holywell La
AL/HA/HU LS17 ....64 E6
Back Hovingham Gv *RHAY* LS8 ....11 J1
Back Hovingham Mt *RHAY* LS8 .....11 J1
Back Hovingham Ter
RHAY * LS8 ....11 J1
Back Hyde Ter *LDSU* LS2 ....9 J6
Back Ibbetson Pl *LDSU* LS2 ....9 L6
Back Ingleby *WOR/ARM* * LS12 ....84 C2
Back Irwell St *BOW* BD4 ....118 B1
Back Ivy Av *OSM* LS9 ....11 K9
Back Ivy Gv *OSM* LS9 ....15 L1
Back Ivy Mt *OSM* LS9 ....11 K9
Back Ivy St *OSM* LS9 ....11 K9
Back John St *CUL/QBY* BD13 ....95 G7
Back Karnac Rd *RHAY* LS8 ....11 H1
Back Kelso Rd *LDSU* LS2 ....9 H5
Back Kendal La *BVRD* * LS3 ....9 J7
Back Kennerleigh Wk
MSTN/BAR LS15 ....105 K4
Back Kensington St *GIR* BD8 ....4 C1

Back Kensington Ter *HDGY* LS6 ....9 G2
Back King's Av *HDGY* * LS6 ....8 F5
Back Kirby St *KGHY* BD21 ....3 J2
Back Kirkgate *SHPY* * BD18 ....77 F5
Back Kitson St *OSM* LS9 ....15 G2
Back Knowle Mt *BULY* LS4 ....8 C3
Back Knowl Rd *MIRF* WF14 ....179 G3
Back Laisteridge La *GTHN* BD7 ......5 H8
Back Lambton Gv *RHAY* LS8 ....11 H1
Back Landseer Av *BRAM* LS13 ....101 H1
Back Landseer Gv *BRAM* LS13 ....101 H2
Back Landseer Ter
BRAM * LS13 ....101 H2
Back La *AIRE* BD20 ....21 F7
AIRE BD20 ....55 G2
BEE/HOL LS11 ....122 E5
BIRK/DRI BD11 ....120 C7
BRAM LS13 ....101 G4
BSPA/BRAM LS23 ....48 C7
CAS WF10 ....148 A4
CUL/QBY BD13 ....95 H6
CUL/QBY BD13 ....116 A4
EARL WF12 ....180 D7
GSLY LS20 ....58 E2
HECK WF16 ....160 A4
HOR/CROF WF4 ....187 F7
HORS LS18 ....80 E4
HTON BD9 ....97 F1
IDLE BD10 ....78 B4
ILK LS29 ....38 A1
LUD/ILL HX2 ....134 A2
MIRF WF14 ....179 F4
OSS WF5 ....182 C4
OT LS21 ....26 B5
PDSY/CALV LS28 ....100 A2
RPDN/SBR HX6 ....172 E5
TAD LS24 ....111 F1
WIL/AL BD15 ....95 H1
WKFDE WF1 ....18 D5
WOR/ARM LS12 ....121 F3
YEA LS19 ....59 H6
Back Langdale Gdns *HDGY* LS6 ..102 B1
Back Langdale Ter *HDGY* LS6 ....102 B1
Back Leatham St *DEWS* WF13 ....160 D7
Back Leeming St *HWTH* BD22 ......92 E4
Back Lime St *KGHY* * BD21 ....73 J1
Back Linden Gv *BEE/HOL* LS11 ...13 M9
Back Lindom St *GTHN* BD7 ....5 G6
Back Lindum St *GIR* BD8 ....97 H3
Back Lodge La *BEE/HOL* LS11 ....123 G3
Back Lombard St *YEA* LS19 ....59 H7
Back Longroyd Ter
BEE/HOL * LS11 ....123 H3
Back Lord St *HFAX* * HX1 ....16 F6
Back Lucas St *HDGY* LS6 ....9 K1
Back Lunan Pl *RHAY* * LS8 ....104 A1
Back Lunan Ter *RHAY* * LS8 ....11 H1
Back Lyon St *CUL/QBY* BD13 ......115 J5
Back Mafeking Av
BEE/HOL * LS11 ....123 F5
Back Mafeking Mt
BEE/HOL LS11 ....123 F5
Back Malt St *HWTH* * BD22 ....53 H7
Back Mannville Rd *KGHY* BD21 ......2 D7
Back Manor Dr *HDGY* LS6 ....8 E2
Back Manor Gv *CHAL* LS7 ....83 J6
Back Manor Ter *ECHL* BD2 ....98 C2
Back Market St *WBSY* * BD6 ....117 H5
Back Markham Av *RHAY* LS8 ......104 A1
Back Marriot St *DEWS* WF13 ......161 G2
Back Marshall St
MSTN/BAR LS15 ....105 K3
Back Marshall Ter
MSTN/BAR LS15 ....105 K3
Back Mary St *EARD/LOFT* WF3 ...143 K7
Back Masham St
WOR/ARM * LS12 ....12 C2
Back Maud Av *BEE/HOL* LS11 ....123 F4
Back Mayville Av *HDGY* LS6 ....8 E3
Back Mayville Pl *HDGY* LS6 ....8 E3
Back Mayville St *HDGY* LS6 ....8 E3
Back Mayville Ter *HDGY* LS6 ....8 E3
Back Meadow Vw *HDGY* LS6 ....8 F3
Back Melbourne Gv
BRAM LS13 ....101 F3
Back Methley Dr *CHAL* LS7 ....83 J6
Back Mexborough Av *CHAL* LS7 ...10 C1
Back Mexborough Dr *CHAL* LS7 ...10 C1
Back Mexborough Gv *CHAL* LS7 ...10 C1
Back Mexborough St *CHAL* LS7 ...10 C1
Back Meynell Av *RTHW* LS26 ......145 F2
Back Middleton Vw
BEE/HOL LS11 ....13 K9
Back Midland Rd *HDGY* LS6 ....9 G2
Back Milan Av *RHAY* LS8 ....11 H2
Back Milan Rd *RHAY* LS8 ....11 H2
Back Milan St *RHAY* LS8 ....11 J2
Back Minnie St *KGHY* * BD21 ....2 E7
Back Mitchell Ter *BGLY* BD16 ....75 J2
Back Mitford Rd
WOR/ARM LS12 ....12 D2
Back Model Rd *WOR/ARM* LS12 ...12 C1
Back Model Ter *WOR/ARM* LS12 ..12 C1
Back Model Vw *WOR/ARM* LS12 ...12 C1
Back Monk Bridge Dr *HDGY* LS6 ..82 E6
Back Montague St
WKFDE WF1 ....185 G6
Back Moorfield St *HFAX* HX1 ....16 C9
Back Moorfield Ter
WOR/ARM LS12 ....101 K5
Back Moorland Ter *LDSU* LS2 ....9 J4
Back Morning St *KGHY* * BD21 .....53 J7
Back Morritt Dr
MSTN/BAR LS15 ....105 G5
Back Mount Pleasant
MID LS10 ....143 H2
WKFDE WF1 ....19 H4
Back Mount Vw *HDGY* LS6 ....9 H1
Back Muff St *BOW* BD4 ....6 E9
Back Myrtle Av *BGLY* BD16 ....75 J2
Back Nansen St *BRAM* LS13 ......100 D3
Back Newport Gdns *HDGY* LS6 .....8 C2
Back Newport Mt *HDGY* LS6 ....8 D2
Back Newport Pl *HDGY* LS6 ....8 D2
Back Newton Gv *CHAL* LS7 ....103 J1
Back Newton La *CAS* WF10 ....129 F7

Back New York St *LDS* LS1 ....14 B1
Back Nice Vw *RHAY* LS8 ....11 H1
Back Norman Mt *KSTL* LS5 ....101 K1
Back Norman Pl *RHAY* LS8 ....84 B2
Back Norman Ter *RHAY* LS8 ....84 B2
Back Northbrook St *CHAL* LS7 .....83 J5
Back Northfield Pl *GIR* * BD8 ....5 H1
Back Northgate *PONT* WF8 ....169 J2
Back North Park Av *RHAY* LS8 .....84 A3
Back North St *LM/WK* * BD12 .....138 B3
Back Norwood Gv *HDGY* LS6 ....8 E2
Back Norwood Pl *HDGY* LS6 ....8 E2
Back Norwood Rd *HDGY* LS6 ....8 E2
Back Nowell Crs *OSM* LS9 ....11 M7
Back Nowell Mt *OSM* LS9 ....11 M7
Back Nowell Pl *OSM* LS9 ....11 M7
Back Nowell Ter *OSM* LS9 ....11 L7
Back Nunington St
WOR/ARM * LS12 ....8 C8
Back Nunington Vw
WOR/ARM LS12 ....8 A7
Back Nunroyd Rd
AL/HA/HU LS17 ....83 J3
Back Nursery Mt *MID* * LS10 ......123 K5
Back Oak Av *BGLY* BD16 ....75 J3
Back Oakfield Ter *HDGY* LS6 ....82 D6
Back Oakley St
EARD/LOFT WF3 ....143 K6
Back Oakley Ter
BEE/HOL * LS11 ....123 H4
Back Oak Rd *CHAL* * LS7 ....83 J7
Back Oakwood Av *RHAY* LS8 ....84 C6
Back Oakwood Dr *RHAY* LS8 ....84 C6
Back Osmondthorpe La
OSM LS9 ....104 D5
Back Otterburn St *KGHY* * BD21 ....3 G2
Back Outwood La *HORS* LS18 ......81 F5
Back Overdale Ter
MSTN/BAR * LS15 ....105 H5
Back Oxford St
EARD/LOFT WF3 ....143 K7
Back Paget St *KGHY* BD21 ....2 D5
Back Parish Ghyll Rd *ILK* LS29 .....24 A6
Back Park Crs *RHAY* LS8 ....84 C2
Back Parkfield Pl
BEE/HOL LS11 ....123 F3
Back Parkfield Rd
BEE/HOL LS11 ....123 F3
Back Park Ter *HFAX* HX1 ....16 C6
Back Park Vw *BEE/HOL* LS11 .....123 F5
Back Park View Av *HDGY* LS6 ....8 D3
Back Parkville Rd
BRAM * LS13 ....101 F2
Back Parnaby Av *MID* LS10 ....124 A5
Back Parnaby Rd *MID* LS10 ....124 A5
Back Parnaby Ter *MID* LS10 ....124 A5
Back Pasture Gv *CHAL* LS7 ....83 J5
Back Pasture Rd *RHAY* LS8 ....103 K1
Back Pawson St
EARD/LOFT WF3 ....143 K7
Back Pleasant St
RPDN/SBR HX6 ....153 K3
Back Pollard La *BRAM* LS13 ....81 F7
Back Pollard St *HUDN* HD2 ....177 G7
Back Poplar Av
MSTN/BAR * LS15 ....106 A3
Back Potternewton La
CHAL LS7 ....83 H6
Back Potters St *CHAL* LS7 ....83 J6
Back Prospect Pl *KGHY* BD21 ....2 F6
Back Prospect Ter *OSM* * LS9 ......15 G1
Back Providence Av
HDGY * LS6 ....9 K1
Back Providence St
BTLY * WF17 ....161 F3
Back Purlwell Hall Rd
BTLY WF17 ....161 F5
Back Quarry Mount Ter
HDGY * LS6 ....9 K1
Back Queen St *GTL/HWG* HX4 ....175 F3
Back Ravenscar Av *RHAY* LS8 .....84 B6
Back Ravens St *DEWS* WF13 ......180 D3
Back Raynville Mt *BRAM* LS13 ....101 H2
Back Regent Park Ter *HDGY* LS6 ...9 H1
Back Regent St *WKFDE* WF1 ......185 F6
Back Regent Ter *HDGY* LS6 ....9 G4
Back Reginald Mt *CHAL* * LS7 .....103 J1
Back Reginald Pl *CHAL* * LS7 ......103 J1
Back Reginald St *CHAL* LS7 ....103 J1
Back Rhodes St *HFAX* HX1 ....16 E6
Back Ribble St *KGHY* BD21 ....54 C3
Back Richardson St
LM/WK BD12 ....138 B3
Back Richmond Mt *HDGY* LS6 ....8 E2
Back Ridge Mount Ter
HDGY LS6 ....103 F1
Back Ridge Vw *CHAL* LS7 ....83 F7
Back Rigging La
RPDN/SBR HX6 ....152 D5
Back Ripley St *AIRE* BD20 ....54 C2
Back Ripon Ter *HIPP* HX3 ....16 F1
Back River St *HWTH* BD22 ....72 E5
Back Rd *LM/WK* BD12 ....137 H3
Back Roberts St *RTHW* * LS26 ....145 K1
Back Rochester Ter *HDGY* LS6 ......8 D1
Back Rokeby Gdns *HDGY* LS6 ......82 B7
Back Roman Av *RHAY* LS8 ....84 B2
Back Roman Gv *RHAY* LS8 ....84 B2
Back Roman Pl *RHAY* LS8 ....84 B2
Back Roman St *RHAY* LS8 ....84 B2
Back Rosebank Crs *HDGY* LS6 ......9 G5
Back Rosemont Wk
BRAM LS13 ....101 F3
Back Rossall Rd *RHAY* LS8 ....11 J1
Back Rossington Gv *RHAY* LS8 ....10 F1
Back Rossington Pl *RHAY* LS8 .....10 F1
Back Rossington Rd *RHAY* LS8 ....10 F1
Back Roundhay Av *RHAY* LS8 ....84 A7
Back Roundhay Crs *RHAY* LS8 .....84 A7
Back Roundhay Gv *RHAY* LS8 ....84 A7
Back Roundhay Pl *RHAY* * LS8 .....84 A7
Back Roundhay Vw *RHAY* * LS8 ....84 A7
Back Row *BEE/HOL* LS11 ....13 M3
Back Rowland Ter
BEE/HOL * LS11 ....123 G3
Back Rupert St *KGHY* BD21 ....3 H2
Back Russell St *WBOW* BD5 ....5 K9
Back Ruthven Vw *RHAY* LS8 ....11 H3

Back Rydal St *HWTH* BD22 ....2 D6
Back Rylstone St *KGHY* BD21 ....3 K2
Back St Alban Crs *OSM* LS9 ....104 D4
Back Saint Ives Mt
WOR/ARM LS12 ....101 K5
Back St Luke's Crs
BEE/HOL * LS11 ....13 K8
Back St Mary's Rd *CHAL* LS7 ....83 J7
Back St Paul's Rd *SHPY* * BD18 ...77 F5
Back Salisbury Gv
WOR/ARM LS12 ....8 A8
Back Salisbury Ter
WOR/ARM LS12 ....8 A8
Back Salisbury Vw
WOR/ARM LS12 ....8 A8
Back Saltaire Rd North
SHPY BD18 ....77 F4
Back Sandhurst Gv *RHAY* LS8 .....11 J2
Back Sandhurst Pl *RHAY* LS8 ....11 J2
Back Sandhurst Rd *RHAY* LS8 .....11 J2
Back Savile Pde *HFAX* HX1 ....154 E3
Back Savile Pl *CHAL* LS7 ....10 C2
Back Savile Rd *CHAL* LS7 ....10 C2
Back School Vw *HDGY* LS6 ....8 F2
Back Seaforth Av *OSM* LS9 ....11 L4
Back Seaforth Pl *OSM* LS9 ....11 K3
Back Seaforth Ter *OSM* LS9 ....11 K3
Back Sefton Av *BEE/HOL* LS11 ...123 F5
Back Sefton Ter *BEE/HOL* LS11 ..123 F4
Back Shaftesbury Av *RHAY* LS8 ...84 B3
Back Shaw La *KGHY* BD21 ....74 A1
Back Shepherd's La *CHAL* LS7 ....103 K1
Back Shepherd's Pl *CHAL* LS7 ......11 G1
Back Sholebroke Av *CHAL* LS7 .....83 J7
Back Sholebroke Mt *CHAL* LS7 ...103 J1
Back Sholebroke Pl *CHAL* LS7 ....103 J1
Back Sholebroke Rw *CHAL* LS7 ..103 H1
Back Sholebroke Ter *CHAL* LS7 ...83 H7
Back Sholebroke Vw *CHAL* LS7 ..103 J1
Back Sidlaw Ter *RHAY* LS8 ....11 G1
Back Simpson St *KGHY* BD21 ....2 D4
Back Sladen St *KGHY* BD21 ....2 D5
Back Slaithwaite Rd
EARL WF12 ....181 F5
Back Smith Rw *WBOW* * BD5 .....117 H3
Back South End Gv *BRAM* LS13 ...101 H3
Back Spencer Mt *RHAY* LS8 ....10 F2
Back Springfield Mt
WOR/ARM LS12 ....101 K6
Back Springfield Rd *ELL* * HX5 ....176 A2
Back Spring Grove Wk *HDGY* LS6 ...8 E5
Back Stanley St *OSM* LS9 ....11 H4
Back Stanmore Pl *BULY* LS4 ....8 A2
Back Stanmore St *BULY* LS4 ....8 A2
Back Station Rd *BTLY* * WF17 ....161 G4
MIRF WF14 ....179 H5
Backstone Gill La
AL/HA/HU LS17 ....64 E2
Back Stone Hall Rd *ECHL* BD2 ......98 C1
Backstone La *ILK* LS29 ....24 B6
Backstone Wy *ILK* LS29 ....24 C5
Back Storey Pl *SCFT* LS14 ....105 F4
Back Stratford Av
BEE/HOL LS11 ....123 F4
Back Stratford St
BEE/HOL * LS11 ....123 H3
Back Stratford Ter
BEE/HOL LS11 ....123 G3
Back Strathmore Dr *OSM* LS9 ......11 K3
Back St *BSPA/BRAM* LS23 ....48 C7
PONT WF8 ....189 H1
Back Sunnydene *SCFT* LS14 ....105 F4
Back Sutton Ap *SCFT* LS14 ....105 F4
Back Swinton St *HFAX* HX1 ....16 A8
Back Sycamore Av *BGLY* BD16 .....75 J2
Back Tamworth St *BOW* BD4 ....7 L8
Back Tempest Rd
BEE/HOL LS11 ....123 G3
Back Temple Vw
BEE/HOL * LS11 ....13 K9
Back the Crs *HDGY* LS6 ....9 H2
Back Thornhill St
PDSY/CALV * LS28 ....79 J6
Back Thornville Rw *HDGY* LS6 ....8 F3
Back Tower Gv *WOR/ARM* LS12 ...101 J5
Back Trafford Av *OSM* LS9 ....11 L4
Back Trentham Pl
BEE/HOL LS11 ....123 G4
Back Trinity Ter *WBOW* BD5 ....5 K9
Back Unity St North *BGLY* BD16 ...75 J2
Back Unity St South *BGLY* BD16 ...75 J2
Back Vicars Rd *RHAY* LS8 ....11 G2
Back Victoria Av *OSM* LS9 ....11 K9
Back Victoria Gv *OSM* LS9 ....11 L9
Back Victoria St *HFAX* HX1 ....17 G5
Back Victor Ter *HFAX* HX1 ....16 C3
Back Walmsley Rd *HDGY* LS6 ....8 E3
Back Walnut St *KGHY* * BD21 ....73 J1
Back Waverley Rd *ELL* HX5 ....175 J4
Back Webster St *DEWS* * WF13 ..181 F1
Back Welton Av *HDGY* LS6 ....8 F2
Back Welton Gv *HDGY* LS6 ....8 F2
Back Welton Mt *HDGY* LS6 ....8 F2
Back Welton Pl *HDGY* LS6 ....8 F2
Back Wesley Rd *WOR/ARM* LS12 ..12 A1
Back Wesley St *CAS* WF10 ....148 C7
Back Westbourne *LDSU* LS2 ....9 J5
Back Westbury St *MID* LS10 ....124 A5
Back Westlock Av *OSM* LS9 ....11 J6
Back Westover Rd *BRAM* LS13 ....101 G2
Back Wetherby Gv *BULY* * LS4 ....8 A2
Back Wetherby Rd *RHAY* LS8 ....84 C6
Back Wharf St
RPDN/SBR HX6 ....153 K4
Back Wickham St
BEE/HOL LS11 ....123 F3
Back William Av
MSTN/BAR * LS15 ....105 F5
Back Wilton Gv *HDGY* * LS6 ....82 D6
Back Winfield Gv *LDSU* * LS2 ....9 M4
Back Winston Gdns *HDGY* LS6 ....82 B7
Back Winterburn St *KGHY* * BD21 ..3 J2
Back Woodbine Ter *HDGY* LS6 .....82 D6
Back Woodland Park Rd
HDGY * LS6 ....82 D7
Back Wood St *EARD/LOFT* WF3 ...143 J7
GIR BD8 ....5 H3

Back Wright Av HWTH BD22 ...72 E1
Back York Pl LDS LS1 ...13 L1
Back York St LDSU LS2 ...14 C1
Bacon Av NORM WF6 ...167 F5
Bacon St GSLY LS20 ...59 G3
Baddeley Gdns IDLE BD10 ...78 B3
Baden Powell Crs PONT WF8 ...189 J2
Baden St HWTH BD22 ...72 C4
Badgergate Av WIL/AL BD15 ...95 F1
Badger Hl HDG6 ...176 C3
Badger La HIPP HX3 ...156 A1
Badgers Mt MSTN/BAR LS15 ...106 C3
Badgers Wk HECK WF16 ...160 B5
Badgers Wy ECHL BD2 ...97 K1
Badger Wood Gld WBY LS22 ...29 H1
Badminton Dr EARD/LOFT WF3 ...143 J4
Baghill Ct PONT WF8 ...190 A1
Baghill Gn EARD/LOFT WF3 ...162 C2
Baghill La PONT WF8 ...169 K7
Baghill Rd EARD/LOFT WF3 ...162 C2
Bagley La PDSY/CALV LS28 ...100 A1
Bagnall Ter WBSY BD6 ...117 G5
Baildon Av GFTH/SHER LS25 ...128 A4
Baildon Cl SCFT LS14 ...85 K6
Baildon Dr SCFT LS14 ...85 K6
Baildon Gn SCFT LS14 ...85 K6
Baildon Holmes BAIL BD17 ...77 H3
Baildon Pl SCFT LS14 ...85 K6
Baildon Rd BAIL BD17 ...77 H2
  SCFT LS14 ...85 K5
Baildon Wood Ct BAIL BD17 ...77 H4
Bailey Hall Bank HIPP HX3 ...17 K6
Bailey Hall Rd HIPP HX3 ...17 K6
Bailey Hills Rd BGLY BD16 ...55 H7
Bailey's Ct SCFT LS14 ...85 H7
Bailey's Hl SCFT LS14 ...85 H7
Bailey's La SCFT LS14 ...85 H7
Baileys Lawn SCFT LS14 ...85 H7
Bailey St BOW BD4 ...118 A1
Bailey Wells Av WBOW BD5 ...117 H3
Bainbrigge Rd HDGY LS6 ...102 C1
Baines St HFAX HX1 ...16 C4
  RTHW * LS26 ...145 F2
Baird St WBOW BD5 ...117 H3
Bairstow Ct LUD/ILL HX2 ...153 K2
Bairstow La LUD/ILL HX2 ...153 K2
Bairstow Mt LUD/ILL HX2 ...153 K3
Bairstow St WIL/AL BD15 ...95 K2
Baker Crs MOR LS27 ...141 K4
Baker Fold HFAX HX1 ...16 D5
Baker La EARD/LOFT WF3 ...164 C1
Baker Rd MOR LS27 ...141 K4
Baker St ECHL BD2 ...98 C3
  MOR LS27 ...141 K4
Baker St North LUD/ILL HX2 ...134 D2
Bakes St GTHN BD7 ...117 F2
Balbec Av HDGY LS6 ...82 D7
Balbec St HDGY LS6 ...82 D7
Balderstone Hall La
  MIRF WF14 ...179 K3
Baldovan Pl RHAY LS8 ...104 A1
Baldovan Pl RHAY LS8 ...104 A1
Baldovan Ter RHAY LS8 ...104 A1
Baldwin La CLAY BD14 ...115 K3
Baldwin Ter HIPP HX3 ...17 K6
Balfour St BGLY BD16 ...75 J2
  BOW BD4 ...118 B2
  KGHY BD21 ...2 E7
The Balk BTLY WF17 ...161 F1
Balk Av EARD/LOFT WF3 ...165 H6
Balkcliffe La MID LS10 ...143 F1
Balk Crs EARD/LOFT WF3 ...165 G6
Balk La EARD/LOFT WF3 ...165 H6
  GTHN BD7 ...117 G2
  WKFDE WF1 ...185 H1
Balkram Dr LUD/ILL HX2 ...133 H2
Balkram Edge LUD/ILL HX2 ...133 G2
Balkram Rd LUD/ILL HX2 ...133 J2
Balks LVSG WF15 ...159 G4
Balk St BTLY WF17 ...160 E3
Ballantyne Rd IDLE BD10 ...78 B2
Ball Royd Rd HUDN HD2 ...177 G7
Ball St CUL/QBY BD13 ...95 H7
Balme La LM/WK BD12 ...137 J4
Balme Rd CLECK BD19 ...138 E7
Balme St BFD BD1 ...6 A5
  LM/WK BD12 ...137 H4
Balme Ter HWTH * BD22 ...72 C6
Balmfield LVSG WF15 ...159 H6
Balmfield Crs LVSG WF15 ...159 H6
Balmoral Cha MID LS10 ...15 G9
Balmoral Cl PONT WF8 ...189 G4
Balmoral Dr KNOT WF11 ...170 C4
Balmoral Pl HFAX HX1 ...16 F7
Balmoral Wy YEA LS19 ...60 A5
Balm Pl BEE/HOL LS11 ...13 J5
Balm Rd MID LS10 ...123 K4
Balm Wk BEE/HOL LS11 ...13 H5
Balne Av WKFDW/WTN WF2 ...18 A3
Balne La WKFDW/WTN WF2 ...18 B3
Bamborough St WKFDE WF1 ...185 G6
Bamburgh Rd MSTN/BAR LS15 ...106 B2
Bamlett Brow HWTH BD22 ...72 E4
Banbury Rd PONT WF8 ...169 K5
Bangor Gv WOR/ARM LS12 ...121 K2
Bangor Pl WOR/ARM LS12 ...121 K2
Bangor St WOR/ARM LS12 ...121 K2
Bangor Ter WOR/ARM LS12 ...121 K2
Bangor Vw WOR/ARM LS12 ...121 K2
Bank IDLE BD10 ...78 E6
Bank Av HORS LS18 ...80 E4
  MOR LS27 ...141 K2
Bank Bottom HBR HX7 ...132 B5
  HFAX HX1 ...17 K6
Bank Bottom La LUD/ILL HX2 ...133 F6
Bank Cl IDLE BD10 ...78 D7
Bank Crest BAIL BD17 ...77 H1
Bank Crest Ri SHPY BD18 ...76 C5
Bank Dr WBSY BD6 ...117 J6
Bank Edge Gdns LUD/ILL HX2 ...134 B4
Bank Edge Rd LUD/ILL HX2 ...134 A4
Banker St BULY LS4 ...8 C6
Bankfield AL/HA/HU LS17 ...46 A6
Bankfield Av SHPY BD18 ...76 C5
Bankfield Cl OSS WF5 ...182 E5
Bankfield Ct MIRF WF14 ...179 G4
  WKFDW/WTN WF2 ...164 A5

Bankfield Dr HWTH BD22 ...53 F4
  SHPY BD18 ...76 C5
  WKFDW/WTN WF2 ...164 A5
Bankfield Flats HWTH * BD22 ...72 C2
Bankfield Gdns BULY LS4 ...8 B4
  HIPP HX3 ...155 J2
Bank Field Gra GTL/HWG HX4 ...175 F2
Bankfield Gv BULY LS4 ...8 A3
Bankfield Mt HWTH BD22 ...53 F4
Bank Field Rd BTLY WF17 ...161 F3
Bankfield Rd BULY LS4 ...8 A4
  HWTH BD22 ...53 F3
  SHPY BD18 ...76 C5
Bankfield St HWTH BD22 ...53 F3
Bankfield Ter BAIL BD17 ...77 J2
  BULY LS4 ...8 B5
Bankfield Vw HIPP HX3 ...16 F2
Bankfield Wk HWTH BD22 ...53 F4
Bankfield Yd HIPP * HX3 ...16 F1
Bank Foot Pl BTLY * WF17 ...161 F3
Bank Foot St BTLY * WF17 ...161 F3
Bank Gdns HORS LS18 ...80 E4
Bank Gv EARL WF12 ...181 K2
Bank Hey Bottom La
  RPDN/SBR HX6 ...173 F6
Bankholme Ct BOW BD4 ...119 G4
Bankhouse PDSY/CALV LS28 ...120 A1
Bankhouse La HIPP HX3 ...155 G6
Bank House La LUD/ILL HX2 ...132 E3
Bankhouse La PDSY/CALV LS28 ...120 A1
Banklands AIRE BD20 ...21 F7
Banklands Av AIRE BD20 ...21 G7
Banklands La AIRE BD20 ...21 G7
Bank La AIRE BD20 ...21 F1
Bank Pde OT LS21 ...39 G3
Bank Rd RPDN/SBR HX6 ...153 J5
Banks Av PONT * WF8 ...189 H1
Banks Buildings
  FEA/AMT * WF7 ...188 C5
Banks End ELL HX5 ...176 B3
Banksfield Av YEA LS19 ...59 J3
Banksfield Cl YEA LS19 ...59 J3
Banksfield Crs YEA LS19 ...59 J3
Banksfield Gv YEA LS19 ...59 J3
Banksfield Mt YEA LS19 ...59 J3
Banksfield Ri YEA LS19 ...59 J3
Bank Side St RHAY LS8 ...11 G3
Banks La AIRE BD20 ...34 B6
  KNOT WF11 ...171 G4
Banks Mt PONT WF8 ...189 H1
Bank Sq MOR LS27 ...141 K2
Banks St BTLY WF17 ...161 F4
Bank St BFD BD1 ...5 M6
  BRIG HD6 ...157 F6
  CAS WF10 ...148 C7
  CLECK BD19 ...158 D1
  EARL WF12 ...181 G1
  LDS LS1 ...14 A1
  MIRF WF14 ...179 F4
  MOR LS27 ...141 K2
  OSS WF5 ...182 C4
  SHPY BD18 ...77 G4
  WBSY * BD6 ...117 H5
  WBY LS22 ...29 H4
  WKFDE WF1 ...18 E5
Bank Ter MOR LS27 ...141 K2
Bank Top HIPP HX3 ...17 M9
Bank Top Dr AIRE BD20 ...54 C1
Bank Top La OT LS21 ...42 C7
Bank Top Wy KGHY BD21 ...54 C5
Bank Vw BAIL BD17 ...77 G2
  EARL WF12 ...181 K2
Bank View Ter CHAL LS7 ...83 G5
Bank Wk BAIL BD17 ...77 H1
Bankwell Fold WBSY BD6 ...117 J5
Bankwood BTLY * WF17 ...140 E3
Bank Wood Rd PONT WF8 ...191 G5
Bankwood Wy BTLY WF17 ...140 E3
Bannerman St LM/WK BD12 ...138 B2
Banner St BFDE BD3 ...6 D7
Bannockburn Ct BOW * BD4 ...118 B5
Bannockburn Wy NORM WF6 ...166 B4
Banstead St East RHAY LS8 ...11 H2
Banstead St West RHAY LS8 ...11 G2
Banstead Ter East RHAY LS8 ...11 H2
Banstead Ter West RHAY LS8 ...11 G2
Bantam Cl MOR LS27 ...142 A3
Bantam Grove La MOR LS27 ...142 C3
Bantam Grove Vw MOR LS27 ...142 C3
Bantree Ct IDLE BD10 ...78 B3
Baptist Fold CUL/QBY BD13 ...115 H5
Baptist La OSS WF5 ...183 G5
Baptist Pl BFD BD1 ...5 K5
Baptist St WKFDE WF1 ...160 D5
Barberry Av BFDE BD3 ...7 M4
Barber Sq HECK WF16 ...159 K4
Barber St BRIG HD6 ...157 F6
Barclay Cl CUL/QBY BD13 ...74 B7
Barclay St CHAL LS7 ...10 C5
Barcroft HWTH BD22 ...73 G4
Barcroft Gv YEA LS19 ...59 H5
Barden Av WBSY BD6 ...116 C5
Barden Cl BTLY WF17 ...160 E1
  WOR/ARM LS12 ...101 K6
Barden Dr BGLY BD16 ...56 B7
Barden Gn WOR/ARM LS12 ...101 K6
Barden Gv WOR/ARM * LS12 ...101 K6
Barden Mt WOR/ARM LS12 ...101 K6
Barden Pl WOR/ARM LS12 ...101 K6
Barden Rd WKFDE WF1 ...19 M4
Barden St GIR BD8 ...4 F2
Barden Ter WOR/ARM LS12 ...101 K6
Bardon Hall Ms
  BHP/TINH * LS16 ...82 C5
Bardsey Crs BFDE BD3 ...6 D6
Bardwell Ct EARD/LOFT WF3 ...165 F3
Bare Head La HIPP HX3 ...135 G2
Barfield Av YEA LS19 ...59 H5
Barfield Crs AL/HA/HU LS17 ...64 A6
Barfield Dr YEA LS19 ...59 H5
Barfield Gv AL/HA/HU LS17 ...64 B6
Barfield Mt AL/HA/HU LS17 ...64 B6
Barfield Rd HIPP HX3 ...156 B1
Bargess Ter GFTH/SHER LS25 ...128 A3
Bargrange Av SHPY BD18 ...77 G6
Barham Ter IDLE BD10 ...98 E1
Bar House La AIRE BD20 ...33 G7

Baring Av BFDE BD3 ...7 J3
Barker Cl HIPP HX3 ...155 H5
Barkerend Rd BFDE BD3 ...6 C5
Barker Pl BRAM LS13 ...101 G4
Barker Rd HOR/CROF WF4 ...182 E7
Barker St EARD/LOFT WF3 ...165 J2
  LVSG WF15 ...159 J4
Barkers Well Fold
  WOR/ARM LS12 ...121 G2
Barkers Well Garth
  WOR/ARM LS12 ...121 H3
Barkers Well Ga
  WOR/ARM LS12 ...121 H3
Barkers Well Lawn
  WOR/ARM LS12 ...121 H3
Bark La ILK LS29 ...22 D1
Barkly Av BEE/HOL LS11 ...123 G5
Barkly Dr BEE/HOL * LS11 ...123 G5
Barkly Gv BEE/HOL LS11 ...123 G4
Barkly Pde BEE/HOL LS11 ...123 G4
Barkly Pl BEE/HOL LS11 ...123 G5
Barkly Rd BEE/HOL LS11 ...122 G4
Barkly St BEE/HOL LS11 ...123 G5
Barkly Ter BEE/HOL LS11 ...123 G5
Barkston Wk WKFDE WF1 ...185 F1
Barley Cl WKFDE WF1 ...165 F2
Barley Cote Av AIRE BD20 ...54 C1
Barley Cote Gv AIRE BD20 ...54 D1
Barley Cote Rd AIRE BD20 ...54 C1
Barley Cft DEWS WF13 ...180 C1
Barleyfield Cl WKFDE WF1 ...185 F1
Barley Field Ct
  MSTN/BAR * LS15 ...105 H5
Barleyfields Cl WBY LS22 ...29 H3
Barleyfields La WBY LS22 ...29 H3
Barleyfields Ms WBY LS22 ...29 H3
Barleyfields Rd WBY LS22 ...29 H3
Barleyfields Ter WBY LS22 ...29 H3
Barleyhill Crs
  GFTH/SHER LS25 ...107 H6
Barleyhill La GFTH/SHER LS25 ...107 H6
Barleyhill Rd GFTH/SHER LS25 ...107 H6
Barley Ms EARD/LOFT WF3 ...144 C4
Barley St HWTH BD22 ...53 H7
Barlow Rd KGHY BD21 ...2 E3
Barlow St BFDE BD3 ...6 E5
Barmby Cl OSS WF5 ...182 E5
Barmby Crs OSS WF5 ...183 F5
Barmby Fold OSS WF5 ...182 E5
Barmby Pl ECHL BD2 ...6 E1
Barmby Rd ECHL BD2 ...6 E1
Barmby St LM/WK BD12 ...137 J3
Bar Mt GFTH/SHER * LS25 ...107 K6
Barmouth Ter BFDE BD3 ...6 A1
The Barn LM/WK BD12 ...137 K1
Barnaby Rd BGLY BD16 ...56 B7
Barnard Cl MSTN/BAR LS15 ...106 B2
Barnard Rd BOW BD4 ...118 B3
Barnard Wy MSTN/BAR LS15 ...106 B2
Barnbow La MSTN/BAR LS15 ...87 F7
  MSTN/BAR LS15 ...106 E1
Barnby Av GIR BD8 ...96 B6
Barncroft Cl SCFT LS14 ...85 G5
Barncroft Dr SCFT LS14 ...85 F6
Barncroft Gdns SCFT LS14 ...85 G6
Barncroft Hts SCFT LS14 ...85 F6
Barncroft Mt SCFT LS14 ...85 G6
Barncroft Ri SCFT LS14 ...85 G6
Barncroft Rd SCFT LS14 ...85 G6
Barnes Av WKFDE WF1 ...164 B5
Barnes Rd CAS WF10 ...168 C2
  GIR BD8 ...4 B4
Barnet Gv MOR LS27 ...141 K5
Barnet Rd WOR/ARM LS12 ...12 C2
Barnsdale Est CAS WF10 ...168 A2
Barnsdale Rd CAS WF10 ...148 C1
  RTHW LS26 ...147 F6
Barnsley Beck Gv BAIL BD17 ...77 J1
Barnsley Rd WKFDE WF1 ...19 H9
Barnstone V WKFDE WF1 ...185 F1
Barn St HWTH BD22 ...92 D3
Barnswick Cl PONT WF8 ...189 J3
Barnswick Vw BHP/TINH LS16 ...61 H7
Baron Cl BRAM LS11 ...13 M8
Baronscourt MSTN/BAR LS15 ...106 A5
Baronsmead MSTN/BAR LS15 ...105 K5
Baronsway MSTN/BAR LS15 ...105 K5
Barrack St CHAL LS7 ...10 D3
Barracks St HECK WF16 ...159 K4
Barrack St CHAL LS7 ...10 C4
Barraclough Sq LM/WK BD12 ...137 G1
Barraclough St LM/WK BD12 ...137 G1
Barran Ct RHAY LS8 ...11 G3
Barras Garth Pl
  WOR/ARM LS12 ...102 A7
Barras Garth Rd
  WOR/ARM LS12 ...102 A7
Barras Pl WOR/ARM LS12 ...102 A7
Barras St WOR/ARM LS12 ...102 A7
Barras Ter WOR/ARM LS12 ...102 A7
Barratt's Rd WKFDE WF1 ...184 D1
Barrett St AIRE BD20 ...32 E1
Barrington Cl HIPP HX3 ...155 K4
Barrington Pde CLECK BD19 ...139 H7
Barrowby Av MSTN/BAR LS15 ...106 B6
Barrowby Crs MSTN/BAR LS15 ...106 C5
Barrowby La MSTN/BAR LS15 ...106 C5
Barrowby Rd MSTN/BAR LS15 ...106 C6
Barrowclough La HIPP HX3 ...155 J1
Barrows La AIRE BD20 ...32 D6
Barr Ter GIR * BD8 ...4 B3
Barry St BFD BD1 ...5 G4
Barsey Green La
  GTL/HWG HX4 ...173 K3
Barstow Fall PONT WF8 ...169 K5
Barstow Sq WKFDE WF1 ...18 E4
Bar St BTLY WF17 ...161 G4
Barthorpe Cl BOW BD4 ...119 G4
Barthorpe Crs CHAL LS7 ...83 H4
Bartle Cl GTHN BD7 ...116 E3

Bartle Fold GTHN BD7 ...117 F2
Bartle Gill Dr BAIL BD17 ...57 K7
Bartle Gill Ri BAIL BD17 ...57 K7
Bartle Gill Vw BAIL * BD17 ...57 K7
Bartle Gv GTHN BD7 ...116 E3
Bartle La GTHN BD7 ...116 E3
Bartle Pl GTHN BD7 ...116 E3
Bartle Sq GTHN BD7 ...117 F2
Barton Ct MSTN/BAR LS15 ...105 K6
Barton Gv BEE/HOL LS11 ...13 K8
Barton Hl BEE/HOL * LS11 ...13 J8
Barton Mt BEE/HOL LS11 ...13 J8
Barton Pl BEE/HOL LS11 ...13 J8
  BTLY WF17 ...161 F4
Barton Rd BEE/HOL LS11 ...13 J8
Barton St BRIG * HD6 ...157 F5
  WBOW BD5 ...117 G3
Barton Ter BEE/HOL LS11 ...13 J8
Barton Vw BEE/HOL LS11 ...13 J8
Barwick Gn WBSY BD6 ...116 D5
Barwick Rd GFTH/SHER LS25 ...107 H4
  SCFT LS14 ...105 J2
Basford Ct WKFDW/WTN * WF2 ...18 A6
Basford St WKFDW/WTN WF2 ...18 A6
Basil St BRAM LS13 ...101 G3
Baslow Gv HTON BD9 ...96 E3
Batcliffe Dr HDGY LS6 ...82 B6
Batcliffe Mt HDGY LS6 ...82 B7
Bateman St GIR BD8 ...5 K1
Bates Av RPDN/SBR HX6 ...153 K1
Bates La PONT WF8 ...190 A4
Bateson St IDLE BD10 ...79 A4
Bath Cl BRAM LS13 ...101 F3
Bath Gv BRAM * LS13 ...101 F3
Bath La BRAM LS13 ...101 F3
Bath Pl CLECK BD19 ...158 E1
  HIPP HX3 ...16 F2
Bath Rd BEE/HOL LS11 ...13 K4
  BRAM LS13 ...101 F3
  CLECK BD19 ...158 E1
  HECK WF16 ...160 A4
  HIPP HX3 ...155 F4
Bath St BFDE BD3 ...6 C6
  BTLY WF17 ...161 G3
  DEWS WF13 ...161 F7
  ELL HX5 ...175 J3
  HFAX * HX1 ...17 J7
  ILK LS29 ...24 B4
  KGHY BD21 ...2 B1
Batley Cl BAIL BD17 ...57 J7
Batley Field Hl BTLY WF17 ...161 J7
Batley Rd BTLY WF17 ...160 C4
  EARD/LOFT WF3 ...162 D3
  WKFDW/WTN WF2 ...163 H7
Batley St HIPP HX3 ...16 D1
Batter La YEA LS19 ...59 K7
Battinson Rd HFAX HX1 ...16 A4
Battinson St HIPP HX3 ...17 M9
Battye St BOW BD4 ...7 H7
  EARL WF12 ...181 G1
Bavaria Pl GIR BD8 ...4 F1
Bawn Ap WOR/ARM LS12 ...121 H1
Bawn Av WOR/ARM LS12 ...101 K4
Bawn Dr WOR/ARM LS12 ...101 K4
Bawn Gdns WOR/ARM LS12 ...101 K4
Bawn La WOR/ARM LS12 ...101 H7
Bawson Ct CLECK BD19 ...139 H6
Baxandall St WBOW BD5 ...117 J3
Baxtergate PONT WF8 ...189 J1
Baxter La HIPP HX3 ...135 K4
Bay Horse La AL/HA/HU LS17 ...65 K1
Bayldons Pl BTLY * WF17 ...161 F3
Bayne Dr BOW BD4 ...118 C4
Bay of Biscay WIL/AL BD15 ...96 A1
Bayswater Crs RHAY LS8 ...11 G3
Bayswater Gv ECHL BD2 ...98 E3
  RHAY LS8 ...11 G3
Bayswater Mt RHAY LS8 ...11 G3
Bayswater Pl RHAY LS8 ...11 G3
Bayswater Rd RHAY LS8 ...11 G4
Bayswater Rw RHAY LS8 ...11 G3
Bayswater Ter HIPP HX3 ...155 F5
  RHAY LS8 ...11 G3
Bayton La YEA LS19 ...60 B5
Beacon Av MOR LS27 ...142 A5
Beacon Brow WBSY BD6 ...116 C4
Beacon Cl BGLY BD16 ...76 A1
Beacon Gv MOR LS27 ...142 A5
  WBSY BD6 ...116 C5
Beacon Hill Rd HIPP HX3 ...17 L8
Beacon Pl WBSY BD6 ...116 D5
Beacon Ri ILK LS29 ...23 H5
Beacon Rd WBSY BD6 ...116 D4
Beaconsfield Ct
  GFTH/SHER LS25 ...107 J5
Beaconsfield Rd CLAY BD14 ...116 B5
Beaconsfield St HIPP HX3 ...17 L8
  GTHN * BD7 ...116 D4
  ILK LS29 ...22 D1
  WBSY BD6 ...117 F5
Beamsley Gv BGLY BD16 ...76 A1
  HDGY * LS6 ...8 E4
Beamsley Mt HDGY LS6 ...8 E4
Beamsley Pl HDGY * LS6 ...8 E4
Beamsley Rd HTON BD9 ...77 G7
  HTON BD9 ...97 G3
Beamsley Ter HDGY * LS6 ...8 E4
Beamsley Vw ILK LS29 ...23 H5
Beancroft Rd CAS WF10 ...168 C3
Beancroft St CAS WF10 ...168 B2
Beanlands Pde ILK LS29 ...24 B4
Bean St HX5 ...176 B3
Bearing Av BEE/HOL LS11 ...123 H4
Bear Pit Gdns HDGY LS6 ...9 G2
Beastfair PONT WF8 ...189 H1
Beatrice St CLECK BD19 ...138 E7
  HWTH BD22 ...92 D3
  KGHY BD21 ...53 K2
Beaufort Gv ECHL BD2 ...98 D3
Beaumont Av RHAY LS8 ...84 D2
Beaumont Cl EARD/LOFT WF3 ...165 G3
Beaumont Pl BTLY WF17 ...160 C4
Beaumont Rd GIR BD8 ...4 C1
Beaumont St BTLY WF17 ...161 F5
  EARD/LOFT WF3 ...165 G3
Beaver Dr DEWS WF13 ...180 C2

Becca La GFTH/SHER LS25 ...88 C4
Beck Bottom PDSY/CALV LS28 ...79 H5
  WKFDW/WTN WF2 ...163 H5
Beckbridge La NORM WF6 ...167 F5
Beckbridge Rd NORM WF6 ...167 F5
Beckbridge Wy NORM WF6 ...167 F6
Beckbury Cl PDSY/CALV LS28 ...100 A3
Beckbury St PDSY/CALV LS28 ...100 A3
Beckenham Pl HFAX HX1 ...134 B7
Beckers Av BTLY * WF17 ...140 E5
Beckett Cl HOR/CROF WF4 ...183 H7
Beckett Crs DEWS WF13 ...180 C1
Beckett Gv DEWS WF13 ...180 C2
Beckett La DEWS WF13 ...180 C2
Beckett Park Campus
  HDGY LS6 ...82 A6
Beckett Rd DEWS WF13 ...160 E6
Beckett's Park Dr HDGY LS6 ...82 A6
Beckett's Park Rd HDGY LS6 ...82 C7
Beckett St BTLY WF17 ...161 F5
  OSM LS9 ...10 F7
Beckett Ter OSM LS9 ...11 G6
Beckett Wk DEWS WF13 ...180 C2
Beckfield La KNOT WF11 ...149 K2
Beckfield Rd BGLY BD16 ...75 K5
Beckfoot La BGLY BD16 ...75 J3
Beck Hl WBSY BD6 ...116 D7
Beckhill Ap CHAL LS7 ...83 F5
Beckhill Av CHAL LS7 ...83 F6
Beckhill Cha CHAL LS7 ...83 F5
Beckhill Cl CHAL * LS7 ...83 F5
Beckhill Dr CHAL LS7 ...83 F5
Beckhill Fold CHAL LS7 ...83 F5
Beckhill Gdns CHAL LS7 ...83 F6
Beckhill Garth CHAL LS7 ...83 F5
Beckhill Ga CHAL LS7 ...83 F6
Beckhill Gn CHAL LS7 ...83 F5
Beckhill Gv CHAL LS7 ...83 F5
Beckhill Lawn CHAL * LS7 ...83 F6
Beckhill Pl CHAL LS7 ...83 F5
Beckhill Rd CHAL LS7 ...83 F5
Beckhill Rw CHAL LS7 ...83 F5
Beckhill V CHAL LS7 ...83 F5
Beckhill Vw CHAL LS7 ...83 F6
Beckhill Wk CHAL LS7 ...83 F5
Beck La BGLY BD16 ...55 J7
  LVSG WF15 ...159 K5
  WBY LS22 ...46 E1
Beckley Rd WKFDW/WTN WF2 ...184 A3
Beck Meadow MSTN/BAR LS15 ...87 H3
Beck Rd BGLY BD16 ...55 H3
  RHAY LS8 ...104 A1
Becks Ct EARL WF12 ...181 J3
Beck Side KGHY BD21 ...3 G6
Beckside Cl ILK LS29 ...22 B1
  ILK LS29 ...38 A1
Beckside Gdns BHP/TINH LS16 ...82 B5
Beckside La GTHN BD7 ...116 E3
Beckside Rd GTHN BD7 ...117 F1
Beckside Vw MOR LS27 ...142 A7
Becks Rd HWTH BD22 ...2 C6
Beck St KGHY BD21 ...3 G5
Beckwith Dr IDLE BD10 ...78 E7
Bective Rd WKFDW/WTN WF2 ...183 H7
Bedale EARD/LOFT WF3 ...142 C7
Bedale Av BRIG HD6 ...176 C7
Bedale Dr WBSY BD6 ...116 D5
Bede Ct WKFDE WF1 ...184 D1
Bede's Cl CUL/QBY BD13 ...95 G7
Bedford Cl BHP/TINH LS16 ...81 J7
  FEA/AMT WF7 ...188 C6
Bedford Ct RHAY LS8 ...84 D6
Bedford Dr BHP/TINH LS16 ...81 H1
Bedford Fld HDGY * LS6 ...103 F1
Bedford Gdns BHP/TINH LS16 ...81 H1
Bedford Garth BHP/TINH LS16 ...81 H1
Bedford Gn BHP/TINH LS16 ...81 H1
Bedford Gv BHP/TINH LS16 ...81 H1
Bedford Mt BHP/TINH LS16 ...81 H1
Bedford Rw MID LS10 ...14 C9
Bedfords Fold
  GFTH/SHER LS25 ...151 J1
Bedford St BOW BD4 ...6 A8
  ELL HX5 ...175 J3
  HFAX HX1 ...16 F6
  KGHY BD21 ...2 E5
  LDS LS1 ...9 M9
Bedford St North HFAX HX1 ...16 F5
Bedford Vw BHP/TINH LS16 ...81 H1
Bedivere Rd GIR BD8 ...96 C6
Bedlam La OT LS21 ...42 E5
Beech Av CUL/QBY BD13 ...93 K2
  EARD/LOFT WF3 ...165 G4
  HORS LS18 ...81 F5
  RPDN/SBR HX6 ...153 J3
  WKFDW/WTN WF2 ...184 A2
  WOR/ARM * LS12 ...8 A9
Beech Cl GFTH/SHER LS25 ...131 G2
  HIPP HX3 ...136 C5
  IDLE BD10 ...78 C2
  ILK LS29 ...38 B4
  OSM LS9 ...104 E2
  PONT WF8 ...189 K3
  TAD LS24 ...51 F7
Beech Ct OSS WF5 ...182 B5
Beech Crs BAIL BD17 ...76 E3
  BFDE BD3 ...6 F2
  CAS WF10 ...169 J2
  PONT WF8 ...190 A4
Beechcroft EARD/LOFT WF3 ...144 A3
Beech Cft PONT WF8 ...169 K5
Beechcroft Cl BEE/HOL LS11 ...122 B5
Beechcroft Md AL/HA/HU LS17 ...64 D7
Beechcroft Vw BEE/HOL LS11 ...122 B5
Beechdale Av BTLY WF17 ...160 D1
Beech Dr CUL/QBY BD13 ...93 K2
  GFTH/SHER LS25 ...131 G2
  WOR/ARM LS12 ...8 A9
Beecher St HIPP HX3 ...134 C5
  KGHY BD21 ...3 L1
The Beeches BAIL BD17 ...57 J7
  GSLY LS20 ...59 F1
  PDSY/CALV LS28 ...99 J3
  WBY LS22 ...29 J3
Beeches End BSPA/BRAM LS23 ...48 D3
Beeches Rd KGHY BD21 ...3 K3
Beechfield WOR/ARM LS12 ...121 G3
Beechfield Dr HOR/CROF WF4 ...186 E5
Beech Gdns CAS WF10 ...169 J2

Beech Gv AIRE BD20 .....32 E1
BFDE BD3.....6 E2
BGLY BD16.....56 B6
CLAY BD14.....116 B2
CLECK BD19.....139 H6
GFTH/SHER LS25.....111 F5
GFTH/SHER LS25.....151 F4
HIPP HX3.....157 F1
NORM WF6.....186 D1
RTHW LS26.....145 G1
Beech Grove Av
GFTH/SHER LS25.....107 H7
Beech Grove Ter
GFTH/SHER LS25.....107 H7
LDSU LS2.....9 K5
Beech HI OT LS21.....39 H2
PONT WF8.....169 K7
Beech La OSM LS9.....104 D2
Beech Lees PDSY/CALV LS28.....99 K1
Beech Mt OSM LS9.....104 E2
Beechmount CI BAIL BD17.....57 J7
Beechnut La PONT WF8.....169 H7
Beech Rd BSPA/BRAM LS23.....48 B2
RPDN/SBR HX6.....153 K4
WBSY BD6.....117 H1
Beech Spinney WBY LS22.....29 J1
Beech Sq CLAY BD14.....116 B2
Beech St AIRE BD20.....32 E5
BGLY BD16.....75 J2
EARD/LOFT WF3.....142 E6
ELL HX5.....175 J3
GTL/HWG HX4.....174 D5
HFAX HX1.....16 E5
KGHY BD21.....3 L3
MIRF WF14.....179 H4
PONT WF8.....189 J7
Beech Ter BFDE BD3.....6 E3
Beechtree CI BAIL BD17.....77 F2
Beechtree Rd TAD LS24.....70 C1
Beech Vw GFTH/SHER LS25.....88 C5
RPDN/SBR * HX6.....153 J3
Beech Wk BHP/TINH LS16.....82 C2
CLECK BD19.....139 J3
OSM LS9.....104 E2
TAD LS24.....50 C7
Beech Wy BTLY WF17.....140 D6
Beechwood PONT WF8.....189 J7
RTHW LS26.....125 K7
Beechwood Av AIRE BD20.....32 E5
BIRK/DRI BD11.....120 A7
BULY LS4.....8 D2
HIPP HX3.....136 A2
LUD/ILL HX2.....134 D2
MIRF WF14.....179 H4
PONT WF8.....189 G1
RPDN/SBR HX6.....153 G5
SHPY BD18.....76 D5
WBSY BD6.....117 F4
WKFDW/WTN WF2.....183 J3
Beechwood CI
GFTH/SHER LS25.....111 F7
HORS LS18.....80 D1
LUD/ILL HX2.....134 C1
Beechwood Ct BHP/TINH LS16.....62 A6
SCFT LS14.....85 F6
Beechwood Crs BULY LS4.....8 C2
PONT WF8.....189 G2
RPDN/SBR HX6.....153 G5
Beechwood Cft
GFTH/SHER * LS25.....111 F7
Beechwood Dr LUD/ILL HX2.....134 C1
RPDN/SBR HX6.....153 G5
WBSY BD6.....117 G4
Beechwood Gld
GFTH/SHER LS25.....111 F7
Beechwood Gv BIRK/DRI BD11.....120 A7
HDGY LS6.....8 D3
HUDN HD2.....177 F4
ILK LS29.....23 J5
LUD/ILL * HX2.....134 C3
SHPY BD18.....76 D5
WBSY BD6.....117 C4
Beechwood Mt BULY LS4.....8 C3
Beechwood Pl BULY LS4.....8 C3
Beechwood Ri WBY LS22.....29 H2
Beechwood Rd BULY LS4.....8 D3
LUD/ILL HX2.....134 C1
MIRF WF14.....179 H3
WBSY BD6.....117 F4
Beechwood Rw HDGY * LS6.....8 D3
Beechwood St BULY LS4.....8 D3
PDSY/CALV LS28.....99 K4
Beechwood Ter BULY LS4.....8 C3
Beechwood Vw BULY LS4.....8 C3
Beechwood Wk BULY LS4.....8 D3
Beecroft CI BRAM LS13.....100 D2
Beecroft Crs BRAM LS13.....100 E2
Beecroft Gdns BRAM LS13.....100 D2
Beecroft Mt BRAM LS13.....100 D3
Beecroft St KGHY BD21.....3 K4
KSTL LS5.....101 K2
Beehive St WBSY BD6.....116 E2
Beehive Yd WBSY * BD6.....116 E2
Beestonley La GTL/HWG HX4.....174 A5
Beeston Park Cft
BEE/HOL * LS11.....122 D4
Beeston Park Garth
BEE/HOL * LS11.....122 D4
Beeston Park Pl BEE/HOL LS11.....122 D4
Beeston Park Ter
BEE/HOL LS11.....122 D4
Beeston Rd BEE/HOL LS11.....123 F3
Bela Rd BOW BD4.....118 D3
Belcross St HIPP HX3.....17 J3
Beldon La WBSY BD6.....116 E5
Beldon Park Av GTHN BD7.....116 E4
Beldon Park CI GTHN BD7.....116 E4
Beldon Pl ECHL BD2.....98 C3
Beldon Rd GTHN BD7.....117 F3
Belfast St HFAX HX1.....16 B8
The Belfry YEA LS19.....59 K5
Belfry Ct WKFDE WF1.....164 D3
Belfry Wy NORM WF6.....167 F7
Belgrave Av HIPP HX3.....17 K3
OSS WF5.....182 D5
Belgrave Crs HIPP HX3.....17 L3

Belgrave Dr HIPP HX3.....17 L3
Belgrave Gdns HIPP HX3.....17 K2
Belgrave Gv HIPP HX3.....17 K3
Belgrave Ms YEA * LS19.....59 H7
Belgrave Mt HIPP HX3.....17 K2
WKFDE WF1.....19 C1
Belgrave Pk HIPP HX3.....17 K3
KGHY BD21.....2 E3
Belgrave Rd BGLY BD16.....75 K1
KGHY BD21.....2 E3
Belgrave St LDSU LS2.....10 A8
OSS WF5.....182 D5
RPDN/SBR HX6.....153 J4
Belgrave Ter WKFDE WF1.....19 C1
Belgravia Gdns RHAY * LS8.....104 C3
Belgravia Rd WKFDE WF1.....18 C1
Belinda St MID LS10.....14 F8
Bell Bank Vw BGLY BD16.....55 H7
Bellbrooke Av OSM LS9.....11 L4
Bellbrooke Gv OSM LS9.....11 L4
Bellbrooke Pl OSM LS9.....11 L4
Bellbrooke St OSM LS9.....11 K4
Bell Dean Rd WIL/AL BD15.....96 A5
Belle Isle Av WKFDE WF1.....19 H9
Belle Isle CI MID LS10.....123 K6
Belle Isle Crs WKFDE WF1.....19 H9
Belle Isle Dr WKFDE WF1.....19 H9
Belle Isle Pde MID LS10.....123 K5
Belle Isle Rd HWTH BD22.....72 D6
MID LS10.....123 K5
Bellerby Brow WBSY BD6.....116 C5
Belle View HIPP HX3.....136 A2
Belle Vue CUL/QBY BD13.....115 H7
GIR BD8.....5 J2
ILK LS29.....24 B6
Belle Vue Av MSTN/BAR LS15.....86 C5
RHAY LS8.....84 E6
Belle Vue Ct BVRD * LS3.....9 H7
Belle Vue Crs HIPP HX3.....136 A2
HUDN HD2.....177 H6
Belle Vue Dr PDSY/CALV LS28.....99 K2
Belle Vue Est MSTN/BAR LS15.....86 C6
Belle Vue Pk HFAX * HX1.....16 D6
Belle Vue Rd HIPP HX3.....136 A2
LDSU LS2.....9 H5
MSTN/BAR LS15.....86 C6
WKFDE WF1.....185 F6
Belle Vue St BTLY WF17.....160 C3
Belle Vue Ter HIPP HX3.....17 M9
KGHY BD21.....3 J6
Bell Hall Mt HFAX HX1.....154 D3
Bell Hall Ter HFAX HX1.....154 D3
Bell House Av BOW BD4.....118 C5
Bellhouse Crs BOW BD4.....118 C6
Bell La BRAM LS13.....101 F2
Bellmont CI BRAM LS13.....100 E1
Bellmont Gdns BRAM LS13.....101 F1
Bellmont Gn BRAM LS13.....101 G2
Bellmont Pl BRAM LS13.....101 F1
Bellmont Vw BRAM LS13.....101 G2
Belloe St WBOW BD5.....117 J2
Bell Rd BRAM LS13.....101 F2
Bellshaw St GIR BD8.....96 D6
Bell Sq GIR BD8.....21 F7
Bell St DEWS WF13.....180 B4
HIPP HX3.....17 J3
LM/WK BD12.....137 H3
OSM LS10.....10 D8
WKFDE WF1.....18 D3
Bellwood Av BSPA/BRAM LS23.....48 C4
Belmont KNOT WF11.....150 D6
Belmont Av BAIL BD17.....77 G1
LM/WK BD12.....117 K7
OT LS21.....39 G1
Belmont CI BAIL BD17.....77 G1
Belmont Crs LM/WK BD12.....117 K7
SHPY BD18.....77 F4
Belmont Gdns WBSY BD6.....117 J7
Belmont Gv LDSU LS2.....9 K7
WBSY BD6.....117 J7
YEA LS19.....59 K6
Belmont Pl HFAX HX1.....16 C8
Belmont Ri BAIL BD17.....77 G1
LM/WK BD12.....117 K7
Belmont Rd ILK LS29.....24 D5
Belmont St ECHL BD2.....78 D7
FEA/AMT WF7.....187 F4
HIPP HX3.....17 J3
RPDN/SBR * HX6.....153 K4
WKFDE WF1.....18 D1
Belmont Ter EARD/LOFT WF3.....144 A5
LUD/ILL HX2.....153 F3
SHPY * BD18.....77 F4
Belton CI GTHN BD7.....117 F3
Belton Gv HUDW HD3.....176 A7
Belton Rd AIRE BD20.....33 F2
Belvedere Av AL/HA/HU LS17.....63 J7
BEE/HOL LS11.....123 G4
Belvedere Ct AL/HA/HU LS17.....63 K7
Belvedere Gv AL/HA/HU LS17.....63 J7
Belvedere Mt BEE/HOL LS11.....123 G4
Belvedere Rd AL/HA/HU LS17.....63 J7
BTLY WF17.....160 E4
Belvedere Ter BEE/HOL LS11.....123 C5
GIR BD8.....4 E3
Belvedere Vw AL/HA/HU LS17.....63 K7
Belvoir Dr KNOT WF11.....171 F4
Belvoir Gdns HIPP HX3.....155 F5
Bembridge Ct
WKFDW/WTN WF2.....183 J1
Bempton Ct GTHN * BD7.....117 G2
Bempton Gv BTLY WF17.....140 C5
Bempton Pl GTHN * BD7.....117 G2
Benbow Av IDLE BD10.....79 F7
Bendigo Rd EARL WF12.....161 J7
Benjamin St LVSG WF15.....159 J5
WKFDW/WTN WF2.....18 A3
Benjamin Sykes Wy
WKFDW/WTN WF2.....183 H5
Benn Av GTHN BD7.....116 E2
Benn Crs GTHN BD7.....116 E2
Bennet Ct MSTN/BAR LS15.....106 A5
Bennett Av EARL WF12.....161 H5
Bennett Rd HDGY LS6.....82 C7
Bennett St HIPP HX3.....17 K8
LVSG WF15.....159 J4
Benns La LUD/ILL HX2.....133 C5
Benny Parr CI BTLY WF17.....161 H3

Ben Rhydding Dr ILK LS29.....24 E6
Ben Rhydding Rd ILK LS29.....24 B6
Benson Gdns WOR/ARM LS12.....102 A7
Benson La NORM WF6.....167 F4
Benson St CHAL LS7.....10 D5
Bentcliffe Av AL/HA/HU LS17.....83 K5
Bentcliffe CI AL/HA/HU LS17.....83 K3
Bentcliffe Dr AL/HA/HU LS17.....83 K2
Bentcliffe Gdns AL/HA/HU LS17.....83 K3
Bentcliffe Gv AL/HA/HU LS17.....83 K3
Bentcliffe La AL/HA/HU LS17.....83 J3
Bentcliffe Mt AL/HA/HU LS17.....83 K3
Bentfield Cottages CLAY BD14.....116 B1
Bent Lea HUDN HD2.....178 A3
Bentley Av BRIG HD6.....157 F1
Bentley CI BAIL BD17.....57 C7
Bentley Gdns CHAL LS7.....82 E6
Bentley Gv HDGY LS6.....82 E6
Bentley La HDGY LS6.....82 E6
Bentley Mt HDGY LS6.....82 E6
RPDN/SBR HX6.....154 A3
Bentley Pde HDGY LS6.....82 E6
Bentley Rd WKFDW/WTN WF2.....183 K5
Bentley Royd CI
RPDN/SBR HX6.....153 H5
Bentley St LM/WK * BD12.....137 J4
Benton Crs HOR/CROF WF4.....183 H7
Benton Park Av YEA LS19.....59 K6
Benton Park Crs YEA LS19.....59 K6
Benton Park Dr YEA LS19.....59 K6
Benton Park Rd YEA LS19.....59 K6
Bents La WIL/AL BD15.....74 D6
Benyon Park Wy
WOR/ARM LS12.....12 D7
Beresford Rd WBSY BD6.....117 G7
Beresford St LM/WK BD12.....138 B2
Berkeley Av RHAY LS8.....11 K3
Berkeley Crs RHAY LS8.....11 K3
Berkeley Mt RHAY LS8.....11 K3
Berkeley Rd RHAY LS8.....11 K3
Berkeley St RHAY LS8.....11 K2
Berkeley Ter RHAY LS8.....11 K3
Berkeley Vw RHAY LS8.....11 K2
Berking Av OSM LS9.....11 H9
Bermondsey Ms OT LS21.....39 J3
Bermondsey St OT LS21.....39 J3
Bernard St HUDN HD2.....177 K6
RTHW LS26.....146 A1
Berne Gv WKFDE WF1.....18 F2
Berners St WKFDE WF1.....19 H5
Berrington Wy HWTH BD22.....72 C1
Berryfield Garth OSS WF5.....182 C1
Berry La HFAX HX1.....17 K6
KGHY BD21.....2 F6
RTHW LS26.....127 H6
Berry Moor Rd RPDN/SBR HX6.....154 A6
Berry St KGHY BD21.....3 J4
Berry's Yd HOR/CROF.....183 H7
Bertha St PDSY/CALV LS28.....100 A3
Bertie St BOW BD4.....118 D3
Bertram Dr BAIL BD17.....77 G2
Bertram Rd GIR BD8.....97 H3
Bertrand St BEE/HOL LS11.....13 J6
Berwick Av HECK WF16.....160 A2
Berwick St HFAX HX1.....17 L4
Bescaby Gv BAIL * BD17.....77 K1
Besha Av LM/WK BD12.....117 J7
Besha Gv LM/WK BD12.....137 J1
Bessingham Gdns WBSY BD6.....116 E6
Best La HWTH BD22.....92 D3
Beswick CI BFDE BD3.....7 J5
Bethel Rd SHPY BD18.....77 J4
Bethel St AIRE BD20.....55 G3
BRIG HD6.....157 G6
HIPP HX3.....134 D5
Betteras Hill Rd
GFTH/SHER LS25.....131 F7
Beulah Gv HDGY LS6.....9 L2
Beulah Mt HDGY * LS6.....9 L2
Beulah Pl LUD/ILL HX2.....153 F3
Beulah St HDGY LS6.....9 L2
Beulah Ter HDGY LS6.....9 L1
Beulah Vw HDGY * LS6.....9 L2
Bevan Av NORM WF6.....186 E1
Bevan Ct GTHN BD7.....116 E3
Bevan Pl WKFDW/WTN WF2.....183 H5
Bevedere Gdns AL/HA/HU LS17.....63 K7
Beverley Av BEE/HOL LS11.....123 G3
LM/WK BD12.....137 J5
Beverley CI ELL HX5.....176 A3
Beverley Dr EARL WF12.....181 J1
LM/WK BD12.....137 J5
Beverley Gdns BTLY WF17.....140 E5
Beverley Mt BEE/HOL LS11.....123 G3
Beverley Pl HIPP HX3.....16 F1
Beverley Ri ILK LS29.....23 K5
Beverley St BOW BD4.....118 E1
Beverley Ter BEE/HOL LS11.....123 G3
HIPP HX3.....16 F1
Beverley Vw BEE/HOL LS11.....13 M9
Bevin CI WKFDE WF1.....164 D3
Bevin Crs WKFDE WF1.....164 D3
Bevor Crs HECK WF16.....160 A3
Bewerley Crs LM/WK BD12.....137 F1
Bewick Ct CUL/QBY BD13.....116 A4
Bewick Gv RTHW LS26.....124 A7
Bexhill CI PONT WF8.....170 A6
Bexley Av RHAY LS8.....11 G4
Bexley Gv OSM LS9.....11 H4
Bexley Mt OSM LS9.....11 G4
Bexley Pl RHAY LS8.....11 H4
Bexley Rd OSM LS9.....11 H4
Bexley Ter OSM LS9.....11 H4
Bexley Vw OSM LS9.....11 H4
Beza Rd MID LS10.....123 J3
Beza St MID LS10.....123 J3
Bickerton Wy OT LS21.....39 F1
Biddenden Rd MSTN/BAR LS15.....106 C3
Bidder Dr EARD/LOFT WF3.....143 H6
Bideford Av RHAY LS8.....84 A1
Bierley Hall Gv BOW BD4.....118 C7
Bierley House Av BOW BD4.....118 C6
Bierley La BOW BD4.....118 C5
Bierley Vw BOW BD4.....118 D5
Big Meadow Dr ILK LS29.....22 A1
Bilberry CI CLAY BD14.....116 B3

Bilberry Ri HWTH BD22.....72 E5
Billams Hl OT LS21.....39 G1
Billey La WOR/ARM LS12.....121 H2
Billing Ct YEA LS19.....80 A1
Billing Dr YEA LS19.....80 B1
Billingham CI
WKFDW/WTN WF2.....183 J1
Billing Vw IDLE BD10.....78 D5
YEA LS19.....80 A1
Billingwood Dr YEA LS19.....80 A1
Bilsdale Gra WBSY BD6.....116 E6
Bilsdale Wy BAIL BD17.....76 E2
Bilton Pl GIR BD8.....5 H4
Binbrook Vw WIL/AL * BD15.....96 A4
Bingley Bank AL/HA/HU LS17.....65 K1
Bingley Rd BAIL BD17.....56 E5
CUL/QBY BD13.....74 B5
HTON BD9.....96 C1
ILK LS29.....57 C1
KGHY BD21.....73 J3
SHPY BD18.....76 C4
Bingley St BVRD LS3.....9 F5
GIR BD8.....4 D5
Binks Fold LM/WK BD12.....137 J5
Binks St WKFDE WF1.....164 D4
Binks Yd OSS * WF5.....182 C3
Binnie St BFDE BD3.....6 E5
Binns Hill La LUD/ILL HX2.....153 J2
Binns La GTHN BD7.....116 E1
Binns St BGLY BD16.....75 K1
Binns Top La HIPP HX3.....156 A5
Birch Av MSTN/BAR LS15.....105 H5
WBOW BD5.....118 A4
Birch CI BRIG HD6.....157 H5
WBOW BD5.....118 A4
Birch Close La BGLY BD16.....56 E3
Birch Crs MSTN/BAR LS15.....105 H5
Birchdale BGLY BD16.....55 J5
Birch Dr GFTH/SHER LS25.....127 K3
Birchen Av OSS WF5.....182 B4
The Birches BHP/TINH LS16.....61 J1
GSLY LS20.....59 F1
Birchfield Av MOR LS27.....141 F1
Birchfield Garth SCFT LS14.....85 K5
Birchfields Av SCFT LS14.....85 K4
Birchfields CI SCFT LS14.....85 K4
Birchfields Ct SCFT LS14.....85 K4
Birchfields Crs SCFT LS14.....85 K4
Birchfields Ri SCFT LS14.....85 K4
Birch Gn PONT WF8.....170 A7
Birch Gv BTLY WF17.....140 D7
CAS WF10.....169 H2
GFTH/SHER LS25.....127 K4
HWTH BD22.....53 H7
WBOW BD5.....117 K5
Birch Hill Ri HORS LS18.....81 H4
Birchington Av HUDW HD3.....175 A7
Birchington CI HUDW HD3.....176 A7
Birchington Dr HUDW HD3.....175 K7
Birchlands Av WIL/AL BD15.....74 E6
Birchlands Gv WIL/AL BD15.....74 E6
Birch La LUD/ILL HX2.....133 G7
WBOW BD5.....117 K3
Birch Ms BHP/TINH LS16.....82 C2
Birch Rd GFTH/SHER LS25.....127 K4
NORM WF6.....186 D1
Birchroyd RTHW LS26.....145 G3
Birchroyd CI HUDN HD2.....176 C7
Birch St GIR BD8.....4 C3
MOR LS27.....142 A5
WKFDE WF1.....19 K9
Birchtree CI WKFDE WF1.....185 J6
Birch Tree Gdns KGHY BD21.....3 L7
Birchtree Wy BHP/TINH * LS16.....81 H2
Birch Wy WBOW BD5.....118 A4
Birchwood Av AIRE BD20.....53 J1
AL/HA/HU LS17.....84 B1
BTLY WF17.....140 C5
LVSG WF15.....159 J5
Birchwood Dr AIRE BD20.....53 H1
Birchwood Hl AL/HA/HU LS17.....64 B7
Birchwood Mt AL/HA/HU LS17.....64 B7
Birchwood Rd AIRE BD20.....53 H1
Birdale Field La WBY LS22.....47 G2
Birdcage Hl HIPP HX3.....154 D5
Birdcage La HIPP HX3.....154 D5
Birdcage Wk OT LS21.....39 H4
Birds Royd La BRIG HD6.....157 H7
Birdswell Av BRIG HD6.....157 J5
The Birdswell Av BTLY WF17.....140 E5
Birfed Crs BULY LS4.....102 A2
Birkby Brow Crs BTLY WF17.....140 E5
Birkby Hvn WBSY BD6.....116 D6
Birkby La BRIG HD6.....157 H1
Birkby Rd HUDW HD3.....176 B7
Birkby St LM/WK BD12.....137 J3
Birkdale CI AL/HA/HU LS17.....63 G7
CUL/QBY BD13.....74 B6
Birkdale Ct AIRE BD20.....33 F2
Birkdale Dr AL/HA/HU LS17.....63 G7
Birkdale Gn AL/HA/HU LS17.....63 G7
Birkdale Gv AL/HA/HU LS17.....63 G7
DEWS WF13.....160 D6
LUD/ILL HX2.....114 C7
Birkdale Mt AL/HA/HU LS17.....63 G7
Birkdale Pl AL/HA/HU LS17.....63 G7
Birkdale Ri AL/HA/HU LS17.....63 G7
Birkdale Rd DEWS WF13.....160 D7
Birkdale Wk AL/HA/HU LS17.....63 F7
Birkenshaw La BIRK/DRI BD11.....139 J2
Birkett St CLECK BD19.....138 D1
Birkhead St HECK WF16.....160 B5
Birkhill CAS WF10.....149 H7
Birkhill Crs BIRK/DRI BD11.....139 J2
Birkhouse La BRIG HD6.....157 J1
Birkhouse Rd BRIG HD6.....157 H1
Birklands Moor CLECK BD19.....139 J4
Birklands Rd HUDN HD2.....176 C7
SHPY BD18.....77 F5
Birklands Ter SHPY BD18.....77 G5
Birk La MOR LS27.....141 H3
Birk Lea St WBOW BD5.....117 K2
Birks Av GTHN BD7.....116 D2
Birks Fold GTHN BD7.....4 A9

Birkshall La BFDE BD3.....6 F8
Birks Hall St HFAX HX1.....16 D4
Birks Hall Ter HFAX HX1.....16 D4
Birksland St BOW BD4.....6 E9
Birks La RPDN/SBR HX6.....172 E1
Birkwith CI SCFT LS14.....85 J4
Birkwood Av HOR/CROF WF4.....186 E7
Birkwood Rd NORM WF6.....165 J5
Birnam Gv BOW BD4.....118 B2
Birr Rd HTON BD9.....97 G2
Birstall La BIRK/DRI BD11.....140 B2
Bishopdale Dr WBY LS22.....46 D1
Bishopdale Holme WBSY BD6.....116 D6
Bishopdike Rd
GFTH/SHER LS25.....111 K5
Bishopgate St LDS LS1.....13 M1
Bishop St HTON BD9.....97 G2
Bishops Wy MIRF WF14.....178 E2
Bishop Wy EARD/LOFT WF3.....142 E7
Bismarck Ct BEE/HOL * LS11.....13 M8
Bismarck Dr BEE/HOL LS11.....13 M8
Bismarck St BEE/HOL LS11.....13 M8
Bitterne Ct CUL/QBY BD13.....116 B4
Bittern Ri MOR LS27.....142 B4
Black Aston Rd BRAM LS13.....101 G3
Blackberry Wy CLAY BD14.....116 A3
Blackbird Gdns GIR BD8.....96 A6
Black Brook Wy GTL/HWG HX4.....175 F3
Black Bull St MID LS10.....14 C4
Blackburn CI GIR BD8.....96 C4
HIPP HX3.....134 C4
Blackburn Ct RTHW LS26.....145 G2
Blackburn La KNOT WF11.....171 K5
Blackburn Pl BTLY WF17.....161 G3
Blackburn Rd BRIG HD6.....156 E4
BTLY WF17.....140 B6
Black Dyke La CUL/QBY BD13.....94 B3
Black Edge La CUL/QBY BD13.....93 K7
Blackers Ct EARL WF12.....180 D5
Blackett St PDSY/CALV LS28.....79 J5
Black Gates Ct
EARD/LOFT WF3.....142 E7
Blackgates Crs
EARD/LOFT WF3.....142 D7
Blackgates Dr
EARD/LOFT WF3.....142 E7
Blackgates Fold
EARD/LOFT * WF3.....142 E7
Black Gates Ri
EARD/LOFT * WF3.....142 E7
Black Hill La AIRE BD20.....52 E2
BHP/TINH LS16.....62 C2
Black Hill Rd OT LS21.....42 B5
Blackhouse Rd HUDN HD2.....177 G7
Blackledge HFAX HX1.....17 J7
Blackley Rd ELL HX5.....175 G4
Blackman La LDSU LS2.....9 M5
Blackmires LUD/ILL HX2.....134 D2
Blackmoor La AL/HA/HU LS17.....65 J1
Black Moor Rd AL/HA/HU LS17.....82 E1
HWTH BD22.....72 E6
Blackpool Gv WOR/ARM LS12.....121 K2
Blackpool Pl WOR/ARM LS12.....121 K2
Blackpool Ter WOR/ARM LS12.....121 K2
Blackpool Vw WOR/ARM LS12.....121 K2
Black Rd WKFDE WF1.....185 J6
Blackshaw Beck La HIPP HX3.....115 K7
Blackshaw Clough Rd
RPDN/SBR HX6.....172 B3
Blackshaw Dr WBSY BD6.....116 C6
Blacksmith GTHN BD7.....117 F2
Blacksmith Fold GTHN BD7.....117 F2
Blacksmith La PONT WF8.....162 E2
Blackstone Av LM/WK BD12.....137 H5
Blackthorn Ct MID LS10.....123 J6
Blackthorn Wy
WKFDW/WTN WF2.....18 A1
Black Wk PONT WF8.....169 K6
Blackwall HFAX HX1.....16 F7
Blackwall La RPDN/SBR HX6.....153 H3
Blackwall Ri RPDN/SBR HX6.....153 J3
Blackwood Av BHP/TINH LS16.....81 G1
Blackwood Gdns
BHP/TINH LS16.....81 G1
Black Wood Gv BHP/TINH LS16.....81 G1
Blackwood Gv HFAX HX1.....16 A4
Blackwood Hall La
LUD/ILL HX2.....152 D2
Black Wood Mt BHP/TINH LS16.....81 G1
Black Wood Ri BHP/TINH LS16.....81 G1
Blacup Moor Vw CLECK BD19.....158 E1
Blairsville Gdns BRAM LS13.....100 E1
Blairsville Gv BRAM LS13.....101 F1
Blaithroyd La HIPP HX3.....17 L8
Blake Crs GSLY LS20.....59 G3
Blake Gv CHAL LS7.....83 J6
Blake Hall Dr MIRF WF14.....179 J5
Blake Hall Rd MIRF WF14.....179 J5
Blake Hl HIPP HX3.....135 H4
Blakehill Av ECHL BD2.....98 D3
Blakehill Ter ECHL BD2.....98 D3
Blakelaw Dr BRIG HD6.....157 H6
Blake Law La BRIG HD6.....158 A6
Blakeley Gv WKFDW/WTN WF2.....184 A3
Blakeney Gv MID LS10.....123 J5
Blakeney Rd MID LS10.....123 J5
Blakeridge La BTLY WF17.....160 E3
Blakey Rd WKFDW/WTN WF2.....184 A1
Blamires Pl GTHN BD7.....116 E3
Blamires St GTHN BD7.....116 E3
Blanche St BOW BD4.....7 J8
Blandford Gdns LDSU LS2.....9 L5
Blandford Gv LDSU LS2.....9 L5
Blands Av CAS WF10.....147 G1
Bland's CI CAS WF10.....168 C1
Blands Crs CAS WF10.....147 G1
Blands Gv CAS WF10.....147 K1
Blands Ter CAS WF10.....147 K2
Bland St HFAX * HX1.....16 F6
Blantyre Ct CUL/QBY BD13.....74 A6
Blayds Garth RTHW LS26.....125 H7
Blayds Ms LDS LS1.....14 A2
LDS * LS1.....14 A2
Blayds St OSM LS9.....15 G1
Blayd's Yd LDS LS1.....14 A2
Bleach Mill La ILK LS29.....37 K5
Bleak St CLECK BD19.....139 K7

Bleak St Lower CLECK BD19 ......139 K7
Bleasdale Av KNOT WF11 ......171 F3
Blencarn Cl SCFT LS14 ......105 G3
Blencarn Garth SCFT LS14 ......105 G1
Blencarn Rd SCFT LS14 ......105 G1
Blencarn Vw SCFT LS14 ......105 G1
Blenheim Av LDSU LS2 ......9 M4
Blenheim Av KNOT WF11 ......170 D4
Blenheim Ct HFAX * HX1 ......16 F4
  LDSU * LS2 ......9 L5
Blenheim Dr BTLY WF17 ......161 F2
  DEWS WF13 ......160 D7
Blenheim Gv LDSU LS2 ......9 M5
Blenheim HI IDLE BD10 ......78 C3
Blenheim Mt GIR BD8 ......97 H3
Blenheim Pl IDLE BD10 ......78 C3
Blenheim Sq LDSU LS2 ......9 M4
Blenheim Ter LDSU LS2 ......9 L5
Blenheim Vw LDSU LS2 ......9 L4
Blenheim Vw LDSU LS2 ......9 L5
Blind La AL/HA/HU LS17 ......65 F7
  BGLY BD16 ......75 G1
  BIRK/DRI BD11 ......120 C7
  EARD/LOFT WF3 ......163 F5
  LUD/ILL HX2 ......132 C2
Blucher St BOW BD4 ......7 K9
Blue Ball Rd RPDN/SBR HX6 ......172 C4
Bluebell Cl PONT WF8 ......189 J2
  SHPY BD18 ......77 J7
  WIL/AL * BD15 ......96 A5
Bluebell Ct BTLY WF17 ......140 D5
Bluebell Wk LUD/ILL HX2 ......133 F7
Bluebird Wk BGLY BD16 ......56 B7
Blue Butts OSS WF5 ......182 C4
Blue Hill Crs WOR/ARM LS12 ......101 K7
Blue Hill Gra WOR/ARM LS12 ......121 K7
Blue Hill Gv WOR/ARM LS12 ......101 K7
Blue Hill La WOR/ARM LS12 ......101 K7
Blundell St LDS LS1 ......9 L7
Blythe Av GIR BD8 ......4 D4
Blythe St GTHN BD7 ......5 H6
Boar La LDS LS1 ......14 A1
Boathouse La MIRF WF14 ......179 K7
Boat La RTHW LS26 ......147 K5
Bobbin Mill Ct AIRE BD20 ......32 D5
Bob La LUD/ILL HX2 ......154 A1
Bodiham HI GFTH/SHER LS25 ......108 A5
Bodley Ter BULY LS4 ......8 D6
Bodmin Ap LS10 ......143 F2
Bodmin Av SHPY BD18 ......77 K5
Bodmin Crs MID LS10 ......143 F2
Bodmin Cft MID LS10 ......143 G3
Bodmin Dr NORM WF6 ......166 E5
Bodmin Gdns MID LS10 ......143 F3
Bodmin Garth MID LS10 ......143 F3
Bodmin Pl MID LS10 ......143 G3
Bodmin Rd MID LS10 ......142 E3
Bodmin St MID LS10 ......143 F3
Boggart HI SCFT LS14 ......85 F6
Boggart Hill Crs SCFT LS14 ......85 F6
Boggart Hill Dr SCFT LS14 ......85 F6
Boggart Hill Gdns SCFT LS14 ......85 F6
Boggart Hill Rd SCFT LS14 ......85 F6
Boggart La HIPP HX3 ......136 C6
  RPDN/SBR HX6 ......153 J5
Bog Green La HUDE HD5 ......178 C4
Bog La MSTN/BAR LS15 ......86 D7
Bogthorn HWTH BD22 ......53 F7
Boland Crs HWTH BD22 ......73 F1
Boldgrove St EARL WF12 ......181 K3
Boldmere Rd MSTN/BAR LS15 ......105 F6
Boldron Holt WBSY BD6 ......116 E6
Boldshay St BFDE BD3 ......6 E4
Bolehill Pk BRIG HD6 ......156 D2
Bolingbroke St WBOW BD5 ......117 J4
Bolland St LM/WK BD12 ......137 K2
Bolling Rd BOW BD4 ......6 B8
  ILK LS29 ......24 C5
Bolsover Cl GFTH/SHER LS25 ......108 A6
Boltby La WBSY BD6 ......116 D6
Bolton LUD/ILL HX2 ......114 B7
Bolton Brow RPDN/SBR HX6 ......153 K4
Bolton Dr ECHL BD2 ......98 C1
Bolton Gra YEA LS19 ......59 K5
Bolton Gv ECHL BD2 ......98 C1
Bolton Hall Rd SHPY BD18 ......77 J7
Bolton La ECHL BD2 ......98 A2
Bolton Rd AIRE BD20 ......21 F7
  BFDE BD3 ......6 A1
  ILK LS29 ......22 C1
  YEA LS19 ......59 K5
Bolton St BFDE BD3 ......6 C5
  LM/WK BD12 ......137 H1
Bolton Ter AIRE BD20 ......21 F7
Bolton Wy BSPA/BRAM LS23 ......48 B3
Bolus Cl WKFDE WF1 ......164 D4
Bolus La WKFDE WF1 ......164 C4
Bond Ct LDS LS1 ......9 M9
Bondgate AL/HA/HU LS17 ......44 B3
  OT LS21 ......39 H3
  PONT WF8 ......189 J1
Bondings Ri GFTH/SHER LS25 ......111 H5
Bond St BRIG HD6 ......157 F5
  BTLY WF17 ......140 B6
  BTLY WF17 ......161 F2
  DEWS WF13 ......181 F1
  HFAX * HX1 ......16 F7
  LDS LS1 ......10 A9
  PONT WF8 ......169 K6
  WKFDE WF1 ......18 D3
Bonegate Av BRIG HD6 ......157 F5
Bonegate Rd BRIG HD6 ......157 F5
Bonn Rd HTON BD9 ......97 F3
Bonwick MI WBSY BD6 ......116 D7
Boocock St PDSY/CALV LS28 ......100 B4
Bookers Fld CLECK BD19 ......159 K1
Bootham Pk HTON BD9 ......96 C3
Booth House La LUD/ILL HX2 ......152 D1
Boothman Wk KGHY BD21 ......2 D9
Booth Royd IDLE BD10 ......78 D3
Boothroyd Dr HDGY LS6 ......82 E7
Booth Royd Dr IDLE BD10 ......78 D3
Boothroyd Gn DEWS WF13 ......180 E1
Boothroyd La DEWS WF13 ......180 E1

Boothroyds Wy FEA/AMT WF7 ......187 K3
Booth St CAS WF10 ......148 C7
  CLECK BD19 ......138 E7
  IDLE BD10 ......78 C5
  ILK LS29 ......25 K7
  SHPY BD18 ......77 J5
Boothtown Rd HIPP HX3 ......134 E4
Boroughgate OT LS21 ......39 H7
Borough Rd WKFDE WF1 ......18 E3
Borrins Wy BAIL BD17 ......77 J1
Borrough Av RHAY LS8 ......83 K4
Borrough Vw RHAY LS8 ......83 K4
Borrowdale Cl WOR/ARM LS12 ......101 J3
Borrowdale Crs
  WOR/ARM LS12 ......101 J3
Borrowdale Cft YEA LS19 ......59 H4
Borrowdale Dr CAS WF10 ......149 G6
Borrowdale Rd EARL WF12 ......161 H6
  WKFDW/WTN WF2 ......183 K2
Borrowdale Ter SCFT LS14 ......105 G2
Boston Av KSTL LS5 ......101 J2
Boston Av WBY LS22 ......29 H5
Boston St CAS WF10 ......148 D7
  HFAX HX1 ......16 B6
  RPDN/SBR HX6 ......153 H5
Boston Wk WBSY BD6 ......116 E6
Bosworth Av NORM WF6 ......166 B4
Bosworth Cl WIL/AL BD15 ......96 A4
Botany Av ECHL BD2 ......98 A1
Botany Dr AIRE BD20 ......55 H1
Bottom Boat Rd
  EARD/LOFT WF3 ......165 J2
Bottomley La GTL/HWG HX4 ......173 K7
Bottomley St BRIG HD6 ......157 G4
  WBOW BD5 ......117 J2
  WBSY BD6 ......116 E7
Bottoms HIPP HX3 ......155 G5
Bottoms La BIRK/DRI BD11 ......139 J3
The Boulevard BEE/HOL LS11 ......12 C9
  PDSY/CALV LS28 ......100 A3
The Boundary GIR BD8 ......96 D4
Boundary Cl BAIL BD17 ......57 J7
  MSTN/BAR LS15 ......106 B6
Boundary Farm Rd
  AL/HA/HU LS17 ......83 F1
Boundary La WKFDE WF1 ......186 C2
Boundary Pl CHAL LS7 ......10 E4
Boundary Rd DEWS WF13 ......160 C6
Boundary St CHAL * LS7 ......10 E4
  LVSC WF15 ......159 K5
Boundary Ter DEWS * WF13 ......160 E6
Bourbon Cl WBSY BD6 ......117 G6
Bourne St IDLE BD10 ......78 C7
The Bourse LDS * LS1 ......14 A1
Bowater Ct BOW BD4 ......119 G4
Bow Beck BOW BD4 ......6 D9
Bowbridge Rd WBOW * BD5 ......117 K3
Bow Bridge Vw TAD LS24 ......51 G5
Bowcliffe Rd BSPA/BRAM LS23 ......68 B1
  MID LS10 ......15 G8
The Bower BTLY WF17 ......140 C7
Bower Gn BFDE BD3 ......7 G6
Bower La DEWS WF13 ......160 C5
Bower Rd MSTN/BAR LS15 ......106 B2
Bower Slack Rd
  RPDN/SBR HX6 ......152 A7
Bowers La GTL/HWG HX4 ......174 A7
Bower St WBOW BD5 ......5 L9
Bowes Nook WBSY BD6 ......116 D7
Bowfell Cl SCFT LS14 ......105 H1
Bow Gn CLAY BD14 ......116 C2
Bowland Cl MSTN/BAR LS15 ......105 F6
Bowland St GIR BD8 ......5 J3
Bowler Cl LM/WK BD12 ......137 H1
Bowling Aly BRIG HD6 ......177 F1
Bowling Av WKFDE * WF1 ......164 A6
Bowling Back La BOW BD4 ......6 D9
Bowling Ct BRIG HD6 ......156 E5
Bowling Dyke HFAX HX1 ......17 H4
Bowling Green Rd
  GTL/HWG HX4 ......174 C6
Bowling Green Ter
  BEE/HOL LS11 ......13 L5
Bowling Hall Rd BOW BD4 ......118 B3
Bowling Old La WBOW BD5 ......117 J4
Bowling Park Cl BOW BD4 ......118 A2
Bowling Park Dr WBOW BD5 ......118 A3
Bowman Av WBSY BD6 ......117 G7
Bowman Gv HFAX HX1 ......16 C5
Bowman La MID LS10 ......14 C2
Bowman Pl HFAX * HX1 ......16 C5
Bowman Rd WBSY BD6 ......117 G7
Bowman St HFAX * HX1 ......16 C5
  WKFDE WF1 ......185 G6
Bowman Ter HFAX * HX1 ......16 D5
Bownas Rd BSPA/BRAM LS23 ......48 B2
Bowness Av CAS WF10 ......149 K6
  IDLE BD10 ......98 E1
Bowood Av CHAL LS7 ......83 F5
Bowood Crs CHAL LS7 ......83 F5
Bowood Gv CHAL LS7 ......83 F5
Bowood La RPDN/SBR HX6 ......152 E7
Bow St KGHY BD21 ......3 G5
  OSM LS9 ......14 E2
Bowwood Dr AIRE BD20 ......54 E3
Boxhill Rd ELL HX5 ......175 J2
Box La PONT WF8 ......169 K6
Box Tree Cl GIR BD8 ......96 D4
Box Tree Gv KGHY BD21 ......3 L7
Box Trees La LUD/ILL HX2 ......134 A4
Boxwood Rd ELL HX5 ......175 J4
Boyd Av BFDE BD3 ......7 M2
Boy La BOW BD4 ......118 C7
  HIPP HX3 ......134 A5
The Boyle MSTN/BAR LS15 ......87 G4
Boyne St HFAX * HX1 ......16 F6
Boynton St WBOW BD5 ......117 J3
Boynton Ter WBOW BD5 ......117 K3
Boys La HIPP HX3 ......155 G5
Bracewell Av WIL/AL BD15 ......95 K5
Bracewell Bank HIPP HX3 ......134 C5
Bracewell Dr HIPP HX3 ......134 C5
Bracewell Gv HIPP HX3 ......16 A1
Bracken Av BRIG HD6 ......157 F3
Bracken Bank Av HWTH BD22 ......73 G1
Bracken Bank Crs HWTH BD22 ......73 G1
Bracken Bank Gv HWTH BD22 ......73 G1
Bracken Bank Wk HWTH BD22 ......73 G1

Bracken Bank Wy HWTH BD22 ......73 G1
Brackenbeck Rd GTHN BD7 ......116 E2
Brackendale Gra LUD/ILL HX2 ......134 B6
Brackenbed La HFAX HX1 ......16 A1
Bracken Cl BRIG HD6 ......157 F3
  ELL HX5 ......176 A2
  MIRF WF14 ......178 E2
Bracken Ct AL/HA/HU LS17 ......83 H3
  WOR/ARM LS12 ......12 D6
Brackendale IDLE BD10 ......78 A2
Brackendale Av IDLE BD10 ......78 B2
Brackendale Dr IDLE BD10 ......78 A2
Brackendale Gv IDLE BD10 ......78 A2
Brackendale Pde IDLE BD10 ......78 A2
Bracken Edge IDLE BD10 ......78 D5
  RHAY LS8 ......84 A7
Bracken Ghyll Dr AIRE BD20 ......20 E7
Bracken Gv HUDN HD2 ......177 G5
  MIRF WF14 ......178 E2
Bracken Hall Rd HUDN HD2 ......177 H6
Bracken HI AL/HA/HU LS17 ......83 H3
  MIRF WF14 ......178 E2
Brackenhill Dr GTHN BD7 ......116 E2
Brackenholme Royd
  WBSY BD6 ......116 C6
Bracken Mt AIRE BD20 ......20 E7
Bracken Pk BGLY BD16 ......76 B1
  SCFT LS14 ......65 H3
Bracken Rd AIRE BD20 ......32 B5
  BRIG HD6 ......157 F3
  HWTH BD22 ......53 H7
Brackens La HIPP HX3 ......116 A3
Bracken Sq HUDN * HD2 ......177 H5
Bracken St KGHY BD21 ......53 J7
Brackenwood Cl ILK LS29 ......24 D5
  RHAY LS8 ......83 K5
Brackenwood Ct WKFDE WF1 ......164 E3
Brackenwood Dr RHAY LS8 ......83 K4
Brackenwood Gn RHAY LS8 ......83 K4
Brackenwood Rd WKFDE WF1 ......164 E3
Bradbeck Rd GTHN BD7 ......4 B6
Bradburn Rd EARD/LOFT WF3 ......144 B4
Bradbury St DEWS WF13 ......180 B4
Bradd Cl LVSG * WF15 ......159 J3
Bradfield Cl HUDN HD2 ......177 K4
Bradford & Wakefield Rd
  BOW BD4 ......119 K7
Bradford La BFDE BD3 ......7 J6
Bradford Old Rd BGLY BD16 ......76 A5
  HIPP HX3 ......135 F4
Bradford Rd BGLY BD16 ......75 K3
  BIRK/DRI BD11 ......139 H3
  BIRK/DRI BD11 ......140 E2
  BRIG HD6 ......157 G4
  BTLY WF17 ......140 A6
  CLAY BD14 ......116 C1
  CLECK BD19 ......138 C4
  DEWS WF13 ......161 F6
  EARD/LOFT WF3 ......142 D6
  EARD/LOFT WF3 ......163 H1
  GSLY LS20 ......58 D2
  HIPP HX3 ......135 J6
  HUDN HD2 ......177 G5
  IDLE BD10 ......78 B7
  ILK LS29 ......38 G3
  KGHY BD21 ......3 J4
  OT LS21 ......38 D4
  PDSY/CALV LS28 ......99 G4
  SHPY BD18 ......77 F4
  WKFDE WF1 ......163 K4
Bradfords Cl MSTN/BAR LS15 ......48 B7
Bradford St DEWS WF13 ......161 G7
  KGHY BD21 ......3 J6
Bradlaugh Rd WBSY BD6 ......117 C5
Bradlaugh Ter WBSY BD6 ......117 H5
Bradley Av AIRE BD20 ......20 E7
  CAS WF10 ......148 B7
Bradley Bvd HUDN HD2 ......177 H6
Bradley Dr AIRE BD20 ......20 E7
Bradley Grange Gdns
  HUDN HD2 ......178 A3
Bradley La GTL/HWG HX4 ......174 C3
  PDSY/CALV LS28 ......99 J6
Bradley Quarry Cl HUDN * HD2 ......178 B3
Bradley Ri AIRE BD20 ......20 E7
  HUDN HD2 ......177 H4
Bradley Vw GTL/HWG HX4 ......174 E5
Bradshaw La CUL/QBY BD13 ......115 F5
Bradshaw Vw CUL/QBY BD13 ......115 F5
Bradstock Gdns MOR LS27 ......141 K1
Brae Av ECHL BD2 ......98 A2
Braemar Dr GFTH/SHER LS25 ......108 A5
Braine Rd WBY LS22 ......29 J3
Braithwaite Av HWTH BD22 ......53 F4
Braithwaite Crs HWTH BD22 ......2 B4
Braithwaite Dr HWTH BD22 ......2 A4
Braithwaite Edge Rd
  HWTH BD22 ......52 E3
Braithwaite Gv HWTH BD22 ......2 A4
Braithwaite Rd HWTH BD22 ......52 E4
Braithwaite Rw MID * LS10 ......123 K4
Braithwaite St BEE/HOL LS11 ......13 H4
Braithwaite Wk HWTH BD22 ......2 A4
Braithwaite Wy HWTH BD22 ......2 A4
Bramble Av BSPA/BRAM LS23 ......48 A3
Bramble Cl CLAY BD14 ......116 A3
  PONT WF8 ......189 G3
Bramble Ct HWTH BD22 ......72 E6
The Brambles ILK LS29 ......23 J5
Bramble Wk BTLY WF17 ......140 C6
Brambling Dr CUL/QBY BD13 ......116 B4
Brambling Ms MOR LS27 ......142 B3
Bramham Dr BAIL BD17 ......57 J7
Bramham La BSPA/BRAM LS23 ......46 D6
  BSPA/BRAM LS23 ......46 E7
Bramham Park Ct
  EARD/LOFT WF3 ......143 J4
Bramham Rd BGLY BD16 ......55 K7
  BSPA/BRAM LS23 ......48 C5
  CAS WF10 ......167 K2
  SCFT LS14 ......66 E5
Bramhope Old La OT LS21 ......40 B6

Bramhope Rd CLECK BD19 ......138 D7
Bramleigh Dr MOR LS27 ......141 K1
Bramleigh Gv MOR LS27 ......141 K1
Bramley Cl HWTH BD22 ......72 C1
Bramley Crs WKFDE WF1 ......164 C6
Bramley Fold HIPP HX3 ......136 C7
Bramley La HWTH BD22 ......136 C7
Bramley St BRAM LS13 ......101 F4
  WBOW BD5 ......117 K2
Bramley Vw HIPP HX3 ......136 D7
Bramstan Av BRAM LS13 ......100 D2
Bramstan Cl BRAM LS13 ......100 D2
Bramstan Gdns BRAM LS13 ......100 D2
Bramston Gdns BRIG HD6 ......177 F1
Bramston St BRIG HD6 ......157 F7
Brancepeth Pl WOR/ARM LS12 ......12 F1
Branch Cl WOR/ARM LS12 ......121 K2
Branch End MOR LS27 ......121 G7
Branch Pl WOR/ARM LS12 ......121 K2
Branch Rd BTLY WF17 ......161 F3
  CLECK BD19 ......138 A6
  DEWS WF13 ......181 F1
  GTL/HWG HX4 ......174 B3
  HUDW HD3 ......175 K5
  WOR/ARM LS12 ......8 A9
  WOR/ARM LS12 ......121 K2
Branch St WOR/ARM LS12 ......121 K2
Brander Ap OSM LS9 ......104 D4
Brander Cl OSM LS9 ......104 E4
Brander Dr OSM LS9 ......104 D4
Brander Gv OSM LS9 ......104 D4
Brander Rd OSM LS9 ......104 D4
Brander St OSM LS9 ......104 E3
Brandfort St GTHN BD7 ......4 D9
Brandon Ct AL/HA/HU LS17 ......64 C6
Brandon Crs AL/HA/HU LS17 ......65 F4
  AL/HA/HU LS17 ......65 G5
Brandon La AL/HA/HU LS17 ......64 C6
  AL/HA/HU LS17 ......65 G4
Brandon Rd BVRD LS3 ......9 J7
Brandon St WOR/ARM LS12 ......13 G1
Brandon Wy CHAL LS7 ......83 J7
Brandy Carr Rd
  WKFDW/WTN WF2 ......163 G6
Branksome Ct HTON * BD9 ......96 E3
Branksome Crs HTON BD9 ......96 E3
Branksome Dr SHPY BD18 ......76 C4
Branksome Gv BGLY BD16 ......76 B4
Branksome Pl HDGY LS6 ......8 F5
Branksome St HDGY LS6 ......8 F5
Branksome Ter HDGY LS6 ......8 F5
Bransby Cl PDSY/CALV LS28 ......100 B3
Bransby Ct PDSY/CALV LS28 ......100 B3
Bransby Ri PDSY/CALV LS28 ......100 B3
Bransdale Cl BAIL BD17 ......77 J2
  NORM WF6 ......166 D4
Bransdale Cl BAIL BD17 ......77 J2
  GSLY LS20 ......59 F3
  NORM WF6 ......166 D4
Bransdale Clough WBSY BD6 ......116 D5
Bransdale Garth GSLY LS20 ......59 F3
Bransdale Ms NORM WF6 ......166 D4
Bransdale Wk NORM WF6 ......166 D4
Branshaw Dr HWTH BD22 ......53 F6
Branshaw Gv HWTH BD22 ......53 F6
Branshaw Mt HWTH BD22 ......53 F6
Branstone Gv OSS WF5 ......162 C7
Bran St HWTH BD22 ......53 H7
Brant Av LUD/ILL HX2 ......134 C3
Brant Bank La ILK LS29 ......23 F3
Brantcliffe Dr BAIL BD17 ......57 G7
Brantdale Cl HTON BD9 ......96 B1
Brantdale Rd HTON BD9 ......96 B1
Brantford St CHAL LS7 ......83 J6
Brant La TAD LS24 ......70 B4
Brantwood Av HTON BD9 ......96 B1
Brantwood Cl HTON BD9 ......96 B1
Brantwood Crs HTON BD9 ......96 A1
Brantwood Dr HTON BD9 ......96 B1
Brantwood Gv HTON BD9 ......96 A1
Brantwood Ov HTON BD9 ......96 A1
Brantwood Rd HTON BD9 ......96 B1
Brantwood Vls HTON BD9 ......96 B1
Branwell Av BTLY WF17 ......140 B4
Branwell Ct HTON BD9 ......96 B1
Branwell Dr HWTH BD22 ......72 D4
Brassey Rd BOW BD4 ......118 B2
Brassey St HFAX HX1 ......16 F8
Brassey Ter BOW BD4 ......118 B2
Brathay Gdns SCFT LS14 ......105 H2
Braybrook Ct GIR BD8 ......97 H2
Bray Cl WBSY * BD6 ......116 C4
Brayshaw Dr GTHN BD7 ......116 C4
Brayshaw Rd EARD/LOFT WF3 ......163 H1
Brayside Av HUDN HD2 ......176 E7
Brayton Ap SCFT LS14 ......85 K7
Brayton Cl SCFT LS14 ......85 K7
Brayton Gn SCFT LS14 ......86 A7
Brayton Gv SCFT LS14 ......85 K7
Brayton Wk SCFT LS14 ......85 K7
Brazil St CAS WF10 ......148 D7
Bread St WKFDE WF1 ......18 E4
Breakmoor Av AIRE BD20 ......21 F7
Break Neck HIPP HX3 ......135 K7
Breaks Rd LM/WK BD12 ......137 J1
Brearcliffe Cl WBSY BD6 ......117 F6
Brearcliffe Dr WBSY BD6 ......117 F6
Brearcliffe Gv WBSY BD6 ......117 F6
Brearcliffe Rd WBSY BD6 ......117 G7
Brearcliffe St WBSY BD6 ......117 F6
Brearley Gdns LVSG WF15 ......159 H5
Brearley La LUD/ILL HX2 ......132 C3
Brearley St BTLY WF17 ......160 E4
Brearton St BFD BD1 ......5 L3
Breary Av HORS LS18 ......81 J3
Breary Ct BHP/TINH LS16 ......41 H7
Breary La BHP/TINH LS16 ......41 H7
Breary La East BHP/TINH LS16 ......41 J7
Breary Ri BHP/TINH LS16 ......61 H1
Breary Ter HORS LS18 ......81 J3
Breary Wk HORS LS18 ......81 J3
Breck Lea RPDN/SBR HX6 ......153 H6
Brecks Gdns GFTH/SHER LS25 ......127 J3
Brecks La GFTH/SHER LS25 ......127 J3
  RTHW LS26 ......127 F2
Brecks Rd CLAY BD14 ......116 C1
Breck Willows RPDN/SBR HX6 ......153 G6

Brecon Ap OSM LS9 ......104 E3
Brecon Cl IDLE BD10 ......78 C5
Bredon Av SHPY BD18 ......78 A5
Breighton Adown WBSY BD6 ......116 C6
Bremner St OT LS21 ......39 J2
Brendon Ct BOW BD4 ......118 E3
  MIRF WF14 ......179 G7
Brendon Wk BOW * BD4 ......118 E4
Brentford Gv WOR/ARM * LS12 ......12 B1
Brentford Rd LM/WK * BD12 ......137 H1
  WBSY BD6 ......117 H7
Brentlea Av WKFDW/WTN WF2 ......184 C6
Brentwood Cl BTLY WF17 ......161 H3
Brentwood Gdns WBSY BD6 ......117 H6
Brentwood Gv WOR/ARM * LS12 ......12 B1
Brentwood St WOR/ARM * LS12 ......12 B1
Brentwood Ter
  WOR/ARM * LS12 ......12 B1
Bretfield Ct EARL WF12 ......181 G4
Brett Gdns BEE/HOL LS11 ......13 L8
Bretton Cl WBSY * BD6 ......116 E6
Bretton St EARL WF12 ......181 G4
Brewerton La DEWS WF13 ......160 C6
Brewery Ct HUDW HD3 ......175 K7
Brewery La CUL/QBY BD13 ......115 F7
  CUL/QBY BD13 ......115 G3
  EARL WF12 ......181 F5
Brewery Rd HWTH BD22 ......73 H1
  ILK LS29 ......24 B5
Brewery St HECK WF16 ......160 A5
  HIPP HX3 ......135 F5
  KGHY BD21 ......3 K4
Brewery Whf MIRF WF14 ......179 H5
Brexdale Av GFTH/SHER LS25 ......127 J3
Brian Crs MSTN/BAR LS15 ......105 J3
Brian Pl MSTN/BAR LS15 ......105 J2
Brian Royd La GTL/HWG HX4 ......174 C2
Brian Vw MSTN/BAR LS15 ......105 J2
Briar Cl ELL HX5 ......175 H4
  HECK WF16 ......160 A3
  PDSY/CALV LS28 ......100 A3
Briardale Rd HTON BD9 ......96 A1
Briardene RTHW * LS26 ......145 K2
Briar Dr HORS LS18 ......81 J3
Briarfield Av IDLE BD10 ......78 B5
Briarfield Cl IDLE BD10 ......78 B5
  ILK LS29 ......24 C5
Briarfield Gdns SHPY BD18 ......77 G6
Briarfield Gv IDLE BD10 ......78 B5
Briarfield Rd SHPY BD18 ......77 H6
Briar Ga WBY LS22 ......29 H5
Briar Gv WKFDE WF1 ......185 F6
Briarlea Cl YEA LS19 ......59 G5
Briarlyn Av HUDW HD3 ......175 K7
Briarlyn Rd HUDW HD3 ......175 K7
Briarmains Rd BTLY WF17 ......140 C5
Briar Rhydding BAIL BD17 ......77 K2
Briarsdale Ct RHAY * LS8 ......104 C2
Briarsdale Garth RHAY LS8 ......11 M3
Briarsdale Hts OSM * LS9 ......104 C2
Briarsdale Ms NORM LS9 ......11 M3
Briar Wd SHPY BD18 ......77 K5
Briarwood Av KGHY BD21 ......54 C2
Briarwood Cl WKFDE WF1 ......164 E3
Briarwood Crs WBSY BD6 ......117 G5
Briarwood Dr WBSY BD6 ......117 G5
Briarwood Gv WBSY BD6 ......117 G4
Briary Cl WKFDE WF1 ......185 G6
Brick & Tile Ter BRIG HD6 ......157 F7
Brickfield Gv LUD/ILL HX2 ......134 D2
Brickfield La LUD/ILL HX2 ......134 D2
Brickfield Ter LUD/ILL HX2 ......134 D2
Brick Mill Rd PDSY/CALV LS28 ......100 B7
Brick Rw LM/WK BD12 ......137 H4
Brick St CLECK BD19 ......158 D1
  OSM LS9 ......14 D1
  WKFDW/WTN WF2 ......183 J2
Brick Ter BRIG HD6 ......157 G7
Brickyard MIRF WF14 ......179 G4
Bridge Cl BSPA/BRAM LS23 ......48 C2
Bridge Ct MOR LS27 ......142 A7
Bridge End BRIG HD6 ......157 F7
  LDS LS1 ......14 B2
Bridge Fold KSTL LS5 ......101 K1
Bridge Foot BSPA/BRAM LS23 ......48 C4
Bridge Garth BSPA/BRAM LS23 ......48 C4
  GFTH/SHER LS25 ......131 G2
Bridgegate Wy IDLE BD10 ......78 E6
Bridgehouse La HWTH BD22 ......72 D2
Bridge La HIPP HX3 ......116 A7
  ILK LS29 ......23 K4
  KNOT WF11 ......171 G3
Bridge Rd BEE/HOL LS11 ......13 J4
  BRAM LS13 ......80 B7
  BRIG HD6 ......157 F5
  BSPA/BRAM LS23 ......48 D2
  HUDN HD2 ......178 C4
  KSTL LS5 ......101 J1
Bridge St AIRE BD20 ......21 F7
  BFD BD1 ......5 L6
  BTLY WF17 ......140 B7
  BTLY WF17 ......161 G3
  CAS WF10 ......148 D7
  HECK WF16 ......159 K4
  HWTH BD22 ......72 C2
  KGHY BD21 ......2 F5
  LDSU LS2 ......10 C8
  MOR LS27 ......142 A5
  NORM WF6 ......167 F6
  OT LS21 ......39 H2
  PONT * WF8 ......189 J1
  TAD LS24 ......50 E7
  WKFDE WF1 ......19 H8
Bridge Vw BRAM LS13 ......80 B7
Bridge View Cl HORS LS18 ......81 G2
Bridgewater HDGY LS6 ......82 D6
Bridgewater Rd OSM LS9 ......14 F5
Bridgeway BOW BD4 ......118 D4
Bridgland Av ILK LS29 ......38 G5
Bridgwater Rd HTON BD9 ......97 F3
Bridle Av OSS WF5 ......182 K1
Bridle Dene HIPP HX3 ......136 B2
Bridle La HORS LS18 ......182 K1
Bridle Pth MSTN/BAR LS15 ......105 H3
Bridle Path Rd AL/HA/HU LS17 ......64 C6
Bridle Path Wk
  MSTN/BAR LS15 ......105 H3

Bridle Pl *OSS* WF5 ....182 C1
Bridle Stile *HIPP* HX3 ....136 B2
Bridle Stile La *CUL/QBY* BD13 .....115 H4
Bierdene *AIRE* BD20 ....21 F7
Brierfield Gdns *MOR* LS27 ....141 F1
Brier Hey Cl *HBR* HX7 ....132 A6
Brier Hey La *HBR* HX7 ....132 A6
Brier Hill Cl *CLECK* BD19 ....158 B2
Brier Hill Vw *HUDN* HD2 ....177 J4
Brierlands Cl *GFTH/SHER* LS25 ....108 A5
Brierlands Fold
  GFTH/SHER LS25 ....108 A5
Brierlands La *GFTH/SHER* LS25 ....108 A5
Brier La *ELL* HX5 ....156 C6
Brierley Cl *SHPY* BD18 ....77 H6
Brier St *HIPP* HX3 ....134 E5
  KGHY BD21 ....53 J7
Briery Cl *ILK* LS29 ....23 H5
Briery Fld *SHPY* BD18 ....77 G7
Briery Gv *MIRF* WF14 ....179 H6
Briggate *AIRE* BD20 ....21 F7
  BAIL BD17 ....77 G4
  BRIG HD6 ....157 F6
  ELL HX5 ....175 J2
  LDS LS1 ....14 A1
Brigg Gdns *HWTH* BD22 ....2 B4
Briggland Ct *WIL/AL* BD15 ....75 F7
Brigglands *WIL/AL* BD15 ....75 F7
Brigg's Av *CAS* WF10 ....168 C2
  WBSY BD6 ....117 F5
Briggs Gv *WBSY* BD6 ....117 F5
Briggs Pl *WBSY* BD6 ....117 F5
Briggs Rw *FEA/AMT* WF7 ....188 C5
Briggs St *CUL/QBY* BD13 ....115 H5
Briggs Yd *OSS* WF5 * 182 B4
Brighouse & Denholme Gate Rd
  HIPP HX3 ....135 K1
Brighouse & Denholme Rd
  CUL/QBY BD13 ....114 D2
Brighouse Rd *CUL/QBY* BD13 ....94 B7
  CUL/QBY BD13 ....115 H5
  HIPP HX3 ....156 B1
  HUDW HD3 ....176 A6
  LM/WK BD12 ....137 J2
Brighouse Wood La *BRIG* HD6 ....156 E5
Brighouse Wood Rw *BRIG* HD6 ...156 E5
Brighton Av *MOR* LS27 ....141 J2
Brighton Cliff *BRAM* LS13 ....101 F3
Brighton Cl *BTLY* WF17 ....160 B2
Brighton Gv *BRAM* LS13 ....101 G4
  HFAX HX1 ....16 C4
Brighton Rd *ILK* LS29 ....24 D6
Brighton St *BAIL* BD17 ....77 G4
  HECK WF16 ....160 A3
  HIPP HX3 ....16 D1
  IDLE BD10 ....78 B3
  WKFDW/WTN WF2 ....18 B7
Brighton Ter *CLECK* BD19 ....138 A7
Bright St *CLAY* BD14 ....116 A2
  CUL/QBY BD13 ....115 J5
  DEWS * WF13 ....161 F7
  EARD/LOFT WF3 ....143 J7
  MIRF WF14 ....179 G1
  MOR LS27 ....141 K3
  PDSY/CALV LS28 ....100 C3
  RPDN/SBR HX6 ....153 J3
  WIL/AL BD15 ....96 A4
Brignall Cft *OSM* LS9 ....11 H7
Brignall Garth *OSM* LS9 ....11 H7
Brignall Wy *OSM* LS9 ....11 H7
Brigshaw Dr *CAS* WF10 ....127 J7
Brigshaw La *CAS* WF10 ....127 K7
Brindle Park Dr *CAS* WF10 ....169 F2
Brindley Gv *GIR* BD8 ....96 B6
Brindley Rd *AIRE* BD20 ....33 G2
Brindley Wy
  WKFDW/WTN WF2 ....164 A4
Brisbane Av *ECHL* BD2 ....97 K2
Briscoe La *GTL/HWG* HX4 ....174 E2
Bristol Av *AIRE* BD20 ....54 E3
Bristol St *CHAL* LS7 ....10 D5
  HIPP HX3 ....155 G5
Britannia Cl *PDSY/CALV* LS28 ....100 C1
Britannia Ct *BRAM* LS13 ....100 D5
Britannia Rd *MOR* LS27 ....141 J5
Britannia St *BGLY* BD16 ....75 K1
  LDS LS1 ....13 L1
  PDSY/CALV LS28 ....100 C3
  WBOW BD5 ....6 A8
Britannia Ter *CLECK* BD19 ....138 E7
Broadacre Rd *OSS* WF5 ....182 D4
Broad Carr La *GTL/HWG* HX4 ....175 F5
Broadcroft Cha
  EARD/LOFT WF3 ....142 D7
Broadcroft Dr
  EARD/LOFT WF3 ....142 D7
Broadcroft Gv
  EARD/LOFT WF3 ....142 D7
Broadcroft Wy
  EARD/LOFT WF3 ....142 D7
Broadfield Cl *BOW* BD4 ....119 F5
Broadfield Wy *ILK* LS29 ....22 A1
Broadfolds *CLAY* BD14 ....116 B2
Broadgate *GTL/HWG* HX4 ....174 C7
  OSS WF5 ....182 D4
Broadgate Av *HORS* LS18 ....81 J3
Broadgate Crs *HORS* LS18 ....81 F4
Broadgate Dr *HORS* LS18 ....81 F3
Broadgate La *HORS* LS18 ....81 F3
Broadgate Ri *HORS* LS18 ....81 G4
Broadgate Wk *HORS* LS18 ....81 F4
Broad Ings Wy *HIPP* HX3 ....136 B3
Broadlands *KGHY* BD21 ....2 C2
Broadlands St *BOW* BD4 ....118 E2
Broadland Wy
  EARD/LOFT WF3 ....144 D7
Broad La *BOW* BD4 ....118 E1
  LUD/ILL HX2 ....152 D3
  PDSY/CALV LS28 ....100 C3
Broad Lane Cl *BRAM* LS13 ....101 H1
Broadlea Av *BRAM* LS13 ....101 H1
Broadlea Crs *BRAM* LS13 ....101 H1
Broadlea Gdns *BRAM* LS13 ....101 H1
Broadlea Hl *BRAM* LS13 ....101 H1

Broadlea Mt *BRAM* LS13 ....101 J2
Broadlea Pl *BRAM* LS13 ....101 H2
Broadlea Rd *BRAM* LS13 ....101 H1
Broadlea St *BRAM* LS13 ....101 H1
Broadlea Ter *BRAM* LS13 ....101 H1
Broadlea Vw *BRAM* LS13 ....101 G1
Bradley Av *LUD/ILL* HX2 ....133 K6
Bradley Cl *LUD/ILL* HX2 ....133 K6
Bradley Gv *LUD/ILL* HX2 ....133 K6
Bradley Rd *LUD/ILL* HX2 ....133 J6
Broadmead *CAS* WF10 ....148 E7
Broad Oak La *HIPP* HX3 ....156 C2
Broadoaks Cl *EARL* WF12 ....181 K2
Broad Oak St *HIPP* HX3 ....156 C2
Broadowler La *OSS* WF5 ....182 D4
Broadstones Pk *BGLY* * BD16 ....76 C1
Broadstone Rd *BOW* BD4 ....119 F2
Broad St *BFD* BD1 ....5 M5
  DEWS WF13 ....180 D3
  HFAX HX1 ....17 H5
  PDSY/CALV LS28 ....99 K2
Broad Tree Rd *HIPP* HX3 ....134 D5
Broad Vw *OSS* WF5 ....182 E4
Broadway *BFD* BD7 ....5 M6
  BGLY BD16 ....75 K1
  GSLY LS20 ....58 D3
  HIPP HX3 ....155 H3
  HORS LS18 ....80 C5
  KSTL LS5 ....81 H5
  MSTN/BAR LS15 ....105 G7
  PONT WF8 ....189 K2
  RPDN/SBR HX6 ....152 E5
  WKFDW/WTN WF2 ....183 H4
Broadway Av *WBOW* BD5 ....117 J4
Broadway Cl *WBOW* BD5 ....117 J4
Broadway Dr *HORS* LS18 ....80 E4
Broadwell Rd *OSS* WF5 ....182 E4
Broadwood Av *LUD/ILL* HX2 ....133 K6
Brockadale Av *PONT* WF8 ....189 J4
Brocklesby Dr *WIL/AL* BD15 ....96 A4
Brockley Cl *TAD* LS24 ....91 K6
Brocks *LUD/ILL* HX2 ....152 D2
Brockstones *GTL/HWG* * HX4 ....174 C2
Brockwell Gdns
  RPDN/SBR HX6 ....153 H5
Brock Well La *RPDN/SBR* HX6 ......153 G6
Brodley Cl *HIPP* HX3 ....136 B7
Brodrick Ct *HDGY* LS6 ....82 C7
Broken Wy *WBOW* * BD5 ....117 J4
Bromet Pl *ECHL* BD2 ....98 C1
Bromford Rd *BOW* BD4 ....118 B2
Bromley Av *BGLY* BD16 ....55 J7
Bromley Mt *WKFDE* WF1 ....19 H9
Bromley Rd *BGLY* BD16 ....55 J7
  SHPY BD18 ....76 D4
Bromley St *BTLY* WF17 ....161 G5
Brompton Av *BOW* BD4 ....118 B3
Brompton Gv *BEE/HOL* LS11 ....123 G4
Brompton Mt *BEE/HOL* LS11 ....123 G4
Brompton Rd *BOW* BD4 ....118 B2
Brompton Rw *BEE/HOL* * LS11 .....123 G4
Brompton Ter *BEE/HOL* LS11 ....123 G4
Brompton Vw *BEE/HOL* LS11 ....123 G4
Bronshill Gv *WIL/AL* BD15 ....96 B4
Bronte Av *KNOT* WF11 ....170 C4
Bronte Cl *CLECK* BD19 ....139 J6
  DEWS WF13 ....160 C6
  HTON BD9 ....96 D3
Bronte Ct *PONT* WF8 ....169 J6
Bronte Dr *HWTH* BD22 ....73 F1
Bronte Gv *MIRF* WF14 ....179 K5
Bronte Old Rd *CUL/QBY* BD13 ....95 H7
Bronte Ri *CAS* WF10 ....169 J3
Bronte Rd *BTLY* WF17 ....140 B5
Bronte St *HWTH* BD22 ....72 C5
  KGHY BD21 ....3 K3
Bronte Vls *HWTH* BD22 ....73 F1
Bronte Wy *BRIG* HD6 ....137 G7
  BRIG HD6 ....157 J4
  CUL/QBY BD13 ....95 J7
  CUL/QBY BD13 ....116 A5
  HWTH BD22 ....72 A7
  MIRF WF14 ....179 K5
Brook Cl *OSS* WF5 ....182 E6
Brookdale Av *OSS* WF5 ....162 B4
Brook Dr *GTL/HWG* HX4 ....175 F5
Brooke St *PONT* WF8 ....189 H4
Brooke St *BRIG* HD6 ....157 F7
  CLECK BD19 ....159 F1
  HECK * WF16 ....160 A5
Brookeville Av *HIPP* HX3 ....156 B1
Brook Fld *MIRF* WF14 ....179 J7
Brookfield Av *BRAM* LS13..............80 A6
  CAS WF10 ....168 E1
  CLECK BD19 ....138 E6
  RHAY LS8 ....104 A1
  SHPY BD18 ....77 J4
Brookfields Av *CLECK* BD19 ....137 K7
Brookfields Rd *LM/WK* BD12 ....137 J6
Brookfield St *MID* LS10 ....14 D5
Brookfield Ter *CLECK* BD19 ....138 E6
  MID * LS10 ....14 D5
Brookfield Vw *CLECK* BD19 ....139 F6
Brookfoot Av *BIRK/DRI* BD11 ......139 H2
Brookfoot La *HIPP* HX3 ....156 D5
Brook Grain Hl *BRIG* HD6 ....177 F1
Brookhill Av *AL/HA/HU* LS17 ....63 K7
Brookhill Cl *AL/HA/HU* LS17 ....63 K7
Brookhill Crs *AL/HA/HU* LS17 ....63 K7
Brookhill Dr *AL/HA/HU* LS17 ....63 K7
Brookhill Gv *AL/HA/HU* LS17 ....63 K7
Brookhouse Gdns *IDLE* BD10 ....79 G4
Brooklands *HUDN* HD2 ....178 A4
Brooklands Av *GTL/HWG* HX4 ....174 E5
  SCFT LS14 ....105 G1
Brooklands Cl *SCFT* LS14 ....105 F1
Brooklands Ct *OSS* WF5 ....182 E5
  SCFT LS14 ....105 G1
Brooklands Crs *SCFT* LS14 ....105 F1
  YEA LS19 ....59 J5

Brooklands Dr *SCFT* LS14 ....105 F1
  YEA LS19 ....59 J5
Brooklands Garth *SCFT* LS14 ....105 F1
Brooklands La *ILK* LS29 ....38 B5
  SCFT LS14 ....105 G1
Brooklands Vw *SCFT* LS14 ....105 G1
Brooklands Wk *ILK* LS29 ....38 C5
Brooklands Wy *ILK* LS29 ....38 B5
Brook La *LVSG* WF15 ....158 D4
Brooklyn Av *WOR/ARM* LS12 ....12 B1
Brooklyn Ct *CLECK* BD19 ....138 E7
Brooklyn Dr *CLECK* BD19 ....138 E7
Brooklyn Pl *WOR/ARM* LS12 ....12 B1
Brooklyn Rd *CLECK* BD19 ....139 F7
Brooklyn St *AIRE* BD20 ....33 H7
  WOR/ARM LS12 ....12 B1
Brooklyn Ter *BRIG* HD6 ....156 D3
  WOR/ARM LS12 ....12 B1
Brook Rd *BEE/HOL* LS11 ....180 C2
Brook Rw *GTL/HWG* * HX4 ....174 C2
Brookroyd Av *BRIG* HD6 ....157 G2
Brookroyd Gdns *BTLY* WF17 ....140 C7
Brookroyd La *BTLY* WF17 ....140 C7
Brooksbank *WKFDW/WTN* WF2 .....18 C5
Brooksbank Av *GTHN* BD7 ....116 D1
Brooksbank Dr
  MSTN/BAR LS15 ....105 H5
Brooksbank Gdns *ELL* HX5 ....175 J2
Brookside *AL/HA/HU* LS17 ....63 K6
  WBY LS22 ....46 E2
Brookside Fold *HWTH* BD22 ....92 D3
Brooks Ter *CUL/QBY* BD13 ....116 A4
Brook St *CAS* WF10 ....149 H4
  DEWS WF13 ....180 C1
  ELL HX5 ....175 K3
  ILK LS29 ....24 A5
  KGHY BD21 ....2 F8
  LM/WK BD12 ....138 C3
  NORM WF6 ....166 C5
  OSS WF5 ....182 C4
  WKFDE WF1 ....18 F5
Brooks Yd *DEWS* WF13 ....180 C2
  HUDN HD2 ....178 B3
Brookway *FEA/AMT* * WF7 ....188 C4
Broombank *HUDN* HD2 ....176 C7
Broom Crs *MID* LS10 ....123 K7
Broomcroft Av *CLAY* BD14 ....116 A2
Broomcroft Rd *OSS* WF5 ....182 C5
Broom Cross *MID* LS10 ....123 K7
Broome Av *ECHL* BD2 ....97 K2
Broome Cl *NORM* WF6 ....166 D4
Broomer St *DEWS* WF13 ....180 B3
Broomfield *BHP/TINH* LS16 ....62 A7
  CLAY BD14 ....115 K3
  GTL/HWG HX4 ....175 G3
Broomfield Av *HIPP* HX3 ....154 E7
Broomfield Crs *HDGY* LS6 ....8 D1
Broomfield Pl *CLAY* BD14 ....115 K3
  HDGY LS6 ....8 D2
  KGHY BD21 ....2 F4
Broomfield Rd *HDGY* LS6 ....8 D1
  HUDN HD2 ....177 F4
  KGHY BD21 ....2 F4
Broomfield St *CUL/QBY* BD13 ....115 H5
  HDGY LS6 ....8 D2
  KGHY BD21 ....2 F4
Broomfield Ter *CLECK* BD19 ....158 C2
  HDGY LS6 ....8 D2
Broomfield Vw *HDGY* LS6 ....8 D2
Broom Gdns *MID* LS10 ....123 K7
Broom Garth *MID* LS10 ....124 A7
Broom Gv *MID* LS10 ....144 A1
Broom Hall Av *WKFDE* WF1 ....164 B6
Broom Hall Crs *WKFDE* WF1 ....164 B6
Broomhill Cl *CAS* WF10 ....169 F2
Broomhill Av *AL/HA/HU* LS17 ....83 J2
  KGHY BD21 ....2 C8
  KNOT WF11 ....171 J5
Broomhill Cl *KNOT* WF11 ....171 J5
Broomhill Crs *AL/HA/HU* LS17 ....83 J2
  KNOT WF11 ....171 J5
Broomhill Dr *AL/HA/HU* LS17 ....83 H3
  KGHY BD21 ....2 D9
  KNOT WF11 ....171 J5
Broomhill Gv *KGHY* BD21 ....2 D9
  KNOT WF11 ....171 J5
Broomhill Mt *KGHY* BD21 ....2 D9
Broomhill Pl *KNOT* WF11 ....171 J5
Broomhill Sq *KNOT* WF11 ....171 J5
Broomhill St *KGHY* * BD21 ....53 H7
Broomhill Wk *KGHY* BD21 ....2 D9
  KNOT WF11 ....171 J5
Broomhill Wy *KGHY* BD21 ....2 D9
Broom Nook *MID* LS10 ....124 A7
Broom Pl *MID* LS10 ....123 K7
Broom Rd *MID* LS10 ....123 K7
  TAD LS24 ....70 C1
Broomsdale Rd *BTLY* WF17 ....161 H5
Broom St *BOW* BD4 ....6 A8
  CLECK BD19 ....158 C2
  KGHY BD21 ....3 H7
Broom Ter *MID* LS10 ....124 A7
Broom Vw *MID* LS10 ....124 A7
Broster Av *HWTH* BD22 ....2 B4
Brotherton Av *WKFDE* WF1 ....19 J5
Brougham Rd *HIPP* HX3 ....16 F1
Brougham St *HIPP* HX3 ....17 G1
Broughton Av *BOW* BD4 ....118 C5
  OSM LS9 ....11 K4
Broughton Ter *OSM* LS9 ....11 K4
  PDSY/CALV LS28 ....100 B5
Brow Bottom La *LUD/ILL* HX2 ......133 J1
Browcliff *AIRE* BD20 ....21 F7
Browfield Vw *HWTH* BD22 ....53 F6
Browfoot *SHPY* BD18 ....77 J5
Browfoot Dr *LUD/ILL* HX2 ....154 A1
Brow Foot Gate La
  LUD/ILL HX2 ....154 A2
Browgate *BAIL* BD17 ....77 H1
Brow La *CLAY* BD14 ....115 K3
  HIPP HX3 ....135 H4
  HIPP HX3 ....136 C1
  LUD/ILL HX2 ....134 D1
Brown Av *BEE/HOL* LS11 ....12 F1
Brown Bank La *AIRE* BD20 ....21 G6
Brownberrie Av *HORS* LS18 ....81 F1
Brownberrie Crs *HORS* LS18 ....80 E1
Brownberrie Dr *HORS* LS18 ....81 F1

Brownberrie Gdns *HORS* LS18 ....80 E1
Brownberrie La *HORS* LS18 ....80 D1
Brownberrie Wk *HORS* LS18 ....81 F1
Brown Hill Av *OSM* LS9 ....11 K5
Brown Hill Cl *BIRK/DRI* BD11 ....119 H7
Brownhill Cl *BTLY* WF17 ....140 C6
Brown Hill Crs *OSM* LS9 ....11 K5
Brown Hill Dr *BIRK/DRI* BD11 ....139 H1
Brownhill Garth *BTLY* WF17 ....140 C6
Brownhill Rd *BTLY* WF17 ....140 C6
Brown Hill Ter *OSM* LS9 ....11 K5
Browning Av *HIPP* * HX3 ....155 G5
Browning Rd *HUDN* HD2 ....177 J6
Browning St *BFDE* BD3 ....6 E6
Brown La East *BEE/HOL* LS11 ....13 G6
Brown La West *WOR/ARM* LS12 ....12 E6
Brown Lee La *WIL/AL* BD15 ....94 D1
Brown Pl *BEE/HOL* LS11 ....12 F7
Brown Rd *BEE/HOL* LS11 ....12 F7
Brown Royd Av *GIR* BD8 ....96 D5
Brownroyd Hill Rd *WBSY* BD6 ....117 G5
Brownroyd St *GTHN* BD7 ....4 E7
Brownroyd Wk *WBSY* BD6 ....117 G4
Brown's Pl *BTLY* WF17 ....160 E4
Brown's St *BTLY* * WF17 ....160 E4
Brown St *KGHY* BD21 ....3 J3
  MIRF WF14 ....179 G4
Brow Rd *HWTH* BD22 ....72 D6
Browsfield Rd *ILK* LS29 ....22 A1
Browsholme St *KGHY* * BD21 ....2 F7
Brow St *KGHY* BD21 ....3 J6
Brow Top Rd *HWTH* BD22 ....73 F5
Brow Wood Crs *ECHL* BD2 ....97 K2
Brow Wood Ri *HIPP* HX3 ....136 C1
Brow Wood Rd *BTLY* WF17 ....140 E6
  HIPP HX3 ....136 C1
Browwood Ter *WBSY* BD6 ....116 E7
Bruce Gdns *WOR/ARM* LS12 ....12 F3
Bruce Lawn *WOR/ARM* LS12 ....12 F3
Bruce St *HFAX* HX1 ....16 B8
Brudenell Cl *HDGY* LS6 ....9 G3
Brudenell Gv *HDGY* LS6 ....9 G3
Brudenell Mt *HDGY* LS6 ....9 F3
Brudenell Rd *HDGY* LS6 ....9 G3
Brudenell St *HDGY* LS6 ....9 G3
Brudenell Vw *HDGY* LS6 ....9 G3
Brunel Cl *HTON* BD9 ....97 F3
Brunel Ct *HIPP* HX3 ....155 J4
Brunel Rd *WKFDW/WTN* WF2 ....164 A3
Brunswick Ct *LDSU* LS2 ....10 C7
Brunswick Dr *DEWS* WF13 ....160 D7
Brunswick Gdns
  GFTH/SHER LS25 ....107 J6
  HFAX HX1 ....16 F6
Brunswick Gv *WKFDE* WF1 ....19 H5
Brunswick Pl *IDLE* BD10 ....78 E5
Brunswick Rd *IDLE* BD10 ....78 E5
  PDSY/CALV LS28 ....100 B5
Brunswick Rw *BGLY* BD16 ....76 A1
  BTLY * WF17 ....161 F3
  CUL/QBY BD13 ....74 B6
  DEWS WF13 ....115 J5
  HECK * WF16 ....160 A5
  MOR LS27 ....141 K2
  WKFDE WF1 ....19 G6
Brunswick St Bungalows
  WKFDE WF1 ....19 H5
Brunswick Ter *LDSU* LS2 ....10 A7
Bruntcliffe Av *MOR* LS27 ....141 H2
Bruntcliffe Cl *MOR* LS27 ....141 J3
Bruntcliffe Dr *MOR* LS27 ....141 J3
Bruntcliffe La *MOR* LS27 ....141 H3
Bruntcliffe Rd *MOR* LS27 ....141 G3
Bruntcliffe Wy *MOR* LS27 ....141 H3
Brunthwaite Br *AIRE* BD20 ....33 H3
Brunthwaite Bridge La
  AIRE BD20 ....33 G2
Brunthwaite La *AIRE* BD20 ....33 H1
Brussels St *OSM* LS9 ....14 D1
Bryan Cl *CAS* WF10 ....147 K7
Bryan Rd *GTL/HWG* HX4 ....175 G3
Bryanstone Rd *BOW* BD4 ....118 E1
Bryan St *BRIG* HD6 ....157 F7
  PDSY/CALV LS28 ....100 A1
Bryan St North
  PDSY/CALV LS28 ....100 A1
Bryer St *DEWS* WF13 ....161 F7
Bryngate *RTHW* LS26 ....145 K1
Bryony Ct *EARD/LOFT* WF3 ....143 K2
Bubwith Gv *LUD/ILL* * HX2 ....154 B2
Buckden Ct *AIRE* BD20 ....21 F7
Buckfast Ct *IDLE* BD10 ....78 C5
Buckingham Av *HDGY* LS6 ....8 F1
Buckingham Crs *CLAY* BD14 ....116 C1
Buckingham Dr *HDGY* LS6 ....8 F1
  WKFDE WF1 ....185 G6
Buckingham Gv *HDGY* LS6 ....8 F1
Buckingham Mt *HDGY* LS6 ....8 F2
Buckingham Pl *HDGY* LS6 ....8 F1
Buckingham Wy *KNOT* WF11 ....170 E7
Buckland Pl *HFAX* HX1 ....154 B2
Buck La *BAIL* BD17 ....78 A1
Buckle La *ILK* LS29 ....38 D6
  NORM WF6 ....166 A4
Buckley La *LUD/ILL* HX2 ....133 K5
Buck Pk *CUL/QBY* BD13 ....93 B3
Buck Mill La *IDLE* BD10 ....78 B1
Buck Stone Av *AL/HA/HU* LS17 ....62 E7
Buck Stone Cl *AL/HA/HU* LS17 ....63 F7
Buck Stone Crs *AL/HA/HU* LS17 .....62 E7
Buckstone Dr *YEA* LS19 ....79 H1
Buck Stone Gdns *AL/HA/HU* LS17 ..62 E7
Buck Stone Garth *AIRE* BD20 ....55 G2
Buck Stone Gn *AL/HA/HU* LS17 ......62 E7
Buck Stone Gv *AL/HA/HU* LS17 ......62 E7
Buck Stone Mt *AL/HA/HU* LS17 ......62 E7
Buck Stone Ov *AL/HA/HU* LS17 ......62 E7
Buck Stone Ri *AL/HA/HU* LS17 ....62 E7
Buck Stone Rd *AL/HA/HU* LS17 ......62 E7
Buck Stone Vw *AL/HA/HU* LS17 ......62 E7
Buck Stone Wy *AL/HA/HU* * LS17 ...62 E7
Buck St *BFDE* BD3 ....6 D4
  CUL/QBY BD13 ....94 B5
Buckthorne Cl
  EARD/LOFT WF3 ....143 J7

Buckthorne Ct
  EARD/LOFT WF3 ....143 J7
Buckthorne Dr
  EARD/LOFT WF3 ....143 J7
Buckthorne Fold
  EARD/LOFT * WF3 ....143 J7
Buckton Cl *BEE/HOL* * LS11 ....13 J8
Buckton Mt *BEE/HOL* LS11 ....13 J8
Buckton Vw *BEE/HOL* LS11 ....13 J8
Bude Rd *BEE/HOL* LS11 ....123 G4
  WBOW BD5 ....118 A5
Bula Cl *GFTH/SHER* LS25 ....128 A4
Bullace Trees La *LVSG* WF15 ....158 E5
Bull Close La *HFAX* HX1 ....16 F7
Buller Cl *OSM* LS9 ....11 M7
Buller Ct *OSM* LS9 ....104 C4
Buller Gv *OSM* LS9 ....11 M6
Buller St *BOW* BD4 ....118 C1
  RTHW LS26 ....145 K1
Bullerthorpe La *RTHW* LS26 ....126 B6
The Bullfield *BGLY* BD16 ....74 E3
Bullfields Cl *EARL* WF12 ....181 H7
Bull Gn *HFAX* HX1 ....17 G7
Bullough La *RTHW* LS26 ....125 G7
Bull Ring *WKFDE* * WF1 ....18 E4
Bull Royd Av *GIR* BD8 ....96 D5
Bull Royd Crs *GIR* BD8 ....96 D5
Bull Royd Dr *GIR* BD8 ....96 D5
Bull Royd La *GIR* BD8 ....96 D5
Bullstyle Rd *PONT* WF8 ....189 H3
Bullytree La *GFTH/SHER* LS25 ......130 H3
Bundria Ct *GIR* BD8 ....97 H3
The Bungalows
  FEA/AMT WF7 ....188 C5
  HIPP * HX3 ....155 H6
  LUD/ILL * HX2 ....134 A6
  NORM WF6 ....166 D3
  OSS * WF5 ....182 B3
  RPDN/SBR * HX6 ....153 H4
  WKFDW/WTN WF2 ....164 A6
Bunkers Hl *GFTH/SHER* LS25 ....88 D7
Bunker's Hill La *HWTH* BD22 ....52 E6
Bunkers La *BTLY* WF17 ....160 C4
Bunting Dr *CUL/QBY* BD13 ....116 B4
Burberry Cl *BOW* BD4 ....118 D6
Burchett Gv *HDGY* LS6 ....9 K1
Burchett Pl *HDGY* LS6 ....9 K1
Burchett Ter *HDGY* LS6 ....9 K1
Burdale Pl *GTHN* BD7 ....4 F8
Burdett Ter *BULY* LS4 ....8 A4
Burdock Wy *HFAX* HX1 ....16 F6
Burghley Ms *EARD/LOFT* WF3 ....143 J4
Burgh Mill Gdns *DEWS* WF13 ....180 D2
Burgh Mill La *DEWS* WF13 ....180 C2
Burkill St *WKFDE* WF1 ....184 E7
Burking Rd *DEWS* WF13 ....180 E1
Burleigh St *HFAX* HX1 ....16 B9
Burley Cl *GFTH/SHER* LS25 ....131 F2
Burley Ct *AIRE* BD20 ....32 C5
Burley Grange Rd *BULY* LS4 ....8 B4
Burley Hill Crs *BULY* LS4 ....102 A2
Burley Hill Dr *BULY* LS4 ....102 A2
Burley La *HORS* LS18 ....80 E5
  ILK LS29 ....38 A5
Burley Lodge Pl *BVRD* LS3 ....8 F6
Burley Lodge Rd *HDGY* LS6 ....8 F6
Burley Lodge St *HDGY* LS6 ....8 F6
Burley Lodge Ter *HDGY* LS6 ....8 E5
Burley Ms *AIRE* BD20 ....32 C5
Burley Rd *BULY* LS4 ....8 A3
  ILK LS29 ....38 B4
Burley St *BVRD* LS3 ....9 H8
  ECHL BD2 ....97 J1
  ELL HX5 ....175 J3
Burley Wk *BTLY* WF17 ....160 E3
Burley Wood Crs *BULY* LS4 ....8 A4
Burley Wood La *BULY* LS4 ....8 A3
Burley Wood Mt *BULY* LS4 ....102 A3
Burley Wood Vw *BULY* LS4 ....8 A3
Burlington Av *BFDE* BD3 ....7 L1
Burlington Pl *BEE/HOL* LS11 ....123 G4
Burlington Rd *BEE/HOL* LS11...........123 G4
Burlington St *GIR* BD8 ....5 K2
  HFAX HX1 ....16 B5
Burmantofts St *OSM* LS9 ....10 E8
Burned Gv *HIPP* HX3 ....116 C7
Burned Rd *HIPP* HX3 ....116 C7
Burneston Gdns *WBSY* BD6 ....116 D6
Burnett Av *WBOW* BD5 ....117 J3
Burnett Pl *WBOW* BD5 ....117 J3
Burnett Ri *CUL/QBY* BD13 ....115 F6
Burnett St *BFD* BD1 ....6 B6
Burnham Av *BOW* BD4 ....118 C5
Burnham Ct *WBY* LS22 ....29 F3
Burnham Rd *GFTH/SHER* LS25......127 J1
Burniston Cl *WIL/AL* BD15 ....95 F1
Burnley Rd *HBR* HX7 ....132 A6
  RPDN/SBR HX6 ....153 J3
Burnleys Cl *RTHW* LS26 ....147 G6
Burnleys Dr *RTHW* LS26 ....147 G6
Burnleys Ms *RTHW* LS26 ....147 G6
Burnleys Vw *RTHW* LS26 ....147 G6
Burnleyville *CLECK* BD19 ....139 J6
Burn Rd *HUDW* HD3 ....176 B7
Burnsall Pl *HUDW* HD3 ....176 B7
Burnsall Cft *WOR/ARM* LS12 ....102 A5
Burnsall Gdns *WOR/ARM* LS12 ....102 A5
Burnsall Gra *WOR/ARM* LS12 ....102 A5
Burnsall Ms *AIRE* BD20 ....21 F7
Burnsall Rd *BFDE* BD3 ....6 F4
  BRIG HD6 ....176 C1
  BTLY WF17 ....160 D3
  LVSG WF15 ....159 G4
Burns Ct *BTLY* WF17 ....140 K5
Burnsdale *WIL/AL* BD15 ....95 K2
Burnshaw Ms *EARD/LOFT* WF3 .....143 H4
Burns Hl *ILK* LS29 ....22 B1
Burnside Cl *BTLY* WF17 ....140 D6
Burns St *HIPP* HX3 ....134 D3
Burns Wy *BSPA/BRAM* LS23 ....48 C3
Burnt Side Rd
  WOR/ARM LS12 ....121 F4
Burnup Gv *CLECK* BD19 ....158 D1
Burnwells Av *IDLE* BD10 ....78 B2
Burrage St *BGLY* BD16 ....75 J1
Burras Av *OT* LS21 ....39 G3
Burras Dr *OT* LS21 ....39 G3

Burras La *OT* LS21 ... 39 G3
Burras Rd *BOW* BD4 ... 118 C4
Burrel Cl *WBY* LS22 ... 29 K4
Burrell St *WKFDE* WF1 ... 19 H5
The Burrows *BTLY* WF17 ... 160 C1
Burrow St *WBOW* BD5 ... 5 L8
Burr Tree Dr *MSTN/BAR* LS15 ... 106 A6
Burr Tree Garth
  MSTN/BAR LS15 ... 106 A6
Burr Tree V *MSTN/BAR* * LS15 ... 106 A6
Burrwood Wy *GTL/HWG* HX4 ... 174 E4
Burton Av *BEE/HOL* LS11 ... 14 A9
Burton Common La
  GFTH/SHER LS25 ... 151 H1
Burton Crs *HDGY* LS6 ... 82 C6
Burton Ms *AL/HA/HU* LS17 ... 63 J6
Burton Rd *BEE/HOL* LS11 ... 14 A9
Burton Rw *BEE/HOL* LS11 ... 14 B8
Burtons Ar *LDS* LS1 ... 14 A1
Burton St *BEE/HOL* LS11 ... 14 A8
  BOW BD4 ... 118 C3
  KGHY BD21 ... 53 J8
  LUD/ILL HX2 ... 134 D2
  PDSY/CALV LS28 ... 100 A2
  WKFDE WF1 ... 18 D3
Burton Ter *BEE/HOL* LS11 ... 123 H3
Burton Wy *OSM* LS9 ... 11 J6
Busely Ct *MOR* LS27 ... 141 J2
Busfield St *BGLY* BD16 ... 75 J1
  BOW BD4 ... 118 C3
Bushill Fold *CUL/QBY* BD13 ... 115 F4
Buslingthorpe Gn *CHAL* LS7 ... 10 A2
Buslingthorpe La *CHAL* LS7 ... 10 C2
Bussey Ct *HDGY* LS6 ... 9 K2
Busy La *SHPY* BD18 ... 77 K3
Butcher Hl *BHP/TINH* LS16 ... 81 J4
Butcher La *RTHW* LS26 ... 145 F2
Butcher St *BEE/HOL* LS11 ... 13 L3
  BFD BD1 ... 5 J7
Bute Av *BRIG* HD6 ... 157 F3
Bute St *SHPY* BD18 ... 97 J1
Butler La *BAIL* BD17 ... 57 J7
Butler St *BFDE* BD3 ... 6 C4
Butler St East *BFDE* BD3 ... 6 D4
Butler St West *BFDE* BD3 ... 6 C4
Butterbowl Dr *WOR/ARM* LS12 ... 121 H1
Butterbowl Gdns
  WOR/ARM LS12 ... 121 J1
Butterbowl Garth
  WOR/ARM LS12 ... 121 H1
Butterbowl Gv *WOR/ARM* LS12 ... 121 H1
Butterbowl Lawn
  WOR/ARM LS12 ... 121 H1
Butterbowl Mt *WOR/ARM* LS12 ... 121 J1
Butterbowl Rd *WOR/ARM* LS12 ... 121 J1
Butterfield Homes *BAIL* * BD17 ... 57 H7
  BGLY * BD16 ... 76 A6
Butterfield St *OSM* LS9 ... 15 G1
Butterley St *MID* LS10 ... 14 B5
Buttermeade Cl *WBSY* BD6 ... 117 F7
Buttermere Av *WBY* LS22 ... 29 F3
Buttershaw Dr *WBSY* BD6 ... 116 D6
Buttershaw La *LVSG* WF15 ... 158 C3
  WBSY BD6 ... 117 G7
Butterwick Gdns *WBY* LS22 ... 29 F4
Butterworth End La
  RPDN/SBR HX6 ... 173 H2
Butterworth La
  RPDN/SBR HX6 ... 153 F7
Butt Hl *GFTH/SHER* LS25 ... 111 F6
Buttholme La *WBSY* BD6 ... 116 E6
Butt La *HWTH* BD22 ... 72 D5
  IDLE BD10 ... 78 C4
  WOR/ARM LS12 ... 101 G7
Button Pk *PONT* WF8 ... 189 H2
Buttress La *LUD/ILL* HX2 ... 133 F6
Butt Rw *WOR/ARM* LS12 ... 101 H7
The Butts *PONT* WF8 ... 169 J7
Butts Ct *LDS* LS1 ... 9 M9
Butts Garth *SCFT* LS14 ... 66 C6
Butts Green La *LUD/ILL* HX2 ... 153 G1
Butts Green Rd *LUD/ILL* HX2 ... 153 G1
Butts Hl *CLECK* BD19 ... 139 H7
Butts La *GFTH/SHER* LS25 ... 130 D6
Butts Mt *WOR/ARM* LS12 ... 12 C2
Butts Yd *CLECK* BD19 ... 158 E1
Buxton Av *HTON* BD9 ... 97 H1
Buxton La *HTON* BD9 ... 97 H1
Buxton Pl *WKFDE* WF1 ... 184 C1
Buxton St *HIPP* HX3 ... 16 C1
  HTON BD9 ... 97 G3
  KGHY BD21 ... 3 J4
Buxton Wy *HIPP* HX3 ... 134 C4
Byeway *GSLY* LS20 ... 58 D2
Byland *LUD/ILL* HX2 ... 134 A1
Byland Cl *BSPA/BRAM* LS23 ... 48 B3
Byland Gv *WIL/AL* BD15 ... 95 J3
Byram Park Av *KNOT* WF11 ... 151 F7
Byram Park Rd *KNOT* WF11 ... 151 F7
Byrl St *KGHY* BD21 ... 3 H2
Byron Av *RPDN/SBR* * HX6 ... 153 J3
  EARD/LOFT WF3 ... 165 F2
Byron Gv *DEWS* WF13 ... 160 B6
Byron Ms *BGLY* BD16 ... 55 K6
Byron St *BFDE* BD3 ... 6 E5
  HFAX HX1 ... 16 A5
  LDSU LS2 ... 10 C7
  RPDN/SBR HX6 ... 153 J3
The Byways *PONT* WF8 ... 189 J3
Bywell Cl *EARL* WF12 ... 161 J7
Bywell Rd *EARL* WF12 ... 161 J7

C

Cabbage Hl *WOR/ARM* LS12 ... 101 K7
Cabin Rd *OT* LS21 ... 40 E5
Cad Beeston Ms
  BEE/HOL * LS11 ... 13 J9
Cadney Cft *HFAX* HX1 ... 17 G7
Caenarvon Cl *BTLY* WF17 ... 140 D6
Caernarvon Av
  GFTH/SHER LS25 ... 108 A6
Cain Cl *OSM* LS9 ... 15 G2
Cain La *HIPP* HX3 ... 155 K4
Cairn Cl *AIRE* BD20 ... 53 H1
Cairns Cl *ECHL* BD2 ... 98 A2

Caister Cl *BTLY* WF17 ... 140 C5
Caister Gv *KGHY* * BD21 ... 53 H7
Caister St *KGHY* BD21 ... 53 H7
Caister Wy *KGHY* BD21 ... 53 J7
Calcaria Crs *TAD* LS24 ... 70 C1
Calcaria Rd *TAD* LS24 ... 70 C1
Calde Ct *LM/WK* BD12 ... 137 K1
Caldene Av *LM/WK* BD12 ... 137 K1
Calder Bank Rd *EARL* WF12 ... 180 E3
Calder Banks *CUL/QBY* BD13 ... 115 K5
Calder Cl *OSS* WF5 ... 182 B4
Caldercroft *ELL* HX5 ... 175 H3
Calderdale Wy *BRIC* HD6 ... 157 H3
  ELL HX5 ... 175 H3
  ELL HX5 ... 176 A5
  GTL/HWG HX4 ... 174 D1
  HIPP HX3 ... 135 K2
Calder Island Wy
  WKFDW/WTN WF2 ... 184 C7
Calder Rd *DEWS* WF13 ... 180 B4
  MIRF WF14 ... 179 H6
Calderstone Av *WBSY* BD6 ... 116 C6
Calder St *BRIG* HD6 ... 157 H7
  CAS WF10 ... 148 A7
  GTL/HWG HX4 ... 175 G2
  HIPP HX3 ... 18 F9
Calder Ter *HIPP* HX3 ... 154 D7
Calder Vale Rd *WKFDE* WF1 ... 19 H6
Calder Vw *BRIC* HD6 ... 156 E7
  OSS WF5 ... 182 A4
Calder Wy *AIRE* BD20 ... 33 F2
Caledonia Ct
  WKFDW/WTN WF2 ... 163 G6
Caledonian Rd *BTLY* WF17 ... 161 F3
  KGHY BD21 ... 3 H7
Caledonia St *WBOW* BD5 ... 5 M9
Calgary Crs *EARD/LOFT* WF3 ... 162 E1
Calgary Pl *CHAL* LS7 ... 83 J6
California Dr *CAS* WF10 ... 167 G3
California La *CLECK* BD19 ... 159 J1
California Ms *MOR* LS27 ... 142 A1
California Mt *MOR* * LS27 ... 142 A3
Call La *LDS* LS1 ... 14 B1
The Calls *LDSU* LS2 ... 14 C1
Calpin Cl *IDLE* * BD10 ... 78 C4
Calton Gv *KGHY* BD21 ... 54 C5
Calton St *KGHY* BD21 ... 2 E8
Calver Av *HWTH* BD22 ... 2 B5
Calver Gv *KGHY* BD21 ... 2 E8
Calverley Av *BFDE* BD3 ... 7 K3
  BRAM LS13 ... 100 E3
Calverley Ct *BRAM* LS13 ... 100 E2
  RTHW LS26 ... 145 J2
Calverley Cutting *IDLE* BD10 ... 79 G4
Calverley Dr *BRAM* LS13 ... 100 E2
Calverley Gdns *BRAM* LS13 ... 100 D1
Calverley Garth *BRAM* LS13 ... 100 E2
Calverley Green Rd
  NORM WF6 ... 166 C5
Calverley Gv *BRAM* LS13 ... 100 E2
Calverley La *BRAM* LS13 ... 100 D2
  HORS LS18 ... 80 B5
  PDSY/CALV LS28 ... 79 K6
Calverley Moor Av
  PDSY/CALV LS28 ... 99 H4
Calverley Rd *RTHW* LS26 ... 145 K2
Calverley St *LDS* LS1 ... 9 M7
Calverley Ter *BRAM* LS13 ... 100 E2
Calver Rd *HWTH* BD22 ... 2 B4
Calversyke St *HWTH* BD22 ... 2 C5
Calvert Cl *GFTH/SHER* LS25 ... 127 K3
Calverts Wk *OSS* WF5 ... 182 B5
Camargue Fold *ECHL* BD2 ... 98 A1
Camberley Cl *PDSY/CALV* LS28 ... 100 B7
Camberley Mt *BOW* BD4 ... 119 F2
Camberley St *BEE/HOL* * LS11 ... 123 H3
Camberley Wy
  PDSY/CALV LS28 ... 100 B7
Camborne Dr *HUDN* HD2 ... 176 E6
Camborne Rd *HUDN* HD2 ... 176 E6
Camborne Wy *HWTH* BD22 ... 53 H6
Cambrian Bar *LM/WK* BD12 ... 137 G1
Cambrian St *BEE/HOL* LS11 ... 13 K7
Cambrian Ter *BEE/HOL* LS11 ... 13 K7
Cambridge Cl *MOR* LS27 ... 142 A2
Cambridge Ct *MOR* LS27 ... 142 A2
Cambridge Crs *HOR/CROF* WF4 ... 185 K7
Cambridge Dr *BRAM* LS13 ... 100 E2
  OT LS21 ... 39 J3
Cambridge Gdns *BRAM* LS13 ... 100 E2
Cambridge Gv
  GFTH/SHER LS25 ... 127 K5
  OT LS21 ... 39 J3
Cambridge Pl *BFDE* BD3 ... 6 B3
  CUL/QBY BD13 ... 115 H5
Cambridge Rd *BTLY* WF17 ... 140 A6
  CHAL LS7 ... 9 M3
Cambridge St *BTLY* WF17 ... 161 F3
  CAS WF10 ... 168 C1
  CLAY * BD14 ... 116 A2
  CUL/QBY BD13 ... 115 J5
  GTHN BD7 ... 117 G2
  HECK WF16 ... 160 B5
  NORM WF6 ... 166 D7
  OT LS21 ... 39 H3
  WKFDW/WTN WF2 ... 184 A4
Cambridge Wy *OT* LS21 ... 39 J3
Camden Rd *CAS* WF10 ... 149 G7
Camden Ter *GIR* BD8 ... 5 J2
Camellia Cl *WKFDW/WTN* WF2 ... 183 J6
Camellia St *SHPY* BD18 ... 77 J7
Camellia Mt *GTHN* BD7 ... 96 D7
Cameron Av *LM/WK* BD12 ... 137 G6
Cameronian Ct *KGHY* BD21 ... 3 H5
Camilla Ct *EARL* WF12 ... 181 J2
Cam La *BRIG* HD6 ... 157 J5
Camm La *MIRF* WF14 ... 179 J5
Camm St *BRIG* HD6 ... 157 F5
Campbell St *CUL/QBY* BD13 ... 115 J5
  KGHY BD21 ... 3 G4
Campion Cl *PONT* WF8 ... 189 J2
Camp Mt *PONT* WF8 ... 189 G1
Camp Ri *PONT* WF8 ... 189 G1
Camp Rd *BHP/TINH* LS16 ... 61 G2
Campus Rd *GTHN* BD7 ... 5 G7
Camroyd St *DEWS* WF13 ... 161 G7

Canada Crs *YEA* LS19 ... 59 K7
Canada Dr *YEA* LS19 ... 59 K6
Canada Rd *YEA* LS19 ... 59 K6
Canada Ter *YEA* LS19 ... 59 K7
Canal Ct *EARD/LOFT* * WF3 ... 164 E2
Canal La *AIRE* BD20 ... 33 H3
  EARD/LOFT WF3 ... 164 E2
Canal Pl *WOR/ARM* LS12 ... 13 H1
Canal Rd *AIRE* BD20 ... 54 B1
  BFDE BD3 ... 6 A3
  BGLY BD16 ... 55 J6
  BRAM LS13 ... 80 B7
  ECHL BD2 ... 97 H1
  RPDN/SBR HX6 ... 154 B4
  WOR/ARM LS12 ... 8 C8
Canal St *BRIG* HD6 ... 157 G6
  HIPP HX3 ... 17 K8
Canal Wk *EARD/LOFT* WF3 ... 165 G2
Canal Whf *BEE/HOL* LS11 ... 13 L2
Canary St *CLECK* BD19 ... 138 E7
Canberra Cl *HWTH* BD22 ... 73 G4
Canberra Dr *HWTH* BD22 ... 73 G4
Cancel St *MID* LS10 ... 14 C6
Canford Dr *WIL/AL* BD15 ... 96 A3
Canford Gv *WIL/AL* BD15 ... 96 A4
Canford Rd *WIL/AL* BD15 ... 96 A3
Canker La *HIPP* HX3 ... 134 D4
Canning Av *WKFDW/WTN* WF2 ... 183 J1
Cannon Gv *HECK* WF16 ... 160 B3
Cannon Hall Cl *BRIG* HD6 ... 157 F6
Cannon Hall Dr *BRIG* HD6 ... 157 J6
Cannon Mill La *GTHN* BD7 ... 117 G2
Cannon St *BGLY* BD16 ... 75 K2
  CAS WF10 ... 168 D3
  HFAX * HX1 ... 16 B9
Cannon Wy *EARL* WF12 ... 181 K2
Canterbury Ter *BEE/HOL* LS11 ... 122 D3
The Canter *MID* LS10 ... 143 J4
Canterbury Av *WBOW* BD5 ... 117 H3
Canterbury Ct *PONT* WF8 ... 169 K5
Canterbury Crs *HIPP* HX3 ... 16 E1
Canterbury Dr *HDGY* LS6 ... 102 B3
Canterbury Rd *EARL* WF12 ... 161 J7
  HDGY LS6 ... 102 B3
Capel Ct *PDSY/CALV* LS28 ... 79 J6
Capel St *BRIG* HD6 ... 157 F7
  PDSY/CALV LS28 ... 79 J6
Cape St *BFD* BD1 ... 5 M3
Capitol Pde *HDGY* LS6 ... 82 D5
Caprington St *NORM* WF6 ... 167 G4
Captain St *BFD* BD1 ... 6 A5
Carberry Pl *HDGY* LS6 ... 8 E5
Carberry Rd *HDGY* * LS6 ... 8 E5
Carberry Ter *HDGY* LS6 ... 8 E5
Cardan Dr *ILK* LS29 ... 24 D5
Carden Av *MSTN/BAR* LS15 ... 105 F5
Carden Rd *BOW* BD4 ... 7 M9
Cardigan Av *MOR* LS27 ... 141 K5
Cardigan Cl *BTLY* WF17 ... 161 H3
Cardigan Ct *HDGY* LS6 ... 8 E1
Cardigan Fields Rd *BULY* LS4 ... 8 B6
Cardigan La *BULY* LS4 ... 8 C5
  OSS WF5 ... 182 A6
Cardigan Rd *HDGY* LS6 ... 8 D1
Cardigan St *CUL/QBY* BD13 ... 115 H5
Cardigan Ter *EARD/LOFT* * WF3 ... 143 K7
  WKFDE WF1 ... 18 D3
Cardinal Av *BEE/HOL* LS11 ... 122 D3
Cardinal Cl *GFTH/SHER* LS25 ... 111 G5
Cardinal Crs *BEE/HOL* LS11 ... 122 E6
Cardinal Gdns *BEE/HOL* LS11 ... 122 D6
Cardinal Gv *BEE/HOL* LS11 ... 122 D6
Cardinal Rd *BEE/HOL* LS11 ... 122 D6
Cardinal Sq *BEE/HOL* LS11 ... 122 D5
Cardinal Wk *BEE/HOL* LS11 ... 122 D5
Cardwell Ter *EARL* WF12 ... 181 F3
Carisbrooke Crs *WBSY* BD6 ... 117 G6
Carisbrooke La
  GFTH/SHER LS25 ... 108 A5
Cariss St *MID* LS10 ... 14 D9
Cark Rd *KGHY* BD21 ... 3 G2
Carlby Gv *HWTH* BD22 ... 2 D6
Carlby St *HWTH* BD22 ... 2 D6
Carleton Cl *BSPA/BRAM* LS23 ... 48 A3
  PONT WF8 ... 189 J2
Carleton Crest *PONT* WF8 ... 189 K3
Carleton Dr *BSPA/BRAM* LS23 ... 48 A3
Carleton Ga *PONT* WF8 ... 189 H3
Carleton Gln *PONT* WF8 ... 189 J2
Carleton Green Cl *PONT* WF8 ... 189 J3
Carleton Park Av *PONT* WF8 ... 189 J2
Carleton Park Rd *PONT* WF8 ... 189 J3
Carleton Rd *PONT* WF8 ... 189 J2
  PONT WF8 ... 190 B5
Carleton St *KGHY* BD21 ... 53 K2
Carleton Vw *PONT* WF8 ... 189 J3
Carling Ct *GTHN* BD7 ... 116 E3
Carlinghow Hl *BTLY* WF17 ... 160 E1
Carlinghow La *BTLY* WF17 ... 160 B1
Carlisle Av *YEA* LS19 ... 59 K5
Carlisle Dr *PDSY/CALV* LS28 ... 100 A3
Carlisle Gv *PDSY/CALV* LS28 ... 100 A3
Carlisle Pl *GIR* BD8 ... 5 G1
Carlisle Rd *GIR* BD8 ... 4 F2
  MID LS10 ... 14 D4
  PDSY/CALV LS28 ... 100 A3
Carlisle St *GIR* BD8 ... 5 G1
  KGHY BD21 ... 3 K5
  LUD/ILL HX2 ... 134 B2
  PDSY/CALV LS28 ... 99 K4
Carlisle Ter *GIR* BD8 ... 5 H1
Carlton Ap *WBY* LS22 ... 29 F3
Carlton Av *BTLY* WF17 ... 160 E5
  CAS WF10 ... 168 E1
  PDSY/CALV LS28 ... 100 B6
  SHPY BD18 ... 76 E4
Carlton Carr *CHAL* LS7 ... 10 A5
Carlton Cl *CHAL* LS7 ... 10 A5
  NORM WF6 ... 166 E6
Carlton Ct *OSS* WF5 ... 182 C5
  WOR/ARM LS12 ... 12 C7
Carlton Cft *CHAL* LS7 ... 10 B4
Carlton Dr *BAIL* BD17 ... 57 H7
  GFTH/SHER LS25 ... 127 J1
  GSLY LS20 ... 59 G1

HTON BD9 ... 97 F1
  NORM WF6 ... 167 F6
Carlton Gdns *CHAL* LS7 ... 10 B5
  CHAL LS7 ... 10 A5
Carlton Garth *AL/HA/HU* LS17 ... 64 B6
  CHAL LS7 ... 10 A5
Carlton Ga *CHAL* LS7 ... 10 A5
Carlton Gv *CHAL* LS7 ... 10 A4
  ELL HX5 ... 176 A2
  SHPY BD18 ... 77 G7
  WBOW BD5 ... 117 J3
Carlton Hl *CHAL* LS7 ... 10 A4
Carlton House Ter *HFAX* HX1 ... 16 D9
Carlton La *EARD/LOFT* WF3 ... 144 D6
  GSLY LS20 ... 59 G1
Carlton Moor Ms
  EARD/LOFT WF3 ... 144 A2
Carlton Mt *YEA* LS19 ... 59 K3
Carlton Pl *CHAL* LS7 ... 10 A4
  HFAX HX1 ... 17 G7
Carlton Ri *CHAL* LS7 ... 10 A5
  PDSY/CALV LS28 ... 100 B6
Carlton Rd *DEWS* WF13 ... 161 F7
  LVSG WF15 ... 159 H5
  SHPY BD18 ... 76 D4
Carlton Rw *WOR/ARM* LS12 ... 101 K6
Carlton St *CAS* WF10 ... 148 C7
  FEA/AMT WF7 ... 188 C2
  GTHN BD7 ... 5 K7
  HFAX HX1 ... 17 G7
  HWTH BD22 ... 72 E5
  NORM WF6 ... 166 E6
  OT LS21 ... 39 J3
  WKFDW/WTN WF2 ... 18 B6
Carlton Ter *HFAX* HX1 ... 17 G7
  CHAL LS7 ... 10 A4
Carlton Vw *CAS* WF10 ... 147 J1
  CHAL LS7 ... 10 A4
Carlton Wk *SHPY* BD18 ... 76 E4
Carlyle Crs *CAS* WF10 ... 169 F1
Carlyle Rd *CAS* WF10 ... 169 F1
Carmel Rd *HIPP* HX3 ... 134 E5
Carmona Av *SHPY* BD18 ... 77 G7
Carmona Gdns *SHPY* BD18 ... 77 G7
Carnaby Rd *GTHN* BD7 ... 116 D4
Carnegie Dr *SHPY* BD18 ... 77 H5
Carnlea Gv *WKFDW/WTN* WF2 ... 184 D6
Carnoustie Gdns *NORM* WF6 ... 167 G7
Carnoustie Gv *BGLY* BD16 ... 75 K5
Caroline St *CLECK* BD19 ... 138 E7
  SHPY BD18 ... 76 E4
Carousel Wk *GFTH/SHER* LS25 ... 111 G6
Carperley Crs *CUL/QBY* BD13 ... 94 B5
Carr Av *GFTH/SHER* LS25 ... 111 F6
Carr Bank *AIRE* BD20 ... 54 E2
Carr Bottom Av *WBOW* BD5 ... 117 H4
Carr Bottom Fold *WBSY* BD6 ... 117 H5
Carr Bottom Gv *WBSY* BD6 ... 117 G4
Carr Bottom Rd *IDLE* BD10 ... 79 F6
  WBOW BD5 ... 117 H4
Carr Bridge Av *BHP/TINH* LS16 ... 81 G1
Carr Bridge Cl *BHP/TINH* LS16 ... 81 G1
Carr Bridge Dr *BHP/TINH* LS16 ... 81 G1
Carr Bridge Vw *BHP/TINH* LS16 ... 81 G1
Carr Cl *YEA* LS19 ... 80 A1
Carr Crofts *WOR/ARM* LS12 ... 102 A6
Carr Crofts Dr
  WOR/ARM LS12 ... 102 A6
Carr Field Dr *LUD/ILL* HX2 ... 133 F7
Carrfield La *MSTN/BAR* LS15 ... 87 G5
Carrfield Dr *MSTN/BAR* LS15 ... 87 G5
Carrfield Rd *MSTN/BAR* LS15 ... 87 G5
Carr Gate Crs
  WKFDW/WTN WF2 ... 163 J3
Carr Gate Dr
  WKFDW/WTN WF2 ... 163 K3
Carr Gate Mt
  WKFDW/WTN WF2 ... 163 J3
Carr Green Av *BHP/TINH* LS16 ... 81 G1
Carr Green Cl *BRIG* HD6 ... 176 E3
Carr Green Dr *BRIG* HD6 ... 176 E3
Carr Green La *BRIG* HD6 ... 176 E3
Carr Gv *AIRE* BD20 ... 54 D2
Carr Hall La *GTL/HWG* HX4 ... 174 D5
Carr Hall Rd *LM/WK* BD12 ... 137 H4
Carr Hill Av *PDSY/CALV* LS28 ... 79 H6
Carr Hill Dr *PDSY/CALV* LS28 ... 79 H6
Carr Hill Gv *PDSY/CALV* LS28 ... 79 H6
Carr Hill Nook *PDSY/CALV* * LS28 ... 79 H6
Carr Hill Ri *PDSY/CALV* LS28 ... 79 H6
Carr Hill Rd *PDSY/CALV* LS28 ... 79 H6
Carrholm Crs *CHAL* LS7 ... 83 G5
Carrholm Dr *CHAL* LS7 ... 83 G5
Carrholm Gn *CHAL* LS7 ... 83 G5
Carrholm Mt *CHAL* LS7 ... 83 G5
Carrholm Rd *CHAL* LS7 ... 83 G5
Carrholm Vw *CHAL* LS7 ... 83 G5
Carr House Gv *LM/WK* BD12 ... 137 H3
Carr House La *HIPP* HX3 ... 116 D7
  LM/WK BD12 ... 137 G2
Carr House Mt *LM/WK* * BD12 ... 137 H3
Carr House Rd *HIPP* HX3 ... 136 C1
The Carriage Dr *GTL/HWG* HX4 ... 174 D5
  GTL/HWG HX4 ... 175 F1
  RHAY LS8 ... 84 D3
Carriage Dr *CLECK* BD19 ... 139 J5
Carricks Cl *LM/WK* BD12 ... 137 K1
Carrington St *BFDE* BD3 ... 7 H5
Carrington Ter *GSLY* LS20 ... 58 E3
Carr La *AIRE* BD20 ... 54 D2
  AL/HA/HU LS17 ... 65 H7
  CAS WF10 ... 168 E3
  CUL/QBY BD13 ... 94 B3
  DEWS WF13 ... 180 B1
  EARD/LOFT WF3 ... 145 F4
  HECK WF16 ... 160 A7
  LM/WK BD12 ... 137 J2
  SHPY BD18 ... 77 J5
  WBY LS22 ... 29 K3
  YEA LS19 ... 80 A1
Carr Manor Av *AL/HA/HU* LS17 ... 83 G4
Carr Manor Crs *AL/HA/HU* LS17 ... 83 G3
Carr Manor Cft *CHAL* LS7 ... 83 G4
Carr Manor Dr *AL/HA/HU* LS17 ... 83 G4
Carr Manor Gdns
  AL/HA/HU LS17 ... 83 G3

Carr Manor Gv *AL/HA/HU* LS17 ... 83 G4
Carr Manor Mt *AL/HA/HU* LS17 ... 83 G4
Carr Manor Pde *AL/HA/HU* LS17 ... 83 G4
Carr Manor Pl *AL/HA/HU* LS17 ... 83 G4
Carr Manor Rd *AL/HA/HU* LS17 ... 83 G4
Carr Manor Vw *AL/HA/HU* LS17 ... 83 G4
Carr Manor Wk *CHAL* LS7 ... 83 G4
Carr Moor Side *BEE/HOL* LS11 ... 123 H5
Carroll St *BFDE* BD3 ... 6 C1
Carr Rd *LM/WK* * BD12 ... 137 H4
  PDSY/CALV LS28 ... 79 G2
Carr Side Crs *BTLY* WF17 ... 160 E5
Carr St *BRIG* HD6 ... 157 F4
  BTLY WF17 ... 140 B7
  CLECK WF13 ... 158 E1
  DEWS WF13 ... 161 F6
  KGHY BD21 ... 3 G5
  LVSG WF15 ... 159 H3
  WBOW BD5 ... 117 J4
Carr Top Cl *DEWS* WF13 ... 160 E6
Carr Wood Gdns
  PDSY/CALV LS28 ... 79 H6
Carr Wood Rd *CAS* WF10 ... 168 C3
Carter Av *MSTN/BAR* LS15 ... 105 K5
Carter La *CUL/QBY* BD13 ... 115 G3
  MSTN/BAR LS15 ... 105 K4
Carter Mt *MSTN/BAR* LS15 ... 105 K5
Carter's La *ILK* LS29 ... 24 D3
Carter St *BFD* BD1 ... 6 B8
  WKFDE WF1 ... 18 D4
Carter Ter *MSTN/BAR* LS15 ... 105 K4
Cartmel La *AIRE* BD20 ... 32 D5
Cartmell Dr *MSTN/BAR* LS15 ... 104 E7
Cartmel Rd *KGHY* BD21 ... 2 D5
Cartwright St *CLECK* BD19 ... 159 G2
Carver St *CLECK* BD19 ... 138 E7
Caryl Rd *BOW* BD4 ... 118 B3
Cashmere St *HWTH* BD22 ... 2 D5
Cass La *GFTH/SHER* LS25 ... 130 E5
Casson Av *EARD/LOFT* WF3 ... 143 G6
Casson Dr *EARD/LOFT* WF3 ... 143 G6
Casson Gv *EARD/LOFT* WF3 ... 143 G6
Cass Yd *WKFDE* * WF1 ... 19 G5
Casterton Gdns *SCFT* LS14 ... 105 H2
Castle Av *BRIG* HD6 ... 176 E1
  WKFDW/WTN WF2 ... 184 E7
Castle Carr Rd *HBR* HX7 ... 112 B5
Castle Cl *AL/HA/HU* LS17 ... 46 A7
  LUD/ILL HX2 ... 132 B3
  BTLY WF17 ... 140 D6
Castle Cft *BGLY* BD16 ... 74 D3
Castlefields *RTHW* LS26 ... 144 C2
Castlefields Crs *BRIG* HD6 ... 176 E1
Castlefields Dr *BRIG* HD6 ... 176 E1
Castlefields La *BGLY* BD16 ... 55 H6
Castlefields Rd *BGLY* BD16 ... 55 G6
  BRIG HD6 ... 176 E1
Castleford Br *CAS* WF10 ... 148 D6
Castleford La *FEA/AMT* WF7 ... 168 A6
  KNOT WF11 ... 170 C1
Castleford Rd *NORM* WF6 ... 166 E6
Castle Garth *PONT* WF8 ... 169 K7
Castle Ga *RTHW* LS26 ... 145 G7
  WBY LS22 ... 29 H4
Castlegate Dr *IDLE* BD10 ... 78 D6
  PONT WF8 ... 189 G4
Castle Gra * LS19 ... 60 A5
Castle Gv *AL/HA/HU* LS17 ... 46 A7
  BGLY BD16 ... 74 D3
Castle Grove Av *HDGY* LS6 ... 82 C5
Castle Grove Dr *HDGY* LS6 ... 82 C5
Castle Head Cl
  EARD/LOFT WF3 ... 144 D6
Castle Head La
  EARD/LOFT WF3 ... 144 B7
Castle Hl *BRIG* HD6 ... 176 E1
  WKFDW/WTN WF2 ... 183 H5
Castle Hill Ct *HWTH* * BD22 ... 2 E1
Castle Hill Rd *CLECK* BD19 ... 159 J2
Castle Hill Vw *HECK* WF16 ... 160 B3
Castle Ings Cl *WOR/ARM* LS12 ... 121 G3
Castle Ings Dr *WOR/ARM* LS12 ... 121 G3
Castle Ings Gdns
  WOR/ARM LS12 ... 121 G4
Castle La *RPDN/SBR* HX6 ... 172 D6
Castlemore Rd *BAIL* BD17 ... 77 J2
Castle Pde *CAS* WF10 ... 168 C2
Castle Rd *ILK* LS29 ... 24 A5
  KGHY BD21 ... 2 F2
  RTHW LS26 ... 144 E2
  SHPY BD18 ... 77 F5
Castle Rd West
  WKFDW/WTN WF2 ... 184 E7
Castle St *LDS* LS1 ... 9 K9
  WBOW BD5 ... 117 K1
Castle Syke Hl *FEA/AMT* WF7 ... 189 G6
Castle Syke Vw *PONT* WF8 ... 189 H7
Castleton Cl *WOR/ARM* LS12 ... 13 G1
Castleton Rd *WOR/ARM* LS12 ... 8 E7
Castle Vw *AL/HA/HU* LS17 ... 83 G3
  MIRF WF14 ... 179 J4
Castle Wood Cl *AL/HA/HU* LS17 ... 46 A7
Castley La *OT* LS21 ... 41 G2
  OT LS21 ... 42 A1
Cater St *BFD* BD1 ... 6 B6
Cathcart St *HDGY* LS6 ... 9 J2
  HIPP HX3 ... 134 C3
Cathedral Cl *WKFDE* WF1 ... 18 D3
Catherine Cl *HUDW* HD3 ... 175 J7
Catherine Gv *BEE/HOL* * LS11 ... 123 G3
Catherine House La *HBR* HX7 ... 132 B1
Catherine Rd *HUDN* HD2 ... 177 G5
Catherine Slack *BRIG* HD6 ... 156 D2
Catherine St *BRIG* HD6 ... 157 F5
  ELL HX5 ... 175 J3
  KGHY BD21 ... 2 E5
Cat La *GTL/HWG* HX4 ... 174 B2
  LUD/ILL HX2 ... 152 C3
Catlow St *CAS* WF10 ... 168 B1
Catterton La *TAD* LS24 ... 51 J3
Cattlelaith La *KNOT* WF11 ... 170 D5
Cattle La *GFTH/SHER* LS25 ... 88 D5
Cattle Market St *OT* LS21 ... 39 H2
Caudle Hl *KNOT* WF11 ... 150 A3
Cauldwell Gdns *WBOW* * BD5 ... 117 K2
Caulms Wood Rd *DEWS* WF13 ... 161 G3
Causeway *GTL/HWG* HX4 ... 173 H7

HFAX HX1 ....17 J6
Causeway Head
*RPDN/SBR * HX6 ....172 C4
Causeway Head La
RPDN/SBR HX6 ....172 C5
Cautley Rd *OSM* LS9 ....15 H4
Cavalier Ap *OSM* LS9 ....15 G4
Cavalier Cl *OSM* LS9 ....15 G4
Cavalier Ct *OSM* LS9 ....15 G3
Cavalier Dr *IDLE* BD10 ....78 E5
Cavalier Gdns *OSM* LS9 ....15 G3
Cavalier Ga *OSM* LS9 ....15 G4
Cavalier Gn *OSM* LS9 ....15 G4
Cavalier Ms *OSM* LS9 ....15 G4
Cavalier Vw *OSM* LS9 ....15 G4
Cave Crs *WKFDW/WTN* WF2 ....183 K5
Cave Hl *HIPP* HX3 ....135 J3
Cave La *EARD/LOFT* WF3 ....163 J1
Cavendish Av *PONT* WF8 ....169 K5
Cavendish Ct *KGHY* * BD21........3 G4
Cavendish Dr *BGLY* BD16 ....56 A7
GSLY LS20..................58 E3
Cavendish Gv *GSLY* LS20.........58 E3
Cavendish Ms *AL/HA/HU* LS17 ....63 J7
Cavendish Pl *PDSY/CALV* LS28 ..100 A4
Cavendish Ri *PDSY/CALV* LS28...100 D6
Cavendish Rd *GSLY* LS20..........58 E3
IDLE BD10..................78 C5
LDS LS1......................9 L5
Cavendish St *BVRD* LS3...........8 F7
HFAX HX1 ....16 E1
KGHY BD21...................3 G4
PDSY/CALV LS28 ....100 D6
YEA LS19....................59 K4
Cavendish Ter *HFAX* * HX1 ....16 E6
Cavewell Cl *OSS* WF5...........182 E6
Cavewell Gdns *OSS* WF5........182 E6
Cawcliffe Dr *BRIG* HD6 ....157 F4
Cawcliffe Rd *BRIG* HD6 ....157 F4
Cawdel Cl *GFTH/SHER* LS25 .....131 G2
Cawdel Wy *GFTH/SHER* LS25 ....131 G2
Cawley Garth *HECK* WF16 ......160 B5
Cawley La *HECK* WF16 ....160 B5
Cawood Hvn *WBSY* * BD6 ....116 D6
Cawthorne Av *HUDN* HD2 ....177 F7
Caxton Gdns *PONT* WF8 ....169 J5
Caxton Rd *OT* LS21 ....39 F4
Caxton St *WBY* LS22 ....29 H4
Caygill Ter *HFAX* HX1 ....17 G9
Caythorne Wk *IDLE* BD10 ....81 F3
Caythorpe Rd *BHP/TINH* LS16 ....82 A5
Cecil Av *BAIL* BD17 ....57 H7
GTHN BD7..................117 G2
HIPP HX3 ....136 D7
Cecil Gv *WOR/ARM* LS12 ....8 A9
Cecil Mt *WOR/ARM* LS12 ....8 A9
Cecil Rd *WOR/ARM* LS12 ....8 B9
Cecil St *HWTH* BD22 ....73 F4
WOR/ARM LS12................8 A9
Cedar Av *OSS* WF5 ....182 D6
WOR/ARM LS12 ....12 A1
Cedar Cl *PONT* WF8 ....189 H4
WOR/ARM LS12 ....12 A2
Cedar Ct *RTHW* LS26 ....126 B7
Cedar Dr *EARL* WF12 ....182 A3
LM/WK BD12.................137 K3
TAD LS24......................50 C7
Cedar Gv *FEA/AMT* WF7 ....188 C2
GTL/HWG HX4 ....174 C2
Cedar Mt *WOR/ARM* LS12 ......102 A6
Cedar Pl *WOR/ARM* LS12 ....102 A6
Cedar Rdg *GFTH/SHER* LS25 ....108 A4
Cedar Rd *EARL* WF12 ....181 K3
NORM WF6..................186 E2
WOR/ARM LS12 ....12 A1
The Cedars *BHP/TINH* LS16 ......61 J2
Cedar St *HFAX* HX1 ....16 B6
KGHY BD21...................53 J7
WOR/ARM LS12 ....102 A6
Cedar Ter *WOR/ARM* LS12 ......102 A6
Cedar Wk *FEA/AMT* WF7.........188 C3
Cedar Wy *CLECK* BD19 ....139 H7
Celandine Cl *PONT* WF8 ....189 J2
Cemetery La *AIRE* BD20 ....53 J1
EARD/LOFT WF3 ....144 D6
RPDN/SBR HX6 ....153 H4
Cemetery Rd *BEE/HOL* LS11 ......13 J8
BGLY BD16....................55 H7
BTLY WF17..................160 E3
DEWS WF13..................180 D2
GIR BD8.......................4 B5
HECK WF16..................160 A4
HWTH BD22...................72 B5
NORM WF6..................167 F6
PDSY/CALV LS28 ....100 A5
WBSY BD6..................117 G2
YEA LS19....................59 K4
Centenary Rd *BAIL* BD17 ....58 A7
Centenary Sq *EARL* WF12.......180 E5
Centenary Wy *BTLY* WF17 ......160 E2
Central Av *BAIL* BD17 ....77 G2
HUDN HD2..................177 G7
HWTH BD22...................73 G1
LVSG WF15..................158 C3
SHPY BD18...................77 G5
WBOW BD5..................117 H2
Central Av East *LVSG* WF15 ....158 C4
Central Cl *HUDN* HD2 ....177 G6
Central Dr *CAS* WF10 ....167 J1
HUDN HD2..................177 G6
HWTH BD22...................73 G1
Central Pde *OSM* LS9 ....124 D3
Central Pk *HFAX* HX1...........16 F9
Central Rd *HUDN* HD2 ....177 G6
Central St *DEWS* WF13 ....181 F1
HFAX HX1...................17 G6
LDS LS1.......................9 J9
Centre La *TAD* LS24 ....50 E7
Centre St *HECK* * WF16 ....159 K4
WBOW * BD5................117 H3
Century Pl *GIR* BD8 ....5 C1
Century Rd *ELL* HX5 ....175 J2
Century St *KGHY* * BD21.........53 J7
Century Wy *MSTN/BAR* LS15 ...106 C6
Ceres Rd *WBY* LS22 ....29 J4
Chaddlewood Cl *HORS* LS18 ......81 F3
Chadwell Springs *BGLY* BD16 ....75 K5

Chadwick Crs *DEWS* WF13 ......160 E7
Chadwick Fold La *MIRF* WF14 ....179 H5
Chadwick Hall Gdns
MIRF WF14..................179 G5
Chadwick La *MIRF* WF14 ....179 G6
Chadwick St *MID* LS10 ....14 D3
Chadwick St South *MID* LS10 ....14 D4
Chaffinch Rd *GIR* BD8 ....96 B6
Chain St *BFD* BD1.................5 K5
CAS WF10..................148 B7
Chalcroft Cl *HECK* WF16 ....160 B3
Chald La *WKFDW/WTN* WF2 ......18 C6
Chalfont Rd *BHP/TINH* * LS16 ....82 A5
Chalice Cl *MID* LS10 ....123 K7
Challenge Wy *BOW* BD4 ....118 E2
BTLY WF17..................161 J4
Challis Gv *WBOW* BD5 ....117 K3
Chalner Av *MOR* LS27 ....141 J5
Chalner Ct *MOR* LS27 ....141 J5
Chalwood *HUDN* HD2 ....177 K5
Champion Av *OSM* LS10 ....168 D3
Chancellor St *HDGY* LS6 ....10 C2
Chancery La *OSS* WF5 ....182 A1
WKFDE WF1...................18 E4
Chancery Rd *EARL* WF12 ....182 A1
The Chandlers *MID* LS10..........14 C2
Chandler Cl *BTLY* WF17 ....140 B6
Chandlers Cl *WKFDE* WF1 ......164 C3
Chandos Av *RHAY* LS8 ....83 K4
Chandos Fold *RHAY* LS8 ....83 K4
Chandos Gdns *RHAY* LS8 ....83 K4
Chandos Garth *RHAY* LS8 ....83 K4
Chandos Gn *RHAY* LS8 ....83 K4
Chandos Pl *RHAY* LS8 ....84 A1
Chandos St *BOW* BD4 ....6 A8
KGHY BD21....................2 F8
Chandos Ter *RHAY* LS8 ....84 A4
Chandos Wk *RHAY* LS8 ....83 K5
Changegate *HWTH* BD22 ....72 C4
Changegate Ct *HWTH* BD22......72 C5
Change La *HIPP* HX3............155 H6
Channing Wy *BFD* BD1.............5 L7
Chantrell Ct *LDSU* LS2 ....14 C1
Chantry Cl *PONT* WF8 ....189 G2
Chantry Cft *MSTN/BAR* LS15 ....106 A6
Chantry Garth *MSTN/BAR* LS15 ..106 A6
Chantry La *TAD* LS24 ....69 H7
TAD LS24......................70 A5
Chantry Rd *WKFDW/WTN* WF2 ...183 K5
Chapel Av *HECK* WF16 ....160 B4
Chapel Cl *EARL* WF12 ....181 G7
GFTH/SHER LS25 ....107 H6
GTL/HWG HX4 ....174 E5
Chapel Ct *MSTN/BAR* LS15 .....105 H5
Chapel Cft *BRIG* HD6 ....176 E2
Chapel Fold *BEE/HOL* LS11 .....122 D4
BTLY WF17..................160 D5
HDGY LS6......................8 D3
LM/WK BD12.................137 H7
MSTN/BAR LS15 ....105 H5
PDSY/CALV * LS28 ....100 B7
WBSY BD6..................117 G5
Chapel Gv *BGLY* BD16 ....55 H6
Chapel Hl *MOR* LS27 ....141 K2
YEA LS19.....................59 J4
Chapel Hill La *OT* LS21 ....42 A2
Chapel House Rd *LM/WK* BD12...117 J7
Chapel La *BAIL* BD17 ....58 C6
BSPA/BRAM LS23 ....48 C4
BTLY WF17..................140 C6
CUL/QBY BD13 ....115 G3
CUL/QBY BD13 ....116 A4
EARL WF12..................181 G7
GFTH/SHER LS25 ....107 H6
GFTH/SHER LS25 ....128 A5
HBR HX7....................132 C5
HDGY LS6......................8 D3
HECK WF16..................160 B4
HIPP HX3 ....155 G6
HIPP HX3 ....156 A4
HWTH BD22...................52 D4
KGHY BD21....................2 F5
MSTN/BAR LS15 ....87 H5
RPDN/SBR HX6 ....154 A4
WIL/AL BD15..................96 B5
WOR/ARM LS12 ....12 B1
WOR/ARM LS12 ....121 G1
YEA LS19.....................59 J4
Chapel Ms *GIR* * BD8 ....96 B5
Chapel Pl *HDGY* LS6 ....82 C7
Chapel Rd *AIRE* BD20 ....32 D5
BGLY BD16....................55 H6
CHAL LS7.....................83 J7
LM/WK BD12.................137 J1
Chapel Rw *WIL/AL* BD15 ....75 F6
Chapel St *AIRE* BD20 ....21 F7
BFD BD1.......................6 B6
BRIG HD6....................156 D3
CLECK BD19..................139 F7
CUL/QBY BD13 ....94 A3
CUL/QBY BD13 ....95 G7
CUL/QBY BD13 ....115 G5
EARD/LOFT WF3 ....142 E6
EARD/LOFT WF3 ....144 E4
EARD/LOFT WF3 ....163 H1
EARD/LOFT WF3 ....165 F3
EARL WF12..................181 F3
ECHL BD2....................98 E1
GFTH/SHER LS25 ....151 K1
GTL/HWG HX4 ....174 E5
HDGY * LS6...................82 C7
ILK LS29......................22 C1
LUD/ILL * HX2................134 B7
LVSG WF15..................158 D3
LVSG WF15..................159 K4
MIRF WF14..................179 H4
MSTN/BAR LS15 ....105 H5
OSS WF5....................183 F5
PDSY/CALV LS28 ....79 J5
PDSY/CALV LS28 ....100 B4
TAD LS24......................50 D7
WBOW * BD5................117 H3
WBSY BD6..................117 H5
YEA * LS19...................59 J7
Chapel St North *LUD/ILL* HX2 ...134 C4
Chapel Ter *HDGY* LS6.............82 C7
WIL/AL * BD15................96 A4
Chapeltown *HFAX* HX1............16 F5

Chapeltown Rd *CHAL* LS7..........10 C4
ECHL BD2.....................98 E1
Chapel Wk *BGLY* BD16 ....75 J1
ECHL BD2.....................98 E1
Chapel Yd *MSTN/BAR* WF15 .....106 A7
Chapman St *BOW* BD4 ....7 J8
OSM LS9......................10 F6
Charles Av *BFDE* BD3 ....7 K5
HIPP HX5....................155 K4
OSM LS9......................15 H3
WKFDE WF1..................164 C3
WKFDE WF1..................185 G6
Charles Cotton Cl
WKFDW/WTN WF2 ....183 J1
Charles Ct *HWTH* * BD22........92 D3
Charles Gdns *BEE/HOL* LS11.....13 J6
Charles Gv *RTHW* LS26 ....145 K1
Charles Jones Ct *BTLY* WF17....160 E3
Charles St *BAIL* BD17 ....77 G4
BFD BD1......................5 M6
BGLY BD16....................75 J1
BTLY WF17..................161 F4
CAS WF10...................168 D1
CLECK BD19..................139 J7
DEWS WF13..................180 D1
DEWS WF13..................180 C1
EARL WF12..................181 H1
ELL HX5......................175 J4
HFAX HX1....................17 J6
HORS LS18....................80 E4
OSS WF5....................182 E5
OT LS21.......................39 H3
PDSY/CALV LS28 ....100 A2
RPDN/SBR HX6 ....153 J3
WKFDE WF1..................19 H6
Charlestown Rd *HIPP* HX3........17 J4
Charlesworth St *EARL* * WF12 ...181 G7
Charlesworth Gv *LUD/ILL* HX2...134 B7
Charlesworth Pl
EARD/LOFT WF3 ....165 J1
Charlesworth Sq *CLECK* BD19 ...139 H7
Charlesworth St *EARL* WF12 ....181 F5
Charlesworth Ter *LUD/ILL* HX2 ..134 B7
Charlesworth Wy
WKFDW/WTN WF2 ....18 D7
Charlotte Cl *BTLY* WF17 ....140 C4
Charlotte Ct *HWTH* BD22 ....72 E4
Charlotte Gv *OSS* * WF5.........182 E5
Charlotte St *WKFDE* WF1 ....18 F6
Charlton Gv *WKFDE* * WF1 ....19 G6
OSM LS9......................15 J2
Charlton Mt *OSM* LS9 ....15 J2
Charlton Pl *OSM* LS9 ....15 J2
Charlton Rd *OSM* LS9 ....15 J2
Charlton St *OSM* LS9 ....15 J2
Charnley Dr *CHAL* LS7 ....83 K6
Charnwood Bank *HECK* WF16 ....160 B3
Charnwood Cl *ECHL* * BD2 ....98 D3
Charnwood Gv *ECHL* BD2.........98 D3
Charnwood Rd *ECHL* BD2.........98 D3
Charterhouse Rd *IDLE* BD10 ......78 C3
Charteris Rd *GIR* BD8 ....96 C6
Chartists Wy *MOR* LS27 ....141 K4
Charville Gdns *AL/HA/HU* LS17 ...85 G1
The Chase *EARD/LOFT* WF3 .....165 H2
GFTH/SHER LS25 ....108 A6
KGHY BD21....................2 E9
WBY LS22.....................29 J3
YEA LS19.....................59 H7
Chase Wy *WBOW* BD5 ....117 K5
Chassum Gv *HTON* BD9 ....97 F3
Chaster St *BTLY* WF17 ....160 D3
Chatham St *BFDE* BD3 ....6 B1
HFAX HX1....................16 E5
RPDN/SBR HX6 ....153 J3
Chat Hill Rd *CUL/QBY* BD13 .....115 J1
Chatswood Av *BEE/HOL* LS11 ...122 E6
Chatswood Crs *BEE/HOL* LS11 ..122 E6
Chatswood Dr *BEE/HOL* LS11 ...122 E5
Chatsworth Av *PDSY/CALV* LS28 ...99 H5
PONT WF8...................169 K5
Chatsworth Cl *RHAY* LS8.........11 K2
Chatsworth Ct *EARL* WF12 ......181 J2
Chatsworth Crs
PDSY/CALV LS28 ....99 H5
Chatsworth Dr *PDSY/CALV* LS28 ...99 H5
WBY LS22.....................29 F3
Chatsworth Fall
PDSY/CALV LS28 ....99 H5
Chatsworth Ms *MOR* * LS27.....142 B4
Chatsworth Pl *GIR* BD8...........97 C3
Chatsworth Ri *PDSY/CALV* LS28 ...99 H5
Chatsworth Rd *PDSY/CALV* LS28 ...99 H5
RHAY LS8.....................11 J2
Chatsworth St *KGHY* BD21 ....3 K4
Chatsworth Ter *EARL* WF12 .....181 J2
Chatts Wood Fold
LM/WK BD12.................138 C2
Chaucer Av *EARD/LOFT* WF3 ...165 F2
PDSY/CALV LS28 ....100 C7
Chaucer Gdns *PDSY/CALV* LS28 ..100 C7
Chaucer Gv *PDSY/CALV* LS28 ...100 C7
Chaucer St *HFAX* HX1 ....16 A7
Cheapside *BFD* BD1 ....5 M5
BTLY WF17..................161 G3
CLECK BD19..................159 F1
HFAX * HX1..................17 H6
HIPP HX3....................136 B1
NORM WF6..................166 E6
WKFDE WF1..................18 D4
Cheddington Gv *WIL/AL* BD15 ....96 A5
Chellow Gdns *WIL/AL* * BD15.....95 K3
Chellow Grange Rd *HTON* BD9 ...96 B2
Chellow La *HTON* BD9.............96 B3
Chellow St *WBOW* BD5...........117 J4
Chellow Wy *EARL* WF12 ....181 F2
Chelmsford Rd *BFDE* BD3 ....7 H4
Chelmsford Ter *BFDE* BD3 ....7 H5
Chelsea Cl *WOR/ARM* LS12 ......12 B3
Chelsea Man *HIPP* HX3 ....135 K5
Chelsea Rd *GTHN* BD7 ....116 E2
Chelsea St *KGHY* BD21 ....2 E8
Chelsfield Wy *MSTN/BAR* LS15 ..106 C2
Cheltenham Av *ILK* LS29 ....24 D5
Cheltenham Ct *HIPP* * HX3 ......155 G4
Cheltenham Gdns *HIPP* HX3 .....155 G4
Cheltenham Pl *HIPP* HX3 ....155 G4

Cheltenham Rd *ECHL* BD2 ....78 A7
Chelwood Av *RHAY* LS8 ....83 K1
Chelwood Crs *RHAY* LS8 ....84 A2
Chelwood Dr *RHAY* LS8 ....84 A2
WIL/AL BD15..................96 A6
Chelwood Gv *RHAY* LS8 ....84 A1
Chelwood Mt *RHAY* LS8 ....84 A1
Chelwood Pl *RHAY* LS8 ....83 K1
Chenies Cl *SCFT* LS14 ....105 F4
Chepstow Cl *GFTH/SHER* LS25 ..108 A6
Chepstow Dr *EARD/LOFT* WF3...143 J4
Chequerfield Av *PONT* WF8 .....190 A1
Chequerfield Cl *CAS* WF10 ......167 K2
Chequerfield Dr *PONT* WF8 .....189 K2
Chequerfield La *PONT* WF8 .....190 A2
Chequerfield Mt *PONT* WF8 .....190 A2
Chequerfield Rd *PONT* WF8 .....189 K2
Chequers Ct *PONT* WF8 ....190 A2
Chequers Ct *PONT* WF8 ....190 A1
Cheriton Dr *CUL/QBY* BD13 .....115 J5
Cherry Ct *HDGY* LS6..............82 E6
HFAX * HX1...................16 D4
OSM LS9......................10 E7
Cherry Flds *ECHL* BD2 ....97 K1
Cherry Gv *HDGY* LS6 ....82 E6
ILK LS29.......................23 J5
Cherry Lea Ct *YEA* LS19 ....59 J7
Cherry Nook Rd *HUDN* HD2 .....177 K6
Cherry Pl *OSM* LS9 ....10 E7
Cherry Ri *SCFT* LS14 ....85 K4
Cherry Rw *OSM* LS9 ....10 E6
Cherry St *HWTH* BD22 ....73 F4
KGHY BD21....................3 L3
Cherry Tree Av *IDLE* * BD10 .....78 E6
Cherry Tree Ct
EARD/LOFT WF3 ....163 H1
Cherry Tree Crs
PDSY/CALV LS28 ....100 A2
Cherry Tree Dr *GTL/HWG* HX4 ...174 E2
PDSY/CALV LS28 ....100 A2
Cherry Tree Gdns *SHPY* BD18 ...78 A3
Cherry Tree Ri *KGHY* BD21 ....3 K8
Cherry Tree Rw *BGLY* BD16 ......74 C5
Cherry Tree Wk
EARD/LOFT WF3 ....163 H1
LDS LS1.......................14 B1
Cherrywood Cl *SCFT* LS14 ....85 J3
Cherrywood Gdns *SCFT* LS14 .....85 J3
Chervana Ct *BOW* BD4 ....119 F2
Cherwell Cft *GFTH/SHER* LS25 ..128 A1
Cherwell Dr *WBSY* BD6 ....116 E7
Chesham St *GTHN* BD7 ....5 H7
KGHY BD21....................3 K4
Chesney Av *MID* * LS10 ....14 C6
Chesnut End *BSPA/BRAM* LS23 ...48 D3
Chester Cl *HIPP* HX3 ....16 F1
Chester Gv *HIPP* * HX3 ....16 F1
Chester Pl *HIPP* HX3 ....16 F1
Chester Rd *HIPP* HX3 ....16 F1
Chester St *GTHN* BD7 ....5 K7
HIPP HX3.....................16 F1
RPDN/SBR HX6 ....153 J4
WOR/ARM LS12................8 B8
Chester Ter *HIPP* * HX3 ....16 F1
Chesterton Ct *HOR/CROF* WF4 ..183 H7
MSTN/BAR LS15 ....106 A7
Chestnut Av *BSPA/BRAM* LS23 ...48 B2
BTLY WF17..................160 D4
HDGY LS6......................8 F2
MSTN/BAR LS15 ....106 A3
WBY LS22.....................29 G3
Chestnut Cl *FEA/AMT* WF7 ......188 C2
GTL/HWG HX4 ....174 E1
HWTH * BD22...................2 B7
ILK LS29......................24 D6
Chestnut Ct *SHPY* BD18 ....76 D5
Chestnut Crs *NORM* WF6 ....186 D1
Chestnut Dr *BHP/TINH* LS16 ......62 D1
Chestnut Gdns *WOR/ARM* LS12 ..12 A3
Chestnut Gn *GFTH/SHER* LS25 ..131 G3
Chestnut Gv *BSPA/BRAM* LS23 ...48 B2
ECHL BD2.....................97 K1
HDGY LS6......................8 F2
PDSY/CALV LS28 ....79 J6
PONT WF8...................189 J3
RTHW LS26..................146 B1
Chestnut Mdw *MIRF* WF14 .....179 G2
Chestnut Pl *HDGY* LS6.............8 F2
Chestnut Ri *WOR/ARM* LS12 ....102 A7
Chestnut Rd *HDGY* LS6 ....8 F3
The Chestnuts *PONT* WF8 ....170 A4
Chestnut St *HDGY* LS6 ....8 F2
HFAX HX1....................16 A8
HUDN HD2..................177 J6
Chestnut Ter *EARL* WF12 ....181 F6
Chestnut Wk *WKFDW/WTN* WF2 ..18 A1
Chestnut Wy *BHP/TINH* LS16 .....62 A6
Chevet Mt *WIL/AL* BD15 ....95 K6
Chevin Av *ILK* LS29 ....38 B5
OT LS21.......................39 J4
Chevin End Rd *ILK* LS29 ....38 D6
Chevington Ct *YEA* * LS19 ....79 H1
Chevins Cl *BTLY* WF17 ....140 C7
Chevin Side *OT* LS21 ....39 H4
Cheviot Ct *GFTH/SHER* LS25 ....127 J5
Cheviot Ga *LM/WK* BD12 ....137 G1
Cheviot Pl *KNOT* WF11 ....171 F1
Cheviot Wy *MIRF* WF14 ....179 G2
Cheyne Wk *KGHY* * BD21 ....2 D7
Chichester St *WOR/ARM* LS12 .....8 B8
Chickenley La *EARL* WF12 ....181 K5
Chidswell Gdns *EARL* WF12 ......162 A5
Chidswell La *EARL* WF12 ....161 K5
Child La *LVSG* WF15 ....159 G6
Childs La *SHPY* BD18 ....77 K6
Childs Rd *WKFDW/WTN* WF2 ....183 J1
Chiltern Av *CAS* WF10 ....167 J3
KNOT WF11..................171 F4
Chiltern Cl *GFTH/SHER* LS25 ....127 J5
Chiltern Ct *BRAM* LS13 ....80 B7
GFTH/SHER LS25 ....127 J5
Chiltern Dr *MIRF* WF14 ....179 G2
Chiltern Rd *EARL* WF12 ....161 J7
Chiltern Wy *LVSG* WF15 ....158 C3
Chilver Dr *BOW* BD4 ....119 H4
Chinewood Av *BTLY* WF17 ......160 E2

Chippendale Ri *GIR* BD8 ....96 C5
OT LS21.......................27 H7
Chirton Gv *RHAY* LS8 ....84 B7
Chislehurst Pl *WBOW* BD5 ......117 H3
Chiswick St *HDGY* LS6 ....8 E6
Chiswick Ter *HDGY* LS6 ....8 E6
Chorley La *BVRD* LS3 ....9 K8
Chrisharben Pk *CLAY* BD14 .....116 B2
Chrismoor *IDLE* BD10 ....78 B5
Christ Church Av
WOR/ARM LS12 ....102 A5
Christ Church Mt
WOR/ARM LS12 ....102 A5
Christ Church Pde
WOR/ARM LS12 ....102 A5
Christ Church Pl
WOR/ARM LS12 ....102 A5
Christ Church Rd
WOR/ARM LS12 ....102 A5
Christ Church Ter
WOR/ARM LS12 ....102 A5
Christ Church Vw
WOR/ARM LS12 ....102 A5
Christopher Rd *HDGY* LS6 ....9 K2
Christopher St *WBOW* * BD5 ....117 H3
Christopher Ter *WBOW* BD5 ....117 H3
Church Ap *GFTH/SHER* LS25 ....107 J7
Church Av *HDGY* LS6 ....82 E5
HORS LS18....................80 E3
MOR LS27...................121 F6
RTHW LS26..................126 D4
WKFDE WF1..................185 G2
Churchbalk Dr *PONT* WF8 ....189 K3
Churchbalk La *PONT* WF8 ....189 K2
Church Bank *BFD* BD1 ....6 A6
LUD/ILL HX2.................154 A2
RPDN/SBR * HX6 ....153 K4
Churchbank Wy *EARL* WF12 .....181 F5
Church Cswy *BSPA/BRAM* LS23 ...48 C1
Church Cl *HECK* WF16 ....160 A4
HOR/CROF WF4 ....186 E7
LUD/ILL HX2.................134 A2
OT LS21.......................41 F3
RTHW LS26..................126 D4
SCFT LS14...................105 J1
Church Ct *GTHN* * BD7 ....116 E1
NORM WF6..................166 D7
YEA LS19.....................59 J5
Church Crs *AL/HA/HU* LS17 ......83 H1
RTHW LS26..................126 E5
TAD LS24......................70 C4
YEA LS19.....................59 H5
Church Cft *TAD* LS24 ....91 F7
Church Dr *AL/HA/HU* LS17 ....45 J5
Church Farm *SCFT* LS14 ....66 C5
Church Farm Cl
EARD/LOFT WF3 ....144 D6
NORM * WF6................166 C4
Churchfarm Garth
AL/HA/HU LS17 ....65 G7
Church Farm Vw
MSTN/BAR * LS15 ....87 H5
Churchfield Cl *LVSG* WF15 ......159 H4
Churchfield Cft *NORM* WF6 .....166 C4
RTHW LS26..................145 G2
Churchfield Gv *RTHW* LS26 .....145 F2
Churchfield La *CAS* WF10 ....168 E2
RTHW LS26..................145 F1
Churchfield Rd *RTHW* LS26 .....145 G2
Church Flds *ECHL* BD2 ....98 E3
NORM WF6..................166 D7
Churchfields *HUDN* HD2 ....178 A6
Churchfields Rd *BRIG* HD6 ......157 F5
Churchfield St *BTLY* * WF17 .....161 F3
Church Gdns *AL/HA/HU* LS17 .....83 J1
GFTH/SHER LS25 ....107 J7
MOR LS27...................121 F7
Church Garth *CAS* WF10 ....168 E2
OT LS21.......................41 F3
Church Ga *HORS* LS18 ....80 E3
Churchgate *BHP/TINH* LS16 ......41 G7
MOR LS27...................121 F7
Church Gn *GIR* BD8 ....4 F1
LUD/ILL * HX2...............134 B6
Church Gv *HDGY* LS6 ....82 D5
HORS LS18....................80 E3
Church Hl *BAIL* BD17 ....57 J7
BHP/TINH LS16 ....41 G7
BSPA/BRAM LS25 ....48 C7
GFTH/SHER LS25 ....130 B1
SCFT LS14....................66 D5
Church Hill Gdns
PDSY/CALV LS28 ....100 C3
Church Hill Gn *PDSY/CALV* LS28 ..100 C3
Church Hill Mt *PDSY/CALV* LS28 ..100 C3
Churchill Gdns *LDSU* LS2 ....9 L5
Churchill Gv *HECK* WF16 ....160 B5
Churchill Rd *CUL/QBY* BD13 ......95 J7
Church La *AL/HA/HU* LS17 ....44 A3
BAIL BD17.....................58 D6
BHP/TINH LS16 ....62 B7
BRIG HD6....................157 F5
CHAL LS7.....................83 J6
CLECK BD19..................139 K7
DEWS WF13..................180 C1
EARD/LOFT WF3 ....162 C1
EARD/LOFT WF3 ....163 H1
EARL WF12..................181 H7
ELL HX5......................176 C2
FEA/AMT WF7 ....168 B7
FEA/AMT WF7 ....187 G1
GFTH/SHER LS25 ....107 J6
GFTH/SHER LS25 ....108 D6
GFTH/SHER LS25 ....128 A5
GFTH/SHER LS25 ....131 J6
GTL/HWG HX4 ....174 D5
HDGY LS6.....................82 E5
HECK WF16..................160 A4
HIPP HX3.....................156 B4
HORS LS18....................80 E3
LUD/ILL HX2.................134 B6
LVSG WF15..................158 C5
LVSG WF15..................159 H3
MIRF WF14..................179 K5
MSTN/BAR LS15 ....105 K3
NORM WF6..................166 D7
OT LS21.......................26 C7
PDSY/CALV LS28 ....100 B6

PONT WF8 ....189 J1
PONT WF8 ....190 E4
RPDN/SBR HX6 ....172 E6
RTHW LS26 ....126 D5
RTHW LS26 ....147 F5
TAD LS24 ....70 C3
WBSY BD6 ....117 G6
WBY LS22 ....46 E1
WKFDE WF1 ....164 C3
Church Lane Av WKFDE WF1 ....164 C3
Church Mdw BSPA/BRAM LS23 ....48 C7
BTLY WF17 ....140 A6
Church Ms BSPA/BRAM LS23 ....48 C7
GFTH/SHER LS25 ....111 F5
Church Mt HORS LS18 ....80 E3
Church Pk LVSG WF15 ....159 F6
Church Pl GFTH/SHER LS25 ....107 J6
HFAX HX1 ....16 E7
Church Rd BTLY WF17 ....140 C7
EARD/LOFT WF3 ....165 G3
HORS LS18 ....80 E4
LVSG WF15 ....159 F6
NORM WF6 ....166 A5
OSM LS9 ....14 E2
RTHW LS26 ....127 H6
WBSY BD6 ....117 G6
WOR/ARM LS12 ....12 B1
Church Rw LDSU LS2 ....14 C1
Church Side RTHW LS26 ....147 F5
Church Side Cl HIPP HX3 ....17 H2
Church Side Dr HIPP HX3 ....17 H2
Churchside Vls RTHW LS26 ....147 F5
Church Sq GFTH/SHER LS25 ....107 J6
Church St BGLY BD16 ....75 K2
BRIG HD6 ....176 E1
BSPA/BRAM LS23 ....48 C3
CAS WF10 ....148 C7
CLECK BD19 ....159 F1
CUL/OBY * BD13 ....74 A6
DEWS WF13 ....180 B4
EARL WF12 ....181 G1
ELL HX5 ....175 J2
GIR BD8 ....4 F1
GSLY LS20 ....59 F2
GTL/HWG HX4 ....175 G2
HECK WF16 ....160 A5
HFAX HX1 ....17 J7
HWTH BD22 ....72 C5
HWTH BD22 ....92 D3
ILK LS29 ....22 D1
KGHY BD21 ....2 F6
KGHY BD21 ....3 J4
KNOT WF11 ....150 D7
KSTL LS5 ....101 K1
LVSG WF15 ....158 D3
LVSG WF15 ....159 H3
MID LS10 ....14 E9
MOR LS27 ....121 F7
MOR LS27 ....141 K2
OSS WF5 ....182 C2
RTHW LS26 ....125 K7
RTHW LS26 ....145 F2
SHPY BD18 ....77 J4
TAD LS24 ....91 F7
TAD LS24 ....91 K6
WBSY BD6 ....116 D7
WBY LS22 ....29 H4
WKFDE WF1 ....18 F8
YEA LS19 ....59 H5
Church Ter LUD/ILL HX2 ....134 A2
Church Vw CLECK BD19 ....138 C7
GFTH/SHER LS25 ....111 F5
GFTH/SHER LS25 ....128 C4
GFTH/SHER LS25 ....131 F3
KSTL LS5 ....102 A1
RPDN/SBR HX6 ....153 K4
WKFDE WF1 ....185 F7
Church View Ms
BSPA/BRAM LS23 ....48 C5
Churchville
GFTH/SHER LS25 ....109 F6
Churchville Av
GFTH/SHER LS25 ....108 E6
Churchville Dr
GFTH/SHER LS25 ....109 F6
Churchville Ter
GFTH/SHER LS25 ....108 E5
Church Wk BTLY WF17 ....160 D5
EARL WF12 ....181 H4
HIPP HX3 ....135 K5
LDSU LS2 ....14 C1
Church Wy KGHY BD21 ....3 G6
MOR * LS27 ....141 K2
Church Wood Av
BHP/TINH LS16 ....82 B6
Church Wood Mt
BHP/TINH LS16 ....82 B6
Church Wood Rd
BHP/TINH LS16 ....82 B6
Churn La LUD/ILL HX2 ....154 A1
Churn Milk La HIPP HX3 ....134 D3
Churwell Av DEWS WF13 ....160 C5
Churwell Cl CAS WF10 ....168 C2
Churwell V EARL WF12 ....161 K6
Cinderhills La HIPP HX3 ....155 H5
Cinder La BSPA/BRAM LS23 ....48 D4
CAS WF10 ....148 B7
The Circle PONT WF8 ....189 K2
City La HIPP HX3 ....134 B6
City Rd GIR BD8 ....5 H4
City Sq LDS LS1 ....13 M1
Clapgate OT LS21 ....39 H2
Clapgate La RPDN/SBR HX6 ....172 E7
Clapham Dene Rd
MSTN/BAR LS15 ....105 J4
Clapham St CUL/OBY BD13 ....94 B5
Clapton Av HFAX HX1 ....16 D8
Clara Dr PDSY/CALV LS28 ....79 H5
Clara Rd ECHL BD2 ....78 A7
Clara St BRIG HD6 ....157 F7
PDSY/CALV LS28 ....100 A3
Clare Crs LM/WK BD12 ....137 H5
Clare Hall La HFAX HX1 ....17 H8
Claremont BVRD * LS3 ....9 J7
PDSY/CALV LS28 ....100 C6
Claremont Av BVRD LS3 ....9 J7
SHPY BD18 ....77 K6
Claremont Ct HDGY LS6 ....82 D6

Claremont Crs HDGY LS6 ....82 E7
SHPY BD18 ....77 K6
Claremont Dr HDGY LS6 ....82 D6
Claremont Gdns BGLY BD16 ....55 K7
Claremont Gv BVRD * LS3 ....9 J7
PDSY/CALV LS28 ....100 B6
SHPY BD18 ....77 K6
Claremont Pl WOR/ARM LS12 ....101 K6
HDGY LS6 ....82 D6
SHPY BD18 ....77 K6
Claremont Rd DEWS WF13 ....160 E7
HDGY LS6 ....82 D6
SHPY BD18 ....77 K6
Claremont St CLECK BD19 ....138 E7
ELL HX5 ....175 K3
RPDN/SBR * HX6 ....153 K3
RTHW * LS26 ....145 K1
WKFDE WF1 ....19 K9
WOR/ARM LS12 ....101 K6
Claremont Ter GTHN BD7 ....5 J8
WKFDW/WTN WF2 ....18 B7
WOR/ARM LS12 ....101 K6
Claremont Vw BVRD * LS3 ....9 J7
Claremont Vls BVRD * LS3 ....9 J7
Claremount HDGY LS6 ....82 D6
Claremount Rd HIPP HX3 ....135 F5
Claremount Ter HIPP HX3 ....135 F5
Clarence Dr HORS LS18 ....80 E5
ILK LS29 ....38 A4
Clarence Gdns HORS LS18 ....80 E5
Clarence Rd HORS LS18 ....80 E5
MID LS10 ....14 E9
SHPY BD18 ....76 E4
WKFDW/WTN WF2 ....184 C6
Clarence St BRAM LS13 ....101 F4
BTLY WF17 ....161 G3
CLECK BD19 ....158 F1
HFAX HX1 ....16 F6
Clarence Ter PDSY/CALV LS28 ....100 A5
Clarence Vw WKFDW/WTN WF2 ....18 A7
Clarendon Ct WKFDE * WF1 ....18 F2
Clarendon Pl CUL/OBY BD13 ....115 F6
HFAX HX1 ....16 C7
LDSU LS2 ....9 J5
Clarendon Rd BGLY BD16 ....56 K7
BSPA/BRAM LS23 ....48 B2
LDSU LS2 ....9 J4
Clarendon St HWTH BD22 ....72 D6
KGHY BD21 ....2 E8
WKFDE WF1 ....18 E2
Clarendon Ter PDSY/CALV LS28 ....100 B7
Clarendon Wy LDSU LS2 ....9 K7
Clare Rd CLECK BD19 ....158 D1
HFAX HX1 ....17 H7
LM/WK BD12 ....137 H5
Clare St HFAX HX1 ....17 H7
Clarges St WBOW BD5 ....117 K4
Clarion St WKFDE WF1 ....19 K9
Clark Av OSM LS9 ....15 H2
Clark Ct HFAX/AMT WF7 ....168 A7
Clark Crs OSM LS9 ....15 H2
Clarke Crs NORM WF6 ....186 D2
Clarke Cl HECK WF16 ....160 B4
Clarke Gv WKFDE WF1 ....165 F7
Clarke Hall Rd EARD/LOFT WF3 ....165 F6
Clarke Dr EARD/LOFT WF3 ....162 D3
Clarke St DEWS WF13 ....160 D7
PDSY/CALV LS28 ....79 J6
Clark Gv OSM LS9 ....15 H3
Clark La OSM LS9 ....15 G2
Clark Mt OSM LS9 ....15 H2
Clark Rd OSM LS9 ....15 H3
Clark Rw OSM LS9 ....15 H3
Clarkson Vw HECK WF16 ....160 B4
Clarkson Cl HECK WF16 ....160 B4
Clarkson Ct NORM WF6 ....167 F7
Clarkson Dr GFTH/SHER LS25 ....151 F4
Clarkson St DEWS WF13 ....180 B3
Clarkson Vw HDGY LS6 ....9 K1
Clark Spring Ri MOR LS27 ....122 A7
Clark Ter OSM LS9 ....15 H2
Clark Vw OSM LS9 ....15 H3
Clayborn Vw CLECK BD19 ....158 E2
Clay Butts HUDN HD2 ....176 D7
Clayfield Dr GTHN BD7 ....117 F4
Clay Hill Dr LM/WK BD12 ....137 J4
Clay House La GTL/HWG HX4 ....175 G2
Claymore Ri AIRE BD20 ....33 G2
Claypit La CAS WF10 ....129 G7
Clay Pit La CHAL LS7 ....10 B6
Claypit La SCFT LS14 ....66 C6
Clay Pits La HFAX HX1 ....16 A4
RPDN/SBR HX6 ....172 C2
Clay St HFAX HX1 ....16 B5
RPDN/SBR HX6 ....153 K4
Clayton Av GFTH/SHER LS25 ....128 A4
Clayton Cl MID LS10 ....124 A4
Clayton Ct FEA/AMT WF7 ....188 B4
MID LS10 ....124 A4
Clayton Dr MID LS10 ....124 A4
Clayton Gv YEA LS19 ....59 J4
Clayton La CLAY BD14 ....116 A3
WBOW BD5 ....117 K2
Clayton Ms NORM WF6 ....166 D4
Clayton Pl NORM WF6 ....166 D4
Clayton Ri KGHY BD21 ....2 D7
WKFDE WF1 ....164 C3
Clayton Rd GTHN BD7 ....116 D2
MID LS10 ....124 A4
Claytons Buildings
FEA/AMT WF7 ....188 C1
Clayton St RTHW * LS26 ....145 G2
WKFDW/WTN WF2 ....18 B6
Clayton Wy MID LS10 ....124 A4
Clayton Wood Bank
BHP/TINH LS16 ....81 J3
Clayton Wood Cl
BHP/TINH LS16 ....81 J3
Clayton Wood Ct
BHP/TINH LS16 ....81 J3
Clayton Wood Ri
BHP/TINH LS16 ....81 J3
Clayton Wood Rd
BHP/TINH LS16 ....81 J3
The Clearings MID LS10 ....123 J6
Cleasby Rd ILK LS29 ....38 B7
Cleavesty La AL/HA/HU LS17 ....45 J3
Cleckheaton Rd WBSY BD6 ....117 J7
Cleeve Hl YEA LS19 ....59 J7
Clegg La GTL/HWG HX4 ....174 C2
Clement St NORM WF6 ....167 G2

Clement St GIR BD8 ....4 A3
RPDN/SBR * HX6 ....153 J4
WKFDW/WTN WF2 ....184 A4
Clement Ter EARL WF12 ....181 F3
WKFDE WF1 ....145 F3
Cleopatra Pl BRAM LS13 ....101 F4
Clerk Green St BTLY WF17 ....160 E4
Clevedon Pl HIPP HX3 ....134 D5
Cleveland Av HIPP * HX3 ....155 H4
KNOT WF11 ....171 H4
WKFDW/WTN WF2 ....183 J7
Cleveland Garth
WKFDW/WTN WF2 ....183 J7
Cleveland Gv
WKFDW/WTN WF2 ....183 J7
Cleveland Rd HTON BD9 ....97 G2
Cleveleys Av BEE/HOL LS11 ....13 H7
Cleveleys Ct BEE/HOL * LS11 ....13 H8
Cleveleys Mt BEE/HOL * LS11 ....13 H7
Cleveleys Rd BEE/HOL LS11 ....13 H7
Cleveleys St BEE/HOL * LS11 ....13 H7
Cleveleys Ter BEE/HOL * LS11 ....13 H7
Cliff Ct LVSG WF15 ....159 H5
Cliff Crs GFTH/SHER LS25 ....127 K1
LUD/ILL HX2 ....154 B3
Cliff Dr DY YEA LS19 ....79 H1
Cliffdale Rd CHAL LS7 ....103 G1
Cliffe Av BAIL BD17 ....77 H1
BGLY BD16 ....74 D3
HIPP HX3 ....157 F1
Cliffe Crs AIRE BD20 ....54 E3
Cliffe Crest HOR/CROF WF4 ....183 G7
Cliffe Dr DY YEA LS19 ....79 H1
Cliffe House Av
GFTH/SHER LS25 ....127 K1
Cliffe La BAIL BD17 ....77 H3
CUL/OBY BD13 ....95 H6
YEA LS19 ....79 K1
Cliffe La South BAIL BD17 ....77 H3
Cliffe La West BAIL BD17 ....77 H2
Cliffe Mill Fold AIRE BD20 ....55 H3
Cliffe Mt CLECK BD19 ....139 H6
Cliffe Pk * MOR * LS27 ....141 G4
Cliffe Park Cha WOR/ARM LS12 ....101 K7
Cliffe Park Cl WOR/ARM LS12 ....101 K7
Cliffe Park Crs WOR/ARM LS12 ....101 K7
Cliffe Park Dr WOR/ARM LS12 ....101 K7
Cliffe Park Mt WOR/ARM LS12 ....101 K7
Cliffe Park Ri WOR/ARM LS12 ....101 J7
Cliffe Park Wy MOR LS27 ....141 G4
Cliffe Rd BFDE BD3 ....98 A3
BRIG HD6 ....157 F6
KGHY BD21 ....53 K7
Cliffestone Dr AIRE BD20 ....55 G3
Cliffe St BTLY WF17 ....160 C4
CUL/OBY BD13 ....95 F6
DEWS WF13 ....161 G7
KGHY BD21 ....2 F3
Cliffe Ter BAIL BD17 ....77 H3
GIR BD8 ....5 K1
KGHY BD21 ....53 K7
RPDN/SBR HX6 ....153 H3
Cliffe Vw MOR LS27 ....141 G4
WIL/AL BD15 ....95 H3
Cliffe Wood Cl HTON BD9 ....96 D2
Cliff Gdns LUD/ILL HX2 ....154 B3
Cliff Hill La LUD/ILL HX2 ....153 J2
Cliff Hollins La LM/WK BD12 ....138 E1
Cliff La HDGY LS6 ....9 H1
RPDN/SBR HX6 ....172 E7
WKFDW/WTN WF2 ....18 D3
Cliff Mt HDGY LS6 ....9 J1
Cliff Mount St HDGY LS6 ....9 J1
Cliff Mount Ter HDGY LS6 ....9 J1
Cliff Rd HDGY LS6 ....9 J1
Cliff Side Gdns HDGY LS6 ....103 F1
Cliff St HWTH BD22 ....72 E5
Cliff Ter HDGY LS6 ....9 J1
Cliff Vale Rd SHPY BD18 ....77 G7
Cliff Villa Ct WKFDE WF1 ....18 C3
Cliff Wood Av SHPY BD18 ....77 G6
Clifton Av EARD/LOFT WF3 ....165 F3
HFAX HX1 ....16 A8
HOR/CROF WF4 ....183 F7
OSM LS9 ....11 K6
PONT WF8 ....189 G1
Clifton Cl HOR/CROF WF4 ....182 E7
Clifton Common BRIG HD6 ....157 H6
Clifton Ct DEWS WF13 ....160 C7
Clifton Crs HOR/CROF WF4 ....183 F7
Clifton Dr HOR/CROF WF4 ....183 F7
PDSY/CALV LS28 ....100 B5
Clifton Gv OSM LS9 ....11 K6
Clifton Hl PDSY/CALV LS28 ....100 B5
Clifton La OT LS21 ....27 F5
Clifton Mt OSM LS9 ....11 K6
Clifton Pl PDSY/CALV LS28 ....100 B5
SHPY BD18 ....77 G6
WKFDE WF1 ....184 C1
Clifton Rd HIPP HX3 ....155 F4
HOR/CROF WF4 ....186 E6
ILK LS29 ....24 C6
PDSY/CALV LS28 ....100 B5
Clifton Side HUDN HD2 ....178 A3
Clifton St GIR BD8 ....5 J1
HIPP HX3 ....16 C1
HWTH BD22 ....72 D6
RPDN/SBR HX6 ....153 K4
Clifton Ter BTLY WF17 ....161 G3
OSM LS9 ....11 K6

Clifton Vls GIR BD8 ....5 J1
Clipstone Av HDGY LS6 ....82 E6
Clipstone St WBOW BD5 ....117 K4
Clipston St HDGY LS6 ....82 E6
Clipston Ter HDGY * LS6 ....82 E6
Clive Pl GTHN BD7 ....4 D7
Clive Ter GTHN BD7 ....4 D7
Cloberry St LDSU LS2 ....9 J5
Clock La CUL/OBY BD13 ....94 A4
Clock View St KGHY BD21 ....53 J2
Clog Br AIRE BD20 ....33 F1
Clog Sole Rd BRIG HD6 ....156 E1
The Cloisters HFAX HX1 ....16 C9
The Close AL/HA/HU LS17 ....45 K5
AL/HA/HU LS17 ....63 F6
BSPA/BRAM LS23 ....48 C2
EARD/LOFT WF3 ....163 J1
GFTH/SHER LS25 ....127 K5
GSLY LS20 ....58 D3
MSTN/BAR LS15 ....87 G6
OSM LS9 ....14 E1
PONT WF8 ....190 A2
SCFT LS14 ....66 C5
TAD LS24 ....90 D7
WBY LS22 ....46 E2
Close Cl WBY LS22 ....29 G1
Close Head Dr CUL/OBY BD13 ....94 D7
Close Head La CUL/OBY BD13 ....94 E6
Close Lea BRIG HD6 ....156 E7
Close Lea Av BRIG HD6 ....156 E7
Close Lea Dr BRIG HD6 ....176 E1
Close Lea Wy BRIG HD6 ....156 E7
Close Rd CAS WF10 ....168 E1
Closes Rd BRIG HD6 ....156 E7
Cloth Hall St DEWS * WF13 ....181 G1
LDS LS1 ....14 B1
Cloudsdale Av WBOW BD5 ....117 K2
The Clough MIRF WF14 ....179 F3
Clough Av AIRE BD20 ....32 D5
Clough Bank LUD/ILL HX2 ....133 J2
Clough Bank La HWTH BD22 ....52 C5
Clough Dr BTLY WF17 ....140 D5
Clough Ga HWTH BD22 ....72 E2
Clough House La
GTL/HWG HX4 ....173 J6
Clough La BRIG HD6 ....157 J3
BRIG HD6 ....176 E3
HBR HX7 ....132 C2
HWTH BD22 ....72 D1
LUD/ILL HX2 ....133 K1
LVSG WF15 ....158 E3
Clough Pl LUD/ILL HX2 ....133 J2
Clough Rd HUDN HD2 ....177 F7
RPDN/SBR HX6 ....154 A6
Clough St MOR LS27 ....142 A3
WBOW BD5 ....117 K3
Clovelly Av BEE/HOL LS11 ....123 G3
Clovelly Gv BEE/HOL LS11 ....123 G3
Clovelly Pl BEE/HOL LS11 ....123 G3
Clovelly Rw BEE/HOL LS11 ....123 G3
Clovelly Ter BEE/HOL LS11 ....123 G3
Clover Cl PDSY/CALV LS28 ....79 H6
Clover Crs PDSY/CALV LS28 ....79 H6
Cloverdale HIPP HX3 ....116 C7
Clover Hl LVSG WF15 ....158 E3
Clover Hill Cl HFAX HX1 ....16 F8
Clover Hill Rd HFAX HX1 ....154 E3
Clover Hill Ter HFAX HX1 ....154 E3
Clover Hill Vw HFAX * HX1 ....154 E3
Clover Ri KGHY BD21 ....3 M5
Clover St BTLY WF17 ....117 G3
Cloverville Ap WBSY BD6 ....117 H7
Club La BRAM LS13 ....80 B7
LUD/ILL HX2 ....134 C4
Club Rw CHAL LS7 ....83 H5
YEA LS19 ....59 K4
Club St GTHN BD7 ....4 B8
Clumber Dr CLECK BD19 ....159 J4
Clunters La LUD/ILL HX2 ....152 C2
Clutton St BTLY WF17 ....161 H3
Clyde Cha WOR/ARM * LS12 ....12 F3
Clyde Ct WOR/ARM LS12 ....12 E2
Clyde Gdns WOR/ARM LS12 ....12 E2
Clyde Gra WOR/ARM LS12 ....12 E3
Clydesdale Dr WBSY BD6 ....116 E7
Clyde St BGLY BD16 ....75 J1
RPDN/SBR HX6 ....153 J5
WKFDE WF1 ....19 K9
Clyde Vw WOR/ARM LS12 ....12 E3
Clyde Wk WOR/ARM LS12 ....12 E3
Coach La CLECK * BD19 ....139 F7
CUL/OBY BD13 ....95 J7
Coach Rd BAIL BD17 ....77 G3
GSLY LS20 ....58 E4
HIPP HX3 ....156 E1
HUDN HD2 ....176 B4
RPDN/SBR HX6 ....172 E5
WKFDE WF1 ....164 D3
WOR/ARM LS12 ....121 H3
Coal Hill Dr BRAM LS13 ....100 C1
Coal Hill Fold BRAM LS13 ....100 C1
Coal Hill Gdns BRAM LS13 ....100 C1
Coal Hill Gn BRAM LS13 ....100 C1
Coal Hill La PDSY/CALV LS28 ....100 B1
Coal La LUD/ILL HX2 ....114 B3
Coal Pit La BRIG HD6 ....157 J7
BTLY WF17 ....160 D2
Coalpit La HIPP HX3 ....155 H4
Coal Pit Ms BTLY WF17 ....160 D2
Coal Rd AL/HA/HU LS17 ....65 H7
AL/HA/HU LS17 ....65 H7
SCFT LS14 ....85 J6
Coates Cl EARL WF12 ....161 H7
Coate's La AIRE BD20 ....20 A3
Coates St WBOW BD5 ....117 J2
Cobb Av WKFDW/WTN WF2 ....184 A5
Cobblers La PONT WF8 ....170 A6
PONT WF8 ....170 A6
Cobden Av WOR/ARM LS12 ....121 J2
Cobden Ct HFAX HX1 ....16 F4
Cobden Gv WOR/ARM LS12 ....121 J2
Cobden Ms MOR LS27 ....141 K3
Cobden Pl WOR/ARM LS12 ....121 K2
Cobden Rd WOR/ARM LS12 ....121 K2
Cobden St CLAY BD14 ....116 A2
CUL/OBY BD13 ....115 J5
IDLE BD10 ....78 C5

WIL/AL BD15 ....96 A4
WOR/ARM LS12 ....121 J2
Cobden Ter ELL * HX5 ....175 J4
WOR/ARM LS12 ....121 J2
Cobham Pde WKFDE * WF1 ....164 C4
Cobham Wk MSTN/BAR LS15 ....106 C3
Cockburn Cl BEE/HOL LS11 ....14 A9
Cockburn Wy BEE/HOL LS11 ....14 B9
Cock Hill La HIPP HX3 ....135 K1
Cocking La ILK LS29 ....21 K4
Cockin La CLAY BD14 ....115 H3
Cockroft Gv BFDE BD3 ....6 C1
Cockshott Cl WOR/ARM LS12 ....101 J4
Cockshott Dr WOR/ARM LS12 ....101 J4
Cockshott La IDLE BD10 ....78 B4
WOR/ARM LS12 ....101 J4
Cockshott Pl ILK LS29 ....22 B1
Coggil St MID LS10 ....124 B4
Colbeck Rw BTLY WF17 ....140 B7
Colbert Av ILK LS29 ....24 C4
Colby Ri MSTN/BAR LS15 ....105 F6
Coldcotes Av OSM LS9 ....11 L4
Coldcotes Crs OSM LS9 ....104 E3
Coldcotes Dr OSM LS9 ....104 D3
Coldcotes Garth OSM LS9 ....104 D3
Coldcotes Gv OSM LS9 ....104 E3
Coldcotes Vw OSM LS9 ....104 E3
Coldcotes Wk OSM LS9 ....104 D3
Cold Edge Rd LUD/ILL HX2 ....112 D1
LUD/ILL HX2 ....133 G2
Coldhill La GFTH/SHER LS25 ....90 A7
GFTH/SHER LS25 ....110 B2
Coldshaw Top HWTH BD22 ....72 D7
Cold St HWTH BD22 ....72 D6
Cold Well Rd MSTN/BAR LS15 ....105 J4
Coldwells Hl GTL/HWG HX4 ....174 B6
Cold Well Sq MSTN/BAR * LS15 ....105 J4
Coleman St BFDE BD3 ....6 A2
WOR/ARM LS12 ....13 G5
Colenso Gdns BEE/HOL LS11 ....13 H7
Colenso Gv BEE/HOL LS11 ....13 H7
KGHY * BD21 ....3 M1
Colenso Mt BEE/HOL LS11 ....13 H7
Colenso Pl BEE/HOL LS11 ....13 H7
Colenso Rd BEE/HOL LS11 ....13 H7
KGHY BD21 ....3 M1
Colenso Ter BEE/HOL LS11 ....13 H7
Colenso Wk KGHY BD21 ....3 M1
Coleridge Crs
WKFDW/WTN WF2 ....164 A5
Coleridge Gdns IDLE BD10 ....78 B4
Coleridge La PDSY/CALV LS28 ....120 C1
Coleridge St HFAX HX1 ....17 H7
Coleridge Wy PONT WF8 ....169 K6
Coles Wy AIRE BD20 ....54 A1
Coley Hall La HIPP HX3 ....136 C5
Coley Rd HIPP HX3 ....136 B4
Coley Vw HIPP HX3 ....135 K4
Colinsway WKFDW/WTN WF2 ....18 A4
Collbrook Av WBSY BD6 ....117 H6
College Farm La WBY LS22 ....28 E6
College Gv CAS WF10 ....167 G2
WKFDE WF1 ....18 E1
College Grove Cl WKFDE WF1 ....18 E1
College Grove Rd WKFDE WF1 ....18 E2
College Grove Vw WKFDE WF1 ....18 E1
College Lawns WOR/ARM LS12 ....101 K5
College Rd BGLY BD16 ....55 K5
CAS WF10 ....169 G1
MOR LS27 ....141 G1
College St BTLY WF17 ....140 B6
College Ter HFAX * HX1 ....154 C3
College Vw WOR/ARM LS12 ....101 K6
Collier La BAIL BD17 ....57 G7
GFTH/SHER LS25 ....108 E1
Colliers Cl SHPY BD18 ....76 B3
Colliers La AL/HA/HU LS17 ....65 F7
Colliery Ap WKFDE WF1 ....164 C3
Collindale Cl IDLE BD10 ....79 F6
Collinfield Ri WBSY BD6 ....136 E1
Collingham Av WBSY BD6 ....116 C6
Collingham Dr
GFTH/SHER LS25 ....107 J3
Collingwood Rd NORM WF6 ....166 D6
Collin Moor La GTL/HWG HX4 ....175 F1
Collin Rd SCFT LS14 ....105 F2
Collins Cl HWTH BD22 ....73 F4
Collinson St CLECK BD19 ....138 E7
Collins St BOW BD4 ....118 C1
GTHN BD7 ....117 G3
Colmore Gv WOR/ARM LS12 ....12 C5
Colmore Rd WOR/ARM LS12 ....12 C4
Colmore St WOR/ARM LS12 ....12 C4
Colne Hurst HUDN HD2 ....177 K5
Colne Rd (Goodley)
HWTH BD22 ....72 C2
Colonel's Wk PONT WF8 ....169 H7
Colorado Wy CAS WF10 ....168 D3
Colston Cl GIR BD8 ....96 D4
Colton Ct MSTN/BAR * LS15 ....106 A6
Colton Cft MSTN/BAR LS15 ....106 A6
Colton Garth MSTN/BAR LS15 ....106 A6
Colton La MSTN/BAR LS15 ....106 A7
Colton Rd MSTN/BAR LS15 ....105 K6
WOR/ARM LS12 ....12 A2
Colton Rd East
MSTN/BAR LS15 ....106 B7
Colton St WOR/ARM LS12 ....12 A1
Coltsfoot Cl PONT WF8 ....189 J2
Columbus St HIPP * HX3 ....16 D1
Colville Ter BEE/HOL LS11 ....13 G6
EARD/LOFT WF3 ....143 K6
Colwyn Av BEE/HOL LS11 ....123 G4
Colwyn Mt BEE/HOL LS11 ....123 G4
Colwyn Pl BEE/HOL LS11 ....123 G4
Colwyn Rd BEE/HOL LS11 ....123 G4
Colwyn Ter BEE/HOL LS11 ....123 G4
Colwyn Vw BEE/HOL LS11 ....123 G4
Colyton Mt WIL/AL BD15 ....95 G4
The Combs EARL WF12 ....181 H6
Combs Rd EARL WF12 ....181 G6
Commerce Ct BOW BD4 ....118 E2
Commercial Buildings
LM/WK BD12 ....138 C3
Commercial Ct LDS LS1 ....14 A2
Commercial Rd DEWS WF13 ....161 F7

KSTL LS5 .....101 K2
Commercial St BFD * BD1 .....6 A5
  BRIG HD6 .....157 F6
  BTLY WF17 .....161 F3
  CAS WF10 .....148 C7
  CLECK BD19 .....159 F1
  CUL/OBY BD13 .....94 A4
  CUL/OBY * BD13 .....95 H7
  DEWS WF13 .....180 C3
  EARL WF12 .....181 J2
  HFAX HX1 .....17 G6
  LDS LS1 .....10 A3
  MOR LS27 .....141 K3
  RTHW LS26 .....145 F2
  SHPY BD18 .....77 G4
  TAD LS24 .....50 E7
  WKFDE WF1 .....19 G8
Commercial Vls
  PDSY/CALV LS28 .....100 A4
The Common EARL WF12 .....181 H6
Commondale Wy BOW BD4 .....138 B1
Common Holme La ILK LS29 .....23 H4
Common La EARD/LOFT WF3 .....143 H6
  GFTH/SHER LS25 .....131 G2
  HIPP HX3 .....155 J2
Common Rd BTLY WF17 .....160 C4
  EARD/LOFT WF3 .....165 G1
  ELL HX5 .....176 B3
  LM/WK BD12 .....137 H1
  TAD LS24 .....91 G7
Commonside BTLY WF17 .....161 G6
  LVSG WF15 .....159 F6
Common Side La
  FEA/AMT WF7 .....187 K4
Como Av GIR BD8 .....4 B2
Como Dr GIR BD8 .....4 A2
Como Gdns GIR BD8 .....4 A2
Como Gv GIR BD8 .....4 B2
Compeigne Av AIRE BD20 .....54 C2
Compton Av OSM * LS9 .....11 J5
Compton Crs OSM LS9 .....11 K5
Compton Gv OSM LS9 .....11 J4
Compton La AL/HA/HU LS17 .....46 C5
Compton Mt OSM LS9 .....11 J4
Compton Pl OSM LS9 .....11 J5
Compton Rd OSM LS9 .....11 J5
Compton Rw OSM LS9 .....11 K5
Compton St BOW BD4 .....118 D4
  KGHY BD21 .....3 J5
  OSM LS9 .....11 J4
Compton Ter OSM LS9 .....11 J5
Compton Vw OSM LS9 .....11 J5
Concordia St LDS LS1 .....14 A2
Concord St LDSU LS2 .....10 C7
Concrete St HIPP HX3 .....16 D1
Condor Cl WBSY BD6 .....116 B5
Conduit St GIR BD8 .....5 G1
Coney La KGHY BD21 .....3 H6
Coney Moor Gv RTHW LS26 .....147 J4
Coney Wk DEWS WF13 .....180 C1
Coney Warren La
  EARD/LOFT WF3 .....145 F7
Conference Pl WOR/ARM LS12 .....101 K6
Conference Rd
  WOR/ARM LS12 .....101 K6
Conference Ter
  WOR/ARM LS12 .....101 K6
Congress Mt WOR/ARM LS12 .....101 K6
Congress St WOR/ARM LS12 .....101 K6
Congreve Ap AL/HA/HU LS17 .....46 B5
Congreve Wy AL/HA/HU LS17 .....46 B4
Conisborough La
  GFTH/SHER LS25 .....108 A6
Coniston Av CUL/OBY BD13 .....115 C5
  HDGY LS6 .....82 D7
Coniston Cl CUL/OBY BD13 .....115 C5
  ELL HX5 .....176 A2
Coniston Ct EARD/LOFT WF3 .....164 C2
Coniston Dr CAS WF10 .....169 K1
Conistone Crs WKFDE WF1 .....185 F1
Coniston Gdns CAS WF10 .....169 K1
  MSTN/BAR LS15 .....105 F7
Coniston Gv HTON BD9 .....96 C3
Coniston Rd EARL WF12 .....161 J6
  GTHN BD7 .....116 D3
  RTHW LS26 .....125 K7
Coniston Wy RTHW LS26 .....125 K7
  WBY LS22 .....28 E3
Connaught Fold HUDN HD2 .....177 K4
Consort St BVRD LS3 .....9 H7
Consort Ter BVRD LS3 .....9 H7
Consort Vw BVRD LS3 .....9 H6
Consort Wk BVRD LS3 .....9 M4
Constable Gv EARD/LOFT WF3 .....165 F2
Constable Rd EARD/LOFT WF3 .....142 E7
  ILK LS29 .....24 C6
Constance Gdns CHAL LS7 .....96 E4
Constance St SHPY * BD18 .....76 E4
Constance Wy CHAL LS7 .....9 M4
Constitutional St HFAX HX1 .....16 B9
Conway Av RHAY LS8 .....11 H3
Conway Crs BTLY WF17 .....161 F6
Conway Dr RHAY LS8 .....11 H3
Conway Gv RHAY LS8 .....11 H3
Conway Mt RHAY LS8 .....11 H3
Conway Pl RHAY LS8 .....11 H3
Conway Rd RHAY LS8 .....11 H2
  WKFDW/WTN WF2 .....183 K2
Conway St HFAX HX1 .....16 C7
  PDSY/CALV LS28 .....100 A4
  RHAY LS8 .....11 H3
Conway Ter RHAY LS8 .....11 H3
Conway Vw RHAY LS8 .....11 H3
Conyers Yd OSS * WF5 .....182 D2
Cooke Crs CLECK BD19 .....139 H7
Cooke La KGHY BD21 .....3 G3
Cooke St KGHY BD21 .....3 G4
Cook La HECK WF16 .....159 K4
Cookridge Av BHP/TINH LS16 .....61 H5
Cookridge Dr BHP/TINH LS16 .....61 G5
Cookridge Gv BHP/TINH LS16 .....61 H5
Cookridge La BHP/TINH LS16 .....61 H5
Cookridge St LDSU LS2 .....9 M7
Cooksland La FEA/AMT WF7 .....187 H1
Cookson Cl CAS WF10 .....169 J3
Cookson St BRIG HD6 .....156 E5
Coombe Hl CUL/OBY BD13 .....116 A4

Co-operative Buildings
  BRIG HD6 .....157 G1
  HIPP HX3 .....134 C5
Co-operative St
  EARD/LOFT WF3 .....144 M6
  EARL WF12 .....182 A1
  MIRF WF14 .....179 H6
  MOR LS27 .....141 K3
  WKFDW/WTN * WF2 .....18 A6
Cooper Bridge Rd HUDN HD2 .....178 C3
Cooper Cl BGLY BD16 .....55 K6
Cooperfields LUD/ILL HX2 .....153 F3
Cooper Gv WBSY BD6 .....116 C7
Cooper La HIPP HX3 .....116 C6
Cooper Rd WBY LS22 .....29 H4
Copeland St BOW BD4 .....118 E1
Copgrove Cl BOW BD4 .....119 F3
Copgrove Ct BOW BD4 .....119 F3
Copgrove Rd BOW BD4 .....119 F3
  RHAY LS8 .....84 B7
Copley Av LUD/ILL HX2 .....154 B3
Copley Gln HIPP HX3 .....154 E6
Copley Gv HIPP HX3 .....154 E6
Copley Hall St HIPP HX3 .....154 E6
Copley Hl BTLY WF17 .....140 C6
  PDSY/CALV LS28 .....99 K3
  WIL/AL BD15 .....95 K4
Copley Hill Wy WOR/ARM LS12 .....12 E5
Copley La EARD/LOFT WF3 .....144 C3
  GFTH/SHER LS25 .....89 H7
  HIPP HX3 .....154 E6
Copley Mt HIPP HX3 .....154 E6
Copley St BTLY WF17 .....160 D1
  WBOW BD5 .....117 G3
  WOR/ARM LS12 .....12 E3
Copley Ter HIPP HX3 .....154 E6
Copley Yd WOR/ARM LS12 .....12 E3
Coplowe La WIL/AL BD15 .....75 G5
Copmanroyd OT LS21 .....29 H7
Copperas Rw GTL/HWG * HX4 .....174 B2
Copperfield Av OSM LS9 .....15 H4
Copperfield Crs OSM LS9 .....15 H4
Copperfield Dr OSM LS9 .....15 H4
Copperfield Gv OSM LS9 .....15 J3
Copperfield Pl OSM * LS9 .....15 H4
Copperfield Rw OSM LS9 .....15 J4
Copperfield Ter OSM LS9 .....15 H3
Copperfield Vw OSM * LS9 .....15 J4
Copperfield Wk OSM * LS9 .....15 H4
Coppertop Ms PONT WF8 .....169 K5
The Coppice GFTH/SHER LS25 .....111 G6
  HFAX * HX1 .....16 E9
  HUDN HD2 .....177 K5
  ILK LS29 .....23 K3
  MIRF * WF14 .....179 J1
  MSTN/BAR LS15 .....87 G6
  YEA LS19 .....59 G6
Coppice Cl WKFDE WF1 .....185 F1
Coppice Gra YEA LS19 .....59 J3
Coppice Head RTHW LS26 .....145 G2
Coppice Vw IDLE BD10 .....78 B4
Coppice Wy HFAX HX3 .....84 B6
Coppice Wood Av GSLY LS20 .....59 H2
  GTHN BD7 .....4 C8
Coppice Wood Cl GSLY LS20 .....59 H2
Coppice Wood Crs YEA LS19 .....59 H3
Coppice Wood Gv GSLY LS20 .....59 H3
  GTHN BD7 .....4 C8
Coppice Wood Ri YEA LS19 .....59 H3
The Coppies LM/WK BD12 .....137 G3
Coppin Hall Gv MIRF WF14 .....178 E3
Coppin Hall La MIRF WF14 .....178 E3
Coppy Cl BGLY BD16 .....75 K6
Coppy La BRAM LS13 .....101 F1
Coppy Rd AIRE BD20 .....32 C5
  ILK LS29 .....22 B1
Coppy Wood Dr ILK LS29 .....24 A2
The Copse BGLY BD16 .....76 C1
  CLECK BD19 .....158 A1
  FEA/AMT WF7 .....168 B7
  ILK LS29 .....37 K2
Copthorne Gdns HUDN HD2 .....178 A4
Copt Royd Gv YEA LS19 .....59 H4
Corban St BOW BD4 .....118 D3
Cordingley Cl BOW BD4 .....119 F5
Cordingley St BOW BD4 .....119 F5
Corfe Cl BTLY WF17 .....140 C5
Corn Ex LDS * LS1 .....14 B1
Cornfield DEWS WF13 .....160 B7
Corn Market HFAX HX1 .....17 H6
Cornmarket PONT WF8 .....189 H1
Corn Ml ILK LS29 .....38 C6
Cornmill Cl AL/HA/HU LS17 .....46 A7
Corn Mill Ct WOR/ARM LS12 .....101 G6
Cornmill Crs LVSG WF15 .....159 J5
Cornmill Dr LVSG WF15 .....159 J5
Cornmill La AL/HA/HU LS17 .....46 A7
Corn Mill La CLAY BD14 .....115 J1
  ILK LS29 .....38 B1
Cornmill La LVSG WF15 .....159 J5
Cornstone Fold
  WOR/ARM LS12 .....101 F6
Corn St HWTH BD22 .....53 H7
Cornus Gdns MID LS10 .....123 J6
Cornwall Av AIRE BD20 .....32 D1
Cornwall Cl RTHW * LS26 .....144 E1
Cornwall Crs BAIL BD17 .....57 C7
  BRIG HD6 .....157 G2
  RTHW LS26 .....144 E1
Cornwall Pl GIR BD8 .....5 K2
Cornwall Rd BGLY BD16 .....76 A2
  GIR BD8 .....5 K2
  KGHY BD21 .....3 M1
Cornwall Ter GIR BD8 .....5 K2
Coronation Av
  GFTH/SHER LS25 .....128 B5
  IDLE BD10 .....58 E7
  NORM WF6 .....166 C5
Coronation Bungalows
  GFTH/SHER LS25 .....128 B5
Coronation Mt HWTH BD22 .....2 B4
Coronation Pde
  MSTN/BAR LS15 .....105 F7
Coronation Rd HIPP HX3 .....155 F4
  HOR/CROF WF4 .....186 E6
Coronation St CAS WF10 .....148 E6
  CAS WF10 .....169 G2
  EARD/LOFT * WF3 .....144 E4

ELL HX5 .....175 J3
GTL/HWG HX4 .....175 G1
LM/WK BD12 .....138 B2
WKFDW/WTN WF2 .....164 A6
Coronation Ter CAS WF10 .....169 F2
  RPDN/SBR HX6 .....173 F3
Coronation Wk HWTH BD22 .....2 B3
Coronation Wy HWTH BD22 .....53 F3
Corporal La CUL/OBY BD13 .....135 H1
Corporation St DEWS WF13 .....181 G1
  ECHL BD2 .....98 D2
  HFAX HX1 .....17 G4
  MOR LS27 .....141 J2
  RPDN/SBR HX6 .....153 J4
Corporation Yd BTLY * WF17 .....160 E3
Corrance Rd LM/WK BD12 .....137 J6
Corrie St CUL/OBY BD13 .....95 H7
Cotchers La TAD LS24 .....90 C4
The Cote PDSY/CALV LS28 .....99 K3
Cote Farm La SHPY BD18 .....78 A4
Cotefields Av PDSY/CALV LS28 .....99 K3
Cote Gap CUL/OBY * BD13 .....95 H6
Cote La HUDN HD2 .....176 C4
  PDSY/CALV LS28 .....99 J3
  WIL/AL BD15 .....95 K4
Cote Rd RPDN/SBR HX6 .....172 C5
Coteroyd Av MOR LS27 .....122 B6
Coteroyd Dr MOR LS27 .....122 B7
Cote Wall Ms MIRF WF14 .....180 A6
Cotewall Rd WBOW BD5 .....117 J3
Cotswold Av SHPY BD18 .....77 K5
Cotswold Dr GFTH/SHER LS25 .....127 J1
  KNOT * WF11 .....171 F4
  LVSG WF15 .....158 E3
  RTHW LS26 .....144 E1
Cotswold Rd RTHW LS26 .....144 E1
  WKFDW/WTN WF2 .....183 J1
Cottage Dr GIR BD8 .....4 A4
Cottage Ms HWTH BD22 .....72 C5
Cottage Rd HDGY LS6 .....82 C6
  IDLE BD10 .....78 E5
Cottam Av GTHN BD7 .....4 F7
Cottam Ter GTHN BD7 .....4 F8
Cotterdale WIL/AL BD15 .....95 K2
Cotterdale Holt WBY LS22 .....46 D1
Cotterdale Vw
  MSTN/BAR LS15 .....105 F7
Cotterill Rd KNOT WF11 .....170 C5
Cottingley Cha BEE/HOL LS11 .....122 B4
Cottingley Cliffe Rd BGLY BD16 .....76 B6
Cottingley Crs BEE/HOL LS11 .....122 C5
Cottingley Dr BEE/HOL LS11 .....122 B5
  BGLY BD16 .....75 K6
Cottingley Fold BEE/HOL LS11 .....122 B4
Cottingley Gdns BEE/HOL LS11 .....122 C5
Cottingley Gn BEE/HOL LS11 .....122 C5
Cottingley Gv BEE/HOL LS11 .....122 C5
Cottingley Manor Pk
  BGLY BD16 .....76 A5
Cottingley Moor Rd BGLY BD16 .....75 K7
Cottingley New Rd BGLY BD16 .....76 A5
Cottingley Rd BEE/HOL LS11 .....122 B4
  WIL/AL BD15 .....95 K2
Cottingley Ter GIR * BD8 .....5 K2
Cottingley V BEE/HOL LS11 .....122 C5
Cotton St OSM LS9 .....14 D2
  WKFDW/WTN WF2 .....18 E8
Couford Gv HUDN HD2 .....178 A5
Coultas Cl ILK LS29 .....38 C6
County Ar LDS LS1 .....10 B9
County Cl BTLY WF17 .....161 F2
Coupe Gv NORM WF6 .....166 C5
Coupland Pl BEE/HOL LS11 .....13 L8
Coupland Rd BEE/HOL LS11 .....13 L8
  GFTH/SHER LS25 .....107 H6
Coupland St BEE/HOL LS11 .....13 L9
The Court AL/HA/HU LS17 .....62 E6
  LVSG WF15 .....159 F4
  SHPY * BD18 .....76 D5
Court Dr KSTL LS5 .....81 H6
Courtenay Cl BFDE BD3 .....7 L5
Courtenays SCFT * LS14 .....105 J1
Courthouse St OT LS21 .....39 H2
Court La LUD/ILL HX2 .....154 A1
Courts Leet LM/WK BD12 .....137 H3
The Courtyard BTLY WF17 .....140 C5
  PONT WF8 .....169 K5
The Courtyards SCFT * LS14 .....85 J5
Cousen Av GTHN BD7 .....116 E1
Cousen Rd GTHN BD7 .....117 G2
Cousin La LUD/ILL HX2 .....134 B3
Coutances Wy ILK LS29 .....25 F5
Coventry St BOW BD4 .....118 C2
  HFAX * HX1 .....154 B1
Coverdale Garth WBY LS22 .....46 D2
Coverdale Wy BAIL BD17 .....57 K7
Cover Dr WBSY BD6 .....117 F6
Coverley Ri YEA LS19 .....59 G4
The Covert BTLY WF17 .....160 C1
The Covert IDLE BD10 .....78 E4
Cowcliffe Hill Rd HUDN HD2 .....176 E7
Cow Close Gv WOR/ARM LS12 .....121 K2
Cow Close La LM/WK BD12 .....137 K5
Cow Close Rd WOR/ARM LS12 .....121 J1
Cowdray Dr CLECK BD19 .....138 A7
Cowdry Cl EARL WF12 .....181 H7
Cowgill St GIR BD8 .....5 G1
Cow Gn HFAX HX1 .....17 G6
Cow Hill Gate La LUD/ILL HX2 .....114 B6
Cow La HIPP HX3 .....155 F6
  HIPP HX3 .....156 C4
  HOR/CROF WF4 .....186 D5
  RPDN/SBR HX6 .....172 C5
Cowley Crs HTON BD9 .....96 B1
Cowley Rd BRAM LS13 .....80 C7
Cowling Br AIRE BD20 .....32 D2
Cowling La HIPP HX3 .....135 J2
Cowpasture Rd ILK LS29 .....24 B6
Cowper Av OSM LS9 .....11 J3
Cowper Crs OSM LS9 .....11 J3
Cowper Gv RHAY LS8 .....11 J4
Cowper Mt OSM LS9 .....11 J3
Cowper Rd OSM LS9 .....11 J4
Cowper St CHAL LS7 .....10 E2
  OSM LS9 .....11 K4
Cowper Ter OSM LS9 .....11 J4
Cowroyd Pl HIPP HX3 .....17 J3
Coxwold Hl WBY LS22 .....29 H2

Coxwold Vw WBY LS22 .....29 H3
Crab Hl PONT WF8 .....189 H1
Crab La WOR/ARM LS12 .....8 B1
Crabtree Av HECK WF16 .....160 B3
Crabtree Gn WBY LS22 .....46 D3
Crabtree La AL/HA/HU LS17 .....45 K3
Crabtree Pl GTHN BD7 .....117 F2
Crabtree St GTHN BD7 .....117 F2
  HFAX HX1 .....16 A6
Crabtree Wy EARD/LOFT WF3 .....162 E1
Crackenedge La DEWS WF13 .....161 G7
Crackenedge Ter DEWS WF13 .....161 G7
Crack La WIL/AL BD15 .....75 G7
Cracoe Rd BFDE BD3 .....6 F7
The Crag BSPA/BRAM LS23 .....68 C3
Crag Cl LUD/ILL HX2 .....134 A3
Crag Gdns BSPA/BRAM LS23 .....68 C3
Cragg Av HORS LS18 .....80 E4
Cragg Cl CUL/OBY BD13 .....114 C1
  GTHN BD7 .....117 F3
Cragg Rd HORS LS18 .....81 F4
Cragg Ter GTHN BD7 .....117 F3
  HORS LS18 .....80 E4
Cragg Top CUL/OBY BD13 .....114 B1
Cragg Vw AIRE BD20 .....21 F7
Cragg Wood Dr YEA LS19 .....79 H1
Craggwood Rd HORS LS18 .....81 F5
Crag Hill Av BHP/TINH LS16 .....61 H4
Crag Hill Rd IDLE BD10 .....78 D2
Crag Hill Vw BHP/TINH LS16 .....61 H4
Crag La AL/HA/HU LS17 .....62 E6
  LUD/ILL HX2 .....134 A3
Crag Mt PONT WF8 .....189 H1
Crag Pl KGHY BD21 .....53 K7
Crag Rd SHPY BD18 .....77 H6
Cragside Cl KSTL LS5 .....81 H5
Cragside Crs KSTL LS5 .....81 H5
Cragside Gdns KSTL LS5 .....81 H5
Cragside Gv KSTL LS5 .....81 H5
Cragside Mt KSTL LS5 .....81 H5
Cragside Pl KSTL LS5 .....81 G5
Cragside Wk KSTL LS5 .....81 H5
Crag Vw IDLE BD10 .....78 D5
Craig Cl BTLY WF17 .....161 F2
Craiglands HIPP HX3 .....136 C7
Craiglands Pk ILK LS29 .....24 B6
Craiglands Rd ILK LS29 .....24 B6
Craiglea Dr LM/WK BD12 .....137 J5
Craigmore Ct BOW BD4 .....119 G4
Craigmore Dr ILK LS29 .....24 D5
Cranbourne Rd HTON BD9 .....96 C3
Cranbrook Av BEE/HOL LS11 .....123 F3
  WBSY BD6 .....117 H6
Cranbrook Pl WBOW BD5 .....117 K3
Cranbrook St CLAY BD14 .....116 A2
  WBOW BD5 .....117 K3
Cranbrook Vw
  PDSY/CALV LS28 .....120 D1
Cranewells Dr MSTN/BAR LS15 .....105 K6
Cranewells Gn MSTN/BAR LS15 .....105 K6
Cranewells Ri MSTN/BAR LS15 .....105 K7
Cranewells V MSTN/BAR LS15 .....105 K7
Cranewells Vw
  MSTN/BAR LS15 .....105 K6
Cranford Pl WIL/AL BD15 .....75 F7
Cranleigh Mt KGHY BD21 .....2 C9
Cranmer Bank AL/HA/HU LS17 .....83 F1
Cranmer Cl AL/HA/HU LS17 .....83 F1
Cranmer Gdns AL/HA/HU LS17 .....83 F1
Cranmer Ri AL/HA/HU LS17 .....63 F7
Cranmer Rd AL/HA/HU LS17 .....83 F1
  BFDE BD3 .....6 A1
Cranmore Crs MID LS10 .....143 K2
Cranmore Dr MID LS10 .....144 A2
Cranmore Gdns MID LS10 .....143 K2
Cranmore Garth MID LS10 .....143 K2
Cranmore Gn MID LS10 .....143 K2
Cranmore Gv EARD/LOFT WF3 .....143 K2
Cranmore La MID LS10 .....144 A2
Cranmore Ri MID LS10 .....144 A2
Cranmore Rd MID LS10 .....143 K2
Craven Av AIRE BD20 .....33 F1
  CUL/OBY BD13 .....95 H7
Craven Cl CLECK BD19 .....139 K7
Craven Ct AIRE BD20 .....33 C1
  GIR BD8 .....4 A4
  HFAX HX1 .....16 C6
Craven Crs ILK LS29 .....22 B1
Cravendale Rd DEWS WF13 .....180 A3
Craven Dr AIRE BD20 .....33 F1
  CLECK BD19 .....139 K7
Craven Edge HFAX HX1 .....16 C7
Craven Gv AIRE BD20 .....33 G1
Craven La CLECK BD19 .....139 K7
Craven Pk ILK LS29 .....38 A5
Craven Rd DEWS WF13 .....180 D3
  HDGY LS6 .....9 M3
  KGHY BD21 .....3 L2
Craven St BFDE * BD3 .....6 B4
  DEWS WF13 .....180 A3
  OT LS21 .....39 J3
  WKFDE WF1 .....18 F3
Craven Ter HFAX HX1 .....16 C7
Crawford Av WBSY BD6 .....117 H6
Crawford Dr
  WKFDW/WTN WF2 .....184 A2
Crawford St BOW BD4 .....118 B2
Crawshaw Av PDSY/CALV LS28 .....100 C6
Crawshaw Gdns
  PDSY/CALV LS28 .....100 B5
Crawshaw Hl PDSY/CALV LS28 .....100 B6
Crawshaw Pk PDSY/CALV LS28 .....100 B6
Crawshaw Ri PDSY/CALV LS28 .....100 B6
Crawshaw Rd PDSY/CALV LS28 .....100 C6
Crawshaw St DEWS WF13 .....180 C3
Crawthorne Crs HUDN HD2 .....177 K5
Cray La GTL/HWG HX4 .....174 A7
Crediton Av WIL/AL BD15 .....96 A3
The Crescent AL/HA/HU LS17 .....62 E5
  BAIL BD17 .....77 H2
  BGLY BD16 .....55 H5
  BHP/TINH LS16 .....61 J3
  BIRK/DRI BD11 .....119 H7
  CAS WF10 .....168 D2
  DEWS WF13 .....180 A4
  EARD/LOFT WF3 .....143 F7

FEA/AMT WF7 .....187 G4
GFTH/SHER LS25 .....107 K5
GFTH/SHER LS25 .....109 F7
GFTH/SHER LS25 .....127 K5
GSLY LS20 .....58 C3
GTL/HWG HX4 .....174 D5
ILK LS29 .....24 D4
ILK LS29 .....37 K5
LVSG WF15 .....158 E3
MSTN/BAR LS15 .....105 J5
NORM WF6 .....166 C4
OT LS21 .....27 H7
PDSY/CALV LS28 .....100 C5
WBSY BD6 .....116 D6
Crescent Av DEWS WF13 .....180 A4
  RTHW LS26 .....125 G4
Crescent Gdns AL/HA/HU LS17 .....63 J7
Crescent Gra BEE/HOL LS11 .....14 B7
Crescent Towers BEE/HOL LS11 .....14 A7
Crescent Vw AL/HA/HU LS17 .....62 E5
  HWTH BD22 .....73 H1
The Crescent HIPP HX3 .....136 C7
Creskeld Crs BHP/TINH LS16 .....41 J7
Creskeld Dr BHP/TINH LS16 .....41 H7
Creskeld Gdns BHP/TINH LS16 .....41 H7
Creskeld Garth BHP/TINH LS16 .....41 J7
Creskeld La BHP/TINH LS16 .....41 J7
Creskeld Pk BHP/TINH LS16 .....41 J7
Creskeld Wy WIL/AL BD15 .....95 J3
Creskell Rd BEE/HOL LS11 .....13 L6
Cresswell Mt GTHN BD7 .....116 D4
Cresswell Pl GTHN BD7 .....116 D4
Cresswell Ter GTHN BD7 .....116 D4
The Crest GFTH/SHER LS25 .....127 K5
  HUDN 177 K3
  RTHW LS26 .....126 D5
Crest Av LM/WK BD12 .....137 H6
Crest Dr PONT WF8 .....189 K3
Crestfield Av ELL HX5 .....175 H4
Crestfield Crs ELL HX5 .....175 H4
Crestfield Dr ELL HX5 .....175 H4
  LUD/ILL HX2 .....154 B3
Crestfield Rd ELL HX5 .....175 H4
Crest Hl RTHW LS26 .....126 D5
Crest Hill Rd HUDN HD2 .....177 G6
Crest Mt PONT WF8 .....189 K3
Crest Rd HUDW HD3 .....175 K5
Crestville Cl CLAY BD14 .....116 C1
Crestville Rd CLAY BD14 .....116 B1
Crestville Ter CLAY BD14 .....116 C1
Crestwood Cl BOW BD4 .....118 C5
Creswell La GFTH/SHER LS25 .....160 C5
Crewe Av KNOT WF11 .....170 C4
Crewe Rd CAS WF10 .....169 H1
Crib La HFAX HX1 .....17 G4
The Cricketers BULY LS4 .....102 A1
Cricketers Ap
  WKFDW/WTN WF2 .....163 K5
Cricketers Cl GFTH/SHER LS25 .....107 K7
Cricketers Fold AL/HA/HU LS17 .....65 F7
Cricketers Gn YEA LS19 .....59 J5
Cricketers Ter WOR/ARM LS12 .....12 A2
Cricketers Vw AL/HA/HU LS17 .....65 F7
Cricketers Wk AIRE BD20 .....32 E5
  MSTN/BAR LS15 .....106 B6
Cricketers Wy
  GFTH/SHER LS25 .....111 F6
Cricklegate MSTN/BAR LS15 .....105 J5
Crimbles Cl PDSY/CALV LS28 .....100 C6
Crimbles Pl PDSY/CALV LS28 .....100 C6
Crimbles Rd PDSY/CALV LS28 .....100 C6
Crimbles Ter PDSY/CALV LS28 .....100 C6
Crimple Gn GFTH/SHER LS25 .....108 A7
Crimshaw La SHPY BD18 .....77 J6
Crinan Ct NORM WF6 .....166 D4
Cringles La AIRE BD20 .....21 F2
Cripplegate HFAX HX1 .....17 K5
The Croft BIRK/DRI BD11 .....140 B2
  CAS WF10 .....168 E2
  EARD/LOFT WF3 .....162 C3
  KNOT WF11 .....171 H3
  MSTN/BAR LS15 .....105 J4
  RTHW LS26 .....145 K2
  SCFT LS14 .....66 A3
  WBY LS22 .....46 D2
Croft Av BGLY BD16 .....55 G5
  EARD/LOFT WF3 .....163 J1
  KNOT WF11 .....171 H3
  NORM WF6 .....166 C5
  NORM WF6 .....167 F5
  OT LS21 .....39 G1
  PDSY/CALV LS28 .....100 A2
Croft Br RTHW LS26 .....145 K2
Croft Cl ILK LS29 .....38 A6
Croft Ct HORS LS18 .....80 E3
  ILK * LS29 .....38 A6
Croftdale Gv MSTN/BAR LS15 .....106 A3
Croft Dr BSPA/BRAM LS23 .....48 C7
  ILK LS29 .....38 B6
Croft End WBY LS22 .....29 F4
Crofters Gn IDLE BD10 .....78 B4
Crofters Lea YEA LS19 .....59 G4
Croft Fld AIRE BD20 .....33 F2
Croft Fold HIPP HX3 .....134 C5
Croft Foulds Ct
  GFTH/SHER LS25 .....107 J6
Croft Head La WKFDE WF1 .....186 B2
Croft House Av MOR LS27 .....142 A1
Croft House Cl MOR LS27 .....142 A1
  WBSY BD6 .....117 G6
Croft House Ct
  PDSY/CALV * LS28 .....100 B5
Croft House Dr MOR LS27 .....142 A2
  OT LS21 .....39 G1
Croft House Fold ILK LS29 .....22 D1
Croft House Gdns MOR LS27 .....142 A2
Croft House Gv MOR LS27 .....142 A2
Croft House La AIRE BD20 .....53 H1
  MOR LS27 .....142 A2
Croft House Ms MOR LS27 .....142 A1
Croft House Mt MOR * LS27 .....142 A1
Croft House Ri MOR LS27 .....142 A2
Croft House Rd MOR LS27 .....142 A2
  WBSY BD6 .....117 G6
Croft House Wk MOR LS27 .....142 A1

Croft House Wy MOR LS27 ....142 A1
Croftlands BTLY WF17 ......161 J5
  IDLE BD10 ......78 B4
  KNOT WF11 ......171 H3
Croft La BSPA/BRAM LS23 ....31 F5
  TAD LS24 ......49 J4
Crofton Ri AL/HA/HU LS17 ....65 H7
Crofton Rd HTON BD9......97 F2
Croft Pk ILK LS29 ......38 A6
Croft Pl BRIG HD6 ......157 G6
Croft Ri HIPP HX3 ......134 C5
  ILK LS29 ......38 B6
Croft Rd AIRE BD20......55 C3
  BSPA/BRAM LS23 ......48 B7
The Crofts BTLY WF17......160 C4
Croft's Ct LDS LS1 ......9 M9
Croftside Cl SCFT LS14 ......105 J2
Croft St AIRE BD20......32 D5
  BIRK/DRI BD11......139 H2
  BRIG HD6 ......157 F6
  DEWS WF13 ......181 F1
  HECK WF16 ......160 A5
  HWTH BD22 ......72 D5
  IDLE BD10 ......78 D4
  KGHY BD21......2 E6
  OT LS21 ......39 J3
  PDSY/CALV LS28 ......100 A2
  RPDN/SBR * HX6 ......153 K4
  SHPY BD18......77 G5
  WBOW BD5 ......5 M8
  WBSY BD6 ......117 H5
Croft Wy ILK LS29 ......38 B6
Croftway GFTH/SHER LS25 ....111 F5
  MSTN/BAR LS15 ......87 H5
Croisdale Cl LVSG WF15......159 F4
Cromack Vw PDSY/CALV LS28 ....99 K6
Cromer Av KGHY * BD21......2 E5
Cromer Gv KGHY * BD21......2 E5
Cromer Pl LDSU LS2 ......9 J5
  LDSU LS2 ......9 J5
Cromer Rd KGHY BD21......2 E5
  LDSU LS2 ......9 J5
Cromer St HFAX HX1 ......16 A9
  LDSU LS2 ......9 J5
Cromer Ter LDSU LS2 ......9 J5
Crompton Dr MOR LS27 ......141 J1
Cromwell Bottom Dr
  BRIG * HD6......157 F4
Cromwell Cl HIPP HX3......155 K4
  KNOT WF11 ......150 E7
Cromwell Ct BGLY BD16 ......96 A1
  BIRK/DRI BD11 ......140 A2
Cromwell Crs PONT WF8 ......189 K1
Cromwell Hts OSM * LS9 ......10 E8
Cromwell Mt MID LS10 ......123 J6
  OSM LS9 ......10 E7
Cromwell Pl OSS WF5 ......182 C2
Cromwell Rd GFTH/SHER LS25 ....127 K6
  HIPP HX3 ......155 K4
Cromwell St OSM LS9 ......10 E8
Cromwell Ter HFAX * HX1 ......16 E6
Crooked La HIPP HX3 ......134 E1
  IDLE BD10 ......78 A3
Crooke La WIL/AL BD15 ......95 F1
Cropper Ga LDS LS1 ......9 J9
Cropredy Cl CUL/QBY BD13 ....115 J5
Cropstones BSPA/BRAM LS23 ....68 C1
Crosby Av BEE/HOL LS11 ......13 H7
Crosby Pl BEE/HOL LS11 ......13 J6
Crosby Rd BEE/HOL LS11 ......13 J6
Crosby St BEE/HOL LS11 ......13 J6
  KGHY BD21......2 E3
Crosby Ter BEE/HOL LS11......13 J6
Crosby Vw BEE/HOL LS11......13 J6
Croscombe Wk WBOW BD5 ......5 L9
Crosland Rd HUDW HD3......175 J7
Crosley Vw BGLY BD16 ......76 A2
Crosley Wood Rd BGLY BD16....76 A2
The Cross MSTN/BAR LS15 ......87 H5
Cross Albert Pl
  WOR/ARM * LS12 ......12 D3
Cross Alcester Rd RHAY LS8....11 G1
Cross Alma St OSM LS9 ......11 G6
Cross Ar LDS * LS1 ......9 M9
Cross Aston Gv BRAM LS13 ....101 H3
Cross Av RTHW LS26 ......125 G7
Cross Bank Rd BTLY WF17 ....160 E2
Cross Banks SHPY BD18 ......77 G5
Cross Bank St MIRF WF14 ....179 H6
Cross Banstead St RHAY * LS8....11 G1
Cross Barstow St
  BEE/HOL LS11 ......14 A4
Crossbeck Cl ILK LS29 ......24 A6
Crossbeck Rd ILK LS29 ......24 A6
Cross Beck Rd RHAY * LS8 ....104 A1
Cross Belgrave St LDSU LS2 ....10 B8
Cross Bellbrooke Av OSM LS9 ....11 L4
Cross Bell St OSM * LS9......10 D8
Cross Bentley La HDGY LS6 ....82 E6
Cross Burley Lodge Rd HDGY LS6....8 E5
Cross Cardigan St BULY LS4....8 B6
Cross Cardigan Ter BULY LS4....8 B6
Cross Catherine St OSM LS9 ....14 F1
Cross Chancellor St HDGY LS6....9 M2
Cross Chapel St HDGY LS6 ....82 C7
Cross Cliff Rd HDGY LS6 ......9 H1
Cross Cowper St CHAL LS7 ....10 D2
Cross Crown St CLECK BD19 ....158 E1
Crossdale Av WBSY BD6 ......116 C6
Cross Dawlish Gv OSM * LS9 ....11 L1
Cross Dikes Rd RPDN/SBR HX6 ....172 B2
Cross Easy Rd OSM LS9 ......11 G3
Cross Elford St RHAY * LS8 ....11 G3
Cross Emily St KGHY * BD21......3 H6
Cross End Fold ILK LS29 ......22 D1
Cross Eric St BRAM LS13 ......81 F7
Cross Evanston Av BULY LS4....8 B5
Cross Farm Ct HWTH BD22 ....92 C2
Cross Fld GTL/HWG HX4 ......174 D5
Crossfield Cl HWTH BD22 ......92 C2
Crossfield Rd HWTH BD22 ....92 C2
Crossfield St LDSU LS2 ......9 K3
Cross Flatts BEE/HOL LS11....123 F5
Cross Flatts Av BEE/HOL LS11....123 F5
Cross Flatts Crs BEE/HOL LS11 ....122 E4
Cross Flatts Dr BEE/HOL LS11 ....122 E4

Cross Flatts Gv BEE/HOL LS11 ....123 F4
Cross Flatts Mt BEE/HOL LS11 ....123 F4
Cross Flatts Pde BEE/HOL LS11....122 E4
Cross Flatts Pl BEE/HOL LS11 ....122 E4
Cross Flatts Rd BEE/HOL LS11 ....122 E4
Cross Flatts Rw BEE/HOL LS11 ....122 E4
Cross Flatts St BEE/HOL LS11 ....122 E4
Cross Flatts Ter BEE/HOL LS11 ....122 E4
Cross Foundry St
  DEWS * WF13 ......180 B4
Cross Fountaine St LDS * LS1....9 M9
Cross Francis St CHAL LS7 ....10 D2
Crossgate OT LS21 ......39 H3
Cross Gates Av
  MSTN/BAR LS15 ......105 K2
Cross Gates La BGLY BD16 ....75 J3
  MSTN/BAR LS15 ......105 J2
Cross Gates Rd
  MSTN/BAR LS15 ......105 H3
Cross Glen Rd BHP/TINH LS16....82 B5
Cross Granby Ter HDGY LS6....82 C7
Cross Grange Av RHAY LS8....10 F2
Cross Grasmere St
  WOR/ARM * LS12 ......12 C2
Cross Gn OT LS21 ......39 J2
Cross Green Ap OSM LS9 ......15 J6
Cross Green Av OSM LS9 ......15 J5
Cross Green Cl OSM LS9 ......15 J5
Cross Green Ct OSM LS9 ......15 K6
Cross Green Crs OSM LS9 ......15 G4
Cross Green Dr OSM LS9 ......15 J5
Cross Green Garth OSM LS9 ....15 J6
Cross Green Gv OSM * LS9 ....15 G4
Cross Green La
  MSTN/BAR LS15 ......105 J5
  OSM LS9 ......14 F3
Cross Green Ri OSM LS9 ......15 K6
Cross Green Rd OSM LS9 ......15 H4
Cross Green Rw HDGY LS6 ....82 D5
Cross Green St OSM LS9 ......15 K7
Cross Green Wy OSM LS9 ......15 L7
Cross Hartley Av HDGY LS6 ....9 L1
Cross Heath Gv BEE/HOL LS11 ....122 D3
Cross Henley Rd BRAM LS13 ....101 F3
Cross HI GTL/HWG HX4 ......175 F2
  HFAX HX1 ......17 H4
  KNOT WF11 ......150 B3
Cross Hill La LVSG WF15 ......158 C7
Cross Hills GFTH/SHER LS25 ....127 K5
  HFAX HX1 ......17 H4
Cross Hills Dr GFTH/SHER LS25 ....127 K5
Crosshills Mt GTL/HWG HX4....175 F2
Cross Hilton Gv RHAY LS8......104 A1
Cross House Ct LM/WK * BD12 ....138 B3
Cross Ingledew Crs RHAY LS8....84 C2
Cross Ingram Rd BEE/HOL LS11 ....13 H5
The Crossings BTLY WF17 ......140 C7
Cross Ivy Mt OSM LS9 ......11 K9
Cross Kelso Rd LDSU LS2 ......9 H6
Cross Keys OSS WF5 ......183 F2
Crossland Ct BEE/HOL * LS11....13 J5
Crossland Rd MOR LS27 ......122 A7
Crossland Ter BEE/HOL LS11....13 M9
Cross La BGLY BD16 ......75 J1
  BIRK/DRI BD11 ......119 J7
  BRIG HD6 ......157 K7
  CUL/QBY BD13 ......115 F6
  ELL HX5 ......175 H5
  GSLY LS20 ......39 G2
  GTHN BD7 ......117 F3
  HIPP HX3 ......135 K1
  HIPP HX3 ......136 A3
  HWTH BD22 ......92 D2
  WIL/AL BD15 ......75 G5
  WKFDW/WTN WF2 ......184 A1
  WOR/ARM LS12 ......102 A6
  WOR/ARM LS12 ......121 H1
Cross Lea Farm Rd KSTL LS5....81 J5
Cross Leeds St KGHY * BD21 ....2 F5
Crossley Cl MIRF WF14 ......179 H1
Crossley Gdns HFAX HX1 ......16 D4
Crossley Gv MIRF WF14 ......179 H1
Crossley Hall Ms GIR BD8 ....96 D6
Crossley Hall St GIR BD8......96 C6
Crossley Hl HIPP HX3 ......155 G5
Crossley La MIRF WF14 ......179 H1
Crossley St BRIG HD6 ......157 G7
  CUL/QBY BD13 ......115 J5
  FEA/AMT WF7 ......188 C4
  GTHN BD7 ......117 G1
  HFAX HX1 ......17 G5
  WBY LS22 ......29 H4
  WKFDE WF1 ......186 C3
Crossley Ter North
  LUD/ILL HX2 ......134 C3
Crossley Ter South
  LUD/ILL HX2 ......134 C3
Crossley Vw MIRF WF14 ......179 J1
Cross Lidgett Pl RHAY LS8 ....84 A4
Cross Louis St CHAL LS7 ......10 D3
Crossman Dr NORM WF6 ......167 F5
Cross Maude St LDSU * LS2 ....14 C1
Cross Milan Rd RHAY LS8......11 J2
Cross Mitford Rd
  WOR/ARM LS12 ......12 D1
Crossmoor Cl AIRE BD20......32 C4
Crossmount St BTLY WF17 ....161 F5
Cross Osmondthorpe La
  OSM LS9 ......11 M8
Cross Park Av CAS WF10......168 E1
Cross Park St BTLY WF17 ......161 G3
  EARL WF12 ......181 J1
  MSTN/BAR LS15 ......105 H5
Cross Peel St MOR LS27 ......142 A3
Cross Pipes Rd
  WKFDW/WTN WF2 ......183 K1
Cross Quarry St HDGY LS6 ......9 K1
Cross Queen St NORM WF6 ....166 D5
Cross Reginald Mt CHAL * LS7 ....10 D1
Cross Rink St BTLY WF17 ......161 G5
Cross River St KGHY * BD21 ....3 L1
Cross Rd EARL WF12 ......181 J7
  GIR BD8 ......4 F1
  HORS LS18 ......80 D4
  IDLE BD10 ......78 D4
  LM/WK BD12 ......138 A2
Cross Roseville Rd RHAY LS8 ....10 F3

Cross Rosse St SHPY * BD18 ....77 G4
Cross Roundhay Av RHAY LS8....84 A7
Cross Rw MSTN/BAR LS15 ......106 D7
Cross Ryecroft St OSS WF5 ....182 C3
Cross Speedwell St HDGY LS6....9 M2
Cross Sq WKFDE WF1 ......18 E4
Cross Stamford St CHAL LS7 ....10 D6
Cross St BRIG HD6 ......157 F4
  BTLY WF17 ......161 F5
  CAS WF10 ......148 B7
  CLAY BD14 ......116 B2
  EARD/LOFT WF3 ......143 K7
  EARL WF12 ......181 G2
  GTL/HWG HX4 ......174 E5
  GTL/HWG * HX4 ......175 G2
  HFAX HX1 ......17 H4
  HFAX * HX1 ......17 J7
  LM/WK BD12 ......138 B3
  LVSG WF15 ......159 H6
  MSTN/BAR LS15 ......105 H5
  OSS WF5 ......182 B7
  PONT * WF8 ......189 J1
  RTHW LS26 ......145 F2
  WBSY * BD6 ......116 E7
  WBY LS22 ......29 H4
  WKFDE WF1 ......18 E4
Cross St West LUD/ILL * HX2....134 B7
Cross Sun St BFD BD1 ......6 A4
Cross Valley Dr
  MSTN/BAR LS15 ......105 H4
Crossway BGLY BD16 ......75 J5
The Crossways OT LS21 ......27 H7
Cross Wells Rd RPDN/SBR HX6 ....172 C4
Cross Westfield Rd BVRD * LS3 ....9 H7
Cross Wingham St CHAL * LS7 ....10 D2
Cross Woodstock St LDSU * LS2 ....9 L4
Cross York St LDSU LS2 ......14 C1
Crowgill Rd SHPY BD18 ......77 G5
Crow Hill End Rd
  RPDN/SBR HX6 ......152 A6
Crow Hill Rd HBR HX7 ......152 A5
Crow La OT LS21 ......39 H3
Crowlees Cl MIRF WF14 ......179 J4
Crowlees Gdns MIRF WF14 ....179 J4
Crowlees Rd MIRF WF14 ......179 H4
Crown & Anchor Yd
  PONT * WF8 ......189 H1
Crown Cl EARL WF12 ......181 K2
Crown Dr LM/WK BD12 ......137 H3
Crow Nest La BEE/HOL LS11 ....122 C4
Crownest La BGLY BD16 ......55 K7
Crow Nest Pk DEWS * WF13 ....180 D2
Crownest Rd BGLY BD16 ......75 K1
Crow Nest Vw DEWS WF13 ....180 D2
Crown Flatt Wy EARL WF12 ....161 H7
Crownlands La OSS WF5 ......182 C3
Crown Point Cl OSS WF5......182 B3
Crown Point Dr OSS WF5......182 B3
Crown Point Rd MID LS10 ......14 C3
Crown Rd HIPP HX3 ......134 C5
Crown St BFD BD1......5 M5
  BRIG HD6 ......157 F5
  CLECK BD19 ......158 E1
  ELL HX5 ......175 J3
  HFAX HX1 ......17 G6
  ILK LS29 ......38 A1
  LDS LS1 ......14 B1
  LM/WK BD12 ......137 H3
  LVSG WF15 ......159 J4
  OSS WF5 ......182 D6
Crowther Av PDSY/CALV LS28....79 G6
Crowther Fold BGLY BD16 ......74 E3
Crowther Pl CAS WF10 ......168 C1
  HDGY LS6 ......9 M2
Crowther Rd HECK WF16 ......160 B3
  MIRF WF14 ......179 H4
Crowther St BTLY WF17 ......160 C3
  CAS WF10 ......168 B1
  CLECK BD19 ......138 E7
  IDLE BD10 ......78 B5
  LM/WK BD12 ......137 H3
Crowther Wk WBOW BD5 ......5 L9
Crow Tree Cl BAIL BD17 ......77 J1
Crow Tree La GIR BD8 ......96 D4
Crowtrees Ct YEA LS19 ......79 J1
Crowtrees Crs BRIG HD6 ......176 E1
Crowtrees La BRIG HD6 ......176 D3
Crow Trees Pk YEA LS19 ......59 J7
Crow Wood La GTL/HWG HX4....173 K7
Crow Wood Pk LUD/ILL HX2 ....154 A3
Croxall Dr EARD/LOFT WF3 ....165 F3
Croydon Rd GTHN BD7 ......116 E2
Croydon St BEE/HOL LS11 ......13 G5
Crumack La HWTH BD22......93 F2
Crystal Ct HFAX HX1 ......16 D5
Crystal Pl WKFDE * WF1 ......19 H5
Crystal Ter BOW BD4......118 D3
Cudbear St MID LS10 ......14 C3
Cullingworth Rd
  CUL/QBY BD13 ......74 A7
Cullingworth St DEWS WF13 ....160 D5
Culpans Rd HBR HX7 ......152 B4
Culver St HFAX HX1 ......17 G5
Cumberland Av HUDN HD2 ....177 H4
Cumberland Cl LUD/ILL HX2 ....134 B3
Cumberland Ct HDGY LS6......8 D2
Cumberland Rd CAS WF10 ....149 K5
  GTHN BD7 ......4 C9
  HDGY LS6 ......9 G1
Cumbrian Wy
  WKFDW/WTN WF2 ......183 J7
Cunliffe Rd BAIL BD17 ......58 C6
Cunliffe Rd GIR BD8......97 H3
  GIR BD8 ......24 A5
Cunliffe Ter GIR BD8 ......97 J2
Cunliffe Vls HTON BD9 ......97 J2
Cure HI HWTH BD22 ......72 C1
Curlew Cl CAS WF10 ......168 C2
  ILK LS29 ......23 H5
Curlew Ct AIRE BD20 ......32 C4
Curlew Ri MOR LS27 ......142 C4
Curlew St WBOW BD5 ......117 H3
Curly HI ILK LS29 ......23 A3
Currer Av BOW BD4 ......118 C5
Currer St BFD BD1 ......6 A6
Currer Wk AIRE BD20 ......32 C4

Curtis Ct CUL/QBY * BD13......74 A6
Curwen Crs HECK WF16 ......160 A3
Curzon Rd BFDE BD3......6 F6
Curzon St HUDN HD2......178 B4
Cuthberts Cl CUL/QBY BD13 ....115 G6
Cutler Heights La BOW BD4....118 D3
Cutler La RTHW LS26 ......147 H4
Cutler Pl BOW BD4......118 E2
Cut Rd KNOT WF11 ......150 D6
  KNOT WF11 ......150 D6
Cutsyke Av CAS WF10 ......168 A2
Cutsyke Crest CAS WF10 ......168 A3
Cutsyke Rd CAS WF10 ......168 A4
Cypress Rd NORM WF6 ......186 E1
Cyprus Av IDLE BD10......78 A3
  WKFDE WF1 ......18 B1
Cyprus Crs MIRF WF14 ......180 A2
Cyprus Dr IDLE BD10......78 A3
Cyprus Gv GFTH/SHER LS25 ....107 H6
  WKFDE WF1 ......184 B1
Cyprus Mt WKFDE WF1 ......184 B1
Cyprus Rd GFTH/SHER LS25 ....107 H6
Cyprus St OSS WF5 ......182 B1
  WKFDE WF1 ......18 C1
Cyprus Ter GFTH/SHER LS25 ....107 H6
Czar St BEE/HOL * LS11 ......13 J5

D

Dacre Av WKFDW/WTN WF2 ....183 H5
Dacre Cl LVSG WF15 ......159 G4
Dacre Ct TAD LS24......90 B6
Daffels Wood Cl BOW BD4 ....118 C6
Daffil Av MOR LS27 ......122 A7
Daffil Grange Ms MOR * LS27 ....122 A7
Daffil Grange Wy MOR LS27 ....122 A7
Daffil Rd MOR LS27 ......122 A7
Daffodil Ct WIL/AL BD15 ......96 A5
Dagenham Rd BOW BD4 ......118 D3
The Dairies NORM * WF6 ......167 F5
Daisy Bank HFAX HX1 ......16 F9
Daisyfield Rd BRAM * LS13 ....101 G4
Daisy Cl BTLY WF17 ......140 E5
  EARL WF12 ......181 F1
  LM/WK BD12 ......137 H4
  MOR LS27 ......142 B2
Daisy Hill Av MOR LS27 ......142 B1
Daisy Hill Back La HTON BD9....96 D3
Daisy Hill Cl MOR * LS27 ......142 B1
Daisy Hill Gv HTON BD9......96 D3
Daisy Hill La HTON BD9 ......96 D3
Daisy Mt RPDN/SBR HX6 ......153 H3
Daisy Rd BRIG HD6 ......177 G1
Daisy St BRIG HD6 ......157 F6
  GTHN BD7 ......117 F3
  HFAX HX1 ......16 E7
  HWTH BD22 ......2 D3
Daisy Vale Ms EARD/LOFT WF3 ....143 K6
Daisy Vale Ter EARD/LOFT WF3 ....143 K6
Dalby Av BFDE BD3......7 H1
Dalcross Gv WBOW BD5 ......118 A2
Dalcross St WBOW BD5......117 K2
The Dale GFTH/SHER LS25 ....88 D4
Dale Cl BTLY WF17 ......161 F6
  GSLY LS20 ......58 C3
  OSS WF5 ......182 D3
Dalecourt ILK * LS29 ......24 D4
Dale Ct OSS * WF5 ......182 C3
  PONT WF8 ......189 J4
Dale Crs AIRE BD20 ......32 D5
Dale Cft GFTH/SHER LS25 ....107 H5
  ILK LS29 ......23 H5
Dale Croft Ri WIL/AL BD15 ....95 K3
Dalefield Av NORM WF6 ......166 C6
Dalefield Rd NORM WF6......166 C6
Dalefield Wy NORM WF6......186 E1
Dale Garth BAIL BD17......77 G1
Dale Gv SHPY BD18......77 K3
Dale La HECK WF16 ......160 A3
Dale Ms PONT WF8 ......189 J4
Dale Park Av BHP/TINH LS16....61 G7
Dale Park Cl BHP/TINH LS16....61 G7
Dale Park Gdns BHP/TINH LS16....61 G7
Dale Park Ri BHP/TINH LS16 ....61 G7
Dale Park Wk BHP/TINH LS16....61 G7
Dale Rd BIRK/DRI BD11 ......120 D6
Dales Dr GSLY LS20......58 C3
Daleside GTL/HWG HX4 ......174 D2
Daleside Av PDSY/CALV LS28....99 H5
Daleside Cl PDSY/CALV LS28 ....99 G4
Daleside Gv LM/WK BD12 ....138 C3
  PDSY/CALV LS28 ......99 H5
Daleside Rd AIRE BD20 ......54 D2
  BFDE BD3 ......99 G4
  SHPY BD18......77 K3
Daleside Wk WBOW BD5 ......118 A4
Daleson Cl HIPP HX3 ......135 K4
Dale Stone Cl KNOT * WF11 ....150 D6
Dale St BFD BD1......5 M5
  KGHY BD21......3 L1
  OSS WF5 ......182 C3
  RPDN/SBR HX6 ......153 J4
  SHPY BD18......77 G5
Dalesway BGLY BD16 ......56 A6
Dales Wy BHP/TINH LS16 ......62 D5
  BHP/TINH LS16 ......82 C4
  GSLY LS20 ......58 C3
  ILK LS29 ......23 H4
Dales Way Link BAIL BD17 ......56 D6
  BHP/TINH LS16 ......41 K7
  BHP/TINH LS16 ......82 C4
  HDGY LS6 ......82 D5
  OT LS21 ......40 C6
Dale Vw AIRE BD20 ......21 J7
  AIRE BD20 ......32 C6
  ILK LS29 ......23 H5
  PONT WF8 ......189 J4
Dale View Cl KGHY BD21......3 M7
Daleview Ct BAIL BD17 ......77 H1
Dale View Gv KGHY BD21......3 M6
Dale View Rd KGHY BD21 ......3 L8
Dallam Av SHPY BD18 ......76 D4
Dallam Rd SHPY BD18......76 D4

Dallam Wk SHPY BD18 ......76 E4
Dalmeny Ter BRAM * LS13......80 B7
Dalton Av BEE/HOL LS11 ......123 F4
Dalton Bank Rd HUDE HD5 ....178 C4
Dalton Gv BEE/HOL LS11 ......123 F4
Dalton La BSPA/BRAM LS23 ....67 H1
  KGHY BD21......3 K4
Dalton Rd BEE/HOL LS11 ......123 F4
  KGHY BD21......3 L4
Dalton St RPDN/SBR HX6 ......153 J3
Dalton Ter CAS WF10......168 C1
  GIR BD8......4 F3
  KGHY BD21......3 L2
Damask St HFAX * HX1 ......16 F4
Damems La HWTH BD22 ......73 G2
Damems Rd HWTH BD22 ......73 H1
Dames La HWTH BD22 ......73 H2
Dam Head Rd RPDN/SBR HX6 ....153 K3
Dam La TAD LS24......90 B6
  YEA LS19 ......59 K4
Damon Av IDLE BD10 ......99 F1
Damside KGHY BD21......2 F1
Damson Ct CLAY BD14 ......116 B3
Danby Av BOW BD4......118 C6
Danby Wk OSM LS9 ......15 G1
Dandy Mill Av PONT WF8 ......170 A6
Dandy Mill Cft PONT WF8 ......170 A6
Dandy Mill Vw PONT WF8 ......170 A6
Danebury Rd BRIG HD6 ......157 G2
Danecourt Rd BOW BD4 ......119 F3
Danefield Ter OT LS21 ......39 J2
Dane Hill Dr BOW BD4 ......119 F2
Danella Crs WKFDW/WTN WF2 ....164 A6
Danella Rd WKFDW/WTN WF2 ....164 A6
Daniel Ct BOW BD4 ......119 C4
Dan La CUL/QBY BD13 ......116 B5
Danny La LUD/ILL HX2 ......152 E1
Dansk Wy ILK LS29 ......24 C1
Danum Dr BAIL BD17 ......77 H2
Darcey Hey La LUD/ILL HX2 ....154 B3
Darfield Av RHAY LS8 ......11 J3
Darfield Crs RHAY LS8 ......11 J3
Darfield Gv RHAY LS8 ......11 H2
Darfield Pl RHAY LS8 ......11 J3
Darfield Rd RHAY LS8 ......11 J3
Darfield St GIR BD8......5 K4
  RHAY LS8 ......11 J3
Darkfield La PONT WF8 ......170 A4
Dark La BTLY WF17 ......140 E4
  BTLY WF17 ......160 E4
  HWTH BD22 ......72 A3
  HWTH BD22 ......92 D2
  LUD/ILL HX2 ......153 J2
  PONT WF8 ......189 H2
Darkwood Cl AL/HA/HU LS17....64 B7
Darkwood Wy AL/HA/HU LS17 ....64 B7
Darley Av MID LS10 ......123 J6
Darley Rd LVSG WF15 ......159 G3
Darley St BFD BD1 ......5 M5
  HECK WF16 ......160 A4
  KGHY BD21......53 J2
Darnell Ter BEE/HOL LS11 ....14 A3
Darnes Av LUD/ILL HX2 ......154 B3
Darnley Av WKFDW/WTN WF2 ....18 A3
Darnley La MSTN/BAR LS15 ....105 K6
Darren St BOW BD4......7 L9
Darrington Rd PONT WF8 ......189 K1
Darryl Dr LUD/ILL HX2 ......154 B3
Dartmouth Av MOR LS27 ......141 K5
Dartmouth Ms MOR LS27 ......141 J4
Dartmouth Ter GIR BD8 ......97 H3
Dartmouth Wy BEE/HOL LS11 ....123 H3
Darwin St WBOW BD5 ......117 H3
David La DEWS WF13 ......161 F6
David St BEE/HOL LS11 ......13 L3
  CAS WF10......168 A1
  WKFDE * WF1 ......19 K9
Davies Av RHAY LS8......84 B4
Davis Av CAS WF10 ......169 J2
Dawlish Av OSM LS9 ......11 L9
Dawlish Crs OSM LS9 ......11 L9
Dawlish Gv OSM LS9 ......15 L1
Dawlish Mt OSM LS9 ......11 L9
Dawlish Pl OSM LS9 ......11 L9
Dawlish Rd OSM LS9 ......11 M8
Dawlish Rw OSM LS9......11 L9
Dawlish St OSM LS9......11 L8
Dawnay Rd WBOW BD5 ......117 H3
Dawson Av WBSY BD6 ......117 H6
Dawson HI MOR LS27 ......141 K2
Dawson La BOW BD4 ......118 C5
  BOW BD4 ......120 B4
Dawson Mt BOW BD4 ......118 D5
Dawson Pl BOW BD4......118 D5
  KGHY BD21......3 H8
Dawson Rd BEE/HOL LS11 ......123 H3
  KGHY BD21......3 H8
Dawsons Meadow
  PDSY/CALV LS28 ......99 K3
Dawson St BOW BD4......118 D5
  EARD/LOFT WF3 ......142 C6
  IDLE BD10 ......78 C2
  PDSY/CALV * LS28 ......100 A4
Dawson Ter BOW BD4 ......118 D5
Dawson Wy KGHY BD21 ......3 H8
Dawtrie Cl CAS WF10......169 J1
Dawtrie St CAS WF10 ......149 J7
Day St DEWS * WF13 ......180 B4
Deacon Cl BFDE * BD3 ......98 C5
Dealburn Rd LM/WK BD12 ....137 J2
Deal St HFAX HX1......17 J7
  KGHY BD21......3 L8
Dean Av RHAY LS8......84 B6
Dean Beck Av WBSY BD6 ......117 K6
Dean Beck Ct WBSY * BD6 ....118 A6
Dean Cl GIR BD8......96 C4
  WKFDW/WTN WF2 ......164 A6
Dean Clough HFAX HX1 ......17 G4
Dean Ct HIPP HX3 ......154 C6
  RHAY LS8 ......84 B6
Dean End GTL/HWG HX4......175 G1
Deanery Gdns IDLE BD10 ......78 D7
Deanfield Av MOR LS27 ......141 J4
Dean Hall Cl MOR * LS27 ......141 J3
Dean Head HORS LS18 ......60 D3
Dean House La LUD/ILL HX2 ....132 E5

Deanhurst Gdns MOR LS27 141 G1
Dean La CUL/QBY BD13 95 F4
GSLY LS20 58 A3
HORS LS18 60 D3
HWTH BD22 52 A5
RPDN/SBR HX6 153 F6
RPDN/SBR HX6 173 F1
Dean Lane Head
CUL/QBY * BD13 95 G4
Dean Park Av BIRK/DRI BD11 120 B7
Dean Park Dr BIRK/DRI BD11 120 B7
Dean Rd WBSY BD6 117 J6
Deanstones Crs
CUL/QBY BD13 115 H6
Deanstones La CUL/QBY BD13 115 H6
Dean St GTL/HWG HX4 175 G2
HWTH BD22 72 E5
ILK LS29 24 B4
Deansway MOR LS27 141 J1
Deanswood Cl AL/HA/HU LS17 83 F1
Deanswood Dr AL/HA/HU LS17 82 E1
Deanswood Gn AL/HA/HU LS17 82 E1
Deanswood Hl AL/HA/HU LS17 82 E1
Deanswood Pl AL/HA/HU LS17 83 F1
Deanswood Ri AL/HA/HU LS17 82 E1
Deanswood Vw AL/HA/HU LS17 83 F1
Deanwood Av WIL/AL BD15 95 K3
Deanwood Crs WIL/AL BD15 95 K3
Deanwood Wk WIL/AL BD15 95 K3
Dearden St OSS WF5 182 C4
RPDN/SBR HX6 153 J3
Dearne Cft WBY LS22 29 H1
Dearnley St DEWS * WF13 180 B3
Dee Ct HWTH BD22 72 D2
Deep Dl BSPA/BRAM LS23 48 B1
Deepdale Cl BAIL BD17 77 F2
Deepdale La BSPA/BRAM LS23 48 A1
Deep La BRIG HD6 157 K6
CLAY BD14 116 B1
CUL/QBY BD13 114 D2
LUD/ILL HX2 153 G1
RPDN/SBR HX6 172 C1
Deer Park Ct GFTH/SHER LS25 131 H6
Deerstone Rdg WBY LS22 29 H1
Defarge Ct WBOW BD5 117 K3
Deganwy Dr HUDE HD5 178 D7
Deighton Av GFTH/SHER LS25 111 F6
Deighton Cl WBY LS22 29 J3
Deighton La BTLY WF17 160 D3
Deighton Rd HUDN HD2 177 J6
WBY LS22 29 H1
De Lacey Ms BOW BD4 118 D4
De Lacies Ct RTHW LS26 125 H7
De Lacies Rd RTHW LS26 125 H7
De Lacy Av BOW * BD4 118 C6
FEA/AMT WF7 168 B7
Delacy Crs CAS WF10 149 J6
De Lacy Mt KSTL LS5 101 K1
De Lacy Ter PONT WF8 189 K1
Delamere St WBOW BD5 117 J4
Delaware Ct BOW BD4 118 C6
Delf Hl BRIG HD6 176 D2
Delfs La RPDN/SBR HX6 172 A1
Delius Av IDLE BD10 78 E7
The Dell AL/HA/HU LS17 46 A7
CAS WF10 167 K3
CUL/QBY BD13 74 B6
HUDN HD2 177 G5
Dell Cft AIRE BD20 20 D7
Dellside Fold CUL/QBY BD13 74 A6
Delmont Cl BTLY WF17 160 B2
The Delph FEA/AMT WF7 188 E4
Delph Ct HDGY LS6 103 F1
Delph Crs CLAY BD14 116 A2
Delph Croft Vw KGHY BD21 3 K7
Delph Dr CLAY BD14 115 K2
Delph Gv CLAY BD14 116 A2
Delph Hl BAIL BD17 57 H7
PDSY/CALV LS28 100 B5
Delph Hill Castle LUD/ILL * HX2 154 A2
Delph Hill La LUD/ILL HX2 132 E5
Delph Hill Rd LUD/ILL HX2 154 C4
Delph Hill Ter LUD/ILL HX2 154 C4
Delph La HDGY LS6 9 K1
Delph Mt HDGY LS6 9 K1
Delph St HFAX HX1 16 F7
Delph Ter CLAY BD14 116 A2
Delph Vw HDGY LS6 9 J1
Delph Wood Cl BGLY BD16 76 B1
Delverne Gv ECHL BD2 98 D2
Denbigh Ap OSM LS9 104 E3
Denbrook Av BOW BD4 119 G6
Denbrook Cl BOW BD4 119 G5
Denbrook Crs BOW BD4 119 G5
Denbrook Wk BOW BD4 119 G5
Denbrook Wy BOW BD4 119 G5
Denbury Mt BOW BD4 119 F4
Denby Cl BTLY WF17 140 A6
LVSG WF15 159 G3
Denby Ct HWTH BD22 72 C3
Denby Crest PONT WF8 190 D4
Denby Dale Rd
WKFDW/WTN WF2 18 D9
Denby Dr BAIL BD17 77 G3
Denby Hill Rd HWTH BD22 72 C2
Denby La WIL/AL BD15 96 A4
Denby Mt HWTH BD22 92 D3
Denby Pl RPDN/SBR HX6 153 J3
Denby Rd KGHY BD21 3 G9
PONT WF8 190 D4
Denby St GIR BD8 5 H3
Dence Gn BOW BD4 7 M9
Dence Pl MSTN/BAR LS15 105 F5
Dendrum Cl HWTH BD22 72 D1
Dene Bank BGLY BD16 55 K5
Dene Cl ELL HX5 175 H4
Dene Crs GTHN BD7 116 D2
Dene Gv AIRE BD20 21 F7
Dene Hl BAIL BD17 76 E1
Denehill HTON BD9 96 C3
Dene House Ct LDSU LS2 9 M4
Dene Mt WIL/AL BD15 96 B4
Dene Pl HFAX HX1 16 F4
Dene Rd WBSY BD6 116 C5
Dene Royd Cl GTL/HWG HX4 174 C6
Dene Royd Ct GTL/HWG HX4 174 C6
Deneside OSS WF5 182 B2
Deneside Mt WBOW BD5 117 H5
Deneside Ter WBOW BD5 117 J4
Denesway GFTH/SHER LS25 127 K1
Dene Vw LUD/ILL HX2 132 E7
Deneway PDSY/CALV LS28 99 K3
Denfield Av HIPP HX3 134 B5
Denfield Crs HIPP HX3 134 C5
Denfield Edge HIPP HX3 134 C5
Denfield Gdns HIPP HX3 134 C5
Denfield La HIPP HX3 134 B5
Denfield Sq HIPP HX3 134 C5
Denhale Av WKFDW/WTN WF2 183 K3
Denham Av MOR LS27 141 K5
Denham St BRIG HD6 157 F7
BTLY WF17 160 D1
Denholme Dr OSS WF5 182 C2
Denholme Gate Rd HIPP HX3 136 B6
Denholme Rd HWTH BD22 92 E4
Denison Rd BVRD LS3 9 J8
Denison St BTLY WF17 161 F4
YEA LS19 59 J4
Denmark St WKFDE WF1 19 J9
Dennil Crs MSTN/BAR LS15 106 A1
Dennil Rd MSTN/BAR LS15 106 A1
Dennis La AIRE BD20 20 B6
Dennison Fold BOW BD4 7 L9
Dennison Hl OT LS21 39 J2
Dennistead Crs HDGY LS6 82 C7
Denshaw Dr MOR LS27 142 B3
Denshaw Gv MOR LS27 142 B3
Denshaw La EARD/LOFT WF3 142 D4
Denstone St WKFDE WF1 19 G3
Dent Dr WKFDE WF1 19 M1
Denton Av RHAY LS8 84 A4
Denton Dr BGLY BD16 56 B7
Denton Gv RHAY * LS8 84 A4
Denton Rd ILK LS29 23 K4
ILK LS29 25 F3
Denton Ter CAS WF10 148 D7
Dent St OSM LS9 15 G2
Denwell Ter PONT WF8 169 J7
Derby Pl BFDE BD3 7 K6
Derby Rd BFDE BD3 7 L6
YEA LS19 59 J7
Derbyshire St MID LS10 15 G9
Derby St CLAY * BD14 116 A2
CUL/QBY BD13 115 G5
GTHN BD7 117 G2
RPDN/SBR HX6 153 K3
Derry Hl ILK LS29 38 A7
Derry Hill Gdns ILK LS29 38 A6
Derry La ILK LS29 38 A6
Derwent Av GFTH/SHER LS25 107 J7
RTHW LS26 145 K1
WIL/AL BD15 95 F1
Derwent Dr BHP/TINH LS16 62 C7
CAS WF10 149 K6
Derwent Gv WKFDW/WTN WF2 184 A3
Derwent Pl BEE/HOL LS11 13 K4
KNOT WF11 171 F6
Derwent Ri WBY LS22 29 G1
Derwent Rd EARL WF12 161 J5
ECHL BD2 98 B2
WKFDW/WTN WF2 184 A3
Derwent St KGHY * BD21 3 M3
Derwentwater Gv HDGY LS6 102 B1
Derwentwater Ter HDGY LS6 82 C7
Detroit Av MSTN/BAR LS15 106 A5
Detroit Dr MSTN/BAR LS15 106 B5
Devon Cl LDSU LS2 9 L4
Devon Rd CHAL LS7 9 M4
Devonshire Av RHAY LS8 84 B2
Devonshire Cl RHAY LS8 84 B2
Devonshire Crs RHAY LS8 84 A3
Devonshire Gdns CHAL LS7 9 M3
Devonshire La RHAY LS8 84 B2
Devonshire St KGHY BD21 2 E4
Devonshire St West KGHY BD21 2 D5
Devonshire Ter GIR BD8 97 H3
Devon St HFAX HX1 16 A8
Devon Wy BRIG HD6 157 G2
Dewar Cl WBY LS22 46 D2
Dewhirst Cl BAIL BD17 77 J2
Dewhirst Pl BOW BD4 7 K9
Dewhirst Rd BAIL BD17 77 J2
BRIG HD6 157 F4
Dewhirst St WIL/AL BD15 75 F7
Dewhurst Rd HUDN HD2 177 G7
Dewsbury Gate Rd
DEWS WF13 160 C5
Dewsbury Ring Rd
DEWS WF13 181 F1
Dewsbury Rd BEE/HOL LS11 14 A7
CLECK BD19 139 J5
CLECK BD19 159 F1
EARL WF12 162 B1
ELL HX5 176 B3
OSS WF5 182 B1
WKFDW/WTN WF2 183 H4
Diadem Dr SCFT LS14 105 F4
Dial St OSM LS9 15 G3
Diamond St BFD BD1 6 A7
BTLY * WF17 160 E2
HFAX HX1 16 C4
HWTH BD22 53 H7
Diamond Ter HFAX HX1 16 C3
Dibb La YEA LS19 59 G4
Dib Cl RHAY LS8 84 E7
Dib La RHAY LS8 84 E7
Dickens Dr CAS WF10 169 J3
Dicken's St LUD/ILL HX2 154 B1
WBOW BD5 117 K3
Dickin Ct RPDN/SBR * HX6 173 F5
Dickinson Ct WKFDE WF1 18 F1
Dickinson St HORS LS18 81 F2
WKFDE WF1 18 F2
Dickinson Ter FEA/AMT WF7 188 C3
Dick La BFDE BD3 99 G5
BOW BD4 119 F1
Dick's Garth Rd ILK LS29 38 A6
Digby Rd ILK LS29 38 B6
Dimple Gdns OSS WF5 182 C5
Dimples La AIRE BD20 55 G3
HWTH BD22 72 B5
Dimple Wells Cl OSS WF5 182 C5
Dimple Wells La OSS WF5 182 C5
Dimple Wells Rd OSS WF5 182 C5
Dirkhill Rd GTHN BD7 117 H1
Dirkhill St GTHN BD7 117 G1
Discovery Rd HFAX HX1 17 J6
Dispensary Wk HFAX HX1 17 J6
Disraeli Gdns BEE/HOL LS11 13 M8
Disraeli Ter BEE/HOL LS11 13 M8
Dixon Av GTHN BD7 4 A9
Dixon Cl AIRE BD20 32 D5
GTL/HWG HX4 174 D1
Dixon La WOR/ARM LS12 12 A5
Dixon Lane Rd WOR/ARM LS12 12 A5
Dixon St FEA/AMT WF7 188 C2
Dixon's Yd WKFDE * WF1 19 G5
Dob La RPDN/SBR HX6 152 E5
Dob Park Rd OT LS21 27 G2
Dobson Av BEE/HOL LS11 14 A9
Dobson Gv BEE/HOL LS11 14 A9
Dobson Pl BEE/HOL LS11 14 A9
Dobson Ter BEE/HOL LS11 14 A9
Dobson Vw BEE/HOL LS11 14 A9
Dockfield Pl BAIL BD17 77 H3
Dockfield Rd BAIL BD17 77 H4
Dockfield Ter BAIL BD17 77 H3
Dock La BAIL BD17 77 H4
Dockroyd La HWTH BD22 72 D2
Dock St MID LS10 14 B2
Doctor Hl IDLE BD10 78 B6
LUD/ILL HX2 134 A6
Doctor La IDLE BD10 78 C3
MIRF WF14 179 H4
Doctors La CAS WF10 147 K1
Dodgeholme Cl LUD/ILL HX2 134 A3
Dodge Holme Gdns
LUD/ILL HX2 134 A3
Dodge Holme Rd LUD/ILL HX2 134 A3
Dodgson Av CHAL LS7 10 E2
Dodgson St ELL HX5 175 J4
Dodsworth Crs NORM WF6 186 E1
Dog Kennel La HIPP HX3 17 M9
Dog La GTL/HWG HX4 174 B7
GTL/HWG HX4 174 B2
Doldram La RPDN/SBR HX6 153 H7
Dole St CUL/QBY BD13 95 H7
Dolfin Pl HUDN HD2 178 A4
Doll La CUL/QBY BD13 74 B7
Dolly La OSM LS9 10 E6
Dolphin Ct OSM LS9 14 F1
Dolphin La EARD/LOFT WF3 143 K5
Dolphin Rd MID LS10 143 K2
Dolphin St OSM LS9 14 F1
Dolphin Ct BRAM LS13 100 E3
Dombey St HFAX HX1 16 D6
Domestic Rd BEE/HOL LS11 12 F5
Domestic St BEE/HOL LS11 13 H5
Dominion Av CHAL LS7 83 J6
Dominion Cl CHAL * LS7 83 J6
Donald Av WBSY BD6 117 H6
Donald St PDSY/CALV LS28 100 A3
Don Av WBY LS22 29 G1
Doncaster Rd HOR/CROF WF4 185 K7
KNOT WF11 170 D4
Doncaster St HIPP HX3 155 G5
Don Ct AIRE BD20 33 F1
Donisthorpe St MID LS10 14 E5
WBOW BD5 117 K3
Don Pedro Av NORM WF6 167 G6
Don Pedro Cl NORM WF6 167 G6
Don St KGHY BD21 2 E3
Dorchester Av PONT WF8 189 G1
Dorchester Ct BOW * BD4 119 F3
Dorchester Crs BAIL BD17 58 A7
BOW BD4 119 F3
Dorchester Dr LUD/ILL HX2 154 B3
YEA LS19 59 K5
Dorchester Rd HUDN HD2 177 G4
TAD LS24 70 C1
Dorian Cl IDLE BD10 78 E6
Dorothy St KGHY BD21 73 H1
Dorset Av RHAY LS8 11 J1
Dorset Cl WBOW BD5 117 H3
Dorset Gv PDSY/CALV * LS28 100 B5
Dorset Mt RHAY LS8 11 J2
Dorset Rd RHAY LS8 11 J1
Dorset St RHAY LS8 11 J1
WBOW BD5 117 J3
Dorset Ter RHAY LS8 11 J2
Dotterel Gln MOR LS27 142 B4
Douglas Av BTLY WF17 161 J3
Douglas Dr BOW * BD4 118 D2
Douglas Rd BOW BD4 118 D2
Douglas St EARL WF12 181 F5
HIPP HX3 134 E5
HWTH BD22 73 F4
Dove Cl WBY LS22 29 H1
Dovecote Cl HOR/CROF WF4 183 G7
Dovecote Dr CAS WF10 148 D1
Dovecote La HOR/CROF WF4 183 F7
Dovedale Cl HIPP HX3 136 A1
Dovedale Gdns
MSTN/BAR LS15 106 C2
Dovedale Garth
MSTN/BAR LS15 106 C2
Dover St BFDE BD3 6 B2
GFTH/SHER LS25 108 A6
Dovesdale Gv WBOW BD5 117 H4
Dovesdale Rd WBOW BD5 117 J4
Dove St SHPY BD18 76 E4
Dowkell La BSPA/BRAM LS23 48 D1
Dowker St HFAX HX1 16 B9
Dowley Gap La BGLY BD16 76 A3
Downham St BFDE BD3 6 D7
Downing Cl BFDE BD3 6 E5
Downland Crs KNOT WF11 171 J6
Downside Crs WIL/AL BD15 95 K4
Dracup Av GTHN BD7 116 D1
Dracup Rd GTHN BD7 116 E3
Dradishaw Rd AIRE BD20 32 E1
Dragon Ct WOR/ARM * LS12 13 H3
Dragon Crs WOR/ARM LS12 12 C6
Dragon Dr WOR/ARM LS12 12 B6
Dragon Rd WOR/ARM LS12 12 B6
Drake La BIRK/DRI BD11 140 B2
Drake St KGHY BD21 3 G3
Draughton Gv WBOW BD5 117 J5
Draughton St WBOW BD5 117 J5
Drayton Manor Yd
BEE/HOL * LS11 14 A7
Dray Vw DEWS WF13 160 C6
Drewry Rd KGHY BD21 2 E3
Drewton Rd BFD BD1 5 K5
Driftholme Rd BIRK/DRI BD11 120 C7
Drill Pde GIR BD8 5 J2
Drill St HWTH BD22 72 D6
KGHY BD21 3 G4
The Drive AL/HA/HU LS17 46 A5
AL/HA/HU LS17 63 F5
BGLY BD16 55 H5
BHP/TINH LS16 61 K7
BTLY WF17 160 D2
GFTH/SHER LS25 127 K5
HIPP HX3 136 C7
IDLE BD10 78 E6
ILK LS29 37 K2
MSTN/BAR LS15 106 A3
OSM LS9 14 E2
RHAY LS8 84 B4
RTHW LS26 126 D5
Driver Pl WOR/ARM LS12 12 F3
Drivers Rw PONT WF8 189 G2
Driver St WOR/ARM LS12 12 F3
Driver Ter AIRE BD20 21 G7
WOR/ARM * LS12 12 F3
Drovers Wy ECHL BD2 97 K2
Drub La CLECK BD19 139 F5
Druggist La ILK LS29 22 C1
Druids St CLAY BD14 116 A2
Drummond Av HDGY LS6 82 B6
Drummond Ct BHP/TINH LS16 82 B6
Drummond Rd BHP/TINH LS16 82 B5
GIR BD8 4 F1
Drury Av HORS LS18 80 E4
Drury Cl HORS LS18 80 E4
Drury La GTL/HWG HX4 174 C5
HORS LS18 80 E4
NORM WF6 166 C5
WKFDE WF1 18 D4
Dry Carr La LUD/ILL HX2 132 D2
Dryclough Cl HIPP HX3 155 F5
Dryclough La HIPP HX3 155 F5
Dryden St BFD BD1 6 B8
BGLY * BD16 75 J1
Dubb La BGLY BD16 75 K1
Duchy Av HTON BD9 96 D2
Duchy Crs HTON BD9 96 D2
Duchy Dr HTON BD9 96 D3
Duchy Gv HTON BD9 96 D2
Duchy Vls HTON BD9 96 D2
Duchywood HTON BD9 96 D2
Ducie St IDLE BD10 78 C3
Duckett Gv PDSY/CALV LS28 99 G5
Duckworth Gv HTON BD9 96 E3
Duckworth La HTON BD9 96 D4
Duckworth Ter HTON BD9 96 E3
Dudley Av BTLY WF17 140 D5
Dudley Crs LUD/ILL HX2 134 A2
Dudley Gv BOW BD4 7 M9
Dudley Hill Rd ECHL BD2 98 C2
Dudley St BOW BD4 7 L9
Dudwell Av HIPP * HX3 155 G6
Dudwell Gv HIPP HX3 155 F6
Dudwell La HIPP HX3 155 F6
Duffield Crs GFTH/SHER * LS25 111 G5
Dufton Ap SCFT LS14 105 H2
Duich Rd WBSY BD6 136 D1
Duinen St WBOW BD5 6 A9
Duke of York Av
WKFDW/WTN WF2 184 E7
Duke of York St WKFDE WF1 19 G2
WKFDW/WTN WF2 164 A6
Dukes Hl ILK * LS29 23 K3
Duke St BFD BD1 5 L5
CAS WF10 148 A7
DEWS WF13 180 B4
ELL HX5 175 J3
HWTH BD22 72 E5
KGHY BD21 53 J2
LUD/ILL HX2 132 E6
OSM LS9 14 D1
Dulverton Cl BEE/HOL LS11 122 C5
PONT WF8 170 A5
Dulverton Gdns BEE/HOL LS11 122 B4
Dulverton Garth
BEE/HOL LS11 122 B5
Dulverton Gn BEE/HOL LS11 122 C5
Dulverton Gv BEE/HOL LS11 122 B5
BOW BD4 118 E3
Dulverton Pl BEE/HOL LS11 122 B5
Dulverton Ri PONT WF8 170 A5
Dulverton Sq BEE/HOL LS11 122 C5
Dulverton Wy PONT WF8 170 A5
Dunbar Cft CUL/QBY BD13 115 J5
Dunbar St WKFDE WF1 19 L9
Dunbottle Cl MIRF WF14 179 J4
Dunbottle La MIRF WF14 179 J3
Dunbottle Wy MIRF WF14 179 K3
Duncan Av OT LS21 38 E4
WKFDW/WTN WF2 185 F7
Duncan St LDS LS1 14 A1
WBOW BD5 5 M9
Dunce Mire Rd
GFTH/SHER LS25 131 J7
Dunce Park Cl ELL HX5 175 J4
Duncombe Rd GIR BD8 4 B5
Duncombe St GIR BD8 4 D5
LDS LS1 9 J8
Duncombe Wy GIR BD8 4 C5
Dundas St HFAX HX1 16 B9
KGHY BD21 3 J6
Dunderdale Crs CAS WF10 149 J6
Dungeon La RTHW LS26 145 H6
Dunhill Crs OSM LS9 105 F5
Dunhill Ri OSM LS9 105 F5
Dunkhill Cft IDLE * BD10 78 C5
Dunkirk Crs HFAX HX1 154 B2
Dunkirk La HFAX HX1 154 B3
Dunkirk Ri AIRE BD20 54 B1
Dunkirk St HFAX HX1 154 B2
Dunkirk Ter HFAX HX1 16 A8
Dunlin Cl MOR LS27 142 C4
Dunlin Ct MID LS10 143 J2
Dunlin Cft MID LS10 143 J2
Dunlin Dr MID LS10 143 J2
Dunlin Fold MID LS10 143 J2
Dunlin Wy GIR BD8 96 B6
Dunmore Av CUL/QBY BD13 115 F5
Dunn Cl WKFDW/WTN WF2 164 A5
Dunningley EARD/LOFT WF3 142 D4
Dunningley La
EARD/LOFT WF3 142 E5
Dunnington Wk LM/WK BD12 137 F1
Dunnock Cft MOR LS27 142 B4
Dunrobin Av GFTH/SHER LS25 108 A6
Dunsford Av BOW BD4 118 C6
Dunstan Cl OSS WF5 182 D5
Dunstarn Dr BHP/TINH LS16 82 C1
Dunstarn Gdns BHP/TINH LS16 82 D1
Dunstarn La BHP/TINH LS16 82 C2
Durban Av BEE/HOL LS11 122 E4
Durban Crs BEE/HOL LS11 122 E4
Durham Rd GIR BD8 4 C1
Durham St CAS WF10 168 D2
LUD/ILL HX2 134 B7
Durham Ter GIR BD8 4 C2
Durkheim Ct BFDE BD3 7 G6
Durley Av HTON BD9 96 E2
Durling Dr SHPY BD18 77 K5
Durlston Gv LM/WK BD12 137 J3
Durlston Ter LM/WK BD12 137 J3
Durrance St HWTH BD22 2 A7
Durrant Cl WBY LS22 29 J4
Dutton Gn SCFT LS14 85 H4
Dutton Wy SCFT LS14 85 H5
Duxbury Ri CHAL LS7 9 M4
Dyehouse Dr CLECK BD19 138 D5
Dyehouse La BRIG HD6 157 H7
PDSY/CALV LS28 120 B2
Dye House La RPDN/SBR HX6 154 B7
WIL/AL BD15 74 D7
Dyehouse Rd LM/WK BD12 138 A2
Dyer La HIPP HX3 16 A1
Dyers Ct HDGY LS6 102 E1
Dyer St LDSU LS2 10 C9
Dyke Cl MIRF WF14 179 H1
Dymond Gv LVSG * WF15 159 H5
Dymond Rd LVSG WF15 159 J5
Dymond Vw LVSG WF15 159 H5
Dyson La RPDN/SBR HX6 172 D6
Dyson Pl HIPP * HX3 155 G5
Dyson Rd HFAX HX1 16 B4
Dyson St BFD BD1 5 J5
BRIG HD6 157 F5
HTON BD9 97 F1

E

Eagle Gv WKFDW/WTN WF2 183 J3
Eaglesfield Dr WBSY BD6 136 E1
Eagle St HWTH BD22 73 F5
KGHY BD21 2 F4
Ealand Av BTLY WF17 160 C1
Ealand Crs BTLY WF17 160 C1
Ealand Rd BTLY WF17 140 C7
Ealing Ct BTLY WF17 160 D2
Earle St FEA/AMT WF7 188 B3
Earlsmere Dr MOR LS27 141 J2
Earls Ter HIPP HX3 134 D5
Earl St EARL WF12 182 A2
HWTH BD22 72 D6
KGHY BD21 2 F2
WBOW BD5 5 L9
WKFDE WF1 19 G3
Earlswood LM/WK * BD12 137 J4
Earlswood Av RHAY LS8 84 A2
Earlswood Cha
PDSY/CALV LS28 100 B7
Earlswood Crs
GFTH/SHER LS25 127 J4
Earlswood Md
PDSY/CALV LS28 120 B1
Earl Ter HIPP HX3 134 D5
Easby Av BTLY WF17 160 C4
Easby Cl ILK LS29 23 J5
Easby Dr ILK LS29 23 J5
Easby Rd WBOW BD5 5 J9
Easdale Cl SCFT LS14 105 G1
Easdale Crs SCFT LS14 85 H7
Easdale Mt SCFT LS14 105 G1
Easdale Rd SCFT LS14 105 G1
East Acres KNOT WF11 171 F1
East Av KGHY BD21 3 H2
PONT WF8 189 G2
East Bank GFTH/SHER LS25 111 G5
East Bath St BTLY WF17 161 G3
East Beck Ct OT LS21 26 A4
East Bolton LUD/ILL HX2 114 A7
Eastborough Crs DEWS WF13 161 G7
Eastbourne Av FEA/AMT WF7 188 D2
Eastbourne Cl PONT WF8 190 B1
Eastbourne Crs PONT WF8 190 B1
Eastbourne Dr PONT WF8 190 B1
Eastbourne Rd HTON BD9 77 G7
Eastbourne Ter PONT WF8 190 A1
Eastbourne Vw PONT WF8 190 A1
Eastbrook Ct
BSPA/BRAM * LS23 68 C1
Eastburn Br AIRE BD20 32 A4
Eastbury Av WBSY BD6 116 C5
East Busk La OT LS21 39 K2
East Byland LUD/ILL HX2 134 B1
East Cswy BHP/TINH LS16 62 C6
East Causeway Cl
BHP/TINH LS16 62 C6
East Causeway Crs
BHP/TINH LS16 62 C7
East Causeway V
BHP/TINH LS16 62 D7
East Chevin Rd OT LS21 40 A5
Eastcliffe HIPP HX3 17 M8
East Cl PONT WF8 189 K4
Eastdean Bank SCFT LS14 85 H6
Eastdean Dr SCFT LS14 85 H6
Eastdean Gdns SCFT LS14 85 J6
Eastdean Ga SCFT LS14 85 J6
Eastdean Gv SCFT LS14 85 J6
Eastdean Ri SCFT LS14 85 J6
Eastdean Rd SCFT LS14 85 H6
East Dene AIRE BD20 21 F7
East Down CAS WF10 149 F7
East Dr GFTH/SHER LS25 128 A1
PONT WF8 190 A2
Easterly Av RHAY LS8 104 B1
Easterly Cl RHAY LS8 11 L2
Easterly Crs RHAY LS8 104 B1

Easterly Cross *RHAY* LS8............11 L1
Easterly Garth *RHAY* LS8...........11 L1
Easterly Mt *RHAY* LS8..............11 L1
Easterly Rd *RHAY* LS8..............84 E7
Easterly Sq *RHAY* LS8..............11 L1
Easterly Vw *RHAY* LS8.............11 M1
Eastfield Av *KNOT* WF11...........171 G5
Eastfield Cl *TAD* LS24..............51 C5
Eastfield Crs *RTHW* LS26..........145 J1
Eastfield Dr *PONT* WF8............190 A1
  RTHW...........................145 H1
Eastfield Gdns *BOW* BD4..........119 F3
Eastfield Gv *NORM* WF6...........167 F5
Eastfield La *CAS* WF10.............148 D7
Eastfield Rd *KNOT* WF11...........171 G5
  MIRF...........................180 A3
East Field St *OSM* LS9..............14 F1
Eastgate *BHP/TINH* LS16...........41 G7
  ELL HX5.......................175 J2
  OSM LS9.........................10 C9
Eastgate Cl *BHP/TINH* LS16........41 G7
East Grange Cl *MID* LS10..........123 K5
East Grange Dr *MID* LS10..........123 K5
East Grange Garth *MID* LS10......123 K5
East Grange Ri *MID* LS10..........123 K5
East Grange Rd *MID* LS10..........123 K5
East Grange Sq *MID* LS10..........123 K5
East Grange Vw *MID* LS10.........123 K5
Easthorpe Ct *ECHL* BD2.............98 E1
East King St *OSM* LS9...............14 E2
Eastland Wk *BRAM* LS13...........101 H4
Eastleigh Ct *EARD/LOFT* WF3......143 F7
Eastleigh Dr *EARD/LOFT* WF3......143 F7
Eastleigh Gv *WBOW* BD5...........117 J3
East Moor Crs *RHAY* LS8............84 A2
East Moor Dr *RHAY* LS8.............84 B3
East Moor La *BHP/TINH* LS16......62 C7
East Moor Rd *RHAY* LS8.............84 A2
Eastmoor Rd *WKFDE* WF1...........18 F1
East Mt *BRIG* HD6...................157 F5
East Pde *RHAY* LS8..................32 E5
  BAIL BD17........................57 J7
  BFD BD1...........................6 B6
  BFDE BD3.........................6 B5
  ILK LS29.........................24 B5
  ILK LS29.........................38 B6
  KGHY BD21........................3 H5
  LDS LS1..........................9 M9
  RPDN/SBR HX6...................154 A3
East Parade Wk *LDS* LS1.............9 M9
East Park Dr *OSM* LS9..............15 H1
East Park Gv *OSM* LS9..............15 J2
East Park Mt *OSM* LS9..............15 J2
East Park Pde *OSM* LS9.............15 J2
East Park Pl *OSM* LS9...............15 J2
East Park Rd *HIPP* HX3.............16 C1
  OSM LS9.........................15 J2
East Park St *MOR* LS27............141 J4
  OSM LS9.........................15 J2
East Park Ter *OSM* LS9.............15 J2
East Park Vw *OSM* LS9.............15 J1
East Rd *LM/WK* BD12...............137 J1
East Royd *HWTH* BD22...............72 C2
East Side Ct *PDSY/CALV* LS28......120 E1
East Squire La *GIR* BD8.............97 H3
East St *BRIG* HD6...................157 F7
  BTLY WF17.......................161 G3
  HIPP HX3.......................157 F1
  OSM LS9.........................14 D1
  RPDN/SBR HX6...................153 F6
  WKFDE WF1......................164 D6
East Ter *HWTH* BD22................73 F4
East Vw *AIRE* BD20.................21 F1
  CAS WF10........................167 K1
  CLECK BD19......................158 B2
  GFTH/SHER LS25.................111 F7
  GFTH/SHER LS25.................128 A5
  KNOT WF11.......................171 H4
  LUD/ILL * HX2...................133 F6
  MIRF WF14.......................179 G3
  MSTN/BAR * LS15.................105 K3
  OSS WF5.........................182 D6
  PDSY/CALV LS28.................120 B1
  RTHW LS26.......................145 K2
  WBD6 BD6........................116 B4
  YEA LS19.........................59 K5
East View Rd *YEA* LS19.............59 K5
East View Ter *LM/WK* BD12........137 J1
Eastville Rd *HOR/CROF* WF4........186 E6
Eastway *MIRF* WF14.................179 G2
Eastway Pk *MIRF* WF14.............179 H2
Eastwick Vw *WIL/AL* * BD15.......96 A4
Eastwood Av *LUD/ILL* HX2..........114 B7
  RPDN/SBR HX6...................153 C5
  WKFDW/WTN WF2.................183 K3
Eastwood Cl *LUD/ILL* HX2..........114 B7
Eastwood Crs *SCFT* LS14...........106 A1
Eastwood Dr *SCFT* LS14.............85 K7
Eastwood Gdns *SCFT* LS14.........105 K1
Eastwood Garth *SCFT* LS14........106 A1
Eastwood Gv *GFTH/SHER* LS25.....127 K1
  LUD/ILL HX2....................114 B7
Eastwood La *SCFT* LS14............106 A1
Eastwood Nook *SCFT* LS14.........106 A1
Eastwood St *BOW* BD4...............118 A1
  BRIG HD6........................157 G5
  HIPP HX3.......................134 D5
Easy Rd *OSM* LS9....................15 G3
Eaton Hl *BHP/TINH* LS16............81 J1
Eaton Ms *MID* LS10.................143 H2
Eaton Rd *ILK* LS29..................23 K6
Eaton Sq *MID* LS10.................143 H3
Eaton St *KGHY* BD21................53 H7
Ebberston Gv *HDGY* LS6.............9 G2
Ebberston Pl *HDGY* LS6.............9 G2
Ebberston Ter *HDGY* LS6............9 G2
Ebenezer Pl *GTHN* BD7.............117 F2
Ebenezer St *BFD* BD1.................6 A7
  EARD/LOFT WF3.................144 C4
  PDSY/CALV LS28.................100 A2
Ebor Gdns *MIRF* WF14..............179 F4
Ebor La *HWTH* BD22.................72 C4
Ebor Mt *GFTH/SHER* LS25...........127 K4
  HDGY LS6.........................9 G4
Ebor Pl *HDGY* LS6....................9 G4
Ebor St *HDGY* LS6....................9 G4
Ebor Wy *AL/HA/HU* LS17............43 H6
  AL/HA/HU LS17..................44 B2

  AL/HA/HU LS17....................45 K2
  ILK LS29.........................37 J4
  ILK LS29.........................38 C6
  OT LS21..........................39 H5
Ebury Cl *BTLY* WF17................161 G2
Ebury St *BTLY* WF17................161 G2
Eccleburn Av *OSM* LS9..............15 K1
Eccleburn Rd *OSM* LS9..............15 K1
Eccleburn St *OSM* LS9..............15 K1
Eccleburn Ter *OSM* * LS9...........15 K1
Eccles Ct *ECHL* BD2.................98 C1
Eccles Parlour *RPDN/SBR* HX6.....172 B2
Eccup Cl *BHP/TINH* LS16............62 C5
  OT LS21..........................43 F6
Eccup Moor Rd *BHP/TINH* LS16.....62 B3
Echo St *LVSG* WF15..................159 G6
Edale Gv *CUL/QBY* BD13............115 F6
Edale Wy *BHP/TINH* LS16............81 J1
Eddercliff Crs *CLECK* BD19.........159 H2
Edderthorpe St *BFDE* BD3............6 D7
Eddison St *BHP/TINH* LS16..........62 C7
Eddison Ter *OSM* LS9...............15 K1
Eden Av *OSS* WF5...................182 C5
  WKFDW/WTN WF2................183 J1
Eden Cl *LM/WK* BD12...............137 J4
Eden Crs *BULY* LS4.................102 A1
Edendale *CAS* WF10.................148 E7
Eden Dr *BULY* LS4...................102 A1
Eden Gdns *BULY* LS4................102 A2
Eden Gv *BULY* LS4...................102 A2
Eden Mt *BULY* LS4...................102 A1
Edensor Rd *KGHY* BD21...............2 D5
Eden Wk *BULY* LS4...................102 A2
Eden Wy *BULY* LS4..................102 A2
Ederoyd Av *PDSY/CALV* LS28........99 J4
Ederoyd Crs *PDSY/CALV* LS28.......99 J4
Ederoyd Dr *PDSY/CALV* LS28........99 J4
Ederoyd Gv *PDSY/CALV* LS28........99 J4
Ederoyd Mt *PDSY/CALV* LS28........99 H4
Ederoyd Ri *PDSY/CALV* LS28.........99 J4
Edgar St *CLAY* BD14.................116 C2
Edgbaston Cl *AL/HA/HU* LS17........63 B7
Edgbaston Wk *AL/HA/HU* LS17.......63 B7
Edgebank Av *WBSY* BD6.............136 E1
Edge End Gdns *WBSY* BD6..........116 D7
Edge End Rd *WBSY* BD6.............116 D7
Edgehill Cl *CUL/QBY* BD13..........115 J5
Edgeholme La *LUD/ILL* HX2.........153 J1
Edgemoor Cl *BOW* BD4.............119 F6
  HIPP............................154 E4
Edgerton Ct *TAD* LS24...............50 C7
Edgerton Cl *TAD* LS24...............50 D7
Edgerton Dr *TAD* LS24...............50 C7
Edgerton Garth *TAD* LS24...........50 C7
Edgerton Rd *BHP/TINH* LS16........82 A5
Edgware Av *RHAY* LS8...............11 G4
Edgware Gv *RHAY* LS8...............11 G4
Edgware Mt *RHAY* LS8..............11 G4
Edgware Pl *RHAY* LS8...............11 G4
Edgware Rw *RHAY* LS8..............11 G4
Edgware St *RHAY* LS8...............10 F4
Edgware Ter *RHAY* LS8.............11 G4
Edgware Vw *RHAY* LS8..............11 G4
Edinburgh Av *WOR/ARM* LS12.......101 K5
Edinburgh Gv *WOR/ARM* LS12......101 K5
Edinburgh Pl *GFTH/SHER* LS25.....108 A6
  WOR/ARM LS12..................101 K5
Edinburgh Rd *WOR/ARM* LS12......101 K5
Edinburgh Ter *WOR/ARM* LS12.....101 K5
Edlington Cl *BOW* BD4.............119 F3
Edmonton Pl *CHAL* LS7..............85 J6
Edmund St *GTHN* BD7.................5 K8
Edrich Cl *LM/WK* BD12..............137 K1
Edroyd Pl *PDSY/CALV* LS28.........100 A2
Edroyd St *PDSY/CALV* LS28.........100 A2
Education Rd *CHAL* LS7..............10 B3
Edward Cl *EARL* WF12..............180 D6
  HIPP............................155 K4
Edward Dr *WKFDE* WF1.............164 C6
Edward Rd *MIRF* WF14..............179 G4
Edwards Rd *LUD/ILL* HX2..........154 B3
Edward St *BOW* BD4...................6 A8
  BOW BD4.........................119 F5
  BRIG HD6........................157 F5
  CLECK BD19......................159 H3
  LDSU LS2.........................10 B9
  NORM WF6.......................166 D3
  RPDN/SBR HX6...................153 J4
  SHPY BD18........................76 E4
  WKFDE * WF1......................19 G2
Edward Turner Cl
  LM/WK BD12.....................137 H1
Edwin Rd *HDGY* LS6...................9 G4
Eel Holme View St *AIRE* BD20......53 J1
Eel Mires Garth *WBY* LS22..........29 J3
Effingham Rd *BGLY* BD16............74 D3
Egerton Gv *WIL/AL* BD15............95 J4
Egerton St *RPDN/SBR* HX6..........153 J4
Eggleston Dr *BOW* BD4.............119 G4
Egglestone Sq *BSPA/BRAM* LS23....48 B3
Eggleston St *BRAM* LS13............80 C7
Egremont Crs *WBSY* BD6............136 E1
Egremont St *RPDN/SBR* HX6........153 H5
Egypt Rd *CUL/QBY* BD13.............95 G5
Eighth Av *LVSG* WF15...............158 C3
  RTHW LS26......................125 H7
  WOR/ARM LS12...................12 D3
Eightlands Av *BRAM* LS13..........101 G3
Eightlands La *BRAM* LS13...........101 G3
Eightlands Rd *DEWS* WF13..........181 F1
Ekota Ri *RHAY* LS8...................11 G1
Elam Wood Rd *AIRE* BD20............33 K7
Elbow La *ECHL* BD2...................98 C3
  LUD/ILL *........................133 F7
Elder Av *WKFDW/WTN* WF2.........18 B3
Elder Cl *BTLY* WF17................140 C5
Elder Cft *BRAM* LS13...............101 F4
Elder Dr *EARL* WF12................181 G6
Elder Garth *GFTH/SHER* LS25.......108 A7
Elder Gn *WKFDW/WTN* WF2..........18 B3
Elder Gv *WKFDW/WTN* WF2.........18 A3
Elder La *HWTH* * HD2...............178 B4
Elder Lea *OSS* * WF5...............182 D5
Elder Mt *BRAM* LS13...............101 F4
Elder Pl *BRAM* LS13................101 F4
Elder Ri *RTHW* LS26................146 A1

  CLECK BD19......................139 H7
  HECK WF16.......................159 K3
  HIPP HX3........................136 C1
  HWTH BD22.......................53 H7
  ILK LS29.........................38 A2
  SHPY BD18........................77 K5
Elderwood Gdns *IDLE* BD10..........79 F7
Eldon Pl *BFD* BD1....................5 K4
  CLECK BD19......................159 F1
Eldon St *HECK* WF16................159 K4
  HIPP HX3.........................17 H3
  OSS WF5.........................182 E2
Eldroth Mt *HFAX* HX1..............154 D3
Eldroth Rd *HFAX* HX1...............154 D3
Eldwick Cft *BGLY* BD16..............56 B6
Eleanor Dr *PDSY/CALV* LS28.........79 G5
Eleanor St *BRIG* HD6................157 F7
Eleventh Av *LVSG* WF15............158 D3
Elford Gv *RHAY* LS8.................11 G3
Elford Pl East *RHAY* LS8............11 H3
Elford Pl West *RHAY* LS8...........11 G3
Elford Rd *RHAY* LS8................11 G3
Elia St *KGHY* BD21...................3 K3
Eliot Gv *GSLY* LS20.................59 G3
Eliots Cl *GFTH/SHER* LS25..........169 H5
Eli St *WBOW* BD5...................118 A3
Elizabethan Ct *PONT* WF8...........169 K6
Elizabeth Av *LM/WK* BD12..........137 H3
Elizabeth Cl *LM/WK* BD12...........137 J3
  CAS WF10.........................149 H7
Elizabeth Crs *LM/WK* BD12..........137 J3
Elizabeth Dr *CAS* WF10.............149 H6
  KNOT WF11......................170 D4
  LM/WK BD12.....................137 J3
Elizabeth Frances St *ELL* HX5.......175 J3
Elizabeth Gdns *WKFDE* WF1........184 D1
Elizabeth Gv *MOR* LS27.............142 B2
Elizabeth Pl *SCFT* LS14.............85 H7
Elizabeth St *BGLY* * BD16...........75 K1
  ELL HX5.........................175 G2
  GTL/HWG HX4....................175 G2
  HDGY LS6..........................8 F3
  KGHY BD21.......................54 C4
  LM/WK BD12.....................137 J3
  LVSG WF15......................159 F4
  WBOW BD5........................5 J9
  WKFDE WF1......................185 F7
Elmwood *MSTN/BAR* LS15...........87 G5
Elmwood Cha *MSTN/BAR* LS15......87 G5
Elmwood Dr *BRIG* HD6..............156 E5
  HWTH BD22.......................53 G5
Elmwood La *LDSU* LS2..............10 B6
  MSTN/BAR LS15...................87 G5
Elmwood Pl *ECHL* BD2................7 G1
  LDSU LS2.........................10 A6
Elm Wood St *BRIG* HD6.............157 G4
Elmwood St *HFAX* HX1.............154 D3
Elmwood Ter *HWTH* BD22...........53 G5
Elsdon Gv *WBOW* BD5..............117 K1
Elsham Ter *BULY* LS4.................8 B4
Elsicker La *WKFDE* WF1............186 C3
Elsie St *HWTH* BD22................73 G4
  KGHY BD21.......................53 J1
Elsinore Av *ELL* HX5...............175 H3
Elsinore Ct *ELL* HX5...............175 H3
Elsworth Av *BFDE* BD3................7 K2
Elsworth St *WOR/ARM* LS12........12 D1
Elsworth Ter *WOR/ARM* LS12.......12 C1
Eltham Cl *HDGY* LS6..................9 L2
Eltham Dr *HDGY* LS6..................9 L2
Eltham Gdns *HDGY* LS6...............9 L2
Eltham Gv *WBSY* BD6................117 F6
Eltham Ri *HDGY* LS6...................9 M2
Elvaston Rd *MOR* LS27.............141 K5
Elvey Cl *ECHL* BD2..................98 E1
Elwell Cl *WBSY* BD6................116 C7
Elwell St *EARD/LOFT* WF3..........143 K6
Elwyn Gv *WBOW* BD5...............117 K3
Elwyn Rd *WBOW* BD5...............118 A3
Ely St *GTL/HWG* HX4...............175 C3
  WOR/ARM LS12....................8 B8
The Embankment *MIRF* WF14......179 H4
Emblem Ter *WKFDE* WF1...........184 B1
Embleton Rd *RTHW* LS26...........147 F6
  HWTH BD22......................53 H7
Emerald St *BTLY* WF17.............160 D2
Emerson Av *HTON* BD9..............96 C2
Emily Hall Gdns *WIL/AL* BD15.....75 F7
Emily St *KGHY* BD21..................3 H3
Emmeline Cl *IDLE* * BD10...........78 C4
Emmfield Dr *HTON* BD9.............97 F1
Emm La *HTON* BD9...................97 F2
Emmott Dr *YEA* LS19................80 J1
Emmott Farm Fold *HWTH* BD22....72 D6
Emscote Av *HFAX* HX1...............16 D9
Emscote Gdns *HFAX* HX1............16 D9
Emscote Gv *HFAX* HX1..............16 D9
Emscote Pl *HFAX* HX1...............16 D9
Emscote St South *HFAX* HX1........16 D9
Emsley Cl *BOW* BD4................118 C6
Emsley Pl *MID* LS10.................14 E6
Emville Av *AL/HA/HU* LS17..........64 D6
Enderby Cl *HIPP* HX3..............134 C4
Enderley Rd *CUL/QBY* BD13.........95 C7
Endor Crs *ILK* LS29..................38 A3
Endor Gv *ILK* LS29..................38 A3
Endsleigh Pl *CLAY* * BD14..........116 A2
Enfield *YEA* LS19....................59 J5
Enfield Av *CHAL* LS7................10 E4
Enfield Cl *BTLY* WF17..............160 C2
Enfield Dr *BTLY* WF17..............160 C2
  GTHN BD7........................116 E5
Enfield Pde *WBSY* BD6..............117 F5
Enfield Rd *BAIL* BD17...............77 H2
Enfield St *CHAL* LS7.................10 D5
  KGHY BD21........................2 E4
Enfield Ter *CHAL* LS7...............10 E4
Enfield Wk *WBSY* BD6..............117 F5
England La *KNOT* WF11.............171 G5
Englefield Cl *BOW* BD4.............119 F4
Englefield Crs *BOW* BD4............119 F4
Ennerdale Av *EARL* WF12..........161 H6
Ennerdale Cl *WBY* LS22.............29 H3
Ennerdale Crs *EARL* WF12..........161 H6
Ennerdale Dr *ECHL* BD2.............98 C2
  ELL HX5.........................176 A2
Ennerdale Rd *EARL* WF12...........161 H6
  ECHL BD2.........................98 B2
  WKFDW/WTN * WF2..............184 D1
  WOR/ARM LS12...................121 G4
Ennerdale Wy
  WOR/ARM * LS12.................121 G4
Enterprise Wy *CAS* WF10...........168 B1
  GFTH/SHER LS25.................111 K6
  IDLE BD10........................78 C6
  MID LS10........................124 A5
Envoy St *BEE/HOL* LS11.............14 D8
Epsom Rd *GFTH/SHER* LS25.........127 J4
Epworth Pl *HWTH* BD22.............72 C1
  MID LS10.........................14 E7

Eric St *BRAM* LS13..................81 F7
  KGHY BD21.........................3 H2
Ernest St *DEWS* WF13...............161 G4
Escroft Cl *LM/WK* BD12.............137 J6
Eshald La *RTHW* LS26...............146 A2
Eshald Pl *RTHW* LS26...............146 A1
Esholt Av *GSLY* LS20................58 E4
Esholt La *BAIL* BD17.................58 B7
Eshton Av *LM/WK* BD12............138 A2
Eskdale Av *HIPP* HX3...............136 A2
  NORM...........................166 D4
Eskdale Cl *EARL* WF12.............161 H5
  NORM...........................166 D4
Eskdale Cft *NORM* WF6.............166 D4
Eskdale Cft *NORM* WF6.............166 D4
Eskdale Gv *GFTH/SHER* LS25........107 K7
Eskdale Mt *SCFT* LS14.............105 K4
Eskdale Ri *WIL/AL* BD15.............96 A5
Eskdale Rd *WKFDW/WTN* WF2.....183 K2
Esk Gdns *WBY* LS22..................29 H1
Eskine Pde *WBSY* BD6..............136 E1
Esmond St *GTHN* BD7..............116 E3
  WOR/ARM * LS12.................12 A1
Esmond Ter *WOR/ARM* LS12........102 A6
Essex St *BOW* BD4....................6 C9
  HFAX HX1.........................16 A7
Estcourt Av *HDGY* LS6..............82 B7
Estcourt Dr *PONT* WF8.............190 E5
Estcourt Gv *GTHN* BD7...............4 D9
Estcourt Rd *PONT* WF8.............190 D4
Estcourt Ter *HDGY* LS6.............82 B7
Esther Av *WKFDW/WTN* WF2.......184 A1
Esther Gv *WKFDW/WTN* WF2.......183 K5
Esthwaite Gdns
  MSTN/BAR * LS15................105 F7
Ethel St *KGHY* BD21................53 J2
Etna St *GTHN* BD7..................116 E3
Eton St *HFAX* HX1...................16 B6
Euston Gv *BEE/HOL* LS11...........13 G7
Euston Mt *BEE/HOL* LS11...........13 G8
Euston Ter *BEE/HOL* LS11...........13 G8
Evanston Av *BULY* LS4................8 B6
Evelyn Av *BFDE* BD3..................7 L4
Evelyn Pl *WOR/ARM* LS12..........12 B3
Evens Ter *WBOW* BD5..............117 K4
Everest Av *SHPY* BD18..............77 K5
Everleigh St *OSM* LS9...............15 J1
Eversley Av *GFTH/SHER* LS25......111 F6
Eversley Ct *GFTH/SHER* LS25.......111 F6
Eversley Dr *BOW* BD4..............119 F2
Eversley Garth Crs
  GFTH/SHER LS25.................111 F6
Eversley Ldg *LUD/ILL* * HX2........154 B2
Eversley Mt *GFTH/SHER* LS25......111 F7
  LUD/ILL *........................154 B2
Eversley Pl *LUD/ILL* HX2...........154 B2
Evesham Gv *IDLE* BD10..............78 C5
Ewart Pl *GTHN* BD7.................117 F3
Ewart St *CUL/QBY* * BD13..........115 H5
  GTHN BD7........................117 F3
Ewood Dr *HBR* HX7.................132 A6
Ewood Hall Av *HBR* HX7...........132 A6
Excelsior Cl *RPDN/SBR* HX6........172 D6
Exchange Sq *BFD* * BD1..............6 A7
Exchange St *CLECK* BD19...........138 E6
  GTL/HWG HX4....................175 C3
  NORM WF6.......................166 D6
Exe St *WBOW* BD5..................117 H3
Exeter Dr *MID* LS10................123 J7
Exeter St *HIPP* HX3................155 G5
  RPDN/SBR HX6...................153 K4
Exhibition Rd *SHPY* BD18...........76 E4
Exley Av *KGHY* BD21................53 H7
Exley Bank *HIPP* HX3..............155 G6
Exley Bank Top *HIPP* HX3..........155 G6
Exley Crs *KGHY* BD21................2 C9
Exley Dr *KGHY* BD21.................2 D9
Exley Gdns *ELL* HX5................155 G7
Exley Gv *KGHY* BD21................53 H7
Exley Head *HWTH* BD22..............2 B9
Exley Head Vw *HWTH* BD22.........53 F5
Exley La *ELL* HX5..................155 H7
Exley Mt *GTHN* BD7..................4 B7
  KGHY BD21........................2 C9
Exley Rd *KGHY* BD21.................2 C9
Exley St *KGHY* BD21.................2 D7
Exley Wy *KGHY* * BD21.............53 H7
Exmoor St *HFAX* HX1................16 A8
Exmouth Pl *BFDE* BD3................6 A1
Express Wy *NORM* WF6.............166 E2
Exton Pl *MSTN/BAR* LS15...........105 F6
Eyres Av *WOR/ARM* LS12.............8 A9
Eyres Gv *WOR/ARM* LS12.............8 A9
Eyres Mill Side *WOR/ARM* LS12.....102 A5
Eyres St *WOR/ARM* LS12.............8 A9
Eyres Ter *WOR/ARM* LS12............8 A9
Eyre St *BTLY* WF17.................161 G4
  EARL WF12.......................180 E5
Eyrie Ap *MOR* LS27.................142 B4

F

Factory La *BOW* BD4................118 C4
Factory St *BOW* BD4.................118 D4
Fagley Crs *ECHL* BD2.................98 D3
Fagley Cft *ECHL* BD2.................98 E3
Fagley Dr *ECHL* BD2.................98 D3
Fagley La *ECHL* BD2..................98 C2
Fagley Pl *ECHL* BD2...................7 H1
Fagley Rd *BFDE* BD3...................7 G1
  ECHL BD2.........................99 F3
Fagley Ter *ECHL* BD2..................7 H1
Fair Bank *SHPY* BD18................77 H6
Fairbank Rd *GIR* BD8.................4 D1
Fairbank Ter *GIR* BD8.................4 D1
Fairburn Ct *HIPP* * HX3............155 K4
Fairburn Dr *GFTH/SHER* LS25.......127 K1
Fairburn Gdns *ECHL* BD2............98 D1
Fairclough Gv *LUD/ILL* HX2.........134 C4
Fairfax Av *BIRK/DRI* BD11...........140 D2
  BOW BD4.........................118 D5
  FEA/AMT WF7....................168 B7
  KNOT WF11......................170 E5
Fairfax Cl *SCFT* LS14...............105 J2
Fairfax Ct *BEE/HOL* * LS11..........13 J4
Fairfax Crs *BOW* BD4...............118 D5

HIPP HX3 .....155 K3
Fairfax Flats OT * LS21 .....39 J3
Fairfax Gdns ILK LS29 .....38 A5
Fairfax Gv YEA LS19 .....59 G4
Fairfax Rd BEE/HOL LS11 .....13 J9
  BGLY BD16 .....55 J6
  CUL/QBY BD13 .....74 A5
  ILK LS29 .....38 A5
  PONT WF8 .....189 K1
Fairfax St AIRE BD20 .....32 E1
  BOW BD4 .....6 B9
  HWTH BD22 .....72 E5
  OT LS21 .....39 H3
Fairfax Vw HORS LS18 .....60 E7
Fairfield CUL/QBY BD13 .....94 A5
  KNOT WF11 .....150 B2
Fairfield Av HECK WF16 .....160 B3
  NORM WF6 .....166 B5
  OSS WF5 .....182 E5
  PDSY/CALV LS28 .....100 C5
  PONT WF8 .....189 G1
Fairfield Cl BRAM LS13 .....100 C3
  CAS WF10 .....149 K6
  GFTH/SHER LS25 .....111 G6
  OSS WF5 .....182 E5
  RTHW LS26 .....144 C3
Fairfield Ct CAS WF10 .....169 F1
  LVSG WF15 .....159 J3
Fairfield Crs BRAM LS13 .....100 C3
  DEWS WF13 .....160 D7
Fairfield Dr BAIL BD17 .....57 K7
  HECK WF16 .....160 B3
  OSS WF5 .....182 E5
  RTHW LS26 .....144 C3
Fairfield Gdns OSS WF5 .....182 E5
  RTHW LS26 .....144 C3
Fairfield Gv BRAM LS13 .....100 C3
  RTHW * LS26 .....144 C3
Fairfield Hl BRAM LS13 .....100 C3
Fairfield La GFTH/SHER LS25 .....151 J3
  RTHW LS26 .....144 C3
Fairfield Link
  GFTH/SHER LS25 .....111 G6
Fairfield Ms DEWS WF13 .....160 D7
Fairfield Mt BRAM LS13 .....100 C3
  OSS WF5 .....182 E5
Fairfield Rd BRAM LS13 .....100 D3
  GIR BD8 .....4 E1
  HECK WF16 .....160 B3
  LM/WK BD12 .....137 J4
  OSS WF5 .....182 D5
  TAD LS24 .....50 D7
Fairfields CAS WF10 .....169 K1
Fairfield Sq BRAM LS13 .....100 C2
Fairfield St BOW BD4 .....118 E5
  BRAM LS13 .....100 E3
Fairfield Ter BRAM LS13 .....100 C3
  EARL WF12 .....181 J1
  OSS WF5 .....182 E5
Fairfield Wy TAD LS24 .....50 D7
Fairford Av BEE/HOL LS11 .....14 A9
Fairford Ter BEE/HOL LS11 .....14 A9
Fairhaven Gn IDLE BD10 .....78 D5
Fairleigh Crs EARD/LOFT WF3 .....143 F7
Fairleigh Rd EARD/LOFT WF3 .....142 E7
Fairless Av HIPP HX3 .....157 F1
Fairmoor Wy HECK WF16 .....160 B3
Fairmount HTON BD9 .....97 H3
Fairmount Pk SHPY BD18 .....76 D5
Fairmount Ter KGHY BD21 .....54 C5
Fair Rd WBSY BD6 .....117 G3
Fair Vw LVSG WF15 .....159 G3
  PONT WF8 .....189 K4
Fairview Av BTLY WF17 .....160 C2
Fairview Ct BAIL BD17 .....77 G3
Fairview Crs BTLY WF17 .....160 D2
Fairview Rd BTLY WF17 .....160 D2
Fairview Ter HIPP HX3 .....16 D1
Fairway GSLY LS20 .....58 C2
  IDLE BD10 .....79 G3
  NORM WF6 .....167 F6
  SHPY BD18 .....76 D5
  WBSY BD6 .....116 E5
The Fairway AL/HA/HU LS17 .....63 H5
  FEA/AMT WF7 .....168 C7
  GFTH/SHER LS25 .....111 G6
  HUDN HD2 .....177 F5
  LUD/ILL HX2 .....114 C7
  PDSY/CALV LS28 .....99 J4
  TAD LS24 .....70 D2
Fairway Ap NORM WF6 .....167 F6
Fairway Cl GTHN BD7 .....116 E4
  NORM WF6 .....167 F6
Fairway Cl GFTH/SHER LS25.....111 G6
  GSLY LS20 .....58 C3
  NORM WF6 .....167 F6
  WBSY BD6 .....116 E5
Fairway Crs HWTH BD22 .....72 E5
Fairway Dr GTHN BD7 .....116 E4
  NORM WF6 .....167 F6
Fairway Gdns NORM WF6 .....167 F6
Fairway Gv GTHN BD7 .....116 E4
Fairway Mdw NORM WF6 .....167 F6
The Fairways AIRE BD20 .....33 H7
  HTON BD9 .....76 D7
Fair Ways MIRF WF14 .....179 G2
Fairway Wk GTHN BD7 .....116 E4
Fairweather Ms GIR * BD8 .....96 D6
Fairy Dell BGLY 75 K5
Fairy Hill La CAS WF10 .....169 J3
Falcon Cliffe AIRE BD20 .....32 C5
Falcon Cl OT LS21 .....39 H3
Falcon Dr CAS WF10 .....168 B2
Falcon Ms GIR * BD8 .....96 B5
  MOR LS27 .....142 B4
Falcon Rd BGLY BD16 .....55 J6
  EARL WF12 .....181 F4
Falcon St GTHN BD7 .....117 F1
  HIPP HX3 .....155 G5
Falkland Crs AL/HA/HU LS17 .....83 H3
Falkland Gdns AL/HA/HU LS17 .....83 H3
Falkland Gv AL/HA/HU LS17 .....83 H3
Falkland Mt AL/HA/HU LS17 .....83 H3
Falkland Ri AL/HA/HU LS17 .....83 H3
Falkland Rd AL/HA/HU LS17 .....83 H3
  IDLE BD10 .....99 F1
Fall Brow Cl CLAY BD14 .....115 K3

Fall Ings Rd WKFDE WF1 .....19 J9
Fall La DEWS WF13 .....180 E3
  EARD/LOFT WF3 .....143 J7
  HIPP HX3 .....135 H3
  LVSG WF15 .....158 E7
  RPDN/SBR HX6 .....154 A5
Fallow Cft HUDN HD2 .....178 A4
Fallowfield Cl BOW BD4 .....118 D6
Fallowfield Dr BOW BD4 .....118 D6
Fallowfield Gdns BOW BD4 .....118 D5
Fallow La HWTH BD22 .....52 B5
Fall Park Ct BRAM LS13 .....81 C7
Fall Rd LVSG WF15 .....159 F7
Fall Spring Gdns
  GTL/HWG HX4 .....174 C5
Fall Spring Gn GTL/HWG HX4 .....174 B5
Fallswood Gv BRAM LS13 .....101 C5
Fall Wood St HWTH BD22 .....72 E6
Falmers Cottages HDGY * LS6 .....9 H1
Falmouth Av BFDE BD3 .....6 B7
  NORM WF6 .....166 E5
Falmouth Crs NORM WF6 .....166 E5
Falmouth Rd NORM WF6 .....166 E5
Falsgrave Av ECHL BD2 .....98 E5
Faltis IDLE BD10 .....78 D7
Fanny La TAD LS24 .....70 C4
Fanny St KGHY BD21 .....2 E6
  SHPY BD18 .....76 E4
Farcliffe Pl GIR BD8 .....4 E1
Farcliffe Rd GIR BD8 .....4 E1
Farcliffe Ter GIR BD8 .....4 E1
Far Common Rd MIRF WF14 .....179 F1
Far Croft Ter WOR/ARM * LS12 .....12 C3
Far Crook IDLE BD10 .....78 A3
Fardene St AIRE BD20 .....20 E7
Farfield Av BTLY * WF17 .....160 C2
  PDSY/CALV LS28 .....99 K2
  WBSY BD6 .....116 D7
Farfield Ct AL/HA/HU LS17 .....63 K6
  GFTH/SHER LS25 .....107 G6
Farfield Crs WBSY BD6 .....116 E7
Farfield Dr PDSY/CALV LS28 .....99 K3
Farfield Gv PDSY/CALV LS28 .....99 K2
  WBSY BD6 .....116 E7
Farfield Ri PDSY/CALV LS28 .....99 K2
Farfield Rd BAIL BD17 .....77 J3
  SHPY BD18 .....77 F5
  WBSY BD6 .....117 F7
Farfield St CLECK BD19 .....138 E6
  HTON BD9 .....97 H3
Farfield Ter HTON BD9 .....97 F3
Far La HBR HX7 .....132 B5
Farlea Dr ECHL BD2 .....98 D2
Farleton Dr ECHL BD2 .....98 E3
Farley Crs HWTH BD22 .....72 C1
Farm Ct MSTN/BAR LS15 .....105 J3
Farm Cft FEA/AMT WF7 .....187 H4
Far Mead Cft ILK LS29 .....25 K7
Farm Gdns FEA/AMT WF7 .....187 H4
Farm Hl Crs CHAL LS7 .....83 F7
Farm Hl North CHAL LS7 .....83 F6
Farm Hill Rd IDLE BD10 .....78 C7
  MOR LS27 .....141 H2
Farm Hl South CHAL LS7 .....83 F7
Farm Hill Wy CHAL LS7 .....83 F7
Farm Mt MSTN/BAR LS15 .....105 K3
Far Moss AL/HA/HU LS17 .....63 K6
Farm Pond Dr BRIG HD6 .....156 D3
Farm Rd FEA/AMT WF7 .....188 C4
  MSTN/BAR LS15 .....105 J3
Farmstead Rd IDLE BD10 .....78 D6
Farndale Ap SCFT LS14 .....85 K7
Farndale Cl SCFT LS14 .....85 K7
  WBY LS22 .....28 E3
Farndale Ct GFTH/SHER LS25.....127 J1
Farndale Garth SCFT LS14 .....85 K6
Farndale Pl SCFT LS14 .....85 K6
Farndale Rd BAIL BD17 .....77 F2
  WIL/AL BD15 .....95 F1
Farne Av WKFDW/WTN WF2 .....184 A4
Farnham Cl BAIL BD17 .....57 J7
  SCFT LS14 .....85 J3
Farnham Cft SCFT LS14 .....85 J3
Farnley Cl ILK LS29 .....38 B6
Farnley La OT LS21 .....39 J1
Farnley Rd ILK LS29 .....38 C6
Farnley Vw BIRK/DRI BD11 .....140 D1
Farrar Av MIRF WF14 .....179 G3
Farrar Ct BRAM LS13 .....101 F2
Farrar Cft MIRF WF14 .....179 F2
Farrar Dr MIRF WF14 .....179 F2
Farrar Gv BHP/TINH LS16 .....61 K7
Farrar Height La
  RPDN/SBR HX6 .....172 C5
Farrar La BHP/TINH LS16 .....61 K7
Farrar Mill La HIPP HX3 .....155 K2
Far Reef Cl HORS LS18 .....81 F2
Farrer La RTHW LS26 .....145 K2
Far Richard Cl OSS WF5 .....182 C2
Farriers Cft ECHL BD2 .....98 A1
Farriers Pl CAS WF10 .....169 G2
Farringdon Cl BOW BD4 .....118 E2
Farringdon Dr BOW BD4 .....119 F3
Farringdon Gv WBSY BD6 .....117 F7
Farrow Bank WOR/ARM LS12 .....101 H6
Farrow Gn WOR/ARM LS12 .....101 H6
Farrow Hl WOR/ARM LS12 .....101 J6
Farrow Rd WOR/ARM LS12 .....101 H6
Farrow V WOR/ARM LS12 .....101 H6
Farside Gn WBOW BD5 .....117 H3
Fartown PDSY/CALV LS28 .....120 B1
Fartown Cl PDSY/CALV LS28 .....120 B1
Farway BOW BD4 .....119 F2
Far Well Fold YEA * LS19 .....80 A1
Favell Av NORM WF6 .....166 E7
Faversham Wk BOW * BD4 .....119 F2
Fawcett Av WOR/ARM LS12 .....122 A1
Fawcett Bank WOR/ARM LS12 .....121 K1
Fawcett Cl WOR/ARM LS12 .....121 K1
Fawcett Dr WOR/ARM LS12 .....121 K1
Fawcett Gdns WOR/ARM LS12 .....121 K1
Fawcett La WOR/ARM LS12 .....121 K1
Fawcett Pl BOW BD4 .....118 D6
Fawcett St WKFDW/WTN WF2 .....18 E9
Fawcett V WOR/ARM LS12 .....121 K1

Fawcett Wy WOR/ARM LS12 .....121 K1
Fawkes Dr OT LS21 .....38 E4
Faxfleet St WBOW BD5 .....117 J5
Faye Gdns BOW BD4 .....118 E5
Fearnley Av OSS WF5 .....182 B2
Fearnley Cl WOR/ARM LS12 .....12 C2
Fearnley Dr OSS WF5 .....182 B2
Fearnley Pl WOR/ARM LS12 .....12 C2
Fearnley St DEWS WF13 .....180 E2
  FEA/AMT WF7 .....188 B4
Fearnside Fold
  HOR/CROF * WF4 .....183 G7
Fearnsides St GIR BD8 .....4 F4
Fearnsides Ter GIR BD8 .....4 F4
Fearnville Av RHAY LS8 .....104 E1
Fearnville Cl RHAY LS8 .....84 E7
Fearnville Dr BOW BD4 .....7 J9
  RHAY LS8 .....104 E1
Fearnville Gv RHAY LS8 .....84 E7
Fearnville Mt RHAY LS8 .....84 E7
Fearnville Pl RHAY LS8 .....85 F7
Fearnville Rd RHAY LS8 .....104 E1
Fearnville Ter RHAY LS8 .....85 F7
Fearnville Vw RHAY LS8 .....104 E1
Feast Fld HORS LS18 .....80 E3
Featherbank Av HORS LS18 .....80 E5
Featherbank Gv HORS LS18 .....80 E4
Featherbank Ter HORS LS18 .....80 E5
Featherbank Wk HORS LS18 .....80 E5
Featherbed Cl GTL/HWG HX4 .....175 G3
Feather Bed La ELL HX5 .....175 G3
Featherbed La TAD LS24 .....31 J3
Featherstone La
  FEA/AMT WF7 .....188 C1
Federation St WBOW BD5 .....118 A4
Felbrigg Av HWTH BD22 .....2 C7
Felcourt Dr BOW BD4 .....119 F3
Felcourt Fold BOW BD4 .....119 F3
Fell Crs HWTH BD22 .....2 A8
Fell Greave Crs HUDN HD2 .....177 H5
Fell Greave Rd HUDN HD2 .....177 G4
Fell Gv HUDN HD2 .....177 G5
  HWTH BD22 .....2 B7
Fell La HWTH BD22 .....2 B7
Fellowsides La OSS WF5 .....182 D4
Fellside Cl WBOW BD5 .....118 A4
Fellwood Av HWTH BD22 .....73 F4
Fellwood Cl HWTH BD22 .....73 F4
Felnex Cl OSM LS9 .....124 D1
Felnex Crs OSM LS9 .....124 D1
Felnex Rd OSM LS9 .....15 M5
Felnex Sq OSM LS9 .....15 M5
Felnex Wy OSM LS9 .....124 D1
Fenby Av BOW BD4 .....118 C2
Fenby Cl BOW BD4 .....118 D3
Fenby Gv BOW BD4 .....118 D2
Fencote Crs ECHL BD2 .....98 E2
Fender Rd WBSY BD6 .....116 E5
Fennec Rd BAIL BD17 .....57 K7
Fenton Av RTHW LS26 .....125 J7
Fenton Cl RTHW LS26 .....125 J7
Fenton La GFTH/SHER LS25 .....111 K3
Fenton Rd EARD/LOFT WF3 .....165 G1
  HFAX HX1 .....16 A9
Fentongate EARD/LOFT WF3 .....144 D6
Fenton St EARD/LOFT WF3 .....142 E6
  ILK LS29 .....38 A1
  LDSU LS2 .....9 M6
  MIRF WF14 .....179 H5
Fenwick Dr WBSY BD6 .....136 E1
Ferguson St HFAX HX1 .....17 G7
Fernbank BRAM LS13 .....100 C3
Fernbank Av HWTH BD22 .....53 G7
Fernbank Cl BRAM LS13 .....100 C2
Fernbank Dr BAIL BD17 .....77 F3
  BGLY BD16 .....75 K1
  BRAM LS13 .....100 C2
Fernbank Gdns BRAM LS13 .....100 C2
Fernbank Pl BRAM LS13 .....100 C2
Fernbank Rd BFDE BD3 .....6 E2
  BRAM LS13 .....100 C2
Fern Cha SCFT LS14 .....65 H4
Ferncliffe Dr AIRE BD20 .....53 G1
  BAIL BD17 .....77 G1
Ferncliffe Rd BGLY BD16 .....75 K1
  SHPY * BD18 .....76 E4
Ferncliffe Ter BRAM LS13 .....100 E3
Fern Ct BTLY WF17 .....161 J3
  AIRE BD20 .....53 H1
Fern Ct LVSG WF15 .....158 D4
  SCFT LS14 .....65 H4
  WKFDW/WTN WF2 .....163 K5
Ferndale Av CLAY BD14 .....115 K3
Ferndale Gv HTON BD9 .....97 H1
Ferndene BGLY BD16 .....76 A1
Ferndene Av BTLY WF17 .....140 C4
Ferndown Gn WBOW BD5 .....117 J3
Fernfield Ter HIPP * HX3 .....134 E5
Fern Gv KSTL LS5 .....101 K1
Fernhill BGLY BD16 .....55 K6
Fern Hill Av SHPY BD18 .....76 E5
Fern Hill Gv SHPY BD18 .....76 E5
Fern Hill Mt SHPY BD18 .....76 E5
Fern Hill Rd SHPY BD18 .....76 E5
Fernhurst Cl MIRF WF14 .....179 H5
Fernhurst Crs MIRF WF14 .....179 J3
Fernhurst Lea MIRF WF14 .....179 J3
Fernhurst Rd MIRF WF14 .....179 J3
Fernhurst Wy MIRF WF14 .....179 H3
Fernlea RTHW LS26 .....145 K1
Fernlea Cl HECK WF16 .....160 B5
Fern Lea St RPDN/SBR HX6 .....153 J3
Fern Lea Vw PDSY/CALV LS28 .....100 B3
Fernleigh Ct
  WKFDW/WTN WF2 .....184 A4
Fernley Gdns LM/WK BD12 .....137 H3
Fernley Green Cl KNOT WF11 .....171 J4
Fernley Green Rd KNOT WF11 .....171 J4
Fernley Hill Dr NORM WF6 .....166 C3
Fern St HFAX HX1 .....118 E3
  HIPP HX3 .....134 C5
  KGHY BD21 .....3 G1
Fern Ter AIRE BD20 .....54 C2
  GIR BD8 .....97 H3
  PDSY/CALV LS28 .....100 B3
Fern Wy SCFT LS14 .....65 H4
Fernwood RHAY LS8 .....84 B3

Ferrand Av BOW BD4 .....118 D6
Ferrand La BGLY BD16 .....75 J1
  CLECK BD19 .....139 H6
Ferrands Cl BGLY BD16 .....74 E3
Ferrands Park Wy BGLY BD16 .....74 E3
Ferrand St BGLY BD16 .....75 K1
Ferriby Cl ECHL BD2 .....98 E2
Ferry Bridge By-Pass
  KNOT WF11 .....170 D2
Ferrybridge Rd CAS WF10 .....148 D7
  KNOT WF11 .....170 E4
  PONT WF8 .....169 K6
Ferry La EARD/LOFT WF3 .....165 G6
Festival Av SHPY BD18 .....77 J6
Feversham St BFDE BD3 .....6 C7
Fewston Av OSM LS9 .....15 G4
  WKFDE WF1 .....19 L1
Fewston Ct OSM LS9 .....15 H3
Fiddle La RPDN/SBR HX6 .....173 G5
Fidler La GFTH/SHER LS25 .....107 H6
Field Cl HECK WF16 .....160 A2
  HIPP HX3 .....16 B1
Fieldcroft Ct MIRF WF14 .....179 C4
Field Dr TAD LS24 .....51 G5
Fieldedge La AIRE BD20 .....54 D1
Field End MSTN/BAR LS15 .....105 H6
Field End Cl MSTN/BAR LS15 .....105 H6
Field End Crs MSTN/BAR LS15 .....105 H6
Field End Gdns
  MSTN/BAR LS15 .....105 H6
Field End Garth
  MSTN/BAR LS15 .....105 H6
Field End Gn MSTN/BAR * LS15 .....105 J3
Field End Gv MSTN/BAR LS15 .....105 J3
Field End Mt MSTN/BAR LS15 .....105 H6
Field End Rd MSTN/BAR LS15 .....105 H6
Fieldens Pl BTLY WF17 .....160 E3
Fieldgate Rd IDLE BD10 .....78 E5
Fieldhead Ct PONT WF8 .....170 A7
Fieldhead Crs BTLY WF17 .....140 B4
Fieldhead Dr GSLY LS20 .....58 E3
  MSTN/BAR LS15 .....87 J5
Fieldhead Gdns EARL WF12 .....162 A5
Field Head La BTLY WF17 .....140 B5
  HWTH BD22 .....72 B7
  LUD/ILL HX2 .....114 A7
Fieldhead Paddock
  BSPA/BRAM LS23 .....48 B3
Fieldhead Rd GSLY LS20 .....58 D3
Fieldhead St GTHN BD7 .....4 F7
Fieldhouse Cl AL/HA/HU LS17 .....83 H2
Field House La WBY LS22 .....29 F4
Fieldhouse Dr AL/HA/HU LS17 .....83 H2
Fieldhouse Gv PDSY/CALV LS28 .....99 K3
Fieldhouse Lawn
  AL/HA/HU LS17 .....83 H2
Fieldhouse St WKFDE WF1 .....185 G6
Fieldhouse Wk AL/HA/HU LS17 .....83 H2
Field Hurst CLECK BD19 .....158 A1
  GTL/HWG HX4 .....173 J4
Fieldhurst Ct BOW BD4 .....118 C6
Fielding Ga WOR/ARM LS12 .....8 C9
Fielding Gate Ms
  WOR/ARM LS12 .....8 B9
Field La BRIG HD6 .....176 E1
  BTLY WF17 .....161 F4
  DEWS WF13 .....180 A3
  GFTH/SHER LS25 .....88 D5
  OSS WF5 .....182 C3
  WKFDW/WTN WF2 .....184 D6
Field Side HFAX HX1 .....16 A3
The Fields EARD/LOFT WF3 .....144 E6
Fields Rd LM/WK BD12 .....137 K2
Field St BFD BD1 .....6 E1
  DEWS * WF13 .....180 B3
Field Ter MSTN/BAR LS15 .....105 H5
Field Top Rd BRIG HD6 .....176 E1
Field Vw CAS WF10 .....167 K2
  HIPP HX3 .....134 C5
Fieldway CLAY BD14 .....116 A2
  ILK LS29 .....24 D5
Fieldway Av BRAM LS13 .....100 D1
Fieldway Cha RTHW LS26 .....146 A2
Fieldway Cl BRAM LS13 .....100 D1
Fieldway Ri BRAM LS13 .....100 C1
Fifth Av BFDE BD3 .....7 G1
  RTHW LS26 .....145 H1
Fifth Av West LVSG WF15 .....158 C4
Filey St BFD BD1 .....6 B7
Filley Royd CLECK BD19 .....158 E2
Fillingfir Dr BHP/TINH LS16 .....81 J4
Fillingfir Rd BHP/TINH LS16 .....81 J4
Fillingfir Wk BHP/TINH LS16 .....81 J4
Finching Gv WKFDW/WTN WF2 .....179 H1
Finchley St WBOW BD5 .....117 J3
Finchley Wy MOR LS27 .....141 K4
Finch St WBOW BD5 .....117 J2
Findon Ter IDLE BD10 .....99 F1
Fine Garth Cl BSPA/BRAM LS23 .....48 C7
Fink Hl HORS LS18 .....80 D4
Finkil St BRIG HD6 .....156 D3
Finkin Av EARD/LOFT WF3 .....165 K6
Finkin Cft EARD/LOFT WF3 .....165 F6
Finkin La EARD/LOFT WF3 .....165 F6
Finkle Hl GFTH/SHER LS25 .....111 F4
Finkle La MOR LS27 .....141 F1
Finkle St LUD/ILL HX2 .....152 E4
  PONT WF8 .....169 J7
Finsbury Dr ECHL BD2 .....78 A6
Finsbury Rd LDS LS1 .....9 L6
Fir Av MIRF WF14 .....180 A4
Firbank Gn ECHL * BD2 .....98 E3
Firbank Gv MSTN/BAR LS15 .....105 F7
Firbeck BGLY BD16 .....74 E4
Firbeck Rd BSPA/BRAM LS23 .....48 C7
Fir Pde DEWS WF13 .....180 A4
The Firs SCFT LS14 .....65 K4
First Av AL/HA/HU LS17 .....46 B5
  BFDE BD3 .....7 H2
  GFTH/SHER LS25 .....111 J4
  HIPP HX3 .....154 D1
  KGHY BD21 .....2 E7
  LVSG WF15 .....158 D3

PDSY/CALV LS28 .....100 B4
RTHW LS26 .....125 G7
WBY LS22 .....29 J4
WKFDE WF1 .....164 C6
WOR/ARM LS12 .....12 C2
YEA LS19 .....59 K6
Fir St HWTH BD22 .....72 D6
  KGHY BD21 .....53 J7
First St LM/WK BD12 .....137 K1
Firth Av BEE/HOL LS11 .....123 F4
  BRIG HD6 .....157 F5
Firthcliffe Dr LVSG WF15 .....159 J3
Firthcliffe Gv LVSG WF15 .....159 J3
Firthcliffe La LVSG WF15 .....159 J3
Firthcliffe Mt LVSG WF15 .....159 J2
Firthcliffe Pde LVSG WF15 .....159 J3
Firthcliffe Pl LVSG WF15 .....159 J3
Firthcliffe Rd LVSG WF15 .....159 J3
Firthcliffe Ter LVSG WF15 .....159 J3
Firthcliffe Vw LVSG WF15 .....159 J3
Firthcliffe Wk LVSG WF15 .....159 J3
Firth Cl EARD/LOFT WF3 .....165 F3
Firthfields GFTH/SHER LS25.....107 K6
Firth Gv BEE/HOL LS11 .....123 F4
Firth House La BRIG HD6 .....177 G2
Firth La WIL/AL BD15 .....75 F7
Firth Mt BEE/HOL LS11 .....123 F4
  HTON BD9 .....97 F2
Firth St BRIG HD6 .....157 F7
  CHAL LS7 .....10 D6
  CUL/QBY BD13 .....95 G7
Firths Yd DEWS * WF13 .....161 F4
Firth Ter OSM LS9 .....10 E6
Firth Vw BEE/HOL LS11 .....123 F4
Fir Tree Ap AL/HA/HU LS17 .....83 G1
Firtree Av GFTH/SHER LS25 .....108 A3
Fir Tree Cl AL/HA/HU LS17 .....63 H7
  IDLE BD10 .....78 E6
Fir Tree Gdns AL/HA/HU LS17 .....63 G7
Fir Tree Gn AL/HA/HU LS17 .....83 H1
Fir Tree Gv AL/HA/HU LS17 .....83 H1
Fir Tree La AL/HA/HU LS17 .....83 H1
Fir Tree Ri AL/HA/HU LS17 .....83 H1
Fir Tree Vw RTHW LS26 .....147 H4
Firville Av NORM WF6 .....166 D7
Firville Crs NORM WF6 .....166 E7
Fir Wk DEWS WF13 .....180 A4
Fishbeck La AIRE BD20 .....21 H5
Fishergate KNOT WF11 .....170 E3
Fisher Gv OSS WF5 .....182 E5
Fisher St KNOT WF11 .....171 F4
Fisher Wy HECK WF16 .....160 B5
Fish St LDS LS1 .....10 B9
Fitts La AL/HA/HU LS17 .....44 B2
Fitzgerald St WBOW BD5 .....5 K9
Fitzroy Dr RHAY LS8 .....84 B6
Fitzroy Rd BFDE BD3 .....6 F6
Fitzwilliam St BOW BD4 .....6 A9
Five Lane Ends BHP/TINH LS16 .....62 C3
Five Oaks BAIL BD17 .....77 F2
Fixby Av LUD/ILL HX2 .....154 B3
Fixby Park Dr HUDN HD2 .....176 D7
Fixby Rd HUDN HD2 .....176 E4
Flagship Sq EARL WF12 .....161 K6
Flanshaw Av
  WKFDW/WTN WF2 .....183 K3
Flanshaw Crs
  WKFDW/WTN WF2 .....183 K3
Flanshaw Gv
  WKFDW/WTN WF2 .....183 K3
Flanshaw La
  WKFDW/WTN WF2 .....183 J3
Flanshaw Rd
  WKFDW/WTN WF2 .....183 K3
Flanshaw St
  WKFDW/WTN WF2 .....183 K3
Flanshaw Vw
  WKFDW/WTN WF2 .....183 K3
Flanshaw Wy
  WKFDW/WTN WF2 .....183 H2
Flasby St KGHY BD21 .....3 G2
Flash La MIRF WF14 .....179 J3
Flass La CAS WF10 .....168 B4
Flat Nook BGLY * BD16 .....76 A1
The Flats YEA * LS19 .....59 K5
Flats La MSTN/BAR LS15 .....87 G6
Flawith Dr ECHL BD2 .....98 E3
Flaxen Ct WBSY BD6 .....117 J5
Flax Meadow HUDW HD3 .....175 K7
Flax Pl OSM LS9 .....14 E2
Flaxton Cl BEE/HOL LS11 .....13 L9
Flaxton Gdns BEE/HOL LS11 .....13 L9
Flaxton Gn ECHL BD2 .....98 E3
Flaxton Pl GTHN BD7 .....4 F7
Flaxton St BEE/HOL LS11 .....13 L9
Flaxton Vw BEE/HOL LS11 .....13 M9
Fledborough Rd WBY LS22 .....29 F4
Fleece St KGHY BD21 .....3 H5
  WBSY BD6 .....116 E7
Fleet La CUL/QBY BD13 .....115 G6
  RTHW LS26 .....146 A2
Fleet Thro Rd HORS LS18 .....80 E6
Fleming St BTLY WF17 .....161 F3
Fletcher Av AIRE BD20 .....21 F7
Fletcher Crs BRIG HD6 .....176 D3
Fletcher La SHPY BD18 .....77 J7
Fletcher Rd WBSY BD6 .....117 G5
Fletton Ter ECHL BD2 .....98 C3
Flexbury Av MOR LS27 .....141 K4
Flight House Rd
  RPDN/SBR HX6 .....172 A5
Flintmill La BSPA/BRAM LS23 .....30 C6
Flinton Gv ECHL BD2 .....98 E2
Flockton Av BOW BD4 .....118 B2
Flockton Cl BOW BD4 .....118 B2
Flockton Crs BOW BD4 .....118 B2
Flockton Dr BOW BD4 .....118 B2
Flockton Gn BOW BD4 .....118 B2
Flockton Gv BOW BD4 .....118 B2
Flockton Rd BOW BD4 .....118 B2
Floral Av CHAL LS7 .....83 H6
Florence Av WIL/AL BD15 .....74 E6
Florence Gv OSM LS9 .....11 J4
Florence Mt OSM LS9 .....11 J4

Hazel Gv *BTLY* WF17 ....160 D4
HIPP HX3 ....157 F1
HUDN HD2 ....177 G4
PONT WF8 ....169 K6
Hazelheads *BAIL* BD17 ....57 H6
Hazelhurst Av *BGLY* BD16 ....75 J4
Hazelhurst Brow *HTON* BD9 ....96 C3
Hazelhurst Ct *BFDE* BD3 ....7 H6
PDSY/CALV LS28 ....100 D3
Hazel Hurst Gv *CUL/OBY* BD13 ....115 G7
Hazel Hurst Rd *CUL/OBY* BD13 ....115 G7
Hazelhurst Rd *HTON* BD9 ....96 C3
Hazelhurst Ter *HTON* BD9 ....96 C3
Hazelmere Av *BGLY* BD16 ....75 K4
Hazel Mt *SHPY* BD18 ....77 H5
Hazel Ri *RTHW* LS26 ....147 F6
Hazel Rd *KNOT* WF11 ....171 F5
Hazel Wk *HTON* BD9 ....96 C3
Hazelwood Av *AIRE* BD20 ....54 C2
GFTH/SHER LS25 ....127 K1
Hazelwood Ct *WKFDE* WF1 ....164 E3
Hazelwood Rd *HTON* BD9 ....96 B2
WKFDE WF1 ....164 E3
Headfield Rd *EARL* WF12 ....181 F3
Headfield Vw *EARL* WF12 ....181 G5
Headingley Av *HDGY* LS6 ....82 B7
Headingley Crs *HDGY* LS6 ....102 C1
Headingley Mt *HDGY* LS6 ....82 B7
Headingley Vw *HDGY* LS6 ....102 C1
Headland Gv *WBSY* BD6 ....116 E5
Headland La *EARL* WF12 ....181 F3
Headlands Av *OSS* WF5 ....182 B4
Headlands Cl *LVSG* WF15 ....159 J5
Headlands Gv *OSS* WF5 ....182 B4
Headlands La *KNOT* WF11 ....171 F4
PONT WF8 ....169 H7
Headlands Pk *OSS* WF5 ....182 B4
Headlands Rd *LVSG* WF15 ....159 H4
OSS WF5 ....182 B4
Headlands St *LVSG* WF15 ....159 H5
Headlands Wk *OSS* WF5 ....182 B4
Headley La *BSPA/BRAM* LS23 ....68 C2
CUL/OBY BD13 ....115 H1
The Headrow *LDS* LS1 ....9 M8
Headwell La *TAD* LS24 ....90 D7
Healdfield Rd *CAS* WF10 ....148 E7
Healds Av *LVSG* WF15 ....159 J4
Healds Rd *DEWS* WF13 ....160 D6
Heald St *CAS* WF10 ....168 B1
Healdwood Cl *CAS* WF10 ....169 F1
Healdwood Rd *CAS* WF10 ....149 F7
Healey Av *BGLY* BD16 ....75 K2
Healey Cl *BTLY* WF17 ....160 E4
Healey Crs *OSS* WF5 ....182 C6
Healey Croft La
EARD/LOFT WF3 ....163 G1
Healey Dr *OSS* WF5 ....182 C6
Healey La *BGLY* BD16 ....75 K2
BTLY WF17 ....160 C4
Healeycliffe *BTLY* WF17 ....140 C4
Healey Rd *OSS* WF5 ....182 B6
Healey St *BTLY* WF17 ....160 C3
Healey Wood Crs *BRIG* HD6 ......177 F1
Healey Wood Gdns *BRIG* HD6 ....177 F1
Healey Wood Gv *BRIG* HD6 ......177 G1
Healey Wood Rd *BRIG* HD6 ......177 F1
Heap La *BFDE* BD3 ....6 C4
Heap St *BFDE* BD3 ....7 G6
HIPP HX3 ....135 F5
Heath Av *HD22* LS22 ....154 E4
Heathcliff *HWTH* BD22 ....72 C5
Heathcliffe Cl *BTLY* WF17 ....140 C4
Heath Cl *EARL* WF12 ....182 A1
Heathcote Ri *HWTH* BD22 ....72 E4
Heath Crs *BEE/HOL* LS11 ....122 D3
Heathcroft Crs *BEE/HOL* LS11 ..122 D4
Heathcroft Dr *BEE/HOL* LS11 ....122 D4
Heathcroft Lawn
BEE/HOL LS11 ....122 D4
Heathcroft Ri *BEE/HOL* LS11 ....122 D4
Heathcroft V *BEE/HOL* LS11 ....122 D4
Heath Dr *BSPA/BRAM* LS23 ......48 A3
Heatherbank *HWTH* BD22 ....53 C7
Heather Bank Cl *CUL/OBY* BD13 ..73 K7
Heather Cl *EARD/LOFT* WF3 ....164 E3
OSS WF5 ....182 E6
Heather Ct *BTLY* WF17 ....140 B5
EARD/LOFT WF3 ....164 E3
Heathercroft *CHAL* LS7 ....83 K6
Heatherdale Ct
EARD/LOFT WF3 ....142 D7
Heatherdale Dr
EARD/LOFT WF3 ....142 D7
Heatherdale Rd
EARD/LOFT WF3 ....142 C7
Heatherdene *TAD* LS24 ....50 E6
Heather Dr *LUD/ILL* HX2 ....133 H4
Heather Gdns *BRAM* LS13 ......101 H5
SCFT LS14 ....65 K4
Heather Gv *BRAM* LS13 ....101 G5
HTON BD9 ....96 A2
KGHY BD21 ....2 B3
Heatherlands Av *CUL/OBY* BD13 ..94 A3
Heather Ri *ILK* LS29 ....37 K2
Heather Rd *BAIL* BD17 ....57 J7
Heather Side *BAIL* BD17 ....57 G7
The Heathers *HOR/CROF* WF4 ..187 F6
Heatherstones *HIPP* HX3 ....154 E4
Heather V *SCFT* LS14 ....65 J4
Heather Vw *BGLY* BD16 ....56 C6
HOR/CROF WF4 ....187 F6
OSS WF5 ....182 C4
Heathfield *BHP/TINH* LS16 ....61 K7
MIRF WF14 ....179 G3
Heathfield Av *ELL* HX5 ....176 A2
Heathfield Cl *BGLY* BD16 ....55 K7
EARD/LOFT WF3 ....162 E1
Heathfield Gv *GTHN* BD7 ....116 D2
HIPP * HX3 ....155 F4
Heathfield La *BSPA/BRAM* LS23 ..48 A2
Heathfield Pl *HIPP* HX3 ....155 F4
Heathfield Rd *OSS* WF5 ....182 B1
Heathfield St *ELL* HX5 ....175 K3
Heathfield Ter *HDGY* LS6 ....82 C6
HFAX * HX1 ....155 F4
Heath Gdns *HIPP* HX3 ....155 F4
Heath Gv *AIRE* BD20 ....55 G3
BEE/HOL LS11 ....122 D3

BTLY WF17 ....161 J4
PDSY/CALV LS28 ....99 K6
Heath Hall *HFAX* HX1 ....155 F4
Heath Hall Av *BOW* BD4 ....118 C5
Heath Hill Rd *LUD/ILL* HX2 ......133 H5
Heath La *HFAX* HX1 ....155 F4
Heath Lea *HFAX* HX1 ....17 G8
Heathmoor Cl *IDLE* BD10 ....78 B5
LUD/ILL HX2 ....134 A1
Heathmoor Mt *LUD/ILL* HX2 ....134 A1
Heathmoor Park Rd
LUD/ILL HX2 ....134 A1
Heathmoor Wy *LUD/ILL* HX2 ....134 A1
Heath Mt *BEE/HOL* LS11 ....122 D3
Heath Mount Rd *BRIG* HD6 ......177 F1
Heath Park Av *HFAX* HX1 ....155 F3
Heath Pk *ILK* LS29 ....23 J6
Heath Pl *BEE/HOL* LS11 ....122 D3
Heath Ri *BEE/HOL* LS11 ....122 D3
Heath Rd *BEE/HOL* LS11 ....122 D3
BFDE BD3 ....6 C9
EARL WF12 ....182 A1
HFAX HX1 ....155 F3
Heath Royd *HIPP* HX3 ....155 F4
BGLY BD16 ....75 K1
HIPP HX3 ....155 F4
LVSG WF15 ....159 H6
Heath Ter *BFDE* BD3 ....7 G6
BGLY BD16 ....75 K1
HIPP HX3 ....155 F4
LVSG WF15 ....159 H6
Heath Vw *HFAX* * HX1 ....17 H8
Heath View St *HFAX* HX1 ....17 H8
Heath Wk *EARL* * WF12 ....182 A1
Heathy Av *LUD/ILL* HX2 ....134 D2
Heathy La *LUD/ILL* HX2 ....134 C1
Heaton Av *AIRE* BD20 ....55 F4
CLECK BD19 ....158 D1
EARL WF12 ....181 H1
WOR/ARM LS12 ....12 A6
Heaton Cl *BGLY* BD16 ....56 A7
Heaton Crs *BGLY* * BD16 ....56 A7
Heaton Dr *BAIL* BD17 ....57 G7
BGLY BD16 ....56 A7
HUDE HD5 ....178 D7
Heaton Gra *BTLY* WF17 ....161 H5
Heaton Gv *CLECK* BD19 ....158 D1
HTON BD9 ....97 G1
SHPY BD18 ....77 H5
Heaton Hl *WBSY* BD6 ....116 D7
Heaton Park Dr *HTON* BD9 ......96 E2
Heaton Park Rd *HTON* BD9 ......96 E2
Heaton Rd *BTLY* WF17 ....161 F1
HTON BD9 ....97 F2
Heaton Royds *SHPY* * BD18 ......76 E7
Heaton Royds La *SHPY* BD18 ....76 E7
Heaton St *BEE/HOL* LS11 ....13 L3
BOW BD4 ....6 C9
BRIG HD6 ....157 H6
CLECK BD19 ....138 E7
Hebble Brook Cl *LUD/ILL* HX2 ..133 K3
Hebble Gdns *LUD/ILL* HX2 ......134 B6
Hebble La *HFAX* HX1 ....16 A1
Hebble St *DEWS* WF13 ....180 C4
Hebble Vale Dr *LUD/ILL* HX2 ..134 B5
Hebb Vw *WBSY* BD6 ....116 D4
Hebden Ap *SCFT* LS14 ....85 J6
Hebden Cl *SCFT* * LS14 ....85 J6
Hebden Gn *SCFT* LS14 ....85 J6
Hebden Pth *SCFT* LS14 ....85 J6
Hebden Pl *SCFT* LS14 ....85 J6
Hebden Rd *HWTH* BD22 ....72 E5
WKFDE WF1 ....19 K1
Heber Cl *AIRE* BD20 ....33 G2
Heber's Ghyll Dr *ILK* LS29 ....23 H6
Heber's Gv *ILK* LS29 ....23 H6
Heber St *KGHY* BD21 ....2 F6
Heckmondwike Rd
DEWS WF13 ....160 C7
Hector Cl *WBOW* BD5 ....117 K1
Heddon Cl *WBOW* BD5 ....117 K1
Heddon Gv *WBOW* BD5 ....5 M9
Heddon St *HDGY* LS6 ....82 D6
Heddon Wk *WBOW* * BD5 ......117 K1
Hedge Cl *GIR* BD8 ....96 C4
Hedge Side *GIR* BD8 ....96 D5
Hedge Top La *HIPP* HX3 ....135 K4
Hedge Wy *GIR* BD8 ....96 D4
Hedley Cha *WOR/ARM* LS12 ....12 F1
Hedley Crs *WKFDE* WF1 ....164 C5
Hedley Gdns *WOR/ARM* LS12 ..12 E1
Hedley Rd *HTON* BD9 ....97 F3
Heidelberg Rd *HTON* BD9 ....97 F3
Height Gn *RPDN/SBR* HX6 ......153 J4
Height La *HWTH* BD22 ....92 E3
Heights Bank *WOR/ARM* LS12 ..101 J6
Heights Cl *WOR/ARM* LS12 ....101 J6
Heights Dr *WOR/ARM* LS12 ....101 J6
Heights Garth *WOR/ARM* LS12 ..101 H6
Heights La *AIRE* BD20 ....20 C5
BGLY BD16 ....55 K4
HECK WF16 ....160 B5
HTON BD9 ....96 C2
WOR/ARM LS12 ....101 J6
Heights Pde *WOR/ARM* LS12 ..101 H6
Heights Wy *WOR/ARM* LS12 ..101 J6
Helena Cl *GFTH/SHER* LS25 ....127 H3
Helena Pl *GFTH/SHER* LS25 ....127 J6
Helena St *GFTH/SHER* LS25 ....127 J6
Helena Wy *BOW* BD4 ....118 C6
Helen Rose Ct *SHPY* BD18 ......77 K3
Helen St *SHPY* BD18 ....76 E4
Hellewell St *WBSY* BD6 ....116 E7
Hell La *WKFDE* WF1 ....186 A5
Hellwood La *SCFT* LS14 ....65 K4
Helm La *HUDE* HD5 ....178 D4
RPDN/SBR HX6 ....172 D1
Helmsley Ct *MID* LS10 ....143 H3
Helmsley Dr *BHP/TINH* LS16 ....82 B3
Helmsley Rd *BHP/TINH* LS16 ....82 B3
BSPA/BRAM LS23 ....48 B3
Helmsley St *BOW* BD4 ....118 B4
Helmsley Cft *MID* LS10 ....143 F2
Helston Garth *MID* LS10 ....143 F2
Helston Pl *MID* LS10 ....143 F2
Helston Rd *MID* LS10 ....143 F1
NORM WF6 ....166 E6
Helston St *MID* LS10 ....142 E1
Helston Wk *MID* LS10 ....142 F1

Helston Wy *MID* LS10 ....143 F1
Hemingway Cl *MID* LS10 ....14 F9
Hemingway Garth *MID* LS10 ....14 F9
Hemingway Gn *MID* LS10 ....14 F9
Hemingway La *IDLE* BD10 ....78 B4
Hemishor Dr *RTHW* LS26 ....127 H6
Hemsby Gv *KGHY* * BD21 ....53 H7
Hemsby Rd *CAS* WF10 ....168 B1
Hemsby St *KGHY* BD21 ....53 H7
Henacrewood Ct
CUL/OBY BD13 ....115 J7
Henbury St *CHAL* LS7 ....10 D6
Henconner Av *CHAL* LS7 ....83 H6
Henconner Crs *CHAL* LS7 ....83 H6
Henconner Dr *CHAL* LS7 ....83 H6
Henconner Gdns *CHAL* LS7 ......83 H6
Henconner La *BRAM* LS13 ......101 C4
CHAL LS7 ....83 H6
Henconner Rd *CHAL* LS7 ....83 H6
Henderson Av *NORM* WF6 ......186 E1
Henderson Pl *WBSY* BD6 ......117 H5
Hendford Dr *BFDE* BD3 ....6 D5
Hen Holme La *AIRE* BD20 ....33 F3
Henley Av *BRAM* LS13 ....101 F3
EARL WF12 ....181 H7
WBOW BD5 ....117 K4
Henley Cl *LS19* LS19 ....80 A1
Henley Ct *WBOW* BD5 ....118 A4
Henley Crs *BRAM* LS13 ....101 F3
YEA LS19 ....80 A1
Henley Dr *FEA/AMT* WF7 ......188 C6
YEA LS19 ....79 K1
Henley Gv *BRAM* LS13 ....101 F3
WBOW BD5 ....117 K4
Henley Hl *YEA* LS19 ....79 K1
Henley Mt *YEA* LS19 ....80 A1
Henley Pl *BRAM* LS13 ....101 F3
Henley Rd *BRAM* LS13 ....101 F3
EARL WF12 ....181 H7
WBOW BD5 ....117 K4
Henley St *BRAM* LS13 ....101 F3
Henley Ter *BRAM* LS13 ....101 F3
Henley Vw *BRAM* LS13 ....101 F3
Henrietta St *BTLY* WF17 ....161 F5
Henry Av *WOR/ARM* LS12 ......12 A6
Henry Moore Ct *CAS* WF10 ....169 G1
Henry St *BRIG* HD6 ....157 F4
BTLY WF17 ....161 F6
CLAY BD14 ....116 B2
CUL/OBY BD13 ....95 G7
HFAX HX1 ....16 F7
KGHY BD21 ....3 G4
WKFDW/WTN WF2 ....18 A5
Henry Ter *YEA* LS19 ....59 G4
Henshaw Av *YEA* LS19 ....59 J5
Henshaw Crs *YEA* LS19 ....59 J5
Henshaw La *YEA* LS19 ....59 J5
Henshaw Ov *YEA* LS19 ....59 J5
Henson Gv *CAS* WF10 ....169 G2
Hepton Ct *OSM* LS9 ....11 M7
Hepworth Av *MOR* LS27 ....122 A6
Hepworth Cl *MIRF* WF14 ....179 K3
Hepworth Crs *MOR* LS27 ....122 A6
Hepworth Dr *MIRF* WF14 ....179 K3
Hepworth La *MIRF* WF14 ....179 K3
Hepworth St *CAS* WF10 ....148 E6
Herbalist St *WOR/ARM* * LS12 ..12 E3
Herbert Pl *BFDE* BD3 ....7 L4
Herbert St *BGLY* BD16 ....75 K1
CAS WF10 ....168 C1
CLAY BD14 ....116 B2
HFAX HX1 ....16 A7
SHPY BD18 ....76 E7
WBOW BD5 ....117 J2
Hereford St *WOR/ARM* LS12 ......8 B8
Hereford Wy *BOW* * BD4 ....118 B2
Heritage Ms *HFAX* * HX1 ....17 J7
Heritage Pk *BGLY* BD16 ....55 K5
Heritage Rd *BTLY* WF17 ....161 F4
Heritage Wy *HWTH* BD22 ....72 D2
Hermit St *HWTH* BD22 ....73 H1
Hermon Av *HFAX* HX1 ....16 C7
Hermon Gv *HFAX* HX1 ....16 C7
Hermon Rd *MSTN/BAR* LS15 ....105 J4
Hermon St *MSTN/BAR* LS15 ....105 J4
Heron Cl *AIRE* BD20 ....32 C4
AL/HA/HU LS17 ....64 A7
CUL/OBY BD13 ....115 F4
Heron Ct *MOR* LS27 ....142 C5
Heron Gv *AL/HA/HU* LS17 ....64 B7
Herriot Ms *CAS* WF10 ....169 J3
Herschel Rd *GIR* BD8 ....96 B6
Hertford Cha *MSTN/BAR* LS15 ..105 K7
Hertford Cl *MSTN/BAR* LS15 ..106 A7
Hertford Cft *MSTN/BAR* LS15 ..106 A7
Hertford Fold
MSTN/BAR LS15 ....105 K7
Hertford Lawn
MSTN/BAR LS15 ....105 K7
Heshbon St *BOW* BD4 ....118 D3
Hesketh Av *EARD/LOFT* WF3 ..142 C7
KSTL LS5 ....101 K1
Hesketh La *EARD/LOFT* WF3 ..142 C7
Hesketh Mt *KSTL* LS5 ....81 K7
Hesketh Rd *KSTL* LS5 ....81 K7
Hesketh Ter *KSTL* LS5 ....101 K1
Hessel Ct *PONT* WF8 ....189 G1
Hessle Av *HDGY* LS6 ....8 E3
Hessle Mt *HDGY* LS6 ....8 F3
Hessle Pl *HDGY* LS6 ....8 E3
Hessle Rd *HDGY* LS6 ....8 E2
Hessle St *HDGY* LS6 ....8 E2
Hessle Ter *HDGY* LS6 ....8 F3
Hessle Vw *HDGY* LS6 ....8 F3
Hessle Wk *HDGY* LS6 ....8 F2
Hetchell Vw *AL/HA/HU* LS17 ....66 A1
Hetton Dr *BFDE* BD3 ....7 L4
Hetton Rd *RHAY* LS8 ....104 C1
Heuthwaite Av *WBY* LS22 ....29 J3
Hew Clews *GTHN* BD7 ....116 D3
Hey Beck La *EARL* WF12 ......162 B3
Heybeck Wk *BOW* BD4 ....119 G4
Heyford Ct *ECHL* BD2 ....97 J2
Heygate Cl *BAIL* BD17 ....57 J7
Heygate La *BAIL* BD17 ....57 J7

BSPA/BRAM LS23 ....48 E6
Heys Av *CUL/OBY* BD13 ....95 J7
Heys Cl *KNOT* WF11 ....171 H4
Heysham Dr *BOW* BD4 ....119 G3
Heys La *CUL/OBY* BD13 ....95 K7
Hey St *BRIG* HD6 ....157 G1
GTHN BD7 ....5 J1
Heywood Cl *HIPP* HX3 ....135 K5
Heywood Pl *HFAX* HX1 ....16 C5
Heywood St *HFAX* HX1 ....16 D5
Hick La *BTLY* WF17 ....161 G3
Hicks La *RTHW* LS26 ....147 G4
Hick St *BFD* * BD1 ....6 B6
Higgin Farm *LUD/ILL* * HX2 ....152 D3
Higgin La *HIPP* HX3 ....155 H3
Higham & Dob La
RPDN/SBR HX6 ....152 D4
Higham Wy *GFTH/SHER* LS25 ..107 J5
High Ash *AL/HA/HU* LS17 ....63 K6
SHPY BD18 ....77 K5
High Ash Av *AL/HA/HU* LS17 ....64 A6
High Ash Dr *AL/HA/HU* LS17 ....63 K6
High Ash Mt *AL/HA/HU* LS17 ....63 K6
High Ash Pk *WIL/AL* BD15 ......95 J4
High Bank Ap *MSTN/BAR* LS15 ..106 A6
High Bank Cl *ILK* * LS29 ....22 C1
MSTN/BAR LS15 ....106 A5
High Bank Gdns
MSTN/BAR LS15 ....106 B6
High Bank Ga
MSTN/BAR * LS15 ....106 A6
High Bank La *SHPY* BD18 ....76 C6
High Banks Cl *AIRE* BD20 ....54 C1
High Bank Vw *MSTN/BAR* LS15 ..106 A6
High Bank Wy *MSTN/BAR* LS15 ..106 A6
High Binns La *HWTH* BD22 ......92 E2
Highbridge Ter *WBOW* BD5 ....118 A5
High Brook Fall
EARD/LOFT WF3 ....164 D2
High Bury Cl *CUL/OBY* BD13 ....115 F6
Highbury Cl *HDGY* LS6 ....82 D6
Highbury La *HDGY* LS6 ....82 D6
Highbury Pl *BRAM* LS13 ....100 D5
HDGY LS6 ....82 D6
Highbury Rd *HDGY* LS6 ....82 D6
Highbury St *HDGY* LS6 ....82 D6
Highbury Ter *HDGY* LS6 ....82 D6
High Busy La *SHPY* BD18 ....77 K4
High Cliffe *BULY* * LS4 ....8 B3
High Cliffe Av *HUDN* HD2 ......176 E7
Highcliffe Dr *LUD/ILL* HX2 ......154 A1
Highcliffe Rd *BTLY* WF17 ....161 F5
MOR LS27 ....141 J3
High Cliffe Ter *WBY* LS22 ....29 H4
High Cl *GSLY* LS20 ....58 C3
OSS WF5 ....162 C7
YEA LS19 ....79 J1
High Ct *LDSU* LS2 ....14 C1
High Court La *LDSU* LS2 ....14 C1
High Cft *CUL/OBY* BD13 ....115 H5
HIPP HX3 ....134 C1
Highcroft *WBY* LS22 ....46 D2
Highcroft Cl *PDSY/CALV* LS28 ..99 K5
Highcroft Gdns *KGHY* BD21 ....54 C5
High Cross La *HIPP* HX3 ....115 K7
Highdale *EARL* WF12 ....161 H6
Highdale Cft *IDLE* BD10 ....78 C4
Higher Brockwell
RPDN/SBR HX6 ....153 G5
Higher Coach Rd *BGLY* BD16 ....76 B2
Higher Downs *GIR* BD8 ....96 B6
Higher Grange Rd
PDSY/CALV LS28 ....100 B5
Higher Intake Rd *ECHL* BD2 ......7 G1
Higher Park Royd Dr
RPDN/SBR HX6 ....173 F2
Higher School St *SHPY* * BD18 ..76 E4
Higherwood Cl *KGHY* BD21 ......3 M5
Highfell Ri *HWTH* BD22 ....53 F6
High Fernley Cl *LM/WK* * BD12 ..137 H3
High Fernley Rd *LM/WK* BD12 ..137 H4
Highfield *BOW* BD4 ....118 C5
EARD/LOFT WF3 ....142 C6
HIPP HX3 ....136 A2
Highfield Av *BRIG* HD6 ....137 G7
GTL/HWG HX4 ....174 E1
HIPP HX3 ....116 C7
IDLE BD10 ....78 B5
PONT WF8 ....170 B4
PONT WF8 ....189 H2
WOR/ARM LS12 ....12 B4
Highfield Cl *AIRE* BD20 ....55 F2
FEA/AMT WF7 ....188 C1
MOR LS27 ....121 H7
WOR/ARM LS12 ....12 C6
Highfield Ct *HWTH* BD22 ....72 D2
LVSG * WF15 ....159 G6
Highfield Crs *BAIL* BD17 ....57 H7
HTON BD9 ....96 C1
PDSY/CALV LS28 ....100 A5
RTHW LS26 ....125 K7
WOR/ARM LS12 ....12 C4
Highfield Dr *BTLY* WF17 ....140 B5
CAS WF10 ....147 J2
GFTH/SHER LS25 ....127 J1
HTON BD9 ....96 C1
LVSG WF15 ....159 F4
MOR LS27 ....121 H7
WKFDW/WTN WF2 ....183 K1
YEA LS19 ....79 K1
Highfield Gdns *EARL* WF12 ....181 G6
HTON BD9 ....96 C1
MOR LS27 ....121 H7
WOR/ARM LS12 ....12 B4
Highfield Garth *WOR/ARM* LS12 ..12 C5
Highfield Gn *CAS* WF10 ....147 J2
GFTH/SHER LS25 ....111 F7
PDSY/CALV LS28 ....100 A5
Highfield Gv *CAS* WF10 ....147 J1
ELL HX5 ....175 H1
IDLE BD10 ....78 B6
High Field La *HWTH* BD22 ......72 D1
RPDN/SBR HX6 ....172 E3
Highfield La *AIRE* BD20 ....21 F7
DEWS WF13 ....160 C5
GFTH/SHER LS25 ....129 J2

KGHY BD21 ....2 D3
MSTN/BAR LS15 ....87 H7
RTHW LS26 ....125 K7
Highfield Ms *AIRE* BD20 ....55 F2
BAIL BD17 ....57 H7
Highfield Mt *RTHW* * LS26 ......145 K1
Highfield Pl *CAS* WF10 ....147 K1
GIR BD8 ....5 H1
HFAX HX1 ....16 B8
MOR LS27 ....142 A4
Highfield Ri *WKFDW/WTN* WF2 ..183 K1
Highfield Rd *BRAM* LS13 ....101 G3
BRIG HD6 ....176 D1
CLECK BD19 ....158 D1
ELL HX5 ....175 J3
GFTH/SHER LS25 ....88 D4
HTON BD9 ....77 H7
IDLE BD10 ....78 B6
KGHY BD21 ....2 C3
LUD/ILL HX2 ....133 F7
PDSY/CALV LS28 ....99 K5
PONT WF8 ....189 H3
High Flds *LUD/ILL* HX2 ....154 B4
Highfield St *BRAM* * LS13 ......101 G3
KGHY BD21 ....2 F4
PDSY/CALV LS28 ....99 K5
Highfield Ter *EARL* WF12 ....181 G6
HFAX * HX1 ....16 B8
PDSY/CALV LS28 ....99 K5
SHPY BD18 ....76 D3
Highfield Vw *MOR* LS27 ....121 H7
Highfield Vls *GFTH/SHER* LS25 ..111 F7
High Fold *HWTH* BD22 ....2 B9
Highfold *YEA* LS19 ....59 H6
High Fold La *AIRE* BD20 ....53 H1
Highgate *HTON* BD9 ....96 E1
Highgate Cl *LUD/ILL* HX2 ......116 B4
Highgate Gdns *LUD/ILL* HX2 ..134 B7
Highgate Gv *CLAY* BD14 ....116 B4
Highgate La *HUDE* HD5 ....178 E7
Highgate Rd *CUL/OBY* BD13 ..116 A4
EARL WF12 ....181 G6
HTON BD9 ....97 F1
Highgate St *BTLY* WF17 ....161 J5
High Green Dr *AIRE* BD20 ....20 E7
High Green Rd *NORM* WF6 ....166 B4
Highgrove Ct *NORM* WF6 ......166 C3
High Grove La *HIPP* HX3 ....17 K1
High Holly Garth *KGHY* BD21 ....3 K7
High House La *LUD/ILL* HX2 ....132 D3
High House Rd *ECHL* BD2 ....98 B1
Highland Cl *PONT* WF8 ....170 A5
The Highlands *LVSG* WF15 ......158 E3
Highlands Cl *GTHN* BD7 ....116 D3
RTHW LS26 ....124 A7
Highlands Dr *RTHW* LS26 ......124 A6
Highlands Gv *GTHN* BD7 ....116 D3
RTHW LS26 ....124 A6
Highlands La *LUD/ILL* HX2 ......134 C1
Highlands Wk *RTHW* LS26 ......124 A6
Highland Ville *HIPP* HX3 ....136 C7
High La *LUD/ILL* HX2 ....133 J7
Highlea Cl *YEA* LS19 ....59 G6
Highlee La *RPDN/SBR* HX6 ......173 G2
High Lees Rd *LUD/ILL* HX2 ......133 J2
High Level Wy *HFAX* HX1 ....16 B3
Highley Hall Cft *BRIG* HD6 ......157 J6
Highley Pk *BRIG* HD6 ....157 K6
High Meadow *KGHY* BD21 ....53 H2
High Mdw *GTL/HWG* HX4 ......174 E2
WIL/AL BD15 ....74 E7
Highmoor *BAIL* BD17 ....77 J1
High Moor Av *AL/HA/HU* LS17 ..83 K2
High Moor Cl *AL/HA/HU* LS17 ..83 K2
High Moor Crs *AL/HA/HU* LS17 ..83 K2
Highmoor Crs *BRIG* HD6 ....157 J3
High Moor Dr *AL/HA/HU* LS17 ..83 K1
High Moor Gv *AL/HA/HU* LS17 ..83 K1
Highmoor La *BRIG* HD6 ....157 J5
CLECK BD19 ....158 B4
Highmoor Wk *BAIL* BD17 ....77 F2
High Oxford St *CAS* WF10 ......168 B1
High Park Crs *HTON* BD9 ....96 C2
High Park Dr *HTON* BD9 ....96 C2
High Park Gv *HTON* BD9 ....96 C2
High Poplars *ECHL* BD2 ....98 A1
High Ridge Av *RTHW* LS26 ......124 E7
High Ridge Ct *RTHW* LS26 ......145 F1
High Ridge Pk *RTHW* LS26 ......125 F7
High Ridge Wy *BHP/TINH* LS16 ..61 J1
High Rd *EARL* WF12 ....181 H2
Highroad Well La *LUD/ILL* HX2 ..153 K1
High Royds Dr *ILK* LS29 ....38 B7
High Spring Gardens La
KGHY BD21 ....2 D1
High Spring Rd *KGHY* BD21 ....54 C5
High St *AIRE* BD20 ....32 D5
BRIG HD6 ....157 G5
BSPA/BRAM LS23 ....48 A2
BSPA/BRAM LS23 ....48 A5
BSPA/BRAM LS23 ....68 C1
BTLY WF17 ....140 B5
BTLY WF17 ....161 J5
CAS WF10 ....168 B1
CLECK BD19 ....138 E7
CUL/OBY BD13 ....95 G7
CUL/OBY BD13 ....115 H5
DEWS WF13 ....180 C4
EARL WF12 ....181 J2
GFTH/SHER LS25 ....128 A5
GFTH/SHER LS25 ....131 F2
GTL/HWG HX4 ....174 B6
GTL/HWG * HX4 ....175 G2
HECK WF16 ....160 A5
HFAX HX1 ....16 F7
HOR/CROF WF4 ....186 B5
IDLE BD10 ....78 C4
KGHY BD21 ....2 F5
KNOT WF11 ....150 E6
KNOT * WF11 ....170 D3
LUD/ILL HX2 ....133 F7
MOR LS27 ....141 K5
NORM WF6 ....166 C5
NORM WF6 ....166 C6
OSS WF5 ....162 B7
PDSY/CALV LS28 ....100 A2

TAD LS24 ....50 D7
WBSY BD6 ....117 H5
WBY LS22 ....29 H4
YEA LS19 ....59 J4
High Street Ct LUD/ILL HX2 ......133 F6
High Sunderland La HIPP HX3 ....17 J1
Highthorne Ct AL/HA/HU LS17 ....64 A7
Highthorne Dr AL/HA/HU LS17 ....64 A7
Highthorne Gv AL/HA/HU LS17 ....64 A7
WOR/ARM * LS12 ....101 K5
Highthorne Mt AL/HA/HU LS17 ....64 A7
Highthorne St
WOR/ARM * LS12 ....101 K5
Highthorne Vw
WOR/ARM * LS12 ....102 A5
Hightown Rd CLECK BD19 ....158 E1
Hightown Vw LVSG WF15 ....158 D3
High Trees Ct GFTH/SHER LS25 ...111 F6
High Trees La GTL/HWG HX4 ......174 A3
Highway GSLY LS20 ....58 C2
High Ways SCFT LS14 ....105 F4
High Weardley La OT LS21 ....43 F4
High Wheatley ILK LS29 ....24 D6
High Wicken Cl CUL/QBY BD13 ....95 F7
High Wd ILK LS29 ....24 E6
Highwood Av AL/HA/HU LS17 .....83 K7
Highwood Crs AL/HA/HU LS17 .....83 H1
Highwood Gv AL/HA/HU LS17 .....83 H1
High Woodlands
EARD/LOFT WF3 ....163 H1
High Wood Ri BTLY WF17 ....140 D3
Hilberoyd Rd BTLY WF17 ....161 G4
Hilda St HTON BD9 ....97 F1
OSS WF5 ....182 D5
Hillam Hall La GFTH/SHER LS25 ..151 J1
Hillam Hall Vw
GFTH/SHER LS25 ....151 J1
Hillam La GFTH/SHER LS25 ....151 F2
Hillam Rd ECHL BD2 ....97 J2
Hillam St WBOW BD5 ....117 C3
Hillary Pl LDSU LS2 ....9 L5
Hillary Rd SHPY BD18 ....77 K5
Hillary St DEWS WF13 ....160 C5
Hillbro Ct BAIL * BD17 ....57 J7
Hillbrook Ri ILK LS29 ....23 J6
Hill Brow CI WIL/AL BD15 ....95 K4
Hill Cl BAIL BD17 ....77 G2
PONT WF8 ....189 J2
Hill Clough Gv HWTH BD22 ....52 D4
Hillcote Dr WBOW BD5 ....117 K2
Hillcourt Av BRAM LS13 ....101 F1
Hillcourt Cft BRAM LS13 ....101 F1
Hill Court Dr BRAM LS13 ....101 F1
Hillcourt Gv BRAM LS13 ....101 F1
Hill Crs BTLY WF17 ....140 D6
ILK LS29 ....38 A3
YEA LS19 ....59 K6
Hillcrest BHP/TINH * LS16 ....40 D6
GFTH/SHER LS25 ....131 J1
NORM WF6 ....166 B4
TAD LS24 ....70 C1
Hill Crest WBY LS22 ....46 B2
Hillcrest Av CUL/QBY BD13 ....94 A4
Hillcrest Av AIRE BD20 ....21 F7
BTLY WF17 ....160 D3
CAS WF10 ....169 J2
CHAL LS7 ....10 F2
CUL/QBY BD13 ....115 J6
FEA/AMT WF7 ....188 A4
OSS WF5 ....182 B1
Hillcrest Cl CAS WF10 ....169 J2
RTHW LS26 ....126 C5
Hillcrest Ct TAD LS24 ....70 C1
Hill Crest Dr CUL/QBY BD13 ....94 A4
Hillcrest Dr CAS WF10 ....169 J2
CUL/QBY BD13 ....115 J6
Hillcrest Mt BHP/TINH LS16 ....61 H7
CAS WF10 ....169 J2
CLECK BD19 ....158 A1
Hill Crest Mt CUL/QBY BD13 ....94 A4
Hillcrest Pl CHAL LS7 ....10 F1
Hillcrest Ri BHP/TINH LS16 ....61 H7
Hill Crest Rd CUL/QBY BD13 ....94 B4
CUL/QBY BD13 ....95 G6
EARL WF12 ....181 F4
Hillcrest Rd CAS WF10 ....169 K2
CUL/QBY BD13 ....115 J6
Hillcrest Vw CHAL LS7 ....10 F1
Hill Cft CUL/QBY BD13 ....95 H6
Hill Croft Cl PONT WF8 ....190 E4
Hill End EARL WF12 ....181 H1
Hill End Cl HIPP HX3 ....137 F5
Hill End Crs WOR/ARM LS12 ......101 J5
Hill End Gv GTHN BD7 ....116 D3
Hill End La CUL/QBY BD13 ....74 B4
CUL/QBY BD13 ....115 G6
Hill End Rd WOR/ARM LS12 ......101 J5
Hillesley Rd EARL WF12 ....161 K5
Hill Foot SHPY BD18 ....76 C5
Hillfoot Av PDSY/CALV LS28 ....99 J3
Hillfoot Crs PDSY/CALV LS28 ....99 J5
Hillfoot Dr PDSY/CALV LS28 ....99 J5
Hillfoot Ri PDSY/CALV LS28 ....99 J5
Hillgarth EARL WF12 ....181 G6
KNOT WF11 ....171 F5
Hill Green Ct BOW BD4 ....120 B4
Hill Gv South MID LS10 ....124 A7
Hillhead Dr BTLY WF17 ....140 D6
Hill House Edge La HWTH BD22 ....92 C5
Hill House La HWTH BD22 ....92 D4
Hilliam Hall Cl GFTH/SHER LS25 ..151 J1
Hillidge Rd MID LS10 ....14 C8
Hillidge Sq MID LS10 ....14 C7
Hillingdon Wy AL/HA/HU LS17 .....63 H6
Hillings La GSLY LS20 ....57 J2
ILK LS29 ....37 J6
Hill Lands LM/WK BD12 ....137 G3
Hill Mount Pleasant MID LS10 ....143 H2
Hill Park Av HIPP HX3 ....16 A1
Hill Ri BTLY WF17 ....161 J4
Hill Rise Av BRAM LS13 ....101 F1
Hill Rise Gv BRAM LS13 ....101 F1
Hill Rd CAS WF10 ....168 C1
Hillside GFTH/SHER LS25 ....107 K7
KNOT WF11 ....170 E1
Hillside Av GSLY LS20 ....38 E7
HUDN HD2 ....177 C2
HWTH BD22 ....72 C2

LUD/ILL HX2 ....152 E1
RPDN/SBR HX6 ....173 F3
Hill Side Buildings
BEE/HOL LS11 ....13 K9
Hillside Cl GFTH/SHER LS25 ......131 J1
ILK LS29 ....22 B1
WKFDW/WTN WF2 ....183 J6
Hillside Ct CHAL LS7 ....83 K5
ILK LS29 ....38 A6
Hillside Gv HWTH BD22 ....72 C2
PDSY/CALV LS28 ....100 C6
Hillside Mt PDSY/CALV LS28 ......100 B3
Hill Side Mt PDSY/CALV LS28 .....100 B3
PONT WF8 ....189 K1
Hillside Ri GSLY LS20 ....58 E1
BGLY BD16 ....75 J1
Hillside Rd CHAL LS7 ....83 J5
PONT WF8 ....189 K1
SHPY BD18 ....77 H6
Hillside Ter BAIL * BD17 ....57 H7
Hillside Vw PDSY/CALV LS28 .....100 C6
RPDN/SBR HX6 ....153 H4
Hill St BEE/HOL LS11 ....13 L9
BOW BD4 ....6 E9
CLECK BD19 ....158 D1
HFAX HX1 ....16 F8
HWTH BD22 ....72 C2
OSM LS9 ....10 F5
WBSY BD6 ....117 F5
Hillthorpe Ct MID LS10 ....143 H4
Hillthorpe Ri PDSY/CALV LS28 ...120 A1
Hillthorpe Rd PDSY/CALV LS28 ..120 A1
Hillthorpe Sq PDSY/CALV LS28 ..120 A1
Hillthorpe St PDSY/CALV * LS28 ..120 B1
Hillthorpe Ter
PDSY/CALV * LS28 ....120 B1
Hill Top CAS WF10 ....167 J1
HFAX HX1 ....154 B3
ILK LS29 ....23 K7
ILK LS29 ....37 K1
KNOT WF11 ....171 G4
Hill Top Av RHAY LS8 ....11 G1
Hilltop Cl CAS WF10 ....149 F6
Hill Top Cl EARD/LOFT WF3 ......162 D2
TAD LS24 ....70 C4
WOR/ARM LS12 ....101 J5
Hill Top Cottages HTON BD9 ....96 D3
Hill Top Ct EARD/LOFT WF3 ......162 D2
Hill Top Est HECK WF16 ....160 B4
Hill Top Gdns
EARD/LOFT * WF3 ....162 D2
Hill Top Gn EARD/LOFT WF3 .....162 C2
Hill Top Gv EARD/LOFT WF3 ......162 D2
WIL/AL BD15 ....95 K4
Hill Top La BGLY BD16 ....55 J3
EARD/LOFT WF3 ....162 C2
WIL/AL BD15 ....95 K4
Hill Top Ms KNOT WF11 ....171 G4
Hill Top Mt RHAY LS8 ....11 G1
Hill Top Pl HDGY LS6 ....9 G4
RHAY LS8 ....11 G1
Hill Top Rd CUL/QBY BD13 ....94 E6
HWTH BD22 ....72 C2
KGHY BD21 ....73 H3
WOR/ARM LS12 ....101 J5
Hill Top St HDGY LS6 ....9 G5
Hill Top Vw EARD/LOFT WF3 .....162 C2
Hill Top Wk HWTH BD22 ....2 A4
Hill Top Wy HWTH BD22 ....2 A4
Hill Vw LUD/ILL HX2 ....114 C7
Hillview Gdns HIPP HX3 ....135 K6
Hill View Pl CHAL * LS7 ....83 J5
Hill View Ter CHAL * LS7 ....83 J5
Hillway GSLY LS20 ....58 D4
Hillworth Village KGHY * BD21 ......2 E6
Hilton Av SHPY BD18 ....77 C7
Hilton Ct BHP/TINH LS16 ....40 D6
Hilton Crs BAIL BD17 ....77 H2
Hilton Dr SHPY BD18 ....77 C7
Hilton Gra BHP/TINH LS16 ....40 D6
Hilton Gv GTHN BD7 ....4 D8
RHAY LS8 ....84 A1
SHPY BD18 ....77 C7
Hilton Ms BHP/TINH LS16 ....40 D7
Hilton Pl RHAY LS8 ....104 A1
Hilton Rd GTHN BD7 ....4 D8
RHAY LS8 ....104 A1
SHPY BD18 ....77 C7
Hilton St RHAY * LS8 ....104 A1
Hilton Ter RHAY LS8 ....104 A1
Hinchliffe Av OSS WF5 ....182 E4
Hinchliffe St BFDE BD3 ....6 E3
Hinchliffe Av BAIL BD17 ....77 J2
Hindle Pl MOR * LS27 ....122 A7
Hindley Rd LVSG WF15 ....159 H5
Hindley Wk GTHN BD7 ....116 C4
Hind St LM/WK BD12 ....137 H5
Hinsley Ct HDGY LS6 ....82 D7
Hinton Cl PONT WF8 ....169 K5
Hinton La KNOT WF11 ....170 B2
Hions Cl BRIG HD6 ....177 F1
Hipswell St BFDE BD3 ....7 H4
Hird Av WBSY BD6 ....117 H6
Hird Rd LM/WK BD12 ....137 J1
Hird St BAIL BD17 ....77 G4
BEE/HOL LS11 ....13 K9
KGHY BD21 ....2 E8
Hirst Av HECK WF16 ....160 A3
Hirstlands Av OSS WF5 ....182 B2
Hirstlands Dr OSS WF5 ....182 B1
Hirst La SHPY BD18 ....76 D1
Hirst Lodge Ct ECHL BD2 ....98 A1
Hirst Mill Crs SHPY BD18 ....76 D3
Hirst Rd DEWS WF13 ....161 F7
WKFDW/WTN WF2 ....183 J4
Hirst St CAS WF10 ....127 H7
Hirst Wood Crs SHPY BD18 ....76 D4
Hirst Wood Rd SHPY BD18 ....76 C4
Hive St HWTH BD22 ....2 D7
Hobart Rd CAS WF10 ....149 J7
EARL WF12 ....181 J6
Hobberley La AL/HA/HU LS17 ......85 G1
Hobb Nook La OT LS21 ....26 B2
Hob Cote La HWTH BD22 ....72 A3
Hob La RPDN/SBR HX6 ....153 J7
RPDN/SBR HX6 ....172 D1
Hockney Rd GIR BD8 ....4 E4

Hodgewood La PONT WF8 ....190 E3
Hodgson Av AL/HA/HU LS17 ....84 B1
BFDE BD3 ....7 K3
Hodgson Crs AL/HA/HU LS17 ......84 B1
Hodgson La BIRK/DRI BD11 ....119 J7
Hodgson's La GFTH/SHER LS25 ..111 H4
Hodgson St MOR LS27 ....142 B6
WKFDE WF1 ....18 C2
Holbeck BEE/HOL LS11 ....13 H4
Holbeck Moor Rd BEE/HOL LS11 ..13 J6
Holbeck Towers BEE/HOL LS11 ...13 J6
Holborn Ct HDGY LS6 ....9 K2
WBSY BD6 ....137 H1
Holborn Gdns HDGY LS6 ....9 K2
Holborn Gn HDGY LS6 ....9 K2
Holborn Gv HDGY LS6 ....9 K3
Holborn St HDGY LS6 ....9 L3
Holborn Ter HDGY LS6 ....9 L3
Holborn Vw HDGY LS6 ....9 K2
Holborn Wk HDGY LS6 ....9 K2
Holby Sq WKFDW/WTN * WF2 ....183 H5
Holden Ing Wy BTLY WF17 ....140 D3
Holden La AIRE BD20 ....33 J3
BAIL BD17 ....57 J7
Holderness Rd KNOT WF11 ....171 F3
Holdforth Cl WOR/ARM LS12 ......12 E2
Holdforth Gdns WOR/ARM LS12 ..12 E2
Holdforth Gn WOR/ARM LS12 ......12 E2
Holdforth Pl WOR/ARM LS12 ....12 E2
Holdsworth Av HECK WF16 ....160 B1
Holdsworth Ct CLECK BD19 ......158 E1
Holdsworth Rd LUD/ILL HX2 ......114 D7
Holdsworth St BFD BD1 ....6 A4
CLECK BD19 ....138 E7
SHPY BD18 ....77 H6
Holdsworth Ter HFAX HX1 ....155 C3
Hole La AIRE BD20 ....20 C5
Holes La KNOT WF11 ....171 F4
Holgate Rd PONT WF8 ....189 H4
Holker St BD8 ....4 F3
KGHY BD21 ....3 C3
Holland Rd GFTH/SHER LS25 ....128 B4
Holland St BTLY WF17 ....161 G3
Hollas La RPDN/SBR HX6 ....154 B6
Hollerton La EARD/LOFT WF3 ....142 E7
The Hollies WOR/ARM * LS12 ......12 B2
Hollinbank La HECK WF16 ....160 B3
Hollin Close La ECHL BD2 ....97 K2
Hollin Ct BHP/TINH * LS16 ....82 C5
Hollin Crs BHP/TINH LS16 ....82 C5
Hollin Dr BHP/TINH LS16 ....82 C5
Hollin Gdns BHP/TINH LS16 ....82 B5
Hollingbourne Rd
MSTN/BAR LS15 ....106 C3
Hollings HWTH * BD22 ....72 B5
Hollings Rd GIR BD8 ....4 F3
Hollings Sq GIR BD8 ....4 F3
Hollings St BGLY BD16 ....76 A5
GIR BD8 ....4 F4
Hollings Ter GIR BD8 ....4 F3
The Hollings RTHW LS26 ....146 E4
Hollingwood Av GTHN BD7 ....116 C3
Hollingwood Dr GTHN BD7 ....116 D2
Hollingwood Ga ILK LS29 ....23 H6
Hollingwood La GTHN BD7 ....116 D3
Hollingwood Mt GTHN BD7 ....116 D2
Hollingwood Ri ILK LS29 ....23 H6
Hollingworth La KNOT WF11 ......171 H4
Hollin Hall Dr ILK LS29 ....23 H6
Hollin Hall La HUDE HD5 ....178 A7
Hollin Hall Rd SHPY BD18 ....76 D6
Hollin Head BAIL BD17 ....58 A7
Hollin Hill Av RHAY LS8 ....84 D7
Hollin La BHP/TINH LS16 ....82 C5
HBR * BD22 ....132 B2
RPDN/SBR HX6 ....153 J7
RPDN/SBR HX6 ....172 B6
SHPY BD18 ....77 J6
Hollin Mt BHP/TINH LS16 ....82 B5
Hollin Park Av RHAY LS8 ....84 E7
Hollin Park Crs PDSY/CALV LS28 ..79 H6
Hollin Park Crs RHAY LS8 ....84 E7
Hollin Park Dr PDSY/CALV LS28 ..79 H6
Hollin Park Mt RHAY LS8 ....84 E7
Hollin Park Pl RHAY LS8 ....84 D7
Hollin Park Rd PDSY/CALV LS28 ..79 H6
RHAY LS8 ....84 D7
Hollin Park Ter RHAY LS8 ....84 D7
Hollin Ri SHPY * BD18 ....77 H6
Hollin Rd BHP/TINH LS16 ....82 C5
SHPY BD18 ....77 H6
Hollinroyd Rd EARL WF12 ....181 H1
Hollins Av DEWS WF13 ....160 C6
Hollins Bank RPDN/SBR HX6 ......153 J4
Hollins Bank La AIRE BD20 ....32 E6
Hollins Beck Cl
GFTH/SHER LS25 ....127 K6
Hollins Bungalows
RPDN/SBR * HX6 ....153 J3
Hollins Cl AIRE BD20 ....53 G1
Hollins Gv CAS WF10 ....147 J1
Hollins Hey Rd GTL/HWG HX4 ....175 C5
Hollins Hl BAIL BD17 ....58 C5
Hollins La AIRE BD20 ....33 G7
LUD/ILL HX2 ....133 K2
LUD/ILL HX2 ....152 C5
RPDN/SBR HX6 ....153 J3
Hollins Mill La RPDN/SBR HX6 ...153 H4
Hollins Pk GFTH/SHER LS25 ....127 K5
Hollins Rd DEWS WF13 ....160 C6
Hollins Row RPDN/SBR HX6 ....153 F7
Hollin Ter SHPY * BD18 ....77 H6
Hollin Vw BHP/TINH LS16 ....82 C5
Hollin Wood Cl SHPY BD18 ....76 D5
Hollinwood Vw AIRE BD20 ....55 G4
Hollis Pl BVRD LS3 ....9 G7
Holly Ap OSS WF5 ....182 C1
Holly Av BHP/TINH LS16 ....81 G1
Holly Bank GFTH/SHER LS25 .....108 A7
HDGY LS6 ....82 C6
Hollybank Av BTLY WF17 ....160 E1
Holly Bank Dr HIPP HX3 ....136 C2
Hollybank Gdns GTHN BD7 ....116 D3
Hollybank Gv GTHN BD7 ....116 D3

Holly Bank Pk BRIG HD6 ....176 E1
Hollybank Rd BRIG HD6 ....176 D1
Hollybank Rd GTHN BD7 ....116 D3
Holly Bush Ct
BSPA/BRAM LS23 ....48 D3
Hollybush Gn WBY LS22 ....47 F2
Holly Cl MID LS10 ....143 G5
Holly Ct EARD/LOFT WF3 ....162 D2
WKFDE WF1 ....164 D3
Holly Crs RPDN/SBR HX6 ....172 D6
Hollycroft Ct BHP/TINH LS16 ....81 K1
Holly Dene OSS WF5 ....182 C1
Holly Gv BTLY WF17 ....160 E1
Holly Gv BHP/TINH LS16 ....81 G1
HFAX HX1 ....16 C7
Holly Hall La LM/WK BD12 ....137 H3
Holly Mede OSS WF5 ....182 C1
Holly Park Dr GTHN BD7 ....116 D3
Holly Park Mills
PDSY/CALV * LS28 ....79 H6
PDSY/CALV * LS28 ....100 B1
Holly Rd BSPA/BRAM LS23 ....48 D2
Hollyshaw Crs MSTN/BAR LS15 ..105 K5
Hollyshaw Gv MSTN/BAR LS15 ..105 K5
Hollyshaw La MSTN/BAR LS15 ..105 K5
Hollyshaw St MSTN/BAR LS15 ...105 K5
Hollyshaw Ter MSTN/BAR LS15 ..105 K5
Hollyshaw Wk MSTN/BAR LS15 ..105 K4
Holly St WBSY BD6 ....116 C4
WKFDW/WTN * WF2 ....184 A2
Holly Tree La MSTN/BAR LS15 ...106 B7
Hollywell Gv WOR/ARM LS12 ....102 A5
Hollywell La WOR/ARM LS12 .....102 A5
Holman Av GFTH/SHER LS25 .....127 J1
Holmdene Dr MIRF WF14 ....179 H3
Holme Dr LUD/ILL HX2 ....153 J2
Holme Farm WBSY BD6 ....116 C5
Holme Farm Ct
WOR/ARM LS12 ....121 G3
Holme Farm La AL/HA/HU LS17 ...66 D1
BSPA/BRAM LS23 ....46 C7
Holme Fld OSS WF5 ....182 B2
Holme Gv WBSY BD6 ....38 A3
Holme House La HWTH BD22 ......52 D6
LUD/ILL HX2 ....133 F3
Holme Ings ILK LS29 ....23 F2
Holme La BOW BD4 ....119 F5
WKFDW/WTN WF2 ....184 C7
Holme Leas Dr OSS WF5 ....182 B2
Holme Mill La HWTH BD22 ....2 A6
Holme Pk ILK LS29 ....38 A3
Holmes Rd LUD/ILL HX2 ....153 J2
Holmes St BEE/HOL LS11 ....14 A4
GIR BD8 ....5 J4
Holmes Ter LUD/ILL HX2 ....134 A7
Holme St BRIG HD6 ....157 F1
HWTH BD22 ....92 D3
LVSG WF15 ....159 J4
WBOW BD5 ....117 J2
Holme Top St WBOW BD5 ....117 J2
Holme Top St WBOW BD5 ....117 J2
Holme Wy OSS WF5 ....182 B2
Holme Well Rd MID LS10 ....143 K2
Holme Wood Rd BOW BD4 ....118 C3
HWTH BD22 ....2 B7
Holmfield Av
WKFDW/WTN WF2 ....184 C6
Holmfield Cha
EARD/LOFT WF3 ....165 J2
Holmfield Dr RHAY LS8 ....84 A3
Holmfield Gv
WKFDW/WTN WF2 ....184 C6
Holmfield La PONT WF8 ....170 A4
WKFDW/WTN WF2 ....184 C7
Holmsley Crest RTHW LS26 ....125 J7
Holmsley Field Ct RTHW LS26 ....145 K1
Holmsley Field La RTHW LS26 ....145 J1
Holmsley Garth RTHW LS26 ......125 J7
Holmsley La RTHW LS26 ....145 J1
Holmwood Av HDGY LS6 ....82 D4
Holmwood Crs HDGY LS6 ....82 D5
Holmwood Dr HDGY LS6 ....82 D4
Holmwood Gv HDGY LS6 ....82 D4
Holmwood Mt HDGY LS6 ....82 E4
Holroyd Hl WBSY BD6 ....117 H5
Holroyd St CHAL LS7 ....10 D5
Holsworthy Rd BOW BD4 ....119 F3
The Holt SHPY BD18 ....77 H5
Holt Av BHP/TINH LS16 ....62 B6
HUDN HD2 ....177 H6
Holtby Gv BRIG HD6 ....157 F1
Holt Cl BHP/TINH LS16 ....62 B7
Holt Crs BHP/TINH LS16 ....61 H6
Holtdale Ap BHP/TINH LS16 ....61 H6
Holtdale Av BHP/TINH LS16 ....61 H6
Holtdale Cl BHP/TINH LS16 ....61 J6
Holtdale Cft BHP/TINH LS16 ....61 H6
Holtdale Dr BHP/TINH LS16 ....61 H6
Holtdale Fold BHP/TINH LS16 ......61 H6
Holtdale Gdns BHP/TINH LS16 ....61 H6
Holtdale Garth BHP/TINH LS16 ...61 H6
Holtdale Gn BHP/TINH LS16 ....61 H6
Holtdale Gv BHP/TINH LS16 ....61 H6
Holtdale Lawn BHP/TINH LS16 ....61 H6
Holtdale Pl BHP/TINH LS16 ....61 H6
Holtdale Rd BHP/TINH LS16 ....61 H6
Holtdale Vw BHP/TINH LS16 ....61 H6
Holtdale Wy BHP/TINH LS16 ....61 H6
Holt Dr BHP/TINH LS16 ....61 K6
Holt Farm Cl BHP/TINH LS16 ......61 K6
Holt Farm Ri BHP/TINH LS16 ......61 H6
Holt Gdns BHP/TINH LS16 ....61 K6
IDLE BD10 ....78 A4
Holt Garth BHP/TINH LS16 ....61 K6
Holt Ga BHP/TINH LS16 ....61 K6
Holt La BHP/TINH LS16 ....61 J6
Holt Park Ap BHP/TINH LS16 ......61 K6
Holt Park Cl BHP/TINH LS16 ....61 K6
Holt Park Crs BHP/TINH LS16 .....61 K6

Holt Park Dr BHP/TINH LS16 ......61 K6
Holt Park Gdns BHP/TINH LS16 ...61 K6
Holt Park Ga BHP/TINH LS16 ......61 K6
Holt Park Gra BHP/TINH LS16 .....61 K6
Holt Park Gn BHP/TINH LS16 ......61 K6
Holt Park Gv BHP/TINH LS16 ......61 J6
Holt Park La BHP/TINH LS16 ....61 K6
Holt Park Ri BHP/TINH LS16 ....61 K6
Holt Park Rd BHP/TINH LS16 ......61 K6
Holt Park V BHP/TINH LS16 ....61 K6
Holt Park Wy BHP/TINH LS16 .....61 K6
Holt Ri BHP/TINH LS16 ....61 K6
Holt Rd BHP/TINH LS16 ....61 K6
Holts La CLAY BD14 ....116 A1
Holts Ter HIPP HX3 ....155 G4
Holt Vw BHP/TINH LS16 ....61 J6
Holt Wy BHP/TINH LS16 ....61 K6
Holybrook Av IDLE BD10 ....78 E6
Holycroft St KGHY BD21 ....2 E7
Holyoake Av BCLY BD16 ....75 J3
BTLY WF17 ....160 D3
Holyrood Crs NORM WF6 ....166 C4
Holy Rood La GFTH/SHER LS25 ..129 K6
Holywell Ash La GIR BD8 ....5 K2
Holywell Gdns CAS WF10 ....168 C2
Holywell La AL/HA/HU LS17 ....64 E6
CAS WF10 ....169 F2
Holywell Mt CAS WF10 ....169 G2
Homefield Av MOR LS27 ....141 K5
Home Lea RTHW LS26 ....124 E7
Home Lea Dr RTHW LS26 ....124 E7
The Homestead HECK WF16 ......160 B4
Homestead Dr
WKFDW/WTN WF2 ....184 A3
Home View Ter GIR BD8 ....4 E1
Honey Pot La BAIL * BD17 ....77 G1
Honeysuckle Cl
WKFDW/WTN WF2 ....183 K2
Honeysuckle Dr EARL WF12 ....181 G6
The Hoods BRIG HD6 ....176 C2
Hopbine Av WBOW BD5 ....117 K4
Hopbine Rd WBOW BD5 ....117 K4
Hope Av SHPY BD18 ....77 J4
WBOW BD5 ....117 H4
Hopefield Cha EARD/LOFT WF3 ..144 C3
Hopefield Cl RTHW LS26 ....144 C3
Hopefield Ct EARD/LOFT WF3 ....144 C3
EARD/LOFT WF3 ....163 H1
Hopefield Crs RTHW LS26 ....144 C3
Hopefield Dr EARD/LOFT WF3 ....144 C3
Hopefield Gdns
EARD/LOFT WF3 ....144 C3
Hopefield Gn RTHW LS26 ....144 C3
Hopefield Gv
EARD/LOFT * WF3 ....144 C3
Hopefield Ms
EARD/LOFT WF3 ....144 C3
Hopefield Pl RTHW LS26 ....144 C3
Hopefield Vw RTHW LS26 ....144 C3
Hopefield Wk RTHW LS26 ....144 C3
Hopefield Wy BOW BD4 ....118 C5
EARD/LOFT * WF3 ....144 C3
Hope Hall St HFAX HX1 ....17 H8
Hope Hall Ter HFAX HX1 ....17 H8
Hope Hill Vw BGLY BD16 ....75 K5
Hope La BAIL BD17 ....77 G1
Hope Pl KGHY BD21 ....2 F8
Hope Rd LDSU LS2 ....10 D8
Hopes Farm Mt RTHW * LS26 ....124 A7
Hopes Farm Rd RTHW LS26 ....124 A7
Hopes Farm Vw RTHW LS26 ......124 A7
Hope St CAS WF10 ....149 H4
DEWS WF13 ....161 F7
HFAX HX1 ....16 C5
MOR LS27 ....141 K3
NORM WF6 ....186 D1
OSS WF5 ....182 B5
RPDN/SBR HX6 ....153 K5
WKFDE WF1 ....18 C2
Hope St East CAS * WF10 ....148 C7
Hope St West CAS * WF10 ....168 B1
Hope Vw SHPY BD18 ....77 H5
Hopewell Pl HDGY * LS6 ....8 F4
Hopewell Ter GFTH/SHER LS25 ..128 A3
Hopewell Vw MID LS10 ....143 J2
Hopkinson Dr BOW BD4 ....118 D6
Hopkinson Rd HUDN HD2 ....177 C5
Hopkinson St LUD/ILL HX2 ....134 C7
Hopkin St BOW BD4 ....119 F5
Hops La HIPP HX3 ....134 B5
Hopton Av BOW BD4 ....118 C5
MIRF WF14 ....179 F7
Hopton Dr MIRF WF14 ....179 F7
Hopton La MIRF WF14 ....179 F7
Hopton Ms WOR/ARM LS12 ......102 A6
Hopton New Rd MIRF WF14 ....179 H6
Hopwood Bank HORS LS18 ....81 F2
Hopwood Cl HORS LS18 ....81 F2
Hopwood Gv CAS WF10 ....169 G1
Hopwood La HFAX HX1 ....16 A7
Hopwood Rd HORS LS18 ....81 F2
Horace Waller VC Pde
EARL WF12 ....161 K6
Horbury Ms HOR/CROF WF4 ......182 E7
Horbury Rd OSS WF5 ....182 D6
WKFDW/WTN WF2 ....18 A6
Horley Green Rd HIPP HX3 ....17 L2
Hornbeam Av
WKFDW/WTN WF2 ....18 A1
Hornbeam Cl WIL/AL BD15 ....95 J1
Hornbeam Gn PONT WF8 ....170 A7
Hornbeam Wy SCFT LS14 ....85 K4
Hornby St HFAX HX1 ....16 B9
Hornby Ter HFAX * HX1 ....16 B8
Horncastle St CLECK BD19 ....159 F1
Horner Av BTLY WF17 ....160 C2
Horner Crs BTLY WF17 ....160 C2
Horne St HFAX HX1 ....16 E5
WKFDW/WTN WF2 ....18 D8
Horn La AIRE BD20 ....20 D4
Hornsea Dr WIL/AL BD15 ....95 F1
Horse Fair PONT WF8 ....189 J1
Horsefair WBY LS22 ....29 H4
Horsfall St HFAX HX1 ....154 D3
MOR LS27 ....141 J1
Horsforth New Rd BRAM LS13 .....80 B6
Horsham Ct HWTH BD22 ....53 F6
Horsham Rd BOW * BD4 ....119 F4

Horsley St *WBSY* BD6 ....117 H5
Horsman St *BOW* BD4 ....119 F5
Horton Cl *BRAM* LS13 ....100 C1
Horton Garth *BRAM* * LS13 ...100 C1
Horton Grange Rd *GTHN* BD7 .....4 E8
Horton Hall Cl *WBOW* BD5 ....117 J1
Horton Park Av *GTHN* BD7 ......117 G1
Horton Ri *BRAM* LS13 ....100 C1
Horton St *HECK* WF16 ....160 A5
HFAX HX1 ....17 H7
OSS WF5 ....182 B3
Hospital Av *BHP/TINH* LS16 ....81 J2
Hospital Rd *AIRE* BD20 ....54 D2
Hothfield St *AIRE* BD20 ....32 E1
Hough *HIPP* HX3 ....135 K5
Hough End Av *BRAM* LS13 ......101 G4
Hough End Cl *BRAM* * LS13 .....101 G4
Hough End Ct *BRAM* LS13 ....101 G4
Hough End Crs *BRAM* LS13 .....101 F4
Hough End Gdns *BRAM* LS13 ...101 G4
Hough End Garth *BRAM* LS13 ...101 G4
Hough End La *BRAM* LS13 ......101 F3
Hough Gv *BRAM* LS13 ....101 F3
Hough La *BRAM* LS13 ....101 F3
Houghley Av *WOR/ARM* LS12 ...101 J3
Houghley Cl *BRAM* LS13 ....101 H3
Houghley Crs *WOR/ARM* LS12 ..101 H3
Houghley La *BRAM* LS13 ....101 H3
Houghley Pl *WOR/ARM* LS12 ....101 J3
Houghley Rd *WOR/ARM* LS12 ...101 J3
Houghley Sq *WOR/ARM* LS12 ...101 J3
Hough Side Cl *PDSY/CALV* LS28 .100 E6
Hough Side La
  PDSY/CALV LS28 ....100 D6
Hough Side Rd
  PDSY/CALV LS28 ....100 D6
Hough Ter *BRAM* LS13 ....101 F3
Houghton Av *KNOT* WF11 ....170 C4
Houghton Pl *BFD* BD1 ....5 K4
Houghton St *BRIG* HD6 ....157 G5
Hough Top *BRAM* LS13 ....100 D5
Hough Tree Rd *BRAM* LS13 .....101 F3
Hoults La *GTL/HWG* HX4 ....174 E1
Houndhill La *FEA/AMT* WF7 .....188 E5
Hovingham Av *RHAY* * LS8 ....11 J1
Hovingham Gv *RHAY* LS8 ....11 K1
Hovingham Mt *RHAY* LS8 ....11 J1
Hovingham Ter *RHAY* LS8 ....11 J1
Howard Av *MSTN/BAR* LS15 .....105 G6
Howard Ct *MSTN/BAR* LS15 .....105 G6
Howard Pl *BTLY* WF17 ....161 F1
Howards Dean *HWTH* BD22 ......72 E3
Howard St *BTLY* WF17 ....161 F5
HFAX HX1 ....16 C4
OSS * WF5 ....182 C2
WBOW BD5 ....5 K8
WKFDE WF1 ....18 E2
Howarth Av *ECHL* BD2 ....78 B7
Howarth Crs *ECHL* * BD2 ....78 B7
Howarth Pl *CHAL* LS7 ....10 B6
Howbeck Av *AIRE* BD20 ....54 D2
Howbeck Dr *AIRE* BD20 ....54 D3
Howcans La *HIPP* HX3 ....134 D3
Howden Av *AIRE* BD20 ....53 H1
Howdenbrook *HIPP* HX3 ....116 C7
Howden Clough Rd *MOR* LS27 ...141 F4
Howden Gdns *HDGY* LS6 ....8 F5
Howden Pl *HDGY* LS6 ....8 F4
Howden Rd *AIRE* BD20 ....33 G1
Howden Wy *WKFDE* WF1 ....19 J5
Howes La *HIPP* HX3 ....135 J4
Howgate *IDLE* BD10 ....78 D4
Howgate Hl *HIPP* HX3 ....155 J3
Howgill Gn *WBSY* BD6 ....137 F1
Howley Mill La *BTLY* WF17 ......161 G1
Howley Park Cl *MOR* LS27 ....141 J5
Howley Park Rd *MOR* LS27 ......141 J5
Howley Park Rd East
  MOR LS27 ....141 K6
Howley St *BTLY* WF17 ....161 G2
Howley Wk *BTLY* WF17 ....161 H3
Howroyd La *GTL/HWG* HX4 ......173 J5
Howroyd's Yd *OSS* WF5 ....162 B7
Howson Cl *GSLY* LS20 ....59 G3
Hoxton Mt *BEE/HOL* LS11 ....13 C9
Hoxton St *GIR* BD8 ....4 C3
Hoylake Av *HUDN* HD2 ....176 E6
Hoyle Court Av *BAIL* BD17 ....77 K1
Hoyle Court Dr *BAIL* BD17 ....77 K1
Hoyle Court Rd *BAIL* BD17 ....77 K1
Hoyle Fold *HWTH* BD22 ....2 A8
Hoyle Ing Rd *CUL/QBY* BD13 .....95 J7
Hubberton Green Rd
  RPDN/SBR HX6 ....152 D5
Hubert St *BFDE* BD3 ....6 F8
  LUD/ILL * HX2 ....154 A1
Huddersfield Rd *BRIG* HD6 ......157 G6
BTLY WF17 ....160 B1
DEWS WF13 ....180 A4
ELL HX5 ....155 G7
ELL HX5 ....175 J2
HUDW HD3 ....175 K5
LM/WK BD12 ....137 G5
MIRF WF14 ....159 G2
MIRF WF14 ....178 E3
Huddleston Ct *EARL* WF12 ......181 J1
Hud Hl *HIPP* HX3 ....136 A3
The Hudson *LM/WK* BD12 ....137 H4
Hudson Av *GTHN* BD7 ....117 G3
Hudson Cl *GTHN* BD7 ....117 G3
  TAD LS24 ....50 E5
  WBY LS22 ....29 H4
Hudson Crs *GTHN* BD7 ....117 G3
Hudson Gdns *GTHN* BD7 ....117 G2
Hudson Gv *OSM* LS9 ....11 K6
Hudson Ms *BSPA/BRAM* LS23 ....48 D3
Hudson Pl *OSM* LS9 ....11 K6
Hudson Rd *OSM* LS9 ....11 K5
Hudson St *BFDE* BD3 ....7 J6
  OSM LS9 ....11 K6
  PDSY/CALV * LS28 ....100 A4
Hudson Vw *TAD* LS24 ....50 E5
Hudson Wy *TAD* LS24 ....50 E5
Hudswell Rd *MID* LS10 ....14 C7
Hudswell St *WKFDE* WF1 ....185 F6
Hughenden Vw *MOR* * LS27 .....141 K1
Hughendon Dr *CUL/QBY* BD13 ...95 K7

Hughendon Wk *CUL/QBY* BD13 ....95 K7
Hugh St *CAS* WF10 ....168 C1
Hugill St *CUL/QBY* BD13 ....95 G7
Hulbert St *BGLY* BD16 ....75 K2
Hullenedge Gdns *ELL* HX5 ......175 G3
Hullenedge La *GTL/HWG* HX4 ...175 G3
Hullenedge Rd *ELL* HX5 ....175 H3
Hullen Rd *ELL* HX5 ....175 G3
Hullett Cl *HBR* HX7 ....132 A6
Hullett Dr *HBR* HX7 ....132 A6
Hull St *MOR* LS27 ....142 A3
Hulme Sq *CAS* WF10 ....149 J6
Humboldt St *BFD* BD1 ....6 C3
Hume Crest *BTLY* WF17 ....161 F3
Hundhill La *PONT* WF8 ....189 J7
Hungate Cl *TAD* LS24 ....90 B6
Hungate La *RTHW* LS26 ....146 C6
Hungate La *GFTH/SHER* LS25 ...111 F5
Hunger Hl *HFAX* HX1 ....17 H8
  ILK LS29 ....24 B2
  MOR LS27 ....141 K4
Hunger Hills Av *HORS* LS18 ......80 D3
Hunger Hills Dr *HORS* LS18 ......80 D3
Hunslet Green Wy *MID* LS10 .....14 C7
Hunslet Hall Rd *BEE/HOL* LS11 ..13 L7
Hunslet La *MID* LS10 ....14 B3
Hunslet Rd *MID* LS10 ....14 B3
Hunsworth La *BIRK/DRI* BD11 ..139 F1
  CLECK BD19 ....138 E6
Hunter Hill Rd *LUD/ILL* HX2 .....133 H2
Huntercombe Ct *BGLY* BD16 .....56 C6
Hunters Ct *HTON* BD9 ....96 B1
Hunters Gn *CUL/QBY* BD13 ......74 A5
Hunters Meadow *AIRE* BD20 .....21 F7
Hunters Park Av *CLAY* BD14 ....116 C1
Hunters Wk *WBY* LS22 ....29 H2
Huntington Av *HUDN* HD2 ....178 A4
Huntingdon Rd *BRIC* HD2 ....157 H7
Huntock Pl *BRIC* HD6 ....156 E3
Huntsman Fold
  WKFDW/WTN WF2 ....183 J3
Huntsmans Cl *BGLY* BD16 ....56 B6
  KGHY BD21 ....2 D3
Hunt St *CAS* WF10 ....148 A7
  CAS WF10 ....148 C7
Huntwick Av *FEA/AMT* WF7 .....188 B5
Huntwick Crs *FEA/AMT* WF7 ....188 A5
Huntwick Dr *FEA/AMT* WF7 .....188 A5
Huntwick La *FEA/AMT* WF7 .....187 J6
Huntwick Rd *FEA/AMT* WF7 ....188 B5
Hurricane Cl *GFTH/SHER* LS25 ..111 K6
Hurst La *MIRF* WF14 ....179 J3
Hurstville Av *BIRK/DRI* BD11 ...139 G1
Hurstwood *HUDN* HD2 ....177 K5
Husler Gv *OSM* LS9 ....10 C3
Husler Pl *CHAL* LS7 ....10 C3
The Hustings *LVSG* * WF15 ......159 H4
Hustlergate *BFD* BD1 ....5 M6
Hustlers Rw *HDGY* LS6 ....82 D4
Hustler St *BFDE* BD3 ....6 E2
Hutchinson's Pl *KSTL* LS5 ......101 K2
Hutson St *WBOW* BD5 ....117 J2
Hutton Dr *HECK* WF16 ....160 B4
Hutton Rd *WBOW* BD5 ....117 H4
Hutton Ter *IDLE* BD10 ....78 E7
  PDSY/CALV LS28 ....100 B6
Hydale Cl *KGHY* BD21 ....3 L8
Hydale Ct *LM/WK* BD12 ....137 H1
Hyde Gv *KGHY* BD21 ....3 J2
Hyde Pk *HFAX* HX1 ....16 D8
Hyde Park Cl *HDGY* LS6 ....9 G4
Hyde Park Cnr *HDGY* LS6 ....9 H2
Hyde Park Pl *HDGY* LS6 ....9 H2
Hyde Park Rd *HDGY* LS6 ....9 H2
  HFAX HX1 ....16 C9
Hyde Park St *HFAX* HX1 ....16 D8
Hyde Park Ter *HDGY* LS6 ....9 H2
Hyde Pl *LDSU* LS2 ....9 J7
Hyde St *IDLE* BD10 ....78 C3
  LDSU LS2 ....9 J7
Hyde Ter *LDSU* LS2 ....9 J6
Hydro Cl *ILK* LS29 ....24 E4
Hyne Av *BOW* BD4 ....118 D5
Hyrst Garth *BTLY* WF17 ....160 E4
Hyrstlands Rd *BTLY* WF17 ......160 E5
Hyrst Wk *BTLY* WF17 ....161 F5

I

Ibbetson Cl *MOR* LS27 ....121 K7
Ibbetson Ct *MOR* LS27 ....121 K7
Ibbetson Cft *MOR* LS27 ....121 K7
Ibbetson Dr *MOR* LS27 ....121 K7
Ibbetson Ov *MOR* LS27 ....121 K7
Ibbetson Ri *MOR* LS27 ....121 K7
Ibbetson Rd *MOR* LS27 ....121 K7
Ibbetson St *MOR* LS27 ....121 K7
Ibbottson St *WKFDE* WF1 ....185 G6
Ida St *MID* LS10 ....124 B4
  WBOW BD5 ....117 H3
Iddesleigh St *BOW* BD4 ....7 H8
Idlecroft Rd *IDLE* BD10 ....78 C4
Idle Rd *ECHL* BD2 ....78 B7
Idlethorp Wy *IDLE* BD10 ....78 D5
Ilbert Av *BOW* BD4 ....118 D5
Ilford St *MOR* LS27 ....142 A3
Ilkersley Rd *BFD* BD1 ....5 G1
The Innings *IDLE* BD10 ....78 B4
Institute Rd *ECHL* BD2 ....78 D7
The Intake *GFTH/SHER* LS25 ...128 A5
Intake Cl *EARD/LOFT* WF3 ......165 C3
Intake Gv *ECHL* BD2 ....98 D3
Intake La *AIRE* BD20 ....32 B6
  BRAM LS13 ....100 C3
  BTLY WF17 ....140 C7
  EARD/LOFT WF3 ....165 G4
  MID LS10 ....143 H4
  OSS WF5 ....182 D4
  SCFT LS14 ....86 A1
  YEA LS19 ....80 A1
Intake Mt *MID* LS10 ....143 H3
Intake Rd *ECHL* BD2 ....98 D3
  PDSY/CALV LS28 ....100 D5
Intake Sq *MID* LS10 ....143 H4
Intake Ter *ECHL* BD2 ....7 H1
Intake Vw *MID* LS10 ....143 H4
Intercity Wy *PDSY/CALV* LS28 ..100 D4
Intermezzo Dr *MID* LS10 ....124 C5

Independent St *WBOW* BD5 .....117 H3
Indus Cl *HECK* WF16 ....160 B4
Industrial Av *BTLY* * WF17 ......140 A6
Industrial Rd *RPDN/SBR* HX6 ...153 J4
Industrial St *BGLY* BD16 ....75 J1
  BRIG HD6 ....157 G5
  CLECK BD19 ....138 A7
  HWTH BD22 ....73 F4
  LVSG WF15 ....159 F4
  OSM LS9 ....11 G6
  WKFDE * WF1 ....18 F3
Industrial Ter *HFAX* HX1 ....154 E3
Infirmary Rd *DEWS* WF13 ....160 E7
Infirmary St *BFD* BD1 ....5 K5
  LDS LS1 ....9 M9
The Ings *BRIG* HD6 ....157 F2
Ing Fld *LM/WK* BD12 ....138 B3
Ingfield Av *OSS* WF5 ....182 D3
Ingham Cl *LUD/ILL* HX2 ....114 C6
Ingham Cft *MIRF* WF14 ....179 K5
Ingham Garth *MIRF* WF14 ....179 K4
Ingham La *LUD/ILL* HX2 ....114 B7
Ingham Rd *EARL* WF12 ....181 G6
Ingham's Av *PDSY/CALV* LS28 ...99 J5
Inghams Ct *HIPP* * HX3 ....16 D1
Inghams Ter *PDSY/CALV* LS28 ...99 J5
Ingham St *MID* LS10 ....14 D5
Ingham's Vw *PDSY/CALV* LS28 ...99 J5
Inghead Gdns *HIPP* HX3 ....136 A3
Ingle Av *MOR* LS27 ....141 J1
Ingleborough Cl *BOW* BD4 ......119 F3
Ingleborough Dr *MOR* LS27 ....142 B5
Ingleby Dr *TAD* LS24 ....50 E6
Ingleby Pl *GTHN* BD7 ....4 D7
Ingleby Rd *GIR* BD8 ....4 D5
Ingleby St *GIR* BD8 ....4 D5
Ingledew Cl *AL/HA/HU* LS17 .....63 J7
Ingledew Crs *RHAY* LS8 ....84 C2
Ingledew Dr *RHAY* LS8 ....84 C3
Ingle Gv *MOR* LS27 ....141 J2
Ingle Rw *CHAL* LS7 ....83 H6
Ingleton Cl *BEE/HOL* LS11 ......123 G4
Ingleton Dr *MSTN/BAR* LS15 ...105 F6
Ingleton Gv *BEE/HOL* LS11 .....123 G4
Ingleton Pl *BEE/HOL* LS11 ......123 G3
Ingleton St *BEE/HOL* LS11 ......123 G5
Inglewood Dr *OT* LS21 ....39 C3
  SCFT LS14 ....85 J2
Inglewood Pl *SCFT* LS14 ....105 J2
Inglewood Ter *HDGY* * LS6 ....9 K1
Ingram Cl *BEE/HOL* LS11 ....13 H5
Ingram Ct *BEE/HOL* LS11 ....13 H5
Ingram Crs *BEE/HOL* * LS11 .....13 C7
  KNOT WF11 ....170 E5
Ingram Gdns *BEE/HOL* LS11 .....13 H5
Ingram Pde *RTHW* LS26 ....145 F2
Ingram Rd *BEE/HOL* LS11 ....13 H7
Ingram Rw *BEE/HOL* LS11 ....13 M4
Ingram Sq *HFAX* HX1 ....154 D1
Ingram St *BEE/HOL* LS11 ....13 M4
  HFAX HX1 ....154 D3
  KGHY BD21 ....73 J1
Ingram Vw *BEE/HOL* LS11 ....13 H6
Ingrow Br *KGHY* * BD21 ....53 J7
Ingrow La *HWTH* BD22 ....53 G7
Ings Av *GSLY* LS20 ....58 E1
Ings Ct *GSLY* LS20 ....58 D1
Ings Crs *EARL* WF12 ....181 F7
  GSLY LS20 ....58 D2
  LVSG WF15 ....159 J4
  OSM LS9 ....15 L1
Ings Dr *RTHW* LS26 ....147 H4
Ings La *BSPA/BRAM* LS23 ....49 F2
  CAS WF10 ....148 C4
  CAS WF10 ....148 E6
  EARL WF12 ....181 F7
  GSLY LS20 ....58 D1
  TAD LS24 ....50 B2
Ings Mere Ct *KNOT* WF11 ....150 B3
Ings Rd *AIRE* BD20 ....32 C3
  BTLY WF17 ....160 E2
  EARL WF12 ....161 H7
  HECK WF16 ....160 A4
  LVSG WF15 ....159 J3
  OSM LS9 ....15 M1
  WKFDE WF1 ....18 D6
Ing St *BFDE* BD3 ....7 K6
Ings Vw *CAS* WF10 ....149 C7
  RTHW LS26 ....147 H4
Ings Vil *LVSG* WF15 ....159 K6
Ings Wy *AIRE* BD20 ....33 C2
  GIR BD8 ....96 D5
Ingthorns La *GFTH/SHER* LS25 .131 H5
Ingthorpe La *GFTH/SHER* LS25 .131 H6
Ingthorpe Wy
  GFTH/SHER LS25 ....131 H5
Ingwell Ct *WKFDE* WF1 ....19 G5
Ingwell St *WKFDE* WF1 ....19 G5
Ingwell Ter *CLECK* BD19 ....159 F1
Inholmes La *TAD* LS24 ....31 H5
  TAD LS24 ....50 C7
Inkerman St *BOW* BD4 ....118 E2
  ECHL BD2 ....98 E1
Imperial Av *WKFDW/WTN* WF2 .164 A6
The Incline *HIPP* HX3 ....17 K4

Invargarry Cl *GFTH/SHER* LS25 .108 A5
Inverness Rd *GFTH/SHER* LS25 .108 A4
Invertrees Av *YEA* LS19 ....59 K7
Iona Pl *HIPP* HX3 ....134 E5
Iona St *HIPP* HX3 ....16 E1
Iqbal Ct *BFDE* BD3 ....7 K6
Ireland Crs *BHP/TINH* LS16 ......81 J1
Ireland St *BGLY* BD16 ....75 H1
Ireland Ter *BGLY* BD16 ....75 H1
Ireton St *GTHN* BD7 ....4 E7
Ireton St *CLECK* BD19 ....158 D1
Iron Rw *ILK* LS29 ....38 C1
Iron St *CLECK* BD19 ....158 D1
Ironwood Ap *SCFT* LS14 ....105 H2
Ironwood Crs *SCFT* LS14 ....105 H1
Ironwood Vw *SCFT* LS14 ....105 H1
Irving St *HFAX* HX1 ....16 A9
Irving Ter *CLAY* BD14 ....116 B3
Irwell St *BOW* BD4 ....118 B1
Irwin Ap *MSTN/BAR* LS15 ......105 G6
Irwin Av *WKFDE* WF1 ....19 K2
Irwin Crs *WKFDE* WF1 ....19 K2
Irwin St *PDSY/CALV* LS28 ......100 A3
Isaac St *GIR* BD8 ....4 E4
Islay Cl *RTHW* LS26 ....145 K2
Isles St *GIR* BD8 ....4 B4
Ivanhoe Rd *GTHN* BD7 ....117 G1
Ivegate *BFD* BD1 ....5 M6
  YEA LS19 ....59 J4
Ive House La *LUD/ILL* HX2 ....133 F7
Iver Wy *SHPY* BD18 ....77 F5
Iveson Ap *BHP/TINH* LS16 ....81 K2
Iveson Cl *BHP/TINH* LS16 ....81 J2
Iveson Ct *BHP/TINH* LS16 ....81 J2
Iveson Crs *BHP/TINH* LS16 ......81 J2
Iveson Dr *BHP/TINH* LS16 ....81 J2
Iveson Gdns *BHP/TINH* LS16 ....81 J2
Iveson Garth *BHP/TINH* LS16 ...81 K2
Iveson Gn *BHP/TINH* LS16 ....81 J2
Iveson Gv *BHP/TINH* LS16 ....81 J2
Iveson Lawn *BHP/TINH* LS16 ....81 K2
Iveson Ri *BHP/TINH* LS16 ....81 K2
Iveson Rd *BHP/TINH* LS16 ....81 J2
Ives St *BAIL* BD17 ....77 C4
Ivory St *BEE/HOL* LS11 ....14 B5
Ivy Av *OSM* LS9 ....11 L9
Ivy Bank La *HWTH* BD22 ....72 D6
Ivy Cha *BRAM* LS13 ....100 E6
Ivy Cl *WKFDE* WF1 ....19 J1
Ivy Crs *HIPP* HX3 ....156 D1
  OSM LS9 ....11 K9
Ivy Gdns *BRAM* LS13 ....101 G1
  CAS WF10 ....169 J3
Ivy Garth *CHAL* LS7 ....83 J6
Ivy Gv *OSM* LS9 ....11 L9
  SHPY BD18 ....76 D5
  WKFDE WF1 ....19 J1
Ivy House Rd *WBOW* BD5 ....117 K5
Ivy La *BSPA/BRAM* LS23 ....48 B2
  LUD/ILL HX2 ....134 A1
  WIL/AL BD15 ....95 K4
  WKFDE WF1 ....19 J1
Ivy Mt *OSM* LS9 ....11 L9
Ivy Pl *BRAM* LS13 ....101 G1
Ivy Rd *KGHY* BD21 ....3 M6
  OSM LS9 ....15 K1
  SHPY BD18 ....76 D5
Ivy St *BRIG* HD6 ....156 E5
  FEA/AMT WF7 ....188 C3
  HFAX HX1 ....154 D3
  KGHY BD21 ....2 F3
  OSM LS9 ....11 K9
Ivy Ter *BRIG* HD6 ....156 E5
  HIPP HX3 ....156 D1
  KGHY BD21 ....54 C5
Ivy Vw *OSM* LS9 ....11 L9

J

Jacana Wy *CUL/QBY* BD13 ......116 B5
Jacinth Ct *HUDN* HD2 ....177 H7
Jackdaw La *BSPA/BRAM* LS23 ...48 B2
Jackie Smart Ct *CHAL* LS7 ....10 C2
Jackie Smart Rd *WBOW* BD5 ...117 K2
Jack La *BEE/HOL* LS11 ....13 L5
  DEWS WF13 ....161 G4
  MID LS10 ....14 C6
Jackman Dr *HORS* LS18 ....81 G5
Jackroyd La *MIRF* WF14 ....179 F7
Jackson Av *RHAY* LS8 ....84 A5
Jackson Hill La *CUL/QBY* BD13 .115 J7
Jackson La *GTL/HWG* HX4 ......173 H4
Jackson Rd *CHAL* LS7 ....10 C3
Jackson Mdw *GTL/HWG* HX4 ...173 H4
Jackson's La *EARL* WF12 ....180 D7
Jackson St *BFDE* BD3 ....6 D8
Jacky La *HWTH* BD22 ....72 D6
Jacobs La *HWTH* BD22 ....72 E4
Jacob St *LDSU* LS2 ....10 B7
  WBOW BD5 ....117 J2
Jacob's Well La *WKFDE* WF1 .....18 F3
Jacques Gv *AIRE* BD20 ....33 G1
Jagger Green La *HUDW* HD3 ...174 H4
Jail Rd *BTLY* WF17 ....160 C3
Jakeman Cl *EARD/LOFT* WF3 ...142 D7
Jakeman Ct *EARD/LOFT* WF3 ...142 D7
Jakeman Dr *EARD/LOFT* WF3 ...142 D7
James Av *AIRE* BD20 ....32 B5
  RHAY LS8 ....84 A4
James Cl *GFTH/SHER* LS25 .....107 K6
James Ct *WBY* LS22 ....46 E2
James Duggan Av
  FEA/AMT WF7 ....188 B3
James Ga *BFD* BD1 ....5 L6
James Gibbs Cl
  FEA/AMT * WF7 ....188 C3
James St *BFD* BD1 ....5 L5
  BIRK/DRI * BD11 ....139 H1
  BRIG HD6 ....157 F4
  BTLY WF17 ....160 E4
  CAS WF10 ....148 C6
  CUL/QBY BD13 ....94 A5
  CUL/QBY BD13 ....95 G7
  DEWS WF13 ....181 F6
  DEWS WF13 ....160 E7
  ELL HX5 ....175 J3
  GTL/HWG HX4 ....175 F1
  HDGY LS6 ....8 F3
  HECK * WF16 ....160 A5
  HFAX HX1 ....17 G6
  HWTH BD22 ....72 E2
  SHPY BD18 ....77 F4
  WKFDE WF1 ....19 H5
  YEA LS19 ....59 J7
John St West *RPDN/SBR* HX6 ..153 J4
John William St *CLECK* BD19 ...138 E7
  ELL HX5 ....175 J3
  LVSG WF15 ....159 K4
Jonathan Garth *ILK* * LS29 ......22 B5
Joseph Av *HIPP* HX3 ....135 K5
Joseph St *BFD* BD1 ....6 C6
  BOW BD4 ....119 F5
  MID LS10 ....14 E7
Josephs Well *LDS* * LS1 ....9 K8
Jowett Park Crs *IDLE* BD10 ......78 B2
Jowett's La *AIRE* BD20 ....20 E1
Jowett St *BFD* BD1 ....5 H1
Jubilee Av *NORM* WF6 ....186 D5
  WKFDE WF1 ....19 H5
Jubilee Ct *SHPY* * BD18 ....77 H4
Jubilee Crs *HOR/CROF* WF4 ....186 E6

MIRF WF14 ....179 H2
WIL/AL BD15 ....96 B4
YEA LS19 ....59 J7
Jamie Ct *IDLE* BD10 ....78 E6
Jane St *CUL/QBY* BD13 ....94 A4
  SHPY BD18 ....76 E4
Janesway *GFTH/SHER* LS25 ....127 J4
Janet St *HWTH* BD22 ....73 F4
Jaques Cl *HDGY* LS6 ....102 A1
Jardine Av *FEA/AMT* WF7 ......188 C3
Jardine Rd *BGLY* BD16 ....75 K1
Jarratt St *GIR* BD8 ....4 D2
Jarrom Cl *BOW* BD4 ....118 E2
Jarvis Sq *EARD/LOFT* WF3 .....144 B4
Jarvis Wk *EARD/LOFT* WF3 ....144 B4
Jasmin Ter *GIR* BD8 ....4 F3
Jason Ter *BTLY* * WF17 ....140 D5
Jasper St *HFAX* HX1 ....16 B6
  IDLE BD10 ....78 C4
Javelin Cl *IDLE* BD10 ....78 C6
Jay House La *BRIG* HD6 ....157 J3
Jay St *HWTH* BD22 ....72 E6
Jean Av *MSTN/BAR* LS15 ....105 H6
Jenkinson Cl *BEE/HOL* LS11 .....13 K5
Jenkinson Lawn *BEE/HOL* LS11 .13 K6
Jenkinsons Pl *MID* LS10 ....123 J6
Jennette St *BTLY* WF17 ....161 F6
Jennetts Crs *OT* LS21 ....39 C3
Jennings Cl *AIRE* BD20 ....33 F2
Jennings Pl *GTHN* BD7 ....117 F2
Jennings St *GTHN* BD7 ....117 F2
Jenny La *BAIL* BD17 ....57 J7
  MIRF WF14 ....179 J2
Jensen Av *DEWS* WF13 ....160 C5
Jepson La *ELL* HX5 ....175 J3
Jeremy La *HECK* WF16 ....160 A4
Jer Gv *WBSY* BD6 ....116 D4
Jer La *WBSY* BD6 ....116 D4
Jermyn St *BFDE* BD3 ....6 A5
Jerry Clay Dr
  WKFDW/WTN WF2 ....163 K6
Jerry Clay La
  WKFDW/WTN WF2 ....163 J5
Jerry Fields Rd *LUD/ILL* HX2 ...152 K2
Jerry La *AIRE* BD20 ....34 C1
  RPDN/SBR HX6 ....153 H5
Jersey Cl *EARL* WF12 ....161 J6
Jerusalem La *LUD/ILL* HX2 .....132 E3
Jervaulx Cl *BSPA/BRAM* LS23 ...48 D3
Jervaulx Crs *GIR* BD8 ....5 H5
Jerwood Hill Cl *HIPP* HX3 ....17 K2
Jerwood Hill Rd *HIPP* HX3 ....17 K2
Jesmond Av *HTON* BD9 ....96 E3
Jesmond Gv *DEWS* WF13 ....160 E7
  HTON BD9 ....96 E3
Jessamine Av *BEE/HOL* LS11 ...122 E5
Jessamine St *DEWS* WF13 ......180 A4
Jesse St *GIR* BD8 ....96 C6
  WBOW BD5 ....117 K1
Jessop St *CAS* WF10 ....148 C7
  WKFDW/WTN WF2 ....18 E9
Jewitt La *WBY* LS22 ....47 F3
Jew La *HWTH* BD22 ....92 D3
Jilley Royd La *HUDN* HD2 ....177 F5
Jill La *MIRF* WF14 ....179 K2
Jim Allen La *LUD/ILL* HX2 ....132 D6
Jinnah Ct *GIR* BD8 ....5 J3
Jinny Moor La *RTHW* LS26 .....126 B6
Jin-whin Hl *CAS* WF10 ....147 J7
Joan Royd *HECK* WF16 ....160 A2
Joba Av *BFDE* BD3 ....6 F6
Joffre Av *CAS* WF10 ....168 D2
John Booth Cl *LVSG* WF15 ......159 G6
John Carr Av *HOR/CROF* WF4 ..183 F7
John Charles Wy
  WOR/ARM LS12 ....12 C8
John Escritt Rd *BGLY* BD16 ......75 J4
John Naylor La *LUD/ILL* HX2 ...153 F3
John Nelson Cl *BTLY* * WF17 ...140 C4
John O'Gaunts Wk *RTHW* LS26 .145 C1
John Ormsby VC Wy
  EARL WF12 ....161 K5
Johns Av *EARD/LOFT* WF3 .....164 D2
John's Crs *WKFDW/WTN* WF2 .163 K6
Johns La *ELL* HX5 ....175 J5
Johnson St *BFDE* BD3 ....7 J1
  BGLY BD16 ....75 J1
  MIRF WF14 ....179 G6
Johnson Ter *MOR* LS27 ....142 A3
Johnston St *HDGY* LS6 ....9 L2
  WKFDE WF1 ....19 H5
John St *BFD* BD1 ....5 L5
  BOW BD4 ....119 F5
  BRIG HD6 ....157 F5
  BTLY WF17 ....140 E4
  CAS WF10 ....168 B2
  CLAY BD14 ....116 B2
  CUL/QBY BD13 ....94 A5
  CUL/QBY BD13 ....95 G7
  DEWS WF13 ....181 F6
  DEWS WF13 ....160 E7
  ELL HX5 ....175 J3
  GTL/HWG HX4 ....175 F1
  HDGY LS6 ....8 F3
  HECK * WF16 ....160 A5
  HFAX HX1 ....17 G6
  HWTH BD22 ....72 E2
  SHPY BD18 ....77 F4
  WKFDE WF1 ....19 H5
  YEA LS19 ....59 J7

WKFDE WF1 ....164 D4
Jubilee Cft BIRK/DRI BD11 ....120 C7
Jubilee Dr KGHY BD21 ....2 C9
Jubilee Pl MOR LS27 ....142 A3
Jubilee Rd HIPP HX3 ....155 C6
HOR/CROF WF4 ....186 E6
Jubilee St GIR BD8 ....5 K2
HIPP HX3 ....17 K8
MOR LS27 ....142 A3
Jubilee St North HIPP HX3 ....134 D3
Jubilee Ter HIPP * HX3 ....17 K8
MOR LS27 ....142 A3
RPDN/SBR HX6 ....173 F3
Jubilee Trees ILK LS29 ....37 H3
Jubilee Wy PONT WF8 ....189 H1
SHPY BD18 ....77 J4
Judy La HUDN HD2 ....177 C6
Julian Dr CUL/OBY BD13 ....116 B4
Jumb Beck Cl ILK LS29 ....38 A2
Jumble Dyke BRIG HD6 ....176 E1
Jumbles Ct EARD/LOFT WF3 ....144 D6
Jumbles La EARD/LOFT WF3 ....144 D6
Jumples LUD/ILL HX2 ....134 A3
Jumples Cl LUD/ILL HX2 ....134 A3
Junction La OSS WF5 ....183 F5
Junction Rd BAIL BD17 ....77 H4
DEWS WF13 ....180 E2
Junction St MID LS10 ....14 B4
June St KGHY BD21 ....3 H2
Juniper Av RTHW LS26 ....126 A3
Juniper Cl GIR * BD8 ....4 D7
Juniper Pl OSM LS9 ....11 L6

K

Karnac Rd RHAY LS8 ....11 H1
Katherine St SHPY BD18 ....76 E4
Katrina Gv FEA/AMT WF7 ....188 C6
Kaycell St BOW BD4 ....118 C4
Kay Cl MOR LS27 ....121 J7
Kaye St EARL WF12 ....181 C3
HECK WF16 ....160 A5
Kay St HTON BD9 ....77 H7
WKFDE WF1 ....19 H5
Keats Cl PONT WF8 ....169 J6
Keats Dr HECK WF16 ....160 B6
Keats Gv EARD/LOFT WF3 ....165 F2
Kebble Ct CLECK BD19 ....159 J1
Keble Garth GFTH/SHER LS25 ...128 B5
Kebroyd La RPDN/SBR HX6 .....173 F2
Kebroyd Mt RPDN/SBR HX6 ....173 F2
Kedleston Rd RHAY LS8 ....84 A1
Keelam Dr YEA LS19 ....59 K7
Keelham La AIRE BD20 ....53 D3
Keel Moorings BRAM LS13 ....80 C7
Keeper La BOW BD4 ....120 A3
Keeton St OSM LS9 ....11 C9
Keighley Cl LUD/ILL HX2 ....134 A1
Keighley Dr LUD/ILL HX2 ....134 B3
Keighley Pl PDSY/CALV LS28 ....100 B3
Keighley Rd AIRE BD20 ....32 E3
BGLY BD16 ....55 H5
BGLY BD16 ....74 D1
CUL/OBY BD13 ....74 A4
CUL/OBY BD13 ....94 A2
HTON BD9 ....97 H2
HWTH BD22 ....73 F1
HWTH BD22 ....92 D2
ILK LS29 ....35 H2
LUD/ILL HX2 ....114 A5
LUD/ILL HX2 ....134 B2
Keir Hardy Cl LVSG * WF15 ......159 J4
Kelburn Gv HWTH BD22 ....72 C1
Kelcbar Cl TAD LS24 ....50 B6
Kelcbar Hl TAD LS24 ....50 B6
Kelcbar Wy TAD LS24 ....50 C6
Kelcliffe Av GSLY LS20 ....59 F2
Kelcliffe La GSLY LS20 ....58 E1
Keldholme Cl BRAM LS13 ....80 C7
Keldholme Rd BRAM * LS13 ......80 C7
Keldregate HUDN HD2 ....177 K5
Kell Beck OT LS21 ....27 C7
Kellett Av WOR/ARM LS12 ....12 A4
Kellett Crs WOR/ARM LS12 ......12 A4
Kellett Dr WOR/ARM LS12 ....12 A4
Kellett Gv WOR/ARM LS12 ....12 A6
Kellett La WOR/ARM LS12 ......122 A1
Kellett Mt WOR/ARM LS12 ....12 B7
Kellett Pl WOR/ARM LS12 ....12 B7
Kellett Rd WOR/ARM LS12 ......122 A1
Kellett Ter WOR/ARM LS12 ....12 A4
Kellett Wk WOR/ARM LS12 ......12 A6
Kell La HIPP HX3 ....135 J5
LUD/ILL HX2 ....133 F1
Kelloe St CLECK BD19 ....138 D6
Kell St BGLY BD16 ....75 K1
Kelmore Gv WBSY BD6 ....136 D1
Kelmscott Av MSTN/BAR LS15 ..106 A2
Kelmscott Crs MSTN/BAR LS15 .106 A2
Kelmscott Gdns
 MSTN/BAR LS15 ....106 B2
Kelmscott Garth
 MSTN/BAR LS15 ....106 B2
Kelmscott Gn MSTN/BAR LS15 ..106 A2
Kelmscott La MSTN/BAR LS15 ...106 A2
Kelsall Av HDGY LS6 ....8 F5
Kelsall Gv HDGY LS6 ....8 F6
Kelsall Pl HDGY LS6 ....8 F5
Kelsall Rd HDGY LS6 ....8 F5
Kelsall Ter HDGY LS6 ....8 F5
Kelsey St HFAX HX1 ....16 B4
Kelso Gdns LDSU LS2 ....9 H6
Kelso Pl LDSU LS2 ....9 H5
Kelso Rd LDSU LS2 ....9 H5
Kelso St LDSU LS2 ....9 G5
Kelvin Av LUD/ILL HX2 ....154 A1
Kelvin Crs LUD/ILL HX2 ....154 A1
Kelvin Hl ELL HX5 ....175 H3
Kelvin Wy ECHL BD2 ....98 D3
Kemp's Br WKFDW/WTN WF2 ...18 A6
Kempton Rd GFTH/SHER LS25 ..127 K4
Kemsing Wk MSTN/BAR LS15 ...106 C2
Ken Churchill Dr
 HOR/CROF WF4 ....183 F7

Kendal Bank BVRD LS3 ....9 H7
Kendal Cl BVRD LS3 ....9 H7
CAS WF10 ....169 K1
Kendal Cft CAS WF10 ....169 K1
Kendal Dr CAS WF10 ....149 J7
HOR/CROF WF4 ....185 K7
MSTN/BAR LS15 ....105 F7
Kendal Gdns CAS WF10 ....169 J1
Kendal Garth CAS WF10 ....169 K1
Kendal Gv BVRD LS3 ....9 J7
Kendal La BVRD LS3 ....9 J7
Kendall Av SHPY BD18 ....76 D4
Kendal Mellor Ct KGHY BD21 .....2 F4
Kendal Ri BVRD LS3 ....9 H8
HOR/CROF WF4 ....185 K7
Kendal Rd BVRD LS3 ....9 J7
Kendell St KGHY BD21 ....3 J6
Kendell St MID LS10 ....14 B2
Kenilworth Av MOR LS27 ....141 G1
Kenilworth Cl MIRF WF14 ....179 G3
Kenilworth Dr BRIG HD6 ....157 F2
Kenilworth Gdns MOR LS27 .....121 G7
Kenilworth Rd WOR/ARM LS12 ...12 A5
Kenilworth St BOW BD4 ....118 B2
Kenley Av WBSY BD6 ....117 F5
Kenley Mt WBSY BD6 ....117 F4
Kenley Pde GTHN BD7 ....116 E4
Kenmore Av CLECK BD19 ....138 D7
Kenmore Cl CLECK BD19 ....138 D7
Kenmore Crs CLECK BD19 ....138 D7
 WBSY BD6 ....117 F4
Kenmore Dr CLECK BD19 ....138 D7
 WBSY BD6 ....117 F4
Kenmore Gv CLECK BD19 ....138 D7
 WBSY BD6 ....117 F4
Kenmore Rd CLECK BD19 ....138 D7
 EARD/LOFT WF3 ....164 A3
 WBSY BD6 ....117 F4
Kenmore Vw CLECK BD19 ....138 D7
Kenmore Wk WBSY BD6 ....117 F4
Kenmore Wy CLECK BD19 ....138 D7
Kennedy Av HUDN HD2 ....177 F4
Kennedy Cl BTLY WF17 ....161 J5
Kennel La RPDN/SBR HX6 ......152 B7
Kennels La SCFT LS14 ....66 C3
Kennerleigh Av
 MSTN/BAR LS15 ....106 A4
Kennerleigh Crs
 MSTN/BAR LS15 ....106 A4
Kennerleigh Dr
 MSTN/BAR LS15 ....105 K4
Kennerleigh Garth
 MSTN/BAR LS15 ....106 A4
Kennerleigh Gln
 MSTN/BAR LS15 ....105 K4
Kennerleigh Gv
 MSTN/BAR LS15 ....106 A4
Kennerleigh Ri
 MSTN/BAR LS15 ....105 K4
Kennerleigh Wk
 MSTN/BAR LS15 ....105 K4
Kenneth St BEE/HOL LS11 ....13 G6
Kennet La GFTH/SHER LS25 ....107 K7
Kennion St WBOW BD5 ....117 J1
Kensington Av SCFT LS14 ....66 D5
Kensington Cl BTLY WF17 ....160 E4
 HIPP HX3 ....154 D4
Kensington Gdns MID LS10 .....124 A7
Kensington Rd HIPP HX3 ....154 D4
 WKFDE WF1 ....18 D1
Kensington St GIR BD8 ....4 D1
 KGHY BD21 ....2 E7
Kensington Ter HDGY LS6 ....9 G2
Kenstone Crs IDLE BD10 ....78 B5
Kent Av AIRE BD20 ....32 E1
 PDSY/CALV LS28 ....100 D6
Kent Cl PDSY/CALV LS28 ....100 D6
Kent Crs PDSY/CALV LS28 ....100 D6
Kent Dr PDSY/CALV LS28 ....100 D6
Kentmere Ap SCFT LS14 ....85 F7
Kentmere Av GFTH/SHER LS25 ..108 A7
 LM/WK BD12 ....137 K6
 SCFT LS14 ....85 G5
Kentmere Cl SCFT LS14 ....85 G6
Kentmere Crs SCFT LS14 ....85 H7
Kentmere Gdns SCFT LS14 ....85 G6
Kentmere Ga SCFT LS14 ....85 G5
Kentmere Gn SCFT LS14 ....85 G6
Kentmere Ri SCFT LS14 ....85 H7
Kent Ms BGLY BD16 ....76 A2
Kenton Wy BOW * BD4 ....119 F3
Kent Rd BGLY BD16 ....76 A1
 PDSY/CALV LS28 ....100 C6
Kent St HFAX HX1 ....16 B4
Kenworthy Cl BHP/TINH LS16 ...61 K6
Kenworthy Gdns
 BHP/TINH LS16 ....61 K6
Kenworthy Garth
 BHP/TINH LS16 ....61 K6
Kenworthy Ga BHP/TINH LS16 ..61 K6
Kenworthy La RPDN/SBR HX6 ..173 F3
Kenworthy Ri BHP/TINH LS16 ...61 K6
Kenworthy V BHP/TINH LS16 ....61 K6
Kenya Mt HWTH BD22 ....24 A3
Kenyon La LUD/ILL HX2 ....154 A1
Kepler Gv RHAY LS8 ....10 F4
Kepler Mt RHAY LS8 ....10 F4
Kepler Ter RHAY LS8 ....10 F4
Kepstorn Cl KSTL LS5 ....81 K7
Kepstorn Ri KSTL LS5 ....81 K7
Kepstorn Rd BHP/TINH LS16 .....82 A7
Keren Gv WKFDW/WTN WF2 ...163 K6
Kerry Garth HORS LS18 ....80 E3
Kerry Hl HORS LS18 ....80 E4
Kerry St HORS LS18 ....80 E3
Kershaw Av CAS WF10 ....169 G1
Kershaw Ct LUD/ILL * HX2 ......132 E7
Kershaw Crs LUD/ILL HX2 ....152 E1
Kershaw Dr LUD/ILL HX2 ....132 E7
Kershaw La KNOT WF11 ....170 E5
Kershaw St BFDE BD3 ....7 K6
Kertland St EARL WF12 ....181 F3
Kester Rd BTLY WF17 ....160 C3
Kesteven Cl BOW BD4 ....119 G4
Kesteven Ct BOW BD4 ....119 G4
Kesteven Rd BOW BD4 ....119 G4
Kestrel Cl AL/HA/HU LS17 ....64 A7

Kestrel Dr ECHL BD2 ....98 B1
Kestrel Garth MOR LS27 ....142 C3
Kestrel Gv AL/HA/HU LS17 ....64 A7
Kestrel Mt ECHL BD2 ....98 B1
Kestrel Vw CLECK BD19 ....138 E6
Keswick Cl HIPP HX3 ....155 H5
 WKFDW/WTN WF2 ....183 K2
Keswick Dr CAS WF10 ....149 K5
Keswick Gra AL/HA/HU LS17 .....45 K5
Keswick La AL/HA/HU LS17 ......45 K6
Keswick Vw BOW BD4 ....7 K9
Keswick Vw AL/HA/HU LS17 .....46 B5
Kettleman Br TAD LS24 ....71 F2
Kettlewell Dr WBOW BD5 ....117 G3
Kew Hl HUDN HD2 ....175 J6
Keystone Av CAS WF10 ....168 D3
Khalaq Ct BFDE BD3 ....6 F4
Khus Wk KGHY BD21 ....53 K7
Kidacre St BEE/HOL LS11 ....14 B5
Kiddal La MSTN/BAR LS15 ....87 H1
Kilburn La DEWS WF13 ....161 F7
Kilburn Rd WOR/ARM LS12 ......12 A2
Kilby St WKFDE WF1 ....18 C2
Kildare Crs WIL/AL BD15 ....95 K4
Kildare Ter WOR/ARM LS12 ......12 F3
Killingbeck Br SCFT LS14 ....105 F4
Killingbeck Dr SCFT LS14 ....105 F4
Killinghall Av ECHL BD2 ....6 F1
Killinghall Dr ECHL BD2 ....6 F1
Killinghall Gv ECHL BD2 ....6 F1
Kilner Rd WBSY * BD6 ....117 F5
Kilners Cft ILK LS29 ....22 C1
Kiln Fold BRIG HD6 ....157 J5
Kiln Hill La AIRE BD20 ....20 B3
Kilnsea Mt BOW BD4 ....119 F3
Kilnsey Fold AIRE BD20 ....20 C7
Kilnsey Gv WKFDE WF1 ....19 K2
Kilnsey Hl BTLY WF17 ....161 G6
Kilnsey Ms BAIL BD17 ....77 G1
Kilnsey Rd BFDE BD3 ....6 F7
 WKFDE WF1 ....19 K1
Kilpin Hill La DEWS WF13 ....160 C5
Kilroyd Av CLECK BD19 ....138 C5
Kilroyd Dr CLECK BD19 ....139 F5
Kimberley Pl HIPP HX3 ....134 D3
 OSM LS9 ....11 M5
Kimberley Rd OSM LS9 ....11 M5
Kimberley St BFDE BD3 ....7 H7
 BRIG HD6 ....157 C5
 FEA/AMT WF7 ....188 B3
 HIPP HX3 ....134 D5
 WKFDE WF1 ....184 E6
Kimberley Vw OSM LS9 ....11 M6
Kinara Ct KGHY BD21 ....3 M1
Kineholme Dr OT LS21 ....38 E4
King Alfred's Dr HDGY LS6 ....83 F3
King Alfred's Wy HDGY LS6 ......83 F3
King Charles St LDS * LS1 ....10 A9
King Cl AL/HA/HU LS17 ....62 E7
King Cross Rd HFAX HX1 ....16 B9
King Cross St HFAX HX1 ....16 C9
King Dr AL/HA/HU LS17 ....62 E7
King Edward Av CAS WF10 .....147 J1
 HORS LS18 ....80 E4
King Edward Crs HORS LS18 ....81 F3
King Edward Rd
 CUL/OBY BD13 ....95 G7
King Edward St EARL WF12 ....180 E6
 HFAX * HX1 ....17 H6
 LDS LS1 ....10 B9
 NORM WF6 ....166 D6
King Edwin's Ct RHAY LS8 ....84 B7
Kingfield GSLY LS20 ....59 G1
Kingfisher Cl AL/HA/HU LS17 ....64 A7
Kingfisher Ct KGHY BD21 ....3 H5
Kingfisher Gv GIR BD8 ....96 B6
Kingfisher Ms MOR LS27 ....142 B4
Kingfisher Reach WBY LS22 ......46 D1
Kingfisher Wy AL/HA/HU LS17 ...64 A7
King George Av CHAL LS7 ....83 J5
 HORS LS18 ....81 F3
 MOR LS27 ....142 A1
King George Cft MOR LS27 .....142 A1
King George Gdns CHAL * LS7 ...83 J5
King George Rd HORS LS18 .....81 F3
King George St WKFDE WF1 ....164 B5
King La AL/HA/HU LS17 ....62 D4
 AL/HA/HU LS17 ....83 G2
Kings Ap BRAM LS13 ....101 H3
Kings Av CAS WF10 ....169 F1
 HDGY LS6 ....8 F6
 ILK LS29 ....23 K5
 NORM WF6 ....166 C3
Kingsbury Pl HFAX HX1 ....16 B6
Kings Cha RTHW LS26 ....145 G1
Kings Cl ILK LS29 ....23 H5
 OSS WF5 ....182 B2
 OT LS21 ....39 K3
 PONT WF8 ....189 H2
Kings Croft Gdns
 AL/HA/HU LS17 ....83 J3
 ECHL BD2 ....98 B2
Kingsdale Cl SCFT LS14 ....85 C6
Kingsdale Crs ECHL BD2 ....98 B2
Kingsdale Dr ECHL BD2 ....98 B2
Kingsdale Gdns BIRK/DRI BD11 .140 B1
Kingsdale Gv ECHL BD2 ....98 A2
King's Dr BTLY WF17 ....140 B5
 ECHL BD2 ....78 A6
 NORM WF6 ....166 C3
Kingsfield RTHW LS26 ....144 C2
King's Ga BFDE BD3 ....5 M1
Kings Gv BGLY BD16 ....55 K7
Kings Head Dr MIRF * WF14 ....179 G3
Kings Head Rd MIRF WF14 ......179 C3
Kings Lea HIPP HX3 ....154 E6
 LVSG WF15 ....159 K6
 OSS WF5 ....182 B1
Kingsley Av BHP/TINH LS16 .....62 A6
 BIRK/DRI BD11 ....139 J3
 ECHL BD2 ....97 K3
 HDGY LS6 ....8 F4
 ILK LS29 ....23 J5
 NORM WF6 ....166 B2

RPDN/SBR HX6 ....153 G5
 WKFDE WF1 ....164 C3
Kingsley Cl BIRK/DRI BD11 .....139 J3
 HOR/CROF WF4 ....186 B7
 WKFDE WF1 ....164 C3
Kingsley Crs BAIL BD17 ....77 H2
 BIRK/DRI BD11 ....139 J3
Kingsley Dr BHP/TINH LS16 .....62 A6
 BIRK/DRI BD11 ....139 J3
 CAS WF10 ....169 J3
Kingsley Garth WKFDE WF1 ....164 C3
Kingsley Pl HFAX HX1 ....16 B8
Kingsley Rd BHP/TINH LS16 .....62 A6
Kings Md RTHW LS26 ....145 H1
Kingsmead OSS WF5 ....182 B1
 SCFT LS14 ....85 H4
Kingsmead Dr SCFT LS14 ....85 C3
Kings Meadow OSS WF5 ....182 B2
Kings Meadow Cl WBY LS22 .....29 G2
Kings Meadow Dr WBY LS22 .....29 G2
Kings Meadow Gv WBY LS22 ....29 G2
Kings Meadow Ms WBY LS22 ....29 G2
Kings Meadow Vw WBY LS22 ....29 G2
Kingsmill Cl MOR LS27 ....141 G2
King's Mt CHAL LS7 ....83 H4
 KNOT WF11 ....170 C3
Kings Paddock OSS WF5 ....182 B2
Kings Pl HDGY LS6 ....102 C1
King's Rd BGLY BD16 ....55 H6
 BHP/TINH LS16 ....61 K2
 ECHL BD2 ....78 A7
 HDGY LS6 ....8 F4
 ILK LS29 ....23 J5
 NORM WF6 ....166 B2
Kingston Cl HFAX HX1 ....16 B7
 WIL/AL BD15 ....95 F1
Kingston Ct HFAX HX1 ....16 B8
Kingston Dr HFAX HX1 ....16 A7
 NORM WF6 ....167 F7
Kingston Gdns
 MSTN/BAR LS15 ....105 J2
Kingston Gv IDLE BD10 ....78 C3
Kingston Rd IDLE BD10 ....78 C3
Kingston St HFAX HX1 ....16 B7
Kingston Ter LDSU LS2 ....9 L4
King St AIRE * BD20 ....33 F1
 BIRK/DRI BD11 ....140 C1
 BRIG HD6 ....157 C6
 CAS WF10 ....168 D2
 CLECK BD19 ....139 F7
 HECK WF16 ....160 A4
 HFAX HX1 ....17 J5
 IDLE BD10 ....78 D7
 KGHY BD21 ....2 F7
 LDS LS1 ....13 L1
 MIRF WF14 ....179 H5
 MOR LS27 ....141 K4
 NORM WF6 ....166 C4
 OSS WF5 ....182 D5
 PDSY/CALV LS28 ....100 A4
 PONT WF8 ....189 H1
 RPDN/SBR * HX6 ....153 F5
 WKFDE WF1 ....18 E4
 YEA LS19 ....59 H7
 YEA LS19 ....59 K4
Kings Vw HIPP HX3 ....155 K4
Kingsway AIRE BD20 ....54 D2
 BGLY BD16 ....75 K2
 BIRK/DRI BD11 ....140 C1
 BTLY WF17 ....140 B5
 EARD/LOFT WF3 ....165 G6
 ECHL BD2 ....78 A6
 GFTH/SHER LS25 ....107 H7
 MSTN/BAR LS15 ....105 K5
 NORM WF6 ....186 B6
 OSS WF5 ....182 B2
 PONT WF8 ....169 J5
Kingsway Cl OSS WF5 ....182 B2
Kingsway Ct OSS WF5 ....182 B2
Kingsway Dr ILK LS29 ....23 K5
Kingsway Garth
 GFTH/SHER LS25 ....107 F7
Kingswear Cl
 MSTN/BAR LS15 ....106 A4
Kingswear Crs
 MSTN/BAR LS15 ....106 A4
Kingswear Garth
 MSTN/BAR LS15 ....106 A4
Kingswear Gln
 MSTN/BAR LS15 ....106 A4
Kingswear Gv
 MSTN/BAR LS15 ....106 A4
Kingswear Pde
 MSTN/BAR LS15 ....106 A4
Kingswear Ri MSTN/BAR LS15 ..106 A4
Kingswear Vw MSTN/BAR LS15 .106 A4
Kingswell Av WKFDE WF1 ......164 D4
Kingswood Av RHAY LS8 ....84 B1
Kingswood Crs RHAY LS8 ....84 A1
Kingswood Dr RHAY LS8 ....84 A1
Kingswood Gdns RHAY LS8 ......84 A1
Kingswood Gn HIPP HX3 ....135 J4
Kingswood Gv RHAY LS8 ....84 B1
Kingswood Pl GTHN BD7 ....117 F2
Kingswood Rd WOR/ARM LS12 ..12 A3
Kingswood St GTHN BD7 ....117 F2
Kingswood Ter GTHN * BD7 .....117 F2
Kinnaird Cl BTLY WF17 ....161 H5
 ELL HX5 ....175 J1
Kipling Ct IDLE BD10 ....78 E5
Kipling Gv PONT WF8 ....169 J6
Kippax Mt OSM LS9 ....15 G2
Kippax Pl OSM LS9 ....15 G2
Kipping La CUL/OBY BD13 ....95 C7
Kipping Pl CUL/OBY BD13 ....95 G7
Kirby St KGHY BD21 ....3 J2
Kirk Beston Cl BEE/HOL LS11 ..122 D4
Kirkbourne Gv BAIL BD17 ....77 K2
Kirkby Av GFTH/SHER LS25 ....127 K1
Kirkby Leas HFAX HX1 ....17 G8
Kirk Cl EARL WF12 ....182 A1
Kirkdale CAS WF10 ....169 H1
Kirkdale Av WOR/ARM LS12 ...122 A2
Kirkdale Crs WOR/ARM LS12 ..122 A3
Kirkdale Dr WOR/ARM LS12 ...122 A2

Kirkdale Gdns WOR/ARM LS12 .121 K2
Kirkdale Gv WOR/ARM LS12 ...121 K2
Kirkdale Mt WOR/ARM LS12 ...122 A3
Kirkdale Ter WOR/ARM LS12 ...122 A3
Kirkdale Vw WOR/ARM LS12 ...122 A3
Kirk Dr BAIL BD17 ....57 J7
Kirkfield Av SCFT LS14 ....66 D5
Kirkfield Crs SCFT LS14 ....66 D5
Kirkfield Dr MSTN/BAR LS15 ...105 K6
Kirkfield Gdns MSTN/BAR LS15 .106 A6
Kirkfield La SCFT LS14 ....66 A5
Kirkfields BAIL BD17 ....57 K7
Kirkfield Vw MSTN/BAR LS15 ...106 A6
Kirkgate AIRE BD20 ....33 F1
 BFD BD1 ....5 M6
 BTLY WF17 ....140 A6
 BTLY WF17 ....161 J5
 GFTH/SHER LS25 ....111 F5
 LDSU LS2 ....14 C1
 OT LS21 ....39 H2
 SHPY BD18 ....77 F5
 TAD LS24 ....50 E7
 WKFDE WF1 ....18 F4
Kirkham Av WKFDW/WTN WF2 .163 G5
Kirkham Rd GTHN BD7 ....4 B1
Kirkham St BRAM LS13 ....80 C7
Kirkhaw La KNOT WF11 ....170 C2
Kirk Ings Yd LDSU * LS2 ....14 C1
Kirklands LVSG WF15 ....159 H4
Kirklands Av BAIL BD17 ....77 K1
Kirklands Cl BAIL BD17 ....77 K2
 YEA LS19 ....59 H4
Kirklands Gdns BAIL BD17 ....77 K1
Kirklands La BAIL BD17 ....77 K1
Kirklands Rd BAIL BD17 ....77 J1
Kirklands Vls BAIL * BD17 ....77 K1
Kirk La HIPP HX3 ....136 B7
 YEA LS19 ....59 H4
Kirklees Cl PDSY/CALV LS28 ...100 B1
Kirklees Cft PDSY/CALV LS28 ..100 A1
Kirklees Dr PDSY/CALV LS28 ...100 A1
Kirklees Garth PDSY/CALV LS28 .100 A1
Kirklees Ri PDSY/CALV LS28 ...100 A1
Kirklees Rd WIL/AL BD15 ....96 A6
Kirklees Wy BIRK/DRI BD11 ....139 G2
 BTLY WF17 ....141 F6
 CLECK BD19 ....138 B4
 EARL WF12 ....181 K2
 HUDN HD2 ....176 E6
 HUDN HD2 ....177 H5
 OSS WF5 ....182 A5
Kirkley Av LM/WK BD12 ....137 H6
Kirkstall Av KSTL LS5 ....101 J2
Kirkstall Hl BULY LS4 ....102 A2
Kirkstall La KSTL LS5 ....102 A1
Kirkstall Mt KSTL LS5 ....101 J2
Kirkstall Rd BULY LS4 ....8 D7
Kirkstone Dr CLECK BD19 ....139 J7
 LUD/ILL HX2 ....133 J7
Kirkthorpe La WKFDE WF1 .....185 J3
Kirkwall Av OSM LS9 ....15 L1
Kirkwall Dr BOW BD4 ....119 F3
Kirkwood Av BHP/TINH LS16 ....61 C7
Kirkwood Cl BHP/TINH LS16 ....61 G7
Kirkwood Crs BHP/TINH LS16 ...61 G6
Kirkwood Dr BHP/TINH LS16 ....61 G6
Kirkwood Gdns BHP/TINH LS16 .61 H7
Kirkwood Gv BHP/TINH LS16 ....61 G7
 EARD/LOFT WF3 ....142 E7
Kirkwood La BHP/TINH LS16 ....61 G6
Kirkwood Ri BHP/TINH LS16 ....61 H6
Kirkwood Vw BHP/TINH LS16 ...61 H6
Kirkwood Wy BHP/TINH LS16 ...61 H6
Kismet Gdns BFDE BD3 ....7 H3
Kitchener Av OSM LS9 ....11 M6
Kitchener Gv OSM LS9 ....11 M5
Kitchener Mt OSM LS9 ....11 M6
Kitchener Pl OSM LS9 ....11 M6
Kitchener St LM/WK BD12 ......138 B2
 OSM LS9 ....11 M6
 RTHW LS26 ....145 K1
Kite Ms GIR BD8 ....96 B6
Kit La AIRE BD20 ....20 D3
Kitson Cl WOR/ARM LS12 ....12 A4
Kitson Gdns WOR/ARM LS12 ....12 A4
Kitson Hill Crs MIRF WF14 ......179 G3
Kitson Hill Rd MIRF WF14 ....179 F3
Kitson La RPDN/SBR HX6 ....154 A7
Kitson Rd MID LS10 ....14 C6
Kitson St EARD/LOFT WF3 .....142 C6
 OSM LS9 ....15 G2
 SHPY BD18 ....77 H5
Kliffen Pl HIPP HX3 ....155 G4
Knaresborough Dr HUDN HD2 ..177 F7
Knavesmire RTHW LS26 ....144 C3
Knightsbridge Wk BOW BD4 ....118 A3
Knightsclose MSTN/BAR LS15 ..105 K5
Knights Cft WBY LS22 ....29 J2
Knightscroft Av RTHW LS26 ....145 F1
Knightscroft Dr RTHW LS26 ....145 F1
Knightshill MSTN/BAR LS15 ....106 A5
Knight St HFAX HX1 ....16 B8
Knightsway EARD/LOFT WF3 ...144 C6
 GFTH/SHER LS25 ....127 C1
 MSTN/BAR LS15 ....105 K5
The Knoll BSPA/BRAM LS23 .....48 B7
 PDSY/CALV LS28 ....99 H2
Knoll Cl OSS WF5 ....182 B1
Knoll Pk EARD/LOFT WF3 ......163 J1
Knoll Park Dr BAIL BD17 ....77 G3
Knoll Wood Pk HORS LS18 ......81 G4
Knottingley Rd PONT WF8 ......170 B6
Knott La AIRE BD20 ....32 A5
 YEA LS19 ....80 B3
Knowle Av BULY LS4 ....8 C3
Knowle Gv BULY LS4 ....8 C3
Knowle La LM/WK BD12 ....137 J5
Knowle Mt BULY LS4 ....8 C3
Knowle Pl BULY LS4 ....8 C3
Knowler Cl LVSG WF15 ....159 H4
Knowler Hl LVSG WF15 ....159 H4
Knowle Rd BULY LS4 ....8 C3
Knowler Wy LVSG WF15 ....159 H3
Knowles Av BOW BD4 ....118 E4
Knowles Hl DEWS * WF13 ......160 C7
Knowles Hill Rd DEWS WF13 ...160 C7

Knowles La *BOW* BD4 ....118 E4
　BTLY * WF17 ....160 E4
　CLECK BD19 ....139 J4
Knowle Spring Rd *KGHY* * BD21 ...2 E8
Knowles Rd *BRIG* HD6 ....177 F1
　BTLY WF17 ....160 E4
Knowles St *BOW* BD4 ....118 D5
　CUL/QBY BD13 ....94 A5
Knowles Vw *BOW* BD4 ....118 E4
Knowle Ter *BULY* LS4 ....8 B4
Knowle Top Dr *HIPP* HX3 ....136 D7
Knowle Top Rd *HIPP* HX3 ....136 D7
Knowl Gv *MIRF* WF14 ....179 F3
Knowl Rd *MIRF* WF14 ....179 H4
Knowsley St *BFDE* BD3 ....6 D7
Knowsthorpe Crs *OSM* LS9 ....15 G5
Knowsthorpe Ga *OSM* LS9 ....15 M7
Knowsthorpe La *OSM* LS9 ....15 H6
Knowsthorpe Rd *OSM* LS9 ....124 D2
Knowsthorpe Wy *OSM* LS9 ....15 L7
Knox St *BRAM* LS13 ....80 C1
Knutsford Dr *BOW* BD4 ....119 F4
Knutsford Ms *BOW* * BD4 ....119 F4
Komla Cl *BFD* BD1 ....6 B5
Kyffin Av *MSTN/BAR* LS15 ....105 F6
Kyffin Pl *BOW* BD4 ....119 F1

L

Laburnum Cl *EARD/LOFT* WF3 ...163 H1
Laburnum Dr *BAIL* BD17 ....57 J7
Laburnum Gv *BRIG* HD6 ....157 F2
　CLECK BD19 ....139 H6
　HWTH BD22 ....73 F4
Laburnum Pl *GIR* BD8 ....5 H2
　IDLE BD10 ....79 F4
Laburnum Rd *DEWS* WF13 ....160 B6
　SHPY BD18 ....77 J7
　WKFDE WF1 ....18 D3
Laburnum St *GIR* BD8 ....5 H2
　PDSY/CALV LS28 ....99 K5
Laceby Cl *IDLE* BD10 ....78 D4
Lacey St *DEWS* WF13 ....180 E1
Lacy Gv *WBY* LS22 ....29 J5
Lacy Wy *ELL* HX5 ....175 K1
Ladbroke Gv *BOW* * BD4 ....119 F5
Ladderbanks La *BAIL* BD17 ....57 J7
Lady Ann Rd *BTLY* WF17 ....161 G4
Lady Balk La *PONT* WF8 ....169 J6
Lady Beck Cl *LDSU* LS2 ....10 D8
Lady Cl *OSS* WF5 ....182 B1
Lady Heton Av *MIRF* WF14 ....179 G3
Lady Heton Cl *MIRF* * WF14 ....179 F3
Lady Heton Dr *MIRF* WF14 ....179 F3
Lady Heton Gv *MIRF* WF14 ....179 F3
Lady La *BGLY* BD16 ....55 K5
　LDSU LS2 ....10 B9
　WKFDE WF1 ....18 D6
Lady Pk *AL/HA/HU* LS17 ....64 A7
Lady Park Av *BGLY* BD16 ....55 K5
Lady Park Ct *AL/HA/HU* * LS17 ....63 K7
Lady Pit La *BEE/HOL* LS11 ....13 L8
Ladyroyd Dr *BIRK/DRI* BD11 ....139 F1
Ladysmith Rd *CUL/QBY* BD13 ....115 F6
Ladywell Cl *WBOW* BD5 ....117 K3
Ladywell La *LVSG* WF15 ....158 C5
Ladywood Gra *RHAY* * LS8 ....84 E6
Ladywood Md *RHAY* LS8 ....84 E6
Lady Wood Rd *RHAY* LS8 ....84 C5
Ladywood Ter *HFAX* HX1 ....16 C3
Ladywood Wy *DEWS* WF13 ....180 A5
Lairum Ri *BSPA/BRAM* LS23 ....48 C5
Laisterdyke *BOW* BD4 ....7 J7
Laisteridge La *GTHN* BD7 ....5 H8
　WBOW BD5 ....117 H1
Laith Cl *BHP/TINH* LS16 ....81 J1
Laithe Cl *AIRE* BD20 ....20 E7
Laithe Croft Rd *BTLY* WF17 ....161 H3
Laithe Gv *WBSY* BD6 ....117 F4
Laithe Rd *WBSY* BD6 ....117 G5
Laithes Cha *WKFDW/WTN* WF2 ....183 J1
Laithes Cl *WKFDW/WTN* WF2 ....183 J2
Laithes Cr *WKFDW/WTN* WF2 ....183 J2
Laithes Crs *WKFDW/WTN* WF2 ....183 J2
Laithes Cft *EARL* WF12 ....181 H2
Laithes Dr *WKFDW/WTN* WF2 ....183 J2
Laithes Fold
　WKFDW/WTN WF2 ....183 J2
Laithes Vw *WKFDW/WTN* WF2 ....183 J2
Laith Gdns *BHP/TINH* LS16 ....81 J1
Laith Garth *BHP/TINH* LS16 ....81 J1
Laith Gn *BHP/TINH* LS16 ....81 J1
Laith Rd *BHP/TINH* LS16 ....81 J1
Laith Staid La *GFTH/SHER* LS25 ....110 C5
Lakeland Cl *AL/HA/HU* LS17 ....63 G5
Lakeland Dr *AL/HA/HU* LS17 ....63 G5
Lake Lock Dr *EARD/LOFT* WF3 ....165 G3
Lake Lock Rd *EARD/LOFT* WF3 ....165 G3
Lake Rw *BOW* BD4 ....6 F9
Lakeside *AIRE* BD20 ....20 E8
Lakeside Cha *YEA* LS19 ....59 K7
Lakeside Cl *ILK* LS29 ....23 K4
Lakeside Gdns *YEA* LS19 ....59 K7
Lakeside Mdw *PONT* WF8 ....169 J5
Lakeside Ter *YEA* LS19 ....59 K7
Lakeside Vw *YEA* LS19 ....59 K7
Lake St *BOW* BD4 ....6 F9
　KGHY BD21 ....3 L1
Lake Ter *MID* LS10 ....123 J4
Lake Vw *HFAX* HX1 ....16 F3
　PONT WF8 ....169 H5
Lake View Ct *RHAY* LS8 ....84 D4
Lamb Cote Rd *HUDN* HD2 ....177 J3
Lambert Av *RHAY* LS8 ....84 A6
Lambert Cl *GTL/HWCG* HX4 ....175 G2
Lambert Dr *RHAY* LS8 ....84 A6
Lambert Pl *ECHL* BD2 ....98 C3
Lambert Pl *GTL/HWCG* HX4 ....175 G2
Lamb Inn Rd *KNOT* WF11 ....171 H4
Lambourne Av *IDLE* BD10 ....78 E7
Lambrigg Crs *SCFT* LS14 ....105 H1
Lambton Gv *RHAY* LS8 ....11 H1
Lambton Pl *RHAY* LS8 ....11 H1

Lambton St *RHAY* LS8 ....11 H1
Lambton Ter *RHAY* LS8 ....11 H1
Lambton Vw *RHAY* LS8 ....11 H1
Lampards Cl *WIL/AL* BD15 ....95 K3
Lamplands *BTLY* WF17 ....161 G1
Lanark Dr *HORS* LS18 ....60 D7
Lancaster Cl *PONT* WF8 ....189 J3
Lancaster Ct *KGHY* BD21 ....2 F8
Lancaster St *CAS* WF10 ....149 J6
Lancastre Av *KSTL* LS5 ....101 J2
Lancastre Gv *KSTL* LS5 ....101 J2
Lancet Ri *EARD/LOFT* WF3 ....144 B4
Landmark Ct *BEE/HOL* LS11 ....13 G9
Landor St *KGHY* BD21 ....3 K3
Lands Beck Wy *LVSG* WF15 ....159 G4
Landscove Av *BOW* BD4 ....119 F4
Landseer Av *BRAM* LS13 ....101 H2
　EARD/LOFT WF3 ....142 D7
Landseer Cl *BRAM* LS13 ....101 G2
Landseer Crs *BRAM* LS13 ....101 H2
Landseer Dr *BRAM* LS13 ....101 G2
Landseer Gdns *BRAM* LS13 ....101 G2
Landseer Gn *BRAM* LS13 ....101 H2
Landseer Gv *BRAM* LS13 ....101 H2
Landseer Mt *BRAM* LS13 ....101 H2
Landseer Ri *BRAM* LS13 ....101 G2
Landseer Rd *BRAM* LS13 ....101 H2
Landseer Ter *BRAM* LS13 ....101 H2
Landseer Vw *BRAM* LS13 ....101 H2
Lands Head La *HIPP* HX3 ....135 J3
Landsholme Ct *BOW* BD4 ....119 G4
Lands La *CSLY* LS20 ....59 G7
　IDLE BD10 ....78 D7
　LDS LS1 ....10 A9
Landsmoor Gv *BGLY* BD16 ....56 A6
Land St *PDSY/CALV* LS28 ....100 A2
The Lane *AL/HA/HU* LS17 ....62 E6
　OSM LS9 ....14 E2
Lane End *CUL/QBY* BD13 ....95 G7
　PDSY/CALV LS28 ....100 C5
Lane End Cl *AL/HA/HU* LS17 ....62 E6
Lane End Cft *AL/HA/HU* LS17 ....62 E6
Lane End Fold *PDSY/CALV* LS28 ....100 C5
Lane End Mt *PDSY/CALV* LS28 ....100 C5
Lane Ends *BEE/HOL* LS11 ....13 L6
Lane Ends Cl *GIR* BD8 ....4 A4
Lane Ends Gn *HIPP* HX3 ....136 A4
Lane Head La *LUD/ILL* HX2 ....134 B5
Lane Head La *LUD/ILL* HX2 ....113 K6
Lane Head Rd *RPDN/SBR* HX6 ....172 D4
The Lanes *PDSY/CALV* LS28 ....100 C5
Lane Side *CUL/QBY* BD13 ....115 G3
　WIL/AL BD15 ....94 E1
Laneside *MOR* LS27 ....122 A7
Lane Side *LM/WK* BD12 ....137 H3
Laneside Cl *MOR* LS27 ....122 A7
Laneside Fold *MOR* LS27 ....122 A7
Laneside Gdns *MOR* LS27 ....142 A1
Lane Top *BRIG* * HD6 ....157 J1
Langbar Ap *SCFT* LS14 ....86 A7
Langbar Av *HTON* BD9 ....96 C2
Langbar Cl *SCFT* LS14 ....86 A6
Langbar Garth *SCFT* LS14 ....86 A6
Langbar Gn *SCFT* LS14 ....86 A7
Langbar Gv *SCFT* LS14 ....86 A7
Langbar Rd *ILK* LS29 ....23 K3
　SCFT LS14 ....86 A7
Langdale Av *EARD/LOFT* WF3 ...164 J3
　GIR BD8 ....96 D5
　HDGY LS6 ....82 B7
　LM/WK BD12 ....137 K6
　NORM WF6 ....166 D4
Langdale Cl *CAS* WF10 ....149 K5
　WBY LS22 ....29 G3
Langdale Ct *BGLY* BD16 ....55 K7
Langdale Crs *LUD/ILL* HX2 ....134 B6
Langdale Dr *CUL/QBY* BD13 ....115 G3
　NORM WF6 ....166 D3
　WKFDW/WTN WF2 ....183 K1
Langdale Gdns *HDGY* LS6 ....102 B1
Langdale Ms *NORM* * WF6 ....166 D4
Langdale Rd *EARL* WF12 ....161 J6
　IDLE BD10 ....99 F1
　RTHW LS26 ....145 J1
Langdale Sq
　WKFDW/WTN WF2 ....184 A3
Langdale St *ELL* HX5 ....175 J3
Langdale Ter *HDGY* LS6 ....102 B1
Langford La *ILK* LS29 ....38 A1
Langford Ride *ILK* LS29 ....38 A1
Langford Rd *ILK* LS29 ....37 K1
Langlands Rd *BGLY* BD16 ....75 K5
Lang La *ECHL* * BD2 ....97 J1
Langley Av *BGLY* BD16 ....55 K7
　BOW BD4 ....118 D5
　BRAM LS13 ....100 D1
Langley Cl *BRAM* LS13 ....100 D1
Langley Crs *BAIL* BD17 ....77 K1
　BRAM LS13 ....100 E2
Langley Garth *BRAM* LS13 ....100 D1
Langley Gv *BGLY* BD16 ....55 K7
Langley La *BAIL* BD17 ....57 K7
Langley Mt *BRAM* LS13 ....100 D1
Langley Pl *BRAM* LS13 ....100 D1
Langley Rd *BGLY* BD16 ....55 K7
　BRAM LS13 ....100 D1
Langport Cl *CUL/QBY* BD13 ....115 J5
Langsett Cft *HUDN* HD2 ....177 K4
Langthorne St *MOR* LS27 ....142 B5
Langton Av *BOW* BD4 ....118 C5
Langton Cl *CLECK* BD19 ....139 H5
Langton Gn *WOR/ARM* LS12 ....12 A4
Langton Rd *RPDN/SBR* HX6 ....153 J3
Langtons Whf *LDSU* LS2 ....14 C2
Langwith Av *WBY* LS22 ....46 B2
Langwith Dr *WBY* LS22 ....46 B2
Langwith Valley Rd *WBY* LS22 ....46 B2
Lansdale Ct *BOW* BD4 ....119 G4
Lansdowne Av *CAS* WF10 ....168 E1
Lansdowne Cl *BAIL* BD17 ....78 A1
　BTLY WF17 ....160 E2
Lansdowne Pl *WBOW* BD5 ....5 K8
Lansdowne St
　WOR/ARM LS12 ....12 B4
Lanshaw Cl *MID* LS10 ....143 K1
Lanshaw Crs *MID* LS10 ....143 K2
Lanshaw Pl *MID* LS10 ....143 K1
Lanshaw Rd *MID* LS10 ....143 K1

Lanshaw Ter *MID* LS10 ....143 K2
Lanshaw Vw *MID* LS10 ....143 K1
Lanshaw Wk *MID* LS10 ....143 K1
Lapage St *BFDE* BD3 ....7 H1
Lapage Ter *BFDE* BD3 ....7 G7
Lapwing Cl *BOW* BD8 ....96 A5
Larch Cl *BTLY* WF17 ....140 D5
　HWTH BD22 ....72 E2
　LVSG WF15 ....159 K5
　NORM WF6 ....186 E1
Larch Dl *HUDN* HD2 ....177 F5
Larch Dr *WBSY* BD6 ....117 H7
Larchfield Rd *MID* LS10 ....14 E7
Larch Gv *BGLY* BD16 ....55 J6
Larch Hl *WBSY* BD6 ....117 J7
Larch Hill Crs *WBSY* BD6 ....117 J6
Larch La *GFTH/SHER* LS25 ....108 A7
Larchmont *CLAY* BD14 ....116 B3
Larch St *KGHY* BD21 ....53 J7
Larch Wd *SCFT* LS14 ....65 K4
Larkfield Av *YEA* LS19 ....59 K7
Larkfield Crs *YEA* LS19 ....59 K7
Larkfield Dr *YEA* LS19 ....59 K7
Larkfield Mt *YEA* LS19 ....59 K7
Larkfield Rd *PDSY/CALV* LS28 ....100 B5
　YEA LS19 ....59 K7
Larkfield Ter *KGHY* BD21 ....3 M6
Lark Hl *BTLY* WF17 ....140 D6
Lark Hill Av *CLECK* BD19 ....158 C2
Larkhill Cl *RHAY* LS8 ....83 K4
Lark Hill Dr *CLECK* BD19 ....158 C1
Larkhill Gn *AL/HA/HU* LS17 ....83 K3
Larkhill Rd *AL/HA/HU* LS17 ....83 K3
Larkhill Vw *RHAY* LS8 ....83 K4
Larkhill Wk *RHAY* LS8 ....83 K3
Larkhill Wy *AL/HA/HU* LS17 ....83 K3
Larks Hl *PONT* WF8 ....189 G3
Larkspur Wy
　WKFDW/WTN WF2 ....183 K2
Lark St *BGLY* BD16 ....75 J1
　HWTH BD22 ....72 E5
　HWTH BD22 ....72 D4
　KGHY BD21 ....2 E4
Larwood Av *IDLE* BD10 ....99 F1
Lascelles Mt *RHAY* * LS8 ....11 H2
Lascelles Rd *HECK* WF16 ....160 B5
Lascelles Rd East *RHAY* LS8 ....11 G2
Lascelles Rd West *RHAY* LS8 ....11 G2
Lascelles St *RHAY* LS8 ....11 G2
Lascelles Ter *RHAY* LS8 ....11 H1
Lascelles Vw *RHAY* LS8 ....11 H2
Lastingham Gn *WBSY* * BD6 ....116 D5
Latchmere Av *BHP/TINH* LS16 ....81 J4
Latchmere Cl *BHP/TINH* LS16 ....81 K4
Latchmere Crest
　BHP/TINH LS16 ....81 J4
Latchmere Cross
　BHP/TINH LS16 ....81 J4
Latchmere Dr *BHP/TINH* LS16 ....81 J4
Latchmere Rd *BHP/TINH* LS16 ....81 J4
Latchmere Vw *BHP/TINH* LS16 ....81 J4
Latchmere Wk *BHP/TINH* LS16 ....81 K3
Latchmore Rd *BEE/HOL* LS11 ....12 E8
Latham St *CLECK* BD19 ....139 J5
Latham La *CLECK* BD19 ....139 H4
Latham Lea *CLECK* BD19 ....139 H6
Latimer St *BFDE* BD3 ....7 J7
Launceston Dr *BOW* BD4 ....119 F4
Launton Wy *WBOW* BD5 ....117 J4
Laura St *BRIG* HD6 ....157 F7
　HIPP HX3 ....17 G2
　WOR/ARM LS12 ....13 H3
Laurel Bank *BGLY* * BD16 ....56 C7
Laurel Bank Cl *LUD/ILL* HX2 ....134 D1
Laurel Bank Ct *BULY* LS4 ....8 A1
Laurel Cl *AL/HA/HU* LS17 ....45 K5
　ELL HX5 ....175 H3
　HIPP HX3 ....116 B7
Laurel Ct *OSS* WF5 ....182 B3
Laurel Crs *KGHY* BD21 ....2 E3
Laurel Dr *BTLY* WF17 ....160 D1
Laurel Fold *WOR/ARM* LS12 ....12 B1
Laurel Gv *AIRE* BD20 ....32 E1
　BGLY BD16 ....55 H6
　BTLY WF17 ....160 C1
　KGHY BD21 ....2 E3
　WOR/ARM * LS12 ....12 B1
Laurel Hill Av *MSTN/BAR* LS15 ....106 A6
Laurel Hill Cft
　MSTN/BAR * LS15 ....106 A6
Laurel Hill Gdns
　MSTN/BAR LS15 ....106 A6
Laurel Hill Gv *MSTN/BAR* LS15 ....106 A6
Laurel Hill Vw *MSTN/BAR* LS15 ....106 A6
Laurel Hill Wy *MSTN/BAR* LS15 ....106 A7
Laurel Mt *CHAL* * LS7 ....83 J7
　HFAX * HX1 ....16 D9
　PDSY/CALV LS28 ....100 B5
Laurel Pk *WIL/AL* BD15 ....95 F1
Laurel Pl *MID* LS10 ....143 G4
　WOR/ARM LS12 ....12 B1
The Laurels *BGLY* * BD16 ....76 A1
　EARL WF12 ....181 K2
　RHAY LS8 ....84 A6
Laurel St *BFDE* BD3 ....7 G7
　HFAX HX1 ....16 D9
　WOR/ARM * LS12 ....12 B1
Laurel Ter *PDSY/CALV* LS28 ....100 B5
　WOR/ARM LS12 ....12 B1
Laurence Ct *RTHW* LS26 ....126 A7
Lavender Cft *HECK* WF16 ....160 B4
Lavender Hl *IDLE* BD10 ....78 D7
Lavender Wk *OSM* LS9 ....15 G1
Laverhills *LVSG* WF15 ....158 E3
Laverock Crs *BRIG* HD6 ....156 E3
Laverock La *BRIG* HD6 ....156 E3
Laverton Rd *BOW* BD4 ....118 C2
Lavinia Ter *CLAY* BD14 ....116 C2
Lawcliffe Crs *HWTH* BD22 ....72 E4
Law Cl *WBY* LS22 ....29 J2
Lawefield Av *RTHW* LS26 ....144 D1
Lawefield Gv *WKFDW/WTN* WF2 ....18 B7
Lawefield La *WKFDW/WTN* WF2 ....18 B7
Lawkholme La *KGHY* BD21 ....3 H2
Law La *HIPP* HX3 ....155 K3
Lawn Av *ILK* LS29 ....38 A1
Lawn Rd *ILK* LS29 ....38 A1
Lawns Av *AL/HA/HU* LS17 ....62 E6

Lawns Cl *NORM* WF6 ....166 B4
　WOR/ARM LS12 ....121 G3
Lawns Ct *WKFDW/WTN* WF2 ....163 K3
Lawns Crs *WOR/ARM* LS12 ....121 G3
Lawns Cft *WOR/ARM* LS12 ....121 G3
Lawns Dene *WOR/ARM* LS12 ....121 G3
Lawns Dr *WOR/ARM* LS12 ....121 G3
Lawns Gn *WOR/ARM* LS12 ....121 G3
Lawns Hall Cl *BHP/TINH* LS16 ....82 A1
Lawn's La *MID* LS10 ....14 E9
　WKFDW/WTN WF2 ....163 K3
Lawns Mt *WOR/ARM* LS12 ....121 G3
Lawns Sq *WOR/ARM* LS12 ....121 G3
Lawns Ter *EARD/LOFT* WF3 ....163 J1
　WOR/ARM LS12 ....121 G3
Lawnswood Gdns
　BHP/TINH LS16 ....82 A2
Lawnswood Rd *KGHY* BD21 ....2 C8
Lawrence Av *PONT* WF8 ....189 G1
　RHAY LS8 ....104 D1
Lawrence Crs *HECK* WF16 ....160 A2
　RHAY LS8 ....104 D1
Lawrence Gdns *RHAY* LS8 ....84 D7
Lawrence Rd *HIPP* HX3 ....154 E5
　RHAY LS8 ....104 D1
Lawrence St *HIPP* * HX3 ....16 D1
Lawrence Wk *RHAY* LS8 ....104 D1
Lawson Rd *BRIG* HD6 ....157 G6
Lawson St *BFDE* BD3 ....6 A3
　WOR/ARM * LS12 ....102 A6
Law St *BOW* BD4 ....118 D4
　BTLY WF17 ....140 C7
　CLECK BD19 ....138 E6
Laycock La *HWTH* BD22 ....52 D5
Laycock Pl *CHAL* LS7 ....10 C3
Lay Garth Cl *RTHW* * LS26 ....145 F2
Lay Garth Gdns *RTHW* LS26 ....144 E3
Lay Garth Md *RTHW* LS26 ....145 F3
Lay Garth Pl *RTHW* LS26 ....145 F3
Lay Garth Sq *RTHW* LS26 ....145 F3
Layton Av *YEA* LS19 ....80 B1
Layton Cl *YEA* LS19 ....80 B2
Layton Crs *YEA* LS19 ....80 A1
Layton Dr *YEA* LS19 ....80 B1
Layton La *YEA* LS19 ....80 B2
Layton Mt *YEA* LS19 ....80 B1
Layton Park Av *YEA* LS19 ....80 B2
Layton Park Cl *YEA* LS19 ....80 A1
Layton Park Cft *YEA* LS19 ....80 A2
Layton Park Dr *YEA* LS19 ....80 B2
Layton Ri *HORS* LS18 ....80 C1
Layton Rd *YEA* LS19 ....80 B1
Lazenby Dr *WBY* LS22 ....29 G3
Lazenby Fold *WBY* LS22 ....29 G3
The Lea *GFTH/SHER* LS25 ....127 J1
Lea Av *HIPP* HX3 ....155 F5
Leabank Av *GFTH/SHER* LS25 ....127 K1
Leach Crs *AIRE* BD20 ....54 B1
Leach Ri *AIRE* BD20 ....54 A1
Leach Rd *AIRE* BD20 ....54 A1
Leach St *AIRE* BD20 ....54 B1
Lea Cl *BRIG* HD6 ....157 F4
Lea Cft *GTHN* BD7 ....116 D4
Lea Farm Crs *KSTL* LS5 ....81 J6
Lea Farm Dr *KSTL* LS5 ....81 J6
Lea Farm Gv *KSTL* LS5 ....81 J6
Lea Farm Mt *KSTL* LS5 ....81 H5
Lea Farm Pl *KSTL* LS5 ....81 J6
Lea Farm Rd *KSTL* LS5 ....81 H5
Lea Farm Rw *KSTL* LS5 ....81 J5
Lea Farm Wk *KSTL* LS5 ....81 J6
Leafield Av *ECHL* BD2 ....98 C2
Leafield Cl *AL/HA/HU* LS17 ....83 G2
　HUDN HD2 ....177 J5
Leafield Crs *ECHL* BD2 ....98 C1
Leafield Dr *AL/HA/HU* LS17 ....83 G2
　ECHL BD2 ....98 D1
Leafield Gra *AL/HA/HU* LS17 ....83 G2
Leafield Gv *ECHL* BD2 ....98 D2
Leafield Ter *ECHL* BD2 ....98 D2
Leafield Wy *ECHL* BD2 ....98 D2
Leafland St *HFAX* HX1 ....16 C6
Leaf St *CAS* WF10 ....168 B1
　HWTH * BD22 ....73 F4
Leafsway *WBSY* * BD6 ....136 E1
Leah Pl *WOR/ARM* LS12 ....13 G4
Leake St *CAS* WF10 ....168 D1
Lea La *FEA/AMT* WF7 ....188 D5
Lea Mill Park Cl *YEA* LS19 ....59 H4
Lea Mill Park Dr *YEA* LS19 ....59 H4
Leamington Dr *IDLE* BD10 ....78 D4
Leamington St *HTON* BD9 ....97 G3
Leamside Wk *BOW* BD4 ....119 G4
Lea Park Cl *RTHW* LS26 ....124 A7
Lea Park Cft *RTHW* LS26 ....124 A7
Lea Park Dr *RTHW* LS26 ....124 A7
Lea Park Gdns *RTHW* LS26 ....124 A7
Lea Park Garth *RTHW* * LS26 ....124 A7
Lea Park Gv *RTHW* LS26 ....124 A7
Lea Park V *RTHW* LS26 ....124 B7
Lea Rd *BTLY* WF17 ....160 C1
Leaside Dr *CUL/QBY* BD13 ....95 G6
Leasowe Av *MID* LS10 ....123 K4
Leasowe Cl *MID* LS10 ....123 K4
Leasowe Gdns *MID* LS10 ....123 K4
Leasowe Garth *MID* LS10 ....123 K4
Leasowe Rd *MID* LS10 ....123 K4
Leatham Av *FEA/AMT* WF7 ....188 D5
Leatham Crs *FEA/AMT* WF7 ....188 D5
Leatham Dr *FEA/AMT* WF7 ....188 E5
Leatham Park Rd
　FEA/AMT WF7 ....188 D5
Leather Bank *ILK* LS29 ....25 K6
Leathley Av *ILK* LS29 ....38 C2
Leathley Br *OT* LS21 ....40 D1
Leathley Crs *ILK* LS29 ....38 C2
Leathley La *ILK* LS29 ....38 C6
　OT LS21 ....41 F2

Leathley Rd *ILK* LS29 ....38 C6
　MID LS10 ....14 B6
Leathley St *MID* LS10 ....14 C5
The Leavens *IDLE* BD10 ....78 E4
Leaventhorpe Av *GIR* BD8 ....96 B6
Leaventhorpe Cl *GIR* BD8 ....96 C6
Leaventhorpe Gv
　CUL/QBY BD13 ....96 B7
Leaventhorpe La
　CUL/QBY BD13 ....96 B7
Leaventhorpe Wy *GIR* BD8 ....96 C6
Lea Vw *BTLY* WF17 ....140 C7
Leavington Cl *LM/WK* BD12 ....137 G3
Ledbury Av *MID* LS10 ....143 K3
Ledbury Cl *MID* LS10 ....144 A3
Ledbury Dr *EARD/LOFT* WF3 ....144 A3
Ledbury Gn *MID* LS10 ....144 A3
Ledbury Gv *MID* LS10 ....144 A3
Ledbury Pl *BOW* BD4 ....118 B2
Ledgard Wy *WOR/ARM* LS12 ....8 B9
Ledgate La *GFTH/SHER* LS25 ....150 E3
Ledger La *EARD/LOFT* WF3 ....144 D6
　WKFDE WF1 ....164 C3
Ledger Pl *WKFDE* WF1 ....164 C4
Ledston Av *GFTH/SHER* LS25 ....127 K1
Ledston Mill La *CAS* WF10 ....128 D7
Lee Bank *HIPP* HX3 ....16 E2
Lee Beck Gv *EARD/LOFT* WF3 ....165 F1
Lee Br *HFAX* HX1 ....16 F3
Lee Brig *NORM* WF6 ....166 C5
Leech La *BGLY* BD16 ....74 C4
Lee Cl *WIL/AL* BD15 ....75 F6
Lee Clough Dr *HBR* HX7 ....132 A6
Lee Ct *KGHY* BD21 ....54 C5
　OSS WF5 ....182 E5
Leeds & Bradford Rd
　PDSY/CALV LS28 ....100 C3
Leeds Barnsdale Rd *CAS* WF10 ....167 K2
Leeds Country Wy
　AL/HA/HU LS17 ....43 J6
　BHP/TINH LS16 ....62 B3
　HORS LS18 ....60 C6
　MOR LS27 ....120 D7
　MOR LS27 ....161 J1
　OSS WF5 ....183 H1
　PDSY/CALV LS28 ....99 G2
　RTHW LS26 ....126 C6
　SCFT LS14 ....66 B4
　SCFT LS14 ....86 E1
　WKFDE WF1 ....164 E6
Leeds La *RTHW* LS26 ....126 E1
Leeds Old Rd *BFDE* BD3 ....7 K4
　HECK WF16 ....159 K3
Leeds Rd *AL/HA/HU* LS17 ....46 A7
　BFD BD1 ....6 B6
　BHP/TINH LS16 ....41 G7
　BTLY WF17 ....140 D5
　CAS WF10 ....147 J1
　CAS WF10 ....168 C3
　EARD/LOFT WF3 ....144 C5
　EARD/LOFT WF3 ....164 C1
　EARL WF12 ....161 H7
　ECHL BD2 ....98 C2
　GFTH/SHER LS25 ....127 J2
　GSLY LS20 ....59 F3
　HIPP HX3 ....135 K6
　HIPP HX3 ....136 C7
　HUDN HD2 ....177 K7
　ILK LS29 ....24 B4
　LVSG WF15 ....159 K3
　MIRF WF14 ....179 F1
　MSTN/BAR LS15 ....106 B1
　OSS WF5 ....162 B7
　OT LS21 ....39 J3
　RTHW LS26 ....124 D6
　RTHW LS26 ....146 E4
　SHPY BD18 ....77 J4
　TAD LS24 ....70 A1
　WBY LS22 ....46 C3
　WKFDE WF1 ....18 D1
　YEA LS19 ....79 K1
Leeds St *KGHY* BD21 ....2 E5
Leefield Rd *HECK* WF16 ....160 B2
Lee Gn *MIRF* WF14 ....179 H3
Leeke Av *HOR/CROF* WF4 ....183 F7
Lee La *BGLY* BD16 ....75 F5
　HIPP HX3 ....135 G4
　HORS LS18 ....80 B1
　HWTH BD22 ....92 A2
　WIL/AL BD15 ....74 E6
Lee La East *HORS* LS18 ....80 E2
Lee La West *HORS* LS18 ....80 C2
Leeming St *BFD* BD1 ....6 A4
Lee Moor La *EARD/LOFT* WF3 ....145 F7
Lee Moor Rd *EARD/LOFT* WF3 ....165 G2
Lee Mount Gdns *HIPP* HX3 ....16 C1
Lee Mount Rd *HIPP* HX3 ....16 C1
Lee Orchards *BSPA/BRAM* LS23 ....48 C2
Lee Rd *DEWS* WF13 ....180 A4
Lees Av *EARL* WF12 ....181 F5
Lees Bank Av *HWTH* BD22 ....73 F4
Lees Bank Dr *HWTH* * BD22 ....73 F4
Lees Bank Hl *HWTH* BD22 ....73 F4
Lees Bank Rd *HWTH* BD22 ....73 F4
Lees Cl *CUL/QBY* BD13 ....73 K6
Lees Dr *EARL* * WF12 ....181 F5
Lees Hall Rd *EARL* WF12 ....180 C5
Lees Holm *EARL* WF12 ....181 F5
Lees House Rd *EARL* WF12 ....181 F5
Leeside Av *HUDN* HD2 ....177 G5
Lees La *HWTH* BD22 ....72 E4
　PDSY/CALV LS28 ....100 A1
Lee Mor Rd *CUL/QBY* BD13 ....73 K6
Lee St *BFD* BD1 ....5 L7
　BRIG HD6 ....157 F4
　CUL/QBY BD13 ....115 G3
　DEWS WF13 ....180 B3
　LVSG WF15 ....159 H3
　WKFDE WF1 ....18 E4
Leesworth Ct *HWTH* * BD22 ....73 F4
Legion St *GFTH/SHER* LS25 ....131 F3
Legrams Av *GTHN* BD7 ....116 E1
Legrams La *GTHN* BD7 ....4 C9
Legrams Mill La *GTHN* BD7 ....4 C7
Legrams St *GTHN* BD7 ....4 F6
Legrams Ter *GTHN* BD7 ....5 G6
Leicester Cl *LDSU* LS2 ....9 M4

Leicester Gv LDSU LS2......9 M4
Leicester Pl LDSU LS2......9 M4
Leicester St BOW BD4......118 B2
Leicester Ter HIPP HX3......154 E4
Leigh Av EARD/LOFT WF3......143 F7
Leigh Rd EARD/LOFT WF3......143 F7
Leigh St RPDN/SBR HX6......153 K3
Leighton La LDS LS1......9 K8
Leighton Pl LDS * LS1......9 L8
Leigh Vw EARD/LOFT WF3......142 E7
Leith St KGHY BD21......2 E3
Lemans Dr DEWS WF13......160 C5
Lemington Av HFAX HX1......16 D8
Lemon St HFAX HX1......16 B6
  WBOW BD5......117 H4
Lemon Tree Cl PONT WF8......189 G3
Lenham Cl MOR LS27......141 K4
Lenhurst Av WOR/ARM LS12......101 K2
Lennie St KGHY BD21......2 E7
Lennon Dr WKFDW/WTN WF2 * 183 J7
Lennox Gdns MSTN/BAR LS15......105 K6
Lennox Rd BULY LS4......8 C6
Lens Dr BAIL BD17......57 H7
Lentilfield St HIPP HX3......134 D5
Lentilfield Ter HIPP HX3......134 D5
Lenton Dr BEE/HOL LS11......123 H4
Lenton Vls IDLE BD10......78 C3
Leodis Ct BEE/HOL LS11......13 L3
Leodis Wy RTHW LS26......124 C6
Leonard's Pl BGLY BD16......75 J2
Leonard St BGLY BD16......75 K2
  LM/WK BD12......137 J4
Leopold Gdns CHAL LS7......10 E3
Leopold Gv CHAL LS7......10 D3
Leopold St CHAL LS7......10 D3
  OSS WF5......183 F5
Lepton Dr MOR LS27......121 G7
Leslie Av YEA LS19......59 J3
Leslie Ter HDGY LS6......9 K2
Lesmere Gv GTHN BD7......116 E4
Lessarna Ct BOW * BD4......7 G9
Leven Gdns WBY LS22......29 G2
Levens Bank MSTN/BAR LS15......104 E7
Levens Cl MSTN/BAR LS15......105 F7
Levens Garth MSTN/BAR LS15......105 F7
Levens Pl MSTN/BAR LS15......105 F7
Leventhorpe Ct RTHW LS26......145 K2
Leventhorpe Wy RTHW LS26......145 K2
Leveret Wy BTLY WF17......140 E6
Lever St WBSY BD6......117 H5
Levita Gv BOW BD4......118 E2
Levita Pl BOW BD4......118 E2
  MSTN/BAR LS15......105 F5
Lewin Gv CAS WF10......149 J7
Lewis Cl CUL/QBY BD13......115 C5
Lewisham Gv MOR LS27......142 A3
Lewisham St MOR LS27......141 H4
Lewis St HFAX HX1......16 F4
Lexington Cl BOW BD4......118 C6
Leyburn Av HECK WF16......160 B3
  HIPP HX3......136 C7
Leyburne St GIR BD8......4 E7
Leyburn Gv BGLY BD16......55 K7
  SHPY BD18......77 F5
Leyden Ri WIL/AL BD15......96 A5
Leyfield BAIL BD17......77 F1
Ley Fleaks Rd IDLE BD10......78 C5
Leyland Cft HUDN HD2......177 K3
Leyland Rd BTLY WF17......140 E4
  CAS WF10......149 J7
Leylands Av HTON BD9......96 C2
Leylands Gv HTON BD9......96 C2
Leylands La HTON BD9......96 C2
  KGHY BD21......3 J6
Leylands Rd LDSU LS2......10 D7
Leylands Ter HTON BD9......96 C2
Ley La WOR/ARM LS12......8 C7
Leys Cl IDLE BD10......78 B3
Leysholme Crs WOR/ARM LS12......102 A3
Leysholme Dr WOR/ARM LS12......102 A3
Leysholme Ter WOR/ARM LS12......102 A3
Leysholme Vw WOR/ARM LS12......101 K7
Leyside Dr WIL/AL BD15......96 A3
Leys La BSPA/BRAM LS23......48 A2
  KNOT WF11......171 G6
Leys Rd PONT WF8......191 G3
Leyton Crs IDLE * BD10......78 C5
Leyton Dr IDLE BD10......78 C5
Leyton Gv IDLE BD10......78 C5
Leyton Ter IDLE BD10......78 C5
Ley Top La WIL/AL BD15......96 B5
Leywell Ter WOR/ARM LS12......101 K5
Libbey St GIR BD8......4 E7
Lichen Cl GTHN BD7......117 F3
Lichfield Mt PDSY/CALV LS28......97 K1
Lichfield Rd EARL WF12......181 J1
Lickless Av HORS LS18......81 G3
Lickless Dr HORS LS18......81 G3
Lickless Gdns HORS LS18......81 G3
Lickless Ter HORS LS18......81 G3
Lidgate Cl DEWS WF13......161 F6
Lidgate La DEWS WF13......161 F6
Lidget Av GTHN * BD7......116 E1
Lidget HI PDSY/CALV LS28......100 B5
Lidget La HOR/CROF WF4......187 C7
Lidget Pl GTHN BD7......4 B9
Lidgett Av RHAY LS8......84 A3
Lidgett Ct GFTH/SHER LS25......107 H7
  RHAY LS8......84 A4
Lidgett Crs RHAY LS8......84 A4
Lidget Ter CLAY BD14......116 C2
Lidgett Gv RHAY LS8......84 A3
Lidgett HI RHAY LS8......84 A4
Lidgett La AL/HA/HU LS17......83 K3
  GFTH/SHER LS25......107 H7
Lidgett Mt RHAY LS8......84 A3
Lidgett Park Av RHAY LS8......84 A3
Lidgett Park Gdns RHAY LS8......84 A4
Lidgett Park Gv RHAY LS8......84 A4
Lidgett Park Ms RHAY LS8......84 B3
Lidgett Park Rd RHAY LS8......84 B3
Lidgett Park Vw RHAY LS8......84 A3
Lidgett Pl RHAY LS8......84 A4
Lidgett Wk RHAY LS8......84 A3
Lifton Pl LDSU LS2......9 J5
Light Bank La AIRE BD20......21 K5
Lightcliffe Rd BRIG HD6......157 F4

Lightcliffe Royd La
  GTL/HWG HX4......173 K3
Lightfoot Av CAS WF10......168 C2
Lightfoot Cl CAS WF10......168 C2
Lighthazles Chapel Rd
  RPDN/SBR HX6......172 B3
Lighthazles Rd RPDN/SBR HX6......172 C2
Light La WKFDW/WTN WF2......183 K2
Lightowler Cl HFAX HX1......16 D5
Lightowler Rd HFAX HX1......16 D5
Lightowler St WBSY BD6......117 H5
Lightridge Cl HUDN......176 E5
Lightridge Rd HUDN HD2......176 E4
The Lilacs GSLY LS20......59 F2
Lilac Av WKFDW/WTN WF2......184 D6
Lilac Cl BRIG HD6......157 H5
  ILK LS29......22 D1
Lilac Gv BOW BD4......7 J8
  CLECK BD19......139 H6
  SHPY BD18......77 J7
Lilac Gv GFTH/SHER LS25......151 J1
Lilac St HIPP HX3......16 D2
Lilian St BOW BD4......118 D3
Lillands Av BRIG HD6......156 E6
Lillands La BRIG HD6......156 E6
Lillands Ter BRIG HD6......156 E6
Lilly La HIPP HX3......17 J7
Lilly St RPDN/SBR HX6......153 J5
Lily Cft GIR BD8......4 E1
Lilycroft Rd GIR BD8......4 A2
Lily St GIR BD8......97 G3
Lilythorne Av IDLE BD10......78 D4
Lime Cl ILK LS29......22 A1
  KGHY BD21......2 C1
Lime Gv YEA LS19......59 H7
Lime Pit La EARD/LOFT WF3......165 G4
Limes Av HIPP HX3......155 F4
Lime St BGLY LS......75 J1
  GTHN BD7......117 F2
  HWTH BD22......72 D6
  KGHY BD21......2 E5
  OSS WF5......182 D5
Lime Tree Av AL/HA/HU LS17......83 K2
  BSPA/BRAM LS23......48 C3
  BTLY WF17......160 D4
  PONT WF8......189 G1
Lime Tree Cl RTHW LS26......126 A7
Lime-tree Crs
  GFTH/SHER LS25......128 B5
Lime Tree Gdns
  BSPA/BRAM LS23......48 D3
Lime Tree Gv BIRK/DRI * BD11......119 H7
  MIRF WF14......179 H1
Limetrees PONT WF8......170 B4
Lime Tree Sq SHPY BD18......76 C4
Limewood Ap SCFT LS14......85 H5
Limewood Rd SCFT LS14......85 H6
Lincoln Av HECK WF16......160 A4
  LVSG WF15......159 G6
Lincoln Dr LVSG WF15......159 H6
Lincoln Green Ct OSM LS9......10 E7
Lincoln Green Rd OSM LS9......10 E7
Lincoln Gv LVSG WF15......159 G6
Lincoln Rd EARL WF12......161 J7
  OSM LS9......10 E6
Lincoln St CAS WF10......148 D7
  WKFDW/WTN WF2......184 A2
Lincoln Wk GFTH/SHER LS25......128 B4
Lincoln Wy HIPP HX3......16 F2
Lincombe Bank RHAY LS8......83 K4
Lincombe Dr RHAY LS8......83 K5
Lincombe Mt RHAY LS8......83 K4
Lincombe Ri RHAY LS8......83 K4
Lincroft Crs BRAM LS13......101 G2
Lincs Wold LVSG WF15......158 C4
Lindale Cl MID LS10......123 J7
Lindale Garth
  WKFDW/WTN WF2......163 H6
Lindale Gv WKFDW/WTN WF2 ...163 J7
Lindale La WKFDW/WTN WF2......163 H6
Lindale Mt WKFDW/WTN WF2......163 H7
Linden Av BEE/HOL LS11......13 M9
  BFDE BD3......7 M4
Linden Cl AL/HA/HU LS17......46 A6
  BRIG HD6......157 H5
  CAS WF10......169 J2
  EARL WF12......182 A2
  KNOT WF11......170 D4
Linden Gdns BEE/HOL LS11......123 H3
Linden Gv BEE/HOL LS11......14 A9
Linden Mt BEE/HOL LS11......13 M9
Linden Pl BEE/HOL LS11......123 H3
Linden Ri KGHY BD21......3 L8
Linden Rd BEE/HOL * LS11......13 M9
  ELL HX5......175 H3
  HIPP HX3......155 F4
Linden Ter PONT WF8......189 H1
Linden Wy WBY LS22......29 G2
Lindisfarne Rd SHPY BD18......76 E5
Lindley Av HUDW HD3......175 K6
Lindley Dr GTHN BD7......116 E4
Lindley Moor Rd HUDW HD3......175 H7
Lindley Rd ELL HX5......175 J5
  WBOW BD5......117 J3
Lindrick Gv LUD/ILL HX2......114 C7
Lindrick Wk LUD/ILL HX2......114 C7
Lindrick Wy LUD/ILL HX2......114 C7
Lindsay Acre EARD/LOFT WF3......143 F7
Lindsay Av WKFDW/WTN WF2......183 H4
Lindsay Rd GFTH/SHER LS25......107 J3
Lindsey Ct OSM LS9......10 F7
Lindsey Gdns OSM LS9......10 E7
Lindsey Mt OSM LS9......10 F6
Lindsey Rd OSM LS9......10 E7
Lindwell Av GTL/HWG HX4......175 F2
Lindwell Gv GTL/HWG HX4......175 F2
Linefield Rd BTLY WF17......161 G3
Lineham Ct LVSG WF15......159 H6
Lineside Cottages
  EARL * WF12......180 D6
Lingard St BFD1......6 A4
Ling Bob LUD/ILL HX2......134 A7
Ling Bob Cft LUD/ILL HX2......134 A6
Ling Cft BSPA/BRAM LS23......48 A2
Lingdale Rd LM/WK BD12......137 F1
Lingfield Ap AL/HA/HU LS17......83 G1
Lingfield Bank AL/HA/HU LS17......83 G1

Lingfield Cl AL/HA/HU LS17......83 H1
Lingfield Crs AL/HA/HU LS17......83 G1
  WBSY BD6......116 B4
Lingfield Dr AL/HA/HU LS17......83 H1
  HWTH BD22......73 H3
Lingfield Gdns AL/HA/HU LS17......83 G1
Lingfield Ga AL/HA/HU LS17......83 G1
Lingfield Gn AL/HA/HU LS17......83 G1
Lingfield Gv AL/HA/HU LS17......83 H1
  WIL/AL BD15......75 G7
Lingfield Mt AL/HA/HU LS17......83 H1
Lingfield Rd AL/HA/HU LS17......83 G1
  WIL/AL BD15......95 F1
Lingfield Ter WBSY BD6......116 B4
Lingfield Vw AL/HA/HU LS17......83 G1
Lingfield Wk AL/HA/HU LS17......83 G1
Ling La AL/HA/HU LS17......65 G4
Ling Park Ap WIL/AL BD15......95 F1
Ling Park Av WIL/AL BD15......95 F1
Ling Royd Av LUD/ILL HX2......134 A7
Lingwell Ap MID LS10......143 H3
Lingwell Av MID LS10......143 H2
Lingwell Cha EARD/LOFT WF3......164 C2
Lingwell Ct EARD/LOFT WF3......164 B3
  MID LS10......143 H3
Lingwell Crs MID LS10......143 H2
Lingwell Gdns MID LS10......143 H3
Lingwell Gate Crs WKFDE WF1......164 C3
Lingwell Gate Dr WKFDE WF1......164 B3
Lingwell Gate La
  EARD/LOFT WF3......144 A6
Lingwell Gn MID LS10......143 H3
Lingwell Gv MID LS10......143 H3
Lingwell Ms MID * LS10......143 H3
Lingwell Nook La
  EARD/LOFT WF3......144 B7
Lingwell Rd MID LS10......143 H2
Lingwell Vw MID * LS10......143 H3
Lingwood Av GIR BD8......4 A2
Lingwood Rd GIR BD8......4 A3
Lingwood Ter GIR BD8......4 A3
The Link PONT WF8......189 H1
  RTHW LS26......126 C5
Link Rd EARL WF12......181 G2
  WKFDE WF1......184 C1
The Links BEE/HOL LS11......123 F7
  FEA/AMT WF7......168 C7
  TAD LS24......70 D1
Links Av CLECK BD19......138 E6
Linkway BGLY BD16......75 K5
Linnet Cl GIR * BD8......96 B5
  MIRF WF14......179 H1
Linnet Ct MOR LS27......142 C4
Linnet St KGHY BD21......3 H3
Linnhe Av WBSY BD6......136 E1
Linton Av AIRE BD20......21 F7
  AL/HA/HU LS17......64 A7
  BTLY WF17......160 C3
  WBY LS22......29 G3
Linton Cl AL/HA/HU LS17......63 K7
  LVSG WF15......159 G3
Linton Common WBY LS22......46 D1
Linton Crs AL/HA/HU LS17......64 A7
Linton Gv AL/HA/HU LS17......63 K7
  BRIG HD6......176 D1
Linton Hills Rd WBY LS22......29 F4
Linton La WBY LS22......28 C2
  WBY LS22......29 F5
Linton Mdw WBY LS22......29 F4
Linton Ri AL/HA/HU LS17......63 K7
  NORM WF6......167 G7
Linton Rd WBY LS22......29 F4
  WBY LS22......46 E1
  WKFDE WF1......19 M4
Linton St BOW BD4......118 A2
  HWTH BD22......2 A9
Linton Vw AL/HA/HU LS17......63 K6
Lionel St OSS WF5......182 D5
Lippersley La AIRE BD20......21 H3
Liquorice Wy PONT WF8......189 H1
Lisbon Sq LDS LS1......9 J9
Lisbon St LDS LS1......9 K9
Lisheen Av CAS WF10......168 C2
Lisheen Gv CAS WF10......168 D1
Lisker Av OT LS21......39 J3
Lisker Ct OT LS21......39 J3
Lisker Dr OT LS21......39 J3
Lismore Cl RTHW LS26......145 G2
Lismore Rd KGHY BD21......2 E1
Lister Av BOW BD4......118 C3
Lister Ct FEA/AMT WF7......188 B4
Lister Ct HFAX HX1......17 G6
Listerdale LVSG WF15......159 H3
Lister Gdns GIR BD8......97 H3
Lister HI HORS LS18......81 F2
Lister La GIR BD8......5 G2
Lister Vw GIR BD8......5 G2
Lister Wk MOR LS27......141 J1
Listing Av LVSG WF15......159 J3
Listing Ct LVSG WF15......159 J3
Listing Dr LVSG WF15......159 J3
Listing La LVSG WF15......159 J3
Litell Royd FEA/AMT WF7......187 G4
Little Baines St HFAX HX1......16 C5
Littlebeck Dr BGLY BD16......76 B1
Little Bradley GTL/HWG HX4......175 F3
Little Catterton La TAD LS24......51 H5
Little Church La RTHW LS26......147 F5
Little Cote IDLE BD10......78 B3
Little Cross St WBOW BD5......117 K4
Littlefield Gv OSS WF5......182 D3
Littlefield Rd OSS WF5......182 D4
Littlefield Wk WBSY BD6......117 G6
Little Fountain St MOR LS27......141 K3
Little Green La HECK WF16......159 K3

Little Hew Royd IDLE BD10......78 A4
Little Horton Gn WBOW BD5......117 H1
Little Horton La WBOW BD5......5 L7
Little King St LDS LS1......13 M1
Littlelands BGLY BD16......75 K5
Littlelands Ct BGLY * BD16......75 K5
Little La AIRE BD20......55 H3
  EARD/LOFT WF3......145 H4
  FEA/AMT WF7......188 D5
  HTON BD9......96 E3
  ILK LS29......24 B5
  MOR LS27......122 B6
Little Lane Ct MOR LS27......122 B6
Littlemoor CUL/QBY BD13......115 K5
Littlemoor Ct
  PDSY/CALV LS28......100 C7
Littlemoor Crs
  PDSY/CALV LS28......120 B1
Littlemoor Crs South
  PDSY/CALV LS28......120 B1
Littlemoor Gdns LUD/ILL HX2......134 B1
  PDSY/CALV LS28......120 B1
Littlemoor Gv MIRF WF14......179 G4
Littlemoor La SCFT LS14......66 C6
Little Moor Pl WOR/ARM LS12......102 A6
Littlemoor Rd LUD/ILL HX2......134 B1
  MIRF WF14......179 G4
  PDSY/CALV LS28......100 B7
Littlemoor Vw
  PDSY/CALV LS28......100 C7
Little Neville St LDS LS1......13 M2
Little Pk IDLE BD10......79 F3
Little Queen St LDS LS1......9 K9
Littlethorpe HI LVSG WF15......158 E6
Littlethorpe Rd LVSG WF15......158 E6
Little Wood Dr CLECK BD19......138 E5
Little Woodhouse BRIG HD6......157 F6
Little Woodhouse St LDSU LS2......9 K7
Litton Cft WKFDE WF1......19 L3
Littondale Cl BAIL BD17......57 K7
Litton Rd HWTH BD22......2 C7
Litton Wy SCFT LS14......85 J4
Liversedge Hall La LVSG WF15......159 H5
Livingstone Cl ECHL BD2......78 A6
Livingstone Rd ECHL BD2......78 A7
  SHPY BD18......97 J1
Livingstone St HIPP HX3......16 D1
Livingstone St North
  LUD/ILL HX2......134 D2
Livinia Gv CHAL LS7......9 M4
Lloyds Dr LM/WK BD12......137 K1
Lobley St HECK WF16......160 B4
Locarno Av HTON BD9......96 D3
Locherbie Gn WIL/AL * BD15......95 K4
Lochy Rd WBSY BD6......136 E1
Lock La CAS WF10......148 C6
  NORM WF6......166 C2
The Locks BGLY BD16......55 J7
Locksley Rd BRIG HD6......157 J7
Lock St EARL WF12......181 G5
  HIPP * HX3......17 K8
Lock Vw ELL HX5......175 K1
Lock Wy DEWS WF13......180 B5
Lockwood Av MIRF WF14......179 J2
Lockwood Cl BEE/HOL LS11......123 G5
Lockwood Ct BEE/HOL LS11......123 H5
Lockwood Pk BEE/HOL LS11......123 H5
Lockwood St LM/WK BD12......137 K2
  SHPY * BD18......76 E4
  WBSY BD6......117 H5
Lockwood Wy BEE/HOL LS11......123 H5
Lode Pit La BGLY BD16......56 C7
Lodge Av CAS WF10......169 H1
  ELL HX5......176 B2
Lodge Dr ELL HX5......176 B2
Lodge Farm Cl EARL WF12......181 G5
Lodge Farm Gdns NORM WF6......166 B5
Lodge Gate Cl CUL/QBY BD13......94 B4
Lodge HI BAIL BD17......76 E1
Lodge Hill Cl WOR/ARM LS12......121 C7
Lodge Hill Rd OSS WF5......182 C1
Lodge La BEE/HOL LS11......13 K9
  HOR/CROF WF4......186 B7
  LUD/ILL * HX2......133 F2
  LVSG WF15......160 A6
Lodge Pl ELL * HX5......176 B2
Lodge Rd PDSY/CALV LS28......100 A5
Lodge St CUL/QBY BD13......74 A6
  LDS LS1......9 L5
Lodge Ter BEE/HOL * LS11......123 C4
Lodore Pl ECHL BD2......98 C2
Lodore Rd ECHL BD2......98 B2
Lofthouse Pl LDSU LS2......9 M5
Lofthouse Ter CHAL LS7......10 A5
Loft St GIR BD8......4 A4
Lolner Ct OSM LS9......124 D1
Lombardi Ct OSS WF5......182 E5
Lombard St HFAX HX1......16 B9
  MSTN/BAR LS15......105 G6
  YEA LS19......59 H7
Lombardy Garth
  WKFDW/WTN WF2......18 A1
Lomond Av HORS LS18......60 E7
Londesboro Gv OSM LS9......15 J1
Londesboro Ter OSM LS9......15 K1
London La YEA LS19......59 H7
London Rd RPDN/SBR HX6......154 A5
London St YEA LS19......59 H7
Long Acre CAS WF10......168 C2
Longacre La HWTH BD22......72 E4
Longacres HWTH BD22......73 F4
Longbottom Av AIRE BD20......33 G1
  RPDN/SBR HX6......153 F5
Longbottom Ter HIPP * HX3......155 J4
Longbow Cl HUDN HD2......177 J4
Long Cswy BHP/TINH LS16......62 C6
  EARD/LOFT WF3......165 G3
  EARL WF12......181 G6
  HWTH BD22......93 H4
  OSM LS9......15 G5
  WKFDE WF1......19 G1
The Long Cswy LUD/ILL HX2......152 B2
Longcauseway EARL WF12......181 G1

Long Cl LM/WK BD12......137 G3
Long Close La OSM LS9......15 G2
Long Crest PONT WF8......189 G3
Longcroft KGHY BD21......3 H6
Longcroft Pl BFD BD1......5 K6
Longcroft Rd ILK LS29......24 D6
Longdike Ct GFTH/SHER LS25 ...128 A5
Longdike La GFTH/SHER LS25......128 B6
Long Edge Low Rd
  RPDN/SBR HX6......152 C6
Long Edge Rd RPDN/SBR HX6......152 C6
Long Fallas Crs BRIG HD6......177 G2
Longfellow Gv
  EARD/LOFT WF3......165 F2
Longfield GTL/HWG HX4......174 E5
Longfield Av HIPP HX3......135 K6
  PDSY/CALV LS28......100 C6
Longfield Ct HECK WF16......160 A4
  PDSY/CALV LS28......100 C6
Longfield Dr BOW BD4......118 D3
  BRAM LS13......100 C1
  MSTN/BAR LS15......105 H5
Longfield Garth BRAM LS13......80 C7
Longfield Gv PDSY/CALV LS28......100 C6
Longfield Mt PDSY/CALV LS28......100 C6
Longfield Rd HECK WF16......160 A4
  PDSY/CALV LS28......100 C6
Longfield Ter PDSY/CALV LS28......100 B6
  WKFDW/WTN WF2......184 A2
Longford Ter GTHN BD7......4 B9
Long Heads La
  GFTH/SHER LS25......131 G5
Long Heys GTL/HWG HX4......175 F3
Long Hill Rd HUDN HD2......177 G5
Longhouse Dr CUL/QBY BD13......94 A5
Longhouse La CUL/QBY BD13......94 A5
Long House Rd LUD/ILL HX2......133 K1
Longlands Av CUL/QBY BD13......94 A4
Longlands Cl OSS WF5......182 D3
Longlands Dr HWTH BD22......72 E4
Longlands Rd DEWS WF13......160 D6
  OSS WF5......182 D3
Longlands St BFD1......5 K5
Long La BGLY BD16......74 D3
  CUL/QBY BD13......115 H7
  EARL WF12......181 J3
  HIPP HX3......134 B5
  HIPP HX3......155 J2
  HTON BD9......76 C7
  MSTN/BAR LS15......87 G5
  PONT WF8......190 A3
  RPDN/SBR HX6......153 H6
  WIL/AL BD15......95 H4
Long Lee La KGHY BD21......3 K8
Long Lee Ter KGHY BD21......3 M8
Longley La RPDN/SBR HX6......173 C1
Long Meadow Ct
  GFTH/SHER LS25......127 K1
Long Meadow Ga
  GFTH/SHER LS25......127 J1
Long Mdw BHP/TINH LS16......61 H7
  ECHL BD2......97 K1
  GFTH/SHER LS25......127 J1
  ILK LS29......25 K7
Long Preston Cha IDLE * BD10......79 F5
Long Reach LUD/ILL HX2......133 H4
Long Rdg BRIG HD6......177 F2
Long Rw HOR/CROF WF4......186 D4
  HORS LS18......81 F3
  LM/WK BD12......137 J2
Longroyd SHPY BD18......78 A4
Longroyd Av BEE/HOL LS11......123 H3
Longroyd Crs BEE/HOL LS11......123 H3
Longroyd Crs North
  BEE/HOL LS11......14 B9
Long Royd Dr BAIL BD17......57 K7
Longroyde Cl BRIG HD6......176 E1
Longroyde Gv BRIG HD6......176 E1
Longroyde Rd BRIG HD6......156 E7
Longroyd Gv BEE/HOL LS11......123 H3
Longroyd Pl BEE/HOL LS11......123 H3
Long Royd Rd RPDN/SBR HX6......152 D6
Longroyd St BEE/HOL LS11......123 H3
Longroyd St North
  BEE/HOL LS11......14 B9
Longroyd Ter MID LS10......123 H3
Longroyd Vw BEE/HOL LS11......123 H3
Longside La GTHN BD7......5 H7
Long St BOW BD4......6 E9
Long Thorpe La
  EARD/LOFT WF3......144 B6
Long Wall ELL HX5......175 H3
Longwood Av BGLY BD16......55 H6
Longwood Cl AL/HA/HU LS17......64 C6
  EARD/LOFT * WF3......142 C7
Longwood Ct EARD/LOFT WF3......142 D7
Longwood Crs AL/HA/HU LS17......64 C6
Longwood Fold
  EARD/LOFT WF3......142 D7
Longwood Garth
  EARD/LOFT WF3......142 D7
Longwood House Rd
  HUDN * HD2......177 F6
Longwood Rd EARD/LOFT WF3...142 C7
Longwood V EARD/LOFT WF3......142 D7
Longwood Vw BGLY BD16......55 H6
Longwood Wy AL/HA/HU LS17......64 C6
Lonsbrough Av HECK WF16......160 A3
Lonsdale Av BTLY WF17......160 C3
Lonsdale Cl MID LS10......123 J5
Lonsdale Mdw
  BSPA/BRAM LS23......48 C3
Lonsdale Ri EARD/LOFT WF3......142 D7
Lonsdale Rd WKFDE WF1......18 C1
Lonsdale St BFDE BD3......6 E1
Lonsdale Ter LVSG * WF15......159 H4
Lord La HWTH BD22......72 C4
Lordsfield Pl BOW BD4......118 C5
Lord's La BRIG HD6......157 G7
Lord St DEWS WF13......160 C4
  EARL * WF12......182 A2
  HFAX HX1......16 F6
  KGHY BD21......3 G4
  RPDN/SBR HX6......153 K3
  WKFDE WF1......185 G6
  WOR/ARM LS12......13 H3
Lord Ter WOR/ARM LS12......13 G3

Loris St *BOW* BD4............................118 E5
Lorne St *BOW* BD4............................118 C3
  HWTH BD22 ....73 G4
  KGHY BD21 ....3 L3
Lorry Bank *CHAL* LS7 ....10 A1
Loscoe Ct *NORM* WF6 ....167 H5
Loscoe La *NORM* WF6 ....167 H6
Lotherton La *GFTH/SHER* LS25 ....88 E6
Lotherton Wy
  GFTH/SHER LS25 ....107 J5
Loughrigg St *WBOW* BD5 ....117 K3
Louisa St *CAS* WF10 ....148 B7
  IDLE * BD10 ....78 C4
Louis Av *WBOW* BD5 ....117 H2
Louis Ct *CHAL* LS7 ....10 D2
Louis Gv *CHAL* LS7 ....10 D3
Louis Le Prince Ct *RHAY* LS8 ....11 L3
Louis St *CHAL* LS7 ....10 D2
Love La *CAS* WF10 ....168 B2
  HFAX HX1 ....16 F8
  OSS WF5...182 B3
  PONT WF8 ....189 G2
  RTHW LS26..145 F2
  WKFDW/WTN WF2 ....18 C4
Love Lane Ter *PONT* WF8 ....189 H1
Lovell Park Cl *CHAL* LS7 ....10 C6
Lovell Park Ct *CHAL* LS7 ....10 B6
Lovell Park Ga *CHAL* LS7 ....10 B6
Lovell Park Gra *CHAL* LS7 ....10 C6
Lovell Park Hts *CHAL* LS7 ....10 C6
Lovell Park Ms *CHAL* LS7 ....10 C6
Lovell Park Rd *CHAL* LS7 ....10 B6
Lovell Park Vw *CHAL* LS7 ....10 C6
Low Ash Av *SHPY* BD18 ....77 J5
Low Ash Crs *SHPY* BD18.....................77 K5
Low Ash Dr *SHPY* BD18.......................77 J5
Low Ash Gv *SHPY* BD18 ....77 J5
Low Ash Rd *SHPY* BD18 ....77 K5
Low Bank Dr *HWTH* BD22 ....72 C1
Low Bank La *HWTH* BD22 ....72 C1
Low Banks *AIRE* * BD20 ....54 C1
Low Bank St *PDSY/CALV* LS28 ....99 K2
Low Cliff Wk *HECK* WF16 ....160 B6
Low Cl *BGLY* BD16 ....76 A2
  ILK LS29 ....24 A3
Low Close St *LDSU* LS2 ....9 K3
Lowcroft *WBY* LS22 ....46 D2
Lowdale *EARL* WF12 ....161 H6
Lowell Av *GTHN* BD7 ....116 E1
Lowell Gv *BRAM* LS13 ....100 D5
Lowell Pl *BRAM* LS13 ....100 D5
Lower Ashgrove *WBOW* BD5................5 K8
Lower Bankhouse
  PDSY/CALV LS28 ....120 A2
Lower Bank Houses
  GTL/HWG * HX4 ....174 A1
Lower Basinghall St *LDS* LS1 ....9 M9
Lower Bower La *DEWS* WF13 ....160 C5
Lower Brock Well La
  RPDN/SBR HX6 ....153 G6
Lower Brunswick St *LDSU* LS2 ....10 C7
Lower Cambridge St
  CAS WF10...148 C7
Lower Clifton St
  RPDN/SBR * HX6...............................153 K4
Lower Clyde St
  RPDN/SBR HX6 ....153 J5
Lower Constable Rd *LM/WK* LS24 ..24 C6
Lower Cow Cl *LM/WK* * BD12 ....138 A5
Lower Cross St *HFAX* HX1 ....17 J4
Lower Crow Nest Dr *BRIG* HD6 ....157 G1
Lower Edge Rd *ELL* HX5 ....176 A2
Lower Ellistones
  GTL/HWG * HX4 ....174 D2
Lower Finkil St *BRIG* HD6 ....156 D3
Lower Fold *BRIG* HD6 ....176 B4
Lower George St *WBSY* * BD6 ....117 G5
Lower Globe St *GIR* BD8 ....5 G4
Lower Gra *HUDN* HD2 ....177 K3
Lower Grattan Rd *BFD* BD1 ....5 J6
Lower Green Av *CLECK* BD19 ....138 A7
Lower Hall Cl *LVSG* WF15 ....159 G4
Lower Hall Dr *LVSG* WF15 ....159 G4
Lower Hall La *LVSG* WF15 ....159 G4
Lower Hall Mt *LVSG* WF15 ....159 G4
Lower Heights Rd
  CUL/QBY BD13 ....95 F5
Lower Holme *BAIL* BD17 ....77 H3
Lower House Cl *SHPY* BD18 ....78 A3
Lower Kipping La
  CUL/QBY BD13 ....95 G7
Lower Kirkgate *HFAX* HX1 ....17 K6
Lower La *BIRK/DRI* BD11 ....138 E2
Lower La *BOW* BD4 ....118 D2
  BOW BD4 ....118 D2
  CLECK BD19 ....159 J1
Lower Langwith *WBY* LS22 ....46 D2
Lower Lark HI *CLECK* BD19 ....158 C1
Lower Mickletown *RTHW* LS26 .....147 H4
Lower Mill Bank Rd
  RPDN/SBR HX6 ....172 C2
Lower Newlands *BRIG* HD6 ....157 G7
Lower North St *BTLY* WF17 ....160 E4
Lower Oxford St *CAS* WF10 ....168 C1
Lower Park Gn *NORM* WF6 ....32 D1
Lower Park Royd Dr
  RPDN/SBR HX6 ....173 F2
Lower Peel St *DEWS* WF13 ....161 F7
Lower Quarry Rd *HUDN* HD2 ....178 B2
Lower Range *HIPP* * HX3 ....17 H2
Lower Rushton Rd *BFDE* BD3 ....7 L5
Lower Sandhills *SCFT* LS14 ....86 B1
Lower School St *LM/WK* BD12 ....137 H1
  SHPY BD18 ....76 E4
Lower Station Rd *NORM* WF6 ....166 D6
Lower Tofts Rd
  PDSY/CALV LS28 ....100 B6
Lowertown *HWTH* BD22 ....92 D3
Lower Town St *BRAM* LS13 ....101 G3
Lower Warrengate *WKFDE* WF1 .....18 F4
Lower Wellington Rd *ILK* LS29 ....24 B5
Lower Westfield Rd *GIR* BD8 ....4 D1
Lower Wortley Rd
  WOR/ARM LS12 ....122 A1
Lower Wyke Gn *LM/WK* BD12 ....137 G7
Lower Wyke La *LM/WK* BD12 ....137 H7
Lower York St *WKFDE* WF1 ....18 E2
Loweswater Av *WBSY* BD6 ....136 E1

Low Farm *RTHW* LS26 ....127 H6
Lowfield Cl *LM/WK* BD12 ....137 K2
Lowfield Crs *AIRE* BD20 ....33 G2
Lowfield Rd *DEWS* WF13 ....180 C1
Low Fields Av *BEE/HOL* LS11 ....12 F8
Lowfields Cl *ELL* HX5 ....175 K1
Low Fields La *WOR/ARM* LS12 ....12 E7
Lowfields Wy *ELL* HX5 ....175 K1
Low Fold *AIRE* BD20 ....32 D4
  CLECK BD19 ....138 A7
  ECHL BD2 ....98 A3
Low Garth Link
  GFTH/SHER LS25 ....111 F6
Low Garth Rd *GFTH/SHER* LS25 ....111 F6
Low Gipton Crs *OSM* LS9 ....104 E2
Low Grange Crs *MID* LS10 ....123 K5
Low Grange Vw *MID* LS10 ....123 K6
Low Gn *BD7* 117 F3
  KNOT WF11 ....171 J4
  YEA LS19 ....79 K1
Low Green Ter *GTHN* BD7................117 G3
Low Hall Pl *BEE/HOL* LS11 ....13 H4
Low Hall Rd *ILK* LS29 ....38 C6
  YEA LS19 ....80 A4
Low Ho Dr *AIRE* BD20 ....33 F3
Low House Fold *LVSG* WF15 ....159 G4
Lowlands Rd *MIRF* WF14 ....179 J5
Low La *AIRE* BD20 ....20 D4
  AIRE BD20 ....33 G3
  BRIG HD6 ....157 H2
  BTLY WF17 ....140 B6
  CLAY BD14 ....115 K1
  CUL/QBY BD13 ....115 F3
  HIPP HX3 ....112 B7
  HORS LS18 ....81 G2
Low MI *ILK* * LS29 ....23 J5
Low Mill La *DEWS* WF13 ....180 B5
  ILK LS29 ....22 E1
  KGHY BD21 ....3 J4
Low Mill Rd *OSS* WF5 ....182 B6
Low Mills *GSLY* * LS20 ....59 F3
Low Mills Rd
  WOR/ARM LS12 ....122 A2
Low Moor Side
  WOR/ARM LS12 ....121 G3
Low Moorside Cl
  WOR/ARM LS12 ....121 H3
Low Moor Side La
  WOR/ARM LS12 ....121 F4
Low Moor St *LM/WK* * BD12 ....137 J1
Low Moor Ter *LUD/ILL* HX2 ....154 A2
Lowood La *BTLY* WF17 ....140 B4
Low Park Rd *ILK* LS29 ....25 G4
Low Rd *DEWS* WF13 ....180 C1
  EARL WF12 ....181 H2
  MID LS10 ....14 F8
Lowry Rd *EARD/LOFT* WF3 ....142 D7
Lowry Vw *KGHY* BD21 ....3 H7
Low Shops La *RTHW* LS26 ....144 D1
Low Spring Rd *KGHY* BD21 ....3 M6
Low St *DEWS* * WF13 ....161 F7
  EARD/LOFT WF3 ....142 D6
  GFTH/SHER LS25 ....111 F6
  GFTH/SHER LS25 ....131 G3
  KGHY BD21 ....3 G5
  KNOT WF11 ....170 D1
Lowswater Rd *KNOT* WF11 ....171 H6
Lowther Av *GFTH/SHER* LS25 ....107 H7
Lowther Crs *RTHW* LS26 ....126 C4
Lowther Dr *GFTH/SHER* LS25 ....107 H7
  RTHW LS26..126 C4
Lowther St *RHAY* LS8 ....11 H1
Lowtown *PDSY/CALV* LS28 ....100 C5
Low Wy *BSPA/BRAM* LS23 ....48 C4
  BSPA/BRAM LS23 ....68 C1
Low Well Rd *WBOW* * BD5 ....117 J3
Low Whitehouse Rw
  MID * LS10 ....14 D6
Low Wd *WIL/AL* BD15 ....95 G1
Low Wood Cl *AIRE* * BD20 ....33 J7
Low Wood Ri *ILK* LS29 ....24 E6
Loxley Gv *WBY* LS22 ....29 G1
Loxley St *BTLY* WF17 ....160 D1
Lucas Ct *CHAL* LS7 ....10 A2
Lucas Pl *HDGY* LS6 ....9 K1
Lucas St *HDGY* LS6 ....9 K1
Lucy Av *MSTN/BAR* LS15 ....105 F5
Lucy Hall Dr *BAIL* BD17 ....76 D2
Lucy St *HIPP* HX3 ....17 K3
Luddenden La *LUD/ILL* HX2 ....152 E1
Ludlam St *WBOW* BD5.......................117 K1
Ludlow Av *GFTH/SHER* LS25 ....108 A6
Ludolf Dr *AL/HA/HU* LS17 ....65 F7
Luke Rd *WBOW* BD5 ....117 H2
Lulworth Av *MSTN/BAR* LS15 ....106 A5
Lulworth Cl *MSTN/BAR* LS15 ....106 A4
Lulworth Crs *MSTN/BAR* LS15 ....106 A4
Lulworth Garth
  MSTN/BAR LS15 ....106 A5
Lulworth Gv *BOW* BD4 ....118 E4
Lulworth Vw *MSTN/BAR* LS15 ....106 A5
Lulworth Wk *MSTN/BAR* LS15 ....106 A5
Lumb Bottom *BIRK/DRI* BD11 ....120 C7
Lumb Gill La *ILK* LS29 ....22 E3
Lumb La *GIR* BD8 ....5 H1
  HIPP HX3 ....134 C6
  LUD/ILL HX2.....................................113 G7
  LVSG WF15 ....159 G6
  RPDN/SBR HX6 ....172 D2
Lumbrook Cl *HIPP* HX3 ....136 B4
Lumby Cl *PDSY/CALV* LS28 ....120 C1
Lumby HI *GFTH/SHER* LS25 ....131 J7
Lumby La *AL/HA/HU* LS17 ....45 H4
  GFTH/SHER LS25 ....131 G4
  PDSY/CALV LS28 ....120 C1
Lumby St *IDLE* * BD10 ....78 C4
Lumley Av *BULY* LS4 ....8 C3
  CAS WF10...167 K1
Lumley HI *CAS* WF10 ....167 K1
Lumley Mt *BULY* LS4 ....8 C3
Lumley Pl *BULY* LS4 ....8 C2
Lumley Rd *BULY* LS4 ....8 C3
Lumley St *BULY* LS4 ....8 C3
Lumley Ter *BULY* LS4 ....8 C3
Lumley Vw *BULY* * LS4 ....8 C3

Lumley Wk *BULY* LS4 ....8 C3
Lunan Pl *RHAY* LS8 ....104 A1
Lunan Ter *RHAY* LS8 ....11 G1
Lund Dr *HECK* WF16 ....160 B5
Lund La *HWTH* BD22 ....52 C5
Lund Sike La *GFTH/SHER* LS25 ......131 H3
Lund St *BGLY* BD16 ....75 K1
  GIR BD8 ....96 D6
  KGHY BD21 ....3 C3
Lunnfields La *KNOT* WF11 ....150 C3
Lupset Crs *WKFDW/WTN* WF2 ......183 H6
Lupton Av *OSM* LS9 ....11 K8
Lupton St *GIR* BD8 ....5 K2
  MID LS10 ....14 E9
Lustre St *KGHY* BD21 ....2 D5
Luther Wy *ECHL* BD2 ....98 A2
Luton St *HFAX* HX1 ....16 B5
  KGHY BD21 ....2 F5
Luttrell Cl *BHP/TINH* LS16 ....81 K2
Luttrell Crs *BHP/TINH* LS16 ....81 K2
Luttrell Gdns *BHP/TINH* LS16 ....81 K2
Luttrell Pl *BHP/TINH* LS16 ....81 K2
Luttrell Rd *BHP/TINH* LS16 ....81 K2
The Lutyens *ILK* LS29 ....23 J5
Luxor Av *RHAY* LS8 ....11 H1
Luxor Rd *RHAY* LS8 ....11 H1
Luxor St *RHAY* LS8 ....11 H1
Luxor Vw *RHAY* LS8 ....11 H1
Lydbrook Pk *HIPP* HX3 ....154 D6
Lyddon Ter *LDSU* LS2 ....9 J5
Lydgate *HIPP* HX3 ....135 K4
  OSM LS9 ....11 H6
Lydgate Pk *HIPP* HX3 ....156 D1
Lydgate Pl *PDSY/CALV* LS28 ....79 H5
Lydgate Rd *BTLY* WF17 ....161 J3
Lydgate St *PDSY/CALV* LS28 ....79 H5
Lydget Ct *AIRE* BD20 ....53 H2
Lydia St *LDSU* LS2 ....10 C8
Lyme Cha *SCFT* LS14 ....105 C3
Lymington Dr *BOW* BD4 ....119 F2
Lynch Av *CUL/QBY* BD13 ....94 D8
Lyncroft *ECHL* BD2 ....98 A1
Lynda Gv *OSS* WF5 ....183 F5
Lyndale *GFTH/SHER* LS25 ....127 K6
Lyndale Crs *HECK* WF16 ....160 B4
Lyndale Dr *SHPY* BD18 ....78 A5
  WKFDW/WTN WF2 ....163 K6
Lyndale Gv *NORM* WF6 ....167 F7
Lyndale Ms *DEWS* WF13 ....160 C5
Lyndale Rd *BGLY* BD16 ....56 C5
Lyndean Gdns *IDLE* BD10 ....78 B5
Lynden Av *SHPY* BD18.........................77 K4
Lynden Ct *WBSY* BD6 ....117 F7
Lyndhurst *BGLY* * BD16 ....55 J7
Lyndhurst Av *BRIG* HD6 ....177 F2
Lyndhurst Cl *MSTN/BAR* LS15 ....86 C5
Lyndhurst Crs *MSTN/BAR* LS15 ....86 C5
Lyndhurst Gv *WIL/AL* BD15 ....96 B4
Lyndhurst Grove Rd *BRIG* HD6 .....177 F2
Lyndhurst Rd *BRIG* HD6 ....177 F1
  MSTN/BAR LS15 ....86 C6
Lyndhurst Vw *MSTN/BAR* LS15 ....86 C6
Lyndon Av *BSPA/BRAM* LS23 ....48 B7
  GFTH/SHER LS25 ....107 H6
Lyndon Cl *BSPA/BRAM* LS23 ....48 B7
Lyndon Crs *BSPA/BRAM* LS23 ....48 B7
Lyndon Rd *BSPA/BRAM* LS23 ....48 B7
Lyndon Sq *BSPA/BRAM* LS23 ....48 B7
Lyndon Ter *BGLY* BD16 ....75 K1
Lyndon Wy *BSPA/BRAM* LS23 ....48 B7
Lyndum Gv *GFTH/SHER* LS25 ....127 K4
Lynfield Dr *HTON* BD9 ....96 C2
  LVSG WF15 ....158 C7
Lynfield Mt *SHPY* BD18 ....77 K4
Lynmoor Ct *IDLE* BD10 ....78 B5
Lynnfield Gdns *MSTN/BAR* LS15 ......86 C6
Lynnwood Gdns
  PDSY/CALV LS28 ....99 K7
Lynsey Gdns *BOW* BD4 ....118 C3
Lynthorne Rd *HTON* BD9 ....97 G1
Lynton Av *BSPA/BRAM* LS23 ....48 C2
  EARD/LOFT WF3 ....143 K5
  HTON BD9 ....96 E2
Lynton Dr *AIRE* BD20 ....54 C2
  HTON BD9 ....96 D3
  SHPY BD18 ....77 F5
Lynton Gv *LUD/ILL* HX2 ....114 C5
Lynton Ter *CLECK* * BD19 ....138 E7
Lynton Vls *HTON* BD9 ....96 E3
Lynwood Av *RTHW* LS26 ....146 A1
  SHPY BD18 ....77 K4
  WOR/ARM LS12 ....12 B7
Lynwood Cl *BIRK/DRI* BD11 ....139 J2
  FEA/AMT WF7 ....187 H5
Lynwood Ct *HWTH* BD22 ....53 F6
Lynwood Crs *HFAX* HX1 ....16 A9
  PONT WF8 ....189 J3
  RTHW LS26..146 A1
  WOR/ARM LS12 ....12 B6
Lynwood Garth *WOR/ARM* LS12 ......12 A6
Lynwood Gv *WOR/ARM* LS12 ....12 B7
Lynwood Ms *BOW* BD4 ....119 G4
Lynwood Mt *WOR/ARM* LS12 ....12 B6
Lynwood Ri *WOR/ARM* LS12 ....12 B6
Lynwood Vw *WOR/ARM* LS12 ....12 A6
Lyon Rd *AIRE* BD20 ....32 A4
Lyon St *CUL/QBY* BD13 ....95 G4
  CUL/QBY BD13 ....115 J5
Lytham Cl *NORM* WF6 ....167 G7
Lytham Dr *CUL/QBY* BD13 ....116 A4
Lytham Gv *WOR/ARM* LS12 ....121 K2
Lytham La *AL/HA/HU* LS17 ....45 H4
Lytham Pl *WOR/ARM* LS12 ....121 K2
Lytton Rd *GIR* BD8 ....4 B3
Lytton St *HIPP* HX3 ....17 H2
  MID LS10 ....14 D9

M

Mabel Royd *GTHN* BD7 ....4 B9
Mabgate *OSM* LS9 ....10 D7
Mabgate Gn *OSM* LS9 ....10 D8
Macaulay St *OSM* LS9 ....10 E8
Mackingstone Dr *HWTH* BD22 ....72 C1
Mackingstone La *HWTH* BD22 ....72 C1
Mackinnon Av *NORM* WF6 ....167 F5

Mackintosh Homes
  LUD/ILL HX2.....................................154 D4
Maddocks St *SHPY* BD18 ....77 F4
Madeley Sq *CAS* WF10 ....149 H6
Madison Av *BOW* BD4 ....119 F5
Madni Cl *HFAX* HX1 ....16 E6
Mafeking Av *BEE/HOL* LS11 ....123 F5
Mafeking Gv *BEE/HOL* LS11 ....123 F5
Mafeking Mt *BEE/HOL* LS11 ....123 F5
Magdalene Cl *BHP/TINH* LS16 ....81 K1
Magdalene Flds *NORM* WF6 ....167 G7
Magdalene Rd
  WKFDW/WTN WF2 ....183 H4
Magnolias *BTLY* WF17 ....160 B5
Magpie Cl *WBSY* BD6..........................116 B5
Magpie La *MOR* LS27 ....142 A4
Maidstone St *BFDE* BD3 ....7 G5
Maidwell Wy *WBSY* BD6 ....137 F1
Mail Cl *MSTN/BAR* LS15 ....106 B2
Main Rd *AIRE* BD20 ....32 B5
  AIRE BD20 ....55 C3
  CUL/QBY BD13 ....94 A5
Mainspring Rd *WIL/AL* BD15 ....75 F7
Main St *AL/HA/HU* LS17 ....45 K5
  AL/HA/HU LS17 ....64 E6
  BAIL BD17 ....58 D6
  BGLY BD16 ....75 J1
  BGLY BD16 ....76 A6
  BSPA/BRAM LS23 ....31 F5
  CAS WF10...148 A3
  EARD/LOFT WF3 ....144 D2
  EARD/LOFT WF3 ....163 J1
  GFTH/SHER LS25 ....88 D7
  GFTH/SHER LS25 ....107 H6
  GFTH/SHER LS25 ....131 H6
  GFTH/SHER LS25 ....151 F4
  GSLY LS20 ....57 K3
  HWTH BD22 ....72 D5
  ILK LS29 ....22 B1
  ILK LS29 ....25 K7
  ILK LS29 ....38 A6
  LM/WK BD12 ....137 H3
  LM/WK BD12 ....137 K5
  MSTN/BAR LS15 ....86 C6
  MSTN/BAR LS15 ....87 G5
  OT LS21 ....27 F3
  RTHW LS26..147 G4
  SCFT LS14 ....66 C7
  TAD LS24 ....49 K3
  TAD LS24 ....90 C6
  TAD LS24 ....90 E7
  WBY LS22 ....28 E7
  WIL/AL BD15 ....75 F7
Maister Pl *HWTH* BD22 ....72 C1
Maitland Cl *WIL/AL* BD15 ....96 A6
Maitland Pl *BEE/HOL* LS11 ....123 K8
Maizebrook *DEWS* WF13 ....180 B1
Maize St *HWTH* BD22 ....53 H7
Major St *WKFDW/WTN* WF2 ....184 D5
Malham Av *BRIG* HD6 ....176 D1
  HTON BD9 ....96 B2
Malham Cl *SCFT* LS14 ....105 H1
Malham Dr *BTLY* WF17 ....160 D3
  LVSG WF15 ....159 G7
Malham Rd *BRIG* HD6 ....176 D2
  WKFDE WF1 ....19 L3
Malham Sq *WKFDE* WF1 ....19 M3
Malin Rd *EARL* WF12 ....161 J6
Mallard Cl *IDLE* BD10 ....78 D7
  RTHW LS26..124 A7
Mallard Ct *GIR* BD8 ....96 B6
Mallard Rd *CAS* WF10 ....168 B2
The Mallards *AIRE* BD20 ....33 F1
Mallard Vw *HWTH* BD22 ....92 D3
Mallard Wy *MOR* LS27 ....142 C3
Mallinson St *DEWS* WF13 ....160 D7
Mallory Cl *GTHN* BD7 ....4 A6
Maltby Ct *MSTN/BAR* * LS15 ....106 A6
Malthouse Cl *SCFT* LS14 ....65 K3
Malting Cl *EARD/LOFT* WF3 ....144 A1
Malting Ri *EARD/LOFT* WF3 ....144 A1
The Maltings *EARD/LOFT* WF3 ....144 C4
  HDGY * LS6 ....8 E4
  MIRF WF14 ....179 G4
  PONT WF8 ....169 J7
Maltings Ct *BEE/HOL* LS11 ....14 A8
Maltings Rd *BEE/HOL* LS11 ....14 B8
  LUD/ILL HX2.....................................134 A5
Maltkiln La *CAS* WF10 ....148 D7
Malt Kiln La *CUL/QBY* BD13 ....114 E1
  GFTH/SHER LS25 ....128 A5
Malt Kiln Ter *TAD* LS24 ....70 C4
Malton St *HIPP* HX3 ....135 F5
  RPDN/SBR HX6 ....153 J3
Malt St *HWTH* BD22 ....53 H7
Malvern Brow *HTON* BD9 ....96 C3
Malvern Cl *CAS* WF10 ....167 J3
Malvern Crs *AIRE* BD20 ....34 A7
Malvern Gv *BEE/HOL* LS11 ....13 K8
  HTON BD9 ....96 C3
Malvern Ri *BEE/HOL* LS11 ....13 K8
Malvern Rd *BEE/HOL* LS11 ....13 K8
  EARL WF12 ....161 H7
  HTON BD9 ....96 C4
  KNOT WF11 ....171 H4
Malvern St *BEE/HOL* LS11 ....13 J8
Malvern Vw *BEE/HOL* LS11 ....13 J8
Manchester Rd *BTLY* WF17 ....117 J6
Mandale Gv *WBSY* BD6 ....116 C6
Mandale Rd *WBSY* BD6 ....116 C6
Mandarin Wy *RTHW* LS26 ....124 A7
Mandeville Crs *WBSY* BD6 ....116 E6
Mangrill La *BSPA/BRAM* LS23 ....67 G5
Manitoba Pl *CHAL* LS7 ....83 K6
Manley Ct *GFTH/SHER* LS25 ....127 J1
Manley Dr *WBY* LS22 ....28 E3
Manley Rd *ILK* LS29 ....24 C6
Manley Ri *ILK* LS29 ....24 C6

Manley St *BRIG* HD6 ....157 F5
Mannerley Gv *CLECK* BD19 ....159 J2
Mannheim Rd *HTON* BD9 ....97 F3
Manningham La *GIR* BD8 ....5 J1
Mannville Gv *HWTH* BD22 ....2 C7
Mannville Pl *HWTH* BD22 ....2 C7
Mannville Rd *KGHY* BD21 ....2 D8
Mannville St *HWTH* BD22 ....2 C7
Mannville Ter *GTHN* BD7 ....5 K8
Mannville Wk *HWTH* * BD22 ....2 C7
Mannville Wy *HWTH* BD22 ....2 C7
Manor Av *HDGY* LS6 ....8 E1
  OSS WF5...182 E6
Manor Cl *BHP/TINH* LS16 ....41 G7
  BIRK/DRI BD11 ....120 B7
  GIR BD8 ....96 C5
  HIPP HX3 ....154 E4
  OSS WF5...182 E6
  RTHW LS26..145 F1
  YEA LS19 ....59 J4
Manor Cottage Ms *SCFT* LS14 ....65 K5
Manor Cft *AL/HA/HU* LS17 ....65 F7
  BGLY * BD16 ....75 K5
  KNOT WF11 ....150 B2
  OSS WF5...182 E6
Manor Crs *OT* LS21 ....41 F3
  RTHW LS26..144 E2
  WKFDW/WTN WF2 ....183 K5
Manor Cft *MSTN/BAR* LS15 ....105 K6
Manor Dr *BGLY* BD16 ....75 K5
  FEA/AMT WF7 ....168 B7
  HDGY LS6 ....8 E2
  HIPP HX3 ....154 E4
  MIRF WF14 ....178 E2
  OSS WF5...182 E6
Manor Farm Cl *BGLY* BD16 ....76 A6
  MID LS10 ....143 J1
Manor Farm Crs *MOR* LS27 ....122 B6
Manor Farm Dr *BTLY* WF17 ....161 J2
  MID LS10 ....143 H1
Manor Farm Gdns *MID* LS10 ....143 H1
Manor Farm Gn *MID* LS10 ....143 H1
Manor Farm Gv *MID* LS10 ....143 H1
Manor Farm Ri *MID* LS10 ....143 J1
Manor Farm Rd *MID* LS10 ....143 H1
Manor Farm Wy *MID* LS10 ....143 H2
Manorfield Dr *HOR/CROF* WF4 ......183 F7
Manor Fold *BGLY* BD16 ....76 A6
Manor Gdns *CUL/QBY* BD13 ....74 A7
  EARL * WF12 ....161 K6
  OT LS21 ....41 F3
  SCFT LS14 ....66 D5
Manor Garth *GFTH/SHER* LS25 ......129 J6
  MSTN/BAR LS15 ....105 K6
Manor Garth Rd *EARL* WF12 ....181 J2
  GFTH/SHER LS25 ....128 A4
Manor Gv *AIRE* BD20 ....54 D3
  CAS WF10...168 D2
  CHAL LS7 ....83 J2
  OSS WF5...182 E6
Manor Haigh Rd
  WKFDW/WTN WF2 ....183 K6
Manor Heath Rd *HIPP* HX3 ....154 E4
Manor House Cft
  BHP/TINH LS16 ....82 C1
Manor House La *AL/HA/HU* LS17 .....41 F6
Manor House Rd *WIL/AL* BD15 ....75 F6
Manor La *OSS* WF5 ....182 E6
  SHPY BD18 ....77 G5
Manorley La *HIPP* HX3 ....136 D1
Manor Mill La *BEE/HOL* LS11 ....148 D1
Manor Pk *CAS* WF10 ....148 D1
  EARL WF12 ....162 A5
  GIR BD8 ....96 C5
  HWTH BD22 ....72 C5
  MIRF WF14 ....178 D2
  PONT WF8 ....190 E4
  SCFT LS14 ....65 K4
Manor Park Av *CAS* WF10 ....148 A3
  PONT WF8 ....170 A5
Manor Park Gdns *CLECK* BD19 ....139 H4
Manor Ri *ILK* LS29 ....24 C5
Manor Rd *AIRE* BD20 ....53 H1
  BEE/HOL LS11 ....13 L4
  BGLY BD16 ....76 A5
  BTLY WF17 ....161 J3
  DEWS WF13 ....180 E2
  HORS LS18 ....80 D4
  MOR LS27 ....122 B6
  OSS WF5...183 F5
  RTHW LS26..144 E1
  TAD LS24 ....50 E6
  TAD LS24 ....70 D3
  WKFDW/WTN WF2 ....184 D4
Manor Rw *BFD* BD1 ....5 L4
  WBSY BD6 ....117 H7
Manor Sq *YEA* LS19 ....59 J4
Manor St *CHAL* LS7 ....10 D3
  CLECK BD19 ....158 A2
  EARL WF12 ....181 G1
  ECHL BD2 ....98 C2
  OT LS21 ....39 H2
Manor Ter *ECHL* BD2 ....98 C2
  HDGY LS6 ....8 E1
Manor Vw *CAS* WF10 ....168 D3
  HDGY LS6 ....8 E1
  PDSY/CALV LS28 ....100 B6
Manor Wy *BTLY* WF17 ....160 E3
Manscombe Rd *WIL/AL* BD15 ....96 B4
Manse Crs *ILK* LS29 ....37 K1
Mansel Ms *BOW* BD4 ....119 F5
Manse Rd *ILK* LS29 ....37 K1
Manse St *BFDE* BD3 ....7 H6
Mansfield Av *BGLY* BD16 ....56 B5
Mansfield Rd *GIR* BD8 ....97 H3
  ILK LS29 ....37 K1
Mansion Ga *CHAL* LS7 ....83 G6
Mansion Gate Dr *CHAL* LS7 ....83 K6
Mansion La *HIPP* HX3 ....155 H4
  RHAY LS8 ....84 C3
Manston Ap *MSTN/BAR* LS15 ....105 K2
Manston Av *MSTN/BAR* LS15 ....105 K2
Manston Crs *MSTN/BAR* LS15 ....105 K2
Manston Dr *MSTN/BAR* LS15 ....105 K2
Manston Gdns *MSTN/BAR* LS15.....106 A2
Manston Gv *MSTN/BAR* LS15 ....105 K2

Manston La *MSTN/BAR* LS15 ......106 B3
Manston Ri *MSTN/BAR* LS15 ......105 K2
Manston Wy *MSTN/BAR* LS15 ......105 K2
Manygates Av *WKFDE* WF1 ......184 E6
Manygates Ct *WKFDE* * WF1 ......184 E6
Manygates Crs *WKFDE* WF1 ......184 E6
Manygates La
  WKFDW/WTN WF2 ......184 E7
Manygates Pk *WKFDE* WF1 ......184 E6
Manywells Brow *CUL/QBY* BD13 ...93 K2
Manywells Crs *CUL/QBY* BD13 ......74 A7
Manywells La *CUL/QBY* BD13 ......73 J7
Maple Av *BFDE* BD3 ......7 M4
  HWTH BD22 ......72 E2
  PONT WF8 ......189 H4
Maple Cl *CAS* WF10 ......168 A3
  GFTH/SHER LS25 ......131 F3
Maple Ct *OSS* WF5 ......182 D6
Maple Cft *AL/HA/HU* LS17 ......83 K1
  WOR/ARM LS12 ......121 C1
Maple Dr *PONT* WF8 ......189 H3
  WBY LS22 ......29 H2
  WOR/ARM LS12 ......121 C1
Maple Fold *WOR/ARM* LS12 ......121 C1
Maple Gdns *AL/HA/HU* LS17 ......46 B3
Maple Gv *CLECK* BD19 ......139 H6
  HUDN HD2 ......177 F5
  KGHY BD21 ......2 C1
  NORM WF6 ......186 D2
  PONT WF8 ......189 H4
  WOR/ARM LS12 ......121 C1
Maple Ri *RTHW* * LS26 ......145 F3
Maple Rd *EARL* WF12 ......182 A2
Maple St *HFAX* HX1 ......16 B3
  WKFDW/WTN WF2 ......184 A1
Maple Wk *EARL* WF12 ......182 A2
Maple Wy *SCFT* LS14 ......85 K4
Maplewell Crs *OSS* WF5 ......182 D4
Maplewell Dr *OSS* WF5 ......182 D4
Marbridge Ct *WBSY* BD6 ......117 G4
Marchant St *CAS* WF10 ......148 B7
March Cote La *BGLY* BD16 ......75 K6
March St *NORM* WF6 ......166 D7
Marchwood Gv *CLAY* BD14 ......116 C1
Mardale Crs *SCFT* LS14 ......105 H2
Mardale Rd *EARL* WF12 ......161 H6
Margaret Av *AL/HA/HU* LS17 ......46 A6
Margaret Cl *MOR* LS27 ......142 B1
Margaret St *HFAX* HX1 ......16 E6
  KGHY BD21 ......2 D1
  WKFDE WF1 ......18 C2
  WKFDE WF1 ......164 B4
Margate *RTHW* * LS26 ......145 K1
Margate Rd *BOW* BD4 ......118 B2
Margate St *RPDN/SBR* HX6 ......153 H5
Margerison Crs *ILK* LS29 ......24 D6
Margerison Rd *ILK* LS29 ......24 D6
Margetson Rd *BIRK/DRI* BD11 ......140 C2
Marian Gv *BEE/HOL* * LS11 ......123 C4
Marian Rd *HDGY* LS6 ......9 L2
Marian Ter *HDGY* LS6 ......9 L2
Maria St *ILK* LS29 ......25 K7
Marina Crs *MOR* LS27 ......141 J4
Marine Villa Rd *KNOT* LS11 ......171 G4
Marion Dr *SHPY* BD18 ......77 H5
Marion Gv *WKFDW/WTN* WF2 ......183 J1
Marion St *BGLY* * BD16 ......75 J2
  BRIG HD6 ......157 F4
  GTHN BD7 ......5 G5
Marizon Gv *WKFDE* WF1 ......19 C2
Mark Cl *IDLE* BD10 ......78 D4
Market Ar *CLECK* * BD19 ......159 F1
Market Balcony *HFAX* * HX1 ......17 H6
Market Cl *CUL/QBY* BD13 ......95 H7
Market Pl *CLECK* BD19 ......159 F1
  HECK WF16 ......160 A5
  KGHY BD21 ......3 C5
  NORM WF6 ......166 D6
  OT LS21 ......39 H2
  PDSY/CALV LS28 ......100 B3
  PONT WF8 ......189 J1
  WBY LS22 ......29 H4
Market Sq *SHPY* BD18 ......77 G4
Market St *AIRE* BD20 ......32 D5
  BFD BD1 ......5 M6
  BGLY BD16 ......75 J1
  BRIG HD6 ......157 G6
  BTLY WF17 ......140 E6
  CLECK BD19 ......159 F1
  CUL/QBY BD13 ......95 H7
  DEWS WF13 ......181 G1
  FEA/AMT WF7 ......188 B3
  HECK WF16 ......160 A5
  HFAX HX1 ......17 H6
  KGHY BD21 ......3 G6
  NORM WF6 ......166 D6
  OT LS21 ......39 H3
  SHPY BD18 ......77 G5
  WBSY * BD6 ......117 H5
  WKFDE WF1 ......18 E5
Market Street Ar *LDS* LS1 ......14 B1
Market Wy *WKFDE* WF1 ......18 F4
Markfield Av *LM/WK* BD12 ......137 H2
Markfield Cl *LM/WK* BD12 ......137 H2
Markfield Crs *LM/WK* BD12 ......137 H2
Markfield Dr *LM/WK* BD12 ......137 H2
Markham Av *RHAY* LS8 ......11 G1
  YEA LS19 ......59 K6
Markham Crs *YEA* LS19 ......59 K6
Markham Cft *YEA* LS19 ......59 K6
Markham St *WKFDW/WTN* WF2 ......18 B5
Markington Pl *MID* LS10 ......143 H4
Mark St *LVSG* WF15 ......159 J4
  WBOW BD5 ......117 K3
  WKFDE WF1 ......18 F8
Marland Rd *KGHY* BD21 ......3 M3
Marlborough Av *HIPP* HX3 ......154 C4
  KNOT WF11 ......170 E1
  TAD LS24 ......70 C1
Marlborough Dr *TAD* LS24 ......70 C1
Marlborough Gdns
  DEWS WF13 ......160 E6
  LDSU LS2 ......9 L5
Marlborough Gra *LDS* LS1 ......9 J8
Marlborough Rd *GIR* BD8 ......5 H1
  HUDN * HD2 ......177 G4
  SHPY BD18 ......77 F5

Marlborough Sq *ILK* LS29 ......24 C6
Marlborough St *KGHY* BD21 ......3 J3
  LDS LS1 ......9 J9
  OSS WF5 ......182 B4
  WKFDW/WTN WF2 ......18 B5
Marlborough Ter
  DEWS * WF13 ......160 E6
Marldon Rd *HIPP* HX3 ......135 K6
Marley Cl *GIR* BD8 ......96 D5
Marley Cottages *KGHY* * BD21 ......54 D4
Marley Ct *AIRE* BD20 ......55 C4
Marley Gv *BEE/HOL* LS11 ......122 E3
Marley La *CUL/QBY* BD13 ......115 H3
Marley Pl *BEE/HOL* LS11 ......122 E3
Marley Rd *KGHY* BD21 ......54 C3
Marley St *BEE/HOL* LS11 ......122 E3
  BFDE BD3 ......6 C6
  KGHY BD21 ......2 F7
Marley Ter *BEE/HOL* LS11 ......122 E3
Marley Vw *AIRE* BD20 ......55 G4
  BEE/HOL LS11 ......122 E3
Marling Rd *HUDW* HD3 ......176 A6
Marlo Rd *EARL* WF12 ......161 K6
Marlott Rd *SHPY* BD18 ......77 J4
Marlowe Cl *PDSY/CALV* LS28 ......120 C1
Marlowe Ct *GFTH/SHER* LS25 ......107 J6
Marlow St *KGHY* BD21 ......3 M3
Marl Pit Hl *PONT* WF8 ......189 D7
Maripit La *PONT* WF8 ......190 C3
Marmion Av *GIR* BD8 ......96 B6
Marne Av *CLAY* BD14 ......116 B3
Marne Crs *IDLE* BD10 ......78 C5
Marquis Av *LM/WK* BD12 ......138 C2
Marriner Rd *KGHY* BD21 ......3 G7
Marriner's Dr *HTON* BD9 ......97 G1
Marriner Wk *KGHY* BD21 ......3 G8
Marsden Av *BEE/HOL* LS11 ......123 F4
Marsden Gv *BEE/HOL* LS11 ......123 F4
Marsden Mt *BEE/HOL* LS11 ......123 F4
Marsden Pl *BEE/HOL* LS11 ......123 F4
Marsden Vw *BEE/HOL* LS11 ......123 F4
Marsett Wy *SCFT* LS14 ......85 J4
Marshall Av *MSTN/BAR* LS15 ......106 A3
Marshall Crs *MOR* LS27 ......142 A5
Marshall St *BEE/HOL* LS11 ......13 L4
  EARD/LOFT WF3 ......165 G3
  KGHY BD21 ......53 J2
  MIRF WF14 ......179 H6
  MOR LS27 ......141 K3
  MSTN/BAR LS15 ......105 K3
  YEA LS19 ......59 J4
Marshall Ter *MSTN/BAR* LS15 ......105 K3
Marsh Ct *PDSY/CALV* LS28 ......99 K6
Marsh Cft *KNOT* WF11 ......170 D1
Marsh Delves La *HIPP* HX3 ......155 J2
Marsh End *KNOT* WF11 ......171 H3
Marshfield Pl *WBOW* BD5 ......117 J3
Marshfield St *WBOW* BD5 ......117 J3
Marsh Gv *WBOW* BD5 ......117 H3
Marsh La *BIRK/DRI* BD11 ......139 H3
  HIPP HX3 ......155 J2
  HWTH BD22 ......92 D1
  KNOT WF11 ......171 G2
  OSM LS9 ......10 E9
  OSM LS9 ......14 D1
Marsh Rd *CAS* WF10 ......167 K3
Marsh St *CLECK* BD19 ......159 F2
  HDGY LS6 ......9 K2
  RTHW LS26 ......145 F3
  WBOW BD5 ......117 J4
Marsh V *HDGY* LS6 ......9 K2
Marshway *HFAX* HX1 ......16 D4
Marsh Wy *WKFDE* WF1 ......18 F3
Marsland Av *WKFDE* WF1 ......19 H5
Marsland Ct *CLECK* BD19 ......138 E5
Marsland Pl *BFDE* BD3 ......7 K5
  WKFDE WF1 ......19 H4
Marsland St *WKFDE* WF1 ......19 H5
Marsland Ter *WKFDE* WF1 ......19 H4
Marston Av *MOR* LS27 ......141 K4
Marston Cl *CUL/QBY* BD13 ......115 J5
Marston Ct *CAS* WF10 ......167 K2
Marston Mt *OSM* LS9 ......10 E6
Marston Wy *WBY* LS22 ......29 F3
Marten Rd *WBOW* BD5 ......117 H3
Martin Cl *MOR* LS27 ......142 B3
Martin Ct *MSTN/BAR* LS15 ......106 A5
Martindale Dr *BRAM* LS13 ......101 H4
Martin Frobisher Dr
  NORM WF6 ......166 C5
Martingale Dr *EARD/LOFT* WF3 ......143 H4
Martin Green La *GTL/HWG* HX4 ......174 D2
Martin St *BRIG* * HD6 ......157 G5
  BTLY WF17 ......140 B6
  NORM WF6 ......186 D1
Martin Ter *BULY* LS4 ......8 B5
Martlett Dr *WBOW* BD5 ......118 A4
Marton Ct *BFDE* BD3 ......7 K6
Marwood Rd *WOR/ARM* LS12 ......101 G4
Maryfield Av *MSTN/BAR* LS15 ......105 H3
Maryfield Cl *MSTN/BAR* LS15 ......105 H3
Maryfield Ct *MSTN/BAR* LS15 ......105 H3
Maryfield Gdns
  MSTN/BAR LS15 ......105 H3
Maryfield Gn *MSTN/BAR* LS15 ......105 H3
Maryfield Ms *MSTN/BAR* LS15 ......105 H3
Maryfield V *MSTN/BAR* LS15 ......105 H3
Marygate *WKFDE* WF1 ......18 E4
Mary St *BOW* BD4 ......7 G9
  BRIG HD6 ......157 F4
  CUL/QBY BD13 ......94 B4
  CUL/QBY BD13 ......95 G7
  EARD/LOFT WF3 ......143 K7
  HWTH BD22 ......92 D3
  LM/WK BD12 ......137 H3
  PDSY/CALV LS28 ......100 B1
  RTHW BD8 ......76 E4
Mary St Caravan Site *BOW* BD4 ......7 G9
Maryville Av *BRIG* HD6 ......156 E3
Masefield St *HTON* BD9 ......96 B2
Masefield St *GSLY* LS20 ......59 G3
Masham Gv *WOR/ARM* LS12 ......12 C3
Masham Pl *HTON* BD9 ......96 E3
Masham St *WOR/ARM* LS12 ......12 C2
Masonic St *HFAX* HX1 ......154 B2

Massey Flds *HWTH* BD22 ......72 E4
Master La *LUD/ILL* HX2 ......154 C4
Matlock St *HIPP* HX3 ......16 C1
Matterdale Cl *EARL* WF12 ......161 H6
Matterdale Rd *EARL* WF12 ......161 H6
Matthew Cl *AIRE* BD20 ......54 B2
Matty Marsden La *OSS* WF5 ......182 D7
Maud Av *BEE/HOL* LS11 ......123 F4
Maude Av *EARL* WF12 ......77 H2
Maude Crs *RPDN/SBR* HX6 ......153 F5
Maude St *GTL/HWG* HX4 ......175 G2
  HIPP HX3 ......134 D3
  LDSU LS2 ......14 C2
Maud Pl *BEE/HOL* LS11 ......123 C3
Maudsley St *BFDE* BD3 ......6 D6
Maud St *BFDE* BD3 ......6 D6
Maufe Wy *ILK* LS29 ......24 A6
Maurice Av *BRIG* HD6 ......156 E4
Mavis Av *BHP/TINH* LS16 ......61 H6
Mavis Dr *DEWS* WF13 ......180 D3
Mavis Gv *BHP/TINH* LS16 ......61 H6
Mavis La *BHP/TINH* LS16 ......61 H6
Mavis Rd *DEWS* WF13 ......160 C5
Mavis St *BFDE* BD3 ......6 E5
  DEWS WF13 ......180 D3
Mawcroft Cl *YEA* LS19 ......59 H6
Mawcroft Grange Dr *YEA* LS19 ......59 H6
Mawson St *SHPY* BD18 ......76 B4
Maw St *BOW* BD4 ......118 A1
Maxwell Av *DEWS* WF13 ......161 H6
Maxwell Rd *ILK* LS29 ......24 C6
  WBSY BD6 ......116 E6
Maxwell St *FEA/AMT* WF7 ......188 B4
May Av *CUL/QBY* BD13 ......95 H7
May Bush Rd *WKFDE* WF1 ......185 F6
Mayfair *WBOW* BD5 ......117 J2
Mayfair Av *GTL/HWG* HX4 ......174 C7
Mayfair Wy *BOW* BD4 ......118 E1
Mayfield Av *BRIG* HD6 ......137 G7
  HFAX HX1 ......16 B4
  ILK LS29 ......24 C5
  LM/WK BD12 ......137 H4
Mayfield Cl *ILK* LS29 ......24 C5
Mayfield Ct *OSS* WF5 ......182 D6
Mayfield Dr *AIRE* BD20 ......55 F3
  HFAX HX1 ......16 C8
Mayfield Gdns *HFAX* HX1 ......16 B4
  OSS WF5 ......182 B1
Mayfield Gv *BAIL* BD17 ......77 J1
  BRIG HD6 ......137 G7
  HFAX HX1 ......16 C8
  WIL/AL BD15 ......74 E6
Mayfield Mt *HFAX* * HX1 ......16 C8
Mayfield Pl *LM/WK* BD12 ......137 H4
Mayfield Ri *LM/WK* BD12 ......137 H4
Mayfield Rd *ILK* LS29 ......24 B5
  KGHY BD21 ......2 E2
  MSTN/BAR LS15 ......105 J5
Mayfield St *HFAX* HX1 ......16 D8
Mayfield Ter *CLAY* BD14 ......116 B2
  HFAX HX1 ......16 B5
  LM/WK BD12 ......137 J4
Mayfield Ter South *HFAX* * HX1 ...16 D8
Mayfield Vw *LM/WK* BD12 ......137 J4
Mayflower St *MID* LS10 ......124 B4
Maylea Dr *OT* LS21 ......38 E4
Mayman Cl *BTLY* WF17 ......160 E3
Mayman La *BTLY* WF17 ......160 E3
Maynes Cl *EARL* WF12 ......181 C7
Mayo Av *WBOW* BD5 ......117 J4
Mayo Cl *RHAY* LS8 ......84 E6
Mayo Crs *WBOW* BD5 ......117 K5
Mayo Dr *WBOW* BD5 ......117 K5
Mayo Gv *WBOW* BD5 ......117 K5
Mayo Rd *WBOW* BD5 ......117 K5
Mayors Wk *CAS* WF10 ......169 K1
  PONT WF8 ......189 J2
Mayor's Walk Av *PONT* WF8 ......189 J2
Mayor's Walk Cl *PONT* WF8 ......189 J2
Maypole Rd *HUDN* HD2 ......177 H6
Mayster Gv *BRIG* HD6 ......176 D2
Mayster Rd *BRIG* HD6 ......176 D2
May St *CLECK* BD19 ......138 E7
  HWTH BD22 ......72 E6
  KGHY BD21 ......3 H2
May Ter *OSM* LS9 ......15 C3
Maythorne Av *BTLY* WF17 ......160 D5
Maythorne Crs *CLAY* BD14 ......116 C2
Maythorne Dr *CLAY* BD14 ......116 C2
May Tree Cl *CLAY* BD14 ......116 C1
Mayville Av *AIRE* BD20 ......54 E3
  HDGY LS6 ......8 E1
Mayville Pl *HDGY* LS6 ......8 E2
Mayville Rd *HDGY* LS6 ......8 E2
Mayville St *HDGY* LS6 ......8 E2
Mayville Ter *HDGY* LS6 ......8 E3
Mazebrook Av *CLECK* BD19 ......139 F5
Mazebrook Crs *CLECK* BD19 ......139 F5
McBride Wy *WBY* LS22 ......29 J4
McLaren Flds *BRAM* LS13 ......101 G3
McMahon Dr *CUL/QBY* BD13 ......116 B4
McMillan Gdns *WBSY* BD6 ......117 J7
Mead Cl *MSTN/BAR* * LS15 ......106 B7
Mead Gv *MSTN/BAR* LS15 ......106 B7
The Meade *GFTH/SHER* LS25 ......107 J6
The Meadow *NORM* WF6 ......186 D2
Meadow Bank *DEWS* WF13 ......180 D1
Meadowbank Av *WIL/AL* BD15 ......96 A4
Meadow Bank Crs *MIRF* WF14 ......179 F4
Meadow Brook Cl *NORM* WF6 ......167 F7
Meadow Cl *AL/HA/HU* LS17 ......46 A5
  BGLY BD16 ......74 E3
  BSPA/BRAM LS23 ......48 B2
  BTLY WF17 ......140 D6
  HIPP HX3 ......136 C1
  LVSG WF15 ......159 G7
  WKFDE WF1 ......164 E3
Meadow Cft *BRIG* HD6 ......157 K6
  CAS WF10 ......169 J2
  OSS WF5 ......182 B2
  WIL/AL BD15 ......95 K1
Meadow Crs *HIPP* HX3 ......134 B5
Meadow Cft *AL/HA/HU* LS17 ......45 K5
  BEE/HOL LS11 ......13 J5
  GTL/HWG HX4 ......173 J5
  HUDN HD2 ......178 A4
  HWTH BD22 ......53 H5
  WKFDE WF1 ......164 D3

Meadowcroft *ILK* LS29 ......38 A7
Meadow Croft Cl *IDLE* BD10 ......78 A4
Meadowcroft Cl *WKFDE* WF1 ......164 E3
Meadowcroft Ct *WKFDE* * WF1 ......164 E3
Meadowcroft Crs *CAS* WF10 ......149 F7
Meadowcroft La
  RPDN/SBR HX6 ......173 F4
Meadowcroft Ms *CAS* WF10 ......149 F7
  OSM * LS9 ......14 F2
Meadowcroft Ri *BOW* BD4 ......118 D6
Meadowcroft Rd *WKFDE* WF1 ......164 E3
Meadow Dr *HIPP* HX3 ......134 B5
Meadow End *BHP/TINH* LS16 ......61 H1
Meadowfield Ri
  EARD/LOFT WF3 ......165 J2
Meadow Garth *BHP/TINH* LS16 ......61 J1
  TAD LS24 ......51 F5
  WKFDE WF1 ......164 D3
Meadowgate *OSS* WF5 ......182 B2
Meadowgate Cft
  EARD/LOFT WF3 ......144 C5
Meadowgate Dr
  EARD/LOFT WF3 ......144 C6
Meadowgate V
  EARD/LOFT WF3 ......144 C6
Meadowhurst Gdns
  PDSY/CALV LS28 ......100 A6
Meadowlands *CLECK* BD19 ......137 K6
Meadow La *BEE/HOL* LS11 ......14 A4
  DEWS WF13 ......161 F7
  HIPP HX3 ......134 B5
  LVSG WF15 ......159 G7
  WKFDW/WTN WF2 ......184 A2
Meadow Pk *HUDE* HD5 ......178 C7
Meadow Park Crs
  PDSY/CALV LS28 ......99 J3
Meadow Park Dr
  PDSY/CALV LS28 ......99 J3
Meadow Rd *BEE/HOL* LS11 ......13 M5
  CAS WF10 ......168 A3
  GFTH/SHER LS25 ......107 K6
  IDLE BD10 ......79 F4
The Meadows *BHP/TINH* LS16 ......82 J7
  GFTH/SHER LS25 ......131 J6
  GFTH/SHER LS25 ......131 F3
  WBSY BD6 ......117 H5
Meadow V *WKFDE* WF1 ......164 D3
Meadow Va *AL/HA/HU* LS17 ......63 F6
Meadow Vw *GFTH/SHER* LS25 ......111 G5
  HDGY LS6 ......8 F3
  HWTH BD22 ......72 E2
  LM/WK BD12 ......137 H6
  MSTN/BAR LS15 ......87 H4
  OSS WF5 ......182 B2
Meadow Wk *CHAL* LS7 ......83 K6
  HIPP HX3 ......134 B5
Meadow Wy *AL/HA/HU* LS17 ......63 F6
  CAS WF10 ......149 F7
  EARD/LOFT WF3 ......162 C1
  TAD LS24 ......51 F6
Mead Rd *MSTN/BAR* LS15 ......106 B7
Mead Vw *BOW* * BD4 ......119 B7
Mead Wy *MSTN/BAR* LS15 ......106 B7
Meadway *FEA/AMT* WF7 ......187 G3
  WBSY BD6 ......136 E1
Meagill Ri *OT* LS21 ......26 E7
Meanwood Cl *CHAL* LS7 ......9 M1
Meanwood Gv *HDGY* LS6 ......82 D7
Meanwood Rd *CHAL* LS7 ......10 C5
  CHAL LS7 ......83 F7
Meanwood St *CHAL* LS7 ......10 B5
Meanwood Valley Dr *CHAL* LS7 ...82 E6
Meanwood Valley Gn *CHAL* LS7 ...82 E6
Meanwood Valley Gv *CHAL* LS7 ...82 E6
Meanwood Valley Mt *CHAL* LS7 ...82 E6
Mearclough Rd
  RPDN/SBR HX6 ......154 A4
Medeway *PDSY/CALV* LS28 ......99 K3
Medhurst Av *GFTH/SHER* LS25 ...128 A3
Medley La *HIPP* HX3 ......135 J3
Medley St *CAS* WF10 ......168 D1
Medway *CUL/QBY* BD13 ......115 J6
  HUDE * HD5 ......178 C7
Medway Av *GFTH/SHER* LS25 ......127 K1
Meggison Gv *WBOW* BD5 ......117 H2
Megnaway *WBOW* BD5 ......117 K2
Melba Rd *GTHN* BD7 ......117 G3
Melbourne Av
  WKFDW/WTN WF2 ......164 A5
Melbourne Gv *BFDE* BD3 ......7 L3
  BRAM LS13 ......101 F3
Melbourne Ms
  WKFDW/WTN WF2 ......163 K4
Melbourne Pl *WBOW* BD5 ......5 K9
Melbourne Rd *WKFDE* WF1 ......18 E3
Melbourne St *HIPP* HX3 ......16 D1
  LDSU LS2 ......10 C7
  LVSG WF15 ......159 J5
  MOR LS27 ......142 A3
  PDSY/CALV LS28 ......100 A3
  SHPY BD18 ......77 F4
Melbourne Ter *WBOW* BD5 ......5 L9
Melcombe Wk *BOW* BD4 ......119 F2
Melford St *BOW* BD4 ......118 D1
Mellor Mill La *GTL/HWG* HX4 ......174 E5
Mellor St *BRIG* * HD6 ......157 G6
  HFAX HX1 ......154 D3
Melrose Dr *ILK* LS29 ......25 K7
Melrose Gv *BFDE* BD3 ......7 L3
Melrose Gv *HORS* LS18 ......81 H4
Melrose Pl *HORS* LS18 ......81 G4
  PDSY/CALV LS28 ......100 A7
Melrose St *GTHN* BD7 ......117 F2
  HIPP HX3 ......16 D1
Melrose Ter *ELL* * HX5 ......175 J3
Melrose Wk *HORS* LS18 ......81 G4
Melton Av *EARD/LOFT* WF3 ......144 A3
Melton Cl *EARD/LOFT* WF3 ......144 A3
Melton Garth *EARD/LOFT* WF3 ...144 A3
Melton Ms *HWTH* BD22 ......72 E5
Melton St *BTLY* WF17 ......160 E2
Melton Ter *IDLE* BD10 ......79 F7
Melton Wy *LVSG* WF15 ......159 G7
Melville Cl *HDGY* LS6 ......9 L2
Melville Gdns *HDGY* LS6 ......9 M2
Melville Gv *ILK* LS29 ......24 D5
Melville Pl *HDGY* LS6 ......9 M1

Melville Rd *HDGY* LS6 ......9 L2
Melville St *GTHN* BD7 ......5 G6
Memorial Cottages
  WOR/ARM * LS12 ......121 C3
Memorial Dr *HDGY* LS6 ......82 E5
Mendip Cl *GFTH/SHER* LS25 ......127 J1
Mendip Rd *EARL* WF12 ......161 J7
Mendip Wy *LM/WK* BD12 ......137 C1
Menin Dr *BAIL* BD17 ......57 G6
Menston Dr *ILK* LS29 ......38 B7
Menston Old La *ILK* LS29 ......38 A4
Merchants Ct *BOW* BD4 ......118 B1
Merchants Quay *OSM* * LS15 ......14 D2
Mercia Wy *MSTN/BAR* LS15 ......106 B2
Mercury Rw *OT* LS21 ......39 H3
Merefield Wy *CAS* WF10 ......168 D3
Merewood Rd *CAS* WF10 ......167 J1
Meriden Av *GFTH/SHER* LS25 ......127 J1
Merlin Cl *MOR* LS27 ......142 B4
Merlin Ct *BTLY* WF17 ......140 C7
  KGHY BD21 ......2 F8
Merlin Gv *GIR* BD8 ......96 B6
Merlinwood Dr *BAIL* BD17 ......57 J7
Merlyn-Rees Av *MOR* LS27 ......141 K3
Merrion Pl *LDS* LS1 ......10 B8
Merrion St *LDSU* LS2 ......10 A8
Merrion Wy *LDSU* LS2 ......10 A7
Merrivale Rd *WIL/AL* BD15 ......95 K5
Merry Bent La *RPDN/SBR* HX6 ...172 B4
Merrydale Rd *BOW* BD4 ......138 B1
Merton Av *PDSY/CALV* LS28 ......100 A3
Merton Cl *GFTH/SHER* LS25 ......128 B4
Merton Dr *PDSY/CALV* LS28 ......99 K3
Merton Fold *WBOW* BD5 ......117 K2
Merton Gdns *PDSY/CALV* LS28 ...99 K3
Merton Rd *GTHN* BD7 ......5 J9
Merville Av *BAIL* BD17 ......57 H6
Metcalfe St *BOW* BD4 ......118 C2
Methley Br *RTHW* LS26 ......147 J7
Methley Dr *CHAL* LS7 ......83 J6
Methley Gv *CHAL* LS7 ......83 H6
Methley La *CHAL* LS7 ......83 J6
  RTHW LS26 ......146 B3
Methley Mt *CHAL* LS7 ......83 J6
Methley Pl *CHAL* LS7 ......83 H6
Methley Rd *CAS* WF10 ......147 K7
Methley Ter *CHAL* LS7 ......83 H6
Methley Vw *CHAL* LS7 ......83 J6
Methuen Ov *LM/WK* BD12 ......137 H6
The Mews *NORM* WF6 ......166 E5
Mews Ct *FEA/AMT* WF7 ......188 C4
Mexborough Av *CHAL* LS7 ......10 C1
Mexborough Dr *CHAL* LS7 ......10 C1
Mexborough Gv *CHAL* LS7 ......10 C1
Mexborough Pl *CHAL* LS7 ......10 C2
Mexborough Rd *CHAL* LS7 ......10 D2
  SHPY BD18 ......77 J7
Mexborough St *CHAL* LS7 ......10 C1
Meynell Ap *BEE/HOL* LS11 ......13 J6
Meynell Av *RTHW* LS26 ......145 F2
Meynell Ct *MSTN/BAR* LS15 ......106 A6
Meynell Hts *BEE/HOL* LS11 ......13 J5
Meynell Mt *RTHW* LS26 ......145 G2
Meynell Rd *MSTN/BAR* LS15 ......106 A7
Meynell Sq *BEE/HOL* LS11 ......13 J5
Meynell Wk *BEE/HOL* LS11 ......13 K6
Meyrick Av *WBY* LS22 ......29 K3
Miall St *HFAX* HX1 ......16 C4
Michael Av *EARD/LOFT* WF3 ......165 F3
Mickle Ct *CAS* WF10 ......168 B1
Mickledore Cl *GTHN* * BD7 ......116 D3
Mickledore Rdg *GTHN* BD7 ......116 D3
Micklefield Ct *YEA* LS19 ......59 J7
Micklefield La *YEA* LS19 ......59 H7
Micklefield Ms *YEA* * LS19 ......59 H7
Micklefield Rd *YEA* LS19 ......59 J7
Micklegate *PONT* WF8 ......169 J7
Micklemoss Dr *CUL/QBY* BD13 ...115 F4
Micklethwaite Dr
  CUL/QBY BD13 ......115 H6
Micklethwaite La *BGLY* BD16 ......55 H5
Micklethwaite Vw *WBY* LS22 ......29 H5
Mickletown Rd *RTHW* LS26 ......147 F4
Mickley St *WOR/ARM* LS12 ......12 B1
Middlebrook Cl *GIR* BD8 ......96 C6
Middlebrook Crs *GIR* BD8 ......96 C6
Middlebrook Dr *GIR* BD8 ......96 C6
Middlebrook Hl *GIR* BD8 ......96 C6
Middlebrook Ri *GIR* BD8 ......96 C6
Middlebrook Vw *GIR* BD8 ......96 C6
Middlebrook Wk *GIR* BD8 ......96 C6
Middlebrook Wy *GIR* BD8 ......96 C7
Middlecroft Cl *RTHW* LS26 ......124 A6
Middlecroft Rd *RTHW* LS26 ......124 A6
Middle Cross St *WOR/ARM* LS12 ...12 C2
Middle Dean St *GTL/HWG* HX4 ...175 F2
Middlegate *BTLY* WF17 ......140 B6
Middlegate Ct *BOW* BD4 ......118 C6
Middle Hall Cl *LVSG* WF15 ......159 G4
Middleham Ct *BOW* * BD4 ......119 F3
Middle La *CLAY* BD14 ......116 B1
  KNOT WF11 ......171 H5
  WBY LS22 ......29 F5
Middlemoor *SCFT* LS14 ......85 J4
Middle Oxford St *CAS* WF10 ......168 D1
Middle Rd *DEWS* WF13 ......180 E2
  EARL WF12 ......181 H2
  OSM LS9 ......124 E3
Middle St *RPDN/SBR* HX6 ......153 F6
Middlethorne Cl
  AL/HA/HU LS17 ......64 C7
Middlethorne Ct
  AL/HA/HU LS17 ......64 B6
Middlethorne Ms
  AL/HA/HU LS17 ......64 C6
Middlethorne Ri
  AL/HA/HU LS17 ......64 B7
Middleton Av *ILK* LS29 ......24 A4
  OSM LS9 ......11 H7
  RTHW LS26 ......144 B2
Middleton Cl *MOR* LS27 ......142 A3
Middleton Ct *LVSG* WF15 ......159 F4
Middleton Gv *BEE/HOL* LS11 ......123 G4
  MOR LS27 ......142 A3
Middleton La *EARD/LOFT* WF3 ...143 J3
  RTHW LS26 ......144 B2
Middleton Park Av *MID* LS10 ......143 G3
Middleton Park Crs *MID* LS10 ......143 H3

Middleton Park Gn MID LS10 ....143 G3
Middleton Park Gv MID LS10 ....143 G3
Middleton Park Mt MID LS10 ....143 G3
Middleton Park Pl MID * LS10 ....143 H3
Middleton Park Rd MID LS10 ....143 H2
Middleton Park Ter MID LS10 ....143 G3
Middleton Rd ILK LS29 ....23 K5
  MID LS10 ....123 K5
  MOR LS27 ....142 A3
Middleton St GIR BD8 ....4 F2
Middleton Ter MOR LS27 ....142 A3
Middleton Wy KNOT WF11 ....171 G4
Middleway AIRE BD20 ....33 G1
Middle Wy KGHY BD21 ....3 J4
Midge Hall Cl ILK LS29 ....37 K1
Midgeham Gv BGLY BD16 ....74 D3
Midgeley Rd BAIL BD17 ....77 F3
Midgley Gdns HDGY LS6 ....9 K2
Midgley Pl HDGY LS6 ....9 L2
Midgley Ri PONT WF8 ....169 J5
Midgley Rd HBR HX7 ....132 B6
  ILK LS29 ....37 K1
Midgley Ter HDGY LS6 ....9 L2
Midland Cl MID LS10 ....124 A3
Midland Garth MID LS10 ....14 F9
Midland Hl BGLY BD16 ....75 J1
Midland Pas HDGY LS6 ....9 K2
Midland Rd BAIL BD17 ....77 J2
  GIR BD8 ....97 J3
  HDGY LS6 ....9 K2
  HTON BD9 ....77 H7
  MID LS10 ....123 K3
  PONT WF8 ....169 K7
Midland St RTHW LS26 ....145 K1
Midland Ter ECHL BD2 ....97 K3
  HTON BD9 ....77 H7
  KGHY * BD21 ....3 G2
Mid Point BFDE BD3 ....99 G5
Midway Av BGLY BD16 ....75 K5
Milan Rd RHAY LS8 ....11 J1
Milan St RHAY LS8 ....11 J2
Mildred Sylvester Wy
  NORM WF6 ....167 H6
Mile Cross Gdns HFAX HX1 ....154 B2
Mile Cross Pl HFAX HX1 ....154 B2
Mile Cross Rd HFAX HX1 ....154 B2
Mile Cross Ter HFAX HX1 ....154 B2
Miles Garth AL/HA/HU LS17 ....46 C4
Miles Hill Av CHAL LS7 ....83 G6
Miles Hill Crs BOW BD4 ....118 D5
  CHAL LS7 ....83 G6
Miles Hill Dr BOW BD4 ....118 D5
Miles Hill Gv CHAL LS7 ....83 G6
Miles Hill Mt CHAL LS7 ....83 F6
Miles Hill Pl CHAL LS7 ....83 G6
Miles Hill Rd CHAL LS7 ....83 G6
Miles Hill St CHAL LS7 ....83 G6
Miles Hill Ter CHAL LS7 ....83 G6
Miles Hill Vw CHAL LS7 ....83 G6
Mile Thorn St HFAX HX1 ....16 B6
Milford Gv CLECK BD19 ....139 H4
Milford Pl BULY LS4 ....8 D7
  HTON BD9 ....97 F2
Milford Rd GFTH/SHER LS25 ....131 G1
Millbank PDSY/CALV LS28 ....100 C7
Mill Bank Cl RPDN/SBR HX6 ....172 C1
Millbank Ct PDSY/CALV LS28 ....120 C1
Mill Bank Rd RPDN/SBR HX6 ....172 C1
Mill Banks AIRE BD20 ....33 F2
Millbeck Ap MOR LS27 ....142 B3
Millbeck Cl GIR BD8 ....96 B7
Millbeck Dr BGLY BD16 ....74 D3
Millbeck Gn WBY LS22 ....46 B6
Millbrook Gdns DEWS WF13 ....160 D6
Mill Carr Hill Rd BOW BD4 ....138 C4
Mill Cl GFTH/SHER LS25 ....131 J7
Mill Ct HWTH BD22 ....92 D5
Mill Cft MOR LS27 ....121 G7
Millcroft EARD/LOFT WF3 ....165 F2
  OT LS21 ....41 G3
Millcroft Cl EARD/LOFT WF3 ....164 E2
Millcroft Ri EARD/LOFT WF3 ....165 F2
Mill Dam La PONT WF8 ....169 K6
Mill Dam La BSPA/BRAM LS23 ....48 D5
Millennium Ct PDSY/CALV * LS28..100 C3
Millennium Sq LDS LS1 ....9 M7
Millennium Wy BEE/HOL LS11 ....123 G6
Miller Av WKFDW/WTN WF2 ....184 E7
Millergate BFD BD1 ....5 L6
Millers Ct LVSG WF15 ....159 J6
Millers Cft BTLY WF17 ....140 E6
Millers Dl MOR LS27 ....141 J1
Millersdale Cl BOW BD4 ....118 B7
Millfield Crs PONT WF8 ....189 H3
Millfields AIRE BD20 ....32 E1
  OSS WF5 ....182 B4
Mill Fold Wy RPDN/SBR HX6 ....172 F5
Mill Forest Wy BTLY WF17 ....161 G4
Mill Garth MOR LS27 ....121 G7
Millgarth Ct WBY LS22 ....46 C6
Millgarth St LDSU LS2 ....10 C9
Millgate ELL HX5 ....175 J2
Mill Grath PONT WF8 ....189 H2
Mill Gn BEE/HOL LS11 ....13 G4
Mill Green Cl SCFT LS14 ....85 K7
Mill Green Gdns SCFT LS14 ....85 K7
Mill Green Garth SCFT * LS14 ....85 K7
Mill Green Pl SCFT LS14 ....105 K1
Mill Green Rd SCFT LS14 ....85 K7
Mill Green Vw SCFT LS14 ....85 J7
Mill Gv BRIG HD6 ....156 E4
Millhaven Ms GIR BD8 ....97 H3
Mill Hey HWTH BD22 ....72 E5
Mill Hl HWTH BD22 ....72 D5
  LDS LS1 ....14 A1
  NORM WF6 ....166 D7
  PDSY/CALV LS28 ....120 B1
  RTHW LS26 ....145 F2
Mill Hill Av PONT WF8 ....189 G2
Mill Hill Cl PONT WF8 ....190 E4
Mill Hill Gn RTHW * LS26 ....145 G4
Mill Hill La BRIG HD6 ....156 E4
  BRIG HD6 ....158 A7
  PONT WF8 ....189 G2
Mill Hill Rd PONT WF8 ....189 H2
Mill Hill Sq RTHW LS26 ....145 F2
Mill Hill Top BGLY BD16 ....74 E4
Mill House La RPDN/SBR HX6 ....153 G6

Mill House Ri BOW * BD4 ....118 C5
Milligan Av ECHL * BD2 ....78 A7
Milligan Ct BGLY BD16 ....74 D7
Mill La AIRE BD20 ....32 D5
  AL/HA/HU LS17 ....46 K1
  BIRK/DRI BD11 ....139 H1
  BOW BD4 ....120 D3
  BRAM LS13 ....100 D3
  BRIG HD6 ....157 G6
  BSPA/BRAM LS23 ....48 D2
  BTLY WF17 ....140 E5
  BTLY WF17 ....161 G4
  CAS WF10 ....148 C6
  CAS WF10 ....167 G4
  CLECK BD19 ....138 E4
  CUL/QBY BD13 ....115 F4
  EARD/LOFT WF3 ....143 J7
  EARL WF12 ....181 K2
  FEA/AMT WF7 ....187 J5
  GFTH/SHER LS25 ....131 F2
  GSLY LS20 ....57 J3
  GTL/HWG HX4 ....175 F5
  HIPP HX3 ....134 E5
  HIPP HX3 ....136 D1
  HUDE HD5 ....178 C4
  HWTH BD22 ....72 C2
  HWTH BD22 ....92 D2
  LUD/ILL HX2 ....113 K7
  MOR LS27 ....121 G7
  OT LS21 ....39 H2
  OT LS21 ....41 G3
  PONT WF8 ....170 A5
  RTHW LS26 ....147 G4
  TAD LS24 ....50 E6
  TAD LS24 ....70 D3
  WBOW BD5 ....117 K1
Millmoor Cl HTON BD9 ....96 C3
Mill Pk MIRF WF14 ....179 G2
Mill Pit La RTHW LS26 ....124 E7
Mill Pond Cl HDGY LS6 ....82 D6
Mill Pond Gv HDGY LS6 ....82 D6
Mill Pond La HDGY LS6 ....82 D6
Mill Pond Sq HDGY LS6 ....82 D5
Mill Rd DEWS WF13 ....161 F6
Mill Rw AIRE BD20 ....32 A4
Mill Royd St BRIG HD6 ....157 G6
Millshaw BEE/HOL LS11 ....122 D5
Millshaw Mt BEE/HOL LS11 ....122 C6
Millshaw Park Av MOR LS27 ....122 C6
Millshaw Park Cl
  BEE/HOL LS11 ....122 C6
Millshaw Park La
  BEE/HOL LS11 ....122 C6
Millshaw Park Wy
  BEE/HOL LS11 ....122 C5
Millshaw Rd BEE/HOL LS11 ....122 D7
Millside Wk MOR LS27 ....142 B3
Millstone Ri LVSG WF15 ....159 J6
Mill St BFD BD1 ....6 A4
  BTLY WF17 ....140 E7
  CAS WF10 ....168 A1
  CUL/QBY BD13 ....74 A6
  HIPP HX3 ....154 D7
  MOR LS27 ....141 K4
  OSM LS9 ....14 E1
  WBSY BD6 ....117 F5
Mill St East EARL WF12 ....181 G3
Mill St West EARL WF12 ....181 F2
Mill Vw ILK LS29 ....25 K7
  KNOT WF11 ....170 C4
Millwater Av EARL WF12 ....180 E4
Millwright St LDSU LS2 ....10 D7
Milne Ct MSTN/BAR LS15 ....106 A7
Milner Bank OT LS21 ....38 E4
Milner Cl GTL/HWG HX4 ....175 F2
Milner Gdns OSM LS9 ....15 G3
Milner Ing LM/WK BD12 ....137 H3
Milner La EARD/LOFT WF3 ....144 B4
  GTL/HWG HX4 ....175 F2
  SCFT LS14 ....66 C3
  TAD LS24 ....90 B5
Milner Rd BAIL BD17 ....77 G3
Milner's La PONT WF8 ....190 E5
Milner's Rd YEA LS19 ....59 G4
Milner St HFAX HX1 ....16 E5
  OSS WF5 ....182 B7
Milner Wy OSS WF5 ....182 D3
Milne's Av WKFDW/WTN WF2 ....184 A6
Milnes Gv CAS WF10 ....169 G1
Milnes St WOR/ARM LS12 ....12 F3
Milne St GTHN BD7 ....5 H6
Milnthorpe Cl BSPA/BRAM LS23 ..48 B7
Milnthorpe Gdns
  BSPA/BRAM LS23 ....48 B7
Milnthorpe Garth
  BSPA/BRAM LS23 ....68 B7
Milnthorpe La
  BSPA/BRAM LS23 ....48 B7
  WKFDW/WTN WF2 ....184 E7
Milnthorpe Wy
  BSPA/BRAM LS23 ....48 B7
Milroyd Crs BTLY WF17 ....140 D5
Milton Av LVSG WF15 ....159 K5
  RPDN/SBR HX6 ....153 K3
Milton Cl LVSG WF15 ....159 K6
Milton Ct EARD/LOFT WF3 ....165 G2
Milton Crs WKFDW/WTN WF2 ....183 H5
Milton Dr LVSG WF15 ....159 K6
  MSTN/BAR LS15 ....86 C5
Milton Gdns LVSG WF15 ....159 K5
Milton Gv DEWS WF13 ....161 F6
Milton Pl HFAX HX1 ....16 E6
  OSS WF5 ....182 C3
Milton Rd LVSG WF15 ....159 K5
  WKFDW/WTN WF2 ....183 H5
Milton Sq HECK WF16 ....160 A4
Milton St CAS WF10 ....148 B7
  CUL/QBY BD13 ....94 A5
  GTHN BD7 ....5 J9
  HECK WF16 ....160 A3
  RPDN/SBR HX6 ....153 J3
Milton Ter CLECK BD19 ....138 D7
  HFAX * HX1 ....16 E6
  KSTL LS5 ....101 K1
Minden Cl PONT WF8 ....189 F2
Minden Wy PONT WF8 ....189 F1
Minnie St HWTH BD22 ....72 D6

  KGHY BD21 ....2 E7
Minorca Mt CUL/QBY BD13 ....94 A4
Mint St ECHL BD2 ....98 C3
Miramar HUDN HD2 ....177 J4
Mirey Butt La KNOT WF11 ....170 A5
Mirey La RPDN/SBR HX6 ....152 C5
Mirfield Av ECHL BD2 ....78 B7
Miry La HBR HX7 ....152 A2
  LVSG WF15 ....158 D3
  MSTN/BAR LS15 ....87 J2
  YEA LS19 ....59 J4
Mission St BRIG HD6 ....157 H7
Mistral Cl LM/WK BD12 ....137 K2
Mistral Gv LVSG WF15 ....158 C3
Mistress La WOR/ARM LS12 ....8 B9
Mitcham Dr HTON BD9 ....97 F3
Mitchell Cl IDLE BD10 ....78 D3
Mitchell La AIRE BD20 ....33 F1
  IDLE BD10 ....78 D3
Mitchell Sq WBOW BD5 ....117 K2
Mitchell St BRIG HD6 ....157 F5
  KGHY BD21 ....3 J4
  RPDN/SBR HX6 ....153 K4
Mitchell Ter BGLY BD16 ....75 J1
Mitford Pl WOR/ARM LS12 ....12 C1
Mitford Rd WOR/ARM LS12 ....12 D2
Mitford Ter WOR/ARM LS12 ....12 C1
Mitford Vw WOR/ARM LS12 ....12 D1
Mitre Ct BOW BD4 ....118 C3
Mitre St DEWS WF13 ....180 D1
Mitton St WBOW BD5 ....117 H5
Mixenden Cl LUD/ILL HX2 ....133 K2
Mixenden La LUD/ILL HX2 ....134 A1
Mixenden Rd LUD/ILL HX2 ....133 K2
Moat Hl BTLY WF17 ....140 C5
Moat Hill Farm Dr BTLY WF17 ....140 D5
Modder Av WOR/ARM LS12 ....102 A6
Modder Pl WOR/ARM LS12 ....102 A6
Model Av WOR/ARM LS12 ....12 C1
Model Rd WOR/ARM LS12 ....12 C1
Model Ter WOR/ARM LS12 ....12 C1
Moderna Wy HBR HX7 ....132 A7
Moffat Cl WBSY BD6 ....116 E5
Mona St WKFDW/WTN WF2 ....183 K3
Monckton Dr CAS WF10 ....169 H2
Monckton Rd
  WKFDW/WTN WF2 ....184 D1
Mond Av BFDE BD3 ....7 J2
Monk Barn Cl BGLY * BD16 ....55 K7
Monk Bridge Av HDGY LS6 ....82 D6
Monk Bridge Dr HDGY LS6 ....82 E6
Monk Bridge Pl HDGY LS6 ....82 D6
Monk Bridge Rd HDGY LS6 ....82 D6
Monk Bridge Ter HDGY LS6 ....82 D6
Monkfield MIRF WF14 ....179 F3
Monkhill Av PONT WF8 ....169 J6
Monkhill Dr PONT WF8 ....169 J6
Monkhill La PONT WF8 ....169 J5
Monkhill Mt PONT WF8 ....169 J6
Monk Ings BTLY WF17 ....140 A6
Monk Ings Av BTLY WF17 ....139 K6
Monkmans Wharfe AIRE BD20 ....32 E1
Monk St GTHN BD7 ....5 H6
  WKFDE WF1 ....19 C6
Monkswood KSTL LS5 ....81 J6
Monkswood Av SCFT LS14 ....85 G4
Monkswood Bank SCFT LS14 ....85 G4
Monkswood Cl SCFT LS14 ....85 G4
Monkswood Dr SCFT LS14 ....85 G4
Monkswood Ga SCFT * LS14 ....85 H4
Monkswood Gn SCFT LS14 ....85 G4
Monkswood Hl SCFT LS14 ....85 G4
Monkswood Ri SCFT LS14 ....85 G4
Monkswood Wk SCFT LS14 ....85 H4
Monkwood Rd WKFDE WF1 ....164 C3
Monson Av PDSY/CALV LS28 ....79 J3
Montagu Av RHAY LS8 ....84 D7
Montagu Ct RHAY LS8 ....84 D7
Montagu Crs RHAY LS8 ....84 D7
Montagu Dr RHAY LS8 ....84 C7
Montague Crs
  GFTH/SHER LS25 ....107 K5
Montague Pl GFTH/SHER LS25 ....107 K6
Montague St RPDN/SBR HX6 ....153 K5
  WBOW BD5 ....117 H3
  WKFDE WF1 ....185 C6
Montagu Gdns RHAY LS8 ....84 C7
Montagu Gv RHAY LS8 ....84 C7
Montagu Pl RHAY LS8 ....84 C7
Montagu Ri RHAY LS8 ....104 D1
Montagu Rd WBY LS22 ....29 K3
Montagu Vw RHAY LS8 ....84 C7
Montcalm Crs EARD/LOFT WF3 ....165 C5
Montfort Cl HORS LS18 ....80 E1
Montpelier Ter HDGY LS6 ....102 E1
Montreal Av CHAL LS7 ....83 J6
Montreal Ter BRAM LS13 ....100 D5
Montrose St ECHL BD2 ....97 J3
Montserrat Rd BOW BD4 ....119 G5
Monument La PONT WF8 ....189 K2
Monument Ms PONT WF8 ....189 K2
Moody St BOW BD4 ....6 A9
Moor Allerton Av
  AL/HA/HU LS17 ....83 K2
Moor Allerton Crs
  AL/HA/HU LS17 ....83 K2
Moor Allerton Dr
  AL/HA/HU LS17 ....84 A2
Moor Allerton Gdns
  AL/HA/HU LS17 ....83 J2
Moor Av BSPA/BRAM LS23 ....48 C4
  EARD/LOFT WF3 ....165 F2
  MSTN/BAR LS15 ....105 G6
Moorbottom CLECK BD19 ....158 C2
Moor Bottom La BGLY BD16 ....75 K1
  GTL/HWG HX4 ....154 D7
  HBR HX7 ....152 B3
  KGHY BD21 ....73 J2
  RPDN/SBR HX6 ....173 H1
Moor Bottom Rd
  GTL/HWG HX4 ....173 G4
  LUD/ILL HX2 ....134 C1
Moorbridge Cft
  GFTH/SHER LS25 ....111 G6
Moor Cl MID LS10 ....123 J4
Moor Close Av CUL/QBY BD13 ..115 F6

Moor Close Farm Ms
  CUL/QBY BD13 ....115 F6
Moor Close La CUL/QBY BD13 ..115 F6
Moor Close Pde
  CUL/QBY BD13 ....115 F5
Moor Crs BEE/HOL LS11 ....14 A8
Moor Crescent Cha
  BEE/HOL LS11 ....14 A7
Moor Cft BGLY BD16 ....56 A6
  BHP/TINH LS16 ....62 C7
Moorcrest DEWS WF13 ....160 D7
Moorcroft Av BFDE BD3 ....7 K2
  DEWS WF13 ....160 E7
Moorcroft Dr BOW BD4 ....119 G5
  DEWS WF13 ....160 D7
Moorcroft Rd BOW BD4 ....119 G6
  DEWS WF13 ....160 D7
Moorcroft Ter BOW BD4 ....119 G6
Moor Dr HDGY LS6 ....82 D6
  HWTH BD22 ....72 D1
  OT LS21 ....40 A2
  PDSY/CALV LS28 ....120 C1
Moore Av GTHN BD7 ....116 E4
Moor Edge High Side
  BGLY BD16 ....74 D2
Moorehouse Gv OSM LS9 ....10 C6
Moor End Av LUD/ILL HX2 ....133 K6
Moor End Gdns LUD/ILL HX2 ....134 A6
Moor End La DEWS WF13 ....160 C6
  RPDN/SBR HX6 ....154 A6
Moor End Rd LUD/ILL HX2 ....133 J5
Moor End Vw LUD/ILL HX2 ....134 B6
Moore Vw GTHN BD7 ....116 E4
Moor Farm Gdns CHAL * LS7 ....83 H5
Moorfield MOR LS27 ....121 F7
Moorfield Av BFDE BD3 ....7 K2
  CLECK BD19 ....157 K1
  ILK LS29 ....38 A6
  WOR/ARM LS12 ....101 K5
Moorfield Cl YEA LS19 ....60 A5
Moorfield Ct YEA LS19 ....60 A5
Moorfield Crs PDSY/CALV LS28 ..100 A7
  WOR/ARM LS12 ....101 K5
  YEA LS19 ....60 A5
Moorfield Cft YEA LS19 ....60 A5
Moorfield Dr BAIL BD17 ....57 H6
  HWTH BD22 ....72 E1
  YEA LS19 ....60 A5
Moorfield Gdns PDSY/CALV LS28..99 K7
Moorfield Gv PDSY/CALV LS28 ....99 K7
  WOR/ARM LS12 ....101 K5
Moorfield Pl IDLE BD10 ....78 C4
Moorfield Rd BGLY BD16 ....75 K5
  ILK LS29 ....24 D5
  WOR/ARM LS12 ....101 K5
  YEA LS19 ....60 A5
Moorfields AL/HA/HU * LS17 ....83 J2
  BRAM LS13 ....101 F2
Moorfield St HFAX HX1 ....16 D9
  LDSU LS2 ....9 K3
  WOR/ARM LS12 ....101 K5
Moorfield Vw LVSG WF15 ....159 F7
Moorfield Wy CLECK BD19 ....157 K1
Moor Flatts Av MID LS10 ....143 H2
Moor Flatts Rd MID LS10 ....143 H2
Moorgarth Av BFDE BD3 ....7 K1
Moorgate BAIL BD17 ....57 H7
Moorgate Av BFDE BD3 ....7 H1
  GFTH/SHER LS25 ....127 K3
Moorgate Cl GFTH/SHER LS25 ....127 K3
Moorgate Dr GFTH/SHER LS25 ..128 A4
Moorgate Ri GFTH/SHER LS25 ....127 K4
Moorgate Rd GFTH/SHER LS25 ....127 K3
Moorgate St HFAX * HX1 ....16 B9
Moor Grange Ri BHP/TINH LS16 ..81 K4
Moor Grange Vw
  BHP/TINH LS16 ....81 K4
Moor Gv EARD/LOFT WF3 ....165 J2
  HIPP HX3 ....116 B7
  PDSY/CALV LS28 ....120 C1
Moorhead Crs SHPY BD18 ....76 D5
Moorhead La SHPY BD18 ....76 D5
Moorhead Ter SHPY BD18 ....76 D5
Moor Hey La ELL HX5 ....176 B4
Moorhouse Av BEE/HOL LS11 ....122 E5
  EARD/LOFT WF3 ....165 J1
  ECHL BD2 ....78 B7
  WKFDW/WTN WF2 ....184 A4
Moorhouse Cl EARD/LOFT WF3 ..165 J1
  HWTH BD22 ....92 D2
  NORM WF6 ....167 F5
Moorhouse Ct
  HWTH BD22 ....92 D2
Moorhouse Crs
  WKFDW/WTN WF2 ....18 A4
Moorhouse Gv
  EARD/LOFT WF3 ....165 J1
Moorhouse La
  HWTH BD22 ....92 C1
Moorhouse Ter
  EARD/LOFT WF3 ....165 J2
Moorhouse Vw
  EARD/LOFT WF3 ....165 J2
The Moorings AL/HA/HU LS17 ....63 K6
  IDLE BD10 ....78 D4
  MID LS10 ....124 C3
Moor Knoll Cl EARD/LOFT WF3 ..143 J7
Moor Knoll Dr EARD/LOFT WF3 ..143 J7
Moor Knoll La EARD/LOFT WF3 ..143 H6
Moorland Av BAIL BD17 ....57 J7
  BGLY BD16 ....56 B5
  GSLY LS20 ....59 F2
  HDGY LS6 ....9 G4
  MOR LS27 ....120 D7
Moorland Cl LUD/ILL HX2 ....134 B4
  MOR LS27 ....121 F7
Moorland Crs AL/HA/HU LS17 ....83 H3
  BAIL BD17 ....57 J7
  GSLY LS20 ....59 F1
  ILK LS29 ....38 B5
  ILK LS29 ....58 C1
  MOR LS27 ....120 E6
Moorland Dr AL/HA/HU LS17 ....83 H3
  BIRK/DRI BD11 ....119 J7
  GSLY LS20 ....59 F1
  PDSY/CALV LS28 ....99 H5
Moorland Gdns AL/HA/HU LS17 ....83 J2

Moorland Garth AL/HA/HU LS17 ..83 H3
Moorland Gv AL/HA/HU LS17 ....83 H2
  PDSY/CALV LS28 ....99 H5
Moorland Ings AL/HA/HU LS17 ..83 H3
Moorland Pl LM/WK BD12 ....137 K2
Moorland Ri AL/HA/HU LS17 ....83 H3
Moorland Rd BHP/TINH LS16 ....61 F1
  BIRK/DRI BD11 ....140 B1
  HDGY LS6 ....9 H1
  PDSY/CALV LS28 ....99 H4
The Moorlands AL/HA/HU LS17 ..63 K7
  WBY LS22 ....29 J4
Moorlands ILK LS29 ....23 K7
Moorlands Av BFDE BD3 ....7 J1
  BIRK/DRI BD11 ....119 H7
  DEWS WF13 ....160 E7
  HWTH BD22 ....53 C7
  LUD/ILL HX2 ....134 A4
  MIRF * WF14 ....179 G3
  OSS WF5 ....182 B1
  YEA LS19 ....60 A5
Moorlands Ct GTL/HWG * HX4 ....174 B7
  WBY LS22 ....29 J4
Moorlands Dr LUD/ILL HX2 ....134 B5
  YEA LS19 ....60 A5
Moorlands Pl HFAX HX1 ....154 E3
Moorlands Rd BIRK/DRI BD11 ....119 H7
  DEWS WF13 ....180 E1
  GTL/HWG HX4 ....174 E1
Moorlands Vw HFAX HX1 ....154 E3
  WBY LS22 ....29 J4
Moorland Ter GFTH/SHER LS25 ..107 F3
  KGHY BD21 ....54 C5
Moorland Vw AL/HA/HU LS17 ....83 H2
  BRAM LS13 ....100 E1
  LM/WK BD12 ....137 K2
  RPDN/SBR HX6 ....153 G5
Moorland Wk AL/HA/HU LS17 ....83 H2
Moor La AIRE BD20 ....32 A5
  AL/HA/HU LS17 ....45 H5
  BSPA/BRAM LS23 ....30 C4
  BTLY WF17 ....140 C7
  CLECK BD19 ....139 J5
  GFTH/SHER LS25 ....111 H5
  GSLY LS20 ....59 F1
  ILK LS29 ....22 A1
  ILK LS29 ....37 J3
  ILK LS29 ....37 K6
  LUD/ILL HX2 ....134 B3
  OT LS21 ....26 C1
  OT LS21 ....26 C6
  PONT WF8 ....189 K5
  PONT WF8 ....190 A4
  TAD LS24 ....51 K1
  TAD LS24 ....70 A3
  WBY LS22 ....47 J2
Moorlea Dr BAIL BD17 ....77 J1
Moorleigh Cl GFTH/SHER LS25 ..128 A4
Moorleigh Dr GFTH/SHER LS25 ..128 A4
Moor Park Av BEE/HOL LS11 ....82 C6
  ILK LS29 ....22 A1
Moor Park Cl BFDE BD3 ....7 J3
  ILK LS29 ....22 A1
Moor Park Ct EARL * WF12 ....161 H7
Moor Park Crs ILK LS29 ....22 A1
Moor Park Dr BFDE BD3 ....7 J3
  HDGY LS6 ....82 C6
  ILK LS29 ....22 A1
Moor Park Gdns EARL WF12 ....181 H5
Moor Park Gv ILK LS29 ....22 B1
Moor Park La EARL WF12 ....181 H4
Moor Park Mt HDGY LS6 ....82 C6
Moor Park Vls HDGY LS6 ....82 D6
Moor Park Wy ILK LS29 ....22 B1
Moor Rd BEE/HOL LS11 ....14 A8
  BHP/TINH LS16 ....61 G1
  EARD/LOFT WF3 ....165 F2
  FEA/AMT WF7 ....188 C4
  GFTH/SHER LS25 ....111 G5
  HDGY LS6 ....82 C6
  ILK LS29 ....36 E1
  MID LS10 ....123 J4
Moor Royd HFAX HX3 ....154 D4
Moorroyd St OSS WF5 ....182 K5
Moor Side BSPA/BRAM LS23 ....48 A2
Moorside BAIL BD17 ....57 J6
  CLECK BD19 ....158 B2
  HTON BD9 ....96 C3
Moorside Ap BIRK/DRI BD11 ....140 C1
Moorside Av AIRE BD20 ....32 B5
  BIRK/DRI BD11 ....119 H7
  BIRK/DRI BD11 ....140 C2
  DEWS WF13 ....160 C6
  ECHL BD2 ....98 E3
Moorside Cl BIRK/DRI BD11 ....140 C1
  ECHL BD2 ....98 D2
Moorside Crs BIRK/DRI BD11 ....140 C2
  DEWS WF13 ....160 C6
Moorside Cft ECHL BD2 ....98 D3
Moorside Dr BIRK/DRI BD11 ....140 C2
  BRAM LS13 ....101 F3
Moorside End DEWS WF13 ....160 C6
Moorside Gdns BIRK/DRI BD11 ..140 C2
  ECHL BD2 ....98 D2
  LUD/ILL HX2 ....134 C3
Moorside Gn BIRK/DRI BD11 ....140 C1
Moor Side La HWTH BD22 ....72 C1
Moorside La BFDE BD3 ....7 J6
  ILK LS29 ....22 B5
  OT LS21 ....26 A2
Moorside Maltings
  BEE/HOL LS11 ....14 A8
Moorside Ms BIRK/DRI BD11 ....140 B2
Moorside Pde BIRK/DRI BD11 ....140 C1
Moorside Pl BFDE BD3 ....7 J6
  DEWS WF13 ....160 C6
Moorside Ri CLECK BD19 ....158 C1
Moorside Rd BIRK/DRI BD11 ....140 B2
  DEWS WF13 ....160 C6
  ECHL BD2 ....98 D2
  HUDE HD5 ....178 D7
  WIL/AL BD15 ....95 F1
Moorside St BRAM LS13 ....101 F1
  LM/WK BD12 ....137 G1
Moorside Ter BIRK/DRI BD11 ....140 B2
  BRAM LS13 ....101 F1
  ECHL BD2 ....98 E3
Moorside V BIRK/DRI BD11 ....140 C1
Moorside Vw BIRK/DRI BD11 ....140 C2

Moorside Wk *BIRK/DRI* BD11......**140** C2
Moor Stone Pl *HIPP* * HX3 ....**136** B2
Moor St *CUL/QBY* * BD13 ....**115** H5
  HWTH BD22 ....**72** E1
Moor Ter *ECHL* * BD2....................**7** C1
Moorthorpe Av *BFDE* BD3........**7** J2
Moortop *BIRK/DRI* BD11........**140** A1
Moor Top *BIRK/DRI* BD11........**140** A2
  MIRF WF14 ....**179** F3
  OT LS21 ....**38** C1
  WOR/ARM LS12 ....**121** F4
Moor Top Gdns *LUD/ILL* HX2 ......**114** B7
Moor Top Rd *HUDE* HD5 ....**178** D7
  LM/WK BD12 ....**137** G1
  LUD/ILL HX2......................**133** J7
Moor Vw *BEE/HOL* LS11 ......**13** K6
  BOW * BD4 ....**119** H6
  HECK WF16 ....**160** B6
  MIRF WF14 ....**159** H7
Moor View Av *SHPY* BD18........**77** F4
Moor View Cl *CAS* WF10........**168** E1
Moor View Ct *AIRE* BD20........**55** F4
  IDLE * BD10 ....**78** B3
Moorview Cft *ILK* LS29 ....**38** A5
Moorview Dr *BGLY* BD16 ....**75** H6
  SHPY BD18........................**78** A5
Moorview Gv *KGHY* BD21 ....**3** K8
Moorville Av *BFDE* BD3............**7** J2
Moorville Cl *BEE/HOL* LS11 ......**13** L8
Moorville Crs *BEE/HOL* LS11 ......**13** K7
Moorville Dr *BIRK/DRI* BD11 ......**119** H7
Moorville Gv *BEE/HOL* LS11 ......**13** K7
Moorville Rd *BEE/HOL* LS11 ......**13** L7
Moorway *GSLY* LS20 ....**58** C2
Moorwell Pl *ECHL* BD2 ....**98** C1
Moravian Pl *WBOW* * BD5 ....**117** J2
Moresby Rd *WBSY* BD6 ....**136** D1
Moresdale La *SCFT* LS14 ....**105** G2
Morlands Cl *DEWS* WF13 ....**160** C5
Morley Av *BFDE* BD3............**7** K2
  KNOT WF11 ....**171** H4
Morley Carr Rd *LM/WK* BD12......**137** J2
Morley Hall La *LUD/ILL* HX2 ......**152** D2
Morley St *GTHN* BD7 ....**5** K8
Morningside *BFDE* BD3............**4** E1
Morning St *KGHY* BD21 ....**53** J7
Mornington Rd *BGLY* BD16 ....**75** K1
  ILK LS29 ....**24** B5
Mornington St *KGHY* BD21........**2** F3
Mornington Vls *GIR* BD8............**5** J1
Morpeth Pl *OSM* LS9 ....**14** E3
Morpeth St *CUL/QBY* BD13 ....**115** H5
  GTHN BD7 ....**5** H6
Morphet Ter *CHAL* * LS7 ....**10** B4
Morrell Crs *WKFDW/WTN* WF2......**164** A3
Morris Av *KSTL* LS5............**81** K7
Morris Gv *KSTL* LS5 ....**101** K1
Morris La *KSTL* LS5............**81** K7
Morris Mt *KSTL* LS5 ....**101** K1
Morrison St *CAS* WF10........**168** D1
Morris Pl *MOR* LS27 ....**141** J2
Morris Vw *KSTL* LS5 ....**101** K1
Morritt Av *MSTN/BAR* LS15 ....**105** J4
Morritt Gv *MSTN/BAR* LS15 ....**105** J5
Mortech Pk *MSTN/BAR* * LS15 ......**87** G5
Mortimer Av *BFDE* BD3............**7** K2
  BTLY WF17 ....**160** C3
Mortimer Ri *OSS* WF5 ....**182** C3
Mortimer Rw *BFDE* BD3............**7** J7
Mortimer St *BTLY* WF17 ....**160** C3
  CLECK * BD19 ....**158** E1
  GIR BD8 ....**4** B4
Mortimer Ter *BTLY* WF17 ....**160** C3
Morton Crs *CAS* WF10 ....**168** E1
Morton Gv *AIRE* BD20 ....**55** G3
  EARL WF12 ....**180** E6
Morton La *AIRE* BD20 ....**55** G4
Morton Pde *WKFDW/WTN* WF2......**18** B5
Morton Rd *BOW* BD4............**7** J9
Mortons Cl *HIPP* HX3........**155** H5
Morwick Gv *MSTN/BAR* LS15 ......**86** B6
Moseley Pl *HDGY* LS6............**9** M2
Moseley Wood Ap
  BHP/TINH LS16 ....**61** G7
Moseley Wood Av
  BHP/TINH LS16 ....**61** G5
Moseley Wood Bank
  BHP/TINH LS16 ....**61** G6
Moseley Wood Cl
  BHP/TINH LS16 ....**61** G7
Moseley Wood Crs
  BHP/TINH LS16 ....**61** G6
Moseley Wood Cft
  HORS LS18 ....**61** F7
Moseley Wood Dr
  BHP/TINH LS16 ....**61** G6
Moseley Wood Gdns
  BHP/TINH LS16 ....**61** G7
Moseley Wood Gn
  BHP/TINH LS16 ....**61** G6
Moseley Wood Gv
  BHP/TINH LS16 ....**61** G6
Moseley Wood La
  BHP/TINH LS16 ....**61** H5
Moseley Wood Ri
  BHP/TINH LS16 ....**61** F6
Moseley Wood Vw
  BHP/TINH LS16 ....**61** H5
Moseley Wood Wk
  BHP/TINH LS16 ....**61** G6
Moseley Wood Wy
  BHP/TINH LS16 ....**61** G5
Moser Av *ECHL* BD2 ....**78** B7
Moser Crs *ECHL* BD2 ....**78** B7
Moss Bridge Rd *BRAM* LS13........**80** C7
Moss Carr Av *KGHY* BD21........**54** C6
Moss Carr Gv *KGHY* * BD21........**54** C6
Moss Carr Rd *KGHY* BD21........**54** C6
Mossdale Av *HTON* BD9........**96** B2
Moss Dr *LUD/ILL* HX2........**134** B1
Moss Gdns *AL/HA/HU* LS17 ....**63** F6
Moss La *LUD/ILL* HX2........**134** B1
Moss Ri *AL/HA/HU* LS17........**63** F6
Moss Rw *WIL/AL* BD15 ....**75** F6
Moss Side *HTON* BD9 ....**96** D3
Moss St *CAS* WF10........**148** A7
  CUL/QBY BD13 ....**95** F6

HWTH BD22 ....**73** F4
Moss Syke *SCFT* LS14 ....**65** K2
Mosstree Cl *CUL/QBY* BD13 ....**115** F4
Moss Va *AL/HA/HU* LS17........**63** F6
Mossy Bank Cl *CUL/QBY* BD13 ......**115** H4
Mostyn Gv *WBSY* BD6........**117** F6
Mostyn Mt *HIPP* HX3........**134** D4
Motley La *GSLY* LS20 ....**59** F1
Moule Ri *GFTH/SHER* LS25 ......**108** A4
Moulson Ct *WBOW* BD5 ....**117** K3
The Mount *AL/HA/HU* LS17 ....**63** G5
  BTLY WF17 ....**140** B5
  CAS WF10 ....**169** H1
  GFTH/SHER LS25 ....**127** K5
  MSTN/BAR LS15 ....**87** G6
  MSTN/BAR LS15 ....**105** J4
  PONT WF8 ....**189** H1
  WKFDW/WTN WF2 ....**163** J7
  WKFDW/WTN WF2 ....**184** A6
  YEA * LS19 ....**80** A1
Mountain Crs *EARL* WF12 ....**181** C7
Mountain Rd *EARL* WF12 ....**181** G7
Mountain Vw *LUD/ILL* HX2........**134** D1
  SHPY BD18........................**77** J6
Mount Av *ECHL* BD2 ....**78** C7
  HECK WF16 ....**160** B2
  LUD/ILL HX2......................**153** K1
  WKFDW/WTN WF2 ....**164** A4
Mountbatten Av *WKFDE* WF1 ......**164** D3
Mountbatten Crs *WKFDE* WF1......**164** D3
Mountbatten Gv *WKFDE* WF1 ......**164** D3
Mountcliffe Vw *MOR* LS27 ....**122** A7
Mount Crs *PDSY/CALV* LS28 ....**100** B5
  LUD/ILL HX2......................**153** K1
Mount Ct *CLECK* BD19 ....**138** E7
  LUD/ILL HX2......................**153** K1
Mount Dr *AL/HA/HU* LS17 ....**63** G5
Mountfields *HIPP* HX3 ....**136** D7
Mount Gdns *AL/HA/HU* LS17 ......**63** G5
  CLECK BD19 ....**138** E7
Mount Gv *ECHL* BD2 ....**78** C7
Mount La *BRIG* HD6 ....**176** D2
Mountleigh Cl *BOW* BD4........**138** B1
Mount Pellon *LUD/ILL* HX2........**16** A3
Mount Pellon Rd *LUD/ILL* HX2......**134** B7
Mount Pl *SHPY* BD18........**77** C4
Mount Royd *GIR* BD8 ....**97** H3
Mount St *BFDE* BD3............**6** D7
  BTLY WF17 ....**161** G5
  CLECK BD19 ....**138** E7
  ECHL BD2 ....**78** C7
  HFAX HX1 ....**16** F6
  HWTH BD22 ....**2** D5
  RPDN/SBR HX6 ....**153** J4
Mount St West *LUD/ILL* * HX2 ......**134** B7
Mount Tabor Rd *LUD/ILL* HX2 ......**133** G3
Mount Tabor St
  PDSY/CALV * LS28 ....**99** K6
Mount Ter *BTLY* WF17 ....**161** F5
  ECHL BD2 ....**78** C7
  LUD/ILL HX2......................**134** B7
Mount Vernon Rd *YEA* LS19........**59** K7
Mount Vw *HWTH* BD22 ....**72** C2
  LUD/ILL HX2......................**133** H4
Mount View Ct *CLECK* BD19........**138** D7
Mount Wk *CAS* WF10 ....**168** C2
Moverley Flatts *PONT* WF8 ....**189** K2
Mowat Ct *LVSG* WF15 ....**158** C3
Mowbray Cha *RTHW* LS26........**125** H7
Mowbray Cl *CUL/QBY* BD13........**73** K7
Mowbray Ct *SCFT* LS14 ....**105** H2
Mowbray Crs *SCFT* LS14 ....**105** H2
Moxon Cl *PONT* WF8 ....**189** J3
Moxon Gv *WKFDW/WTN* WF2 ......**183** H4
Moxon Pl *WKFDW/WTN* WF2 ......**183** H4
Moxon Sq *WKFDE* WF1 ....**164** D4
Moxon St *WKFDE* WF1 ....**164** D4
Moxon Wy *WKFDE* WF1 ....**164** D4
Moynihan Cl *RHAY* LS8 ....**11** M1
Mozley Dr *LUD/ILL* HX2........**134** C1
Mucky La *CLECK* BD19 ....**140** A7
Muddy La *WBY* LS22 ....**28** E6
Muffit La *CLECK* BD19 ....**140** A7
Muff St *BOW* BD4............**6** D9
Muir Ct *HDGY* LS6........**102** C1
Muirfield Av *FEA/AMT* WF7........**168** B7
Muirfield Dr *WKFDW/WTN* WF2......**184** B7
Muirhead Ct *BOW* BD4........**119** F4
Muirhead Dr *BOW* BD4........**119** F4
Muirhead Fold *BOW* BD4........**119** F4
The Muirlands *HUDN* HD2........**177** K4
Mulberry Av *BHP/TINH* LS16 ......**82** C1
  BSPA/BRAM LS23 ....**48** D2
Mulberry Garth *BHP/TINH* LS16 ......**82** C1
Mulberry Ri *BHP/TINH* LS16 ....**62** C1
Mulberry St *KGHY* BD21............**3** J3
  MID LS10 ....**14** C5
  PDSY/CALV LS28 ....**100** B6
Mulberry Vw *BHP/TINH* LS16........**82** C1
Mulcture Hall Rd *HFAX* HX1 ....**17** J5
Mulgrave St *BFDE* BD3............**6** E8
Mullberry Gdns *RTHW* LS26 ....**146** E5
Mullins Ct *OSM* LS9 ....**15** C2
Mumford St *WBOW* BD5........**117** K3

Munby St *GIR* BD8 ....**96** D6
Muncaster Rd
  GFTH/SHER LS25 ....**108** A5
Munster St *BOW* BD4 ....**118** C3
Munton Cl *WBSY* BD6 ....**136** D1
Murdoch St *KGHY* BD21 ....**54** C3
Murgatroyd St *SHPY* BD18 ....**77** G4
  WBOW BD5 ....**117** K3
Murray St *WBOW* * BD5 ....**117** H3
Murton Cl *SCFT* LS14 ....**105** H1
Museum Ct *ECHL* BD2 ....**98** D3
Museum St *OSM* LS9 ....**11** C6
Musgrave Bank *BRAM* LS13 ....**101** H3
Musgrave Buildings
  PDSY/CALV LS28 ....**100** C5
Musgrave Dr *ECHL* BD2 ....**98** D3
Musgrave Gv *ECHL* BD2 ....**98** D3
Musgrave Mt *BRAM* LS13 ....**101** H3
  ECHL BD2 ....**98** D3
Musgrave Ri *BRAM* LS13 ....**101** H3
Musgrave Rd *ECHL* BD2 ....**98** D3
Musgrave St *BTLY* * WF17 ....**140** B6
Musgrave Vw *BRAM* LS13 ....**101** H3
Mushroom St *CHAL* LS7 ....**10** D6
Musselburgh St *GTHN* BD7 ....**5** C5
Mutton La *WIL/AL* BD15 ....**95** C3
Myers Av *ECHL* BD2 ....**98** B1
Myers Cft *OT* LS21 ....**39** H3
Myers La *ECHL* BD2 ....**98** B1
Myrtle Av *BGLY* * BD16 ....**75** J2
  DEWS WF13 ....**180** B4
  LUD/ILL HX2......................**134** B3
Myrtle Ct *BGLY* BD16 ....**75** J2
Myrtle Dr *HWTH* BD22 ....**73** G3
  LUD/ILL HX2......................**134** B3
Myrtle Gdns *LUD/ILL* HX2 ....**134** B5
Myrtle Gv *BGLY* BD16 ....**75** J2
  LUD/ILL HX2......................**134** B3
Myrtle Pl *BGLY* BD16 ....**75** J1
Myrtle Rd *DEWS* * WF13 ....**180** B4
  ELL HX5 ....**175** J4
Myrtle St *BFDE* BD3............**7** F7
  BGLY BD16 ....**75** K1
Myson Av *PONT* WF8 ....**170** A4
Mytholmes La *HWTH* BD22 ....**72** D5

N

The Nab *MIRF* WF14 ....**179** F4
Nab End La *GTL/HWG* HX4 ....**175** C2
Nab La *BTLY* WF17 ....**140** D5
  MIRF WF14 ....**179** G3
  SHPY BD18 ....**76** C5
Naburn Ap *SCFT* LS14 ....**85** J3
Naburn Cl *SCFT* LS14 ....**85** J5
Naburn Dr *SCFT* LS14 ....**85** J5
Naburn Gn *SCFT* LS14 ....**85** J5
Naburn Pl *SCFT* LS14 ....**85** J4
Naburn Rd *SCFT* LS14 ....**85** J5
Naburn Vw *SCFT* LS14 ....**85** K5
Nab Vw *AIRE* BD20 ....**21** C6
Nab Water La *HWTH* BD22 ....**92** D7
Nab Wood Bank *SHPY* BD18 ....**76** D5
Nab Wood Cl *SHPY* * BD18 ....**76** D5
Nab Wood Crs *SHPY* BD18 ....**76** D5
Nab Wood Dr *BGLY* BD16 ....**76** C6
Nab Wood Gdns *SHPY* BD18 ....**76** D5
Nab Wood Gv *SHPY* BD18 ....**76** D5
Nab Wood Mt *SHPY* BD18 ....**76** D5
Nab Wood Pl *SHPY* BD18 ....**76** D5
Nab Wood Ri *SHPY* BD18 ....**76** D5
Nab Wood Rd *SHPY* BD18 ....**76** C6
Nab Wood Ter *SHPY* BD18 ....**76** D5
Nancroft Crs *WOR/ARM* LS12 ....**12** B1
Nancroft Mt *WOR/ARM* LS12 ....**12** B1
Nancroft Ter *WOR/ARM* LS12 ....**12** B1
Nanny Goat La
  GFTH/SHER LS25 ....**107** H5
Nansen Av *BRAM* LS13 ....**100** E3
Nansen Gv *BRAM* LS13 ....**100** E3
Nansen Mt *BRAM* LS13 ....**100** E3
Nansen Pl *BRAM* LS13 ....**100** E3
Nansen St *BRAM* LS13 ....**100** D3
Nansen Ter *BRAM* LS13 ....**100** E3
Nansen Vw *BRAM* LS13 ....**100** E3
Napier Rd *BFDE* BD3............**7** J5
  ELL HX5 ....**175** H3
Napier St *BFDE* BD3............**7** K6
  CUL/QBY BD13 ....**115** J5
  KGHY BD21 ....**3** J6
Napier Ter *BFDE* BD3............**7** J6
Naples St *GIR* BD8............**4** E2
Nares St *HWTH* BD22 ....**73** F4
  KGHY BD21 ....**2** E4
Narrow La *BGLY* BD16 ....**74** E3
The Narrows *BGLY* BD16........**74** E3
Naseby Gdns *OSM* * LS9 ....**10** E7
Naseby Garth *OSM* LS9 ....**10** E7
Naseby Gra *OSM* LS9 ....**10** E8
Naseby Pl *OSM* LS9 ....**10** E8
Naseby Ri *CUL/QBY* BD13 ....**115** J5
Naseby Ter *OSM* LS9 ....**10** E8
Naseby Vw *OSM* * LS9 ....**10** E8
Naseby Wk *OSM* LS9 ....**10** E8
Nashville Rd *HWTH* BD22 ....**2** D7
Nashville St *HWTH* BD22 ....**2** D7
Nashville Ter *HWTH* BD22 ....**2** D7
Nassau Pl *CHAL* LS7 ....**10** D4
Nathan La *RPDN/SBR* HX6 ....**172** D2
National Rd *MID* LS10 ....**14** F7
Natty Fields Cl *LUD/ILL* HX2 ....**114** B7
Natty La *LUD/ILL* HX2 ....**114** A7
Nature Wy *WBSY* BD6 ....**116** D7
Navigation Cl *ELL* HX5........**175** K1
Navigation Rd *CAS* WF10 ....**148** C6
  EARL WF12 ....**180** E5
  HIPP HX3 ....**17** K7
Navigation Wk *MID* LS10........**14** B2
Naylor Ct *DEWS* WF13........**161** G7
Naylor La *LUD/ILL* HX2 ....**132** D7
Naylors Garth *HDGY* LS6........**82** E7
Naylor St *DEWS* WF13 ....**160** E6
  HFAX HX1 ....**16** A1
  OSS WF5 ....**182** B1
Neal St *WBOW* BD5............**5** L8

Nearcliffe Rd *HTON* BD9 ....**97** F3
Near Crook *SHPY* BD18........**78** A3
Neath Gdns *OSM* LS9........**104** E2
Necropolis Rd *GTHN* BD7 ....**4** A9
Ned Hill Rd *LUD/ILL* HX2........**114** B4
Needles Inn La *RTHW* LS26........**125** K7
Nelson Cft *MOR* LS27 ....**141** J5
Nelson Gv *GFTH/SHER* LS25 ....**107** G7
Nelson Pl *CUL/QBY* BD13........**115** H5
  MOR LS27 ....**141** K2
Nelson Rd *ILK* LS29 ....**24** A5
Nelson St *BFD* BD1 ....**5** M7
  BTLY WF17 ....**140** C6
  BTLY * WF17 ....**160** D3
  CUL/QBY BD13 ....**115** H5
  DEWS * WF13 ....**181** F1
  HWTH BD22 ....**73** F4
  LVSG WF15 ....**159** J5
  NORM WF6 ....**167** F5
  OT LS21 ....**39** H3
  RPDN/SBR HX6 ....**154** A4
  WIL/AL BD15 ....**96** A4
Nene St *WBOW* BD5 ....**117** H2
Nepshaw La *MOR* LS27 ....**141** J2
Nepshaw La North *MOR* LS27 ......**141** H2
Nepshaw La South *MOR* LS27 ......**141** C3
Neptune St *OSM* LS9 ....**14** D2
Nesfield Cl *MID* LS10 ....**144** A1
Nesfield Crs *MID* LS10 ....**144** A1
Nesfield Gdns *MID* LS10 ....**143** K1
Nesfield Garth *MID* LS10........**143** K1
Nesfield Rd *ILK* LS29 ....**23** J4
  MID LS10 ....**143** K1
Nesfield St *BFD* BD1............**5** K3
Nesfield Vw *ILK* LS29 ....**23** H5
  MID LS10 ....**143** K1
Nesfield Wk *MID* LS10 ....**143** K1
Nessfield Dr *HWTH* BD22 ....**2** B8
Nessfield Gv *HWTH* BD22 ....**2** B8
Nessfield Rd *HWTH* BD22 ....**2** B8
Nestfield Cl *PONT* WF8 ....**169** J5
Neston Wy *OSS* * WF5 ....**162** C7
Netherby St *BFDE* BD3............**6** F6
Nethercliffe Rd *GSLY* LS20 ....**58** F3
Netherdale Ct *WBY* LS22 ....**29** K3
Netherfield Cl *CAS* WF10........**167** J3
  YEA LS19 ....**59** J4
Netherfield Dr *GSLY* LS20 ....**58** E1
Netherfield Pl *CLECK* BD19 ....**159** F1
Netherfield Rd *DEWS* WF13 ....**180** B4
  ILK LS29 ....**38** D7
Netherhall Rd *BAIL* BD17 ....**77** J1
Netherlands Av *WBSY* BD6........**117** H7
Netherlands Sq *WBSY* BD6........**117** J7
Netherly Brow *OSS* WF5........**182** D6
Nether Moor Vw *BGLY* BD16 ....**75** K1
Netheroyd *FEA/AMT* WF7 ....**187** F4
Netheroyd Hill Rd *HUDN* HD2 ......**176** E6
Netheroyd Pl *HOR/CROF* WF4 ......**186** E6
Nether St *PDSY/CALV* LS28........**100** A1
Netherwood Cl *HUDN* HD2........**177** F6
Nettle Gv *HIPP* HX3 ....**135** J6
Nettleton Av *MIRF* WF14........**179** G4
Nettleton Cha *OSS* WF5........**162** B7
Nettleton Cl *BOW* BD4 ....**120** B4
Nettleton Ct *MSTN/BAR* LS15 ......**106** A5
Nettleton Rd *MIRF* WF14 ....**179** G4
Nettleton St *EARD/LOFT* WF3 ......**165** J2
  OSS WF5............................**182** D5
Neville Ap *OSM* LS9 ....**104** D7
Neville Av *BOW* BD4 ....**118** C5
  OSM LS9 ....**104** E5
Neville Cl *OSM* LS9 ....**104** D7
Neville Crs *OSM* LS9 ....**104** E5
Neville Garth *OSM* LS9 ....**104** E5
Neville Mt *OSM* LS9 ....**104** D7
Neville Pde *OSM* LS9 ....**104** D7
Neville Pl *OSM* LS9 ....**104** E5
Neville Rd *BOW* BD4 ....**118** C2
  OSM LS9 ....**104** E5
  OT LS21 ....**39** J5
  RTHW LS26 ....**126** D4
Neville Mt *OSM* LS9 ....**104** D7
Neville Rw *OSM* LS9 ....**104** D7
Neville Sq *OSM* LS9 ....**104** E6
Neville St *BEE/HOL* LS11........**13** M2
  CLECK BD19 ....**159** F2
  KGHY * BD21 ....**3** J3
  NORM WF6 ....**166** E7
  WKFDE WF1 ....**19** L9
Neville Ter *OSM* LS9 ....**104** D7
Neville Vw *OSM* LS9 ....**104** D7
Neville Wk *OSM* LS9 ....**104** D7
Nevill Gv *HTON* BD9 ....**96** C2
Nevins Rd *DEWS* WF13 ....**180** A3
Nevison Av *PONT* WF8 ....**169** K5
New Adel Av *BHP/TINH* LS16 ....**81** K1
New Adel Gdns *BHP/TINH* LS16 ......**81** K1
New Adel La *BHP/TINH* LS16 ....**81** K1
Newall Av *OT* LS21 ....**39** G1
Newall Carr Rd *OT* LS21 ....**27** F3
Newall Cl *ILK* LS29 ....**38** C5
  OT LS21 ....**39** G1
Newall Hall Pk *OT* LS21........**39** H1
Newall Rd *BGLY* BD16 ....**55** H6
Newark Rd *BOW* BD4 ....**6** D9
Newark St *BOW* BD4 ....**6** D9
Newark V *EARD/LOFT* WF3........**144** B4
New Augustus St *BFD* BD1 ....**6** B7
New Bank *HIPP* HX3............**17** J3
New Bank Ri *BOW* BD4 ....**118** E3
New Bank St *MOR* LS27 ....**142** A2
New Bbrighton *BGLY* BD16 ....**76** B6
New Bond St *HFAX* HX1 ....**16** F6
New Briggate *LDSU* LS2 ....**10** B8
New Brook St *ILK* LS29 ....**24** A4
New Brunswick St *HFAX* HX1 ....**16** F5
  WKFDE WF1 ....**18** F8
Newburn Rd *GTHN* BD7 ....**117** G1
Newbury Rd *BRIG* HD6 ....**176** D7
Newby Garth *AL/HA/HU* LS17 ....**64** C6
Newcastle Cl *BIRK/DRI* BD11 ....**140** A2
Newcastle Farm Ct
  KNOT WF11 ....**150** B3
New Cl *SHPY* BD18 ....**76** C5
New Close Av *AIRE* * BD20 ....**33** F1

New Close Rd *SHPY* BD18 ....**76** C5
New Clough Rd
  RPDN/SBR HX6 ....**154** A6
Newcombe St *ELL* HX5 ....**175** K4
New Cottages *OSS* * WF5........**182** C4
New Craven Ga *BEE/HOL* LS11 ......**14** B7
New Crs *HORS* LS18 ....**80** E4
New Cft *HORS* LS18 ....**80** E4
New Cross St *LM/WK* BD12 ....**138** C2
  WBOW BD5 ....**117** K4
New Farmers Hl *RTHW* LS26 ....**126** A7
Newfield Av *CAS* WF10 ....**168** D1
  NORM WF6 ....**167** F7
Newfield Cl *NORM* WF6 ....**167** F7
Newfield Ct *NORM* WF6 ....**167** F7
Newfield Crs *GFTH/SHER* LS25........**128** A2
  NORM WF6 ....**167** F7
Newfield Dr *GFTH/SHER* LS25 ....**128** A1
  ILK LS29 ....**38** B2
Newfield La *GFTH/SHER* LS25 ......**129** J6
New Fold *WBSY* BD6 ....**116** D7
Newforth Gv *WBOW* * BD5 ....**117** H4
Newgate *MIRF* WF14 ....**179** H5
  PONT WF8 ....**189** H1
Newgate St *BTLY* WF17........**161** J5
Newhall Bank *MID* LS10........**143** J1
Newhall Cha *MID* LS10........**143** J1
Newhall Cl *MID* LS10 ....**143** J1
Newhall Crs *MID* LS10 ....**143** J1
Newhall Cft *MID* LS10 ....**143** J1
Newhall Dr *WBSY* BD6........**118** A6
Newhall Gdns *MID* LS10........**143** J2
Newhall Garth *MID* LS10........**143** J2
Newhall Ga *MID* LS10 ....**123** J7
Newhall Gn *MID* LS10 ....**143** J1
Newhall La *MIRF* WF14........**179** J7
Newhall Mt *MID* LS10 ....**143** J2
  WBSY BD6 ....**118** A6
Newhall Rd *BOW* * BD4 ....**118** C5
  MID LS10 ....**143** J1
New Hall Rd *PONT* WF8 ....**169** K5
New Hey Rd *BOW* BD4 ....**118** B2
  HUDE HD3 ....**176** A5
Newhold *GFTH/SHER* LS25........**107** K5
New Holme Rd *HWTH* BD22 ....**72** E6
New House La *CUL/QBY* BD13 ......**116** A6
New House Rd *HUDN* HD2........**177** H5
New Houses *CUL/QBY* * BD13 ......**115** J1
Newill Cl *WBOW* BD5 ....**118** A4
New Inn St *WOR/ARM* LS12 ....**101** K6
New John St *BFD* * BD1 ....**5** L6
New Kirkgate *SHPY* * BD18........**77** G4
New Laithe Rd *WBSY* * BD6 ....**117** F5
Newlaithes Crs *NORM* WF6........**167** F6
Newlaithes Gdns *HORS* LS18 ....**80** E5
Newlaithes Garth *HORS* LS18 ......**80** D6
Newlaithes Rd *HORS* LS18 ....**80** E6
Newland Ct *WKFDE* WF1 ....**185** F7
Newland La *NORM* WF6 ....**166** B7
The Newlands *RPDN/SBR* HX6 ......**153** F6
Newlands *PDSY/CALV* LS28 ....**100** A3
  YEA LS19 ....**59** H4
Newlands Cl *BRIG* HD6 ....**157** G7
Newlands Crs *MOR* LS27 ....**142** C3
Newlands Dr *BGLY* BD16 ....**55** H6
  EARD/LOFT WF3 ....**165** H7
  HIPP HX3 ....**135** K4
  MOR LS27 ....**142** C3
Newlands Gv *HIPP* HX3........**135** K4
Newlands Pl *BFDE* BD3............**6** D3
Newlands Ri *YEA* LS19 ....**59** H4
Newlands Rd *LUD/ILL* HX2 ....**153** J1
Newland St *KNOT* WF11 ....**170** C3
  WKFDE WF1 ....**185** F7
Newlands Wk *EARD/LOFT* WF3 ......**165** F7
Newland Vw *NORM* WF6........**166** C6
New La *AIRE* BD20 ....**20** A7
  BEE/HOL LS11 ....**13** M3
  BOW BD4 ....**7** K8
  BOW BD4 ....**119** J4
  CLECK BD19 ....**158** B2
  EARD/LOFT WF3 ....**143** H7
  GFTH/SHER LS25 ....**110** E7
  HIPP HX3 ....**154** E6
  HIPP HX3 ....**155** C4
  KNOT WF11 ....**150** E4
  LUD/ILL HX2......................**152** C3
  MID LS10 ....**143** G2
  MOR LS27 ....**120** D6
Newlay Cl *IDLE* BD10 ....**79** F5
Newlay Gv *HORS* LS18 ....**80** E6
Newlay La *BRAM* LS13 ....**101** F1
  HORS LS18 ....**80** E6
Newlay Lane Pl *BRAM* LS13 ....**101** F1
Newlay Wood Av *HORS* LS18 ......**81** F5
Newlay Wood Cl *HORS* LS18........**81** F5
Newlay Wood Crs *HORS* LS18 ......**81** F5
Newlay Wood Dr *HORS* LS18 ....**81** F5
Newlay Wood Gdns
  HORS * LS18......................**81** F5
Newlay Wood Ri *HORS* LS18 ....**80** E5
Newlay Wood Rd *HORS* LS18........**80** E5
Newley Av *BTLY* WF17........**140** C7
Newley Mt *HORS* LS18 ....**80** E6
New Line *IDLE* BD10 ....**79** F5
New Longley La
  RPDN/SBR HX6 ....**153** H7
Newlyn Dr *WKFDW/WTN* WF2 ......**184** D2
Newlyn Rd *AIRE* BD20 ....**54** D2
Newman St *BOW* BD4 ....**118** C4
Newmarket Ap *OSM* LS9 ....**15** L5
Newmarket Gn *OSM* LS9 ....**15** K4
Newmarket La
  EARD/LOFT WF3 ....**145** K7
  OSM LS9 ....**15** M5
New Market St *LDS* LS1 ....**14** B1
New Mill La *BSPA/BRAM* LS23 ......**48** D5
New North Rd *HECK* WF16........**159** K3
New Occupation La
  PDSY/CALV LS28 ....**99** K7
New Otley Rd *BFDE* BD3............**6** C4
New Park Av *PDSY/CALV* LS28........**100** B2
New Park Cl *PDSY/CALV* LS28 ......**100** B2

New Park Cft PDSY/CALV LS28 ....100 B2
New Park La OSS WF5 ....183 G1
New Park Pl PDSY/CALV LS28 ....100 B2
New Park Rd CUL/QBY BD13 ....115 C5
New Park St MOR LS27 ....141 J4
New Park V PDSY/CALV LS28 ....100 B2
New Park Vw PDSY/CALV LS28 ..100 A3
New Park Wk
  PDSY/CALV * LS28 ....100 A2
New Park Wy PDSY/CALV LS28 ..100 B2
New Popplewell La
  CLECK BD19 ....138 A7
Newport Av BRAM LS13 ....100 D3
Newport Crs HDGY LS6 ....8 C2
Newport Gdns HDGY LS6 ....8 C2
Newport Mt HDGY LS6 ....8 C2
Newport Pl GIR BD8 ....5 G3
Newport Rd GIR BD8 ....5 G3
  HDGY LS6 ....8 D2
Newport St PONT WF8 ....169 H7
Newport Vw HDGY LS6 ....8 C1
New Princess St BEE/HOL LS11 ..13 L5
New Pudsey Sq
  PDSY/CALV LS28 ....99 K4
New Rd AIRE BD20 ....33 J5
  BSPA/BRAM LS23 ....48 C7
  CUL/QBY BD13 ....94 A5
  EARD/LOFT WF3 ....144 E4
  FEA/AMT WF7 ....187 G1
  GFTH/SHER LS25 ....129 J4
  GTL/HWG HX4 ....174 D2
  HFAX HX1 ....17 H7
  HUDE HD5 ....178 C7
  HUDW HD3 ....175 F7
  KNOT WF11 ....170 B3
  LUD/ILL HX2 ....132 E6
  PONT WF8 ....191 K7
  TAD LS24 ....71 J6
  YEA LS19 ....59 G4
New Rd East CLECK BD19 ....137 K7
New Road Side HORS LS18 ....80 D5
  YEA LS19 ....59 J7
New Road Sq BRIG * HD6 ....176 D3
New Rw HTON BD9 ....96 B3
  WKFDW/WTN WF2 ....163 G6
Newroyd Rd WBOW BD5 ....117 K4
Newsam Ct MSTN/BAR * LS15 ..105 H6
Newsam Dr MSTN/BAR LS15 ....105 H6
Newsam Green Rd
  MSTN/BAR LS15 ....126 A4
Newsholme New Rd
  HWTH BD22 ....52 B7
Newsome St DEWS WF13 ....160 E7
New Station St LDS LS1 ....13 M1
  WKFDE WF1 ....164 B4
Newstead Av HFAX HX1 ....154 B1
  WKFDE WF1 ....164 B4
Newstead Gdns HFAX HX1 ....154 B1
Newstead Heath HFAX HX1 ......154 B1
Newstead Pl HFAX HX1 ....154 B1
Newstead Rd WKFDE WF1 ....18 D3
Newstead Ter HFAX HX1 ....154 B1
Newstead Wk WBOW * BD5 .....117 K4
New St BOW BD4 ....118 C6
  BRIG HD6 ....157 G1
  BRIG HD6 ....157 J6
  BTLY WF17 ....161 H5
  CAS WF10 ....148 D7
  CLECK BD19 ....159 G2
  CUL/QBY BD13 ....94 A5
  EARL WF12 ....181 J2
  GFTH/SHER LS25 ....128 A5
  GTL/HWG HX4 ....174 C6
  HIPP HX3 ....155 K4
  HORS LS18 ....80 E4
  HWTH BD22 ....72 D6
  IDLE BD10 ....78 C4
  LM/WK BD12 ....138 C2
  LUD/ILL * HX2 ....134 B7
  OSS WF5 ....182 D4
  PDSY/CALV LS28 ....100 A4
  PDSY/CALV LS28 ....100 B7
  TAD LS24 ....50 E7
New Street Cl
  PDSY/CALV LS28 ....100 B7
New Street Gdns
  PDSY/CALV LS28 ....100 B7
New Street Gv
  PDSY/CALV LS28 ....100 B7
New Sturton La
  GFTH/SHER LS25 ....108 A6
New Tanhouse
  MIRF WF14 ....179 G4
New Temple Ga
  MSTN/BAR LS15 ....105 H7
Newton Av WKFDE WF1 ....164 C4
Newton Cl AIRE BD20 ....32 E1
  RTHW LS26 ....144 C3
  WKFDE WF1 ....164 C7
Newton Ct RHAY LS8 ....84 D6
  WKFDE WF1 ....164 C4
Newton Dr CAS WF10 ....169 J4
  WKFDE WF1 ....164 C6
Newton Garth CHAL LS7 ....83 K7
Newton Gn WKFDE WF1 ....164 C7
Newton Gv CHAL LS7 ....83 J1
Newton Hill Rd CHAL LS7 ....83 J7
Newton La CAS WF10 ....148 C3
  WKFDE WF1 ....164 C6
Newton Lodge Cl CHAL LS7 ....83 H7
Newton Lodge Dr CHAL LS7 ....83 H7
Newton Pde CHAL * LS7 ....83 J7
Newton Pk BRIG HD6 ....156 E2
Newton Park Ct CHAL * LS7 ....83 K7
Newton Park Dr CHAL LS7 ....83 K7
Newton Park Vw CHAL LS7 ....103 K1
Newton Pl WBOW BD5 ....117 J2
Newton Rd CHAL LS7 ....83 J7
Newton St RPDN/SBR * HX6 .....153 J4
  WBOW BD5 ....117 K3
Newton Vw CHAL LS7 ....83 J1
Newton Vls CHAL * LS7 ....83 H6
Newton Wk CHAL LS7 ....83 J1
Newton Wy BAIL * BD17 ....57 H7
New Town Ct HWTH BD22 ....2 D5
New Wk RHAY LS8 ....84 B1
New Wy BTLY WF17 ....161 F3
  GSLY LS20 ....58 D2

New Wellgate CAS WF10 ....168 E2
New Wls WKFDE WF1 ....18 F6
New Wells Ter WKFDE * WF1 ....18 F6
New Windsor Dr RTHW LS26 ......145 G1
New Works Rd LM/WK BD12 ......137 H2
New York La YEA LS19 ....80 A2
New York Rd LDSU LS2 ....10 C8
New York St LDSU LS2 ....14 B1
Nibshaw La CLECK BD19 ....139 H7
Nibshaw Rd CLECK BD19 ....139 H7
Nice Av RHAY LS8 ....11 H1
Nice St RHAY LS8 ....11 H1
Nice Vw RHAY LS8 ....11 H1
Nicholas Cl GTHN * BD7 ....4 B1
Nicholson Ct RHAY * LS8 ....84 B6
Nicholson St CAS WF10 ....168 B1
Nichols Wy WBY LS22 ....28 E4
Nickleby Rd OSM LS9 ....11 J9
Nicolsons Pl AIRE BD20 ....33 F1
Nidd Ap WBY LS22 ....29 G1
Nidd Ct AIRE BD20 ....33 F2
Nidderdale Cl GFTH/SHER LS25 ...128 A7
Nidderdale Wk BAIL BD17 ....57 K7
Nidd St BFDE BD3 ....7 H1
Nighthorne Av BFDE BD3 ....7 H1
Nightingale Crest
  WKFDW/WTN WF2 ....183 H5
Nightingale Dr KGHY * BD21 ....3 H2
Nightingale Wk BGLY BD16 ....56 B7
Nijinsky Wy MID LS10 ....124 C5
Nile Crs HWTH BD22 ....2 A7
Nile St HWTH * BD22 ....73 F4
  HWTH BD22 ....73 F4
  LDSU LS2 ....10 C8
Nina Rd GTHN BD7 ....116 E3
Ninelands La GFTH/SHER LS25 ...127 K1
Ninelands Sp GFTH/SHER LS25 ...107 J7
Ninelands Vw GFTH/SHER LS25 ...107 K6
Ninevah La CAS WF10 ....147 J2
Nineveh Gdns BEE/HOL LS11 ....13 K5
Nineveh Pde BEE/HOL LS11 ....13 K6
Nineveh Rd BEE/HOL LS11 ....13 J5
Ninth Av LVSG WF15 ....158 C3
Nippet La OSM LS9 ....10 F8
Nixon Av OSM LS9 ....15 M1
Noble St GTHN BD7 ....117 G1
Nog La HTON BD9 ....97 F1
The Nook AL/HA/HU LS17 ....63 J6
  CLECK BD19 ....139 F7
  EARD/LOFT WF3 ....162 D2
  GFTH/SHER LS25 ....131 F2
  RPDN/SBR HX6 ....153 J5
The Nooking
  WKFDW/WTN WF2 ....163 G5
Nook La RPDN/SBR HX6 ....172 A1
Nook Rd MSTN/BAR LS15 ....86 C4
The Nooks MOR LS27 ....121 G7
Nook Wk DEWS WF13 ....180 C1
Noon Cl EARD/LOFT WF3 ....165 F3
Nora Pl BRAM LS13 ....100 D2
Nora Rd BRAM LS13 ....100 D2
Nora Ter BRAM LS13 ....100 D2
Norbeck Dr HWTH BD22 ....73 F4
Norbury Rd IDLE BD10 ....79 F7
Norcliffe La HIPP HX3 ....155 K2
Norcroft Brow GTHN BD7 ....5 J7
Norcroft St BFD BD1 ....5 H6
Norfield HUDN HD2 ....177 F5
Norfolk Av BTLY WF17 ....160 E5
Norfolk Cl CHAL LS7 ....83 J5
  KNOT WF11 ....150 C7
  RTHW LS26 ....146 A2
Norfolk Dr RTHW LS26 ....146 A2
Norfolk Gdns BFD BD1 ....5 M7
  CHAL LS7 ....83 J5
Norfolk Gn CHAL LS7 ....83 J5
Norfolk Mt CHAL LS7 ....83 J5
Norfolk Pl CHAL LS7 ....83 J5
  HFAX HX1 ....16 D8
Norfolk St BGLY BD16 ....75 K1
  BTLY WF17 ....160 E4
Norfolk Ter CHAL * LS7 ....83 J5
Norfolk Vw CHAL LS7 ....83 J5
Norfolk Wk CHAL LS7 ....83 J5
Norgarth Cl BTLY WF17 ....161 J5
Norham Gv LM/WK BD12 ....137 J5
Norland Rd RPDN/SBR HX6 ....153 J5
  RPDN/SBR HX6 ....154 A7
Norland St GTHN BD7 ....116 E3
Norland Town Rd
  RPDN/SBR HX6 ....154 A6
Norland Vw RPDN/SBR HX6 ....154 A4
Norman Av ECHL BD2 ....78 C7
  ELL HX5 ....175 K3
Norman Crs ECHL BD2 ....78 C7
Norman Dr MIRF WF14 ....179 G3
Norman Gv ECHL BD2 ....78 C7
  ELL * HX5 ....175 K3
  KSTL LS5 ....101 K1
Norman La ECHL BD2 ....78 C7
Norman Mt ECHL BD2 ....78 C7
  KSTL LS5 ....101 K1
Normanon Pl BEE/HOL LS11 ....13 K7
Norman Pl RHAY LS8 ....84 B1
Norman Rd MIRF WF14 ....179 G3
Norman Rw KSTL LS5 ....101 K1
Norman St BGLY * BD16 ....75 K1
  ELL HX5 ....175 K3
  HFAX HX1 ....16 A9
  KSTL LS5 ....101 K1
  SHPY BD18 ....77 J5
Norman Ter ECHL BD2 ....78 C7
  ELL HX5 ....175 K3
  RHAY LS8 ....84 B2
Normanton Gv BEE/HOL LS11 ......13 J7
Normanton Vw NORM WF6 ....186 E1
Norman Vw KSTL LS5 ....101 K1
Norristhorpe La LVSG WF15 ....159 H6
Nortech Cl CHAL LS7 ....10 D5
Northallerton Rd BFDE BD3 ....6 B2
North Ap TAD LS24 ....69 F7
North Av CAS WF10 ....167 J1
  HTON BD9 ....97 J2
  OT LS21 ....39 H2

PONT WF8 ....189 F1
WKFDE WF1 ....184 D1
North Baileygate PONT WF8 ......169 J7
North Bank Rd BGLY BD16 ....75 K7
  BTLY WF17 ....160 D3
North Bolton LUD/ILL HX2 ....114 A7
North Bridge St HFAX HX1 ....17 H4
North Broadgate La HORS LS18 ....81 F3
Northbrook Cft CHAL * LS7 ....83 J5
Northbrook Pl CHAL LS7 ....83 J5
North Brook St BD1 ....6 A4
Northbrook St CHAL LS7 ....83 J5
North Byland LUD/ILL HX2 ....114 B7
North Cliffe Av CUL/QBY BD13 .....95 J7
North Cliffe Cl CUL/QBY * BD13 ...95 H7
North Cliffe Dr CUL/QBY BD13 .....95 H7
North Cliffe Gv CUL/QBY BD13 .....95 H6
North Cliffe La CUL/QBY BD13 ......95 J6
Northcliffe Rd SHPY BD18 ....77 F6
North Ct LDSU LS2 ....10 B8
North Court Gv WBY LS22 ....29 H3
North Crs GFTH/SHER LS25 ....111 F4
North Croft Grove Rd ILK LS29 .....23 K5
Northcroft Ri HTON BD9 ....96 D4
North Cross Rd HUDN HD2 ....176 D7
North Cut BRIG HD6 ....156 D6
Northdale Av WBOW BD5 ....117 H4
Northdale Crs WBOW BD5 ....117 H4
Northdale Mt WBOW BD5 ....117 H4
Northdale Rd HTON BD9 ....77 G7
North Dean Av HWTH BD22 ....53 F4
North Dean Rd GTL/HWG HX4 ....154 C7
North Dene Rd AIRE BD20 ....21 F7
North Dr BHP/TINH LS16 ....61 J1
  GFTH/SHER LS25 ....111 F4
Northedge La AIRE BD20 ....136 C5
Northedge Meadow
  IDLE BD10 ....78 C6
Northedge Pk HIPP HX3 ....136 C5
Northern Cl GTHN BD7 ....116 E4
Northern St LDS LS1 ....13 K1
North Farm Rd RHAY LS8 ....11 M2
Northfield Av KNOT WF11 ....171 G4
  OSS WF5 ....182 C3
  RTHW LS26 ....144 D3
Northfield Cl ELL * HX5 ....175 J4
Northfield Crs BGLY BD16 ....75 K5
Northfield Dr PONT WF8 ....170 A7
Northfield Gdns WBSY BD6 ....117 H5
Northfield Gv WBSY BD6 ....117 H5
Northfield La GFTH/SHER LS25 ...130 E1
Northfield Pl DEWS WF13 ....160 E7
  GIR BD8 ....5 H1
  RTHW LS26 ....144 C3
  WBY LS22 ....29 H3
Northfield Rd DEWS WF13 ....160 E7
  HOR/CROF WF4 ....186 A6
  KNOT WF11 ....171 G4
  OSS WF5 ....182 C3
  WBSY BD6 ....117 H5
Northfields BSPA/BRAM LS23 ......31 F6
Northfield St DEWS WF13 ....161 F7
Northfield Ter CUL/QBY BD13 .....115 K5
  HOR/CROF * WF4 ....183 H7
North Fold LUD/ILL HX2 ....78 C4
North Ga MIRF WF14 ....178 E7
Northgate BAIL BD17 ....57 H7
  BFD BD1 ....5 L5
  CLECK BD19 ....159 F1
  DEWS WF13 ....181 G1
  ELL HX5 ....175 J2
  GTL/HWG HX4 ....174 E5
  HECK WF16 ....159 K4
  HFAX HX1 ....17 H5
  HOR/CROF WF4 ....183 F7
  PONT WF8 ....169 J7
  RTHW LS26 ....145 K1
  WKFDE WF1 ....18 D2
Northgate Cl PONT WF8 ....169 J7
Northgate La WBY LS22 ....28 D5
Northgate Ldg PONT WF8 ....169 J7
Northgate Ri WBY LS22 ....28 E7
Northgates WBY LS22 ....29 H4
North Grange Ms HDGY LS6 ....9 G1
North Grange Mt HDGY LS6 ....82 D7
North Gv WBY LS22 ....29 H3
North Grove Av WBY LS22 ....29 H2
North Grove Cl RHAY LS8 ....84 B6
North Grove Crs WBY LS22 ....29 H2
North Grove Dr RHAY LS8 ....84 E6
  WBY LS22 ....29 H2
North Grove Mt WBY LS22 ....29 H3
North Grove Ri RHAY LS8 ....84 E6
North Grove Wy WBY LS22 ....29 H2
North Hall Av IDLE BD10 ....78 B2
North Hill Cl HDGY LS6 ....84 D6
North Hill Rd HDGY LS6 ....9 G1
North Holme St BFD BD1 ....5 M4
North King St BTLY WF17 ....161 G4
North La RHAY LS8 ....84 E6
  RTHW LS26 ....145 K1
Northlea Av IDLE BD10 ....78 B3
North Lingwell Rd MID LS10 ....143 H2
North Lodge Fold DEWS WF13 ....160 C5
North Lodge La PONT WF8 ....191 G5
North Md BHP/TINH LS16 ....61 J1
North Moor La HUDE HD5 ....178 D7
Northolme Av BHP/TINH LS16 ......82 A5
Northolme Crs BHP/TINH LS16 .....82 A5
Northorpe La MIRF WF14 ....179 K2
Northorpe Vw MIRF WF14 ....179 K2
Northowram Gn HIPP HX3 ....135 K3
North Pde BFD BD1 ....5 L5
  BHP/TINH LS16 ....81 K4
  HFAX HX1 ....17 G5
  ILK LS29 ....24 B5
  ILK LS29 ....25 K7

OT LS21 ....39 H2
WIL/AL BD15 ....95 J3
North Park Av RHAY LS8 ....84 A4
North Park Gv RHAY LS8 ....84 B4
North Park Rd HTON BD9 ....97 G2
  RHAY LS8 ....84 B4
North Park St DEWS WF13 ....160 D7
North Park Ter HTON BD9 ....97 H3
North Pkwy SCFT LS14 ....85 F7
North Pollard St HFAX HX1 ....17 H4
North Queen St BTLY WF17 ....3 G4
North Rd DEWS WF13 ....180 A3
  HORS LS18 ....80 E1
  KNOT WF11 ....150 B3
  MSTN/BAR * LS15 ....105 K3
  OSM LS9 ....124 D3
  WBSY BD6 ....117 G6
North Road Ter WKFDE WF1 ....18 D2
Northrop Cl GIR BD8 ....4 B2
Northside Av GTHN BD7 ....4 B7
Northside Rd GTHN BD7 ....4 B7
Northside Ter GTHN BD7 ....4 B7
North St AIRE BD20 ....21 F7
  BFD BD1 ....6 B5
  CAS WF10 ....148 B7
  CAS WF10 ....149 H5
  CHAL LS7 ....10 C5
  DEWS WF13 ....161 F7
  GFTH/SHER LS25 ....111 F4
  GTL/HWG HX4 ....174 D5
  HECK WF16 ....175 G2
  HIPP HX3 ....136 A5
  HWTH BD22 ....72 C5
  IDLE BD10 ....78 C2
  ILK LS29 ....22 D1
  KGHY BD21 ....3 C5
  LM/WK BD12 ....138 B3
  MIRF WF14 ....179 G3
  NORM WF6 ....186 D1
  OT LS21 ....39 H2
  PDSY/CALV LS28 ....100 B5
  WBY LS22 ....29 H4
  YEA LS19 ....59 J7
North Ter BTLY WF17 ....140 C6
  MSTN/BAR * LS15 ....105 K3
  YEA LS19 ....59 J4
North Vw AIRE BD20 ....32 A4
  AL/HA/HU LS17 ....63 H7
  ELL HX5 ....181 G3
  ILK LS29 ....38 B6
  KNOT WF11 ....171 F3
  WIL/AL BD15 ....75 F7
  WIL/AL BD15 ....95 K4
North View Rd BFDE BD3 ....98 A3
  BOW BD4 ....119 H7
North View St KGHY BD21 ....53 K2
  PDSY/CALV LS28 ....100 B3
North View Ter DEWS * WF13 .....160 E6
  HWTH BD22 ....72 D4
  PDSY/CALV LS28 ....100 B3
North Wk BGLY BD16 ....74 D3
North Wy HUDN HD2 ....177 K5
  RHAY LS8 ....84 E6
Northway MIRF WF14 ....179 G2
Northway Crs MIRF WF14 ....179 G1
Northway Gdns MIRF WF14 ....179 G1
Northwell Ga OT LS21 ....39 F1
North West Rd HDGY LS6 ....9 M3
North Wing BFDE BD3 ....6 B4
Northwood Cl PDSY/CALV LS28 ..120 C1
  RTHW LS26 ....125 K7
Northwood Crs IDLE BD10 ....78 D5
Northwood Falls RTHW LS26 ....125 K7
Northwood Gdns
  MSTN/BAR LS15 ....106 B6
Northwood Mt
  PDSY/CALV LS28 ....120 C1
Northwood Pk RTHW LS26 ....125 K7
Northwood Vw
  PDSY/CALV LS28 ....120 C1
Norton Cl ELL HX5 ....175 J4
  LUD/ILL HX2 ....153 J1
Norton Dr LUD/ILL HX2 ....153 J1
Norton Fold ECHL * BD2 ....78 C7
Norton Rd RHAY LS8 ....84 B1
Norton St AIRE BD20 ....32 E1
  ELL HX5 ....175 J4
  WKFDE WF1 ....19 K9
Norton Wy MOR LS27 ....141 J1
Norville Ter HDGY * LS6 ....8 F1
Norwich Av MID LS10 ....123 J4
Norwood PONT WF8 ....190 B4
Norwood Av BIRK/DRI BD11 ....136 E5
  ILK LS29 ....38 A1
  SHPY BD18 ....77 G6
Norwood Cl ILK LS29 ....38 A1
Norwood Crs CLECK BD19 ....139 J3
  PDSY/CALV LS28 ....100 C3
Norwood Dr BIRK/DRI BD11 ....139 J3
  BTLY WF17 ....140 C7
Norwood Green Hl HIPP HX3 ......136 E5
Norwood Gv BIRK/DRI BD11 ....139 J3
  HDGY LS6 ....8 E2
Norwood Mt HDGY LS6 ....8 E2
Norwood Pl HDGY LS6 ....8 E2
  SHPY BD18 ....77 G6
Norwood Rd HDGY LS6 ....8 E2
  HUDN HD2 ....176 D7
  SHPY BD18 ....77 G6
Norwood St NORM WF6 ....167 G5
  SHPY BD18 ....77 G6
  WBOW BD5 ....117 J4
Norwood Ter HDGY LS6 ....8 E2
  ILK LS29 ....38 A1
  SHPY BD18 ....77 G6
Norwood Vw HDGY LS6 ....8 E2
Nostell Cl GIR BD8 ....5 J3
Noster Gv BEE/HOL LS11 ....13 H9
Noster Hl BEE/HOL LS11 ....122 H9
Noster Pl BEE/HOL LS11 ....13 H9
Noster Rd BEE/HOL LS11 ....122 H9
Noster St BEE/HOL LS11 ....13 H9
Noster Ter BEE/HOL LS11 ....13 H9
Noster Vw BEE/HOL LS11 ....13 H9
Nottingham Cl
  EARD/LOFT * WF3 ....144 B4

Nottingham St BFDE BD3 ....7 L6
Nova La BTLY WF17 ....140 A5
Nowell Ap OSM LS9 ....11 L6
Nowell Av OSM LS9 ....11 L6
Nowell Crs OSM LS9 ....11 M7
Nowell End Rw OSM LS9 ....11 M7
Nowell Gdns OSM LS9 ....11 L6
Nowell Gv OSM LS9 ....11 L6
Nowell La OSM LS9 ....11 L6
Nowell Mt OSM LS9 ....11 L7
Nowell Pde OSM LS9 ....11 L7
Nowell Pl OSM LS9 ....11 L7
Nowell St DEWS WF13 ....160 E7
  OSM LS9 ....11 L6
Nowell's Yd DEWS WF13 ....180 E1
Nowell Ter OSM LS9 ....11 L6
Nowell Vw OSM LS9 ....11 M7
Nowell Wk OSM LS9 ....11 L6
Nunburnholme Wk IDLE BD10 ......78 D6
Nunington Av WOR/ARM LS12 ......8 B8
Nunington St WOR/ARM LS12 ......8 B8
Nunington Ter WOR/ARM LS12 .....8 B8
Nunington Vw WOR/ARM LS12 .....8 A7
Nunlea Royd BRIG HD6 ....157 F2
Nunnery La BRIG HD6 ....176 C2
Nunns Av FEA/AMT WF7 ....188 B5
Nunns Cl FEA/AMT WF7 ....188 B6
Nunns Ct FEA/AMT WF7 ....188 B6
Nunns Cft FEA/AMT WF7 ....188 C5
Nunns Gn FEA/AMT WF7 ....188 C5
Nunns La FEA/AMT WF7 ....188 C5
Nunroyd HECK WF16 ....160 A3
Nunroyd Av GSLY LS20 ....59 J3
Nunroyd Gv AL/HA/HU LS17 ....83 J3
Nunroyd Lawn
  AL/HA/HU * LS17 ....83 J3
Nunroyd Rd AL/HA/HU LS17 ....83 J3
Nunroyd Ter AL/HA/HU LS17 ....83 J3
Nunthorpe Rd BRAM LS13 ....80 C7
Nurser La WBOW BD5 ....117 H2
Nurser Pl WBOW BD5 ....117 H2
Nursery Av LUD/ILL HX2 ....134 C4
Nursery Cl AIRE BD20 ....33 H7
  AL/HA/HU LS17 ....63 H7
  BAIL * BD17 ....76 D2
Nursery Garth WBY LS22 ....29 J3
Nursery Gv AL/HA/HU LS17 ....63 H7
  LUD/ILL HX2 ....134 C4
Nursery La AL/HA/HU LS17 ....63 H7
  HIPP HX3 ....134 C4
  ILK LS29 ....22 D1
  RPDN/SBR HX6 ....172 C6
Nursery Mt MID LS10 ....123 K5
Nursery Mount Rd MID LS10 ....123 K5
Nursery Rd GSLY LS20 ....38 E7
  GTHN BD7 ....116 E4
Nursery St EARL WF12 ....181 F5
Nursery Wy BSPA/BRAM LS23 ......48 C5
  BSPA/BRAM LS23 ....48 C5
Nursery Wood Rd BTLY WF17 .....161 G4
Nussey Av BTLY WF17 ....140 B5
Nuttall Rd BFDE BD3 ....6 C5
Nutter La CLECK BD19 ....139 K5
Nutter St CLECK BD19 ....158 C1
Nutting Grove Ter
  WOR/ARM LS12 ....121 H1
Nutwood Wk WBSY BD6 ....136 D1

O

Oak Av BGLY BD16 ....75 J3
  EARD/LOFT WF3 ....165 G4
  GFTH/SHER LS25 ....107 J6
  GIR BD8 ....97 H3
  ILK LS29 ....38 A2
  MOR LS27 ....142 A4
  NORM WF6 ....186 D1
  RPDN/SBR HX6 ....153 J5
Oak Bank BGLY BD16 ....75 J3
  SHPY BD18 ....77 J7
Oakbank Av HWTH BD22 ....2 A9
Oakbank Broadway
  HWTH BD22 ....53 G7
Oakbank Ct HWTH BD22 ....53 G7
Oakbank Crs HWTH BD22 ....53 G7
Oakbank Dr HWTH BD22 ....2 A9
Oakbank Gv HWTH BD22 ....2 B9
Oakbank La HWTH BD22 ....53 G7
Oakbank Mt HWTH BD22 ....53 G7
Oakburn Rd ILK LS29 ....23 K6
Oak Crs GFTH/SHER LS25 ....107 J6
  MSTN/BAR LS15 ....105 G6
Oakdale BGLY BD16 ....55 K6
Oakdale Av SHPY BD18 ....77 J6
  WBSY BD6 ....117 G5
Oakdale Cl EARD/LOFT WF3 ....164 C2
  HIPP HX3 ....134 D5
  IDLE BD10 ....99 F2
Oakdale Crs WBSY BD6 ....117 G5
Oakdale Dr IDLE BD10 ....99 F2
  SHPY BD18 ....77 K6
Oakdale Garth SCFT LS14 ....85 J7
Oakdale Gv SHPY BD18 ....77 K6
Oakdale Meadow SCFT LS14 ....85 J7
Oakdale Pk OT LS21 ....41 G4
Oakdale Rd SHPY BD18 ....77 K6
Oakdale Ter WBSY BD6 ....117 G5
Oakdean HUDN HD2 ....177 F5
Oakdene Cl PDSY/CALV LS28 .....120 C1
Oakdene Ct AL/HA/HU LS17 ....64 B7
Oakdene Dr AL/HA/HU LS17 ....64 B7
Oakdene Gdns AL/HA/HU LS17 .....64 B7
Oakdene V AL/HA/HU LS17 ....64 B7
Oakdene Vw AL/HA/HU LS17 ....64 B7
Oak Dr GFTH/SHER LS25 ....107 J6
Oakenshaw Ct LM/WK BD12 ....137 H5
Oakenshaw La CLECK BD19 ....138 B4
Oakenshaw St WKFDE WF1 ....185 G6
Oakes St WKFDW/WTN WF2 ......183 J3
Oakfield HDGY LS6 ....82 D7
Oakfield Av BGLY BD16 ....76 B2
  RTHW * LS26 ....145 F1
Oakfield Cl ELL HX5 ....175 H3
  GFTH/SHER LS25 ....107 J7
  ILK LS29 ....38 B4

Oakfield Crs *KNOT* WF11.................171 G5
Oakfield Dr *BAIL* BD17.......................77 J2
  MIRF WF14...............................179 G6
Oakfield Gv *HTON* BD9.......................97 H3
Oakfield Rd *HWTH* BD22.....................53 H7
Oakfield Ter *SHPY* BD18.....................77 J5
Oak Gv *GFTH/SHER* LS25..................107 K6
  HWTH BD22................................73 H1
  MOR LS27..................................142 A4
Oakhall Pk *CUL/QBY* BD13..................95 G6
Oakhall Park Av *CUL/QBY* BD13 ....95 G6
Oakhampton Ct *RHAY* LS8..................84 D5
Oakham Wk *BOW* BD4......................118 B2
Oak Hl *RPDN/SBR* HX6.....................173 F1
Oak Hill Rd *BRIG* HD6.......................157 G5
Oakhurst Av *BEE/HOL* LS11...............122 C5
Oakhurst Gv *BEE/HOL* LS11...............122 C5
Oakhurst Mt *BEE/HOL* LS11...............122 C5
Oakhurst Rd *BEE/HOL* LS11................123 F5
Oakhurst St *BEE/HOL* LS11................122 C5
Oakland Rd *WKFDE* WF1....................185 F6
Oaklands *BRIG* HD6..........................156 E7
  EARD/LOFT WF3.........................144 B4
  IDLE BD10.................................78 B4
  ILK LS29...................................23 J7
  SHPY BD18................................76 C5
Oaklands Av *BHP/TINH* LS16..............82 C1
  BRAM LS13................................80 B7
  HIPP HX3.................................135 K4
Oaklands Cl *BHP/TINH* LS16...............82 C1
Oaklands Dr *BHP/TINH* LS16...............82 C1
  BTLY WF17...............................161 J3
Oaklands Fold *BHP/TINH* LS16............82 C1
Oaklands Gv *BHP/TINH* LS16..............82 C1
Oaklands Rd *BRAM* LS13.....................80 B7
Oakland St *AIRE* BD20........................32 E1
Oak La *GIR* BD8.................................97 H3
  HFAX HX1.................................16 C5
  RPDN/SBR HX6.........................173 F1
Oaklea Gdns *BHP/TINH* LS16..............82 C2
Oaklea Hall Cl *BHP/TINH* LS16 ....82 C2
Oaklea Rd *MSTN/BAR* LS15..................86 C6
Oakleigh Av *CLAY* BD14....................116 A3
  HIPP HX3.................................155 F5
  WKFDW/WTN WF2....................183 K4
Oakleigh Cl *CLAY* BD14....................116 A2
  HOR/CROF WF4.........................187 F5
Oakleigh Gdns *CLAY* * BD14..............116 A3
Oakleigh Gv *CLAY* BD14....................116 A3
Oakleigh Rd *CLAY* BD14....................116 A3
Oakleigh Ter *CLAY* BD14....................116 A2
Oakleigh Vw *BAIL* BD17......................77 G1
Oakley Gv *BEE/HOL* LS11..................123 H5
Oakley St *EARD/LOFT* WF3................143 K6
Oakley Ter *BEE/HOL* LS11.................123 H4
Oakley Vw *BEE/HOL* LS11..................123 H4
Oak Mt *GIR* BD8.................................97 J3
  HIPP * HX3...............................156 D1
Oak Pl *GFTH/SHER* LS25...................107 H6
  HFAX HX1.................................16 C6
  RPDN/SBR HX6.........................153 J3
Oak Rdg *WBY* LS22.............................29 F4
Oakridge Av *ILK* LS29.........................38 C6
Oakridge Ct *BGLY* BD16......................55 K7
Oak Ri *CLECK* BD19...........................138 E5
Oak Rd *CHAL* LS7..............................83 J7
  GFTH/SHER LS25......................107 H6
  HUDN HD2...............................178 B4
  MOR LS27................................141 J5
  MSTN/BAR LS15........................105 G6
  WOR/ARM LS12.........................12 E1
Oak Royd *GFTH/SHER* LS25...............107 J6
Oakroyd *RTHW* LS26.........................145 G3
Oakroyd Av *WBSY* BD6......................139 F6
  BRIG HD6................................157 G3
Oakroyd Cl *BIRK/DRI* BD11................139 H2
  BRIG HD6................................157 G3
Oakroyd Dr *BIRK/DRI* BD11................139 H3
  BRIG HD6................................157 G3
Oakroyd Fold *MOR* * LS27.................122 B6
Oakroyd Mt *PDSY/CALV* LS28............100 B5
Oakroyd Rd *WBSY* BD6.....................117 H6
Oakroyd Ter *BAIL* BD17......................77 J2
  GIR BD8....................................97 J3
  MOR * LS27..............................122 B6
  PDSY/CALV LS28.......................100 B5
Oakroyd Vls *GIR* BD8.........................97 J3
The Oaks *HOR/CROF* WF4.................186 E5
  MOR LS27................................122 A7
Oaks Dr *GIR* BD8................................96 B5
Oaksfield *RTHW* LS26........................147 G5
Oaks Fold *WBOW* BD5.......................117 K3
Oaks Green Mt *BRIG* HD6..................176 E2
Oaks La *BSPA/BRAM* LS23...................48 C2
  GIR BD8....................................96 B5
Oaks Rd *BTLY* WF17..........................161 H4
Oak St *CLAY* BD14............................116 A2
  ELL HX5....................................175 J3
  HECK WF16...............................159 K4
  HWTH BD22...............................72 E5
  HWTH BD22...............................92 D2
  MOR LS27................................122 A7
  PDSY/CALV LS28.........................99 K5
  RPDN/SBR HX6.........................153 J3
  WKFDE WF1.............................164 D4
Oak Ter *HFAX* * HX1...........................16 C5
Oak Tree Cl *OSM* LS9.......................104 D2
Oak Tree Ct *BEE/HOL* BD20................20 E7
Oak Tree Crs *OSM* LS9......................104 D2
Oak Tree Dr *RHAY* LS8........................84 D2
Oak Tree Gv *OSM* LS9.......................104 D2
Oak Tree Mt *OSM* LS9.......................104 D2
Oak Tree Pl *OSM* LS9.........................104 D2
Oak Tree Wk *OSM* LS9......................104 D2
Oak Vw *AIRE* BD20.............................21 F7
Oak Vls *GIR* BD8.................................97 J3
Oakway *BIRK/DRI* BD11.....................139 J3
Oakwell Av *BTLY* WF17.....................160 C2
  PONT WF8................................189 H3
  RHAY LS8...................................84 B6
  WOR/ARM LS12..........................12 C1
Oakwell Cl *BIRK/DRI* BD11.................140 D2
  GTHN BD7...............................117 G3
Oakwell Ct *BRAM* LS13......................100 E2
Oakwell Crs *RHAY* LS8........................84 B6
Oakwell Dr *RHAY* LS8..........................84 B6
Oakwell Gdns *RHAY* LS8......................84 B6
Oakwell Gv *BRAM* LS13......................100 E2

Oakwell Mt *RHAY* LS8.........................84 B6
Oakwell Ov *RHAY* LS8.........................84 B6
Oakwell Rd *BIRK/DRI* BD11................140 D2
Oakwell Ter *PDSY/CALV* * LS28..........100 A2
Oakwell Wy *BTLY* WF17.....................140 D2
Oakwood *WKFDW/WTN* * WF2...........183 J6
  ECHL BD2..................................97 J1
  RHAY LS8..................................84 C6
  WKFDW/WTN WF2....................183 J4
Oakwood Av *BIRK/DRI* BD11..............139 H2
  RHAY LS8..................................84 C6
Oakwood Boundary Rd
  RHAY LS8..................................84 C6
Oakwood Cl *NORM* WF6....................166 C4
  TAD LS24...................................91 K6
Oakwood Cottages
  BGLY * BD16...............................55 K5
Oakwood Ct *GIR* BD8...........................5 G4
  RHAY LS8..................................84 D6
Oakwood Dr *BGLY* BD16......................55 J6
  NORM WF6...............................166 C4
  RHAY LS8..................................84 C6
  RTHW LS26..............................124 E7
Oakwood Gdns *RHAY* LS8...................84 C6
Oakwood Garth *RHAY* LS8...................84 D6
Oakwood Gra *RHAY* LS8......................84 D6
Oakwood Grange La *RHAY* LS8 ....84 D6
Oakwood Gn *RHAY* LS8.......................84 D6
Oakwood Gv *GIR* BD8...........................4 D1
  RHAY LS8..................................84 C6
Oakwood La *OSM* LS9........................104 E2
  RHAY LS8..................................84 C6
Oakwood Mt *RHAY* LS8.......................84 C6
Oakwood Nook *RHAY* LS8....................84 C6
Oakwood Pk *RHAY* LS8........................84 D7
Oakwood Pl *RHAY* LS8.........................84 C6
Oakwood Ri *RHAY* LS8.........................84 D6
Oakwood Rd *BTLY* WF17...................161 H3
Oak Wood Rd *WBY* LS22......................29 F4
Oakwood Ter *PDSY/CALV* LS28...........100 B7
Oakwood Vw *RHAY* * LS8....................84 D6
Oakwood Wk *RHAY* LS8.......................84 C6
Oakworth Hall *HWTH* BD22.................72 D2
Oakworth Rd *HWTH* BD22...................53 G7
  KGHY BD21.................................2 B7
Oasby Cft *BOW* BD4..........................119 F5
Oast House Cft
  EARD/LOFT WF3.......................144 C4
Oastler Pl *LM/WK* BD12.....................137 J1
Oastler Rd *PDSY/CALV* LS28................79 J6
  SHPY BD18................................76 E4
Oastler St *DEWS* WF13......................180 E1
Oates St *DEWS* WF13.........................181 G1
Oatland Cl *CHAL* LS7..........................10 B4
Oatland Ct *CHAL* LS7..........................10 B5
Oatland Dr *CHAL* LS7..........................10 B5
Oatland Gdns *CHAL* LS7......................10 B4
Oatland Gn *CHAL* LS7.........................10 B4
Oatland Hts *CHAL* LS7.........................10 C5
Oatland La *CHAL* LS7..........................10 A4
Oatland Pl *CHAL* LS7...........................10 A3
Oatland Rd *CHAL* LS7.........................10 A4
Oatlands Dr *OT* LS21...........................39 C1
Oat St *HWTH* * BD22...........................53 H7
Oban Cl *EARD/LOFT* WF3..................142 C6
Oban Pl *WOR/ARM* LS12....................102 A5
Oban St *WOR/ARM* LS12...................102 A5
Oban Ter *WOR/ARM* LS12..................102 A5
Occupation La *BHP/TINH* LS16 ....40 E7
  DEWS WF13.............................160 C5
  HWTH BD22...............................52 E7
  LUD/ILL HX2............................134 B1
  PDSY/CALV LS28........................99 K7
  TAD LS24...................................68 C7
Occupation Rd *HUDN* * HD2...............177 H6
Ochrewell Av *HUDN* HD2...................177 K6
Octagon Ter *LUD/ILL* HX2..................154 B4
Odda La *GSLY* LS20.............................57 K2
Oddfellows' Ct *BFD* BD1........................5 L6
Oddfellows St *BRIG* HD6....................157 G5
  CLECK BD19............................138 A7
  MIRF WF14...............................179 H4
Oddfellow St *MOR* LS27....................141 K3
Oddy Pl *WBSY* BD6...........................117 G5
Oddy's Fold *HDGY* LS6........................82 D4
Oddy St *BOW* BD4.............................119 F5
Odsal Pl *WBSY* BD6...........................117 G5
Odsal Rd *WBSY* BD6..........................117 H5
Ogden Crs *CUL/QBY* BD13...................94 A3
Ogden La *BRIG* HD6..........................176 E1
  CUL/QBY BD13..........................94 A3
  LUD/ILL HX2............................114 A4
Ogden St *RPDN/SBR* HX6..................153 H5
Ogden View Cl *LUD/ILL* HX2..............114 A7
Ogilby Ct *RTHW* LS26........................125 J7
Ogilby Ms *RTHW* LS26.......................125 J7
O'Grady Sq *OSM* LS9...........................15 G2
Old Allen Rd *CUL/QBY* BD13...............94 D2
Old Bank *HIPP* HX3.............................17 K5
Old Bank Rd *EARL* WF12....................181 H1
  MIRF WF14...............................179 J2
Old Barn Cl *AL/HA/HU* LS17................63 F6
Old Bell Ct *HFAX* * HX1........................17 H6
Old Brandon La *AL/HA/HU* LS17 ....65 F7
Old Brewery Gdns *TAD* LS24................51 F6
Old Bridge Ri *ILK* LS29........................23 K5
Old Canal Rd *BFD* BD1.........................5 M2
Old Cawsey *RPDN/SBR* HX6...............153 K4
Old Church St *OSS* WF5......................182 C4
Old Cl *BEE/HOL* LS11.........................122 C6
Old Cock Yd *HFAX* * HX1.....................17 H6
Old Corn Mill La *GTHN* * BD7.............117 F2
Old Crown Rd
  WKFDW/WTN WF2....................183 J6
Old Dalton La *KGHY* BD21.....................3 J4
Old Earth *ELL* HX5.............................176 A2
Oldfarm Ap *BHP/TINH* LS16.................81 J4
Oldfarm Cl *BHP/TINH* LS16..................81 K4
Old Farm Crs *BOW* * BD4...................118 C3
Oldfarm Cross *BHP/TINH* LS16.............81 K4
Oldfarm Dr *BHP/TINH* LS16..................81 K4
Oldfarm Garth *BHP/TINH* LS16.............81 K4
Oldfarm Pde *BHP/TINH* LS16................81 J4
Oldfarm Wk *BHP/TINH* LS16.................81 J4
Oldfield Av *WOR/ARM* LS12..................12 A4
Oldfield Ct *CHAL* LS7...........................83 K6
Old Fieldhouse La *HUDN* HD2 ....177 J7
Oldfield La *HECK* WF16......................160 A5
  HWTH BD22...............................72 B5

  WBY LS22..................................47 H1
  WOR/ARM LS12..........................12 A4
Oldfield St *HIPP* HX3..........................134 D3
  WOR/ARM LS12..........................12 B3
Old Forge Ms *BHP/TINH* LS16.............41 G7
Old Garth Cft *KNOT* WF11..................150 B3
Oldgate La *GFTH/SHER* LS25...............110 D1
Old Great North Rd
  KNOT WF11.............................150 C6
Old Guy Rd *CUL/QBY* BD13...............114 E4
Old Hall Cl *HWTH* * BD22....................72 D6
Old Hall Ms *BTLY* * WF17..................161 F1
Old Hall Rd *BTLY* WF17.....................161 F1
  EARD/LOFT WF3......................142 A7
Old Haworth La *YEA* LS19....................59 J4
Old Hollings Hl *BAIL* BD17....................58 D5
Old La *BEE/HOL* LS11.........................122 E4
  BHP/TINH LS16..........................40 E7
  BIRK/DRI BD11........................120 D7
  BIRK/DRI BD11........................139 H2
  BRIG HD6................................157 G5
  GSLY LS20.................................57 K3
  HIPP HX3...................................16 E1
  HUDN HD2...............................177 J5
  ILK LS29...................................23 F3
  ILK LS29...................................24 C6
  LUD/ILL HX2............................132 E6
Old Langley La *BAIL* BD17.....................57 K7
Old Lee Bank *HIPP* HX3........................16 E2
Old Lindley Rd *HUDW* HD3..................175 F7
Old London Rd *TAD* LS24......................70 B5
Old Main St *BGLY* BD16.......................75 J1
Old Manse Cft *HWTH* * BD22...............92 D2
Old Market *HFAX* HX1..........................17 H6
Old Marsh *PDSY/CALV* LS28..................99 K6
Old Mill Cl *ILK* LS29............................26 A7
Old Mill La *BSPA/BRAM* LS23................48 D5
  MID LS10...................................14 F8
Old Mill Rd *BAIL* * BD17.......................77 F4
Old Mill Vw *EARL* WF12......................180 E4
Old Mill Yd *OSS* * WF5.......................182 B6
Old Oak Cl *BHP/TINH* LS16..................81 K5
Old Oak Dr *BHP/TINH* LS16..................81 J5
Old Oak Garth *BHP/TINH* LS16.............81 J5
Old Oak Lawn *BHP/TINH* LS16.............81 K5
The Old Orch *OT* LS21..........................41 F3
Old Oxenhope La *HWTH* BD22..............72 C7
Old Park Rd *IDLE* BD10........................78 D5
  RHAY LS8..................................84 B5
Old Pool Bank *BHP/TINH* LS16.............40 E6
Old Popplewell La *CLECK* BD19...........137 K7
Old Power Wy *ELL* HX5......................175 K1
Old Quarry La *GFTH/SHER* LS25..........130 E5
Old Riding La *LUD/ILL* HX2.................133 G4
Old Rd *CUL/QBY* BD13........................94 A5
  CUL/QBY BD13..........................95 J7
  GTHN BD7...............................116 D4
  MOR LS27................................122 B6
Oldroyd Crs *BEE/HOL* LS11.................122 D4
Oldroyd Wy *DEWS* WF13....................180 E1
Old Run Rd *MID* LS10.........................123 J4
  MID LS10.................................123 J6
Old Schools *CAS* WF10.......................168 B3
Old School Ms *MOR* LS27...................122 B6
Old Schools Gdns *HIPP* HX3.................17 H2
Old Side Ct *AIRE* BD20.........................55 H2
Old Souls Wy *BGLY* BD16.....................55 H5
Old Station Rd *LUD/ILL* HX2................152 E1
Old Station Wy *ILK* LS29......................22 C1
Old Vicarage La
  GFTH/SHER LS25......................131 J6
Old Well Head *HFAX* HX1.....................17 G8
Old Westgate *EARL* WF12...................181 F1
Old Whack House La *YEA* LS19.............59 G5
Old Wood La *BGLY* BD16.....................57 F1
Olicana Pk *ILK* LS29............................23 K4
Olive Gv *GIR* BD8................................96 D5
Oliver Gdns *MIRF* WF14......................179 G2
Oliver Hl *HORS* LS18............................81 F5
Oliver Mdw *ELL* HX5...........................175 K1
Oliver Rd *HECK* WF16........................160 B3
Olivers Mt *PONT* WF8.........................189 K1
Oliver St *BOW* BD4...............................6 C9
Ollerdale Av *WIL/AL* BD15....................95 K2
Ollerdale Cl *WIL/AL* BD15.....................95 K3
Olympic Pk *LM/WK* BD12...................137 K2
Omar St *HECK* WF16..........................159 K4
Onslow Crs *BOW* BD4.........................118 C4
Ontario Pl *CHAL* LS7............................83 J6
Opal St *HWTH* BD22............................53 H7
Orange St *BFDE* BD3.............................7 H7
  HFAX HX1.................................17 G5
Orange Tree Gv
  EARD/LOFT WF3......................163 H1
The Orchard *FEA/AMT* WF7................168 C7
  KGHY BD21.................................54 C4
  MIRF WF14...............................179 J2
  NORM WF6...............................186 D1
  OSS WF5.................................182 C4
  PONT WF8...............................190 A4
  WKFDW/WTN WF2....................164 A5
Orchard Av *EARD/LOFT* WF3..............165 G3
Orchard Cl *EARD/LOFT* WF3...............163 J2
  GFTH/SHER LS25......................131 J6
  GFTH/SHER LS25......................131 F3
  HOR/CROF WF4.........................183 F7
  LUD/ILL HX2............................154 A2
  TAD LS24...................................90 E7
  WKFDW/WTN WF2....................163 K5
Orchard Ct *BSPA/BRAM* LS23...............68 C4
Orchard Cft *WKFDW/WTN* WF2...........163 K6
Orchard Dr *KNOT* WF11.....................150 C2
  WBY LS22..................................28 E6
Orchard Gv *IDLE* BD10.........................78 E5
  ILK LS29...................................38 B6
Orchard Head Crs *PONT* WF8..............169 K4
Orchard Head Dr *PONT* WF8...............169 K5
Orchard Head La *PONT* WF8................169 K4
Orchard La *ILK* LS29............................22 D1
  PONT WF8...............................190 D5
  TAD LS24.................................111 F1
Orchard Mt *MSTN/BAR* LS15..............105 K3
Orchard Ri *RPDN/SBR* HX6.................153 G6
Orchard Rd *MSTN/BAR* LS15...............105 J3
The Orchards *BGLY* BD16.....................55 K6
  CLECK BD19............................139 K7

  MSTN/BAR LS15.......................105 J3
  RTHW LS26..............................147 F5
Orchard Sq *MSTN/BAR* LS15...............105 J3
Orchard St *EARL* WF12.......................181 F1
  OT LS21....................................39 J3
Orchard Wk *HBR* HX7.........................132 A6
Orchard Wy *BRIG* HD6.......................157 F4
  RTHW LS26..............................145 F1
Orchid Cl *SHPY* BD18..........................77 J7
Orchid Ct *EARD/LOFT* WF3................144 C5
Oriental St *WOR/ARM* * LS12.............12 A1
Orion Crs *MID* LS10...........................123 K7
Orion Dr *MID* LS10............................123 K7
Orion Gdns *MID* LS10.........................124 A7
Orion Vw *MID* LS10...........................124 A7
Orion Wk *MID* LS10...........................124 A6
Orlando Cl *MIRF* WF14.......................179 G2
Orleans St *WBSY* BD6........................116 E7
Ormonde Dr *WIL/AL* BD15....................95 K5
Ormond St *WBSY* BD6.......................117 G6
Ormondroyd Av *WBSY* BD6................117 H6
Ormond St *GTHN* BD7........................117 F2
Orville Gdns *HDGY* LS6......................102 D1
Orwell Cl *CAS* WF10..........................169 H3
Osborne Av *HOR/CROF* WF4..............183 H6
Osborne Gv *HFAX* HX1.........................16 B4
  WBOW BD5.............................117 J1
Osborne Ct *BRAM* LS13......................101 G4
Osbourne Dr *CUL/QBY* BD13...............115 H5
Osmondthorpe Cottages
  OSM LS9..................................15 M1
Osmondthorpe La *OSM* LS9...............104 D6
Osmondthorpe Ter *OSM* * LS9..............11 L8
Osprey Cl *AL/HA/HU* LS17....................64 A7
  WBY LS22..................................46 E1
Osprey Ct *GIR* * BD8............................96 B6
Osprey Gv *AL/HA/HU* LS17...................64 A7
Osprey Meadow *MOR* LS27.................142 C3
Ossett La *EARL* WF12.........................181 J2
Osterley Gv *IDLE* BD10.........................79 F7
Oswald St *SHPY* BD18...........................77 J5
Oswaldthorpe Av *BFDE* BD3...................7 K2
Otley La *YEA* LS19...............................59 J4
Otley Mt *AIRE* * BD20..........................55 C3
Otley Old Rd *BHP/TINH* LS16................61 H6
  HORS LS18................................60 D2
Otley Rd *BAIL* BD17.............................78 A1
  BFDE BD3....................................6 B5
  BGLY BD16................................55 K2
  BGLY BD16................................56 E2
  BHP/TINH LS16..........................62 A4
  GSLY LS20.................................58 D2
  ILK LS29...................................38 B2
  OT LS21....................................43 F3
  SHPY BD18................................77 G6
Otley St *HFAX* HX1..............................16 A5
  KGHY BD21.................................2 F7
Ottawa Pl *CHAL* LS7............................83 J6
Otterburn Cl *WBOW* BD5...................117 J1
Otterburn Gdns *BHP/TINH* LS16 ....82 A1
Otterburn St *KGHY* * BD21....................3 G1
Otter Lee La *RPDN/SBR* HX6...............172 D1
Otterwood Bank *WBY* LS22...................29 J2
Ouchthorpe La *WKFDE* WF1................164 D5
Oulton Dr *RTHW* LS26........................145 K4
Oulton La *RTHW* LS26.........................125 K7
  RTHW LS26..............................145 H2
Oulton Ter *GTHN* BD7...........................5 G9
Ounsworth St *BOW* BD4.....................118 C2
Ouse Dr *WBY* LS22..............................29 G1
Ouston Cl *TAD* LS24.............................51 F7
Ouston La *TAD* LS24.............................51 F7
Out Gang *BRAM* LS13.........................101 G2
Outgang La *BRAM* LS13.......................101 F1
Outlands Ri *IDLE* BD10.........................78 E4
Outside La *HWTH* BD22........................92 A3
Outwood Av *HORS* LS18.......................81 G5
Outwood Cha *HORS* LS18.....................81 G4
Outwood La *HORS* LS18........................81 F5
Outwood Park Ct *WKFDE* WF1............164 C5
Outwood Wk *HORS* LS18......................81 F5
Ouzelwell Crs *EARL* WF12...................180 D6
Ouzelwell La *EARL* WF12.....................180 D6
Ouzelwell Rd *EARL* WF12....................180 E5
Ouzelwell Gn *EARD/LOFT* WF3............144 E5
The Oval *BGLY* BD16............................76 A2
  GIR BD8....................................96 D3
  GSLY LS20.................................58 D3
  LVSG WF15..............................158 D3
  MID LS10...................................14 D8
  OT LS21....................................39 G1
  RTHW LS26..............................145 G3
  SCFT LS14...............................105 G3
Ovenden Av *HIPP* * HX3.......................16 C1
Ovenden Cl *HIPP* * HX3........................16 D1
Ovenden Crs *HIPP* HX3......................134 D5
Ovenden Gn *HIPP* HX3.......................134 D5
Ovenden Pk *LUD/ILL* * HX2................134 C3
Ovenden Rd *HIPP* HX3........................134 D4
Ovenden Road Ter *HIPP* HX3..............134 D5
Ovenden Ter *HIPP* HX3.......................134 D5
Ovenden Wy *HIPP* HX3.......................134 C5
Ovenden Wood Rd
  LUD/ILL HX2............................133 K5
Overdale *RPDN/SBR* HX6....................173 F2
Overdale Av *AL/HA/HU* LS17................64 B6
Overdale Cl *WBY* LS22.........................29 G3
Overdale Dr *SHPY* BD18........................78 A3
Overdale Mt *LUD/ILL* HX2...................154 A3
Overdale Ter *HWTH* * BD22..................72 D5
  MSTN/BAR LS15.......................105 H5
Over Hall Cl *MIRF* WF14.....................179 J3
Over Hall Pk *MIRF* WF14.....................179 J3
Over Hall Rd *MIRF* WF14.....................179 J3
Overland Crs *IDLE* BD10.......................78 E4
Over La *YEA* LS19................................79 K1
Overthorpe Rd *EARL* WF12.................181 G7
Overton Dr *WBSY* BD6.......................116 C4
Ovington Dr *BOW* BD4.......................119 F4
Owen Ct *BGLY* BD16............................55 K5
Owlcotes Dr *PDSY/CALV* LS28.............99 K5
Owlcotes Gdns *PDSY/CALV* LS28.........99 K5
Owlcotes Garth
  PDSY/CALV LS28........................99 J5
Owlcotes La *PDSY/CALV* LS28.............99 J4
Owlcotes Rd *PDSY/CALV* LS28.............99 J5
Owlcotes Ter *PDSY/CALV* LS28.............99 K5
Owler Ings Rd *BRIG* HD6....................157 F6

Owler La *BTLY* WF17.........................140 B4
Owler Mdw *HECK* WF16.....................159 K3
Owler Park Rd *ILK* LS29.......................23 J3
Owlers Cl *HUDN* HD2.........................178 A4
Owlet Hurst La *LVSG* WF15................159 J6
Owlet Md *EARD/LOFT* WF3.................143 K6
Owlett Mead Cl
  EARD/LOFT WF3......................143 K7
Owl La *EARL* WF12............................161 K6
Owl Rdg *MOR* LS27............................142 B4
Owl St *KGHY* BD21................................3 J5
Oxford Av *GSLY* LS20...........................58 C2
Oxford Cl *CLECK* BD19.......................139 J7
  CUL/QBY BD13.........................115 F7
Oxford Court Gdns *CAS* * WF10...........168 B1
Oxford Crs *CLAY* BD14.......................116 A2
  HIPP HX3.................................155 G4
Oxford Dr *CLECK* BD19......................139 J7
  GFTH/SHER LS25......................127 G5
Oxford La *HIPP* HX3...........................155 G4
Oxford Pl *BAIL* BD17............................77 J2
  BFDE BD3....................................6 B3
  LDS LS1.....................................9 L8
  PDSY/CALV LS28......................100 B4
Oxford Rd *CHAL* LS7...........................10 A3
  CLECK BD19............................139 J5
  CUL/QBY BD13.........................115 F6
  DEWS WF13............................160 D7
  ECHL BD2..................................98 B3
  GSLY LS20.................................58 C2
  HFAX HX1.................................17 C8
Oxford Rw *LDS* LS1..............................9 L8
Oxford St *BTLY* WF17.........................160 E4
  CLAY BD14...............................116 A2
  EARD/LOFT WF3.......................143 K7
  FEA/AMT WF7..........................188 C4
  GSLY LS20.................................59 F2
  HWTH BD22................................2 D6
  NORM WF6...............................167 F5
  RPDN/SBR HX6.........................154 A3
  WKFDE WF1.............................185 F6
Oxford Ter *BTLY* WF17.......................161 G4
Oxford Wk *CLECK* BD19.....................139 J7
Ox Heys Mdw *CUL/QBY* BD13.............95 K7
Oxley Gdns *WBSY* BD6......................117 H7
Oxley Rd *HUDN* HD2..........................177 H5
Oxley St *GIR* BD8..................................5 H4
  OSM LS9...................................15 H3
Oxton Dr *TAD* LS24.............................51 F7
Oxton La *TAD* LS24.............................51 F7
Oxton Mt *OSM* LS9.............................11 H8
Oxton Wy *OSM* LS9............................11 H9
Oyster Cl *MOR* LS27..........................142 B4
Ozar St *BEE/HOL* LS11.........................13 J5

P

Pacaholme Rd
  WKFDW/WTN WF2....................183 J1
Padan St *HIPP* HX3.............................155 G4
The Paddock *AIRE* BD20.......................33 F1
  AL/HA/HU LS17..........................45 K4
  BAIL BD17..................................58 A7
  CAS WF10...............................169 H2
  CLECK * BD19..........................138 A7
  CUL/QBY BD13..........................74 A6
  EARL WF12..............................181 J3
  GFTH/SHER LS25......................151 F3
  HDGY LS6.................................82 E5
  KNOT WF11.............................171 G5
  NORM WF6...............................166 E7
  RTHW LS26..............................145 F2
  SCFT LS14................................66 C6
  WKFDE * WF1...........................164 B6
Paddock *HTON* BD9.............................97 H1
Paddock Br *WBY* LS22..........................46 E1
Paddock Cl *GFTH/SHER* LS25..............107 K7
  LM/WK BD12...........................137 H6
Paddock Dr *BIRK/DRI* BD11................140 B2
Paddock Gn *AL/HA/HU* LS17.................45 K5
Paddock La *BGLY* BD16........................56 C5
  LUD/ILL HX2............................133 K7
Paddock Rd *HIPP* HX3.........................135 H2
Paddocks Church Rd *HDGY* HD6..........157 K6
Paddock Vw *CAS* WF10......................169 G7
Padgum *BAIL* BD17...............................57 H7
Padma Cl *GTHN* BD7.............................4 E6
Padstow Gdns *MID* LS10.....................143 F2
Page Hl *LUD/ILL* HX2..........................134 B5
Paget St *KGHY* BD21.............................2 B5
Pagewood Ct *IDLE* BD10.......................78 B3
Paisley Gv *WOR/ARM* * LS12...............102 A5
Paisley Pl *WOR/ARM* * LS12................102 A5
Paisley Rd *WOR/ARM* LS12.................102 A5
Paisley St *WOR/ARM* LS12..................102 A5
Paisley Ter *WOR/ARM* * LS12.............102 A5
Pakington St *WBOW* BD5...................117 J2
Paleside La *OSS* WF5..........................182 C2
Palesides Av *OSS* WF5........................182 C1
Paley Rd *BOW* BD4............................118 B2
Paley Ter *BOW* BD4............................118 B2
Palin Av *BFDE* BD3................................7 J2
Palm Cl *WBSY* BD6.............................117 G6
Palmer Rd *BFDE* BD3.............................6 F4
Palmerston St *ECHL* * BD2....................98 C3
Palm St *HIPP* HX3..............................134 E5
Panelagh Av *IDLE* BD10........................79 F7
Pannal Av *WKFDE* WF1.........................19 K1
Pannal St *GTHN* BD7..........................117 F3
Panorama Dr *ILK* LS29..........................23 H7
The Parade *BGLY* BD16........................75 K5
  BRAM * LS13...........................101 F3
  BTLY * WF17...........................140 C4
  BTLY * WF17...........................160 D4
  HDGY LS6.................................82 C7
  OSM LS9...................................14 E2
  YEA * LS19...............................59 G5
Paradise La *LUD/ILL* HX2.....................153 J2
  TAD LS24...................................69 G6
Paradise Rd *HTON* BD9.........................96 E1
Paradise St *BFD* BD1..............................5 J5
  HFAX HX1.................................16 F7
  PDSY/CALV LS28......................100 A2
Parish Ghyll Dr *ILK* LS29......................23 J6
Parish Ghyll La *ILK* LS29.......................23 J6

Parish Ghyll Rd *ILK* LS29 ....23 K6
Parish Ghyll Wk *ILK* LS29 ....23 K6
Park Av *BGLY* BD16 ....75 J2
  BIRK/DRI BD11 ....140 B1
  CAS WF10 ....148 B3
  CAS WF10 ....168 C1
  DEWS WF13 ....180 E1
  EARD/LOFT WF3 ....164 D1
  ELL HX5 ....175 H3
  GFTH/SHER LS25 ....110 E6
  GFTH/SHER LS25 ....128 B5
  HWTH BD22 ....72 E2
  IDLE BD10 ....78 C2
  KGHY BD21 ....2 E7
  LVSG WF15 ....159 H6
  MIRF WF14 ....179 J5
  MOR LS27 ....141 J4
  MSTN/BAR LS15 ....106 A3
  NORM WF6 ....166 E6
  PONT WF8 ....189 G1
  PONT WF8 ....190 D4
  RHAY LS8 ....84 C5
  RTHW LS26 ....126 D5
  SHPY BD18 ....77 H4
  WKFDE WF1 ....164 B4
  WKFDE WF1 ....186 A2
  WKFDW/WTN WF2 ....18 D8
  WOR/ARM LS12 ....102 A5
  YEA LS19 ....59 H4
Park Cliffe Rd *ECHL* BD2 ....98 B3
Park Cl *BGLY* BD16 ....55 K7
  BIRK/DRI BD11 ....140 B1
  BRAM LS13 ....101 F2
  BTLY WF17 ....160 E5
  CUL/QBY BD13 ....115 G5
  HIPP HX3 ....156 D1
  IDLE BD10 ....78 D7
  KGHY BD21 ....3 G9
  LUD/ILL HX2 ....133 J6
  PONT WF8 ....190 D4
Park Copse *HORS* LS18 ....80 D3
Park Ct *OSS* WF5 ....182 E5
  OT LS21 ....41 G4
Park Crs *BFDE* BD3 ....98 B3
  CAS WF10 ....169 H1
  GSLY LS20 ....58 D3
  HIPP HX3 ....16 C1
  ILK LS29 ....22 D1
  MOR LS27 ....141 C1
  RHAY LS8 ....84 C3
  RTHW LS26 ....145 H1
  WOR/ARM LS12 ....102 A5
Park Cft *BTLY* WF17 ....160 D4
  DEWS WF13 ....180 D1
Parkcroft *PDSY/CALV* LS28 ....100 A3
Park Cross St *LDS* LS1 ....9 L9
Park Dl *CAS* WF10 ....149 H6
  ILK LS29 ....38 B6
Parkdale Dr *RPDN/SBR* HX6 ....173 F2
Park Dene *HFAX* HX1 ....16 C7
Park Dr *BGLY* BD16 ....56 A6
  BTLY WF17 ....160 D1
  EARD/LOFT WF3 ....164 D1
  HORS LS18 ....80 C4
  HTON BD9 ....97 G1
  MIRF WF14 ....179 J5
Park Drive Rd *KGHY* BD21 ....3 C8
Park Edge Cl *RHAY* LS8 ....84 D5
Parker Av *NORM* WF6 ....166 B4
Parker La *MIRF* WF14 ....179 J4
Parker Rd *EARL* WF12 ....181 F6
Parker's La *AIRE* BD20 ....33 H7
Parker St *EARD/LOFT* WF3 ....163 H1
  LVSG WF15 ....159 K5
Park Fld *ILK* LS29 ....38 B6
Parkfield Av *BEE/HOL* LS11 ....123 F3
  ELL HX5 ....175 J3
  MIRF WF14 ....179 K5
Parkfield Cl *GFTH/SHER* LS25.......................128 A4
  PDSY/CALV LS28 ....100 A6
Parkfield Ct *SCFT* LS14 ....105 F2
Parkfield Crs *MIRF* WF14 ....179 J5
Parkfield Cft *MIRF* WF14 ....179 K5
Parkfield Dr *BSPA/BRAM* LS23.......................48 B2
  CUL/QBY BD13 ....115 G5
  RPDN/SBR HX6 ....153 H6
Parkfield Gv *BEE/HOL* LS11 ....123 F3
Parkfield La *FEA/AMT* WF7 ....168 B6
  RPDN/SBR HX6 ....154 A5
Parkfield Mt *BEE/HOL* LS11 ....122 E3
  PDSY/CALV LS28 ....100 B6
Parkfield Pl *BEE/HOL* LS11.......................123 F3
Parkfield Rd *BEE/HOL* LS11 * 123 F3
  GIR BD8 ....97 J3
  SHPY BD18 ....76 D4
Parkfield Rw *BEE/HOL* LS11.......................123 F3
Park Flds *LUD/ILL* HX2 ....133 J3
Parkfield St *BEE/HOL* LS11 ....14 A6
Parkfield Ter *PDSY/CALV* LS28 ....100 B4
Parkfield Vw *BEE/HOL* LS11 ....123 F3
  OSS WF5 ....183 F4
Parkfield Wy *MIRF* WF14 ....179 J5
  SCFT LS14 ....105 F2
Park Gdns *LUD/ILL* HX2 ....154 A3
  OSS WF5 ....182 E5
Parkgate Av *WKFDE* WF1 ....19 K4
Park Gate Cl *HORS* LS18 ....80 C4
Park Ga West *HIPP* * HX3 ....155 H6
Park Gn *AIRE* BD20 ....20 D7
  NORM WF6 ....166 C7
Park Gv *CUL/QBY* BD13.......................115 G5
  HDGY LS6 ....82 C6
  HIPP HX3 ....135 J6
  HOR/CROF WF4.......................182 E7
  HORS LS18 ....80 C4
  HTON BD9 ....97 H1
  MIRF WF14 ....179 K5
  MOR LS27 ....141 G1
  RTHW LS26 ....126 E6
  SHPY BD18 ....76 E4
  YEA LS19 ....59 H4
Park Grove Rd
  WKFDW/WTN WF2 ....18 A7
Park Hl *HUDN* HD2.......................178 A3
Park Hill Cl *GIR* BD8 ....96 C4
Parkhill Crs *WKFDE* WF1 ....19 K4
Park Hill Dr *GIR* BD8 ....96 C4

Park Hill Gv *WKFDE* WF1.......................19 L5
Park Hill La *WKFDE* WF1.......................19 J4
Parkhome Est *RTHW* * LS26.......................126 C5
Park House Cl *LM/WK* BD12.......................117 K7
Park House Crs *LM/WK* BD12 ....117 K7
Park House Dr *EARL* WF12.......................181 G5
Park House Gv *LM/WK* BD12.......................117 K7
Park House Rd *LM/WK* BD12.......................137 J1
Park House Wk *LM/WK* BD12.......................117 K7
Parkin Hall La *RPDN/SBR* HX6.......................152 C6
Parkin La *IDLE* BD10 ....79 G4
Parkinson Ap *GFTH/SHER* LS25.......................107 J5
Parkinson Cl *WKFDE* WF1.......................19 K3
Parkinson Rd *CUL/QBY* BD13.......................94 B4
Parkinson St *WBOW* BD5 ....117 J2
Parkin St *LVSG* WF15.......................158 D3
Parkland Av *MOR* LS27 ....141 H4
Parkland Crs *HDGY* LS6 ....83 F3
Parkland Dr *HDGY* LS6 ....83 F3
  IDLE BD10 ....78 D5
  TAD LS24 ....51 F6
Parkland Gdns *HDGY* LS6 ....83 F4
Parklands *BHP/TINH* LS16 ....41 G7
  CAS WF10 ....168 D1
  ILK LS29 ....24 C5
  OSS WF5 ....182 E5
Parklands Crs *BHP/TINH* LS16.......................41 H7
Parklands Dr *RPDN/SBR* HX6.......................153 F7
Parklands Ga *BHP/TINH* LS16.......................41 H7
Parkland Ter *HDGY* LS6 ....82 E4
Parkland Vw *YEA* LS19 ....59 J5
Park La *BAIL* BD17 ....58 A7
  BVRD LS3 ....9 H8
  CAS WF10 ....148 A2
  CLAY BD14 ....116 A2
  CUL/QBY BD13 ....115 J5
  GFTH/SHER LS25 ....128 B6
  GFTH/SHER LS25 ....129 H6
  GSLY LS20 ....58 D4
  HIPP HX3 ....155 H6
  KGHY BD21 ....3 H8
  PONT WF8 ....168 D7
  RHAY LS8 ....84 C2
  RTHW LS26 ....145 C2
  RTHW LS26 ....146 D6
  WBOW BD5 ....117 J2
Park Lane Ms *AL/HA/HU* LS17.......................64 C7
Park Lea *HUDN* HD2 ....178 B3
  MID * LS10 ....143 H2
Park Lodge Ct *WKFDE* WF1.......................19 H4
Park Lodge Crs *WKFDE* WF1.......................19 J4
Park Lodge Gv *WKFDE* WF1.......................19 H4
Park Lodge La *WKFDE* WF1.......................19 H4
Park Md *IDLE* BD10 ....78 C2
Parkmere Cl *BOW* BD4 ....118 C7
Park Ms *OT* LS21 ....41 G4
Park Mill La *OSS* WF5 ....183 F2
Park Mt *KSTL* LS5 ....102 A1
  OT LS21 ....40 E5
  WOR/ARM LS12 ....101 K5
Park Mount Av *BAIL* BD17 ....77 K1
Park Pde *DEWS* WF13 ....180 E2
  MOR * LS27 ....141 J4
  OSM LS9 ....15 J3
Park Pl *HFAX* * HX1 ....16 C8
  IDLE BD10 ....78 C2
  LDS LS1.......................9 K9
  PONT WF8 ....189 G1
Park Pl East *HIPP* HX3.......................156 D1
Park Pl West *HIPP* HX3.......................156 D1
Park Ri *BRAM* LS13 ....101 F1
  CAS WF10 ....168 C1
Park Rd *BGLY* BD16 ....75 J1
  BRAM LS13.......................101 F2
  BSPA/BRAM LS23 ....48 B2
  BTLY WF17 ....161 G3
  CAS WF10 ....169 F3
  DEWS WF13 ....160 D7
  DEWS WF13 ....180 C3
  EARL WF12 ....181 F3
  EARL WF12 ....181 J2
  ELL HX5 ....175 J1
  GSLY LS20 ....58 E4
  HECK WF16 ....160 A4
  HFAX HX1 ....16 E7
  IDLE BD10 ....78 C2
  IDLE BD10 ....78 E7
  ILK LS29 ....38 B6
  MSTN/BAR LS15 ....126 A1
  PONT WF8 ....169 F5
  RPDN/SBR HX6 ....153 K4
  SHPY BD18 ....77 H5
  WBOW BD5 ....117 H7
  WBSY BD6 ....117 H7
  WOR/ARM LS12 ....101 K5
  YEA LS19 ....59 J7
  YEA LS19 ....59 H4
Park Rw *BRIG* * HD6 ....157 G6
  LDS LS1.......................9 M9
  PDSY/CALV LS28 ....100 B4
Parkside *BGLY* BD16 ....55 K7
  CLECK BD19 ....158 E1
Park Side *CLECK* BD19.......................159 H1
  HORS LS18 ....80 D4
Parkside Av *CUL/QBY* BD13.......................115 G5
  HDGY LS6 ....82 E5
Parkside Cl *HDGY* LS6 ....82 E4
Parkside Ct *HWTH* BD22 ....73 F4
Parkside Crs *HDGY* LS6.......................82 E4
Parkside Gdns *HDGY* LS6.......................82 E5
Parkside Gn *HDGY* LS6.......................82 E5
Parkside Gv *HTON* BD9.......................97 F2
Parkside La *BEE/HOL* LS11.......................123 H5
  EARD/LOFT WF3 ....165 F6
Parkside Lawns *HDGY* LS6.......................82 E5
Parkside Mt *BEE/HOL* LS11.......................123 F5
Parkside Pde *BEE/HOL* LS11.......................123 F5
Parkside Pl *HDGY* LS6.......................82 E4
Parkside Rd *HDGY* LS6.......................82 D5
  PDSY/CALV LS28 ....100 A3
  WBOW BD5 ....117 K4
Parkside Rw *BEE/HOL* LS11.......................123 F5
Parkside Ter *CUL/QBY* BD13 ....054 A6
Parkside Vw *HDGY* LS6.......................82 E4
Parkside Wk *PDSY/CALV* LS28.......................100 B3
Park Spring Gdns *BRAM* LS13 ....100 E4
Park Spring Ri *BRAM* LS13 ....100 E5

Park Sq *EARD/LOFT* WF3 ....164 D2
  OSS WF5.......................182 E5
  OT LS21 ....41 G4
  WBSY BD6 ....116 E6
Park Sq East *LDS* LS1.......................9 L9
Park Sq North *LDS* LS1.......................9 L9
Park Sq South *LDS* LS1.......................9 L9
Park Sq West *LDS* LS1.......................9 L9
Parkstone *HUDN* HD2.......................178 A3
Parkstone Av *BHP/TINH* LS16 ....81 K3
Parkstone Dr *IDLE* BD10 ....78 D7
Parkstone Gn *BHP/TINH* LS16.......................81 K3
Parkstone Mt *BHP/TINH* LS16.......................81 K3
Parkstone Pl *BHP/TINH* * LS16.......................81 K3
Park Stone Ri *HIPP* HX3 ....136 A1
Park St *BRIG* HD6 ....157 C6
  BTLY WF17.......................140 B7
  CLECK BD19.......................139 K7
  CLECK BD19.......................158 C2
  DEWS WF13.......................161 G7
  HECK WF16.......................160 A4
  HWTH BD22.......................72 E5
  LDS LS1.......................9 L8
  MOR LS27.......................122 B6
  MSTN/BAR LS15.......................105 J5
  OSS WF5.......................182 E5
  RPDN/SBR HX6.......................153 K4
  SHPY BD18.......................77 H4
  WKFDE WF1.......................19 G6
  WOR/ARM LS12.......................101 K5
  YEA LS19.......................59 H4
Park Ter *HDGY* LS6.......................82 C6
  HFAX * HX1.......................16 C6
  HIPP HX3.......................135 J6
  KGHY BD21.......................3 J7
  OT LS21.......................40 D5
  SHPY BD18.......................77 H4
Park Top *PDSY/CALV* LS28.......................100 B4
The Park Towngate *HIPP* HX3.......................155 K5
Park Vw *BEE/HOL* LS11.......................123 F3
  BRAM LS13.......................101 F2
  CAS WF10.......................169 H2
  CLECK BD19.......................138 D7
  EARD/LOFT WF3.......................164 D2
  HFAX HX1.......................16 C7
  HIPP HX3.......................156 D1
  PDSY/CALV LS28.......................100 B6
  RTHW LS26.......................126 D5
  WKFDW/WTN * WF2.......................183 K3
Park View Av *HDGY* LS6.......................8 D3
  HIPP HX3.......................135 K6
  HWTH BD22.......................73 F4
Parkview Ct *RHAY* LS8.......................84 C2
  SHPY * BD18.......................77 F5
Park View Crs *RHAY* LS8.......................84 C3
Park View Gv *BULY* LS4.......................8 D3
Park View Rd *BULY* LS4.......................8 D4
  HTON BD9.......................97 G3
Park View Ter *HTON* BD9.......................97 C2
  YEA LS19.......................59 J7
Park Vls *RHAY* LS8.......................84 B2
Park Villas Dr *PONT* WF8.......................169 G7
Parkville Pl *BRAM* LS13.......................101 F2
Park Wy *BAIL* BD17.......................76 E3
  ILK LS29.......................38 B6
  OT LS21.......................41 G4
Parkway *AIRE* BD20.......................32 C5
  CUL/QBY BD13.......................115 G5
  HOR/CROF WF4.......................186 C7
  KGHY BD21.......................3 G9
  MOR LS27.......................141 F1
  WBOW BD5.......................118 A5
Parkway Cl *SCFT* LS14.......................105 F1
Parkways *RTHW* LS26.......................145 J1
Parkways Av *RTHW* LS26.......................145 J2
Parkways Cl *RTHW* LS26.......................145 J1
Parkways Ct *RTHW* LS26.......................145 J1
Parkways Dr *RTHW* LS26.......................145 J1
Parkways Garth *RTHW* * LS26.......................145 J2
Parkways Gv *RTHW* LS26.......................145 J1
Park West *RTHW* LS26.......................145 C2
Park Willow *HIPP* HX3.......................136 C1
Park Wood Av *BEE/HOL* LS11.......................122 E7
Parkwood Av *RHAY* LS8.......................84 B4
Parkwood Ct *RHAY* LS8.......................84 B4
Park Wood Crs *BEE/HOL* LS11.......................122 E6
Park Wood Dr *BEE/HOL* LS11.......................122 E6
Parkwood Gdns
  PDSY/CALV LS28.......................79 H6
  RHAY LS8.......................84 B5
Parkwood Ri *KGHY* BD21.......................3 H7
Park Wood Rd *BEE/HOL* LS11.......................122 E7
Parkwood Rd *PDSY/CALV* LS28.......................79 H6
  SHPY BD18.......................76 E5
Parkwood St *KGHY* BD21.......................3 J6
Parkwood Vw *RHAY* LS8.......................84 B4
Parkwood Wy *RHAY* LS8.......................84 B5
Parliament Pl *WOR/ARM* LS12.......................8 C9
Parliament Rd *WOR/ARM* LS12.......................12 C1
Parliament St
  WKFDW/WTN WF2.......................18 C5
Parlington Ct *MSTN/BAR* LS15.......................87 H5
Parlington Dr *GFTH/SHER* LS25.......................88 D3
Parlington La *GFTH/SHER* LS25.......................88 D6
  GFTH/SHER LS25.......................107 K1
Parlington Meadow
  MSTN/BAR LS15.......................87 H6
Parlington Vls
  GFTH/SHER LS25.......................88 C5
Parma St *WBOW* BD5.......................117 K1
Parnaby Av *MID* LS10.......................124 A5
Parnaby Rd *MID* LS10.......................124 A5
Parnaby St *MID* LS10.......................124 A5
Parnaby Ter *MID* LS10.......................124 A5
Parratt Rw *BFDE* BD3.......................7 J6
Parrott St *BOW* BD4.......................118 C5
Parry Cl *BGLY* * BD16.......................74 D3
Parry La *BOW* BD4.......................118 D1
Parsonage Rd *BRIG* HD6.......................157 F6
Parsonage Rd *RTHW* LS26.......................147 G4
  WBOW BD5.......................117 K3
Parsonage St *HIPP* HX3.......................17 J2
Parsons Gn *WBY* LS22.......................29 J4
Parson's La *ILK* LS29.......................21 K1
Parsons Rd *HTON* BD9.......................97 F1
Parson St *KGHY* BD21.......................3 J3
Partons Pl *EARD/LOFT* WF3.......................164 D2

Partridge Cl *MOR* LS27.......................142 C3
Pasture Av *CHAL* LS7.......................83 J5
  GFTH/SHER LS25.......................111 H5
  HWTH BD22.......................72 D3
Pasture Cl *CLAY* BD14.......................116 C2
Pasture Ct *GFTH/SHER* LS25.......................111 G6
Pasture Crs *CHAL* LS7.......................83 J5
Pasture Dr *CAS* WF10.......................167 K2
Pasture Fold *ILK* LS29.......................25 K7
Pasture Gv *CHAL* LS7.......................83 J5
  CLAY BD14.......................116 C2
  WBY LS22.......................45 F1
Pasture Mt *WOR/ARM* LS12.......................102 A5
Pasture Pde *CHAL* LS7.......................83 J5
Pasture Pl *CHAL* LS7.......................83 J5
Pasture Ri *CLAY* BD14.......................116 C2
Pasture Rd *BAIL* BD17.......................77 J2
  RHAY LS8.......................103 K1
Pasture Side Ter East
  CLAY BD14.......................116 C2
Pasture Side Ter West
  CLAY BD14.......................116 B2
Pasture St *CHAL* * LS7.......................83 J5
Pasture Ter *CHAL* LS7.......................83 J5
Pasture Vw *GFTH/SHER* LS25.......................111 G5
  WOR/ARM LS12.......................102 A5
Pasture View Rd *RTHW* LS26.......................144 E2
Pasture Wk *CLAY* BD14.......................116 B2
Pasture Wy *CAS* WF10.......................167 K2
  GFTH/SHER LS25.......................111 H5
Pateley Crs *HUDN* HD2.......................176 E7
Patent St *HTON* BD9.......................97 G3
Paternoster La *GTHN* BD7.......................117 G2
Paterson Av *WKFDW/WTN* WF2.......................18 B5
Patience La *NORM* WF6.......................166 B5
Patricia Gdns *RPDN/SBR* HX6.......................154 C4
Patterdale Ap *WBY* LS22.......................28 E4
Patterdale Rd *EARL* WF12.......................161 H6
Patterson Ct
  WKFDW/WTN WF2.......................164 A5
Pattie St *KGHY* BD21.......................53 J2
Pauline Ter *CAS* WF10.......................168 B1
Paul La *HUDE* HD5.......................178 D4
Pavement La *LUD/ILL* HX2.......................114 B7
Pavilion Ms *HDGY* LS6.......................8 C2
Paw La *CUL/QBY* BD13.......................115 J7
Pawson St *BOW* BD4.......................7 J8
  EARD/LOFT WF3.......................143 K7
  EARD/LOFT WF3.......................144 C5
  MOR LS27.......................141 H4
Peabody St *HIPP* HX3.......................16 C1
Peace St *BOW* BD4.......................7 H9
Peach Tree Cl *PONT* * WF8.......................189 G3
Peacock Av *WKFDW/WTN* WF2.......................184 A2
Peacock Ct *YEA* LS19.......................59 K7
Peacock Gn *WKFDW/WTN* WF2.......................184 A2
Peak Vw *DEWS* WF13.......................160 C6
Pearl St *BTLY* WF17.......................160 D2
  HWTH BD22.......................53 H7
Pearson Av *HDGY* LS6.......................8 F3
Pearson Gv *HDGY* LS6.......................8 F3
Pearson La *HTON* BD9.......................96 C4
Pearson Rd *WBSY* BD6.......................117 J6
Pearson Rw *LM/WK* BD12.......................137 J4
Pearson St *BFDE* BD3.......................7 H7
  CLECK BD19.......................158 C2
  MID LS10.......................14 C6
  NORM WF6.......................166 D3
  PDSY/CALV LS28.......................79 J5
Pearson Ter *HDGY* LS6.......................8 F3
Pear St *HFAX* HX1.......................16 A7
  HWTH BD22.......................73 H1
  HWTH * BD22.......................92 D3
Pear Tree Acre
  BSPA/BRAM LS23.......................48 D1
Pear Tree Cl *PONT* WF8.......................189 G3
Pear Tree Ct *AIRE* BD20.......................21 F7
Pear Tree Gdns *MSTN/BAR* LS15.......................87 H6
Pear Tree Wk
  WKFDW/WTN WF2.......................18 A1
Peasborough Vw *ILK* LS29.......................38 A3
Pease Cl *PONT* WF8.......................189 J3
Peasefold *GFTH/SHER* LS25.......................128 A5
Peasehill Cl *YEA* LS19.......................59 K7
Peasehill Pk *YEA* LS19.......................59 K7
Peaseland Av *CLECK* BD19.......................158 D1
Peaseland Cl *CLECK* BD19.......................158 E1
Peaseland Rd *CLECK* BD19.......................158 E1
Peckover Dr *PDSY/CALV* LS28.......................99 G4
Peckover St *BFD* BD1.......................6 B6
Peel Av *BTLY* WF17.......................161 F5
Peel Cl *BOW* BD4.......................7 L8
Peel Park Dr *ECHL* BD2.......................98 C3
Peel Park Ter *ECHL* BD2.......................98 B5
Peel Park Vw *BFDE* BD3.......................7 L8
Peel Pl *ILK* LS29.......................37 K1
Peel Rw *GTHN* BD7.......................117 F3
Peel Sq *BFD* BD1.......................5 K4
Peel St *BGLY* BD16.......................76 A1
  CUL/QBY BD13.......................95 G7
  CUL/QBY BD13.......................115 J5
  HECK WF16.......................159 K4
  MOR LS27.......................142 A3
  RPDN/SBR * HX6.......................153 J4
  WIL/AL BD15.......................95 F1
Peep Green Rd *LVSG* WF15.......................158 D5
Pegholme Dr *OT* LS21.......................38 E4
Pelham Ct *EARD/LOFT* * WF3.......................143 J4
  ECHL BD2.......................98 C2
Pelham Pl *CHAL* LS7.......................83 H5
Pelham Rd *ECHL* BD2.......................98 C2
Pellon La *HFAX* HX1.......................16 A3
Pellon New Rd *LUD/ILL* HX2.......................134 B7
Pellon Ter *IDLE* BD10.......................78 C3
Pellon Wk *IDLE* BD10.......................78 C3
Pemberton Dr *GTHN* BD7.......................5 J8
Pemberton Rd *CAS* WF10.......................149 G7
Pembroke Cl *MOR* LS27.......................141 J2
Pembroke Ri *GFTH/SHER* LS25.......................128 B4
Pembroke Rd *PDSY/CALV* LS28.......................100 B5
Pembroke St *WBOW* BD5.......................117 H2
Pembury Mt *MSTN/BAR* LS15.......................106 C2
Penarth Rd *MSTN/BAR* LS15.......................105 J3
Penda's Dr *MSTN/BAR* LS15.......................106 A4
Penda's Gv *MSTN/BAR* LS15.......................106 A3
Penda's Wk *MSTN/BAR* LS15.......................106 A3

Penda's Wy *MSTN/BAR* LS15.......................106 B3
Pendil Cl *MSTN/BAR* LS15.......................105 K5
Pendle Ct *CUL/QBY* BD13.......................115 H7
Pendle Rd *BGLY* BD16.......................76 A1
Pendragon *ECHL* * BD2.......................98 B2
Pendragon La *ECHL* BD2.......................98 C2
Penfield Gv *CLAY* BD14.......................116 B2
Penfield Rd *BIRK/DRI* BD11.......................140 C1
Pengarth *BGLY* BD16.......................56 A6
Penistone Ms *HWTH* * BD22.......................72 D5
Penlands Crs *MSTN/BAR* LS15.......................106 A6
Penlands Lawn
  MSTN/BAR LS15.......................106 A6
Penlands Wk *MSTN/BAR* LS15.......................106 A6
Penn Cl *ECHL* BD2.......................98 C2
Penn Dr *CLECK* BD19.......................158 E2
Penn Gv *CLECK* BD19.......................158 E2
Pennine Cl *CUL/QBY* BD13.......................115 G7
  WKFDW/WTN WF2.......................183 K7
Pennine Rd *EARL* WF12.......................181 K5
Pennine Vw *BTLY* WF17.......................140 D5
  HUDE HD5.......................178 D7
Pennington Gv *HDGY* LS6.......................9 K2
Pennington La *RTHW* LS26.......................145 J5
Pennington Pl *HDGY* LS6.......................9 K2
Pennington St *HDGY* LS6.......................9 K1
Pennington Ter *HDGY* LS6.......................9 K2
  WBOW * BD5.......................117 H2
Pennithorne Av *BAIL* BD17.......................57 H7
Penn St *HFAX* HX1.......................16 C4
Pennwell Fold *SCFT* LS14.......................86 B7
Pennwell Garth *SCFT* LS14.......................86 A7
Pennwell Gn *SCFT* LS14.......................86 A7
Pennwell Lawn *SCFT* LS14.......................86 A7
Pennygate *BGLY* BD16.......................56 C5
Penny Hill Dr *CLAY* BD14.......................116 C2
Penny Lane Wy *MID* LS10.......................14 C8
Penraevon Av *CHAL* LS7.......................10 A2
Penraevon St *CHAL* LS7.......................10 A2
Penrith Crs *CAS* WF10.......................149 K5
Penrith Gv *WOR/ARM* LS12.......................12 A3
Penrose Dr *GTHN* BD7.......................116 E3
Pentland Av *CLAY* BD14.......................116 C2
  KNOT WF11.......................171 F4
Pentland Cl *HWTH* * BD22.......................2 D6
Pentland Dr *GFTH/SHER* LS25.......................127 J1
Pentland Gv
  WKFDW/WTN WF2.......................183 K6
Pentland Rd *EARL* WF12.......................181 G3
Pentland Wy *MOR* LS27.......................141 K4
Penzance Ct *GIR* BD8.......................4 F3
Pepper Gdns *BRAM* LS13.......................101 F4
Pepper La *BRAM* LS13.......................101 G1
  MID LS10.......................124 A3
Pepper Rd *MID* LS10.......................124 A4
Pepper Royd St *DEWS* WF13.......................161 G7
Percival St *BFDE* BD3.......................6 D6
  LDSU LS2.......................9 M7
Percy St *BGLY* BD16.......................75 K1
  KGHY BD21.......................53 J7
  WOR/ARM LS12.......................12 C3
Peregrine Av *MOR* LS27.......................142 C3
Peregrine Wy *WBSY* BD6.......................116 B5
Peridot Fold *HUDN* HD2.......................177 H7
Per La *LUD/ILL* HX2.......................114 A7
Perry Cl *HWTH* BD22.......................73 H1
Perseverance La *GTHN* BD7.......................117 F3
Perseverance Rd
  CUL/QBY BD13.......................114 C2
Perseverance St *BAIL* * BD17.......................57 J7
  CAS WF10.......................148 B7
  LM/WK BD12.......................137 H3
  PDSY/CALV LS28.......................99 K6
  RPDN/SBR HX6.......................153 J4
Perseverance Ter *HFAX* HX1.......................154 D3
  RTHW LS26.......................145 F3
Perth Av *ECHL* BD2.......................97 K2
Perth Dr *EARD/LOFT* WF3.......................142 E7
Perth Mt *HORS* LS18.......................60 F7
Peterborough Pl *ECHL* BD2.......................98 C2
Peterborough Rd *ECHL* BD2.......................98 C3
Peterborough Ter *ECHL* BD2.......................98 C2
Petergate *BFD* BD1.......................6 C7
Peter Hl *BTLY* WF17.......................161 G6
Peterhouse Dr *OT* LS21.......................39 K3
Peter La *LUD/ILL* HX2.......................153 J1
  MOR LS27.......................142 C2
Petersfield Av *MID* LS10.......................123 K7
Peterson Rd *WKFDE* WF1.......................19 G5
Pether Hl *GTL/HWG* HX4.......................174 C6
Petrel Cl *WBSY* BD6.......................116 B5
Petrel Wy *MOR* LS27.......................142 B4
Petrie Crs *BRAM* LS13.......................80 A7
Petrie Gv *BFDE* BD3.......................7 L5
Petrie Rd *BFDE* BD3.......................7 L6
Petrie St *BRAM* LS13.......................80 A7
Peverell Cl *BOW* BD4.......................119 F3
Peverill Mt *ECHL* BD2.......................98 C8
Pheasant Dr *BTLY* WF17.......................140 D4
Pheasant St *KGHY* BD21.......................3 J3
Philip Garth *WKFDE* WF1.......................164 C3
Philippa Wy *WOR/ARM* LS12.......................12 B9
Philip's Gv *EARD/LOFT* WF3.......................164 D2
Philip's La *PONT* WF8.......................190 D4
Phillips St *CAS* WF10.......................148 A7
Phil May Ct *WOR/ARM* * LS12.......................12 E3
Phoebe La *HIPP* HX3.......................155 C4
  WKFDW/WTN WF2.......................18 A5
Phoenix Ct *BTLY* WF17.......................161 J3
Phoenix Wy *BOW* BD4.......................7 M7
Piccadilly *BFD* BD1.......................5 M5
  WKFDW/WTN WF2.......................18 D5
Pickard Bank *HDGY* LS6.......................82 C7
Pickard Ct *MSTN/BAR* LS15.......................105 K5
Pickard La *AIRE* BD20.......................21 F7
Pickard Wy *DEWS* WF13.......................160 E7
Pickering Av *GFTH/SHER* LS25.......................108 A3
Pickering Dr *OSS* WF5.......................162 B7
Pickering La *OSS* WF5.......................162 A7
Pickering Mt *WOR/ARM* LS12.......................8 C8
The Pickerings *CUL/QBY* BD13.......................115 H6
Pickering St *WOR/ARM* LS12.......................8 C8
Pickersgill St *OSS* WF5.......................182 B1
Picklesfield *DEWS* WF13.......................160 E6
Pickles La *GTHN* BD7.......................116 E3
Pickles St *DEWS* WF13.......................160 E6
  KGHY BD21.......................2 F8

Pickwood La *RPDN/SBR* HX6......154 B6
Picton St *LUD/ILL* BD8 ....5 J2
Pictureville *BFD* BD1...................5 L7
Piece Wood Rd *BHP/TINH* LS16....81 G1
Pigeon Cote Cl *SCFT* LS14...........85 H6
Pigeon Cote Rd *SCFT* LS14...........85 G6
Piggott St *BRIG* HD6..................157 H5
Pildacre Brow *OSS* WF5 ....182 B3
Pildacre Cft *OSS* WF5................182 B3
Pildacre La *EARL* WF12.............182 A3
Pilden La *EARD/LOFT* WF3..........163 H1
Pilgrim Av *DEWS* WF13...............180 C2
Pilgrim Crs *DEWS* WF13.............180 C2
Pilgrim Dr *DEWS* WF13...............180 C2
Pilmer Ct *WKFDW/WTN* WF2 ......183 J5
Pilot St *OSM* LS9.........................10 E6
Pincheon St *WKFDE* WF1............19 G4
Pinder Av *WOR/ARM* LS12..........121 J2
Pinderfields Rd *WKFDE* WF1........18 F2
Pinder Gv *WOR/ARM* LS12..........121 J1
Pinders Crs *KNOT* WF11..............170 D3
Pinders Garth *KNOT* WF11...........170 D3
Pinders Gn *RTHW* LS26..............147 F6
Pinders Green Ct *RTHW* LS26.....147 F6
Pinders Green Dr *RTHW* LS26.....147 F6
Pinders Green Fold
  RTHW LS26.............................147 F6
Pinder's Gv *WKFDE* WF1.............185 F1
Pinder St *WOR/ARM* LS12..........121 J2
Pinebury Dr *CUL/QBY* BD13........115 F5
Pine Cl *CAS* WF10......................168 D2
  WBY LS22.................................29 H2
Pine Ct *LDSU* LS2........................14 C1
Pine Cft *KGHY* BD21......................2 C1
Pinedale *BGLY* BD16....................55 J6
Pine Gv *BTLY* WF17...................160 E4
Pines Gdns *ILK* LS29...................23 J6
Pine St *BFD* BD1............................6 B5
  HFAX HX1................................17 G7
  HWTH BD22..............................72 D6
Pine Tree Av *BSPA/BRAM* LS23...48 D2
  PONT WF8................................189 D3
Pine Tree La *GFTH/SHER* LS25 .....151 J1
Pinewood Av
  WKFDW/WTN WF2 ....183 J5
Pinewood Cl *ILK* LS29.................23 K6
Pinewood Gdns *GTL/HWG* HX4 ...174 D5
Pinewood Pl *KNOT* WF11 ....171 F5
Pinfold Av *GFTH/SHER* LS25.......111 G5
Pinfold Ct *EARL* WF12.................181 H7
  GFTH/SHER LS25 ....111 G5
  GTL/HWG HX4 ....173 H4
  KNOT WF11..............................170 D3
  MIRF WF14...............................179 J4
Pinfold Ct *GFTH/SHER* LS25.......111 G5
  *MSTN/BAR * LS15.......................105 J3
Pinfold Cft *CLAY* BD14................116 B2
Pinfold Garth *GFTH/SHER* LS25 ..111 H5
Pinfold Gv *MSTN/BAR* LS15.......105 H5
Pinfold Hl *DEWS* WF13...............180 C2
  MSTN/BAR LS15........................105 J4
Pinfold La *BHP/TINH* LS16...........61 H5
  ELL HX5...................................176 C3
  GFTH/SHER LS25 ....107 J6
  MIRF WF14...............................179 J4
  MSTN/BAR LS15........................105 H5
  RPDN/SBR HX6.........................152 E4
  RTHW LS26...............................147 H5
  WOR/ARM LS12........................102 A3
Pinfold Mt *MSTN/BAR* LS15.......105 J6
Pinfold Ri *GFTH/SHER* LS25........88 E7
Pinfold Rd *MSTN/BAR* LS15.......105 J6
Pinfold Sq *MSTN/BAR* LS15.......105 H5
Pinfold Wy *GFTH/SHER* LS25.....111 H5
Pin Hill La *LUD/ILL* HX2.............132 E5
Pink St *HWTH* BD22......................72 D6
Pinnar La *HIPP* HX3....................155 J3
Pioneer St *EARL* WF12...............181 F6
Pioneer Wy *CAS* WF10...............167 H3
Pipe & Nook La
  WOR/ARM LS12........................101 J3
Pipercroft *WBSY* BD6.................136 D1
Piper Hl *KNOT* WF11..................150 B2
Piper La *OT* LS21.........................39 G3
Pipit Meadow *MOR* LS27............142 B4
Pippin's Ap *NORM* WF6..............166 E5
Pippins Green Av
  WKFDW/WTN WF2 ....163 G6
Pirie Cl *ECHL* BD2........................98 A2
Pitchstone Ct *WOR/ARM* LS12...101 C6
Pitcliffe Wy *WBOW* BD5.............117 K2
Pitfall St *LDS* LS1.........................14 B2
Pit Field Rd *EARD/LOFT* WF3......144 E5
Pit Hl *HIPP* HX3............................17 K8
Pit La *CLECK* BD19......................139 J5
  CUL/QBY BD13...........................93 K4
  CUL/QBY BD13.........................115 F2
  DEWS WF13...............................160 C6
  GFTH/SHER LS25 ....109 F7
  GFTH/SHER LS25.......................107 J6
  RTHW LS26...............................147 C4
Pits La *CLECK* BD19....................157 K2
Pitt Hill La *GTL/HWG* HX4...........173 K7
Pitt Rw *LDS* LS1............................14 A2
Pitts St *BOW* BD4........................118 E2
Pitt St *KGHY* BD21..........................3 J5
  LVSG WF15...............................159 H6
Place's Rd *OSM* LS9.....................14 F2
Plaid Rw *OSM* LS9.......................10 F9
Plain La *RPDN/SBR* HX6............150 C6
Plains La *ELL* HX5.......................155 J7
Plane Gn *PONT* WF8...................170 A7
Plane Tree Av *AL/HA/HU* LS17.....64 A7
Plane Tree Cl *AL/HA/HU* LS17.....64 A7
Plane Tree Cft *AL/HA/HU* LS17....64 A7
Plane Tree Gdns *AL/HA/HU* LS17..64 A7
Plane Tree Gv *YEA* LS19..............60 A5
Plane Tree Nest La
  LUD/ILL HX2.............................154 B2
Plane Tree Ri *AL/HA/HU * LS17 ....64 A7
Plane Tree Rd *RPDN/SBR* HX6....153 J3
Plane Trees *LUD/ILL* HX2...........134 C4
Plane Trees Cl *CLECK* BD19........138 E4
Plane Tree Vw *AL/HA/HU* LS17.....64 A7
Plantation Av *AL/HA/HU* LS17.....64 B6
  MSTN/BAR LS15........................105 G6

Plantation Gdns *AL/HA/HU* LS17....64 C6
Plantation Pl *BOW* BD4..............118 D2
Plantation Wy *BAIL* BD17............77 J1
Playfair Rd *MID* LS10.................123 J4
Playfair Sq *OSM* LS9...................10 D9
The Pleasance *RTHW* LS26.......126 D5
Pleasant Ct *HDGY* LS6...................9 J2
Pleasant Mt *BEE/HOL* LS11.........13 J5
Pleasant Pl *BEE/HOL* LS11..........13 J5
Pleasant St *BEE/HOL* LS11..........13 H5
  GTHN BD7.................................117 F2
Pleasant Ter *BEE/HOL* LS11........13 J5
Plevna St *MID* LS10....................124 B4
Plevna Ter *BGLY* BD16.................55 J7
Plimsoll St *BOW* BD4..................118 B2
Ploughcroft La *HIPP* HX3............134 E5
Ploughmans Cft *ECHL* BD2..........97 K1
Plover Dr *BTLY* WF17..................160 C3
Plover St *KGHY* BD21.....................3 H2
  WBOW BD5...............................117 H3
Plover Wy *MOR* LS27..................142 B4
Plumpton Cl *ECHL* BD2................78 A6
Plumpton Dr *ECHL* BD2................78 A6
Plumpton End *ECHL* BD2.............78 B6
Plumpton Gdns *ECHL* BD2...........78 A6
Plumpton Lea *ECHL* BD2..............78 A6
Plumpton Md *ECHL* BD2..............78 A6
Plumpton Pl *WKFDW/WTN* WF2 ..18 B5
Plumpton Rd
  WKFDW/WTN WF2 ....18 B5
Plumpton St *GIR* BD8....................4 D4
  WKFDW/WTN WF2 ....18 B6
Plumpton Ter
  WKFDW/WTN WF2 ....18 B6
Plumpton Wk *ECHL* BD2..............78 A6
Plum St *HFAX* HX1.......................16 B8
  HWTH BD22..............................73 H1
Plum Tree Cl *PONT* WF8.............189 G3
Plymouth Gv *HFAX * HX1..............16 C3
Poet's Pl *HORS* LS18....................81 F2
Pohlman St *HFAX* HX1.................16 B9
Pole Rd *HWTH* BD22.....................52 A3
Pollard Av *BGLY* BD16..................56 A6
  CLECK BD19.............................139 J6
Pollard Cl *CLECK* BD19...............139 J6
Pollard La *BFDE* BD3......................6 F1
  BRAM LS13.................................81 F6
Pollard St *BOW* BD4......................6 A9
  EARD/LOFT WF3........................164 D3
  HUDN HD2................................177 G7
Pollard Wy *CLECK* BD19.............139 J6
Pollit Av *RPDN/SBR* HX6............153 C5
Polperro Cl *NORM* WF6..............166 E5
Pomfret Pl *GFTH/SHER* LS25.......108 A5
Ponderosa Cl *RHAY* LS8................11 G2
Pondfields Cl *GFTH/SHER* LS25...128 A5
Pondfields Crest
  GFTH/SHER LS25.......................128 A5
Pondfields Dr *GFTH/SHER* LS25...128 A4
Pondfields Ri *GFTH/SHER* LS25...128 A5
Pond St *KGHY* BD21.......................3 H4
Pontefract La *OSM* LS9.................11 G9
  OSM LS9...................................124 E1
Pontefract Lane Cl *OSM* LS9........15 J1
Pontefract La *MSTN/BAR* LS15...125 K4
Pontefract Rd *CAS* WF10............168 D1
  FEA/AMT WF7............................188 B5
  HOR/CROF WF4..........................186 C1
  MID LS10..................................124 B4
  NORM WF6................................167 G5
  PONT WF8.................................170 B4
Pontefract St *OSM* LS9.................15 G2
Pool Bank Cl *OT* LS21..................41 G3
Pool Bank Ct *OT* LS21..................41 G4
Pool Bank New Rd
  BHP/TINH LS16...........................40 E6
Pool Br *OT* LS21...........................41 F2
Pool Ct *BFDE* BD3..........................6 D4
Poole Crs *MSTN/BAR* LS15.........105 J3
Poole La *GFTH/SHER* LS25.........151 F4
Poole Mt *MSTN/BAR* LS15..........105 J4
Poole Rd *MSTN/BAR* LS15..........105 J4
Poole Sq *MSTN/BAR* LS15..........105 J4
Pool Rd *OT* LS21...........................39 K2
  OT LS21....................................40 C2
Pool St *KGHY* BD21........................3 L1
Popeley Rd *HECK* WF16..............159 K2
Pope St *KGHY* BD21.......................3 K3
  NORM WF6................................166 E3
Poplar Av *CAS* WF10...................169 H1
  GFTH/SHER LS25 ....107 H6
  GTHN BD7.................................116 E4
  MSTN/BAR LS15........................106 A3
  RPDN/SBR HX6.........................153 J3
  SHPY BD18.................................77 H7
  WBY LS22...................................29 H2
  WKFDW/WTN WF2 ....183 J4
Poplar Cl *BRAM* LS13..................101 J5
  ILK LS29....................................38 A2
Poplar Cft *ELL * HX5....................175 J3
Poplar Crs *EARD/LOFT* WF3.......142 B6
  LUD/ILL HX2.............................114 C7
  SHPY BD18.................................77 H7
Poplar Cft *BRAM* LS13................101 H5
Poplar Dr *AIRE* BD20....................55 F4
  HORS LS18.................................80 D3
  NORM WF6................................166 D3
  SHPY BD18.................................77 H7
Poplar Gdns *BRAM* LS13.............101 H5
Poplar Garth *BRAM* LS13............101 H5
Poplar Ga *WOR/ARM* LS12.........101 H5
Poplar Ga *PONT* WF8..................170 A7
Poplar Gv *BGLY* BD16...................74 D3
  CLECK BD19.............................158 D2
  GTHN BD7.................................116 E4
  KNOT WF11..............................171 F6
  PONT WF8.................................189 G1
  SHPY BD18.................................77 H7
Poplar Rd *BRAM* LS13.................101 H4
  GTHN BD7.................................117 F4
  SHPY BD18.................................77 H7
The Poplars *BHP/TINH* LS16.......61 J1
  GSLY LS20.................................59 F1
  HDGY LS6................................102 D1
  *HIPP * HX3.................................137 F5

Poplars Park Rd *ECHL* BD2..........97 J6
Poplar Sq *PDSY/CALV* LS28........100 A3
Poplar St *EARD/LOFT* WF3.........164 D2
  HIPP HX3....................................17 G3
Poplar Ter *AIRE* BD20...................55 G4
Poplar Vw *AL/HA/HU * LS17..........85 G1
  BRAM LS13................................101 H5
  BRIG HD6..................................157 F2
  GTHN BD7.................................116 D4
Poplar Wy *BRAM* LS13................101 H5
Poplarwood Gdns *IDLE* BD10.......79 F7
Popples Dr *LUD/ILL* HX2............114 C7
Poppleton Ct *EARD/LOFT* WF3 ...142 D6
Poppleton Dr *EARD/LOFT* WF3 ...142 D6
Poppleton Ri *EARD/LOFT* WF3 ...142 D7
Poppleton Rd *EARD/LOFT* WF3 ...142 D6
Poppleton Wy
  EARD/LOFT WF3........................142 D7
Popple Wells La *LUD/ILL* HX2.....153 C1
Poppy Cl *MIRF* WF14...................179 H1
Porritt St *CLECK * BD19...............138 E6
Portage Av *MSTN/BAR* LS15......105 G6
Portage Crs *MSTN/BAR* LS15.....105 G6
Portal Crs *MIRF* WF14.................159 H7
Portal Dr *MIRF* WF14..................179 H1
Portland Av *PONT* WF8................169 G7
Portland Crs *LDSU* LS2...................9 M7
Portland Ga *LDSU* LS2....................9 M7
Portland Pl *BGLY* BD16................75 K2
  HFAX HX1...................................17 H8
  WOR/ARM LS12..........................12 A3
Portland Rd *HIPP* HX3.................17 H5
Portland St *HFAX* HX1..................17 H5
  HWTH BD22................................72 E5
  LDS LS1......................................9 L8
  *PDSY/CALV * LS28.......................100 D6
  WBOW BD5...................................5 M8
  WKFDE WF1...............................185 G6
Portland Wy *LDSU* LS2...................9 M7
Portman St *PDSY/CALV* LS28.......79 J6
Portobello Gv
  WKFDW/WTN WF2 ....184 E6
Portobello Rd
  WKFDW/WTN WF2 ....184 E6
Portsmouth Av *BFDE* BD3.............6 B2
Portwood St *HTON* BD9................96 C3
Post Hill Ct *WOR/ARM* LS12......101 G6
Post Office Rd *FEA/AMT* WF7.....188 C4
  IDLE BD10..................................78 D7
Post Office St *CLECK* BD19.........159 G2
Pothouse Rd *WBSY* BD6.............117 G6
Pot La *AIRE* BD20.........................32 B2
Potovens La
  WKFDW/WTN WF2 ....164 A5
Potter Av *WKFDW/WTN* WF2.....183 K5
Potter Brow Rd *BAIL* BD17..........57 H4
Potternewton Av *CHAL* LS7.........83 G6
Potternewton Ct *CHAL* LS7.........83 G7
Potternewton Crs *CHAL* LS7........83 G7
Potternewton Gdns *CHAL * LS7 ....83 H6
Potternewton Hts *CHAL* LS7........83 H6
Potternewton La *CHAL* LS7..........83 F6
Potternewton Mt *CHAL* LS7.........83 G6
Potternewton Vw *CHAL * LS7........83 G6
Potters Cft *EARD/LOFT* WF3.......164 D2
Potterton Br *MSTN/BAR* LS15......87 H3
Potterton Cl *MSTN/BAR* LS15......87 H4
Potterton La *MSTN/BAR* LS15......87 H5
Pottery La *KNOT* WF11...............170 E3
  RTHW LS26...............................126 A7
Pottery Rd *MID* LS10....................14 C7
Pottery St *CAS* WF10..................148 A7
Potts' Ter *NORM* WF6.................186 D1
Poulton Pl *BEE/HOL* LS11............14 B9
Poverty La *RPDN/SBR* HX6.........152 B7
Powell Av *WBOW* BD5................117 H2
Powell Rd *BGLY* BD16...................75 K1
  SHPY BD18.................................77 J7
Powell St *CAS* WF10...................148 C7
  HECK WF16...............................160 A5
  HFAX HX1...................................17 G6
Prail Cl *PONT* WF8......................170 A7
Pratt La *MIRF* WF14....................179 H1
  SHPY BD18.................................77 H6
Premiere Pk *ILK* LS29...................23 H6
Prescott St *HFAX* HX1...................17 H8
Prescott Ter *WIL/AL* BD15............96 A4
Preston La *LUD/ILL* HX2.............133 K5
  RTHW LS26...............................127 H1
Preston Pde *BEE/HOL* LS11........123 F4
Preston Pl *HFAX* HX1....................16 D6
Preston St *BTLY* WF17................161 F4
  EARL WF12...............................181 H7
  GTHN BD7....................................5 G5
Preston Vw *RTHW* LS26..............126 E5
Prestwich Dr *HUDN* HD2............176 E7
Prestwick Cl *OT* LS21...................38 E4
Prestwick Fold *OSS* WF5............182 C2
Pretoria St *CAS* WF10.................168 D1
  FEA/AMT WF7............................188 B3
  WKFDE WF1...............................184 E6
Priest Hill Gdns *WBY* LS22...........29 G2
Priesthorpe Av *PDSY/CALV* LS28..99 J3
Priesthorpe Ct
  PDSY/CALV LS28.......................100 A1
Priesthorpe La *PDSY/CALV* LS28 ..99 J2
Priesthorpe Rd *PDSY/CALV* LS28..99 K1
Priest La *RPDN/SBR* HX6............173 F5
Priestley Av *HECK* WF16............160 A2
  WBSY BD6.................................117 G6
Priestley Cl *PDSY/CALV* LS28.....100 C5
Priestley Ct *PDSY/CALV* LS28.....100 C5
Priestley Dr *PDSY/CALV* LS28.....100 C5
Priestley Gdns *HECK* WF16........159 K3
  PDSY/CALV LS28.......................100 C5
Priestley Pl *RPDN/SBR* HX6.......153 H5
Priestley Sq *BTLY* WF17..............140 B5
Priestley Ter *WBSY* BD6.............117 H5
Priestley Vw *PDSY/CALV* LS28...100 C5
Priestley Wk *PDSY/CALV* LS28...100 C5
Priestman Cl *GIR* BD8....................5 G1
Priestman St *GIR* BD8...................5 G2
Priestthorpe Cl *BGLY* BD16.........55 K7
Priestthorpe La *BGLY* BD16.........55 K7
Priestthorpe Rd *BGLY* BD16........75 K1
Primitive St *EARD/LOFT* WF3.....144 E4

Primley Gdns *AL/HA/HU* LS17.....63 H7
Primley Park Av *AL/HA/HU* LS17...63 H7
Primley Park Cl *AL/HA/HU* LS17...63 H7
Primley Park Ct *AL/HA/HU* LS17...63 H6
Primley Park Crs *AL/HA/HU* LS17 ..63 H7
Primley Park Dr
  AL/HA/HU LS17...........................63 H7
Primley Park Garth
  AL/HA/HU LS17...........................63 J6
Primley Park Gn
  AL/HA/HU LS17...........................63 J6
Primley Park La
  AL/HA/HU LS17...........................63 J7
Primley Park Mt
  AL/HA/HU LS17...........................63 J7
Primley Park Ri
  AL/HA/HU LS17...........................63 J7
Primley Park Rd
  AL/HA/HU LS17...........................63 H7
Primley Park Vw
  AL/HA/HU LS17...........................63 H6
Primley Park Wk
  AL/HA/HU LS17...........................63 H6
Primley Park Wy
  AL/HA/HU LS17...........................63 H6
Primrose Av *MSTN/BAR* LS15....105 G6
  RTHW LS26...............................126 E5
Primrose Bank *BGLY* BD16..........76 B3
Primrose Cl *MSTN/BAR* LS15.....105 H5
  PONT WF8.................................189 J2
Primrose Crs *MSTN/BAR* LS15...105 H4
Primrose Ct *AL/HA/HU * LS17.......63 J6
Primrose Dene *KNOT* WF11.......170 E1
Primrose Dr *BGLY* BD16..............76 B2
  CAS WF10.................................169 G2
  MSTN/BAR LS15........................105 H5
Primrose Gdns *BTLY* WF17.........161 H2
  MSTN/BAR LS15........................105 H5
Primrose Garth
  MSTN/BAR LS15........................105 G5
Primrose Gv *KGHY* BD21...............3 M4
Primrose Hill Cl *RTHW* LS26.......126 E5
Primrose Hill Dr *RTHW* LS26......126 E6
Primrose Hill Gn *RTHW* LS26......126 E6
Primrose La *BEE/HOL* LS11.........14 B9
  BGLY BD16.................................76 A3
  BSPA/BRAM LS23.......................48 B3
  ECHL BD2...................................97 J1
  LVSG WF15...............................159 G4
  MIRF WF14...............................179 K2
  MSTN/BAR LS15........................105 G6
Primrose St *GIR* BD8......................5 H3
  KGHY BD21..................................3 M4
Primrose Wk *MOR* LS27.............122 B6
Primrose Wy *HIPP* HX3...............116 C7
Prince Edward Gv
  WOR/ARM LS12........................121 K2
Prince Edward Rd
  WOR/ARM LS12........................121 K2
Prince Henry Rd *OT* LS21.............39 H1
Princeroyd Wy *GTHN* BD7.............4 D6
Prince's Av *RHAY* LS8...................84 C5
Prince's Ct *AL/HA/HU * LS17........83 H3
Prince's Crs *ECHL* BD2................97 K2
Prince's Ga *HIPP* HX3.................154 C4
Prince's Gv *HDGY* LS6..................82 C7
Princess Av *EARL* WF12.............181 K1
Princess Cl *AL/HA/HU* LS17.........83 J1
  NORM WF6................................167 F7
Princess Crs *EARL* WF12............181 K2
Princess Flds *MSTN/BAR* LS15...106 A7
Princess La *EARL* WF12..............181 K1
Princes Sq *LDS* LS1......................13 L2
Princess Rd *EARL* WF12..............181 K1
  ILK LS29....................................23 K6
Princess St *BRIG* HD6................157 G6
  BTLY WF17...............................161 F2
  CAS WF10.................................148 D6
  EARL WF12...............................181 K1
  GTL/HWG HX4 ....175 G2
  HFAX HX1...................................17 H5
  NORM WF6................................166 E6
  RPDN/SBR HX6.........................153 K4
  WKFDE WF1...............................164 C4
  WKFDE WF1...............................184 E7
  YEA LS19...................................59 H7
Princes St *HECK* WF16...............160 B4
  WBSY BD6................................116 D7
  WBSY BD6................................117 G6
Prince St *AIRE* BD20....................32 E1
  BOW BD4.................................118 D5
  *BTLY * WF17..............................161 F2
  CAS WF10.................................127 H7
  DEWS WF13..............................181 G1
  HWTH BD22................................72 E5
Prince's Wy *WBOW* BD5................5 L7
Princeville Rd *GTHN* BD7...............4 E6
Princeville St *GTHN* BD7...............4 E6
Prince Wood La *HUDN* HD2........176 B7
Priordale Rd *FEA/AMT* WF7........188 A5
Priors Ter *GTL/HWG * HX4...........174 C5
Prior St *KGHY* BD21.......................3 K2
Priory Cl *BGLY* BD16....................55 K7
  MIRF WF14...............................179 F3
  NORM WF6................................166 C4
  OSS WF5...................................182 C5
  WBY LS22...................................29 J3
Priory Ct *GIR * BD8..........................5 J3
Priory Gv *BGLY* BD16...................55 K7
Priory Ms *EARD/LOFT* WF3........165 G2
Priory Park Gv
  GFTH/SHER LS25......................131 J6
Priory Pl *HUDN* HD2...................178 A4
Priory Rd *BRIC* HD6.....................157 H7
  FEA/AMT WF7............................188 B5
Priory Wk *MIRF* WF14.................179 F3
Priory Wy *MIRF* WF14.................179 F3
Privilege St *WOR/ARM* LS12......102 A7
Proctor St *BOW* BD4...................118 E5
Prod Ga *BAIL* BD17.......................76 D2
Prod La *BAIL* BD17........................76 D2

Progress Av *BGLY* BD16...............74 D3
Prospect Av *BRAM* LS13.............101 F2
  GFTH/SHER LS25......................111 G6
  LUD/ILL HX2.............................154 B4
  NORM WF6................................166 D5
  PDSY/CALV LS28.......................100 A5
  SHPY BD18.................................77 H5
Prospect Bank
  BSPA/BRAM LS23.......................48 C7
Prospect Cl *LUD/ILL* HX2............154 B4
  SHPY BD18.................................77 H5
Prospect Ct *LUD/ILL* HX2...........133 J7
  TAD LS24...................................50 E7
Prospect Crs *HWTH* BD22............53 F6
  MID LS10..................................123 J4
Prospect Dr *HWTH* BD22.............53 F6
  TAD LS24...................................50 E6
Prospect Gdns
  MSTN/BAR LS15........................105 H5
Prospect Gv *PDSY/CALV* LS28....100 A5
  SHPY BD18.................................77 H5
Prospect La *BIRK/DRI* BD11........139 J2
Prospect Mt *HWTH* BD22.............53 F6
  SHPY BD18.................................77 H5
Prospect Pl *BRIG* HD6.................157 F6
  EARD/LOFT WF3........................144 C5
  ECHL BD2...................................98 D3
  HORS LS18.................................80 E4
  HTON BD9....................................4 B1
  LUD/ILL HX2.............................134 C4
  *RPDN/SBR * HX6.........................152 E5
  RTHW LS26...............................145 G3
Prospect Rd *BFDE* BD3...................6 D3
  BGLY BD16.................................56 B6
  CLECK BD19.............................138 E7
  HECK WF16...............................159 K2
  ILK LS29....................................38 A2
  LVSG WF15...............................158 E6
  OSS WF5...................................182 C4
Prospect Sq *PDSY/CALV* LS28....100 A3
Prospect St *BOW* BD4....................6 B9
  *BTLY * WF17..............................161 F2
  CLECK BD19.............................158 E1
  CUL/QBY BD13...........................95 H7
  HIPP HX3...................................17 J3
  HWTH BD22..................................2 A7
  HWTH BD22................................72 D6
  IDLE BD10..................................78 D7
  *PDSY/CALV * LS28.......................99 K5
  PDSY/CALV LS28.......................100 A2
  SHPY BD18.................................77 H5
  WBSY BD6................................116 E7
  YEA LS19...................................79 K1
Prospect Ter *BRAM* LS13............101 F2
  CLECK BD19.............................138 E7
  GFTH/SHER LS25......................109 F7
  LVSG WF15...............................159 H4
  RTHW LS26...............................145 G3
  WIL/AL BD15..............................96 B4
Prospect Vw *BRAM* LS13............101 F2
  LVSG WF15...............................158 E6
Prospect Wk *SHPY* BD18..............77 H5
Prosper St *MID* LS10.....................14 E7
Providence Av *BAIL* BD17.............57 H7
  HDGY LS6....................................9 K1
Providence Ct *MOR * LS27...........141 K2
Providence Crs *HWTH* BD22........72 D2
Providence Gn *PONT* WF8...........169 K5
Providence La *HWTH* BD22..........72 D2
Providence Pl *BRIG * HD6............157 H7
  GFTH/SHER LS25......................107 H6
  *PDSY/CALV * LS28.......................100 B4
  RTHW LS26...............................148 A4
Providence Rd *HDGY* LS6...............9 K1
Providence Rw *BAIL* BD17............57 H7
  LUD/ILL HX2.............................134 C4
Providence St *BFD* BD1..................5 K6
  BTLY WF17...............................161 F3
  *CLECK * BD19.............................137 K7
  *CLECK * BD19.............................139 F7
  EARL WF12...............................181 J2
  ELL HX5...................................175 J2
  OSM LS9....................................14 F1
  PDSY/CALV LS28.......................100 A3
  WKFDE WF1...............................18 E4
Providence Ter *CUL/QBY* BD13....95 G7
  LDSU LS2....................................9 K3
Prune Park La *WIL/AL* BD15.........95 K4
Pudsey Rd *BRAM* LS13................100 E6
Pugneys Rd *WKFDW/WTN* WF2...184 D7
Pule Green La *HIPP* HX3..............134 E4
Pullan Av *ECHL* BD2.....................98 D1
Pullan Dr *ECHL* BD2.....................98 D1
Pullan Gv *ECHL* BD2.....................98 D1
Pullan La *BAIL* BD17.....................58 D6
Pullan St *WBOW* BD5..................117 J1
Pumphouse La *MIRF* WF14.........179 J3
Pump La *DEWS* WF13..................180 C1
  EARD/LOFT WF3........................162 D3
Purbeck Ct *BOW * BD4.................119 F4
Purbeck Gv *GFTH/SHER* LS25.....107 J7
Purcell Dr *AIRE* BD20....................20 E7
Purley Wk *WBSY* BD6.................117 G6
Purlwell Av *BTLY* WF17...............160 E5
Purlwell Crs *BTLY* WF17..............160 E5
Purlwell Hall Rd *BTLY* WF17.......161 F5
Purlwell La *BTLY* WF17...............160 E5
Purston Park Ct *FEA/AMT* WF7...188 C5
Pye Nest Av *LUD/ILL* HX2...........154 A3
Pye Nest Ct *LVSG* WF15.............158 E4
Pye Nest Dr *LUD/ILL* HX2...........154 B4
Pye Nest Gdns *LUD/ILL* HX2.......154 B3
Pye Nest Gv *LUD/ILL* HX2...........154 A3
Pye Nest Ri *LUD/ILL* HX2............154 B4
Pye Nest Rd *RPDN/SBR* HX6......154 A4
Pyenot Av *CLECK* BD19...............159 F2
Pyenot Dr *CLECK* BD19...............159 F2
Pyenot Gdns *CLECK* BD19..........159 F2
Pyenot Hall La *CLECK* BD19........159 F1
Pymont Ct *EARD/LOFT* WF3........144 D6
Pymont Dr *RTHW* LS26................125 J7
Pymont Gv *RTHW* LS26...............125 J7
Pym St *MID* LS10..........................14 E6
Pynate Rd *BTLY* WF17................160 D2
Pyrah Rd *LM/WK* BD12...............117 J7
Pyrah St *DEWS* WF13.................161 F7
  LM/WK BD12.............................137 J3

Q

Quail St *KGHY* * BD21 ....3 J3
Quaker La *CLECK* BD19 ....158 E2
  WBOW BD5 ....117 K5
Quakers La *RPDN/SBR* HX6 ......172 E7
  YEA LS19 ....59 J6
Quarrie Dene Ct *CHAL* * LS7 ......83 H6
The Quarry *AL/HA/HU* LS17 ....63 F5
Quarry Av *KNOT* WF11 ....171 H5
Quarry Bank Ct *KSTL* LS5 ....81 J5
Quarry Ct *CAS* WF10 ....168 C2
Quarry Dene *BHP/TINH* LS16 .....82 B4
Quarrydene Dr *CAS* LS7 ....169 G2
Quarry Dene Pk *BHP/TINH* LS16 ...82 B4
Quarry Farm Rd *OT* LS21 ....40 D5
Quarryfields *MIRF* WF14 ....179 J2
Quarry Gdns *AL/HA/HU* LS17 ......63 F5
Quarry HI *OSM* LS9 ....10 D9
  RPDN/SBR HX6 ....153 J5
  RTHW LS26 ....145 K1
Quarry Hill La *WBY* LS22 ....29 G3
Quarry La *BTLY* WF17 ....140 C6
  MOR LS27 ....142 A5
  MOR LS27 ....161 K1
Quarry Mt *HDGY* LS6 ....103 F1
Quarry Mount St *HDGY* LS6 ....9 K1
Quarry Mount Ter *HDGY* LS6 ....9 K1
Quarry PI *ECHL* BD2 ....98 C3
  HDGY LS6 ....9 K2
  MIRF WF14 ....178 E3
Quarry Rd *CLECK* BD19 ....158 D1
  CLECK BD19 ....159 J1
  DEWS WF13 ....180 B2
  HIPP HX3 ....134 B5
  LVSG WF15 ....159 H4
  OT LS21 ....40 D5
  RTHW LS26 ....146 A1
Quarryside Rd *MIRF* WF14 ....179 F3
Quarry St *HDGY* LS6 ....9 K1
  HTON BD9 ....97 F1
  KGHY BD21 ....3 K5
Quarry Vw *DEWS* WF13 ....160 C7
Quayside *BAIL* BD17 ....77 G4
Quebec St *ELL* HX5 ....175 K3
  KGHY BD21 ....2 F5
  LDS LS1 ....9 L9
  WKFDE/WTN WF2 ....18 C5
Queen Elizabeth Dr
  NORM WF6 ....186 D1
Queen Elizabeth Gv
  WKFDE WF1 ....19 J2
Queen Elizabeth Rd
  WKFDE WF1 ....19 J2
Queen Elizabeth St
  WKFDE WF1 ....164 B4
Queen Margarets Av
  KNOT WF11 ....150 E7
Queen Margarets Cl
  KNOT * WF11 ....150 E7
Queen Margaret's Dr
  KNOT WF11 ....150 E7
Queens Ar *KNOT* LS10 ....10 A9
Queen's Av *ECHL* BD2 ....98 C4
  PONT WF8 ....189 F2
Queensbury Av *WKFDE* WF1 ....164 D3
Queensbury Ct *NORM* WF6 ....167 F7
Queensbury Rd *HIPP* HX3 ....134 C2
Queensbury Sq
  CUL/QBY * BD13 ....115 H5
Queens Cl *BGLY* BD16 ....76 A2
  CHAL LS7 ....83 H4
Queenscourt *MOR* * LS27 ....141 K3
Queen's Crs *HOR/CROF* WF4 ......187 F5
  OSS WF5 ....182 C4
Queen's Dr *EARD/LOFT* WF3 ......144 E4
  ILK LS29 ....23 J6
  OSS WF5 ....182 D5
  PDSY/CALV LS28 ....100 A3
  WKFDW/WTN WF2 ....163 K7
Queens Drive Cl *OSS* WF5 ....182 C5
Queen's Drive La *ILK* LS29 ....23 J6
Queen's Gdns *ILK* LS29 ....23 K6
  OSS WF5 ....182 C4
  TAD LS24 ....70 D1
Queensgate *BFD* BD1 ....5 M6
Queen's Ga *HIPP* HX3 ....154 E4
Queens Gv *KGHY* BD21 ....2 E5
  MOR LS27 ....141 J4
Queenshill Av *AL/HA/HU* LS17 .....83 H2
Queenshill Cl *AL/HA/HU* * LS17 ....83 H2
Queenshill Ct *AL/HA/HU* * LS17 ....83 H1
Queenshill Crs *AL/HA/HU* LS17 ....83 H1
Queenshill Dr *AL/HA/HU* LS17 .....83 H2
Queenshill Gdns *AL/HA/HU* LS17 ...83 G2
Queenshill Garth
  AL/HA/HU LS17 ....83 H2
Queenshill Rd *AL/HA/HU* LS17 .....83 H2
Queenshill Vw *AL/HA/HU* LS17 ....83 H1
Queenshill Wk *AL/HA/HU* LS17 ....83 H1
Queenshill Wy *AL/HA/HU* LS17 ....83 H1
Queens Md *HIPP* * HX3 ....135 K4
Queens Park Cl *CAS* WF10 ....149 G7
Queen's Park Dr *CAS* WF10 ....169 F1
Queen's PI *MOR* LS27 ....141 K3
  OT LS21 ....39 H3
  SHPY BD18 ....76 E2
Queen's Prom *MOR* LS27 ....141 K3
Queen's Ri *ECHL* BD2 ....98 A2
Queen Sq *LDSU* LS2 ....10 A7
Queen's Ri *ECHL* BD2 ....98 A2
Queen Sq *LDSU* LS2 ....10 A7
Queen's Rd *BGLY* BD16 ....55 H5
  BSPA/BRAM LS23 ....48 B2
  CAS WF10 ....169 F1
  ECHL BD2 ....97 K3
  HDGY LS6 ....8 F4
  HFAX HX1 ....16 B4
  HIPP HX3 ....136 E5
  ILK LS29 ....23 K6
  KGHY BD21 ....2 E5
  MOR LS27 ....141 J4
  PONT WF8 ....189 F2
  SHPY BD18 ....76 E2
Queen's Ct *LDS* LS1 ....9 H7
Queen's Sq *PONT* WF8 ....189 F2
Queen's Ter *OSS* WF5 ....182 C4

Queensthorpe Av *BRAM* LS13 ....101 G5
Queensthorpe Cl *BRAM* LS13 ....101 H5
Queensthorpe Ri *BRAM* LS13.....101 G5
Queen St *AIRE* BD20 ....32 D5
  AIRE BD20 ....33 F1
  BAIL BD17 ....77 H3
  BGLY BD16 ....75 J1
  CAS WF10 ....148 D6
  CLECK BD19 ....139 J6
  CLECK BD19 ....159 F2
  DEWS WF13 ....180 B3
  EARD/LOFT WF3 ....143 J7
  EARD/LOFT WF3 ....144 E4
  EARL WF12 ....181 K1
  GTL/HWG HX4 ....175 J4
  HECK WF16 ....159 K5
  IDLE BD10 ....78 E5
  LDS LS1 ....13 K1
  MID LS10 ....124 B4
  MIRF WF14 ....179 H5
  MOR LS27 ....141 K3
  NORM WF6 ....166 D6
  OSS WF5 ....182 C4
  PONT WF8 ....189 G1
  RPDN/SBR HX6 ....153 F5
  RTHW LS26 ....147 H1
  WBSY BD6 ....116 D7
  WIL/AL BD15 ....95 F1
  WKFDE WF1 ....18 E5
  WKFDE WF1 ....164 C4
  YEA LS19 ....59 J7
Queens Vw *SCFT* * LS14 ....85 J7
Queen's Wk *OSS* WF5 ....182 E4
Queensway *BGLY* BD16 ....76 A2
  GFTH/SHER LS25 ....107 G6
  GSLY LS20 ....59 G2
  HIPP HX3 ....134 B5
  LVSG WF15 ....159 H4
  MOR LS27 ....141 K3
  MSTN/BAR LS15 ....105 K5
  NORM WF6 ....186 D2
  PONT WF8 ....170 A5
  RTHW LS26 ....145 F1
Queenswood Cl *HDGY* LS6 ....81 K5
Queenswood Ct *HDGY* LS6 ....102 A1
Queenswood Dr *HDGY* LS6 ....81 K6
Queenswood Gdns *HDGY* LS6 ....102 A1
Queenswood Gn *HDGY* LS6 ....81 K5
Queenswood Hts *HDGY* LS6 ....82 A7
Queenswood Mt *HDGY* LS6 ....82 A7
Queenswood Ri *HDGY* LS6 ....102 A1
Queenswood Rd *HDGY* LS6 ....81 K5
Queen Victoria Crs *HIPP* HX3 .....136 A4
Queen Victoria St *LDS* LS1 ....10 B9
Quincy Cl *ECHL* BD2 ....98 D1

R

Raby Av *CHAL* LS7 ....10 C2
Raby Pk *WBY* LS22 ....29 G4
Raby St *CHAL* LS7 ....10 C2
Raby Ter *CHAL* LS7 ....10 C2
Racca Av *KNOT* WF11 ....171 J4
Racca Gn *KNOT* WF11 ....171 H4
Race Moor La *HWTH* BD22 ....72 C1
Radcliffe Av *ECHL* BD2 ....78 B7
Radcliffe Gdns
  PDSY/CALV LS28 ....100 B6
Radcliffe La *LUD/ILL* HX2 ....132 D5
  PDSY/CALV LS28 ....100 B6
Radcliffe Pl *WKFDE* WF1 ....18 E4
Radcliffe Rd
  WKFDW/WTN WF2 ....183 J5
Radfield Dr *WBSY* BD6 ....117 K6
Radnor St *BFDE* BD3 ....7 J9
  WOR/ARM LS12 ....12 F3
Radwell Dr *WBOW* BD5 ....117 F7
Raeburn Dr *WBSY* BD6 ....117 F7
Rae Ct *EARD/LOFT* WF3 ....165 F3
Rae Rd *SHPY* BD18 ....77 F6
Raglan Av *HWTH* BD22 ....2 B6
Raglan Cl *HFAX* HX1 ....16 D5
Raglan Ct *HDGY* LS6 ....9 K2
Raglan Rd *HDGY* LS6 ....9 K2
Raglan St *BFDE* BD3 ....7 K6
  CUL/QBY BD13 ....115 H5
  HFAX HX1 ....16 D5
  HWTH BD22 ....2 B6
Raglan Ter *BFDE* BD3 ....7 L6
Raikes La *BOW* BD4 ....119 F7
  BOW BD4 ....119 H4
  BTLY WF17 ....140 B5
Raikes Wood Dr *BOW* BD4 ....119 F5
Railes Cl *LUD/ILL* HX2 ....132 E6
Railsfield Mt *BRAM* LS13 ....101 F3
Railsfield Ri *BRAM* LS13 ....101 F4
Railsfield Wy *BRAM* LS13 ....101 F3
Railway Av *PONT* WF8 ....169 H7
Railway Rd *IDLE* BD10 ....78 C4
  MSTN/BAR LS15 ....106 A3
Railway St *BOW* BD4 ....118 D5
  BRIG HD6 ....157 G7
  CLECK BD19 ....158 E1
  DEWS WF13 ....180 C3
  EARL WF12 ....181 G1
  HECK WF16 ....160 A5
  KGHY * BD21 ....53 K2
  OSM LS9 ....14 E1
Railway Ter *EARD/LOFT* WF3 ....143 H6
  HIPP HX3 ....154 D6
  NORM WF6 ....166 D6
Railway Vw *CAS* WF10 ....168 A1
Rainbow Ms *WBSY* * BD6 ....136 E1
Raincliffe Gv *OSM* LS9 ....11 J9
Raincliffe Mt *OSM* * LS9 ....15 K1
Raincliffe Rd *OSM* LS9 ....11 J9
Raincliffe St *OSM* LS9 ....15 K1
Raincliffe Ter *OSM* LS9 ....15 K1
Rainsborough Av *KNOT* WF11 .....170 E6
Raistrick Wy *SHPY* BD18 ....77 J4
Rakehill Rd *MSTN/BAR* LS15 ....86 C5
Raleigh St *HFAX* * HX1 ....16 B9
Rampart Rd *HDGY* LS6 ....9 J2
Ramsden Av *GTHN* BD7 ....116 D1
Ramsden Cl *KNOT* WF11 ....150 D7
Ramsden Ct *GTHN* BD7 ....117 D1
Ramsden Pl *CLAY* BD14 ....116 A1

Ramsden St *CAS* WF10 ....168 B3
  GFTH/SHER LS25 ....127 J6
  HIPP HX3 ....134 B5
Ramsey St *WBOW* BD5 ....117 J3
Ramsgate Ap *SCFT* LS14 ....85 H6
Ramsgate Crs *EARD/LOFT* WF3 ...144 C6
Ramsgate St *HFAX* HX1 ....16 A5
Ramshead Ap *SCFT* LS14 ....85 H6
Ramshead Cl *SCFT* LS14 ....85 H5
Ramshead Crs *SCFT* LS14 ....85 G5
Ramshead Dr *SCFT* LS14 ....85 H5
Ramshead Gdns *SCFT* LS14 ....85 G5
Ramshead Gv *SCFT* LS14 ....85 H6
Ramshead Hl *SCFT* LS14 ....85 H6
Ramshead Pl *SCFT* LS14 ....85 H6
Ramshead Rd *SCFT* LS14 ....85 H6
Ramshead Ter *BRAM* LS13 ....101 J2
Ramshead Vw *SCFT* LS14 ....85 H6
Randall Pl *HTON* BD9 ....97 F2
Randall Well St *BFD* BD1 ....5 K7
Randolph St *BFDE* BD3 ....7 L3
  BRAM LS13 ....100 D3
  HIPP HX3 ....17 G3
Random Cl *HWTH* BD22 ....2 A9
Rand Pl *GTHN* BD7 ....5 G9
Rand St *GTHN* BD7 ....5 G9
Ranelagh Av *IDLE* BD10 ....79 F7
Range Bank *HIPP* HX3 ....17 H2
Range Bank Top *HIPP* HX3 ....17 H1
Range Ct *HIPP* HX3 ....17 G2
Range Gdns *HIPP* HX3 ....17 H3
Range La *HIPP* HX3 ....17 H3
Range St *HIPP* HX3 ....17 G1
Ransdale Dr *WBOW* BD5 ....117 J3
Ransdale Gv *WBOW* BD5 ....117 J3
Ransdale Rd *WBOW* BD5 ....117 J3
Raper Vw *GFTH/SHER* LS25 ....88 D4
Rastrick Common *BRIG* HD6 ....177 F1
Rathlin Rd *EARL* WF12 ....181 H6
Rathmell Rd *MSTN/BAR* LS15 .....105 G7
Rathmell St *WBOW* BD5 ....117 J5
Ratten Row Rd
  RPDN/SBR HX6 ....152 D7
Raven Cl *FEA/AMT* WF7 ....168 A7
Raven Rd *HDGY* LS6 ....8 E1
Ravens Av *DEWS* WF13 ....180 D3
Ravenscar Av *RHAY* LS8 ....84 B6
Ravenscar Mt *RHAY* LS8 ....84 B6
Ravenscar Ter *RHAY* LS8 ....84 B6
Ravenscar Vw *RHAY* LS8 ....84 B6
Ravenscar Wk *RHAY* * LS8 ....84 B6
Ravenscliffe Av *IDLE* BD10 ....79 F7
Ravenscliffe Rd
  PDSY/CALV LS28 ....79 F6
Ravens Crs *DEWS* WF13 ....180 D3
Ravensfield Rd *DEWS* WF13 ....180 D3
Ravens Gv *DEWS* WF13 ....180 D3
Ravenshouse Rd *DEWS* WF13 .....180 C2
Ravens Lodge Ter
  DEWS * WF13 ....180 D3
Ravensmead *FEA/AMT* WF7 ....188 E4
Ravens Mt *PDSY/CALV* LS28 ....100 C6
Ravens St *DEWS* WF13 ....180 D3
Ravensthorpe Rd *EARL* WF12 ......180 C5
Ravenstone Dr *GTL/HWG* HX4 .....175 F3
Raven St *BGLY* BD16 ....75 K1
  HFAX HX1 ....16 B5
  KGHY BD21 ....2 F4
Ravens Wk *DEWS* WF13 ....180 D3
Ravenswharf Rd *DEWS* WF13 ......180 D3
Ravensworth Cl
  MSTN/BAR LS15 ....106 C2
Ravensworth Wy
  MSTN/BAR LS15 ....106 C2
Raven Ter *GIR* BD8 ....96 B6
Rawden Hl *OT* LS21 ....42 D4
Rawdon Dr *YEA* LS19 ....79 J1
Rawdon Hall Dr *YEA* LS19 ....79 J1
Rawdon Rd *HORS* LS18 ....80 B3
  HWTH BD22 ....72 D5
Rawdon St *HWTH* BD22 ....2 C7
Raw End Rd *LUD/ILL* HX2 ....133 H7
Rawfield La *GFTH/SHER* LS25 .....150 D1
Rawfolds Av *BTLY* WF17 ....140 C5
Rawfolds Wy *CLECK* BD19 ....159 F2
Rawgate Av *CAS* WF10 ....147 J7
Raw Hl *BRIG* * HD6 ....176 E1
Raw La *LUD/ILL* HX2 ....134 A2
  TAD LS24 ....71 F7
Rawling St *KGHY* BD21 ....2 E9
Rawling Wy *HDGY* LS6 ....82 E7
Raw Nook *LM/WK* BD12 ....138 A2
Rawroyds *GTL/HWG* HX4 ....175 F5
Rawson Av *BFDE* BD3 ....7 K3
  HIPP HX3 ....154 E5
Rawson Pl *BFD* BD1 ....5 L5
  RPDN/SBR HX6 ....153 H5
Rawson Rd *BFD* BD1 ....5 K5
Rawson Sq *BFD* BD1 ....5 L5
  IDLE BD10 ....78 C3
Rawson St *HFAX* HX1 ....17 G6
  LM/WK BD12 ....137 J3
Rawson St North *HIPP* HX3 ....16 E1
Rawson Ter *BEE/HOL* * LS11 ....123 H3
Rayfield *WKFDW/WTN* WF2 ....184 A4
Ray Ga *HBP* HX7 ....112 A7
Raygill Cl *AL/HA/HU* LS17 ....64 C6
Raylands Ct *MID* LS10 ....144 A1
Raylands Fold *MID* LS10 ....144 A1
Raylands Garth *MID* LS10 ....144 A1
Raylands La *MID* LS10 ....144 A1
Raylands Pl *MID* LS10 ....144 A1
Raylands Rd *MID* LS10 ....144 A1
Raylands Wy *MID* LS10 ....144 A2
Rayleigh St *BOW* BD4 ....118 B2
Raymond Dr *WBOW* BD5 ....117 K4
Raymond St *WBOW* BD5 ....117 K5
Raynbron Crs *WBOW* BD5 ....118 A4
Raynel Ap *BHP/TINH* LS16 ....81 J1
Raynel Cl *BHP/TINH* LS16 ....61 J7
Raynel Dr *BHP/TINH* LS16 ....81 K1
Raynel Gdns *BHP/TINH* LS16 ....61 K7
Raynel Garth *BHP/TINH* LS16.......81 K1
Raynel Gn *BHP/TINH* LS16 ....81 K1
Raynel Mt *BHP/TINH* LS16 ....81 K1
Raynel Wy *BHP/TINH* LS16 ....61 J7
Rayner Av *GIR* BD8 ....4 B1
  HECK WF16 ....160 A2

Rayner Dr *BRIG* HD6 ....157 F4
Rayner Mt *WIL/AL* BD15 ....96 A5
Rayner Rd *BRIG* HD6 ....157 F4
Rayners Av *LVSG* WF15 ....158 D4
Raynham Crs *HWTH* BD22 ....53 F5
Raynville Ap *BRAM* LS13 ....101 H3
Raynville Av *BRAM* LS13 ....101 J2
Raynville Crs *WOR/ARM* LS12 .....101 J3
Raynville Dr *BRAM* LS13 ....101 H2
Raynville Gn *BRAM* LS13 ....101 H3
Raynville Mt *BRAM* LS13 ....101 H2
Raynville Pl *BRAM* LS13 ....101 J2
Raynville Ri *BRAM* LS13 ....101 H3
Raynville Rd *WOR/ARM* LS12 ......101 J2
Raynville Ter *BRAM* LS13 ....101 H2
Raynville Wk *BRAM* LS13 ....101 H3
Raynville Wy *BRAM* LS13 ....101 H3
Raywood Cl *YEA* LS19 ....59 J1
Reap Hirst Rd *HUDN* HD2 ....176 C7
Rebecca St *GIR* BD8 ....5 J4
Recreation Av *BEE/HOL* * LS11 .....13 J7
Recreation Crs *BEE/HOL* LS11 ....13 H7
Recreation La *ELL* HX5 ....175 H3
Recreation Pl *BEE/HOL* LS11 ....13 H7
Recreation Rd *RPDN/SBR* HX6 ....153 J4
Recreation St *BEE/HOL* LS11 ....13 H7
Recreation Ter *BEE/HOL* LS11 ....13 H7
Recreation Vw *BEE/HOL* LS11 ....13 H7
Rectory Cl *GFTH/SHER* LS25 ....107 J6
Rectory Dr *BTLY* WF17 ....140 D6
Rectory Rw *KGHY* BD21 ....2 F5
Rectory St *CAS* WF10 ....148 C7
  OSM LS9 ....10 F6
Rectory Vw *EARL* WF12 ....181 H6
Red Beck Rd *HIPP* HX3 ....135 J6
Red Beck V *SHPY* BD18 ....77 F7
Red Brink La *RPDN/SBR* HX6 ....152 C6
Redburn Av *SHPY* BD18 ....77 F7
Redburn Dr *SHPY* BD18 ....77 F7
Redburn Rd *SHPY* BD18 ....77 F7
Redcar La *AIRE* BD20 ....52 C1
Redcar Rd *IDLE* BD10 ....79 F6
Redcar St *HFAX* HX1 ....16 A5
Redcliffe Av *KGHY* BD21 ....2 D4
Redcliffe Gv *KGHY* BD21 ....2 D4
Redcliffe St *KGHY* BD21 ....2 C4
Redcote La *BULY* LS4 ....8 A6
Red Doles Rd *HUDN* HD2 ....177 H7
Redesdale Gdns *BHP/TINH* LS16 ...82 A1
Redfearn Av *HECK* WF16 ....160 A3
Red Hall Ap *SCFT* LS14 ....85 H3
Red Hall Av *AL/HA/HU* LS17 ....85 G3
Redhall Cl *BEE/HOL* LS11 ....122 D5
Red Hall Ct *SCFT* LS14 ....85 H3
Redhall Crs *BEE/HOL* LS11 ....122 D5
Red Hall Cft *SCFT* LS14 ....85 H4
Red Hall Dr *SCFT* LS14 ....85 H3
Red Hall Gdns *AL/HA/HU* LS17 .....85 H3
Red Hall Garth *SCFT* LS14 ....85 H3
Redhall Ga *BEE/HOL* LS11 ....122 D5
Red Hall La *AL/HA/HU* LS17 ....85 G3
  WKFDE WF1 ....164 B7
Red Hall Vw *SCFT* * LS14 ....85 H3
Red Hall Wk *SCFT* LS14 ....85 H3
Red Hall Wy *SCFT* LS14 ....85 H3
Redhill Av *CAS* WF10 ....168 E2
Redhill Cl *EARD/LOFT* WF3 ....162 D3
Redhill Crs *EARD/LOFT* WF3 ....162 D3
Redhill Dr *CAS* WF10 ....169 F1
  EARD/LOFT WF3 ....162 D3
Redhill Gdns *CAS* WF10 ....169 F1
Red Hill La *GFTH/SHER* LS25 ....130 D5
Redhill Mt *CAS* WF10 ....169 F1
Redhill Rd *CAS* WF10 ....169 F1
Redhill Vw *CAS* WF10 ....169 F2
Redhouse La *CHAL* * LS7 ....83 K5
Red Laithes La *DEWS* WF13 ....180 B3
Red La *FEA/AMT* WF7 ....187 H4
  PDSY/CALV LS28 ....99 K2
  WKFDE WF1 ....186 B4
Red Lodge Cl *RHAY* LS8 ....104 E1
Redman Garth *HWTH* BD22 ....72 C5
Redmayne Gv *KNOT* WF11 ....170 E4
Redmire Ct *SCFT* LS14 ....105 H1
Redmire Dr *SCFT* LS14 ....105 H1
Redmire St *BFDE* BD3 ....7 L6
Redmire Vw *SCFT* LS14 ....105 H1
Redruth Dr *NORM* WF6 ....166 E5
Redshaw Rd *WOR/ARM* LS12 ....12 C3
Red V *CLECK* BD19 ....139 J5
Redvers Cl *BHP/TINH* LS16 ....81 K3
Redwood Av *EARD/LOFT* WF3 .....143 F7
Redwood Gv *HOR/CROF* WF4 ......187 F5
Redwood Wy *YEA* LS19 ....59 G4
Reedling Dr *MOR* LS27 ....142 B4
Reed Rd *WOR/ARM* LS12 ....12 B3
Reedsdale Av *MOR* LS27 ....121 F7
Reedsdale Dr *MOR* LS27 ....121 F7
Reedsdale Gdns *MOR* LS27 ....121 F7
Rees Wy *BFDE* BD3 ....6 B3
Reeth Rd *BRIG* HD6 ....176 D1
Reevy Av *WBSY* BD6 ....116 E6
Reevy Crs *WBSY* BD6 ....116 D7
Reevy Dr *WBSY* BD6 ....117 F6
Reevylands Dr *WBSY* BD6 ....117 F6
Reevy Rd *WBSY* BD6 ....116 D6
Reevy Rd West *WBSY* BD6 ....116 D6
Reevy St *WBSY* BD6 ....116 E6
Reform St *CLECK* BD19 ....139 J6
Regency Ct *GIR* BD8 ....4 D3
  HDGY LS6 ....8 E1
  ILK LS29 ....23 K6
Regency Gdns
  EARD/LOFT WF3 ....143 F7
Regency Park Gv
  PDSY/CALV LS28 ....120 B1
Regency Park Rd
  PDSY/CALV LS28 ....120 B1
Regency Rd *MIRF* WF14 ....179 H5
Regency Vw *BFDE* BD3 ....98 B3

Regent Av *HORS* LS18 ....81 F5
Regent Cl *BRIG* HD6 ....176 D3
Regent Ct *LDS* * LS1 ....14 B1
Regent Crs *HORS* LS18 ....80 E5
Regent Ms *BTLY* WF17 ....161 J4
Regent Park Av *HDGY* LS6 ....9 H1
Regent Park Cross Av *HDGY* LS6 ....9 H1
Regent Park Ter *HDGY* LS6 ....9 H1
Regent Pl *IDLE* BD10 ....78 B3
  RPDN/SBR HX6 ....153 J3
Regent Rd *HORS* LS18 ....80 E5
  HUDE HD5 ....178 D7
  ILK LS29 ....23 K5
Regents Pk *WKFDE* WF1 ....19 J5
Regent St *CAS* WF10 ....168 D5
  CHAL LS7 ....83 H5
  CUL/QBY BD13 ....115 G3
  FEA/AMT WF7 ....188 C4
  HECK WF16 ....159 K5
  HFAX HX1 ....16 F7
  IDLE BD10 ....78 E5
  IDLE * BD10 ....78 E5
  MIRF WF14 ....179 H6
  NORM WF6 ....167 F5
  OSM LS9 ....10 D8
  WKFDE WF1 ....19 K9
Regent Ter *HDGY* LS6 ....9 G5
Regina Dr *CHAL* LS7 ....83 J6
Reginald Mt *CHAL* LS7 ....103 J1
Reginald Pl *CHAL* LS7 ....103 J1
Reginald Rw *CHAL* LS7 ....103 J1
Reginald St *CHAL* LS7 ....103 J1
  WBOW BD5 ....117 J3
Reginald Ter *CHAL* LS7 ....103 J1
Reginald Vw *CHAL* LS7 ....103 J1
Reighton Cft *IDLE* BD10 ....79 F6
The Rein *SCFT* LS14 ....85 C6
Rein Closet *GFTH/SHER* LS25 ....88 D4
Rein Gdns *EARD/LOFT* WF3 ....142 E7
Rein Ms *EARD/LOFT* WF3 ....142 E7
Rein Rd *BRAM* LS13 ....81 F6
  EARD/LOFT WF3 ....142 E7
Reins Av *BAIL* BD17 ....77 G3
Reins Rd *BRIG* HD6 ....176 D1
Rein St *MOR* LS27 ....142 B6
Reinwood Av *RHAY* LS8 ....84 C1
Rembrandt Av
  EARD/LOFT WF3 ....142 E7
Renee Cl *BOW* BD4 ....118 D6
Renfield Gv *NORM* WF6 ....167 G5
Renshaw St *IDLE* BD10 ....78 C3
Renton Av *GSLY* LS20 ....58 E2
Renton Dr *GSLY* LS20 ....58 E3
Reservoir Pl *CUL/QBY* BD13 ....115 F4
Reservoir Rd *LUD/ILL* HX2 ....134 B7
Reservoir St *DEWS* WF13 ....160 D7
Reservoir Vw *CUL/QBY* BD13 ....95 F7
Restmore Av *GSLY* LS20 ....38 C7
Retford Pl *GTHN* BD7 ....5 H9
Reuben St *LVSG* WF15 ....159 H3
Reva Cl *BGLY* BD16 ....56 A7
Reva Syke Rd *CLAY* BD14 ....116 A3
Revie Rd *BEE/HOL* LS11 ....13 G9
Reydon Wk *WBSY* BD6 ....116 E5
Reyhill Gv *WBOW* BD5 ....5 M9
Reyner House Ms *WBOW* BD5 ....5 M9
Reynolds Av *GTHN* BD7 ....116 D1
Rhine St *BOW* BD4 ....118 B1
Rhodes Av *HECK* WF16 ....160 A2
Rhodes Crs *PONT* WF8 ....189 J3
Rhodes Gdns *EARD/LOFT* WF3 ....164 C1
Rhode's Hill La
  BSPA/BRAM LS23 ....48 D7
Rhodesia Av *HIPP* HX3 ....155 F5
  WIL/AL BD15 ....96 B5
Rhodes La *BSPA/BRAM* LS23 ....48 A5
Rhodes Pl *SHPY* BD18 ....77 G4
Rhodes St *CAS* WF10 ....168 A1
  HFAX HX1 ....16 F6
  LVSG WF15 ....159 K4
  SHPY BD18 ....77 F4
Rhodes Ter *WOR/ARM* LS12 ....12 E3
Rhodes Wy *GIR* BD8 ....96 C4
Rhodesway *GIR* BD8 ....96 C6
Rhondda Pl *HFAX* HX1 ....154 B1
Rhum Cl *WBSY* BD6 ....136 E1
Rhylstone Mt *GTHN* BD7 ....4 B6
Rhyl St *FEA/AMT* WF7 ....188 D2
Ribblesdale Av
  GFTH/SHER LS25 ....108 A3
Ribble St *KGHY* BD21 ....3 M3
Ribbleton Gv *BFDE* BD3 ....6 C4
Riccall Nook *IDLE* BD10 ....78 E6
Richardshaw La
  PDSY/CALV LS28 ....100 B4
Richardshaw Rd
  PDSY/CALV LS28 ....100 C4
Richardson Av *WBSY* BD6 ....117 H6
Richardson Crs *OSM* LS9 ....15 M2
Richardson Rd *OSM* LS9 ....15 M1
Richardson St *LM/WK* BD12 ....138 D3
Richard St *BFDE* BD3 ....6 C6
  BRIG HD6 ....157 F7
  WKFDE WF1 ....19 K6
Richard Thorpe Av *MIRF* WF14 ....179 J4
Richmond Av *HDGY* LS6 ....8 E2
  HUDN HD2 ....177 J7
  KNOT WF11 ....170 C3
  RPDN/SBR HX6 ....153 C5
Richmond Cl *BRAM* LS13 ....100 D3
  HFAX HX1 ....16 F4
  MOR LS27 ....141 K4
  RTHW LS26 ....125 G7
Richmond Ct *RTHW* * LS26 ....145 G1
Richmond Cft *OSM* * LS9 ....15 H2
Richmondfield Av
  MSTN/BAR LS15 ....87 H6
Richmondfield Cl
  MSTN/BAR LS15 ....87 H6
Richmondfield Crs
  MSTN/BAR LS15 ....87 H6
Richmondfield Cross
  MSTN/BAR LS15 ....87 H6
Richmondfield Dr
  MSTN/BAR LS15 ....87 H6
Richmondfield Garth
  MSTN/BAR LS15 ....87 H5

Richmondfield Gv
  MSTN/BAR LS15 ....87 H6
Richmondfield La
  MSTN/BAR LS15 ....87 H6
Richmondfield Mt
  MSTN/BAR LS15 ....87 H6
Richmondfield Wy
  MSTN/BAR LS15 ....87 H6
Richmond Gdns
  PDSY/CALV LS28 ....100 D6
  RPDN/SBR HX6 ....153 G5
Richmond Garth OSS WF5 ....182 E5
Richmond Green St OSM LS9 ....14 F2
Richmond Gv CLECK BD19 ....139 J5
Richmond Hill Ap OSM LS9 ....14 F2
Richmond Hill Cl OSM LS9 ....14 F2
Richmond Lea MIRF WF14 ....179 H3
Richmond Ms SHPY BD18 ....76 E4
Richmond Mt HDGY LS6 ....8 E2
Richmond Park Av LVSG WF15 ....159 H5
Richmond Pl SHPY BD18 ....76 E4
Richmond Rd GTHN BD7 ....5 H6
  HDGY LS6 ....8 F1
  HECK WF16 ....160 B2
  HFAX HX1 ....16 F4
  PDSY/CALV LS28 ....99 K3
  SHPY * BD18 ....76 E4
  WKFDE WF1 ....184 C1
Richmond St CLECK BD19 ....158 E1
  HFAX HX1 ....16 F4
  KCHY BD21 ....2 E3
  OSM LS9 ....14 E2
Richmond Ter OT LS21 ....39 C3
  PDSY/CALV LS28 ....100 D6
Richmond Wy
  GFTH/SHER LS25 ....127 J1
Rickard St WOR/ARM LS12 ....13 C3
Ridding Ga OT LS21 ....39 F1
Riddings Cl HUDN HD2 ....177 J6
Riddings Ri HUDN HD2 ....177 J6
Riddings Rd HUDN HD2 ....177 K6
Riddlesden St * AIRE BD20 ....54 C2
Rider Rd HDGY LS6 ....9 L1
Rider St OSM LS9 ....10 E8
The Ridge WBY LS22 ....28 E6
Ridge Cl GSLY LS20 ....58 D3
Ridgedale Mt PONT WF8 ....169 H4
Ridgefield St CAS WF10 ....168 C1
Ridge Gv CHAL LS7 ....103 F1
Ridge Hl BRIG HD6 ....156 D7
Ridge La AIRE BD20 ....20 D2
Ridge Lea BRIG HD6 ....156 E7
Ridge Mt HDGY LS6 ....9 M1
Ridgemount Rd AIRE BD20 ....54 B1
Ridge Rd GFTH/SHER LS25 ....128 C4
  HDGY LS6 ....9M1
Ridge Ter HDGY LS6 ....82 D7
Ridge Vw BRAM LS13 ....101 F5
Ridge View Dr HUDN HD2 ....176 D7
Ridge View Gdns IDLE BD10 ....78 D5
Ridge View Rd BRIC * HD6 ....157 F7
Ridge Wy RHAY LS8 ....84 A6
The Ridgeway KNOT WF11 ....171 G5
Ridgeway CUL/QBY BD13 ....115 J6
  GSLY LS20 ....58 C3
  SHPY BD18 ....77 K6
Ridgeway Cl RHAY LS8 ....84 A6
Ridgeway Dr BTLY WF17 ....140 D6
Ridgeway Gdns BRIG HD6 ....156 D3
Ridgeway Mt HWTH BD22 ....2 A9
Ridgeway Sq KNOT WF11 ....171 G5
Ridgeway Ter HDGY * LS6 ....9 K1
Ridgewood Cl BAIL BD17 ....77 K1
Riding Head La LUD/ILL HX2 ....133 F6
Riding Hl HIPP HX3 ....136 D1
Riding La LUD/ILL HX2 ....133 K4
The Ridings AIRE BD20 ....33 J7
Ridings Cl EARD/LOFT WF3 ....164 C2
Ridings Ct EARD/LOFT WF3 ....164 C2
Ridings Gdns EARD/LOFT WF3 ....164 C2
Ridings La EARD/LOFT WF3 ....164 C2
Ridings Ms EARD/LOFT WF3 ....164 C2
Ridings Rd EARL WF12 ....181 C1
Riding St BTLY WF17 ....160 B2
Ridings Wy EARD/LOFT WF3 ....164 C2
  WBSY BD6 ....116 D6
Ridleys Fold ILK LS29 ....22 C1
Rievaulx Av GIR BD8 ....5 H3
Rievaulx Cl BSPA/BRAM LS23 ....48 B3
Rigton Ap OSM LS9 ....10 F8
Rigton Bank AL/HA/HU LS17 ....46 A6
Rigton Cl OSM LS9 ....11 G8
Rigton Dr OSM LS9 ....11 G8
Rigton Gn AL/HA/HU LS17 ....46 B6
  OSM LS9 ....10 F8
Rigton Lawn OSM LS9 ....10 F8
Rigton Ms OSM LS9 ....11 M5
Rigton St WBOW BD5 ....117 J3
Riley La LUD/ILL HX2 ....114 C6
Rillbank La BVRD LS3 ....8 F6
Rillbank St BVRD LS3 ....9 G6
Rillington Md IDLE BD10 ....78 E6
Rills Md OT LS21 ....39 H3
Rilston St GTHN BD7 ....4 E7
Rimswell Holt IDLE BD10 ....79 F6
Ringby La HIPP HX3 ....134 E5
Ringby Ter HIPP * HX3 ....134 E5
Ring Rd WOR/ARM LS12 ....12 A8
Ring Rd Adel BHP/TINH LS16 ....82 C2
Ring Rd Beeston
  WOR/ARM LS12 ....12 B8
Ring Rd Beeston Pk
  BEE/HOL LS11 ....142 E1
Ring Rd Bramley BRAM LS13 ....101 G5
Ring Rd Cross Gates
  MSTN/BAR LS15 ....105 K2
Ring Rd Farnley
  WOR/ARM LS12 ....101 G6
Ring Rd Farsley
  PDSY/CALV LS28 ....99 K2
Ring Rd Halton
  MSTN/BAR LS15 ....105 M2
Ring Rd Horsforth HORS LS18 ....81 H4
Ring Rd Low Wortley
  WOR/ARM LS12 ....12 A8
Ring Rd Meanwood
  BHP/TINH LS16 ....82 D2
Ring Rd Middleton MID LS10 ....143 J2

Ring Rd Moortown
  AL/HA/HU LS17 ....83 F2
Ring Rd Seacroft SCFT LS14 ....85 H4
Ring Rd Shadwell
  AL/HA/HU LS17 ....84 D2
Ring Rd Weetwood
  BHP/TINH LS16 ....82 B3
Ring Rd West Pk
  BHP/TINH LS16 ....81 K3
Ringway GFTH/SHER LS25 ....107 G7
Ringwood Av SCFT LS14 ....85 G4
Ringwood Ct WKFDE * WF1 ....164 E3
Ringwood Crs SCFT LS14 ....85 H3
Ringwood Dr SCFT LS14 ....85 H3
Ringwood Edge GTL/HWG HX4 ....175 F3
Ringwood Gdns SCFT LS14 ....85 H4
Ringwood Mt SCFT LS14 ....85 H4
Ringwood Rd WBOW BD5 ....117 G3
Rink St BTLY WF17 ....161 C5
Ripley Cl NORM WF6 ....167 G6
Ripley Ct NORM WF6 ....186 E1
Ripley Dr NORM WF6 ....167 G6
Ripley La GSLY LS20 ....59 F1
Ripley Rd BOW BD4 ....118 A2
  LVSG WF15 ....159 G4
Ripley St AIRE BD20 ....54 C2
  HIPP HX3 ....157 F1
  WBOW BD5 ....117 K2
  WIL/AL BD15 ....95 K3
Ripon Av HUDN HD2 ....177 F7
Ripon Rd EARL WF12 ....181 J1
Ripon St HFAX HX1 ....154 B2
Ripon Ter HIPP HX3 ....16 F1
Rippondene New Bank
  RPDN/SBR HX6 ....173 F5
Rippondene Old Bank
  RPDN/SBR HX6 ....173 F5
Rippondene Old La
  RPDN/SBR HX6 ....172 B6
The Rise HIPP HX3 ....135 K5
  KNOT WF11 ....150 D7
  KSTL LS5 ....81 K7
  PONT WF8 ....189 K7
Risedale Av BTLY WF17 ....140 E5
Risedale Cl BTLY WF17 ....140 E5
Rishworth Cl
  WKFDW/WTN WF2 ....163 K6
Rishworthian Ct HIPP * HX3 ....154 D7
Rishworth Rd EARL WF12 ....181 G1
  GTL/HWG HX4 ....173 H6
Rishworth St EARL WF12 ....181 G1
  HWTH BD22 ....2 B7
  WKFDE WF1 ....18 E3
Rivadale Vw ILK LS29 ....24 A5
Rivelin Rd CAS WF10 ....168 K3
Riverdale WBY LS22 ....29 J5
Riverdale Av EARD/LOFT WF3 ....165 G6
Riverdale Cl EARD/LOFT WF3 ....165 G6
Riverdale Crs EARD/LOFT WF3 ....165 G6
Riverdale Dr EARD/LOFT WF3 ....165 G6
Riverdale Gdns OT LS21 ....39 H2
Riverdale Rd EARD/LOFT WF3 ....165 G6
  OT LS21 ....39 H2
Rivermead WKFDW/WTN WF2 ....184 C6
River Mt AIRE BD20 ....54 C2
Riverside KGHY BD21 ....3 L4
Riverside Av OT LS21 ....27 J7
Riverside Cl OT LS21 ....39 J1
Riverside Ct LDS LS1 ....14 B2
Riverside Crs OT LS21 ....39 J1
Riverside Dr CLECK BD19 ....138 E6
  OT LS21 ....27 J7
Riverside Est BAIL BD17 ....77 F4
Riverside Pk OT LS21 ....39 J1
Riverside Vls
  WKFDW/WTN WF2 ....184 E7
Riverside Wk ILK LS29 ....23 J4
River St BRIG HD6 ....157 F1
  HWTH * BD22 ....72 E5
  KGHY BD21 ....3 L1
River Vw BSPA/BRAM LS23 ....48 E3
  MIRF WF14 ....178 E3
River Wk BGLY BD16 ....75 J1
Riverwood Dr HIPP HX3 ....154 E6
Riviera Gdns CHAL LS7 ....83 H6
Rivock Av AIRE BD20 ....32 E4
  AIRE BD20 ....33 G7
Rivock Gv AIRE BD20 ....53 G1
Roach Grange Av
  GFTH/SHER LS25 ....127 G1
Roans Brae IDLE BD10 ....79 F6
Robb Av BEE/HOL LS11 ....123 F5
Robbins Ter FEA/AMT WF7 ....188 C3
Robb St BEE/HOL LS11 ....123 F5
Roberson Ter CLECK BD19 ....139 H7
Roberts Av OSM LS9 ....11 M5
Roberts Ct OSM LS9 ....11 M5
Robertsgate EARD/LOFT WF3 ....144 C6
Robertson Av BRIG HD6 ....177 F1
Roberts Pl BFD BD1 ....5 K5
  OSM LS9 ....11 M6
Robert's St CLECK BD19 ....158 D1
  HWTH BD22 ....52 D5
  PDSY/CALV LS28 ....100 A4
  RTHW * LS26 ....145 K1
Robert St BFDE BD3 ....6 C7
  HIPP HX3 ....134 D5
  HWTH BD22 ....73 G4
Robert St North HIPP HX3 ....135 F5
Roberttown La LVSG WF15 ....159 F7
Robin Cha PDSY/CALV LS28 ....100 C6
Robin Cl ECHL BD2 ....98 D1
  PONT WF8 ....169 J5
Robin Dr AIRE BD20 ....32 C4
  ECHL BD2 ....98 D1
Robin Hl BTLY WF17 ....140 C7
Robin Hood Crs
  WKFDW/WTN WF2 ....183 J5
Robin Hood Gv HUDN HD2 ....177 H5
Robin Hood Rd HUDN HD2 ....177 H5
Robin Hood St CAS * WF10 ....168 D1
Robin Hood Wy BRIG HD6 ....157 K6
Robinia Wk WKFDW/WTN WF2 ....18 A1
Robin La DEWS WF13 ....160 C5
  PDSY/CALV LS28 ....100 B6
Robin Royd Av MIRF WF14 ....179 H1
Robin Royd Cft MIRF WF14 ....179 H1
Robin Royd Dr MIRF WF14 ....179 H1

Robin Royd Garth
  MIRF * WF14 ....179 H1
Robin Royd Gv MIRF * WF14 ....179 H1
Robin Royd La MIRF WF14 ....179 H2
The Robins ILK LS29 ....37 K2
Robinson Ct GTHN BD7 ....4 A7
Robinson St CAS WF10 ....148 A4
  PONT LS9 ....169 J7
Robin St WBOW * BD5 ....117 H2
Robin Wk SHPY BD18 ....77 J6
Robson Cl PONT WF8 ....189 J3
Rochdale Rd GTL/HWG HX4 ....174 B2
  LUD/ILL HX2 ....154 A3
  RPDN/SBR HX6 ....153 G6
  RPDN/SBR HX6 ....173 F4
Rocheford Cl MID LS10 ....15 G9
Rocheford Gdns MID LS10 ....15 G9
Rocheford Gv MID LS10 ....15 G9
Rocheford Wk MID LS10 ....15 G9
Rochester Ct HOR/CROF WF4 ....183 H6
Rochester Dr HOR/CROF WF4 ....183 H6
Rochester Gdns BRAM LS13 ....100 C1
Rochester Pl ELL * HX5 ....175 J3
Rochester Rd BTLY WF17 ....140 B4
Rochester St BFDE BD3 ....7 G6
  SHPY BD18 ....77 H6
Rochester Ter HDGY LS6 ....8 D1
Rochester Wynd
  AL/HA/HU LS17 ....64 B7
Rockcliffe Av BAIL BD17 ....77 H3
Rock Edge LVSG WF15 ....159 H3
Rockery Cft HORS LS18 ....81 F7
Rockery Rd HORS LS18 ....81 F2
Rockfield Ter YEA LS19 ....59 K4
Rock Hl CAS WF10 ....169 F2
Rockhill Cl BTLY WF17 ....140 C5
Rockhill La BOW BD4 ....118 B7
Rock House Dr DEWS WF13 ....161 F6
Rockingham Cl
  MSTN/BAR LS15 ....106 C2
Rockingham St TAD LS24 ....70 E7
Rockingham Rd
  MSTN/BAR LS15 ....106 C2
Rockingham Wy
  MSTN/BAR LS15 ....106 C2
Rockland Crs GTHN BD7 ....116 D1
Rocklands Av BAIL BD17 ....57 H7
Rocklands Pl BAIL BD17 ....57 H7
Rock La BRAM LS13 ....100 E1
  CUL/QBY BD13 ....95 F5
Rockley Grange Gdns
  GFTH/SHER LS25 ....127 G1
Rockley St EARL WF12 ....181 C1
Rocks La HIPP HX3 ....154 D5
Rock Rd BRIG HD6 ....157 F5
Rocks Vw LUD/ILL HX2 ....154 D4
Rock Ter CUL/QBY BD13 ....95 G7
  EARL * WF12 ....162 A2
  GIR BD8 ....5 K1
  HUDW HD3 ....175 K7
  MOR LS27 ....142 A2
  MSTN/BAR LS15 ....105 G6
Rock Vw GTL/HWG HX4 ....175 F5
Rockville Ter HFAX HX1 ....154 D3
Rockwell La IDLE BD10 ....78 D6
Rockwood Cl HUDN HD2 ....177 K3
Rockwood Crs
  PDSY/CALV LS28 ....99 H2
Rockwood Gv PDSY/CALV LS28 ....99 J3
Rockwood Hill Ct
  PDSY/CALV LS28 ....99 H3
Rockwood Rd PDSY/CALV LS28 ....99 H3
Roderick St WOR/ARM LS12 ....102 A6
Rodger La WKFDW/WTN WF2 ....164 A6
Rodin Av GIR BD8 ....96 C6
Rodley La PDSY/CALV LS28 ....79 K6
Rodney Yd WKFDE WF1 ....18 F5
Rods Mills La MOR LS27 ....142 A4
Roebuck La OT LS21 ....27 H5
Roebuck St BTLY WF17 ....140 C6
Roger Ct ECHL BD2 ....6 F1
Roger Fold GFTH/SHER LS25 ....128 A5
Rogers Ct EARD/LOFT WF3 ....165 G2
Rogerson Sq BRIG HD6 ....157 F5
Rogers Pl PDSY/CALV LS28 ....100 C5
Roils Head Rd LUD/ILL HX2 ....153 J1
Rokeby Gdns HDGY LS6 ....82 B7
  IDLE BD10 ....79 F6
Roker La PDSY/CALV LS28 ....120 C1
Rolling Br TAD LS24 ....51 J5
Roman Av RHAY LS8 ....84 B1
Romanby Shaw IDLE BD10 ....78 E6
Roman Cl TAD LS24 ....50 E6
Roman Crs RHAY LS8 ....84 C2
Roman Dr RHAY LS8 ....84 C2
Roman Gdns RHAY LS8 ....84 B2
Roman Gv RHAY LS8 ....84 B2
Roman Pl RHAY LS8 ....84 B2
Roman Ri PONT WF8 ....189 H4
Roman Rd BTLY WF17 ....140 C7
Roman Ter RHAY LS8 ....84 B2
Roman Vw RHAY LS8 ....84 C2
Rombalds Av ILK LS29 ....24 D6
Rombalds Crs AIRE BD20 ....33 G2
  WOR/ARM LS12 ....8 A7
Rombalds Dr BGLY BD16 ....76 A1
Rombalds La ILK LS29 ....24 D6
Rombalds Pl WOR/ARM LS12 ....8 A7
Rombalds St WOR/ARM LS12 ....8 A7
Rombalds Ter WOR/ARM LS12 ....8 A7
Rombald's Vw ILK LS29 ....24 C4
  OT LS21 ....26 E7
  WOR/ARM LS12 ....8 A7
Romford Av MOR LS27 ....141 K4
Romney Mt PDSY/CALV LS28 ....120 D1
Romsey Gdns BOW BD4 ....118 E3
Romsey Ms BOW BD4 ....118 E3
Rona Cft RTHW LS26 ....145 H2
Ronald Dr GTHN BD7 ....4 D6
Rookery Cottages OSS * WF5 ....182 C6
Rookery La HIPP HX3 ....155 C5
Rookes Av WBSY BD6 ....117 H6
Rookes La HIPP HX3 ....137 F6

Rookhill Dr PONT WF8 ....189 K2
Rookhill Mt PONT WF8 ....190 A2
Rookhill Rd PONT WF8 ....190 A3
Rook La BOW BD4 ....118 C4
Rooks Av CLECK BD19 ....138 D7
Rooks Cl LM/WK BD12 ....137 J6
Rook's Nest Rd WKFDE WF1 ....164 D4
Rook St BGLY BD16 ....75 J1
Rookwith Pde IDLE BD10 ....78 E6
Rookwood Av
  GFTH/SHER LS25 ....127 K6
  OSM LS9 ....104 D5
Rookwood Crs OSM LS9 ....104 D5
Rookwood Gdns OSM LS9 ....104 D6
Rookwood Hl OSM LS9 ....104 D5
Rookwood Mt OSM LS9 ....104 D5
Rookwood Pde OSM LS9 ....104 E5
Rookwood Pl OSM LS9 ....104 E5
Rookwood Rd OSM LS9 ....104 D6
Rookwood Sq OSM LS9 ....104 E5
Rookwood Ter OSM LS9 ....104 E5
Rookwood V OSM LS9 ....104 D6
Rookwood Vw OSM LS9 ....104 D6
Rooley Av WBSY BD6 ....117 J6
Rooley Cl WBOW BD5 ....117 K6
Rooley Crs WBSY BD6 ....117 K6
Rooley Hts RPDN/SBR HX6 ....152 E5
Rooley La RPDN/SBR HX6 ....152 E6
  WBOW BD5 ....117 J5
Rooms Fold MOR LS27 ....141 K1
Rooms La MOR LS27 ....121 J6
Roper Av RHAY LS8 ....84 A4
Ropergate PONT WF8 ....189 A1
Ropergate Service Rd
  PONT WF8 ....189 H1
Roper Gn LUD/ILL HX2 ....134 A3
Roper Gv RHAY LS8 ....84 A4
Roper La LUD/ILL HX2 ....114 C6
Rope Wk KNOT WF11 ....171 H4
  LUD/ILL HX2 ....113 C7
Roscoe St CHAL LS7 ....10 D4
Roseate Gn MOR LS27 ....142 B4
Rose Av GFTH/SHER LS25 ....111 F7
  HORS LS18 ....80 D4
Rose Bank GIR BD8 ....5 H1
  ILK LS29 ....37 K2
Rosebank Crs HDGY LS6 ....9 G5
Rosebank Gdns BVRD LS3 ....9 G6
Rose Bank Pl GIR BD8 ....96 D6
Rosebank Rd BVRD LS3 ....9 G6
Rosebank Rw BVRD LS3 ....9 G6
Rosebank St BTLY WF17 ....160 E2
Roseberry Ter HFAX HX1 ....16 C3
Rosebery Mt SHPY BD18 ....77 H5
Rosebery Rd GIR BD8 ....97 H3
Rosebery St ELL HX5 ....175 J3
  PDSY/CALV LS28 ....99 K5
Rosebery Ter HFAX HX1 ....16 C3
Rosebud Wk RHAY LS8 ....10 E4
Rosechapel Cl WBSY * BD6 ....136 E1
Rosecliffe Mt BRAM LS13 ....100 E3
Rosecliffe Ter BRAM LS13 ....100 E3
Rose Cottages GTL/HWG * HX4 ....174 B7
Rose Ct GFTH/SHER LS25 ....107 K6
Rose Cft AL/HA/HU LS17 ....45 K4
Rose Crs GFTH/SHER LS25 ....111 F7
Rosedale RTHW LS26 ....145 G2
Rosedale Av LVSG WF15 ....158 E6
  WIL/AL BD15 ....95 J3
Rosedale Bank MID LS10 ....123 J5
Rosedale Cl BAIL BD17 ....77 F2
  NORM WF6 ....167 G7
Rosedale Gdns MID LS10 ....123 J5
Rosedale Ri BSPA/BRAM LS23 ....48 B3
Rosedale Ri MID LS10 ....123 J5
Rose Farm Ap NORM WF6 ....166 C4
Rose Farm Cl NORM WF6 ....166 C3
Rose Farm Fold NORM WF6 ....166 C3
Rose Farm Ri NORM WF6 ....166 C3
Rose Garth ILK LS29 ....37 H3
Rose Gv RPDN/SBR HX6 ....153 G3
  RTHW LS26 ....144 E1
Rose Heath LUD/ILL HX2 ....114 A7
Rosehill Crs LM/WK BD12 ....137 H5
Rose La TAD LS24 ....91 J6
Rose Lea Cl GFTH/SHER LS25 ....151 J1
Roselee Cl HIPP HX3 ....155 H5
Rosemary Av WOR/ARM LS12 ....12 C1
Rosemary Ct TAD LS24 ....50 E6
Rosemary La BRIC HD6 ....177 F1
  HIPP HX3 ....155 H5
Rosemary Rw TAD LS24 ....50 E6
Rose Mdw HWTH BD22 ....53 F6
Rosemont Av BRAM * LS13 ....101 F3
  PDSY/CALV LS28 ....100 C5
Rosemont Dr PDSY/CALV LS28 ....100 C5
Rosemont Gdns BRAM LS13 ....100 E3
Rosemont La BAIL BD17 ....77 J2
Rosemont Pl BRAM LS13 ....100 E3
Rosemont Rd BRAM LS13 ....101 F3
Rosemont St BRAM LS13 ....101 F3
  PDSY/CALV LS28 ....100 C5
Rosemont Ter BRAM LS13 ....101 F3
  PDSY/CALV LS28 ....100 C5
Rosemont Vw BRAM LS13 ....100 E3
Rosemont Wk BRAM LS13 ....101 F3
Rose Mt BOW * BD4 ....119 H6
  ECHL BD2 ....98 B2
  LUD/ILL * HX2 ....154 D4
Rosemount Av ELL HX5 ....175 K3
Rosemount Cl KGHY * BD21 ....2 F4
Rose Mount Pl WOR/ARM LS12 ....12 D3
Rosemount Wk KGHY * BD21 ....2 F4
Roseneath Pl WOR/ARM LS12 ....12 C4
Roseneath St WOR/ARM LS12 ....12 C3
Roseneath Ter WOR/ARM LS12 ....12 C3
Rose Pl LUD/ILL HX2 ....153 F3
Rose St GIR BD8 ....4 F1
  HFAX HX1 ....16 B6
  HORS LS18 ....80 D4
  KGHY BD21 ....54 C4
Rose Ter BTLY * WF17 ....140 D5

HFAX HX1 ....16 C5
  ILK LS29 ....22 C1
  LUD/ILL * HX2 ....154 D4
Roseville Rd RHAY LS8 ....10 E5
Roseville St RHAY LS8 ....10 F4
Roseville Wy RHAY LS8 ....10 E5
Rosewood Av GFTH/SHER LS25 ....127 J3
  KGHY BD21 ....54 C2
Rosewood Ct RTHW LS26 ....125 C7
Rosewood Gv BOW BD4 ....118 E1
Rosgill Dr SCFT LS14 ....85 G7
Rosgill Wk SCFT LS14 ....85 G7
Rosley Mt WBSY BD6 ....136 E1
Rossall Gv RHAY LS8 ....11 H1
Rossall Rd RHAY LS8 ....11 H1
Rossefield Ap BRAM LS13 ....101 G4
Rossefield Av BRAM LS13 ....101 G3
Rossefield Cha BRAM LS13 ....101 G3
Rossefield Cl BRAM * LS13 ....101 G3
Rossefield Dr BRAM LS13 ....101 G3
Rossefield Gv BRAM LS13 ....101 G3
Rossefield Lawn BRAM LS13 ....101 G3
Rossefield Pk HTON BD9 ....97 G1
Rossefield Pl BRAM LS13 ....101 G3
Rossefield Rd HTON BD9 ....97 F1
Rossefield Ter BRAM LS13 ....101 G3
Rossendale Pl SHPY BD18 ....77 F5
Rosse St GIR BD8 ....4 D5
  SHPY BD18 ....77 G4
Ross Gv BRAM LS13 ....100 E1
Rossington Av RHAY LS8 ....10 F1
Rossington Pl RHAY LS8 ....10 F1
Rossington Rd RHAY LS8 ....84 B7
Rossington St LDSU LS2 ....9 M8
Rossiter Dr KNOT WF11 ....170 E5
Rosslyn Ct EARL WF12 ....181 J2
Rosslyn Gv HWTH BD22 ....72 D6
Rossmore Dr WIL/AL BD15 ....96 B4
Rosy St HWTH BD22 ....73 G4
Rothbury Gdns BHP/TINH LS16 ....82 A1
Rothery Ct HFAX * HX1 ....16 C3
Rothesay Ter GTHN BD7 ....5 G9
Roth St HWTH BD22 ....73 F4
Rothwell La RTHW LS26 ....145 H2
Rothwell Mt HFAX HX1 ....16 E9
Rothwell Rd HTON BD9 ....16 E9
Rough Hall La LUD/ILL HX2 ....133 F2
Roundell Av BOW BD4 ....118 C6
Roundhay Av RHAY LS8 ....84 A7
Roundhay Crs RHAY LS8 ....84 A7
Roundhay Gdns RHAY * LS8 ....84 A7
Roundhay Gv RHAY LS8 ....84 A7
Roundhay Mt RHAY LS8 ....84 A7
Roundhay Park La
  AL/HA/HU LS17 ....64 C6
Roundhay Pl RHAY LS8 ....103 K1
Roundhay Vw RHAY * LS8 ....84 A7
Roundhead Fold IDLE BD10 ....79 F4
Round Hl LUD/ILL HX2 ....134 C1
Roundhill Av BGLY BD16 ....76 A5
Round Hill Cl CUL/QBY BD13 ....116 A4
Roundhill Mt BGLY BD16 ....76 A5
Roundhill Pl BFD BD1 ....5 K5
Roundhill Rd CAS WF10 ....168 C1
Roundhill St WBOW BD5 ....117 J2
Round St WBOW BD5 ....117 K3
  WKFDE WF1 ....19 K9
Round Thorn Pl GIR BD8 ....4 C4
The Roundway MOR LS27 ....141 J4
Roundwell Rd LVSG WF15 ....158 D3
Roundway SHPY BD18 ....76 D5
Roundwood Av BAIL BD17 ....78 A1
  IDLE BD10 ....79 F7
Roundwood Crs
  WKFDW/WTN WF2 ....183 H4
Roundwood Gln IDLE BD10 ....79 F6
Roundwood Ri
  WKFDW/WTN WF2 ....183 J5
Roundwood Rd BAIL BD17 ....57 J7
  OSS WF5 ....183 F5
Roundwood Vw IDLE BD10 ....79 F6
Rouse Fold BOW BD4 ....6 B9
Rouse Mill La BTLY WF17 ....161 C4
Rouse St LVSG WF15 ....159 H4
Rowan Av AIRE BD20 ....53 H1
Rowanberry Cl ECHL BD2 ....98 C1
Rowan Cl BTLY WF17 ....140 D5
Rowan Ct ECHL * BD2 ....7 H1
  RTHW LS26 ....146 B1
  WKFDW/WTN WF2 ....184 A1
  YEA LS19 ....59 J6
Rowan Dr BRIC HD6 ....157 H5
Rowan Gn PONT WF8 ....170 A7
Rowan Pl GFTH/SHER LS25 ....108 A7
The Rowans BAIL BD17 ....76 E1
  BHP/TINH LS16 ....61 J1
  BRAM LS13 ....100 C2
Rowan St AIRE BD20 ....53 H1
Rowantree Av BAIL BD17 ....57 G7
Rowantree Dr IDLE BD10 ....78 D6
Rowanwood Gdns IDLE * BD10 ....79 F7
Rowland Pl BEE/HOL LS11 ....123 G3
Rowland Rd BEE/HOL LS11 ....123 H3
Rowland Ter BEE/HOL LS11 ....123 H3
Row La RPDN/SBR HX6 ....152 E5
Rowlestone Ri IDLE BD10 ....79 F6
Rowley Dr ILK LS29 ....24 E6
Rowsley St KGHY BD21 ....3 J4
Rowton Thorpe IDLE BD10 ....79 F6
Roxburghe Dl NORM WF6 ....167 G2
Roxburgh Gv WIL/AL BD15 ....96 A5
Roxby Cl OSM LS9 ....10 F7
Roxby St WBOW BD5 ....117 J5
Roxholme Av CHAL LS7 ....83 K7
Roxholme Gv CHAL LS7 ....83 K7
Roxholme Pl CHAL LS7 ....83 K7
Roxholme Ter CHAL LS7 ....83 K7
Royal Cl GTHN BD7 ....116 E3
  MID LS10 ....123 J4
Royal Ct MID LS10 ....123 J4
  PONT WF8 ....189 C4
Royal Dr MID LS10 ....123 J4
Royal Gdns MID LS10 ....123 J4
Royal Park Av HDGY LS6 ....9 G4
Royal Park Gv HDGY LS6 ....9 G3
Royal Park Mt HDGY LS6 ....9 G3

Royal Park Rd HDGY LS6 ......8 F4
Royal Park Ter HDGY LS6 ......9 G3
Royal Park Vw HDGY LS6 ......9 G3
Royal Pl MID LS10 ......123 J4
Royal Ter BSPA/BRAM LS23 ......48 D2
Royd Av BGLY BD16 ......76 A1
  HECK WF16 ......160 A2
  HUDW HD3 ......175 K6
Royd Crs HBR HX7 ......132 A6
  HFAX * HX1 ......16 A4
Royden Gv HTON BD9 ......97 F3
Roydfield St HUDN HD2 ......177 G7
Royd Head Farm OSS WF5 ......182 B4
Royd House Gv KGHY BD21 ......3 L8
Royd House Rd KGHY BD21 ......3 M8
Royd House Wk KGHY BD21 ......3 M8
Royd House Wy KGHY BD21 ......3 L8
Royd Ings Av KGHY BD21 ......3 J1
Roydlands St HIPP HX3 ......136 C7
Royd La HIPP HX3 ......134 D4
  KGHY BD21 ......53 J3
  LUD/ILL HX2 ......114 B7
  RPDN/SBR HX6 ......172 D4
Royd Moor Rd BOW BD4 ......119 G5
Royd Mt HIPP HX3 ......135 F5
Roydon Gv HTON BD9 ......97 F3
Royd Pl HIPP HX3 ......135 F5
Royds Av BIRK/DRI BD11 ......139 J2
  BRIG HD6 ......137 G7
  CAS WF10 ......149 H7
  OSS WF5 ......182 B1
Roydscliffe Dr HTON BD9 ......96 E1
Roydscliffe Rd HTON BD9 ......96 D2
Royds Cl WOR/ARM LS12 ......12 A8
Royds Crs BRIG HD6 ......157 G1
Roydsdale Wy BOW BD4 ......138 B1
Royds Farm Rd BEE/HOL LS11 ......122 B4
Royds Gv WKFDE WF1 ......164 D3
Royds Hall Av WBSY BD6 ......117 H6
Royds Hall La LM/WK BD12 ......137 F2
Royds Hall Rd WOR/ARM LS12 ......12 A8
Royds La RTHW LS26 ......145 H3
  WOR/ARM LS12 ......12 A8
Royds Park Crs LM/WK BD12 ......137 J3
Roydstone Ter BFDE BD3 ......7 J3
Royd St BTLY WF17 ......161 H5
  CUL/QBY BD13 ......95 F7
  KGHY BD21 ......53 J1
  WIL/AL BD15 ......75 F7
Royd Wy KGHY BD21 ......3 H1
Royd Wd CLECK BD19 ......158 E2
Roydwood Ter CUL/QBY BD13 ......74 A6
Roydwood Ter Back
  CUL/QBY BD13 ......74 A6
Royle Fold HECK WF16 ......160 A4
Roy Rd WBSY BD6 ......116 C5
Royston Cl EARD/LOFT WF3 ......163 J2
Royston Hl EARD/LOFT WF3 ......163 J2
Ruby St BTLY WF17 ......160 D2
  CHAL LS7 ......10 E6
  HWTH BD22 ......53 H7
Rudding Av WIL/AL BD15 ......95 K4
Rudding Crs WIL/AL BD15 ......95 K3
Rudding Dr BTLY WF17 ......160 C2
Rudd St GTHN BD7 ......117 F3
Rudgate TAD LS24 ......31 H5
  TAD LS24 ......49 J5
Rudgate Pk BSPA/BRAM LS23 ......31 F6
Rudstone Gv GFTH/SHER LS25 ......111 J3
Ruffield Side LM/WK BD12 ......137 F2
Rufford Av YEA LS19 ......59 J5
Rufford Bank YEA LS19 ......59 K5
Rufford Cl YEA LS19 ......59 K5
Rufford Crs YEA LS19 ......59 K5
Rufford Dr YEA LS19 ......59 K5
Rufford Pl HFAX * HX1 ......154 E4
Rufford Rdg YEA LS19 ......59 K5
Rufford Ri YEA LS19 ......59 J5
Rufford Rd ELL HX5 ......175 H3
  HIPP HX3 ......154 E4
Rufford St BFDE BD3 ......7 G6
  WKFDW/WTN WF2 ......184 A3
Rufford Vls HIPP HX3 ......154 E4
Rufus St KGHY BD21 ......3 H2
  WBOW BD5 ......117 H5
Rugby Av HIPP HX3 ......134 C4
Rugby Dr HIPP HX3 ......134 C4
Rugby Gdns HIPP HX3 ......134 C4
Rugby Mt HIPP HX3 ......134 C4
Rugby Pl GTHN BD7 ......4 E8
Rugby Ter HIPP HX3 ......134 C4
Rumble Rd EARL WF12 ......161 J7
Rumple Cft OT LS21 ......27 F7
The Runtlings OSS WF5 ......182 A4
Runtlings La OSS WF5 ......182 B5
Rupert Rd ILK LS29 ......23 K4
Rupert St HWTH BD22 ......73 G4
  KGHY * BD21 ......3 H2
Rush Cft IDLE BD10 ......78 A3
Rushdene Ct LM/WK BD12 ......137 H6
Rushmoor Rd BOW BD4 ......118 E4
Rusholme Rd PDSY/CALV LS28 ......99 K2
Rushton Av BFDE BD3 ......7 L3
Rushton Hill Cl LUD/ILL HX2 ......133 K6
Rushton Rd BFDE BD3 ......7 K4
Rushton St HFAX HX1 ......16 B4
  PDSY/CALV LS28 ......79 J6
Rushton Ter BFDE BD3 ......7 L5
Ruskin Av HTON BD9 ......96 C2
  WKFDE WF1 ......164 B6
Ruskin Ct CAS WF10 ......149 G7
Ruskin Ct WKFDE WF1 ......164 A6
Ruskin Crs GSLY LS20 ......59 G3
Ruskin Dr CAS WF10 ......149 G7
Ruskin Gv HUDN HD2 ......177 J6
Ruskin Pl CAS WF10 ......149 G7
Ruskin St PDSY/CALV LS28 ......99 K4
Ruskin Ter HIPP HX3 ......16 D1
Russell Av CUL/QBY BD13 ......115 H6

Russell Cl BTLY WF17 ......161 F3
  HECK WF16 ......160 B5
Russell Hall La CUL/QBY BD13 ......115 H5
Russell Rd CUL/QBY BD13 ......115 C6
Russell St CUL/QBY BD13 ......115 H5
  DEWS WF13 ......160 D7
  HFAX HX1 ......17 H6
  KGHY BD21 ......2 F5
  LDS LS1 ......9 M9
  SHPY BD18 ......77 H7
  WBOW BD5 ......5 K9
  WKFDE WF1 ......18 F8
Russell Wy BRIG HD6 ......157 G4
Rustic Av HIPP HX3 ......155 K4
Ruswarp Crs IDLE BD10 ......78 E6
Ruthven Vw RHAY LS8 ......11 K3
Rutland Av PONT WF8 ......189 J4
  WKFDW/WTN WF2 ......184 D7
Rutland Cl GFTH/SHER LS25 ......128 A4
  RTHW LS26 ......146 A1
Rutland Dr GFTH/SHER LS25 ......128 A4
  HOR/CROF WF4 ......185 K6
Rutland Mt BVRD LS3 ......9 H8
Rutland Rd BTLY WF17 ......161 G2
Rutland St BOW BD4 ......118 B2
  KGHY BD21 ......2 F8
  LDS LS1 ......9 J8
Rutland Ter BVRD LS3 ......9 H8
Ryan Gv HWTH BD22 ......52 E3
Ryan Pl RHAY LS8 ......11 J1
Ryan St WBOW BD5 ......117 J3
Ryburn Ct HFAX HX1 ......16 B5
Ryburn La RPDN/SBR HX6 ......173 F4
Ryburn Pl WKFDW/WTN WF2 ......18 D8
Ryburn St RPDN/SBR HX6 ......153 J5
Ryburn Ter HFAX HX1 ......16 B5
Ryburn Vw LUD/ILL HX2 ......154 B3
  RPDN/SBR HX6 ......172 D6
Rycroft Av BGLY BD16 ......75 K6
  BRAM LS13 ......100 E4
Rycroft Cl BRAM LS13 ......100 E4
Rycroft Dr BRAM LS13 ......100 E4
Rycroft Gdns BRAM LS13 ......100 E4
Rycroft Gn BRAM LS13 ......100 E4
Rycroft St SHPY BD18 ......77 J6
Rycroft Towers BRAM LS13 ......100 D4
Rydal Av GFTH/SHER LS25 ......107 H7
  HTON BD9 ......97 H1
Rydal Crs MOR LS27 ......142 C2
  WKFDW/WTN WF2 ......183 K2
Rydal Dr MOR LS27 ......142 C2
  WKFDW/WTN WF2 ......183 K2
Rydale Ct OSS WF5 ......182 C5
Rydale Ms OSS WF5 ......182 C5
Rydal Gv LVSG WF15 ......159 H7
Rydall Pl BEE/HOL LS11 ......13 H6
Rydall St BEE/HOL LS11 ......13 H6
Rydall Ter BEE/HOL LS11 ......13 H6
Rydal St CAS WF10 ......149 J7
  HWTH BD22 ......2 D6
Ryder Cl PONT WF8 ......189 C1
Ryder Gdns RHAY LS8 ......84 B5
Rydings Av BRIG HD6 ......157 F5
Rydings Cl BRIG HD6 ......157 F5
Rydings Dr BRIG HD6 ......156 E5
Ryebread CAS WF10 ......148 D6
Ryecroft BGLY BD16 ......74 C3
Rye Cft LUD/ILL HX2 ......134 C1
Ryecroft Cl WKFDE WF1 ......164 C3
Ryecroft Crs LUD/ILL HX2 ......134 A6
Ryecroft La LUD/ILL HX2 ......134 A7
Ryecroft Rd BGLY BD16 ......74 A2
Ryecroft St OSS WF5 ......182 B3
Ryecroft Ter LUD/ILL HX2 ......134 A6
Ryedale HUDE HD5 ......178 C7
  WOR/ARM LS12 ......122 A2
Ryedale Cl KNOT WF11 ......171 F6
Ryedale Ct SCFT LS14 ......85 G7
Ryedale Holt WOR/ARM LS12 ......122 A1
Ryedale Pk ILK LS29 ......24 C6
Ryedale Pl NORM * WF6 ......166 D3
Ryedale Wy EARD/LOFT WF3 ......162 D1
  WIL/AL BD15 ......95 K3
Ryefield Av CLAY BD14 ......116 A1
Rye Garth WBY LS22 ......29 G1
Rye La LUD/ILL HX2 ......133 K6
Rye Pl SCFT LS14 ......105 G4
Rye St HWTH BD22 ......53 J7
Rylands Av BGLY BD16 ......76 A1
Rylands Meadow HWTH BD22 ......73 F4
Rylstone Gdns BFDE BD3 ......6 D1
Rylstone Gv WKFDE WF1 ......185 F1
Rylstone Rd BAIL BD17 ......76 E2
Rylstone St KGHY BD21 ......3 K2
Ryshworth Av AIRE BD20 ......55 G4
Ryton Dl IDLE BD10 ......79 F6

S

Sable Crest ECHL BD2 ......98 A1
Sackville Ap CHAL LS7 ......10 B3
Sackville Rd AIRE BD20 ......21 F7
Sackville St BFD BD1 ......5 L6
  CHAL LS7 ......10 B3
  DEWS WF13 ......180 B4
Saddlers Cft CAS WF10 ......169 G2
Saddlers La KNOT WF11 ......150 D7
Saddler St LM/WK BD12 ......137 H3
Saddleworth Rd GTL/HWG HX4 ......173 J4
  GTL/HWG HX4 ......175 H2
Sadler Cl BHP/TINH LS16 ......62 B7
Sadler Copse BHP/TINH LS16 ......62 B7
Sadler Wy BHP/TINH LS16 ......62 B7
Saffron Dr WIL/AL BD15 ......95 K4
Sagar Pl HDGY LS6 ......102 C1
Sagar St CAS WF10 ......148 C7
Sage St WBOW BD5 ......117 H2
Sahara Ct GIR BD8 ......97 J3
St Abbs Cl WBSY BD6 ......117 H7
St Abbs Dr WBSY BD6 ......117 H7
St Abbs Fold WBSY BD6 ......117 H7
St Abbs Ga WBSY BD6 ......117 H7
St Abbs Wk WBSY BD6 ......117 H7
St Abbs Wy WBSY BD6 ......117 H7
St Aidan's Rd BAIL BD17 ......77 J2

  RTHW LS26 ......127 H6
St Aiden's Wk OSM WF5 ......183 H5
St Alban Ap OSM LS9 ......11 M7
St Alban Cl OSM LS9 ......104 D4
St Alban Crs OSM LS9 ......104 D4
St Alban Gv OSM * LS9 ......104 D4
St Alban Mt OSM LS9 ......104 D4
St Alban Rd OSM LS9 ......104 D4
St Alban's Av HIPP HX3 ......155 F5
St Albans Cft HIPP HX3 ......155 G4
St Albans Pl LDSU LS2 ......10 B7
St Alban's Rd HIPP HX3 ......155 F5
St Alban Vw OSM LS9 ......104 D4
St Andrew's Av MOR LS27 ......141 J4
St Andrew's Cl BRAM LS13 ......80 B7
  MOR LS27 ......141 H4
  YEA LS19 ......59 K4
St Andrews Ct BVRD LS3 ......9 H8
St Andrew's Crs LM/WK BD12 ......138 B3
St Andrews Cft AL/HA/HU LS17 ......63 G7
St Andrews Dr AL/HA/HU LS17 ......63 F7
  FEA/AMT WF7 ......168 B7
  KNOT WF11 ......170 D3
St Andrew's Gv MOR LS27 ......141 J4
St Andrew's Pl BVRD LS3 ......9 H8
  GTHN BD7 ......5 G7
St Andrew's Rd CAS WF10 ......149 H6
  YEA LS19 ......59 K4
St Andrew's St BVRD LS3 ......9 H8
St Andrews Vls GTHN BD7 ......5 G6
St Andrews Wk AL/HA/HU LS17 ......63 F7
St Anne's Cl EARL WF12 ......181 G5
St Anne's Dr BULY LS4 ......8 A1
St Anne's Gn BULY LS4 ......8 A1
  HIPP HX3 ......155 F6
St Anne's La LDS LS1 ......9 M8
St Ann's Av BULY LS4 ......8 A2
St Ann's Cl BRAM LS13 ......8 A1
St Ann's Gdns BULY LS4 ......8 A1
St Ann's La BULY LS4 ......8 A2
St Ann's Mt BULY LS4 ......8 A3
St Ann's Ri BULY LS4 ......8 A2
St Ann's Sq BULY LS4 ......8 A2
  OSM * LS9 ......10 E9
  RPDN/SBR HX6 ......153 K4
St Ann's Wy BULY LS4 ......8 A2
St Anthony's Dr BEE/HOL LS11 ......122 K4
St Anthony's Rd BEE/HOL LS11 ......122 D4
St Anuil GIR BD8 ......4 F1
St Augustine's Ter BFDE BD3 ......6 C2
  HFAX * HX1 ......16 C5
St Barnabas Rd BEE/HOL LS11 ......13 M4
  LVSG WF15 ......158 D3
St Bartholomew's Cl
  WOR/ARM * LS12 ......12 A2
St Bartholomews Ct
  WKFDW/WTN WF2 ......183 H5
St Benedicts Cha BRAM LS13 ......81 G7
St Benedicts Dr BRAM LS13 ......81 G7
St Bernard's Av PONT WF8 ......189 C1
St Bevan's Rd HIPP HX3 ......155 F5
St Blaise Ct WBOW BD5 ......5 M8
St Blaise Wy BFD BD1 ......5 M5
St Boltophs Cl KNOT * WF11 ......171 H4
St Catherine's Crs BRAM LS13 ......101 C1
St Catherine's Dr BRAM LS13 ......101 G1
St Catherine's Gn BRAM LS13 ......101 G1
St Catherine's Hl BRAM LS13 ......101 G1
St Catherine St WKFDE WF1 ......185 G6
St Catherines Vls WKFDE WF1 ......185 G6
St Catherine's Wk RHAY LS8 ......84 B6
St Chad's Av BRIG * HD6 ......156 D3
  HDGY LS6 ......82 B6
St Chad's Dr HDGY LS6 ......82 B6
St Chad's Ri HDGY LS6 ......82 B6
St Chad's Rd GIR BD8 ......4 E1
  HDGY LS6 ......82 C6
St Chad's Vw HDGY LS6 ......82 B7
St Christopher's Av RTHW LS26 ......145 C2
St Christophers Dr ILK LS29 ......22 C2
St Clair Gn WKFDW/WTN WF2 ......183 J1
St Clair Rd OT LS21 ......39 J3
St Clair St OT LS21 ......39 J2
  WKFDE WF1 ......19 C5
St Clare's Av ECHL BD2 ......98 E3
St Clements Av RTHW LS26 ......145 F2
St Clements Cl RTHW LS26 ......144 E3
St Clements Ri RTHW LS26 ......144 E2
St Cyprians Gdns OSM LS9 ......11 L4
St Davids Rd OT LS21 ......39 J2
St Edmunds Cl CAS WF10 ......149 H7
St Edwards Cl KNOT WF11 ......171 F1
St Elmo Gv OSM * LS9 ......11 K9
St Eloi Av BAIL BD17 ......57 H7
St Enoch's Rd WBSY BD6 ......117 H8
St Francis Gdns HUDN HD2 ......177 H4
St Francis Pl BEE/HOL LS11 ......13 L3
St George's Av HUDW HD3 ......175 K6
  RTHW LS26 ......124 D7
St George's Crs HFAX HX1 ......124 D7
St George's Pl WBOW BD5 ......5 L9
St George's Rd HIPP HX3 ......16 D2
  LDS LS1 ......9 L7
  WKFDW/WTN WF2 ......183 J6
St Giles Av WKFDW/WTN WF2 ......189 G1
St Giles Cl BRIG HD6 ......156 D3
St Giles Garth BHP/TINH LS16 ......41 G7
St Giles Rd HIPP HX3 ......156 D2
St Helena Rd WBSY BD6 ......117 G5
St Helens Av BHP/TINH LS16 ......82 C1
St Helens Cl BHP/TINH LS16 ......82 C1
St Helens Cft BHP/TINH LS16 ......82 B1
St Helen's Dr GFTH/SHER LS25 ......108 C5
St Helens Gdns BHP/TINH LS16 ......82 B1
St Helen's La BHP/TINH LS16 ......82 A1
St Helen's Pl CAS WF10 ......168 D1
St Helens St MID LS10 ......14 D6
St Helens Wy BHP/TINH LS16 ......82 C1
  ILK LS29 ......24 C1
St Helier Gv BAIL BD17 ......57 J7
St Hilda's Av OSM LS9 ......15 H4
St Hilda's Crs OSM LS9 ......15 G4
St Hilda's Gv OSM LS9 ......15 H4

St Hilda's Mt OSM LS9 ......15 H4
St Hilda's Pl OSM LS9 ......15 H4
St Hilda's Rd OSM LS9 ......15 H4
St Hilda's Ter BFDE BD3 ......7 L4
St Ians Cft ILK LS29 ......22 C2
St Ives Cl PONT WF8 ......169 J3
St Ives CAS WF10 ......169 H3
St Ive's Gdns HIPP * HX3 ......155 F5
St Ives Gv BGLY BD16 ......75 F2
  WOR/ARM LS12 ......101 K5
St Ives Mt WOR/ARM LS12 ......101 K5
St Ives Pl BGLY BD16 ......75 F2
St Ives Rd BGLY BD16 ......75 F2
  HIPP HX3 ......154 E5
St James Ap SCFT LS14 ......105 H1
St James Av HORS LS18 ......81 F3
St James Cl WOR/ARM LS12 ......101 H5
St James Ct HFAX HX1 ......17 G5
St James Crs PDSY/CALV LS28 ......99 J6
St James Dr HORS LS18 ......81 G3
St James Ms WOR/ARM LS12 ......101 H5
St James Ri WKFDW/WTN WF2 ......183 H5
St James Rd HFAX HX1 ......17 G5
  ILK LS29 ......23 K6
St James's Ct OSM LS9 ......10 F4
  WKFDW/WTN WF2 ......18 D8
St James's Market BFDE * BD3 ......6 C8
St James's Ms WOR/ARM LS12 ......101 J4
St James's Pk WKFDE WF1 ......19 J5
St James's Sq WBOW * BD5 ......117 K1
St James's St WBY LS22 ......29 H4
St James St BTLY WF17 ......161 F3
  HECK WF16 ......160 A5
  HFAX HX1 ......17 G5
St James Ter HORS LS18 ......81 G3
St James Wk HORS LS18 ......81 G3
St John Pde OSM WF13 ......180 E1
St John's Av HDGY LS6 ......9 H5
  ILK LS29 ......22 C1
  OSS WF5 ......183 F4
  PDSY/CALV LS28 ......100 A3
  SCFT LS14 ......66 C6
  WKFDE WF1 ......18 C1
St John's Cha WKFDE WF1 ......18 C1
St Johns Cl CLECK * BD19 ......159 F1
  DEWS * WF13 ......180 E1
  GFTH/SHER LS25 ......88 D3
  HDGY LS6 ......9 G5
  OSS WF5 ......183 F4
St John's Ct BAIL BD17 ......77 K2
  SCFT * LS14 ......66 C6
  WKFDE WF1 ......18 C2
  YEA LS19 ......59 H5
St John's Cft WKFDE WF1 ......18 C2
St John's Dr YEA LS19 ......59 H5
St John's Garth
  GFTH/SHER LS25 ......88 D4
St John's Gv HDGY LS6 ......9 G4
  WKFDE WF1 ......18 F1
St John's La HFAX HX1 ......17 G8
St Johns Ms WKFDE WF1 ......18 C1
St John's Mt WKFDE WF1 ......18 B1
St John's North WKFDE WF1 ......18 D2
St John's Pk BIRK/DRI * BD11 ......139 H1
  HFAX * HX1 ......17 G8
St John's Rd AIRE BD20 ......53 H1
  BSPA/BRAM LS23 ......48 C4
  BVRD LS3 ......9 H6
  ILK LS29 ......24 D5
  YEA LS19 ......59 H5
St John's Sq WKFDE WF1 ......18 C2
St John's St AIRE BD20 ......33 F1
  RTHW LS26 ......145 K2
St Johns Ter HDGY LS6 ......9 H5
St John St BRIG HD6 ......157 F7
  DEWS WF13 ......180 E1
St John's Vw BSPA/BRAM LS23 ......48 B3
St Johns Wy HWTH BD22 ......2 B7
  YEA LS19 ......59 H5
St John Wk DEWS WF13 ......180 E1
St Joseph's Mt PONT WF8 ......189 G2
St Joseph's St TAD LS24 ......50 D7
St Jude's Pl GIR BD8 ......5 K3
St Jude's St BFD BD1 ......5 K3
  HFAX * HX1 ......154 E3
St Laurence's Cl SHPY BD18 ......77 J7
St Lawrence Cl
  PDSY/CALV LS28 ......100 A6
St Lawrence Md
  PDSY/CALV LS28 ......100 A7
St Lawrence St CHAL * LS7 ......83 J6
St Lawrence Ter
  PDSY/CALV LS28 ......100 B7
St Leonards Cl ILK LS29 ......22 C2
St Leonards Ct HTON BD9 ......4 A1
St Leonard's Gv GIR BD8 ......4 A1
St Leonard's Rd GIR BD8 ......4 A1
St Luke's Cl BSPA/BRAM LS23 ......48 C5
  BTLY * WF17 ......161 H4
  CLECK BD19 ......158 C1
  WBOW BD5 ......117 J1
St Luke's Crs BEE/HOL LS11 ......13 K7
St Luke's Gn BEE/HOL LS11 ......13 K8
St Luke's Rd BEE/HOL LS11 ......13 K8
St Luke's St BEE/HOL LS11 ......13 K8
St Luke's Vw BEE/HOL LS11 ......13 K8
St Margaret's Av BOW BD4 ......118 E4
  HORS LS18 ......80 E3
  RHAY LS8 ......84 B6
  RTHW LS26 ......147 G4
St Margaret's Cl HORS LS18 ......80 E2
St Margaret's Dr HORS LS18 ......80 E2
  RHAY LS8 ......84 B6
St Margaret's Gv RHAY LS8 ......84 B6
St Margaret's Pl GTHN BD7 ......4 E9
St Margaret's Rd GTHN BD7 ......4 E9
  HORS LS18 ......80 E2
  RTHW LS26 ......147 G4
St Margaret's Ter GTHN BD7 ......4 E9
  ILK LS29 ......24 A6
St Margaret's Vw RHAY LS8 ......84 B6
St Mark's Av LDSU LS2 ......9 K4
  LM/WK BD12 ......137 H2
St Mark's Rd LDSU LS2 ......9 K3

St Mark's St LDSU LS2 ......9 K4
  WKFDE WF1 ......19 G1
St Mark's Ter LM/WK BD12 ......137 H2
St Martin's Av CHAL LS7 ......83 H7
  GTHN BD7 ......5 G6
  OT LS21 ......27 G7
St Martins Cl FEA/AMT WF7 ......188 D5
St Martin's Crs CHAL LS7 ......83 J7
St Martin's Dr CHAL * LS7 ......83 J6
St Martin's Gdns CHAL LS7 ......83 J7
St Martin's Gv CAS WF10 ......168 A2
  CHAL LS7 ......83 J7
St Martin's Rd CHAL LS7 ......83 J7
St Martins Ter CHAL * LS7 ......83 J7
St Martin's Vw BRIG HD6 ......157 F5
  CHAL LS7 ......83 J7
St Mary Magdalenes Cl
  GIR * BD8 ......5 H3
St Mary's Av BTLY WF17 ......160 D5
  LM/WK BD12 ......137 H5
  MIRF WF14 ......179 K3
  NORM WF6 ......166 C4
  RTHW LS26 ......126 D5
St Mary's Cl CHAL LS7 ......83 J7
  EARD/LOFT WF3 ......162 B1
  GFTH/SHER LS25 ......107 J3
  ILK LS29 ......24 B5
  LM/WK BD12 ......137 G5
  WOR/ARM LS12 ......12 D3
St Mary's Ct CAS WF10 ......148 A3
  CHAL LS7 ......83 J7
St Mary's Crs LM/WK BD12 ......137 G6
St Mary's Dr LM/WK BD12 ......137 H5
St Mary's Gdns LM/WK BD12 ......137 H5
St Mary's Garth AL/HA/HU LS17 ......45 J5
St Marys Ga ELL HX5 ......175 J2
St Mary's La OSM LS9 ......10 E8
St Mary's Mt LM/WK BD12 ......137 G6
St Mary's Park Ap
  WOR/ARM LS12 ......101 J5
St Mary's Park Ct
  WOR/ARM LS12 ......101 J5
St Mary's Park Crs
  WOR/ARM LS12 ......101 J5
St Mary's Park Gn
  WOR/ARM LS12 ......101 J5
St Mary's Pl EARL WF12 ......181 F3
St Mary's Rd AIRE BD20 ......54 C1
  BOW BD4 ......7 J9
  CHAL LS7 ......83 J7
  HTON BD9 ......97 H3
  NORM WF6 ......166 C5
St Mary's Sq LM/WK BD12 ......137 G5
  MOR * LS27 ......141 K3
St Mary's St BSPA/BRAM LS23 ......48 C2
  OSM LS9 ......10 D8
St Mary St HFAX HX1 ......16 E7
St Mary's Wk GFTH/SHER LS25 ......108 C6
  MIRF WF14 ......179 K5
St Matthew Rd DEWS WF13 ......180 E1
St Matthews Cl WIL/AL BD15 ......94 E1
St Matthew's Dr HIPP HX3 ......135 K4
St Matthews Gv WIL/AL BD15 ......94 E1
St Matthew's Rd WBSY BD6 ......117 J5
St Matthews St BEE/HOL LS11 ......13 J5
St Matthew's Wk CHAL LS7 ......83 H4
St Matthias' Gv BULY LS4 ......8 C5
St Matthias' St BULY LS4 ......8 C5
St Matthias Ter BULY LS4 ......8 C5
St Merrion Crs HIPP HX3 ......17 M9
St Michaels Av PONT WF8 ......189 G1
St Michael's Cl CAS WF10 ......168 C1
  EARL WF12 ......181 H7
  WKFDW/WTN WF2 ......18 A6
St Michael's Crs HDGY LS6 ......102 C1
St Michaels Gn NORM WF6 ......166 D3
St Michael's Gv HDGY LS6 ......102 C1
St Michael's La BULY LS4 ......8 C3
St Michael's Mt EARL WF12 ......181 H7
St Michael's Rd GIR BD8 ......5 H4
  HDGY LS6 ......102 C1
St Michael's Ter HDGY LS6 ......102 C1
St Michaels Vls HDGY LS6 ......102 C1
St Michaels Wy ILK LS29 ......22 C1
St Nicholas Rd ILK LS29 ......23 K4
St Nicholas St CAS WF10 ......168 C1
St Oswald Av PONT WF8 ......189 G1
St Oswald Rd
  WKFDW/WTN WF2 ......183 H4
St Oswalds Garth GSLY LS20 ......59 G7
St Oswalds Pl OSS WF5 ......182 D2
St Oswald St CAS * WF10 ......148 C7
St Paulinus Cl DEWS WF13 ......180 E1
St Paul's Av BIRK/DRI BD11 ......139 J2
  WBSY BD6 ......117 G6
St Pauls Cl GIR * BD8 ......5 G1
St Pauls Ct PONT WF8 ......169 K5
St Paul's Dr WKFDW/WTN WF2 ......183 J1
St Paul's Gv ILK LS29 ......24 C5
  WBSY BD6 ......117 G6
St Paul's Pl LDS * LS1 ......9 L9
St Pauls Ri ILK LS29 ......22 C1
St Paul's Rd BIRK/DRI BD11 ......139 H2
  GIR BD8 ......97 H3
  HFAX HX1 ......16 A9
  KGHY BD21 ......3 J6
  MIRF WF14 ......179 H5
  SHPY BD18 ......77 F5
  WBSY BD6 ......117 G6
St Paul's St LDS LS1 ......9 K9
  MOR * LS27 ......141 K4
St Paul's Ter MIRF WF14 ......179 H5
St Paul's Wk
  WKFDW/WTN WF2 ......183 J1
St Peg Cl CLECK BD19 ......159 F1
St Peg La CLECK BD19 ......159 F1
St Peter's Av RPDN/SBR HX6 ......153 C5
  RTHW LS26 ......145 G2
St Peter's Cl BTLY WF17 ......140 E4
  MIRF * WF14 ......179 C4
St Peters Ct BEE/HOL LS11 ......14 A1
  BRAM LS13 ......101 G2
  HOR/CROF WF4 ......183 F7
  ILK LS29 ......22 C2
St Peter's Crs EARD/LOFT WF3 ......165 J2
  MOR LS27 ......141 K4

St Peter's Gdns *BRAM* LS13 ....**101** F2
St Peter's Garth *SCFT* LS14..........**66** D5
St Peters Ga *OSS* WF5..........**182** C2
St Peter's Mt *BRAM* LS13 ....**101** F3
St Peter's Sq *LS9*..........**10** D9
St Peter's Wy *ILK* LS29..........**38** A6
St Philip's Av *MID* LS10..........**143** G2
St Philip's Cl *DEWS* * WF13..........**161** G7
  ILK LS29..........**38** A2
  MID LS10..........**143** H2
St Philips Ct *HUDW* HD3..........**176** A7
St Philip's Dr *ILK* LS29..........**38** A2
St Philip's Wy *ILK* LS29..........**38** A1
St Phillips Ct *GIR* BD8..........**4** C2
St Richards Rd *OT* LS21..........**27** G7
St Stephen's Ct *AIRE* BD20..........**32** D4
  HIPP * HX3..........**154** D6
  OSM LS9..........**11** G8
St Stephen's Rd *AIRE* BD20..........**32** D5
  OSM LS9..........**11** G8
  PDSY/CALV LS28..........**79** H5
  WBOW BD5..........**117** K3
St Stephen's St *HIPP* HX3..........**154** D6
St Stephen's Ter *WBOW* * BD5.....**117** K3
Saint St *GTHN* BD7..........**117** F2
St Swithins Dr *EARD/LOFT* WF3..*165* C6
St Swithins Gv
  EARD/LOFT * WF3..........**165** C6
St Thomas Gdns *HUDN* HD2..........**178** A3
St Thomas Rd *FEA/AMT* WF7 ....**188** C4
St Thomas Rw *LDSU* LS2..........**10** C7
St Vincent Rd *PDSY/CALV* LS28 ....**100** B7
St Wilfred's St *PDSY/CALV* LS28....**79** J5
St Wilfrid's Av *RHAY* LS8..........**11** K1
St Wilfrid's Circ *RHAY* LS8..........**11** L2
St Wilfrid's Cl *GTHN* BD7..........**116** E1
  RHAY LS8..........**11** L1
St Wilfrid's Crs *GTHN* BD7..........**116** E1
  RHAY LS8..........**11** L1
St Wilfrid's Dr *RHAY* LS8..........**11** K1
St Wilfrid's Garth *RHAY* LS8..........**11** L2
St Wilfrid's Gv *RHAY* LS8..........**11** L1
St Wilfrid's Rd *GTHN* BD7..........**116** E1
St Winifred's Cl *LUD/ILL* * HX2 ....**134** C2
Salcombe Pl *BOW* BD4..........**119** F4
Salem Pl *GFTH/SHER* LS25 ....**107** H6
  MID LS10..........**14** B3
Salem St *BFDE* BD1..........**5** L5
  CUL/QBY * BD13..........**115** G5
Salisbury Av *BAIL* BD17..........**77** H1
  WOR/ARM LS12..........**8** A8
Salisbury Cl *EARL* WF12..........**181** J1
  NORM WF6..........**166** E5
Salisbury Gv *WOR/ARM* LS12 ....**8** A9
Salisbury Ms *HORS* LS18..........**81** G2
Salisbury Pl *HIPP* HX3..........**16** F1
  PDSY/CALV LS28..........**79** H6
Salisbury Rd *CLECK* BD19 ....**138** A7
  HTON BD9..........**77** H7
  HWTH BD22..........**2** D7
  LM/WK BD12..........**137** H1
  WOR/ARM LS12..........**8** B8
Salisbury St *PDSY/CALV* LS28..........**79** H6
  RPDN/SBR HX6..........**153** H5
  YEA LS19..........**59** J7
Salisbury Ter *HIPP* HX3..........**16** F1
  WOR/ARM LS12..........**8** A8
Salisbury Vw *WOR/ARM* LS12 ....**8** A8
Salmon Crs *HORS* LS18..........**81** F3
Sal Nook Cl *LM/WK* BD12..........**117** J7
Sal Royd Rd *LM/WK* BD12..........**137** K2
Saltaire Rd *BGLY* BD16..........**56** C6
  SHPY BD18..........**77** F4
Saltburn Pl *HTON* BD9..........**96** E3
Saltburn St *HFAX* HX1..........**16** A5
Salt Drake *RPDN/SBR* HX6..........**172** C1
Salterhebble Hl *HIPP* HX3..........**155** G6
Salterlee *HIPP* HX3..........**135** H5
Salter Rw *PONT* WF8..........**189** J1
Saltersgate Av *KNOT* WF11..........**171** F7
Salter St *DEWS* WF13..........**160** E6
Salt Horn Cl *LM/WK* BD12..........**138** A2
Saltonstall La *LUD/ILL* HX2..........**132** E2
Salt Pie Aly *WKFDW/WTN* WF2 ....**18** C6
Salts Mill Rd *BAIL* BD17..........**77** G4
Salt St *GIR* BD8..........**5** G2
  HFAX HX1..........**16** C4
Sampson St *LVSG* WF15..........**159** J4
Samuel Dr *EARD/LOFT* WF3 ....**165** F3
Samuel St *KGHY* * BD21..........**3** G3
Sandale Wk *WBSY* BD6..........**116** E7
Sandall Cl *GFTH/SHER* LS25 ....**128** A4
Sandall Magna *WBSY* BD6..........**116** D7
Sandals Rd *BAIL* BD17..........**77** H2
Sandal Wy *BTLY* WF17..........**140** C6
Sandbeck La *WBY* LS22..........**29** J2
Sandbeck Pk *WBY* LS22..........**29** J2
Sandbeck Wy *WBY* LS22..........**29** J2
Sandbed Ct *MSTN/BAR* LS15 ....**106** A2
Sandbed La *MSTN/BAR* LS15 ....**106** A2
Sand Beds *CUL/QBY* BD13..........**115** H5
Sandbeds Crs *LUD/ILL* HX2..........**134** B6
Sandbeds Rd *LUD/ILL* HX2..........**134** B7
Sandbeds Ter *LUD/ILL* HX2..........**134** B6
Sanderling Ct *GIR* * BD8..........**96** B6
Sanderling Garth *MID* LS10..........**143** G2
Sanderling Wy *MID* LS10..........**143** G2
Sanderson Av *NORM* WF6..........**166** D7
  WBSY BD6..........**117** H5
Sanderson La *RTHW* LS26..........**145** H5
Sanderson St *WKFDE* WF1..........**19** H5
Sandfield Av *HDGY* LS6..........**82** D6
Sandfield Garth *HDGY* LS6..........**82** D6
Sandfield Rd *IDLE* BD10..........**78** C6
Sandfield Ter *TAD* LS24..........**51** F6
Sandfield Vw *HDGY* LS6..........**82** D6
Sandford Rd *BFDE* BD3..........**7** G6
  KSTL LS5..........**102** A2
Sandforth Av *HIPP* HX3..........**135** F5
Sandgate Dr *GFTH/SHER* LS25..........**128** A4
Sandgate La *GFTH/SHER* LS25 ....**128** B5
Sandgate Ri *GFTH/SHER* LS25 ....**128** B4
Sandgate Ter *GFTH/SHER* LS25 ....**128** B5
Sandhall Av *LUD/ILL* HX2..........**154** A1
Sandhall Dr *LUD/ILL* HX2..........**154** A1
Sandhall Gn *LUD/ILL* HX2..........**134** A7
Sandhall La *LUD/ILL* HX2..........**154** A1

Sandhill Cl *PONT* WF8 ....**169** J4
Sandhill Crs *AL/HA/HU* LS17..........**63** K7
Sandhill Dr *AL/HA/HU* LS17..........**63** K7
Sandhill Fold *IDLE* BD10..........**78** B5
Sand Hill La *AL/HA/HU* LS17..........**83** J1
Sandhill Lawn *PONT* WF8..........**189** H2
Sand Hill Lawns *AL/HA/HU* LS17 ....**83** J1
Sandhill Mt *AL/HA/HU* LS17..........**63** J6
  IDLE BD10..........**78** C6
Sandhill Ov *AL/HA/HU* LS17..........**63** K6
Sandhill Ri *PONT* WF8..........**169** J5
Sandholme Crs *HIPP* HX3..........**156** C1
Sandholme Dr *IDLE* BD10..........**78** D6
  ILK LS29..........**38** A3
  OSS WF5..........**182** C4
Sandhurst Av *RHAY* LS8..........**11** K1
Sandhurst Gv *RHAY* LS8..........**11** J1
Sandhurst Mt *RHAY* LS8..........**11** K1
Sandhurst Pl *RHAY* LS8..........**11** J1
Sandhurst Rd *RHAY* LS8..........**11** J2
Sandhurst Ter *RHAY* LS8..........**11** K1
Sandiford Cl *MSTN/BAR* LS15 ....**106** A2
Sandiford Ter *MSTN/BAR* LS15 ....**106** A2
Sand La *GFTH/SHER* LS25 ....**131** F5
Sandleas Wy *MSTN/BAR* LS15 ....**106** C3
Sandlewood Cl *BEE/HOL* LS11..........**13** K6
Sandlewood Gn *BEE/HOL* LS11 ....**13** K6
Sandmead Cl *BOW* BD4 ....**119** F3
  MOR LS27..........**141** K1
Sandmead Cft *MOR* LS27..........**141** K1
Sandmead Wy *MOR* LS27..........**141** K1
Sandmoor Av *AL/HA/HU* LS17..........**63** J5
Sandmoor Cha *AL/HA/HU* LS17..........**63** J6
Sandmoor Cl *AL/HA/HU* LS17..........**63** J6
  CUL/QBY BD13..........**95** H7
Sandmoor Dr *AL/HA/HU* LS17 ....**63** J5
Sandmoor Gdns *HIPP* HX3..........**136** A3
Sandmoor Garth *IDLE* BD10..........**78** C3
Sandmoor Gn *AL/HA/HU* LS17..........**63** H5
Sandmoor La *AL/HA/HU* LS17..........**63** J5
Sandmoor Ms *AL/HA/HU* LS17..........**63** J6
Sandon Gv *MID* * LS10..........**123** K4
Sandon Mt *MID* LS10..........**123** K4
Sandown Av *LUD/ILL* HX2..........**134** B3
Sandown Rd *LUD/ILL* HX2..........**134** B3
Sandpiper Ap *MOR* LS27..........**142** B4
Sandpiper Ms *GIR* BD8..........**96** B6
Sandringham *HUDN* HD2..........**177** K4
Sandringham Ap
  AL/HA/HU LS17..........**83** K1
Sandringham Av *KNOT* WF11..........**170** D4
Sandringham Cl *CLAY* * BD14..........**116** C1
  MOR LS27..........**142** B2
  PONT WF8..........**189** H4
Sandringham Ct *CLAY* BD14..........**116** C1
Sandringham Crs
  AL/HA/HU LS17..........**83** J1
  PDSY/CALV LS28..........**100** B7
Sandringham Dr
  AL/HA/HU LS17..........**83** J1
Sandringham Gdns
  AL/HA/HU LS17..........**83** J1
Sandringham Gn
  AL/HA/HU * LS17..........**83** K1
Sandringham Mt
  AL/HA/HU LS17..........**83** K1
Sandringham Rd *CLAY* BD14..........**116** C1
  KNOT WF11..........**170** E1
  WBY LS22..........**29** H3
Sandringham Wy
  AL/HA/HU LS17..........**83** J1
Sandrock Rd *PONT* WF8..........**169** K6
Sandside Cl *WBOW* BD5..........**118** A4
Sands La *EARL* WF12..........**181** G2
  MIRF WF14..........**180** A6
Sands Rd *EARL* WF12..........**181** H3
Sands Ter *HUDN* * HD2..........**177** K7
Sandstone Dr *WOR/ARM* LS12.....**101** F6
Sand St *HWTH* BD22..........**72** D6
  KGHY BD21..........**3** G3
Sandwath La *TAD* LS24..........**91** J5
Sandway *MSTN/BAR* LS15 ....**105** J3
Sandway Gdns
  MSTN/BAR LS15 ....**105** J3
Sandway Gv *MSTN/BAR* LS15 ....**105** J3
Sandwich Crs *HUDN* HD2..........**178** E6
Sandyacres *RTHW* LS26..........**145** G1
Sandyacres Crs *RTHW* LS26..........**145** G1
Sandyacres Dr *RTHW* LS26..........**145** G1
Sandy Bank Av *RTHW* LS26..........**145** G1
Sandy Banks *BGLY* BD16..........**74** E4
Sandy Beck *WIL/AL* BD15..........**95** K2
Sandy Dyke La *RPDN/SBR* HX6 ..**173** F1
Sandyfoot *GTL/HWG* HX4..........**173** J5
Sandy Ga *AL/HA/HU* LS17..........**43** J3
  KGHY BD21..........**2** E1
Sandy Gate La *FEA/AMT* WF7 ....**189** H6
Sandygate Ter *BOW* BD4..........**118** E1
Sandy Gv *RTHW* LS26..........**145** G1
Sandy Lobby *OT* LS21..........**41** F4
Sandymoor *WIL/AL* BD15..........**95** K1
Sandy Wk *BHP/TINH* LS16..........**61** J1
  WKFDE WF1..........**18** C3
Sandy Wy *YEA* LS19..........**59** J4
Sandywood St *KGHY* BD21..........**3** F3
Sangster Wy *WBOW* BD5..........**118** B5
Santa Monica Crs *IDLE* BD10..........**78** B5
Santa Monica Gv *IDLE* BD10..........**78** B5
Santa Monica Rd *IDLE* BD10..........**78** B5
Sapgate La *CUL/QBY* BD13..........**95** H7
Saplin St *GIR* BD8..........**4** E2
Sapphire Cl *BTLY* WF17..........**160** D2
Sarah St *EARD/LOFT* WF3 ....**143** J7
Sardinia St *MID* LS10..........**14** C6
Saunters Wy *NORM* WF6..........**166** D4
Savile Av *CHAL* LS7..........**10** C2
  IDLE BD10..........**78** D6
Savile Cl *BRIG* HD6..........**157** J5
Savile Ct *MIRF* * WF14..........**179** H3
Savile Crs *HFAX* HX1..........**16** F8
Savile Dr *CHAL* LS7..........**10** C2
  HFAX HX1..........**16** E8
  HOR/CROF WF4..........**183** F7
Savile Gln *HFAX* HX1..........**16** F8
Savile Gn *HFAX* HX1..........**17** G8

Savile Gv *EARL* WF12..........**181** F2
Savile La *BRIG* HD6..........**157** J5
Savile Lea *HFAX* HX1..........**16** F8
Savile Ms *EARL* WF12..........**181** F4
Savile Mt *CHAL* LS7..........**10** C2
Savile Pde *HFAX* HX1..........**154** E3
Savile Pk *HFAX* HX1..........**154** D3
Savile Park Gdns *HFAX* HX1..........**154** E3
Savile Park Rd *CLECK* BD19 ....**138** E4
  HFAX HX1..........**16** F8
Savile Park St *HFAX* HX1..........**154** D3
Savile Park Ter *HFAX* * HX1..........**154** D3
Savile Pit La *EARL* WF12..........**161** K7
Savile Pl *CHAL* LS7..........**10** C2
  MIRF WF14..........**179** H3
Savile Rd *CAS* WF10..........**148** B7
  CHAL LS7..........**10** C2
  EARL WF12..........**181** F4
  ELL HX5..........**175** J3
  HFAX HX1..........**16** F8
  RTHW LS26..........**147** G4
Savile Royd *HFAX* HX1..........**16** E9
Savile St *CLECK* BD19..........**138** E6
  DEWS WF13..........**161** F6
Savile Ter *HFAX* HX1..........**16** D9
Saville Cl *EARD/LOFT* WF3 ....**144** D6
Saville Ct *OT* LS21..........**39** C3
Saville Pk *OSS* WF5..........**182** E5
Saville Park Rd *HFAX* HX1..........**16** E9
Saville St *OSS* WF5..........**182** E5
  WKFDE WF1..........**18** E2
Savins Mill Wy *KSTL* LS5..........**101** K1
Sawley Cl *WKFDE* WF1..........**19** K1
Sawley St *KGHY* BD21..........**2** E7
Saw Mill St *BEE/HOL* LS11..........**13** L3
Sawood La *HWTH* BD22..........**93** G5
Sawrey Pl *WBOW* BD5..........**5** K8
Saw Wells La *TAD* LS24..........**111** F1
Saw Yd *WKFDE* WF1..........**18** E5
Sawyers Garth *ILK* LS29..........**22** D1
Saxon Ga *AL/HA/HU* LS17..........**83** G2
Saxon Gn *AL/HA/HU* LS17..........**83** F2
Saxon Gv *AL/HA/HU* LS17..........**83** F2
Saxon Mt *AL/HA/HU* LS17..........**83** G1
Saxon Rd *AL/HA/HU* LS17..........**83** F2
Saxon St *GIR* BD8..........**5** G4
  HFAX HX1..........**16** A5
Saxon Wy *CAS* WF10..........**149** F7
Saxton Av *WBSY* BD6..........**116** E5
Saxton Ct *GFTH/SHER* LS25 ....**107** J5
  TAD LS24..........**90** C5
Saxton Gdns *OSM* * LS9..........**14** E1
Saxton La *OSM* LS9..........**14** D1
  TAD LS24..........**90** C6
Saxton St *LVSG* WF15..........**159** K3
Sayers Cl *KSTL* LS5..........**102** A1
Sayle Av *BOW* BD4..........**118** C6
Sayner La *MID* LS10..........**14** D4
Sayner Rd *MID* LS10..........**14** C4
Scalebor Park Cl *ILK* LS29..........**37** K2
Scale Hl *HUDN* HD2..........**177** F7
Scaley St *BFDE* * BD3..........**7** J6
Scammonden Rd
  GTL/HWG HX4..........**173** H4
Scarboro Mdw *MIRF* * WF14 ....**179** H4
Scarborough Gv *SHPY* BD18..........**77** F5
Scarborough La
  EARD/LOFT WF3..........**142** C7
Scarborough Rd *SHPY* BD18..........**77** F5
Scarborough St
  EARD/LOFT WF3..........**142** C6
  EARL WF12..........**181** G3
Scarborough Ter *EARL* WF12..........**181** G3
Scar Bottom La *GTL/HWG* HX4 ....**174** C2
Scarbro' Jct *BRAM* LS13..........**101** G4
Scarcroft Ct *SCFT* LS14..........**66** A3
Scargill Cl *OSM* LS9..........**11** G7
Scargill Gra *OSM* LS9..........**11** H8
Scar Head Rd *RPDN/SBR* HX6 ....**153** F7
Scarlet Hts *CUL/QBY* BD13..........**115** J5
Scarr Bottom Rd *LUD/ILL* HX2....**154** C4
Scarr End La *DEWS* WF13..........**160** C6
  EARL WF12..........**181** J4
Scarr End Vw *DEWS* WF13..........**160** C6
Scarsdale La *AL/HA/HU* LS17..........**46** B4
Scarsdale Rdg *AL/HA/HU* LS17 ....**46** B4
Scarth Av *OSM* LS9..........**11** J4
Scarthingwell Crs *TAD* LS24..........**90** C5
Scarthingwell La *TAD* LS24..........**90** C5
Scarth Ter *EARD/LOFT* WF3 ....**165** J2
Scar Top *GTL/HWG* * HX4..........**174** C2
Scarwood Cl *BGLY* BD16..........**55** K7
Scatcherd Gv *MOR* LS27..........**141** J3
Scatcherd La *MOR* LS27..........**141** J4
Scatcherd Park Av *MOR* LS27 ....**141** K2
Scawthorpe Cl *PONT* WF8..........**170** A7
Schofield Cl *MOR* * LS27..........**141** K3
Scholars Wk *ECHL* BD2..........**98** C2
Scholebrook La *BOW* BD4..........**119** K3
Scholemoor Av *GTHN* BD7..........**116** D1
Scholemoor La *GTHN* BD7..........**116** D1
Scholemoor Rd *GTHN* BD7..........**4** A9
Scholes La *CLECK* BD19..........**138** A7
  GTL/HWG HX4..........**154** D7
  HWTH BD22..........**72** A3
  MSTN/BAR LS15..........**86** B4
Scholes Rd *CAS* WF10..........**149** J6
  HUDN HD2..........**177** H7
Scholes St *WBOW* BD5..........**117** J4
Scholey Av *BRIG* HD6..........**177** F1
Scholey Rd *BRIG* HD6..........**177** F1
School Av *DEWS* WF13..........**160** C7
School Cl *HOR/CROF* WF4..........**186** E5
  LUD/ILL HX2..........**114** C7
  RPDN/SBR HX6..........**173** F5
  WOR/ARM LS12..........**121** G3
School Cote Brow *LUD/ILL* HX2 ..**134** E1
School Crs *DEWS* WF13..........**160** C7
  LUD/ILL HX2..........**114** C7
  WKFDW/WTN WF2..........**183** J5
School Cft *KNOT* WF11..........**150** D7
  RTHW LS26..........**145** F1
School Dr *KNOT* WF11..........**170** D3
Schoolgate *MSTN/BAR* LS15..........**87** H5
School Gn *BHP/TINH* LS16..........**61** H1
  BRIG HD6..........**177** F1
  CUL/QBY BD13..........**95** K7

School Green Av *CUL/QBY* BD13....**95** J7
School Gv *DEWS* WF13 ....**160** C7
School La *AL/HA/HU* LS17..........**45** K5
  AL/HA/HU LS17..........**64** C3
  BSPA/BRAM LS23..........**30** E5
  CAS WF10..........**168** E2
  CHAL LS7..........**83** H5
  DEWS WF13..........**160** C7
  GFTH/SHER LS25..........**88** D5
  GFTH/SHER LS25..........**131** F3
  HDGY LS6..........**82** D6
  HIPP HX3..........**155** K5
  ILK LS29..........**22** B1
  LUD/ILL HX2..........**114** C6
  LUD/ILL HX2..........**134** C1
  LVSG WF15..........**158** E3
  MSTN/BAR LS15..........**105** H5
  MSTN/BAR LS15..........**106** B6
  WBY LS22..........**46** E2
  WKFDW/WTN WF2..........**163** K6
School Pl *LM/WK* * BD12 ....**137** H3
School Rd *HWTH* BD22..........**2** A5
  PONT WF8..........**189** K2
  WBY LS22..........**29** J3
  WKFDW/WTN WF2..........**183** J6
School Sq *BFDE* * BD3..........**7** J5
School St *AIRE* BD20..........**32** D5
  AIRE BD20..........**53** H1
  BGLY BD16..........**76** A5
  BOW BD4..........**118** C6
  BOW BD4..........**118** D3
  BTLY WF17..........**140** C6
  CAS WF10..........**148** B7
  CAS WF10..........**148** D6
  CLAY BD14..........**116** A2
  CLECK BD19..........**158** D2
  CUL/QBY * BD13..........**94** B5
  DEWS WF13..........**180** A4
  EARD/LOFT WF3..........**162** C3
  EARL WF12..........**181** F1
  EARL WF12..........**182** A1
  GTL/HWG HX4..........**174** E1
  HFAX HX1..........**17** J7
  LM/WK BD12..........**137** H1
  LM/WK BD12..........**138** B3
  LVSG WF15..........**159** F6
  LVSG WF15..........**159** J6
  MOR LS27..........**122** B6
  MOR LS27..........**142** A3
  OSS WF5..........**162** B7
  PDSY/CALV LS28..........**100** A2
  PDSY/CALV LS28..........**100** A5
  WIL/AL BD15..........**75** F7
School Vw *HDGY* LS6..........**8** F2
School Wk *HWTH* BD22 ....**2** B5
School Yard Vw *HIPP* * HX3..........**17** H2
Sconce La *BAIL* BD17..........**57** F3
Score Hl *HIPP* HX3..........**135** K3
Scoresby St *BFD* BD1..........**6** B6
Scotchman La *MOR* LS27..........**141** J3
Scotchman La *MOR* LS27..........**141** H7
Scotchman Rd *HTON* BD9..........**96** D3
Scotland Cl *HORS* LS18..........**80** E1
Scotland La *HORS* LS18..........**60** D4
Scotland Mill La *BHP/TINH* LS16....**82** E2
Scotland St *CLECK* BD19..........**139** K6
Scotland Wy *HORS* LS18..........**60** D7
Scotland Wood Rd
  AL/HA/HU LS17..........**82** E2
Scott Av *HECK* WF16..........**160** A2
Scott Cl *HECK* * WF16..........**160** B4
  RTHW LS26..........**126** D5
Scott Gn *MOR* LS27..........**120** E6
Scott Green Crs *MOR* LS27..........**120** E6
Scott Green Dr *MOR* LS27..........**120** E6
Scott Green Gv *MOR* * LS27 ....**121** F6
Scott Green Mt *MOR* LS27..........**120** E6
Scott Green Vw *MOR* LS27..........**121** F6
Scott Hall Av *CHAL* LS7..........**103** H1
Scott Hall Dr *CHAL* LS7..........**10** B2
Scott Hall Gn *CHAL* LS7..........**83** H7
Scott Hall Gv *CHAL* LS7..........**83** H7
Scott Hall Pl *CHAL* LS7..........**83** H7
Scott Hall Rd *CHAL* LS7..........**83** G6
Scott Hall Rw *CHAL* LS7..........**10** C1
Scott Hall Sq *CHAL* LS7..........**83** H7
Scott Hall St *CHAL* LS7..........**10** A1
Scott Hall Ter *CHAL* LS7..........**83** H7
Scott Hall Wk *CHAL* LS7..........**103** H1
Scott Hall Wy *CHAL* LS7..........**83** H6
Scott La *AIRE* BD20..........**54** B1
  CLECK BD19..........**138** E7
  CLECK BD19..........**139** J6
  MOR LS27..........**141** H4
  WBY LS22..........**29** H4
Scott La West *AIRE* BD20..........**54** A1
Scott Ms *WBY* LS22..........**29** H4
Scotts Hill Cl *SCFT* LS14..........**66** C6
Scott St *KGHY* BD21..........**2** F4
  PDSY/CALV LS28..........**100** B7
Scott V *HUDN* HD2..........**177** J6
Scott Wood La *CHAL* LS7..........**83** G7
Scotty Bank *BRIG* HD6..........**157** F6
Scotty Croft La *BRIG* HD6..........**157** H6
Scout Bottom La *HBR* HX7..........**132** A7
Scout Cl *HBR* HX7..........**132** A7
Scout Hill Rd *DEWS* WF13..........**180** D3
Seacroft Av *SCFT* LS14..........**85** J7
Seacroft Cl *SCFT* LS14..........**85** J7
Seacroft Crs *SCFT* LS14..........**85** J7
Seacroft Ga *SCFT* * LS14..........**85** J7
Seaforth Av *OSM* LS9..........**11** K4
Seaforth Gv *OSM* LS9..........**11** K3
Seaforth Mt *OSM* LS9..........**11** K3
Seaforth Pl *OSM* LS9..........**11** K3
Seaforth Rd *OSM* LS9..........**11** K3
Seaforth Ter *OSM* LS9..........**11** K3
Seaton St *BFDE* BD3..........**6** E5
Second Av *AL/HA/HU* LS17..........**46** B5
  BFDE BD3..........**7** H2
  HIPP HX3..........**154** E4
  KGHY BD21..........**2** E7
  LVSG WF15..........**158** C4
  RTHW LS26..........**125** G7
  WBY LS22..........**29** J4
  WKFDE WF1..........**164** C6
  WOR/ARM LS12..........**12** E2

  YEA LS19..........**59** K6
Second St *LM/WK* BD12..........**137** K1
Sedan St *HFAX* * HX1..........**17** G7
Sedbergh Cl *MSTN/BAR* LS15..........**104** E6
Sedbergh Dr *ILK* LS29..........**24** B6
Sedbergh Pk *ILK* LS29..........**24** B6
Sedburgh Rd *HIPP* HX3..........**17** J9
Sedge Gv *HWTH* BD22..........**72** C4
Sedge Ri *TAD* LS24..........**70** B1
Sedgewick St *BTLY* WF17..........**140** B6
Sedgwick Cl *GIR* BD8..........**5** J4
Seed Hill Ter *LUD/ILL* HX2..........**133** K1
Seed St *LM/WK* BD12..........**137** J1
Sefton Av *BEE/HOL* LS11..........**123** F5
  BRIG HD6..........**156** E3
Sefton Ct *HDGY* LS6..........**82** C5
Sefton Crs *BRIG* HD6..........**156** E3
Sefton Dr *BRIG* HD6..........**156** E3
  ILK LS29..........**24** A6
Sefton Gv *ECHL* BD2..........**98** C2
Sefton Pl *KGHY* BD21..........**3** G3
Sefton Ri *EARL* WF12..........**181** G5
Sefton St *BEE/HOL* LS11..........**123** G3
  HFAX HX1..........**16** D4
  KGHY BD21..........**3** G2
Sefton Ter *BEE/HOL* LS11..........**123** F3
  HFAX HX1..........**16** D4
Selborne Gv *HTON* BD9..........**97** G2
  KGHY BD21..........**2** D8
Selborne Mt *HTON* BD9..........**97** H3
Selborne Ter *HTON* BD9..........**97** G3
  SHPY BD18..........**77** G6
Selborne Vls *CLAY* BD14..........**116** B3
  HTON BD9..........**97** G3
Selbourne Av *EARL* WF12..........**181** F3
Selbourne Dr *EARL* WF12..........**181** F4
Selbourne Rd *EARL* WF12..........**181** F4
Selby *LUD/ILL* HX2..........**114** A7
Selby Av *OSM* LS9..........**105** F5
Selby Rd *GFTH/SHER* LS25 ....**127** G1
  GFTH/SHER LS25..........**127** K2
  GFTH/SHER LS25..........**129** F2
  MSTN/BAR LS15..........**106** D7
  SCFT LS14..........**104** E4
Selby St *WKFDE* WF1..........**18** F2
Seldon St *WBOW* BD5..........**117** G3
Selene Cl *CLECK* BD19..........**139** K5
Sellars Fold *GTHN* * BD7..........**117** F2
Sellerdale Av *LM/WK* BD12..........**137** J6
Sellerdale Dr *LM/WK* BD12..........**137** J5
Sellerdale Ri *LM/WK* BD12..........**137** J5
Sellerdale Wy *LM/WK* BD12..........**137** J6
Selso Rd *EARL* WF12..........**161** J7
Seminary St *LDSU* LS2..........**9** K6
Semon Av *ECHL* BD2..........**78** A7
Senior St *DEWS* WF13..........**180** E2
Senior Wy *WBOW* BD5..........**5** L8
Serpentine Rd *CLECK* BD19 ....**138** E7
Servia Dr *CHAL* LS7..........**9** M3
Servia Gdns *CHAL* LS7..........**10** A3
Servia Hl *CHAL* LS7..........**9** M3
Servia Rd *HDGY* LS6..........**9** M3
Service Rd *OSM* LS9..........**124** E3
Sessions House Yd *PONT* WF8 ..**169** H7
Sevenoaks Md *WIL/AL* BD15 ....**96** A4
Seventh Av *LVSG* WF15..........**158** C3
  RTHW LS26..........**145** H1
Severn Dr *GFTH/SHER* LS25 ....**128** A1
Severn Rd *ECHL* BD2..........**98** B3
  MID LS10..........**15** G9
Severn Wy *MID* LS10..........**15** H8
Sewage Works Rd *OSM* LS9..........**124** D3
Sewell Rd *BFDE* BD3..........**6** F7
Sewerbridge La *FEA/AMT* WF7 ...**167** J7
Seymour St *BFDE* BD3..........**6** F9
  WKFDW/WTN WF2..........**18** E9
Shadwell La *AL/HA/HU* LS17..........**83** J2
Shadwell Park Av
  AL/HA/HU LS17..........**64** D6
Shadwell Park Cl
  AL/HA/HU LS17..........**64** D6
Shadwell Park Ct
  AL/HA/HU LS17..........**64** D7
Shadwell Park Dr
  AL/HA/HU LS17..........**64** D7
Shadwell Park Gdns
  AL/HA/HU LS17..........**64** D6
Shadwell Park Gv
  AL/HA/HU LS17..........**64** D6
Shadwell Wk *AL/HA/HU* LS17.....**83** K1
Shaftesbury Av *BRIG* HD6 ....**177** G2
  HTON BD9..........**96** C3
  RHAY LS8..........**84** B3
  SHPY BD18..........**77** H5
Shaftesbury Pde *OSM* * LS9 ....**104** D4
Shaftesbury Rd *RHAY* LS8..........**84** B2
Shafton La *BEE/HOL* LS11..........**13** H6
Shafton Pl *BEE/HOL* LS11..........**13** J6
Shafton St *BEE/HOL* LS11..........**13** J6
Shafton Vw *BEE/HOL* LS11..........**13** H6
Shakespeare Ap *OSM* LS9..........**11** G6
Shakespeare Av *NORM* WF6 ....**186** D2
  OSM LS9..........**11** G6
Shakespeare Cl *OSM* LS9..........**11** G6
Shakespeare Ct *OSM* LS9..........**11** G6
Shakespeare Crs *CAS* WF10 ....**169** J3
Shakespeare Gdns *OSM* LS9 ....**11** H6
Shakespeare Gra *OSM* LS9..........**11** G6
Shakespeare Lawn *OSM* LS9 ....**11** G6
Shakespeare Rd *CSLY* LS20..........**59** F3
Shakespeare St *HFAX* HX1..........**17** H7
Shakespeare Tower *OSM* LS9 ....**11** G5
Shalimar St *HFAX* HX1..........**16** A5
The Shambles *WBY* LS22..........**29** H4
Shann Av *KGHY* BD21..........**2** B3
Shann Crs *KGHY* BD21..........**2** B3
Shann La *KGHY* BD21..........**2** B1
Shannon Cl *BRIG* HD6..........**176** D2
  ILK LS29..........**23** J6
Shannon Rd *BRIG* HD6..........**176** D2
  OSM LS9..........**10** F9
Shannon St *OSM* LS9..........**10** E9
Shann St *SHPY* BD18..........**97** J1
Shapla Cl *HWTH* BD22..........**2** C6
Sharp Av *WBSY* BD6..........**117** H6
Sharpe St *BFD* BD1..........**5** L8
  HECK WF16..........**160** A5

Sharp House Rd *MID* LS10 ....143 K3
Sharp La *MID* LS10 ....143 K2
Sharp Ms *HDGY* LS6 ....82 E7
Sharp Rw *PDSY/CALV* LS28 ....100 C7
Sharp St *DEWS* WF13 ....181 G1
   WBSY BD6 ....117 H5
Shaw Av *NORM* WF6 ....167 F6
Shaw Barn Cft *WBY* LS22 ....29 F4
Shaw Barn La *WBY* LS22 ....29 F4
Shaw Booth La *LUD/ILL* HX2 ....133 C3
Shaw Cl *GFTH/SHER* LS25 ....127 K1
   GTL/HWG HX4 ....175 F5
   NORM WF6 ....167 F6
Shaw HI *HFAX* HX1 ....17 J9
Shaw Hill La *HIPP* HX3 ....17 J9
Shaw La *ELL* HX5 ....176 B2
   CSLY LS20 ....59 G2
   GTL/HWG HX4 ....174 E5
   HDGY LS6 ....82 C6
   HIPP HX3 ....135 J1
   HIPP HX3 ....155 H5
   KGHY BD21 ....74 A1
   RPDN/SBR HX6 ....153 K7
   RPDN/SBR HX6 ....172 D7
Shaw Lane Gdns *CSLY* LS20 ....59 G2
Shaw Leys *YEA* LS19 ....59 H3
Shaw Ri *NORM* WF6 ....167 F6
Shaw Royd *YEA* LS19 ....59 H3
Shaws La *MSTN/BAR* LS15 ....87 F6
   RPDN/SBR HX6 ....152 B7
Shaw St *CLECK* BD19 ....158 C1
   GTL/HWG HX4 ....175 F5
   LM/WK BD12 ....137 C1
   MIRF WF14 ....179 H4
Shay Cl *HTON* BD9 ....96 E1
Shay Ct *LDSU* LS2 ....9 L3
Shay Crs *HTON* BD9 ....96 D1
Shay Dr *HTON* BD9 ....96 D1
Shayfield La *EARD/LOFT* WF3 ....144 E4
Shay Fold *HTON* BD9 ....96 D1
Shay Gap Rd *HWTH* BD22 ....52 D4
Shay Ga *WIL/AL* BD15 ....95 H1
Shay Gra *HTON* BD9 ....96 D7
Shay Gv *HTON* BD9 ....96 E1
Shay La *HTON* BD9 ....96 D1
   LUD/ILL HX2 ....134 D3
   WIL/AL BD15 ....95 H1
Shay St *HDGY* LS6 ....9 L3
Shay Syke *HFAX* HX1 ....17 J8
Sheaf St *MID* LS10 ....14 C7
Shearbridge Gn *GTHN* BD7 ....5 H8
Shearbridge Rd *GTHN* BD7 ....5 G7
Shearbridge Ter *GTHN* BD7 ....5 H9
Shed St *KGHY* BD21 ....3 C4
Sheep Hill La *CUL/QBY* BD13 ....116 A4
Sheepridge Gv *HUDN* HD2 ....177 H6
Sheepridge Rd *HUDN* HD2 ....177 H6
Sheepscar Gv *CHAL* LS7 ....10 C6
Sheepscar St North *CHAL* LS7 ....10 D5
Sheepscar St South *CHAL* LS7 ....10 D5
Sheepscar Wy *CHAL* LS7 ....10 C3
Sheepwalk La *CAS* WF10 ....169 J2
Sheldon Rdg *BOW* BD4 ....118 C7
Sheldrake Av *CAS* WF10 ....96 B6
Sheldrake Rd *CAS* WF10 ....168 C2
Shelf Hall La *HIPP* HX3 ....136 A2
Shelf Moor *HIPP* HX3 ....116 B7
Shelf Moor Rd *HIPP* HX3 ....116 B7
Shelldrake Dr *MID* LS10 ....143 J2
Shelley Av *HECK* WF16 ....160 B6
Shelley Cl *RTHW* LS26 ....145 K4
Shelley Ct *BGLY* BD16 ....75 K1
   HOR/CROF WF4 ....183 H7
Shelley Crs *RTHW* LS26 ....145 K4
Shelley Dr *KNOT* WF11 ....170 C4
Shelley Gv *GIR* BD8 ....96 D5
Shell La *PDSY/CALV* LS28 ....99 J7
Shepcote Cl *BHP/TINH* LS16 ....81 J1
Shepcote Crs *BHP/TINH* LS16 ....81 J1
Shepherds Gv *HUDN* HD2 ....177 K6
   RHAY LS8 ....10 F1
Shepherd's La *CHAL* LS7 ....103 K1
   RHAY LS8 ....10 F1
Shepherd's Pl *RHAY* LS8 ....104 A1
Shepherds Thorn La
   HUDN HD2 ....177 H3
Shepley Mt *MIRF* WF14 ....179 J3
Shepley St *WKFDE* WF1 ....19 J4
Sherborne Dr *HWTH* BD22 ....53 F6
Sherborne Rd *GTHN* BD7 ....5 H8
   IDLE BD10 ....78 C3
Sherbrooke Av
   MSTN/BAR LS15 ....105 G6
Sherburn Ap *SCFT* LS14 ....85 K6
Sherburn Ct *BIRK/DRI* BD11 ....139 J5
Sherburn Ct *SCFT* LS14 ....85 K6
Sherburn Dr *BIRK/DRI* BD11 ....139 J1
Sherburn Pl *SCFT* LS14 ....85 K6
Sherburn Rd *BRIG* HD6 ....176 C1
   SCFT LS14 ....85 K6
Sherburn Rd North *SCFT* LS14 ....85 J4
Sheridan Cl *PDSY/CALV* LS28 ....100 C7
Sheridan Ct *PDSY/CALV* LS28 ....100 C7
Sheridan St *BOW* BD4 ....118 B2
   WKFDE WF1 ....164 E3
Sheridan Wy *PDSY/CALV* LS28 ....100 B7
Sheriff La *BGLY* BD16 ....56 B7
Sherwell Gv *WIL/AL* BD15 ....96 B4
Sherwell Ri *WIL/AL* BD15 ....96 B4
Sherwood Av *CLECK* BD19 ....139 G5
   HUDN HD2 ....178 A4
Sherwood Cl *BGLY* BD16 ....56 B6
   CLECK BD19 ....139 G5
   DEWS WF13 ....160 C5
Sherwood Gdns
   EARD/LOFT WF3 ....144 B4
Sherwood Gn *EARD/LOFT* WF3 ....144 B4
Sherwood Gv *SHPY* BD18 ....76 D4
   WKFDW/WTN WF2 ....183 D4
Sherwood Pl *ECHL* BD2 ....98 C3
Sherwood Rd *BRIG* HD6 ....157 H6
Shetcliffe La *BOW* BD4 ....118 D6
Shetcliffe Rd *BOW* BD4 ....118 C6
Shetland Cl *ECHL* BD2 ....98 A1
Shibden Dr *BTLY* WF17 ....160 B2
Shibden Garth *HIPP* HX3 ....135 K7
Shibden Hall Cft *HIPP* HX3 ....135 J7

Shibden Hall Rd *HIPP* HX3 ....135 J7
Shibden Head La
   CUL/QBY BD13 ....115 G7
Shibden Vw *CUL/QBY* BD13 ....115 G7
Shield Cl *MSTN/BAR* LS15 ....106 B2
Shield Hall La *RPDN/SBR* HX6 ....152 D4
Shill Bank Av *MIRF* WF14 ....179 K5
Shill Bank La *MIRF* WF14 ....179 K5
Shillbank Vw *MIRF* WF14 ....179 K5
Shilling St *WKFDE* WF1 ....19 G1
Shipley Airedale Rd *BFDE* BD3 ....6 C4
Shipley Fields Rd *SHPY* BD18 ....77 G7
Ship St *BRIC* HD6 ....157 F6
Shipton Ms *MOR* LS27 ....142 A4
Shire Cl *WBSY* BD6 ....116 E7
Shire Oak Rd *HDGY* LS6 ....82 C7
Shire Oak St *HDGY* LS6 ....82 C7
Shires Gv *EARD/LOFT* WF3 ....165 G3
Shirley Av *CLECK* BD19 ....139 J7
   LM/WK BD12 ....137 G6
Shirley Cl *OT* LS21 ....39 J3
Shirley Crs *LM/WK* BD12 ....137 G6
Shirley Dr *BRAM* LS13 ....101 F1
Shirley Gv *CLECK* BD19 ....139 J7
   HIPP HX3 ....157 F1
Shirley Mt *CLECK* BD19 ....139 J7
Shirley Pde *CLECK* BD19 ....139 H7
Shirley Pl *CLECK* BD19 ....139 H7
   LM/WK BD12 ....137 H6
Shirley Rd *BOW* BD4 ....118 E5
   CLECK BD19 ....139 J7
   GTHN BD7 ....4 B8
Shirley St *HWTH* BD22 ....72 C5
   SHPY BD18 ....76 E4
Shirley Ter *CLECK* BD19 ....139 J7
Shirley Wk *CLECK* BD19 ....139 J7
Shoebridge Av *AIRE* BD20 ....32 A4
Shoe Market *PONT* WF8 ....189 H1
Sholebroke Av *CHAL* LS7 ....103 H1
Sholebroke Mt *CHAL* LS7 ....103 H1
Sholebroke Pl *CHAL* LS7 ....103 J1
Sholebroke St *CHAL* LS7 ....103 H1
Sholebroke Ter *CHAL* LS7 ....83 J7
Sholebroke Vw *CHAL* LS7 ....103 J1
Shoolaboards La *PONT* WF8 ....190 A1
Shop La *EARD/LOFT* WF3 ....144 C7
Shore End La *HBR* HX7 ....112 B7
Shoreham Rd *WOR/ARM* LS12 ....12 A2
Short Cl *LM/WK* BD12 ....137 G2
Short La *CHAL* LS7 ....83 H5
Short St *EARL* WF12 ....181 K2
   FEA/AMT WF7 ....188 B4
Shortway *CUL/QBY* BD13 ....95 K7
   PDSY/CALV LS28 ....99 H4
Showfield Cl *GFTH/SHER* LS25 ....111 H4
Shroggs Rd *HFAX* HX1 ....16 D3
Shroggs St *HFAX* HX1 ....16 D4
Shroggs Vue Ter *HFAX* HX1 ....16 D4
Shuttleworth La *GIR* BD8 ....96 D5
Shuttocks Cl *GFTH/SHER* LS25 ....127 K3
Shuttocks Fold
   GFTH/SHER LS25 ....128 A3
Shutts La *HIPP* HX3 ....136 D5
Sickleholme Ct *HUDN* HD2 ....177 K4
Sickle St *CLECK* BD19 ....139 F7
Sicklinghall Rd *WBY* LS22 ....28 C3
Siddal Gv *HIPP* HX3 ....155 G4
Siddal La *HIPP* HX3 ....155 H4
Siddall St *BEE/HOL* LS11 ....13 L4
Siddal New Rd *HIPP* HX3 ....155 G3
Siddal St *HIPP* HX3 ....155 H5
Siddal Top La *HIPP* HX3 ....155 H4
Side Copse *OT* LS21 ....39 J2
Sides Rd *PONT* WF8 ....189 J2
The Sidings *CSLY* LS20 ....58 E2
   SHPY BD18 ....77 H4
Sidney St *LDS* LS1 ....10 B9
Siegen Cl *MOR* LS27 ....141 K3
Silcoates Av *WKFDW/WTN* WF2 ....163 K7
Silcoates Ct *WKFDW/WTN* WF2 ....183 K1
Silcoates Dr *WKFDW/WTN* WF2 ....163 K7
Silcoates La *WKFDW/WTN* WF2 ....163 J5
Silcoates St *WKFDW/WTN* WF2 ....184 A1
Silk Mill Ap *BHP/TINH* LS16 ....81 H2
Silk Mill Av *BHP/TINH* LS16 ....81 G1
Silk Mill Bank *BHP/TINH* LS16 ....81 G2
Silk Mill Cl *BHP/TINH* LS16 ....81 G1
Silk Mill Dr *BHP/TINH* LS16 ....81 G2
Silk Mill Gdns *BHP/TINH* LS16 ....81 G2
Silk Mill Gn *BHP/TINH* LS16 ....81 G2
Silk Mill Ms *BHP/TINH* LS16 ....81 J2
Silk Mill Rd *BHP/TINH* LS16 ....81 G2
Silk Mill Wy *BHP/TINH* LS16 ....81 H2
Silkstone Cl *GFTH/SHER* LS25 ....108 A4
Silkstone Ct *MSTN/BAR* LS15 ....105 K4
Silkstone Crs *NORM* WF6 ....166 C4
Silkstone Wy *MSTN/BAR* LS15 ....105 K4
Silk St *HTON* BD9 ....97 F3
Silsden Br *AIRE* BD20 ....32 E3
Silsden Rd *AIRE* BD20 ....34 C6
   ILK LS29 ....21 J2
Silson La *BAIL* BD17 ....57 K7
Silver Birch Av *LM/WK* BD12 ....137 H3
Silver Birch Cl *LM/WK* BD12 ....137 H3
Silver Birch Dr *LM/WK* BD12 ....137 H3
Silver Birch Gv *LM/WK* BD12 ....137 H3
Silverdale Av *AIRE* BD20 ....54 B2
   AL/HA/HU LS17 ....64 C6
   CSLY LS20 ....59 F3
Silverdale Cl *CSLY* LS20 ....59 F4
Silverdale Dr *CSLY* LS20 ....59 F4
Silverdale Gra *CSLY* LS20 ....59 F4
Silverdale Gv *CSLY* LS20 ....58 E4
Silverdale Mt *CSLY* LS20 ....59 F4
Silverdale Rd *CSLY* LS20 ....58 E4
   WBOW BD5 ....117 H4
Silverhill Dr *BFDE* BD3 ....7 J1
Silverhill Rd *BFDE* BD3 ....7 H1
Silver La *YEA* LS19 ....59 J4
Silver Mill Hl *OT* LS21 ....39 H5
Silver Royd Av
   WOR/ARM LS12 ....101 J7
Silver Royd Cl
   WOR/ARM LS12 ....101 J7
Silver Royd Garth
   WOR/ARM LS12 ....101 J7

Silver Royd Gv
   WOR/ARM LS12 ....101 J7
Silver Royd Hl
   WOR/ARM LS12 ....101 J7
Silver Royd Pl
   WOR/ARM LS12 ....101 J7
Silver Royd Rd
   WOR/ARM LS12 ....101 J7
Silver Royd St
   WOR/ARM LS12 ....101 J7
Silver Royd Ter
   WOR/ARM LS12 ....101 J7
Silver St *BEE/HOL* LS11 ....13 L5
   GIR BD8 ....4 F1
   HFAX HX1 ....17 G6
   KNOT WF11 ....150 B4
   WKFDE WF1 ....18 E4
   WKFDE WF1 ....164 C5
Silverwood Av *LUD/ILL* HX2 ....133 K6
Silwood Dr *ECHL* BD2 ....98 D2
Simes St *BFD* BD1 ....5 K5
Simm Carr La *HIPP* HX3 ....135 G3
Simmonds La *HFAX* HX1 ....17 J9
Simmons Wy *RHAY* LS8 ....11 M1
Simms Dene *WIL/AL* BD15 ....95 K1
Simon Cl *BOW* BD4 ....119 G4
Simpson Gv *IDLE* BD10 ....78 D3
Simpson St *EARD/LOFT* WF3 ....143 K7
   HIPP HX3 ....134 E5
   KGHY BD21 ....2 D4
Sinclair Rd *ECHL* BD2 ....78 A7
Sinden Ms *IDLE* BD10 ....78 C2
Singleton St *BFD* BD1 ....5 M3
Sion Hl *HIPP* HX3 ....155 H5
Sir George Martin Dr
   BHP/TINH LS16 ....62 C6
Sir Isaac Holden Pl *GTHN* BD7 ....4 E1
Sir John's La *GFTH/SHER* LS25 ....110 E5
Sir Karl Cohen Sq
   WOR/ARM LS12 ....102 A6
Sir Wilfred Pl *IDLE* BD10 ....78 A6
Siskin Cl *MOR* LS27 ....142 A4
Sissons Av *MID* LS10 ....143 G4
Sissons Crs *MID* LS10 ....143 G4
Sissons Dr *MID* LS10 ....143 G4
Sissons Gn *MID* LS10 ....143 G3
Sissons Gv *MID* LS10 ....143 G3
Sissons La *MID* LS10 ....143 G3
Sissons Mt *MID* LS10 ....143 F4
Sissons Pl *MID* LS10 ....143 G3
Sissons Rd *MID* LS10 ....143 F4
Sissons Rw *MID* LS10 ....143 G3
Sissons St *MID* LS10 ....143 G3
Sissons Ter *MID* LS10 ....143 G3
Sissons Vw *MID* LS10 ....143 F4
Sixth Av *BFDE* BD3 ....7 G1
   LVSG WF15 ....158 C3
   RTHW LS26 ....125 H7
Sizers Ct *YEA* LS19 ....59 H6
Skelbrooke Dr *PONT* WF8 ....189 J4
Skelda Ri *ILK* LS29 ....24 A6
Skelton Av *OSM* LS9 ....11 L9
Skelton Crs *OSM* LS9 ....11 M9
Skelton Grange Rd *MID* LS10 ....124 C4
Skelton Mt *OSM* LS9 ....11 L8
Skelton Pl *OSM* LS9 ....11 L8
Skelton Rd *OSM* LS9 ....11 M9
Skeltons La *SCFT* LS14 ....85 J3
Skelton St *OSM* LS9 ....11 L8
Skelton Ter *OSM* LS9 ....11 M8
Skelton Wk *IDLE* BD10 ....78 E5
Skelwith Ap *SCFT* LS14 ....105 H3
Skinner La *GIR* BD8 ....97 K3
   LDSU LS2 ....10 D6
Skinner St *LDS* LS1 ....9 J9
Skipton Av *HUDN* HD2 ....177 C7
Skipton Ri *GFTH/SHER* LS25 ....108 A6
Skipton Rd *AIRE* BD20 ....32 C1
   AIRE BD20 ....33 G7
   ILK LS29 ....22 B1
   ILK LS29 ....23 G4
   KGHY BD21 ....3 G1
Skipton St *BTLY* WF17 ....161 F6
Skircoat Gn *HIPP* HX3 ....155 G6
Skircoat Green Rd *HIPP* HX3 ....155 F6
Skircoat Moor Cl *LUD/ILL* HX2 ....154 D4
Skircoat Moor Rd *LUD/ILL* HX2 ....154 D4
Skircoat Rd *HFAX* HX1 ....17 H9
Skirrow St *BGLY* BD16 ....76 A6
Skye Rd *HTON* BD9 ....97 F2
Skye Vw *RTHW* LS26 ....145 G2
Slack Bottom Rd *WBSY* BD6 ....117 F6
Slack La *GTL/HWG* HX4 ....173 H6
   HBR HX7 ....132 C3
   HWTH BD22 ....72 C1
   RPDN/SBR HX6 ....152 A7
   RPDN/SBR HX6 ....172 A4
Sladdin Rw *CUL/QBY* BD13 ....115 F6
Slade Cl *BSPA/BRAM* LS23 ....48 C3
Slade La *AIRE* BD20 ....54 B1
   BRIC HD6 ....176 E3
Sladen St *KGHY* BD21 ....2 D5
Slade Wk *BTLY* WF17 ....140 C6
Slaithwaite Av *EARL* WF12 ....181 F5
Slaithwaite Cl *EARL* WF12 ....181 F5
Slaithwaite Rd *EARL* WF12 ....181 G5
Slaters Rd *PDSY/CALV* LS28 ....100 A4
Slates La *ILK* LS29 ....24 A2
Slaymaker La *HWTH* BD22 ....72 D1
Slead Av *BRIC* HD6 ....156 E4
Slead Ct *BRIC* HD6 ....156 E4
Slead Crs *BRIC* HD6 ....156 E4
Slead Gv *BRIC* HD6 ....156 E4
Slead Rd *BRIC* HD6 ....156 E4
Sledmere Cft *SCFT* LS14 ....85 K6
Sledmere Garth *SCFT* LS14 ....85 K6
Sledmere La *SCFT* LS14 ....85 K6
Sledmere Pl *SCFT* LS14 ....85 K6
Sleights La *AL/HA/HU* LS17 ....44 C5
Sleningford Rd *SHPY* BD18 ....76 D4
Sleningford Ri *BGLY* BD16 ....55 H6
Sleningford Rd *BGLY* BD16 ....55 H6
   SHPY BD18 ....76 D4
Slice La *TAD* LS24 ....51 J7

Slingsby Cl *IDLE* BD10 ....78 E4
Slipper La *MIRF* WF14 ....179 F1
Slippy La *LUD/ILL* HX2 ....133 K2
Sloan Sq *GIR* BD8 ....4 E3
Slutwell La *PONT* WF8 ....189 J1
Smalewell Cl *PDSY/CALV* LS28 ....100 A7
Smalewell Dr *PDSY/CALV* LS28 ....99 K7
Smalewell Gdns
   PDSY/CALV LS28 ....99 K7
Smalewell Gn *PDSY/CALV* LS28 ....100 A7
Smalewell Rd *PDSY/CALV* LS28 ....99 J7
Small Lees Rd *RPDN/SBR* HX6 ....172 E6
Small Page Fold
   CUL/QBY BD13 ....115 H5
Smallpage Yd *WKFDE* WF1 ....18 H5
Smallwood Gdns *EARL* WF12 ....161 K5
Smallwood Rd *EARL* WF12 ....161 K6
Smawthorne Av *CAS* WF10 ....168 C1
Smawthorne Gv *CAS* WF10 ....168 C1
Smawthorne La *CAS* WF10 ....168 C1
Smeaton Ap *MSTN/BAR* LS15 ....106 D2
Smeaton Gv *RTHW* LS26 ....126 D4
Smiddles La *WBOW* BD5 ....117 H4
Smiddy Hl *BSPA/BRAM* LS23 ....31 F5
Smirthwaite St *WKFDE* WF1 ....18 F1
Smirthwaite Vw *NORM* WF6 ....166 D7
Smith Av *WBSY* BD6 ....117 H6
Smith Crs *BRIG* HD6 ....176 D3
Smitherds St *KGHY* BD21 ....2 F7
Smithfield Av *HIPP* HX3 ....136 D3
Smith House Crs *BRIG* HD6 ....156 E3
Smith House Gv *BRIC* HD6 ....157 F3
Smith House La *BRIG* HD6 ....157 F3
Smithies La *BTLY* WF17 ....140 D3
   LVSG WF15 ....159 K6
Smithies Moor Crs *BTLY* WF17 ....140 D3
Smithies Moor La *BTLY* WF17 ....160 B1
Smithies Moor Ri *BTLY* WF17 ....140 D3
Smith La *HTON* BD9 ....96 D3
Smith Rd *DEWS* WF13 ....160 D3
   GTHN BD7 ....117 C3
Smithson Av *CAS* WF10 ....169 G2
Smithville *AIRE* BD20 ....54 C2
Smith Wy *RTHW* LS26 ....145 C3
Smithy Carr La *BRIC* HD6 ....157 F4
Smithy Clough La
   RPDN/SBR HX6 ....172 B6
Smithy Hl *CUL/QBY* BD13 ....94 B7
   WBSY BD6 ....117 H5
Smithy La *AL/HA/HU* LS17 ....65 K1
   BHP/TINH LS16 ....61 H5
   EARD/LOFT WF3 ....142 E7
   ILK LS29 ....25 G2
   ILK LS29 ....37 K2
   WIL/AL BD15 ....75 F6
Smithy Mills La *BHP/TINH* LS16 ....82 C7
Smithy St *HFAX* HX1 ....17 J5
Smyth St *WKFDE* WF1 ....18 D5
Snaith Wood Dr *YEA* LS19 ....79 K3
Snaith Wood Ms *YEA* LS19 ....79 K3
Snape Dr *GTHN* BD7 ....116 C4
Snape St *KGHY* BD21 ....53 K7
Snapethorpe Crs
   WKFDW/WTN WF2 ....183 J5
Snapethorpe Ga
   WKFDW/WTN WF2 ....183 H5
Snapethorpe Rd
   WKFDW/WTN WF2 ....183 J5
Snelsins La *CLECK* BD19 ....138 D6
Snelsins Rd *CLECK* BD19 ....138 D6
Snowden Ap *BRAM* LS13 ....101 H2
Snowden Cl *BRAM* LS13 ....101 H3
Snowden Crs *BRAM* LS13 ....101 H3
Snowden Fold *BRAM* LS13 ....101 G3
Snowden Gv *BRAM* LS13 ....101 G3
Snowden Lawn *BRAM* LS13 ....101 G3
Snowden Rd *SHPY* BD18 ....77 J6
Snowden Royd *BRAM* LS13 ....101 G3
Snowden St *BFD* BD1 ....5 L4
Snowdens Wk *CLAY* BD14 ....116 C2
Snowden V *BRAM* LS13 ....101 G3
Snowdon Av *KNOT* WF11 ....170 D4
Snowdon St *BTLY* WF17 ....160 E4
Snowdrop Ms *WIL/AL* BD15 ....96 A5
Snow Hill Cl *WKFDE* WF1 ....164 B7
Snow Hill Ri *WKFDE* WF1 ....164 B7
Snydale Av *NORM* WF6 ....167 F7
Snydale Cl *NORM* WF6 ....167 F7
Snydale Ct *NORM* WF6 ....167 F7
Snydale Gv *NORM* WF6 ....167 F7
Snydale Rd *NORM* WF6 ....166 E7
Soaper House La *HIPP* HX3 ....136 B5
Soaper La *HIPP* HX3 ....116 C7
Sod House Gn *HIPP* HX3 ....134 D4
Soho Gv *WKFDW/WTN* WF2 ....18 A5
Soho St *BFD* BD1 ....5 K6
   HFAX HX1 ....16 B6
Solomon Hl *LUD/ILL* HX2 ....132 E6
Solway Rd *BTLY* WF17 ....161 J3
Somerdale Cl *BRAM* LS13 ....101 G4
Somerdale Gdns *BRAM* LS13 ....101 G4
Somerdale Gv *BRAM* LS13 ....101 G4
Somerdale Wk *BRAM* LS13 ....101 G4
Somerset Av *BAIL* BD17 ....57 G7
   BRIG HD6 ....156 E4
Somerset Rd *PDSY/CALV* LS28 ....100 B5
Somers Pl *LDS* LS1 ....9 K9
Somers St *LDS* LS1 ....9 K9
Somerton Dr *BOW* BD4 ....118 E4
Somerville Av *SCFT* LS14 ....105 G4
   WBSY BD6 ....117 G7
Somerville Dr *SCFT* LS14 ....105 G2
Somerville Gn *SCFT* LS14 ....105 G4
Somerville Gv *SCFT* LS14 ....105 G3
Somerville Mt *SCFT* LS14 ....105 G4
Somerville Pk *WBSY* BD6 ....117 G7
Somerville Vw *SCFT* LS14 ....105 G3
Sonning Rd *WIL/AL* BD15 ....96 A5
Soothill La *BTLY* WF17 ....161 J3

Sorrel Cl *PONT* WF8 ....189 J2
Sorrin Cl *IDLE* BD10 ....78 B5
Sotheron Cft *PONT* WF8 ....190 A4
Soureby Cross Wy *BOW* BD4 ....119 G7
South Accommodation Rd
   MID LS10 ....14 D5
Southampton St *BFDE* BD3 ....6 E1
South Ap *BSPA/BRAM* LS23 ....67 J3
   GFTH/SHER LS25 ....88 D2
South Av *CAS* WF10 ....167 J1
   PONT WF8 ....189 F2
South Baileygate *PONT* WF8 ....169 K1
South Bank *AL/HA/HU* LS17 ....45 K4
   CUL/QBY BD13 ....115 J5
South Bank Rd *BTLY* WF17 ....160 D2
South Brook Ter *GTHN* BD7 ....5 K7
South Cliffe *CUL/QBY* BD13 ....95 G7
Southcliffe *HIPP* HX3 ....17 M9
Southcliffe Dr *BAIL* BD17 ....77 H3
Southcliffe Wy *BAIL* BD17 ....77 H3
South Cl *CSLY* LS20 ....58 C3
South Clough Head
   LUD/ILL HX2 ....153 H1
Southcote Pl *IDLE* BD10 ....78 C4
South Croft Av *BIRK/DRI* BD11 ....139 H1
South Croft Dr *BIRK/DRI* BD11 ....119 H7
South Croft Ga *BIRK/DRI* BD11 ....139 H1
South Cross Rd *HUDN* HD2 ....176 E7
Southdale Gdns *OSS* WF5 ....182 A5
Southdale Rd *OSS* WF5 ....182 C5
Southdown Cl *HTON* BD9 ....96 D1
Southdown Rd *BAIL* BD17 ....77 G3
South Dr *CSLY* LS20 ....58 C3
   PDSY/CALV LS28 ....100 A2
South Edge *KGHY* BD21 ....2 C3
   SHPY BD18 ....76 D5
Southedge Cl *HIPP* HX3 ....156 B1
South End Av *BRAM* LS13 ....101 G5
South End Gv *BRAM* LS13 ....101 G5
South End Mt *BRAM* LS13 ....101 G5
South End Ter *BRAM* LS13 ....101 G5
South Farm Crs *OSM* LS9 ....104 D3
South Farm Rd *OSM* LS9 ....104 D3
Southfield *BHP/TINH* LS16 ....61 J7
Southfield Av *AIRE* BD20 ....54 C1
   AL/HA/HU LS17 ....83 K2
   FEA/AMT WF7 ....188 A3
   WBSY BD6 ....117 H5
Southfield Cl
   WKFDW/WTN WF2 ....163 K7
Southfield Dr *AIRE* BD20 ....54 D1
   AL/HA/HU LS17 ....83 K2
Southfield La *GTHN* BD7 ....117 F3
   ILK LS29 ....22 C1
Southfield Mt *AIRE* BD20 ....54 D1
   WOR/ARM LS12 ....12 B2
Southfield Rd *BGLY* BD16 ....75 K3
   HOR/CROF WF4 ....186 E5
   ILK LS29 ....22 C1
   ILK LS29 ....37 K1
   KNOT WF11 ....171 G5
   WBOW BD5 ....117 H3
Southfield Sq *GIR* BD8 ....5 H2
Southfield St *WOR/ARM* LS12 ....12 B2
Southfield Ter *BIRK/DRI* BD11 ....139 H1
   HIPP HX3 ....136 B5
   ILK LS29 ....22 C1
Southfield Wy *AIRE* BD20 ....54 D1
Southgate *BFD* BD1 ....5 L7
   EARL WF12 ....181 F1
   ELL HX5 ....175 J2
   CSLY LS20 ....58 C4
   HFAX HX1 ....17 H6
   PONT WF8 ....189 J1
   RTHW LS26 ....145 K1
   WKFDE WF1 ....18 E5
South Gv *BRIC* HD6 ....156 C3
   SHPY BD18 ....76 C5
South Hill Cl *MID* LS10 ....124 A7
South Hill Cft *MID* LS10 ....124 A7
South Hill Dr *BGLY* BD16 ....76 A1
South Hill Gdns *RTHW* LS26 ....124 A7
South Hill Gv *MID* LS10 ....124 A7
South Hill Ri *MID* LS10 ....124 A7
South Hill Wy *MID* LS10 ....124 A7
Southlands *BAIL* BD17 ....77 G3
   LUD/ILL HX2 ....114 C5
Southlands Av *AIRE* BD20 ....54 D2
   AL/HA/HU LS17 ....83 H4
   BGLY BD16 ....75 K3
   CUL/QBY BD13 ....96 B7
   YEA LS19 ....80 A2
Southlands Cl *GFTH/SHER* LS25 ....131 G3
Southlands Crs *AL/HA/HU* LS17 ....83 H4
Southlands Dr *AIRE* BD20 ....54 D2
   AL/HA/HU LS17 ....83 H4
   HUDN HD2 ....177 F6
Southlands Gv *AIRE* BD20 ....54 D2
   BGLY BD16 ....75 J3
   CUL/QBY BD13 ....96 B7
Southlands Gv West *AIRE* BD20 ....54 D1
Southlands Mt *AIRE* BD20 ....54 D2
Southlands Rd *AIRE* BD20 ....54 D1
South La *ELL* HX5 ....175 J5
   HIPP HX3 ....116 A7
South Lane Gdns *ELL* HX5 ....175 J4
South Lea *EARD/LOFT* WF3 ....142 E4
Southlea Av *HWTH* BD22 ....73 F2
Southlea Cl *LM/WK* BD12 ....138 B2
South Lee *HORS* LS18 ....80 C3
Southleigh Av *BEE/HOL* LS11 ....123 F6
Southleigh Crs *BEE/HOL* LS11 ....123 F6
Southleigh Cft *BEE/HOL* LS11 ....123 G6
Southleigh Dr *BEE/HOL* LS11 ....123 F6
Southleigh Gdns
   BEE/HOL LS11 ....123 F6
Southleigh Gra *BEE/HOL* LS11 ....123 G6
Southleigh Gv *BEE/HOL* LS11 ....123 F6
Southleigh Rd *BEE/HOL* LS11 ....123 F6
Southleigh Vw *BEE/HOL* LS11 ....123 F6
South Md *BHP/TINH* LS16 ....61 J7
Southmere Av *GTHN* BD7 ....117 F3
Southmere Crs *GTHN* BD7 ....117 F3
Southmere Dr *GTHN* BD7 ....116 E3
Southmere Gv *GTHN* BD7 ....117 F3
Southmere Ov *GTHN* BD7 ....116 E4
Southmere Rd *GTHN* BD7 ....117 F3
Southmere Ter *GTHN* BD7 ....117 F3

Southmoor La *KNOT* WF11....171 K6
South Mt *AL/HA/HU* LS17....45 J4
South Nelson St *MOR* LS27....142 A3
Southolme Cl *KSTL* LS5....81 J7
Southowram Bank *HIPP* HX3....17 L6
South Pde *CLECK* BD19....138 D7
  ELL HX5....175 J4
  GIR BD8....5 K2
  GTL/HWG HX4....174 C6
  HDGY LS6....82 C7
  HFAX HX1....17 J8
  ILK LS29....23 K5
  LDS LS1....9 M9
  MOR LS27....142 A3
  OSS WF5....183 F5
  PDSY/CALV LS28....100 B7
  WKFDE WF1....18 L1
South Parade Cl
  PDSY/CALV LS28....100 A7
South Pkwy *SCFT* LS14....105 G2
South Park Wy
  WKFDW/WTN WF2....164 A4
South Parkway Ap *OSM* LS9....105 F2
South Point *MID* * LS10....14 E5
South Queen St *MOR* LS27....142 A4
South Rdg *GFTH/SHER* LS25....127 K5
South Rd *CUL/OBY* BD13....74 A7
  HTON BD9....97 H1
  OSM LS9....124 D3
South Royde Av *HIPP* HX3....155 F5
Southroyd Ri *PDSY/CALV* LS28....120 B1
South Sq *CUL/OBY* BD13....95 G7
South St *BRIG* HD6....157 F5
  CUL/OBY BD13....94 A3
  CUL/OBY BD13....95 F6
  EARL WF12....181 F1
  EARL WF12....181 G3
  HFAX HX1....16 F7
  KGHY BD21....53 J7
  LM/WK BD12....138 B3
  LVSG WF15....159 J4
  MIRF WF14....179 G6
  MOR LS27....142 A3
  NORM WF6....186 D2
  OSS WF5....182 C5
  WBOW BD5....117 H3
  WKFDE WF1....19 H6
South Ter *OSS* WF5....182 D6
South Vw *AIRE* BD20....54 E2
  BAIL BD17....77 H1
  CAS WF10....149 H5
  CAS WF10....168 D3
  FEA/AMT WF7....188 C3
  HIPP HX3....155 K4
  HWTH BD22....72 D5
  IDLE BD10....78 E5
  ILK LS29....38 B7
  PDSY/CALV LS28....99 K4
  PDSY/CALV LS28....100 C6
  RTHW LS26....144 E1
  WBY LS22....29 H1
  YEA LS19....59 G4
South View Cl *BOW* BD4....119 F7
  YEA LS19....59 F4
South View Cottages
  AL/HA/HU * LS17....85 G1
South View Ct *HIPP* HX3....156 C5
South View Dr *BOW* BD4....119 G7
South View Gdns *PONT* WF8....190 A1
South View Gv *CLECK* * BD19....159 J1
South View Rd *BOW* BD4....119 G7
  MID LS10....123 K5
  YEA LS19....59 F4
South View Ter *AIRE* BD20....32 E1
  BAIL * BD17....77 H1
  HFAX HX1....16 B4
  YEA LS19....59 K5
Southwaite La *SCFT* LS14....105 G1
Southwaite Pl *SCFT* LS14....105 G1
South Wk *BGLY* BD16....74 D3
South Wy *BOW* BD4....119 F7
  SHPY BD18....76 C5
Southway *BGLY* BD16....56 B6
  GSLY LS20....58 C3
  HORS LS18....80 D1
  ILK LS29....24 C6
  MIRF WF14....179 G2
Southwood Cl *SCFT* LS14....105 K1
Southwood Crs *SCFT* LS14....105 K1
Southwood Ga
  MSTN/BAR LS15....105 K1
Sovereign Cl *BTLY* WF17....140 E3
Sovereign Ct *AL/HA/HU* LS17....63 K5
Sovereign Gdns *NORM* WF6....166 C6
Sovereign Quay *LDS* * LS1....14 B2
Sovereign St *HFAX* * HX1....16 E5
  LDS LS1....13 M2
Sovereign's Wy *EARL* WF12....180 E6
Sowden Buildings *ECHL* BD2....98 C3
Sowden Gra *CUL/OBY* BD13....95 G7
Sowden Rd *HTON* BD9....96 C2
Sowden St *GTHN* * BD7....117 G3
Sowden's Yd *HDGY* * LS6....82 C6
Sowerby Croft La
  RPDN/SBR HX6....153 J5
Sowerby La *LUD/ILL* HX2....152 C2
Sowerby New Rd
  RPDN/SBR HX6....153 F5
Sowerby St *RPDN/SBR* HX6....153 J5
Sowgate La *PONT* WF8....170 B5
Sowood Av *OSS* WF5....182 D6
Sowood Ct *OSS* WF5....182 E6
Sowood Gdns *OSS* WF5....182 D6
Sowood Gra *OSS* WF5....182 D6
Sowood La *OSS* WF5....182 G6
Sowood St *BULY* LS4....82 E5
Sowood Vw *OSS* WF5....182 E5
Soyland Town Rd
  RPDN/SBR HX6....172 E3
Spa Croft Rd *OSS* WF5....183 F5
Spa Gv *WKFDW/WTN* WF2....183 K3
Spa La *BGLY* BD16....55 K6
  BSPA/BRAM LS23....48 D3
  OSS WF5....183 F6
Spa Ms *BSPA/BRAM* LS23....48 D3
Sparable La *WKFDE* WF1....185 F6
Spark House La
  RPDN/SBR HX6....153 K5

Spartal La *GFTH/SHER* LS25....128 D6
Spartan Rd *LM/WK* BD12....137 J2
Spa St *BTLY* WF17....161 F3
  OSS WF5....183 G5
Spawd Bone La *KNOT* WF11....171 F5
Speak Cl *WKFDE* WF1....185 G1
Speakers Ct *DEWS* WF13....180 E1
Spear Fir *AL/HA/HU* LS17....65 H1
Spearhead Wy *KGHY* BD21....3 H5
Speedwell Mt *HDGY* LS6....9 M7
Speedwell Rd *CAS* WF10....167 H2
Speedwell St *HDGY* LS6....9 M7
Speeton Av *WBSY* BD6....116 D4
Speeton Gv *GTHN* BD7....116 C4
Spen Ap *BHP/TINH* LS16....81 J5
Spen Bank *BHP/TINH* LS16....81 J5
  CLECK BD19....159 G1
Spence La *WOR/ARM* LS12....13 G3
Spenceley St *LDSU* LS2....9 K4
Spencer Av *AIRE* BD20....21 F7
  GTHN BD7....117 F1
  MOR LS27....141 K5
Spencer Mt *RHAY* LS8....10 F2
Spencer Pl *RHAY* LS8....10 F3
Spencer Rd *GSLY* LS20....59 G3
  GTHN BD7....4 C3
Spencer St *KGHY* BD21....2 D4
  MIRF WF14....179 H4
Spen Cl *BOW* BD4....118 C7
Spen Common La *TAD* LS24....68 D5
Spen Crs *BHP/TINH* LS16....81 J5
Spen Dr *BHP/TINH* LS16....81 K4
Spenfield Ct *LVSG* WF15....159 H6
Spen Gdns *BHP/TINH* LS16....82 A4
Spen Gv *BHP/TINH* LS16....81 J5
Spen La *CLECK* BD19....139 G2
  HDGY LS6....81 K6
Spen Ms *BHP/TINH* LS16....81 K5
Spennithorne Av
  BHP/TINH LS16....81 K3
Spennithorne Dr
  BHP/TINH LS16....81 K3
Spen Rd *BHP/TINH* LS16....82 A4
Spenser Ri *GSLY* LS20....59 G3
Spenser Rd *GSLY* LS20....59 G3
Spenslea Gv *MOR* LS27....141 K5
Spen Vale St *HECK* WF16....160 A5
Spen Valley Heritage Trail
  BTLY....140 A4
  CLECK BD19....139 F5
Spen Valley Rd *DEWS* WF13....180 B3
Spen Vw *DEWS* WF13....180 B1
Spen View La *BOW* BD4....118 C7
Spen Wk *BHP/TINH* LS16....81 K6
Spibey Crs *RTHW* LS26....124 E7
Spibey La *RTHW* LS26....124 E7
Spicer St *WBOW* * BD5....117 H3
Spiers Garth *WBSY* BD6....117 J5
Spindle St *LUD/ILL* HX2....134 D2
Spink La *PONT* WF8....169 J7
Spink Pl *GIR* BD8....5 H4
Spinks Gdns *SCFT* LS14....105 J1
Spink Well La *EARD/LOFT* WF3....142 E6
Spinkwell Rd *DEWS* WF13....161 F7
The Spinners *HWTH* BD22....72 D6
Spinners Cha *PDSY/CALV* LS28....100 B6
Spinners Wy *CLECK* BD19....138 A7
  MIRF WF14....179 H6
The Spinney *AIRE* BD20....55 C3
  AL/HA/HU LS17....83 K2
  BRIG HD6....157 F3
  IDLE BD10....79 H2
  OSM * LS9....14 F2
  WBY LS22....29 G3
Spinneyfield *HUDN* HD2....177 F6
Spinney St *OSM* LS9....14 F2
Spinning Mill Ct *SHPY* BD18....76 D4
Spion Kop *SCFT* LS14....66 C6
Spitalgap La *PONT* WF8....190 C2
Spitfire Wy *GFTH/SHER* LS25....111 J6
Spittal Hardwick La *CAS* WF10....169 H3
Spofforth Hl *WBY* LS22....29 F3
Spofforth Wk *GFTH/SHER* LS25....108 A6
Spout Fold *WKFDW/WTN* WF2....183 J3
Spout Hl *BRIG* HD6....176 D3
Spout House La *BRIG* HD6....156 D2
Spring Av *KGHY* BD21....3 M7
  MOR LS27....121 F6
Springbank *GFTH/SHER* LS25....127 F1
Spring Bank *LUD/ILL* HX2....133 F7
Springbank Av *MOR* LS27....121 F7
  PDSY/CALV LS28
Springbank Cl *PDSY/CALV* LS28....100 B2
Springbank Crs
  GFTH/SHER LS25....107 F7
Springbank Crs *MOR* LS27....121 F6
Springbank Dr *LVSG* WF15....159 J6
Springbank Dr
  PDSY/CALV LS28....100 B2
Springbank Gv
  PDSY/CALV LS28....100 B2
Spring Bank Pl *GIR* BD8....5 J1
Spring Bank Ri *KGHY* BD21....53 K7
Springbank Rd *MOR* LS27....121 F6
  PDSY/CALV LS28....100 A2
Springcliffe *GIR* BD8....4 E1
Springcliffe St *GIR* BD8....4 E1
Spring Cl *BGLY* BD16....76 A2
  GFTH/SHER LS25....107 K5
  GFTH/SHER LS25....108 A7
  KGHY BD21....3 M7
  MOR LS27....121 G7
Spring Close Av *OSM* LS9....14 F3
Spring Close Gdns *OSM* LS9....15 G3
Spring Close St *OSM* LS9....14 F3
Spring Close Wk *OSM* LS9....15 G3
Spring Ct *WIL/AL* * BD15....95 K2
Springdale Crs *IDLE* BD10....78 D4
Spring Dr *KGHY* BD21....3 M7
Spring Edge North *HFAX* HX1....16 C9
Spring Edge South *HFAX* HX1....154 C3
Spring Edge West *HFAX* HX1....154 D3
Spring End Rd *OSS* WF5....183 G6
Spring Farm La *BGLY* BD16....74 D3
Spring Farm Ms *WIL/AL* BD15....75 F7

Springfield *BSPA/BRAM* LS23....48 B2
  BSPA/BRAM LS23....48 C5
  RPDN/SBR HX6....153 H5
Springfield Av *BTLY* WF17....160 E3
  GTHN BD7....116 E1
  ILK LS29....24 B5
  MOR LS27....141 K1
  PONT WF8....169 K7
Springfield Bungalows
  CLECK * BD19....159 F1
Springfield Cl *HORS* LS18....81 H3
  MID LS10....124 B4
Springfield Ct *GFTH/SHER* LS25....111 G4
  KGHY BD21....2 C2
Springfield Crs *MOR* LS27....141 K1
Springfield Dr *LVSG* WF15....158 D3
Springfield Gdns *HORS* LS18....81 G3
  KGHY BD21....2 D2
Springfield Gra
  WKFDW/WTN WF2....183 J3
Springfield Gn *MID* * LS10....123 K4
Springfield Gv *BGLY* BD16....55 J7
  BRIG HD6....157 F4
Springfield La *BOW* BD4....120 B4
  LVSG WF15....159 F3
  MOR LS27....141 K1
Springfield Mt *HORS* LS18....81 F3
  LDSU LS2....9 J6
  WOR/ARM * LS12....101 K6
Springfield Pk *MIRF* WF14....179 J4
Springfield Pl *GIR* BD8....5 K3
  MID LS10....123 K4
Springfield Ri *HORS* LS18....81 G3
  RTHW LS26....145 G3
Springfield Rd *BAIL* BD17....57 G7
  ELL HX5....176 A2
  GFTH/SHER LS25....111 G4
  GSLY LS20....59 F3
  KGHY BD21....2 D2
  MOR LS27....141 K1
Springfield Ter *CLECK* BD19....138 A6
  DEWS WF13....161 F7
  GIR * BD8....5 H3
  GSLY LS20....59 F2
  PDSY/CALV LS28....100 A4
Springfields *KNOT* WF11....171 J5
Springfields *KNOT* WF11....171 J4
Springfield St *CUL/OBY* BD13....95 H7
  GIR BD8....5 H3
  RTHW LS26....145 G3
Springfield Wk *CLECK* BD19....138 A6
Spring Gdns *AL/HA/HU* LS17....44 B3
  BFD BD1....5 K3
  BIRK/DRI BD11....140 C3
  BRIG * HD6....157 F4
  BTLY * WF17....160 E3
  MOR LS27....122 B7
Spring Gardens La *KGHY* BD21....2 E7
Spring Gardens Mt *KGHY* BD21....2 E1
Spring Gardens Rd *HTON* BD9....97 F2
Spring Garden St
  CUL/OBY BD13....115 H5
Spring Gv *HFAX* HX1....154 B1
Spring Grove Ter *HDGY* LS6....8 E5
Spring Grove Vw *HDGY* LS6....8 E5
Spring Grove Wk *HDGY* LS6....8 E5
Spring Hall Cl *HIPP* HX3....136 A2
Spring Hall Dr *HFAX* HX1....134 B7
Spring Hall Gdns *HFAX* HX1....154 B1
Spring Hall Gv *LUD/ILL* HX2....154 B1
Spring Hall La *HFAX* HX1....154 B2
Spring Hall Pl *HFAX* HX1....154 B1
Spring Head Rd *CUL/OBY* BD13....95 H7
  HWTH BD22....72 D4
Springhead Rd *RTHW* LS26....145 H1
Spring Hl *BAIL* BD17....76 E1
  BHP/TINH LS16....62 D7
  CHAL LS7....10 A1
  SHPY BD18....77 K5
Springhill Cl *WKFDE* WF1....164 B3
Springhill Ct *TAD* LS24....50 E6
Springhills *WKFDE* WF1....164 B3
Spring Hill Ter *HDGY* LS6....82 D6
Spring Holes La *CUL/OBY* BD13....95 F6
Springhurst Rd *SHPY* BD18....77 F5
Spring La *BGLY* BD16....56 C5
  BTLY WF17....160 E1
  GTL/HWG HX4....174 D2
  WBY LS22....30 B4
Springlodge Pl *GIR* BD8....5 K2
Springmead Dr
  GFTH/SHER LS25....107 J7
Spring Mill La *OSS* WF5....182 E3
Spring Mill St *WBOW* BD5....117 K1
Spring Mt *KGHY* BD21....3 M8
Spring Park Rd *WIL/AL* BD15....75 F7
Spring Pl *GTHN* BD7....5 H9
  KGHY BD21....3 M8
Spring Ri *KGHY* BD21....3 M7
Spring Rd *HDGY* LS6....8 D1
Spring Rw *BGLY* BD16....74 E3
  KGHY BD21....2 F7
Springroyd Ter *GIR* BD8....4 A3
The Springs *WKFDE* WF1....18 F4
Springs La *BSPA/BRAM* LS23....30 C5
  ILK LS29....24 A5
Springs Pavement *ILK* * LS29....24 A5
Springs Rd *BAIL* BD17....59 F6
Springstone Av *OSS* WF5....182 C2
Spring St *BRIG* HD6....157 F6
  DEWS WF13....161 F7
  IDLE BD10....78 C6
  KGHY BD21....3 H2
  LVSG WF15....159 J4
  RPDN/SBR HX6....172 E5
Springswood Av *SHPY* BD18....77 F5
Springswood Pl *SHPY* BD18....77 F5
Springswood Rd *SHPY* BD18....77 F5
Spring Ter *HIPP* HX3....17 J8
  KGHY BD21....3 M6
  RPDN/SBR HX6....153 K6
Springvale Cl *HOR/CROF* WF4....186 E6
Spring Va *PDSY/CALV* LS28....100 B4
Spring Valley Av *BRAM* LS13....101 F4
Spring Valley Cl *BRAM* LS13....101 F4
Spring Valley Cft *BRAM* LS13....101 F4
Spring Valley Dr *BRAM* LS13....101 F4

Spring Valley St *LVSG* WF15....159 H3
Spring Valley Vw *BRAM* LS13....101 F4
Spring Valley Wk *BRAM* LS13....101 F4
Spring Vw *MOR* LS27....121 G6
  OSS WF5....182 E3
Spring Wy *KGHY* BD21....3 M7
Springwell Av *RTHW* LS26....126 D5
Springwell Cl *YEA* LS19....59 K5
Springwell Ct *BEE/HOL* LS11....13 H3
  EARD/LOFT WF3....142 D6
Springwell Dr *WBOW* BD5....117 K2
Springwell Rd *RTHW* LS26....126 D5
  WOR/ARM LS12....13 H3
Springwell St *BEE/HOL* LS11....13 H3
Springwell Vw *BEE/HOL* LS11....13 J4
Spring Wood Av *HIPP* HX3....154 E6
Springwood Av *WBOW* BD5....118 A3
Spring Wood Dr *HIPP* HX3....154 E6
Spring Wood Gdns *HIPP* * HX3....154 E7
Spring Wood Gdns *RHAY* LS8....84 C6
Spring Wood Gv *WBOW* BD5....118 A4
Springwood Gv *RHAY* LS8....84 C6
Springwood Rd *RHAY* LS8....84 C6
  YEA LS19....79 H1
Springwood Ter *ECHL* BD2....97 K3
Sprinkwell Cl *BFDE* BD3....6 A2
Spruce Hts *BRIG* HD6....157 F2
Spruce St *KGHY* BD21....3 J3
Spur Dr *MSTN/BAR* LS15....106 B2
Spurrier's Av *KNOT* WF11....170 D5
Spurr St *BTLY* WF17....161 G4
The Square *BSPA/BRAM* LS23....48 D3
  CAS WF10....169 H1
  GFTH/SHER LS25....127 K5
  GIR BD8....96 B6
  KNOT WF11....170 D2
  TAD LS24....51 F6
Square Rd *HFAX* HX1....17 J6
Square St *BOW* BD4....118 B1
Squire Gn *GIR* BD8....4 A2
Squire La *HTON* BD9....4 A2
Squirrel Cl *DEWS* WF13....160 C5
Squirrel Ct *HUDN* HD2....176 B7
Squirrel Hall Dr *DEWS* WF13....160 C5
Squirrel La *CUL/OBY* BD13....114 E1
Squirrel Wk *DEWS* WF13....160 C5
Stable Fold *LM/WK* BD12....137 J3
Stableford Gdns *HUDN* HD2....176 C7
Stable La *HIPP* HX3....16 C7
Stablers Wk *NORM* WF6....166 D4
Stables La *BSPA/BRAM* LS23....48 D3
Stackgarth *BRIG* HD6....177 F1
Stacks La *HBR* HX7....152 A3
Stadium Rd *WBSY* BD6....117 J6
Stadium Wy *BEE/HOL* LS11....12 F7
Stafford Av *HIPP* HX3....155 F4
Stafford Pde *HIPP* HX3....155 F5
Stafford Rd *HIPP* HX3....155 F5
Stafford Sq *HIPP* HX3....155 G5
Stafford St *BOW* BD4....118 C2
  CAS WF10....148 B6
  MID LS10....14 E7
Stafford Ter *WKFDW/WTN* WF2....184 A3
Stainbeck Av *CHAL* LS7....82 E6
Stainbeck Cnr *CHAL* LS7....83 H5
Stainbeck Gdns *CHAL* LS7....83 G6
  WBSY BD6....116 C6
Stainbeck La *CHAL* LS7....83 F5
Stainbeck Rd *CHAL* LS7....83 F6
Stainbeck Wk *CHAL* LS7....83 G6
Stainburn Av *AL/HA/HU* LS17....83 F3
  CAS WF10....169 H1
Stainburn Crs *AL/HA/HU* LS17....83 F3
Stainburn Dr *AL/HA/HU* LS17....83 J3
Stainburn Gdns *AL/HA/HU* LS17....83 K3
Stainburn Mt *AL/HA/HU* LS17....83 J4
Stainburn Rd *AL/HA/HU* LS17....83 J4
Stainburn Ter *AL/HA/HU* LS17....83 J4
Stainburn Vw *AL/HA/HU* LS17....83 K3
Staincliffe Cl *SCFT* LS14....105 H2
Staincliffe Crs *DEWS* WF13....160 C6
Staincliffe Hall Rd *BTLY* WF17....160 C5
Staincliffe Mill Yd
  DEWS * WF13....160 D5
Staincliffe Rd *DEWS* WF13....160 C6
Stainland Rd *GTL/HWG* HX4....173 H5
  GTL/HWG HX4....174 C6
Stainmore Cl *SCFT* LS14....105 H2
Stainmore Pl *SCFT* LS14....105 H2
Stainton Cl *WBSY* BD6....116 D6
Stainton La *EARD/LOFT* WF3....144 E3
Staircase La *OT* LS21....41 C5
Stairfoot Cl *BHP/TINH* LS16....62 C6
Stair Foot La *BHP/TINH* LS16....62 C6
Stairfoot Vw *BHP/TINH* LS16....62 C6
Staithe Av *MID* LS10....143 J2
Staithe Cl *MID* LS10....143 J2
Staithe Gdns *MID* LS10....143 J2
Staithgate La *WBSY* BD6....118 A6
Stallabrass St *GIR* BD8....5 H4
Stamford Av *CAS* WF10....167 K2
Stamford St *BOW* BD4....6 E9
Stammergate La *WBY* LS22....28 E7
Stamp Hill Cl *ILK* LS29....22 A1
Stanacre Pl *BFDE* BD3....6 B2
Standale Av *PDSY/CALV* LS28....100 A5
Standale Crs *PDSY/CALV* LS28....100 A5
Standale Ri *PDSY/CALV* LS28....100 A5
Stanhall Av *PDSY/CALV* LS28....100 A4
Stanhope Av *HORS* LS18....81 F2
Stanhope Cl *HORS* LS18....81 F2
Stanhope Dr *HORS* LS18....80 E2
Stanhope Gdns
  EARD/LOFT WF3....143 K6
Stanhope Gv *EARD/LOFT* WF3....143 K6

Stanks Ri *SCFT* LS14....106 B1
Stanks Rd *SCFT* LS14....106 A1
Stanks Wy *SCFT* LS14....106 A1
Stanley Av *OSM* LS9....11 H4
Stanley Cottages *NORM* WF6....166 D6
Stanley Dr *RHAY* LS8....84 C7
Stanley Garth *HECK* * WF16....160 B4
Stanley La *GTL/HWG* HX4....174 C6
  LVSG WF15....159 H3
  WKFDE WF1....164 C6
Stanley Pl *BTLY* WF17....161 G3
  OSM LS9....11 H4
Stanley Rd *CHAL* LS7....10 B2
  ECHL BD2....97 J1
  HFAX HX1....16 A8
  HUDW HD3....175 K5
  HWTH BD22....53 H7
  LVSG WF15....159 H6
  OSM LS9....11 H4
  WKFDE WF1....19 H2
Stanley St *BGLY* BD16....75 K1
  BRIG HD6....157 G5
  CAS WF10....148 D7
  CLECK BD19....138 D7
  FEA/AMT WF7....188 C2
  HWTH BD22....73 F4
  IDLE BD10....78 C4
  KGHY * BD21....2 F3
  RPDN/SBR HX6....153 K4
  SHPY BD18....77 H7
  WKFDE WF1....19 H4
Stanley Ter *OSM* LS9....11 H4
  WOR/ARM LS12....12 A1
Stanley Vw *WOR/ARM* LS12....12 A1
Stanmoor Dr *EARD/LOFT* WF3....165 F2
Stanmore Av *BULY* LS4....8 B3
Stanmore Crs *BULY* LS4....8 B2
Stanmore Gv *BULY* LS4....8 B3
Stanmore Hl *BULY* LS4....8 C3
Stanmore Mt *BULY* LS4....8 B3
Stanmore Pl *BULY* LS4....8 B3
  GTHN BD7....4 C9
Stanmore Rd *BULY* LS4....8 B2
Stanmore St *BULY* LS4....8 B2
Stanmore Ter *BULY* LS4....8 B2
Stanmore Vw *BULY* LS4....8 B3
Stannard Well Dr
  HOR/CROF WF4....183 G7
Stannard Well La
  HOR/CROF WF4....183 G7
Stannary Pl *HFAX* HX1....16 F4
Stannery End La *HBR* HX7....152 A1
Stanningley Av *LUD/ILL* HX2....133 J2
Stanningley By-Pass
  PDSY/CALV LS28....99 K4
Stanningley Dr *LUD/ILL* HX2....133 J2
Stanningley Gv *HECK* WF16....160 A5
Stanningley Rd *LUD/ILL* HX2....133 J2
  PDSY/CALV LS28....100 D3
Stansfield Cl *CAS* WF10....149 G6
  HFAX HX1....16 D5
Stansfield Ct *RPDN/SBR* HX6....153 J5
Stansfield Dr *CAS* WF10....149 H7
Stansfield Mill La
  RPDN/SBR HX6....153 G7
Stansfield Rd *CAS* WF10....149 G7
Stapper Gn *WIL/AL* BD15....74 E6
Starbeck Rd *WKFDE* WF1....19 J1
Starkie St *KGHY* BD21....2 F6
Star St *WBOW* BD5....117 H3
Starwort Cl *PONT* WF8....189 J2
Station Ap *ILK* LS29....37 K2
Station Av *BRAM* LS13....100 E3
Station Ct *GSLY* * LS20....58 E2
Station Crs *WOR/ARM* LS12....102 A4
Station Est *TAD* * LS24....50 D7
Station Flds *GFTH/SHER* LS25....107 J6
Station Forecourt *BFD* * BD1....5 M6
Station La *BIRK/DRI* BD11....139 J1
  EARD/LOFT WF3....142 D6
  EARD/LOFT WF3....143 J3
  FEA/AMT WF7....188 B4
  LVSG WF15....159 K6
  PONT WF8....189 J1
  RTHW LS26....126 A7
  SCFT LS14....66 C5
  WBY LS22....46 E1
Station Mt *BRAM* LS13....101 F3
Station Pde *KSTL* LS5....101 K1
Station Pl *BRAM* LS13....101 F3
Station Rd *AIRE* BD20....32 E4
  BAIL BD17....58 C5
  BAIL BD17....77 J1
  BFD BD1....97 J3
  BIRK/DRI BD11....140 B1
  BRIG HD6....157 H6
  BTLY WF17....161 G4
  CAS WF10....148 B3
  CAS WF10....148 C7
  CLAY BD14....116 B2
  CUL/OBY BD13....73 K6
  CUL/OBY BD13....94 B5
  CUL/OBY BD13....115 H5
  EARL WF12....181 F4
  EARL WF12....181 J3
  GFTH/SHER LS25....127 J6
  GSLY LS20....58 E2
  GTL/HWG HX4....174 C6
  HECK WF16....159 K5
  HIPP HX3....137 F5
  HIPP HX3....156 B1
  HORS LS18....81 F2
  HUDN HD2....178 B4
  HWTH BD22....72 D5
  HWTH BD22....72 E2
  HWTH BD22....92 D5
  ILK LS29....24 A5
  ILK LS29....37 K2
  ILK LS29....38 B6
  KNOT * WF11....170 D5
  LM/WK BD12....137 K2
  LUD/ILL HX2....152 E1
  MIRF WF14....179 H5
  MOR LS27....141 J2
  MSTN/BAR LS15....86 C5
  MSTN/BAR LS15....105 K3
  NORM WF6....166 C5
  OSS WF5....182 C4

OT LS21 .....39 H3
OT LS21 .....41 J5
RPDN/SBR HX6 .....153 K5
RTHW LS26 .....146 E4
SHPY BD18 .....77 G4
TAD LS24 .....50 D7
TAD LS24 .....91 K6
WIL/AL BD15 .....94 C2
WOR/ARM LS12 .....102 A6
Station St PDSY/CALV LS28 .....100 A7
WKFDE WF1 .....185 F7
Station Ter BRAM LS13 .....101 F3
CAS WF10 .....148 B3
Station Vw AIRE BD20 .....32 E5
HWTH BD22 .....92 D2
MSTN/BAR LS15 .....105 K4
Station Wy WOR/ARM LS12 .....102 A6
Staups La HIPP HX3 .....135 J6
Staveley Dr SHPY BD18 .....76 C5
Staveley Gv HWTH BD22 .....73 H1
Staveley Ms BGLY * BD16 .....55 K7
Staveley Rd BGLY BD16 .....55 J7
GTHN BD7 .....4 E8
HWTH BD22 .....73 H1
SHPY BD18 .....76 C4
Staveley Wy HWTH BD22 .....53 H7
Stavely Ms BGLY * BD16 .....55 K7
Staverton Gv CUL/QBY BD13 .....95 H6
Staverton St LUD/ILL HX2 .....154 B1
Staybrite Av BGLY BD16 .....75 K5
Staygate Gn WBSY BD6 .....117 K5
Staynton Crs HUDN HD2 .....178 A4
Stead La ILK LS29 .....37 G2
RPDN/SBR HX6 .....172 D7
SCFT LS14 .....66 D6
Steadman St BFDE BD3 .....6 F7
Steadman Ter BFDE BD3 .....6 F7
Stead Rd BOW BD4 .....119 F6
Stead St BAIL BD17 .....77 G4
HFAX * HX1 .....16 F6
Stead's Yd HORS LS18 .....81 F2
Steanard La MIRF WF14 .....179 K6
Steander OSM LS9 .....14 D2
Steeplands HUDN HD2 .....178 A3
Steep La HBR HX7 .....152 B4
Steeton Gv AIRE BD20 .....32 D4
Steeton Hall Gdns AIRE BD20 .....32 C4
Steeton Wy GFTH/SHER LS25 .....130 D3
Steincroft Rd GFTH/SHER LS25 .....131 G3
Stella Gdns PONT WF8 .....170 A6
Stell HI HWTH BD22 .....52 E6
Stennard Island WKFDE WF1 .....19 H7
Stephen Cl HIPP HX3 .....135 K6
Stephen Crs ECHL BD2 .....97 K2
Stephen Rd WBSY BD6 .....116 E4
Stephenson Cl EARL WF12 .....161 H7
Stephenson Dr
    WOR/ARM * LS12 .....121 G3
Stephenson Rd WIL/AL BD15 .....95 G3
Stephenson St GTHN BD7 .....117 G3
Stephenson Wy
    WKFDW/WTN WF2 .....164 A3
    WOR/ARM LS12 .....121 G3
Stepping Stones AIRE BD20 .....55 H3
Sterling Cl EARD/LOFT WF3 .....142 D5
Sterling Wy EARD/LOFT WF3 .....142 D5
Sterne HI LUD/ILL HX2 .....154 C4
Stevenson Av CAS WF10 .....169 H3
Stewart Cl ECHL BD2 .....78 D7
    MSTN/BAR LS15 .....105 K6
Stewart Pl BEE/HOL * LS11 .....13 K9
Stewart Royd HECK * WF16 .....160 B4
Stewart St HWTH BD22 .....73 F4
Sticker La BOW BD4 .....118 D3
Stile Hill Wy MSTN/BAR LS15 .....106 B6
Stirling Crs BOW BD4 .....119 F3
    HORS LS18 .....60 D7
Stirling Rd ILK LS29 .....37 J1
Stirling St AIRE BD20 .....21 F7
    HFAX HX1 .....16 E7
Stirling Wy GFTH/SHER LS25 .....108 A7
Stirrup Gv ECHL BD2 .....98 A1
Stirton St WBOW BD5 .....117 J3
Stithy St OSS WF5 .....182 B1
Stockeld La WBY LS22 .....28 A3
Stockeld Rd ILK LS29 .....23 K5
Stockeld Wy ILK LS29 .....23 K4
Stockheld La MSTN/BAR LS15 .....86 C3
Stockhill Fold IDLE BD10 .....78 E4
Stockhill Rd IDLE BD10 .....78 E5
Stockhill St DEWS WF13 .....180 D1
Stockinger La ILK LS29 .....22 C2
Stocking La GFTH/SHER LS25 .....88 E6
    GFTH/SHER LS25 .....151 K1
    KNOT WF11 .....171 K4
Stock La LUD/ILL HX2 .....153 J2
Stocks Ap SCFT LS14 .....105 J1
Stocksbank Dr MIRF WF14 .....178 E3
Stocks Bank Rd MIRF WF14 .....178 E2
Stocks HI BEE/HOL LS11 .....13 J5
    ILK LS29 .....38 A6
    WOR/ARM LS12 .....8 A3
Stocks Hill Cl AIRE * BD20 .....55 G2
Stocks Ri BTLY WF17 .....161 F3
    CUL/QBY BD13 .....116 A5
    LUD/ILL HX2 .....133 F6
    RPDN/SBR HX6 .....153 F5
Stocks Ri SCFT LS14 .....105 J1
Stocks Rd SCFT LS14 .....105 J1
Stocks St CHAL LS7 .....10 C1
Stockwell Dr BTLY WF17 .....161 G2
Stod Fold LUD/ILL HX2 .....113 H6
Stone Arches WBOW BD5 .....117 K2
Stonebridge Ap
    WOR/ARM * LS12 .....101 H7
Stonebridge Av
    WOR/ARM LS12 .....101 J7
Stonebridge Gv
    WOR/ARM LS12 .....101 H7
Stonebridge La
    WOR/ARM LS12 .....101 H7
Stone Brig Gn RTHW LS26 .....144 E3
Stone Brig La RTHW LS26 .....145 F3
Stonechat Ri MOR LS27 .....142 B3
Stonecliffe LUD/ILL HX2 .....154 D4
Stonecliffe Crs WOR/ARM LS12 .....101 H7

Stonecliffe Dr WOR/ARM LS12 .....101 H7
Stonecliffe Garth
    WOR/ARM LS12 .....101 H7
Stonecliffe Gv WOR/ARM LS12 .....101 H7
Stonecliffe Mt WOR/ARM LS12 .....101 H7
Stonecliffe Ter WOR/ARM LS12 .....101 H7
Stonecliffe Wy WOR/ARM LS12 .....121 G1
Stone Ct AIRE BD20 .....55 G3
Stonecroft EARD/LOFT WF3 .....165 F3
    ECHL BD2 .....98 D1
Stonecroft Mt LUD/ILL HX2 .....153 K1
Stonedale Cl OT LS21 .....41 H4
Stonedene Pk WBY LS22 .....29 H3
Stonefield Cl IDLE BD10 .....78 C7
Stonefield Pl BTLY WF17 .....140 C6
Stonefield St CLECK BD19 .....158 B2
    DEWS 161 F7
Stonegate BGLY BD16 .....55 K6
    CHAL LS7 .....10 B2
    OSS WF5 .....182 D6
Stonegate Ap CHAL LS7 .....82 E6
Stonegate Cha CHAL LS7 .....82 E5
Stonegate La AL/HA/HU LS17 .....83 J1
Stonegate Crs CHAL LS7 .....83 F5
Stonegate Dr PONT WF8 .....189 H3
Stonegate Farm Cl CHAL LS7 .....82 E5
Stonegate Gdns CHAL LS7 .....82 E5
Stonegate Gn CHAL LS7 .....82 E6
Stonegate La CHAL LS7 .....82 E5
Stonegate Ms CHAL LS7 .....82 E6
Stonegate Pl CHAL * LS7 .....82 E6
Stonegate Rd AL/HA/HU LS17 .....83 F7
    IDLE BD10 .....78 D6
Stonegate Wk CHAL LS7 .....82 E5
Stoneleigh CUL/QBY BD13 .....115 J5
Stone Gv AIRE BD20 .....32 D5
Stone Hall Rd ECHL BD2 .....98 C1
Stone HI BGLY BD16 .....56 A7
Stonehouse Dr CUL/QBY BD13 .....115 F6
Stonehurst MSTN/BAR LS15 .....106 A1
Stonehurst Rd MIRF WF14 .....179 H3
Stonehyrst Av DEWS WF13 .....161 G7
Stone La HWTH BD22 .....92 C3
Stonelea Cl CHAL LS7 .....83 F5
Stonelea Ct CHAL LS7 .....83 F5
    HDGY LS6 .....82 C7
Stone Mill Ap HDGY LS6 .....82 D5
Stone Mill Ct HDGY LS6 .....82 D5
Stone Mill Wy HDGY LS6 .....82 D5
Stone Pits La MOR LS27 .....141 G2
Stones Dr RPDN/SBR HX6 .....172 C7
Stone St BAIL BD17 .....77 K2
    BFD BD1 .....5 M5
    WIL/AL BD15 .....95 K2
Stone Vis HDGY LS6 .....82 C2
Stoney Bank St DEWS WF13 .....180 D3
Stoney Battery HFAX HX1 .....17 G4
Stoney Cft CLECK BD19 .....159 J1
Stoneycroft La AIRE BD20 .....53 J1
Stoney HI BRIG HD6 .....157 F6
Stoneyhurst Sq BOW BD4 .....119 F3
Stoney La AL/HA/HU LS17 .....65 H6
    BTLY WF17 .....161 G2
    HIPP HX3 .....134 C4
    HIPP HX3 .....157 F1
    HORS LS18 .....80 E4
    ILK LS29 .....37 H4
    WKFDW/WTN WF2 .....163 J3
Stoney Ridge Av WIL/AL BD15 .....96 A1
Stoney Ridge Rd BGLY BD16 .....76 B7
Stoney Ri HORS LS18 .....80 E4
Stoney Rock Ct OSM LS9 .....11 G7
Stoney Rock Gv OSM LS9 .....11 G7
Stoney Rock La OSM LS9 .....11 G7
Stoney Royd Ter HIPP HX3 .....155 G4
Stoneys Fold WIL/AL BD15 .....74 E6
Stoney St AIRE BD20 .....53 J1
Stoneythorpe HORS LS18 .....80 E4
Stony Croft La GTL/HWG HX4 .....173 J5
Stony La ECHL BD2 .....78 D7
    GTL/HWG HX4 .....174 D1
    HIPP HX3 .....156 B4
    RPDN/SBR HX6 .....172 E4
    WIL/AL BD15 .....95 J3
Stony Royd PDSY/CALV LS28 .....99 K2
Stoodley Ter LUD/ILL HX2 .....154 A3
Storey Pl SCFT LS14 .....105 F4
Storie Crs WKFDW/WTN WF2 .....183 K5
Stormer Hill La RPDN/SBR HX6 .....144 A6
Storr HI LM/WK BD12 .....137 H3
Storrs Hill Rd OSS WF5 .....182 D7
Stott HI BFD BD1 .....6 A5
Stott Rd HDGY LS6 .....8 E2
Stott St WOR/ARM LS12 .....12 C1
Stott Ter ECHL BD2 .....98 E1
Stourton Rd ILK LS29 .....23 J4
Stowe Gv OSM LS9 .....104 D5
Stowell Mill St WBOW BD5 .....117 J2
Stradmore Rd CUL/QBY BD13 .....94 B5
Strafford Wy IDLE BD10 .....78 E4
Straightacres La IDLE BD10 .....78 E7
Straight La ILK LS29 .....22 A4
    LUD/ILL HX2 .....134 A2
Straits BAIL BD17 .....57 H7
Stralau St BTLY WF17 .....161 F2
Strangford Ct IDLE BD10 .....78 E4
Stranglands La KNOT WF11 .....170 B4
Stratford Av BEE/HOL LS11 .....123 F4
Stratford Rd GTHN BD7 .....117 G1
Stratford St BEE/HOL LS11 .....123 F4
Stratford Ter BEE/HOL LS11 .....123 G3
Strathallan Dr BAIL BD17 .....77 J1
Stratheden Rd
    WKFDW/WTN WF2 .....18 B3
Strathmore Av OSM LS9 .....11 K4
Strathmore Dr BAIL BD17 .....57 J6
    OSM LS9 .....11 K3
Strathmore Rd ILK LS29 .....24 D5
Strathmore St OSM LS9 .....11 L4
Strathmore Ter OSM LS9 .....11 K4
Strathmore Vw OSM LS9 .....11 K4
Stratton Cl BRIG HD6 .....157 F7
Stratton Pk BRIG HD6 .....157 G7
Stratton Rd BRIG HD6 .....157 G7
Stratton Vw BOW * BD4 .....119 F2
Strawberry Av
    GFTH/SHER LS25 .....107 G7

Strawberry Bank LVSG WF15 .....159 H4
Strawberry Flds KGHY BD21 .....3 G3
Strawberry La WOR/ARM LS12 .....12 B1
Strawberry Rd WOR/ARM LS12 .....12 B1
Strawberry St AIRE BD20 .....32 E1
    KGHY BD21 .....3 G3
Stream Head Rd CUL/QBY BD13 .....94 B3
Streamside HDGY LS6 .....82 D6
The Street ILK LS29 .....22 A1
Street 1 BSPA/BRAM LS23 .....49 F2
Street 2 BSPA/BRAM LS23 .....49 G2
Street 3 BSPA/BRAM LS23 .....49 G1
Street 5 BSPA/BRAM LS23 .....31 G7
Street 6 BSPA/BRAM LS23 .....31 G6
Street 7 BSPA/BRAM LS23 .....31 G6
Street 8 BSPA/BRAM LS23 .....31 H7
Street Furlong La PONT WF8 .....190 C2
Street La AIRE BD20 .....34 E7
    AIRE BD20 .....55 C2
    AL/HA/HU LS17 .....83 J2
    MOR * LS27 .....121 F7
Strensall Gn WBSY BD6 .....116 D6
Stretchgate La LUD/ILL HX2 .....134 B7
Stretton Cl FEA/AMT WF7 .....167 K7
Strickland Av AL/HA/HU LS17 .....65 G5
Strickland Cl AL/HA/HU LS17 .....65 G7
Strickland Crs AL/HA/HU LS17 .....65 G5
Strong Close Gv KGHY BD21 .....3 L4
Strong Close Rd KGHY BD21 .....3 L4
Strong Close Wy KGHY BD21 .....3 L4
Stuart Gv NORM WF6 .....166 D4
Stuart Pl HUDN HD2 .....178 A4
Stuart Rd PONT WF8 .....169 H7
Stuart St CAS WF10 .....148 D7
    PONT WF8 .....169 H7
Stubbing La GTL/HWG HX4 .....174 B4
    RPDN/SBR HX6 .....173 F1
Stubbings Rd BAIL BD17 .....76 E2
Stubbing Wy SHPY BD18 .....77 H6
Stubbs La EARD/LOFT WF3 .....163 K1
    KNOT WF11 .....191 H2
Stubham Ri ILK LS29 .....23 K4
Stubley Farm Rd HECK WF16 .....159 K2
Stubley Rd HECK WF16 .....159 K2
Stubley St WKFDE * WF1 .....18 D5
Stubs Beck La CLECK BD19 .....138 D5
Studfold Vw SCFT LS14 .....105 F4
Studio Rd BVRD LS3 .....8 F7
Studley Av WBSY BD6 .....117 G7
Studley Cl AIRE BD20 .....55 G2
Studley Crs BGLY BD16 .....76 A1
Studley Rd ECHL BD2 .....98 A3
Stump Cross HIPP HX3 .....135 J6
Stumpcross Ct PONT WF8 .....170 A5
Stumpcross La PONT WF8 .....170 B5
Stumpcross Wy PONT WF8 .....170 A5
Stunsteds Rd CLECK BD19 .....138 E7
Sturges Gv ECHL BD2 .....98 C3
Sturton Av GFTH/SHER LS25 .....107 K5
Sturton Grange La
    GFTH/SHER LS25 .....108 A6
Sturton Gv LUD/ILL HX2 .....114 B7
Sturton La GFTH/SHER LS25 .....107 K5
    LUD/ILL HX2 .....134 B1
Stutely Gv HUDN HD2 .....177 K4
Stutton Rd TAD LS24 .....70 C3
Styebank La RTHW LS26 .....145 G1
Styes La LUD/ILL HX2 .....152 E4
Sty La BGLY BD16 .....55 J5
Styveton Wy AIRE BD20 .....32 C4
Suffield Cl MOR LS27 .....120 E6
Suffield Dr MOR LS27 .....120 E6
Suffield Rd MOR LS27 .....120 E6
Suffolk Av BTLY WF17 .....160 D5
Suffolk Ct YEA LS19 .....59 J4
Suffolk Pl ECHL BD2 .....98 A1
Suffolk St BTLY WF17 .....160 E4
Sugar HI ILK LS29 .....22 C1
Sugar Hill Cl RTHW LS26 .....145 K4
Sugar La EARL WF12 .....181 H1
    WKFDE WF1 .....19 J9
Sugar Well Ap CHAL * LS7 .....83 F7
Sugar Well Crs CHAL * LS7 .....103 G1
Sugar Well Mt CHAL LS7 .....83 F7
Sugar Well Rd CHAL LS7 .....83 F7
Sugden Cl BRIG HD6 .....177 F1
Sugden St BFD BD1 .....5 H5
    LM/WK BD12 .....138 A3
Sulby Gv IDLE BD10 .....79 F6
Summerbank Cl
    BIRK/DRI BD11 .....120 C7
Summerbridge Cl BTLY WF17 .....160 D2
Summerbridge Crs
    CLECK BD19 .....139 J5
    IDLE BD10 .....78 E7
Summerbridge Dr IDLE BD10 .....78 E7
Summerdale CLECK BD19 .....139 J5
Summerfield Av BRAM LS13 .....100 D2
    BRIG HD6 .....157 G2
Summerfield Cl BAIL BD17 .....77 F1
    KNOT WF11 .....151 F7
Summerfield Dr BAIL BD17 .....77 G1
    BRAM LS13 .....100 D2
    KNOT WF11 .....150 E7
Summerfield Gdns BRAM LS13 .....100 D3
Summerfield Gn BAIL BD17 .....77 G1
    BRAM LS13 .....100 D2
Summerfield Gv BAIL BD17 .....77 F1
Summerfield Pk BAIL BD17 .....77 G1
Summerfield Pl BRAM LS13 .....100 D2
Summerfield Rd BRAM LS13 .....100 D3
    IDLE BD10 .....78 D6
Summergate Pl HFAX HX1 .....16 A8
Summergate St HFAX HX1 .....16 A8
Summer Hall Ing LM/WK BD12 .....137 G3
Summerhill Av AIRE BD20 .....32 E4
Summerhill Dr AIRE BD20 .....32 E4
Summerhill Gdns RHAY LS8 .....84 C1
Summerhill La
    GFTH/SHER LS25 .....107 G7
Summerhill La AIRE BD20 .....32 E4
Summerhill Pl RHAY LS8 .....84 C1
Summerhill Rd
    GFTH/SHER LS25 .....107 G6
Summer Hill St GTHN BD7 .....117 H1
Summer Hill St GTHN BD7 .....117 H1
Summerlands Gv WBOW BD5 .....118 B4

Summer Lea IDLE BD10 .....78 B4
Summer Meadow PONT * WF8 .....189 H2
Summerscale St HFAX * HX1 .....16 C4
Summerseat Pl GTHN BD7 .....4 F7
Summer St HFAX HX1 .....16 B9
Summerville Rd GTHN BD7 .....5 G7
    PDSY/CALV LS28 .....99 K3
Summit St KGHY * BD21 .....2 F3
Sunbeam Av BEE/HOL LS11 .....123 G3
Sunbeam Gv BEE/HOL LS11 .....123 G3
Sunbeam Pl BEE/HOL LS11 .....123 G3
Sunbeam Ter BEE/HOL LS11 .....123 G3
    EARD/LOFT * WF3 .....142 D6
Sunbridge Rd BFD BD1 .....5 H4
Sun Ct FEA/AMT WF7 .....168 D7
Sunderland Ct BRIG HD6 .....157 F5
Sunderland Rd HTON BD9 .....97 G3
Sunderland St HFAX HX1 .....16 F6
    HWTH BD22 .....73 C4
    KGHY BD21 .....2 F7
Sundown Av GTHN BD7 .....116 D2
Sun Fld PDSY/CALV LS28 .....100 A4
Sunfield Cl PDSY/CALV LS28 .....100 A3
Sunfield Dr PDSY/CALV LS28 .....100 A3
Sunfield Gdns
    PDSY/CALV * LS28 .....100 A3
Sunfield Pl PDSY/CALV LS28 .....100 A3
Sun Fold HFAX HX1 .....17 J8
Sun Hill Dr BAIL BD17 .....76 D1
Sunhurst Cl HWTH BD22 .....72 D2
Sunhurst Dr HWTH BD22 .....72 D2
Sun La ILK LS29 .....25 J7
    WKFDE WF1 .....19 C5
Sunningdale GFTH/SHER LS25 .....108 E6
    GIR BD8 .....96 C5
Sunningdale Av AL/HA/HU LS17 .....63 F7
Sunningdale Crs CUL/QBY BD13 .....74 B7
Sunningdale Cft HUDN HD2 .....176 E6
Sunningdale Dr AL/HA/HU LS17 .....63 F7
Sunningdale Gn AL/HA/HU LS17 .....63 F7
Sunninglands NORM WF6 .....167 G2
Sunny Bank CHAL LS7 .....84 A7
    KNOT WF11 .....171 H4
    NORM WF6 .....186 D1
    SHPY BD18 .....77 G5
Sunnybank Av BFDE BD3 .....99 G4
    HORS LS18 .....80 E5
Sunny Bank Av MIRF WF14 .....179 H2
    WBOW * BD5 .....117 J5
Sunnybank Cl CLECK BD19 .....158 A2
Sunnybank Ct YEA LS19 .....60 A4
Sunnybank Crs GTL/HWG HX4 .....174 D2
    YEA LS19 .....60 A4
Sunnybank Dr GTL/HWG HX4 .....174 E2
Sunny Bank Dr MIRF WF14 .....179 C1
    RPDN/SBR HX6 .....153 K4
Sunnybank Gv BFDE BD3 .....99 G4
Sunny Bank Gv CHAL LS7 .....83 K7
    MIRF WF14 .....179 H2
Sunnybank La BFDE BD3 .....99 G4
Sunny Bank La BTLY WF17 .....161 G1
Sunnybank La GTL/HWG HX4 .....174 E2
Sunny Bank La HIPP HX3 .....156 A3
Sunny Bank Pde MIRF WF14 .....179 G1
Sunny Bank Rd BRIG HD6 .....156 E5
    BTLY WF17 .....161 G2
    LUD/ILL HX2 .....133 J2
    MIRF WF14 .....179 H1
    WBOW BD5 .....117 J5
Sunnybank Rd
    GFTH/SHER LS25 .....109 G7
    GTL/HWG HX4 .....174 D2
    HORS LS18 .....80 E5
Sunnybank St OSS WF5 .....182 B4
Sunny Bank St RPDN/SBR HX6 .....153 K4
Sunny Bank Ter HIPP * HX3 .....17 G2
Sunny Bank Vw RHAY * LS8 .....84 A7
Sunny Bank Wk MIRF WF14 .....179 H1
Sunnybank Woods BTLY WF17 .....161 G2
Sunnybrae Crs BGLY BD16 .....76 A2
Sunny Brow La HTON BD9 .....96 C3
Sunnycliffe AIRE BD20 .....55 G3
Sunnydale Av BRIG HD6 .....177 F1
Sunnydale Crs OT LS21 .....38 E4
Sunnydale Cft OSS * WF5 .....182 D5
Sunnydale Gv KGHY BD21 .....3 G6
Sunnydale Pk AIRE BD20 .....55 H2
    OSS WF5 .....182 D4
Sunnydale Rdg OT LS21 .....38 E4
Sunnydale Rd OSS WF5 .....182 D4
Sunnydale Ter OSS WF5 .....182 D4
Sunnydene SCFT LS14 .....105 G4
Sunnyfield EARD/LOFT WF3 .....163 H1
Sunny Gv MOR LS27 .....122 B6
Sunnyhill Av WKFDW/WTN WF2 .....163 J7
Sunny Hill Av HWTH BD22 .....2 B8
Sunny Hill Cl
    WKFDW/WTN * WF2 .....163 K6
Sunnyhill Crs
    WKFDW/WTN WF2 .....163 J7
Sunnyhill Cft
    WKFDW/WTN WF2 .....163 J6
Sunny Hill Gv HWTH BD22 .....2 B8
Sunny Lea Ter WBSY * BD6 .....117 H3
Sunny Mt AIRE BD20 .....55 F4
    BGLY BD16 .....74 E3
    KGHY BD21 .....2 E3
Sunnymount HWTH BD22 .....52 E3
Sunnyridge Av PDSY/CALV LS28 .....99 J6
    HECK WF16 .....160 A5
Sunnyside Av EARD/LOFT WF3 .....142 C7
    LVSG WF15 .....159 G4
Sunnyside La BFDE BD3 .....6 B1
Sunnyside Rd BRAM LS13 .....100 E4
Sunny Side St HIPP * HX3 .....17 G2
Sunnyview EARD/LOFT WF3 .....163 H1
Sunny View BEE/HOL LS11 .....122 E3
Sunny View Gdns
    BEE/HOL LS11 .....122 E3
Sunny View Ter CUL/QBY BD13 .....115 F6
Sunroyd Av HOR/CROF WF4 .....183 G7
Sunroyd HI HOR/CROF WF4 .....183 G7
Sunset Av HDGY LS6 .....82 D4

Sunset Dr HDGY LS6 .....82 D5
    ILK LS29 .....24 C4
Sunset Hilltop HDGY LS6 .....82 D4
Sunset Mt HDGY LS6 .....82 D5
Sunset Ri HDGY LS6 .....82 D4
Sunset Rd HDGY LS6 .....82 D4
Sunset Vw HDGY LS6 .....82 D4
Sunshine Ct WBSY BD6 .....116 E7
Sun St AIRE BD20 .....32 A5
    BFDE BD3 .....6 B4
    KGHY BD21 .....3 G6
    PDSY/CALV LS28 .....100 A4
    YEA LS19 .....59 K4
Sun Wy HIPP HX3 .....155 J3
Sunways MIRF WF14 .....179 F2
Sun Wood Av HIPP HX3 .....136 A3
Suresnes Rd KGHY BD21 .....2 F5
Surgery St HWTH BD22 .....72 D6
Surrey Gv PDSY/CALV LS28 .....100 B5
    WBOW BD5 .....117 K2
Surrey Rd PDSY/CALV LS28 .....100 B5
Surrey St BTLY WF17 .....161 G3
    HFAX HX1 .....154 B2
    KGHY BD21 .....3 L2
Sussex Av HORS LS18 .....81 F1
    MID LS10 .....124 A3
Sussex Crs CAS WF10 .....169 K1
Sussex Gdns MID LS10 .....124 A3
Sussex Gn MID LS10 .....124 A3
Sussex Pl MID LS10 .....124 A3
Sussex St BTLY WF17 .....161 G3
    KGHY BD21 .....3 L2
    OSM LS9 .....14 F2
Sutcliffe St LUD/ILL HX2 .....134 B7
Sutcliffe Wood La HIPP HX3 .....156 B2
Sutherland Av RHAY LS8 .....84 B3
Sutherland Crs RHAY LS8 .....84 B2
Sutherland Mt OSM LS9 .....11 K5
Sutherland Rd HIPP HX3 .....136 D7
    OSM LS9 .....11 K5
Sutherland St WOR/ARM LS12 .....12 E3
Sutherland Ter OSM LS9 .....11 K5
Sutton Ap SCFT LS14 .....105 F4
Sutton Crs BOW BD4 .....78 A7
Sutton Crs BOW BD4 .....119 F2
    SCFT LS14 .....105 F4
Sutton Dr CUL/QBY BD13 .....74 A7
Sutton Gv BOW BD4 .....119 F1
    MOR * LS27 .....141 K4
Sutton La KNOT WF11 .....170 E1
Sutton Rd BOW BD4 .....7 L9
Sutton St WOR/ARM LS12 .....13 L3
Swaine Hill Crs YEA LS19 .....59 H4
Swaine Hill St YEA LS19 .....59 H4
Swaine Hill Ter YEA LS19 .....59 H4
Swain House Crs ECHL BD2 .....78 B7
Swain House Rd ECHL BD2 .....78 B7
Swain Mt ECHL BD2 .....78 B7
Swale Crs GFTH/SHER LS25 .....108 A7
Swales Moor Rd HIPP HX3 .....135 F2
Swales' Yd PONT WF8 .....189 H1
Swallow Av WOR/ARM LS12 .....101 K7
Swallow Cl AL/HA/HU * LS17 .....64 A7
    OT LS21 .....41 G4
Swallow Crs WOR/ARM LS12 .....101 K7
Swallow Dr AL/HA/HU LS17 .....64 A7
    OT LS21 .....41 G4
Swallow Fold GIR BD8 .....96 B6
Swallow HI BTLY WF17 .....140 E5
Swallow Mt WOR/ARM LS12 .....101 K6
Swallow St HECK WF16 .....159 K5
    KGHY BD21 .....3 J3
Swallow V MOR LS27 .....142 C3
Swan Av BGLY BD16 .....76 B1
Swan Bank La HIPP HX3 .....17 K9
Swanhill La PONT WF8 .....189 J2
Swan St WBOW BD5 .....5 L9
Swarcliffe Ap SCFT LS14 .....105 K1
Swarcliffe Av SCFT LS14 .....105 K1
Swarcliffe Bank SCFT LS14 .....85 K7
Swarcliffe Dr SCFT LS14 .....105 K1
Swarcliffe Dr East
    MSTN/BAR LS15 .....106 A1
Swarcliffe Gn SCFT LS14 .....106 A1
Swarcliffe Rd SCFT LS14 .....85 K7
Swardale Gn SCFT LS14 .....105 K1
Swardale Rd SCFT LS14 .....105 K1
Swarland Gv WBOW BD5 .....117 K2
Swartha La AIRE BD20 .....21 H6
Sweet St BEE/HOL LS11 .....13 M4
Sweet St West BEE/HOL LS11 .....13 K4
Swillington La RTHW LS26 .....126 C5
Swincar Av YEA LS19 .....59 J4
Swincliffe Cl CLECK BD19 .....139 H3
Swincliffe Crs CLECK BD19 .....139 H4
Swincroft OSS WF5 .....182 B4
Swindon Rd DEWS WF13 .....181 F1
Swinegate LDS 14 A2
Swine La AIRE BD20 .....54 E3
Swine Lane Br AIRE BD20 .....55 F3
Swinnow Av BRAM LS13 .....100 D4
Swinnow Cl BRAM LS13 .....100 D4
Swinnow Crs PDSY/CALV LS28 .....100 D3
Swinnow Dr BRAM LS13 .....100 D4
Swinnow Gdns BRAM LS13 .....100 D4
Swinnow Garth
    PDSY/CALV LS28 .....100 D5
Swinnow Gn PDSY/CALV LS28 .....100 D5
Swinnow Gv BRAM LS13 .....100 D4
Swinnow La BRAM LS13 .....100 D4
Swinnow Pl PDSY/CALV LS28 .....100 D5
Swinnow Rd PDSY/CALV LS28 .....100 D5
Swinnow Vw BRAM LS13 .....100 D4
Swinnow Wk BRAM LS13 .....100 D4
Swinton Pl GTHN BD7 .....4 F9
Swinton Ter HFAX HX1 .....16 A8
Swires Rd ECHL BD2 .....6 F1
    HFAX HX1 .....16 E8
Swires Ter HFAX HX1 .....16 F8
Swiss St CAS WF10 .....148 D6
Swithenbank Av OSS WF5 .....182 B1
Swithenbank St OSS WF5 .....162 B7
Swithens Ct RTHW LS26 .....145 F3
Swithens Dr RTHW LS26 .....145 F3
Swithens Gv RTHW LS26 .....145 F3
Swithen's La RTHW LS26 .....145 G5
Swithen's St RTHW LS26 .....145 G4

Swordfish Wy
GFTH/SHER LS25 ....**111** J6
Sycamore Av *BGLY* BD16 ......**75** J2
GFTH/SHER LS25 ....**127** K8
GTHN BD7 ....**4** A6
KNOT WF11 ....**170** E5
MSTN/BAR LS15 ....**105** H5
RHAY LS8 ....**84** A7
WKFDW/WTN * WF2 ....**164** A6
WKFDW/WTN WF2 ....**184** A2
Sycamore Cha
PDSY/CALV LS28 ....**100** C6
Sycamore Cl *BFDE* BD3 ....**6** C3
BHP/TINH LS16 ....**61** J2
CHAL LS7 ....**82** E5
HDGY LS6 ....**9** J1
KNOT WF11 ....**170** E6
Sycamore Copse
WKFDW/WTN WF2 ....**184** A4
Sycamore Ct *PONT* WF8 ....**169** K6
RHAY LS8 ....**84** D6
Sycamore Cft *BEE/HOL* LS11 ...**13** L9
Sycamore Dr *BRIG* HD6 ....**157** F2
CLECK BD19 ....**158** C1
ELL HX5 ....**175** G3
ILK LS29 ....**22** D1
Sycamore Fold *BEE/HOL* LS11 ..**13** L9
Sycamore Gn *PONT* WF8 ......**170** C4
Sycamore Gv *AIRE* BD20 ......**32** A5
NORM WF6 ....**186** D1
WKFDW/WTN WF2 ....**184** A2
Sycamore Rw *BRAM* LS13 ....**100** D1
The Sycamores *BHP/TINH* LS16 ..**61** J2
DEWS WF13 ....**160** A4
GSLY LS20 ....**59** F1
WIL/AL * BD15 ....**95** J5
Sycamore St *WKFDE* WF1 .....**19** K9
Sycamore Vw *HWTH* BD22 ......**2** B7
Sycamore Wk *PDSY/CALV* LS28 ..**100** A3
Sycamore Wy *BTLY* WF17 ....**140** C6
FEA/AMT WF7 ....**188** C3
Sydenham Pl *BFDE* BD3 ....**98** B3
Sydenham Rd *BEE/HOL* LS11 ...**13** G4
Sydenham St *BEE/HOL* LS11 ...**13** G4
Sydney St *BGLY* BD16 ....**75** K1
LVSG WF15 ....**159** J3
PDSY/CALV LS28 ....**100** A3
RTHW LS26 ....**146** A1
Syke Av *EARD/LOFT* WF3 ....**162** C1
EARL WF12 ....**181** J1
Syke Cl *EARD/LOFT* WF3 ....**162** B1
Syke Gdns *EARD/LOFT* WF3 ..**162** C1
Syke Gn *SCFT* LS14 ....**65** K3
Syke Gv *EARL* WF12 ....**181** J1
Syke House La *GTL/HWG* HX4 ..**174** C1
Syke Ing Cl *EARL* WF12 ....**181** K2
Syke La *CUL/QBY* BD13 ....**115** H7
EARL WF12 ....**181** J2
HIPP HX3 ....**136** D6
LUD/ILL HX2 ....**114** A4
RPDN/SBR HX6 ....**153** H5
SCFT LS14 ....**65** H3
Syke Pde *EARD/LOFT* * WF3 ..**142** B7
Syke Rd *EARD/LOFT* WF3 ....**162** C1
EARL WF12 ....**181** J1
WBY LS22 ....**29** K4
Sykes Av *MIRF* WF14 ....**179** K3
Sykes Cl *BTLY* WF17 ....**161** H2
Syke Side *AIRE* BD20 ....**53** J1
Sykes La *AIRE* BD20 ....**32** E2
EARL WF12 ....**161** K4
HWTH BD22 ....**72** E1
LM/WK BD12 ....**138** B3
Sykes Rd *BTLY* WF17 ....**161** H2
Sykes St *CAS* WF10 ....**148** C2
CLECK BD19 ....**158** E1
Syke St *EARL* WF12 ....**181** J2
Syke Ter *EARD/LOFT* * WF3 ..**162** B1
Syke Vw *EARL* WF12 ....**181** J1
Sylhet Cl *BFD* BD1 ....**5** K4
Sylvan Av *CUL/QBY* BD13 ...**115** C6
Sylvester Av *NORM* WF6 .....**186** C2
Symons St *WKFDW/WTN* WF2 ..**18** D8
Syringa Av *WIL/AL* BD15 ......**95** K1

T

Tabbs Ct *CLECK* BD19 ....**138** A6
Tabbs La *CLECK* BD19 ....**137** K6
Tadman St *WKFDE* WF1 ....**18** F8
Tagore Ct *BOW* BD4 ....**7** K7
Talbot & Falcon Yd *WKFDE* WF1 ..**18** E4
Talbot Av *AL/HA/HU* LS17 ....**83** K2
BULY LS4 ....**8** B3
Talbot Ct *RHAY* LS8 ....**84** A3
Talbot Crs *RHAY* LS8 ....**84** A2
Talbot Fold *RHAY* LS8 ....**84** A3
Talbot Gdns *RHAY* LS8 ....**84** A2
Talbot Gv *RHAY* LS8 ....**84** A2
Talbot Mt *BULY* LS4 ....**8** B3
Talbot Ri *RHAY* LS8 ....**84** A2
Talbot Rd *RHAY* LS8 ....**84** A2
Talbot Rw *BTLY* WF17 ....**161** G4
Talbot St *BTLY* WF17 ....**161** F4
GTHN BD7 ....**4** F6
KCHY BD21 ....**2** C5
NORM WF6 ....**166** D6
Talbot Ter *BULY* LS4 ....**8** B3
RTHW LS26 ....**145** F3
Talbot Vw *BULY* LS4 ....**8** B3
Tall Trees *AL/HA/HU* LS17 .....**83** H1
Tall Trees Dr *FEA/AMT* WF7 ..**188** A7
Tamar St *WBOW* BD5 ....**117** H2
Tammy Hall St *WKFDE* * WF1 ..**18** E4
Tamworth St *BOW* BD4 ....**7** L8
Tanfield Dr *ILK* LS29 ....**24** A3
Tanglewood Ct *WBSY* BD6 ...**117** F5
Tanhouse Hl *HIPP* HX3 ....**156** B1
HORS LS18 ....**81** H4
Tan House La *HIPP* HX3 ....**135** K3
WIL/AL BD15 ....**74** D7
Tanhouse Pk *HIPP* HX3 ....**156** B1
Tanhouse Vw *HIPP* * HX3 .....**156** B1
Tan La *BOW* BD4 ....**138** C1
Tannerbrook Cl *CLAY* BD14 ..**116** C2

Tanner Hill Rd *GTHN* BD7 ......**116** D3
Tanner St *LVSG* WF15 ....**158** C3
Tannery Ct *IDLE* BD10 ....**78** E4
PDSY/CALV * LS28 ....**100** C6
Tannery Sq *HDGY* LS6 ....**82** D5
Tanton Crs *CLAY* BD14 ....**116** C2
Tanton Wk *CLAY* BD14 ....**116** C2
Tarn *BAIL* * BD17 ....**58** B7
Tarn Cl *CAS* WF10 ....**149** K6
Tarn Ct *HWTH* BD22 ....**2** A2
WKFDE WF1 ....**164** C5
Tarnhill Ms *WBOW* BD5 ....**117** K2
Tarn La *AL/HA/HU* LS17 ....**64** E4
AL/HA/HU LS17 ....**65** F4
HWTH BD22 ....**52** D3
Tarn Rd *FEA/AMT* WF7 ....**188** D5
Tarnside Dr *SCFT* LS14 ....**105** G2
Tarn View Rd *YEA* LS19 ....**59** K4
Tarn Vls *ILK* * LS29 ....**24** B6
Tatefield Gv *GFTH/SHER* LS25 ..**127** K6
Tatefield Pl *GFTH/SHER* LS25 ..**127** K6
Tateley Cl *OSS* WF5 ....**162** C7
Tateley La *OSS* WF5 ....**162** B7
Tate Naylor St *DEWS* * WF13 ..**160** E6
Tatham Wy *RHAY* LS8 ....**84** D6
Tatton St *WKFDE* * WF1 ......**185** G6
Taunton St *WKFDE* WF1 ....**18** F2
Tavern St *WKFDE* WF1 ....**19** H6
Tavora St *WKFDE* WF1 ....**18** F2
Tawny Beck *WOR/ARM* LS12 ..**101** F6
Tawny Cl *BOW* BD4 ....**119** F5
MOR LS27 ....**142** C3
Taylor Av *AIRE* BD20 ....**32** E1
Taylor Cl *OSS* WF5 ....**182** E5
Taylor Crs *OSS* WF5 ....**182** E5
Taylor Dr *OSS* WF5 ....**182** E5
Taylor Gv *RTHW* LS26 ....**147** H4
Taylor Hall La *MIRF* WF14 ....**159** F7
MIRF WF14 ....**179** G2
Taylor La *LUD/ILL* HX2 ....**114** D4
MSTN/BAR LS15 ....**86** E6
Taylor Rd *WBSY* BD6 ....**117** J6
Taylors Cl *SCFT* LS14 ....**105** J1
Taylor St *BTLY* WF17 ....**161** F4
CLECK BD19 ....**158** D1
Tealbeck Ap *OT* LS21 ....**39** J3
Tealby Cl *BHP/TINH* LS16 ......**81** H2
Teal Cl *CAS* WF10 ....**168** C2
Teal Ct *AIRE* BD20 ....**32** C4
Teal Dr *MOR* LS27 ....**142** C3
Teall Ct *OSS* WF5 ....**183** F4
Teall St *OSS* WF5 ....**183** F5
WKFDE WF1 ....**18** F3
Teal Ms *MID* LS10 ....**143** J2
Teal St *WKFDE* WF1 ....**18** F4
Teasdale St *BOW* BD4 ....**118** C3
Teasel Cl *LM/WK* BD12 ....**138** B3
Tebbet Pl *HECK* * WF16 ......**160** B4
Technology Dr *BTLY* WF17 ...**161** H4
Tees St *WBOW* BD5 ....**117** H3
Telephone Pl *CHAL* LS7 ....**10** D6
Telford Cl *AIRE* BD20 ....**33** C2
CAS WF10 ....**168** A1
Telford Pl *MID* LS10 ....**123** K4
Telford Ter *MID* LS10 ....**123** K3
Telford Wy *WKFDW/WTN* WF2 ..**163** K3
Telscombe Dr *BOW* BD4 ......**118** C4
Temperance Flds *CLECK* BD19 ..**138** A7
Tempest Rd *BEE/HOL* LS11 ...**13** K9
Templar Gdns *WBY* LS22 ....**29** J2
Templar La *LDSU* LS2 ....**10** C9
MSTN/BAR LS15 ....**106** A1
Templar Pl *LDSU* LS2 ....**10** C9
Templars Cl *GTL/HWG* HX4 ..**174** D2
Templar St *LDSU* LS2 ....**10** C8
WKFDE WF1 ....**185** G6
Templars Wy *GFTH/SHER* LS25 ..**107** J7
GIR BD8 ....**96** D5
Temple Av *MSTN/BAR* LS15 ..**105** H7
RTHW LS26 ....**125** G7
Temple Bank Flats *HTON* BD9 ..**96** D4
Temple Cl *MSTN/BAR* LS15 ..**105** H6
Temple Ct *MSTN/BAR* LS15 ..**105** G6
RTHW LS26 ....**125** G7
Temple Crs *BEE/HOL* LS11 ....**13** J9
Temple Gdns *NORM* WF6 .....**166** C4
Temple Ga *MSTN/BAR* LS15 ..**105** J6
Temple Gate Dr
MSTN/BAR LS15 ....**105** H6
Templegate Gn
MSTN/BAR LS15 ....**105** J6
Templegate Ri
MSTN/BAR LS15 ....**105** H7
Templegate Rd
MSTN/BAR LS15 ....**105** H7
Templegate Vw
MSTN/BAR LS15 ....**105** H7
Templegate Wk
MSTN/BAR LS15 ....**105** J6
Templegate Wy
MSTN/BAR LS15 ....**105** J7
Temple Gn *RTHW* LS26 ......**125** H7
Temple Gv *MSTN/BAR* LS15 ..**105** H6
Temple La *MSTN/BAR* LS15 ..**105** J6
Temple Lea *MSTN/BAR* LS15 ..**105** H6
Temple Moor
MSTN/BAR * LS15 ....**105** J5
Templenewsam Rd
MSTN/BAR LS15 ....**105** G6
Templenewsam Vw
MSTN/BAR LS15 ....**105** G7
Temple Park Cl
MSTN/BAR LS15 ....**105** H6
Temple Park Gdns
MSTN/BAR LS15 ....**105** H6
Temple Park Gn
MSTN/BAR LS15 ....**105** H6
Temple Rhydding Dr *BAIL* BD17 ..**77** H2
Temple Ri *MSTN/BAR* LS15 ..**105** H7
Temple Rd *DEWS* WF13 ......**180** D2

Temple Row Cl
MSTN/BAR LS15 ....**106** B7
Templestowe Crs
MSTN/BAR LS15 ....**105** K4
Templestowe Dr
MSTN/BAR LS15 ....**105** K5
Templestowe Gdns
MSTN/BAR LS15 ....**105** J5
Templestowe Hl
MSTN/BAR LS15 ....**105** J4
Temple St *WF10* WF10 ....**168** B1
HTON BD9 ....**97** G3
KCHY BD21 ....**2** F5
Temple Vw *EARD/LOFT* WF3 ..**144** D6
Temple View Gv *OSM* LS9 ......**11** H9
Temple View Pl *OSM* LS9 ....**15** H2
Temple View Rd *OSM* LS9 .....**11** H9
Temple View Ter *OSM* LS9 .....**15** H2
Temple Vue *HDGY* LS6 ....**82** C6
Temple Wk *MSTN/BAR* LS15 ..**105** J5
Tenbury Fold *BOW* BD4 ....**119** F3
Tenby Ter *HFAX* * HX1 ....**16** B4
Tennis Av *BOW* BD4 ....**119** F5
Tennis Wy *BAIL* BD17 ....**77** J1
Tennyson Av *EARD/LOFT* WF3 ..**165** F2
RPDN/SBR HX6 ....**153** C5
Tennyson Cl *PDSY/CALV* LS28 ..**100** C7
Tennyson Pl *BFDE* BD3 ....**6** C3
CLECK BD19 ....**138** E7
Tennyson Rd *WBSY* BD6 ......**117** K6
Tennyson St *GSLY* LS20 ....**59** G3
HIPP HX3 ....**16** D1
KCHY BD21 ....**2** F8
MOR LS27 ....**142** A3
PDSY/CALV LS28 ....**100** A3
PDSY/CALV LS28 ....**100** C7
Tennyson Ter *MOR* * LS27 ....**142** A3
Tennyson Wy *PONT* WF8 ......**169** J5
Tenter Cl *BTLY* WF17 ....**161** F2
Tentercroft Ct *DEWS* WF13 ...**161** G7
Tenterden Wy *MSTN/BAR* LS15 ..**106** C2
Tenterfield Ri *HIPP* HX3 ....**135** K6
Tenterden Wy *OSS* WF5 ....**182** D4
Tenterfields *IDLE* BD10 ....**79** F4
LUD/ILL HX2 ....**153** F3
Tenter Hl *BSPA/BRAM* LS23 ...**68** A1
CLAY BD14 ....**116** A2
Tenter Hl La *HUDN* HD2 ....**177** J5
Tenters Cl *KNOT* WF11 ....**170** D3
Tenters Gv *HUDN* HD2 ....**177** H6
Tenth Av *LVSG* WF15 ....**158** C3
Terminus Pde
MSTN/BAR * LS15 ....**105** K3
Ternhill Gv *WBOW* BD5 ....**5** L9
Tern Pk *WBY* LS22 ....**46** D1
Tern St *WBOW* BD5 ....**117** H3
The Terrace *PDSY/CALV* LS28 ..**120** B2
Terrace Gdns *HIPP* HX3 ....**16** E2
Terrington Crest *CLAY* BD14 ..**116** C2
Terry Rd *LM/WK* BD12 ....**137** K2
Tetley Dr *BIRK/DRI* BD11 .....**139** J3
Tetley La *HIPP* HX3 ....**135** K5
Tetley Pl *ECHL* BD2 ....**98** A2
Tetley St *BFD* BD1 ....**5** K6
Teville Ct *BOW* BD4 ....**118** B2
Tewit Cl *LUD/ILL* HX2 ....**114** C7
Tewit Gn *LUD/ILL* HX2 ....**114** C7
Tewit Hall Gdns *LUD/ILL* HX2 ..**134** C1
Tewit Hall Rd *BFDE* BD3 ....**7** H4
Tewit La *LUD/ILL* HX2 ....**114** C7
Tewitt Cl *AIRE* BD20 ....**32** C4
Tewitt La *BGLY* BD16 ....**56** A5
Tew St *WKFDW/WTN* WF2 .....**18** E8
Texas St *MOR* LS27 ....**142** A5
Thackeray Rd *IDLE* BD10 ....**98** E1
Thacker Gate Rd *HBR* HX7 ...**152** C4
Thackley Av *IDLE* BD10 ....**78** B2
Thackley Ct *BAIL* BD17 ....**77** H4
Thackley Old Rd *SHPY* BD18 ...**77** J4
Thackley Rd *IDLE* BD10 ....**78** B2
Thackley Vw *IDLE* BD10 ....**78** B2
Thackray Av *HECK* WF16 ......**160** B6
Thackray La *PONT* WF8 ....**169** J7
Thackray St *LUD/ILL* HX2 .....**154** A1
MOR LS27 ....**141** K4
Thames Dr *GFTH/SHER* LS25 ..**107** K7
Thanes Cl *HUDN* HD2 ....**176** D7
Thanet Garth *AIRE* BD20 ....**33** C2
Thane Wy *MSTN/BAR* LS15 ..**106** B2
Thatchers Wy *CLECK* BD19 ...**139** H6
Theaker La *WOR/ARM* LS12 ....**8** A9
Theakston Md *CLAY* BD14 ....**116** B1
Thealby Cl *OSM* LS9 ....**10** E8
Thealby Lawn *OSM* LS9 ....**10** E7
Thealby Pl *OSM* LS9 ....**10** E7
Thearne Gn *CLAY* BD14 ....**116** C2
Theodore St *BEE/HOL* LS11 ..**123** F5
Third Av *BFDE* BD3 ....**7** H2
HIPP HX3 ....**154** A4
KCHY BD21 ....**2** E7
LVSG WF15 ....**158** C3
RTHW LS26 ....**125** G7
WBY LS22 ....**29** J4
WKFDE WF1 ....**164** C6
WOR/ARM LS12 ....**12** D3
Third St *LM/WK* BD12 ....**137** K1
Thirkleby Royd *CLAY* BD14 ..**116** B2
Thirlmere Av *ELL* HX5 ....**176** A2
LM/WK BD12 ....**137** K6
Thirlmere Cl *BEE/HOL* LS11 ..**122** D6
Thirlmere Dr *CAS* WF10 ......**169** J1
EARD/LOFT WF3 ....**143** F7
WBY LS22 ....**28** E4
Thirlmere Gdns *BEE/HOL* LS11 ..**122** D6
ECHL BD2 ....**98** C3
Thirlmere Rd *EARL* WF12 .....**161** J6
WKFDW/WTN WF2 ....**183** K3
Thirsk Dr *GFTH/SHER* LS25 ..**127** K4
Thirsk Gra *CLAY* BD14 ....**116** B2
Thirsk Gv *EARD/LOFT* WF3 ..**143** J4
Thirsk Rw *LDS* LS1 ....**13** L1
Thistle Cl *HUDN* HD2 ....**176** D7
Thistle Wy *MOR* LS27 ....**141** G2
Thistlewood Rd
EARD/LOFT WF3 ....**164** E3

Thomas Ct *WBSY* BD6 ....**117** H5
Thomas St *BRIG* HD6 ....**157** F7
BTLY WF17 ....**160** E2
CAS WF10 ....**148** C6
ELL HX5 ....**175** K3
HDGY LS6 ....**9** K2
HECK WF16 ....**160** A5
HFAX HX1 ....**17** H6
HWTH BD22 ....**72** E6
LVSG WF15 ....**159** H4
Thomas St South *HFAX* HX1 ..**16** B7
Thomas St West *HFAX* HX1 ..**154** D1
Thompson Av *CAS* WF10 .....**169** K2
ECHL BD2 ....**78** A7
Thompson Dr
WKFDW/WTN WF2 ....**164** A5
Thompson Gn *BAIL* BD17 ......**77** F2
Thompson La *BAIL* BD17 ....**77** F3
Thompson St *HFAX* HX1 ....**16** F5
SHPY BD18 ....**77** F4
Thompson's Yd *WKFDE* WF1 ..**18** D4
Thoresby Dr *CLAY* BD14 ......**116** B2
Thoresby Gv *GTHN* BD7 ......**116** D3
Thoresby Pl *LDS* LS1 ....**9** L8
Thornaby Dr *CLAY* BD14 .....**116** B2
Thornacre Crs *SHPY* BD18 .....**77** K5
Thornacre Rd *SHPY* BD18 .....**77** K5
Thorn Av *EARL* WF12 ....**181** G4
HTON BD9 ....**96** B1
Thorn Bank Av *HWTH* BD22 ...**53** F7
Thornberry Dr *LVSG* WF15 ..**158** C3
Thornbridge Ms *ECHL* BD2 ....**98** C1
Thornbury Av *BFDE* BD3 ....**7** K4
Thornbury Crs *BFDE* BD3 ....**7** K4
Thornbury Dr *BFDE* BD3 ....**7** K4
Thornbury Gv *BFDE* BD3 ....**7** K4
Thornbury Pk
WKFDW/WTN WF2 ....**184** A5
Thornbury Rd *BFDE* BD3 ....**7** J5
WKFDW/WTN WF2 ....**184** A5
Thornbury St *BFDE* BD3 ....**7** K6
Thorncliffe Est *BTLY* WF17 ...**160** D5
Thorncliffe Rd *BTLY* WF17 ...**160** D5
GIR BD8 ....**5** K1
HWTH BD22 ....**2** A6
Thorn Cl *RHAY* LS8 ....**11** M3
SHPY BD18 ....**77** K6
Thorn Crs *RHAY* LS8 ....**11** M2
Thorncroft Rd *WBSY* BD6 ....**117** H5
Thorndale Ri *ECHL* BD2 ....**97** K1
Thorndene Wy *BOW* BD4 .....**119** H7
Thorn Dr *CUL/QBY* BD13 ....**115** F7
HTON BD9 ....**96** C1
RHAY LS8 ....**11** M3
Thorne Cl *NORM* WF6 ....**167** F7
PDSY/CALV LS28 ....**99** J5
Thornefield Crs
EARD/LOFT WF3 ....**142** C7
Thorne Gv *RTHW* LS26 ....**145** C1
Thorner Gv *AIRE* BD20 ....**21** F7
Thorner La *BSPA/BRAM* LS23 ..**67** F1
SCFT LS14 ....**66** A3
SCFT LS14 ....**86** B2
Thorner Rd *BSPA/BRAM* LS23 ..**67** G3
Thornes Farm Ap *OSM* LS9 ..**124** E1
Thornes Farm Wy *OSM* LS9 ..**124** E1
Thornes La *WKFDW/WTN* WF2 ..**18** E9
Thornes Lane Whf *WKFDE* WF1 ..**19** G8
Thornes Moor Av
WKFDW/WTN WF2 ....**184** B6
Thornes Moor Cl
WKFDW/WTN WF2 ....**184** B6
Thornes Moor Dr
WKFDW/WTN WF2 ....**184** B6
Thornes Moor Rd
WKFDW/WTN WF2 ....**184** B7
Thornes Pk *BRIG* HD6 ....**157** F7
SHPY BD18 ....**77** J7
Thornes Park Ct
WKFDW/WTN * WF2 ....**184** C6
Thornes Rd *WKFDW/WTN* WF2 ..**184** B6
Thorne St *GTL/HWG* HX4 ....**174** D5
Thorney La *LUD/ILL* HX2 .....**132** E5
Thornfield *BGLY* BD16 ....**55** H7
Thornfield Av *PDSY/CALV* LS28 ..**99** K2
WBSY BD6 ....**117** H6
Thornfield Cl *MSTN/BAR* LS15 ..**105** J3
Thornfield Ct *MSTN/BAR* LS15 ..**105** J3
MSTN/BAR LS15 ....**105** J3
Thornfield Mt *BTLY* WF17 ....**140** D6
Thornfield Pl *ECHL* BD2 ....**98** D2
Thornfield Ri *GTL/HWG* HX4 ..**174** E2
Thornfield Rd *BHP/TINH* LS16 ..**82** A4
Thornfield St *GTL/HWG* HX4 ..**174** E2
Thornfield Wy *MSTN/BAR* LS15 ..**105** J3
Thorn Garth *CLECK* BD19 ....**158** D2
KCHY BD21 ....**53** H2
Thorn Gv *HTON* BD9 ....**96** C1
RHAY LS8 ....**11** M2
Thorn Hl *GTL/HWG* HX4 ......**174** C7
Thornhill Av *HWTH* BD22 ......**73** F1
SHPY BD18 ....**77** J7
Thornhill Bridge La *BRIG* HD6 ..**157** F5
Thornhill Cl *PDSY/CALV* LS28 ..**79** J5
Thornhill Ct *WOR/ARM* LS12 ..**12** A3
Thornhill Dr *PDSY/CALV* LS28 ..**79** H4
SHPY BD18 ....**77** J7
Thornhill Hey *GTL/HWG* HX4 ..**174** C7
Thornhill Park Av *EARL* WF12 ..**181** G5
Thornhill Pl *BFDE* BD3 ....**7** L4
WOR/ARM LS12 ....**102** A7
Thornhill Rd *AIRE* BD20 ....**32** C4
BRIG HD6 ....**176** E1
CAS WF10 ....**168** C4
EARL WF12 ....**180** E3
WOR/ARM LS12 ....**102** A6

Thornhill St Bungalows
WKFDE WF1 ....**18** F6
Thornhill Ter *BFDE* BD3 ....**7** J4
Thornie Bank *EARL* * WF12 ..**181** G3
Thorn La *HTON* BD9 ....**96** C1
RHAY LS8 ....**84** A6
Thornlea Cl *YEA* LS19 ....**59** G6
Thornleigh *EARL* WF12 ....**181** G3
Thornleigh Av
WKFDW/WTN WF2 ....**18** F9
Thornleigh Crs
WKFDW/WTN WF2 ....**18** E9
Thornleigh Cft
WKFDW/WTN WF2 ....**18** E9
Thornleigh Dr *LVSG* WF15 ...**159** J3
WKFDW/WTN WF2 ....**184** D6
Thornleigh Gdns *OSM* LS9 ....**15** H3
Thornleigh Garth
WKFDW/WTN WF2 ....**184** D6
Thornleigh Gv *OSM* LS9 ....**15** H3
WKFDW/WTN WF2 ....**184** D6
Thornleigh Mt *OSM* LS9 ....**15** H3
Thornleigh Rd
WKFDW/WTN WF2 ....**18** E9
Thornleigh St *OSM* LS9 ....**15** H3
Thornleigh Vw *OSM* LS9 ....**15** H3
Thornmead Rd *BAIL* BD17 ......**77** J2
Thorn Mt *RHAY* LS8 ....**104** D1
Thorn Royd Dr *BOW* BD4 ....**119** G4
Thornsgill Av *BOW* BD4 ....**118** D3
Thorn St *BTLY* * WF17 ....**140** E6
GIR BD8 ....**4** B2
HWTH BD22 ....**73** F4
Thorn Ter *RHAY* LS8 ....**11** M1
Thornton Av *WOR/ARM* LS12 ..**101** K6
Thornton Cl *BTLY* WF17 ......**140** C4
Thornton Ct *GIR* BD8 ....**4** A4
Thornton Gdns
WOR/ARM LS12 ....**101** K6
Thornton Gv *WOR/ARM* LS12 ..**101** K6
Thornton La *WBOW* BD5 .....**117** H3
Thornton Moor Rd *HWTH* BD22 ..**93** H6
Thornton Old Rd *GIR* BD8 ......**96** C6
Thornton Rd *BRIG* HD6 ....**176** D1
CUL/QBY BD13 ....**95** J7
CUL/QBY BD13 ....**114** C1
EARL WF12 ....**180** E5
GIR BD8 ....**4** B4
Thorntons Ar *LDS* LS1 ....**10** A9
Thorntons Di *HORS* LS18 ......**80** E6
Thornton St *BFD* BD1 ....**5** H5
CLECK BD19 ....**158** B2
CLECK BD19 ....**159** G1
DEWS WF13 ....**180** E2
HFAX HX1 ....**16** A9
ILK LS29 ....**25** K7
Thornton Ter *HFAX* HX1 ....**16** A9
Thornton View Rd *CLAY* BD14 ..**116** B2
Thorntonville *CLECK* BD19 ...**159** G2
Thorntree Cl *PONT* WF8 ......**190** E5
Thorn Tree St *HFAX* HX1 ....**16** B9
Thorn Vw *HIPP* HX3 ....**135** F5
RHAY LS8 ....**11** M2
Thornville *MOR* LS27 ....**122** A7
Thornville Av *HDGY* LS6 ....**8** F3
Thornville Ct *HDGY* LS6 ....**8** E4
Thornville Crs *HDGY* LS6 ....**8** E3
Thornville Gv *HDGY* LS6 ....**8** E4
Thornville Mt *DEWS* WF13 ..**180** D3
HDGY LS6 ....**8** E3
Thornville Pl *DEWS* * WF13 ..**180** D3
HDGY LS6 ....**8** F4
Thornville Rd *HDGY* LS6 ....**8** E5
Thornville Rw *HDGY* LS6 ....**8** E4
Thornville St *DEWS* * WF13 ..**180** D3
HDGY LS6 ....**8** F5
Thornville Ter *DEWS* * WF13 ..**180** D3
HDGY LS6 ....**8** F3
Thornville Vw *HDGY* LS6 ....**8** E4
Thornville Wk *DEWS* WF13 ..**180** D3
Thorn Wk *RHAY* LS8 ....**104** D2
Thorp Arch Pk *BSPA/BRAM* LS23 ..**48** D2
Thorpe Av *CUL/QBY* BD13 ...**95** K7
Thorpe Cl *GSLY* LS20 ....**58** C3
Thorpe Ct *MID* LS10 ....**143** H4
Thorpe Crs *MID* LS10 ....**143** H4
Thorpe Dr *GSLY* LS20 ....**58** C2
Thorpe Gdns *MID* LS10 ....**143** H4
Thorpe Garth *MID* LS10 ....**143** G4
Thorpe Gv *CUL/QBY* BD13 ...**96** A7
MID LS10 ....**143** H3
Thorpe La *EARD/LOFT* WF3 ..**142** D6
GSLY LS20 ....**58** B3
Thorpe Lower La
EARD/LOFT WF3 ....**144** A5
Thorpe Mill Ct
RPDN/SBR * HX6 ....**173** F2
Thorpe Mt *MID* LS10 ....**143** G4
Thorpe Pl *MID* LS10 ....**143** H3
Thorpe Rd *CUL/QBY* BD13 ....**95** K7
EARD/LOFT WF3 ....**163** J1
MID LS10 ....**143** H3
PDSY/CALV LS28 ....**100** A5
Thorpe Sq *MID* LS10 ....**143** J4
Thorpe St *HIPP* HX3 ....**134** E5
KCHY BD21 ....**3** G2
MID LS10 ....**143** H3
MSTN/BAR LS15 ....**105** H5
Thorpe Ter *MID* LS10 ....**143** H3
Thorpe Vw *EARD/LOFT* WF3 ..**143** K5
MID LS10 ....**143** H4
OSS WF5 ....**182** C1
WKFDW/WTN WF2 ....**184** A3
Thorp Garth *IDLE* BD10 ....**78** C5
Thorverton Dr *BOW* BD4 .....**119** F6
Thorverton Gv *BOW* BD4 .....**119** F6
Threshfield Crs *BIRK/DRI* BD11 ..**139** H1
Thrice Fold *IDLE* BD10 ....**78** A3
Thrift Wy *BGLY* BD16 ....**75** J5
Throstle Av *MID* LS10 ....**143** G4
Throstle Bank *LUD/ILL* HX2 ..**154** C3
Throstle Crest *FEA/AMT* WF7 ..**187** K1
Throstle Dr *MID* LS10 ....**143** F4
Throstle Hl *MID* LS10 ....**143** H4
Throstle La *MID* LS10 ....**143** H4
Throstle Mt *LUD/ILL* HX2 ....**153** G3
MID LS10 ....**143** G4
Throstle Nest *BTLY* WF17 ....**160** D4

Throstle Nest Cl *OT* LS21 ....26 E7
Throstle Nest Rd *AIRE* * BD20 ......20 E7
Throstle Nest Vw *HORS* LS18.....81 F5
Throstle Pde *MID* LS10..............143 F5
Throstle Pl *MID* LS10................143 G4
Throstle Rd *MID* LS10................143 H4
Throstle Rw *MID* LS10................143 G4
Throstle Sq *MID* LS10................143 J5
Throstle St *MID* LS10.................143 G4
Throstle Ter *MID* LS10...............143 H4
Throstle Vw *MID* LS10................143 J4
Throstle Wk *MID* LS10...............143 H4
Throxenby Wy *CLAY* BD14...........116 B2
Thrum Hall Cl *HFAX* HX1.............154 B1
Thrum Hall Dr *HFAX* HX1..............16 A5
Thrum Hall La *HFAX* HX1..............16 A5
Thrush St *KGHY* BD21.....................3 J2
Thryberg St *BFDE* BD3....................6 D7
Thunderton La *RPDN/SBR* HX6....152 C6
Thurley Dr *BOW* BD4..................118 C4
Thurley Rd *BOW* BD4...................118 C4
Thurnscoe Rd *BFD* BD7...................5 K3
Thursby St *BFDE* BD3......................6 E6
Thurston Gdns *WIL/AL* BD15........96 A5
Thwaite Ga *MID* LS10....................15 H9
Thwaite La *MID* LS10...................124 C3
Thwaites Av *ILK* LS29....................24 B5
Thwaites Br *KGHY* BD21.................3 M4
Thwaites Brow Rd *KGHY* BD21.....54 C4
Thwaites La *KGHY* BD21.................3 M4
Tib Garth *WBY* LS22......................28 E6
Tichborne Rd *LVSG* WF15............159 F4
Tichborne Rd West
    WBOW BD5................................117 K3
Tichborne St *BTLY* WF17.............160 C4
Tickhill St *BFDE* BD3........................6 E7
Tidswell St *HECK* WF16...............160 B4
Tilbury Av *BEE/HOL* LS11.............13 H8
Tilbury Gv *BEE/HOL* LS11.............13 H8
Tilbury Mt *BEE/HOL* LS11.............13 H8
Tilbury Pde *BEE/HOL* LS11...........13 H8
Tilbury Rd *BEE/HOL* LS11.............13 H8
Tilbury Rw *BEE/HOL* LS11............13 G8
Tilbury Ter *BEE/HOL* LS11............13 H8
Tilbury Vw *BEE/HOL* * LS11..........13 H8
Tile La *BHP/TINH* LS16.................82 C1
Tile St *GIR* BD8................................4 F2
Tiley Sq *WBOW* BD5.....................117 K2
Till Carr La *HIPP* HX3..................157 F1
Tillotson Av *RPDN/SBR* HX6........153 J7
Tillotson St *AIRE* * BD20...............20 E7
Timber St *ELL* HX5.......................175 J3
    KGHY * BD21..................................3 L3
Timble Dr *BGLY* BD16...................56 A7
Tim La *HWTH* BD22......................72 D7
Timmey La *RPDN/SBR* HX6.........153 H3
Timothy La *BTLY* WF17................161 G1
Tingley Av *EARD/LOFT* WF3........142 D6
Tingley Common *MOR* LS27.........142 A5
Tingley Crs *EARD/LOFT* WF3......142 D6
Tinkerfield La *WBY* LS22..............31 H1
Tinkler Stile *SHPY* BD18...............78 A4
Tinsel Rd *EARL* WF12..................161 J7
Tinshill Av *BHP/TINH* LS16...........81 H1
Tinshill Cl *BHP/TINH* LS16............81 H1
Tinshill Crs *BHP/TINH* LS16..........61 H7
Tinshill Dr *BHP/TINH* LS16............61 H7
Tinshill Garth *BHP/TINH* LS16......61 H7
Tinshill Gv *BHP/TINH* LS16...........61 H7
Tinshill La *BHP/TINH* LS16............81 G1
Tinshill Mt *BHP/TINH* LS16...........61 H7
Tinshill Rd *BHP/TINH* LS16...........61 H7
Tinshill Vw *BHP/TINH* LS16..........61 H7
Tintagel Ct *NORM* WF6...............166 E5
Tintern Av *GIR* BD8.......................96 C6
Tippaty La *KNOT* WF11................171 H1
Tisma Dr *BOW* BD4......................118 D6
Tithe Barn La *AL/HA/HU* LS17......65 J1
Tithe Barn Rd *KNOT* WF11..........171 H4
Tithe Barn St *EARL* WF12............181 G1
Tithe Barn Vw *BRIG* HD6.............177 H1
Tithe House Wy *HUDN* HD2.........177 K3
Titus St *SHPY* BD18......................76 E4
Tivoli Pl *ILK* LS29..........................24 B6
    WBOW BD5................................117 H3
Toby La *GTHN* BD7......................117 F1
Todd Ter *GTHN* * BD7.................117 G2
Todley Hall Rd *HWTH* BD22..........52 A5
Todwell La *WBOW* BD5................117 H3
Tofts Av *LM/WK* BD12.................137 H5
Tofts Gv *BRIG* HD6......................176 E2
Tofts Grove Gdns *BRIG* HD6........176 E2
Toftshaw Fold *BOW* BD4.............118 E6
Toftshaw La *BOW* BD4................119 F6
Toftshaw New Rd *BOW* BD4.......118 E6
Tofts House Cl *PDSY/CALV* LS28..100 B6
Tofts Rd *CLECK* BD19..................158 E1
    PDSY/CALV LS28.......................100 A6
Toft St *WOR/ARM* LS12...............12 C4
Toll Bar La *WKFDW/WTN* WF2....163 J7
Toll Bar Rd *CAS* WF10.................167 J1
Toll Bar Wy *TAD* LS24..................51 G5
Toller Dr *HTON* BD9......................96 D2
Toller Gv *HTON* BD9.....................96 E2
Toller La *GIR* BD8...........................4 D1
    HTON BD9....................................96 E2
Toller Pk *HTON* BD9.....................96 E2
Tolson St *DEWS* * WF13.............161 F7
    OSS WF5.....................................182 A1
Tolworth Fold *WIL/AL* BD15..........95 K5
Tomahawk Trail *CAS* WF10.........168 C4
Tom Dando Cl *NORM* WF6...........166 E2
Tomling Cote La *AIRE* BD20..........33 H2
Tomlinson Wy
    GFTH/SHER LS25......................110 E6
Tonbridge Cl *WBSY* BD6...............117 G6
Tonbridge St *LDS* LS1.....................9 K6
Tong Ap *WOR/ARM* S12..............101 G7
Tong Dr *WOR/ARM* LS12.............101 G7
Tong Ga *WOR/ARM* LS12............101 G5
Tong Gn *WOR/ARM* LS12.............101 G5
Tong La *BOW* BD4.......................119 K6
Tong Rd *WOR/ARM* LS12.............120 E2
Tong St *BOW* BD4.........................99 G6
Tongue La *HDGY* LS6....................82 E3
Tong Wy *WOR/ARM* LS12............101 G6
Tootal St *WKFDE* WF1...................19 G8

Toothill Av *BRIG* HD6...................177 F2
Toothill Bank *BRIG* HD6...............177 F2
Toothill La *BRIG* HD6...................177 F2
Toot Hill La *HUDN* HD2................176 E4
Topaz Cl *HUDN* HD2....................177 H7
Topcliffe Av *MOR* LS27................142 C3
Topcliffe Gv *MOR* LS27................142 B5
Topcliffe La *MOR* LS27.................142 C5
Topcliffe Ms *MOR* LS27...............142 C3
Topfield Fold *MOR* LS27..............142 B5
Top Fold *KNOT* WF11..................150 B5
Top House Farm Ms
    KNOT * WF11............................150 B5
Top Meadow *MIRF* WF14.............179 G7
Top Moor Side *BEE/HOL* LS11......13 J6
Top Stone Cl *GFTH/SHER* LS25....151 F4
Tor Av *LM/WK* BD12....................137 H6
Torcote Crs *HUDN* HD2................177 H4
Tordoff Av *GTHN* BD7..................116 D1
Tordoff Rd *LM/WK* BD12.............137 K1
Tordoff Ter *KSTL* * LS5................101 K1
Toronto Pl *CHAL* LS7.....................83 J6
Torre Cl *OSM* LS9............................11 J8
Torre Crs *OSM* LS9.........................11 L8
    WBSY BD6................................116 C5
Torre Dr *OSM* LS9...........................11 K7
Torre Gv *OSM* LS9..........................11 K6
    WBSY BD6................................116 C5
Torre Hl *OSM* LS9............................11 L8
Torre La *OSM* LS9...........................11 L8
Torre Mt *OSM* LS9..........................11 K6
Torre Pl *OSM* LS9............................11 K8
Torre Rd *OSM* LS9..........................11 J8
    WBSY BD6................................116 C5
Torre Sq *OSM* LS9...........................11 L7
Torre Vw *OSM* LS9.........................11 L7
Torre Wk *OSM* LS9.........................11 L7
Torridon Crs *WBSY* BD6..............136 D3
Torridon Rd *EARL* WF12..............161 H6
Toulston La *TAD* LS24....................68 E1
Tower Cft *TAD* LS24.......................50 C6
The Tower Dr *OT* LS21...................41 H4
Tower Gdns *LUD/ILL* HX2............154 C4
Tower Gv *WOR/ARM* LS12...........101 K5
Tower Hl *RPDN/SBR* HX6.............153 J4
Tower House St *LDSU* LS2.............10 A7
Tower La *WOR/ARM* LS12...........101 J5
Tower Pl *WOR/ARM* LS12............101 J5
Tower Rd *OSM* LS9.......................124 E2
    SHPY BD18..................................76 D4
The Towers *WOR/ARM* LS12.......101 K5
Towers Paddock *CAS* WF10.........169 F1
Towers Sq *HDGY* LS6....................83 F4
Tower St *ECHL* BD2........................98 C3
Towers Wy *HDGY* LS6...................83 F4
Tower Vw *HFAX* HX1....................154 B2
Towlerton La
    WKFDW/WTN WF2....................163 K6
The Town *EARL* WF12..................181 G7
Town Cl *HORS* LS18........................80 E3
Towncliose Wy
    GFTH/SHER LS25......................127 J6
Town End *GFTH/SHER* LS25.........107 H5
    GTHN BD7.................................117 F2
    MOR LS27.................................121 G7
    OSS WF5....................................182 C4
Townend Ct *PDSY/CALV* LS28.....100 C5
Town End Rd *CLAY* BD14............116 A1
Townend Wk *WOR/ARM* LS12......122 A1
Townfield *WIL/AL* BD15.................75 F7
Town Fields Rd *ELL* HX5..............175 H3
Townfold *OSS* WF5......................182 D3
Town Ga *CLECK* BD19..................138 A7
    GSLY LS20...................................59 F2
    HIPP HX3...................................135 K4
    LUD/ILL HX2.............................132 C6
    PDSY/CALV LS28.........................79 J3
    RPDN/SBR HX6..........................152 E5
Towngate *BRIG* HD6....................157 J5
    HIPP HX3...................................136 B7
    HIPP HX3...................................155 K4
    LM/WK BD12.............................137 H5
    MIRF WF14................................179 J3
    OSS WF5....................................182 D4
    SHPY BD18..................................77 J5
Towngate Av *BRIG* HD6...............157 J5
Town Gate Cl *GSLY* LS20...............59 F2
Towngate Gv *MIRF* WF14............179 J4
Towngate Rd *BTLY* WF17.............160 D3
Town Hall Sq *YEA* LS19.................59 J4
Town Hall St *ELL* HX5..................175 J3
    KGHY BD21....................................3 G5
    MIRF * WF14.............................179 H5
    RPDN/SBR HX6..........................153 J5
Town Hall St East *HFAX* * HX1.......17 H5
Town Hall Wy *EARL* * WF12........181 G1
Townhead Fold *ILK* LS29...............22 B1
Town Hl *BSPA/BRAM* LS23...........68 C1
Town Hill St *BGLY* * BD16.............76 A6
Town La *IDLE* BD10.......................78 C4
Townley Av *HIPP* HX3..................155 K4
Townley Rd *WKFDW/WTN* WF2...183 J4
Town St *BEE/HOL* LS11................122 E4
    BIRK/DRI BD11...........................139 H1
    BRAM LS13...................................80 C7
    CHAL LS7.....................................83 J5
    DEWS WF13...............................161 F6
    EARD/LOFT WF3........................144 A4
    EARL WF12.................................181 J2
    GSLY LS20...................................59 F2
    HORS LS18...................................80 E4
    MID LS10...................................143 H2
    MOR LS27...................................121 G7
    PDSY/CALV LS28.......................100 B3
    WOR/ARM LS12.........................101 K5
    YEA LS19.....................................59 J4
    YEA LS19.....................................80 A1
Town Street Ms *CHAL* LS7............83 J5
Town Street Wk *CHAL* LS7...........83 J5
Town Wells Dr *PDSY/CALV* LS28...79 J6
Towton Dr *CAS* WF10..................167 K2
Track Mt *BTLY* WF17...................160 E4
Track Rd *BTLY* WF17...................160 E6
Trafalgar Cl *HUDN* HD2...............177 G5
Trafalgar Gdns *MOR* LS27............141 K4
Trafalgar Rd *DEWS* WF13............160 E7

    ILK LS29.......................................24 A5
Trafalgar Sq *HFAX* HX1..................16 C9
Trafalgar St *BFD* BD1......................5 L4
    BTLY WF17.................................160 D3
    HFAX * HX1.................................16 C9
    LDSU LS2......................................10 C8
Trafford Av *OSM* LS9.....................11 L4
Trafford Gv *OSM* LS9.....................11 K3
Trafford Ter *OSM* LS9....................11 L4
Traith Ct *BTLY* * WF17................160 B2
Tramways *LM/WK* BD12...............138 A1
Tranbeck Rd *GSLY* LS20................58 C2
Tranfield Av *GSLY* LS20.................58 D2
Tranfield Cl *GSLY* LS20..................58 D2
Tranfield Gdns *GSLY* LS20.............58 D2
Tranmere Cl *GSLY* LS20.................58 D2
Tranmere Dr *GSLY* LS20................58 C2
Tranquility *MSTN/BAR* LS15.........105 K3
Tranquility Ct *MSTN/BAR* LS15....105 K3
Trans Pennine Trail
    EARD/LOFT WF3........................165 H5
    MID LS10......................................14 D2
    RTHW LS26................................126 B7
    RTHW LS26................................166 C1
    WKFDE WF1...............................185 H5
Transperience Wy
    LM/WK BD12..............................138 A1
Transvaal Ter *BTLY* WF17............160 C4
Tranter Gv *BOW* BD4...................119 F1
Tranter Pl *MSTN/BAR* LS15..........105 F5
Tredgold Av *BHP/TINH* LS16..........61 H1
Tredgold Cl *BHP/TINH* LS16...........61 H1
Tredgold Crs *BHP/TINH* LS16.........61 H1
Tredgold Garth *BHP/TINH* LS16.....61 H1
Tree La *LUD/ILL* HX2...................133 G2
Trees St *GIR* BD8............................5 G1
Tree Tops Ct *BTLY* LS8..................84 D5
Tree Top Vw *CUL/QBY* BD13.......115 F4
Trelawn Av *HDGY* LS6...................82 C7
Trelawn Pl *HDGY* LS6....................82 C7
Trelawn St *HDGY* LS6....................82 C7
Trelawn Ter *HDGY* LS6..................82 C7
Tremont Gdns *MID* LS10..............123 K4
Trenance Dr *SHPY* BD18................78 E5
Trenance Gdns *GTL/HWG* HX4.....174 C2
Trenholme Av *LM/WK* BD12........137 G1
Trenic Crs *HDGY* LS6.......................8 D2
Trenic Dr *HDGY* LS6........................8 D2
Trent Av *GFTH/SHER* LS25..........127 K1
    NORM WF6................................166 D4
Trentham Av *BEE/HOL* LS11........123 K4
Trentham Gv *BEE/HOL* LS11.......123 C4
Trentham Pl *BEE/HOL* LS11.........123 C4
Trentham Rw *BEE/HOL* LS11.......123 C4
Trentham St *BEE/HOL* LS11.........123 C4
Trenton Dr *GIR* BD8........................5 H2
Trenton Rd *EARL* WF12...............161 J6
Trent Rd *OSM* LS9..........................11 H8
Trent St *BEE/HOL* LS11..................13 L5
Trescoe Av *WOR/ARM* LS12........101 H4
Tresham Ct *EARL* WF12...............161 J6
Trevelyan Sq *LDS* * LS1.................14 A1
Trevelyan St *BRIG* HD6................157 F3
Triath Ct *BTLY* WF17...................160 B2
Trilby St *WKFDE* WF1....................19 G5
Trimmingham La *LUD/ILL* HX2.....154 A2
Trimmingham Rd
    LUD/ILL HX2.............................154 A2
Trimmingham Vls
    LUD/ILL * HX2..........................154 B2
Trinity Church Ga *WKFDE* WF1.....18 F5
Trinity Cl *LUD/ILL* HX2.................134 D1
Trinity Fold *HFAX* * HX1................17 C7
Trinity Mt *DEWS* * WF13............161 F6
Trinity Pl *BGLY* BD16....................75 K2
    HFAX HX1....................................17 G7
Trinity Ri *OT* LS21..........................39 J3
Trinity Rd *HFAX* HX1......................17 G7
    WBOW BD5....................................5 J9
Trinity St *BTLY* WF17...................161 F6
    HFAX HX1....................................17 G7
    KGHY BD21....................................3 H2
    MIRF WF14................................179 H5
    PONT WF8..................................169 J7
    WKFDE WF1...............................185 G6
Trinity Street Ar *LDS* LS1...............10 A9
Trinity Ter *BTLY* WF17.................160 A6
Trinity Vw *HIPP* HX3......................17 K8
    LM/WK BD12..............................117 K7
    OSS WF5....................................182 C2
Trinity Wk *LM/WK* BD12.............117 K7
Trip Garth *WBY* LS22.....................28 C7
Trip La *WBY* LS22...........................28 C7
Tristram Av *WBOW* BD5..............118 B4
Triumph Cl *BEE/HOL* LS11............13 L4
Troon Dr *HUDN* HD2....................176 E6
Troon Wy *WKFDW/WTN* WF2.....184 B7
Trooper La *HIPP* HX3.....................17 K8
Trooper Ter *HIPP* HX3....................17 K8
Trough La *HWTH* BD22..................93 H4
Trough Well La
    WKFDW/WTN WF2....................163 K5
Troydale La *PDSY/CALV* LS28......120 C1
Troydale Gv *PDSY/CALV* LS28.....120 C1
Troydale La *PDSY/CALV* LS28......100 D7
Troy Hl *MOR* * LS27....................141 G1
Troy Ri *MOR* LS27.......................142 A2
Troy Rd *HORS* LS18.......................81 F2
    MOR LS27...................................141 G1
Trueman Av *HECK* WF16.............160 B4
Trueman Ct *LM/WK* BD12...........137 K1
Truncliffe *WBSY* BD6...................117 J5
Trundles La *KNOT* WF11..............171 J4
Truro Dr *NORM* WF6...................166 E5
Truro St *WOR/ARM* LS12...............8 B7
Truro Wk *NORM* WF6..................166 E5
Trust Fold *GFTH/SHER* LS25........150 K4
Tudor Barn Ct *SHPY* BD18............77 J5
Tudor Cl *PDSY/CALV* LS28.............99 K3
    PONT WF8..................................189 H4
Tudor Cft *HUDN* HD2...................178 A4
Tudor Gdns *BEE/HOL* LS11..........122 D4
Tudor Lawns *RHAY* LS8.................84 C5
    WKFDW/WTN WF2....................163 K3
Tudor St *WBOW* BD5...................117 J2
Tudor Wy *EARL* WF12..................180 E6

Tuel La *RPDN/SBR* HX6................153 K4
Tufton St *AIRE* BD20......................20 E7
Tulip St *HWTH* BD22......................72 D7
    MID LS10...................................123 J3
Tumbling Cl *OSS* WF5..................182 D3
Tumbling Hl *PONT* WF8................190 B4
Tumbling Hill St *GTHN* BD7..............5 J7
Tunnel St *CUL/QBY* BD13..............94 A3
Tunnicliffe Pl *AIRE* BD20...............32 E1
Tunstall Gn *BOW* BD4...................119 F3
Tunstall Rd *BEE/HOL* LS11...........123 H3
Tunwell La *ECHL* BD2.....................98 D1
Tunwell St *ECHL* BD2.....................98 D1
Turbary Av *PDSY/CALV* LS28.......100 B3
Turbury Gv *GTL/HWG* HX4...........174 B1
Turf Ct *CUL/QBY* BD13...................73 K7
Turf La *CUL/QBY* BD13...................73 K6
Turgate La *RPDN/SBR* HX6...........152 A7
Turlow Ct *OSM* LS9........................14 D2
Turnberry Av *AL/HA/HU* LS17.......63 G7
Turnberry Cl *AL/HA/HU* LS17........63 G7
Turnberry Ct *AIRE* BD20................33 H7
    NORM WF6................................167 G7
Turnberry Dr *AL/HA/HU* LS17.......63 G7
Turnberry Gdns
    EARD/LOFT WF3........................142 C7
Turnberry Gv *AL/HA/HU* LS17.......63 G7
    GTHN BD7.....................................4 B9
Turnberry Pl *AL/HA/HU* LS17........63 G7
Turnberry Ri *AL/HA/HU* LS17........63 G7
Turnberry Vw *AL/HA/HU* LS17.......63 G7
Turner Av *BTLY* * WF17...............161 F3
    GTHN BD7.................................117 G1
Turner Av North *LUD/ILL* HX2.....134 A3
Turner Av South *LUD/ILL* HX2......134 B3
Turner Cl *EARD/LOFT* WF3..........142 C7
Turners Ct *OT* LS21........................39 H1
Turner Dr *EARD/LOFT* WF3..........142 C7
Turner La *HIPP* HX3........................17 K2
    ILK LS29.......................................21 K1
Turner Pl *GTHN* BD7....................117 G1
    LUD/ILL HX2..............................134 B3
Turner's Ct *HIPP* HX3...................134 E5
Turners Rd *PDSY/CALV* LS28.......100 A2
Turners Yd *PDSY/CALV* LS28.......100 A2
Turner Vw *LUD/ILL* * HX2............134 B3
Turney St *HIPP* HX3......................134 D5
Turn o'the Nook *OSS* WF5...........182 B3
Turnpike Rd *TAD* LS24...................51 C5
Turnpike St *ELL* HX5.....................175 K2
Turnshaw Rd *HWTH* BD22............72 A2
Turnsteads Av *CLECK* BD19.........138 C7
Turnsteads Cl *CLECK* BD19..........138 C7
Turnsteads Crs *CLECK* BD19........138 C7
Turnsteads Dr *CLECK* BD19..........138 C7
Turnsteads Mt *CLECK* BD19.........138 C7
Turnstone Ct *MID* LS10................143 J2
The Turnways *HDGY* LS6................8 B1
Turpin La *GFTH/SHER* LS25..........131 J3
Turton Gn *MOR* LS27...................121 G7
Turton St *WKFDE* WF1...................19 G5
Turton V *MOR* LS27....................141 G1
Tuscany Wy *NORM* WF6..............166 E2
Twain Crs *DEWS* WF13................169 H3
Tweedale Gdns *DEWS* WF13........180 E1
Tweedale St *DEWS* * WF13.........180 E1
Tweed Cl *BTLY* WF17...................140 D6
Tweedy St *WIL/AL* BD15................75 F7
Twelfth Av *LVSG* WF15................158 C3
Twickenham Ct *GIR* BD8................97 J3
Twivey St *CAS* WF10....................168 B1
Tyas Gv *OSM* LS9..........................15 M1
Tyersal Av *BOW* BD4.....................99 G6
Tyersal Cl *BOW* BD4......................99 G6
Tyersal Ct *BOW* BD4......................7 M8
Tyersal Crs *BOW* BD4....................99 G7
Tyersal Dr *BOW* BD4.....................99 G7
Tyersal Garth *BOW* BD4................99 G7
Tyersal Gn *BOW* BD4.....................99 G7
Tyersal Gv *BOW* BD4.....................99 G6
Tyersal La *BOW* BD4....................119 F2
    PDSY/CALV LS28..........................99 K7
Tyersal Pk *BOW* BD4.....................99 G7
Tyersal Rd *BOW* BD4.....................99 G7
Tyersal Ter *BOW* BD4.....................7 M7
Tyersal Vw *BOW* BD4.....................7 M8
Tyersal Wk *BOW* BD4....................99 G7
Tyler Cl *NORM* WF6.....................167 H6
Tyndale Av *HOR/CROF* WF4.........183 H1
Tyndale Wk *BTLY* WF17...............160 B3
Tynedale Ct *CHAL* LS7...................83 F6
Tyne St *BFDE* BD3...........................6 B4
    KGHY BD21....................................3 G5
Tynwald Cl *AL/HA/HU* * LS17........83 F2
Tynwald Dr *AL/HA/HU* LS17..........83 F1
Tynwald Gn *AL/HA/HU* LS17.........83 F1
Tynwald Hl *AL/HA/HU* LS17...........83 F1
Tynwald Mt *AL/HA/HU* LS17.........83 F1
Tynwald Rd *AL/HA/HU* LS17.........83 F2
Tynwald Wk *AL/HA/HU* LS17........83 F1
Tyrrell Ct *WKFDW/WTN* WF2......183 J2
Tyrrel St *BFD* BD1...........................5 M6
Tyson St *HFAX* HX1......................154 B2

U

Ullswater Av *EARL* WF12.............161 H5
Ullswater Cl *EARL* WF12..............161 H5
Ullswater Crs *MSTN/BAR* LS15....105 J7
    RTHW LS26................................145 K1
Ullswater Dr *WBSY* BD6..............136 E1
    WBY LS22....................................29 F3
Ullswater Ri *WBY* LS22..................29 F3
Ullswater Rd *EARL* WF12.............161 H6
Undercliffe La *BFDE* BD3.................6 E1
Undercliffe Old Rd *ECHL* BD2........6 C1
Undercliffe Ri *ILK* LS29..................24 D7
Undercliffe Rd *ECHL* BD2..............98 C2
Undercliffe St *BFDE* BD3.................6 E1
Underwood Dr *YEA* LS19...............79 J3
Union Gv *LVSG* WF15...................159 J5
Union House La *CLAY* BD14.........116 B4
Union La *LUD/ILL* HX2.................114 A5
Union Pl *BEE/HOL* LS11..................13 L4
Union Rd *GTHN* BD7....................117 G1
    LVSG WF15................................159 J5

    WBSY BD6.................................117 H7
Union Sq *WKFDE* WF1....................18 F5
Union St *BAIL* BD17........................77 J2
    BGLY BD16...................................55 H4
    BTLY WF17.................................140 B6
    CUL/QBY * BD13.......................115 H5
    DEWS WF13...............................181 C1
    GTL/HWG HX4..........................175 G2
    HFAX HX1....................................17 H7
    LDSU LS2......................................10 B9
    LVSG WF15................................159 K5
    MOR * LS27...............................122 B6
    OSS WF5....................................182 C3
    OT LS21.......................................39 G3
    RPDN/SBR HX6..........................153 F7
    RPDN/SBR HX6..........................153 K3
    WKFDE WF1................................18 F4
Union St South *HFAX* * HX1...........17 H8
Union Ter *CHAL* LS7.......................83 H6
Union Yd *IDLE* BD10......................78 C4
Unity Cl *HDGY* LS16........................9 L1
Unity Ct *DEWS* WF13...................180 E1
Unity St *AIRE* BD20.......................54 C1
    EARD/LOFT WF3........................144 E4
Unity St North *BGLY* BD16.............75 J2
Unity St South *BGLY* BD16.............75 J2
Unity Ter *HFAX* HX1.....................154 B2
University Rd *LDSU* LS2....................9 J5
University St *CAS* WF10................168 C1
Unwin Pl *HTON* BD9......................96 D3
Upland Crs *RHAY* LS8....................84 B7
Upland Gdns *RHAY* LS8................104 B1
Upland Gv *RHAY* LS8......................84 B7
Upland Rd *RHAY* LS8....................104 B1
Uplands *KGHY* BD21.......................53 H2
Uplands Av *CUL/QBY* BD13..........116 A4
Uplands Cl *CUL/QBY* BD13...........116 A4
Uplands Crs *CUL/QBY* BD13.........116 A4
Uplands Dr *MIRF* WF14................179 H3
Uplands Gv *CUL/QBY* BD13..........116 A4
The Uplands *PONT* WF8................189 H2
Upper Accommodation Rd
    OSM LS9......................................14 F1
Upper Ada St *SHPY* BD18..............76 D7
Upper Addison St *BOW* BD4............6 A1
Upper Allerton La *WIL/AL* BD15.....95 H5
Upper Ashley La *SHPY* * BD18......77 G4
Upper Bank Houses
    GTL/HWG * HX4........................174 A5
Upper Barker St *LVSG* WF15........159 H4
Upper Basinghall St *LDS* LS1...........9 M9
Upper Batley La *BTLY* WF17.........140 E7
Upper Batley Low La
    BTLY WF17................................140 E5
Upper Battye St *HECK* WF16.......160 A3
Upper Bell Hall *HFAX* HX1............154 D3
Upper Bolton Brow
    RPDN/SBR HX6..........................154 A4
Upper Bonegate *BRIG* HD6...........157 H2
Upper Brig Royd
    RPDN/SBR HX6..........................172 E5
Upper Butts *CLECK* BD19.............158 E1
Upper Calton St *KGHY* BD21...........2 E8
Upper Camroyd St
    DEWS WF13...............................161 G7
Upper Carr La *PDSY/CALV* LS28....79 H6
Upper Carr St *LVSG* WF15...........159 H5
Upper Castle St *WBOW* BD5.........117 K1
Upper Chelsea St *KGHY* BD21.........2 E5
Upper Commercial St
    BTLY WF17................................161 F3
Upper Croft Rd *BTLY* WF17.........160 C4
Upper Cross St *DEWS* * WF13.....161 F7
Upper Ellistones Ct
    GTL/HWG HX4..........................174 D3
Upper Ferndown Gn
    WIL/AL * BD15............................95 K4
Upper Field House La
    RPDN/SBR HX6..........................152 E6
Upper Forge *HFAX* HX1..................17 G6
Upper Fountaine St *LDS* LS1............9 M9
Upper Fountain St
    RPDN/SBR HX6..........................153 J4
Upper Fyfe La *BAIL* BD17...............77 K1
Upper George St *HECK* WF16.......160 A4
    WBSY * BD6...............................117 G5
Upper Grange Av *WIL/AL* BD15.....96 A5
Upper Green Av *CLECK* * BD19....138 C7
    EARD/LOFT WF3........................162 C1
Upper Green La *BRIG* HD6............156 D7
Upper Green Wy
    EARD/LOFT WF3........................162 C1
Upper Hall Fold *GTL/HWG* HX4....173 J5
Upper Hall Vw *HIPP* HX3..............135 K4
Upper Haugh Shaw *HFAX* HX1......16 D9
Upper Headley
    CUL/QBY * BD13.......................115 G1
Upper Heaton La *HUDE* HD5........178 D4
Upper Heights Rd
    CUL/QBY BD13............................95 F5
Upper House La *LVSG* WF15.........158 D4
Upper House St *BOW* BD4...........118 C4
Upper Kirkgate *HFAX* HX1.............17 J6
Upper La *CLECK* BD19..................159 J1
    HIPP HX3...................................135 J3
Upper Langwith *WBY* LS22............46 B2
Upper Lombard St *YEA* LS19.........59 H7
Upper Marsh *HIPP* HX3................155 J3
Upper Marsh La *HWTH* BD22........72 A7
Upper Martin Gn
    GTL/HWG HX4..........................174 D2
Upper Mary St *SHPY* BD18............76 D7
Upper Mdw *CUL/QBY* BD13..........115 H6
Uppermoor *PDSY/CALV* LS28........99 K6
Uppermoor Cl *PDSY/CALV* LS28...100 A7
Upper Mosscar St *BFDE* BD3...........6 D6
Upper Mount St *BTLY* WF17........161 G1
Upper Nidd St *BFDE* BD3.................6 F7
Upper North St *BTLY* WF17..........160 E4
    LDSU LS2......................................9 M7
Upper Parish Ghyll La *ILK* LS29....23 J4
Upper Park Gate *BFD* BD1...............6 B5
Upper Peel St *DEWS* * WF13........161 G7
Upper Piccadilly *BFD* * BD1..............5 L5
Upper Quarry Rd *HUDN* HD2........178 B3
Upper Range *HIPP* HX3..................17 H1
Upper Rd *DEWS* WF13.................160 E6
Upper Royd *HIPP* * HX3...............136 B7

Upper Rushton Rd *BFDE* BD3 ....7 J1
Upper School St *AIRE* BD20 ....32 D5
Upper Seymour St *BFDE* BD3 ....6 E7
Upper South St *WF13* 161 F7
Upper Station Rd *BTLY* WF17 ....161 G4
Upper St *EARD/LOFT* * WF3 ....142 E6
Upper Sutherland Rd *HIPP* HX3 ....136 D7
Upper Town St *BRAM* LS13 ....101 F3
Upper Warrengate *WKFDE* WF1 ....19 G4
Upper Washer La *LUD/ILL* HX2 ....154 C3
Upper Westlock Av *OSM* LS9 ....11 J8
Upper West St *BTLY* * WF17 ....161 H3
Upper Willow Hall *LUD/ILL* HX2 ....154 A2
Upper Woodlands Rd *GIR* BD8 ....4 C1
Upper Woodview Pl
  BEE/HOL * LS11 ....123 G4
Upper Wortley Dr
  WOR/ARM * LS12 ....102 A6
Upper Wortley Rd
  WOR/ARM LS12 ....102 A6
Upper York St *WKFDE* WF1 ....18 E3
Upton La *BTLY* WF17 ....160 E2
Upwood La *AIRE* BD20 ....55 G1
Ure Crs *GIR* BD8 ....5 H3
Ure Gv *WBY* LS22 ....29 G1
Usher St *BOW* BD4 ....118 B1
Uttley St *HIPP* HX3 ....134 E5

V

The Vale *HDGY* LS6 ....82 E7
Vale Av *KNOT* WF11 ....170 E4
  RHAY LS8 ....84 B1
Vale Crs *KNOT* WF11 ....170 E4
Vale Crest *KNOT* WF11 ....170 E4
Vale Gv *AIRE* BD20 ....32 E1
  CUL/QBY BD13 ....115 J6
Vale Head Gv *KNOT* WF11 ....170 E4
Vale Head Mt *KNOT* WF11 ....170 E4
Vale Mill La *HWTH* BD22 ....72 E3
Valentine Ct *CUL/QBY* BD13 ....95 H6
Vale St *BRIG* HD6 ....157 F5
  KGHY BD21 ....3 L1
  WBY LS22 ....46 D2
The Valley *AL/HA/HU* LS17 ....63 F5
Valley Av *HIPP* HX3 ....136 F2
Valley Cl *AL/HA/HU* LS17 ....63 F6
Valley Ct *AL/HA/HU* LS17 ....83 J4
  BFD BD1 ....5 M1
  CAS WF10 ....167 K3
Valley Crs *WKFDW/WTN* WF2 ....164 A6
Valley Dr *ILK* LS29 ....24 D5
  MSTN/BAR LS15 ....105 J4
  RTHW LS26 ....127 H6
  WKFDW/WTN WF2 ....164 A7
Valley Farm Rd *RTHW* LS26 ....124 B5
Valley Farm Wy *RTHW* LS26 ....124 B5
Valley Fold *CUL/QBY* BD13 ....115 H6
Valley Gdns *CHAL* LS7 ....83 H4
  PONT WF8 ....191 F5
Valley Gn *PDSY/CALV* LS28 ....100 C7
Valley Gv *LUD/ILL* HX2 ....114 C7
  PDSY/CALV LS28 ....100 C7
Valley Head *HUDW* HD2 ....176 B7
Valley Mt *BRAM* LS13 ....100 D5
  GFTH/SHER LS25 ....127 K4
Valley Pl *BFD* BD1 ....5 L1
Valley Rdg *GFTH/SHER* LS25 ....127 J4
Valley Ri *BRAM* LS13 ....81 F7
Valley Ri *BFD* BD1 ....5 M2
  BRAM LS13 ....81 F7
  CLECK BD19 ....139 F7
  GFTH/SHER LS25 ....127 J4
  ILK LS29 ....24 C4
  LVSG WF15 ....159 H3
  MOR LS27 ....142 A2
  OSS WF5 ....182 C5
  PDSY/CALV LS28 ....100 C7
  PONT WF8 ....191 F5
  SHPY BD18 ....77 G6
Valley Sq *PDSY/CALV* LS28 ....100 C7
Valley Ter *AL/HA/HU* LS17 ....84 A1
Valley Vw *BAIL* BD17 ....77 G3
  BGLY BD16 ....74 D3
  LUD/ILL HX2 ....114 C7
Valley View Cl *HWTH* BD22 ....73 F1
Valley View Gdns *HWTH* * BD22 ....73 F4
Valley View Gv *ECHL* BD2 ....98 B3
Valley View Rd *OSS* WF5 ....182 C5
Valley Wy *LUD/ILL* HX2 ....114 C7
Vancouver Pl *CHAL* LS7 ....83 K6
Varley St *PDSY/CALV* LS28 ....100 A4
Vaughan St *BFD* BD1 ....5 J5
  HFAX HX1 ....16 A9
Ventnor Cl *CLECK* BD19 ....139 J5
  OSS WF5 ....182 C4
Ventnor Dr *OSS* WF5 ....182 C4
Ventnor St *BFDE* BD3 ....6 D6
Ventnor Ter *HIPP* HX3 ....154 E4
Ventnor Wy *OSS* WF5 ....182 C4
Vento Cl *WBSY* BD6 ....117 G6
Verdun Rd *WBSY* BD6 ....117 F6
Vere Sq *SCFT* LS14 ....105 F5
Verity Sp *BOW* BD4 ....119 G7
Verity St *BOW* BD4 ....119 G7
Verity Vw *SCFT* LS14 ....105 F4
Vermont St *BRAM* LS13 ....100 D3
Verner St *FEA/AMT* WF7 ....188 A4
Vernon Ct *KGHY* BD21 ....2 F5
Vernon Pl *ECHL* BD2 ....98 C3
  PDSY/CALV LS28 ....100 B3
  WKFDW/WTN WF2 ....184 D5
Vernon Rd *LDS* LS1 ....9 L6
  LVSG WF15 ....159 J4
Vernon St *HWTH* BD22 ....73 G4
  LDSU LS2 ....9 M7
Vesper Cl *KSTL* LS5 ....81 J5
Vesper Ct *KSTL* LS5 ....81 J5
Vesper Gdns *KSTL* LS5 ....81 J7
Vesper Gate Crs *KSTL* LS5 ....81 J5
Vesper Gate Dr *KSTL* LS5 ....81 H6
Vesper Gate Mt *KSTL* LS5 ....81 J6
Vesper Gv *KSTL* LS5 ....101 K1
Vesper La *KSTL* LS5 ....81 J7
Vesper Mt *KSTL* LS5 ....101 K1

Vesper Pl *KSTL* LS5 ....101 K1
Vesper Ri *KSTL* LS5 ....81 H6
Vesper Rd *KSTL* LS5 ....81 H6
Vesper Ter *KSTL* LS5 ....101 K1
Vesper Wk *KSTL* LS5 ....81 H6
Vesper Wy *KSTL* LS5 ....81 G6
Vestry St *BOW* BD4 ....118 C3
Viaduct Rd *WOR/ARM* LS12 ....8 D7
Vicarage Av *KSTL* LS5 ....102 A1
  MOR LS27 ....141 F1
Vicarage Cl *LM/WK* BD12 ....137 H5
  WKFDE WF1 ....164 C3
Vicarage Ct *CLECK* BD19 ....138 E7
Vicarage Dr *PDSY/CALV* LS28 ....100 A6
Vicarage Gdns *BIRK/DRI* BD11 ....139 H2
  BRIG HD6 ....176 E1
  FEA/AMT WF7 ....188 C1
  OT LS21 ....39 H5
Vicarage La *BSPA/BRAM* LS23 ....68 C1
  FEA/AMT WF7 ....188 C4
Vicarage Meadow *MIRF* WF14 ....179 K4
Vicarage Rd *EARL* WF12 ....181 F4
  EARL WF12 ....181 G1
  HDGY LS6 ....9 G4
  SHPY BD18 ....77 K4
Vicarage St *KSTL* LS5 ....102 A1
Vicarage St North *WKFDE* WF1 ....19 G3
  WKFDE WF1 ....19 G3
Vicarage St South *WKFDE* WF1 ....19 G3
Vicarage Ter *KSTL* LS5 ....102 A1
Vicarage Vw *KSTL* LS5 ....102 A1
Vicar La *BFD* BD1 ....6 A7
  LDS LS1 ....10 B9
  OSS WF5 ....182 D5
Vicar Park Dr *LUD/ILL* HX2 ....133 J7
Vicars Rd *RHAY* LS8 ....11 G2
Vicars Ter *CAS* WF10 ....148 A3
  RHAY LS8 ....11 G1
Vickerman St *HFAX* HX1 ....16 B8
Vickers Av *KSTL* LS5 ....101 J2
Vickersdale *PDSY/CALV* LS28 ....100 B3
Vickers St *CAS* WF10 ....168 C1
  MOR LS27 ....141 J5
Victor Dr *GSLY* LS20 ....59 F3
Victoria Av *BRIG* HD6 ....157 H5
  BTLY WF17 ....161 F4
  CLECK * BD19 ....158 E1
  ECHL BD2 ....98 E1
  ELL HX5 ....175 H3
  HFAX HX1 ....16 A8
  HORS LS18 ....80 D5
  HWTH BD22 ....72 D4
  ILK LS29 ....23 J5
  ILK LS29 ....38 A5
  KGHY BD21 ....3 H2
  MOR LS27 ....141 K2
  OSM LS9 ....15 K2
  RPDN/SBR HX6 ....153 K3
  RTHW LS26 ....145 F3
  SHPY BD18 ....76 E4
  WKFDW/WTN WF2 ....18 A4
  YEA LS19 ....60 A4
Victoria Cl *CAS* WF10 ....148 A3
  HORS LS18 ....80 D5
  ILK LS29 ....23 J5
  YEA LS19 ....60 A4
Victoria Court Ms *HDGY* * LS6 ....8 F7
Victoria Crs *DEWS* WF13 ....160 D6
  ELL HX5 ....175 J3
  HORS LS18 ....80 D5
  PDSY/CALV LS28 ....99 K6
Victoria Dr *EARL* WF12 ....181 F5
  ECHL BD2 ....98 E1
  HIPP HX3 ....136 A4
  HORS LS18 ....80 D5
  ILK LS29 ....23 J5
  MOR LS27 ....142 A1
Victoria Gdns *HORS* LS18 ....80 D5
  ILK LS29 ....23 J5
  PDSY/CALV LS28 ....99 K6
Victoria Grange *MOR* LS27 ....141 K2
Victoria Gv *HORS* LS18 ....80 D6
  ILK LS29 ....23 J5
  OSM LS9 ....11 K9
  WKFDW/WTN WF2 ....183 J6
Victoria Houses *KSTL* * LS5 ....101 K1
Victoria Ms *ELL* * HX5 ....175 J3
  HORS LS18 ....80 D5
  KGHY BD21 ....2 D4
  MOR LS27 ....141 K2
Victoria Mt *HORS* LS18 ....80 D5
Victoria Pk *HFAX* * HX1 ....16 C5
  SHPY BD18 ....76 E5
Victoria Park Av *BRAM* LS13 ....101 F3
Victoria Park Gv *BRAM* LS13 ....101 F2
Victoria Park St *KGHY* * BD21 ....3 J3
Victoria Park Vw *KGHY* BD21 ....3 J2
Victoria Pl *BEE/HOL* LS11 ....13 M3
  BRIG HD6 ....157 G7
  CAS WF10 ....148 C7
  MIRF WF14 ....179 G4
  YEA LS19 ....59 H4
Victoria Ri *PDSY/CALV* LS28 ....99 K6
Victoria Rd *BEE/HOL* LS11 ....13 M3
  BRIG HD6 ....157 G7
  CLECK BD19 ....139 K7
  DEWS WF13 ....161 F7
  EARL WF12 ....181 F5
  ECHL BD2 ....98 D1
  ELL HX5 ....175 H3
  GSLY LS20 ....58 E3
  HDGY LS6 ....8 E2
  HFAX HX1 ....16 C5
  HIPP HX3 ....156 C1
  HWTH BD22 ....72 E5
  HWTH BD22 ....72 E2
  ILK LS29 ....23 J5
  KSTL LS5 ....101 K1
  LVSG WF15 ....159 H5
  MOR LS27 ....141 K2
  PDSY/CALV LS28 ....99 K6
  PDSY/CALV * LS28 ....100 A2
  RPDN/SBR HX6 ....153 J5
  RTHW LS26 ....144 E1
  SHPY BD18 ....76 E4
  WBSY BD6 ....117 F6
Victoria Sq *LDS* LS1 ....10 B9
Victoria St *BAIL* BD17 ....77 G4
  BFD BD1 ....5 K3
  BRIG HD6 ....157 G2
  BTLY WF17 ....140 C6
  BTLY WF17 ....160 E2
  BVRD LS3 ....9 H7
  CAS WF10 ....148 A3
  CAS WF10 ....148 A7
  CHAL LS7 ....83 H5
  CLAY BD14 ....116 A2
  CLECK BD19 ....138 E7
  CUL/QBY BD13 ....74 B6
  CUL/QBY BD13 ....115 J5
  DEWS WF13 ....180 B3
  ECHL BD2 ....98 D3
  FEA/AMT WF7 ....188 C4
  GTL/HWG HX4 ....175 G2
  HECK WF16 ....160 A4
  HFAX HX1 ....17 G5
  HUDN HD2 ....177 K6
  IDLE BD10 ....78 C2
  MID LS10 ....14 D4
  MOR LS27 ....122 B7
  MOR LS27 ....141 J2
  PDSY/CALV LS28 ....79 H6
  PONT WF8 ....169 H5
  RPDN/SBR HX6 ....153 J5
  WBY LS22 ....29 H4
  WIL/AL BD15 ....95 F1
  WIL/AL BD15 ....95 K2
  WKFDE WF1 ....164 C4
  WKFDW/WTN WF2 ....18 A3
Victoria Wk *HORS* LS18 ....80 D5
Victoria Wy *WKFDE* WF1 ....164 C5
Victor Rd *HTON* BD9 ....97 G3
Victor St *BFDE* BD3 ....7 L5
  BTLY WF17 ....161 G3
  CAS WF10 ....168 B3
  HTON BD9 ....97 G3
Victor Ter *HFAX* HX1 ....16 C3
  HTON BD9 ....97 G3
Victory La *EARD/LOFT* WF3 ....165 H6
The View *AL/HA/HU* LS17 ....62 E5
  RHAY LS8 ....84 A4
View Croft Rd *BAIL* BD17 ....77 G4
Viewlands *HUDN* HD2 ....177 H5
Viewlands Mt *ILK* LS29 ....38 C5
View Rd *KGHY* BD21 ....2 D2
Vignola Ter *CLAY* BD14 ....116 B1
Viking Rd *PONT* WF8 ....189 K1
The Village *BSPA/BRAM* LS23 ....48 D1
Village Av *BULY* LS4 ....8 C4
Village Ms *WIL/AL* * BD15 ....75 F7
Village Pl *BULY* LS4 ....8 C4
Village Rd *BHP/TINH* LS16 ....62 E1
The Village St *BULY* LS4 ....8 C4
Village St *HIPP* HX3 ....136 E5
Village Ter *BULY* LS4 ....8 D4
Villa Gv *BGLY* BD16 ....55 K7
Villa Mt *LM/WK* BD12 ....137 H6
Villa Rd *BGLY* BD16 ....55 K7
Villa St *RPDN/SBR* HX6 ....153 K4
Villier Ct *WIL/AL* BD15 ....96 A4
Vincent Av *BFDE* BD20 ....32 B5
Vincent St *BFD* * BD1 ....5 K6
  HFAX HX1 ....16 B7
Vine Av *CLECK* BD19 ....138 D7
Vine Cl *BRIG* HD6 ....157 J6
Vine Ct *BRIG* HD6 ....157 J6
Vine Crs *CLECK* BD19 ....138 D7
Vine Garth *BRIG* HD6 ....157 J6
Vine Gv *BRIG* HD6 ....157 J6
Vinery Av *OSM* LS9 ....11 K9
Vinery Gv *OSM* LS9 ....11 K9
Vinery Mt *OSM* LS9 ....15 J1
Vinery Pl *OSM* LS9 ....15 J1
Vinery Rd *BULY* LS4 ....8 C5
Vinery St *OSM* LS9 ....11 J9
Vinery Ter *OSM* LS9 ....15 J1
Vinery Vw *OSM* LS9 ....15 K1
Vine St *CLECK* BD19 ....138 E7
  GTHN BD7 ....117 G1
  HFAX HX1 ....16 F8
Vine Ter East *GIR* BD8 ....96 C5
Vine Ter West *GIR* BD8 ....96 D5
Violet St *HFAX* HX1 ....16 C5
  HWTH BD22 ....72 D7
Violet St North *HFAX* HX1 ....16 C4
Virginia Cl *EARD/LOFT* WF3 ....164 B2
Virginia Ct *EARD/LOFT* WF3 ....164 B2
Virginia Dr *EARD/LOFT* WF3 ....164 B2
Virginia Gdns *EARD/LOFT* WF3 ....164 B2
Virginia St *CLAY* BD14 ....116 B3
Vivian Pl *GTHN* BD7 ....117 F3
Vivien Rd *GIR* BD8 ....96 B5
Vulcan Cl *DEWS* WF13 ....181 F1
Vulcan Gdns *DEWS* * WF13 ....181 F1
Vulcan Rd *DEWS* WF13 ....180 E1
Vulcan St *BOW* BD4 ....118 E5
  BRIG HD6 ....157 H7

W

Waddington St *KGHY* * BD21 ....3 G7
Wade House Av *HIPP* HX3 ....136 B1
Wade House Rd *HIPP* HX3 ....136 B2
Wade La *LDSU* LS2 ....10 A7
Wade St *BFD* BD1 ....5 L7
  HFAX HX1 ....17 H5
  PDSY/CALV LS28 ....100 A2
Wadlands Cl *PDSY/CALV* LS28 ....99 K1
Wadlands Dr *PDSY/CALV* LS28 ....99 K2
Wadlands Gv *PDSY/CALV* LS28 ....99 K1
Wadlands Ri *PDSY/CALV* LS28 ....99 K2
Wadsworth St *HFAX* HX1 ....16 B4
Wagon La *BGLY* BD16 ....75 K3
Waincliffe Crs *BEE/HOL* LS11 ....122 E5
Waincliffe Dr *BEE/HOL* LS11 ....122 E6

Waincliffe Garth
  BEE/HOL LS11 ....122 D5
Waincliffe Mt *BEE/HOL* LS11 ....122 E6
Waincliffe Pl *BEE/HOL* LS11 ....122 E5
Waincliffe Ter *BEE/HOL* LS11 ....122 E6
Wain Cl *GFTH/SHER* LS25 ....130 E3
Waindale Cl *LUD/ILL* HX2 ....133 H4
Waindale Crs *LUD/ILL* HX2 ....133 H4
Waindyke Wy *NORM* WF6 ....167 G6
Wainhouse Rd *HFAX* HX1 ....16 A9
Wainman St *BAIL* BD17 ....57 J7
  BAIL BD17 ....77 G4
  HFAX HX1 ....16 B5
Wainstalls La *LUD/ILL* HX2 ....133 F2
Wainstalls Lodge La
  LUD/ILL 133 F2
Wainstalls Rd *LUD/ILL* HX2 ....133 G1
Waites Cft *WKFDW/WTN* * WF2 ....163 G6
Waite St *WKFDW/WTN* WF2 ....183 K3
Wakefield Av *SCFT* LS14 ....105 G4
Wakefield Crs *EARL* WF12 ....181 J1
Wakefield Ga *LUD/ILL* HX2 ....154 C4
Wakefield Old Rd *EARL* * WF12 ....181 G1
Wakefield Rd *BFD* BD1 ....6 B8
  BIRK/DRI BD11 ....140 D2
  BOW BD4 ....118 C2
  BRIG HD6 ....157 J7
  EARL WF12 ....181 H1
  FEA/AMT WF7 ....187 J4
  GFTH/SHER LS25 ....107 F7
  HIPP HX3 ....154 D6
  HIPP HX3 ....156 F1
  HOR/CROF WF4 ....183 H7
  LVSG WF15 ....159 J4
  MID LS10 ....124 A4
  MOR LS27 ....141 F2
  NORM WF6 ....166 D7
  OSS WF5 ....183 G3
  PONT WF8 ....189 G2
  RPDN/SBR HX6 ....154 B4
  RTHW LS26 ....126 C6
  RTHW LS26 ....144 C2
Walden Dr *HTON* BD9 ....96 B2
Walden St *CAS* WF10 ....168 C1
Waldorf Wy *WKFDW/WTN* WF2 ....18 E7
Walesby Ct *BHP/TINH* LS16 ....81 H2
Walford Av *OSM* LS9 ....11 J9
Walford Gv *OSM* LS9 ....11 J9
Walford Mt *OSM* LS9 ....11 J9
Walford Rd *OSM* LS9 ....11 J8
Walford Ter *OSM* LS9 ....11 J9
The Walk *KGHY* BD21 ....3 H6
  PDSY/CALV LS28 ....99 J3
Walker Av *GTHN* BD7 ....116 D1
  WKFDW/WTN WF2 ....184 A2
Walker Dr *GIR* BD8 ....4 D3
Walkergate *OT* LS21 ....39 H3
  PONT WF8 ....169 K7
Walker La *RPDN/SBR* HX6 ....154 A4
Walker Pl *MOR* * LS27 ....122 A7
  SHPY BD18 ....77 J4
Walker Rd *HORS* LS18 ....80 E3
  LM/WK BD12 ....138 A3
Walkers Gn *WOR/ARM* LS12 ....12 A7
Walker's La *AIRE* BD20 ....20 E2
  WOR/ARM LS12 ....12 A7
Walkers Mt *BTLY* WF17 ....161 F5
  HDGY LS6 ....82 E7
Walkers Rw *YEA* LS19 ....59 H5
Walker's Pl *AIRE* BD20 ....33 F2
Walker's Ter *WKFDE* * WF1 ....18 D4
Walker St *BOW* BD4 ....118 C6
  CLECK BD19 ....138 A6
  CLECK BD19 ....138 E7
  DEWS WF13 ....180 A5
  EARL WF12 ....181 G5
Walker Ter *BOW* BD4 ....118 B2
  CUL/QBY BD13 ....74 A7
Walker Wd *BAIL* BD17 ....76 C2
Walkley Av *HECK* WF16 ....160 A4
Walkley Gv *HECK* WF16 ....160 A5
Walkley La *HECK* WF16 ....160 A4
Walkley Ter *HECK* WF16 ....160 B6
Wallace Gdns *EARD/LOFT* WF3 ....164 C2
Wallace St *HFAX* HX1 ....16 A7
Wallbank Dr *SHPY* BD18 ....77 H6
Wallingford Mt *WIL/AL* BD15 ....96 A4
Wallis St *GIR* BD8 ....4 C5
  RPDN/SBR HX6 ....153 J4
Wall St *HWTH* BD22 ....2 B7
Walmer Gv *PDSY/CALV* LS28 ....120 C1
Walmer Vls *GIR* BD8 ....5 J1
Walmsley Rd *HDGY* LS6 ....8 E3
Walnut Av *EARL* WF12 ....181 K2
  WKFDW/WTN WF2 ....184 A2
Walnut Cl *EARL* WF12 ....181 K3
  SCFT LS14 ....85 K4
  TAD LS24 ....90 C6
Walnut Crs *EARL* WF12 ....181 K2
  WKFDW/WTN WF2 ....184 A2
Walnut Dr *EARL* WF12 ....182 A2
  NORM WF6 ....186 D2
  PONT WF8 ....189 G3
Walnut Gv *EARL* WF12 ....182 A2
Walnut La *EARL* WF12 ....181 K3
Walnut Pl *EARL* WF12 ....181 K3
Walnut Rd *EARL* WF12 ....181 K2
Walnut St *BFDE* BD3 ....7 J7
  HFAX HX1 ....16 C6
  KGHY BD21 ....53 J7
Walsden *BGLY* BD16 ....55 J5
  HIPP HX3 ....16 E2
  WOR/ARM LS12 ....121 F4
Walsh Sq *HFAX* * HX1 ....154 E3
Walsh St *HFAX* HX1 ....16 B6
Walter Clough La *HIPP* HX3 ....156 A3
Walter Crs *OSM* LS9 ....15 G2
Walter St *BULY* LS4 ....8 C6
  ECHL BD2 ....97 J1
  IDLE BD10 ....78 C4
Walton Cha *BSPA/BRAM* LS23 ....30 E6
Walton Dr *BIRK/DRI* BD11 ....140 C1
Walton Garth *BIRK/DRI* BD11 ....140 C2
Walton La *BRIG* HD6 ....157 K3
Walton Rd *BSPA/BRAM* LS23 ....30 E7
  WBY LS22 ....29 J4
Walton St *BEE/HOL* LS11 ....13 L4

Bow BD4 ....6 B9
  MID LS10 ....14 E8
  RPDN/SBR HX6 ....153 J4
Waltroyd Rd *CLECK* BD19 ....158 D1
Wansford Cl *BOW* BD4 ....119 F4
Wanstead Crs *WIL/AL* BD15 ....96 A5
Wapping Nick La *HUDW* HD3 ....175 H6
Wapping Rd *BFDE* BD3 ....6 A3
Ward La *EARD/LOFT* WF3 ....165 H6
  MID LS10 ....123 J5
Wardle Crs *HWTH* BD22 ....2 B3
Wardman St *KGHY* BD21 ....3 L1
Ward's End *HFAX* HX1 ....17 H7
Wards Hill *BTLY* WF17 ....161 F3
Wards Hill Ct *BTLY* * WF17 ....161 F3
Ward St *DEWS* WF13 ....161 G7
  GTHN BD7 ....117 F3
  KGHY BD21 ....2 E7
  MID LS10 ....14 C5
Wareham Cnr *BOW* BD4 ....119 G4
Warehouse St *BTLY* WF17 ....161 G4
Warhurst Rd *ELL* HX5 ....175 K1
Waring Wy *EARL* WF12 ....181 H7
Warlbeck *ILK* LS29 ....23 J5
Warley Av *BFDE* BD3 ....7 J4
Warley Dene *LUD/ILL* HX2 ....153 J2
Warley Dr *BFDE* BD3 ....7 J5
Warley Edge La *LUD/ILL* HX2 ....153 J1
  LUD/ILL HX2 ....154 A1
Warley Gv *LUD/ILL* HX2 ....154 A2
Warley Rd *LUD/ILL* HX2 ....153 J2
Warley St *HFAX* HX1 ....16 C7
Warley Town La *LUD/ILL* HX2 ....153 H1
Warley Vw *LUD/ILL* HX2 ....154 A1
Warley Wood Av *LUD/ILL* HX2 ....153 G3
Warley Wood La *LUD/ILL* HX2 ....153 G3
Warmfield La *WKFDE* WF1 ....186 B2
Warmfield Vw *WKFDE* WF1 ....19 L2
Warm La *YEA* LS19 ....59 H6
Warnleigh Pk *CUL/QBY* BD13 ....114 E5
Warneford Av *OSS* WF5 ....182 C2
Warrel's Av *BRAM* LS13 ....101 F3
Warrel's Ct *BRAM* LS13 ....101 F3
Warrel's Gv *BRAM* LS13 ....101 F3
Warrel's Mt *BRAM* LS13 ....101 F3
Warrel's Pl *BRAM* LS13 ....101 F3
Warrel's Rd *BRAM* LS13 ....101 F2
Warrel's Rw *BRAM* * LS13 ....101 F3
Warrel's St *BRAM* LS13 ....101 F3
Warrel's Ter *BRAM* LS13 ....101 F3
Warren Av *BGLY* BD16 ....56 A6
  KNOT WF11 ....170 E5
  WKFDW/WTN WF2 ....184 E7
Warren Cl *LVSG* WF15 ....159 J6
Warren Ct *WKFDE* WF1 ....19 H4
Warren Dr *BGLY* BD16 ....56 A7
  FEA/AMT WF7 ....187 K1
Warrenfield Ct *HUDN* HD2 ....177 J6
Warren House La *HUDW* HD3 ....175 K6
  YEA LS19 ....60 A2
Warren La *BGLY* BD16 ....56 A7
  OT LS21 ....41 K3
  TAD LS24 ....69 G2
Warren Pk *BRIG* HD6 ....156 D2
Warren Park Cl *BRIG* HD6 ....156 D3
Warren Rd *FEA/AMT* WF7 ....188 A4
Warrenside *HUDN* HD2 ....177 K5
Warrens La *BTLY* WF17 ....140 A2
Warren St *EARL* WF12 ....181 G3
Warrenton Pl *GTHN* BD7 ....4 D9
Warton Av *BOW* BD4 ....118 C5
Warwick Cl *BOW* BD4 ....118 C2
  HFAX * HX1 ....154 E3
Warwick Dr *BOW* BD4 ....118 C2
Warwick Rd *BOW* BD4 ....118 C2
  BTLY WF17 ....161 F5
Warwick St *WKFDE* WF1 ....185 G6
Wasdale Crs *WKFDW/WTN* WF2 ....183 K2
Wasdale Rd *WKFDW/WTN* WF2 ....183 K2
Washburn Ct *WBY* LS22 ....29 G1
Washer La *LUD/ILL* HX2 ....154 C4
Washington Pl *BRAM* LS13 ....100 D5
Washington St *BRAM* LS13 ....100 D5
  BVRD LS3 ....8 F8
  GIR BD8 ....4 B1
  HIPP BD8 ....16 D1
Washington Ter *BRAM* LS13 ....100 D5
Waste La *MIRF* WF14 ....179 H6
Wastwater Dr *WBSY* BD6 ....136 E1
Watercock St *BOW* BD4 ....118 B1
Waterfall Fold *PONT* WF8 ....169 K4
Waterfront Ms *IDLE* BD10 ....79 H4
Watergate *HIPP* HX3 ....156 E1
  PONT WF8 ....189 H1
  RTHW LS26 ....146 F2
Watergate Rd *DEWS* WF13 ....180 E2
Water Green La
  RPDN/SBR HX6 ....172 B3
Water Hill La *RPDN/SBR* HX6 ....153 H3
Waterhouse Gv
  WKFDW/WTN WF2 ....18 B5
Waterhouse St *HFAX* HX1 ....17 G6
  KGHY BD21 ....2 E4
Water La *BEE/HOL* LS11 ....13 K3
  BFD BD1 ....5 J5
  EARD/LOFT WF3 ....165 G4
  EARL WF12 ....180 E3
  EARL WF12 ....181 K2
  GFTH/SHER LS25 ....131 J6
  HFAX HX1 ....17 J8
  HORS LS18 ....80 B3
  KGHY BD21 ....2 F6
  PDSY/CALV LS28 ....100 A2
  PONT WF8 ....170 A5
  PONT WF8 ....189 J7
  WOR/ARM LS12 ....101 G6
Waterloo Cl *CAS* WF10 ....167 J3
Waterloo Crs *BRAM* LS13 ....101 G2
  IDLE BD10 ....79 G4
Waterloo Fold *LM/WK* BD12 ....137 J4
Waterloo Gv *PDSY/CALV* LS28 ....99 J5
Waterloo La *BRAM* LS13 ....101 G2
Waterloo Mt *PDSY/CALV* LS28 ....99 J5
Waterloo Rd *BGLY* BD16 ....75 J1
  BRIG HD6 ....157 F5
  PDSY/CALV LS28 ....99 J5
Waterloo St *MID* LS10 ....14 B2
  WKFDE WF1 ....19 G8

Waterloo Ter LUD/ILL HX2 ....153 K2
Waterloo Wy BRAM LS13 ....101 G2
Water Royd Av MIRF WF14 ....179 H3
Water Royd Crs MIRF * WF14 ...179 H3
Water Royd Dr MIRF WF14 ....179 H3
Water Royd La MIRF WF14 ...179 H3
Waterside AIRE BD20 ....33 G2
 BGLY BD16 ....55 G6
 HIPP HX3 ....17 J8
 HWTH BD22 ....92 D3
Waterside Rd MID LS10 ...124 C4
Waterside Wk HUDE HD5 ...178 E4
Watersole La WBY LS22 ...30 C1
Water St BRIG HD6 ....157 G5
 RPDN/SBR HX6 ...153 J5
Waterton Gv
 WKFDW/WTN WF2 ...184 A4
Waterton Rd
 WKFDW/WTN WF2 ...183 K5
Water Vw CAS WF10 ...148 C7
Waterwood Cl
 EARD/LOFT WF3 ...162 E1
Waterworks Rd BTLY WF17 ...160 C4
Watford Av HIPP HX3 ...136 E4
Watkin Av CUL/QBY BD13 ...95 J7
Watkinson Av LUD/ILL HX2 ...134 C3
Watkinson Dr LUD/ILL HX2 ...134 C3
Watkinson Rd LUD/ILL HX2 ...134 C3
Watling Rd CAS WF10 ...149 J6
Watmough St GTHN BD7 ...117 F3
Watson Av EARL WF12 ...182 A1
Watson Crs WKFDE WF1 ...19 J2
Watson Mill La RPDN/SBR HX6 ...153 J5
Watson Rd SCFT LS14 ...105 G4
Watson's La TAD LS24 ...49 J5
Watson St MOR LS27 ...141 J4
 NORM WF6 ...166 D6
Wattle Syke WBY LS22 ...47 G1
Watts St CLAY BD14 ...116 A2
Watt St BOW BD4 ...7 K9
Watty Hall Av WBSY BD6 ...117 F4
Watty Hall La WBSY BD6 ...117 G4
Watty Hall Rd WBSY BD6 ...117 F4
Wauchope St
 WKFDW/WTN WF2 ...18 D8
Wauds Gates BAIL BD17 ...77 H3
Waveney Rd WOR/ARM LS12 ...12 B4
Waverley Av AIRE BD20 ...54 E3
 GTHN BD7 ...4 E9
Waverley Crs HIPP HX3 ...156 B1
Waverley Garth BEE/HOL LS11 ...13 L8
Waverley Pl GTHN BD7 ...117 G1
Waverley Rd ELL HX5 ...175 J4
 GTHN BD7 ...4 E9
Waverley St EARL WF12 ...181 F2
Waverley Ter GTHN BD7 ...4 E9
Waverton Gn WBSY BD6 ...116 D7
Wavertree Park Gdns
 LM/WK BD12 ...137 H3
Wayland Ap BHP/TINH LS16 ...62 C2
Wayland Dr BHP/TINH LS16 ...62 C2
Wayne Cl BTLY WF17 ...161 F2
Wayside Av SCFT LS14 ...66 A2
Wayside Crs IDLE * BD10 ...78 C7
 SCFT LS14 ...66 A1
Wayside Mt SCFT LS14 ...66 A2
Weardale Cl BOW BD4 ...118 D5
Weardley La HU/HU LS17 ...43 G4
Weatherhead Pl AIRE BD20 ...33 G1
Weatherhill Crs HUDW HD3 ...175 K7
Weather Hill Rd HUDW HD3 ...175 K6
Weatherhouse Ter
 LUD/ILL HX2 ...134 A6
Weaver Cottages
 HWTH * BD22 ...92 D3
Weaver Gdns MOR LS27 ...142 C4
Weavers Ct WOR/ARM LS12 ...102 A6
Weavers Cft IDLE BD10 ...78 B2
 PDSY/CALV LS28 ...100 C7
Weavers Gra GSLY LS20 ...59 F2
Weavers Rd PONT WF8 ...169 K7
Weavers Rw PDSY/CALV LS28 ...100 C7
Weaver St BULY LS4 ...8 C6
Weavers Wk AIRE BD20 ...21 F7
Weaverthorpe Rd BOW BD4 ...119 F6
Webb Dr ECHL BD2 ...98 B3
Webb's Ter HIPP HX3 ...17 K3
Weber Ct BFDE BD3 ...7 G6
Webster Hl EARL WF12 ...181 F1
Webster Pl NORM WF6 ...166 D6
Webster Rw WOR/ARM LS12 ...102 A7
Webster St BFDE BD3 ...6 E4
 DEWS * WF13 ...181 F1
Wedgemoor Cl LM/WK BD12 ...137 H3
Wedgewood Dr RHAY LS8 ...84 B4
Wedgewood Gv RHAY LS8 ...84 B4
Weedling Ga TAD LS24 ...70 C3
Weeland Av HOR/CROF WF4 ...186 E6
Weeland Ct KNOT WF11 ...171 J4
Weeland Crs HOR/CROF WF4 ...187 F5
Weeland Dr HOR/CROF WF4 ...187 F6
Weeland Rd HOR/CROF WF4 ...186 D7
Weetlands Cl GFTH/SHER LS25 ...128 A4
Weetwood Av BHP/TINH LS16 ...82 C5
Weetwood Ct BHP/TINH LS16 ...82 B4
Weetwood Crs BHP/TINH LS16 ...82 C4
Weetwood Grange Gv
 BHP/TINH LS16 ...82 A4
Weetwood House Ct
 BHP/TINH LS16 ...82 A4
Weetwood La
 BHP/TINH LS16 ...82 B3
Weetwood Mill La
 BHP/TINH LS16 ...82 C4
Weetwood Park Dr
 BHP/TINH LS16 ...82 A4
Weetwood Rd BHP/TINH LS16 ...82 A4
 GIR BD8 ...4 D3
Weetwood Wk BHP/TINH LS16 ...82 B5
Weetworth Av CAS WF10 ...168 D2
Weetworth Pk CAS WF10 ...168 D2
Weir Vw CAS WF10 ...148 C7
Welbeck Dr GTHN BD7 ...116 C2
Welbeck Ri GTHN BD7 ...116 C2
Welbeck Rd BTLY WF17 ...140 C5
 OSM LS9 ...15 J1
Welbeck St CAS * WF10 ...148 C7

WKFDE WF1 ....19 L9
Welburn Av BHP/TINH LS16 ...82 A5
 HIPP HX3 ...156 C1
Welburn Dr BHP/TINH LS16 ...82 A5
Welburn Gv BHP/TINH LS16 ...82 A5
Welburn Mt WBSY BD6 ...116 D6
Welbury Dr GIR BD8 ...97 H3
Weldon Ct BOW BD4 ...119 F2
Welfare Av MSTN/BAR LS15 ...87 H5
Welham Wk BFDE BD3 ...7 G5
Welland Dr GFTH/SHER LS25 ...107 K7
Wellands Gn CLECK BD19 ...158 C1
Wellands La CLECK BD19 ...138 A7
Wellands Ter BFDE BD3 ...7 G5
 YEA LS19 ...79 K1
Well Cl RTHW LS26 ...127 H6
Well Close Ri LDSU LS2 ...10 A5
Well Close St BRIG HD6 ...157 F5
Wellcroft OT LS21 ...39 H3
Well Cft SHPY BD18 ...77 G5
Wellcroft Gv EARD/LOFT WF3 ...162 E1
Wellesley Gn
 WKFDW/WTN WF2 ...183 K2
Wellfield La ILK LS29 ...25 K7
Wellgarth HFAX HX1 ...16 F9
Well Garth MSTN/BAR LS15 ...105 A3
Well Garth Bank BRAM LS13 ...100 E1
Well Garth Mt MSTN/BAR LS15 ...105 K3
Wellgarth Rd FEA/AMT WF7 ...188 D5
Well Garth Vw BRAM LS13 ...101 F1
Well Green La BRIG * HD6 ...156 E3
Well Gv BRIG HD6 ...156 E3
 HUDN HD2 ...177 H6
Wellhead Cl BHP/TINH LS16 ...41 H6
Well Head Dr HFAX HX1 ...17 G8
Well Head La HFAX HX1 ...17 G8
 RPDN/SBR HX6 ...152 D6
Well Heads CUL/QBY BD13 ...94 D7
Well Hl OT LS21 ...39 G3
 YEA LS19 ...59 J4
Wellholme BRIG HD6 ...157 G5
Well Holme Md
 WOR/ARM LS12 ...121 H3
Wellhouse Av MIRF WF14 ...179 J2
Well House Av RHAY LS8 ...84 B7
Wellhouse Cl MIRF WF14 ...179 H2
Well House Crs RHAY LS8 ...84 B7
Well House Dr RHAY LS8 ...84 B7
Well House Gdns RHAY LS8 ...84 B7
Wellhouse La MIRF WF14 ...179 J2
Well House Rd RHAY LS8 ...84 B7
Wellington Ar BRIG * HD6 ...176 C2
Wellington Br WOR/ARM LS12 ...13 G1
Wellington Bridge St BVRD LS3 ...9 H9
 LDS LS1 ...13 H1
Wellington Ct BIRK/DRI BD11 ...139 H1
 BTLY * WF17 ...160 E3
 LUD/ILL * HX2 ...134 B6
Wellington Crs SHPY BD18 ...77 F5
Wellington Gdns BRAM LS13 ...101 G1
Wellington Garth BRAM LS13 ...101 G1
Wellington Gv BRAM LS13 ...101 G1
 ECHL BD2 ...98 C3
 PDSY/CALV LS28 ...99 K6
Wellington Hl SCFT LS14 ...85 H2
Wellington Mt BRAM LS13 ...101 G1
Wellington Pl KNOT WF11 ...170 E4
Wellington Rd EARL WF12 ...181 F1
 ECHL BD2 ...98 C3
 KGHY BD21 ...3 H6
 WIL/AL BD15 ...95 F1
 WOR/ARM LS12 ...12 F3
Wellington Rd East
 DEWS * WF13 ...181 F1
Wellington Rd West BFD BD1 ...6 A5
 BGLY BD16 ...75 J1
 BOW BD4 ...7 J8
 BTLY WF17 ...160 E3
 BTLY WF17 ...161 F4
 BVRD LS3 ...9 H9
 CAS WF10 ...148 A7
 CUL/QBY BD13 ...115 J5
 DEWS WF13 ...181 F1
 ECHL BD2 ...98 C2
 IDLE BD10 ...78 C5
 LVSG WF15 ...159 J5
 MOR LS27 ...141 K3
 WIL/AL BD15 ...96 B4
 WKFDW/WTN WF2 ...183 K2
Wellington St South HFAX HX1 ...17 J7
Wellington St West HFAX HX1 ...16 E8
Wellington Ter BRAM LS13 ...101 C1
Well La BRIG HD6 ...157 K6
 BTLY WF17 ...161 G3
 CHAL LS7 ...83 J5
 DEWS WF13 ...180 C1
 GFTH/SHER LS25 ...127 K5
 GFTH/SHER LS25 ...131 F2
 GSLY LS20 ...59 F2
 HFAX HX1 ...17 J5
 YEA LS19 ...59 J5
 YEA LS19 ...79 K1
Well Road Cl LUD/ILL HX2 ...154 K1
Well Royd Av LUD/ILL HX2 ...153 K1
The Wells LUD/ILL HX2 ...153 K1
 LUD/ILL * HX2 ...154 B3
Wells Ct OSS WF5 ...182 B4
Wells Cft HDGY LS6 ...82 D5
Wells Prom ILK LS29 ...24 A6
Wells Rd EARL WF12 ...181 G7
 GSLY LS20 ...59 F2
 ILK LS29 ...23 K7
Wellstone Av BRAM LS13 ...100 E5
Wellstone Dr BRAM LS13 ...100 E5
Wellstone Gdns BRAM LS13 ...100 E5
Wellstone Garth BRAM LS13 ...100 E4
Wellstone Gn BRAM LS13 ...100 E5
Wellstone Ri BRAM LS13 ...100 E5
Wellstone Rd BRAM LS13 ...100 E4
Wellstone Wy BRAM LS13 ...100 E5
Well St BFD BD1 ...6 A4
 CUL/QBY BD13 ...94 A5
 EARL WF12 ...181 H1
 GTL/HWG HX4 ...174 C5
 KGHY BD21 ...2 D1

LVSG WF15 ...159 H3
WIL/AL BD15 ...75 F7
Wells Wk ILK LS29 ...24 A6
Well Vw GSLY LS20 ...59 F2
Welton Gv HDGY LS6 ...8 F2
Welton Mt HDGY LS6 ...8 F2
Welton Pl HDGY LS6 ...8 F2
Welton Rd HDGY LS6 ...8 F2
Welwyn Av BTLY WF17 ...160 C2
 SHPY BD18 ...78 A5
Welwyn Dr BAIL BD17 ...77 H2
 SHPY BD18 ...78 A5
Welwyn Rd EARL WF12 ...161 J5
Wembly Av CUL/QBY BD13 ...95 J7
Wenborough La BOW BD4 ...119 G3
Wendel Av MSTN/BAR LS15 ...87 G5
Wendron Cl LVSG WF15 ...159 G2
Wendron Wy IDLE BD10 ...78 C5
Wenlock St BFDE BD3 ...6 C7
Wenning St KGHY BD21 ...3 M3
Wensley Av CHAL LS7 ...83 H5
 SHPY BD18 ...77 H5
Wensley Bank CUL/QBY BD13 ...95 F7
Wensley Bank Ter
 CUL/QBY BD13 ...95 F7
Wensley Bank West
 CUL/QBY BD13 ...95 F7
Wensley Crs CHAL LS7 ...83 H5
Wensleydale Av
 WOR/ARM LS12 ...101 J3
Wensleydale Crs
 WOR/ARM LS12 ...101 J3
Wensleydale Dr
 WOR/ARM LS12 ...101 J3
Wensleydale Ms
 WOR/ARM LS12 ...101 J3
Wensleydale Ri BAIL BD17 ...57 K7
 WOR/ARM * LS12 ...101 J3
Wensleydale Rd BFDE BD3 ...7 L5
Wensley Dr CHAL LS7 ...83 G4
 PONT WF8 ...189 K3
Wensley Gn CHAL LS7 ...83 G5
Wensley Gv BRIG HD6 ...176 D1
 CHAL LS7 ...83 G4
Wensley Lawn MID LS10 ...143 H5
Wensley Rd CHAL LS7 ...83 G4
Wensley Vw CHAL LS7 ...83 H5
Went Av FEA/AMT WF7 ...188 B6
Wentbridge Rd FEA/AMT WF7 ...188 D5
Wentcliffe Rd KNOT WF11 ...170 C4
Went Cft PONT WF8 ...189 J4
Went-Dale Rd PONT WF8 ...189 H4
Went Fold PONT WF8 ...189 J4
Went Garth PONT WF8 ...189 J4
Went Gv FEA/AMT WF7 ...189 H4
Wentwell Rd FEA/AMT WF7 ...187 F4
Wentworth Av AL/HA/HU LS17 ...63 G7
Wentworth Cl ILK LS29 ...38 B6
Wentworth Ct BRIG HD6 ...176 E2
Wentworth Crs AL/HA/HU LS17 ...63 H7
Wentworth Dr LUD/ILL HX2 ...114 C7
Wentworth Ga WBY LS22 ...28 E3
Wentworth Gv LUD/ILL HX2 ...114 C7
Wentworth Park Ri PONT WF8 ...190 E4
Wentworth Rd FEA/AMT WF7 ...188 A5
Wentworth St WKFDE WF1 ...18 C1
Wentworth Ter WKFDE WF1 ...18 D2
Wentworth Wy AL/HA/HU LS17 ...63 H7
Wepener Mt OSM LS9 ...11 M6
Wepener Pl OSM LS9 ...11 M6
Wesleyan Ter BOW * BD4 ...118 D3
Wesley Ap BEE/HOL LS11 ...122 E4
Wesley Av LM/WK BD12 ...117 J7
 WOR/ARM * LS12 ...12 A1
Wesley Av South LM/WK BD12 ...137 K1
Wesley Cl BTLY WF17 ...140 B6
Wesley Cft BEE/HOL LS11 ...122 E4
 HDGY LS6 ...9 L2
 HFAX * HX1 ...17 H5
 OSS WF5 ...182 B3
Wesley Cft BEE/HOL LS11 ...13 C9
Wesley Dr LM/WK BD12 ...117 K7
Wesley Garth BEE/HOL LS11 ...122 E3
Wesley Gn BEE/HOL LS11 ...122 E4
Wesley Gv IDLE BD10 ...78 D3
Wesley Hall Ct
 EARD/LOFT * WF3 ...165 G6
Wesley Pl AIRE BD20 ...33 F1
 DEWS * WF13 ...181 F1
 FEA/AMT WF7 ...188 C5
 KGHY BD21 ...73 J1
 OSM LS9 ...14 F1
Wesley Rd PDSY/CALV LS28 ...99 K4
 WOR/ARM LS12 ...12 A1
Wesley Rw PDSY/CALV * LS28 ...100 B5
Wesley Sq PDSY/CALV LS28 ...100 B5
Wesley St BRAM LS13 ...80 B7
 CAS WF10 ...148 C7
 CAS WF10 ...168 B3
 CLECK BD19 ...138 E7
 MOR LS27 ...141 K3
 OSS WF5 ...182 B3
 OT LS21 ...39 H2
 PDSY/CALV LS28 ...100 A2
 WKFDE WF1 ...185 F6
Wesley Ter BRAM LS13 ...80 C7
 BRAM LS13 ...101 G2
 PDSY/CALV LS28 ...100 B5
Wesley Vw BRAM * LS13 ...80 C7
 PDSY/CALV LS28 ...100 B6
West Acres KNOT WF11 ...150 F7
West Av BAIL BD17 ...57 H7
 BSPA/BRAM LS23 ...48 B2
 HIPP HX3 ...154 A1
 HIPP HX3 ...157 F1
 PONT WF8 ...189 J1
 RHAY LS8 ...84 D4
West Bank HWTH BD22 ...2 B5
 LUD/ILL HX2 ...134 A3
West Bank Cl HWTH BD22 ...2 A3
West Bank Gv HWTH BD22 ...54 B1
West Bank Ri HWTH BD22 ...2 A3
West Bank Rd HWTH BD22 ...54 A1
West Bolton LUD/ILL HX2 ...114 A7
Westborough Dr LUD/ILL HX2 ...154 A1
Westbourne Av BEE/HOL LS11 ...123 G3
 GFTH/SHER LS25 ...107 G7
 PONT WF8 ...189 G2
Westbourne Cl OT LS21 ...39 F4

Westbourne Crs
 GFTH/SHER LS25 ...107 G7
 PONT WF8 ...189 G2
Westbourne Dr
 GFTH/SHER LS25 ...107 G7
 CSLY LS20 ...58 D2
 ILK LS29 ...38 B5
Westbourne Gdns
 GFTH/SHER LS25 ...107 G7
Westbourne Gv
 GFTH/SHER LS25 ...107 G7
 HIPP HX3 ...155 G5
 OT LS21 ...39 F3
Westbourne Mt BEE/HOL LS11 ...123 G3
Westbourne Pl BEE/HOL LS11 ...123 G3
 PDSY/CALV LS28 ...100 A3
Westbourne Rd GIR * BD8 ...97 G3
 PONT WF8 ...189 H2
Westbourne St BEE/HOL LS11 ...123 G3
Westbourne Ter
 GFTH/SHER LS25 ...107 F7
 HIPP HX3 ...155 G5
Westbrook Cl HORS LS18 ...80 E2
West Brook Ct HFAX HX1 ...16 F4
Westbrook La HORS LS18 ...80 E2
Westburn Av HWTH BD22 ...2 A8
Westburn Crs HWTH BD22 ...2 A8
Westburn Gv HWTH BD22 ...2 A8
Westburn Wy HWTH BD22 ...2 A8
Westbury Cl BOW BD4 ...118 E1
Westbury Gv MID LS10 ...124 A4
Westbury Mt RTHW LS26 ...124 A5
Westbury Pl HFAX HX1 ...154 B2
Westbury Pl North MID LS10 ...124 A4
Westbury Pl South RTHW LS26 ...124 A5
Westbury Rd WBSY BD6 ...116 C5
Westbury St BOW BD4 ...118 E1
 ELL HX5 ...175 K2
 MID LS10 ...124 A5
Westbury Ter HFAX HX1 ...154 B2
 RTHW LS26 ...124 A5
West Busk La OT LS21 ...38 E4
West Byland LUD/ILL HX2 ...114 A7
West Chevin Rd OT LS21 ...38 E5
Westcliffe Av BAIL BD17 ...57 G7
Westcliffe Dr LUD/ILL HX2 ...154 A1
Westcliffe Ri CLECK BD19 ...158 D1
Westcliffe Rd CLECK BD19 ...138 D7
 SHPY BD18 ...77 G5
West Cl HUDN HD2 ...177 H7
 NORM WF6 ...166 D6
 PONT WF8 ...189 K4
Westcombe Av RHAY LS8 ...84 B2
Westcombe Ct LM/WK BD12 ...137 H3
West Cote Dr IDLE BD10 ...78 A3
West Ct RHAY LS8 ...84 D5
West Cft ILK LS29 ...22 C1
 LM/WK BD12 ...137 H4
Westcroft Av HIPP HX3 ...136 A3
Westcroft Rd GTHN BD7 ...117 F2
West Dl BSPA/BRAM LS23 ...48 B1
Westdale Dr PDSY/CALV LS28 ...100 A5
Westdale Gdns
 PDSY/CALV LS28 ...100 A5
Westdale Gv PDSY/CALV LS28 ...100 A5
Westdale Ri PDSY/CALV LS28 ...100 A5
Westdale Rd PDSY/CALV LS28 ...100 A5
West Dene AIRE BD20 ...21 F7
West Dr HWTH BD22 ...92 D2
 PONT WF8 ...189 K2
West End Ap MOR LS27 ...141 H4
West End Av FEA/AMT WF7 ...187 K1
West End Cl HORS LS18 ...80 D3
West End Dr CLECK BD19 ...158 C2
 HORS LS18 ...80 D3
West End Gv HORS LS18 ...80 D3
West End La HORS LS18 ...80 C2
West End Pl BEE/HOL LS11 ...13 J4
West End Ri HORS LS18 ...80 C3
West End Rd HFAX HX1 ...154 B2
 PDSY/CALV LS28 ...79 J6
Westend St BFD BD1 ...5 K5
West End Ter ECHL BD2 ...78 C7
 GSLY LS20 ...58 D2
 SHPY BD18 ...77 F4
Westercroft La HIPP HX3 ...136 A4
Westercroft Vw HIPP HX3 ...136 A4
Westerley Crs AIRE BD20 ...32 D1
Westerly Cft WOR/ARM LS12 ...8 B9
Westerly Ri FEA/AMT * WF7 ...188 C5
Westerman Cl FEA/AMT WF7 ...188 C5
Westerman St WKFDE WF1 ...185 G7
Western Av AIRE BD20 ...34 A7
 BTLY WF17 ...140 D6
 PONT WF8 ...170 A7
Western Ct PONT WF8 ...170 A7
Western Gales Wy NORM WF6 ...167 G7
Western Gv WOR/ARM LS12 ...122 A1
Western Mt WOR/ARM LS12 ...122 A1
Western Pl CUL/QBY BD13 ...116 A5
Western Rd WOR/ARM LS12 ...122 A1
Western St WOR/ARM LS12 ...122 A1
Western Wy WBSY BD6 ...117 F7
Westerton Cl EARD/LOFT WF3 ...143 G1
Westerton Ct LM/WK BD12 ...138 C2
Westerton Rd EARD/LOFT WF3 ...162 C1
Westerton Wk
 EARD/LOFT WF3 ...143 G7
West Farm Av MID LS10 ...143 H4
Westfell Cl HWTH BD22 ...2 B7
Westfell Rd HWTH BD22 ...2 B7
Westfell Wy HWTH BD22 ...2 B7
Westfield CUL/QBY BD13 ...95 K7
 PDSY/CALV LS28 ...100 A4
Westfield Av CAS WF10 ...168 B4
 EARL WF12 ...181 K1
 GFTH/SHER LS25 ...127 K4
 HIPP HX3 ...156 C1
 KNOT WF11 ...171 G5
 PONT WF8 ...189 H3

WOR/ARM LS12 ...101 J5
 YEA LS19 ...59 G5
Westfield Cl GFTH/SHER LS25 ...130 E3
 HECK * WF16 ...159 K3
 RTHW LS26 ...144 D3
 YEA LS19 ...59 G5
Westfield Crs GFTH/SHER LS25 ...131 G3
 HOR/CROF WF4 ...182 E7
 MIRF WF14 ...179 H4
 RTHW LS26 ...144 D3
Westfield Crs AIRE BD20 ...54 C1
 ECHL BD2 ...6 E1
 HDGY LS6 ...9 G5
 OSS WF5 ...182 B4
 SHPY BD18 ...77 K6
 TAD LS24 ...50 D7
 WKFDW/WTN WF2 ...163 G6
Westfield Dr AIRE BD20 ...54 C2
 HIPP HX3 ...156 C1
 OSS WF5 ...182 B4
 YEA LS19 ...59 F5
Westfield Farm OSS WF5 ...182 B3
Westfield Gdns
 GFTH/SHER LS25 ...127 J4
 HIPP HX3 ...156 C1
Westfield Gv CAS WF10 ...147 K1
 CAS WF10 ...168 B4
 DEWS WF13 ...180 C1
 IDLE BD10 ...78 B4
 SHPY * BD18 ...77 K6
 WKFDE WF1 ...184 D1
Westfield La ECHL BD2 ...78 A5
 GFTH/SHER LS25 ...127 J4
 GFTH/SHER LS25 ...130 E3
 LM/WK BD12 ...137 J6
 PONT WF8 ...190 D6
Westfield Mt YEA LS19 ...59 F5
Westfield Ov YEA LS19 ...59 F5
Westfield Pk WKFDE WF1 ...184 D1
Westfield Pl CLECK BD19 ...137 K6
 HFAX HX1 ...16 C8
 WKFDW/WTN WF2 ...163 G6
Westfield Rd AIRE BD20 ...54 C2
 BVRD LS3 ...9 G6
 CLAY BD14 ...116 A2
 HECK WF16 ...159 K3
 HOR/CROF WF4 ...182 E7
 HTON BD9 ...97 F3
 KNOT WF11 ...171 G5
 MOR * LS27 ...141 K3
 RTHW LS26 ...144 D3
 WKFDE WF1 ...18 E1
Westfield Sq TAD LS24 ...50 D6
Westfields CAS WF10 ...168 B3
Westfields Av MIRF WF14 ...179 H4
Westfield Sq TAD LS24 ...50 D6
Westfields Rd MIRF WF14 ...179 H4
Westfield St HECK WF16 ...159 K3
 HFAX HX1 ...16 E7
 OSS WF5 ...182 B4
Westfield Ter BAIL BD17 ...57 H7
 BFDE BD2 ...6 E1
 BVRD LS3 ...8 F6
 CAS WF10 ...147 K2
 CHAL LS7 ...83 H4
 CLAY BD14 ...116 A2
 ECHL BD2 ...6 E1
 HFAX HX1 ...16 C8
 TAD LS24 ...50 D6
 WKFDE WF1 ...18 E1
Westfield Vw WKFDE WF1 ...164 D7
Westgarth WBY LS22 ...28 E6
West Ga WBY LS22 ...29 H4
Westgate BAIL BD17 ...57 H7
 BRIG HD6 ...157 K6
 CLECK BD19 ...158 D1
 EARL WF12 ...181 G1
 ECHL BD2 ...98 D1
 ELL HX5 ...175 J2
 GIR BD8 ...5 J4
 GSLY LS20 ...58 C3
 HFAX HX1 ...17 H6
 LDS LS1 ...9 J9
 LVSG WF15 ...159 K4
 OT LS21 ...39 G3
 SHPY BD18 ...77 G4
 TAD LS24 ...50 D7
 WKFDW/WTN WF2 ...18 D5
Westgate Cl EARD/LOFT WF3 ...144 C7
Westgate Ct EARD/LOFT WF3 ...144 D7
Westgate End
 WKFDW/WTN WF2 ...18 B6
Westgate Gdns KGHY BD21 ...2 F6
Westgate Gv EARD/LOFT WF3 ...144 D7
Westgate Hill St BOW BD4 ...119 H6
Westgate La EARD/LOFT WF3 ...144 C7
Westgate Market HFAX HX1 ...17 H6
Westgate Ter BOW BD4 ...119 H6
West Grange Cl MID LS10 ...123 J5
West Grange Dr MID LS10 ...123 J5
West Grange Fold MID LS10 ...123 J5
West Grange Gdns MID LS10 ...123 J5
West Grange Garth MID LS10 ...123 J5
West Grange Rd MID LS10 ...123 J5
West Grange Wk MID LS10 ...123 J5
West Gv BAIL BD17 ...57 H7
West Grove St
 PDSY/CALV * LS28 ...100 A4
West Grove Ter HFAX HX1 ...16 C8
West Hill Av CHAL LS7 ...83 H5
Westhill Av CUL/QBY BD13 ...74 D7
West Hill St HFAX HX1 ...16 D6
Westholme Rd HFAX HX1 ...16 C8
Westholme St BFD BD1 ...5 K7
West Ings Cl KNOT WF11 ...171 J3
West Ings Crs KNOT WF11 ...171 J3
West Ings La KNOT WF11 ...171 J3
West Ings Ms KNOT WF11 ...171 J3
West Ings Wy KNOT WF11 ...171 J3
Westland Rd BEE/HOL LS11 ...123 F5
Westlands Dr WIL/AL BD15 ...96 B4
Westlands Gv WIL/AL BD15 ...96 B4
Westland Sq BEE/HOL LS11 ...123 G6
West La BAIL BD17 ...77 F2
 BSPA/BRAM LS23 ...48 B1
 CLECK BD19 ...139 J6
 CUL/QBY BD13 ...95 G7
 HIPP HX3 ...155 J5

HOR/CROF WF4........186 E7
HWTH BD22........2 A3
HWTH BD22........72 C5
OT LS21........25 K4
Westlea Mz KCHY BD21........54 C2
West Lea Cl AL/HA/HU LS17........83 G3
West Lea Crs EARD/LOFT WF3........162 C1
YEA LS19........59 G5
West Lea Dr AL/HA/HU LS17........83 G3
EARD/LOFT WF3........162 C1
West Lea Gdns AL/HA/HU LS17........83 G3
West Lea Garth AL/HA/HU LS17........83 G3
West Lea Gv YEA LS19........59 G5
West Leeds St HWTH BD22........2 D5
Westleigh BGLY BD16........55 K7
Westleigh Cl BAIL * BD17........77 F2
Westleigh Dr BAIL BD17........77 F2
Westleigh Rd BAIL BD17........77 F2
Westleigh Wy BAIL BD17........76 E2
Westlock Av OSM LS9........11 H6
West Ldg ILK * LS29........37 K2
West Lodge Crs HUDW HD3........176 A3
West Lodge Gdns CHAL LS7........83 H6
West Md CAS WF10........169 F1
Westminster Av CLAY BD14........115 K2
Westminster Cl BRAM LS13........100 C1
Westminster Crs CLAY BD14........115 K2
MSTN/BAR LS15........105 F7
Westminster Dr BRAM LS13........100 C1
CLAY BD14........115 K2
Westminster Gdns CLAY BD14........115 K2
Westminster Pl BFDE BD3........6 B2
Westminster Rd BFDE BD3........6 B2
Westminster Ter BFDE BD3........6 B3
Westmoor Av BAIL BD17........57 G7
Westmoor Cl BAIL * BD17........57 G7
West Moorlands Av
DEWS * WF13........160 E7
Westmoor Pl BRAM LS13........100 C2
Westmoor Ri BRAM LS13........100 C2
Westmoor St BRAM LS13........100 C2
Westmoreland Mt
BRAM * LS13........101 G1
Westmorland St WKFDE WF1........18 F4
West Mt TAD LS24........70 C1
West Mount Pl HFAX HX1........16 C4
West Mount St HFAX * LS11........13 K9
Westmount St PONT WF8........189 H1
Weston Av CUL/QBY BD13........115 G6
Weston Crs OT LS21........39 F1
Weston Dr OT LS21........26 E7
Weston La OT LS21........39 F1
OT LS21........38 E1
Weston Moor Rd OT LS21........26 C3
Weston Park Vw OT LS21........26 E7
Weston Rdg OT LS21........27 F7
Weston St HWTH BD22........2 A9
Weston Vale Rd
CUL/QBY BD13........115 F6
Westover Gdns
PDSY/CALV LS28........99 K6
Westover Gn BRAM * LS13........101 F2
Westover Gv BRAM * LS13........101 F2
Westover Mt BRAM * LS13........101 F2
Westover Rd BRAM LS13........101 F2
Westover St BRAM LS13........101 F2
Westover Ter BRAM LS13........101 F2
Westover Vw BRAM LS13........101 F2
West Pde BHP/TINH LS16........81 K4
HFAX HX1........16 E7
ILK LS29........24 B5
RPDN/SBR HX6........154 A4
RTHW LS26........145 G2
WKFDE WF1........18 F5
West Parade Ct WKFDE WF1........18 E6
West Parade Flats HFAX HX1........16 F7
West Parade St WKFDE WF1........18 F5
West Pk BHP/TINH LS16........81 K4
GSLY LS20........58 D1
West Park Av RHAY LS8........84 C1
West Park Cl RHAY LS8........84 B1
West Park Crs RHAY LS8........84 C1
West Park Dr BHP/TINH LS16........81 K4
PONT WF8........190 E7
West Park Dr East RHAY LS8........84 B1
West Park Dr West RHAY LS8........84 A1
West Park Dr BTLY WF17........160 D3
RHAY LS8........84 B1
West Park Pl RHAY LS8........84 C2
West Park Rd BTLY WF17........160 C4
GIR BD8........4 A3
RHAY LS8........84 C2
West Parks PDSY/CALV LS28........100 A6
West Park St BRIG HD6........157 G6
DEWS WF13........160 E7
West Park Ter BTLY WF17........160 D3
GIR BD8........4 B4
West Pasture Cl HORS LS18........80 C3
West Rd OSM LS9........124 D3
West Rd North OSM LS9........124 D3
Westroyd PDSY/CALV LS28........99 K7
West Royd WIL/AL BD15........75 F7
West Royd Av ECHL * BD2........98 C1
HFAX HX1........16 B9
MIRF WF14........179 H4
SHPY BD18........77 J4
Westroyd Av CLECK BD19........138 E4
PDSY/CALV LS28........99 K7
West Royd Cl HFAX HX1........16 C9
SHPY BD18........77 J4
Westroyd Crs PDSY/CALV LS28........99 K7
West Royd Crs SHPY BD18........77 K4
West Royd Dr MIRF WF14........179 H3
SHPY BD18........77 K4
Westroyd Gdns
PDSY/CALV LS28........99 K7
West Royd Gv MIRF WF14........179 H3
SHPY BD18........77 K4
West Royd Mt SHPY BD18........77 K4
West Royd Pk MIRF WF14........179 H3
West Royd Rd SHPY BD18........77 K4
West Royd Ter SHPY BD18........77 K4
West Royd Vls HFAX HX1........16 C9
West Royd Wk SHPY BD18........77 K4
West Scausby Pk LUD/ILL HX2........114 B7
West Shaw La HWTH BD22........92 B2
West Side Ct GIR BD8........4 B3

West St BAIL BD17........57 H7
BFD BD1........6 A7
BIRK/DRI BD11........140 B2
BRIG HD6........157 F5
BRIG HD6........157 G1
BTLY WF17........161 H3
BVRD LS3
CAS WF10........148 B7
CLECK BD19........139 H6
CLECK BD19........158 E1
EARL WF12........181 F2
ECHL BD2........98 C2
GTL/HWG HX4........174 E5
HECK WF16........159 K4
HFAX HX1........16 C5
HIPP HX3........136 A3
MOR LS27........142 A4
NORM WF6........166 D6
PDSY/CALV LS28........100 B5
RPDN/SBR HX6........153 J5
WKFDW/WTN WF2........184 A4
West V WOR/ARM LS12........12 E6
Westvale Ms BRAM LS13........101 H4
West Vw AIRE BD20........21 F7
BEE/HOL LS11........13 K9
BOW BD4........118 B2
DEWS WF13........160 E6
GFTH/SHER LS25........109 G7
GFTH/SHER LS25........111 F7
GFTH/SHER LS25........128 A4
GTL/HWG HX4........174 D5
HIPP HX3........134 E5
NORM WF6........166 C3
OT LS21........39 J2
OT LS21........41 J4
RTHW LS26........145 K2
WKFDW/WTN WF2........163 G6
YEA LS19........59 G4
West View Av CAS WF10........169 F1
HFAX HX1........154 B1
ILK LS29........37 K1
SHPY BD18........77 K5
Westview Av KCHY BD21........2 B1
West View Cl SHPY BD18........77 K5
Westview Ct KCHY BD21........2 D2
West View Crs YEA LS19........59 G4
West View Dr LUD/ILL HX2........154 A1
Westview Gv KCHY BD21........2 D2
West View Rd HIPP * HX3........134 E5
ILK LS29........37 K1
West View Ter GIR * BD8........96 D6
LUD/ILL * HX2........134 B7
Westview Wy KCHY BD21........2 E2
West Villa Rd GSLY LS20........59 F2
Westville Av ILK LS29........23 K5
Westville Cl ILK LS29........23 K5
Westville Rd ILK LS29........23 K5
Westville Wy CUL/QBY BD13........95 G7
Westward Cft HUDW HD3........176 B7
Westward Ho HIPP LS12........134 D3
Westway BTLY WF17........161 J5
GFTH/SHER LS25........107 G7
GSLY LS20........58 C3
HTON BD9........96 B3
KGHY BD21........2 B1
MIRF WF14........179 G2
PDSY/CALV LS28........99 K7
West Wy SHPY BD18........76 C5
Westways WKFDW/WTN WF2........164 A5
Westways Cl
WKFDW/WTN WF2........164 A6
Westways Dr RHAY LS8........84 D5
Westways Ri
WKFDW/WTN WF2........164 A6
West Wells Crs OSS WF5........182 B4
West Wells Rd OSS WF5........182 B4
West Winds ILK LS29........37 K5
Westwinn Garth SCFT LS14........85 K4
Westwinn Vw SCFT LS14........85 K3
Westwood Av ECHL BD2........78 C7
Westwood Cl FEA/AMT WF7........188 C2
MOR LS27........142 A1
West Wood Ct MID LS10........143 F2
Westwood Crs BGLY BD16........75 K4
Westwood Gv ECHL BD2........78 C7
Westwood Ri BRAM LS13........23 J7
MOR LS27........141 K1
West Wood Rd MOR LS27........142 E3
Westwood Rd CAS WF10........168 A3
OSS WF5........182 E4
Westwoodside MOR LS27........121 K7
Westwoodside MOR LS27........122 A7
Westwood St HUDN * HD2........178 B3
Westwood Wy
BSPA/BRAM LS23........48 C3
Wetherby Grange Pk
WBY * LS22........29 K6
Wetherby Gv BULY LS4........8 B4
Wetherby Pl BULY LS4........8 C4
Wetherby Rd AL/HA/HU LS17........46 A6
BSPA/BRAM LS23........30 D5
BSPA/BRAM LS23........48 B7
RHAY LS8........84 C5
SCFT LS14........85 H1
TAD LS24........50 C6
WBY LS22........28 A4
WBY LS22........29 H1
WBY LS22........29 H5
WBY LS22........47 G1
Wetherby Ter BULY LS4........8 B4
Wetherill St BTLY WF17........160 E3
Wetton Ct BFDE BD3........7 K6
Weyhill Dr WIL/AL BD15........96 A5
Weymouth Av AL/HA/HU LS17........45 H5
Whack House Cl YEA LS19........59 H5
Whalley La CUL/QBY BD13........94 A3
Wharfe Bank WBY LS22........46 B2
Wharfe Cl BHP/TINH LS16........62 C7
Wharfe Ct AIRE BD20........33 F1
Wharfe Crs OT LS21........41 C3
Wharfedale Av CHAL LS7........103 G1
Wharfedale Cl OT LS21........39 J2
SCFT LS14........85 G2
Wharfedale Crs
GFTH/SHER LS25........127 J1
Wharfedale Dr ILK LS29........24 B6

NORM WF6........166 D4
Wharfedale Gdns BAIL BD17........57 K7
Wharfedale Gv HDGY LS6........9 L1
Wharfedale Lawns WBY LS22........29 H4
Wharfedale Ms OT LS21........39 J2
Wharfedale Mt HIPP HX3........136 A1
Wharfedale Pl HDGY LS6........9 L1
Wharfedale Ri
EARD/LOFT WF3........162 C1
HTON BD9........96 B3
Wharfedale Rd BOW BD4........118 B7
Wharfedale St HDGY LS6........9 L1
Wharfedale Vw HDGY LS6........103 G1
ILK LS29........22 B1
ILK LS29........38 B6
Wharfe Gra WBY LS22........29 G4
Wharfe Gv WBY LS22........29 G4
Wharfe Ms ILK * LS29........38 C6
WBY * LS22........29 H4
Wharfe Pk ILK LS29........22 D1
Wharfe Rein WBY LS22........46 B2
Wharfeside La ILK LS29........24 B4
Wharfe St OT LS21........39 J2
Wharfe Vw WBY LS22........29 G4
Wharfe View Rd ILK LS29........24 A5
Wharf St BAIL BD17........77 C2
BFDE BD3........6 A4
BRIG HD6........157 C6
EARL WF12........181 G2
LDSU LS2........14 C1
RPDN/SBR HX6........153 K4
Wharncliffe Crs ECHL BD2........98 E1
Wharncliffe Dr ECHL BD2........98 E1
Wharncliffe Gv ECHL BD2........98 E1
SHPY BD18........77 G6
Wharncliffe Rd SHPY BD18........77 G7
The Whartons OT LS21........27 H7
Wharton St LVSG WF15........159 J4
Wheat Cl DEWS WF13........180 C1
Wheatcroft CAS WF10........169 G2
Wheatcroft Av BTLY WF17........161 F4
Wheatfield Ct PDSY/CALV LS28........100 A7
Wheathead Crs HWTH BD22........53 F6
Wheat Head Dr HWTH BD22........2 A8
Wheathead La HWTH BD22........53 F6
The Wheatings OSS WF5........182 K4
Wheatlands ILK LS29........24 B4
PDSY/CALV LS28........99 K2
Wheatlands Av HTON BD9........96 D3
Wheatlands Crs HTON BD9........96 D3
Wheatlands Dr HTON BD9........96 D3
LVSG * WF15........159 G6
Wheatlands Gv HTON BD9........96 D3
Wheatlands Sq HTON BD9........96 D3
Wheatley Av ILK LS29........24 D6
NORM WF6........166 E7
Wheatley Dr MIRF WF14........179 H6
Wheatley Gdns ILK LS29........24 D6
Wheatley Gv ILK LS29........24 D6
Wheatley Ri HIPP HX3........16 C1
ILK LS29........24 D6
Wheatley Ri ILK LS29........24 D6
Wheatley Rd HIPP HX3........134 C5
ILK LS29........24 B6
Wheaton Av MSTN/BAR LS15........105 H5
Wheatroyd Crs OSS WF5........182 K6
Wheat St HWTH BD22........53 H7
Wheelwright Av
WOR/ARM LS12........121 K1
Wheelwright Cl
WOR/ARM LS12........121 K1
Wheelwright Dr DEWS WF13........160 E6
Wheelwright St EARL * WF12........181 F1
Wheldale La CAS WF10........149 K5
Wheldon Rd CAS WF10........148 D7
CAS WF10........149 J4
Whernside Mt CTHN BD7........116 D4
Whernside Wy LUD/ILL HX2........133 H4
Wherwell Rd BRIG HD6........157 G2
Whetley Cl GIR BD8........5 G3
Whetley Gv GIR BD8........4 D2
Whetley Hl GIR BD8........4 F2
Whetley La GIR BD8........4 D3
Whetley Ter GIR BD8........5 H3
Whewell St BTLY WF17........140 B6
Whiddon Cft ILK LS29........38 A5
Whimbrel Cl GIR BD8........96 B6
Whimbrel Ms MOR LS27........142 B4
Whinbeck Av NORM WF6........167 G7
Whinberry Pl FEA/AMT WF7........140 C4
Whinbrook Crs AL/HA/HU LS17........83 H3
Whinbrook Gdns
AL/HA/HU LS17........83 H3
Whinbrook Gv AL/HA/HU LS17........83 H3
Whincop Av CAS WF10........167 J1
Whincover Cl WOR/ARM LS12........121 J1
Whincover Cross
WOR/ARM LS12........121 J1
Whincover Dr WOR/ARM LS12........121 H1
Whincover Gdns
WOR/ARM LS12........121 J1
Whincover Gv WOR/ARM LS12........121 J1
Whincover Hl WOR/ARM LS12........121 J1
Whincover Mt WOR/ARM LS12........121 J1
Whincover Rd WOR/ARM LS12........121 H1
Whincover Vw WOR/ARM LS12........121 J1
Whinfield BHP/TINH LS16........62 A7
Whinfield Cl HWTH BD22........53 F3
Whinfield Dr HWTH BD22........2 A3
Whinfield Dr HWTH BD22........53 F3
Whingate WOR/ARM LS12........101 K5
Whingate Av WOR/ARM LS12........101 K6
Whingate Cl WOR/ARM LS12........101 K6
Whingate Gn WOR/ARM LS12........101 K6
Whingate Gv WOR/ARM LS12........101 K6
Whingate Rd WOR/ARM LS12........101 K6
Whin Knoll Av KGHY BD21........2 B3
Whin La GFTH/SHER LS25........130 B3
Whinmoor Ct SCFT LS14........85 H3
Whinmoor Crs SCFT LS14........85 H3
Whinmoor Gdns SCFT LS14........85 G3
Whinmoor La AL/HA/HU LS17........85 F1
Whinmore Gdns CLECK BD19........159 K1
Whin Mt NORM WF6........187 F1
Whinney Brow IDLE BD10........78 A4
Whinney Hill Pk BRIG HD6........157 F3

Whinney La FEA/AMT WF7........187 G4
Whinney Moor Av
WKFDW/WTN WF2........183 J6
Whinney Royd La HIPP HX3........135 K2
Whins La BSPA/BRAM LS23........48 E1
Whin St HWTH BD22........2 C4
Whiskers La HIPP HX3........135 H4
Whisperwood Cl
WKFDE * WF1........164 E3
Whisperwood Rd
WKFDE WF1........164 E3
Whitacre Cl HUDN HD2........177 K6
Whitacre St HUDN HD2........177 K6
Whitaker Av ECHL BD2........98 D2
Whitaker Cl ECHL BD2........98 D2
Whitaker St BTLY WF17........161 G4
PDSY/CALV LS28........100 A3
Whitaker Wk HWTH * BD22........92 D3
Whitby Av HUDN HD2........177 F7
Whitby Crs EARL WF12........181 J1
Whitby Rd GIR BD8........4 C1
Whitby Ter GIR BD8........4 D2
Whitcliffe Rd CLECK BD19........138 D7
Whitcliffe Sq CLECK BD19........138 E7
White Abbey Rd GIR BD8........5 H3
Whitebeam La MID LS10........123 J6
Whitebeam Pk HUDN HD2........176 C7
White Birch Ter HIPP HX3........134 C5
Whitebridge Crs OSM LS9........105 F4
Whitebridge Sp SCFT LS10........105 F4
Whitebridge Vw OSM LS9........105 F4
White Castle Ct CUL/QBY BD13........114 E4
Whitechapel Cl RHAY LS8........84 C6
Whitechapel Gv CLECK BD19........138 B7
Whitechapel Rd CLECK BD19........138 B7
Whitechapel Wy RHAY LS8........84 C6
Whitecliffe Crs RTHW LS26........126 A4
Whitecliffe Dr RTHW LS26........126 D4
Whitecliffe Ri RTHW LS26........126 D4
Whitecote Gdns BRAM LS13........100 E1
Whitecote Hl BRAM LS13........100 E1
Whitecote La BRAM LS13........80 E7
GFTH/SHER LS25........130 C2
Whitecote Ri BRAM LS13........100 E1
White Cross HUDN HD2........177 K4
White Cross Rd EARL WF12........161 H7
Whitefield Pl GIR BD8........4 D3
Whitegate AL/HA/HU LS17........45 K4
HIPP HX3........155 G4
White Ga LUD/ILL HX2........114 A7
Whitegate Dr HIPP HX3........155 G3
White Gate Rd HIPP HX3........155 G3
Whitegates Cl
WKFDW/WTN WF2........164 A7
Whitegate Ter HIPP HX3........155 H4
Whitegate Top HIPP HX3........155 H4
White Gv RHAY LS8........84 B4
Whitehall Av LM/WK BD12........137 H6
MIRF WF14........179 H2
WKFDE WF1........164 B7
Whitehall Crs WKFDE WF1........164 B7
Whitehall Est WOR/ARM * LS12........121 J2
Whitehall Gv BIRK/DRI BD11........139 J2
Whitehall Quay LDS LS1........13 L1
Whitehall Ri WKFDE WF1........184 B1
Whitehall Rd LM/WK BD12........137 K6
WOR/ARM LS12........12 A7
Whitehall Rd East
BIRK/DRI BD11........139 J2
Whitehall Rd West
CLECK BD19........138 E5
Whitehall St HIPP HX3........136 C7
WKFDW/WTN WF2........184 A3
Whitehall Wy DEWS WF13........181 G1
White Hart Fold
RPDN/SBR HX6........172 D6
Whitehaven Cl WBSY BD6........116 E7
Whitehead Pl ECHL BD2........98 D3
Whitehead's Ter HFAX * HX1........16 B5
Whitehead St BFDE BD3........6 F7
Whitehill Cottages
LUD/ILL * HX2........134 B2
Whitehill Crs LUD/ILL HX2........134 B2
Whitehill Dr LUD/ILL HX2........134 B1
Whitehill Gn LUD/ILL HX2........134 C1
Whitehill Rd LUD/ILL HX2........134 B2
White Holme Dr OT LS21........41 H4
White Horse Cl BTLY WF17........140 E6
White Horse Fold CAS WF10........148 D2
White Horse Yd WKFDE WF1........18 E5
Whitehouse Av RTHW LS26........127 G6
Whitehouse Bungalows
WKFDW/WTN WF2........184 C6
Whitehouse Crs RTHW LS26........127 H6
Whitehouse Dr RTHW LS26........127 G6
Whitehouse La RTHW LS26........127 F3
YEA LS19........60 C3
Whitehouse St MID LS10........14 D6
White Laith Av SCFT LS14........85 J4
White Laithe Ap SCFT LS14........85 J4
White Laithe Cl SCFT LS14........85 J4
White Laithe Cft SCFT LS14........85 J4
White Laithe Gdns SCFT * LS14........85 K4
White Laithe Garth SCFT LS14........85 J3
White Laithe Gn SCFT LS14........85 J4
White Laithe Gv SCFT LS14........85 K4
White Laithe Rd SCFT LS14........85 J4
White Laithe Wk SCFT LS14........85 K4
White Lands YEA LS19........59 H7
Whitelands Crs BAIL BD17........77 J1
Whitelands Rd BAIL BD17........77 J1
White La HWTH BD22........72 A2
WBSY BD6........117 J6
White Lee Cl BTLY WF17........160 B2
White Lee Gdns HBR HX7........132 A6
White Lee Rd BTLY WF17........160 B2
White Lee Side HECK WF16........160 B2
Whiteley Av RPDN/SBR HX6........153 C5
Whiteley Cft OT LS21........39 H3
Whiteley Croft Ri OT LS21........39 H3
Whiteley Croft Rd OT LS21........39 H3
Whiteley St FEA/AMT WF7........188 B4
HFAX HX1........16 F7
Whitelock St CHAL LS7........10 C6
White Rose Av
GFTH/SHER LS25........107 J6

Whiterose Md
GFTH/SHER * LS25........107 K6
White Rose Wy
GFTH/SHER LS25........107 K6
White's Rd WKFDE WF1........19 G4
White's Ter GIR BD8........4 F2
Whitestone Crs YEA LS19........59 J4
Whitestone Dr AIRE BD20........55 G2
White St RTHW LS26........146 A1
White's Vw GIR BD8........4 F3
Whiteways BFDE BD2........97 K2
Whitfield Av MID LS10........14 E8
Whitfield Gdns MID * LS10........14 E8
Whitfield Pl MID LS10........14 E8
Whitfield Sq MID LS10........14 E8
Whitfield St CLECK BD19........138 E7
RHAY LS8........11 G2
Whitfield Wy MID LS10........14 E8
Whitham Cl BSPA/BRAM LS23........48 C2
Whitkirk Cl MSTN/BAR LS15........106 B5
Whitkirk La MSTN/BAR LS15........106 A5
Whitlam St SHPY BD18........76 E4
Whitley Dr LUD/ILL HX2........134 C1
Whitley Gdns RHAY LS8........10 F3
Whitley La HIPP HX3........155 K3
Whitley Pl CAS WF10........148 A3
Whitley Rd KGHY BD21........2 C8
Whitley Spring Crs OSS WF5........182 E3
Whitley Spring Rd OSS WF5........182 E3
Whitley St BFDE BD3........6 C5
BGLY BD16........75 J1
Whittle Crs CLAY BD14........116 A1
Whitty La LUD/ILL HX2........153 J2
Whitwell Av ELL HX5........176 A2
Whitwell Dr ELL HX5........176 A2
Whitwell Gv ELL HX5........176 A2
Whitwell St BOW BD4........118 B3
Whitwood Common La
CAS WF10........167 J3
Whitwood La CAS WF10........167 H2
CLECK BD19........157 H1
Whitworth Rd DEWS * WF13........180 E2
Whytecote End LM/WK BD12........137 H3
Wibsey Bank WBSY BD6........117 J5
Wibsey Park Av WBSY BD6........116 E6
Wicken Cl IDLE BD10........78 D6
Wicken La CUL/QBY BD13........95 F6
The Wickets BTLY WF17........160 E6
HDGY LS6........82 E5
MSTN/BAR LS15........106 B6
Wickets Cl WBSY BD6........117 J6
Wickham Av BSPA/BRAM LS23........48 B2
WBSY * BD6........117 H6
Wickham Cl BSPA/BRAM LS23........48 B2
Wickham St BEE/HOL LS11........13 K9
CLECK BD19........138 A6
Wicking La RPDN/SBR HX6........172 B1
Wide La HWTH BD22........72 B1
MOR LS27........142 C3
Wigan St BFD BD1........5 K5
Wigeon Ap MOR LS27........142 B3
Wiggan La HUDN HD2........177 J6
Wighill Garth TAD LS24........50 E5
Wighill La BSPA/BRAM LS23........31 H7
TAD LS24........50 C3
Wightman St BFDE BD3........98 B3
Wignall St KGHY BD21........53 J2
Wigton Cha AL/HA/HU LS17........64 C6
Wigton Ga AL/HA/HU LS17........63 K5
Wigton Gn AL/HA/HU LS17........64 A5
Wigton Gv AL/HA/HU LS17........63 K5
Wigton La AL/HA/HU LS17........63 K5
Wigton Park Cl AL/HA/HU LS17........64 C7
Wike La AL/HA/HU LS17........44 C7
Wike Ridge Av AL/HA/HU LS17........64 B6
Wike Ridge Cl AL/HA/HU LS17........64 B5
Wike Ridge Ct AL/HA/HU LS17........64 C5
Wike Ridge Fold AL/HA/HU LS17........64 B5
Wike Ridge Gv AL/HA/HU LS17........64 C6
Wike Ridge La AL/HA/HU LS17........64 C6
Wike Ridge Ms AL/HA/HU LS17........64 C6
Wike Ridge Mt AL/HA/HU LS17........64 C6
Wike Ridge Vw AL/HA/HU LS17........64 B6
Wilcock La AIRE BD20........20 A5
Wild Gv PDSY/CALV LS28........99 H6
Wild's Yd WKFDE WF1........18 F6
Wilfred Av MSTN/BAR LS15........105 J5
Wilfred St CLAY BD14........116 C2
MSTN/BAR LS15........105 J5
Wilfrid Ter MSTN/BAR LS15........121 K2
Wilkinson Fold LM/WK * BD12........137 H5
Wilkinson Ter BD7........4 B8
Wilkinson Wy OT LS21........39 F1
Wilkin St KGHY BD21........2 F4
Willans Av RTHW LS26........125 F7
Willan's Rd DEWS WF13........181 F1
Willerton Cl EARL WF12........162 A5
Willgutter La HWTH BD22........72 A3
William Av MSTN/BAR LS15........105 F5
William Henry St BRIG * HD6........157 F5
SHPY * BD18........76 E4
William Hey Ct OSM LS9........11 L5
William Prince Gv WKFDE WF1........19 K9
William Ri MSTN/BAR LS15........105 F5
Williams Dr AIRE BD20........32 C5
Williamson St HFAX HX1........16 C4
Williams Rd AIRE BD20........32 C5
William St BOW BD4........7 J9
BOW BD4........118 C5
BRIG HD6........157 F7
CAS WF10........148 D6
CAS WF10........149 H5
CUL/QBY * BD13........94 A4
DEWS WF13........160 C5
DEWS WF13........180 B4
EARL * WF12........161 F7
HDGY LS6........8 F3
LVSG WF15........159 H4
MOR LS27........122 B6
PDSY/CALV LS28........100 A4
WBOW * BD5........5 L8
WBSY BD6........116 E7
WKFDE WF1........19 G6
William Vw MSTN/BAR LS15........105 F5
Willis St OSM LS9........14 F2
Willoughby Ter BEE/HOL LS11........13 H6
Willow Ap BULY LS4........8 C5

Willow Av BSPA/BRAM LS23......48 C4
BULY LS4......8 E6
ECHL BD2......78 B6
Willow Bank HFAX HX1......16 C9
Willow Bank Dr PONT WF8......169 K6
Willowbridge La CAS WF10......167 J2
Willowbridge Wy CAS WF10......167 J2
Willow Cl BULY LS4......8 F6
CLECK BD19......159 J1
ILK LS29......37 K1
LUD/ILL HX2......154 A2
WBSY BD6......117 H7
Willow Clough RPDN/SBR HX6......172 E7
Willow Ct BTLY WF17......161 F2
FEA/AMT WF7......168 B7
OT LS21......41 G4
WKFDW/WTN WF2......183 J2
Willow Crs BSPA/BRAM LS23......48 C4
ECHL BD2......78 B6
MSTN/BAR LS15......105 G6
NORM WF6......186 D1
RPDN/SBR HX6......153 K3
Willow Cft CLECK BD19......158 D1
Willow Dene Av LUD/ILL HX2......154 A3
Willowdene La PONT WF8......169 J5
Willow Dr LUD/ILL HX2......154 A2
WBSY BD6......117 H7
Willowfield Av LUD/ILL HX2......154 A3
Willowfield Cl LUD/ILL HX2......154 A2
Willowfield Crs IDLE BD10......78 B6
LUD/ILL HX2......154 A2
Willowfield Dr LUD/ILL HX2......154 A3
Willowfield Rd LUD/ILL HX2......154 B3
Willowfield St GTHN BD7......4 E7
Willowfield Ter LUD/ILL HX2......154 B3
Willowfield Vw LUD/ILL HX2......154 A2
Willow Gdns CAS WF10......169 J2
ECHL BD2......78 B6
GSLY LS20......59 F2
WKFDW/WTN WF2......183 J2
Willow Garth BULY LS4......8 E6
Willow Gld BSPA/BRAM LS23......48 C5
Willow Gn WKFDE WF1......164 C5
Willow Gv BSPA/BRAM LS23......48 C4
ECHL BD2......78 B6
GFTH/SHER LS25......127 J3
OSS WF5......182 D5
WKFDE WF1......185 F7
Willow Hall Dr RPDN/SBR HX6......153 K3
Willow Hall La RPDN/SBR HX6......153 K3
Willow La BSPA/BRAM LS23......48 C4
FEA/AMT WF7......168 B7
NORM WF6......186 A2
WKFDW/WTN WF2......183 J2
Willow La East FEA/AMT WF7......168 B7
Willow Ms WKFDW/WTN WF2......183 J2
Willow Mt WKFDW/WTN WF2......183 J2
Willow Pk PONT WF8......190 A1
WKFDE WF1......164 C6
Willow Ri LUD/ILL HX2......154 A2
TAD LS24......70 C1
Willow Rd BTLY WF17......161 H4
BULY LS4......8 E6
CAS WF10......168 C2
KNOT WF11......171 H3
PDSY/CALV LS28......99 K3
WKFDW/WTN WF2......183 J1
The Willows AL/HA/HU LS17......83 H2
BGLY BD16......74 E3
LUD/ILL HX2......114 B7
Willow St CLECK BD19......138 E6
GIR BD8......5 K8
HFAX HX1......16 C6
RPDN/SBR HX6......153 K4
Willow Terrace Rd LDSU LS2......9 K6
Willow Tree Cl KGHY BD21......3 K8
Willow Tree Gdns BGLY BD16......56 B6
ILK LS29......38 A1
Willow V WBY LS22......29 G2
Willow Vis IDLE BD10......78 B6
Willow Wk LVSG WF15......159 H5
Willow Well Rd MSTN/BAR LS15......105 G5
Wills Gill GSLY LS20......59 G2
Wilman Dr OSS WF5......182 B3
Wilman Post OSS WF5......182 B3
Wilmer Dr HTON BD9......97 F1
SHPY BD18......77 F7
Wilmer Rd HTON BD9......97 F2
Wilmington Gv CHAL LS7......10 B3
Wilmington St CHAL LS7......10 B4
Wilmington Ter CHAL LS7......10 B4
Wilmot Rd ILK LS29......24 B5
Wilsden Hill Rd WIL/AL BD15......74 E7
Wilsden Old Rd BGLY BD16......74 E3
Wilsden Rd BGLY BD16......74 E3
WIL/AL BD15......95 H2
Wilson Av AIRE BD20......32 C4
MIRF WF14......179 G4
OSS WF5......185 F5
Wilson Ct WKFDE WF1......164 C4
Wilson Dr WKFDE WF1......164 C4
Wilson Rd BGLY BD16......56 E5
HFAX HX1......16 A9
LM/WK BD12......137 J3
MIRF WF14......179 G4
Wilson St CAS WF10......148 B7
FEA/AMT WF7......188 B4
GIR * BD8......5 H1
PONT * WF8......169 J7
Wilsons Yd PDSY/CALV LS28......100 A4
Wilson Ter MIRF WF14......179 G4
Wilson Wood St BTLY WF17......160 E5
Wilton Av HUDN HD2......177 K3
Wilton Gv HDGY LS6......82 D6
Wilton Rd ILK LS29......23 K6
Wilton St BRIG HD6......156 E5
EARL WF12......181 G2
GTHN BD7......5 K8
Wilton Ter CLECK BD19......158 E1
Wimborne Dr HWTH BD22......53 F3
WIL/AL BD15......96 B4
Winbrooke Ter WBSY BD6......117 F5
Winburg Rd GTHN BD7......4 D9
Winchester Cl WKFDW/WTN WF2......163 J7
Winchester St WOR/ARM LS12......12 D1
Winden Cl WKFDE WF1......164 D3

Winden Gv WKFDE * WF1......164 C3
Windermere Av ILK LS29......38 B4
Windermere Dr AL/HA/HU LS17......62 E5
GFTH/SHER LS25......107 J7
KNOT WF11......171 F6
Windermere Rd CAS WF10......169 J1
EARL WF12......161 H5
GTHN BD7......116 D3
WKFDW/WTN WF2......183 K2
Windermere Ter GTHN BD7......116 D3
Winders Dl MOR LS27......141 J1
Windgate AIRE BD20......33 G2
Windhill Ct WKFDE WF1......19 L1
Windhill Crs WKFDE WF1......19 L1
Windhill Old Rd IDLE BD10......78 A2
Windhill Rd WKFDE WF1......19 L1
Windhill Vw WKFDE WF1......19 H2
Winding Rd HFAX HX1......17 H5
Winding Wy AL/HA/HU LS17......63 G6
Windle Royd La LUD/ILL HX2......153 K1
Windmill Ap MID LS10......123 K6
Windmill Cha RTHW LS26......145 F3
Windmill Cl MID LS10......123 K7
Windmill Ct SCFT LS14......85 J2
Windmill Crs HIPP HX3......135 K5
Windmill Dr HIPP HX3......135 J5
Windmill Field Rd RTHW LS26......145 F3
Windmill Gdns MSTN/BAR LS15......106 A6
Windmill Gn RTHW LS26......145 F3
Windmill Gv CLECK BD19......159 J2
TAD LS24......70 C1
Windmill Hl PDSY/CALV LS28......99 K7
WBSY BD6......117 H5
Windmill La BTLY WF17......140 D6
ILK LS29......38 E6
RTHW LS26......145 F3
WBSY BD6......117 H5
YEA LS19......59 K5
Windmill Ri GFTH/SHER LS25......88 D6
TAD LS24......70 C2
Windmill Rd BSPA/BRAM LS23......48 D7
MID LS10......123 K6
Windrose Cl NORM WF6......166 D4
Windsor Av AIRE BD20......20 E7
MSTN/BAR LS15......105 J5
Windsor Cl EARL WF12......162 A5
GFTH/SHER LS25......127 K4
NORM WF6......167 F7
Windsor Ct AL/HA/HU LS17......83 K2
LUD/ILL HX2......134 B6
RTHW LS26......145 F1
WKFDE WF1......164 A7
Windsor Crs HWTH BD22......72 C2
LUD/ILL HX2......134 B6
RTHW LS26......145 F1
WKFDE WF1......164 A7
Windsor Dr KNOT WF11......170 C3
LVSG WF15......159 J6
Windsor Gdns EARL WF12......162 A5
Windsor Gn GFTH/SHER LS25......108 A6
Windsor Gv CUL/QBY BD13......95 F7
HWTH BD22......72 C2
Windsor Mt MSTN/BAR LS15......105 J5
Windsor Pl HUDN HD2......177 K4
Windsor Ri PONT WF8......189 G4
Windsor Rd BTLY WF17......140 D6
EARL WF12......161 K6
HWTH BD22......72 C2
SHPY * BD18......77 G4
WKFDE WF1......164 A6
Windsor St BOW BD4......6 C9
HFAX HX1......17 G8
Windsor Vw EARL WF12......161 K6
Windsor Wk BRIG HD6......157 F2
Windy Bank La HIPP HX3......134 E1
LVSG WF15......158 C4
Windy Gv WIL/AL BD15......95 G2
Windy Rdg CUL/QBY BD13......95 F6
Wine Tavern La LDS LS1......9 M9
Wine Tavern La RPDN/SBR HX6......152 C5
Wine Tavern Rd RPDN/SBR HX6......152 C5
Winfield Gv LDSU * LS2......9 M4
Winfield Pl LDSU LS2......9 M4
Winfield Rd BIRK/DRI BD11......139 F1
Winfield Ter LDSU LS2......9 L4
Wingate Av HWTH BD22......2 B7
Wingate Wy HWTH BD22......2 B6
Wingfield Ct BGLY BD16......55 K7
Wingfield Mt BFDE BD3......6 E3
Wingfield St BFDE BD3......6 E4
Winnard Rw WBOW * BD5......118 A3
Winnipeg Pl CHAL LS7......83 J6
Winnow La BSPA/BRAM LS23......48 A3
Winrose Ap MID LS10......123 K7
Winrose Av MID LS10......123 J6
Winrose Cl LM/WK BD12......137 H3
Winrose Crs MID LS10......123 J6
Winrose Dr MID LS10......123 J6
Winrose Garth MID LS10......123 J6
Winrose Gv MID LS10......123 K6
Winrose Hl MID LS10......123 K5
Winslow Rd IDLE BD10......99 F1
Winstanley Ter HDGY * LS6......8 E2
Winston Gdns HDGY LS6......82 B7
Winston Mt HDGY LS6......82 B7
Winston Ter GTHN BD7......4 C9
Winterbourne Av MOR LS27......142 A1
Winterburn La LUD/ILL HX2......153 H2
Winterburn St KGHY * BD21......3 G2
Winter Ct WIL/AL BD15......95 K2
Winter St HFAX HX1......16 B9
Winterton Dr LM/WK BD12......137 H2
Winthorpe Av EARD/LOFT WF3......143 J4
Winthorpe Crs EARD/LOFT WF3......143 J5
Wintoun St CHAL LS7......10 C6
Wistons La ELL HX5......175 K2
Witchfield Hl HIPP HX3......136 C1
Witham Rd SHPY BD18......76 D4
Witham Wy GFTH/SHER LS25......107 K7
Withens Hill Cft LUD/ILL HX2......114 A7
Withens New Rd LUD/ILL HX2......113 G4
Withens Rd BTLY WF17......140 B5
LUD/ILL HX2......113 G4
Within Flds HIPP HX3......155 K4
Withins Cl GTHN BD7......117 G4
Witton St WKFDE WF1......18 F3
Woburn Ter CLAY BD14......116 A2

Wold Cl CUL/QBY BD13......95 G7
Wolley Av WOR/ARM LS12......121 G3
Wolley Ct WOR/ARM LS12......121 G3
Wolley Dr WOR/ARM LS12......121 G3
Wolley Gdns WOR/ARM LS12......121 G3
Wolseley Rd BULY LS4......8 D6
Wolseley St CLAY BD14......116 A1
Wolseley Ter HFAX HX1......16 B5
Wolsey Av PONT WF8......189 G1
Wolsey Cl GFTH/SHER LS25......111 G5
Wolsey Cft GFTH/SHER LS25......111 G5
Wolsey Gdns GFTH/SHER LS25......111 G5
Wolston Cl BOW BD4......119 F4
Womersley Pl PDSY/CALV LS28......100 A7
Womersley Rd KNOT WF11......171 H5
Womersley St HFAX HX1......16 B5
Wonder St WKFDE WF1......19 G6
Woodacre Crs AL/HA/HU LS17......45 K7
Woodacre Gn AL/HA/HU LS17......45 K6
Woodacre La AL/HA/HU LS17......45 K6
Woodale Av HTON BD9......96 C2
Wood Av HECK WF16......160 A3
Woodbine Av PONT WF8......189 H1
Woodbine Gv IDLE BD10......78 C5
Woodbine St BFDE BD3......6 C5
HFAX * HX1......16 C9
OSS WF5......182 C2
Woodbine Ter BRAM * LS13......101 F2
HDGY LS6......82 D6
HFAX * HX1......16 C9
IDLE BD10......78 C5
Wood Bottom La BRIG HD6......156 D3
Woodbourne Av AL/HA/HU LS17......83 H3
Woodbridge Av GFTH/SHER LS25......108 B4
Woodbridge Cl HDGY LS6......82 A7
WKFDE WF1......19 K5
Woodbridge Crs HDGY LS6......81 K6
Woodbridge Fold HDGY LS6......81 K7
Woodbridge Gdns HDGY LS6......81 K6
Woodbridge Garth HDGY LS6......82 A7
Woodbridge Gn HDGY LS6......81 K7
Woodbridge Lawn HDGY LS6......81 K7
Woodbridge Pl HDGY LS6......81 K7
Woodbridge Rd HDGY LS6......81 K7
Woodbridge V HDGY LS6......81 K7
Woodbrook Av LUD/ILL HX2......133 K2
Woodbrook Cl LUD/ILL HX2......133 K2
Woodbrook Pl LUD/ILL HX2......133 K2
Woodbrook Rd LUD/ILL HX2......133 K2
Woodburn Av EARL WF12......181 J4
Woodbury Rd GIR BD8......97 G3
Wood Cl BAIL BD17......77 G2
BHP/TINH LS16......82 C1
CHAL LS7......83 H5
NORM WF6......166 B5
RTHW LS26......144 E1
Woodcock St WKFDE WF1......184 E6
Woodcot Av BAIL BD17......77 J2
Wood Crs RTHW LS26......144 E1
Wood Cft BRIG HD6......156 E7
RPDN/SBR HX6......153 F5
Woodcross MOR LS27......141 K1
Woodcross End MOR LS27......121 K7
Woodcross Fold MOR LS27......141 K1
Woodcross Gdns MOR LS27......141 K1
Woodcross Garth MOR LS27......121 K7
Wood Dr RTHW LS26......144 D1
Woodend CAS WF10......147 J1
Wood End Cl HIPP HX3......154 E5
Woodend Cottages MIRF * WF14......179 J5
Woodend Crs CAS WF10......147 J2
Wood End Crs SHPY BD18......77 J4
Woodend Rd MIRF WF14......179 G5
Woodfield Av BTLY WF17......160 D4
GTL/HWG HX4......174 E2
Woodfield Cl IDLE BD10......78 C4
Woodfield Cottages HIPP * HX3......16 E1
Woodfield Dr GTL/HWG HX4......174 E3
Woodfield Rd CUL/QBY BD13......74 B5
Woodford Av HIPP HX3......155 G4
Woodford Cl WIL/AL BD15......95 K5
Woodgarth Gdns BOW BD4......119 G3
Wood Gn CAS WF10......167 J3
Wood Gv OSS WF5......182 C1
WOR/ARM LS12......101 G6
Woodhall Av BFDE BD3......7 M2
KSTL LS5......81 H6
Woodhall Cl PDSY/CALV LS28......99 H3
Woodhall Ct MSTN/BAR LS15......106 A7
PDSY/CALV LS28......79 H7
Woodhall Cft PDSY/CALV LS28......99 H3
Woodhall Dr BTLY WF17......160 D4
KSTL LS5......81 H6
Woodhall Gv RTHW LS26......147 G4
Woodhall La PDSY/CALV LS28......99 H2
Woodhall Park Av PDSY/CALV LS28......99 H3
Woodhall Park Crs West PDSY/CALV LS28......99 H4
Woodhall Park Cft PDSY/CALV * LS28......99 J4
Woodhall Park Dr PDSY/CALV LS28......99 H4
Woodhall Park Gv PDSY/CALV LS28......99 H4
Woodhall Park Mt PDSY/CALV LS28......99 H3
Woodhall Pl BFDE BD3......7 M2
Woodhall Rd BFDE BD3......7 M3
PDSY/CALV LS28......99 F2
Woodhall Ter BFDE BD3......7 M3
Woodhall Vw BFDE BD3......99 G4
Woodhead Cl HUDN HD2......177 H6
Woodhead La BRIG HD6......157 K7
MOR LS27......121 F7
Woodhead Rd BTLY WF17......140 E4
GTHN BD7......4 F8
Woodhead St CLECK BD19......159 F2
LUD/ILL HX2......134 D7
Wood Hl RTHW LS26......144 E1
Wood Hill Ct BHP/TINH LS16......61 G7
Wood Hill Crs BHP/TINH LS16......81 F1
Wood Hill Gdns BHP/TINH LS16......61 G7
Wood Hill Ri BHP/TINH LS16......61 G7

Woodhill Ri IDLE BD10......79 F4
Wood Hill Rd BHP/TINH LS16......61 G7
Woodhill Vw WBY LS22......29 H3
Woodhouse Av HUDN HD2......177 H7
KGHY BD21......3 H9
Woodhouse Cliff HDGY LS6......9 J1
Woodhouse Cl EARD/LOFT WF3......163 G2
KGHY BD21......3 H9
Woodhouse Crs NORM WF6......186 E1
Woodhouse Dr KGHY BD21......53 K7
Woodhouse Gdns BRIG HD6......177 H1
Woodhouse Gv HUDN HD2......177 G7
KGHY BD21......3 G9
Woodhouse Hall Rd HUDN HD2......177 H7
Woodhouse Hl HUDN HD2......177 H7
Woodhouse Hill Av MID * LS10......123 K4
Woodhouse Hill Gv MID * LS10......123 K4
Woodhouse Hill Pl MID * LS10......123 K4
Woodhouse Hill Rd MID * LS10......123 K4
Woodhouse Hill Ter MID * LS10......123 K4
Woodhouse La BRIG HD6......177 H1
HDGY LS6......9 J2
HIPP HX3......154 D5
WKFDW/WTN WF2......163 F5
Woodhouse Mt NORM WF6......186 D1
Woodhouse Rd KGHY BD21......53 K7
WKFDE WF1......19 J4
Woodhouse Sq BVRD LS3......9 K8
Woodhouse St HDGY LS6......9 J2
Woodhouse Ter WBSY BD6......117 J6
Woodhouse Wk KGHY BD21......3 H9
Woodhouse Wy KGHY BD21......3 H9
Woodkirk Av EARD/LOFT WF3......142 B7
Woodkirk Gdns EARL WF12......162 A3
Woodkirk Gv EARD/LOFT WF3......142 C7
LM/WK BD12......137 H6
Woodland Av RTHW LS26......126 C5
Woodland Cl HTON BD9......96 B1
MSTN/BAR LS15......105 K5
Woodland Ct BGLY BD16......55 G6
RHAY LS8......84 A7
Woodland Crs BGLY BD16......96 A1
RTHW LS26......124 E7
RTHW LS26......126 D5
Woodland Dr BRIG HD6......156 E5
CHAL LS7......83 J5
LUD/ILL HX2......154 A3
RTHW LS26......126 C5
Woodland Hl MSTN/BAR LS15......105 J5
Woodland La CHAL LS7......83 J5
MSTN/BAR * LS15......105 K5
Woodland Pk RTHW LS26......145 K2
Woodland Park Rd HDGY LS6......82 D7
Woodland Ri MSTN/BAR LS15......105 K5
WKFDW/WTN WF2......183 J4
Woodland Rd HUDN HD2......178 A7
MSTN/BAR LS15......105 J5
WKFDW/WTN WF2......183 J3
Woodlands BAIL * BD17......57 K7
EARD/LOFT WF3......163 H1
HOR/CROF WF4......183 H7
HWTH * BD22......72 C2
ILK LS29......24 C5
OSS WF5......182 C2
RPDN/SBR HX6......153 G6
Woodlands Cl EARD/LOFT WF3......163 H1
CLECK BD19......139 H6
HIPP HX3......17 G1
PDSY/CALV LS28......99 K4
TAD LS24......70 D1
Woodlands Ct BHP/TINH LS16......82 A3
Woodlands Dr CLECK BD19......139 H6
EARD/LOFT WF3......163 G1
GFTH/SHER LS25......108 A7
IDLE BD10......79 G3
MOR LS27......141 J1
Woodlands Cft GFTH/SHER LS25......128 A6
Woodlands Fold BIRK/DRI BD11......139 J2
Woodlands La BAIL BD17......76 E2
BGLY BD16......76 A5
CUL/QBY BD13......115 K5
GFTH/SHER LS25......128 B6
HIPP HX3......17 G1
ILK LS29......23 H5
PDSY/CALV LS28......99 K4
The Woodlands PONT WF8......189 K3
RTHW * LS26......145 K2
Woodlands La DEWS WF13......180 C1
Woodlands Mt HIPP HX3......135 F5
Woodlands Pk CLECK BD19......138 C4
SCFT LS14......65 K3
Woodlands Park Rd PDSY/CALV LS28......120 A1
Woodland Sq BRIG * HD6......157 H7
WOR/ARM LS12......101 J3
Woodlands Ri HWTH BD22......72 D6
Woodlands St BGLY BD16......56 B7
BTLY WF17......140 D7
CLECK BD19......139 H6
CUL/QBY BD13......115 K5
ELL HX5......175 J1
GIR BD8......4 D2
HIPP HX3......17 G1
Woodlands St GIR BD8......5 H4
Woodlands Ter GIR BD8......4 C2
PDSY/CALV LS28......99 K4
Woodlands Vw GFTH/SHER LS25......128 B6
HIPP HX3......17 G2
TAD LS24......70 C1
Woodland Ter CHAL LS7......83 F5

Woodland Vw PDSY/CALV LS28......79 H6
PONT WF8......189 K3
Wood La AL/HA/HU LS17......46 A7
BRAM LS13......101 F1
BRAM LS13......101 G5
BSPA/BRAM LS23......30 D6
CAS WF10......167 J3
CHAL LS7......83 H5
DEWS WF13......161 F6
ECHL BD2......78 A7
HBR HX7......132 C1
HDGY LS6......82 D7
HIPP HX3......136 A6
HIPP HX3......156 C6
HORS LS18......81 F5
HUDE HD5......178 E5
LUD/ILL HX2......134 A6
MSTN/BAR LS15......86 B6
PDSY/CALV LS28......79 J5
RPDN/SBR HX6......153 F4
RTHW LS26......144 E1
RTHW LS26......147 H1
WOR/ARM LS12......121 J4
Wood Lane Ct HDGY LS6......82 D7
Woodlea BSPA/BRAM LS23......48 C2
Wood Lea HDGY LS6......82 E7
Woodlea Ap HDGY LS6......82 E7
YEA LS19......59 G5
Woodlea Av HDGY LS6......82 E7
Woodlea Cha HDGY LS6......82 E4
Woodlea Cl YEA LS19......59 G6
Woodlea Ct HDGY LS6......82 E7
Woodlea Cft HDGY LS6......82 E7
Woodlea Dr HDGY LS6......82 E3
YEA LS19......59 G6
Woodlea Fold HDGY LS6......82 E4
Woodlea Gdns HDGY LS6......82 E4
Woodlea Garth HDGY LS6......82 E3
Woodlea Ga HDGY LS6......82 E3
Woodlea Gn HDGY LS6......82 E3
Woodlea Gv BEE/HOL * LS11......122 E3
HDGY LS6......82 E4
YEA LS19......59 G5
Woodlea Holt HDGY LS6......82 E3
Woodlea La HDGY LS6......82 E3
Woodlea Lawn HDGY LS6......82 E3
Woodlea Mt BEE/HOL LS11......122 E3
YEA LS19......59 G5
Woodlea Pk HDGY LS6......82 E4
Woodlea Pl BEE/HOL LS11......122 E3
Woodlea Rd YEA LS19......59 G5
Woodlea Sq HDGY * LS6......82 E4
Woodlea St BEE/HOL LS11......122 E3
Woodlea Vw HDGY LS6......82 E4
Woodleigh EARL * WF12......181 G7
Woodleigh Av GFTH/SHER LS25......107 H6
WBOW BD5......117 K5
Woodleigh Hall Vw YEA * LS19......80 B3
Woodlesford Crs LUD/ILL HX2......133 J3
Woodliffe Ct CHAL LS7......83 H5
Woodliffe Dr CHAL LS7......83 H5
Woodman Av ELL HX5......175 J4
HUDN HD2......178 A4
Woodman Ct WBSY BD6......136 D1
Woodman St MSTN/BAR LS15......105 H5
Wood Mt RTHW LS26......144 D1
Woodnook Cl BHP/TINH LS16......81 G4
Woodnook Dr BHP/TINH LS16......81 G4
Woodnook Garth BHP/TINH LS16......81 G2
Wood Nook La RPDN/SBR HX6......153 K3
Woodnook Rd BHP/TINH LS16......81 G4
Wood Nook Ter PDSY/CALV LS28......99 G4
Woodpecker Rd ILK LS29......25 J1
Wood Pl BEE/HOL * LS11......13 K9
GIR BD8......5 H1
Wood Rd HTON BD9......97 H1
WBOW BD5......117 K2
Wood Rw RTHW LS26......146 E4
Woodrow Crs RTHW LS26......146 E4
Woodrow Dr LM/WK BD12......137 K2
Woodroyd Av WBOW * BD5......118 A4
Woodroyd Dr HIPP HX3......134 B5
Woodroyd Gdns ILK LS29......24 E6
RPDN/SBR HX6......153 G3
Woodroyd Rd WBOW BD5......117 K4
Woodroyd Ter WBOW BD5......118 A3
Woodside CAS WF10......149 H7
KGHY BD21......53 H2
SHPY BD18......77 J4
WKFDW/WTN WF2......163 K6
Woodside Av BGLY BD16......75 J5
BULY LS4......8 A4
CHAL LS7......82 E5
HOR/CROF WF4......187 F6
SHPY BD18......76 D4
WKFDW/WTN WF2......163 K6
Woodside Cl MOR LS27......141 K1
Woodside Ct CUL/QBY BD13......74 A4
HORS LS18......81 H4
Woodside Crs BGLY BD16......75 J5
BTLY WF17......160 D4
HIPP HX3......16 E1
HOR/CROF WF4......186 E5
Woodside Dr BGLY BD16......75 J5
MOR LS27......121 K7
WKFDW/WTN WF2......163 K6
Woodside Gdns MOR LS27......121 K7
Woodside Gv CAS WF10......147 J1
GTL/HWG HX4......175 F3
HIPP HX3......17 G2
Woodside Hill Cl HORS LS18......81 G4
Woodside La HUDN HD2......177 G5
MOR LS27......121 K7
Woodside Ms CHAL LS7......82 E5
Woodside Mt HFAX HX1......16 F5
Woodside Park Av HORS LS18......81 G4
Woodside Park Dr HORS LS18......81 G4
Woodside Pl BULY LS4......8 A4
HIPP HX3......16 F2
Woodside Rd AIRE BD20......32 D1
BSPA/BRAM LS23......48 A3
HFAX HX1......16 F2
LM/WK BD12......137 H3
Woodside St CAS WF10......147 J1
Woodside Ter BULY LS4......8 A4

HIPP HX3 ....16 F2
Woodside Vw BGLY BD16 ....75 J5
BULY LS4 ....8 A4
HIPP HX3 ....16 F2
Woodsley Gn HDGY LS6 ......9 G5
Woodsley Rd HDGY LS6 ......9 G5
IDLE BD10 ....78 B6
Woodsley Ter LDSU LS2 ......9 J6
Woodsome Av MIRF WF14 ...179 F3
Woodsome Dr MIRF WF14 ...179 G3
Wood Sq HIPP HX3 ....134 E5
Wood's Rw PDSY/CALV LS28 ..100 B4
Woodstock Wk WBOW * BD5 ..117 K1
Wood St AIRE BD20 ....32 D5
BAIL BD17 ....77 H3
BGLY BD16 ....55 H5
BRIG HD6 ....157 C6
BTLY WF17 ....161 F4
CAS WF10 ....148 B7
CLECK BD19 ....158 D1
DEWS WF13 ....161 G7
EARD/LOFT WF3 ....143 J7
ELL HX5 ....175 K3
HOR/CROF WF4 ....186 E5
KGHY BD21 ....3 H7
MOR LS27 ....141 J2
OSS WF5 ....182 C2
WIL/AL BD15 ....96 B4
WKFDE WF1 ....18 E4
Wood St North HIPP * HX3 ..134 E5
Woodthorne Cft
AL/HA/HU LS17 ....64 D7
Wood Top BRIG HD6 ....156 D3
Woodvale Cl BOW BD4 ......119 F1
Woodvale Crs BGLY BD16 ....55 K6
Woodvale Gv GTHN BD7 .....116 D1
Woodvale Rd BRIG HD6 .....157 G5
Woodvale Wy CLAY BD14 ....116 D1
Woodview BIRK/DRI BD11 ...120 D4
Wood Vw HUDN HD2 ....176 C7
HWTH * BD22 ....53 G7
MOR LS27 ....122 B6
Woodview Av BAIL BD17 ......58 A7
Wood View Av CAS WF10 ....167 K1
Wood View Cl CAS WF10 ....167 K1
Woodview Cl HORS LS18 .....81 F2
Wood View Crs CAS WF10 ...147 K7
Wood View Dr ECHL BD2 .....98 D3
Woodview Gv BEE/HOL LS11 ..123 G4
Wood View Gv BRIG HD6 ....156 E4
Woodview Mt BEE/HOL LS11 ..123 G4
Woodview Rd BEE/HOL LS11 ..123 G4
HWTH BD22 ....53 G7
Woodview Ter BEE/HOL LS11 ..123 G4
Wood View Ter KGHY BD21 ...53 J7
Woodville Av HORS LS18 .....81 G4
Woodville Ct RHAY LS8 ......84 B3
WKFDW/WTN WF2 ....184 D7
Woodville Crs HORS LS18 ....81 G4
Woodville Gv HORS * LS18 ...81 G4
HWTH BD22 ....73 G4
MID * LS10 ....125 K5
Woodville Pl HORS LS18 .....81 H3

HTON BD9 ....96 E1
HUDN HD2 ....177 K3
Woodville Rd EARL WF12 ...181 G1
KGHY BD21 ....2 E3
Woodville Sq MID LS10 .....123 K5
Woodville St HIPP HX3 ......16 D1
HORS LS18 ....81 H3
SHPY BD18 ....77 J4
Woodville Ter HORS LS18 ....81 G4
WBOW BD5 ....5 K9
Wood Vine Rd PDSY/CALV LS28 ...99 K4
Woodward Ct MIRF WF14 ...179 J2
Woodway BGLY BD16 ....75 J5
HORS LS18 ....81 F5
Woodway Dr HORS LS18 .....81 F5
Woolcomb Ct HTON BD9 .....97 F3
Woolcroft Gv KGHY BD21 ....73 J1
Wooler Av BEE/HOL LS11 ...123 F4
Wooler Dr BEE/HOL LS11 ...123 F4
Wooler Gv BEE/HOL LS11 ...123 F4
Wooler Pl BEE/HOL LS11 ....122 F4
Wooler Rd BEE/HOL * LS11 ..122 G4
Wooler St BEE/HOL LS11 ...122 F4
The Wool Ex BFD BD1 ....5 M6
Woolford Wy EARD/LOFT WF3 ..164 E2
Woollin Av EARD/LOFT WF3 ..162 D3
Woollin Crs EARD/LOFT WF3 ..162 D2
Woolmarket PONT WF8 .....189 J7
Woolpack's Yd WKFDE WF1 ...18 D4
Woolrow La BRIG HD6 ......157 H2
Woolshops Sq HFAX HX1 .....17 H6
Wool St HECK WF16 ....160 A5
Wootton St WBOW BD5 .....117 J2
Worcester Av EARD/LOFT WF3 ..144 A3
Worcester Cl EARD/LOFT WF3 ..143 H6
Worcester Dr EARD/LOFT WF3 ..144 A3
Worcester Pl BOW BD4 ......118 C5
Worden Gv CLAY BD14 .....116 D2
Wordsworth Ap PONT WF8 ..169 J4
Wordsworth Ct RTHW LS26 ..145 K4
Wordsworth Dr KNOT WF11 ..170 C3
RTHW LS26 ....145 K4
Wordsworth Gv
EARD/LOFT WF3 ....165 F3
Workhouse La GTL/HWG HX4 ..175 D3
LUD/ILL HX2 ....153 H1
Wormald Rw LDS LS1 ....10 A8
Wormald St DEWS WF13 ....181 F1
LVSG WF15 ....159 K5
Worrall St MOR LS27 ....141 J4
Worsnop Buildings
LM/WK BD12 ....137 H3
Worsnop St LM/WK BD12 ...137 J1
Worstead Rd HWTH BD22 ....73 G4
Worth Av KGHY BD21 ....3 M1
Worth Bridge Rd KGHY BD21 ..3 L3
Worthing Head Cl
LM/WK BD12 ....137 J4
Worthing Head Rd
LM/WK BD12 ....137 H4
Worthington St GIR BD8 .....5 H4
Worthville Cl KGHY BD21 .....3 H9

Worth Wy HWTH BD22 ....73 H4
HWTH BD22 ....92 E1
KGHY BD21 ....3 G7
Wortley Hts WOR/ARM LS12 ..12 D3
Wortley La WOR/ARM LS12 ...13 G4
Wortley Moor La
WOR/ARM LS12 ....101 K6
Wortley Moor Rd
WOR/ARM LS12 ....101 K6
Wortley Pk WOR/ARM LS12 ..12 E3
Wortley Rd WOR/ARM LS12 ..102 A6
Wortley St BGLY BD16 ....76 A1
Wrangthorn Av HDGY LS6 .....9 G3
Wrangthorn Pl HDGY LS6 ......9 G3
Wrangthorn Ter HDGY LS6 .....9 G3
Wren Av GTHN BD7 ....116 D1
Wrenbeck Av OT LS21 ....27 H7
Wrenbeck Cl OT LS21 ....27 H7
Wrenbeck Dr OT LS21 ....27 H7
Wrenbury Av BHP/TINH LS16 ..61 G6
Wrenbury Crs BHP/TINH LS16 ..61 G6
Wrenbury Gv BHP/TINH LS16 ..61 H6
Wren Cft PONT WF8 ....169 J5
Wren Dr MOR LS27 ....142 C4
Wren Hl BTLY WF17 ....140 D7
Wren Nest Rd RPDN/SBR HX6 ..172 B5
Wren St KGHY BD21 ....3 H3
Wrenthorpe La
WKFDW/WTN WF2 ....163 H7
Wrenthorpe Rd
WKFDW/WTN WF2 ....164 A7
Wrexhall Rd EARL WF12 ....161 H6
Wrexham Rd ILK LS29 ....37 J1
Wright Av HWTH BD22 ....72 E1
Wright St HWTH BD22 ....72 E1
Wrigley Av BOW BD4 ....118 C5
Wrigley Hl LUD/ILL HX2 ....134 B1
Wroe Crs LM/WK BD12 .....137 H4
Wroe Pl LM/WK BD12 ......137 H4
Wroe St DEWS WF13 ....160 C7
Wroe Ter LM/WK BD12 .....137 H4
Wrose Av SHPY BD18 ....77 J6
Wrose Brow Rd SHPY BD18 ..77 J4
Wrosecliffe Gv SHPY BD18 ....78 A4
Wrose Dr SHPY BD18 ....77 J6
Wrose Gv SHPY BD18 ....77 J6
Wrose Hill Pl SHPY BD18 .....77 J7
Wrose Mt SHPY BD18 ....77 K6
Wrose Rd SHPY BD18 ....77 J6
Wrose Vw SHPY BD18 ....77 J6
Wycliffe Cl BRAM LS13 ......80 A7
Wycliffe Dr AL/HA/HU LS17 ..83 J2
Wycliffe Gdns SHPY BD18 ....77 F4
Wycliffe Rd SHPY BD18 ......77 F4
Wycliffe St OSS WF5 ....182 B2
Wycoller Rd LM/WK BD12 ...137 H3
Wycombe Gn BOW BD4 ....119 F3
Wykebeck Av OSM LS9 ....104 E6
Wykebeck Crs OSM LS9 ....104 E5
Wykebeck Gdns OSM LS9 ...104 E5
Wykebeck Gv OSM LS9 ....104 E5
Wykebeck Mt OSM LS9 ....104 E5
Wykebeck Pl OSM LS9 .....105 F5
Wykebeck Rd OSM LS9 ....104 E5

Wykebeck Sq OSM LS9 ....104 E5
Wykebeck St OSM LS9 ....104 E5
Wykebeck Ter OSM LS9 ....104 E5
Wykebeck Valley Rd OSM LS9 ..104 E3
Wykebeck Vw OSM LS9 ....104 E5
Wyke Crs LM/WK BD12 ....137 J5
Wyke La LM/WK BD12 .....137 J5
Wykelea Cl LM/WK BD12 ...137 J5
Wyke Old La BRIG HD6 ....157 G1
Wyncliffe Gdns AL/HA/HU LS17 ..83 J2
Wyncroft Gv BHP/TINH LS16 ..61 J7
Wyncroft Ri SHPY BD18 ......77 J7
Wyndham Av ECHL BD2 .....98 A2
Wynford Av BHP/TINH LS16 ..82 A3
Wynford Gv BHP/TINH LS16 ..82 A3
Wynford Mt BHP/TINH LS16 ..81 J3
Wynford Ri BHP/TINH LS16 ..81 K3
Wynford Ter BHP/TINH LS16 ..81 K3
Wynford Wy WBSY BD6 ....117 K6
Wynmore Av BHP/TINH LS16 ..61 H1
Wynmore Crs BHP/TINH LS16 ..61 J1
Wynmore Dr BHP/TINH LS16 ..61 H1
Wynyard Dr MOR LS27 .....141 J3
Wyther Park Av
WOR/ARM LS12 ....101 J4
Wyther Park Cl
WOR/ARM LS12 ....101 J4
Wyther Park Crs
WOR/ARM LS12 ....101 J4
Wyther Park Gv
WOR/ARM LS12 ....101 J4
Wyther Park Hl
WOR/ARM LS12 ....101 J3
Wyther Park Pl
WOR/ARM LS12 ....101 J3
Wyther Park Rd BRAM LS13 ..101 H4
Wyther Park Sq
WOR/ARM LS12 ....101 H3
Wyther Park St
WOR/ARM LS12 ....101 J4
Wyther Park Ter
WOR/ARM LS12 ....101 J4
Wyther Park Vw
WOR/ARM LS12 ....101 J3
Wyvern Cl BTLY WF17 .....161 F2
GTHN BD7 ....4 A8
Wyvern Pl LUD/ILL HX2 ....134 B7
Wyvern Ter LUD/ILL HX2 ...134 B7
Wyvil Crs ILK LS29 ....24 D5
Wyvil Rd ILK LS29 ....24 D4

Yeadon Dr HIPP HX3 ....155 K4
Yeadon Moor Rd YEA LS19 ..60 B5
Ye Farre Cl BRIG HD6 ......156 E4
Yewbank Cl ILK LS29 ....23 K5
Yewbank Ter ILK LS29 ....23 K5
Yewdall Rd BRAM LS13 .....80 A7
Yewdall Wy IDLE BD10 ......78 D6
Yew La GFTH/SHER LS25 ...108 A7
Yew Tree Av GIR BD8 ....96 C4
Yew Tree Cl SHPY BD18 .....77 H6
Yew Tree Crs GIR BD8 ....96 C4
Yew Tree Dr RTHW LS26 ...146 B1
Yew Tree La MSTN/BAR LS15 ..106 B6
WIL/AL BD15 ....95 H5
Yew Tree Rd HUDW HD3 ...175 K7
Yew Trees Av HIPP HX3 ....135 K4
Yew Trees Cft LUD/ILL HX2 ..132 C6
Yew Tree St WKFDE WF1 ....19 K9
York Av HUDN HD2 ....177 F7
York Crs BGLY * BD16 ....75 K2
York Dr BTLY WF17 ....161 G2
HECK WF16 ....160 A2
York Ga OT LS21 ....39 F6
OT LS21 ....39 K6
York Gv BTLY WF17 ....161 F2
York Pl CLECK BD19 ....138 E7
LDS LS1 ....9 L9
WBY LS22 ....29 H3
York Rd BTLY WF17 ....161 G2
EARL WF12 ....161 J7
ILK LS29 ....38 A1
OSM LS9 ....10 F9
SCFT LS14 ....85 J7
SCFT LS14 ....105 J2
TAD LS24 ....51 F6
WBY LS22 ....30 B2
Yorkshire Wy GTHN BD7 ...117 G3
York St BGLY LS16 ....75 K2
BRIG HD6 ....157 F7
CAS WF10 ....148 D7
CUL/QBY BD13 ....115 H5
GIR BD8 ....96 D6
HFAX HX1 ....16 F7
LDSU LS2 ....14 C1
NORM * WF6 ....166 C5
York Ter HIPP HX3 ....16 F1
York Vls NORM WF6 ....166 E6
Young's Ct GFTH/SHER LS25 ..88 D6
Young St GIR BD8 ....4 B4

Zealand St BOW BD4 ......118 E2
Zermatt Gv CHAL LS7 ....83 H6
Zermatt Mt CHAL * LS7 .....83 H6
Zermatt St CHAL LS7 ....83 J6
Zermatt Ter CHAL LS7 ....83 J6
Zetland Pl RHAY LS8 ....11 H1
Zetland St WKFDE WF1 ......18 F4
Zoar St MOR LS27 ....141 K3

Index - featured places

A1 Business Park
KNOT WF11 ....170 D5
Abbey Grange CE High School
BHP/TINH LS16 ....81 J4
Abbey House Museum
KSTL LS5 ....81 J7
Abbey Park School
LUD/ILL HX2 ....134 A1
ABC Cinema
HFAX HX1 ....17 H7
Aberford CE Primary School
GFTH/SHER LS25 ....88 D5
Ackton Pastures
Primary School
CAS WF10 ....168 A2
Acorn Business Park
SCFT LS14 ....105 F4
Acorn Park Industrial Estate
BAIL BD17 ....77 K2
Addingham Cricket Club
ILK LS29 ....22 B1
Adel Primary School
BHP/TINH LS16 ....82 D1
Adult Education Centre
BRIG HD6 ....157 F5
Adwalton Cricket Club
BIRK/DRI BD11 ....140 C2
Adwalton Moor
Business Park
BOW BD4 ....119 J7
Agnes Stewart CE High School
OSM LS9 ....10 E8
Ainley Industrial Estate
ELL HX5 ....175 K4
Aireborough Leisure Centre
GSLY LS20 ....59 F2
Aire & Calder Industrial Park
CAS WF10 ....148 D6
The Aire & Calder
Industrial Park
CAS WF10 ....148 C6
Airedale Centre
KGHY BD21 ....3 G5
Airedale Clinic
CAS WF10 ....169 H1
Airedale Community
Business Centre
CAS WF10 ....149 G7
Airedale Community Campus
CAS WF10 ....169 J1
Airedale General Hospital
AIRE BD20 ....32 B4
Airedale Junior School
CAS WF10 ....169 H1
Aireside Business Centre
LDS LS1 ....13 L1

Aireside Retail Park
LDS LS1 ....13 K1
Aire Valley Business Centre
KGHY BD21 ....3 G3
Aire Valley Clinic
AIRE BD20 ....32 D5
Aireview Business Centre
BAIL BD17 ....77 F4
Aire View Infant School
AIRE BD20 ....32 E1
Aireville Primary School
BRAM LS13 ....100 B1
Albion Mills Retail Park
WKFDW/WTN WF2 ....18 C5
Alhambra Theatre
BFD BD1 ....5 L7
Allerton Bywater
Business Park
CAS WF10 ....148 C3
Allerton Bywater
Infant School
CAS WF10 ....148 A3
Allerton Bywater
Primary School
CAS WF10 ....148 A2
Allerton Clinic
WIL/AL BD15 ....96 A5
Allerton First & Middle School
WIL/AL BD15 ....96 A4
Allerton Grange High School
AL/HA/HU LS17 ....84 A3
Allerton High School
AL/HA/HU LS17 ....63 F7
All Saints CE Infant School
OT LS21 ....39 K3
All Saints CE Junior School
OT LS21 ....39 H2
All Saints CE First School
WBOW BD5 ....117 J2
All Saints CE J & I School
HIPP HX3 ....155 F6
All Saints First School
ILK LS29 ....24 A5
All Saints High School
HUDN HD2 ....177 H4
All Saints Industrial Estate
PONT WF8 ....169 K7
All Saints Infant School
PONT WF8 ....169 K7
Alston Retail Park
KGHY BD21 ....3 K1
Altofts Middle School
NORM WF6 ....166 C5
Altofts Sports Club
NORM WF6 ....166 D3
Alwoodley Golf Club
AL/HA/HU LS17 ....63 K5

Alwoodley Primary School
AL/HA/HU LS17 ....83 F1
Amateurs FC
ELL HX5 ....176 A1
AMF Bowling
LDSU LS2 ....10 A7
Apex Business Centre
BEE/HOL LS11 ....14 A5
Apex Business Park
BEE/HOL LS11 ....14 A5
Archbishop Cranmer CE
Primary School
AL/HA/HU LS17 ....83 G1
Arlington Business Centre
MOR LS27 ....122 C6
Armley Clinic
WOR/ARM LS12 ....8 A9
Armley Link Trading Estate
WOR/ARM LS12 ....8 D9
Armley Primary School
WOR/ARM LS12 ....8 A8
Armley Sports &
Leisure Centre
WOR/ARM LS12 ....102 A6
Armytage Road
Industrial Estate
BRIG HD6 ....157 G1
Arndale Centre
HDGY LS6 ....82 C7
Arndale Shopping Centre
SHPY BD18 ....77 G5
A S B & S Sports Club
FEA/AMT WF7 ....188 B4
Ashbrow Junior School
HUDN HD2 ....177 G6
Ashfield Medical Centre
MSTN/BAR LS15 ....105 K3
Ashfield School
IDLE BD10 ....78 D3
Ashlands First School
ILK LS29 ....24 B5
Ashley Business Centre
LDSU LS2 ....10 C8
Ashley Industrial Estate
CHAL LS7 ....10 B3
HUDN HD2 ....178 B5
OSS WF5 ....182 D2
Ashton Road Industrial Estate
RHAY LS8 ....11 J3
Ashton View Medical Centre
RHAY LS8 ....11 H4
Ash Tree County Infant School
LUD/ILL HX2 ....133 K2
Askwith CP School
OT LS21 ....26 A4
Astley Lane Industrial Estate
RTHW LS26 ....126 E6

Astra Business Park
BEE/HOL LS11 ....123 H4
Athelstan Primary School
GFTH/SHER LS25 ....111 F7
Atlas First School
GIR BD8 ....5 G2
Austhorpe Primary School
MSTN/BAR LS15 ....106 B5
Aylesham Industrial Estate
LM/WK BD12 ....137 J1
Bagshaw Museum
BTLY WF17 ....140 E7
Baildon CE First School
BAIL BD17 ....57 J7
Baildon Golf Club
BAIL BD17 ....57 H6
Baildon Recreation Centre
BAIL BD17 ....77 G3
Baileygate Industrial Estate
PONT WF8 ....169 K7
Bailiff Bridge Primary School
BRIG HD6 ....157 G1
Balm Road Industrial Estate
MID LS10 ....14 D9
Bankfield Museum
HIPP HX3 ....17 G2
Bankfoot First School
WBOW BD5 ....117 J4
Bankside Primary School
RHAY LS8 ....11 G2
Bardsey Primary School
AL/HA/HU LS17 ....45 K6
Barkerend First School
BFDE BD3 ....6 D4
Barkisland CE J & I School
GTL/HWG HX4 ....173 H4
Barkisland Cricket Club
GTL/HWG HX4 ....173 H5
Barkston Ash
Catholic Primary
TAD LS24 ....90 E7
Barplas Industrial Park
WBOW BD5 ....117 K3
Barras Garth Industrial Estate
WOR/ARM LS12 ....102 A7
Barwick In Elmet CE
Primary School
MSTN/BAR LS15 ....87 H5
Batley Boys High School
BTLY WF17 ....161 F2
Batley Business Centre
BTLY WF17 ....160 E2
Batley Business &
Technology Centre
BTLY WF17 ....161 H4
Batley Bus Station
BTLY WF17 ....161 F3

Batley Grammar School
BTLY WF17 ....160 E1
Batley Parish CE
(A) J I & N School
BTLY WF17 ....160 E2
Batley RLFC
BTLY WF17 ....161 F4
Batley Sports Centre
BTLY WF17 ....140 E6
Battyeford CE
(c) J & I School
MIRF WF14 ....179 F3
Batty Street School
HECK WF16 ....160 A4
BBC North Studios
BFD BD1 ....5 M7
LDSU LS2 ....9 M6
Beacon Business Centre
HIPP HX3 ....17 L8
The Beaconsfield Centre
HIPP HX3 ....17 L9
Beckett Park Athletics Centre
HDGY LS6 ....81 K6
Beckett Park Primary School
HDGY LS6 ....82 A7
Beckfoot Upper School
BGLY BD16 ....75 K3
Beech Hill County
Primary School
HFAX HX1 ....16 E4
Beechwood Primary School
SCFT LS14 ....85 H7
Beeston Hill St Lukes CE
Primary School
BEE/HOL LS11 ....13 L7
Beeston Primary School
BEE/HOL LS11 ....122 D4
Beeston Royds
Industrial Estate
BEE/HOL LS11 ....122 B3
Belle Isle Medical Centre
RTHW LS26 ....124 A6
Belle Vue Boys School
HTON BD9 ....96 C1
Belle Vue Girls Upper School
BGLY BD16 ....76 B7
Belmont Business Centre
BFD BD1 ....6 A6
Belmont Middle School
BAIL BD17 ....77 G1
Ben Rhydding Golf Club
ILK LS29 ....24 E7
Ben Rhydding Sports Club
ILK LS29 ....25 F4
Bentley Primary School
HDGY LS6 ....82 E6

Benton Park School
 YEA LS19 .... 59 J6
Bero Bu School
 LDSU LS2 .... 10 A6
Bierley CE First School
 BOW BD4 .... 118 C5
Bilton Medical Centre
 GIR BD8 .... 5 G4
Bingley Grammar School
 BGLY BD16 .... 55 H7
Bingley Health Centre
 BGLY BD16 .... 75 K1
Bingley Hospital
 BGLY BD16 .... 75 K1
Bingley Little Theatre
 BGLY BD16 .... 75 J1
Bingley St Ives Golf Club
 BGLY BD16 .... 75 F1
Birchfield Primary School
 MOR LS27 .... 141 F1
Birch Lane Medical Centre
 WBOW BD5 .... 117 K3
Birkenshaw C E F & N School
 BIRK/DRI BD11 .... 139 H1
Birkenshaw Health Centre
 BIRK/DRI BD11 .... 139 H1
Birkenshaw Middle School
 BIRK/DRI BD11 .... 139 J3
Birksland Industrial Estate
 BOW BD4 .... 6 F9
Birstall Cricket Club
 BTLY WF17 .... 140 D6
Birstall J & I School
 BTLY WF17 .... 140 D6
Blackburn Industrial Estate
 GFTH/SHER LS25 .... 111 J5
Blackgates Infant School
 EARD/LOFT WF3 .... 142 E6
Blackgates Junior School
 EARD/LOFT WF3 .... 142 E7
Blakehill First School
 IDLE BD10 .... 78 B6
Blenheim Primary School
 LDSU LS2 .... 9 M5
BMK Industrial Estate
 LVSG WF15 .... 159 J4
Bolling Hall
 BOW BD4 .... 118 B3
Bolling Road First School
 ILK LS29 .... 24 C5
Bolton Brow Primary School
 RPDN/SBR HX6 .... 154 A4
Bolton Lane First School
 ECHL BD2 .... 98 B2
Bolton Royd College of Further
 Education
 GIR BD8 .... 97 J3
Bolton Royd Primary School
 PDSY/CALV LS28 .... 99 J3
Bolton Villas Cricket Club
 IDLE BD10 .... 78 B6
Bolton Woods First School
 SHPY BD18 .... 77 J7
Bondgate Industrial Estate
 PONT WF8 .... 169 K7
Borough Market
 HFAX HX1 .... 17 H6
Boston Spa
 Comprehensive School
 BSPA/BRAM LS23 .... 48 A3
Bowers Mill Industrial Estate
 GTL/HWG HX4 .... 174 A4
Bowling Community College &
 Swimming Pool
 BOW BD4 .... 118 B3
Bowling Court Industrial Estate
 BOW BD4 .... 7 G9
Bowling Green Primary School
 GTL/HWG HX4 .... 174 C6
Bowling Park First School
 WBOW BD5 .... 118 A3
Bowling Special School
 BOW BD4 .... 118 C3
Bracken Edge Primary School
 CHAL LS7 .... 83 K7
Brackenhill First School
 GTHN BD7 .... 116 E2
Bradford Area Health Authority
 GTHN BD7 .... 117 F2
Bradford & Bingley RFC
 BGLY BD16 .... 76 A3
Bradford Bulls RLFC
 (Odsal Stadium)
 WBSY BD6 .... 117 K6
Bradford Business Park
 BFDE BD3 .... 5 M2
Bradford Cathedral Community
 College
 BOW BD4 .... 118 C3
Bradford City FC
 (Bradford & Bingley Stadium)
 GIR BD8 .... 5 K1
Bradford Girls
 Grammar School
 GIR BD8 .... 96 D4
Bradford Golf Club
 GSLY LS20 .... 58 B4
Bradford Grammar School
 HTON BD9 .... 97 H2
Bradford & Ilkley College
 BFD BD1 .... 5 K7
 WBOW BD5 .... 5 J9
Bradford & Ilkley
 Community College
 GTHN BD7 .... 5 H8
 ILK LS29 .... 24 A6
Bradford Industrial &
 Horses at Work Museum
 ECHL BD2 .... 98 D2
Bradford Moor First School
 BFDE BD3 .... 7 H4
Bradford Moor Golf Club
 BFDE BD3 .... 7 G1
Bradford Royal Infirmary
 HTON BD9 .... 96 E3
Bradford Royal Infirmary
 Remedial Unit
 HTON BD9 .... 96 D3

Bradford Salem RFC
 HTON BD9 .... 96 D1
Bradford University
 PDSY/CALV LS28 .... 99 H4
Bradley Junction
 Industrial Estate
 HUDN HD2 .... 178 A5
Bradley Park Golf Club
 HUDN HD2 .... 177 J3
Bradshaw School
 LUD/ILL HX2 .... 114 B6
Braim Wood High
 School For Boys
 RHAY LS8 .... 84 E5
Braithwaite Special School
 HWTH BD22 .... 53 F3
Bramall Business Park
 WBOW BD5 .... 117 K2
Bramham Park
 BSPA/BRAM LS23 .... 67 J3
Bramham Primary School
 BSPA/BRAM LS23 .... 48 C6
Bramhope Primary School
 BHP/TINH LS16 .... 61 H1
Bramley Business Centre
 BRAM LS13 .... 100 E4
Bramley Grange College
 SCFT LS14 .... 85 K3
Bramley Health Centre
 BRAM LS13 .... 101 F2
Bramley RUFC
 BRAM LS13 .... 101 F2
Bramley St Peters CE
 Primary School
 BRAM LS13 .... 101 F3
Brandon Golf Club
 AL/HA/HU LS17 .... 64 E6
Branshaw Golf Club
 HWTH BD22 .... 72 E1
Branshaw School
 HWTH BD22 .... 2 D6
Branxholme Industrial Estate
 BRIG HD6 .... 157 H1
Bretton Hall College
 WKFDE WF1 .... 184 E6
Bridge Court Business Park
 BEE/HOL LS11 .... 13 J5
Brighouse High School
 BRIG HD6 .... 157 F5
Brighouse Sports Centre
 BRIG HD6 .... 156 E3
Brighouse Sports Club
 BRIG HD6 .... 157 G5
Brigshaw High School
 CAS WF10 .... 127 J7
Britannia Business
 Enterprise Centre
 EARL WF12 .... 182 A3
The British Library
 Document Supply Centre
 BSPA/BRAM LS23 .... 31 G6
Broadgate Primary School
 HORS LS18 .... 81 F3
Brodetsky Primary School
 AL/HA/HU LS17 .... 63 H7
Bronte House School
 IDLE BD10 .... 79 G2
Bronte Parsonage Museum
 HWTH BD22 .... 72 C5
Bronte School
 HWTH BD22 .... 73 F1
Brookfield Infant School
 IDLE BD10 .... 79 F6
Brookfoot Industrial Estate
 BRIG HD6 .... 156 E6
The Brooksbank School
 ELL HX5 .... 175 H4
Brookwoods Industrial Estate
 GTL/HWG HX4 .... 175 F4
Broomwood Middle School
 BOW BD4 .... 118 D5
Brotherton & Byram CP School
 KNOT WF11 .... 150 D7
Brownhill Infant School
 BTLY WF17 .... 140 D6
Brownhill Primary School
 OSM LS9 .... 11 K7
Brow Quarry
 Industrial Estate
 HIPP HX3 .... 156 C2
Brudenell Primary School
 HDGY LS6 .... 8 E2
Brunswick Industrial Estate
 HFAX HX1 .... 16 E8
Bull Royd Industrial Estate
 GIR BD8 .... 96 D5
Burley FC
 KSTL LS5 .... 81 J6
Burley Hill Trading Estate
 BULY LS4 .... 8 B4
Burley In Wharfedale School
 ILK LS29 .... 37 K1
Burley Middle School
 ILK LS29 .... 38 A2
Burley Park Medical Centre
 BULY LS4 .... 8 C5
Burley St Mathias CE
 Primary School
 BULY LS4 .... 8 C5
Burley Woodhead CE School
 ILK LS29 .... 38 A2
Burmantofts Health Centre
 OSM LS9 .... 10 F7
Burton Salmon Primary School
 GFTH/SHER LS25 .... 151 F3
Business Enterprise Centre
 BFDE BD3 .... 6 A5
Butterfield Industrial Estate
 BAIL BD17 .... 77 J3
Buttershaw Middle School
 WBSY BD6 .... 116 E6
Buttershaw Upper School
 WBSY BD6 .... 116 E6
Byram Industrial Park
 KNOT WF11 .... 150 E7
Byron Primary School
 BFDE BD3 .... 6 F4

Bywell CE Junior School
 EARL WF12 .... 161 J6
Calderdale Business Centre
 HFAX HX1 .... 16 B6
Calderdale Business Park
 LUD/ILL HX2 .... 134 C4
Calderdale Industrial Museum
 HFAX HX1 .... 17 J3
The Calderdale
 Royal Hospital
 HIPP HX3 .... 155 F5
Calder High School
 HBR HX7 .... 132 A6
Calder Industrial Estate
 BRIG HD6 .... 157 G2
Calder Trading Estate
 HUDN HD2 .... 178 B3
 RPDN/SBR HX6 .... 153 K5
Calverley CE Primary School
 PDSY/CALV LS28 .... 79 J3
Calverley Golf Club
 PDSY/CALV LS28 .... 99 H2
Calverley Medical Centre
 PDSY/CALV LS28 .... 79 H6
Calverley Parkside
 Primary School
 PDSY/CALV LS28 .... 79 H6
Calversyke Middle School
 HWTH BD22 .... 2 A5
Cape Industrial Estate
 PDSY/CALV LS28 .... 100 B2
Cardigan Trading Estate
 BULY LS4 .... 8 C5
Cardinal Heenan RC
 High School
 HDGY LS6 .... 82 E3
Carleton Park Primary School
 PONT WF8 .... 189 J3
Carlinghow J I & N School
 BTLY WF17 .... 160 D1
Carlisle Mills Business Centre
 GIR BD8 .... 5 G1
Carlton Bolling College &
 Sports Centre
 BFDE BD3 .... 6 D3
Carlton Cricket Club
 EARD/LOFT WF3 .... 144 C5
Carlton High School
 PONT WF8 .... 189 K4
Carlton J & I School
 DEWS WF13 .... 160 E6
Carlton Lanes Shopping Area
 CAS WF10 .... 148 C7
Carlton Mills Trading Estate
 WOR/ARM LS12 .... 8 C8
Carlton Northfield AFC
 EARD/LOFT WF3 .... 144 E5
Carr Gate Hospital
 WKFDW/WTN WF2 .... 163 K5
Carr Green County
 Primary School
 BRIG HD6 .... 176 B2
Carr Manor High School
 AL/HA/HU LS17 .... 83 F4
Carr Manor Primary School
 AL/HA/HU LS17 .... 83 F4
Carr Wood Industrial Estate
 CAS WF10 .... 168 C3
Cartwright Hall Art Gallery
 HTON BD9 .... 97 H2
Castlefields Industrial Estate
 BGLY BD16 .... 55 G6
Castleford Health Centre
 CAS WF10 .... 148 C7
Castleford High School
 CAS WF10 .... 148 C7
Castleford RUFC
 CAS WF10 .... 167 J3
Castleford Swimming Pool
 CAS WF10 .... 148 A2
Castleford Tigers RLFC
 (The Jungle)
 CAS WF10 .... 148 E6
Castle Grove Infant School
 WKFDW/WTN WF2 .... 185 K1
Castle Hall School
 MIRF WF14 .... 179 J4
The Castle Special School
 CAS WF10 .... 169 H1
Castleton Primary School
 WOR/ARM LS12 .... 12 D2
Cas Whitwood Mere
 Middle School
 CAS WF10 .... 147 K7
Cathedral Retail Park
 WKFDW/WTN WF2 .... 18 D7
The Cathedral School
 WKFDW/WTN WF2 .... 184 B6
Cawley J I & N School
 HECK WF16 .... 160 B4
Central Library,
 Museum & Art Gallery
 LDS LS1 .... 9 M8
Centre 27 Business Park
 BTLY WF17 .... 140 E4
Chantry Bridge
 Industrial Estate
 WKFDE WF1 .... 18 F7
Chapel Allerton Hospital
 CHAL LS7 .... 83 K7
Chapel Allerton
 Medical Centre
 CHAL LS7 .... 83 J6
Chapel Allerton Primary School
 CHAL LS7 .... 83 H6
Chapel Grange Special School
 GIR BD8 .... 96 B5
Chapeltown Business Centre
 CHAL LS7 .... 10 D1
Chapeltown Health Centre
 CHAL LS7 .... 10 E3
Chel House Business Centre
 HIPP HX3 .... 136 B7
Chellow Dene Middle School
 GIR BD8 .... 96 C5
Chequerfield Infant School
 PONT WF8 .... 190 A2

Chesham Building
 GTHN BD7 .... 5 H8
Chesney Park Industrial Estate
 MID LS10 .... 14 C7
Chevet Business Centre
 KNOT WF11 .... 170 D5
Chevin Forest Park
 OT LS21 .... 40 A5
Chickenley Community
 J & I School
 EARL WF12 .... 181 K2
Chickenley Medical Clinic &
 Health Centre
 EARL WF12 .... 181 K2
Chippendale Junior School
 OT LS21 .... 27 G7
Chohan Medical Centre
 WBOW BD5 .... 117 J2
Christ Church J & I School
 LUD/ILL HX2 .... 134 A7
Christ Church Junior School
 RPDN/SBR HX6 .... 153 K3
Christ Church Primary School
 WOR/ARM LS12 .... 102 A5
Christ Church Woodhouse
 J & I School
 HUDN HD2 .... 177 J5
Christ the King RC
 Primary School
 BRAM LS13 .... 101 H4
Church School
 CUL/QBY BD13 .... 95 H7
Churwell Primary School
 MOR LS27 .... 122 A7
Cineworld
 BFD BD1 .... 6 A6
 WKFDW/WTN WF2 .... 18 C7
City Link Industrial Park
 BOW BD4 .... 7 M7
City of Leeds School
 HDGY LS6 .... 103 F1
City of Wakefield Golf Club
 WKFDW/WTN WF2 .... 183 K7
City Park Industrial Estate
 WOR/ARM LS12 .... 122 B3
City Varieties Music Hall
 LDS LS1 .... 10 A9
Civic Theatre
 DEWS WF13 .... 161 F6
 HFAX HX1 .... 17 G7
Clapgate Primary School
 MID LS10 .... 144 A2
Clayton CE First School
 CLAY BD14 .... 116 B2
Clayton Cemetery
 CLAY BD14 .... 116 C1
Clayton CE First School
 CLAY BD14 .... 116 A2
Clayton Golf Club
 CLAY BD14 .... 116 B3
Clayton Hospital
 WKFDE WF1 .... 18 D2
Clayton Middle School
 CLAY BD14 .... 116 B2
Cleckheaton & District
 Golf Club
 CLECK BD19 .... 138 C5
Cleckheaton Sports Club
 CLECK BD19 .... 138 D5
Clevedon House School
 ILK LS29 .... 25 F7
Cliffe Castle Museum & Gallery
 KGHY BD21 .... 2 F1
Cliffe Hill School
 HIPP HX3 .... 157 F2
Cliffe Middle School
 BFDE BD3 .... 6 B1
Cliff School
 WKFDE WF1 .... 18 D1
Clifton Cemetery
 BRIG HD6 .... 157 K6
Clifton Forge Business Park
 KNOT WF11 .... 171 F4
Clifton Infant School
 HOR/CROF WF4 .... 182 E6
Cobblers Lane J & I School
 PONT WF8 .... 190 B1
Cobden Primary School
 WOR/ARM LS12 .... 121 J2
Cockburn High School
 BEE/HOL LS11 .... 123 F7
Cocksford Golf Club
 TAD LS24 .... 70 B7
College of Art & Design
 LDSU LS2 .... 9 M7
College of Technology
 LDSU LS2 .... 9 M7
College of Technology (Annexe)
 OSM LS9 .... 14 E2
The College
 WKFDE WF1 .... 18 E2
Colour Museum
 BFD BD1 .... 5 K6
Colton Primary School
 MSTN/BAR LS15 .... 106 B7
Colton Retail Park
 MSTN/BAR LS15 .... 106 C6
Common Road
 Industrial Estate
 LM/WK BD12 .... 137 J1
Community Clinic
 HORS LS18 .... 80 E3
Conway Medical Centre
 RHAY LS8 .... 11 J3
Cookridge Hall
 Golf & Country Club
 BHP/TINH LS16 .... 61 J5
Cookridge Hospital
 BHP/TINH LS16 .... 81 H1
Cookridge Primary School
 BHP/TINH LS16 .... 61 H7
Co-operative Shopping Parade
 HIPP HX3 .... 136 B7
Cooper Lane First School
 WBSY BD6 .... 116 B5
Copley Hill Trading Estate
 WOR/ARM LS12 .... 12 E5

Copley Primary School
 HIPP HX3 .... 154 E7
Copperfields College
 OSM LS9 .... 15 J4
Copthorne First School
 GTHN BD7 .... 117 H1
Copwood Mental Health Clinic
 BOW BD4 .... 119 F2
Coronation Business Centre
 KGHY BD21 .... 3 J1
Corpus Christi Primary School
 OSM LS9 .... 104 E6
Corpus Christi RC High School
 OSM LS9 .... 105 F5
Cottage Road Picture House
 HDGY LS6 .... 82 B6
Cottingley Clinic
 BGLY BD16 .... 75 K5
Cottingley Community
 Health Centre
 BEE/HOL LS11 .... 122 C5
Cottingley First School
 BGLY BD16 .... 76 A5
Cottingley Hall Crematorium
 BEE/HOL LS11 .... 122 C4
Cottingley Primary School
 BEE/HOL LS11 .... 122 B5
Covered Market
 KGHY BD21 .... 3 G5
Craven Road Medical Centre
 HDGY LS6 .... 9 M2
Crawshaw School
 PDSY/CALV LS28 .... 100 C6
Crossflatts Cricket Club
 BGLY BD16 .... 55 G5
Crossflatts First School
 BGLY BD16 .... 55 H5
Cross Flatts Park
 Primary School
 BEE/HOL LS11 .... 123 F4
Cross Gates Primary School
 SCFT LS14 .... 105 H3
Crossgates Shopping Centre
 MSTN/BAR LS15 .... 105 K3
Cross Green Industrial Estate
 OSM LS9 .... 15 K5
Cross Hall Infant School
 MOR LS27 .... 141 J4
Cross Lane Business Park
 LVSG WF15 .... 159 H4
Crosslane Industrial Estate
 LVSG WF15 .... 159 H4
Cross Lane Primary School
 ELL HX5 .... 175 H4
Crossley Hall First &
 Middle School
 GIR BD8 .... 96 D6
Crossley Heath School
 HFAX HX1 .... 154 E4
Crossley Retail Park
 HFAX HX1 .... 16 E4
Crossley Street
 Primary School
 WBY LS22 .... 29 H3
Crowlees CE School
 MIRF WF14 .... 179 H4
Crown Point Retail Park
 MID LS10 .... 14 B4
Cuckoo Nest Industrial Estate
 GTHN BD7 .... 5 G6
Cullingworth First School
 CUL/QBY BD13 .... 74 A6
Cullingworth Medical Centre
 CUL/QBY BD13 .... 74 A6
Dales Bank Holiday Park
 AIRE BD20 .... 20 E4
Dansk Way
 ILK LS29 .... 24 B4
Darrington CE J & I School
 PONT WF8 .... 190 E4
Deanfield County
 Primary School
 LUD/ILL HX2 .... 134 B4
Delf Hill Middle School
 LM/WK BD12 .... 137 H1
Denholme Clinic
 CUL/QBY BD13 .... 94 A4
Denholme First School
 CUL/QBY BD13 .... 94 A4
Dental Institute
 LDSU LS2 .... 9 K7
Dewsbury Bus Station
 EARL WF12 .... 181 F2
Dewsbury Cemetery
 DEWS WF13 .... 180 D2
Dewsbury College
 DEWS WF13 .... 160 E7
Dewsbury District Golf Club
 MIRF WF14 .... 180 A6
Dewsbury & District Hospital
 DEWS WF13 .... 160 D6
Dewsbury Moor Crematorium
 DEWS WF13 .... 180 D1
Dewsbury Moor
 Infant & Nursery School
 DEWS WF13 .... 160 C6
Dewsbury Museum &
 Art Gallery
 DEWS WF13 .... 180 D2
Dewsbury Sports Centre
 EARL WF12 .... 181 G1
Dimplewell Infant School
 OSS WF5 .... 182 C5
District Archives Office
 WKFDE WF1 .... 18 C2
Dixon Lane Medical Centre
 WOR/ARM LS12 .... 12 D7
Dixons City
 Technology College
 WBOW BD5 .... 117 K2
Dockfield Industrial Estate
 BAIL BD17 .... 77 H4
Domestic Street
 Industrial Estate
 BEE/HOL LS11 .... 13 G4
Dominion Industrial Park
 HIPP HX3 .... 136 B7

Drakes Industrial Estate
LUD/ILL HX2 .... 134 D3
Drighlington Junior School
BIRK/DRI BD11 .... 120 C7
Drug Addiction Clinic
LDSU LS2 .... 9 J1
Drummond Middle School
GIR BD8 .... 5 G2
Drummond Trading Estate
GIR BD8 .... 5 J3
Dudley Hill First School
BOW BD4 .... 118 D3
Eagles Yard Business Park
WKFDE WF1 .... 18 F5
Earlsheaton High School
EARL WF12 .... 181 H1
Earlsheaton Infant School
EARL WF12 .... 181 J2
East Ardsley Health Centre
EARD/LOFT WF3 .... 163 G1
East Ardsley J I & N School
EARD/LOFT WF3 .... 143 J7
East Ardsley Primary School
EARD/LOFT WF3 .... 143 J7
East Ardsley United Cricket
& Athletic Club
EARD/LOFT WF3 .... 163 H2
East Bierley CE First School
BOW BD4 .... 119 G7
East Bierley Cricket Club
BIRK/DRI BD11 .... 139 F1
East Bierley Golf Club
BOW BD4 .... 119 F7
Eastborough J I & N School
EARL WF12 .... 181 G1
Eastburn J & I School
AIRE BD20 .... 32 A4
East Garforth Primary School
GFTH/SHER LS25 .... 108 A5
East Leeds Clinic
OSM LS9 .... 11 M7
East Leeds Leisure Centre
MSTN/BAR LS15 .... 105 F6
Eastmoor Health Centre
WKFDE WF1 .... 19 L1
East Morton First School
AIRE BD20 .... 55 F2
Eastwood First School
KGHY BD21 .... 3 J2
Eccleshill Clinic & Health Centre
IDLE BD10 .... 78 E6
Eccleshill Cricket Club
IDLE BD10 .... 78 E7
Eccleshill North Middle School
IDLE BD10 .... 79 F6
Eccleshill School
IDLE BD10 .... 79 F7
Eccleshill United Sports Club
ECHL BD2 .... 78 A6
Eldwick First School
BGLY BD16 .... 56 B6
Elizabeth Industrial Estate
HFAX HX1 .... 16 D3
Elland CE School
ELL HX5 .... 175 J2
Elland Old Earth School
ELL HX5 .... 176 B2
Elland Road Industrial Park
BEE/HOL LS11 .... 122 C3
Ellen Royde Health Centre
ELL HX5 .... 175 H2
Elmfield Business Park
GFTH/SHER LS25 .... 107 K5
Emmanuel Trading Estate
WOR/ARM LS12 .... 13 H3
Empire Business Centre
LUD/ILL HX2 .... 134 D2
England Lane J & I School
KNOT WF11 .... 171 H5
English Martyrs RC
Primary School
WKFDW/WTN WF2 ...... 183 J4
Enterprise Park
Industrial Estate
BEE/HOL LS11 .... 122 E5
Environmental Business Centre
MOR LS27 .... 141 K3
Esholt & Aire
Bronians Sports Club
BAIL BD17 .... 58 C6
Essex Park Industrial Estate
BFDE BD3 .... 6 C8
Eureka the Museum
for Children
HIPP HX3 .... 17 J7
Euroway Trading Estate
BOW BD4 .... 138 B1
The Eye Clinic
GTHN BD7 .... 5 H6
Fagley First School
ECHL BD2 .... 98 E3
Fairburn Community School
KNOT WF11 .... 150 B3
Fairburn Sports &
Recreation Centre
KNOT WF11 .... 150 B3
Fairfield Special School
HECK WF16 .... 160 B3
Fairway Industrial Estate
BTLY WF17 .... 140 C5
Farfield Primary School
PDSY/CALV LS28 .... 99 K3
Farnham First School
GTHN BD7 .... 4 D9
Farnley CE Primary School
OT LS21 .... 27 K4
Farnley Park High School
WOR/ARM LS12 .... 121 H2
Farrow Medical Centre
BFDE BD3 .... 6 B3
Farsley Celtic AFC
PDSY/CALV LS28 .... 100 B3
Farsley Community Clinic
PDSY/CALV LS28 .... 99 K2
Fartown High School
HUDN HD2 .... 177 H7
Fearnville Sports Centre
RHAY LS8 .... 104 E1

Featherbank Infant School
HORS LS18 .... 80 E4
Featherstone Cemetery
FEA/AMT WF7 .... 168 A6
Featherstone High School
FEA/AMT WF7 .... 188 E4
Featherstone Sports Centre
FEA/AMT WF7 .... 188 E5
Felnex Trading Estate
OSM LS9 .... 124 D1
Fentham Industrial Estate
BRIC HD6 .... 157 F7
Ferniehurst First School
BAIL BD17 .... 77 H2
Fernley Green
Industrial Estate
KNOT WF11 .... 171 J4
Ferrybridge Infant School
KNOT WF11 .... 170 D3
Feversham College
BFDE BD3 .... 6 C7
Feversham Street First School
BFDE BD3 .... 6 F6
Fieldhead Carr Primary School
SCFT LS14 .... 85 J3
Field Head Hospital
WKFDE WF1 .... 164 E6
Fieldhead J & I School
BTLY WF17 .... 140 C4
Field Lane Infant School
BTLY WF17 .... 161 G4
First Avenue Industrial Estate
PDSY/CALV LS28 .... 100 B5
Fir Tree Primary School
AL/HA/HU LS17 .... 83 J1
Fixby J & I School
HUDN HD2 .... 177 F5
Flanshaw J & I School
WKFDW/WTN WF2 ...... 184 A2
Flushdyke Primary School
OSS WF5 .... 182 E2
Forster Square Retail Park
BFD BD1 .... 5 L3
Foundry Industrial Estate
KNOT WF11 .... 170 D3
PDSY/CALV LS28 .... 100 B4
The Fountain Medical Centre
MOR LS27 .... 141 K4
Four Lanes Business Park
GIR BD8 .... 4 A4
Fowler Street Industrial Estate
BOW BD4 .... 118 C1
Foxhill First School
CUL/QBY BD13 .... 115 C4
Friars Industrial Estate
IDLE BD10 .... 78 C5
Frizinghall First &
Middle School
HTON BD9 .... 77 H7
Frizinghall Medical Centre
HTON BD9 .... 97 G1
The Froebelian School
HORS LS18 .... 80 E5
Frost Hill Business Park
LVSG WF15 .... 159 J4
Fulford Grange Hospital
YEA LS19 .... 79 H1
Fulneck Golf Club
PDSY/CALV LS28 .... 120 A2
Fulneck School
PDSY/CALV LS28 .... 120 B2
Garforth Clinic
GFTH/SHER LS25 .... 107 H7
Garforth Community College
GFTH/SHER LS25 .... 107 H7
Garforth Golf Club
GFTH/SHER LS25 .... 107 J2
Garforth Leisure Centre
GFTH/SHER LS25 .... 107 K6
Garforth Medical Centre
GFTH/SHER LS25 .... 107 H6
Gateways School
AL/HA/HU LS17 .... 44 B4
Gawthorpe Primary School
OSS WF5 .... 162 B7
Gelderd Business Park
WOR/ARM LS12 .... 12 C8
Gelderd Trading Estate
WOR/ARM LS12 .... 12 F6
Gemini Business Park
CHAL LS7 .... 10 C3
Ghyll Royd School
ILK LS29 .... 23 J6
Gibson Lane Junior School
GFTH/SHER LS25 .... 128 A5
Gildersome Junior School
MOR LS27 .... 121 F7
Gilstead Middle School
BGLY BD16 .... 56 B7
Girlington First School
GIR BD8 .... 4 C2
Girlington Industrial Centre
GIR BD8 .... 4 C4
Girnhill Infant School
FEA/AMT WF7 .... 188 B5
Glasshoughton Infant School
CAS WF10 .... 168 D1
The Gleddings School
HIPP HX3 .... 154 D5
Gledhow Primary School
RHAY LS8 .... 84 A4
Glenaire First School
BAIL BD17 .... 77 F2
Glen Cable Tramway
BAIL BD17 .... 76 E2
Glenfield Caravan Park
AL/HA/HU LS17 .... 65 G2
Golden Acre Park & Gardens
BHP/TINH LS16 .... 62 A3
Gomersal CE Middle School
CLECK BD19 .... 139 K6
Gomersal First School
CLECK BD19 .... 139 J6
The Good Health Centre
RHAY LS8 .... 84 B2
Gordon Street J & I School
FEA/AMT WF7 .... 188 C2

Gotts Park Golf Club
WOR/ARM LS12 .... 101 K4
Grafton School
HDGY LS6 .... 9 M2
Grand Theatre & Opera House
LDSU LS2 .... 10 A8
Grangefield Industrial Estate
PDSY/CALV LS28 .... 100 C4
The Grange Medical Centre
SCFT LS14 .... 85 J7
Grange Middle School
AIRE BD20 .... 54 B2
Grange Road Business Park
BTLY WF17 .... 161 H5
Grange Road First School
GTHN BD7 .... 4 D9
Grange Road Industrial Estate
BTLY WF17 .... 161 H4
Grange Upper School
WBOW BD5 .... 117 G4
Great Horton Cricket Club
GTHN BD7 .... 117 F3
Great Horton Industrial Estate
WBSY BD6 .... 116 C4
Great Horton Middle School
GTHN BD7 .... 117 F2
Great & Little Preston CE
Infants School
RTHW LS26 .... 127 H7
Great & Little Preston
Junior School
RTHW LS26 .... 127 H7
Greenfield Primary School
GFTH/SHER LS25 .... 127 K4
Greenfield School
IDLE BD10 .... 78 C3
Greengates First School
IDLE BD10 .... 79 F5
Greenhead Athletics Track
KGHY BD21 .... 53 J2
Greenhead Grammar School
AIRE BD20 .... 53 H1
Greenhill CP School
BRAM LS13 .... 101 G5
Greenhill Infant & Juniors School
WKFDE WF1 .... 19 J3
Green Lane Industrial Estate
FEA/AMT WF7 .... 187 K3
Green Lane Primary School
GFTH/SHER LS25 .... 108 A4
Green Leas School
PONT WF8 .... 189 K4
Green Meadows School
GSLY LS20 .... 58 D2
Greenmount Primary School
BEE/HOL LS11 .... 13 L9
Green Mount Retail Park
HFAX HX1 .... 16 E5
Greenwood Primary School
BEE/HOL LS11 .... 13 M8
Greetland Cricket &
Bowling Club
GTL/HWG HX4 .... 175 F2
Greetland J & I School
GTL/HWG HX4 .... 174 D2
Greetland Mixed School
GTL/HWG HX4 .... 174 E2
Gregory Middle School
WBOW BD5 .... 118 B5
Gresley Road Industrial Estate
KGHY BD21 .... 3 H5
Grove House First School
ECHL BD2 .... 98 B1
Grove Mills Industrial Estate
ELL HX5 .... 175 K2
Guiseley AFC
GSLY LS20 .... 58 D2
Guiseley Cemetery
ILK LS29 .... 38 D7
Guiseley County Infant School
GSLY LS20 .... 59 F2
Guiseley School
GSLY LS20 .... 58 E3
Gulsyke Medical Centre
MSTN/BAR LS15 .... 105 H6
Haigh Hall Medical Centre
IDLE BD10 .... 78 E5
Haigh Road Infant School
RTHW LS26 .... 145 F1
Hainsworth Moor J & I School
CUL/QBY BD13 .... 115 G6
Half Acres J & I School
CAS WF10 .... 168 B1
Halfpenny Lane J & I School
PONT WF8 .... 189 G1
Halifax Blue Sox RLFC
(The Shay Stadium)
HFAX HX1 .... 17 H9
Halifax Bradley Hall Golf Club
GTL/HWG HX4 .... 174 D4
Halifax Building Society
HFAX HX1 .... 17 G7
Halifax Catholic High School
LUD/ILL HX2 .... 134 D1
Halifax Cricket Ground
HFAX HX1 .... 154 B1
Halifax Golf Club
LUD/ILL HX2 .... 113 K5
Halifax High School
HFAX HX1 .... 17 G8
Halifax Industrial Centre
HFAX HX1 .... 16 D4
Halifax Leisure Centre
HFAX HX1 .... 17 H7
Halifax RUFC
LUD/ILL HX2 .... 134 C3
Halifax Swimming Pool
HFAX HX1 .... 17 H8
Halifax Town FC
(The Shay Stadium)
HFAX HX1 .... 17 H9
Halton Building
GTHN BD7 .... 5 J7
Hambleton First School
BOW BD4 .... 118 C6
Hanging Heaton CE J & I School
BTLY WF17 .... 161 J5

Hanging Heaton Golf Club
EARL WF12 .... 161 H6
Hanson Upper School
ECHL BD2 .... 98 A1
Harden First School
BGLY BD16 .... 74 D3
Harehills Middle School
RHAY LS8 .... 11 H3
Harehills Primary School
RHAY LS8 .... 11 J3
Harewood CE Primary School
AL/HA/HU LS17 .... 44 B3
Harewood House &
Bird Garden
AL/HA/HU LS17 .... 43 K4
Hartington Middle School
HWTH BD22 .... 72 D5
Hartshead J & I School
LVSG WF15 .... 158 D6
Hatfield Hall Golf Club
EARD/LOFT WF3 .... 165 F5
Hawksworth CE School
GSLY LS20 .... 57 K3
Hawksworth Wood
Primary School
KSTL LS5 .... 81 H5
Haworth School
HWTH BD22 .... 72 D5
Haycliffe Special School
WBSY BD6 .... 117 G4
Headfield CE Junior School
EARL WF12 .... 181 F4
Headingley Golf Club
BHP/TINH LS16 .... 62 C6
Headingley Primary School
HDGY LS6 .... 82 C7
Headlands CE J & I School
LVSG WF15 .... 159 H4
Headley Golf Club
CUL/QBY BD13 .... 115 G1
Headrow Shopping Centre
LDS LS1 .... 10 A9
Headway Business Park
WKFDW/WTN WF2 ...... 184 C6
Healey J & I School
BTLY WF17 .... 160 C4
Heather Grove First School
HTON BD9 .... 96 C2
Heathfield Industrial Estate
ELL HX5 .... 175 K3
Heathfield-Rishworth School
RPDN/SBR HX6 .... 172 D7
Heath View Community School
WKFDE WF1 .... 19 K3
Heaton Middle School
HTON BD9 .... 96 C1
Heaton Royds Hospital
HTON BD9 .... 76 C7
Heaton Royds Special School
SHPY BD18 .... 77 F7
Hebble Brook Business Park
LUD/ILL HX2 .... 113 K7
Heckmondwike
Grammar School
HECK WF16 .... 160 A4
Heckmondwike Sports Club
HECK WF16 .... 160 A4
Henry Moore Clinic
CAS WF10 .... 168 C1
Highbank First School
LVSG WF15 .... 158 C3
Highcliffe Industrial Estate
MOR LS27 .... 141 J2
High Crags First School
SHPY BD18 .... 77 H6
High Fernley First School
LM/WK BD12 .... 137 H4
Highfield Middle School
KGHY BD21 .... 2 D4
Highfield Primary School
AL/HA/HU LS17 .... 63 K7
Highfield School
OSS WF5 .... 162 C7
The Highfields
Medical Centre
BRAM LS13 .... 101 G3
High Royds Hospital
ILK LS29 .... 58 C1
Hightown School
LVSG WF15 .... 158 D3
High Trees School
BSPA/BRAM LS23 .... 48 D4
Hillcrest Primary School
CHAL LS7 .... 10 F1
Hillside Works
Industrial Estate
CLECK BD19 .... 138 E5
Hill Top CE First School
LM/WK BD12 .... 137 H1
Hill Top Infant School
EARD/LOFT WF3 .... 162 C3
Hipperholme Clinic
HIPP HX3 .... 136 C7
Hipperholme Grammar School
HIPP HX3 .... 136 B7
Hipperholme & Lightcliffe
High School
HIPP HX3 .... 156 E1
HM Prison
BSPA/BRAM LS23 .... 31 F7
WKFDW/WTN WF2 ...... 18 B4
HM Prison Service College
WKFDW/WTN WF2 ...... 18 C4
HM Young Offender Institution
WBY LS22 .... 30 A2
Hockney Road Industrial Estate
GIR BD8 .... 4 D3
IDLE BD10 .... 78 C7
Hollingwood First School
GTHN BD7 .... 116 D3
Hollywood Bowl
BULY LS4 .... 8 B6
Holmefield First School
BOW BD4 .... 119 G2
Holme Middle School
BOW BD4 .... 118 D3
Holme Wood Health Centre
BOW BD4 .... 119 F3

Holmfield Industrial Estate
LUD/ILL HX2 .... 114 D7
Holycroft First School
KGHY BD21 .... 2 E7
Holy Family RC Primary School
WOR/ARM LS12 .... 12 C1
Holy Family & St Michaels RC
Primary School
PONT WF8 .... 170 B7
Holy Family School
KGHY BD21 .... 2 D1
Holy Name RC Primary School
BHP/TINH LS16 .... 81 J1
Holy Rosary & St Annes RC
Primary School
CHAL LS7 .... 10 D3
Holy Trinity CE First School
BGLY BD16 .... 75 K2
Holy Trinity CE J & I School
OSS WF5 .... 182 C3
Holy Trinity CE Primary School
BHP/TINH LS16 .... 61 G6
Holy Trinity CE Senior School
LUD/ILL HX2 .... 134 C1
Holy Trinity Infant School
HFAX HX1 .... 16 E8
Holy Trinity Junior School
HFAX HX1 .... 16 E8
Holywell Green
Primary School
GTL/HWG HX4 .... 174 E5
Homestead Clinic
WKFDW/WTN WF2 ...... 184 A3
Hopton Junior Infant &
Nursery School
MIRF WF14 .... 179 G5
The Horsefair Centre
WBY LS22 .... 29 H4
Horsfall Stadium
WBSY BD6 .... 117 G7
Horsforth Golf Club
HORS LS18 .... 80 C1
Horsforth Hall Park
Cricket Club
HORS LS18 .... 81 H4
Horsforth Newlaithes
Junior School
HORS LS18 .... 80 D6
Horsforth School
HORS LS18 .... 80 E2
Horsforth Village Museum
HORS LS18 .... 80 D4
Horsforth Woodside CE
Primary School
HORS LS18 .... 81 G3
Horton Bank Top First School
GTHN BD7 .... 116 D4
Horton Park First School
WBOW BD5 .... 117 G2
Hothfield Street Junior School
AIRE BD20 .... 32 E1
Hovingham Primary School
RHAY LS8 .... 11 K1
Howden Clough High School
BTLY WF17 .... 140 E6
Howden Clough
Industrial Estate
BTLY WF17 .... 140 E4
Howland Centre
EARL WF12 .... 181 F1
Howley Hall Golf Club
MOR LS27 .... 161 H1
Howley Park Trading Estate
MOR LS27 .... 141 K5
Hoyle Court First School
BAIL BD17 .... 77 F1
Hoyle Head Mills
Industrial Estate
EARL WF12 .... 181 J2
Huddersfield Crematorium
HUDN HD2 .... 177 F3
Huddersfield Golf Club
(Fixby Hall)
HUDN HD2 .... 176 D6
Huddersfield Technical College
HUDN HD2 .... 177 J7
Hugh Gaitskell Primary School
BEE/HOL LS11 .... 122 D4
Hungate Primary School
GFTH/SHER LS25 .... 111 F5
Hunslet Business Park
MID LS10 .... 14 E6
Hunslet Carr Primary School
MID LS10 .... 123 K4
Hunslet Hall Shopping Centre
BEE/HOL LS11 .... 13 M8
Hunslet Health Centre
MID LS10 .... 14 F8
Hunslet Moor
Primary School
BEE/HOL LS11 .... 14 A9
Hunslet St Josephs RC
Primary School
MID LS10 .... 14 E7
Hunslet St Marys CE
Primary School
MID LS10 .... 14 E9
Hunslet Trading Estate
MID LS10 .... 15 H9
Hutton J & I School
IDLE BD10 .... 78 D7
Hutton Middle School
ECHL BD2 .... 78 D7
Hyde Park Picture House
HDGY LS6 .... 8 F3
Hyrstmount Junior School
BTLY WF17 .... 161 F5
Ida & Robert
Arthington Hospital
BHP/TINH LS16 .... 81 H2
Idle CE School
IDLE BD10 .... 78 C3
Idle Cricket Club
IDLE BD10 .... 78 C5
Idle Medical Centre
IDLE BD10 .... 78 C4
Ilkley Golf Club
ILK LS29 .... 23 J3

Ilkley Grammar School
ILK LS29 .... 24 B6
Ilkley Health Centre
ILK LS29 .... 24 B6
Ilkley Middle School
ILK LS29 .... 24 D5
Ilkley Swimming Baths
ILK LS29 .... 24 A4
Immaculate Heart of
Mary Primary School
AL/HA/HU LS17 .... 83 H3
Industrial & Commercial Centre
LDSU LS2 .... 10 D7
Industrial Avenue
BTLY WF17 .... 140 B6
Industrial Light Estate
CHAL LS7 .... 103 G1
Ingfield Business Centre
HUDN HD2 .... 177 K6
Inglebrook Business Centre
PONT WF8 .... 169 J7
Ingram Road Primary School
BEE/HOL LS11 .... 13 G6
Ingrow First & Infant School
HWTH BD22 .... 53 H7
Intake High School
BRAM LS13 .... 100 D2
Ireland Wood Primary School
BHP/TINH LS16 .... 61 K7
Iveson Primary School
BHP/TINH LS16 .... 81 K2
Jacksons Estate
OSS WF5 .... 182 D2
Jawbone Industrial Estate
RTHW LS26 .... 124 C7
Jerry Clay Lane
Primary School
WKFDW/WTN WF2 .... 163 J6
Joe Dean Recreation Centre
WOR/ARM LS12 .... 101 J6
John Jamieson School
RHAY LS8 .... 84 D7
John O'Gaunts Trading Estate
RTHW LS26 .... 125 F7
John Smeaton High School
MSTN/BAR LS15 .... 106 B2
John Smeaton Sports Centre
MSTN/BAR LS15 .... 106 B1
John Street Market
BFD BD1 .... 5 L5
Joseph Priestley College
MOR LS27 .... 142 A3
Junction 25 Business Park
MIRF WF14 .... 179 G4
Junction 1 Retail Park
BEE/HOL LS11 .... 122 C4
Keelham First School
CUL/QBY BD13 .... 114 C1
Keighley Business Centre
KGHY BD21 .... 2 F8
Keighley College
KGHY BD21 .... 3 K3
KGHY BD21 .... 3 G4
Keighley Crematorium
HWTH BD22 .... 72 B1
Keighley Cricket Club
KGHY BD21 .... 3 H1
Keighley Golf Club
AIRE BD20 .... 33 J6
Keighley Industrial Park
KGHY BD21 .... 53 K2
Keighley Leisure Centre
KGHY BD21 .... 3 J2
Keighley Retail Park
KGHY BD21 .... 3 H1
Keighley RUFC
AIRE BD20 .... 33 G7
Keighley St Andrew's
Primary School
HWTH BD22 .... 2 D5
Keighley & Worth
Valley Railway
HWTH BD22 .... 72 D5
HWTH BD22 .... 73 G2
KGHY BD21 .... 3 G8
KGHY BD21 .... 53 J7
Kensington Street
Health Centre
GIR BD8 .... 4 C3
Kents Sports Club
ECHL BD2 .... 98 C1
Kerr Mackie Primary School
RHAY LS8 .... 84 B5
Kershaw Drive Health Centre
LUD/ILL HX2 .... 132 E7
Killingbeck Retail Park
SCFT LS14 .... 105 G3
Killinghall First School
BFDE BD3 .... 7 G2
Kings High School
PONT WF8 .... 189 H2
Kippax Health Centre
GFTH/SHER LS25 .... 128 A4
Kippax Infant School
GFTH/SHER LS25 .... 127 K5
Kippax Leisure Centre
GFTH/SHER LS25 .... 127 J5
Kippax North Primary School
GFTH/SHER LS25 .... 127 J2
Kirk Fenton Primary School
TAD LS24 .... 91 K5
Kirkfields Business Centre
YEA LS19 .... 59 H4
Kirkgate Business Centre
WKFDE WF1 .... 19 H7
Kirkgate Market
LDS LS1 .... 10 B9
Kirkgate Shopping
Centre & Market
BFD BD1 .... 5 L6
Kirkhamgate Primary School
WKFDW/WTN WF2 .... 163 G6
Kirkstall Abbey (remains of)
KSTL LS5 .... 81 J7
Kirkstall Health Clinic
KSTL LS5 .... 101 K1
Kirkstall Industrial Park
BULY LS4 .... 8 C6

Kirkstall Leisure Centre
KSTL LS5 .... 101 K1
Kirkstall Valley Primary School
BULY LS4 .... 8 A5
Knottingley CE (C) J & I School
KNOT WF11 .... 171 H4
Knottingley Vale J & I School
KNOT WF11 .... 170 E4
Knowle Spring
Industrial Estate
KGHY BD21 .... 2 F9
LA Bowl
BEE/HOL LS11 .... 13 L4
Ladderbank Middle School
BAIL BD17 .... 57 K7
Lady Anne Business Park
BTLY WF17 .... 161 G2
Lady E Hastings CE
Primary School
BSPA/BRAM LS23 .... 48 D1
Lady Elizabeth Hastings CE
Primary School
WBY LS22 .... 46 D1
Lady Lane Park School
BGLY BD16 .... 55 K6
Laisterdyke Clinic
BFDE BD3 .... 7 J6
Laisterdyke Middle School
BFDE BD3 .... 7 K5
Lakeside Industrial Estate
WOR/ARM LS12 .... 101 H6
Langdale Primary School
RTHW LS26 .... 125 J7
Lapage Middle School
BFDE BD3 .... 7 G4
Larks Hill Primary School
PONT WF8 .... 189 G3
Latchmere Industrial Park
WOR/ARM LS12 .... 12 D8
WOR/ARM LS12 .... 12 B9
Laura Mitchell Health Centre
HFAX HX1 .... 17 G5
Lawefield First School
WKFDW/WTN WF2 .... 18 B6
Lawns Park Primary School
WOR/ARM LS12 .... 121 H1
Lawnswood Business Park
BHP/TINH LS16 .... 81 K3
Lawnswood Cemetery
BHP/TINH LS16 .... 82 A1
Lawnswood Crematorium
BHP/TINH LS16 .... 82 A1
Lawnswood School
BHP/TINH LS16 .... 82 A4
Laycock First School
HWTH BD22 .... 52 D4
Leaventhorpe Middle School
WIL/AL BD15 .... 96 A6
Lee Bridge Industrial Estate
HFAX HX1 .... 16 D3
Lee Brigg First School
NORM WF6 .... 166 D4
Leeds & Bradford Airport
Industrial Estate
YEA LS19 .... 60 B2
Leeds Bradford
International Airport
YEA LS19 .... 60 C4
The Leeds Business Centre
MOR LS27 .... 141 H3
Leeds College of Art & Design
LDSU LS2 .... 9 L4
Leeds College of Building
LDSU LS2 .... 10 C7
Leeds College of Music
OSM LS9 .... 10 D9
Leeds College of Technology
BEE/HOL LS11 .... 123 F4
Leeds Community &
Mental Health Services
PDSY/CALV LS28 .... 100 B6
Leeds Community &
Mental Health Services
Teaching NHS Trust
WOR/ARM LS12 .... 12 E3
Leeds General Infirmary
LDSU LS2 .... 9 K7
Leeds Girls High School
HDGY LS6 .... 9 G1
Leeds Golf Centre
AL/HA/HU LS17 .... 64 D2
Leeds Golf Club
RHAY LS8 .... 84 E4
Leeds Grammar Junior School
AL/HA/HU LS17 .... 64 A4
Leeds Grammar School
AL/HA/HU LS17 .... 64 A5
HDGY LS6 .... 9 H5
Leeds & Hull Business Centre
LDSU LS2 .... 9 L5
Leeds 27 Industrial Estate
MOR LS27 .... 141 G3
Leeds Industrial Museum
WOR/ARM LS12 .... 8 C8
Leeds International
Swimming Pool
LDS LS1 .... 9 K9
Leeds Islamia Girls School
CHAL LS7 .... 83 J6
Leeds Metropolitan University
HDGY LS6 .... 82 B6
KSTL LS5 .... 101 J1
LDSU LS2 .... 9 M6
Leeds Plaza Shopping Centre
LDS LS1 .... 14 A1
Leeds Rhinos RLFC
(Headingley Stadium)
HDGY LS6 .... 8 B1
Leeds Road Hospital
BFDE BD3 .... 6 E6
The Leeds Teaching Hospitals
NHS Trust
BVRD LS3 .... 9 K8
Leeds Tykes RUFC
(Headingley Stadium)
HDGY LS6 .... 8 B1
Leeds United AFC (Elland Road)
BEE/HOL LS11 .... 12 E9

Leeds University
LDSU LS2 .... 9 J5
Lee Mills Industrial Estate
HFAX HX1 .... 16 E3
Lee Mount County
Primary School
HIPP HX3 .... 16 C2
Lees First School
HWTH BD22 .... 73 F4
Leeside J I & N School
HECK WF16 .... 160 B2
Leisure Centre
BGLY BD16 .... 74 E4
Leopold Primary School
CHAL LS7 .... 10 E3
Library Headquarters
WKFDW/WTN WF2 .... 18 B3
Lidget Green First School
GTHN BD7 .... 4 A7
Lidget Green Middle School
GTHN BD7 .... 4 B8
Lightcliffe CE Primary School
HIPP HX3 .... 156 D1
Lightcliffe Golf Club
HIPP HX3 .... 136 D7
Lightcliffe Preparatory School
HIPP HX3 .... 136 C7
Light Waves Sports Centre
WKFDE WF1 .... 18 F3
Lilycroft First School
HTON BD9 .... 97 G3
Little London CP School
CHAL LS7 .... 10 B4
Littlemoor Primary School
YEA LS19 .... 59 K7
Littletown J & I School
CLECK BD19 .... 159 H3
Liversedge Cricket Club
LVSG WF15 .... 159 G6
Lofthousegate J & I School
EARD/LOFT WF3 .... 164 E2
Longclose Industrial Estate
OSM LS9 .... 10 F5
Longlands Trading Estate
OSS WF5 .... 182 D3
Long Lee J & I School
KGHY BD21 .... 3 M8
Longroyde Junior School
BRIG HD6 .... 156 E7
Lorne First School
BOW BD4 .... 118 C2
Lotherton Hall
GFTH/SHER LS25 .... 89 H7
Lounge Cinema
HDGY LS6 .... 82 C7
Low Ash First School
SHPY BD18 .... 77 J6
Lowerfields Middle School
BOW BD4 .... 118 D2
Lower Grange Medical Centre
GIR BD8 .... 96 B6
Lower Wortley CP School
WOR/ARM LS12 .... 122 A1
Lowfields Business Park
ELL HX5 .... 176 A1
Low Laithes Golf Club
OSS WF5 .... 183 G1
Low Mills Industrial Estate
DEWS WF13 .... 180 A5
Low Moor Business Park
LM/WK BD12 .... 137 K1
Low Moor CE First School
LM/WK BD12 .... 137 J1
Low Road Primary School
MID LS10 .... 14 F8
Lowtown Primary School
PDSY/CALV LS28 .... 100 C6
Luddendenfoot J & I School
LUD/ILL HX2 .... 153 F3
Luddenden Primary School
LUD/ILL HX2 .... 132 E7
Lupset Group Medical Centre
WKFDW/WTN WF2 .... 183 J1
Lupset Hall (Club House)
WKFDW/WTN WF2 .... 184 A7
Lydgate J & I School
BTLY WF17 .... 161 J3
Lynfield Mount Hospital
HTON BD9 .... 96 C3
M1 Industrial Estate
MID LS10 .... 14 E8
Madni Muslim Girls High School
EARL WF12 .... 181 G3
Magnet Sports Club
TAD LS24 .... 70 D1
Mandale Middle School
WBSY BD6 .... 116 C6
Manningham Baths &
Sports Centre
GIR BD8 .... 4 F2
Manningham Clinic
GIR BD8 .... 5 J1
Manningham Middle School
GIR BD8 .... 5 J2
Manorfield Infant School
BTLY WF17 .... 160 D4
Manor House Gallery & Museum
ILK LS29 .... 24 A5
Manor Leisure Centre
YEA LS19 .... 59 H4
Manor Park Industrial Estate
BIRK/DRI BD11 .... 120 B7
Manor Street
Industrial Estate
CHAL LS7 .... 10 E4
Manston Primary School
MSTN/BAR LS15 .... 105 K2
Manston St James CE
Primary School
MSTN/BAR LS15 .... 106 A2
Mantra House Business Centre
KGHY BD21 .... 2 F6
Manywells Brow
Industrial Estate
CUL/QBY BD13 .... 74 A7
Margaret McMillan First School
HTON BD9 .... 97 F3

Margram Business Centre
HFAX HX1 .... 16 E5
Marley Mills Industrial Estate
KGHY BD21 .... 3 G6
Marriott Hollins Hall
Hotel & Country Club
GSLY LS20 .... 58 B5
Marshfield First School
WBOW BD5 .... 117 H3
Martin Frobisher First School
NORM WF6 .... 166 C4
Matthew Murray High School
BEE/HOL LS11 .... 13 G7
Maybrook Industrial Park
WOR/ARM LS12 .... 8 E9
WOR/ARM LS12 .... 13 C1
Meanwood CE Primary School
HDGY LS6 .... 82 D5
Meanwood Health Centre
HDGY LS6 .... 82 E6
Meanwood Park Hospital
HDGY LS6 .... 82 D3
Menston Cricket Club
ILK LS29 .... 38 C5
Menston Primary School
ILK LS29 .... 38 B6
Merrion Shopping Centre
LDSU LS2 .... 10 A7
Methley Infant School
RTHW LS26 .... 147 F5
Methley Junior School
RTHW LS26 .... 147 H4
Methley Park Hospital
RTHW LS26 .... 146 D4
Methley Road Industrial Park
CAS WF10 .... 168 A1
Micklefield CE Primary School
GFTH/SHER LS25 .... 109 F6
Middleton Park High School
MID LS10 .... 143 J3
Middleton Park Leisure Centre
MID LS10 .... 143 J2
Middleton Park Municipal
Golf Club
MID LS10 .... 143 F2
Middleton Primary School
MID LS10 .... 143 G3
Middleton Railway
MID LS10 .... 123 H5
Middleton St Marys CE
Primary School
MID LS10 .... 143 H2
Mid Point Business Park
PDSY/CALV LS28 .... 99 G5
Mid Yorkshire Golf Club
PONT WF8 .... 191 F4
Mid Yorkshire Nuffield Hospital
HORS LS18 .... 81 G4
Miles Hill First School
CHAL LS7 .... 83 F5
Milestone School
PDSY/CALV LS28 .... 100 B3
Milford RUFC
KSTL LS5 .... 101 K1
Millbridge J & I School
LVSG WF15 .... 159 J4
Millennium Business Park
AIRE BD20 .... 32 D4
Mill Lane J & I School
BTLY WF17 .... 161 G5
Millshaw Park Trading Estate
MOR LS27 .... 122 D6
Minerva Industrial Estate
RTHW LS26 .... 126 B7
Mirfield Parish Cricket Club
MIRF WF14 .... 179 J3
Miriam Lord First School
GIR BD8 .... 4 F1
Mixenden Clinic
LUD/ILL HX2 .... 134 A3
Mixenden County
Primary School
LUD/ILL HX2 .... 133 J1
Moderna Business Park
HBR HX7 .... 132 A7
Monckton Road
Industrial Estate
WKFDW/WTN WF2 .... 184 B7
Monk Fryston CE
Primary School
GFTH/SHER LS25 .... 131 J6
Moor Allerton Golf Club
AL/HA/HU LS17 .... 65 F3
Moor Allerton Hall
Primary School
AL/HA/HU LS17 .... 84 A3
Moorfield Business Park
YEA LS19 .... 60 A5
Moorfield First School
BFDE BD3 .... 7 H5
Moorfield School
ILK LS29 .... 24 B6
Moorlands School
BHP/TINH LS16 .... 82 C3
Moorlands Small
Business Centre
CLECK BD19 .... 138 E6
Moor Lane Trading Estate
GFTH/SHER LS25 .... 111 J6
Moor Lodge Park
AL/HA/HU LS17 .... 65 H2
Moor Park Business Centre
WKFDW/WTN WF2 .... 184 B6
Moorside School
LUD/ILL HX2 .... 134 C3
The Moors Shopping Centre
ILK LS29 .... 23 K5
Moortown Golf Club
AL/HA/HU LS17 .... 63 J6
Moortown Primary School
AL/HA/HU LS17 .... 83 J2
Moortown RUFC
AL/HA/HU LS17 .... 63 F6
Moorview Business Park
IDLE BD10 .... 78 B3
Morley Bruntcliffe
High School
MOR LS27 .... 141 H3

Morley High School
MOR LS27 .... 141 J4
Morley Leisure Centre
MOR LS27 .... 141 J3
Morley Victoria
Primary School
MOR LS27 .... 141 K2
Moslem School
BTLY WF17 .... 161 F4
The Mount J & I School
WKFDW/WTN WF2 .... 184 A6
Mount Pellon J & I School
HFAX HX1 .... 16 A4
Mount St Marys High School
OSM LS9 .... 14 F2
Mount St Marys RC
Primary School
OSM LS9 .... 11 J9
Municipal Baths
BRIG HD6 .... 157 G6
Myrtle Park Primary School
BGLY BD16 .... 75 J2
Nab Wood Cemetery
SHPY BD18 .... 76 C4
Nab Wood Grammar School
BGLY BD16 .... 76 B5
Nab Wood Middle School
BGLY BD16 .... 76 B5
Napoleon Business Park
BOW BD4 .... 118 C1
National Film Theatre North
LDS LS1 .... 14 B2
National Museum of
Photography, Film
& Television
WBOW BD5 .... 5 L8
Neil Hunt Memorial Ground &
Rugby Club
BOW BD4 .... 118 D1
Nessfield First School
HWTH BD22 .... 2 A8
Netherfield Industrial Park
DEWS WF13 .... 180 B4
Netherleigh School
HTON BD9 .... 96 E3
Newbridge Industrial Estate
KGHY BD21 .... 3 J5
Newby First School
WBOW BD5 .... 117 J3
New College
PONT WF8 .... 169 G7
New Cross Street
Health Centre
WBOW BD5 .... 117 J3
New Hold Industrial Estate
GFTH/SHER LS25 .... 107 K5
Newlands County
Junior School
RPDN/SBR HX6 .... 153 J5
Newlands Industrial Estate
BAIL BD17 .... 77 H4
Newlands Primary School
MOR LS27 .... 142 C3
New Line Clinic
IDLE BD10 .... 79 F5
Newspaper Office
BFD BD1 .... 6 A6
Newton Hill Primary School
WKFDE WF1 .... 164 D6
Newton Ings
CAS WF10 .... 149 H3
Ninelands Lane
Primary School
GFTH/SHER LS25 .... 107 K4
Norcroft Industrial Estate
BFD BD1 .... 5 H6
Norland CE J & I School
RPDN/SBR HX6 .... 154 A6
Normanton CE First School
NORM WF6 .... 166 E6
Normanton Common First
NORM WF6 .... 167 F4
Normanton Freeston
High School
NORM WF6 .... 166 E6
Normanton Health Centre
NORM WF6 .... 166 D7
Normanton Industrial Estate
NORM WF6 .... 167 H4
NORM WF6 .... 167 G5
Normanton Public Baths
NORM WF6 .... 166 E6
Normanton Town
Middle School
NORM WF6 .... 166 D7
Norquest Industrial Park
BTLY WF17 .... 140 D4
Norristhorpe Primary School
LVSG WF15 .... 159 J4
North Bridge Leisure Centre
HFAX HX1 .... 17 H4
Northcliffe Golf Club
SHPY BD18 .... 76 D6
North Dean Business Park
GTL/HWG HX4 .... 175 G1
North Dean RFC
GTL/HWG HX4 .... 175 G1
Northern Ballet Theatre
BHP/TINH LS16 .... 81 K4
BRAM LS13 .... 101 J4
Northern School of
Contemporary Dance
CHAL LS7 .... 10 C2
The North Halifax
Grammar School
LUD/ILL HX2 .... 134 C1
North Leeds Cricket Club
RHAY LS8 .... 84 B4
The North of England Higher
Secretarial College
LDS LS1 .... 10 A9
Northowram Hall Hospital
HIPP HX3 .... 135 H3
Northowram School
HIPP HX3 .... 135 K4
Northside Business Park
CHAL LS7 .... 10 C4

Northside Retail Park
  CHAL LS7 .... 82 K5
Northwest Business Park
  HDGY LS6 .... 9 M3
Norwood Business Park
  LM/WK BD12 .... 137 G5
Notre Dame Sixth Form College
  LDSU LS2 .... 9 L3
Nova Scotia Medical Centre
  CAS WF10 .... 147 K2
Oakbank School
  HWTH BD22 .... 53 G7
Oakdale First School
  SHPY BD18 .... 77 J6
Oaktree Business Park
  SCFT LS14 .... 85 H5
Oakwell Hall
  BTLY WF17 .... 139 K4
Oakwell Industrial Park
  BTLY WF17 .... 140 C3
Oakwood Primary School
  RHAY LS8 .... 104 D2
Oakworth Health Centre
  HWTH BD22 .... 72 E2
Oakworth J & I School
  HWTH BD22 .... 72 D2
Odeon Cinema
  BFD BD1 .... 5 L7
  BFDE BD3 .... 99 G5
  LDS LS1 .... 10 A8
Old Bank J I & N School
  MIRF WF14 .... 179 H2
Old Mill Business Park
  MID LS10 .... 15 G8
Old Rishworthians RUFC
  HIPP HX3 .... 154 D6
Old Roundhegians RUFC
  AL/HA/HU LS17 .... 83 K2
The Open University
  LDS LS1 .... 14 A1
Optimax Eye Clinic
  LDS LS1 .... 9 J8
Orchard Head Primary School
  PONT WF8 .... 169 K4
Osmondthorpe Primary School
  OSM LS9 .... 104 E6
Ossett Cricket & Athletic Club
  OSS WF5 .... 182 C5
Ossett Dimplewell
  Junior School
  OSS WF5 .... 182 D5
Ossett Health Centre
  OSS WF5 .... 182 C4
Ossett School
  OSS WF5 .... 182 C6
Otley Golf Club
  OT LS21 .... 38 D4
Otley RUFC
  OT LS21 .... 39 J2
Otley Town FC &
  Old Otliensians RUFC
  OT LS21 .... 39 K2
Oulton Health Centre
  RTHW LS26 .... 145 K1
Oulton Park Golf Course
  RTHW LS26 .... 145 J3
Oulton Primary School
  RTHW LS26 .... 145 J1
Our Lady of Lourdes
  CP School
  HUDN HD2 .... 177 H5
Our Lady of Victories
  RC J & I School
  HWTH BD22 .... 2 B4
Outwood Grange School
  WKFDE WF1 .... 164 B4
Outwood Ledger Lane
  J & I School
  WKFDE WF1 .... 164 C4
Overland Industrial Estate
  MOR LS27 .... 141 F2
Overthorpe CE J & I School
  EARL WF12 .... 181 F7
The Owlcotes Centre
  PDSY/CALV LS28 .... 100 A4
Oxenhope CE First School
  HWTH BD22 .... 92 C2
Oyster Park Infant School
  CAS WF10 .... 149 J6
Oyster Park Middle School
  CAS WF10 .... 149 J7
Parkhouse Industrial Estate
  LM/WK BD12 .... 137 K1
Parkinson Lane School
  HFAX HX1 .... 16 C8
Park Junior School
  CAS WF10 .... 168 D1
Parkland First & Middle School
  IDLE BD10 .... 78 E5
Parklands County
  Primary School
  SCFT LS14 .... 105 H1
Parklands Girls High School
  SCFT LS14 .... 105 J1
Park Lane College
  HORS LS18 .... 80 C5
  LDSU LS2 .... 10 B8
Park Lane College of Further
  Education
  BVRD LS3 .... 9 J8
  CHAL LS7 .... 83 K7
Park Road J I & N School
  BTLY WF17 .... 161 G3
Park Road Medical Centre
  WBOW BD5 .... 117 K1
Park Road Retail Park
  PONT WF8 .... 169 H6
Parkside Industrial Estate
  BEE/HOL LS11 .... 123 H5
Parkside Middle School
  CUL/QBY BD13 .... 74 B6
The Park Special School
  WKFDW/WTN WF2 .... 18 C7
Park Spring CP School
  BRAM LS13 .... 101 F5
Park Wood Crematorium
  ELL HX5 .... 155 J7

Parkwood First School
  KGHY BD21 .... 3 J6
Parkwood Primary School
  KGHY BD21 .... 3 J6
Parkwood Street
  Industrial Estate
  KGHY BD21 .... 3 M4
Parl Lane College
  PDSY/CALV LS28 .... 100 B5
Pavilion Business Centre
  PDSY/CALV LS28 .... 100 C3
Pecketwell College
  HFAX HX1 .... 16 F5
Peel Mill Business Centre
  MOR LS27 .... 142 A3
Pellon Industrial Estate
  HFAX HX1 .... 16 B4
Penistone Hill
  HWTH BD22 .... 72 B6
Pennine Industrial Estate
  WOR/ARM LS12 .... 102 A6
Penny Field School
  HDGY LS6 .... 82 E3
Penraevon Industrial Estate
  CHAL LS7 .... 10 B3
Pentland Infant School
  EARL WF12 .... 181 C4
Pentland Road Clinic
  EARL WF12 .... 181 G3
Percival Whitley
  College of Education
  (Halifax New College)
  HFAX HX1 .... 16 D7
Peter Laycock Industrial Estate
  CHAL LS7 .... 10 B3
Phoebe Lane Industrial Estate
  HIPP HX3 .... 155 G4
Pickup Business Park
  PDSY/CALV LS28 .... 100 B3
Picture House Cinema
  CHAL LS7 .... 10 D5
  NORM WF6 .... 166 D6
  KGHY BD21 .... 3 G4
  WKFDE WF1 .... 19 G3
Pictureville Cinema
  BFD BD1 .... 5 L8
Piece Hall Art Gallery
  HFAX HX1 .... 17 J6
Pilot Theatre
  CAS WF10 .... 168 E2
Pinderfield Hospital
  WKFDE WF1 .... 164 E7
Pinderfields & Pontefract
  Hospital NHS Trust
  EARD/LOFT WF3 .... 165 C7
Pioneer Business Park
  CAS WF10 .... 167 J4
Pitt Street Business Centre
  KGHY BD21 .... 3 K5
Playhouse & Film Theatre
  BFD BD1 .... 6 B7
Playhouse Theatre
  HFAX HX1 .... 16 F6
Police Sports Ground
  RHAY LS8 .... 84 A5
Pollard Park Health Centre
  BFDE BD3 .... 6 C3
Pollard Park Middle School
  BFDE BD3 .... 6 F4
Pontefract Castle
  PONT WF8 .... 169 J7
Pontefract Crematorium
  PONT WF8 .... 189 F3
Pontefract & District Golf Club
  PONT WF8 .... 168 D7
Pontefract General Infirmary
  PONT WF8 .... 189 J1
Pontefract Museum
  PONT WF8 .... 169 H7
Pontefract Racecourse
  PONT WF8 .... 169 F2
Pontefract RFC
  PONT WF8 .... 190 A5
Pontefract Squash &
  Leisure Centre
  PONT WF8 .... 169 H7
Pontefract Swimming Pool
  PONT WF8 .... 169 H7
Pool CE Primary School
  OT LS21 .... 41 G3
Poplars Farm First School
  ECHL BD2 .... 97 K1
Potternewton Primary School
  CHAL LS7 .... 83 G7
Powerhouse Showcase Theatre
  WKFDE WF1 .... 18 D5
Priesthorpe School
  PDSY/CALV LS28 .... 99 J3
Priestley Centre
  BFD BD1 .... 6 B6
Priestman Middle School
  WBOW BD5 .... 117 H4
Priestthorpe First School
  BGLY BD16 .... 75 K1
Priestthorpe Medical Centre
  BGLY BD16 .... 55 J7
Primrose Hill High School
  OSM LS9 .... 10 F6
Primrose Hill Primary School
  PDSY/CALV LS28 .... 100 A4
Primrose Lane Primary School
  BSPA/BRAM LS23 .... 48 C3
Prince Henrys Grammar School
  OT LS21 .... 39 H1
Prince of Wales Business Park
  BRIG HD6 .... 157 G6
Princes Mary Campus
  (Halifax New College)
  HFAX HX1 .... 16 C7
Princess Mary Stadium
  CLECK BD19 .... 159 G3
Princeville First School
  GTHN BD7 .... 4 E6
Princeville Road
  Industrial Estate
  GIR BD8 .... 4 D5

Public Baths &
  Recreation Centre
  BTLY WF17 .... 161 F3
Public Health Laboratory
  Service Seacroft Hospital
  SCFT LS14 .... 105 G3
Pudsey Business Centre
  PDSY/CALV LS28 .... 100 C6
Pudsey Grangefield School
  PDSY/CALV LS28 .... 100 B5
Pudsey Greenside J & I School
  PDSY/CALV LS28 .... 100 A7
Pudsey Leisure Centre
  PDSY/CALV LS28 .... 100 B6
Pudsey St Lawrence
  Cricket Club
  PDSY/CALV LS28 .... 100 A6
Pudsey Tyersal
  Primary School
  BOW BD4 .... 119 G1
Purlwell Infant School
  BTLY WF17 .... 160 E4
QBM Business Park
  BTLY WF17 .... 140 C5
Q F Industrial Estate
  BOW BD4 .... 118 C2
Quality Foods Industrial Park
  BOW BD4 .... 7 K9
Quarry House
  OSM LS9 .... 10 D9
Quarry Mount Primary School
  HDGY LS6 .... 9 K1
Queen Elizabeth
  Grammar School
  WKFDE WF1 .... 18 E1
Queensbury Golf Club
  CUL/QBY BD13 .... 115 J6
Queensbury Health Centre
  CUL/QBY BD13 .... 115 G5
Queensbury School
  CUL/QBY BD13 .... 115 H6
Queens Road School
  HFAX HX1 .... 16 A5
Queens Sports Club
  HFAX HX1 .... 16 E9
Queen Street Infant School
  MOR LS27 .... 141 K3
Queen Street J & I School
  NORM WF6 .... 166 E6
Queensway Primary School
  GSLY LS20 .... 59 H3
Raglan Industrial Estate
  CAS WF10 .... 148 A7
Ralph Thoresby High School
  BHP/TINH LS16 .... 61 J7
Ramgarhia Sikh Sports Centre
  CHAL LS7 .... 10 C4
Rastrick High School
  BRIG HD6 .... 156 E7
Rastrick Squash Centre
  BRIG HD6 .... 157 F7
Ravensbridge Industrial Estate
  DEWS WF13 .... 180 C3
Ravenscliffe First School
  IDLE BD10 .... 99 F1
Ravenscliffe High School
  HIPP HX3 .... 154 E6
Ravensthorpe CE Junior School
  DEWS WF13 .... 180 A4
Ravensthorpe Infant School
  DEWS WF13 .... 180 A3
Rawdon CE Primary School
  YEA LS19 .... 80 A1
Rawdon Cricket Club
  YEA LS19 .... 59 K7
Rawdon Golf & Lawn
  Tennis Club
  YEA LS19 .... 79 H1
Rawfolds Industrial Estate
  CLECK BD19 .... 159 G2
Rawson J & I School
  HIPP HX3 .... 134 E5
Rawson Market
  BFD BD1 .... 5 K5
Raynville Primary School
  BRAM LS13 .... 101 H3
Redhill Infant School
  CAS WF10 .... 149 H7
Red House
  CLECK BD19 .... 139 J6
Reevy Hill Primary School
  WBSY BD6 .... 116 E5
Revival Industrial Estate
  BOW BD4 .... 6 C9
Rex Cinema
  ELL HX5 .... 175 J3
Rhodesway School
  GIR BD8 .... 96 B5
Richard Dunn Sports Centre
  WBOW BD5 .... 117 J5
Richmond Building
  GTHN BD7 .... 5 J7
Richmond Hill Primary School
  OSM LS9 .... 15 G3
Richmond House School
  BHP/TINH LS16 .... 82 B5
Richmond Medical Centre
  OSM LS9 .... 14 F2
Riddlesden CE School
  AIRE BD20 .... 54 C1
Riddlesden Golf Club
  AIRE BD20 .... 33 J6
Riddlesden Infants School
  AIRE BD20 .... 54 C1
Ridings Business Park
  HFAX HX1 .... 16 A7
The Ridings School
  LUD/ILL HX2 .... 134 B4
Ridings Shopping Centre
  WKFDE WF1 .... 18 F5
Ripponden J & I School
  RPDN/SBR HX6 .... 173 F4
Riverside Business Park
  BAIL BD17 .... 77 H4
  ILK LS29 .... 24 B4
Riverside Industrial Estate
  EARL WF12 .... 181 F2

Riverside Medical Centre
  CAS WF10 .... 148 B7
Riverside Primary School
  TAD LS24 .... 50 D6
Rock Hill Sports Club
  CAS WF10 .... 169 F2
Rodillian School
  EARD/LOFT WF3 .... 144 D6
Rodley Primary School
  BRAM LS13 .... 80 C7
The Rookeries Carleton
  J & I School
  PONT WF8 .... 190 A3
Rooks Nest Primary School
  WKFDE WF1 .... 164 D4
Roseville Business Park
  RHAY LS8 .... 10 F4
Rossefield School
  HTON BD9 .... 97 F1
Rossett Business Park
  BRAM LS13 .... 100 E1
Rothwell CE Primary School
  RTHW LS26 .... 145 F1
Rothwell Health Centre
  RTHW LS26 .... 145 F2
Rothwell Methley CP
  Infant School
  RTHW LS26 .... 147 F5
Rothwell Primary School
  RTHW LS26 .... 145 F3
Rothwell Sports Centre
  RTHW LS26 .... 145 K3
Rothwell West Junior School
  RTHW LS26 .... 144 E3
Roundhay Golf Club
  RHAY LS8 .... 84 D2
Roundhay Park Site
  RHAY LS8 .... 84 E5
Roundhay St Johns
  Primary School
  RHAY LS8 .... 84 D6
Roundhay School
  RHAY LS8 .... 84 B5
Roundhill Junior School
  KNOT WF11 .... 170 C3
Roundhouse Business Park
  WOR/ARM LS12 .... 13 H2
Roundwood Industrial Estate
  OSS WF5 .... 183 G4
Royal Armouries Museum
  MID LS10 .... 14 D3
Royal Halifax Infirmary
  HFAX HX1 .... 155 F3
Royal Industrial Park
  HFAX HX1 .... 16 E6
The Royal London
  Industrial Estate
  BEE/HOL LS11 .... 122 E5
Royal Park Primary School
  HDGY LS6 .... 8 F4
Royd Mill Business Park
  BRIG HD6 .... 157 G6
Royd Mount Middle School
  CUL/QBY BD13 .... 95 F7
Royds School
  RTHW LS26 .... 145 J5
RSPB Nature Reserve
  (Fairburn Ings)
  KNOT WF11 .... 149 J3
Russell Hall First School
  CUL/QBY BD13 .... 115 H5
Rutland Industrial Estate
  WKFDE WF1 .... 19 G8
Ryan Middle School
  BOW BD4 .... 118 A3
Ryburn County
  Secondary School
  RPDN/SBR HX6 .... 153 F6
Ryburn Golf Club
  RPDN/SBR HX6 .... 153 K7
Ryecroft First School
  BOW BD4 .... 119 G4
Ryecroft Primary School
  WOR/ARM LS12 .... 101 H7
Ryshworth Middle School
  BGLY BD16 .... 55 H4
Sacred Heart Catholic
  Primary School
  BULY LS4 .... 102 A2
Sai Medical Centre
  GIR BD8 .... 97 H3
St Agnes PNEU School
  HDGY LS6 .... 82 C6
St Andrew CE Infant School
  BRIG HD6 .... 157 F4
St Andrews CE Junior School
  BRIG HD6 .... 157 F5
St Annes Cathedral
  LDSU LS2 .... 9 M8
St Annes RC School
  KGHY BD21 .... 2 F3
St Anthonys RC First School
  CLAY BD14 .... 116 C1
St Anthonys RC J & I School
  SHPY BD18 .... 78 A4
St Anthonys RC
  Primary School
  BEE/HOL LS11 .... 122 E4
St Augustines CE First School
  BFDE BD3 .... 6 C2
St Augustines CE
  Primary School
  HFAX HX1 .... 16 C4
St Augustines RC
  Primary School
  RHAY LS8 .... 11 L2
St Austins RC Primary School
  WKFDE WF1 .... 19 G2
St Barnabas CE School
  HTON BD9 .... 97 F1
St Bartholomews CE
  Primary School
  WOR/ARM LS12 .... 12 B3
St Bedes Grammar School
  HTON BD9 .... 97 F2
St Benedicts RC
  Primary School
  GFTH/SHER LS25 .... 107 J6

St Catherines
  Business Complex
  BRAM LS13 .... 101 G1
St Chads CE Primary School
  BRIG HD6 .... 156 D3
  BHP/TINH LS16 .... 81 K5
St Clares Roman
  Catholic School
  ECHL BD2 .... 98 E3
St Columbas RC
  Primary School
  BOW BD4 .... 118 E4
St Cuthberts & First
  Martyrs First School
  HTON BD9 .... 97 F3
St Edwards RC Primary School
  BSPA/BRAM LS23 .... 48 B2
St Francis of Assisi RC
  Primary School
  BEE/HOL LS11 .... 13 M9
St Francis RC First School
  ECHL BD2 .... 98 B1
St Francis RC Primary School
  MOR LS27 .... 141 J3
St George's Hall
  BFD BD1 .... 6 A7
St Giles CE VA Primary School
  PONT WF8 .... 169 J7
St Gregorys RC Primary School
  SCFT LS14 .... 86 A7
St Hildas School
  HOR/CROF WF4 .... 183 F7
St Ignatius RC Primary School
  OSS WF5 .... 182 C6
St James Business Park
  BFD BD1 .... 6 B7
St James CE Primary School
  WBY LS22 .... 29 J3
St James Market
  BFDE BD3 .... 6 C8
St James's University Hospital
  OSM LS9 .... 11 H5
St John Fisher RC High School
  DEWS WF13 .... 160 E7
St Johns Catholic School
  BSPA/BRAM LS23 .... 48 C3
St Johns CE Infant School
  DEWS WF13 .... 180 D1
St Johns CE J & I School
  WKFDE WF1 .... 18 C1
St Johns CE Primary School
  BRIG HD6 .... 157 K6
St Johns CE First School
  BOW BD4 .... 118 E5
St Johns Health Centre
  HFAX HX1 .... 16 C5
St Johns Shopping Centre
  LDSU LS2 .... 10 A8
St Johns the Baptist
  Catholic Primary School
  NORM WF6 .... 166 E6
St John the Baptist
  CE Primary School
  BHP/TINH LS16 .... 62 B7
St John the Evangelist
  RC School
  WBSY BD6 .... 116 D5
St Josephs Catholic
  Primary School
  WBY LS22 .... 29 H3
St Josephs College
  HTON BD9 .... 97 H2
St Josephs RC First School
  WBOW BD5 .... 117 J2
St Josephs RC Primary School
  CAS WF10 .... 148 D7
  DEWS WF13 .... 160 D6
  PDSY/CALV LS28 .... 100 C5
  PONT WF8 .... 189 H1
  TAD LS24 .... 50 D6
St Josephs RC School
  BGLY BD16 .... 75 K1
  HIPP HX3 .... 17 J3
  KGHY BD21 .... 2 E9
St Jospehs RC Primary School
  BRIG HD6 .... 156 E3
St Lukes CE First School
  CLECK BD19 .... 158 C1
St Lukes Eccleshill CE
  First School
  ECHL BD2 .... 98 E1
St Lukes Hospital
  WBOW BD5 .... 117 J2
St Malachys RC School
  LUD/ILL HX2 .... 134 B4
St Margarets CE
  Primary School
  HORS LS18 .... 80 E3
St Marys Catholic School
  ILK LS29 .... 24 C5
St Marys CE J & I School
  WKFDE WF1 .... 19 H5
St Marys CE Primary School
  RPDN/SBR HX6 .... 172 D2
St Marys Hospital
  WOR/ARM LS12 .... 101 J5
St Marys RC Infant School
  HFAX HX1 .... 16 D7
St Marys RC J I & N School
  BTLY WF17 .... 160 E3
St Marys RC Primary School
  BFD BD1 .... 6 A5
  HORS LS18 .... 81 F3
  RTHW LS26 .... 145 G3
St Marys RC School
  ILK LS29 .... 38 D7
St Matthews CE
  Primary School
  CHAL LS7 .... 83 H5
St Matthews CE First School
  WBOW BD5 .... 117 K5
St Matthews RC
  Primary School
  WIL/AL BD15 .... 96 A5
St Michael & All Angels CE
  Primary School
  HIPP HX3 .... 136 C1

St Michaels CE
Primary School
HDGY LS6 .... 82 D7
St Michaels College
BVRD LS3 .... 9 H6
St Nicholas RC Primary School
OSM LS9 .... 104 E2
St Oswald's CE Primary School
WBOW BD5 .... 117 H3
St Oswalds CE Junior School
GSLY LS20 .... 59 F3
St Patricks RC Primary School
BTLY WF17 .... 140 B5
St Patricks R C Primary School
ELL HX5 .... 175 G3
St Patricks RC Primary School
OSM LS9 .... 11 J8
St Paulinus RC J & I School
DEWS WF13 .... 180 D2
St Pauls J & I CE School
WKFDW/WTN WF2 .... 183 J1
St Pauls RC Primary School
AL/HA/HU LS17 .... 63 F7
St Peter CE Primary School
OSM LS9 .... 10 D8
St Peters Cathedral
BFD BD1 .... 6 A5
St Peters CE J & I School
BTLY WF17 .... 140 B5
St Peters CE Infant School
RPDN/SBR HX6 .... 153 F5
St Peters RC First School
BFDE BD3 .... 6 F5
St Philips C E First School
GIR BD8 .... 4 B3
St Philips CE First School
WIL/AL BD15 .... 95 K3
St Philips RC Primary School
MID LS10 .... 143 G2
St Saviours CE Junior School
BTLY WF17 .... 140 D6
St Stephens CE
Primary School
KSTL LS5 .... 101 K1
St Stephens Special School
WBOW BD5 .... 117 K3
St Theresas RC
Primary School
MSTN/BAR LS15 .... 105 K2
St Thomas CE Junior School
FEA/AMT WF7 .... 188 B4
St Urbans RC Primary School
HDGY LS6 .... 83 F7
St Walburgas RC First School
SHPY BD18 .... 76 E5
St Wilfrids Catholic
High (VA) School
FEA/AMT WF7 .... 168 B6
St Williams RC
Primary School
GIR BD8 .... 4 C5
Saltaire First School
SHPY BD18 .... 76 E4
Saltaire Medical Centre
SHPY BD18 .... 76 E4
Salterhebble School
HIPP HX3 .... 155 G5
Salter Lee School
HIPP HX3 .... 135 J5
Salt Grammar School
BAIL BD17 .... 76 E2
Sandal First School
BAIL BD17 .... 77 H1
Sandal Magna J & I School
WKFDE WF1 .... 185 F7
Sandbeck Industrial Estate
WBY LS22 .... 29 J2
Sandbeck Park
Industrial Estate
WBY LS22 .... 29 J2
Sandbeds Trading Estate
OSS WF5 .... 182 C2
Sand Moor Golf Club
AL/HA/HU LS17 .... 63 H5
Sandy Lane First School
WIL/AL BD15 .... 95 K1
Savile Business Centre
EARL WF12 .... 181 G2
Savile Park J & I School
HFAX HX1 .... 154 D3
Savile Town CE
Infant School &
Nursery School
EARL WF12 .... 181 F3
Saxton CE Primary School
TAD LS24 .... 90 B6
Scalebor Park Hospital
ILK LS29 .... 37 J2
Scarcroft Golf Club
SCFT LS14 .... 65 J3
Scarthingwell Golf Club
TAD LS24 .... 91 F5
Scholemoor Cemetery
GTHN BD7 .... 96 D7
Scholemoor Crematorium
GTHN BD7 .... 96 D7
Scholes Elmete Junior School
MSTN/BAR LS15 .... 86 B6
School Lane Health Centre
DEWS WF13 .... 160 C7
Schreiber Business Centre
WKFDE WF1 .... 19 H7
Scotchman Middle School
HTON BD9 .... 97 F3
Scotch Park Trading Estate
WOR/ARM LS12 .... 8 D8
Scout Road County
Primary School
HBR HX7 .... 132 A7
S D H Industrial Estate
RPDN/SBR HX6 .... 153 J5
Seacroft Clinic
SCFT LS14 .... 85 J7
Seacroft Industrial Estate
SCFT LS14 .... 85 J5
Seemore Shopping Centre
OSS WF5 .... 182 C3

Selby Gas & Leisure Centre
KNOT WF11 .... 150 D7
Seven Hills Primary School
MOR LS27 .... 142 A3
Shadwell Medical Centre
AL/HA/HU LS17 .... 83 K1
Shadwell Primary School
AL/HA/HU LS17 .... 65 G7
Shakespeare Primary School
OSM LS9 .... 11 G7
Sharlston Primary School
HOR/CROF WF4 .... 186 E5
Sharma Park Industrial Estate
RHAY LS8 .... 10 E5
Shawcross Business Park
EARL WF12 .... 161 J6
Shaw Cross Health Centre
EARL WF12 .... 161 K5
Shaw Cross Infant School
EARL WF12 .... 161 K5
Shaw House School
HTON BD9 .... 97 F2
Sheibarg Industrial Estate
BOW BD4 .... 118 E2
Shelf Health Centre
HIPP HX3 .... 136 B1
Sherburn High School
GFTH/SHER LS25 .... 111 F7
Sherwood Industrial Estate
EARD/LOFT WF3 .... 144 C4
Shibden Hall & Folk Museum
HIPP HX3 .... 135 J7
Shibden Head First School
CUL/QBY BD13 .... 115 F7
Shipley Baths
SHPY BD18 .... 77 G5
Shipley CE First School
SHPY BD18 .... 77 G6
Shipley College
SHPY BD18 .... 77 F4
Shipley College of Education
SHPY BD18 .... 76 E3
Shipley Golf Club
BGLY BD16 .... 75 J3
Shipley Health Centre
SHPY BD18 .... 77 F5
Shipley Hospital
SHPY BD18 .... 77 F5
Shires Business Park
GTHN BD7 .... 117 F2
Showcase Cinemas
BTLY WF17 .... 140 E3
Siddal Infant School
HIPP HX3 .... 155 H5
Siddal Junior School
HIPP HX3 .... 155 H5
Silcoates School
WKFDW/WTN WF2 .... 163 K7
Silsden Cricket Club
AIRE BD20 .... 32 E2
Silsden Golf Club
AIRE BD20 .... 33 H1
Silsden Health Centre
AIRE BD20 .... 32 E1
Silver Blades Ice Rink
WBOW BD5 .... 5 L8
Simpson Lane J & I School
KNOT WF11 .... 170 E5
Sirdar Business Park
WKFDW/WTN WF2 .... 183 K2
Smawthorne Infant School
CAS WF10 .... 168 C2
Snapethorpe Junior School
WKFDW/WTN WF2 .... 183 H5
Soothill Cricket Club
BTLY WF17 .... 161 H3
South Bradford Golf Club
WBSY BD6 .... 117 K6
Southdale CE Junior School
OSS WF5 .... 182 D4
South Halifax High School
HIPP HX3 .... 155 H6
South Leeds Business Park
MID LS10 .... 14 C7
South Leeds Golf Club
BEE/HOL LS11 .... 123 F7
South Leeds Sports Centre
BEE/HOL LS11 .... 13 M6
South Leeds Stadium
BEE/HOL LS11 .... 123 H6
Southmere First School
GTHN BD7 .... 117 F3
South Milford Primary School
GFTH/SHER LS25 .... 131 F3
South Ossett Infant School
OSS WF5 .... 182 D5
South Parade Junior School
OSS WF5 .... 182 E5
Southroyd Primary School
PDSY/CALV LS28 .... 100 B7
South Side Aviation Centre
YEA LS19 .... 60 B4
South View Business Centre
GSLY LS20 .... 59 F1
Southview Business Park
GSLY LS20 .... 59 F4
GSLY LS20 .... 59 F1
South View Infant School
YEA LS19 .... 59 J5
South View Junior School
YEA LS19 .... 59 J5
Sovereign Business Park
MID LS10 .... 14 B5
Sowerby Bridge Clinic
RPDN/SBR HX6 .... 153 K5
Sowerby Bridge CE
Junior School
RPDN/SBR HX6 .... 153 J4
Sowerby Bridge Cricket Club
RPDN/SBR HX6 .... 153 H4
Sowerby Bridge High School
RPDN/SBR HX6 .... 153 K3
Spa Baths
BSPA/BRAM LS23 .... 48 D2
Spenborough Industrial Estate
LVSG WF15 .... 159 K5

Spenborough Moorend
CE School
CLECK BD19 .... 138 D6
Spenborough Whitcliffe
Mount School
CLECK BD19 .... 138 C7
Spen Trading Estate
CLECK BD19 .... 159 G1
Spen Valley High School
LVSG WF15 .... 159 H5
Spen Valley Industrial Park
CLECK BD19 .... 159 F2
Spen Victoria Cricket
Bowling & Athletic Club
CLECK BD19 .... 139 C7
Spring Bank Industrial Estate
RPDN/SBR HX6 .... 153 H6
Springbank Junior School
PDSY/CALV LS28 .... 100 A3
Spring Bank Primary School
HDGY LS6 .... 8 D1
Spring Ram Business Park
BTLY WF17 .... 140 D3
Springwell Health Clinic
WKFDW/WTN WF2 .... 185 F7
Springwood First School
GIR BD8 .... 5 H2
Staincliffe CE Junior School
BTLY WF17 .... 160 D5
Standard Industrial Estate
ECHL BD2 .... 98 D2
Stanley Grove J & I School
EARD/LOFT WF3 .... 165 G5
Stanley Health Centre
EARD/LOFT WF3 .... 165 F3
Stanley St Peters J & I School
EARD/LOFT WF3 .... 165 G3
Stanley Sports & Social Club
EARD/LOFT WF3 .... 165 G2
Stanningley Industrial Centre
PDSY/CALV LS28 .... 100 A4
Stanningley Primary School
PDSY/CALV LS28 .... 100 C2
Stanningley RLFC
PDSY/CALV LS28 .... 100 D3
Station Industrial Park
LUD/ILL HX2 .... 152 E1
Station Road Industrial Estate
GFTH/SHER LS25 .... 127 J7
Station Works Industrial Park
KGHY BD21 .... 3 L4
Steeton Hallgatehouse
GFTH/SHER LS25 .... 130 D3
Steeton Health Centre
AIRE BD20 .... 32 D5
Steeton Junior &
Infants School
AIRE BD20 .... 32 E5
Sterling Industrial Park
CAS WF10 .... 168 E2
Stocks Lane First School
CUL/QBY BD13 .... 116 A4
Stonegate School
AL/HA/HU LS17 .... 83 F4
Stoney Lee Middle School
BGLY BD16 .... 76 A6
Stoney Ridge Hospital
BGLY BD16 .... 76 B7
Stoney Royd Cemetery
HIPP HX3 .... 155 G3
Streethouse J & I School
HOR/CROF WF4 .... 187 H4
Summerfield Primary School
BRAM LS13 .... 100 C2
Sunfield Medical Centre
PDSY/CALV LS28 .... 100 A3
Sunny Hill House School
WKFDW/WTN WF2 .... 163 K7
Surgery Savile Centre
EARL WF12 .... 181 G2
Swain House Middle School
ECHL BD2 .... 98 B1
Swillington Primary School
RTHW LS26 .... 126 D4
Swinnow Primary School
PDSY/CALV LS28 .... 100 D5
Swinnow Shopping Centre
BRAM LS13 .... 100 D5
Swire Smith Middle School
KGHY BD21 .... 3 K7
Sycamore Industrial Estate
HECK WF16 .... 160 A6
Tadcaster Albion FC
TAD LS24 .... 50 E7
Tadcaster Cricket Club
TAD LS24 .... 50 D7
Tadcaster East Primary School
TAD LS24 .... 51 F7
Tadcaster Grammar School
TAD LS24 .... 69 J7
Tadcaster Sports &
Leisure Centre
TAD LS24 .... 50 D7
Tainton Park Trading Estate
WOR/ARM LS12 .... 12 F4
Taison Industrial Park
GTHN BD7 .... 116 E3
Takalani Dance Theatre
RHAY LS8 .... 104 D1
Talbot Primary School
RHAY LS8 .... 84 A3
The Tandy Trading Estate
WOR/ARM LS12 .... 8 C7
Tannery Business Park
HIPP HX3 .... 135 K4
Tanshelf Industrial Estate
PONT WF8 .... 169 H7
Temple Bank Special School
HTON BD9 .... 96 D3
Temple Moor High School
MSTN/BAR LS15 .... 105 J6
Temple Newsam
MSTN/BAR LS15 .... 125 J1
Temple Newsam Country Park
MSTN/BAR LS15 .... 105 J7
Temple Newsam Golf Club
MSTN/BAR LS15 .... 105 G7

Temple Newsam Halton
Primary School
MSTN/BAR LS15 .... 105 H5
Tenterfields Business Park
LUD/ILL HX2 .... 153 F3
Tetley Brewery Wharf
MID LS10 .... 14 C2
Thackley AFC
IDLE BD10 .... 78 B2
Thackley Cricket Club
IDLE BD10 .... 78 C2
Thackley First School
IDLE BD10 .... 78 C2
Thackray Medical Museum
OSM LS9 .... 11 H5
Thomas Danby College
CHAL LS7 .... 10 D4
Thomas Park Athletics Stadium
WKFDW/WTN WF2 .... 18 A7
Thornbury First School
BFDE BD3 .... 7 K3
Thornbury Middle School
BFDE BD3 .... 7 L3
Thorncliffe Park
Industrial Estate
GIR BD8 .... 5 K1
Thorncliffe Square
Industrial Estate
GIR BD8 .... 5 J1
Thornes Industrial Estate
WKFDE WF1 .... 18 F8
Thornhill Lees CE Infant School
EARL WF12 .... 181 F5
Thorn Park School
HTON BD9 .... 96 C1
Thornton Baths
CUL/QBY BD13 .... 95 H7
Thornton First School
CUL/QBY BD13 .... 95 G7
Thornton Medical Centre
CUL/QBY BD13 .... 95 H7
Thornton Upper School
CUL/QBY BD13 .... 96 A7
Thorp Arch Trading Estate
BSPA/BRAM LS23 .... 31 F6
Thorpe First & Middle School
IDLE BD10 .... 78 C4
Thorpe Primary School
EARD/LOFT WF3 .... 143 K5
Three Lane Ends
Business Centre
CAS WF10 .... 147 K7
Throstle Farm J & I School
KNOT WF11 .... 171 G6
Thrum Hall Industrial Park
LUD/ILL HX2 .... 154 B1
Thwaite Mills Watermill
OSM LS9 .... 15 M9
Tinshill Primary School
BHP/TINH LS16 .... 81 H1
Tong Park First School
BAIL BD17 .... 58 A7
Tong Sports Centre
BOW BD4 .... 119 H6
Top Rank Theatre
HFAX HX1 .... 17 G5
Towngate Primary School
OSS WF5 .... 182 D3
Towton 1461
TAD LS24 .... 90 C4
Tranmere Park Primary School
GSLY LS20 .... 58 C3
Treefield Industrial Estate
MOR LS27 .... 141 G2
Triangle Business Park
BTLY WF17 .... 140 D4
Triangle CE Primary School
RPDN/SBR HX6 .... 153 F7
Trinity Business Centre
WKFDE WF1 .... 19 H6
Trinity Medical Centre
WKFDE WF1 .... 18 F5
Tropical World
RHAY LS8 .... 84 C3
Tuel Lane County
Primary School
RPDN/SBR HX6 .... 153 J4
Tulip Street Retail Park
MID LS10 .... 123 J3
Tyersal Family Clinic
BOW BD4 .... 99 G7
Tyersal First School
BOW BD4 .... 7 K9
Undercliffe Cemetery
BFDE BD3 .... 6 D1
Undercliffe Cricket Club
ECHL BD2 .... 98 D3
Undercliffe First School
ECHL BD2 .... 6 E1
Union Business Centre
ECHL BD2 .... 98 E1
University of Bradford
GTHN BD7 .... 5 H7
University of Leeds
BHP/TINH LS16 .... 82 B3
HDGY LS6 .... 9 J4
HDGY LS6 .... 102 E1
LDSU LS2 .... 9 K6
University of Leeds Trinity &
All Saints College
HORS LS18 .... 80 D1
University Sports Centre
LDSU LS2 .... 9 K6
Upper Wortley
Primary School
WOR/ARM LS12 .... 102 A7
Utley J & I School
AIRE BD20 .... 53 J1
Valley Mills Industrial Estate
IDLE BD10 .... 79 F4
Valley Road Business Park
LVSG WF15 .... 159 H4
Vehicle Testing Centre
BSPA/BRAM LS23 .... 31 F5
Venlo Industrial Estate
BOW BD4 .... 118 D4
Victoria Baths
ELL HX5 .... 175 K3

Victoria Centre
EARL WF12 .... 181 F1
Victoria Industrial Estate
ECHL BD2 .... 98 D1
Victoria Industrial Park
SCFT LS14 .... 85 J4
Victoria Junior School
RTHW LS26 .... 144 E1
Victoria Park School
BRAM LS13 .... 101 G3
Victoria Primary School
OSM LS9 .... 11 M8
Victoria Spring Business Park
LVSG WF15 .... 159 G3
The Victoria Theatre
HFAX HX1 .... 17 G6
Vine Industrial Estate
BRIG HD6 .... 156 E5
Vintage Railway
Carriage Museum
HWTH BD22 .... 72 D5
Wainstalls School
LUD/ILL HX2 .... 133 G2
Wakefield Art Gallery
WKFDE WF1 .... 18 D2
Wakefield Cathedral
WKFDE WF1 .... 18 F4
Wakefield City Baths
WKFDE WF1 .... 19 G4
Wakefield City High School
WKFDE WF1 .... 19 M2
Wakefield College
CAS WF10 .... 168 A2
FEA/AMT WF7 .... 188 C4
WKFDE WF1 .... 18 C2
Wakefield Girls High School
WKFDE WF1 .... 18 D3
Wakefield Girls
High School (Junior)
WKFDE WF1 .... 18 C2
Wakefield Health Authority
WKFDE WF1 .... 164 C3
Wakefield 41 Industrial Park
EARD/LOFT WF3 .... 164 A3
Wakefield Methodist
First School
WKFDW/WTN WF2 .... 184 C1
Wakefield Museum
WKFDE WF1 .... 18 E4
Wakefield Music School
WKFDE WF1 .... 18 D4
Wakefield RUFC
WKFDE WF1 .... 18 F1
Wakefield Superbowl 2000
WKFDE WF1 .... 185 G6
Wakefield Theatre Royal &
Opera House
WKFDW/WTN WF2 .... 18 C4
Wakefield Trinity RLFC
WKFDE WF1 .... 185 G6
Wakefield Tutorial
Preparatory School
MOR LS27 .... 141 K3
Walnut Business Park
HFAX HX1 .... 16 C6
Wapping First School
BFDE BD3 .... 6 B3
Warley Road J & I School
LUD/ILL HX2 .... 154 B2
Warley Town School
LUD/ILL HX2 .... 153 J2
Warner Village
BULY LS4 .... 8 B6
Warwick Road J & I School
BTLY WF17 .... 161 F5
Waterloo Infant School
PDSY/CALV LS28 .... 99 K6
Waterloo Junior School
PDSY/CALV LS28 .... 99 K6
Waterside Industrial Estate
OSM LS9 .... 124 C2
Waterton J & I School
WKFDW/WTN WF2 .... 183 J5
Waverley Middle School
GTHN BD7 .... 4 E9
Wax Museum
BFD BD1 .... 5 K5
Weetwood Primary School
BHP/TINH LS16 .... 82 C5
Wellhouse Middle School
MIRF WF14 .... 179 J2
Wellington Business Centre
ELL HX5 .... 175 K2
Wellington First School
ECHL BD2 .... 98 C2
Wellington Middle School
ECHL BD2 .... 98 C2
Wellington Road
Industrial Estate
WOR/ARM LS12 .... 9 H9
Wellington Shopping Arcade
BRIG HD6 .... 157 F6
Wellington Street
Business Park
CAS WF10 .... 148 B7
Well Lane Business Centre
BTLY WF17 .... 161 F5
Wellwoman Clinic
HFAX HX1 .... 17 G7
Westborough High School
DEWS WF13 .... 160 D7
West Bowling Golf Club
WBOW BD5 .... 118 B5
West Bradford Golf Club
HTON BD9 .... 96 A2
Westbrook Lane
Primary School
HORS LS18 .... 80 D1
Westcliffe Medical Centre
SHPY BD18 .... 77 F5
West End Golf Club (Halifax)
LUD/ILL HX2 .... 133 K7
West End Industrial Estate
MOR LS27 .... 141 G4
West End Middle School
CLECK BD19 .... 158 C1
West End Primary School
HORS LS18 .... 80 C2

Westerton Primary School
EARD/LOFT WF3...................... **162** C1
Westfield Industrial Estate
YEA LS19 .... **59** H5
Westfield Medical Centre
CHAL LS7 .... **83** J7
Westfield Primary School
BVRD LS3 .... **9** G7
West Garforth Junior School
GFTH/SHER LS25..................... **107** H7
Westgate Hill First School
BOW BD4 .... **119** H7
Westgate Infant School
OT LS21 .... **39** F3
Westgate Retail &
Leisure Park
WKFDW/WTN WF2...................... **18** C6
West Hall Special School
EARD/LOFT WF3...................... **165** J2
West Leeds High School
WOR/ARM LS12 .... **101** J6
Westmoor Junior School
DEWS WF13 .... **160** C7
West Oaks School
BSPA/BRAM LS23..................... **48** B3
West Park Bramhope RUFC
BHP/TINH LS16........................... **61** K2
West Riding Magistrates Court
BTLY WF17 .... **140** B6
Westroyd Infant School
PDSY/CALV LS28..................... **100** A3
West Side Retail Park
GSLY LS20 .... **59** G4
West Vale J & I School
GTL/HWG HX4........................... **175** G2
Westville House
Preparatory School
ILK LS29 .... **24** C2
Westwood Primary School
MID LS10 .... **143** F3
West Yorkshire College of
Health Studies
WKFDE WF1 .... **165** F7
West Yorkshire
Industrial Estate
BOW BD4 .... **118** E5
West Yorkshire Playhouse
OSM LS9 .... **10** D9
West Yorkshire Retail Park
BTLY WF17 .... **140** E3
West Yorks Police HQ
WKFDE WF1 .... **18** D3

Wetherby Business Park
WBY LS22 .... **29** J3
Wetherby Golf Club
WBY LS22 .... **29** F5
Wetherby High School
WBY LS22 .... **29** J4
Wetherby Leisure Centre
WBY LS22 .... **29** H5
Wetherby Racecourse
WBY LS22 .... **30** B3
Wharfebank Business Centre
OT LS21 .... **39** F3
Wharfedale Business Park
BOW BD4 .... **118** E5
Wharfedale General Hospital
OT LS21 .... **27** C7
The Whartons Primary School
OT LS21 .... **27** H7
Wheldon Infant School
CAS WF10 .... **148** D7
Whetley First School
GIR BD8 .... **4** D2
Whetley Middle School
GIR BD8 .... **4** D3
Whinburn Residential School
AIRE BD20 .... **53** G1
Whingate Business Centre
WOR/ARM LS12 .... **101** K6
Whingate Business Park
WOR/ARM LS12 .... **102** A6
Whingate Primary School
WOR/ARM LS12 .... **101** K6
Whitebridge Primary School
MSTN/BAR LS15..................... **105** F6
Whitechapel Middle School
CLECK BD19 .... **138** D6
Whitecote Primary School
BRAM LS13 .... **101** F1
Whitehall Industrial Estate
WOR/ARM LS12 .... **121** J2
Whitehall Trading Estate
WOR/ARM LS12 .... **121** H2
Whitehill County Infant School
LUD/ILL HX2 .... **134** B1
White Horse Leisure Centre
WKFDE WF1 .... **18** D5
White Laith Primary School
SCFT LS14 .... **85** K5
White Rose House
WKFDE WF1 .... **18** F6
White Rose Shopping Centre
MOR LS27 .... **122** D7

Whitkirk Medical Centre
MSTN/BAR LS15..................... **106** A5
Whitkirk Primary School
MSTN/BAR LS15..................... **105** J6
Whitwood Business Centre
CAS WF10 .... **147** K7
Whitwood Golf Club
CAS WF10 .... **167** H2
Wibsey First School
WBSY BD6..................................... **117** G5
Wibsey Middle School
WBSY BD6..................................... **117** G5
Wiggan Lane Trading Estate
HUDN HD2 .... **177** J5
Wigton Moor Primary School
AL/HA/HU LS17 .... **64** A6
William Henry Smith School
BRIG HD6 .... **176** D1
Willow Industrial Complex
RPDN/SBR HX6 .... **153** J5
The Willows Medical Centre
CUL/QBY BD13 .... **115** H5
Willow Valley Golf &
Country Club
BRIG HD6 .... **157** K3
Wilsden Primary School
WIL/AL BD15............................... **75** F7
Windhill CE First School
SHPY BD18 .... **77** J4
Windhill Cricket Club
SHPY BD18 .... **77** J3
Windhill Green Medical Centre
SHPY BD18 .... **77** H4
Windmill Primary School
MID LS10 .... **123** K6
Windsor Medical Centre
EARL WF12 .... **181** H1
Wira Business Park
BHP/TINH LS16........................... **81** J3
Withinfields Junior &
Infants School
HIPP HX3..................................... **155** J3
Woodbank Special School
LUD/ILL HX2 .... **133** F7
Woodhall Hills Golf Club
PDSY/CALV LS28....................... **99** G1
Woodhill Middle School
SHPY BD18 .... **77** J4
Woodhouse Business Centre
NORM WF6 .... **166** D7
Woodhouse Cricket Club
CHAL LS7 .... **82** E6

Woodhouse First School
NORM WF6 .... **186** D1
Woodhouse Grove School
IDLE BD10 .... **79** G3
Woodhouse Health Centre
HDGY LS6 .... **9** M3
Woodhouse Primary School
BRIG HD6 .... **177** G1
Woodkirk High School
EARD/LOFT WF3...................... **142** B6
Woodland Glade Leisure Centre
HUDN HD2 .... **177** J4
Woodlands CE First School
LM/WK BD12 .... **138** B2
Woodlands Cricket Club
LM/WK BD12 .... **138** A2
Woodlands Primary School
OSM LS9 .... **11** L3
Woodroyd Industrial Estate
LM/WK BD12 .... **137** K2
Woodroyd Middle School
WBOW BD5 .... **117** K3
Woodside Clinic
WBSY BD6..................................... **137** F1
Woodside First School
WBSY BD6..................................... **137** F1
Woodside Middle School
WBSY BD6..................................... **137** F1
Woodside Trading Estate
HORS LS18 .... **81** H3
Woodsley Health Centre
HDGY LS6 .... **9** G5
Woolshops Shopping Centre
HFAX HX1..................................... **17** H6
Worthinghead First School
LM/WK BD12 .... **137** J4
Worth Valley Middle School
HWTH BD22 .... **73** H1
Wortley High School
WOR/ARM LS12 .... **101** J7
Wortley Moor Lane
Trading Estate
WOR/ARM LS12 .... **102** A7
Wrenthorpe Health Centre
WKFDW/WTN WF2.................. **163** K6
Wrenthorpe Primary School
WKFDW/WTN WF2.................. **164** A6
Wrenthorpe Sports Club
WKFDW/WTN WF2.................. **164** A5
Wrose Health Centre
ECHL BD2 .... **78** A7

Wycliffe Middle School
SHPY BD18 .... **77** F4
Wykebeck Infant School
OSM LS9 .... **104** E3
Wykebeck Primary School
OSM LS9 .... **104** E3
Wyke Manor Upper School
LM/WK BD12 .... **137** J4
Wyke Middle School
LM/WK BD12 .... **137** H4
Wyther Lane
Industrial Estate
KSTL LS5 .... **101** K2
Wyther Park Primary School
KSTL LS5 .... **101** J2
Yarnbury RUFC
HORS LS18 .... **80** D1
Yeadon Airport
Industrial Estate
YEA LS19 .... **60** B2
Yeadon Cemetery
YEA LS19 .... **59** K3
Yeadon Cricket Club
YEA LS19 .... **59** K4
Yeadon Health Centre
YEA LS19 .... **59** J4
Yeadon Westfield Junior School
YEA LS19 .... **59** G5
York Road Industrial Estate
WBY LS22 .... **29** J3
Yorkshire Amateurs FC
CHAL LS7 .... **84** A6
Yorkshire Bank Sports Ground
AL/HA/HU LS17 .... **83** J2
Yorkshire CCC
(Headingley Cricket Ground)
HDGY LS6 .... **102** C1
Yorkshire Clinic
BGLY BD16 .... **76** B5
Yorkshire Martyrs
Collegiate School
BOW BD4 .... **119** H6
Yorkshire Post Sports Club
BHP/TINH LS16........................... **82** B5
Yorkshire Television Studios
BVRD LS3 .... **8** F7
Young Street Industrial Estate
GIR BD8 .... **4** B4
Zakaria Muslim Girls
High School
BTLY WF17 .... **161** G4

Notes

Notes

Notes

Notes